ectures and keep up with their reading
houldn't end when class is over.

.ectures and Office Hours Leave Off

Students choose MyEconLab:

In a recent study, 87 percent of students who used MyEconLab regularly felt it improved their grade.

"It was very useful because it had EVERYTHING, from practice exams to exercises to reading. Very helpful."

—student, Northern Illinois University

"I like how every chapter is outlined by vocabulary and flash cards. It helped me memorize equations and definitions. It was like having a study partner."

—student, Temple University

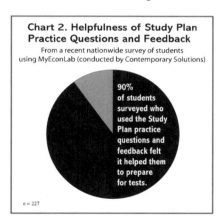

Chart 2. Helpfulness of Study Plan Practice Questions and Feedback
From a recent nationwide survey of students using MyEconLab (conducted by Contemporary Solutions)

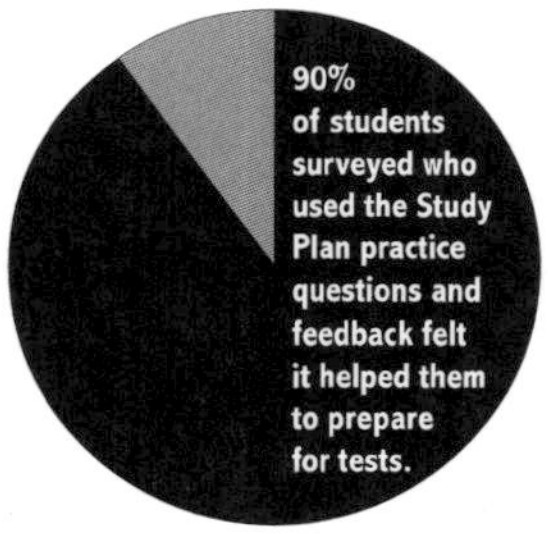

90% of students surveyed who used the Study Plan practice questions and feedback felt it helped them to prepare for tests.

n = 227

"It made me look through the book to find answers so I did more reading."

—student, Northern Illinois University

"It was very helpful to get instant feedback. Sometimes I would get lost reading the book, and these individual problems would help me focus and see if I understood the concepts."

—student, Temple University

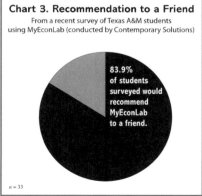

Chart 3. Recommendation to a Friend
From a recent survey of Texas A&M students using MyEconLab (conducted by Contemporary Solutions)

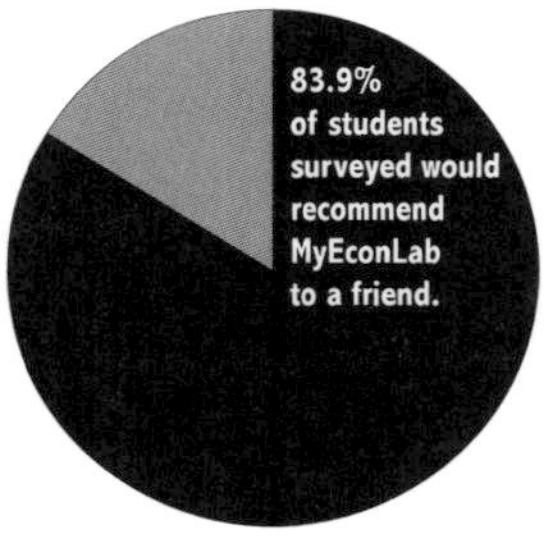

83.9% of students surveyed would recommend MyEconLab to a friend.

n = 33

"I really like the way MyEconLab took me through the graphs step-by-step. The Fast Track tutorials were the most helpful for the graph questions. I used the 1-2-3 buttons all the time."

—student, Stephen F. Austin State University

"I would recommend MyEconLab to a friend. It was really easy to use and helped in studying the material for class."

—student, Northern Illinois University

"I would recommend taking the quizzes on MyEconLab because it gives you a true account of whether or not you understand the material."

—student, Montana Tech

macroeconomics

Second Edition

R. Glenn Hubbard
Columbia University

Anthony Patrick O'Brien
Lehigh University

PEARSON
Prentice Hall

Upper Saddle River, New Jersey 07458

Library of Congress Cataloging-in-Publication Data

Hubbard, R. Glenn.
Macroeconomics / R. Glenn Hubbard, Anthony Patrick O'Brien.—2nd ed.
p. cm.
Includes bibliographical references and index.
ISBN-13: 978-0-13-235669-5
ISBN-10: 0-13-235669-4
1. Macroeconomics. I. O'Brien, Anthony Patrick. II. Title.
HB172.5.H86 2008
339—dc22
2007032939

AVP/Executive Editor: David Alexander
Senior Development Editor: Lena Buonanno
VP/Director of Development: Steve Deitmer
Project Manager: Christina Volpe
Editorial Assistant: Valerie Patruno
Marketing Manager: Lori DeShazo
Marketing Assistant: Justin Jacob
Senior Managing Editor, Production: Judy Leale
Project Manager, Production: Suzanne Grappi
Permissions Project Manager: Charles Morris
Senior Operations Supervisor: Arnold Vila
Designer: Blair Brown
Interior Design: Blair Brown
Cover Design: Blair Brown
Cover Illustration/Photo: iStockphoto/Oliver Hoffmann
Illustration (Interior): Fernando Quijano
Director, Image Resource Center: Melinda Patelli
Manager, Rights and Permissions: Zina Arabia
Manager: Visual Research: Beth Brenzel
Manager, Cover Visual Research & Permissions: Karen Sanatar
Image Permission Coordinator: Kathy Gavilanes
Photo Researcher: Rachel Lucas
Composition: GGS Book Services
Full-Service Project Management: GGS Book Services
Printer/Binder: RR Donnelley-Willard
Typeface: 10.5/12 Minion

Credits and acknowledgments borrowed from other sources and reproduced, with permission, in this textbook appear on page C-1.

Pearson Education LTD
Pearson Education Singapore, Pte. Ltd
Pearson Education, Canada, Ltd
Pearson Education–Japan
Pearson Education Australia PTY, Limited
Pearson Education North Asia Ltd
Pearson Educación de Mexico, S.A. de C.V.
Pearson Education Malaysia, Pte. Ltd.

PEARSON
Prentice Hall

10 9 8 7 6 5 4 3 2
ISBN-13: 978-0-13-235669-5
ISBN-10: 0-13-235669-4

For Constance, Raph, and Will
—R. Glenn Hubbard

For Cindy, Matthew, Andrew, and Daniel
—Anthony Patrick O'Brien

About the Authors

Glenn Hubbard, policymaker, professor, and researcher. R. Glenn Hubbard is the dean and Russell L. Carson Professor of Finance and Economics in the Graduate School of Business at Columbia University and professor of economics in Columbia's Faculty of Arts and Sciences. He is also a research associate of the National Bureau of Economic Research and a director of Automatic Data Processing, Black Rock Closed-End Funds, Duke Realty, Information Services Group, KKR Financial Corporation, MetLife, and Ripplewood Holdings. He received his Ph.D. in economics from Harvard University in 1983. From 2001 to 2003, he served as chairman of the White House Council of Economic Advisers and chairman of the OECD Economy Policy Committee, and from 1991 to 1993, he was deputy assistant secretary of the U.S. Treasury Department. He currently serves as co-chair of the nonpartisan committee on Capital Markets Regulation. Hubbard's fields of specialization are public economics, financial markets and institutions, corporate finance, macroeconomics, industrial organization, and public policy. He is the author of more than 100 articles in leading journals, including *American Economic Review, Brookings Papers on Economic Activity, Journal of Finance, Journal of Financial Economics, Journal of Money, Credit,* and *Banking, Journal of Political Economy, Journal of Public Economics, Quarterly Journal of Economics, RAND Journal of Economics,* and *Review of Economics and Statistics.* His research has been supported by grants from the National Science Foundation, the National Bureau of Economic Research, and numerous private foundations.

Tony O'Brien, award-winning professor and researcher. Anthony Patrick O'Brien is a professor of economics at Lehigh University. He received his Ph.D. from the University of California, Berkeley, in 1987. He has taught principles of economics for more than 15 years, in both large sections and small honors classes. He received the Lehigh University Award for Distinguished Teaching. He was formerly the director of the Diamond Center for Economic Education and was named a Dana Foundation Faculty Fellow and Lehigh Class of 1961 Professor of Economics. He has been a visiting professor at the University of California, Santa Barbara, and the Graduate School of Industrial Administration at Carnegie Mellon University. O'Brien's research has dealt with such issues as the evolution of the U.S. automobile industry, the sources of U.S. economic competitiveness, the development of U.S. trade policy, the causes of the Great Depression, and the causes of black–white income differences. His research has been published in leading journals, including *American Economic Review, Quarterly Journal of Economics, Journal of Money, Credit, and Banking, Industrial Relations, Journal of Economic History,* and *Explorations in Economic History.* His research has been supported by grants from government agencies and private foundations. In addition to teaching and writing, O'Brien also serves on the editorial board of the *Journal of Socio-Economics.*

Preface

When George Lucas was asked why he made *Star Wars*, he replied, "It's the kind of movie I like to see, but no one seemed to be making them. So, I decided to make one." We realized that no one seemed to be writing the kind of textbook we wanted to use in our classes. So, after years of supplementing texts with fresh, lively, real-world examples from newspapers, magazines, and professional journals, we decided to write an economics text that delivers complete economics coverage with many real-world business examples. Our goal was to keep our classes "widget free."

NEW TO THIS EDITION

The core ideas of economics remain unchanged: opportunity costs, comparative advantage, demand and supply, marginal analysis, the role of the entrepreneur in the market system, aggregate demand and aggregate supply, the importance of long-run economic growth to rising living standards, and the role of economic incentives in the design of policy. What does change is the context in which professors present these ideas in class and the policy debates of the time. In the past three years, to take just a few examples, we have witnessed the runaway success of Apple's iPod, companies such as MySpace entering China, renewed debate over policies toward health care, immigration, and the environment, the appointment of a new Federal Reserve chairman, and the bursting of the housing bubble. This new edition helps students understand these changing economic realities.

We were pleased by the success of the first edition and grateful for the many suggestions for improvement we received from instructors and students. In this second edition, we retained the focus of presenting economics in the context of real-world businesses and real-world policy debates that proved so popular. But we have made a number of significant improvements that we hope will make the text an even more effective teaching tool. In addition to the changes listed next, we literally worked through the text line by line, making hundreds of small changes to improve clarity and readability. The second edition includes the following key changes:

- A more streamlined approach to presenting demand and supply in Chapter 3, "Where Prices Come From: The Interaction of Demand and Supply"
- A clearer development of consumer surplus and producer surplus in Chapter 4, "Economic Efficiency, Government Price Setting, and Taxes"
- A new, more flexible presentation of aggregate demand and aggregate supply in Chapter 12, "Aggregate Demand and Aggregate Supply Analysis"
- A new layered, full-color acetate figure for the dynamic aggregate demand and aggregate supply model in Chapter 12
- A new feature titled *Economics in Your Life* that relates a key idea in each chapter to the students' personal lives and experiences
- Updated and new chapter-opening cases covering such topics as the introduction of the iPod and the end of the housing bubble
- Dozens of new examples, including several new *Making the Connection* features
- A new *An Inside Look* newspaper article and analysis in every chapter

- Many additions to the end-of-chapter *Review Questions* and *Problems and Applications* sections
- *Review Questions* and *Problems and Applications* sections are now organized according to chapter learning objectives to improve learning assessment

New Streamlined Approach to **CHAPTER 3**

We have streamlined Chapter 3, "Where Prices Come From: The Interaction of Demand and Supply," to make the chapter more accessible to students encountering demand and supply curves for the first time.

Chapter 3 now opens with a discussion of Apple and its iPod and iTunes, a company and products that the majority of students are familiar with. We return to the company and its products in the graphs, a *Making the Connection* feature, and the end-of-chapter *An Inside Look* to provide students with continuity as they read and learn about new concepts.

We added a new table, Table 3-3, "How Shifts in Demand and Supply Affect Equilibrium Price (*P*) and Quantity (*Q*)." This table provides an important summary of a key topic that many students find challenging.

A Clearer Development of Consumers Surplus and Producer Surplus in **CHAPTER 4**

Adopters of the first edition praised our use of consumer surplus and producer surplus to analyze the efficiency of competitive markets and the economic effects of price ceilings and price floors. But some instructors and students found our introduction of these important concepts to be a little too terse. In this edition, we proceed more slowly, employing three new graphs in our expanded explanation.

A New, More Flexible Presentation of Aggregate Demand and Aggregate Supply in **CHAPTER 12**

We received much positive feedback on our approach to the aggregate demand–aggregate supply model in the first edition. We also received some recommendations on how to make the discussion more flexible. In this second edition, we retain our approach of making the *AD-AS* model dynamic by emphasizing two points: First, changes in the position of the short-run (upward-sloping) aggregate supply curve depend mainly on the state of expectations of the inflation rate. Second, the existence of growth in the economy means that the long-run (vertical) aggregate supply curve shifts to the right every year. This dynamic *AD-AS* model makes it possible for instructors to provide students with a more realistic account of the business cycle. In particular, it is now possible for instructors to show that in a recession, the price level does not decline but increases less than it otherwise would have.

We know, however, that some instructors believe that students need more help in understanding the dynamic *AD-AS* model, while other instructors would prefer to use the basic *AD-AS* model in order to free up class time for other macroeconomic topics. To address these two concerns, we made the following revisions to our discussion of aggregate demand and aggregate supply.

New Layered, Full-Color Acetate for the Dynamic *AD-AS* Model

Chapter 12, "Aggregate Demand and Aggregate Supply Analysis," now includes a three-layer, full-color acetate for the key introductory dynamic *AD-AS* graph (Figure 12-8, "A Dynamic Aggregate Demand and Aggregate Supply Model," on **page 408**). We created this acetate to help students see how the graph builds step by step and to help make the graph more accessible to students and easier for instructors to present. The acetate will help instructors who want to use dynamic *AD-AS* in class but believe the model needs to be developed carefully.

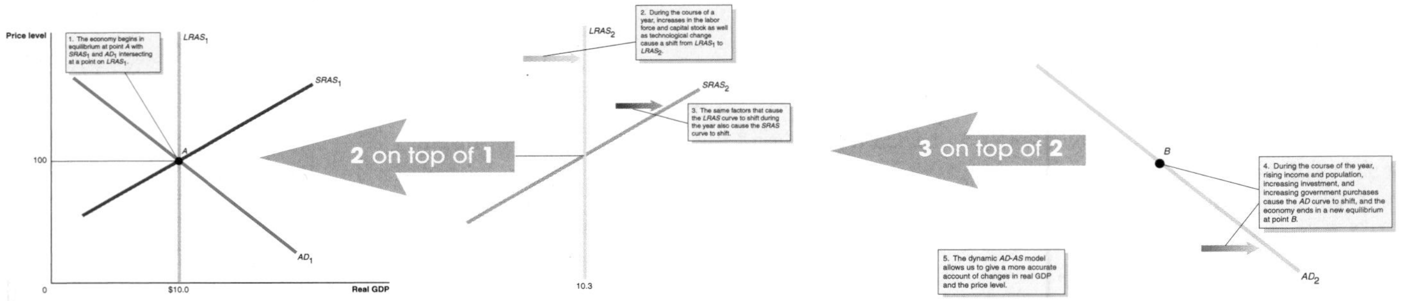

LAYER 1 LAYER 2 first acetate overlay LAYER 3 second acetate overlay

New Basic *AD-AS* Graphs That Make It Possible to Omit Dynamic *AD-AS*

As in the first edition, we introduce aggregate demand and aggregate supply in Chapter 12 by devoting most of the chapter to discussing the basic *AD-AS* model, turning to the dynamic *AD-AS* model only in a final, self-contained section. Instructors who do not wish to cover the dynamic *AD-AS* model can skip this last section in Chapter 12. Chapter 14, "Monetary Policy," includes a new graph, Figure 14-7, "Monetary Policy," that shows expansionary and contractionary policy using only the basic *AD-AS* model, which makes it possible to skip the dynamic *AD-AS* discussion of monetary policy, which is in a self-contained section. Chapter 15, "Fiscal Policy," also includes a new graph, Figure 15-5, "Fiscal Policy," that shows expansionary and contractionary policy using only the basic *AD-AS* model, which makes it possible to skip the dynamic *AD-AS* discussion of fiscal policy, which again is in a self-contained section. Chapter 16, "Inflation, Unemployment, and Federal Reserve Policy," now uses only the basic *AD-AS* model in discussing the Phillips curve. Instructors may now safely omit the sections on the dynamic *AD-AS* model without any loss in continuity to the discussion of macroeconomic theory and policy.

New Personal Dimension: *Economics in Your Life*

Each chapter opens with a discussion of a real-world business that is familiar to students. To pique the interest of students and emphasize the connection between the material they are learning and their own experiences, we have added a personal dimension to the chapter opener with a new feature titled *Economics in Your Life*, which asks students to consider questions about how economics affects their personal lives. At the end of the chapter, we use the concepts covered to answer the questions. Here are examples of the topics we cover in the real-world business case and the new *Economics in Your Life* feature:

Chapter 3: "Where Prices Come From: The Interaction of Demand and Supply"

Business case: Apple and the Demand for iPods

Economics in Your Life: Will you buy an iPod or a Zune?

Chapter 10: "Long-Run Economic Growth: Sources and Policies"

Business case: MySpace Meets the Chinese Economic Miracle

Economics in Your Life: Would you be better off without China?

Chapter 12: "Aggregate Demand and Aggregate Supply Analysis"

Business case: The Fortunes of FedEx Follow the Business Cycle

Economics in Your Life: Is an employer likely to cut your pay during a recession?

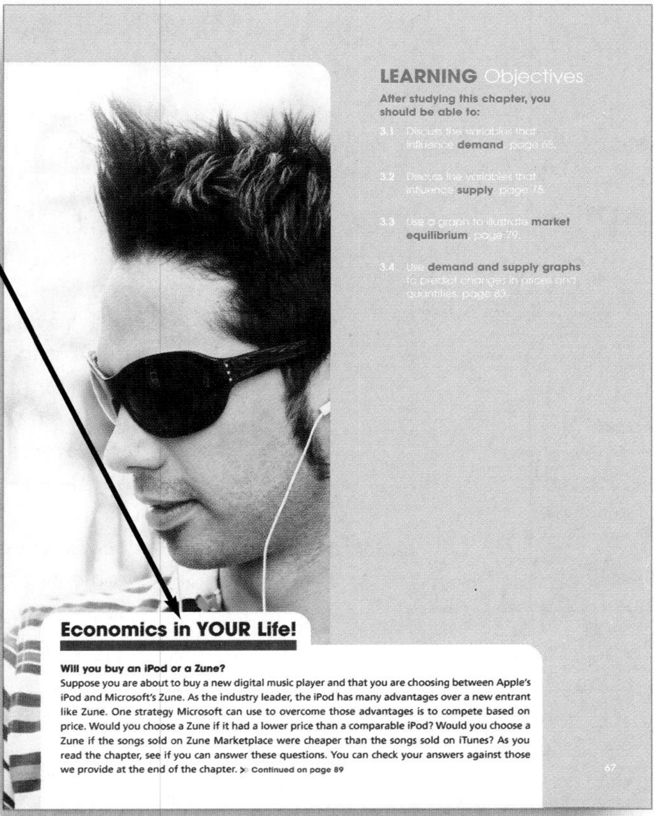

LEARNING Objectives
After studying this chapter, you should be able to:
3.1 demand
3.2 supply
3.3 market equilibrium
3.4 demand and supply graphs
Economics in YOUR Life!
Will you buy an iPod or a Zune?
Suppose you are about to buy a new digital music player and that you are choosing between Apple's iPod and Microsoft's Zune. As the industry leader, the iPod has many advantages over a new entrant like Zune. One strategy Microsoft can use to overcome those advantages is to compete based on price. Would you choose a Zune if it had a lower price than a comparable iPod? Would you choose a Zune if the songs sold on Zune Marketplace were cheaper than the songs sold on iTunes? As you read the chapter, see if you can answer these questions. You can check your answers against those we provide at the end of the chapter. > Continued on page 89
67

Updated and New Chapter-Opening Business Cases

As in the previous edition, each chapter-opening business case provides a real-world context for learning, sparks students' interest in economics, and helps unify the chapter. Each case describes an actual company facing a real situation. The company is integrated in the narrative, graphs, and pedagogical features of the chapter. Many of the chapter openers focus on the role of the entrepreneur in developing new products and bringing them to the market. See the fold-out at the back of the book for a complete list of the new cases.

New *Making the Connection* Feature

Each chapter includes two to four *Making the Connection* features that present real-world reinforcement of key concepts and help students learn how to interpret what they read on the Web or in newspapers. One-third of the *Making the Connection* features are new to this edition, and most others have been updated. Several *Making the Connection* features discuss health care, which remains a pressing policy issue. Each *Making the Connection* now has at least one supporting end-of-chapter problem to allow students to test their understanding of the topic discussed. See the fold-out at the back of the book for a complete list of the new *Making the Connections.*

All New *An Inside Look* Newspaper Articles and Analyses

For this edition, the *An Inside Look* newspaper articles and analyses are all new. Select articles deal with policy issues and are titled *An Inside Look at Policy.* We use articles from sources such as the *Wall Street Journal,* the *Economist,* and *BusinessWeek.* The feature consists of an excerpt of an article, analysis of the article, graph(s), and critical thinking questions. See the fold-out at the back of the book for a complete list of the *Inside Look* articles.

New Review Questions and Problems and Applications—Grouped by Learning Objective to Improve Assessment

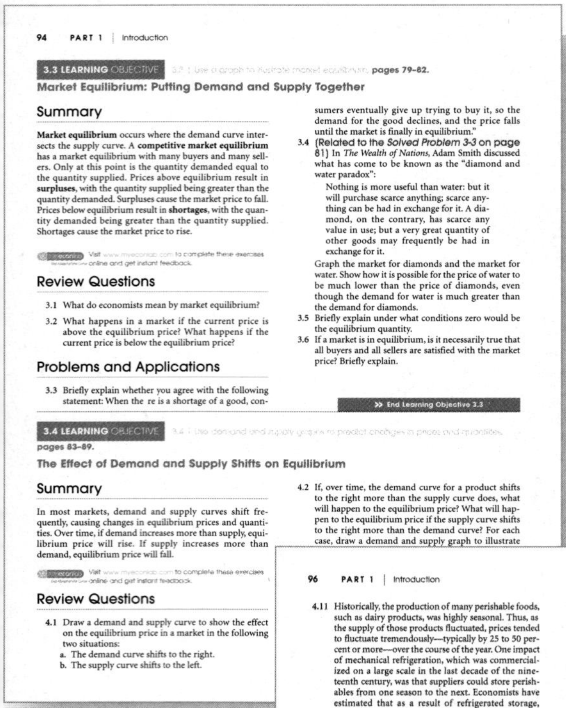

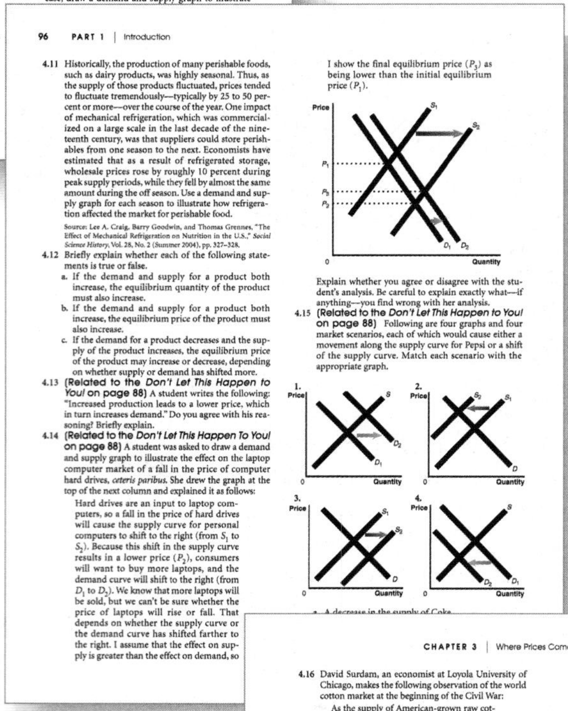

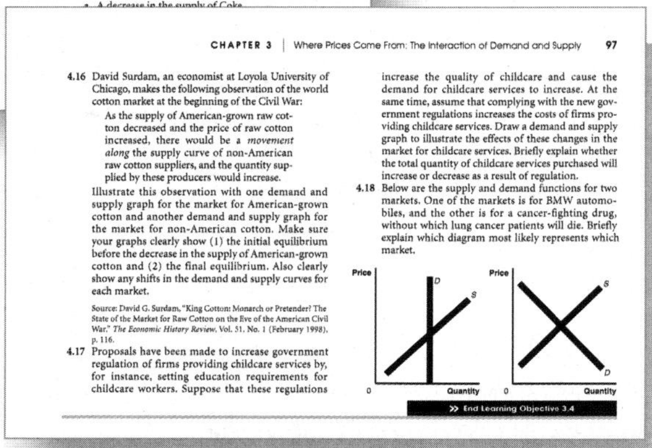

At least one-third of the *Review Questions* and *Problems and Applications* are new, and many others have been revised and updated. In this edition, all the end-of-chapter material—summary, review questions, and review problems—is grouped under learning objectives. The goals of this new organization are to make it easier for professors to assign problems based on learning objectives, both in the book and in MyEconLab and to help students efficiently review material that they find difficult. If students have difficulty with a particular learning objective, a professor can easily identify which end-of-chapter questions and problems support that objective and assign them for homework and discuss them in class. Every exercise in a chapter's *Problems and Applications* section is available in MyEconLab. Students can complete these and many other exercises online, get tutorial help, and receive instant feedback and assistance on those exercises they answer incorrectly. Also, student learning will be enhanced by having the summary material and questions and problems grouped together by learning objective, which will allow them to focus on the parts of the chapter they found most challenging. Each major section of the chapter, paired with a learning objective, has at least two review questions and three problems.

As in the first edition, we include one or more end-of-chapter problems that test the students' understanding of the content presented in the *Solved Problem*, *Making the Connection*, and *Don't Let This Happen to You!* special features in the chapter. Professors can cover the feature in class and assign the corresponding problem for homework. The test banks also include test questions that pertain to these special features.

The Foundation:
Contextual Learning and Modern Organization

Students come to study macroeconomics with a strong interest in understanding events and developments in the economy. We try to capture that interest and develop students' economic intuition and understanding in this text. We present macroeconomics in a way that is modern and based in the real world of business and economic policy. And we believe we achieve this presentation without making the analysis more difficult. We avoid the recent trend of using simplified versions of intermediate models, which are often more detailed and more complex than what students need to understand the basic macroeconomic issues. Instead, we use a more realistic version of the familiar aggregate demand and aggregate supply model to analyze short-run fluctuations and monetary and fiscal policy. We also avoid the "dueling schools of thought" approach often used to teach macroeconomics at the principles level. We emphasize the many areas of macroeconomics where most economists agree. And we present throughout real business and policy situations to develop students' intuition.

Here are a few highlights of our approach to macroeconomics:

- **A BROAD DISCUSSION OF MACRO STATISTICS.** Many students pay at least some attention to the financial news and know that the release of statistics by federal agencies can cause movements in stock and bond prices. A background in macroeconomic statistics helps clarify some of the policy issues encountered in later chapters. In Chapter 7, "GDP: Measuring Total Production and Income," and Chapter 8, "Unemployment and Inflation," we provide students with an understanding of the uses and potential shortcomings of the key macroeconomic statistics, without getting bogged down in the minutiae of how the statistics are constructed. So, for instance, we discuss the important differences between the payroll survey and the household survey for understanding conditions in the labor market. We explain why the financial markets react more strongly to news from the payroll survey. Chapter 14, "Monetary Policy," discusses why the Federal Reserve prefers to measure inflation using the personal consumption expenditures price index rather than the consumer price index.
- **EARLY COVERAGE OF LONG-RUN TOPICS.** We place key macroeconomic issues in their long-run context in Chapter 9, "Economic Growth, the Financial System, and Business Cycles," and Chapter 10, "Long-Run Economic Growth: Sources and Policies." Chapter 9 puts the business cycle in the context of underlying long-run growth and discusses what actually happens during the phases of the business cycle. We believe this material is important if students are to have the understanding of business cycles they will need to interpret economic events, yet this material is often discussed only briefly or omitted entirely in other books. We know that many instructors prefer to have a short-run orientation to their macro courses, with a strong emphasis on policy. Accordingly, we have structured Chapter 9 so that its discussion of long-run growth would be sufficient for instructors who want to move quickly to short-run analysis. Chapter 10 uses a simple neoclassical growth model to explain important growth issues. We apply the model to topics such as the decline of the Soviet economy, the surprisingly strong growth performance of Botswana, and the failure of many developing countries to sustain high growth rates. And we challenge students with the discussion "Why Isn't the Whole World Rich?"
- **A DYNAMIC MODEL OF AGGREGATE DEMAND AND AGGREGATE SUPPLY.** We take a fresh approach to the standard aggregate demand and aggregate supply model. We realize there is no good, simple alternative to using the *AD-AS* model when explaining movements in the price level and in real GDP. But we know that more

instructors are dissatisfied with the *AD-AS* model than with any other aspect of the macro principles course. The key problem, of course, is that *AD-AS* is a static model that attempts to account for dynamic changes in real GDP and the price level. Our approach retains the basics of the *AD-AS* model but makes it more accurate and useful by making it more dynamic. We emphasize two points: First, changes in the position of the short-run (upward-sloping) aggregate supply curve depend mainly on the state of expectations of the inflation rate. Second, the existence of growth in the economy means that the long-run (vertical) aggregate supply curve shifts to the right every year. This "dynamic" *AD-AS* model provides students with a more accurate understanding of the causes and consequences of fluctuations in real GDP and the price level. We introduce this model in Chapter 12, "Aggregate Demand and Aggregate Supply Analysis," and use it to discuss monetary policy in Chapter 14, "Monetary Policy," and fiscal policy in Chapter 15, "Fiscal Policy." Note, though, that as discussed earlier, in this edition the sections on dynamic *AD-AS* are self-contained so they can be omitted without any loss of continuity in the discussion of macroeconomic theory and policy.

- **EXTENSIVE COVERAGE OF MONETARY POLICY.** Because of the central role monetary policy plays in the economy and in students' curiosity about business and financial news, we devote two chapters—Chapters 14, "Monetary Policy," and 6, "Inflation, Unemployment, and Federal Reserve Policy"—to the topic. We emphasize the issues involved in the Fed's choice of monetary policy targets, and we include coverage of the Taylor rule. Our discussion of inflation targeting is particularly pertinent since Ben Bernanke succeeded Alan Greenspan as Fed chair.
- **COVERAGE OF BOTH THE DEMAND-SIDE AND SUPPLY-SIDE EFFECTS OF FISCAL POLICY.** Our discussion of fiscal policy in Chapter 15, "Fiscal Policy," carefully distinguishes between automatic stabilizers and discretionary fiscal policy. We also provide significant coverage of the supply-side effects of fiscal policy.
- **A SELF-CONTAINED BUT THOROUGH DISCUSSION OF THE KEYNESIAN INCOME-EXPENDITURE APPROACH.** The Keynesian income-expenditure approach (the "45°-line diagram," or "Keynesian cross") is useful for introducing students to the short-run relationship between spending and production. Many instructors, however, prefer to omit this material. Therefore, we use the 45°-line diagram only in Chapter 11, "Output and Expenditure in the Short Run." The discussion of monetary and fiscal policy in later chapters uses only the *AD-AS* model, making it possible to omit Chapter 11.
- **EXTENSIVE INTERNATIONAL COVERAGE.** We include three chapters devoted to international topics: Chapter 6, "Comparative Advantage and the Gains from International Trade," Chapter 17, "Macroeconomics in an Open Economy," and Chapter 18, "The International Financial System." Having a good understanding of the international trading and financial systems is essential to understanding the macroeconomy and to satisfying students' curiosity about the economic world around them. In addition to the material in our three international chapters, we weave international comparisons into the narratives of several chapters, including our discussion of labor market policies in Chapter 16 "Inflation, Unemployment, and Federal Reserve Policy," and central banking in Chapter 13, "Money, Banks, and the Federal Reserve System."
- **FLEXIBLE CHAPTER ORGANIZATION.** Because we realize that there are a variety of approaches to teaching principles of macroeconomics, we have structured our chapters for maximum flexibility. For example, our discussion of long-run economic growth in Chapter 9, "Economic Growth, the Financial System, and Business Cycles," makes it possible for instructors to omit the more thorough discussion of these issues in Chapter 10, "Long-Run Economic Growth: Sources and Policies." Our discussion of the Keynesian 45°-line diagram is confined to Chapter 11 so that instructors who do not use this approach can proceed directly to aggregate demand and aggregate supply analysis in Chapter 12, "Aggregate Demand and Aggregate Supply Analysis." While we devote two chapters to monetary policy, the first of these—Chapter 14, "Monetary Policy"—is a

self-contained discussion, so instructors may safely omit the material in Chapter 16, "Inflation, Unemployment, and Federal Reserve Policy," if they choose to. Finally, instructors may choose to omit all three of the international chapters (Chapter 6, "Comparative Advantage and the Gains from International Trade," Chapter 17, "Macroeconomics in an Open Economy," and Chapter 18, "The International Financial System"), cover just Chapter 6 on international trade; cover just Chapter 17; or cover Chapter 17 and Chapter 18, while omitting Chapter 6.

Please refer to the flexibility chart on **pages xlv–xlvi** of this preface to help select the chapters and order best suited to your classroom needs.

Special Features:

A Real-World, Hands-on Approach to Learning Economics

Business Cases and *Inside Look* News Articles

Each chapter-opening case provides a real-world context for learning, sparks students' interest in economics, and helps to unify the chapter. The case describes an actual company facing a real situation. The company is integrated in the narrative, graphs, and pedagogical features of the chapter. Many of the chapter openers focus on the role of the entrepreneur in developing new products and bringing them to the market. For example, Chapter 3 covers Steve Jobs of Apple, Chapter 10 covers Tom Anderson and Chris DeWolfe of MySpace.com, and Chapter 12 covers Fred Smith of Fedex. Here are a few examples of companies we explore in this second edition:

- Can Apple's iPod continue to dominate the market? (**Chapter 3**, "Where Prices Come From: The Interaction of Demand and Supply")
- Will MySpace succeed in China? (**Chapter 10**, "Long-Run Economic Growth: Sources and Policies")
- How does the business cycle affect FedEx? (**Chapter 12**, "Aggregate Demand and Aggregate Supply Analysis")

Chapter 3

Where Prices Come From: The Interaction of Demand and Supply

Apple and the Demand for iPods

During the last three months of 2006, Apple sold \$3.43 billion worth of iPods. iPods seemed to be everywhere, but during 2007 it became clear that the market for digital music players was becoming much more competitive.

Steve Jobs and Steve Wozniak started Apple in 1976. Working out of Jobs's parents' garage, the two friends created the Apple I computer. By 1980, although Jobs was still only in his mid-twenties, Apple had become the first firm in history to join the Fortune 500 list of largest U.S. firms in less than five years. Apple's success in the computer business has been up and down, but when the company introduced the iPod digital music player in 2001, it had a runaway success on its hands. The most obvious reasons for the iPod's success are its ease of use and sleek design. But also important has been iTunes, Apple's online music store. Apple decided to offer individual songs, as well as whole albums, for download at a price of just \$0.99 per song. After paying a royalty to the record company, Apple makes very little profit from the songs it sells on iTunes. Apple was willing to accept a small profit on the sale of each song to make the purchase of the iPod more attractive to consumers.

At a price of several hundred dollars, the iPod might be relatively expensive, but purchasing the music is very inexpensive. In addition, the songs on iTunes are playable only on iPods, and iPods can only play songs downloaded from iTunes (although with enough technical skill, it's possible to get around both restrictions). So, owners of other digital music players do not have easy access to iTunes, and iPod owners have little incentive to download music from other online sites. In addition, because Apple makes the iPod and owns iTunes, the two systems work smoothly together, which is not the case for many of Apple's competitors. Microsoft's Vice President Bryan Lee says, "That's something that Apple has played up very well. One brand, one device, one service."

By early 2007, more than 100 million iPods had been sold and more than 2 billion songs had been downloaded from iTunes. Clearly, the strategy of selling an expensive digital music player and selling the music cheaply has been very successful for Apple. But how long will the iPod's dominance last? By 2007, competitors were flooding into the market. New digital music players, such as Microsoft's Zune, Toshiba's Gigabeat, and iRiver's H10, among many others, were rapidly gaining customers. In addition, firms were introducing new "music phones" that combined the features of a cell phone with the features of a digital music player. Although this wave of competition might be bad news for Apple, it could be good news for consumers by increasing the choices available and lowering prices. AN INSIDE LOOK on page 90 discusses how Apple responded to competition by teaming with AT&T to create its own music phone, the iPhone.

Economics in YOUR Life!

Will you buy an iPod or a Zune?
Suppose you are about to buy a new digital music player and that you are choosing between Apple's iPod and Microsoft's Zune. As the industry leader, the iPod has many advantages over a new entrant like Zune. One strategy Microsoft can use to overcome those advantages is to compete based on price. Would you choose a Zune if it had a lower price than a comparable iPod? Would you choose a Zune if the songs sold on Zune Marketplace were cheaper than the songs sold on iTunes? As you read the chapter, see if you can answer these questions. You can check your answers against those we provide at the end of the chapter. Continued on page 89

LEARNING Objectives

After studying this chapter, you should be able to:

3.1 … demand …
3.2 … supply …
3.3 … market equilibrium …
3.4 … demand and supply graphs …

An Inside Look is a two-page newspaper feature that shows students how to apply the concepts of a chapter to the analysis of an article they may read either on the Web or in a newspaper. Select articles deal with policy issues and are titled An Inside Look at Policy. Articles are from sources such as the Wall Street Journal, the Economist, and BusinessWeek. The feature presents an excerpt from an article, analysis of the article, graph(s), and critical thinking questions.

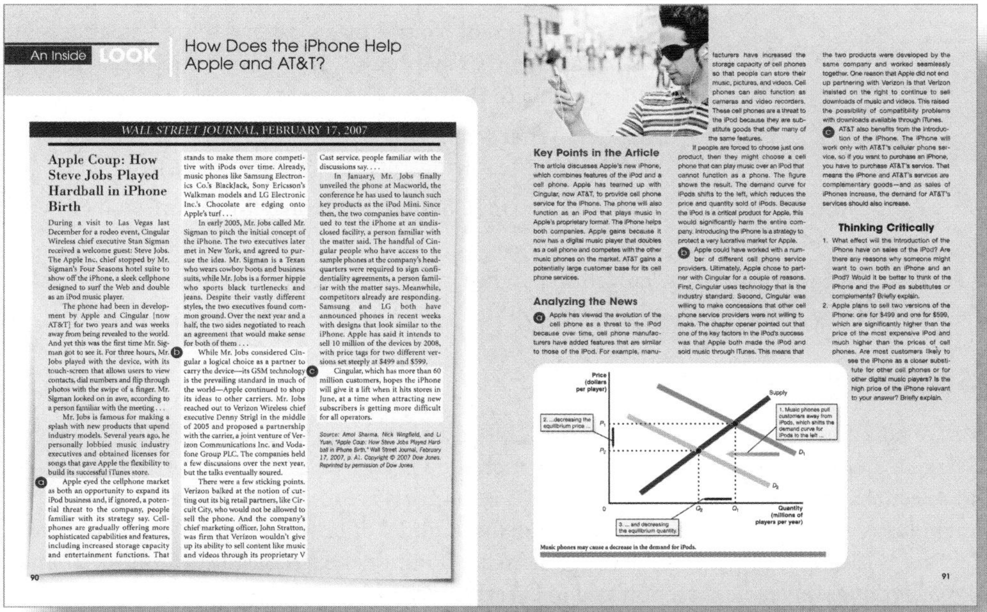

An Inside LOOK | How Does the iPhone Help Apple and AT&T?

WALL STREET JOURNAL, FEBRUARY 17, 2007

Apple Coup: How Steve Jobs Played Hardball in iPhone Birth

During a visit to Las Vegas last December for a rodeo event, Cingular Wireless chief executive Stan Sigman received a welcome guest: Steve Jobs. The Apple Inc. chief stopped by Mr. Sigman's Four Seasons hotel suite to show off the iPhone, a sleek cellphone designed to surf the Web and double as an iPod music player.

The phone had been in development by Apple and Cingular [now AT&T] for two years and was weeks away from being revealed to the world. And yet this was the first time Mr. Sigman got to see it. For three hours, Mr. (b) Jobs played with the device, with its touch-screen that allows users to view contacts, dial numbers and flip through photos with the swipe of a finger. Mr. Sigman looked on in awe, according to a person familiar with the meeting . . .

Mr. Jobs is famous for making a splash with new products that upend industry models. Several years ago, he personally lobbied music industry executives and obtained licenses for songs that gave Apple the flexibility to build its successful iTunes store.

(a) Apple eyed the cellphone market as both an opportunity to expand its iPod business and, if ignored, a potential threat to the company, people familiar with its strategy say. Cellphones are gradually offering more sophisticated capabilities and features, including increased storage capacity and entertainment functions. That stands to make them more competitive with iPods over time. Already, music phones like Samsung Electronics Co.'s BlackJack, Sony Ericsson's Walkman models and LG Electronic Inc.'s Chocolate are edging onto Apple's turf . . .

In early 2005, Mr. Jobs called Mr. Sigman to pitch the initial concept of the iPhone. The two executives later met in New York, and agreed to pursue the idea. Mr. Sigman is a Texan who wears cowboy boots and business suits, while Mr. Jobs is a former hippie who sports black turtlenecks and jeans. Despite their vastly different styles, the two executives found common ground. Over the next year and a half, the two sides negotiated to reach an agreement that would make sense for both of them . . .

While Mr. Jobs considered Cingular a logical choice as a partner to carry the device—its GSM technology (c) is the prevailing standard in much of the world—Apple continued to shop its ideas to other carriers. Mr. Jobs reached out to Verizon Wireless chief executive Denny Strigl in the middle of 2005 and proposed a partnership with the carrier, a joint venture of Verizon Communications Inc. and Vodafone Group PLC. The companies held a few discussions over the next year, but the talks eventually soured.

There were a few sticking points. Verizon balked at the notion of cutting out its big retail partners, like Circuit City, who would not be allowed to sell the phone. And the company's chief marketing officer, John Stratton, was firm that Verizon wouldn't give up its ability to sell content like music and videos through its proprietary V Cast service, people familiar with the discussions say. . . .

In January, Mr. Jobs finally unveiled the phone at Macworld, the conference he has used to launch such key products as the iPod Mini. Since then, the two companies have continued to test the iPhone at an undisclosed facility, a person familiar with the matter said. The handful of Cingular people who have access to the sample phones at the company's headquarters were required to sign confidentiality agreements, a person familiar with the matter says. Meanwhile, competitors already are responding. Samsung and LG both have announced phones in recent weeks with designs that look similar to the iPhone. Apple has said it intends to sell 10 million of the devices by 2008, with price tags for two different versions set steeply at $499 and $599.

Cingular, which has more than 60 million customers, hopes the iPhone will give it a lift when it hits stores in June, at a time when attracting new subscribers is getting more difficult for all operators.

Source: Amol Sharma, Nick Wingfield, and Li Yuan, "Apple Coup: How Steve Jobs Played Hardball in iPhone Birth," Wall Street Journal, February 17, 2007, p. A1. Copyright © 2007 Dow Jones. Reprinted by permission of Dow Jones.

90

Key Points in the Article

The article discusses Apple's new iPhone, which combines features of the iPod and a cell phone. Apple has teamed up with Cingular, now AT&T, to provide cell phone service for the iPhone. The phone will also function as an iPod that plays music in Apple's proprietary format. The iPhone helps both companies. Apple gains because it now has a digital music player that doubles as a cell phone and competes with the other music phones on the market. AT&T gains a potentially large customer base for its cell phone services.

Analyzing the News

(a) Apple has viewed the evolution of the cell phone as a threat to the iPod because over time, cell phone manufacturers have added features that are similar to those of the iPod. For example, manufacturers have increased the storage capacity of cell phones so that people can store their music, pictures, and videos. Cell phones can also function as cameras and video recorders. These cell phones are a threat to the iPod because they are substitute goods that offer many of the same features.

If people are forced to choose just one product, then they might choose a cell phone that can play music over an iPod that cannot function as a phone. The figure shows the result. The demand curve for iPods shifts to the left, which reduces the price and quantity sold of iPods. Because the iPod is a critical product for Apple, this would significantly harm the entire company. Introducing the iPhone is a strategy to protect a very lucrative market for Apple.

(b) Apple could have worked with a number of different cell phone service providers. Ultimately, Apple chose to partner with Cingular for a couple of reasons. First, Cingular uses technology that is the industry standard. Second, Cingular was willing to make concessions that other cell phone service providers were not willing to make. The chapter opener pointed out that one of the key factors in the iPod's success was that Apple both made the iPod and sold music through iTunes. This means that the two products were developed by the same company and worked seamlessly together. One reason that Apple did not end up partnering with Verizon is that Verizon insisted on the right to continue to sell downloads of music and videos. This raised the possibility of compatibility problems with downloads available through iTunes.

(c) AT&T also benefits from the introduction of the iPhone. The iPhone will work only with AT&T's cellular phone service, so if you want to purchase an iPhone, you have to purchase AT&T's service. That means the iPhone and AT&T's services are complementary goods—and as sales of iPhones increase, the demand for AT&T's services should also increase.

Thinking Critically

1. What effect will the introduction of the iPhone have on sales of the iPod? Are there any reasons why someone might want to own both an iPhone and an iPod? Would it be better to think of the iPhone and the iPod as substitutes or complements? Briefly explain.
2. Apple plans to sell two versions of the iPhone: one for $499 and one for $599, which are significantly higher than the price of the most expensive iPod and much higher than the prices of cell phones. Are most customers likely to see the iPhone as a closer substitute for other cell phones or for other digital music players? Is the high price of the iPhone relevant to your answer? Briefly explain.

Music phones may cause a decrease in the demand for iPods.

91

Here are some examples of the articles featured in An Inside Look:

- "Apple Coup: How Steve Jobs Played Hardball in iPhone Birth," *Wall Street Journal*, (**Chapter 3**, "Where Prices Come From: The Interaction of Demand and Supply")
- "Feeling Brighter: Entrepreneurship and Sustained Growth in Europe," *Economist*, (**Chapter 10**, "Long-Run Economic Growth: Sources and Policies")
- "Freight Carrier Weakness Shows Retailer Uncertainty," *Wall Street Journal*, (**Chapter 12**, "Aggregate Demand and Aggregate Supply Analysis")

Economics in Your Life Feature

After the chapter-opening real-world business case, we have added a personal dimension to the chapter opener with a new feature titled *Economics in Your Life*, which asks students to consider how economics affects their own lives. The feature piques the interest of students and emphasizes the connection between the material they are learning and their own experiences.

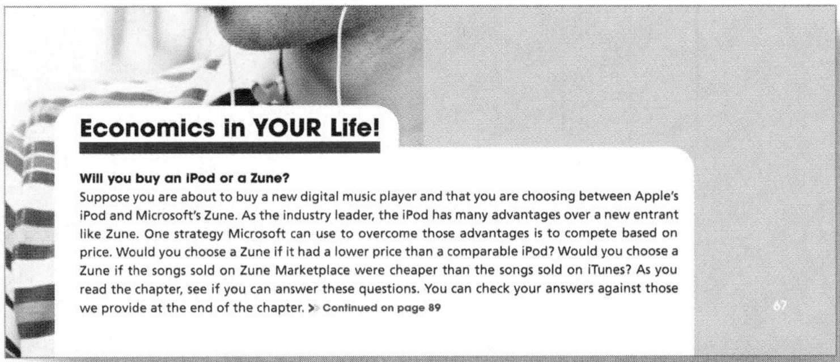

Economics in YOUR Life!

Will you buy an iPod or a Zune?

Suppose you are about to buy a new digital music player and that you are choosing between Apple's iPod and Microsoft's Zune. As the industry leader, the iPod has many advantages over a new entrant like Zune. One strategy Microsoft can use to overcome those advantages is to compete based on price. Would you choose a Zune if it had a lower price than a comparable iPod? Would you choose a Zune if the songs sold on Zune Marketplace were cheaper than the songs sold on iTunes? As you read the chapter, see if you can answer these questions. You can check your answers against those we provide at the end of the chapter. ➤ Continued on page 89

67

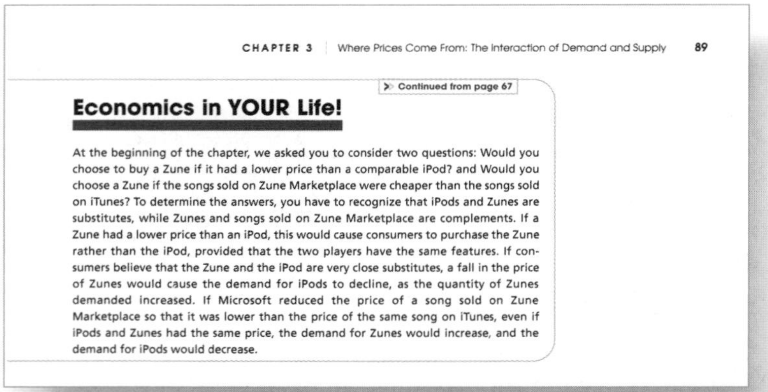

CHAPTER 3 | Where Prices Come From: The Interaction of Demand and Supply 89

>> Continued from page 67

Economics in YOUR Life!

At the beginning of the chapter, we asked you to consider two questions: Would you choose to buy a Zune if it had a lower price than a comparable iPod? and Would you choose a Zune if the songs sold on Zune Marketplace were cheaper than the songs sold on iTunes? To determine the answers, you have to recognize that iPods and Zunes are substitutes, while Zunes and songs sold on Zune Marketplace are complements. If a Zune had a lower price than an iPod, this would cause consumers to purchase the Zune rather than the iPod, provided that the two players have the same features. If consumers believe that the Zune and the iPod are very close substitutes, a fall in the price of Zunes would cause the demand for iPods to decline, as the quantity of Zunes demanded increased. If Microsoft reduced the price of a song sold on Zune Marketplace so that it was lower than the price of the same song on iTunes, even if iPods and Zunes had the same price, the demand for Zunes would increase, and the demand for iPods would decrease.

At the end of the chapter, we use the concepts covered in the chapter to answer the questions. Here are examples of the topics we cover in the new "Economics in Your Life" feature:

- Will you buy an iPod or a Zune? (**Chapter 3**, "Where Prices Come From: The Interaction of Demand and Supply")
- Does rent control make it easier to find an affordable apartment? (**Chapter 4**, "Economic Efficiency, Government Price Setting, and Taxes")
- What's the best country to work in? (**Chapter 7**, "GDP: Measuring Total Production and Income")
- Would you be better off without China? (**Chapter 10**, "Long-Run Economic Growth: Sources and Policies")
- Is an employer likely to cut your pay during a recession? (**Chapter 12**, "Aggregate Demand and Aggregate Supply Analysis")

Solved Problems

As we all know, many students have great difficulty handling applied economics problems. We help students overcome this hurdle by including two or three worked-out problems tied to select chapter-opening learning objectives. Our goals are to keep students focused on the main ideas of each chapter and to give students a model of how to solve an economic problem by breaking it down step by step. There are additional exercises in the end-of-chapter *Problems and Applications* section tied to every *Solved Problem.*

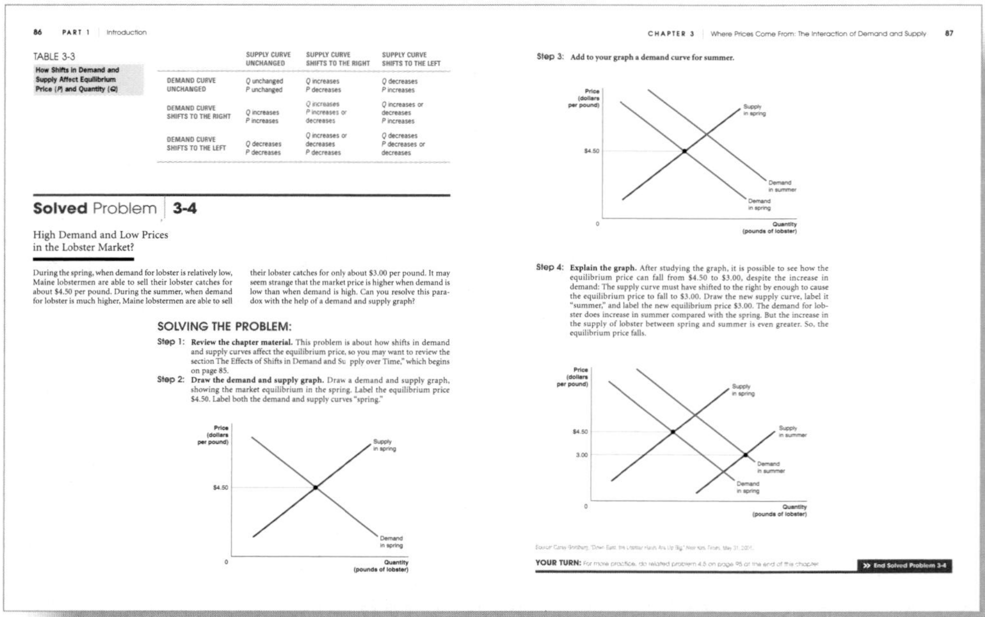

86 PART 1 | Introduction

TABLE 3-3 **How Shifts in Demand and Supply Affect Equilibrium Price (P) and Quantity (Q)**

	SUPPLY CURVE UNCHANGED	SUPPLY CURVE SHIFTS TO THE RIGHT	SUPPLY CURVE SHIFTS TO THE LEFT
DEMAND CURVE UNCHANGED	Q unchanged P unchanged	Q increases P decreases	Q decreases P increases
DEMAND CURVE SHIFTS TO THE RIGHT	Q increases P increases	Q increases P increases or decreases	Q increases or decreases P increases
DEMAND CURVE SHIFTS TO THE LEFT	Q decreases P decreases	Q increases or decreases P decreases	Q decreases P decreases or decreases

Solved Problem | 3-4

High Demand and Low Prices in the Lobster Market?

During the spring, when demand for lobster is relatively low, Maine lobstermen are able to sell their lobster catches for about $4.50 per pound. During the summer, when demand for lobster is much higher, Maine lobstermen are able to sell their lobster catches for only about $3.00 per pound. It may seem strange that the market price is higher when demand is low than when demand is high. Can you resolve this paradox with the help of a demand and supply graph?

SOLVING THE PROBLEM:

Step 1: **Review the chapter material.** This problem is about how shifts in demand and supply curves affect the equilibrium price, so you may want to review the section The Effects of Shifts in Demand and Su pply over Time," which begins on page 85.

Step 2: **Draw the demand and supply graph.** Draw a demand and supply graph, showing the market equilibrium in the spring. Label the equilibrium price $4.50. Label both the demand and supply curves "spring."

CHAPTER 3 | Where Prices Come From: The Interaction of Demand and Supply 87

Step 3: **Add to your graph a demand curve for summer.**

Step 4: **Explain the graph.** After studying the graph, it is possible to see how the equilibrium price can fall from $4.50 to $3.00, despite the increase in demand: The supply curve must have shifted to the right by enough to cause the equilibrium price to fall to $3.00. Draw the new supply curve, label it "summer," and label the new equilibrium price $3.00. The demand for lobster does increase in summer compared with the spring. But the increase in the supply of lobster between spring and summer is even greater. So, the equilibrium price falls.

YOUR TURN: For more practice, do related problem 4.5 on page 95 at the end of this chapter.

>> End Solved Problem 3-4

Additional *Solved Problems* appear in the following areas:

- The *Instructor's Manual*
- PowerPoint slides
- The print Study Guide
- The Test Item File includes problems tied to the *Solved Problems* in the main book.

Don't Let This Happen to You!

We know from many years of teaching which concepts students find most difficult. Each chapter contains a box feature called *Don't Let This Happen to You!* that alerts students to the most common pitfalls in that chapter's material. We follow up with a related question in the end-of-chapter *Problems and Applications* section.

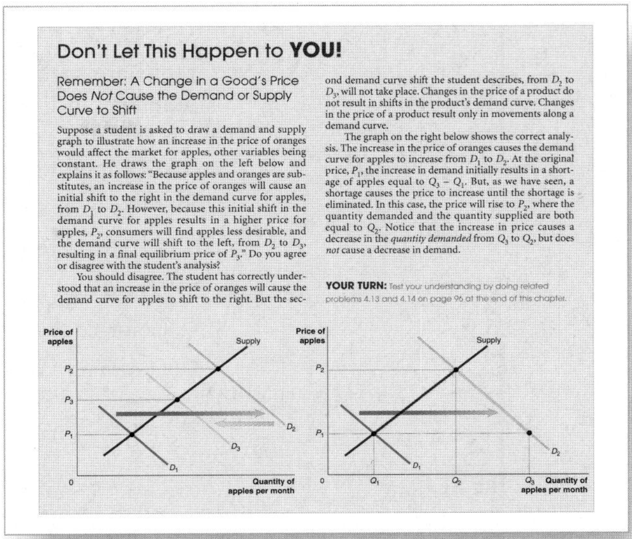

Don't Let This Happen to **YOU!**

Remember: A Change in a Good's Price Does *Not* Cause the Demand or Supply Curve to Shift

Suppose a student is asked to draw a demand and supply graph to illustrate how an increase in the price of oranges would affect the market for apples, other variables being constant. He draws the graph on the left below and explains it as follows: "Because apples and oranges are substitutes, an increase in the price of oranges will cause an initial shift to the right in the demand curve for apples, from D_1 to D_2. However, because this initial shift in the demand curve for apples results in a higher price for apples, P_2, consumers will find apples less desirable, and the demand curve will shift to the left, from D_2 to D_3, resulting in a final equilibrium price of P_3." Do you agree or disagree with the student's analysis?

You should disagree. The student has correctly understood that an increase in the price of oranges will cause the demand curve for apples to shift to the right. But the second demand curve shift the student describes, from D_2 to D_3, will not take place. Changes in the price of a product do not result in shifts in the product's demand curve. Changes in the price of a product result only in movements along a demand curve.

The graph on the right below shows the correct analysis. The increase in the price of oranges causes the demand curve for apples to increase from D_1 to D_2. At the original price, P_1, the increase in demand initially results in a shortage of apples equal to $Q_3 - Q_1$. But, as we have seen, a shortage causes the price to increase until the shortage is eliminated. In this case, the price will rise to P_2, where the quantity demanded and the quantity supplied are both equal to Q_2. Notice that the increase in price causes a decrease in the *quantity demanded* from Q_3 to Q_2, but does *not* cause a decrease in demand.

YOUR TURN: Test your understanding by doing related problems 4.13 and 4.14 on page 96 at the end of this chapter.

Making the Connection

Each chapter includes two to four *Making the Connection* features that present real-world reinforcement of key concepts and help students learn how to interpret what they read on the Web or in newspapers. Most *Making the Connection* features use relevant, stimulating, and provocative news stories focused on businesses and policy issues. One-third of the *Making the Connection* features are new to this edition, and most others have been updated. Several *Making the Connection* features discuss health care, which remains a pressing policy issue. Each *Making the Connection* has at least one supporting end-of-chapter problem to allow students to test their understanding of the topic discussed. Here are some of the new *Making the Connection* features:

- The Market System in Action: How Do You Make an iPod? **Chapter 2**, "Trade-offs, Comparative Advantage, and the Market System")
- How Apple Computer Inc. Forecasts the Demand for Consumer Electronics (**Chapter 3**, "Where Prices Come From: The Interaction of Demand and Supply")
- How Expanding International Trade Has Helped Boeing (**Chapter 6**,")
- Do Oil Shocks Still Cause Recessions? (**Chapter 12**, "Aggregate Demand and Aggregate Supply Analysis")
- In a Global Economy, How Can You Tell the Imports from the Domestic Goods? (**Chapter 12**)
- Do We Still Need the Penny? (**Chapter 13**, "Money, Banks, and the Federal Reserve System")
- How Does the Fed Measure Inflation? (**Chapter 14**, "Monetary Policy")
- Is Losing Your Job Good for Your Health? (**Chapter 15**, "Fiscal Policy")
- Was the Euro Undervalued or Overvalued in 2007? (**Chapter 18**, "The International Financial System")

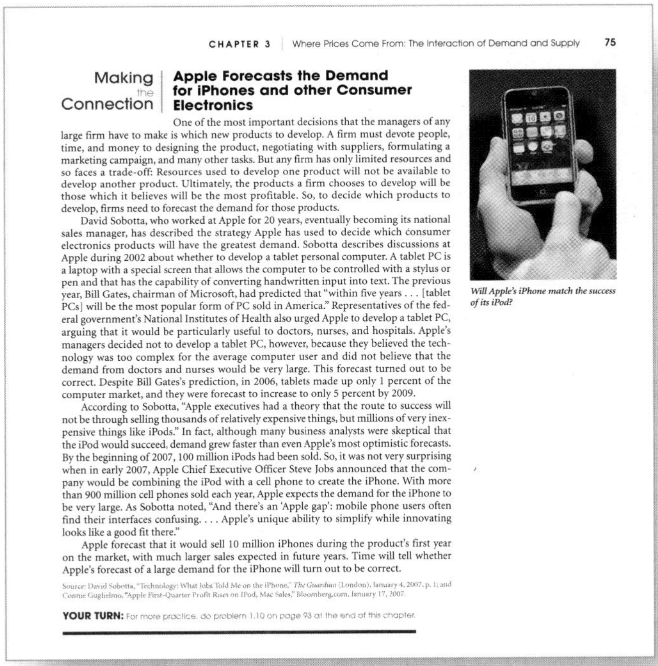

CHAPTER 3 | Where Prices Come From: The Interaction of Demand and Supply 75

Making the Connection | **Apple Forecasts the Demand for iPhones and other Consumer Electronics**

One of the most important decisions that the managers of any large firm have to make is which new products to develop. A firm must devote people, time, and money to designing the product, negotiating with suppliers, formulating a marketing campaign, and many other tasks. But any firm has only limited resources and so faces a trade-off: Resources used to develop one product will not be available to develop another product. Ultimately, the products a firm chooses to develop will be those which it believes will be the most profitable. So, to decide which products to develop, firms need to forecast the demand for those products.

David Sobotta, who worked at Apple for 20 years, eventually becoming its national sales manager, has described the strategy Apple has used to decide which consumer electronics products will have the greatest demand. Sobotta describes discussions at Apple during 2002 about whether to develop a tablet personal computer. A tablet PC is a laptop with a special screen that allows the computer to be controlled with a stylus or pen and that has the capability of converting handwritten input into text. The previous year, Bill Gates, chairman of Microsoft, had predicted that "within five years . . . [tablet PCs] will be the most popular form of PC sold in America." Representatives of the federal government's National Institutes of Health also urged Apple to develop a tablet PC, arguing that it would be particularly useful to doctors, nurses, and hospitals. Apple's managers decided not to develop a tablet PC, however, because they believed the technology was too complex for the average computer user and did not believe that the demand from doctors and nurses would be very large. This forecast turned out to be correct. Despite Bill Gates's prediction, in 2006, tablets made up only 1 percent of the computer market, and they were forecast to increase to only 5 percent by 2009.

According to Sobotta, "Apple executives had a theory that the route to success will not be through selling thousands of relatively expensive things, but millions of very inexpensive things like iPods." In fact, although many business analysts were skeptical that the iPod would succeed, demand grew faster than even Apple's most optimistic forecasts. By the beginning of 2007, 100 million iPods had been sold. So, it was not very surprising when in early 2007, Apple Chief Executive Officer Steve Jobs announced that the company would be combining the iPod with a cell phone to create the iPhone. With more than 900 million cell phones sold each year, Apple expects the demand for the iPhone to be very large. As Sobotta noted, "And there's an 'Apple gap': mobile phone users often find their interfaces confusing. . . . Apple's unique ability to simplify while innovating looks like a good fit there."

Apple forecast that it would sell 10 million iPhones during the product's first year on the market, with much larger sales expected in future years. Time will tell whether Apple's forecast of a large demand for the iPhone will turn out to be correct.

Source: David Sobotta, "Technology: What Jobs Told Me on the iPhone," *The Guardian* (London), January 4, 2007, p. 1; and Connie Guglielmo, "Apple First-Quarter Profit Rises on IPod, Mac Sales," Bloomberg.com, January 17, 2007.

YOUR TURN: For more practice, do problem 1.10 on page 93 at the end of this chapter.

Will Apple's iPhone match the success of its iPod?

Graphs and Summary Tables

Graphs are an indispensable part of the principles of economics course but are a major stumbling block for many students. Every chapter except Chapter 1 includes end-of-chapter problems that require students to draw, read, and interpret graphs. Interactive graphing exercises appear on the book's supporting Web site. We use four devices to help students read and interpret graphs:

1. Detailed captions
2. Boxed notes
3. Color-coded curves
4. Summary tables with graphs

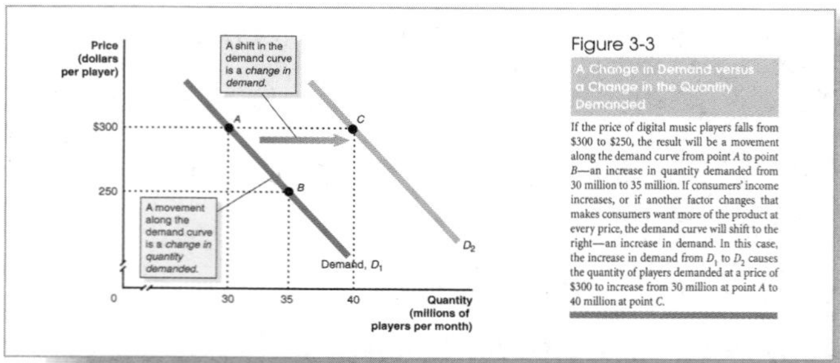

Price (dollars per player)
A shift in the demand curve is a *change in demand*.
A movement along the demand curve is a *change in quantity demanded*.
$300
250
0
30
35
40
Demand, D_1
D_2
Quantity (millions of players per month)
Figure 3-3
A Change in Demand versus a Change in the Quantity Demanded
If the price of digital music players falls from $300 to $250, the result will be a movement along the demand curve from point A to point B—an increase in quantity demanded from 30 million to 35 million. If consumers' income increases, or if another factor changes that makes consumers want more of the product at every price, the demand curve will shift to the right—an increase in demand. In this case, the increase in demand from D_1 to D_2 causes the quantity of players demanded at a price of $300 to increase from 30 million at point A to 40 million at point C.

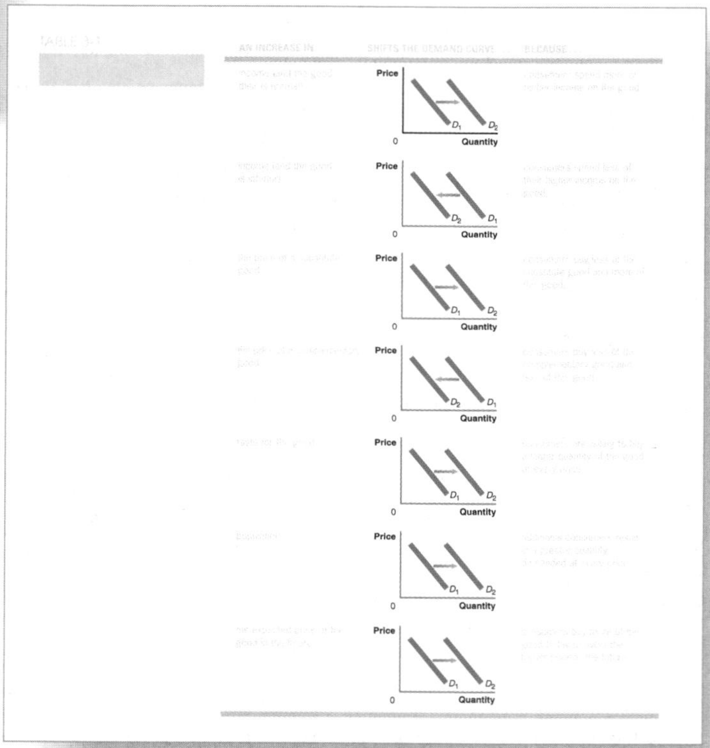

Integrated Supplements

The authors and Prentice Hall have worked together to integrate the text, print, and media resources to make teaching and learning easier. The process of revising the supplements began with the Test Item File Review Board, which consisted of 30 professors who reviewed each question in the first edition's Test Item files. Many of these professors became part of the second edition team. We are grateful to both the Test Item Review Board and our creative and generous supplement authors. They met with us for a two-day meeting to discuss ideas on how to improve the supplements and how to ensure that they are consistent with the main book. Ben Paris, Prentice Hall's Executive Producer of Assessment Programs, evaluated test bank questions and provided the test bank authors guidance on how to write effective questions.

The supplement author team from left to right: Iordanis Petsas, Cathleen Leue, Fernando Quijano, Yvonn Quijano, Ed Scahill, main book authors Glenn Hubbard and Tony O'Brien, Kelly Blanchard, and Ratha Ramoo. Not pictured here are Robert Gillette, Wendine Thompson-Dawson, Nick Noble, Robert Holland, Rebecca Stein, and Jim Lee.

Resources for the Instructor

Instructor's Manual

Iordanis Petsas of the University of Scranton prepared the *Instructor's Manual* to accompany macroeconomics. This supplement includes chapter-by-chapter summaries, learning objectives, extended examples and class exercises, teaching outlines incorporating key terms and definitions, teaching tips, topics for class discussion, new *Solved Problems*, new *Making the Connections*, new *Economics in Your Life* scenarios, and solutions to all review questions and problems in the book. The *Instructor's Manual* is available in print and for download from the Instructor's Resource Center. Jim Lee of Texas A&M University and the authors prepared the solutions to the end-of-chapter review questions and problems.

Two Test Banks

Cathleen Leue of the University of Oregon, Robert Gillette of the University of Kentucky, Kelly Blanchard of Purdue University, and Robert Holland of Purdue University prepared two test banks to accompany macroeconomics. Each test bank includes 2,000 multiple-choice questions, true/false, short-answer, and graphing questions. There are questions to support each key feature in the book. Test questions are annotated with the following information:

- **Difficulty:** 1 for straight recall, 2 for some analysis, 3 for complex analysis
- **Type:** multiple-choice, true/false, short-answer, essay
- **Topic:** the term or concept the question supports

- **Skill:** fact, definition, analytical, conceptual
- **Learning objective**
- **AACSB** (see description that follows)
- **Page number**
- **Special feature in the main book:** chapter-opening business example, *Economics in Your Life, Solved Problem, Making the Connection, Don't Let this Happen to You!* and *An Inside Look.*

The test banks were checked for accuracy by Thomas C. Kinnaman of Bucknell University; Randy Methenitis of Richland College; Norman C. Miller of Miami University; Brian Rosario of the University of California, Davis; Rachel Small of the University of Colorado, Boulder

AACSB

The Association to Advance Collegiate Schools of Business (AACSB)

The test bank authors have connected select test bank questions to the general knowledge and skill guidelines found in the AACSB standards.

What is the AACSB?

AACSB is a not-for-profit corporation of educational institutions, corporations, and other organizations devoted to the promotion and improvement of higher education in business administration and accounting. A collegiate institution offering degrees in business administration or accounting may volunteer for AACSB accreditation review. The AACSB makes initial accreditation decisions and conducts periodic reviews to promote continuous quality improvement in management education. Pearson Education is a proud member of the AACSB and is pleased to provide advice to help you apply AACSB Learning Standards.

What are AACSB Learning Standards?

One of the criteria for AACSB accreditation is the quality of the curricula. Although no specific courses are required, the AACSB expects a curriculum to include learning experiences in such areas as:

- Communication
- Ethical Reasoning
- Analytic Skills
- Use of Information Technology
- Multicultural and Diversity Reflective Thinking

These six categories are AACSB Learning Standards. Questions that test skills relevant to these standards are tagged with the appropriate standard. For example, a question testing the moral questions associated with externalities would receive the Ethical Reasoning tag.

How Can Instructors Use the AACSB Tags?

Tagged questions help you measure whether students are grasping the course content that aligns with the AACSB guidelines noted above. In addition, the tagged questions may help instructors identify potential applications of these skills. This in turn may suggest enrichment activities or other educational experiences to help students achieve these skills.

TestGen

The computerized TestGen package allows instructors to customize, save, and generate classroom tests. The test program permits instructors to edit, add, or delete questions from the test banks; edit existing graphics and create new graphics; analyze test results; and organize a database of tests and student results. This software allows for extensive flexibility and ease of use. It provides many options for organizing and displaying tests, along with search and sort features. The software and the test banks can be downloaded from the Instructor's Resource Center (www.prenhall.com/hubbard).

Acetates

All figures and tables from the text are reproduced and provided as full-page, four-color acetates.

PowerPoint Lecture Presentation

There are two sets of PowerPoint slides, prepared by Fernando and Yvonn Quijano, for instructors to use:

1. A comprehensive set of PowerPoint slides that can be used by instructors for class presentations or by students for lecture preview or review. The presentation includes all the graphs, tables, and equations in the textbook. It displays figures in step-by-step, automated mode, using a single click per graph curve.
2. A comprehensive set of PowerPoint slides with Classroom Response Systems (CRS) questions built in so instructors can incorporate CRS "clickers" into their classroom lectures. For more information on Prentice Hall's partnership with CRS, see the facing page.

Instructors may download these PowerPoint presentations from the Instructor's Resource Center (www.prenhall.com/hubbard).

Instructor's Resource CD-ROM

The Instructor's Resource CD-ROM contains all the faculty and student resources that support this text. Instructors have the ability to access and edit the *Instructor's Manuals*, test banks, and PowerPoint presentations. By simply clicking on a chapter or searching for a keyword, faculty can access an interactive library of resources. Faculty can pick and choose from the various supplements and export them to their hard drives.

Classroom Response Systems

Classroom Response Systems (CRS) is an exciting new wireless polling technology that makes large and small classrooms even more interactive because it enables instructors to pose questions to their students, record results, and display the results instantly. Students can answer questions easily, using compact remote-control transmitters. Prentice Hall has partnerships with leading classroom response systems providers and can show you everything you need to know about setting up and using a CRS system. We'll provide the classroom hardware, text-specific PowerPoint slides, software, and support, and we'll also show you how your students can benefit! Learn more at www.prenhall.com/crs.

Blackboard and WebCT Course Content

Prentice Hall offers fully customizable course content for the Blackboard and WebCT Course Management Systems.

Resources for the Student

Study Guide

Nicholas Noble of Miami University prepared the study guide to accompany macroeconomics. The study guide reinforces the textbook and provides students with the following:

- Chapter summary
- Discussion of each learning objective
- Section-by-section review of the concepts presented

- Helpful study hints
- Additional *Solved Problems* to supplement those in the text
- Key terms with definitions
- A self-test, including 40 multiple-choice questions, plus a number of short-answer and true/false questions, with accompanying answers and explanations

Companion Web Site

The free companion Web site, www.prenhall.com/hubbard, gives students access to an interactive study guide that provides instant feedback, economics updates, student PowerPoint slides, and many other resources to promote success in the principles of economics course.

PowerPoint Slides

For student use as a study aide or note-taking guide, PowerPoint slides, prepared by Fernando and Yvonn Quijano, may be downloaded from the companion Web site, at www.prenhall.com/hubbard. The slides include:

- All graphs, tables, and equations in the text
- Figures in step-by-step, automated mode, using a single click per graph curve
- End-of-chapter key terms with hyperlinks to relevant slides

CourseSmart
Learn Smart. Choose Smart.

CourseSmart is an exciting new *choice* for students looking to save money. As an alternative to purchasing the print textbook, students can purchase an electronic version of the same content and save up to 50 percent off the suggested list price of the print text. With a CourseSmart etextbook, students can search the text, make notes online, print out reading assignments that incorporate lecture notes, and bookmark important passages for later review. For more information, or to purchase access to the CourseSmart eTextbook, visit www.coursesmart.com.

vango notes
Hear it. Get it.
www.vangonotes.com

Vango Notes

Study on the go with VangoNotes (www.VangoNotes.com), detailed chapter reviews in downloadable MP3 format. Now, wherever you are and whatever you're doing, you can study on the go by listening to the following for each chapter of your textbook:

- **Big Ideas:** Your "need to know" for each chapter
- **Practice Questions:** A gut check for the Big Ideas—tells you if you need to keep studying
- **Key Terms:** Audio "flashcards"—help you review key concepts and terms
- **Rapid Review:** Quick-drill sessions—use it right before your test

VangoNotes are **flexible**: Download all the material (or only the chapters you need) directly to your player. And *VangoNotes* are **efficient**: Use them in your car, at the gym, walking to class, wherever you go. So get yours today, and get studying.

Get Ahead of the Curve

For the Instructor

MyEconLab is an online course management, testing, and tutorial resource. Instructors can choose how much, or how little, time to spend setting up and using MyEconLab.

Each chapter contains two Sample Tests, Study Plan Exercises, and Tutorial Resources. Student use of these materials requires no initial set-up by their instructor. The online Gradebook records each student's performance and time spent on the Tests and Study Plan and generates reports by student or by chapter.

Instructors can assign Tests, Quizzes, and Homework in MyEconLab using four resources:

- pre-loaded Sample Test questions
- Problems similar to the end-of-chapter problems
- Test Bank questions
- Self-authored questions using Econ Exercise Builder

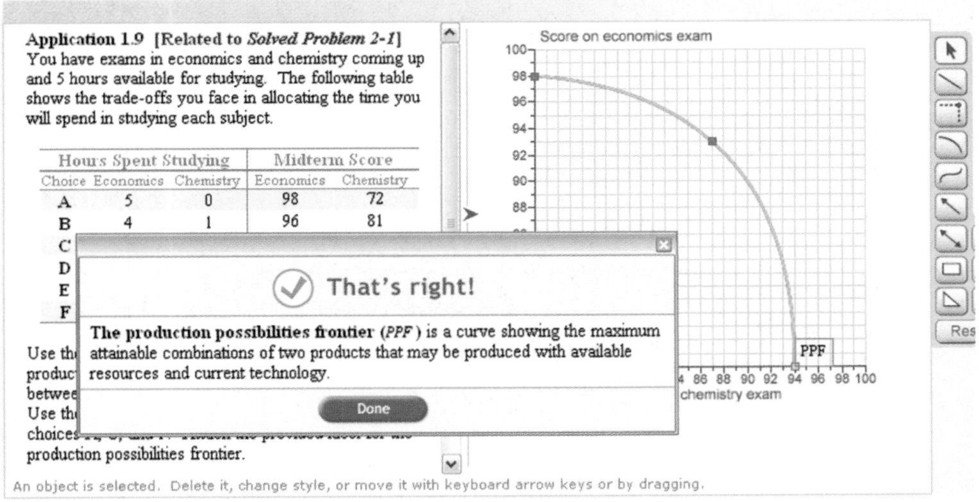

Exercises use multiple-choice, graph drawing, and free-response items, many of which are generated algorithmically so that they present differently each time a student works them.

MyEconLab grades every problem, even those with graphs. When working homework exercises students receive immediate feedback with links to additional learning tools.

Customization and Communication

MyEconLab in CourseCompass provides additional optional customization and communication tools. Instructors who teach distance-learning courses or very large lecture sections find the CourseCompass format useful because they can upload course documents and assignments, customize the order of chapters, and use communication features such as Digital Dropbox and Discussion Board.

For the Student

MyEconLab puts students in control of their learning through a collection of testing, practice, and study tools tied to the online, interactive version of the textbook and other medial resources.

Within MyEconLab's structured environment, students practice what they learn, test their understanding, and pursue a personalized Study Plan generated from their performance on Sample Tests and tests created by their instructors. At the core of MyEconLab are the following features:

- Sample Tests, two per chapter
- Personal Study Plan
- Tutorial Instruction
- Graphing Tool

Sample Tests

Two Sample Tests for each chapter are pre-loaded in MyEconLab, enabling students to practice what they have learned, test their understanding, and identify areas in which they need to do further work. Students can study on their own, or they can complete assignments created by their instructor.

Personal Study Plan

Based on a student's performance on tests, MyEconLab generates a personal Study Plan that shows where he or she needs further study. The Study Plan consists of a series of additional practice exercises with detailed feedback and guided solutions and keyed to other tutorial resources.

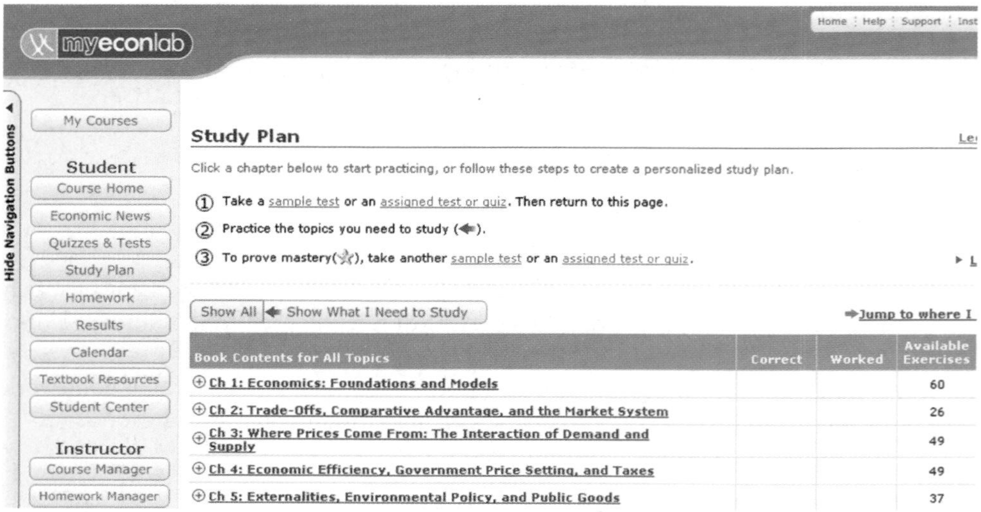

Tutorial Instruction

Launched from many of the exercises in the Study Plan, MyEconLab provides tutorial instruction in the form of step-by-step solutions and other media-based explanations.

Graphing Tool

A graphing tool is integrated into the Tests and Study Plan exercises to enable students to make and manipulate graphs. This feature helps students understand how concepts, numbers, and graphs connect.

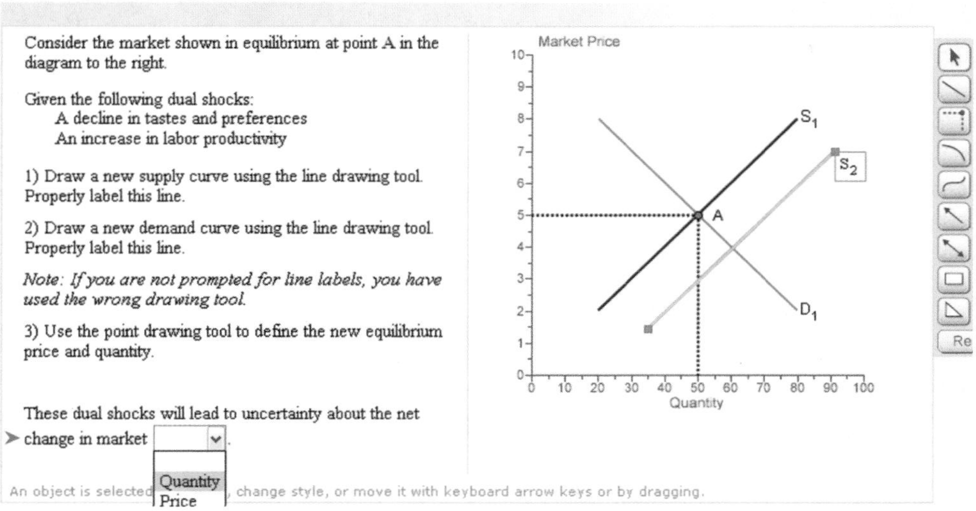

Additional MyEconLab Tools

MyEconLab also includes the following additional features:

1. **Economics in the News**—weekly news article updates during the school year of news items with links to sources for further reading and discussion questions
2. **eText**—While working in the Study Plan or completing homework assignments, part of the tutorial resources available is a link directly to the relevant page of the text so the student can review the appropriate material to help them complete the exercise.
3. **Glossary**—a searchable version of the textbook glossary with additional examples and links to related terms
4. **Glossary Flashcards**—every key term is available as a flashcard, allowing students to quiz themselves on vocabulary from one or more chapters at a time.
5. **Ask the Author**—email economic related questions to the author
6. **Research Navigator (CourseCompass version only)**—extensive help on the research process and four exclusive databases of credible and reliable source material, including *The New York Times*, the *Financial Times*, and peer-reviewed journals

MyEconLab content has been created through the efforts of: Chris Annala, State University of New York–Geneseo; Charles Baum, Middle Tennessee State University; Sarah Ghosh, University of Scranton; Chris Kauffman, University of Tennessee–Knoxville; Russell Kellogg, University of Colorado–Denver; Noel Lotz, Middle Tennessee State University; Woo Jung, University of Colorado; Katherine McCann, University of Delaware; Christine Polek, University of Massachusetts–Boston; Leonie L. Stone, State University of New York–Geneseo; Bert G. Wheeler, Cedarville University; and Douglas A. Ruby, Pearson Education.

Consultant Board, Accuracy Review Board, and Reviewers

The guidance and recommendations of the following professors helped us develop the revision plans for this new edition and the supplement package. While we could not incorporate every suggestion from every consultant board member, reviewer, or accuracy checker, we do thank each and every one of you, and acknowledge that your feedback was indispensable in developing this text. We greatly appreciate your assistance in making this the best text it could be—you have helped teach a whole new generation of students about the exciting world of economics.

Consultant Board

Kate Antonovics, University of California–San Diego
Robert Beekman, University of Tampa
Valerie Bencivenga, University of Texas–Austin
Kelly Blanchard, Purdue University
Robert Gillette, University of Kentucky
Robert Godby, University of Wyoming
William Goffe, State University of New York–Oswego
Jane S. Himarios, University of Texas–Arlington
Michael Potepan, San Francisco State University
Robert Whaples, Wake Forest University
Jonathan B. Wight, University of Richmond

Accuracy Review Board

Our accuracy checkers did a particularly painstaking and thorough job of helping us proof the graphs, equations, and features of the second edition of the text and the supplements. We are grateful for their time and commitment:

Fatma Abdel-Raouf, Goldey-Beacom College
Mohammad S. Bajwa, Northampton Community College
Hamid Bastin, Shippensburg University
Kelly Blanchard, Purdue University
Don Bumpass, Sam Houston State University
Mark S. Chester, Reading Area Community College
Kenny Christianson, Binghamton University
Ishita Edwards, Oxnard College
Harry Ellis, University of North Texas
Can Erbil, Brandeis University
Marc Fusaro, East Carolina University
Sarah Ghosh, University of Scranton
Maria Giuili, Diablo Valley College
Carol Hogan, University of Michigan–Dearborn
Aaron Jackson, Bentley College
Nancy Jianakoplos, Colorado State University
Thomas C. Kinnaman, Bucknell University
Mary K. Knudson, University of Iowa
Stephan Kroll, California State University–Sacramento
Tony Lima, California State University–Hayward
Randy Methenitis, Richland College
Norman C. Miller, Miami University
Michael Potepan, San Francisco State University
Mary L. Pranzo, California State University–Fresno
Brian Rosario, University of California–Davis
Joseph M. Santos, South Dakota State University
Mark V. Siegler, California State University–Sacramento
Rachel Small, University of Colorado–Boulder
Stephen Smith, Bakersfield College
Rajeev Sooreea, Pennsylvania State University–Altoona
Rebecca Stein, University of Pennsylvania
Wendine Thompson-Dawson, Monmouth College
Robert Whaples, Wake Forest University

Reviewers

The guidance and thoughtful recommendations of many professors helped us develop and implement a revision plan that expanded the book's content, improved the figures, and strengthened assessment features. We extend special thanks to Joseph Santos of South Dakota State University, Matthew Rafferty of Quinnipiac University, and David Eaton of Murray State University for helping us revise the chapter openers and *Inside Look* features. We are grateful for the comments and many helpful suggestions received from the following reviewers:

ALABAMA

Doris Bennett, Jacksonville State University
Harold W. Elder, University of Alabama–Tuscaloosa
Wanda Hudson, Alabama Southern Community College

ARIZONA

Price Fishback, University of Arizona

ARKANSAS

Jerry Crawford, Arkansas State University

CALIFORNIA
Maneeza Aminy, Golden Gate University
Becca Arnold, Mesa College
Anoshua Chaudhuri, San Francisco State University
Jose Esteban, Palomar College
Craig Gallet, California State University–Sacramento
Maria Giuili, Diablo Valley College
Lisa Grobar, California State University–Long Beach
Dewey Heinsma, Mt. San Jacinto Community College
Jessica Howell, California State University–Sacramento
Greg Hunter, California State University–Pomona
Jonathan Kaplan, California State University–Sacramento
Philip King, San Francisco State University
Lori Kletzer, University of California, Santa Cruz
Stephan Kroll, California State University–Sacramento
David Lang, California State University–Sacramento
Carsten Lange, California State Polytechnic University–Pomona
Rose LeMont, Modesto Junior College
Kristen Monaco, California State University–Long Beach
Mary L. Pranzo, California State University–Fresno
Scott J. Sambucci, California State University–East Bay
Stephen Smith, Bakersfield College
Lea Templer, College of the Canyons
Kristin Vangaasbeck, California State University–Sacramento
Michael Visser, Sonoma State University
Kevin Young, Diablo Valley College
COLORADO
Dale DeBoer, University of Colorado–Colorado Springs
William G. Mertens, University of Colorado–Boulder
Rachael Small, University of Colorado–Boulder
CONNECTICUT
Matthew Rafferty, Quinnipiac University
DELAWARE
Fatma Abdel-Raouf, Goldey-Beacom College
Ali Ataiifar, Delaware County Community College
FLORIDA
Herman Baine, Broward Community College
Robert L. Beekman, University of Tampa
Eric P. Chiang, Florida Atlantic University
Brad Kamp, University of South Florida
Brian Kench, University of Tampa
Barbara A. Moore, University of Central Florida
Deborah Paige, Santa Fe Community College
Bob Potter, University of Central Florida
Zhiguang Wang, Florida International University
Joan Wiggenhorn, Barry University
GEORGIA
Constantin Ogloblin, Georgia Southern University
Dr. Greg Okoro, Georgia Perimeter College–Clarkston
ILLINOIS
Ali Akarca, University of Illinois at Chicago
Zsolt Becsi, Southern Illinois University–Carbondale
David Gordon, Illinois Valley Community College
Rosa Lea Danielson, College of DuPage
Scott Gilbert, Southern Illinois University
Rajeev K. Goel, Illinois State University
Alan Grant, Eastern Illinois University
Alice Melkumian, Western Illinois University
Jeff Reynolds, Northern Illinois University
Thomas R. Sadler, Western Illinois University
Kevin Sylwester, Southern Illinois University–Carbondale
Wendine Thompson-Dawson, Monmouth College
INDIANA
Robert B. Harris, Indiana University–Purdue University–Indianapolis
James K. Self, Indiana University–Bloomington
Arun K. Srinivasan, Indiana University–Southeast Campus
IOWA
John Solow, University or Iowa
Jonathan Warner, Dordt College
KANSAS
Guatam Bhattacharya, University of Kansas
Dipak Ghosh, Emporia State University
Alan Grant, Baker University
Wayne Oberle, St. Ambrose University
Martin Perline, Wichita State University
Joel Potter, Kansas State University
Joshua Rosenbloom, University of Kansas
Shane Sanders, Kansas State University
Bhavneet Walia, Kansas State University
KENTUCKY
David Eaton, Murray State University
Ann Eike, University of Kentucky
Barry Haworth, University of Louisville
Donna Ingram, Eastern Kentucky University
Waithaka Iraki, Kentucky State University
Martin Milkman, Murray State University
David Shideler, Murray State University
LOUISIANA
Sung Chul No, Southern University and A&M College
MARYLAND
Jill Caviglia-Harris, Salisbury University
Dustin Chambers, Salisbury University
Karl Einolf, Mount Saint Mary's University
Bruce Madariaga, Montgomery College
Gretchen Mester, Anne Arundel Community College
MASSACHUSETTS
Michael Enz, Western New England College
Can Erbil, Brandeis University
Lou Foglia, Suffolk University

Aaron Jackson, Bentley College
Ahmad Saranjam, Bridgewater State College
Howard Shore, Bentley College
Janet Thomas, Bentley College

MICHIGAN
Eric Beckman, Delta College
Jared Boyd, Henry Ford Community College
Victor Claar, Hope College
Dr. Sonia Dalmia, Grand Valley State University
Daniel Giedeman, Grand Valley State University
Gregg Heidebrink, Washtenaw Community College
Carol Hogan, University of Michigan–Dearborn
Marek Kolar, Delta College
Susan J. Linz, Michigan State University
James Luke, Lansing Community College
Ilir Miteza, University of Michigan–Dearborn
Norman P. Obst, Michigan State University
Laudo M. Ogura, Grand Valley State University
Michael J. Ryan, Western Michigan University
Charles A. Stull, Kalamazoo College
Michael J. Twomey, University of Michigan–Dearborn
Mark Wheeler, Western Michigan University
Wendy Wysocki, Monroe County Community College

MINNESOTA
Mary Edwards, Saint Cloud State University
Phillip J. Grossman, Saint Cloud State University
David J. O'Hara, Metropolitan State University–Minneapolis
Ken Rebeck, Saint Cloud State University
Kwang Woo (Ken) Park, Minnesota State University–Mankato

MISSISSIPPI
Becky Campbell, Mississippi State University

MISSOURI
Chris Azevedo, University of Central Missouri
Ariel Belasen, Saint Louis University
Catherine Chambers, University of Central Missouri
Paul Chambers, University of Central Missouri
Ben Collier, Northwest Missouri State University
John R. Crooker, University of Central Missouri
Mark Karscig, Central Missouri State University
Nicholas D. Peppes, Saint Louis Community College–Forest Park

MONTANA
Jeff Bookwalter, University of Montana–Missoula
Agnieszka Bielinska-Kwapisz, Montana State University–Bozeman

NEBRASKA
Allan Jenkins, University of Nebraska–Kearney
Kim Sosin, University of Nebraska–Omaha

NEVADA
Bernard Malamud, University of Nevada–Las Vegas

NEW JERSEY
Giuliana Campanelli-Andreopoulos, William Paterson University
Donna Thompson, Brookdale Community College

NEW MEXICO
Kate Krause, University of New Mexico
Curt Shepherd, University of New Mexico

NEW YORK
Seemi Ahmad, Dutchess Community College
Chris Annala, State University of New York–Geneseo
John Bockino, Suffolk County Community College–Ammerman
Sean Corcoran, New York University
Debra Dwyer, Stony Brook University
Glenn Gerstner, Saint John's University–Queens
Susan Glanz, Saint John's University–Queens
Leonie Stone, State University of New York–Geneseo

NORTH CAROLINA
Marc Fusaro, East Carolina University
Melissa Hendrickson, North Carolina State University
Jeff Sarbaum, University of North Carolina–Greensboro
Catherine Skura, Sandhills Community College

OHIO
Bolong Cao, Ohio University–Athens
Harley Gill, Ohio State University
Leroy Gill, Ohio State University
Steven Heubeck, Ohio State University
Ida A. Mirzaie, Ohio State University
Dennis C. O'Neill, University of Cincinnati
Joseph Palardy, Youngstown State University
Bert Wheeler, Cedarville University
Kathryn Wilson, Kent State University

OKLAHOMA
Ed Price, Oklahoma State University
Abdulhamid Sukar, Cameron University

PENNSYLVANIA
Bradley Andrew, Juniata College
Mohammad Bajwa, Northampton Community College
Howard Bodenhorn, Lafayette College
Milica Bookman, St Joseph's University
Eric Brucker, Widener University
Scott J. Dressler, Villanova University
Satyajit Ghosh, University of Scranton
Anthony Gyapong, Pennsylvania State University–Abington
Andrew Hill, Federal Reserve Bank of Philadelphia
James Jozefowicz, Indiana University of Pennsylvania
Stephanie Jozefowicz, Indiana University of Pennsylvania
Nicholas Karatjas, Indiana University of Pennsylvania
Mary Kelly, Villanova University
Thomas C. Kinnaman, Bucknell University
Christopher Magee, Bucknell University
Judy McDonald, Lehigh University

Ranganath Murthy, Bucknell University
Hong V. Nguyen, University of Scranton
Cristian Pardo, Saint Joseph's University
Rajeev Sooreea, Pennsylvania State University–Altoona
Rebecca Stein, University of Pennsylvania
Sandra Trejos, Clarion University
Ann Zech, Saint Joseph's University
Lei Zhu, West Chester University of Pennsylvania

RHODE ISLAND
Leonard Lardaro, University of Rhode Island
Nazma Latif-Zaman, Providence College

SOUTH CAROLINA
Calvin Blackwell, College of Charleston
Ward Hooker, Orangeburg-Calhoun Technical College
Woodrow W. Hughes, Jr., Converse College
John McArthur, Wofford College

SOUTH DAKOTA
Joseph M. Santos, South Dakota State University
Jason Zimmerman, South Dakota State University

TENNESSEE
Charles Baum, Middle Tennessee State University
Michael J. Gootzeit, University of Memphis

TEXAS
Carlos Aguilar, El Paso Community College
William Beaty, Tarleton State University
Klaus Becker Texas Tech University
Jack A. Bucco, Austin Community College–Northridge and Saint Edward's University
Don Bumpass, Sam Houston State University
Marilyn M. Butler, Sam Houston State University
Cesar Corredor, Texas A&M University
Patrick Crowley, Texas A&M University–Corpus Christi
Mark Frank, Sam Houston State University
Tina J. Harvell, Blinn College–Bryan Campus
Jane S. Himarios, University of Texas–Arlington
James Holcomb, University of Texas–El Paso
Jamal Husein, Angelo State University
Karen Johnson, Baylor University
Kathy Kelly, University of Texas–Arlington
Jim Lee, Texas A&M University–Corpus Christi
Ronnie W. Liggett, University of Texas–Arlington
Kimberly Mencken, Baylor University
Randy Methenitis, Richland College
Charles Newton, Houston Community College–Southwest College
Sara Saderion, Houston Community College–Southwest College
George E. Samuels, Sam Houston State University
Roger Wehr, University of Texas–Arlington
Jim Wollscheid, Texas A&M University–Kingsville
Dr. J. Christopher Wreh, I, North Central Texas College
David W. Yoskowitz, Texas A&M University–Corpus Christi
Inske Zandvliet, Brookhaven College

VERMONT
Nancy Brooks, University of Vermont

VIRGINIA
Philip Heap, James Madison University
George E. Hoffer, Virginia Commonwealth University
Oleg Korenok, Virginia Commonwealth University
Frances Lea, Germanna Community College
John Min, Northern Virginia Community College
Susanne Toney, Hampton University
George Zestos, Christopher Newport University

WASHINGTON
Stacey Jones, Seattle University
Dean Peterson, Seattle University

WISCONSIN
Marina Karabelas, Milwaukee Area Technical College
Elizabeth Sawyer Kelly, University of Wisconsin–Madison
John R. Stoll, University of Wisconsin–Green Bay

DISTRICT OF COLUMBIA
Michael Bradley, George Washington University
Colleen M. Callahan, American University

INTERNATIONAL
Minh Quang Dao, Carleton University–Ottawa, Canada

Previous Edition Class Testers, Accuracy Reviewers, and Consultants

Class Testers

We are grateful to both the professors who class tested manuscript of the first edition and their students for providing clear-cut recommendations on how to make chapters interesting, relevant, and comprehensive:

Charles A. Bennett, Gannon University
Anne E. Bresnock, University of California, Los Angeles and California State Polytechnic University–Pomona
Linda Childs-Leatherbury, Lincoln University, Pennsylvania
John Eastwood, Northern Arizona University
David Eaton, Murray State University
Paul Elgatian, St. Ambrose University
Patricia A. Freeman, Jackson State University
Robert Godby, University of Wyoming
Frank Gunter, Lehigh University
Ahmed Ispahani, University of LaVerne
Brendan Kennelly, Lehigh University and National University of Ireland–Galway
Ernest Massie, Franklin University
Carol McDonough, University of Massachusetts–Lowell
Shah Mehrabi, Montgomery College
Sharon Ryan, University of Missouri–Columbia
Bruce G. Webb, Gordon College
Madelyn Young, Converse College
Susan Zumas, Lehigh University

Accuracy Review Board

We are grateful to the following first edition accuracy checkers for their hard work on the book and supplements:

Kelly Hunt Blanchard, Purdue University
Harold Elder, University of Alabama
Marc Fusaro, East Carolina University
Robert Gillette, University of Kentucky
William L. Goffe, State University of New York–Oswego
Travis Hayes, University of Tennessee–Chattanooga
Anisul M. Islam, University of Houston–Downtown
Faik A. Koray, Louisiana State University
Tony Lima, California State University–Hayward
James A. Moreno, Blinn College
Matthew Rafferty, Quinnipiac University
Jeff Reynolds, Northern Illinois University
Brian Rosario, University of California–Davis
Joseph M. Santos, South Dakota State University
Edward Scahill, University of Scranton
Robert Whaples, Wake Forest University

Consultant Board

We received guidance during the first edition development at several critical junctures from a dedicated consultant board. We relied on the board for input on content, figure treatment, and design:

Susan Dadres, Southern Methodist University
Harry Ellis, Jr., University of North Texas
Robert Godby, University of Wyoming
William L. Goffe, State University of New York–Oswego
Donn M. Johnson, Quinnipiac University
Mark Karscig, Central Missouri State University
Jenny Minier, University of Kentucky
Nicholas Noble, Miami University
Matthew Rafferty, Quinnipiac University
Helen Roberts, University of Illinois–Chicago
Robert Rosenman, Washington State University
Joseph M. Santos, South Dakota State University
Martin C. Spechler, Indiana University–Purdue University–Indianapolis
Robert Whaples–Wake Forest University

Reviewers

The guidance and recommendations of the following professors helped us shape the first edition over the course of three years. We extend special thanks to Joseph Santos of South Dakota State University for helping prepare some of the *Inside Look* features and Robert Gillette of the University of Kentucky, Robert Whaples of Wake Forest University, Nicholas Noble of Miami University, and Lee Craig of North Carolina State University preparing some of the review questions and problems and applications that appear at the ends of chapters.

ALABAMA

Doris Bennett, Jacksonville State University
Harold W. Elder, University of Alabama–Tuscaloosa
James L. Swofford, University of Southern Alabama

ARIZONA
Doug Conway, Mesa Community College
John Eastwood, Northern Arizona University
Price Fishback, University of Arizona
CALIFORNIA
Renatte Adler, San Diego State University
Robert Bise, Orange Coast Community College
Victor Brajer, California State University–Fullerton
Anne E. Bresnock, University of California, Los Angeles and California State Polytechnic University–Pomona
David Brownstone, University of California, Irvine
Maureen Burton, California State Polytechnic University–Pomona
James G. Devine, Loyola Marymount University
Roger Frantz, San Diego State University
Andrew Gill, California State University–Fullerton
Lisa Grobar, California State University–Long Beach
Steve Hamilton, California State University–Fullerton
Ahmed Ispahani, University of LaVerne
George A. Jouganatos, California State University–Sacramento
Philip King, San Francisco State University–Chico
Don Leet, California State University–Fresno
Rose LeMont, Modesto Junior College
Solina Lindahl, California Polytechnic State University–San Luis Obispo
Kristen Monaco, California State University–Long Beach
W. Douglas Morgan, University of California, Santa Barbara
Joseph M. Pogodzinksi, San Jose State University
Michael J. Potepan, San Francisco State University
Ratha Ramoo, Diablo Valley College
Ariane Schauer, Marymount College
Frederica Shockley, California State University–Chico
Mark Siegler, California State University–Sacramento
Lisa Simon, California Polytechnic State University–San Louis Obispo
Rodney B. Swanson, University of California, Los Angeles
Kristin A. Van Gaasbeck, California State University–Sacramento
Anthony Zambelli, Cuyamaca College
COLORADO
Rhonda Corman, University of Northern Colorado
Dale DeBoer, University of Colorado–Colorado Springs
Murat Iyigun, University of Colorado at Boulder
Nancy Jianakoplos, Colorado State University
Jay Kaplan, University of Colorado–Boulder
Stephen Weiler, Colorado State University
CONNECTICUT
Christopher P. Ball, Quinnipiac University
Donn M. Johnson, Quinnipiac University
Judith Mills, Southern Connecticut State University
Matthew Rafferty, Quinnipiac University
DELAWARE
Fatma Abdel-Raouf, Goldey-Beacom College
Andrew T. Hill, University of Delaware
FLORIDA
Herm Baine, Broward Community College–Central
Martine Duchatelet, Barry University
Hadley Hartman, Santa Fe Community College
Richard Hawkins, University of West Florida
Barbara Moore, University of Central Florida
Augustine Nelson, University of Miami
Jamie Ortiz, Florida Atlantic University
Robert Pennington, University of Central Florida
Jerry Schwartz, Broward Community College–North
William Stronge, Florida Atlantic University
Nora Underwood, University of Central Florida
IDAHO
Don Holley, Boise State University
ILLINOIS
Teshome Abebe, Eastern Illinois University
Ali Akarca, University of Illinois–Chicago
James Bruehler, Eastern Illinois University
Louis Cain, Loyola University Chicago and Northwestern University
Rik Hafer, Southern Illinois University–Edwardsville
Alla A. Melkumian, Western Illinois University
Christopher Mushrush, Illinois State University
Jeff Reynolds, Northern Illinois University
Helen Roberts, University of Illinois–Chicago
Eric Schulz, Northwestern University
Charles Sicotte, Rock Valley Community College
Neil T. Skaggs, Illinois State University
Mark Witte, Northwestern University
Laurie Wolff, Southern Illinois University–Carbondale
Paula Worthington, Northwestern University
INDIANA
Kelly Blanchard, Purdue University
Cecil Bohanon, Ball State University
Thomas Gresik, University of Notre Dame
Fred Herschede, Indiana University–South Bend
James K. Self, Indiana University–Bloomington
Esther-Mirjam Sent, University of Notre Dame
Virginia Shingleton, Valparaiso University
Martin C. Spechler, Indiana University–Purdue University–Indianapolis
Geetha Suresh, Purdue University–West Lafayette
IOWA
Terry Alexander, Iowa State University
Paul Elgatian, St. Ambrose University
KANSAS
Jodi Messer Pelkowski, Wichita State University
Josh Rosenbloom, University of Kansas

KENTUCKY
Tom Cate, Northern Kentucky University
Nan-Ting Chou, University of Louisville
David Eaton, Murray State University
Robert Gillette, University of Kentucky
Hak Youn Kim, Western Kentucky University
Jenny Minier, University of Kentucky
John Vahaly, University of Louisville
LOUISIANA
Faik Koray, Louisiana State University
Paul Nelson, University of Louisiana–Monroe
Tammy Parker, University of Louisiana–Monroe
Wesley A. Payne, Delgado Community College
MASSACHUSETTS
William L. Casey, Jr., Babson College
Arthur Schiller Casimir, Western New England College
Michael Enz, Western New England College
Todd Idson, Boston University
Russell A. Janis, University of Massachusetts–Amherst
Anthony Laramie, Merrimack College
Carol McDonough, University of Massachusetts–Lowell
William O'Brien, Worcester State College
Gregory H. Wassall, Northeastern University
Bruce G. Webb, Gordon College
Gilbert Wolpe, Newbury College
MARYLAND
Carey Borkoski, Anne Arundel Community College
Kathleen A. Carroll, University of Maryland–Baltimore County
Dustin Chambers, Salisbury University
Shah Mehrabi, Montgomery College
David Mitch, University of Maryland–Baltimore County
John Neri, University of Maryland
Henry Terrell, University of Maryland
MICHIGAN
John Nader, Grand Valley State University
Robert J. Rossana, Wayne State University
Mark Wheeler, Western Michigan University
MISSOURI
Jo Durr, Southwest Missouri State University
Julie H. Gallaway, Southwest Missouri State University
Terrel Galloway, Southwest Missouri State University
Mark Karscig, Central Missouri State University
Steven T. Petty, College of the Ozarks
Sharon Ryan, University of Missouri–Columbia
Ben Young, University of Missouri–Kansas City
MINNESOTA
Monica Hartman, University of St. Thomas
MISSISSIPPI
Randall Campbell, Mississippi State University
Patricia A. Freeman, Jackson State University
NEBRASKA
James Knudsen, Creighton University
Craig MacPhee, University of Nebraska–Lincoln
Mark E. Wohar, University of Nebraska–Omaha
NEW HAMPSHIRE
Evelyn Gick, Dartmouth College
Neil Niman, University of New Hampshire
NEW JERSEY
Len Anyanwu, Union County College
Maharuk Bhiladwalla, Rutgers University–New Brunswick
Gary Gigliotti, Rutgers University–New Brunswick
John Graham, Rutgers University–Newark
Berch Haroian, William Paterson University
Paul Harris, Camden County College
NEW MEXICO
Donald Coes, University of New Mexico
NEW YORK
Erol Balkan, Hamilton College
Ranjit S. Dighe, City University of New York–Bronx Community College
William L. Goffe, State University of New York–Oswego
Wayne A. Grove, LeMoyne College
Christopher Inya, Monroe Community College
Clifford Kern, State University of New York–Binghampton
Mary Lesser, Iona College
Howard Ross, Baruch College
Leonie Stone, State University of New York–Geneseo
Ganti Subrahmanyam, University of Buffalo
Jogindar S. Uppal, State University of New York–Albany
Susan Wolcott, Binghamton University
NORTH CAROLINA
Otilia Boldea, North Carolina State University
Robert Burrus, University of North Carolina–Wilmington
Lee A. Craig, North Carolina State University
Kathleen Dorsainvil, Winston-Salem State University
Marc Fusaro, East Carolina University
Salih Hakeem, North Carolina Central University
Haiyong Liu, East Carolina University
Kosmas Marinakis, North Carolina State University
Todd McFall, Wake Forest University
Shahriar Mostashari, Campbell University
Peter Schuhmann, University of North Carolina–Wilmington
Carol Stivender, University of North Carolina–Charlotte
Vera Tabakova, East Carolina University
Robert Whaples, Wake Forest University
Gary W. Zinn, East Carolina University
OHIO
John P. Blair, Wright State University
Kyongwook Choi, Ohio University
Darlene DeVera, Miami University
Tim Fuerst, Bowling Green University

Ernest Massie, Franklin University
Mike Nelson, University of Akron
Nicholas Noble, Miami University
Rochelle Ruffer, Youngstown State University
Kate Sheppard, University of Akron
Steve Szheghi, Wilmington College
Melissa Thomasson, Miami University
Yaqin Wang, Youngstown State University
Sourushe Zandvakili, University of Cincinnati

OKLAHOMA

David Hudgins, University of Oklahoma

OREGON

Bill Burrows, Lane Community College
Tom Carroll, Central Oregon Community College
Larry Singell, University of Oregon
Ayca Tekin-Koru, Oregon State University

PENNSYLVANIA

Gustavo Barboza, Mercyhurst College
Charles A. Bennett, Gannon University
Howard Bodenhorn, Lafayette College
Milica Bookman, St. Joseph's University
Robert Brooker, Gannon University
Linda Childs-Leatherbury, Lincoln University
Satyajit Ghosh, University of Scranton
Mehdi Haririan, Bloomsburg University
Nicholas Karatjas, Indiana University of Pennsylvania
Brendan Kennelly, Lehigh University
Iordanis Petsas, University of Scranton
Adam Renhoff, Drexel University
Edward Scahill, University of Scranton
Rajeev Sooreea, Pennsylvania State University–Altoona
Sandra Trejos, Clarion University
Peter Zaleski, Villanova University
Susan Zumas, Lehigh University

SOUTH CAROLINA

Calvin Blackwell, College of Charleston
Chad Turner, Clemson University
Madelyn Young, Converse College

SOUTH DAKOTA

Joseph M. Santos, South Dakota State University
Jason Zimmerman, South Dakota State University

TENNESSEE

Bichaka Fayissa, Middle Tennessee State University
Travis Hayes, University of Tennessee–Chattanooga
Christopher C. Klein, Middle Tennessee State University
Milicent Sites, Carson-Newman College

TEXAS

Rashid Al-Hmoud, Texas Tech University
Mike Cohick, Collin County Community College
Cesar Corredor, Texas A&M University
Susan Dadres, Southern Methodist University
Harry Ellis, Jr., University of North Texas
Paul Emberton, Texas State University
Diego Escobari, Texas A&M University
Nicholas Feltovich, University of Houston–Main
Charles Harold Fifield, Baylor University
Richard Gosselin, Houston Community College–Central
James W. Henderson, Baylor University
Ansul Islam, University of Houston–Downtown
Sheila Amin Gutierrez de Pineres, University of Texas–Dallas
James W. Henderson, Baylor University
Ansul Islam, University of Houston–Downtown
Kathy Kelly, University of Texas–Arlington
Thomas Kemp, Tarrant County College–Northwest
Akbar Marvasti, University of Houston–Downtown
James Mbata, Houston Community College
Carl Montano, Lamar University
James Moreno, Blinn College
John Pisciotta, Baylor University
Sara Saderion, Houston Community College–Southwest
Ivan Tasic, Texas A&M University

UTAH

Lowell Glenn, Utah Valley State College
Aric Krause, Westminster College
Arden Pope, Brigham Young University

VIRGINIA

Lee Badgett, Virginia Military Institute
Lee A. Coppock, University of Virginia
Carrie Meyer, George Mason University
James Roberts, Tidewater Community College–Virginia Beach
Araine A. Schauer, Mary Mount College
Sarah Stafford, The College of William & Mary
Michelle Vachris, Christopher Newport University
James Wetzel, Virginia Commonwealth University

WASHINGTON

Robert Rosenman, Washington State University

WASHINGTON, DC

Leon Battista, American Enterprise Institute

WISCONSIN

Pascal Ngoboka, University of Wisconsin–River Falls
Kevin Quinn, St. Norbert College
John R. Stoll, University of Wisconsin–Green Bay

WYOMING

Robert Godby, University of Wyoming

A Word of Thanks

Once again, we benefited greatly from the dedication and professionalism of the Prentice Hall team. Executive Editor David Alexander's energy and support were indispensable. David helped mold the presentation and provided words of encouragement whenever our energy flagged. Developmental Editor Lena Buonanno worked tirelessly to ensure that this text was as good as it could be. We remain literally astonished at the amount of time, energy, and unfailing good humor she brings to this project. As we worked on the first edition, Director of Key Markets David Theisen provided invaluable insight into how best to structure a principles text. His advice helped shape nearly every chapter. Executive Marketing Manager Sharon Koch and Marketing Development Manager Kathleen McLellan helped develop a unique and innovative marketing plan for the first edition, and we sincerely appreciate the upcoming efforts of Lori DeShazo, who is the Executive Marketing Manager for the Second Edition. Steve Deitmer, Director of Development, brought sound judgment to the many decisions required to create this book. Christina Volpe managed the extensive supplement package that accompanies the book. Suzanne Grappi and Blair Brown turned our manuscript pages into a beautiful published book. Ben Paris, executive producer of assessment programs, evaluated test bank questions and provided the test bank authors guidance on how to write effective questions. Valerie Patruno, editorial assistant, was involved in many aspects of the book, including coordinating the review program and assisting with the supplements. Photo researcher Rachel Lucas located photographs that captured the essence of key concepts. We received excellent research assistance from Ed Timmons, David Van Der Goes, and Jason Hockenberry.

A good part of the burden of a project of this magnitude is borne by our families. We appreciate the patience, support, and encouragement of our wives and children. We extend special thanks to Constance Hubbard for her diligent reading of page proofs.

Brief Contents

Contents

CHAPTER 3: Where Prices Come From: The Interaction of Demand and Supply 66

CHAPTER 4: Economic Efficiency, Government Price Setting, and Taxes 98

CHAPTER 4 Appendix: Quantitative Demand and Supply Analysis 131

PART 2: Firms in the Domestic and International Economies

PART 5: Monetary and Fiscal Policy

CHAPTER 13: Money, Banks, and the Federal Reserve System 430

CHAPTER 14: Monetary Policy 466

FLEXIBILITY CHART

The following chart helps you organize your syllabus based on your teaching preferences and objectives:

Core

CHAPTER 1: Economics: Foundations and Models
Uses the debate of outsourcing to discuss the role of models in economic analysis.

CHAPTER 2: Trade-offs, Comparative Advantage, and the Market System
Includes coverage of the role of the entrepreneur, property rights, and the legal system in a market system.

CHAPTER 7: GDP: Measuring Total Production and Income
Covers how total production is measured and the difference between real and nominal variables.

CHAPTER 8: Unemployment and Inflation
Covers the three types of unemployment, how inflation is measured, and the difference between real and nominal interest rates.

CHAPTER 9: Economic Growth, the Financial System, and Business Cycles
Provides an overview of key macroeconomic issues by discussing the business cycle in the context of long-run growth. Discusses the roles of entrepreneurship, financial institutions, and policy in economic growth.

CHAPTER 10: Long-Run Economic Growth: Sources and Policies
Highlights the importance of institutions, policies, and technological change for economic growth.

CHAPTER 12: Aggregate Demand and Aggregate Supply Analysis
Carefully develops the AD-AS model and then makes the model dynamic to better account for actual movements in real GDP and the price level.

CHAPTER 13: Money, Banks, and the Federal Reserve System
Explores the role of money in the economy, the money supply process, and the structure of the Federal Reserve.

Policy

CHAPTER 4: Economic Efficiency, Government Price Setting, and Taxes

CHAPTER 14: Monetary Policy
Uses the aggregate demand and aggregate supply model to show the effects of monetary policy on real GDP and the price level. Chapter 14 is a self-contained discussion, so instructors may safely omit the material in Chapter 16.

CHAPTER 15: Fiscal Policy
Uses the aggregate demand and aggregate supply model to show how taxes and government spending affect the economy. Includes significant coverage of the supply-side effects of fiscal policy.

Optional

CHAPTER 1 Appendix: Using Graphs and Formulas

CHAPTER 4 Appendix: Quantitative Demand and Supply Analysis
Provides a quantitative analysis of rent control.

CHAPTER 5: Firms, the Stock Market, and Corporate Governance
Unique chapter that includes coverage of the Sarbanes-Oxley Act.

CHAPTER 5 Appendix: Tools to Analyze Firms Financial Information
Covers present value and financial statements.

CHAPTER 6: Comparative Advantage and the Gains from International Trade
This chapter may be delayed until after Chapter 16.

CHAPTER 6 Appendix: Multinational Firms
Covers the benefits and challenges of operating overseas businesses.

CHAPTER 11: Output and Expenditure in the Short Run
Uses the Keynesian 45°-line aggregate expenditure model to introduce students to the short-run relationship between spending and production. The discussion of monetary and fiscal policy in later chapters uses only the aggregate demand and aggregate supply model, which allows instructors to omit Chapter 11.

CHAPTER 11 Appendix: The Algebra of Macroeconomic Equilibrium
Uses equations to represent the aggregate expenditure model described in the chapter.

CHAPTER 12 Appendix: Macroeconomic Schools of Thought
Covers the monetarist model, the new classical model, and the real business cycle model.

Core	Policy	Optional
		CHAPTER 16: Inflation, Unemployment, and Federal Reserve Policy *Discusses the short-run and long-run Phillips curves. Also covers the roles of expectations formation and central bank credibility in monetary policy.* **CHAPTER 17:** Macroeconomics in an Open Economy *Explains the linkages among countries at the macroeconomic level and how policymakers in all countries take these linkages into account when conducting monetary and fiscal policy.* **CHAPTER 18:** The International Financial System *Covers the international financial system and explores the role central banks play in the system.*

macroeconomics

Second Edition

Chapter 1

Economics: Foundations and Models

What Happens When U.S. High-Technology Firms Move to China?

You have probably seen the words "Made in China" on a variety of the products you own, including running shoes, clothing, towels, and sheets. It may not be surprising that relatively simple products are manufactured in China, where workers receive much lower wages than in the United States. Until recently, though, most people would not have expected sophisticated, high-technology products to be designed and manufactured in China. That is why the movement of high-technology manufacturing and even high-technology research and development (R&D) to China has surprised many people. In recent years, U.S. firms such as Oracle, IBM, and Motorola have all opened R&D facilities in China. Harry Shum, who runs Microsoft's research center in Beijing, said, "For us, it's always been about finding the best people. China has 1.3 billion brains. The question is how you make them truly creative, truly innovative. This is the key to China becoming a real superpower in science."

3Com is a leading U.S. high-technology firm. The firm introduced a new network switch for corporate computer systems that not only was manufactured in China but had been designed by Chinese engineers. 3Com was able to charge a much lower price for the switch than competitors that designed and manufactured similar products in the United States. Because the salaries of engineers are so much lower in China, 3Com was able to use four times as many engineers to design its switch than did competing firms employing engineers in the United States. The cost to manufacture the switch was also much lower in China, where the average factory worker earns the equivalent of about $2.10 per hour, including benefits, compared with about $24.00 per hour earned by the average factory worker in the United States.

Many U.S., Japanese, and European firms have been moving the production of goods and services outside their home country, a process called *outsourcing* (sometimes also referred to as *off-shoring*). Articles on outsourcing appear frequently in business magazines and the financial pages of newspapers, and the issue has also been the subject of heated debate among political commentators, policymakers, and presidential candidates. The focus of the debate has been the question "Has outsourcing been good or bad for the U.S. economy?" This question is one of many that cannot be answered without using economics. In this chapter and the remainder of this book, we will see how economics helps in answering important questions about outsourcing, as well as many other issues. Economics provides us with tools for understanding why outsourcing has increased, why some firms are more likely to move production to other countries, and what the effects of outsourcing will be on the wages of U.S. workers, the profits of U.S. firms, and the overall ability of the U.S. economy to produce more and better goods and services. **AN INSIDE LOOK** on **page 18** discusses how developments in China and India are affecting the high-technology sector in the United States.

Sources: Charles Leadbeater and James Wilson, "Do Not Fear the Rise of World-Class Science Asia," *Financial Times*, October 12, 2005, p. 19; Pete Engardio and Dexter Roberts, "The China Price," *BusinessWeek*, December 6, 2004; and Judith Banister, "Manufacturing Earnings and Compensation in China," *Monthly Labor Review*, August 2006, pp. 22–40.

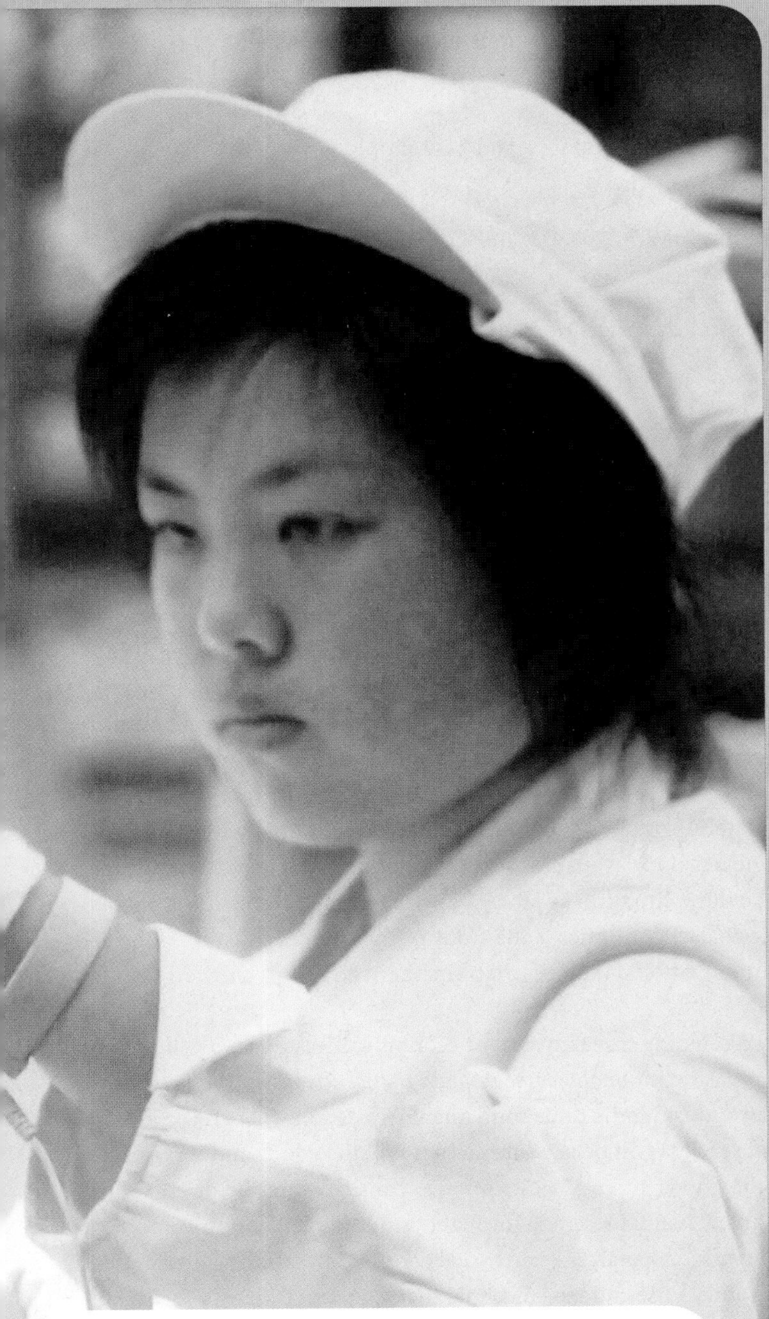

LEARNING Objectives

After studying this chapter, you should be able to:

1.1 Explain these three key economic ideas: *People are* **rational**. *People respond to* **incentives**. *Optimal decisions are made at the* **margin**, page 4.

1.2 Discuss how an economy answers these questions: **What** goods and services will be produced? **How** will the goods and services be produced? **Who** will receive the goods and services? page 8.

1.3 Understand the role of **models** in economic analysis, page 11.

1.4 Distinguish between **microeconomics** and **macroeconomics**, page 15.

1.5 Become familiar with important **economic terms**, page 15.

APPENDIX Review the use of **graphs** and **formulas**, page 24.

Economics in YOUR Life!

Are You Likely to Lose Your Job to Outsourcing?

An estimated 3.3 million jobs in the United States will have been outsourced between 2000 and 2015, according to a report by John McCarthy of Forrester Research, a private research firm. Other estimates of the number of U.S. jobs likely to be outsourced have been in the same range. More than 3 million jobs seems like a large number. Suppose you plan on working as an accountant, a software engineer, a lawyer, a business consultant, a financial analyst, or in another industry where some jobs have already been outsourced. Is it likely that during your career, your job will be outsourced to China, India, or some other foreign country? As you read the chapter, see if you can answer this question. You can check your answer against the one we provide at the end of the chapter.

>> Continued on page 17

In this book, we use economics to answer questions such as the following:

- How are the prices of goods and services determined?
- How does pollution affect the economy, and how should government policy deal with these effects?
- Why do firms engage in international trade, and how do government policies affect international trade?
- Why does government control the prices of some goods and services, and what are the effects of those controls?

Economists do not always agree on the answers to every question. In fact, as we will see, economists engage in lively debate on some issues. In addition, new problems and issues are constantly arising. So, economists are always at work developing new methods to analyze and answer these questions.

All the questions we discuss in this book illustrate a basic fact of life: People must make choices as they try to attain their goals. We must make choices because we live in a world of **scarcity**, which means that although our wants are unlimited, the resources available to fulfill those wants are limited. You might like to have a 60-inch plasma television in every room of your home, but unless you are a close relative of Bill Gates, you probably lack the money to purchase them. Every day, you must make choices about how to spend your limited income on the many goods and services available. The finite amount of time available to you also limits your ability to attain your goals. If you spend an hour studying for your economics midterm, you have one less hour available to study for your history midterm. Firms and the government are in the same situation as you: They have limited resources available as they attempt to attain their goals. **Economics** is the study of the choices consumers, business managers, and government officials make to attain their goals, given their scarce resources.

Scarcity The situation in which unlimited wants exceed the limited resources available to fulfill those wants.

Economics The study of the choices people make to attain their goals, given their scarce resources.

We begin this chapter by discussing three important economic ideas that we will return to many times in the book: *People are rational. People respond to incentives. Optimal decisions are made at the margin.* Then we consider the three fundamental questions that any economy must answer: *What* goods and services will be produced? *How* will the goods and services be produced? *Who* will receive the goods and services? Next we consider the role of *economic models* in helping analyze the many issues presented throughout this book. **Economic models** are simplified versions of reality used to analyze real-world economic situations. Later in this chapter, we explore why economists use models and how they construct them. Finally, we discuss the difference between microeconomics and macroeconomics, and we preview some important economic terms.

Economic model A simplified version of reality used to analyze real-world economic situations.

1.1 LEARNING OBJECTIVE

1.1 | Explain these three key economic ideas: *People are rational. People respond to incentives. Optimal decisions are made at the margin.*

Three Key Economic Ideas

As you try to achieve your goals, whether they are buying a new computer or finding a part-time job, you will interact with other people in *markets*. A **market** is a group of buyers and sellers of a good or service and the institution or arrangement by which they come together to trade. Most of economics involves analyzing what happens in markets.

Market A group of buyers and sellers of a good or service and the institution or arrangement by which they come together to trade.

Throughout this book, as we study how people make choices and interact in markets, we will return to three important ideas:

1 People are rational.

2 People respond to economic incentives.

3 Optimal decisions are made at the margin.

People Are Rational

Economists generally assume that people are rational. This assumption does *not* mean that economists believe everyone knows everything or always makes the "best" decision. It means that economists assume that consumers and firms use all available information as they act to achieve their goals. Rational individuals weigh the benefits and costs of each action, and they choose an action only if the benefits outweigh the costs. For example, if Microsoft charges a price of $239 for a copy of Windows, economists assume that the managers at Microsoft have estimated that a price of $239 will earn Microsoft the most profit. The managers may be wrong; perhaps a price of $265 would be more profitable, but economists assume that the managers at Microsoft have acted rationally on the basis of the information available to them in choosing the price. Of course, not everyone behaves rationally all the time. Still, the assumption of rational behavior is very useful in explaining most of the choices that people make.

People Respond to Economic Incentives

Human beings act from a variety of motives, including religious belief, envy, and compassion. Economists emphasize that consumers and firms consistently respond to *economic* incentives. This fact may seem obvious, but it is often overlooked. For example, according to an article in the *Wall Street Journal*, the FBI couldn't understand why banks were not taking steps to improve security in the face of an increase in robberies: "FBI officials suggest that banks place uniformed, armed guards outside their doors and install bullet-resistant plastic, known as a 'bandit barrier,' in front of teller windows." FBI officials were surprised that few banks took their advice. But the article also reported that installing bullet-resistant plastic costs $10,000 to $20,000, and a well-trained security guard receives $50,000 per year in salary and benefits. The average loss in a bank robbery is only about $1,200. The economic incentive to banks is clear: It is less costly to put up with bank robberies than to take additional security measures. That banks respond as they do to the threat of robberies may be surprising to the FBI—but not to economists.

In each chapter, the *Making the Connection* feature discusses a news story or another application related to the chapter material. Read the following *Making the Connection* for a discussion of whether people respond to economic incentives even when making the decision to have children.

Making the Connection

Will Women Have More Babies if the Government Pays Them To?

The populations of the United States, Japan, and most European countries are aging as birthrates decline and the average person lives longer. The governments of these countries have programs to pay money to retired workers, such as the Social Security system in the United States. Most of the money for these programs comes from taxes paid by people currently working. As the population ages, there are fewer workers paying taxes relative to the number of retired people receiving government payments. The result is a funding crisis that countries can solve only by either reducing government payments to retired workers or by raising the taxes paid by current workers.

In some European countries, birthrates have fallen so low that the total population will soon begin to decline, which will make the funding crisis for government retirement programs even worse. For the population of a country to be stable, the average woman must have 2.1 children, which is enough to replace both parents and account for children who die before reaching adulthood. In recent years, the birthrates in a number of countries, including France, Germany, and Italy, have fallen below this replacement level. The concern about falling birthrates has been particularly strong in the small European country of Estonia. In 2001, the United Nations issued a report in which it forecast that, given its current birthrate, by 2050, the population of Estonia would decline from 1.4 million to only about 700,000. The Estonian government responded by using economic incentives in an attempt to increase the birthrate. Beginning in 2004, the government began paying working women who take time off after having a baby their entire salary for up to 15 months. Women who do not work receive $200 per month, which is a substantial amount, given that the average income in Estonia is only $650 per month.

Will women actually have more babies as a result of this economic incentive? As the graph below shows, the birthrate in Estonia has increased from 1.3 children per woman in the late 1990s to 1.5 children per woman in 2006. This is still below the replacement level birthrate of 2.1 children, and it is too early to tell whether the increased birthrate is due to the economic incentives. But the Estonian government is encouraged by the results and is looking for ways to provide additional economic incentives to raise the birthrate further. And Estonia is not alone; more than 45 other countries in Europe and Asia have taken steps to try to raise their birthrates. People may respond to economic incentives even when making the very personal decision of how many children to have.

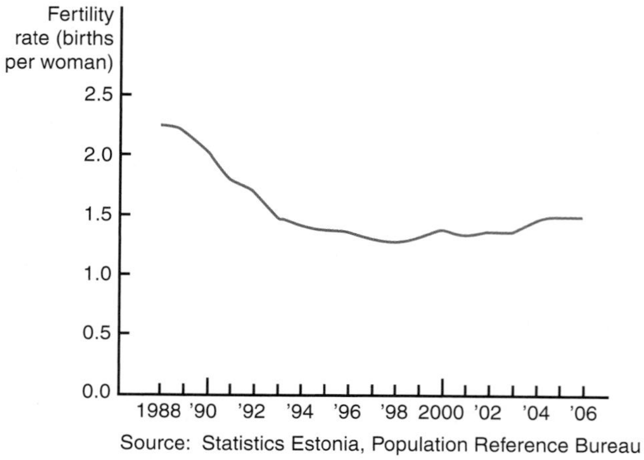

Source: Marcus Walker, "In Estonia, Paying Women to Have Babies Is Paying Off," *Wall Street Journal*, October 20, 2006, p. A1. Copyright © 2006 Dow Jones. Reprinted by permission of Dow Jones via Copyright Clearance Center; and Sharon Lerner, "The Motherhood Experiment," *New York Times*, March 4, 2007.

YOUR TURN: Test your understanding by doing related problem 1.7 on page 21 at the end of this chapter.

Optimal Decisions Are Made at the Margin

Some decisions are "all or nothing": An entrepreneur decides whether to open a new restaurant. He or she either starts the new restaurant or doesn't. You decide whether to enter graduate school or to take a job instead. You either enter graduate school or you don't. But most decisions in life are not all or nothing. Instead, most decisions involve doing a little more or a little less. If you are trying to decrease your spending and increase your saving, the decision is not really a choice between saving every dollar you earn or spending it all. Rather, many small choices are involved, such as whether to buy a caffè mocha at Starbucks every day or to cut back to three times per week.

Economists use the word *marginal* to mean an extra or additional benefit or cost of a decision. Should you watch another hour of TV or spend that hour studying? The *marginal benefit* (or, in symbols, *MB*) of watching more TV is the additional enjoyment you receive. The *marginal cost* (or *MC*) is the lower grade you receive from having studied a little less. Should Apple Computer produce an additional 300,000 iPods? Firms receive *revenue* from selling goods. Apple's marginal benefit is the additional revenue it receives from selling 300,000 more iPods. Apple's marginal cost is the additional cost—for wages, parts, and so forth—of producing 300,000 more iPods. *Economists reason that the optimal decision is to continue any activity up to the point where the marginal benefit equals the marginal cost—in symbols, where* MB = MC. Often we apply this rule without consciously thinking about it. Usually you will know whether the additional enjoyment from watching a television program is worth the additional cost involved in not spending that hour studying, without giving it a lot of thought. In business situations, however, firms often have to make careful calculations to determine, for example, whether the additional revenue received from increasing production is greater or less than the additional cost of the production. Economists refer to analysis that involves comparing marginal benefits and marginal costs as **marginal analysis.**

Marginal analysis Analysis that involves comparing marginal benefits and marginal costs.

In each chapter of this book, you will see the special feature *Solved Problem.* This feature will increase your understanding of the material by leading you through the steps of solving an applied economic problem. After reading the problem, you can test your understanding by working the related problems that appear at the end of the chapter and in the study guide that accompanies this book.

Solved Problem 1-1

Apple Computer Makes a Decision at the Margin

Suppose Apple is currently selling 3,000,000 iPods per year. Managers at Apple are considering whether to raise production to 3,300,000 iPods per year. One manager argues, "Increasing production from 3,000,000 to 3,300,000 is a good idea because we will make a total profit of $100 million if we produce 3,300,000." Do you agree with her reasoning? What, if any, additional information do you need to decide whether Apple should produce the additional 300,000 iPods?

SOLVING THE PROBLEM:

Step 1: **Review the chapter material.** The problem is about making decisions, so you may want to review the section "Optimal Decisions Are Made at the Margin," which begins on page 6. Remember to think "marginal" whenever you see the word "additional" in economics.

Step 2: **Explain whether you agree with the manager's reasoning.** We have seen that any activity should be continued to the point where the marginal benefit is equal to the marginal cost. In this case, that involves continuing to produce iPods up to the point where the additional revenue Apple receives from selling more iPods is equal to the marginal cost of producing them. The Apple manager has not done a marginal analysis, so you should not agree with her reasoning. Her statement about the *total* profit of producing 3,300,000 iPods is not relevant to the decision of whether to produce the last 300,000 iPods.

Step 3: **Explain what additional information you need.** You will need additional information to make a correct decision. You will need to know the additional revenue Apple would earn from selling 300,000 more iPods and the additional cost of producing them.

YOUR TURN: For more practice, do related problems 1.4, 1.5, and 1.6 on pages 20–21 at the end of this chapter.

>> End Solved Problem 1-1

1.2 LEARNING OBJECTIVE

1.2 | Discuss how an economy answers these questions: *What* goods and services will be produced? *How* will the goods and services be produced? *Who* will receive the goods and services?

The Economic Problem That Every Society Must Solve

Trade-off The idea that because of scarcity, producing more of one good or service means producing less of another good or service.

Opportunity cost The highest-valued alternative that must be given up to engage in an activity.

We have already noted the important fact that we live in a world of scarcity. As a result, any society faces the economic problem that it has only a limited amount of economic resources—such as workers, machines, and raw materials—and so can produce only a limited amount of goods and services. Therefore, society faces **trade-offs**: Producing more of one good or service means producing less of another good or service. In fact, the best way to measure the cost of producing a good or service is the value of what has to be given up to produce it. The **opportunity cost** of any activity—such as producing a good or service—is the highest-valued alternative that must be given up to engage in that activity. The concept of opportunity cost is very important in economics and applies to individuals as much as it does to firms or to society as a whole. Consider the example of someone who could receive a salary of $80,000 per year working as a manager at a firm but opens her own firm instead. In that case, the opportunity cost of her managerial services to her own firm is $80,000, even if she does not explicitly pay herself a salary.

Trade-offs force society to make choices, particularly when answering the following three fundamental questions:

1. *What* goods and services will be produced?
2. *How* will the goods and services be produced?
3. *Who* will receive the goods and services produced?

Throughout this book, we will return to these questions many times. For now, we briefly introduce each question.

What Goods and Services Will Be Produced?

How will society decide whether to produce more economics textbooks or more HD-DVD players? More daycare facilities or more football stadiums? Of course, "society" does not make decisions; only individuals make decisions. The answer to the question of what will be produced is determined by the choices made by consumers, firms, and the government. Every day, you help decide which goods and services will be produced when you choose to buy an iPod rather than an HD-DVD player or a caffè mocha rather than a chai tea. Similarly, Apple must choose whether to devote its scarce resources to making more iPods or more MacBook laptop computers. The federal government must choose whether to spend more of its limited budget on breast cancer research or on homeland security. In each case, consumers, firms, and the government face the problem of scarcity by trading off one good or service for another. And each choice made comes with an opportunity cost measured by the value of the best alternative given up.

How Will the Goods and Services Be Produced?

Firms choose how to produce the goods and services they sell. In many cases, firms face a trade-off between using more workers or using more machines. For example, a local service station has to choose whether to provide car repair services using more diagnostic computers and fewer auto mechanics or more auto mechanics and fewer diagnostic computers. Similarly, movie studios have to choose whether to produce animated films using highly skilled animators to draw them by hand or fewer animators and more computers. In deciding whether to move production offshore to China, firms may be choosing between a production method in the United States that uses fewer workers and more machines and a production method in China that uses more workers and fewer machines.

Who Will Receive the Goods and Services Produced?

In the United States, who receives the goods and services produced depends largely on how income is distributed. Individuals with the highest income have the ability to buy the most goods and services. Often, people are willing to give up some of their income—and, therefore, some of their ability to purchase goods and services—by donating to charities to increase the incomes of poorer people. Each year, Americans donate more than $250 billion to charity, or an average donation of $2,100 for each household in the country. An important policy question, however, is whether the government should intervene to make the distribution of income more equal. Such intervention already occurs in the United States, because people with higher incomes pay a larger fraction of their incomes in taxes and because the government makes payments to people with low incomes. There is disagreement over whether the current attempts to redistribute income are sufficient or whether there should be more or less redistribution.

Centrally Planned Economies versus Market Economies

Societies organize their economies in two main ways to answer the three questions of what, how, and who. A society can have a **centrally planned economy** in which the government decides how economic resources will be allocated. Or a society can have a **market economy** in which the decisions of households and firms interacting in markets allocate economic resources.

Centrally planned economy An economy in which the government decides how economic resources will be allocated.

Market economy An economy in which the decisions of households and firms interacting in markets allocate economic resources.

From 1917 to 1991, the most important centrally planned economy in the world was that of the Soviet Union, which was established when Vladimir Lenin and his Communist Party staged a revolution and took over the Russian Empire. In the Soviet Union, the government decided what goods to produce, how to produce them, and who would receive them. Government employees managed factories and stores. The objective of these managers was to follow the government's orders rather than to satisfy the wants of consumers. Centrally planned economies like the Soviet Union have not been successful in producing low-cost, high-quality goods and services. As a result, the standard of living of the average person in a centrally planned economy tends to be quite low. All centrally planned economies have also been political dictatorships. Dissatisfaction with low living standards and political repression finally led to the collapse of the Soviet Union in 1991. Today, only a few small countries, such as Cuba and North Korea, still have completely centrally planned economies.

All the high-income democracies, such as the United States, Canada, Japan, and the countries of western Europe, are market economies. Market economies rely primarily on privately owned firms to produce goods and services and to decide how to produce them. Markets, rather than the government, determine who receives the goods and services produced. In a market economy, firms must produce goods and services that meet the wants of consumers, or the firms will go out of business. In that sense, it is ultimately consumers who decide what goods and services will be produced. Because firms in a market economy compete to offer the highest-quality products at the lowest price, they are under pressure to use the lowest-cost methods of production. For example, in the past 10 years, some U.S. firms, particularly in the electronics and furniture industries, have been under pressure to reduce their costs to meet competition from Chinese firms.

In a market economy, the income of an individual is determined by the payments he receives for what he has to sell. If he is a civil engineer and firms are willing to pay a salary of $85,000 per year for engineers with his training and skills, that is the amount of income he will have to purchase goods and services. If the engineer also owns a house that he rents out, his income will be even higher. One of the attractive features of markets is that they reward hard work. Generally, the more extensive the training a person has received and the longer the hours the person works, the higher the person's income will be. Of course, luck—both good and bad—also plays a role here, as elsewhere in life. We can conclude that market economies answer the question "Who receives the goods and services produced?" with the answer "Those who are most willing and able to buy them."

The Modern "Mixed" Economy

In the nineteenth and early twentieth centuries, the U.S. government engaged in relatively little regulation of markets for goods and services. Beginning in the middle of the twentieth century, government intervention in the economy dramatically increased in the United States and other market economies. This increase was primarily caused by the high rates of unemployment and business bankruptcies during the Great Depression of the 1930s. Some government intervention was also intended to raise the incomes of the elderly, the sick, and people with limited skills. For example, in the 1930s, the United States established the Social Security system, which provides government payments to retired and disabled workers, and minimum wage legislation, which sets a floor on the wages employers can pay in many occupations. In more recent years, government intervention in the economy has also expanded to meet such goals as protection of the environment and the promotion of civil rights.

Some economists argue that the extent of government intervention makes it no longer accurate to refer to the U.S., Canadian, Japanese, and western European economies as pure market economies. Instead, they should be referred to as *mixed economies*. A **mixed economy** is still primarily a market economy with most economic decisions resulting from the interaction of buyers and sellers in markets, but in a mixed economy the government plays a significant role in the allocation of resources. As we will see in later chapters, economists continue to debate the role government should play in a market economy.

Mixed economy An economy in which most economic decisions result from the interaction of buyers and sellers in markets but in which the government plays a significant role in the allocation of resources.

One of the most important developments in the international economy in recent years has been the movement of China from being a centrally planned economy to being a more mixed economy. The Chinese economy had suffered decades of economic stagnation following the takeover of the government by Mao Zedong and the Communist Party in 1949. Although China remains a political dictatorship, production of most goods and services is now determined in the market rather than by the government. The result has been rapid economic growth that in the near future may lead to total production of goods and services in China surpassing total production in the United States.

Efficiency and Equity

Market economies tend to be more efficient than centrally planned economies. There are two types of efficiency: *productive efficiency* and *allocative efficiency*. **Productive efficiency** occurs when a good or service is produced at the lowest possible cost. **Allocative efficiency** occurs when production is in accordance with consumer preferences. Markets tend to be efficient because they promote competition and facilitate voluntary exchange. **Voluntary exchange** refers to the situation in which both the buyer and seller of a product are made better off by the transaction. We know that the buyer and seller are both made better off because, otherwise, the buyer would not have agreed to buy the product or the seller would not have agreed to sell it. Productive efficiency is achieved when competition among firms in markets forces the firms to produce goods and services at the lowest cost. Allocative efficiency is achieved when the combination of competition among firms and voluntary exchange between firms and consumers results in firms producing the mix of goods and services that consumers prefer most. Competition will force firms to continue producing and selling goods and services as long as the additional benefit to consumers is greater than the additional cost of production. In this way, the mix of goods and services produced will be in accordance with consumer preferences.

Productive efficiency The situation in which a good or service is produced at the lowest possible cost.

Allocative efficiency A state of the economy in which production is in accordance with consumer preferences; in particular, every good or service is produced up to the point where the last unit provides a marginal benefit to society equal to the marginal cost of producing it.

Voluntary exchange The situation that occurs in markets when both the buyer and seller of a product are made better off by the transaction.

Although markets promote efficiency, they don't guarantee it. Inefficiency can arise from various sources. To begin with, it may take some time to achieve an efficient outcome. When DVD players were introduced, for example, firms did not instantly achieve productive efficiency. It took several years for firms to discover the lowest-cost method of producing this good. As we will discuss in Chapter 4, governments sometimes reduce efficiency by interfering with voluntary exchange in markets. For example, many governments limit the imports of some goods from foreign countries. This limitation reduces efficiency by keeping goods from being produced at the lowest cost. The production of some goods damages the environment. In this case, government intervention can increase efficiency because without such intervention, firms may ignore the costs of environmental damage and thereby fail to produce the goods at the lowest possible cost.

Just because an economic outcome is efficient does not necessarily mean that society finds it desirable. Many people prefer economic outcomes that they consider fair or equitable, even if those outcomes are less efficient. **Equity** is harder to define than efficiency, but it usually involves a fair distribution of economic benefits. For some people, equity involves a more equal distribution of economic benefits than would result from an emphasis on efficiency alone. For example, some people support taxing people with higher incomes to provide the funds for programs that aid the poor. Although governments may increase equity by reducing the incomes of high-income people and increasing the incomes of the poor, efficiency may be reduced. People have less incentive to open new businesses, to supply labor, and to save if the government takes a significant amount of the income they earn from working or saving. The result is that fewer goods and services are produced, and less saving takes place. As this example illustrates, *there is often a trade-off between efficiency and equity*. In this case, the total amount of goods and services produced falls, although the distribution of the income to buy those goods and services is made more equal. Government policymakers often confront this trade-off.

Equity The fair distribution of economic benefits.

1.3 LEARNING OBJECTIVE

1.3 | Understand the role of models in economic analysis.

Economic Models

Economists rely on economic theories, or *models* (the words *theory* and *model* are used interchangeably), to analyze real-world issues, such as the economic effects of outsourcing. As mentioned earlier, economic models are simplified versions of reality. Economists are certainly not alone in relying on models: An engineer may use a computer model of a bridge to help test whether it will withstand high winds, or a biologist may make a physical model of a nucleic acid to better understand its properties. One purpose of economic models is to make economic ideas sufficiently explicit and concrete so that individuals, firms, or the government can use them to make decisions. For example, we will see in Chapter 3 that the model of demand and supply is a simplified version of how the prices of products are determined by the interactions among buyers and sellers in markets.

Economists use economic models to answer questions. For example, consider the question from the chapter opener: Has outsourcing been good or bad for the U.S. economy? For a complicated issue such as the effects of outsourcing, economists often use several models to examine different aspects of the issue. For example, they may use a model of how wages are determined to analyze how outsourcing affects wages in particular industries. They may use a model of international trade to analyze how outsourcing affects income growth in the countries involved. Sometimes economists use an existing model to analyze an issue, but in other cases, they must develop a new model. To develop a model, economists generally follow these steps:

1. Decide on the assumptions to be used in developing the model.
2. Formulate a testable hypothesis.
3. Use economic data to test the hypothesis.
4. Revise the model if it fails to explain well the economic data.
5. Retain the revised model to help answer similar economic questions in the future.

The Role of Assumptions in Economic Models

Any model is based on making assumptions because models have to be simplified to be useful. We cannot analyze an economic issue unless we reduce its complexity. For example, economic models make *behavioral assumptions* about the motives of consumers and firms. Economists assume that consumers will buy the goods and services that will maximize their well-being or their satisfaction. Similarly, economists assume that firms act to maximize their profits. These assumptions are simplifications because they do not describe the motives of every consumer and every firm. How can we know if the assumptions in a model are too simplified or too limiting? We discover this when we form hypotheses based on these assumptions and test these hypotheses using real-world information.

Forming and Testing Hypotheses in Economic Models

Economic variable Something measurable that can have different values, such as the wages of software programmers.

A *hypothesis* in an economic model is a statement that may be either correct or incorrect about an *economic variable*. An **economic variable** is something measurable that can have different values, such as the wages paid to software programmers. An example of a hypothesis in an economic model is the statement that outsourcing by U.S. firms reduces wages paid to software programmers in the United States. An economic hypothesis is usually about a *causal relationship*; in this case, the hypothesis states that outsourcing causes, or leads to, lower wages for software programmers.

Before accepting a hypothesis, we must test it. To test a hypothesis, we must analyze statistics on the relevant economic variables. In our example, we must gather statistics on the wages paid to software programmers, and perhaps on other variables as well. Testing a hypothesis can be tricky. For example, showing that the wages paid to software programmers fell at a time when outsourcing was increasing would not be enough to demonstrate that outsourcing *caused* the wage fall. Just because two things are *correlated*—that is, they happen at the same time—does not mean that one caused the other. For example, suppose that the number of workers trained as software engineers greatly increased at the same time that outsourcing was increasing. In that case, the fall in wages paid to software engineers might have been caused by the increased competition among workers for these jobs rather than by the effects of relocating programming jobs from the United States to India or China. Over a period of time, many economic variables change, which complicates testing hypotheses. In fact, when economists disagree about a hypothesis, such as the effect of outsourcing on wages, it is often because of disagreements over interpreting the statistical analysis used to test the hypothesis.

Note that hypotheses must be statements that could, in principle, turn out to be incorrect. Statements such as "Outsourcing is good" or "Outsourcing is bad" are value judgments rather than hypotheses because it is not possible to disprove them.

Economists accept and use an economic model if it leads to hypotheses that are confirmed by statistical analysis. In many cases, the acceptance is tentative, however, pending the gathering of new data or further statistical analysis. In fact, economists often refer to a hypothesis having been "not rejected," rather than having been "accepted," by statistical analysis. But what if statistical analysis clearly rejects a hypothesis? For example, what if a model leads to a hypothesis that outsourcing by U.S. firms lowers wages of U.S. software programmers, but this hypothesis is rejected by the data? In that case, the model must be reconsidered. It may be that an assumption used in the model was too simplified or too limiting. For example, perhaps the model used to determine the effect of outsourcing on wages paid to software programmers assumed that software programmers in China and India had the same training and experience as software programmers in the United States. If, in fact, U.S. software programmers have more training and experience than Chinese and Indian programmers, this difference may explain why our hypothesis was rejected by the economic statistics.

The process of developing models, testing hypotheses, and revising models occurs not just in economics but also in disciplines such as physics, chemistry, and biology. This process is often referred to as the *scientific method*. Economics is a *social science* because it applies the scientific method to the study of the interactions among individuals.

Making the Connection

When Economists Disagree: A Debate over Outsourcing

Does outsourcing by U.S. firms raise or lower incomes in the United States?

There is an old saying in the newspaper business that it's not news when a dog bites a man, but it is news when a man bites a dog. In 2004, many newspapers ran a "man bites dog" story concerning economics.

Most economists believe that international trade—including the trade that results when firms move production offshore—increases economic efficiency and raises incomes. It was news, then, when Paul Samuelson, an MIT economist and a winner of the Nobel Prize in Economics, wrote an article in the *Journal of Economic Perspectives* questioning whether incomes in the United States will be higher as a result of the outsourcing of jobs to India and China. Samuelson presented a model of the effects of outsourcing that can be illustrated with the following hypothetical case: Suppose a bank in New York has been using a company in South Dakota to handle its telephone customer service. The bank then switches to using a company in Bangalore, India, that pays its workers much lower wages. Samuelson argued that even when the workers fired by the South Dakota firm eventually find new jobs, the jobs may pay lower wages. If outsourcing becomes widespread enough, Samuelson argued, it may result in a significant decline in U.S. incomes.

Many economists objected to Samuelson's argument. One economist who wrote a rebuttal to Samuelson was Jagdish Bhagwati, a former student of Samuelson's and a professor of economics at Columbia University. Bhagwati argued that in Samuelson's example, the wages of South Dakota call center workers were reduced by outsourcing, but the costs to the bank were also reduced, which would allow the bank to reduce the prices it charged its customers. In Bhagwati's model, these gains to consumers from lower prices more than offset the loss to workers from lower wages, so the United States experiences a net gain from outsourcing. Samuelson argued, though, that if the United States exports the product—in this case banking services—to other countries, the lower price hurts the exporting firms. In that case, the United States might still be hurt by outsourcing.

This brief summary does not do full justice to the models of Samuelson and Bhagwati, which are too complicated for us to cover in this chapter. We can, however, discuss the sources of the disagreement between these two economists. We have seen that economists sometimes differ about the assumptions that should be used in building a model. That is not the case here: Samuelson and Bhagwati basically agree on the model and the assumptions to be used. Instead, they disagree over how to interpret the relevant economic statistics. Bhagwati argues that the number of U.S. jobs moving to other countries has been relatively small, amounting to about 1 percent of the jobs created in the U.S. economy each year. He also argues that the jobs lost to outsourcing tend to be low-wage jobs, such as telephone customer service or data entry, and are likely to be replaced by higher-wage jobs. Samuelson argues that the impact of outsourcing is greater than Bhagwati believes, and he is less optimistic that newly created jobs in the United States will pay higher wages than the jobs lost to outsourcing.

The debate between Samuelson and Bhagwati demonstrates that economics is an evolving discipline. New models are continually being introduced, and new hypotheses are being formulated and tested. We can expect the debate over the economic impact of outsourcing to continue to be lively.

Sources: Paul A. Samuelson, "Where Ricardo and Mill Rebut and Confirm Arguments of Mainstream Economists Supporting Globalization," *Journal of Economic Perspectives*, Vol. 18, No. 3, Summer 2004, pp. 135–146; Jagdish Bhagwati, Arvind Panagariya, and T. N. Srinivasan, "The Muddles Over Outsourcing," *Journal of Economic Perspectives*, Vol. 18, No. 4, Fall 2004, pp. 93–114; and Steve Lohr, "An Elder Challenges Outsourcing's Orthodoxy," *New York Times*, September 9, 2004, p. C1.

YOUR TURN: Test your understanding by doing related problem 3.7 on page 22 at the end of this chapter.

Normative and Positive Analysis

Positive analysis Analysis concerned with what is.

Normative analysis Analysis concerned with what ought to be.

Throughout this book, as we build economic models and use them to answer questions, we need to bear in mind the distinction between *positive analysis* and *normative analysis*. **Positive analysis** is concerned with *what is*, and **normative analysis** is concerned with *what ought to be*. Economics is about positive analysis, which measures the costs and benefits of different courses of action.

We can use the federal government's minimum wage law to compare positive and normative analysis. In 2008, under this law, it was illegal for an employer to hire a worker at a wage less than \$6.55 per hour (the minimum wage is scheduled to increase to \$7.25 per hour in 2009). Without the minimum wage law, some firms and some workers would voluntarily agree to a lower wage. Because of the minimum wage law, some workers have difficulty finding jobs, and some firms end up paying more for labor than they otherwise would have. A positive analysis of the federal minimum wage law uses an economic model to estimate how many workers have lost their jobs because of the law, its impact on the costs and profits of businesses, and the gains to workers receiving the minimum wage. After economists complete this positive analysis, the decision as to whether the minimum wage law is a good idea or a bad idea is a normative one and depends on how people evaluate the trade-off involved. Supporters of the law believe that the losses to employers and to workers who are unemployed as a result of the law are more than offset by the gains to workers who receive higher wages than they would without the law. Opponents of the law believe the losses are greater than the gains. The assessment by any individual would depend, in part, on that person's values and political views. The positive analysis provided by an economist would play a role in the decision but can't by itself decide the issue one way or the other.

In each chapter, you will see a *Don't Let This Happen to You!* box like the one below. These boxes alert you to common pitfalls in thinking about economic ideas. After reading the box, test your understanding by working the related problem that appears at the end of the chapter.

Economics as a Social Science

Because economics is based on studying the actions of individuals, it is a social science. Economics is therefore similar to other social science disciplines, such as psychology, political science, and sociology. As a social science, economics considers human behavior—particularly decision-making behavior—in every context, not just in the context of business. Economists have studied such issues as how families decide the number of children

Don't Let This Happen to **YOU!**

Don't Confuse Positive Analysis with Normative Analysis

"Economic analysis has shown that the minimum wage law is a bad idea because it causes unemployment." Is this statement accurate? As of 2008, the federal minimum wage law prevents employers from hiring workers at a wage of less than \$6.55 per hour. This wage is higher than some employers are willing to pay some workers. If there were no minimum wage law, some workers who currently cannot find any firm willing to hire them at \$6.55 per hour would be able to find employment at a lower wage. Therefore, positive economic analysis indicates that the minimum wage law causes unemployment (although economists disagree about how much unemployment is caused by the minimum wage). *But,* those workers who still have jobs benefit from the minimum wage because they are paid a higher wage than they otherwise would be. In other words, the minimum wage law creates both losers (the workers who become unemployed and the firms that have to pay higher wages) and winners (the workers who receive higher wages).

Should we value the gains to the winners more than we value the losses to the losers? The answer to that question involves normative analysis. Positive economic analysis can only show the consequences of a particular policy; it cannot tell us whether the policy is "good" or "bad." So, the statement at the beginning of this box is inaccurate.

YOUR TURN: Test your understanding by doing related problem 3.9 on page 23 at the end of this chapter.

to have, why people have difficulty losing weight or attaining other desirable goals, and why people often ignore relevant information when making decisions. Economics also has much to contribute to questions of government policy. As we will see throughout this book, economists have played an important role in formulating government policies in areas such as the environment, health care, and poverty.

1.4 LEARNING OBJECTIVE

1.4 | Distinguish between microeconomics and macroeconomics.

Microeconomics and Macroeconomics

Economic models can be used to analyze decision making in many areas. We group some of these areas together as *microeconomics* and others as *macroeconomics*. **Microeconomics** is the study of how households and firms make choices, how they interact in markets, and how the government attempts to influence their choices. Microeconomic issues include explaining how consumers react to changes in product prices and how firms decide what prices to charge. Microeconomics also involves policy issues, such as analyzing the most efficient way to reduce teenage smoking, analyzing the costs and benefits of approving the sale of a new prescription drug, and analyzing the most efficient way to reduce air pollution.

Microeconomics The study of how households and firms make choices, how they interact in markets, and how the government attempts to influence their choices.

Macroeconomics is the study of the economy as a whole, including topics such as inflation, unemployment, and economic growth. Macroeconomic issues include explaining why economies experience periods of recession and increasing unemployment and why over the long run, some economies have grown much faster than others. Macroeconomics also involves policy issues, such as whether government intervention can reduce the severity of recessions.

Macroeconomics The study of the economy as a whole, including topics such as inflation, unemployment, and economic growth.

The division between microeconomics and macroeconomics is not hard and fast. Many economic situations have *both* a microeconomic and a macroeconomic aspect. For example, the level of total investment by firms in new machinery and equipment helps to determine how rapidly the economy grows—which is a macroeconomic issue. But to understand how much new machinery and equipment firms decide to purchase, we have to analyze the incentives individual firms face—which is a microeconomic issue.

1.5 LEARNING OBJECTIVE

1.5 | Become familiar with important economic terms.

A Preview of Important Economic Terms

In the following chapters, you will encounter certain important terms again and again. Becoming familiar with these terms is a necessary step in learning economics. Here we provide a brief introduction to some of these terms. We will discuss them all in greater depth in later chapters:

- ***Entrepreneur.*** An entrepreneur is someone who operates a business. In a market system, entrepreneurs decide what goods and services to produce and how to produce them. An entrepreneur starting a new business puts his or her own funds at risk. If an entrepreneur is wrong about what consumers want or about the best way to produce goods and services, the entrepreneur's funds can be lost. This is not an unusual occurrence: In the United States, about half of new businesses close within four years. Without entrepreneurs willing to assume the risk of starting and operating businesses, economic progress would be impossible in a market system.
- ***Innovation.*** There is a distinction between an *invention* and *innovation*. An invention is the development of a new good or a new process for making a good. An innovation is the practical application of an invention. (*Innovation* may also be used more broadly to refer to any significant improvement in a good or in the

means of producing a good.) Much time often passes between the appearance of a new idea and its development for widespread use. For example, the Wright brothers first achieved self-propelled flight at Kitty Hawk, North Carolina, in 1903, but the Wright brothers' plane was very crude, and it wasn't until the introduction of the DC-3 by Douglas Aircraft in 1936 that regularly scheduled intercity airline flights became common in the United States. Similarly, the first digital electronic computer—the ENIAC—was developed in 1945, but the first IBM personal computer was not introduced until 1981, and widespread use of computers did not have a significant effect on the productivity of American business until the 1990s.

- ***Technology.*** A firm's technology is the processes it uses to produce goods and services. In the economic sense, a firm's technology depends on many factors, such as the skill of its managers, the training of its workers, and the speed and efficiency of its machinery and equipment.
- ***Firm, company, or business.*** A firm is an organization that produces a good or service. Most firms produce goods or services to earn profits, but there are also nonprofit firms, such as universities and some hospitals. Economists use the terms *firm*, *company*, and *business* interchangeably.
- ***Goods.*** Goods are tangible merchandise, such as books, computers, or DVD players.
- ***Services.*** Services are activities done for others, such as providing haircuts or investment advice.
- ***Revenue.*** A firm's revenue is the total amount received for selling a good or service. It is calculated by multiplying the price per unit by the number of units sold.
- ***Profit.*** A firm's profit is the difference between its revenue and its costs. Economists distinguish between *accounting profit* and *economic profit.* In calculating accounting profit, we exclude the cost of some economic resources that the firm does not pay for explicitly. In calculating economic profit, we include the opportunity cost of all resources used by the firm. When we refer to *profit* in this book, we mean economic profit. It is important not to confuse *profit* with *revenue.*
- ***Household.*** A household consists of all persons occupying a home. Households are suppliers of factors of production—particularly labor—used by firms to make goods and services. Households also demand goods and services produced by firms and governments.
- ***Factors of production or economic resources.*** Firms use factors of production to produce goods and services. The main factors of production are labor, capital, human capital, natural resources—including land—and entrepreneurial ability. Households earn income by supplying the factors of production to firms.
- ***Capital.*** The word *capital* can refer to *financial capital* or to *physical capital.* Financial capital includes stocks and bonds issued by firms, bank accounts, and holdings of money. In economics, though, *capital* refers to physical capital, which includes manufactured goods that are used to produce other goods and services. Examples of physical capital are computers, factory buildings, machine tools, warehouses, and trucks. The total amount of physical capital available in a country is referred to as the country's *capital stock.*
- ***Human capital.*** Human capital refers to the accumulated training and skills that workers possess. For example, college-educated workers generally have more skills and are more productive than workers who have only high school degrees.

» Continued from page 3

Economics in YOUR Life!

At the beginning of the chapter, we posed the question: "Is it likely that during your career, your job will be outsourced to China, India, or some other foreign country?" Some information helpful in answering this question appears in the *Making the Connection* on page 13. Economist Jagdish Bhagwati notes that the number of jobs moving to other countries each year is relatively small—probably less than 1 percent of the total jobs created in the U.S. economy each year. In fact, the U.S. economy is constantly creating and eliminating jobs as new firms open their doors and as existing firms get larger or smaller or go out of business. For example, from June 2005 to June 2006, the U.S. economy created 31.2 million jobs and eliminated 28.8 million jobs. The Forrester Research report cited at the beginning of the chapter indicated that as many as 3.3 million jobs might be lost to outsourcing between 2000 and 2015. But that number is very small compared with the more than 450 million jobs the economy is likely to create over that period, or in comparison with the more than 430 million jobs that will be lost due to all causes. So, you may lose your job one or more times during your career, but probably not because of outsourcing.

Conclusion

The best way to think of economics is as a group of useful ideas about how individuals make choices. Economists have put these ideas into practice by developing economic models. Consumers, business managers, and government officials use these models every day to help make choices. In this book, we explore many key economic models and give examples of how to apply them in the real world.

Most students taking an introductory economics course do not major in economics or become professional economists. Whatever your major may be, the economic principles you will learn in this book will improve your ability to make choices in many aspects of your life. These principles will also improve your understanding of how decisions are made in business and government.

Reading the newspaper and other periodicals is an important part of understanding the current business climate and learning how to apply economic concepts to a variety of real-world events. At the end of each chapter, you will see a two-page feature entitled *An Inside Look.* This feature consists of an excerpt of an article that relates to the company introduced at the start of the chapter and also to the concepts discussed throughout the chapter. A summary and analysis and supporting graphs highlight the economic key points of the article. Read *An Inside Look* on the next page to learn why some economists argue that fears about outsourcing to China are unjustified. Test your understanding by answering the *Thinking Critically* questions.

An Inside **LOOK**

Should the United States Worry about High-Tech Competition from India and China?

ECONOMIST, OCTOBER 7, 2006

Nightmare Scenarios

India's high-tech enclaves exude euphoria. Proud techies take their parents on tours of company campuses. Proud parents boast that their children earn more than the rest of the family combined. Mr Nilekani of Infosys says that his company's greatest achievement is not its $2 billion turnover but the fact that it has taught Indians to redefine the possible.

The mood in America, the country that is driving the outsourcing boom, could hardly be more different. People view the global war for talent with foreboding. Their fears take two forms. The first is that well-paying jobs in services will follow manufacturing jobs to the developing world. Norman Augustine, a former boss of Lockheed Martin, says that "virtually no one's job seems safe." Craig Barrett, the chairman of Intel, admits that "I worry for my grandchildren." The second fear is that America may no longer be able to attract more than its fair share of the world's brains. . . .

a Are Americans right to worry? One misconception is that the number of jobs is fixed, so if some of them go abroad there must be fewer left at home. If a farmer in Palo Alto in 1900 had been told that in a hundred years' time agricultural workers would account for only 2% of the American workforce, he would have expected the Valley to become a desert rather than a global technological hub. But even if the number of good jobs were fixed, the fears of a great job migration are exaggerated.

b The McKinsey Global Institute has conducted a large-scale study of the offshoring market and concluded that constraints on both the demand and the supply side will keep the number of service jobs moving offshore much lower than is widely believed. It will probably rise from 1.5m in 2003 to 4.1m in 2008, or 1.2% of the demand for labour in the developed world. That figure is dwarfed by the normal job churn in America, where 4.6m Americans start with a new employer every month.

There is clearly plenty of eager talent in the developing world. But McKinsey argues that only about 13% of that talent is capable of working for a Western multinational in a high-grade job at the moment (although the stock of suitable professionals is expanding a lot faster in developing than in rich countries). There are problems with cultural and language skills, particularly in China. The quality of education is often inadequate. China may have twice as many engineering graduates as America, but only 10% of them are equipped to work for a Western multinational. Geography also imposes limits. In large countries such as India and China many graduates live far away from international airports. In China only about half the talent pool is accessible to multinationals, according to McKinsey. . . .

India's difficulties have more to do with another intractable problem: poor government. The country's infrastructure is crumbling and the education system is hugely uneven. The Indian Institutes of Technology are very good at producing a highly educated elite, but run-of-the-mill colleges are often of poor quality. The result is graduate unemployment of 17% at a time when the high-tech economy is booming.

Americans are right to worry about losing out in the international competition for talented people, particularly as highly qualified Indians and Chinese based in America go home. America's immigration system is hopelessly antiquated, geared more towards reuniting families than attracting high-quality workers. The 2005 allocation for H1B visas for skilled workers ran out on the first day of the fiscal year. . . .

c But again these worries are exaggerated. America remains the world's number one destination for foreign students, soaking up almost 30% of the global supply. There is every reason to think that the absolute number of people from India and China who want to study in America will rise as those countries get richer. It is true that some foreigners who might have stayed in America a few years ago are going home. But David Zweig, of the Hong Kong University of Science and Technology, argues that the best Chinese students remain abroad. The pattern of geographical mobility is likely to get more complicated in the future as people divide their careers between the developed and the developing world, but America is unlikely to be denuded of talent. . . .

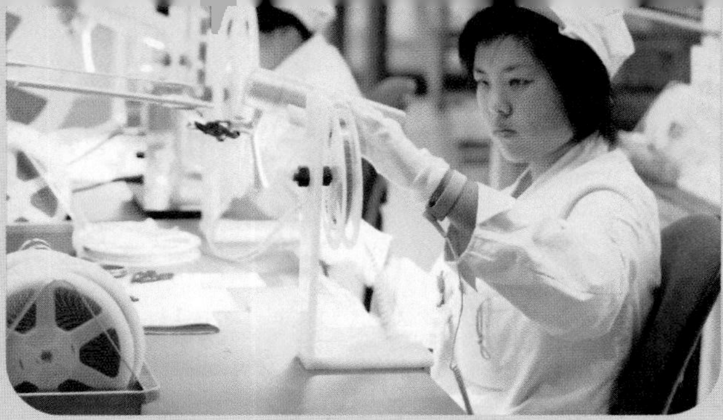

Key Points in the Article

This article discusses fears in the United States that as the Chinese and Indian economies grow, well-paying jobs will move overseas, and it will also become more difficult to attract high-skilled foreign workers to the United States. A decline in the number of high-skilled jobs in the United States could undermine economic growth and reduce increases in living standards. The article argues that these fears are exaggerated and that the United States has many advantages that should allow it to retain many high-skilled, high-wage jobs.

Analyzing the News

a We have seen in this chapter that economists use models to analyze economic issues such as the effects of outsourcing. One advantage of economic models is that they make explicit the assumptions being made. Models also generate hypotheses that can be tested against the real world. According to the article, people who fear competition from China believe that it will result in a loss of jobs in the United States. People who make this argument are also using a model, but it is a model that is not explicitly stated. This model assumes "that the number of jobs is fixed, so if some of them go abroad there must be fewer left at home." We know this model is not useful because for many years the United States has been trading goods and services with other countries, and U.S. firms have had operations in other countries, and the total number of jobs available in the United States has continued to increase.

b The *Making the Connection* on page 13 presents the debate between economists Paul Samuelson and Jagdish Bhagwati over whether outsourcing has helped or hurt the U.S. economy. One key aspect of the debate concerns whether workers who lose their jobs because of outsourcing are eventually likely to find comparable or better jobs. The article cites a study from the McKinsey Global Institute that points out that the number of jobs lost to outsourcing is small relative to the total number of new jobs created in the United States each month.

c The figure below shows the trend in foreign-born doctoral scientists and engineers employed in the United States from 1993 to 2004. Although the relative number of permanent resident scientists and engineers has declined somewhat, the relative number of scientists and engineers who were born in other countries but who have become naturalized citizens of the United States has increased over time. In fact, the share of foreign-born scientists and engineers in the United States increased from 17.9 percent in 1993 to 24.8 percent in 2004. The United States has retained the ability to attract scientists and engineers from other countries.

Thinking Critically

1. The article points out that a total of 4.1 million well-paying service-sector jobs will have moved from the developed world to China and India by 2008. However, the article argues that there are limits to the number of jobs that can move from developed countries to China and India. What determines those limits?
2. According to the article, some Americans worry that the United States is having more difficulty attracting highly skilled workers from China and India and that this will undermine the U.S. high-tech sector. What evidence from the article suggests that the lead of the United States in the high-tech sector is relatively secure?

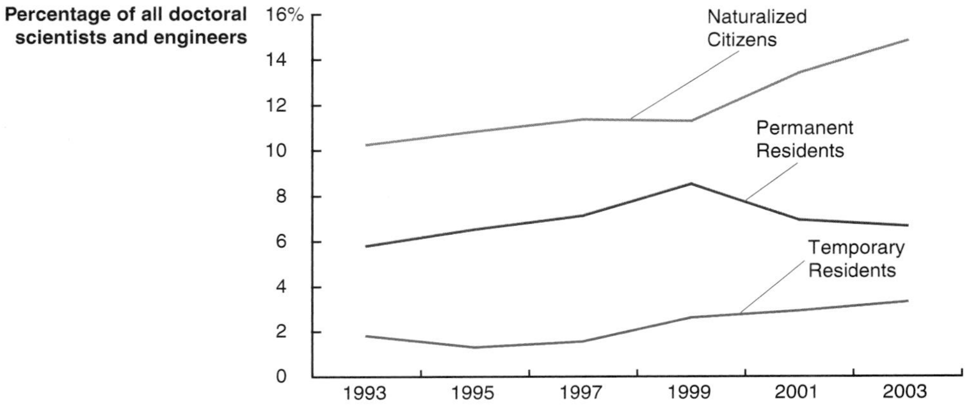

The United States has continued to attract foreign-born scientists and engineers.
Source: National Science Foundation, Division of Science Resources Statistics, *Characteristics of Doctoral Scientists and Engineers in the United States: 2003*, NSF 06-320, Project Officer, John Tsapogas (Arlington, VA, 2006).

Key Terms

1.1 LEARNING OBJECTIVE 1.1 | Explain these three key economic ideas: *People are rational. People respond to incentives. Optimal decisions are made at the margin,* **pages 4–7.**

Three Key Economic Ideas

Summary

Economics is the study of the choices consumers, business managers, and government officials make to attain their goals, given their scarce resources. We must make choices because of **scarcity**, which means that although our wants are unlimited, the resources available to fulfill those wants are limited. Economists assume that people are rational in the sense that consumers and firms use all available information as they take actions intended to achieve their goals. Rational individuals weigh the benefits and costs of each action and choose an action only if the benefits outweigh the costs. Although people act from a variety of motives, ample evidence indicates that they respond to economic incentives. Economists use the word **marginal** to mean extra or additional. The optimal decision is to continue any activity up to the point where the marginal benefit equals the marginal cost.

myeconlab Get Ahead of the Curve — Visit www.myeconlab.com to complete these exercises online and get instant feedback.

Review Questions

1.1 Briefly discuss each of the following economic ideas: People are rational. People respond to incentives. Optimal decisions are made at the margin.

1.2 What is scarcity? Why is scarcity central to the study of economics?

Problems and Applications

1.3 In the first six months of 2003, branches of Commerce Bank in New York City were robbed 14 times. The New York City Police Department recommended steps the bank could take to deter robberies, including the installation of plastic barriers called "bandit barriers." The police were surprised that the bank did not take their advice. According to a deputy commissioner of police, "Commerce does very little of what we recommend. They've told our detectives they have no interest in ever putting in the barriers." Wouldn't Commerce Bank have a strong incentive to install bandit barriers to deter robberies? Why, then, wouldn't it do so?

Source: Dan Barry, "Friendly Bank Makes It Easy for Robbers," *New York Times*, July 5, 2003.

1.4 **(Related to *Solved Problem 1-1* on page 7)** Suppose Dell is currently selling 250,000 Pentium 4 laptops per month. A manager at Dell argues, "The last 10,000 laptops we produced increased our revenue by \$8.5 million and our costs by \$8.9 million. However, because we are making a substantial total profit of \$25 million from producing 250,000 laptops, I think we are producing the optimal number of laptops." Briefly explain whether you agree with the manager's reasoning.

1.5 **(Related to *Solved Problem 1-1* on page 7)** Two students are discussing Solved Problem 1-1:

Joe: "I think the key additional information you need to know in deciding whether to produce 300,000 more iPods is the amount of profit you currently are making while producing 3,000,000. Then you can compare the profit earned from selling 3,300,000 iPods with the profit earned from selling 3,000,000. This information is more important than the additional revenue and additional cost of the last 300,000 iPods produced."

Jill: "Actually, Joe, knowing how much profits change when you sell 300,000 more iPods is exactly the same as knowing the additional revenue and the additional cost."

Briefly evaluate their arguments.

1.6 **(Related to *Solved Problem 1-1* on page 7)** Late in the semester, a friend tells you, "I was going to drop my psychology course so I could concentrate on my other courses, but I had already put so much time into the course that I decided not to drop it." What do you think of your friend's reasoning? Would it make a difference to your answer if your friend has to pass the psychology course at some point to graduate? Briefly explain.

1.7 **(Related to the *Making the Connection* on page 5)** Estonia has attempted to increase the country's birthrate by making payments to women who have babies. According to an article in the *Wall Street Journal*, "Some demographers argue that paying people to have a baby simply makes them have one earlier; it doesn't necessarily make them have more." Reread the description of Estonia's programs. Could the program be changed in ways that might make it more likely that Estonian women will have more children, rather than simply changing the timing of when they have children? What information would we need to have to resolve the question of whether Estonian women are responding to the government's incentives by having more children or simply by having them earlier?

Source: Marcus Walker, "In Estonia, Paying Women to Have Babies Is Paying Off," *Wall Street Journal*, October 20, 2006, p. A1.

1.8 In a column in the *Wall Street Journal*, Robert McTeer, Jr., former president of the Federal Reserve Bank of Dallas, wrote, "My take on training in economics is that it becomes increasingly valuable as you move up the career ladder. I can't think of a better major for corporate CEOs [chief executive officers], congressmen or American presidents." Why might studying economics be particularly good preparation for being the top manager of a corporation or a leader in government?

Source: Robert D. McTeer, Jr., "The Dismal Science? Hardly!" *Wall Street Journal*, June 4, 2003.

>> End Learning Objective 1.1

1.2 LEARNING OBJECTIVE 1.2 | Discuss how an economy answers these questions: *What* goods and services will be produced? *How* will the goods and services be produced? *Who* will receive the goods and services? **pages 8–11.**

The Economic Problem That Every Society Must Solve

Summary

Society faces **tradeoffs**: Producing more of one good or service means producing less of another good or service. The **opportunity cost** of any activity—such as producing a good or service—is the highest-valued alternative that must be given up to engage in that activity. The choices of consumers, firms, and governments determine what goods and services will be produced. Firms choose how to produce the goods and services they sell. In the United States, who receives the goods and services produced depends largely on how income is distributed in the marketplace. In a **centrally planned economy**, most economic decisions are made by the government. In a **market economy**, most economic decisions are made by consumers and firms. Most economies, including that of the United States, are **mixed economies** in which most economic decisions are made by consumers and firms but in which the government also plays a significant role. There are two types of efficiency: productive efficiency and allocative efficiency. **Productive efficiency** occurs when a good or service is produced at the lowest possible cost. **Allocative efficiency** occurs when production is in accordance with consumer preferences. **Voluntary exchange** is the situation that occurs in markets when both the buyer and seller of a product are made better off by the transaction. **Equity** is more difficult to define than efficiency, but it usually involves a fair distribution of economic benefits. Government policymakers often face a tradeoff between equity and efficiency.

myeconlab Get Ahead of the Curve — Visit www.myeconlab.com to complete these exercises online and get instant feedback.

Review Questions

2.1 What are the three economic questions that every society must answer? Briefly discuss the differences in how centrally planned, market, and mixed economies answer these questions.

2.2 What is the difference between productive efficiency and allocative efficiency?

2.3 What is the difference between efficiency and equity? Why do government policymakers often face a trade-off between efficiency and equity?

Problems and Applications

2.4 Does Bill Gates, the richest person in the world, face scarcity? Does everyone? Are there any exceptions?

2.5 Would you expect new and better machinery and equipment to be adopted more rapidly in a market economy or in a centrally planned economy? Briefly explain.

2.6 Centrally planned economies have been less efficient than market economies.
  a. Has this happened by chance, or is there some underlying reason?
  b. If market economies are more economically efficient than centrally planned economies, would there ever be a reason to prefer having a centrally planned economy rather than a market economy?

2.7 Thomas Sowell, an economist at the Hoover Institution at Stanford University, has written, "All economic systems not only provide people with goods and services, but also restrict or prevent them from getting as much of these goods and services as they wish." Why is it necessary for all economic systems to do this? How does a market system prevent people from getting as many goods and services as they wish?

Source: Thomas Sowell, *Applied Economics: Thinking Beyond Stage One*, New York: Basic Books, 2004, p. 16.

2.8 Suppose that your local police department recovers 100 tickets to a big NASCAR race in a drug raid. It decides to distribute these to residents and announces that tickets will be given away at 10 A.M. Monday at City Hall.
  a. What groups of people will be most likely to try to get the tickets? Think of specific examples and then generalize.
  b. What is the opportunity cost of distributing the tickets this way?
  c. Productive efficiency occurs when a good or service (such as the distribution of tickets) is produced at the lowest possible cost. Is this an efficient way to distribute the tickets? If possible, think of a more efficient method of distributing the tickets.
  d. Is this an equitable way to distribute the tickets? Explain.

>> End Learning Objective 1.2

1.3 LEARNING OBJECTIVE

1.3 | Understand the role of models in economic analysis, **pages 11–15.**

Economic Models

Summary

Economists rely on economic models when they apply economic ideas to real-world problems. **Economic models** are simplified versions of reality used to analyze real-world economic situations. Economists accept and use an economic model if it leads to hypotheses that are confirmed by statistical analysis. In many cases, the acceptance is tentative, however, pending the gathering of new data or further statistical analysis. Economics is a **social science** because it applies the scientific method to the study of the interactions among individuals. Economics is concerned with positive analysis rather than normative analysis. **Positive analysis** is concerned with what is. **Normative analysis** is concerned with what ought to be. Because economics is based on studying the actions of individuals, it is a social science. As a social science, economics considers human behavior in every context of decision making, not just in business.

myeconlab Get Ahead of the Curve Visit www.myeconlab.com to complete these exercises online and get instant feedback.

Review Questions

3.1 Why do economists use models? How are economic data used to test models?

3.2 Describe the five steps by which economists arrive at a useful economic model.

3.3 What is the difference between normative analysis and positive analysis? Is economics concerned mainly with normative analysis or mainly with positive analysis? Briefly explain.

Problems and Applications

3.4 Do you agree or disagree with the following assertion: "The problem with economics is that it assumes consumers and firms always make the correct decision. But we know everyone's human, and we all make mistakes."

3.5 Suppose an economist develops an economic model and finds that "it works great in theory, but it fails in practice." What should the economist do next?

3.6 Dr. Strangelove's theory is that the price of mushrooms is determined by the activity of subatomic particles that exist in another universe parallel to ours. When the subatomic particles are emitted in profusion, the price of mushrooms is high. When subatomic particle emissions are low, the price of mushrooms also is low. How would you go about testing Dr. Strangelove's theory? Discuss whether this theory is useful.

3.7 **(Related to the *Making the Connection* on page 13)** The *Making the Connection* that discusses the debate between Paul Samuelson and Jahdish Bhagwati over outsourcing mentions that the two economists disagree over how to interpret the relevant economic statistics. What economic statistics would be most useful in evaluating the positions these economists hold? Assuming these statistics are available or could be gathered, are they likely to finally resolve the debate?

3.8 **(Related to the *Chapter Opener* on page 2)** Many large firms have begun outsourcing work to China.
   a. Why have large firms done this?
   b. Is outsourcing work to low-wage Chinese workers a risk-free proposition for large firms?

3.9 **(Related to the *Don't Let This Happen to You!* on page 14)** Explain which of the following statements represent positive analysis and which represent normative analysis.
   a. A 50-cent-per-pack tax on cigarettes will reduce smoking by teenagers by 12 percent.
   b. The federal government should spend more on AIDS research.
   c. Rising paper prices will increase textbook prices.
   d. The price of coffee at Starbucks is too high.

3.10 The American Bar Association has proposed a law that would prohibit anyone except lawyers from giving legal advice. Under the proposal, income tax preparers, real estate agents, hospitals, labor unions, and anyone else who offered legal advice would be penalized. One critic of the proposal argued that the proposal would protect attorneys more than it would protect consumers.
   a. How might the proposal protect consumers?
   b. Why did the critic of the proposal argue that it would protect attorneys more than it would protect consumers?
   c. Briefly discuss whether you consider the proposed law to be a good idea.

Source: Adam Liptak, "U.S. Opposes Proposal to Limit Who May Give Legal Advice," *The New York Times*, February 3, 2003.

>> End Learning Objective 1.3

1.4 LEARNING OBJECTIVE 1.4 | Distinguish between microeconomics and macroeconomics, **page 15.**

Microeconomics and Macroeconomics

Summary

Microeconomics is the study of how households and firms make choices, how they interact in markets, and how the government attempts to influence their choices. **Macroeconomics** is the study of the economy as a whole, including topics such as inflation, unemployment, and economic growth.

myeconlab Get Ahead of the Curve — Visit www.myeconlab.com to complete these exercises online and get instant feedback.

Review Question

4.1 Briefly discuss the difference between microeconomics and macroeconomics.

Problems and Applications

4.2 Briefly explain whether each of the following is primarily a microeconomic issue or a macroeconomic issue.
   a. The effect of higher cigarette taxes on the quantity of cigarettes sold.
   b. The effect of higher income taxes on the total amount of consumer spending.
   c. The reasons for the economies of East Asian countries growing faster than the economies of sub-Saharan African countries.
   d. The reasons for low rates of profit in the airline industry.

4.3 Briefly explain whether you agree with the following assertion: "Microeconomics is concerned with things that happen in one particular place, such as the unemployment rate in one city. In contrast, macroeconomics is concerned with things that affect the country as a whole, such as how the rate of teenage smoking in the United States would be affected by an increase in the tax on cigarettes."

>> End Learning Objective 1.4

1.5 LEARNING OBJECTIVE 1.5 | Become familiar with important economic terms, **pages 15–16.**

A Preview of Important Economic Terms

Summary

Becoming familiar with important terms is a necessary step in learning economics. These important economic terms include *capital, entrepreneur, factors of production, firm, goods, household, human capital, innovation, profit, revenue,* and *technology.*

Appendix

Using Graphs and Formulas

LEARNING OBJECTIVE

Review the use of **graphs** and **formulas**.

Graphs are used to illustrate key economics ideas. Graphs appear not just in economics textbooks but also on Web sites and in newspaper and magazine articles that discuss events in business and economics. Why the heavy use of graphs? Because they serve two useful purposes: (1) They simplify economic ideas, and (2) they make the ideas more concrete so they can be applied to real-world problems. Economic and business issues can be complicated, but a graph can help cut through complications and highlight the key relationships needed to understand the issue. In that sense, a graph can be like a street map.

For example, suppose you take a bus to New York City to see the Empire State Building. After arriving at the Port Authority Bus Terminal, you will probably use a map similar to the one shown below to find your way to the Empire State Building.

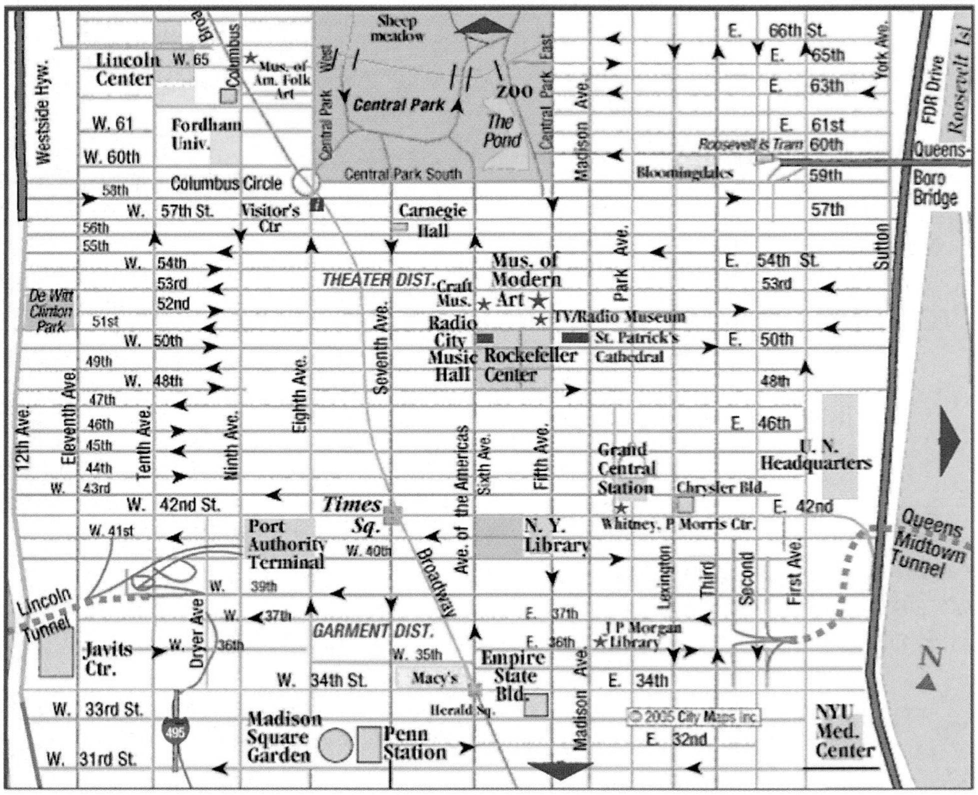

Maps are very familiar to just about everyone, so we don't usually think of them as being simplified versions of reality, but they are. This map does not show much more than the streets in this part of New York City and some of the most important buildings. The names, addresses, and telephone numbers of the people who live and work in the area aren't given. Almost none of the stores and buildings those people work and live in are shown either. The map doesn't tell which streets allow curbside parking and which don't. In fact, the map tells almost nothing about the messy reality of life in this section of New York City, except how the streets are laid out, which is the essential information you need to get from the Port Authority to the Empire State Building.

Think about someone who says, "I know how to get around in the city, but I just can't figure out how to read a map." It certainly is possible to find your destination in a city without a map, but it's a lot easier with one. The same is true of using graphs in economics. It is possible to arrive at a solution to a real-world problem in economics and business without using graphs, but it is usually a lot easier if you do use them.

Often, the difficulty students have with graphs and formulas is a lack of familiarity. With practice, all the graphs and formulas in this text will become familiar to you. Once you are familiar with them, you will be able to use them to analyze problems that would otherwise seem very difficult. What follows is a brief review of how graphs and formulas are used.

Graphs of One Variable

Figure 1A-1 displays values for *market shares* in the U.S. automobile market, using two common types of graphs. Market shares show the percentage of industry sales accounted for by different firms. In this case, the information is for groups of firms: the "Big Three"—Ford, General Motors, and DaimlerChrysler—as well as Japanese firms, European firms, and Korean firms. Panel (a) displays the information on market shares as a *bar graph*, where the market share of each group of firms is represented by the

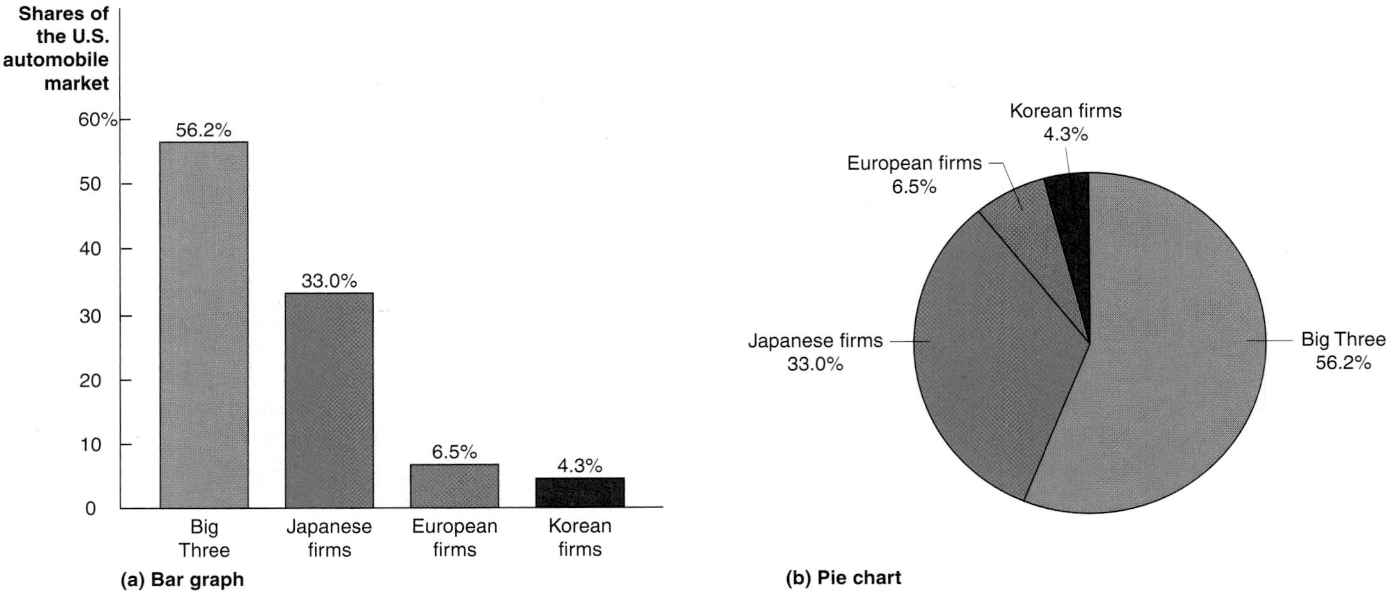

Figure 1A-1 | Bar Graphs and Pie Charts

Values for an economic variable are often displayed as a bar graph or as a pie chart. In this case, panel (a) shows market share data for the U.S. automobile industry as a bar graph, where the market share of each group of firms is represented by the height of its bar. Panel (b) displays the same information as a pie chart, with the market share of each group of firms represented by the size of its slice of the pie.

Source: "Auto Sales," *Wall Street Journal*, March 1, 2007.

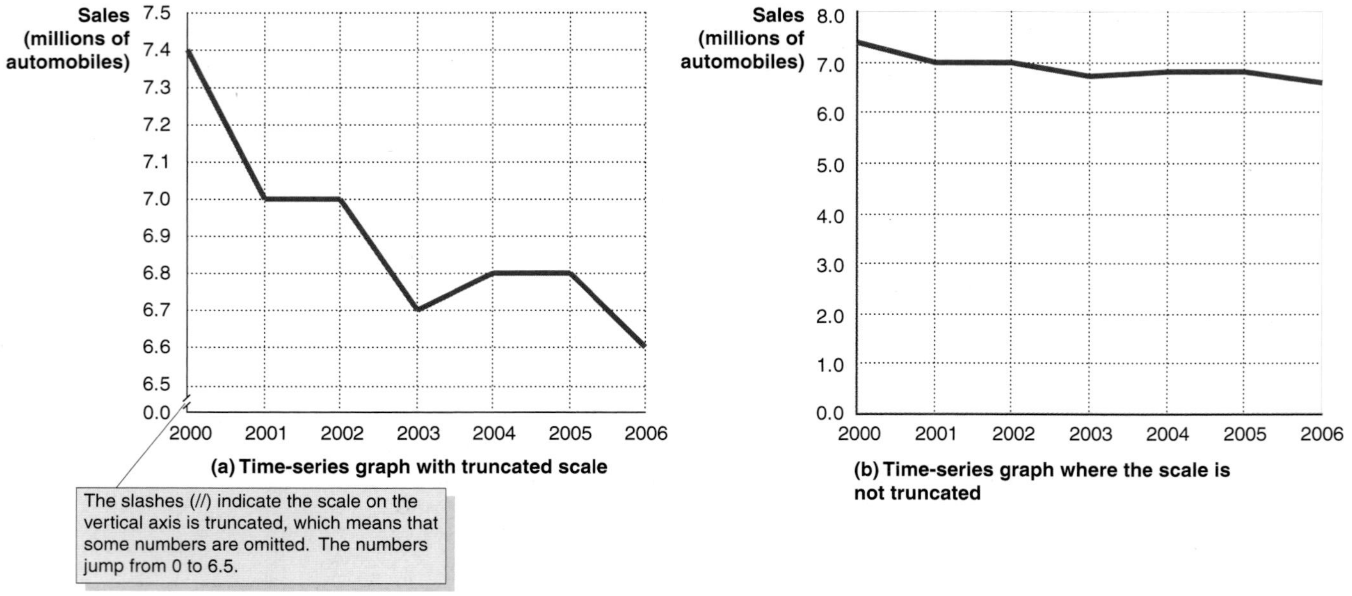

Figure 1A-2 | Time-Series Graphs

Both panels present time-series graphs of Ford Motor Company's worldwide sales during each year from 2000–2006. Panel (a) has a truncated scale on the vertical axis, and panel (b) does not. As a result, the fluctuations in Ford's sales appear smaller in panel (b) than in panel (a).
Source: Ford Motor Company, *Annual Report*, various years.

height of its bar. Panel (b) displays the same information as a *pie chart*, with the market share of each group of firms represented by the size of its slice of the pie.

Information on economic variables is also often displayed in *time-series graphs.* Time-series graphs are displayed on a coordinate grid. In a coordinate grid, we can measure the value of one variable along the vertical axis (or *y*-axis), and the value of another variable along the horizontal axis (or *x*-axis). The point where the vertical axis intersects the horizontal axis is called the *origin.* At the origin, the value of both variables is zero. The points on a coordinate grid represent values of the two variables. In Figure 1A-2, we measure the number of automobiles and trucks sold worldwide by the Ford Motor Company on the vertical axis, and we measure time on the horizontal axis. In time-series graphs, the height of the line at each date shows the value of the variable measured on the vertical axis. Both panels of Figure 1A-2 show Ford's worldwide sales during each year from 2000 to 2006. The difference between panel (a) and panel (b) illustrates the importance of the scale used in a time-series graph. In panel (a), the scale on the vertical axis is truncated, which means that it does not start with zero. The slashes (//) near the bottom of the axis indicate that the scale is truncated. In panel (b), the scale is not truncated. In panel (b), the decline in Ford's sales since 2000 appears smaller than in panel (a). (Technically, the horizontal axis is also truncated because we start with the year 2000, not the year 0.)

Graphs of Two Variables

We often use graphs to show the relationship between two variables. For example, suppose you are interested in the relationship between the price of a pepperoni pizza and the quantity of pizzas sold per week in the small town of Bryan, Texas. A graph showing the relationship between the price of a good and the quantity of the good demanded at each price is called a *demand curve.* (As we will discuss later, in drawing a demand curve for a good, we have to hold constant any variables other than price that might affect the

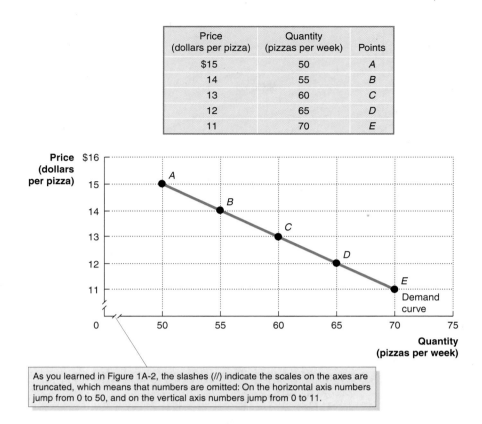

Price (dollars per pizza)	Quantity (pizzas per week)	Points
$15	50	*A*
14	55	*B*
13	60	*C*
12	65	*D*
11	70	*E*

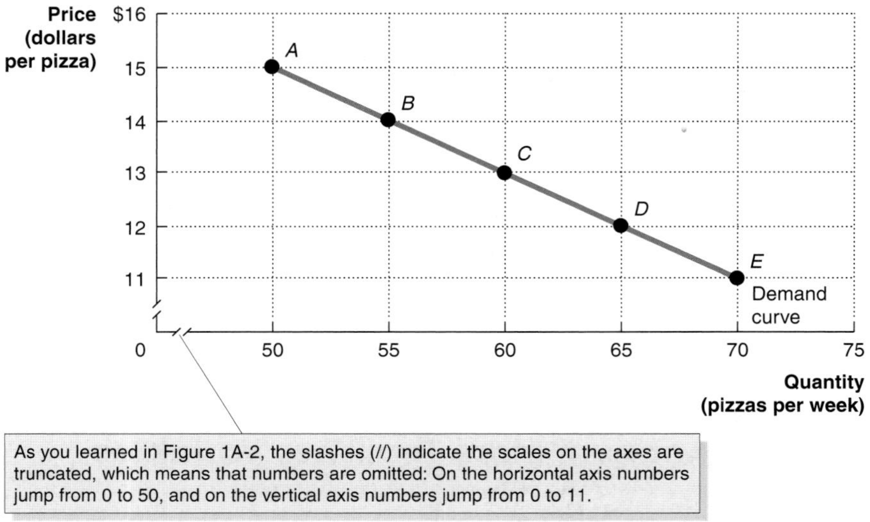
Price (dollars per pizza)
$16
15
14
13
12
11
0
A
B
C
D
E
Demand curve
50
55
60
65
70
75
Quantity (pizzas per week)
As you learned in Figure 1A-2, the slashes (//) indicate the scales on the axes are truncated, which means that numbers are omitted: On the horizontal axis numbers jump from 0 to 50, and on the vertical axis numbers jump from 0 to 11.

Figure 1A-3

Plotting Price and Quantity Points in a Graph

The figure shows a two-dimensional grid on which we measure the price of pizza along the vertical axis (or *y*-axis) and the quantity of pizza sold per week along the horizontal axis (or *x*-axis). Each point on the grid represents one of the price and quantity combinations listed in the table. By connecting the points with a line, we can better illustrate the relationship between the two variables.

willingness of consumers to buy the good.) Figure 1A-3 shows the data you have collected on price and quantity. The figure shows a two-dimensional grid on which we measure the price of pizza along the *y*-axis and the quantity of pizza sold per week along the *x*-axis. Each point on the grid represents one of the price and quantity combinations listed in the table. We can connect the points to form the demand curve for pizza in Bryan, Texas. Notice that the scales on both axes in the graph are truncated. In this case, truncating the axes allows the graph to illustrate more clearly the relationship between price and quantity by excluding low prices and quantities.

Slopes of Lines

Once you have plotted the data in Figure 1A-3, you may be interested in how much the quantity of pizza sold increases as the price decreases. The *slope* of a line tells us how much the variable we are measuring on the *y*-axis changes as the variable we are measuring on the *x*-axis changes. We can use the Greek letter delta (Δ) to stand for the change in a variable. The slope is sometimes referred to as the rise over the run. So, we have several ways of expressing slope:

$$\text{Slope} = \frac{\text{Change in value on the vertical axis}}{\text{Change in value on the horizontal axis}} = \frac{\Delta y}{\Delta x} = \frac{\text{Rise}}{\text{Run}}.$$

Figure 1A-4 reproduces the graph from Figure 1A-3. Because the slope of a straight line is the same at any point, we can use any two points in the figure to calculate the slope of the line. For example, when the price of pizza decreases from $14 to $12, the quantity of pizza sold increases from 55 per week to 65 per week. Therefore, the slope is:

$$\text{Slope} = \frac{\Delta\text{Price of pizza}}{\Delta\text{Quantity of pizza}} = \frac{(\$12 - \$14)}{(65 - 55)} = \frac{-2}{10} = -0.2.$$

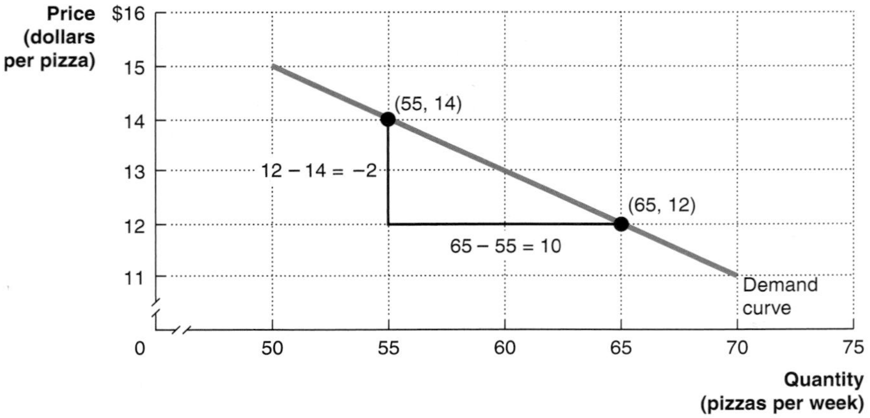

Figure 1A-4

Calculating the Slope of a Line

We can calculate the slope of a line as the change in the value of the variable on the *y*-axis divided by the change in the value of the variable on the *x*-axis. Because the slope of a straight line is constant, we can use any two points in the figure to calculate the slope of the line. For example, when the price of pizza decreases from \$14 to \$12, the quantity of pizza demanded increases from 55 per week to 65 per week. So, the slope of this line equals −2 divided by 10, or −0.2.

The slope of this line gives us some insight into how responsive consumers in Bryan, Texas, are to changes in the price of pizza. The larger the value of the slope (ignoring the negative sign), the steeper the line will be, which indicates that not many additional pizzas are sold when the price falls. The smaller the value of the slope, the flatter the line will be, which indicates a greater increase in pizzas sold when the price falls.

Taking into Account More Than Two Variables on a Graph

The demand curve graph in Figure 1A-4 shows the relationship between the price of pizza and the quantity of pizza sold, but we know that the quantity of any good sold depends on more than just the price of the good. For example, the quantity of pizza sold in a given week in Bryan, Texas, can be affected by such other variables as the price of hamburgers, whether an advertising campaign by local pizza parlors has begun that week, and so on. Allowing the values of any other variables to change will cause the position of the demand curve in the graph to change.

Suppose, for example, that the demand curve in Figure 1A-4 was drawn holding the price of hamburgers constant at \$1.50. If the price of hamburgers rises to \$2.00, then some consumers will switch from buying hamburgers to buying pizza, and more pizzas will be sold at every price. The result on the graph will be to shift the line representing the demand curve to the right. Similarly, if the price of hamburgers falls from \$1.50 to \$1.00, some consumers will switch from buying pizza to buying hamburgers, and fewer pizzas will be sold at every price. The result on the graph will be to shift the line representing the demand curve to the left.

The table in Figure 1A-5 shows the effect of a change in the price of hamburgers on the quantity of pizza demanded. For example, suppose at first we are on the line labeled *Demand curve*$_1$. If the price of pizza is \$14 (point *A*), an increase in the price of hamburgers from \$1.50 to \$2.00 increases the quantity of pizzas demanded from 55 to 60 per week (point *B*) and shifts us to *Demand curve*$_2$. Or, if we start on *Demand curve*$_1$ and the price of pizza is \$12 (point *C*), a decrease in the price of hamburgers from \$1.50 to \$1.00 decreases the quantity of pizzas demanded from 65 to 60 per week (point *D*) and shifts us to *Demand curve*$_3$. By shifting the demand curve, we have taken into account the effect of changes in the value of a third variable—the price of hamburgers. We will use this technique of shifting curves to allow for the effects of additional variables many times in this book.

Positive and Negative Relationships

We can use graphs to show the relationships between any two variables. Sometimes the relationship between the variables is *negative*, meaning that as one variable increases in value, the other variable decreases in value. This was the case with the

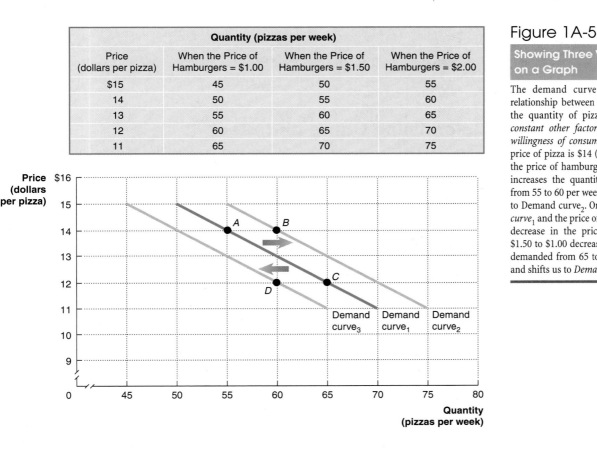

Price (dollars per pizza)	Quantity (pizzas per week)		
	When the Price of Hamburgers = \$1.00	When the Price of Hamburgers = \$1.50	When the Price of Hamburgers = \$2.00
\$15	45	50	55
14	50	55	60
13	55	60	65
12	60	65	70
11	65	70	75

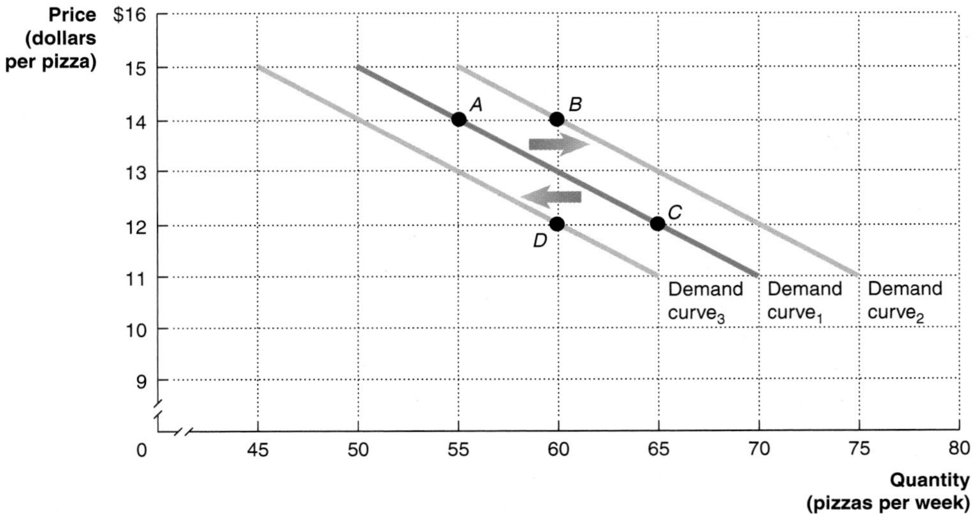

Figure 1A-5

Showing Three Variables on a Graph

The demand curve for pizza shows the relationship between the price of pizzas and the quantity of pizzas demanded, *holding constant other factors that might affect the willingness of consumers to buy pizza.* If the price of pizza is \$14 (point *A*), an increase in the price of hamburgers from \$1.50 to \$2.00 increases the quantity of pizzas demanded from 55 to 60 per week (point *B*) and shifts us to Demand curve$_2$. Or, if we start on *Demand curve*$_1$ and the price of pizza is \$12 (point *C*), a decrease in the price of hamburgers from \$1.50 to \$1.00 decreases the quantity of pizza demanded from 65 to 60 per week (point *D*) and shifts us to *Demand curve*$_3$.

price of pizza and the quantity of pizzas demanded. The relationship between two variables can also be *positive*, meaning that the values of both variables increase or decrease together. For example, when the level of total income—or *disposable personal income*—received by households in the United States increases, the level of total *consumption spending*, which is spending by households on goods and services, also increases. The table in Figure 1A-6 shows the values for income and consumption spending for the years 2003–2006 (the values are in billions of dollars). The graph

Year	Disposable Personal Income (billions of dollars)	Consumption Spending (billions of dollars)
2003	\$8,163	\$7,704
2004	8,682	8,212
2005	9,036	8,742
2006	9,523	9,269

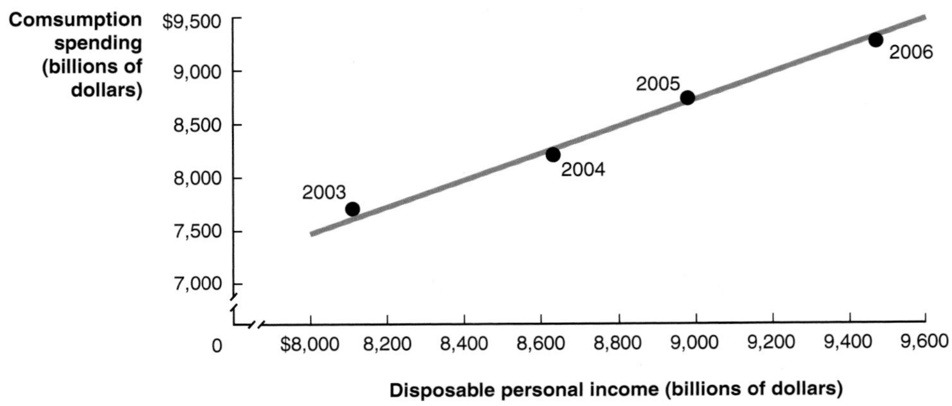

Figure 1A-6

Graphing the Positive Relationship between Income and Consumption

In a positive relationship between two economic variables, as one variable increases, the other variable also increases. This figure shows the positive relationship between disposable personal income and consumption spending. As disposable personal income in the United States has increased, so has consumption spending.

Source: U.S. Department of Commerce, Bureau of Economic Analysis.

plots the data from the table, with national income measured along the horizontal axis and consumption spending measured along the vertical axis. Notice that the four points do not all fall exactly on the line. This is often the case with real-world data. To examine the relationship between two variables, economists often use the straight line that best fits the data.

Determining Cause and Effect

When we graph the relationship between two variables, we often want to draw conclusions about whether changes in one variable are causing changes in the other variable. Doing so, however, can lead to incorrect conclusions. For example, suppose you graph the number of homes in a neighborhood that have a fire burning in the fireplace and the number of leaves on trees in the neighborhood. You would get a relationship like that shown in panel (a) of Figure 1A-7: The more fires burning in the neighborhood, the fewer leaves the trees have. Can we draw the conclusion from this graph that using a fireplace causes trees to lose their leaves? We know, of course, that such a conclusion would be incorrect. In spring and summer, there are relatively few fireplaces being used, and the trees are full of leaves. In the fall, as trees begin to lose their leaves, fireplaces are used more frequently. And in winter, many fireplaces are being used and many trees have lost all their leaves. The reason that the graph in Figure 1A-7 is misleading about cause and effect is that there is obviously an *omitted variable* in the analysis—the season of the year. An omitted variable is one that affects other variables, and its omission can lead to false conclusions about cause and effect.

Although in our example the omitted variable is obvious, there are many debates about cause and effect where the existence of an omitted variable has not been clear. For instance, it has been known for many years that people who smoke cigarettes suffer from higher rates of lung cancer than do nonsmokers. For some time, tobacco companies and some scientists argued that there was an omitted variable—perhaps psychological temperament—that made some people more likely to smoke and more likely to develop lung cancer. If this omitted variable existed, then the finding that smokers were

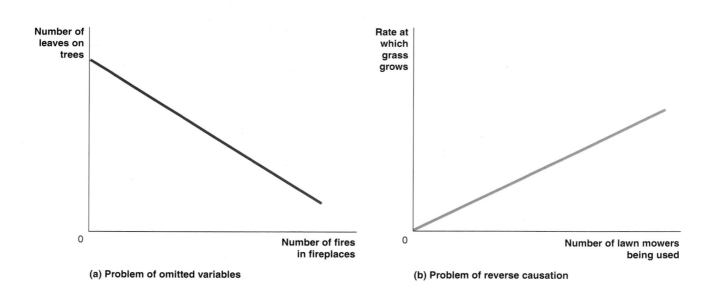

(a) Problem of omitted variables

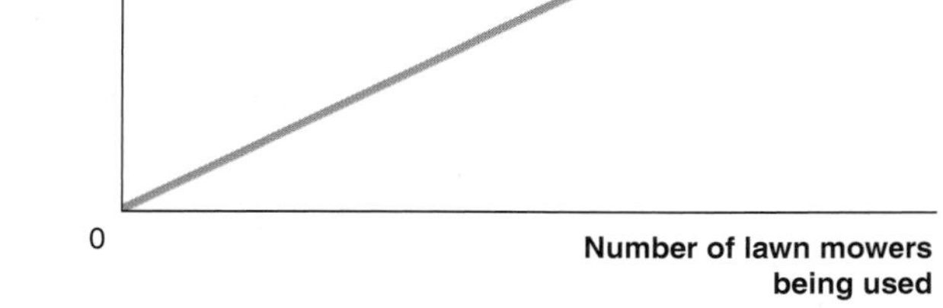

(b) Problem of reverse causation

Figure 1A-7 | Determining Cause and Effect

Using graphs to draw conclusions about cause and effect can be hazardous. In panel (a), we see that there are fewer leaves on the trees in a neighborhood when many homes have fires burning in their fireplaces. We cannot draw the conclusion that the fires cause the leaves to fall because we have an *omitted variable*—the season of the year. In panel (b), we see that more lawn mowers are used in a neighborhood during times when the grass grows rapidly and fewer lawn mowers are used when the grass grows slowly. Concluding that using lawn mowers *causes* the grass to grow faster would be making the error of *reverse causality*.

more likely to develop lung cancer would not have been evidence that smoking *caused* lung cancer. In this case, however, nearly all scientists eventually concluded that the omitted variable did not exist and that, in fact, smoking does cause lung cancer.

A related problem in determining cause and effect is known as *reverse causality*. The error of reverse causality occurs when we conclude that changes in variable X cause changes in variable Y when, in fact, it is actually changes in variable Y that cause changes in variable X. For example, panel (b) of Figure 1A-7 plots the number of lawn mowers being used in a neighborhood against the rate at which grass on lawns in the neighborhood is growing. We could conclude from this graph that using lawn mowers *causes* the grass to grow faster. We know, however, that in reality, the causality is in the other direction: Rapidly growing grass during the spring and summer causes the increased use of lawn mowers. Slowly growing grass in the fall or winter or during periods of low rainfall causes decreased use of lawn mowers.

Once again, in our example, the potential error of reverse causality is obvious. In many economic debates, however, cause and effect can be more difficult to determine. For example, changes in the money supply, or the total amount of money in the economy, tend to occur at the same time as changes in the total amount of income people in the economy earn. A famous debate in economics was about whether the changes in the money supply caused the changes in total income or whether the changes in total income caused the changes in the money supply. Each side in the debate accused the other side of committing the error of reverse causality.

Are Graphs of Economic Relationships Always Straight Lines?

The graphs of relationships between two economic variables that we have drawn so far have been straight lines. The relationship between two variables is *linear* when it can be represented by a straight line. Few economic relationships are actually linear. For example, if we carefully plot data on the price of a product and the quantity demanded at each price, holding constant other variables that affect the quantity demanded, we will usually find a curved—or *nonlinear*—relationship rather than a linear relationship. In practice, however, it is often useful to approximate a nonlinear relationship with a linear relationship. If the relationship is reasonably close to being linear, the analysis is not significantly affected. In addition, it is easier to calculate the slope of a straight line, and it also is easier to calculate the area under a straight line. So, in this textbook, we often assume that the relationship between two economic variables is linear even when we know that this assumption is not precisely correct.

Slopes of Nonlinear Curves

In some situations, we need to take into account the nonlinear nature of an economic relationship. For example, panel (a) of Figure 1A-8 shows the hypothetical relationship between Apple's total cost of producing iPods and the quantity of iPods produced. The relationship is curved, rather than linear. In this case, the cost of production is increasing at an increasing rate, which often happens in manufacturing. Put a different way, as we move up the curve, its slope becomes larger. (Remember that with a straight line, the slope is always constant.) To see this effect, first remember that we calculate the slope of a curve by dividing the change in the variable on the y-axis by the change in the variable on the x-axis. As we move from point A to point B, the quantity produced increases by 1 million iPods, while the total cost of production increases by \$50 million. Farther up the curve, as we move from point C to point D, the change in quantity is the same—1 million iPods—but the change in the total cost of production is now much larger: \$250 million. Because the change in the y variable has increased, while the change in the x variable has remained the same, we know that the slope has increased.

To measure the slope of a nonlinear curve at a particular point, we must measure the slope of the *tangent line* to the curve at that point. A tangent line will only touch the curve at that point. We can measure the slope of the tangent line just as we would

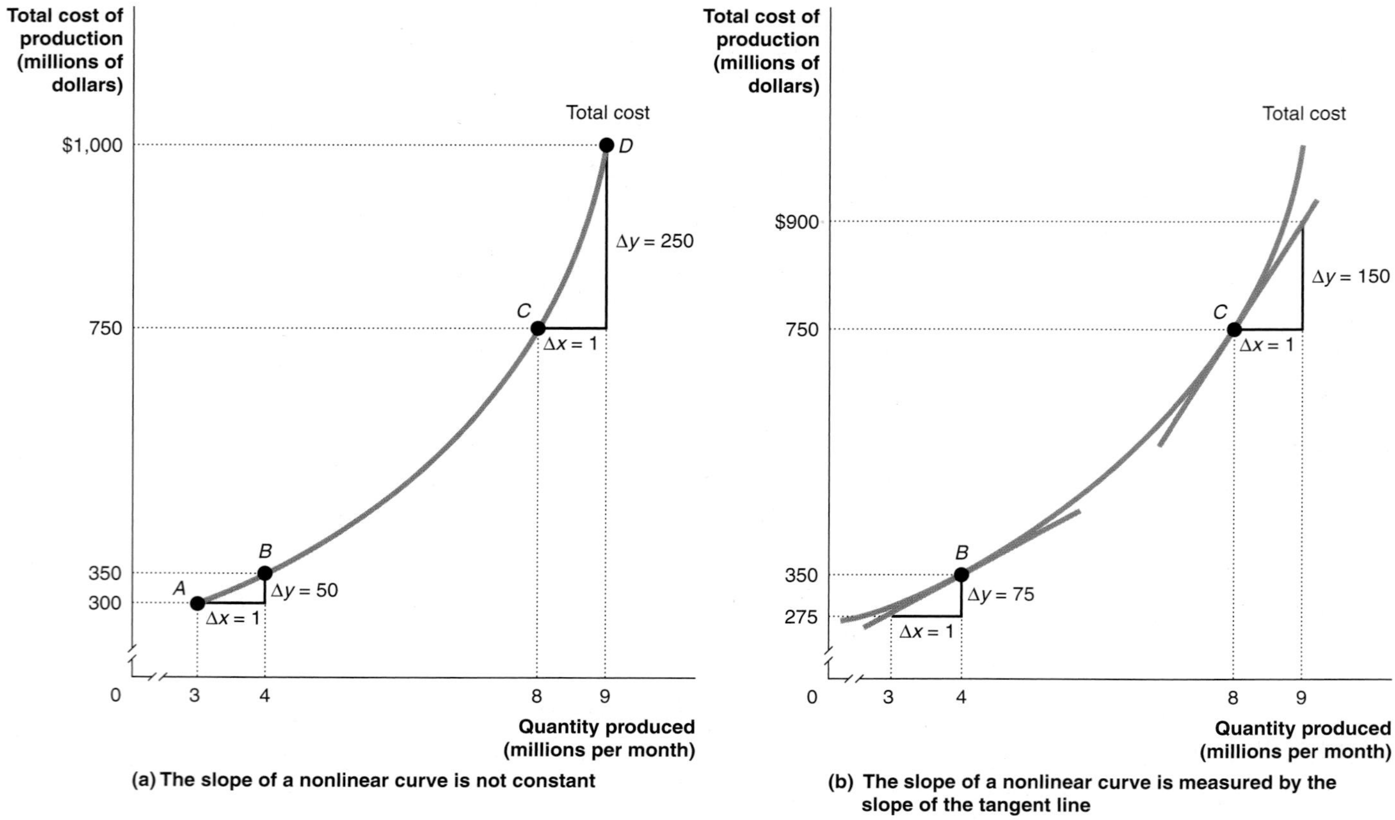

Figure 1A-8 | The Slope of a Nonlinear Curve

The relationship between the quantity of iPods produced and the total cost of production is curved, rather than liner. In panel (a), in moving from point *A* to point *B*, the quantity produced increases by 1 million iPods, while the total cost of production increases by $50 million. Farther up the cure, as we move from point *C* to point *D*, the change in quantity is the same—1 million iPods—but the change in the total cost of production is now much larger: $250 million. Because the change in the *y* variable has increased, while the change in the *x* variable has remained the same, we know that the slope has increased. In panel (b), we measure the slope of the curve at a particular point by the slope of the tangent line. The slope of the tangent line at point *B* is 75, and the slope of the tangent line at point *C* is 150.

the slope of any straight line. In panel (b), the tangent line at point *B* has a slope equal to:

$$\frac{\Delta\text{Cost}}{\Delta\text{Quantity}} = \frac{75}{1} = 75.$$

The tangent line at point *C* has a slope equal to:

$$\frac{\Delta\text{Cost}}{\Delta\text{Quantity}} = \frac{150}{1} = 150.$$

Once again, we see that the slope of the curve is larger at point *C* than at point *B*.

Formulas

We have just seen that graphs are an important economic tool. In this section, we will review several useful formulas and show how to use them to summarize data and to calculate important relationships.

Formula for a Percentage Change

One important formula is the percentage change. The *percentage change* is the change in some economic variable, usually from one period to the next, expressed as a percentage. An important macroeconomic measure is the real gross domestic product (GDP). *GDP* is the value of all the final goods and services produced in a country during a year. "Real" GDP is corrected for the effects of inflation. When economists say that the U.S. economy grew 3.3 percent during 2006, they mean that real GDP was 3.3 percent higher in 2006 than it was in 2005. The formula for making this calculation is:

$$\left(\frac{\text{GDP}_{2006} - \text{GDP}_{2005}}{\text{GDP}_{2005}}\right) \times 100$$

or, more generally, for any two periods:

$$\text{Percentage change} = \frac{\text{Value in the second period} - \text{Value in the first period}}{\text{Value in the first period}} \times 100.$$

In this case, real GDP was $11,049 billion in 2005 and $11,415 billion in 2006. So, the growth rate of the U.S. economy during 2006 was:

$$\left(\frac{\$11{,}415 - \$11{,}049}{\$11{,}049}\right) \times 100 = 3.3\%.$$

Notice that it didn't matter that in using the formula, we ignored the fact that GDP is measured in billions of dollars. In fact, when calculating percentage changes, *the units don't matter.* The percentage increase from $11,049 billion to $11,415 billion is exactly the same as the percentage increase from $11,049 to $11,415.

Formulas for the Areas of a Rectangle and a Triangle

Areas that form rectangles and triangles on graphs can have important economic meaning. For example, Figure 1A-9 shows the demand curve for Pepsi. Suppose that the price is currently $2.00 and that 125,000 bottles of Pepsi are sold at that price. A firm's *total revenue* is equal to the amount it receives from selling its product, or the quantity sold multiplied by the price. In this case, total revenue will equal 125,000 bottles times $2.00 per bottle, or $250,000.

The formula for the area of a rectangle is:

$$\text{Area of a rectangle} = \text{Base} \times \text{Height}$$

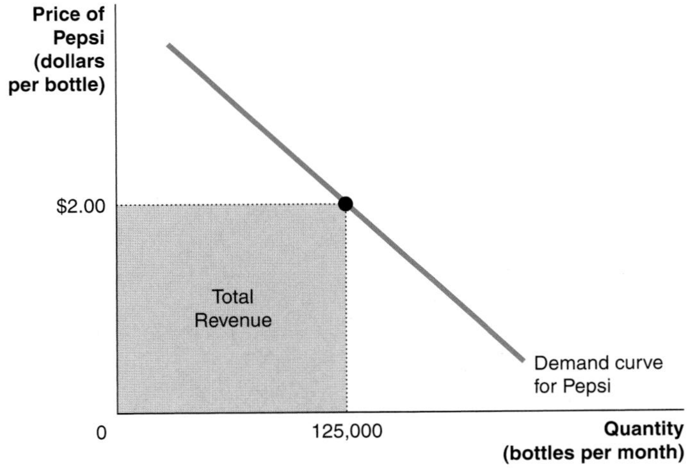

Figure 1A-9

Showing a Firm's Total Revenue on a Graph

The area of a rectangle is equal to its base multiplied by its height. Total revenue is equal to quantity multiplied by price. Here, total revenue is equal to the quantity of 125,000 bottles times the price of $2.00 per bottle, or $250,000. The area of the green-shaded rectangle shows the firm's total revenue.

Figure 1A-10

The Area of a Triangle

The area of a triangle is equal to ½ multiplied by its base multiplied by its height. The area of the blue-shaded triangle has a base equal to 150,000 − 125,000, or 25,000, and a height equal to $2.00 − $1.50, or $0.50. Therefore, its area equals ½ × 25,000 × $0.50, or $6,250.

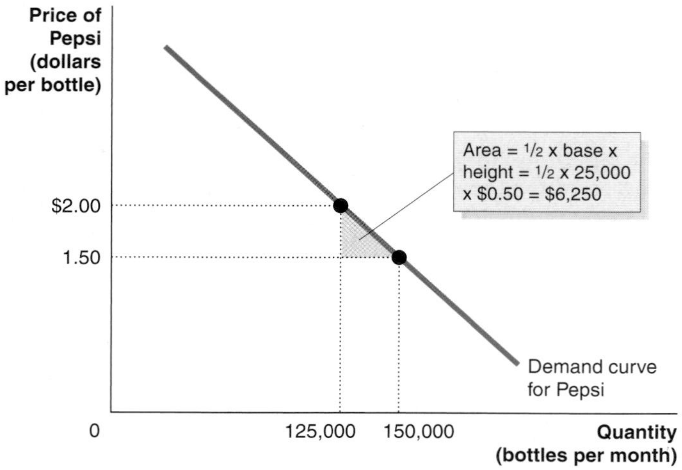

In Figure 1A-9, the green-shaded rectangle also represents the firm's total revenue because its area is given by the base of 125,000 bottles multiplied by the price of $2.00 per bottle.

We will see in later chapters that areas that are triangles can also have economic significance. The formula for the area of a triangle is:

$$\text{Area of a triangle} = \frac{1}{2} \times \text{Base} \times \text{Height}.$$

The blue-shaded area in Figure 1A-10 is a triangle. The base equals 150,000 − 125,000, or 25,000. Its height equals $2.00 − $1.50, or $0.50. Therefore, its area equals ½ × 25,000 × $0.50, or $6,250. Notice that the blue area is a triangle only if the demand curve is a straight line, or linear. Not all demand curves are linear. However, the formula for the area of a triangle will usually still give a good approximation, even if the demand curve is not linear.

Summary of Using Formulas

You will encounter several other formulas in this book. Whenever you must use a formula, you should follow these steps:

1. Make sure you understand the economic concept that the formula represents.
2. Make sure you are using the correct formula for the problem you are solving.
3. Make sure that the number you calculate using the formula is economically reasonable. For example, if you are using a formula to calculate a firm's revenue and your answer is a negative number, you know you made a mistake somewhere.

LEARNING OBJECTIVE Review the use of graphs and formulas, **pages 24–34.**

Problems and Applications

1A.1 The following table gives the relationship between the price of custard pies and the number of pies Jacob buys per week.

PRICE	QUANTITY OF PIES	WEEK
$3.00	6	July 2
2.00	7	July 9
5.00	4	July 16
6.00	3	July 23
1.00	8	July 30
4.00	5	August 6

a. Is the relationship between the price of pies and the number of pies Jacob buys a positive relationship or a negative relationship?
b. Plot the data from the table on a graph similar to Figure 1A-3. Draw a straight line that best fits the points.
c. Calculate the slope of the line.

1A.2 The following table gives information on the quantity of glasses of lemonade demanded on sunny and overcast days. Plot the data from the table on a graph similar to Figure 1A-5. Draw two straight lines representing the two demand curves—one for sunny days and one for overcast days.

PRICE (DOLLARS PER GLASS)	QUANTITY (GLASSES OF LEMONADE PER DAY)	WEATHER
$0.80	30	Sunny
0.80	10	Overcast
0.70	40	Sunny
0.70	20	Overcast
0.60	50	Sunny
0.60	30	Overcast
0.50	60	Sunny
0.50	40	Overcast

1A.3 Using the information in Figure 1A-2, calculate the percentage change in auto sales from one year to the next. Between which years did sales fall at the fastest rate?

1A.4 Real GDP in 1981 was $5,292 billion. Real GDP in 1982 was $5,189 billion. What was the percentage change in real GDP from 1981 to 1982? What do economists call the percentage change in real GDP from one year to the next?

1A.5 Assume that the demand curve for Pepsi passes through the following two points:

PRICE PER BOTTLE OF PEPSI	NUMBER OF BOTTLES OF PEPSI SOLD
$2.50	100,000
1.25	200,000

a. Draw a graph with a linear demand curve that passes through these two points.
b. Show on the graph the areas representing total revenue at each price. Give the value for total revenue at each price.

1A.6 What is the area of the blue triangle shown in the following figure?

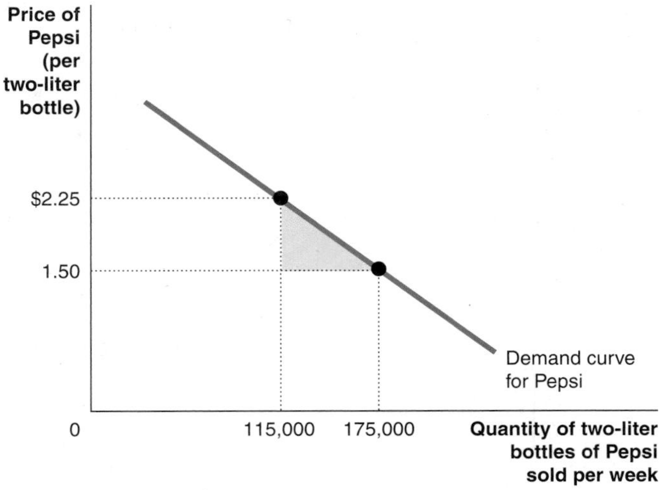

1A.7 Calculate the slope of the total cost curve at point *A* and at point *B* in the following figure.

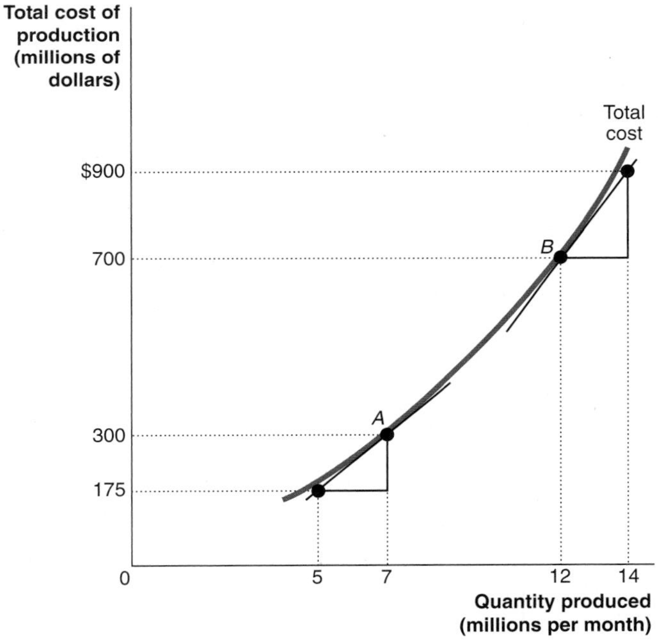

>> End Appendix Learning Objective

Chapter 2

Trade-offs, Comparative Advantage, and the Market System

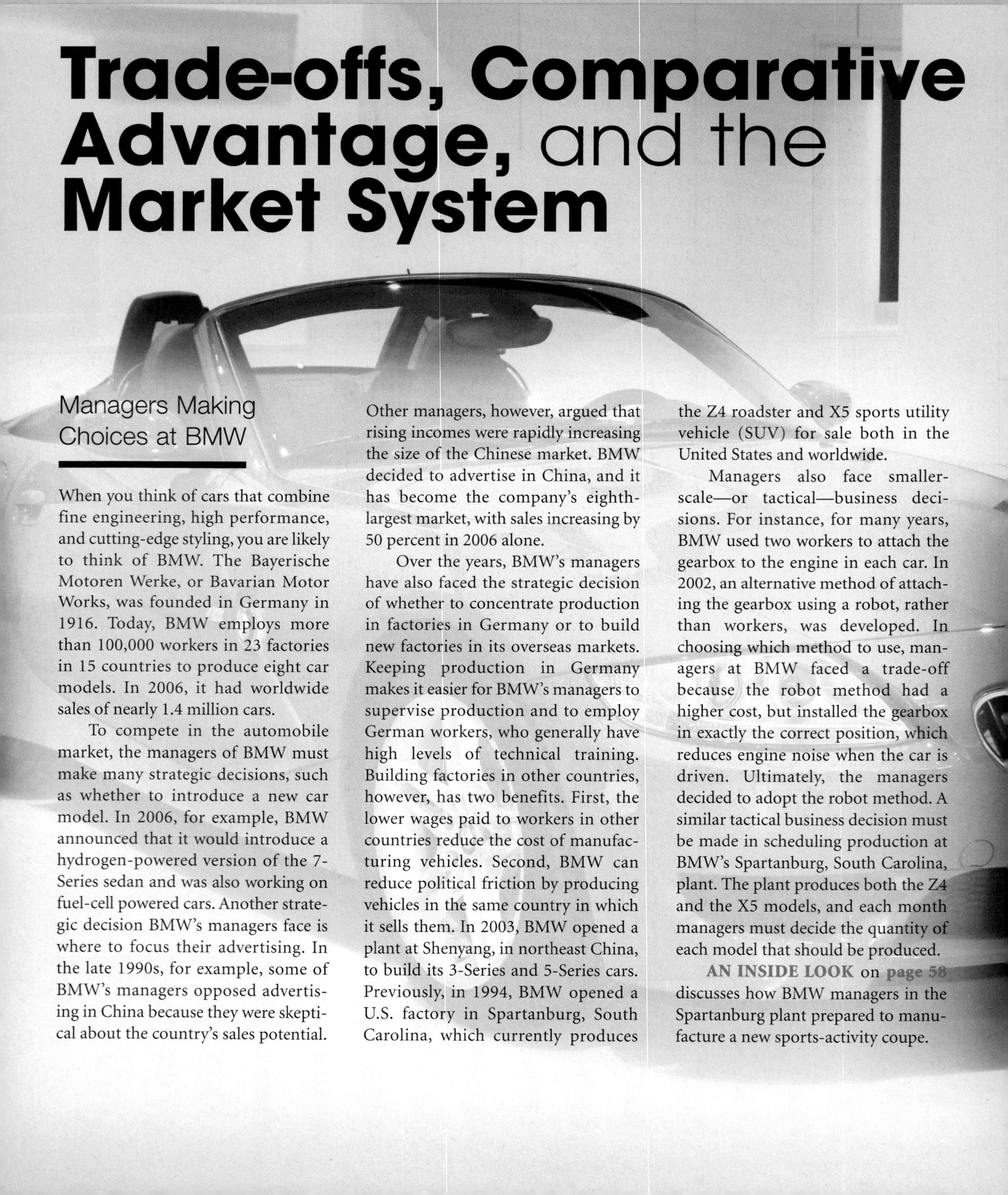

Managers Making Choices at BMW

When you think of cars that combine fine engineering, high performance, and cutting-edge styling, you are likely to think of BMW. The Bayerische Motoren Werke, or Bavarian Motor Works, was founded in Germany in 1916. Today, BMW employs more than 100,000 workers in 23 factories in 15 countries to produce eight car models. In 2006, it had worldwide sales of nearly 1.4 million cars.

To compete in the automobile market, the managers of BMW must make many strategic decisions, such as whether to introduce a new car model. In 2006, for example, BMW announced that it would introduce a hydrogen-powered version of the 7-Series sedan and was also working on fuel-cell powered cars. Another strategic decision BMW's managers face is where to focus their advertising. In the late 1990s, for example, some of BMW's managers opposed advertising in China because they were skeptical about the country's sales potential. Other managers, however, argued that rising incomes were rapidly increasing the size of the Chinese market. BMW decided to advertise in China, and it has become the company's eighth-largest market, with sales increasing by 50 percent in 2006 alone.

Over the years, BMW's managers have also faced the strategic decision of whether to concentrate production in factories in Germany or to build new factories in its overseas markets. Keeping production in Germany makes it easier for BMW's managers to supervise production and to employ German workers, who generally have high levels of technical training. Building factories in other countries, however, has two benefits. First, the lower wages paid to workers in other countries reduce the cost of manufacturing vehicles. Second, BMW can reduce political friction by producing vehicles in the same country in which it sells them. In 2003, BMW opened a plant at Shenyang, in northeast China, to build its 3-Series and 5-Series cars. Previously, in 1994, BMW opened a U.S. factory in Spartanburg, South Carolina, which currently produces the Z4 roadster and X5 sports utility vehicle (SUV) for sale both in the United States and worldwide.

Managers also face smaller-scale—or tactical—business decisions. For instance, for many years, BMW used two workers to attach the gearbox to the engine in each car. In 2002, an alternative method of attaching the gearbox using a robot, rather than workers, was developed. In choosing which method to use, managers at BMW faced a trade-off because the robot method had a higher cost, but installed the gearbox in exactly the correct position, which reduces engine noise when the car is driven. Ultimately, the managers decided to adopt the robot method. A similar tactical business decision must be made in scheduling production at BMW's Spartanburg, South Carolina, plant. The plant produces both the Z4 and the X5 models, and each month managers must decide the quantity of each model that should be produced.

AN INSIDE LOOK on **page 58** discusses how BMW managers in the Spartanburg plant prepared to manufacture a new sports-activity coupe.

LEARNING Objectives

After studying this chapter, you should be able to:

2.1 Use a **production possibilities frontier** to analyze opportunity costs and trade-offs, page 38.

2.2 Understand **comparative advantage** and explain how it is the basis for **trade**, page 44.

2.3 Explain the basic idea of how a **market system** works, page 50.

Economics in YOUR Life!

The Trade-offs When You Buy a Car

When you buy a car, you probably consider factors such as safety and gas mileage. To increase gas mileage, automobile manufacturers make cars small and light. Large cars absorb more of the impact of an accident than do small cars. As a result, people are usually safer driving large cars than small cars. What can we conclude from these facts about the relationship between safety and gas mileage? Under what circumstances would it be possible for car manufacturers to make cars safer and more fuel efficient? As you read the chapter, see if you can answer these questions. You can check your answer against those provided at the end of the chapter. » **Continued on page 56**

Scarcity The situation in which unlimited wants exceed the limited resources available to fulfill those wants.

In a market system, managers at most firms must make decisions like those made by BMW's managers. The decisions managers face reflect a key fact of economic life: *Scarcity requires trade-offs.* **Scarcity** exists because we have unlimited wants but only limited resources available to fulfill those wants. Goods and services are scarce. So, too, are the economic resources, or *factors of production*—workers, capital, natural resources, and entrepreneurial ability—used to make goods and services. Your time is scarce, which means you face trade-offs: If you spend an hour studying for an economics exam, you have one less hour to spend studying for a psychology exam or going to the movies. If your university decides to use some of its scarce budget funds to buy new computers for the computer labs, those funds will not be available to buy new books for the library or to resurface the student parking lot. If BMW decides to devote some of the scarce workers and machinery in its Spartanburg assembly plant to producing more Z4 roadsters, those resources will not be available to produce more X5 SUVs.

Many of the decisions of households and firms are made in markets. One key activity that takes place in markets is trade. Trade involves the decisions of millions of households and firms spread around the world. By engaging in trade, people can raise their standard of living. In this chapter, we provide an overview of how the market system coordinates the independent decisions of these millions of households and firms. We begin our analysis of the economic consequences of scarcity and the working of the market system by introducing an important economic model: the *production possibilities frontier.*

2.1 LEARNING OBJECTIVE

2.1 | Use a production possibilities frontier to analyze opportunity costs and trade-offs.

Production Possibilities Frontiers and Opportunity Costs

Production possibilities frontier (*PPF*) A curve showing the maximum attainable combinations of two products that may be produced with available resources and current technology.

As we saw in the opening to this chapter, BMW operates an automobile factory in Spartanburg, South Carolina, where it assembles Z4 roadsters and X5 SUVs. Because the firm's resources—workers, machinery, materials, and entrepreneurial skills—are limited, BMW faces a trade-off: Resources devoted to producing Z4s are not available for producing X5s and vice versa. Chapter 1 explained that economic models can be useful in analyzing many questions. We can use a simple model called the *production possibilities frontier* to analyze the trade-offs BMW faces in its Spartanburg plant. A **production possibilities frontier (*PPF*)** is a curve showing the maximum attainable combinations of two products that may be produced with available resources and current technology. In BMW's case, the two products are Z4 roadsters and X5 SUVs, and the resources are BMW's workers, materials, robots, and other machinery.

Graphing the Production Possibilities Frontier

Figure 2-1 uses a production possibilities frontier to illustrate the trade-offs that BMW faces. The numbers from the table are plotted in the graph. The line in the graph is BMW's production possibilities frontier. If BMW uses all its resources to produce roadsters, it can produce 800 per day—point *A* at one end of the production possibilities frontier. If BMW uses all its resources to produce SUVs, it can produce 800 per day—point *E* at the other end of the production possibilities frontier. If BMW devotes resources to producing both vehicles, it could be at a point like *B*, where it produces 600 roadsters and 200 SUVs.

All the combinations either on the frontier—like *A*, *B*, *C*, *D*, and *E*—or inside the frontier—like point *F*—are *attainable* with the resources available. Combinations on

BMW's Production Choices at Its Spartanburg Plant

Choice	Quantity of Roadsters Produced	Quantity of SUVs Produced
A	800	0
B	600	200
C	400	400
D	200	600
E	0	800

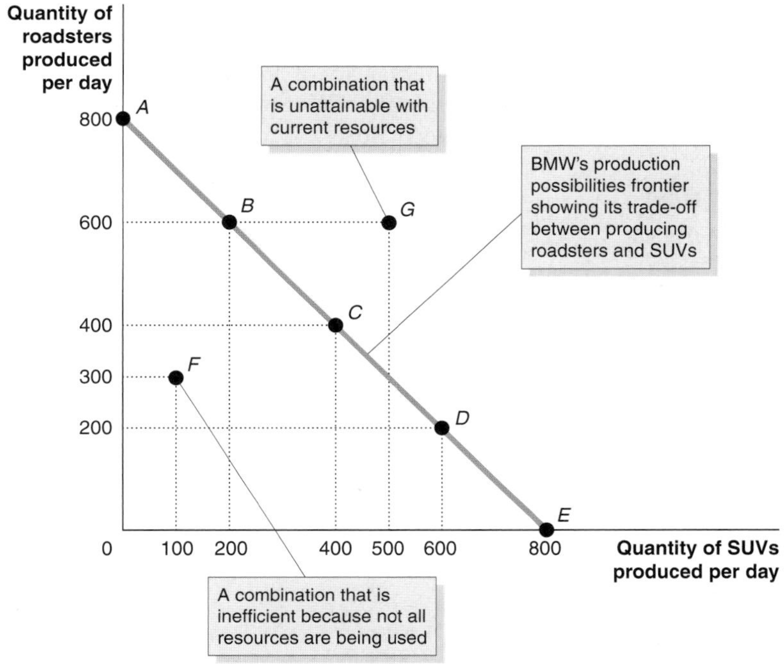

Figure 2-1

BMW's Production Possibilities Frontier

BMW faces a trade-off: To build one more roadster, it must build one less SUV. The production possibilities frontier illustrates the trade-off BMW faces. Combinations on the production possibilities frontier—like points *A, B, C, D,* and *E*—are *technically efficient* because the maximum output is being obtained from the available resources. Combinations inside the frontier—like point *F*—are *inefficient* because some resources are not being used. Combinations outside the frontier—like point *G*—are *unattainable* with current resources.

the frontier are *efficient* because all available resources are being fully utilized, and the fewest possible resources are being used to produce a given amount of output. Combinations inside the frontier—like point *F*—are *inefficient* because maximum output is not being obtained from the available resources—perhaps because the assembly line is not operating at capacity. BMW might like to be beyond the frontier—at a point like *G*, where it would be producing 600 roadsters and 500 SUVs—but points beyond the production possibilities frontier are *unattainable*, given the firm's current resources. To produce the combination at *G*, BMW would need more machines or more workers.

Notice that if BMW is producing efficiently and is on the production possibilities frontier, the only way to produce more of one vehicle is to produce less of the other vehicle. Recall from Chapter 1 that the **opportunity cost** of any activity is the highest valued alternative that must be given up to engage in that activity. For BMW, the opportunity cost of producing one more SUV is the number of roadsters the company will not be able to produce because it has shifted those resources to producing SUVs. For example, in moving from point *B* to point *C*, the opportunity cost of producing 200 more SUVs per day is the 200 fewer roadsters that can be produced.

Opportunity cost The highest-valued alternative that must be given up to engage in an activity.

What point on the production possibilities frontier is best? We can't tell without further information. If consumer demand for SUVs is greater than demand for roadsters, the company is likely to choose a point closer to *E*. If demand for roadsters is greater than demand for SUVs, the company is likely to choose a point closer to *A*.

Solved Problem 2-1

Drawing a Production Possibilities Frontier for Rosie's Boston Bakery

Rosie's Boston Bakery specializes in cakes and pies. Rosie has 5 hours per day to devote to baking. In 1 hour, Rosie can prepare 2 pies or 1 cake.

a. Use the information given to complete the following table:

	HOURS SPENT MAKING		QUANTITY MADE	
CHOICE	CAKES	PIES	CAKES	PIES
A	5	0		
B	4	1		
C	3	2		
D	2	3		
E	1	4		
F	0	5		

b. Use the data in the table to draw a production possibilities frontier graph illustrating Rosie's trade-offs between making cakes and making pies. Label the vertical axis "Quantity of cakes made." Label the horizontal axis "Quantity of pies made." Make sure to label the values where Rosie's production possibilities frontier intersects the vertical and horizontal axes.

c. Label the points representing choice *D* and choice *E*. If Rosie is at choice *D*, what is her opportunity cost of making more pies?

SOLVING THE PROBLEM:

Step 1: Review the chapter material. This problem is about using production possibilities frontiers to analyze trade-offs, so you may want to review the section "Graphing the Production Possibilities Frontier," which begins on page 38.

Step 2: Answer question (a) by filling in the table. If Rosie can produce 1 cake in 1 hour, then with choice *A*, she will make 5 cakes and 0 pies. Because she can produce 2 pies in 1 hour, with choice *B*, she will make 4 cakes and 2 pies. Using similar reasoning, you can fill in the remaining cells in the table as follows:

	HOURS SPENT MAKING		QUANTITY MADE	
CHOICE	CAKES	PIES	CAKES	PIES
A	5	0	5	0
B	4	1	4	2
C	3	2	3	4
D	2	3	2	6
E	1	4	1	8
F	0	5	0	10

Step 3: Answer question (b) by drawing the production possibilities frontier graph. Using the data in the table in Step 2, you should draw a graph that looks like this:

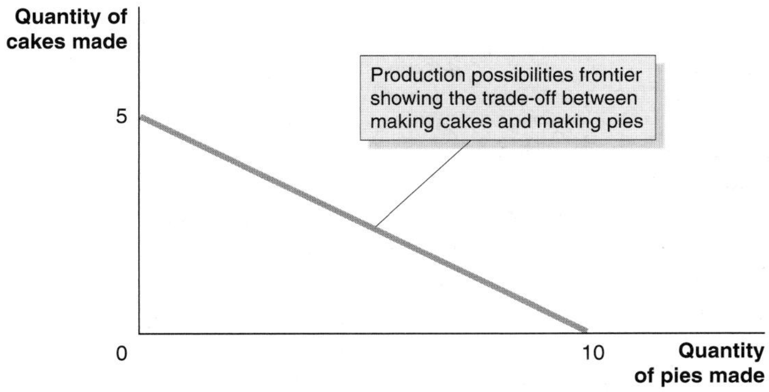

If Rosie devotes all 5 hours to making cakes, she will make 5 cakes. Therefore, her production possibilities frontier will intersect the vertical axis at 5 cakes made. If Rosie devotes all 5 hours to making pies, she will make 10 pies. Therefore, her production possibilities frontier will intersect the horizontal axis at 10 pies made.

Step 4: **Answer question (c) by showing choices *D* and *E* on your graph.** The points for choices *D* and *E* can be plotted using the information from the table:

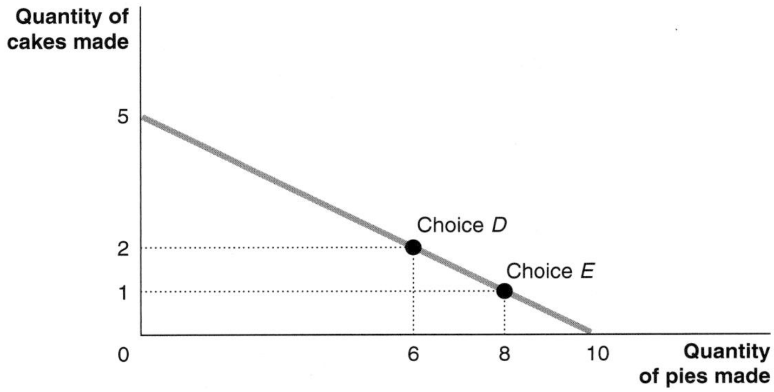

Moving from choice *D* to choice *E* increases Rosie's production of pies by 2 but lowers her production of cakes by 1. Therefore, her opportunity cost of making 2 more pies is making 1 less cake.

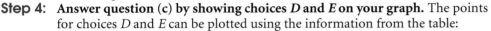

YOUR TURN: For more practice, do related problem 1.9 on page 61 at the end of this chapter. **>> End Solved Problem 2-1**

Making the Connection | Trade-offs: Hurricane Katrina, Tsunami Relief, and Charitable Giving

When Hurricane Katrina hit the Gulf Coast region in August 2005, it resulted in massive flooding that destroyed large sections of New Orleans and other towns in Louisiana, Mississippi, Alabama, and Texas. More than 1,800 people lost their lives. In response, there was a massive outpouring of charitable donations to aid the victims. More than two-thirds of Americans donated money to hurricane relief. Although these funds helped to reduce the suffering of many hurricane victims, donations to some other causes actually declined. For instance, the head of the United Way in Alleghany County, Pennsylvania, indicated that it had suffered a decline in donations during 2005: "We're seeing declines this year, not all entirely due to the economy but also due to the effect of so much fund raising in August and September for hurricanes Katrina and Rita." The director of the Women's Center and Shelter of Great Pittsburgh

More funds for Katrina relief meant less funds for other charities.

had a similar experience: "What they've told us is there are so many important causes that they are aware of that they want to support. The choices are greater than what they've been faced with before."

Unfortunately, the trade-off of an increase in charitable giving to one cause resulting in a decrease in charitable giving to other causes is common following a disaster. In December 2004, an earthquake caused a tidal wave—or tsunami—to flood coastal areas of Indonesia, Thailand, Sri Lanka, and other countries bordering the Indian Ocean. More than 280,000 people died, and billions of dollars worth of property was destroyed. Governments and individuals around the world moved quickly to donate to relief efforts. The U.S. government donated $950 million, and individual U.S. citizens donated an additional $500 million. Both governments and individuals face limited budgets, however, and funds used for one purpose are unavailable to be used for another purpose. Although governments and individuals did increase their total charitable giving following the tsunami disaster, much of the funds spent on tsunami relief appear to have been diverted from other uses. A difficult trade-off resulted: Giving funds to victims of the tsunami meant fewer funds were available to aid other good causes.

For example, some of the funds provided by the U.S. government for reconstruction in the tsunami-devastated areas came from existing aid programs. As a result, spending on other aid projects in the region declined. Similarly, nonprofit organizations in New York City reported sharp declines in donations to the homeless and the poor, as donors gave funds for tsunami relief instead. According to a report in the newspaper *Crain's New York Business*, "Some groups such as Bailey House, which helps homeless people who have AIDS, have even started receiving letters from longtime donors warning that this year's gifts are being redirected to the tsunami relief effort." As one commentator observed, "The milk of human kindness is probably flowing at the usual rate in the United States. It's just getting channeled in different directions."

Source: Steve Levin, "Disaster Aid Is Extra Giving," *Pittsburgh Post Gazette*, April 22, 2006; Jacqueline L. Salmon, "Katrina Compassion Drives Disaster Donations to a Record," *Washington Post*, June 19, 2006, p. A05; and Daniel Gross, "Zero-Sum Charity," *Slate*, January 20, 2005.

YOUR TURN: Test your understanding by doing related problem 1.10 on page 61 at the end of this chapter.

Increasing Marginal Opportunity Costs

We can use the production possibilities frontier to explore issues related to the economy as a whole. For example, suppose we divide all the goods and services produced in the economy into just two types: military goods and civilian goods. In Figure 2-2, we let tanks represent military goods and automobiles represent civilian goods. If all the coun-

Figure 2-2

Increasing Marginal Opportunity Cost

As the economy moves down the production possibilities frontier, it experiences *increasing marginal opportunity costs* because increasing automobile production by a given quantity requires larger and larger decreases in tank production. For example, to increase automobile production from 0 to 200—moving from point *A* to point *B*—the economy has to give up only 50 tanks. But to increase automobile production by another 200 vehicles—moving from point *B* to point *C*—the economy has to give up 150 tanks.

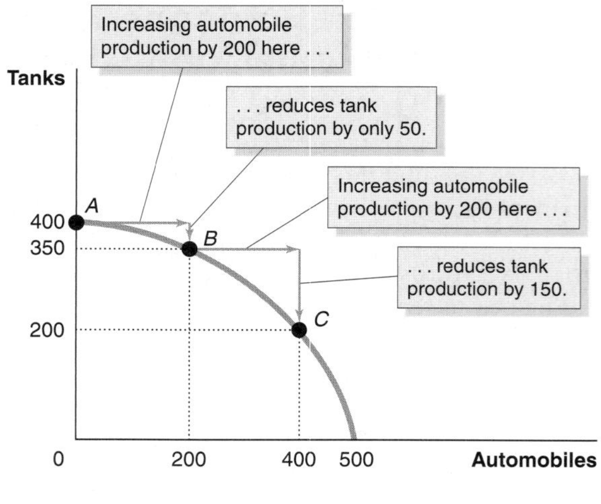

try's resources are devoted to producing military goods, 400 tanks can be produced in one year. If all resources are devoted to producing civilian goods, 500 automobiles can be produced in one year. Devoting resources to producing both goods results in the economy being at other points along the production possibilities frontier.

Notice that this production possibilities frontier is bowed outward rather than being a straight line. Because the curve is bowed out, the opportunity cost of automobiles in terms of tanks depends on where the economy currently is on the production possibilities frontier. For example, to increase automobile production from 0 to 200—moving from point *A* to point *B*—the economy has to give up only 50 tanks. But to increase automobile production by another 200 vehicles—moving from point *B* to point *C*—the economy has to give up 150 tanks.

As the economy moves down the production possibilities frontier, it experiences *increasing marginal opportunity costs* because increasing automobile production by a given quantity requires larger and larger decreases in tank production. Increasing marginal opportunity costs occurs because some workers, machines, and other resources are better suited to one use than to another. At point *A*, some resources that are well suited to producing automobiles are forced to produce tanks. Shifting these resources into producing automobiles by moving from point *A* to point *B* allows a substantial increase in automobile production, without much loss of tank production. But as the economy moves down the production possibilities frontier, more and more resources that are better suited to tank production are switched into automobile production. As a result, the increases in automobile production become increasingly smaller, while the decreases in tank production become increasingly larger. We would expect in most situations that production possibilities frontiers will be bowed outward rather than linear, as in the BMW example discussed earlier.

The idea of increasing marginal opportunity costs illustrates an important economic concept: *The more resources already devoted to any activity, the smaller the payoff to devoting additional resources to that activity.* For example, the more hours you have already spent studying economics, the smaller the increase in your test grade from each additional hour you spend—and the greater the opportunity cost of using the hour in that way. The more funds a firm has devoted to research and development during a given year, the smaller the amount of useful knowledge it receives from each additional dollar—and the greater the opportunity cost of using the funds in that way. The more funds the federal government spends cleaning up the environment during a given year, the smaller the reduction in pollution from each additional dollar—and, once again, the greater the opportunity cost of using the funds in that way.

Economic Growth

At any given time, the total resources available to any economy are fixed. Therefore, if the United States produces more automobiles, it must produce less of something else—tanks in our example. Over time, though, the resources available to an economy may increase. For example, both the labor force and the capital stock—the amount of physical capital available in the country—may increase. The increase in the available labor force and the capital stock shifts the production possibilities frontier outward for the U.S. economy and makes it possible to produce both more automobiles and more tanks. Panel (a) of Figure 2-3 shows that the economy can move from point *A* to point *B*, producing more tanks and more automobiles.

Similarly, technological advance makes it possible to produce more goods with the same amount of workers and machinery, which also shifts the production possibilities frontier outward. Technological advance need not affect all sectors equally. Panel (b) of Figure 2-3 shows the results of technological advance in the automobile industry that increases the quantity of automobile workers can produce per year while leaving unchanged the quantity of tanks that can be produced.

Shifts in the production possibilities frontier represent **economic growth** because they allow the economy to increase the production of goods and services, which ultimately raises the standard of living. In the United States and other high-income countries, the

Economic growth The ability of the economy to produce increasing quantities of goods and services.

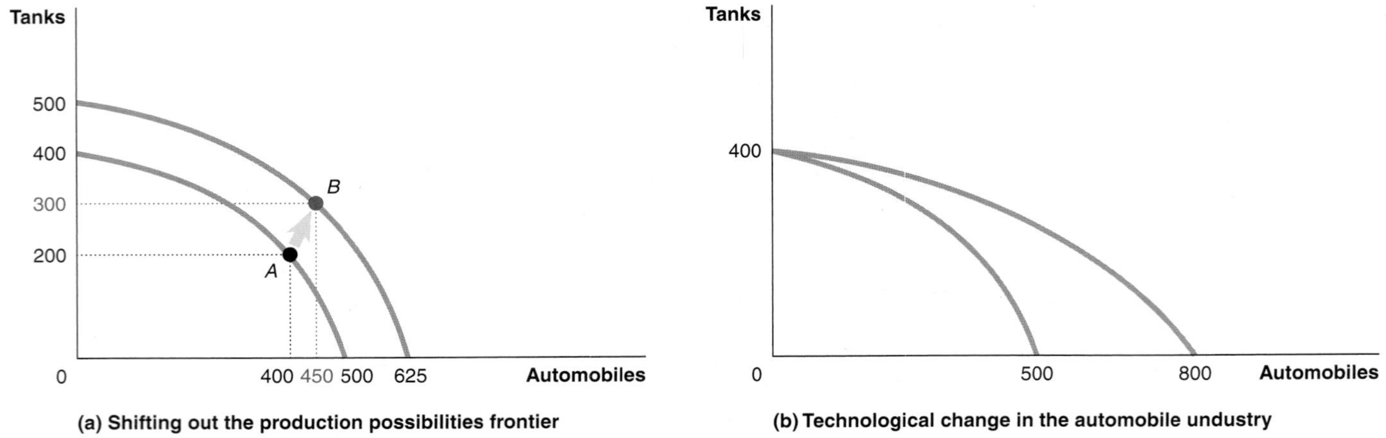

Figure 2-3 | Economic Growth

Panel (a) shows that as more economic resources become available and technological change occurs, the economy can move from point *A* to point *B*, producing more tanks and more automobiles. Panel (b) shows the results of technological advance in the automobile industry that increases the quantity of vehicles workers can produce per year while leaving the maximum quantity of tanks that can be produced unchanged. Shifts in the production possibilities frontier represent *economic growth*.

market system has aided the process of economic growth, which over the past 200 years has greatly increased the well-being of the average person.

2.2 LEARNING OBJECTIVE

2.2 | Understand comparative advantage and explain how it is the basis for trade.

Comparative Advantage and Trade

Trade The act of buying or selling.

We can use the ideas of production possibilities frontiers and opportunity costs to understand the basic economic activity of *trade*. Markets are fundamentally about **trade**, which is the act of buying and selling. Sometimes we trade directly, as when children trade one baseball card for another baseball card. But often we trade indirectly: We sell our labor services as, say, an accountant, a salesperson, or a nurse for money, and then we use the money to buy goods and services. Although in these cases, trade takes place indirectly, ultimately the accountant, salesperson, or nurse is trading his or her services for food, clothing, and other goods and services. One of the great benefits to trade is that it makes it possible for people to become better off by increasing both their production and their consumption.

Specialization and Gains from Trade

Consider the following situation: You and your neighbor both have fruit trees on your property. Initially, suppose you have only apple trees and your neighbor has only cherry trees. In this situation, if you both like apples and cherries, there is an obvious opportunity for both of you to gain from trade: You trade some of your apples for some of your neighbor's cherries, making you both better off. But what if there are apple and cherry trees growing on both of your properties? In that case, there can still be gains from trade. For example, your neighbor might be very good at picking apples, and you might be very good at picking cherries. It would make sense for your neighbor to concentrate on picking apples and for you to concentrate on picking cherries. You can then trade some of the cherries you pick for some of the apples your neighbor picks. But what if your neighbor is actually better at picking both apples and cherries than you are?

We can use production possibilities frontiers (*PPFs*) to show how your neighbor can benefit from trading with you even though she is better than you are at picking both apples and cherries. (For simplicity, and because it will not have any effect on the conclusions we draw, we will assume that the *PPF*s in this example are straight lines.) The table in Figure 2-4 shows how many apples and how many cherries you and your neighbor can pick in one week. The graph in the figure uses the data from the table to construct *PPF*s. Panel (a) shows your *PPF*. If you devote all your time to picking apples, you can pick 20 pounds of apples per week. If you devote all your time to picking cherries, you can pick 20 pounds per week. Panel (b) shows that if your neighbor devotes all her time to picking apples, she can pick 30 pounds. If she devotes all her time to picking cherries, she can pick 60 pounds.

The production possibilities frontiers in Figure 2-4 show how many apples and cherries you and your neighbor can consume, *without trade*. Suppose that when you don't trade with your neighbor, you pick and consume 8 pounds of apples and 12 pounds of cherries per week. This combination of apples and cherries is represented by point *A* in panel (a) of Figure 2-5, on page 46. When your neighbor doesn't trade with you, she picks and consumes 9 pounds of apples and 42 pounds of cherries per week. This combination of apples and cherries is represented by point *B* in panel (b) of Figure 2-5.

After years of picking and consuming your own apples and cherries, suppose your neighbor comes to you one day with the following proposal: She offers to trade you 15 pounds of her cherries for 10 pounds of your apples next week. Should you accept this offer? You should accept because you will end up with more apples and more cherries to consume. To take advantage of her proposal, you should specialize in picking only apples rather than splitting your time between picking apples and picking cherries. We know this will allow you to pick 20 pounds of apples. You can trade 10 pounds of apples to your neighbor for 15 pounds of her cherries. The result is that you will be able to consume 10 pounds of apples and 15 pounds of cherries (point *A*' in panel (a) of Figure 2-5). You are clearly better off as a result of trading with your neighbor: You now can consume 2 more pounds of apples and 3 more pounds of cherries than you were consuming without trading. You have moved beyond your *PPF*!

	You		Your Neighbor	
	Apples	Cherries	Apples	Cherries
Devote all time to picking apples	20 pounds	0 pounds	30 pounds	0 pounds
Devote all time to picking cherries	0 pounds	20 pounds	0 pounds	60 pounds

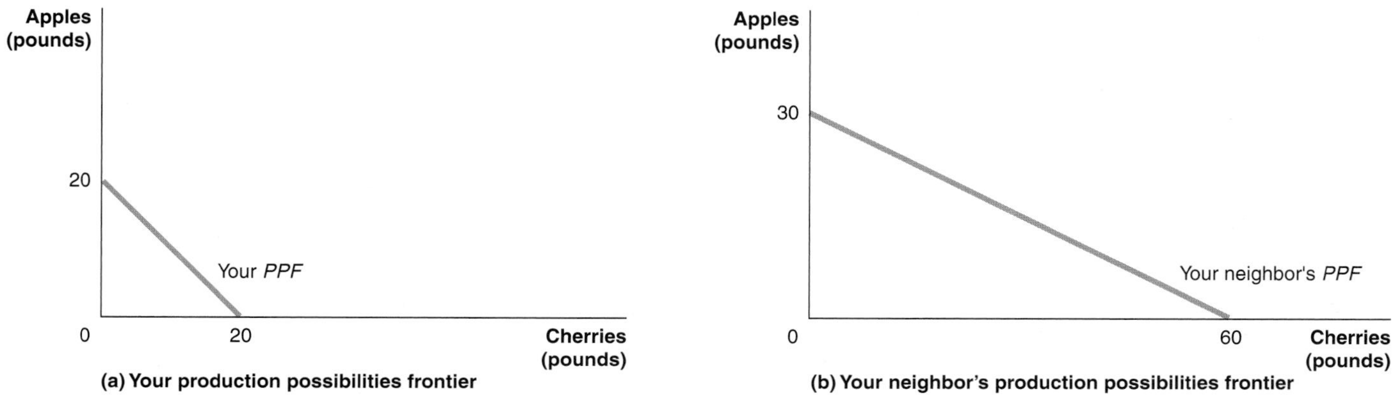

Figure 2-4 | Production Possibilities for You and Your Neighbor, without Trade

The table in this figure shows how many pounds of apples and how many pounds of cherries you and your neighbor can each pick in one week. The graphs in the figure use the data from the table to construct production possibilities frontiers (*PPF*s) for you and your neighbor. Panel (a) shows your *PPF*. If you devote all your time to picking apples and none of your time to picking cherries, you can pick 20 pounds. If you devote all your time to picking cherries, you can pick 20 pounds. Panel (b) shows that if your neighbor devotes all her time to picking apples, she can pick 30 pounds. If she devotes all her time to picking cherries, she can pick 60 pounds.

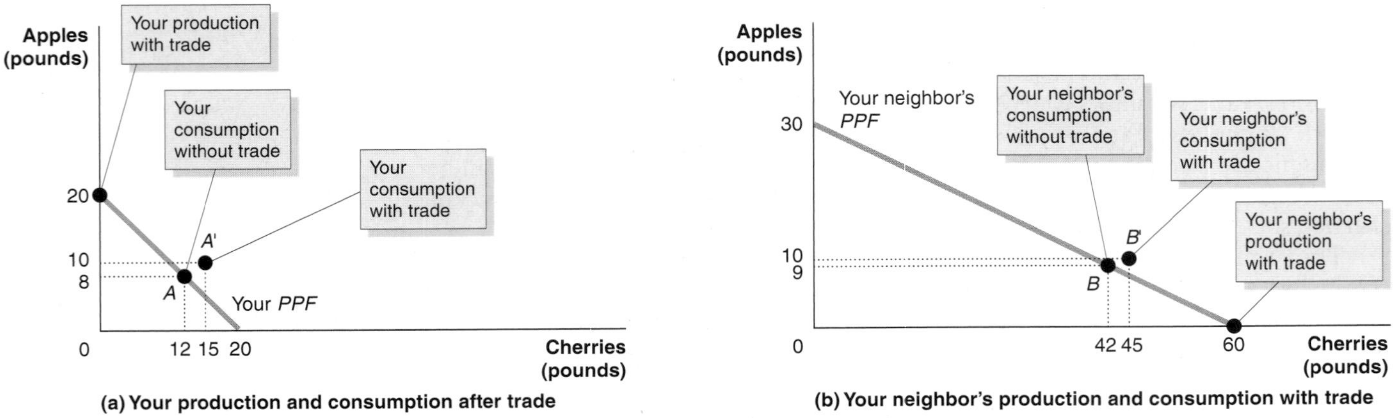

Figure 2-5 | Gains from Trade

When you don't trade with your neighbor, you pick and consume 8 pounds of apples and 12 pounds of cherries per week—point *A* in panel (a). When your neighbor doesn't trade with you, she picks and consumes 9 pounds of apples and 42 pounds of cherries per week—point *B* in panel (b). If you specialize in picking apples, you can pick 20 pounds. If your neighbor specializes in picking cherries, she can pick 60 pounds. If you trade 10 pounds of your apples for 15 pounds of your neighbor's cherries, you will be able to consume 10 pounds of apples and 15 pounds of cherries—point *A'* in panel (a). Your neighbor can now consume 10 pounds of apples and 45 pounds of cherries—point *B'* in panel (b). You and your neighbor are both better off as a result of trade.

Your neighbor has also benefited from the trade. By specializing in picking only cherries, she can pick 60 pounds. She trades 15 pounds of cherries to you for 10 pounds of apples. The result is that she can consume 10 pounds of apples and 45 pounds of cherries (point *B'* in panel (b) of Figure 2-5). This is 1 more pound of apples and 3 more pounds of cherries than she was consuming before trading with you. She also has moved beyond her *PPF*. Table 2-1 summarizes the changes in production and consumption that result from your trade with your neighbor. (In this example, we chose one specific rate of trading cherries for apples—15 pounds of cherries for 10 pounds of apples. There are, however, many other rates of trading cherries for apples that would also make you and your neighbor better off.)

Absolute advantage The ability of an individual, a firm, or a country to produce more of a good or service than competitors, using the same amount of resources.

Absolute Advantage versus Comparative Advantage

Perhaps the most remarkable aspect of the preceding example is that your neighbor benefits from trading with you even though she is better than you at picking both apples and cherries. **Absolute advantage** is the ability of an individual, a firm, or a country to

TABLE 2-1

A Summary of the Gains from Trade

	YOU		YOUR NEIGHBOR	
	APPLES (IN POUNDS)	CHERRIES (IN POUNDS)	APPLES (IN POUNDS)	CHERRIES (IN POUNDS)
Production *and* consumption *without* trade	8	12	9	42
Production *with* trade	20	0	0	60
Consumption *with* trade	10	15	10	45
Gains from trade (increased consumption)	2	3	1	3

produce more of a good or service than competitors, using the same amount of resources. Your neighbor has an absolute advantage over you in producing both apples and cherries because she can pick more of each fruit than you can in the same amount of time. Although it seems that your neighbor should pick her own apples *and* her own cherries, we have just seen that she is better off specializing in cherry picking and leaving the apple picking to you.

We can consider further why both you and your neighbor benefit from specializing in picking only one fruit. First, think about the opportunity cost to each of you of picking the two fruits. We saw from the *PPF* in Figure 2-4 that if you devoted all your time to picking apples, you would be able to pick 20 pounds of apples per week. As you move down your *PPF* and shift time away from picking apples to picking cherries, you have to give up 1 pound of apples for each pound of cherries you pick (the slope of your *PPF* is −1). (For a review of calculating slopes, see the appendix to Chapter 1.) Therefore, your opportunity cost of picking 1 pound of cherries is 1 pound of apples. By the same reasoning, your opportunity cost of picking 1 pound of apples is 1 pound of cherries. Your neighbor's *PPF* has a different slope, so she faces a different trade-off: As she shifts time from picking apples to picking cherries, she has to give up 0.5 pound of apples for every 1 pound of cherries she picks (the slope of your neighbor's *PPF* is −0.5). As she shifts time from picking cherries to picking apples, she gives up 2 pounds of cherries for every 1 pound of apples she picks. Therefore, her opportunity cost of picking 1 pound of apples is 2 pounds of cherries, and her opportunity cost of picking 1 pound of cherries is 0.5 pound of apples.

Table 2-2 summarizes the opportunity costs for you and your neighbor of picking apples and cherries. Note that even though your neighbor can pick more apples in a week than you can, the *opportunity cost* of picking apples is higher for her than for you because when she picks apples, she gives up more cherries than you do. So, even though she has an absolute advantage over you in picking apples, it is more costly for her to pick apples than it is for you. The table also shows that her opportunity cost of picking cherries is lower than your opportunity cost of picking cherries. **Comparative advantage** is the ability of an individual, a firm, or a country to produce a good or service at a lower opportunity cost than competitors. In apple picking, your neighbor has an *absolute advantage* over you, but you have a *comparative advantage* over her. Your neighbor has both an absolute and a comparative advantage over you in picking cherries. As we have seen, you are better off specializing in picking apples, and your neighbor is better off specializing in picking cherries.

Comparative advantage The ability of an individual, a firm, or a country to produce a good or service at a lower opportunity cost than competitors.

Comparative Advantage and the Gains from Trade

We have just derived an important economic principle: *The basis for trade is comparative advantage, not absolute advantage.* The fastest apple pickers do not necessarily do much apple picking. If the fastest apple pickers have a comparative advantage in some other activity—picking cherries, playing major league baseball, or being industrial engineers—they are better off specializing in that other activity. Individuals, firms, and countries are better off if they specialize in producing goods and services for which they have a comparative advantage and obtain the other goods and services they need by trading. We will return to the important concept of comparative advantage in Chapter 8, which is devoted to the subject of international trade.

TABLE 2-2

Opportunity Costs of Picking Apples and Cherries

	OPPORTUNITY COST OF PICKING 1 POUND OF APPLES	OPPORTUNITY COST OF PICKING 1 POUND OF CHERRIES
YOU	1 pound of cherries	1 pound of apples
YOUR NEIGHBOR	2 pounds of cherries	0.5 pound of apples

Don't Let This Happen to **YOU!**

Don't Confuse Absolute Advantage and Comparative Advantage

First, make sure you know the definitions:

- ***Absolute advantage.*** The ability of an individual, a firm, or a country to produce more of a good or service than competitors, using the same amount of resources. In our example, your neighbor has an absolute advantage over you in both picking apples and picking cherries.
- ***Comparative advantage.*** The ability of an individual, a firm, or a country to produce a good or service at a lower opportunity cost than competitors. In our example, your neighbor has a comparative advantage in picking cherries, but you have a comparative advantage in picking apples.

Keep these two key points in mind:

1. It is possible to have an absolute advantage in producing a good or service without having a comparative advantage. This is the case with your neighbor picking apples.
2. It is possible to have a comparative advantage in producing a good or service without having an absolute advantage. This is the case with you picking apples.

YOUR TURN: Test your understanding by doing related problem 2.7 on page 63 at the end of this chapter.

Solved Problem | 2-2

Comparative Advantage and the Gains from Trade

Suppose that Canada and the United States both produce maple syrup and honey. These are the combinations of the two goods that each country can produce in one day:

CANADA		UNITED STATES	
HONEY (IN TONS)	MAPLE SYRUP (IN TONS)	HONEY (IN TONS)	MAPLE SYRUP (IN TONS)
0	60	0	50
10	45	10	40
20	30	20	30
30	15	30	20
40	0	40	10
		50	0

a. Who has a comparative advantage in producing maple syrup? Who has a comparative advantage in producing honey?

b. Suppose that Canada is currently producing 30 tons of honey and 15 tons of maple syrup and the United States is currently producing 10 tons of honey and 40 tons of maple syrup. Demonstrate that Canada and the United States can both be better off if they specialize in producing only one good and engage in trade.

c. Illustrate your answer to question (b) by drawing a *PPF* for the United States and a *PPF* for Canada. Show on your *PPF*s the combinations of honey and maple syrup produced and consumed in each country before and after trade.

SOLVING THE PROBLEM:

Step 1: Review the chapter material. This problem concerns comparative advantage, so you may want to review the section "Absolute Advantage versus Comparative Advantage," which begins on page 46.

Step 2: Answer question (a) by calculating who has a comparative advantage in each activity. Remember that a country has a comparative advantage in producing a good if it can produce the good at the lowest opportunity cost. When

Canada produces 1 more ton of honey, it produces 1.5 fewer tons of maple syrup. On the one hand, when the United States produces 1 more ton of honey, it produces 1 less ton of maple syrup. Therefore, the United States's opportunity cost of producing honey—1 ton of maple syrup—is lower than Canada's—1.5 tons of maple syrup. On the other hand, when Canada produces 1 more ton of maple syrup, it produces 0.67 ton less of honey. When the United States produces 1 more ton of maple syrup, it produces 1 less ton of honey. Therefore, Canada's opportunity cost of producing maple syrup—0.67 ton of honey—is lower than that of the United States—1 ton of honey. We can conclude that the United States has a comparative advantage in the production of honey and Canada has a comparative advantage in the production of maple syrup.

Step 3: Answer question (b) by showing that specialization makes Canada and the United States better off. We know that Canada should specialize where it has a comparative advantage and the United States should specialize where it has a comparative advantage. If both countries specialize, Canada will produce 60 tons of maple syrup and 0 tons of honey, and the United States will produce 0 tons of maple syrup and 50 tons of honey. After both countries specialize, the United States could then trade 30 tons of honey to Canada in exchange for 40 tons of maple syrup. (Other mutually beneficial trades are possible as well.) We can summarize the results in a table:

	BEFORE TRADE		AFTER TRADE	
	HONEY (IN TONS)	MAPLE SYRUP (IN TONS)	HONEY (IN TONS)	MAPLE SYRUP (IN TONS)
CANADA	30	15	30	20
UNITED STATES	10	40	20	40

The United States is better off after trade because it can consume the same amount of maple syrup and 10 more tons of honey. Canada is better off after trade because it can consume the same amount of honey and 5 more tons of maple syrup.

Step 4: Answer question (c) by drawing the *PPF*s.

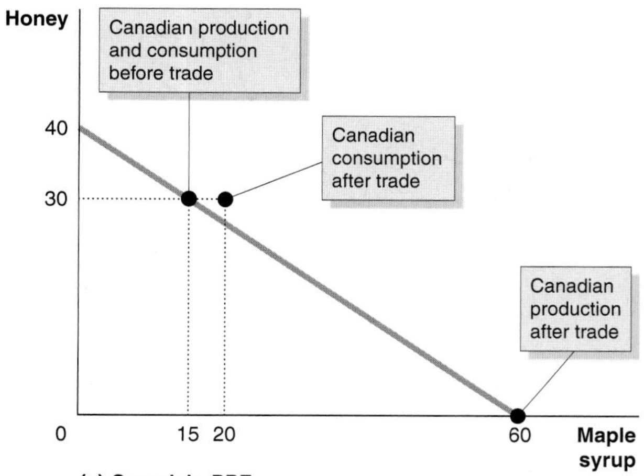

(a) Canada's *PPF*

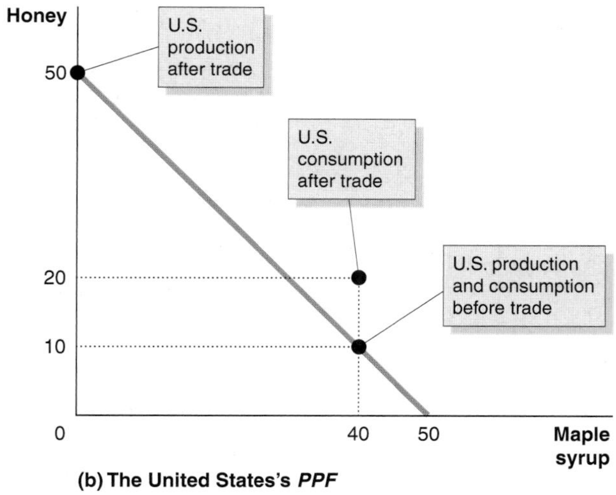

(b) The United States's *PPF*

YOUR TURN: For more practice, do related problems 2.5 and 2.6 on pages 62 and 63 at the end of this chapter.

>> End Solved Problem 2-2

2.3 LEARNING OBJECTIVE

2.3 | Explain the basic idea of how a market system works.

The Market System

We have seen that households, firms, and the government face trade-offs and incur opportunity costs because of the scarcity of resources. We have also seen that trade allows people to specialize according to their comparative advantage. By engaging in trade, people can raise their standard of living. Of course, trade in the modern world is much more complex than the examples we have considered so far. Trade today involves the decisions of millions of people spread around the world. But how does an economy make trade possible, and how are the decisions of these millions of people coordinated? In the United States and most other countries, trade is carried out in markets. Markets also determine the answers to the three fundamental questions discussed in Chapter 1: *What* goods and services will be produced? *How* will the goods and services be produced? and *Who* will receive the goods and services?

Market A group of buyers and sellers of a good or service and the institution or arrangement by which they come together to trade.

Product markets Markets for goods—such as computers—and services—such as medical treatment.

Factor markets Markets for the factors of production, such as labor, capital, natural resources, and entrepreneurial ability.

Factors of production The inputs used to make goods and services.

Recall that the definition of **market** is a group of buyers and sellers of a good or service and the institution or arrangement by which they come together to trade. Markets take many forms: They can be physical places, like a local pizza parlor or the New York Stock Exchange, or virtual places, like eBay. In a market, the buyers are demanders of goods or services, and the sellers are suppliers of goods or services. Households and firms interact in two types of markets: *product markets* and *factor markets*. **Product markets** are markets for goods—such as computers—and services—such as medical treatment. In product markets, households are demanders, and firms are suppliers. **Factor markets** are markets for the *factors of production*. **Factors of production** are the inputs used to make goods and services. Factors of production are divided into four broad categories:

- *Labor* includes all types of work, from the part-time labor of teenagers working at McDonald's to the work of top managers in large corporations.
- *Capital* refers to physical capital, such as computers and machine tools, that is used to produce other goods.
- *Natural resources* include land, water, oil, iron ore, and other raw materials (or "gifts of nature") that are used in producing goods.
- An *entrepreneur* is someone who operates a business. *Entrepreneurial ability* is the ability to bring together the other factors of production to successfully produce and sell goods and services.

The Circular Flow of Income

Two key groups participate in markets:

- A *household* consists of all the individuals in a home. Households are suppliers of factors of production—particularly labor—used by firms to make goods and services. Households use the income they receive from selling the factors of production to purchase the goods and services supplied by firms. We are used to thinking of households as suppliers of labor because most people earn most of their income by going to work, which means they are selling their labor services to firms in the labor market. But households own the other factors of production, as well, either directly or indirectly, by owning the firms that have these resources. All firms are owned by households. Small firms, like a neighborhood restaurant, might be owned by one person. Large firms, like Microsoft or BMW, are owned by millions of households who own shares of stock in them. (We discuss the stock market in Chapter 7.) When firms pay profits to the people who own them, the firms are paying for using the capital and natural resources that are supplied to them by those owners. So, we can generalize by saying that in factor markets, households are suppliers, and firms are demanders.

- *Firms* are suppliers of goods and services. Firms use the funds they receive from selling goods and services to buy the factors of production needed to make the goods and services.

We can use a simple economic model called the **circular-flow diagram** to see how participants in markets are linked. Figure 2-6 shows that in factor markets, households supply labor and other factors of production in exchange for wages and other payments from firms. In product markets, households use the payments they earn in factor markets to purchase the goods and services supplied by firms. Firms produce these goods and services using the factors of production supplied by households. In the figure, the blue arrows show the flow of factors of production from households through factor markets to firms. The red arrows show the flow of goods and services from firms through product markets to households. The green arrows show the flow of funds from firms through factor markets to households and the flow of spending from households through product markets to firms.

Circular-flow diagram A model that illustrates how participants in markets are linked.

Like all economic models, the circular-flow diagram is a simplified version of reality. For example, Figure 2-6 leaves out the important role of government in buying goods from firms and in making payments, such as Social Security or unemployment insurance payments, to households. The figure also leaves out the roles played by banks, the stock and bond markets, and other parts of the *financial system* in aiding the flow of funds from lenders to borrowers. Finally, the figure does not show that some goods and services purchased by domestic households are produced in foreign countries and some goods and services produced by domestic firms are sold to foreign households. The government, the financial system, and the international sector are explored further in later chapters. Despite these simplifications, the circular-flow diagram in Figure 2-6 is useful for seeing how product markets, factor markets, and their participants are linked

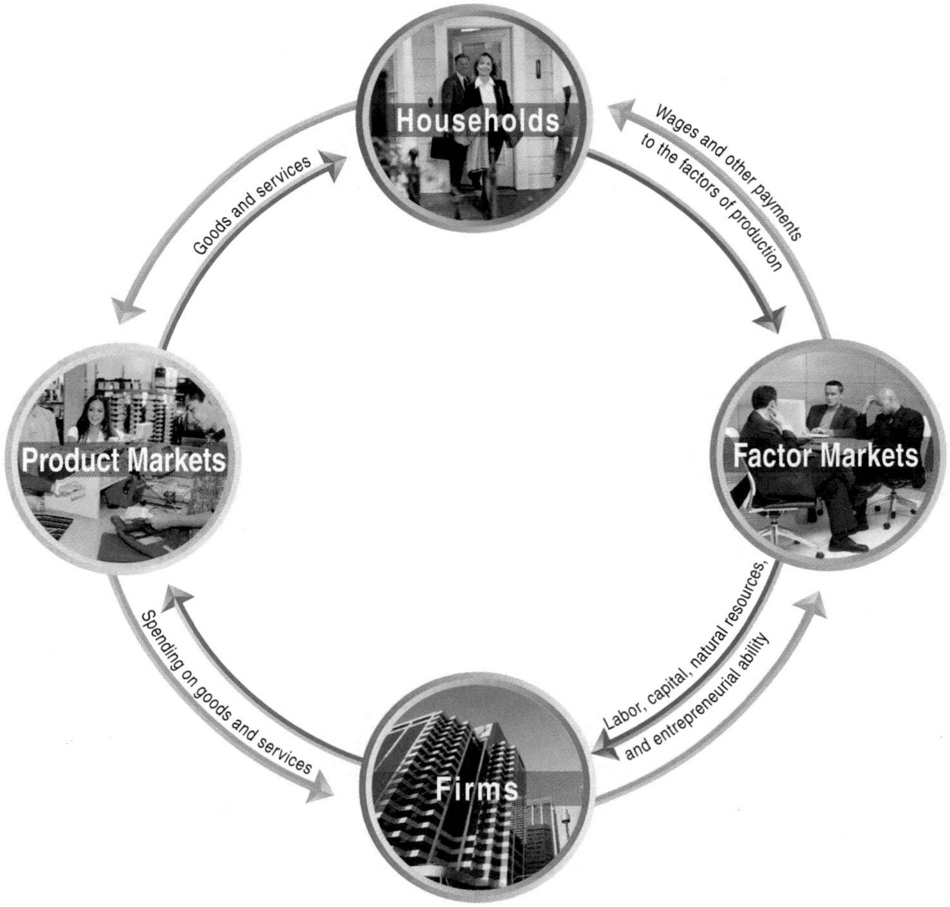

Figure 2-6

The Circular-Flow Diagram

Households and firms are linked together in a circular flow of production, income, and spending. The blue arrows show the flow of the factors of production. In factor markets, households supply labor, entrepreneurial ability, and other factors of production to firms. Firms use these factors of production to make goods and services that they supply to households in product markets. The red arrows show the flow of goods and services from firms to households. The green arrows show the flow of funds. In factor markets, households receive wages and other payments from firms in exchange for supplying the factors of production. Households use these wages and other payments to purchase goods and services from firms in product markets. Firms sell goods and services to households in product markets, and they use the funds to purchase the factors of production from households in factor markets.

together. One of the great mysteries of the market system is that it manages to successfully coordinate the independent activities of so many households and firms.

The Gains from Free Markets

Free market A market with few government restrictions on how a good or service can be produced or sold or on how a factor of production can be employed.

A **free market** exists when the government places few restrictions on how a good or a service can be produced or sold or on how a factor of production can be employed. Governments in all modern economies intervene more than is consistent with a fully free market. In that sense, we can think of the free market as being a benchmark against which we can judge actual economies. There are relatively few government restrictions on economic activity in the United States, Canada, the countries of Western Europe, Hong Kong, Singapore, and Estonia. So these countries come close to the free market benchmark. In countries such as Cuba and North Korea, the free market system has been rejected in favor of centrally planned economies with extensive government control over product and factor markets. Countries that come closest to the free-market benchmark have been more successful than countries with centrally planned economies in providing their people with rising living standards.

The Scottish philosopher Adam Smith is considered the father of modern economics because his book *An Inquiry into the Nature and Causes of the Wealth of Nations*, published in 1776, was an early and very influential argument for the free market system. Smith was writing at a time when extensive government restrictions on markets were still very common. In many parts of Europe, the *guild system* still prevailed. Under this system, governments would give guilds, or organizations of producers, the authority to control the production of a good. For example, the shoemakers' guild controlled who was allowed to produce shoes, how many shoes they could produce, and what price they could charge. In France, the cloth makers' guild even dictated the number of threads in the weave of the cloth.

Smith argued that such restrictions reduced the income, or wealth, of a country and its people by restricting the quantity of goods produced. Some people at the time supported the restrictions of the guild system because it was in their financial interest to do so. If you were a member of a guild, the restrictions served to reduce the competition you faced. But other people sincerely believed that the alternative to the guild system was economic chaos. Smith argued that these people were wrong and that a country could enjoy a smoothly functioning economic system if firms were freed from guild restrictions.

The Market Mechanism

In Smith's day, defenders of the guild system worried that if, for instance, the shoemakers' guild did not control shoe production, either too many or too few shoes would be produced. Smith argued that prices would do a better job of coordinating the activities of buyers and sellers than the guilds could. A key to understanding Smith's argument is the assumption that *individuals usually act in a rational, self-interested way.* In particular, individuals take those actions most likely to make themselves better off financially. This assumption of rational, self-interested behavior underlies nearly all economic analysis. In fact, economics can be distinguished from other fields that study human behavior—such as sociology and psychology—by its emphasis on the assumption of self-interested behavior. Adam Smith understood—as economists today understand—that people's motives can be complex. But in analyzing people in the act of buying and selling, the motivation of financial reward usually provides the best explanation for the actions people take.

For example, suppose that a significant number of consumers switch from buying regular gasoline-powered cars to buying gasoline/electric-powered hybrid cars, such as the Toyota Prius, as in fact happened in the United States during the 2000s. Firms will find that they can charge relatively higher prices for hybrid cars than they can for regular cars. The self-interest of these firms will lead them to respond to consumers' wishes by producing more hybrids and fewer regular cars. Or suppose that consumers decide that they want to eat less bread, pasta, and other foods high in carbohydrates, as many did following the increase in popularity of the Atkins and South Beach diets. Then the prices firms can charge for bread and pasta will fall. The self-interest of firms will lead them to produce less bread and pasta, which in fact is what happened.

In the case where consumers want more of a product, and in the case where they want less of a product, the market system responds without a guild or the government giving orders about how much to produce or what price to charge. In a famous phrase, Smith said that firms would be led by the "invisible hand" of the market to provide consumers with what they wanted. Firms would respond to changes in prices by making decisions that ended up satisfying the wants of consumers.

Making the Connection

A Story of the Market System in Action: How Do You Make an iPod?

The market coordinates the activities of the many people spread around the world who contribute to the making of an iPod.

The iPod is a product of Apple, which has its headquarters in Cupertino, California. It seems reasonable to assume that iPods are also manufactured in California. In fact, Apple produces none of the components of the iPod, nor does it assemble the components into a finished product. Far from being produced entirely by one company in one place, the iPod requires the coordinated activities of thousands of workers and dozens of firms, spread around the world.

Several Asian firms, including Asustek, Inventec Appliances, and Foxconn, assemble the iPod, which is then shipped to Apple for sale in the United States. But the firms doing final assembly don't make any of the components. For example, the iPod's hard drive is manufactured by the Japanese firm, Toshiba, although Toshiba actually assembles the hard drive in factories in China and the Philippines. Apple purchases the controller chip that manages the iPod's functions from PortalPlayer, which is based in Santa Clara, California. But PortalPlayer actually has the chip manufactured for it by Taiwan Semiconductor Manufacturing Corporation, and the chip's processor core was designed by ARM, a British company. Taiwan Semiconductor Manufacturing Corporation's factories are for the most part not in Taiwan, but in mainland China and Eastern Europe.

All told, the iPod contains 451 parts, designed and manufactured by firms around the world. Many of these firms are not even aware of which other firms are also producing components for the iPod. Few of the managers of these firms have met managers of the other firms or shared knowledge of how their particular components are produced. In fact, no one person from Steve Jobs, the head of Apple, on down possesses the knowledge of how to produce all of the components that are assembled into an iPod. Instead, the invisible hand of the market has led these firms to contribute their knowledge to the process that ultimately results in an iPod available for sale in a store in the United States. Apple has so efficiently organized the process of producing the iPod that you can order a custom iPod with a personal engraving and have it delivered from an assembly plant in China to your doorstep in the United States in as little as three days.

Hal Varian, an economist at the University of California, Berkeley, has summarized the iPod story: "Those clever folks at Apple figured out how to combine 451 mostly generic parts into a valuable product. They may not make the iPod, but they created it."

Sources: Hal Varian,"An iPod Has Global Value. Ask the (Many) Countries That Make It," *New York Times*, June 28, 2007; and Greg Linden, Kenneth L. Kraemer, Jaon Dedrick, "Who Captures Value in a Global Innovation System? The Case of Apple's iPod," Personal Computing Industry Center, June 2007.

YOUR TURN: Test your understanding by doing related problem 3.8 on page 64 at the end of this chapter.

The Role of the Entrepreneur

Entrepreneurs are central to the working of the market system. An **entrepreneur** is someone who operates a business. Entrepreneurs must first determine what goods and services they believe consumers want, and then they must decide how to produce those goods and services most profitably. Entrepreneurs bring together the factors of production—labor, capital, and natural resources—to produce goods and services. They put their own funds

Entrepreneur Someone who operates a business, bringing together the factors of production—labor, capital, and natural resources—to produce goods and services.

at risk when they start businesses. If they are wrong about what consumers want or about the best way to produce goods and services, they can lose those funds. In fact, it is not unusual for entrepreneurs who eventually achieve great success to fail at first. For instance, early in their careers, both Henry Ford and Sakichi Toyoda, who eventually founded the Toyota Motor Corporation, started companies that quickly failed.

The Legal Basis of a Successful Market System

In a free market, government does not restrict how firms produce and sell goods and services or how they employ factors of production, but the absence of government intervention is not enough for a market system to work well. Government has to provide secure rights to private property for a market system to work at all. In addition, government can aid the working of the market by enforcing contracts between private individuals through an independent court system. Many economists would also say the government has a role in facilitating the development of an efficient financial system as well as systems of education, transportation, and communication. The protection of private property and the existence of an independent court system to impartially enforce the law provide a *legal environment* that will allow a market system to succeed.

Protection of Private Property For a market system to work well, individuals must be willing to take risks. Someone with $250,000 can be cautious and keep it safely in a bank—or even in cash, if the person doesn't trust the banking system. But the market system won't work unless a significant number of people are willing to risk their funds by investing them in businesses. Investing in businesses is risky in any country. Many businesses fail every year in the United States and other high-income countries. But in the high-income countries, someone who starts a new business or invests in an existing business doesn't have to worry that the government, the military, or criminal gangs might decide to seize the business or demand payments for not destroying the business. Unfortunately, in many poor countries, owners of businesses are not well protected from having their businesses seized by the government or from having their profits taken by criminals. Where these problems exist, opening a business can be extremely risky. Cash can be concealed easily, but a business is difficult to conceal and difficult to move.

Property rights The rights individuals or firms have to the exclusive use of their property, including the right to buy or sell it.

Property rights are the rights individuals or firms have to the exclusive use of their property, including the right to buy or sell it. Property can be tangible, physical property, such as a store or factory. Property can also be intangible, such as the right to an idea.

Two amendments to the U.S. Constitution guarantee property rights: The 5th Amendment states that the federal government shall not deprive any person "of life, liberty, or property, without due process of law." The 14th Amendment extends this guarantee to the actions of state governments: "No state . . . shall deprive any person of life, liberty, or property, without due process of law." Similar guarantees exist in every high-income country. Unfortunately, in many developing countries, such guarantees do not exist or are poorly enforced.

In any modern economy, *intellectual property rights* are very important. Intellectual property includes books, films, software, and ideas for new products or new ways of producing products. To protect intellectual property, the federal government grants a *patent* that gives an inventor—which is often a firm—the exclusive right to produce and sell a new product for a period of 20 years from the date the product was invented. For instance, because Microsoft has a patent on the Windows operating system, other firms cannot sell their own versions of Windows. The government grants patents to encourage firms to spend money on the research and development necessary to create new products. If other companies could freely copy Windows, Microsoft would not have spent the funds necessary to develop it. Just as a new product or a new method of making a product receives patent protection, books, films, and software receive *copyright* protection. Under U.S. law, the creator of a book, film, or piece of music has the exclusive right to use the creation during the creator's lifetime. The creator's heirs retain this exclusive right for 50 years after the death of the creator.

Making the Connection

Property Rights in Cyberspace: YouTube and MySpace

The development of the Internet has led to new problems in protecting intellectual property rights. People can copy and e-mail songs, newspaper and magazine articles, and even entire motion pictures and television programs or post them on Web sites. Controlling unauthorized copying is more difficult today than it was when "copying" meant making a physical copy of a book, CD, or DVD. The popularity of YouTube and MySpace highlights the problem of unauthorized copying of videos and music. YouTube, founded in 2005, quickly became an enormous success because it provided an easy way to upload videos, which could then be viewed by anyone with an Internet connection. By 2007, thousands of new videos were being uploaded each day, and the site was receiving more than 20 million visitors per month. YouTube earned substantial profits from selling online advertising. Unfortunately, many of the videos on the site contained copyrighted material.

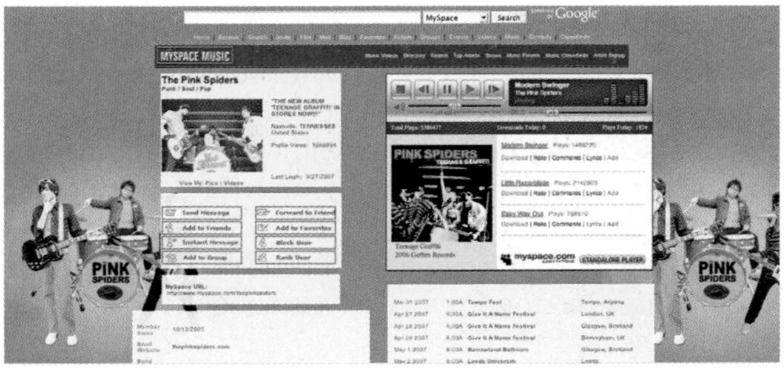

Some recording artists worry that the copyrights for their songs are not being protected on the Internet.

At first, YouTube's policy was to remove any video containing unauthorized material if the holder of the copyright complained. Then YouTube began to negotiate with the copyright holders to pay a fee in return for allowing the copyrighted material to remain on the site. For music videos, YouTube was usually able to obtain the needed permission directly from the recording company. Things were more complicated when videos on YouTube used copyrighted songs as background music. In those cases, YouTube needed to obtain permissions from the songwriters as well as the record company, which could be a time-consuming process. Obtaining permission to use videos that contained material from television shows or movies was even more complicated because sometimes dozens of people—including the actors, directors, and composers of music—held rights to the television show or movie. YouTube's vice president for business development was quoted as saying, "It's almost like technology has pushed far beyond the business practices and the law, and now everything needs to kind of catch up." In November 2006, YouTube agreed to be purchased by Google for $1.65 billion, which made the young entrepreneurs who started the company very wealthy. The willingness of YouTube's owners to sell their company to Google was motivated at least partly by the expectation that Google had the resources to help them resolve their copyright problems.

MySpace had similar problems because many Web pages on the site contained copyrighted music or videos. Universal Music sued MySpace after music from rapper Jay-Z's latest album started appearing on the site even before the album was released. In its lawsuit, Universal claimed that the illegal use of its copyrighted music had "created hundreds of millions of dollars of value for the owners of MySpace."

Music, television, and movie companies believe that the failure to give the full protection of property rights to the online use of their material reduces their ability to sell CDs and DVDs.

Sources: Kevin J. Delaney, Ethan Smith, and Brooks Barnes, "YouTube Finds Signing Rights Deals Complex, Frustrating," *Wall Street Journal*, November 3, 2006, p. B1; and Ethan Smith and Julia Angwin, "Universal Music Sues MySpace Claiming Copyright Infringement," *Wall Street Journal*, November 18, 2006, p. A3.

YOUR TURN: Test your understanding by doing related problem 3.14 on page 64 at the end of this chapter.

Enforcement of Contracts and Property Rights Much business activity involves someone agreeing to carry out some action in the future. For example, you may borrow $20,000 to buy a car and promise the bank—by signing a loan contract—that you will pay back the money over the next five years. Or Microsoft may sign a licensing agreement with a small technology company, agreeing to use that company's technology for a period of several years in return for a fee. Usually these agreements take the form of legal contracts. For a market system to work, businesses and individuals have to rely on these contracts being carried out. If one party to a legal contract does not fulfill its obligations—perhaps the small company had promised Microsoft exclusive use of its technology but then began licensing it to other companies—the other party could go to court to have the agreement enforced. Similarly, if property owners in the United States believe that the federal or state government has violated their rights under the 5th or 14th Amendments, they can go to court to have their rights enforced.

But going to court to enforce a contract or private property rights will be successful only if the court system is independent and judges are able to make impartial decisions on the basis of the law. In the United States and other high-income countries, the court systems have enough independence from other parts of the government and enough protection from intimidation by outside forces—such as criminal gangs—that they are able to make their decisions based on the law. In many developing countries, the court systems lack this independence and will not provide a remedy if the government violates private property rights or if a person with powerful political connections decides to violate a business contract.

If property rights are not well enforced, fewer goods and services will be produced. This reduces economic efficiency, leaving the economy inside its production possibilities frontier.

>> Continued from page 37

Economics in YOUR Life!

At the beginning of the chapter, we asked you to think about two questions: When buying a new car, what is the relationship between safety and gas mileage? and Under what circumstances would it be possible for car manufacturers to make cars safer and more fuel efficient? To answer the first question, you have to recognize that there is a trade-off between safety and gas mileage. With the technology available at any particular time, an automobile manufacturer can increase gas mileage by making a car smaller and lighter. But driving a lighter car increases your chances of being injured if you have an accident. The trade-off between safety and gas mileage would look much like the relationship in Figure 2-1. To get more of both safety and gas mileage, automobile makers would have to discover new technologies that allow them to make the car lighter and safer at the same time. Such new technologies would make points like *G* in Figure 2-1 attainable.

Conclusion

We have seen that by trading in markets, people are able to specialize and pursue their comparative advantage. Trading on the basis of comparative advantage makes all participants in trade better off. The key role of markets is to facilitate trade. In fact, the market system is a very effective means of coordinating the decisions of millions of consumers, workers, and firms. At the center of the market system is the consumer. To be successful, firms must respond to the desires of consumers. These desires are communicated to firms through prices. To explore how markets work, we must study the behavior of consumers and firms. We continue this exploration of markets in Chapter 3, when we develop the model of demand and supply.

Before moving on to Chapter 3, read *An Inside Look* on the next page to learn how BMW managers reallocate scarce resources in the firm's South Carolina plant to prepare to manufacture a new sports-activity coupe.

An Inside **LOOK**

BMW Managers Change Production Strategy

KNIGHT RIDDER TRIBUNE BUSINESS NEWS, JANUARY 25, 2007

Redesigned X5 to lead increase; new coupe to debut in 2008

a BMW expects production to rise 58 percent this year, nearly reaching its record production of 2002 and ending the string of production declines since then. The plant's 4,500 workers [based in Spartanburg, South Carolina] are expected to make 165,000 vehicles this year, up from 104,632 in 2006, spokesman Bob Nitto said Wednesday. The redesigned X5 sport utility vehicle is expected to drive the increase, with its production nearly doubling to about 130,000 vehicles. Production of the Z4 and related coupes is expected to decline slightly to 35,000 cars, down from 38,756 last year.

And in 2008, the plant is expected to add a new coupe to the production line, one that BMW now refers to as a sports-activity coupe. The term is a variation of the moniker BMW adopted in 1999 for the X5—a sports-activity vehicle. The automotive press is referring to the new car as the BMW X6, the crossover vehicle company officials have said previously would be built at Greer.

But even with a third vehicle, plant employment is not likely to increase substantially, plant spokeswoman Bunny Richardson said. Production workers at the plant earn about $25 to $26 per hour.

b Richardson and Nitto spoke with about a dozen area journalists allowed to see the plant for the first time since November 2005. That winter, the facility was shut down for two months as its separate assembly lines for the X5 and Z4 were merged into a single line.

One reason for the change was the increasing imbalance in production. The Z4s are smaller cars with fewer parts than the large, complex X5s. Also, Z4 sales have flattened, while X5 sales have risen. As a result, X5s are expected to account for 80 percent of the cars made at the plant this year.

The plant continues to become more dense. When it opened in 1994, aisles were wide and heavy equipment thin. Now many parts move overhead, and robots have become more numerous.

c The appearance has changed as the plant's production has climbed:

- At the end of 1995, the first full year of production, the plant had 1,556 workers and made 13,943 cars, or about nine cars per worker.
- At the end of 2000—the first full year of production of the original X5—the plant had 4,058 workers and made 83,672 vehicles, about 21 vehicles per worker.
- Production peaked in 2003, when the plant's work force swelled to 4,700, making 166,090 vehicles, or about 35 per worker.
- This year, the plant is expected to exceed 2003 in productivity, with production of 37 cars per worker.

This will be all the more challenging because of the size and complexity of the new X5, which first reached U.S. dealers in November, and is being rolled out to the European market this year. The X5 is filled with gizmos designed to allow it to shift from trips to the grocery store to fording creeks. Even the tires are complex: Run-flat tires now are standard equipment. Those supplied by Michelin are made at its Lexington plant, Richardson said.

Journalists were allowed to test the cars driving on a test track and off-road trail near the plant. Some versions carried an option that BMW calls Active Steering, a form of power steering that varies response depending on speed.

In a parking lot, only a slight motion is needed to steer into a space, while at higher speeds, sharp turns require more turning.

"You don't want to sneeze and change lanes," said Larry Parmele, a 55-year-old former race car driver and instructor at BMW's Performance Center test tracks in Greer.

Source: Jim Duplessis, "BMW Expects Turnaround," Knight Ridder Tribune Business News, *January 25, 2007, p.1. Reprinted by permission of the Permissions Group.*

Key Points in the Article

The article discusses the trade-offs that BMW managers face when making production decisions, given the size of the manufacturing plant and the technology used at the plant. The article also points out that these production decisions depend on the characteristics of the cars being produced, the number of workers at the plant, the technology of production, and the sales of the different car models.

Analyzing the News

a BMW plans to produce about 60,000 more automobiles at the Spartanburg, South Carolina plant during 2007. Even though the total number of automobiles produced is going to increase, BMW is going to cut back on the production of the Z4 and other coupes. Figure 1 shows the increase in total production as a movement toward the production possibilities frontier. Notice that even though BMW is producing more automobiles, it is choosing to produce fewer coupes, so total production of coupes is declining as the production at the plant is moving toward the frontier.

b Production at plants frequently responds to changes in the marketplace. If sales of one model decline, then automobile companies often reduce production of that model and expand production of the models that are selling. At this plant, production of the Z4 model is declining, while production of the X5 model is expanding. These changes in production decisions are a direct response to changes in the sales of these models. In addition, managers sometimes have to stop production so that they can retool the plant. In this case, managers closed the plant for two months during 2005, so that they could introduce a new assembly line that produced both the X5 and Z4 models. This allowed the managers to expand production at the plant and make it easier to introduce a new "sports-activity coupe" model that will begin production in 2008. The managers may have to close the plant again to prepare for production of the new sports-activity couple. In effect, the managers would be giving up production of existing models in 2007 while the plant is closed so that they can increase production of the new model in the future. Sometimes the trade-offs that managers face are trade-offs between the present and the future.

c As the demand for BMW models has increased, the automobile factory has changed. Managers introduced more machinery and workers and changed the layout of the factory. Moving the X5 and Z4 to the same assembly line so the plant can produce the new sports-activity coupe model is just the latest in a long line of changes that the managers have made. These changes provide the plant with more resources for producing BMW cars. We show this by shifting out the production possibilities frontier in Figure 2. You should also notice that as output at the plant expanded, BMW increased employment and the number of robots. As output at a firm or a plant expands, BMW tends to use more of all types of inputs, including labor.

Thinking Critically

1. Launching the new sports-activity coupe may require that the BMW managers shut down the Spartanburg plant for some period. Besides the direct costs of installing a new assembly line and new machinery, what would be the costs to BMW of shutting down the plant for a period of months? If shutting down the plant is costly, why would BMW do it?
2. Some BMWs are made in Germany, some in South Carolina, and some in other places. Should the United States government encourage the domestic production of BMWs by banning imports of BMWs?

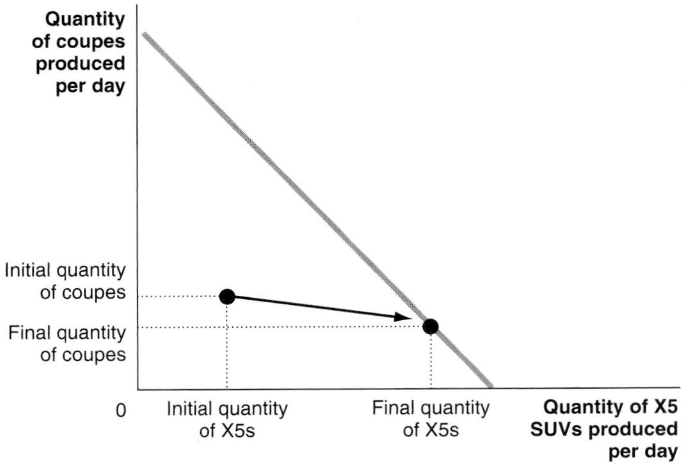

Figure 1. The increase in production at the plant in 2008.

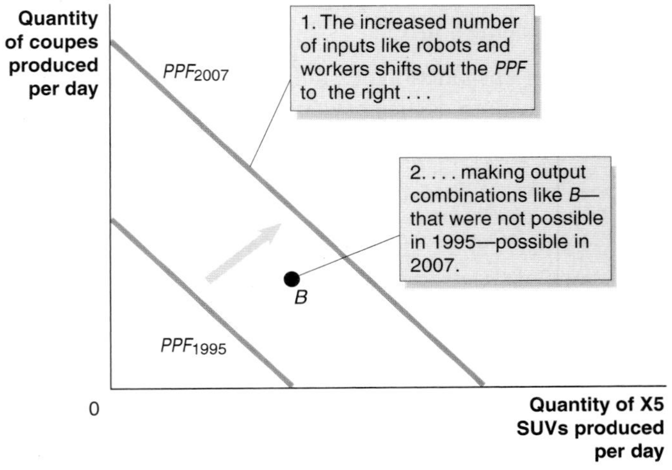

Figure 2. The effect of increasing inputs on output at the plant.

Key Terms

Absolute advantage, p. 46	Entrepreneur, p. 53	Market, p. 50	Property rights, p. 54
Circular-flow diagram, p. 51	Factor markets, p. 50	Opportunity cost, p. 39	Scarcity, p. 38
Comparative advantage, p. 47	Factors of production, p. 50	Product markets, p. 50	Trade, p. 44
Economic growth, p. 43	Free market, p. 52	Production possibilities frontier (*PPF*), p. 38	

2.1 LEARNING OBJECTIVE 2.1 | Use a production possibilities frontier to analyze opportunity costs and trade-offs, **pages 38–44.**

Production Possibilities Frontiers and Opportunity Costs

Summary

The **production possibilities frontier (*PPF*)** is a curve that shows the maximum attainable combinations of two products that may be produced with available resources. The *PPF* is used to illustrate the trade-offs that arise from **scarcity**. Points on the frontier are technically efficient. Points inside the frontier are inefficient, and points outside the frontier are unattainable. The **opportunity cost** of any activity is the highest valued alternative that must be given up to engage in that activity. Because of increasing marginal opportunity costs, production possibilities frontiers are usually bowed out rather than straight lines. This illustrates the important economic concept that the more resources that are already devoted to any activity, the smaller the payoff to devoting additional resources to that activity is likely to be. **Economic growth** is illustrated by shifting a production possibilities frontier outward.

myeconlab Get Ahead of the Curve Visit www.myeconlab.com to complete these exercises online and get instant feedback.

Review Questions

1.1 What do economists mean by scarcity? Can you think of anything that is not scarce according to the economic definition?

1.2 What is a production possibilities frontier? How can we show economic efficiency on a production possibilities frontier? How can we show inefficiency? What causes a production possibilities frontier to shift outward?

1.3 What does increasing marginal opportunity costs mean? What are the implications of this idea for the shape of the production possibilities frontier?

Problems and Applications

1.4 Draw a production possibilities frontier that shows the trade-off between the production of cotton and the production of soybeans.
   a. Show the effect that a prolonged drought would have on the initial production possibilities frontier.
   b. Suppose genetic modification makes soybeans resistant to insects, allowing yields to double. Show the effect of this technological change on the initial production possibilities frontier.

1.5 **(Related to the *Chapter Opener* on page 36)** One of the trade-offs BMW faces is between safety and gas mileage. For example, adding steel to a car makes it safer but also heavier, which results in lower gas mileage. Draw a hypothetical production possibilities frontier that BMW engineers face that shows this trade-off.

1.6 Suppose you win free tickets to a movie plus all you can eat at the snack bar for free. Would there be a cost to you to attend this movie? Explain.

1.7 Suppose we can divide all the goods produced by an economy into two types: consumption goods and capital goods. Capital goods, such as machinery, equipment, and computers, are goods used to produce other goods.
   a. Use a production possibilities frontier graph to illustrate the trade-off to an economy between producing consumption goods and producing capital goods. Is it likely that the production possibilities frontier in this situation would be a straight line (as in Figure 2-1 on page 39) or bowed out (as in Figure 2-2 on page 42)? Briefly explain.
   b. Suppose a technological advance occurs that affects the production of capital goods but not consumption goods. Show the effect on the production possibilities frontier.
   c. Suppose that country A and country B currently have identical production possibilities frontiers but that country A devotes only 5 percent of its resources to producing capital goods over each of the next 10 years, whereas country B devotes 30 percent. Which country is likely to experience more rapid economic growth in the future? Illustrate using a production possibilities frontier graph. Your graph should include production possibilities frontiers for country A today and in 10 years and production possibilities frontiers for country B today and in 10 years.

1.8 Use the production possibilities frontier for a country to answer the following questions.

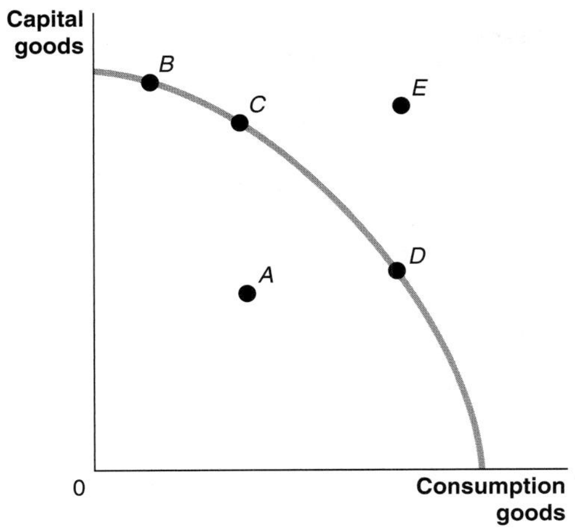

a. Which point(s) are unattainable? Briefly explain why.
b. Which point(s) are efficient? Briefly explain why.
c. Which point(s) are inefficient? Briefly explain why.
d. At which point is the country's future growth rate likely to be the highest? Briefly explain why.

1.9 **(Related to *Solved Problem 2-1* on page 40)** You have exams in economics and chemistry coming up and five hours available for studying. The following table shows the trade-offs you face in allocating the time you will spend in studying each subject.

	HOURS SPENT STUDYING		MIDTERM SCORE	
CHOICE	ECONOMICS	CHEMISTRY	ECONOMICS	CHEMISTRY
A	5	0	95	70
B	4	1	93	78
C	3	2	90	84
D	2	3	86	88
E	1	4	81	90
F	0	5	75	91

a. Use the data in the table to draw a production possibilities frontier graph. Label the vertical axis "Score on economics exam" and label the horizontal axis "Score on chemistry exam." Make sure to label the values where your production possibilities frontier intersects the vertical and horizontal axes.
b. Label the points representing choice *C* and choice *D*. If you are at choice *C*, what is your opportunity cost of increasing your chemistry score?
c. Under what circumstances would *A* be a sensible choice?

1.10 **(Related to the *Making the Connection* on page 41)** Suppose the president is attempting to decide whether the federal government should spend more on research to find a cure for heart disease. He asks you, one of his economic advisors, to prepare a report discussing the relevant factors he should consider. Discuss the main issues you would deal with in your report.

1.11 Lawrence Summers served as secretary of the treasury in the Clinton administration and later as the president of Harvard University. He has been quoted as giving the following moral defense of the economic approach:

> There is nothing morally unattractive about saying: We need to analyze which way of spending money on health care will produce more benefit and which less, and using our money as efficiently as we can. I don't think there is anything immoral about seeking to achieve environmental benefits at the lowest possible costs.

Would it be more moral to reduce pollution without worrying about the cost or by taking the cost into account? Briefly explain.

Source: David Wessel, "Precepts from Professor Summers," *Wall Street Journal*, October 17, 2002.

1.12 In *The Wonderful Wizard of Oz* and his other books about the Land of Oz, L. Frank Baum observed that if people's wants were modest enough, most goods would not be scarce. According to Baum, this was the case in Oz:

> There were no poor people in the Land of Oz, because there was no such thing as money. . . . Each person was given freely by his neighbors whatever he required for his use, which is as much as anyone may reasonably desire. Some tilled the lands and raised great crops of grain, which was divided equally among the whole population, so that all had enough. There were many tailors and dressmakers and shoemakers and the like, who made things that any who desired them might wear. Likewise there were jewelers who made ornaments for the person, which pleased and beautified the people, and these ornaments also were free to those who asked for them. Each man and woman, no matter what he or she produced for the good of the community, was supplied by the neighbors with food and clothing and a house and furniture and ornaments and games. If by chance the supply ever ran short, more was taken from the great storehouses of the Ruler, which were afterward filled up again when there was more of any article than people needed. . . .

You will know, by what I have told you here, that the Land of Oz was a remarkable country. I do not suppose such an arrangement would be practical with us.

Do you agree with Baum that the economic system in Oz wouldn't work in the contemporary United States? Briefly explain why or why not.

Source: L. Frank Baum, *The Emerald City of Oz*, pp. 30–31. First edition published in 1910.

>> End Learning Objective 2.1

2.2 LEARNING OBJECTIVE 2.2 | Understand comparative advantage and explain how it is the basis for trade, **pages 44–49.**

Comparative Advantage and Trade

Summary

Fundamentally, markets are about **trade**, which is the act of buying or selling. People trade on the basis of comparative advantage. An individual, a firm, or a country has a **comparative advantage** in producing a good or service if it can produce the good or service at the lowest opportunity cost. People are usually better off specializing in the activity for which they have a comparative advantage and trading for the other goods and services they need. It is important not to confuse comparative advantage with absolute advantage. An individual, a firm, or a country has an **absolute advantage** in producing a good or service if it can produce more of that good or service from the same amount of resources. It is possible to have an absolute advantage in producing a good or service without having a comparative advantage.

Review Questions

2.1 What is absolute advantage? What is comparative advantage? Is it possible for a country to have a comparative advantage in producing a good without also having an absolute advantage? Briefly explain.

2.2 What is the basis for trade? What advantages are there to specialization?

Problems and Applications

2.3 Look again at the information in Figure 2-4 on page 45. Choose a rate of trading cherries for apples different than the rate used in the text (15 pounds of cherries for 10 pounds of apples) that will allow you and your neighbor to benefit from trading apples and cherries. Prepare a table like Table 2-1 on page 46 to illustrate your answer.

2.4 Using the same amount of resources, the United States and Canada can both produce lumberjack shirts and lumberjack boots, as shown in the following production possibilities frontiers.

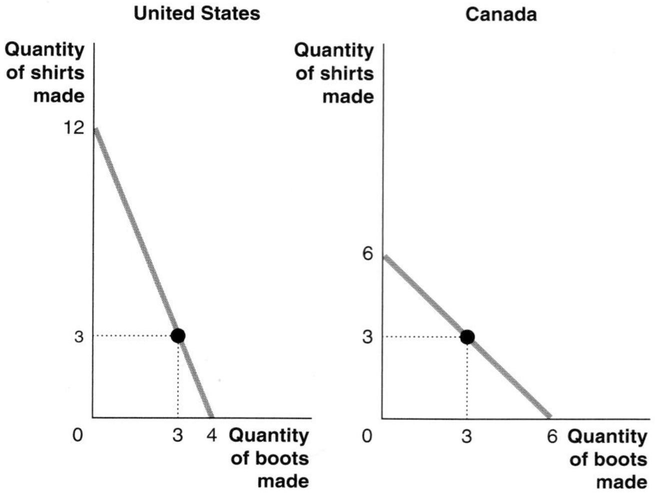

a. Who has a comparative advantage in producing lumberjack boots? Who has a comparative advantage in producing lumberjack shirts? Explain your reasoning.
b. Does either country have an absolute advantage in producing both goods? Explain.
c. Suppose that both countries are currently producing three pairs of boots and three shirts. Show that both can be better off if they specialize in producing one good and then engage in trade.

2.5 (Related to *Solved Problem 2-2* on page 48) Suppose Iran and Iraq both produce oil and olive oil. The following table shows combinations of both goods that each country can produce in a day, measured in thousands of barrels.

IRAQ		IRAN	
OIL	OLIVE OIL	OIL	OLIVE OIL
0	8	0	4
2	6	1	3
4	4	2	2
6	2	3	1
8	0	4	0

a. Who has the comparative advantage in producing oil? Explain.
b. Can these two countries gain from trading oil and olive oil? Explain.

2.6 **(Related to *Solved Problem 2-2* on page 48)** Suppose that France and Germany both produce schnitzel and wine. The following table shows combinations of the goods that each country can produce in a day.

FRANCE		GERMANY	
WINE (BOTTLES)	SCHNITZEL (POUNDS)	WINE (BOTTLES)	SCHNITZEL (POUNDS)
0	8	0	15
1	6	1	12
2	4	2	9
3	2	3	6
4	0	4	3
		5	0

a. Who has a comparative advantage in producing wine? Who has a comparative advantage in producing schnitzel?
b. Suppose that France is currently producing 1 bottle of wine and 6 pounds of schnitzel, and Germany is currently producing 3 bottles of wine and 6 pounds of schnitzel. Demonstrate that France and Germany can both be better off if they specialize in producing only one good and then engage in trade.

2.7 **(Related to *Don't Let This Happen to You!* on page 48)** In the 1950s, the economist Bela Balassa compared 28 manufacturing industries in the United States and Britain. In every one of the 28 industries, Balassa found that the United States had an absolute advantage. In these circumstances, would there have been any gain to the United States from importing any of these products from Britain? Explain.

2.8 In colonial America, the population was spread thinly over a large area, and transportation costs were very high because it was difficult to ship products by road for more than short distances. As a result, most of the free population lived on small farms where they not only grew their own food but also usually made their own clothes and very rarely bought or sold anything for money. Explain why the incomes of these farmers were likely to rise as transportation costs fell. Use the concept of comparative advantage in your answer.

2.9 During the 1928 presidential election campaign, Herbert Hoover, the Republican candidate, argued that the United States should only import those products that could not be produced here. Do you believe that this would be a good policy? Explain.

>> End Learning Objective 2.2

2.3 LEARNING OBJECTIVE 2.3 | Explain the basic idea of how a market system works, **pages 50–56.**

The Market System

Summary

A **market** is a group of buyers and sellers of a good or service and the institution or arrangement by which they come together to trade. **Product markets** are markets for goods and services, such as computers and medical treatment. **Factor markets** are markets for the **factors of production**, such as labor, capital, natural resources, and entrepreneurial ability. A **circular-flow diagram** shows how participants in product markets and factor markets are linked. Adam Smith argued in his 1776 book *The Wealth of Nations* that in a **free market** where the government does not control the production of goods and services, changes in prices lead firms to produce the goods and services most desired by consumers. If consumers demand more of a good, its price will rise. Firms respond to rising prices by increasing production. If consumers demand less of a good, its price will fall. Firms respond to falling prices by producing less of a good. An **entrepreneur** is someone who operates a business. In a market system, entrepreneurs are responsible for organizing the production of goods and services. A market system will work well only if there is protection for **property rights**, which are the rights of individuals and firms to use their property.

myeconlab Get Ahead of the Curve Visit www.myeconlab.com to complete these exercises online and get instant feedback.

Review Questions

3.1 What is the circular-flow diagram, and what does it demonstrate?

3.2 What are the two main categories of participants in markets? Which participants are of greatest importance in determining what goods and services are produced?

3.3 What is a free market? In what ways does a free market economy differ from a centrally planned economy?

3.4 What is an entrepreneur? Why do entrepreneurs play a key role in a market system?

3.5 Under what circumstances are firms likely to produce more of a good or service? Under what circumstances are firms likely to produce less of a good or service?

3.6 What are private property rights? What role do they play in the working of a market system? Why are independent courts important for a well-functioning economy?

Problems and Applications

3.7 Identify whether each of the following transactions will take place in the factor market or in the product market and whether households or firms are supplying the good or service or demanding the good or service:

a. George buys a BMW X5 SUV.
b. BMW increases employment at its Spartanburg plant.
c. George works 20 hours per week at McDonald's.
d. George sells land he owns to McDonald's so it can build a new restaurant.

3.8 **(Related to the *Making the Connection* on page 53)** In *The Wealth of Nations*, Adam Smith wrote the following (Book I, Chapter II): "It is not from the benevolence of the butcher, the brewer, or the baker, that we expect our dinner, but from their regard to their own interest." Briefly discuss what he meant by this.

3.9 In a commencement address to economics graduates at the University of Texas, Robert McTeer, Jr., who was then the president of the Federal Reserve Bank of Dallas, argued, "For my money, Adam Smith's invisible hand is the most important thing you've learned by studying economics." What's so important about the idea of the invisible hand?

Source: Robert D. McTeer, Jr., "The Dismal Science? Hardly!" *Wall Street Journal*, June 4, 2003.

3.10 Evaluate the following argument: "Adam Smith's analysis is based on a fundamental flaw: He assumes that people are motivated by self-interest. But this isn't true. I'm not selfish, and most people I know aren't selfish."

3.11 Writing in the *New York Times*, Michael Lewis argued that "a market economy is premised on a system of incentives designed to encourage an ignoble human trait: self-interest." Do you agree that self-interest is an "ignoble human trait"? What incentives does a market system provide to encourage self-interest?

Source: Michael Lewis, "In Defense of the Boom," *New York Times*, October 27, 2002.

3.12 An editorial in *BusinessWeek* magazine offered this opinion: "Economies should be judged on a simple measure: their ability to generate a rising standard of living for all members of society, including people at the bottom." Briefly discuss whether you agree.

Source: "Poverty: The Bigger Picture," *BusinessWeek*, October 7, 2002.

3.13 An estimated 400 million to 600 million people worldwide are squatters who live on land to which they have no legal title, usually on the outskirts of cities in developing countries. Economist Hernando de Soto persuaded Peru's government to undertake a program to make it cheap and easy for such squatters to obtain a title to the land they had been occupying. How would this creation of property rights be likely to affect the economic opportunities available to these squatters?

Source: Alan B. Krueger, "A Study Looks at Squatters and Land Title in Peru," *New York Times*, January 9, 2003.

3.14 **(Related to the *Making the Connection* on page 55)** A columnist for the *Wall Street Journal* argued that most copyright holders are not damaged by having their material shown on YouTube:

> It's [laughable] to suggest that content owners are hurt by videos of teenagers lip-synching to hip-hop songs, that the market for sports DVDs is destroyed by fans being allowed to relive a team's great moment, or that artists reusing footage of famous televised events destroys interest in documentaries.

Do you agree with the argument that the copyright owners of the material mentioned should not be paid a fee if their material is on YouTube? Are there other types of material not mentioned by this columnist with which the copyright holders might suffer significant financial damages by having their material available on YouTube?

Source: Jason Fry, "The Revolution May Be Briefly Televised," *Wall Street Journal*, November 13, 2006.

>> End Learning Objective 2.3

Chapter 3

Where Prices Come From: The Interaction of Demand and Supply

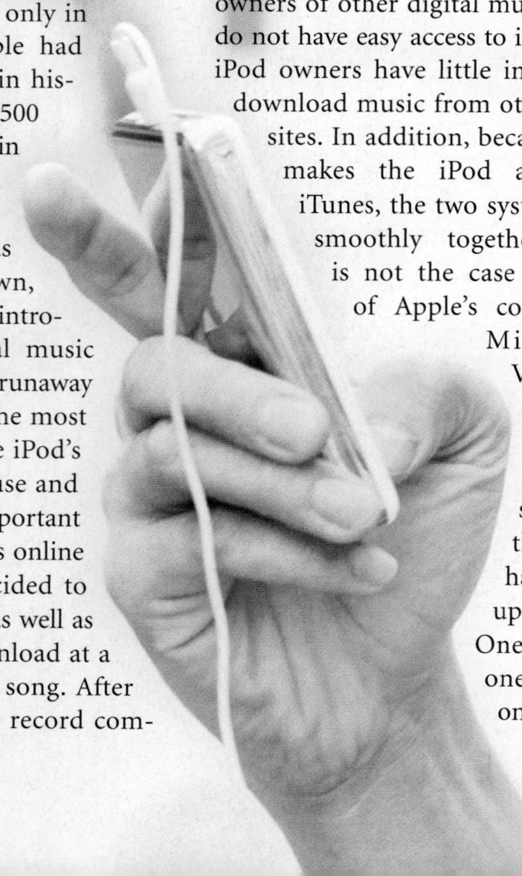

Apple and the Demand for iPods

During the last three months of 2006, Apple sold $3.43 billion worth of iPods. iPods seemed to be everywhere, but during 2007 it became clear that the market for digital music players was becoming much more competitive.

Steve Jobs and Steve Wozniak started Apple in 1976. Working out of Jobs's parents' garage, the two friends created the Apple I computer. By 1980, although Jobs was still only in his mid-twenties, Apple had become the first firm in history to join the Fortune 500 list of largest U.S. firms in less than five years. Apple's success in the computer business has been up and down, but when the company introduced the iPod digital music player in 2001, it had a runaway success on its hands. The most obvious reasons for the iPod's success are its ease of use and sleek design. But also important has been iTunes, Apple's online music store. Apple decided to offer individual songs, as well as whole albums, for download at a price of just $0.99 per song. After paying a royalty to the record company, Apple makes very little profit from the songs it sells on iTunes. Apple was willing to accept a small profit on the sale of each song to make the purchase of the iPod more attractive to consumers.

At a price of several hundred dollars, the iPod might be relatively expensive, but purchasing the music is very inexpensive. In addition, the songs on iTunes are playable only on iPods, and iPods can only play songs downloaded from iTunes (although with enough technical skill, it's possible to get around both restrictions). So, owners of other digital music players do not have easy access to iTunes, and iPod owners have little incentive to download music from other online sites. In addition, because Apple makes the iPod and owns iTunes, the two systems work smoothly together, which is not the case for many of Apple's competitors. Microsoft's Vice President Bryan Lee says, "That's something that Apple has played up very well. One brand, one device, one service."

By early 2007, more than 100 million iPods had been sold and more than 2 billion songs had been downloaded from iTunes. Clearly, the strategy of selling an expensive digital music player and selling the music cheaply has been very successful for Apple. But how long will the iPod's dominance last? By 2007, competitors were flooding into the market. New digital music players, such as Microsoft's Zune, Toshiba's Gigabeat, and iRiver's H10, among many others, were rapidly gaining customers. In addition, firms were introducing new "music phones" that combined the features of a cell phone with the features of a digital music player. Although this wave of competition might be bad news for Apple, it could be good news for consumers by increasing the choices available and lowering prices. **AN INSIDE LOOK** on **page 90** discusses how Apple responded to competition by teaming with AT&T to create its own music phone, the iPhone.

Sources: Nick Wingfield and Robert Guth, "iPod, TheyPod: Rivals Imitate Apple's Success," *Wall Street Journal*, September 18, 2006, p. B1; and Nick Wingfield, "iPod Demand Lifts Apple's Results," *Wall Street Journal*, January 18, 2007, p. A2.

LEARNING Objectives

After studying this chapter, you should be able to:

3.1 Discuss the variables that influence **demand**, page 68.

3.2 Discuss the variables that influence **supply**, page 75.

3.3 Use a graph to illustrate **market equilibrium**, page 79.

3.4 Use **demand and supply graphs** to predict changes in prices and quantities, page 83.

Economics in YOUR Life!

Will you buy an iPod or a Zune?

Suppose you are about to buy a new digital music player and that you are choosing between Apple's iPod and Microsoft's Zune. As the industry leader, the iPod has many advantages over a new entrant like Zune. One strategy Microsoft can use to overcome those advantages is to compete based on price. Would you choose a Zune if it had a lower price than a comparable iPod? Would you choose a Zune if the songs sold on Zune Marketplace were cheaper than the songs sold on iTunes? As you read the chapter, see if you can answer these questions. You can check your answers against those we provide at the end of the chapter. » **Continued on page 89**

In Chapter 1, we explored how economists use models to predict human behavior. In Chapter 2, we used the model of production possibilities frontiers to analyze scarcity and trade-offs. In this chapter and the next, we explore the model of demand and supply, which is the most powerful tool in economics, and use it to explain how prices are determined.

Recall from Chapter 1 that economic models rely on assumptions and that these assumptions are simplifications of reality. In some cases, the assumptions of the model may not seem to describe exactly the economic situation being analyzed. For example, the model of demand and supply assumes that we are analyzing a *perfectly competitive market.* In a **perfectly competitive market**, there are many buyers and sellers, all the products sold are identical, and there are no barriers to new firms entering the market. These assumptions are very restrictive and apply exactly to only a few markets, such as the markets for wheat and other agricultural products. Experience has shown, however, that the model of demand and supply can be very useful in analyzing markets where competition among sellers is intense, even if there are relatively few sellers and the products being sold are not identical. In fact, in recent studies the model of demand and supply has been successful in analyzing markets with as few as four buyers and four sellers. In the end, the usefulness of a model depends on how well it can predict outcomes in a market. As we will see in this chapter, the model of demand and supply is often very useful in predicting changes in quantities and prices in many markets.

Perfectly competitive market A market that meets the conditions of (1) many buyers and sellers, (2) all firms selling identical products, and (3) no barriers to new firms entering the market.

We begin considering the model of demand and supply by discussing consumers and the demand side of the market, then we turn to firms and the supply side. As you will see, we will apply this model throughout this book to understand business, the economy, and economic policy.

3.1 LEARNING OBJECTIVE

3.1 | Discuss the variables that influence demand.

The Demand Side of the Market

Chapter 2 explained that in a market system, consumers ultimately determine which goods and services will be produced. The most successful businesses are the ones that respond best to consumer demand. But what determines consumer demand for a product? Certainly, many factors influence the willingness of consumers to buy a particular product. For example, consumers who are considering buying a digital music player, such as Apple's iPod or Microsoft's Zune, will make their decisions based on, among other factors, the income they have available to spend and the effectiveness of the advertising campaigns of the companies that sell digital music players. The main factor in consumer decisions, though, will be the price of the digital music player. So, it makes sense to begin with price when analyzing the decisions of consumers to buy a product. It is important to note that when we discuss demand, we are considering not what a consumer *wants* to buy but what the consumer is both willing and *able* to buy.

Demand schedule A table showing the relationship between the price of a product and the quantity of the product demanded.

Quantity demanded The amount of a good or service that a consumer is willing and able to purchase at a given price.

Demand curve A curve that shows the relationship between the price of a product and the quantity of the product demanded.

Market demand The demand by all the consumers of a given good or service.

Demand Schedules and Demand Curves

Tables that show the relationship between the price of a product and the quantity of the product demanded are called **demand schedules**. The table in Figure 3-1 shows the number of players consumers would be willing to buy over the course of a month at five different prices. The amount of a good or a service that a consumer is willing and able to purchase at a given price is referred to as the **quantity demanded**. The graph in Figure 3-1 plots the numbers from the table as a **demand curve**, a curve that shows the relationship between the price of a product and the quantity of the product demanded. (Note that for convenience, we made the demand curve in Figure 3-1 a straight line, or linear. There is no reason that all demand curves need to be straight lines.) The demand curve in Figure 3-1 shows the **market demand**, or the demand by all the consumers of a

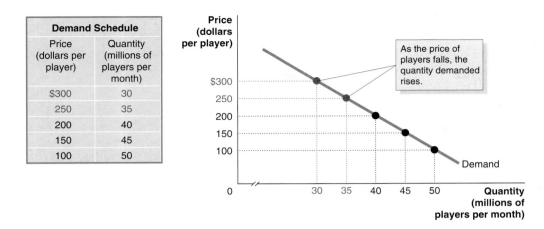

Demand Schedule	
Price (dollars per player)	Quantity (millions of players per month)
$300	30
250	35
200	40
150	45
100	50

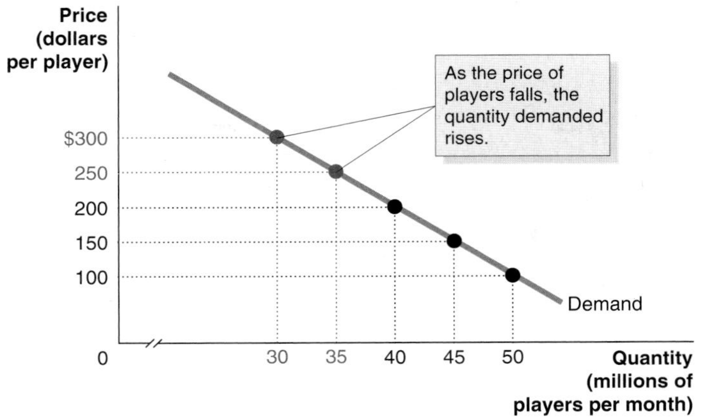

Figure 3-1

A Demand Schedule and Demand Curve

As the price changes, consumers change the quantity of digital music players they are willing to buy. We can show this as a *demand schedule* in a table or as a *demand curve* on a graph. The table and graph both show that as the price of players falls, the quantity demanded rises. When the price of a player is $300, consumers buy 30 million. When the price drops to $250, consumers buy 35 million. Therefore, the demand curve for digital music players is downward sloping.

given good or service. The market for a product, such as restaurant meals, that is purchased locally would include all the consumers in a city or a relatively small area. The market for a product that is sold internationally, such as digital music players, would include all the consumers in the world.

The demand curve in Figure 3-1 slopes downward because consumers will buy more players as the price falls. When the price of players is $300, consumers buy 30 million players per month. If the price of players falls to $250, consumers buy 35 million players. Buyers demand a larger quantity of a product as the price falls because the product becomes less expensive relative to other products and because they can afford to buy more at a lower price.

The Law of Demand

The inverse relationship between the price of a product and the quantity of the product demanded is known as the **law of demand**: Holding everything else constant, when the price of a product falls, the quantity demanded of the product will increase, and when the price of a product rises, the quantity demanded of the product will decrease. The law of demand holds for any market demand curve. Economists have never found an exception to it. In fact, Nobel Prize–winning economist George Stigler once remarked that the surest way for an economist to become famous would be to discover a market demand curve that sloped upward rather than downward.

Law of demand The rule that, holding everything else constant, when the price of a product falls, the quantity demanded of the product will increase, and when the price of a product rises, the quantity demanded of the product will decrease.

What Explains the Law of Demand?

It makes sense that consumers will buy more of a good when the price falls and less of a good when the price rises, but let's look more closely at why this is true. When the price of digital music players falls, consumers buy a larger quantity because of the *substitution effect* and the *income effect.*

Substitution Effect The **substitution effect** refers to the change in the quantity demanded of a good that results from a change in price, making the good more or less expensive *relative* to other goods that are *substitutes.* When the price of digital music players falls, consumers will substitute buying music players for buying other goods, such as radios or compact stereos.

Substitution effect The change in the quantity demanded of a good that results from a change in price, making the good more or less expensive relative to other goods that are substitutes.

The Income Effect The **income effect** of a price change refers to the change in the quantity demanded of a good that results from the effect of a change in the good's price on consumers' purchasing power. Purchasing power is the quantity of goods a consumer can buy with a fixed amount of income. When the price of a good falls, the increased purchasing power of consumers' incomes will usually lead them to purchase a larger quantity of the good. When the price of a good rises, the decreased purchasing power of consumers' incomes will usually lead them to purchase a smaller quantity of the good.

Income effect The change in the quantity demanded of a good that results from the effect of a change in the good's price on consumers' purchasing power.

Note that although we can analyze them separately, the substitution effect and the income effect happen simultaneously whenever a price changes. Thus, a fall in the price of digital music players leads consumers to buy more players, both because the players are now cheaper relative to substitute products and because the purchasing power of the consumers' incomes has increased.

Holding Everything Else Constant: The *Ceteris Paribus* Condition

Notice that the definition of the law of demand contains the phrase *holding everything else constant.* In constructing the market demand curve for digital music players, we focused only on the effect that changes in the price of players would have on the quantity of players consumers would be willing and able to buy. We were holding constant other variables that might affect the willingness of consumers to buy players. Economists refer to the necessity of holding all variables other than price constant in constructing a demand curve as the ***ceteris paribus*** condition; *ceteris paribus* is Latin for "all else equal."

***Ceteris paribus* ("all else equal")** The requirement that when analyzing the relationship between two variables—such as price and quantity demanded—other variables must be held constant.

What would happen if we allowed a change in a variable—other than price—that might affect the willingness of consumers to buy music players? Consumers would then change the quantity they demand at each price. We can illustrate this effect by shifting the market demand curve. A shift of a demand curve is *an increase or a decrease in demand.* A movement along a demand curve is *an increase or a decrease in the quantity demanded.* As Figure 3-2 shows, we shift the demand curve to the right if consumers decide to buy more of the good at each price, and we shift the demand curve to the left if consumers decide to buy less at each price.

Variables That Shift Market Demand

Many variables other than price can influence market demand. These five are the most important:

- Income
- Prices of related goods
- Tastes
- Population and demographics
- Expected future prices

We next discuss how changes in each of these variables affect the market demand curve for digital music players.

Figure 3-2

Shifting the Demand Curve

When consumers increase the quantity of a product they wish to buy at a given price, the market demand curve shifts to the right, from D_1 to D_2. When consumers decrease the quantity of a product they wish to buy at any given price, the demand curve shifts to the left, from D_1 to D_3.

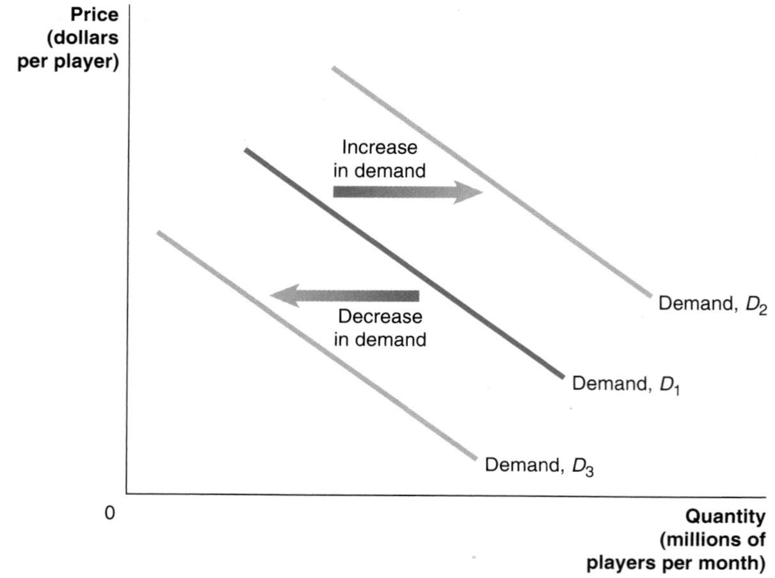

Income The income that consumers have available to spend affects their willingness and ability to buy a good. Suppose that the market demand curve in Figure 3-1 represents the willingness of consumers to buy digital music players when average household income is $43,000. If household income rises to $45,000, the demand for players will increase, which we show by shifting the demand curve to the right. A good is a **normal good** when demand increases following a rise in income and decreases following a fall in income. Most goods are normal goods, but the demand for some goods falls when income rises and rises when income falls. For instance, as your income rises, you might buy less canned tuna fish or fewer hot dogs and buy more shrimp or prime rib. A good is an **inferior good** when demand decreases following a rise in income and increases following a fall in income. So, for you hot dogs and tuna fish would be examples of inferior goods—not because they are of low quality but because you buy less of them as your income increases.

Normal good A good for which the demand increases as income rises and decreases as income falls.

Inferior good A good for which the demand increases as income falls and decreases as income rises.

Prices of Related Goods The prices of other goods can also affect consumers' demand for a product. Suppose that the market demand curve in Figure 3-1 represents the willingness and ability of consumers to buy digital music players during a year when the average price of compact stereos, such as the Bose Wave music system, is $500. If the average price of these stereo systems falls to $400, how will the market demand for digital music players change? Fewer players will be demanded at every price. We show this by shifting the demand curve for players to the left.

Goods and services that can be used for the same purpose—such as digital music players and compact stereos—are **substitutes**. When two goods are substitutes, the more you buy of one, the less you will buy of the other. A decrease in the price of a substitute causes the demand curve for a good to shift to the left. An increase in the price of a substitute causes the demand curve for a good to shift to the right.

Substitutes Goods and services that can be used for the same purpose.

Many consumers play songs downloaded from a Web site, such as iTunes or Zune Marketplace, on their digital music players. Suppose the market demand curve in Figure 3-1 represents the willingness of consumers to buy players at a time when the average price to download a song is $0.99. If the price to download a song falls to $0.49, consumers will buy more song downloads *and* more digital music players: The demand curve for music players will shift to the right.

Products that are used together—such as digital music players and song downloads—are **complements**. When two goods are complements, the more consumers buy of one, the more they will buy of the other. A decrease in the price of a complement causes the demand curve for a good to shift to the right. An increase in the price of a complement causes the demand curve for a good to shift to the left.

Complements Goods and services that are used together.

Making the Connection | Why Supermarkets Need to Understand Substitutes and Complements

Supermarkets sell what sometimes seems like a bewildering variety of goods. The first row of the following table shows the varieties of eight products stocked by five Chicago supermarkets.

	COFFEE	FROZEN PIZZA	HOT DOGS	ICE CREAM	POTATO CHIPS	REGULAR CEREAL	SPAGHETTI SAUCE	YOGURT
Varieties in five Chicago supermarkets	391	337	128	421	285	242	194	288
Varieties introduced in a 2-year period	113	109	47	129	93	114	70	107
Varieties removed in a 2-year period	135	86	32	118	77	75	36	51

Source: Juin-Kuan Chong, Teck-Hua Ho, and Christopher S. Tang, "A Modeling Framework for Category Assortment Planning," *Manufacturing & Service Operations Management*, 2001, Vol. 3, No. 3, pp. 191–210.

Supermarkets are also constantly adding new varieties of goods to their shelves and removing old varieties. The second row of the table shows that these five Chicago supermarkets added 113 new varieties of coffee over a two-year period, while the third row shows that they eliminated 135 existing varieties. How do supermarkets decide which varieties to add and which to remove?

Christopher Tang is a professor at the Anderson Graduate School of Management at the University of California, Los Angeles (UCLA). In an interview with the *Baltimore Sun*, Tang argues that supermarkets should not necessarily remove the slowest-selling goods from their shelves but should consider the relationships among the goods. In particular, they should consider whether the goods being removed are substitutes or complements with the remaining goods. A lobster bisque soup, for example, could be a relatively slow seller but might be a complement to other soups because it can be used with them to make a sauce. In that case, removing the lobster bisque would hurt sales of some of the remaining soups. Tang suggests the supermarket would be better off removing a slow-selling soup that is a substitute for another soup. For example, the supermarket might want to remove one of two brands of cream of chicken soup.

Source: Lobster bisque example from Lorraine Mirabella, "Shelf Science in Supermarkets," *Baltimore Sun*, March 17, 2002, p. 16.

YOUR TURN: For more practice, do problem 1.5 on page 92 at the end of this chapter.

Tastes Consumers can be influenced by an advertising campaign for a product. If Apple, Microsoft, Toshiba, and other makers of digital music players begin to heavily advertise on television and online, consumers are more likely to buy players at every price, and the demand curve will shift to the right. An economist would say that the advertising campaign has affected consumers' *taste* for digital music players. Taste is a catchall category that refers to the many subjective elements that can enter into a consumer's decision to buy a product. A consumer's taste for a product can change for many reasons. Sometimes trends play a substantial role. For example, the popularity of low-carbohydrate diets caused a decline in demand for some goods, such as bread and donuts, and an increase in demand for beef. In general, when consumers' taste for a product increases, the demand curve will shift to the right, and when consumers' taste for a product decreases, the demand curve for the product will shift to the left.

Demographics The characteristics of a population with respect to age, race, and gender.

Population and Demographics Population and demographic factors can affect the demand for a product. As the population of the United States increases, so will the number of consumers, and the demand for most products will increase. The **demographics** of a population refers to its characteristics, with respect to age, race, and gender. As the demographics of a country or region change, the demand for particular goods will increase or decrease because different categories of people tend to have different preferences for those goods. For instance, in 2006, a record 17 percent of the U.S. population was 60 years of age or older increasing the demand for health care and other products heavily used by older people.

Making the Connection | Companies Respond to a Growing Hispanic Population

The spending power of Hispanic Americans is rapidly increasing. So, it is no surprise that firms have begun to respond: When Apple announced in early 2007 that it would sell a 90-minute video of highlights of the 2007 Super Bowl on its iTunes store, the download was made available in Spanish as well as in English. In late 2006, "Coffee Break Spanish," a weekly Spanish language podcast, was one of the most frequently downloaded podcasts on iTunes. Today, more than one third of all DVDs are sold to consumers whose first language is Spanish, and Blockbuster has responded by increasing its offerings of Spanish-language films. Kmart sells a clothing line named after Thalia, a Mexican singer. The Ford Motor Company hired Mexican actress Salma Hayek to appear in commercials. A used car dealer in Pennsylvania displayed a sign stating "Salga Manejando Hoy Mismo" (or "Drive Out Today" in English).

Blockbuster responds to a growing Hispanic population by featuring DVDs dubbed in Spanish.

The increase in spending by Hispanic households was due partly to increased population growth and partly to rising incomes. By 2020, the Hispanic share of the U.S. consumer market is expected to grow to more than 13 percent—almost twice what it was in 2000. The Selig Center for Economic Growth at the University of Georgia has forecast that spending by Hispanic households will increase about 70 percent more between 2006 and 2011 than spending by non-Hispanic households.

As the demand for goods purchased by Hispanic households increases, a larger quantity can be sold at every price. Firms have responded by devoting more resources to serving this demographic group.

Sources: "Apple Completes Pass for Super Bowl Highlights," *St. Petersburg* (Florida) *Times*, February 1, 2007; Catherine E. Shoichet and John Martin, "Downloading," *Houston Chronicle*, January 7, 2007; Jeffrey M. Humphreys, "The Multicultural Economy 2006," *Georgia Business and Economic Conditions*, Third Quarter 2006, Vol. 66, No. 3; and Eduardo Porter, "Buying Power of Hispanics Is Set to Soar," *Wall Street Journal*, April 18, 2003, p. B1.

YOUR TURN: For more practice, do problem 1.8 on page 93 at the end of this chapter.

Expected Future Prices Consumers choose not only which products to buy but also when to buy them. If enough consumers become convinced that digital music players will be selling for lower prices three months from now, the demand for players will decrease now, as some consumers postpone their purchases to wait for the expected price decrease. Alternatively, if enough consumers become convinced that the price of players will be higher three months from now, the demand for players will increase now, as some consumers try to beat the expected price increase.

Table 3-1 on page 74 summarizes the most important variables that cause market demand curves to shift. You should note that the table shows the shift in the demand curve that results from an *increase* in each of the variables. A *decrease* in these variables would cause the demand curve to shift in the opposite direction.

A Change in Demand versus a Change in Quantity Demanded

It is important to understand the difference between a *change in demand* and a *change in quantity demanded.* A change in demand refers to a shift of the demand curve. A shift occurs if there is a change in one of the variables, *other than the price of the product,* that affects the willingness of consumers to buy the product. A change in quantity demanded refers to a movement along the demand curve as a result of a change in the product's price. Figure 3-3 illustrates this important distinction. If the price of digital music players falls from $300 to $250, the result will be a movement along the demand curve from

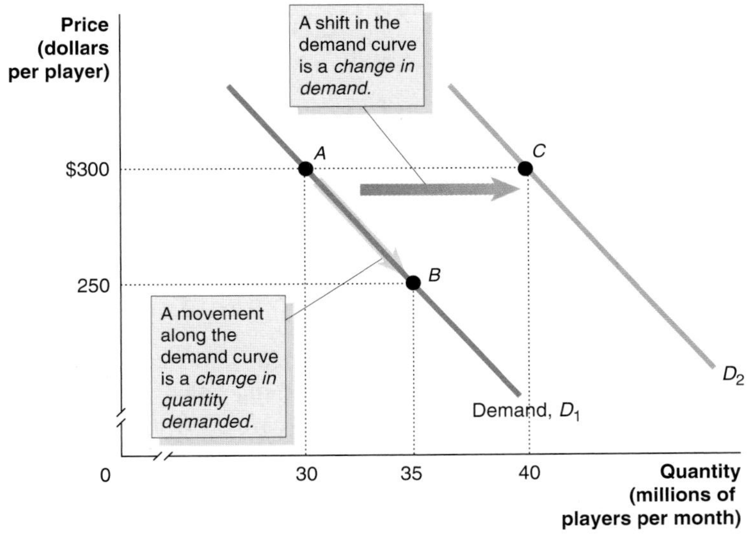

Figure 3-3

A Change in Demand versus a Change in the Quantity Demanded

If the price of digital music players falls from $300 to $250, the result will be a movement along the demand curve from point *A* to point *B*—an increase in quantity demanded from 30 million to 35 million. If consumers' income increases, or if another factor changes that makes consumers want more of the product at every price, the demand curve will shift to the right—an increase in demand. In this case, the increase in demand from D_1 to D_2 causes the quantity of players demanded at a price of $300 to increase from 30 million at point *A* to 40 million at point *C*.

TABLE 3-1

Variables That Shift Market Demand Curves

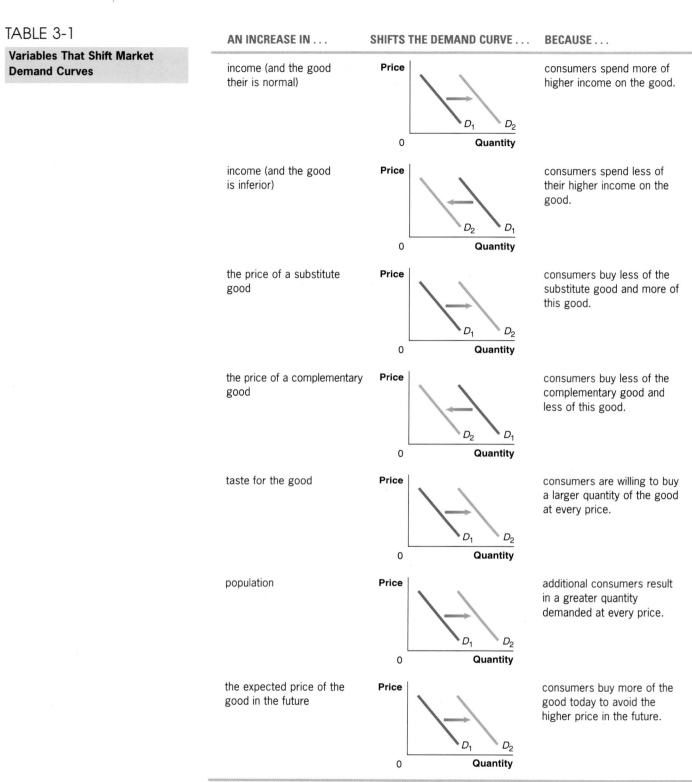

AN INCREASE IN . . .	SHIFTS THE DEMAND CURVE . . .	BECAUSE . . .
income (and the good their is normal)	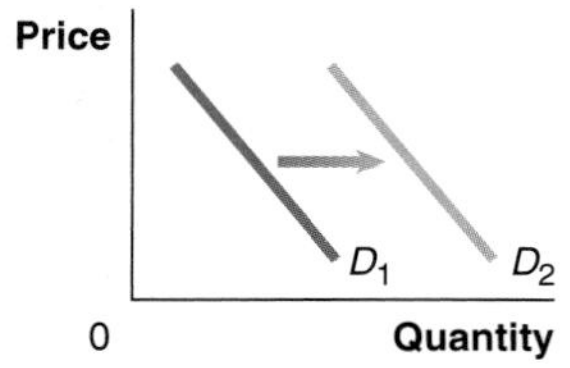	consumers spend more of higher income on the good.
income (and the good is inferior)	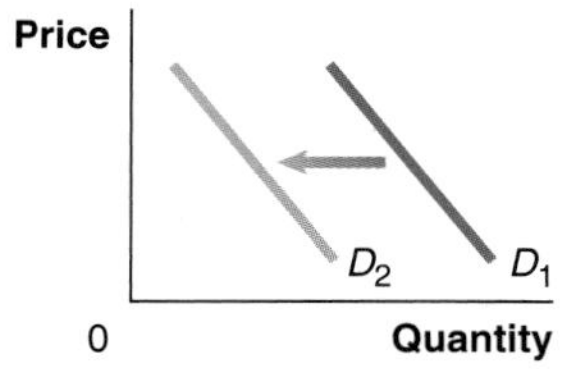	consumers spend less of their higher income on the good.
the price of a substitute good	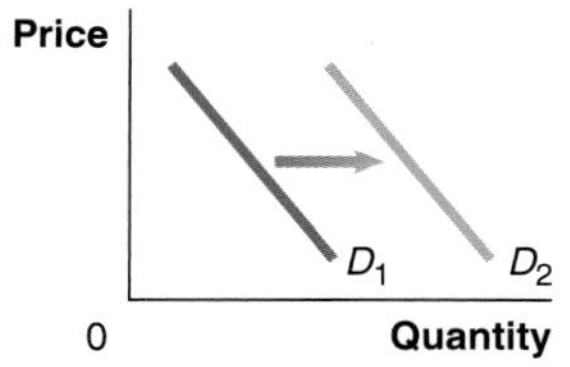	consumers buy less of the substitute good and more of this good.
the price of a complementary good	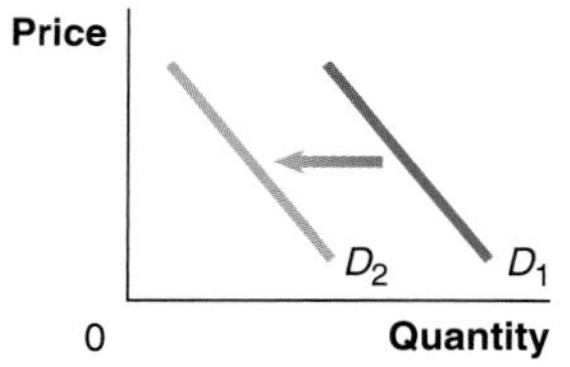	consumers buy less of the complementary good and less of this good.
taste for the good	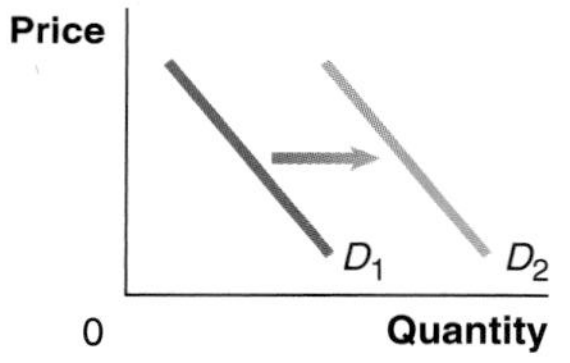	consumers are willing to buy a larger quantity of the good at every price.
population	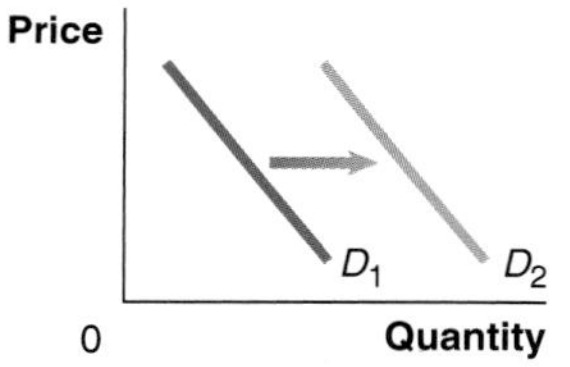	additional consumers result in a greater quantity demanded at every price.
the expected price of the good in the future	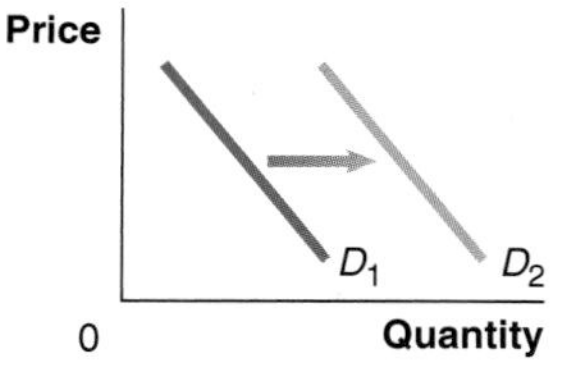	consumers buy more of the good today to avoid the higher price in the future.

point *A* to point *B*—an increase in quantity demanded from 30 million to 35 million. If consumers' incomes increase, or if another factor changes that makes consumers want more of the product at every price, the demand curve will shift to the right—an increase in demand. In this case, the increase in demand from D_1 to D_2 causes the quantity of digital music players demanded at a price of \$300 to increase from 30 million at point *A* to 40 million at point *C*.

Making the Connection | Apple Forecasts the Demand for iPhones and other Consumer Electronics

Will Apple's iPhone match the success of its iPod?

One of the most important decisions that the managers of any large firm have to make is which new products to develop. A firm must devote people, time, and money to designing the product, negotiating with suppliers, formulating a marketing campaign, and many other tasks. But any firm has only limited resources and so faces a trade-off: Resources used to develop one product will not be available to develop another product. Ultimately, the products a firm chooses to develop will be those which it believes will be the most profitable. So, to decide which products to develop, firms need to forecast the demand for those products.

David Sobotta, who worked at Apple for 20 years, eventually becoming its national sales manager, has described the strategy Apple has used to decide which consumer electronics products will have the greatest demand. Sobotta describes discussions at Apple during 2002 about whether to develop a tablet personal computer. A tablet PC is a laptop with a special screen that allows the computer to be controlled with a stylus or pen and that has the capability of converting handwritten input into text. The previous year, Bill Gates, chairman of Microsoft, had predicted that "within five years . . . [tablet PCs] will be the most popular form of PC sold in America." Representatives of the federal government's National Institutes of Health also urged Apple to develop a tablet PC, arguing that it would be particularly useful to doctors, nurses, and hospitals. Apple's managers decided not to develop a tablet PC, however, because they believed the technology was too complex for the average computer user and did not believe that the demand from doctors and nurses would be very large. This forecast turned out to be correct. Despite Bill Gates's prediction, in 2006, tablets made up only 1 percent of the computer market, and they were forecast to increase to only 5 percent by 2009.

According to Sobotta, "Apple executives had a theory that the route to success will not be through selling thousands of relatively expensive things, but millions of very inexpensive things like iPods." In fact, although many business analysts were skeptical that the iPod would succeed, demand grew faster than even Apple's most optimistic forecasts. By the beginning of 2007, 100 million iPods had been sold. So, it was not very surprising when in early 2007, Apple Chief Executive Officer Steve Jobs announced that the company would be combining the iPod with a cell phone to create the iPhone. With more than 900 million cell phones sold each year, Apple expects the demand for the iPhone to be very large. As Sobotta noted, "And there's an 'Apple gap': mobile phone users often find their interfaces confusing. . . . Apple's unique ability to simplify while innovating looks like a good fit there."

Apple forecast that it would sell 10 million iPhones during the product's first year on the market, with much larger sales expected in future years. Time will tell whether Apple's forecast of a large demand for the iPhone will turn out to be correct.

Source: David Sobotta, "Technology: What Jobs Told Me on the iPhone," *The Guardian* (London), January 4, 2007, p. 1; and Connie Guglielmo, "Apple First-Quarter Profit Rises on IPod, Mac Sales," Bloomberg.com, January 17, 2007.

YOUR TURN: For more practice, do problem 1.10 on page 93 at the end of this chapter.

3.2 LEARNING OBJECTIVE

3.2 | Discuss the variables that influence supply.

The Supply Side of the Market

Just as many variables influence the willingness and ability of consumers to buy a particular good or service, many variables also influence the willingness and ability of firms to sell a good or service. The most important of these variables is price. The amount of a good or service that a firm is willing and able to supply at a given price is the **quantity supplied**. Holding other variables constant, when the price of a good rises, producing

Quantity supplied The amount of a good or service that a firm is willing and able to supply at a given price.

the good is more profitable, and the quantity supplied will increase. When the price of a good falls, the good is less profitable, and the quantity supplied will decrease. In addition, as we saw in Chapter 2, devoting more and more resources to the production of a good results in increasing marginal costs. So, if, for example, Apple, Microsoft, and Toshiba increase production of digital music players during a given time period, they are likely to find that the cost of producing the additional players increases as they run existing factories for longer hours and pay higher prices for components and higher wages for workers. With higher marginal costs, firms will supply a larger quantity only if the price is higher.

Supply Schedules and Supply Curves

Supply schedule A table that shows the relationship between the price of a product and the quantity of the product supplied.

Supply curve A curve that shows the relationship between the price of a product and the quantity of the product supplied.

A **supply schedule** is a table that shows the relationship between the price of a product and the quantity of the product supplied. The table in Figure 3-4 is a supply schedule showing the quantity of digital music players that firms would be willing to supply per month at different prices. The graph in Figure 3-4 plots the numbers from the supply schedule as a *supply curve.* A **supply curve** shows the relationship between the price of a product and the quantity of the product supplied. The supply schedule and supply curve both show that as the price of players rises, firms will increase the quantity they supply. At a price of $250 per player, firms will supply 45 million players per year. At the higher price of $300, they will supply 50 million. (Once again, we are assuming for convenience that the supply curve is a straight line, even though not all supply curves are actually straight lines.)

The Law of Supply

Law of supply The rule that, holding everything else constant, increases in price cause increases in the quantity supplied, and decreases in price cause decreases in the quantity supplied.

The *market supply curve* in Figure 3-4 is upward sloping. We expect most supply curves to be upward sloping according to the **law of supply**, which states that, holding everything else constant, increases in price cause increases in the quantity supplied, and decreases in price cause decreases in the quantity supplied. Notice that the definition of the law of supply—like the definition of the law of demand—contains the phrase *holding everything else constant.* If only the price of the product changes, there is a movement along the supply curve, which is *an increase or a decrease in the quantity supplied.* As Figure 3-5 shows, if any other variable that affects the willingness of firms to supply a good changes, the supply curve will shift, which is *an increase or decrease in supply.* When firms increase the quantity of a product they wish to sell at a given price, the supply curve shifts to the right. The shift from S_1 to S_3 represents *an increase in supply.* When firms decrease the quantity of a product they wish to sell at a given price, the supply curve shifts to the left. The shift from S_1 to S_2 represents *a decrease in supply.*

Figure 3-4

Supply Schedule and Supply Curve

As the price changes, Apple, Microsoft, Toshiba, and the other firms producing digital music players change the quantity they are willing to supply. We can show this as a *supply schedule* in a table or as a *supply curve* on a graph. The supply schedule and supply curve both show that as the price of players rises, firms will increase the quantity they supply. At a price of $250, firms will supply 45 million players. At a price of $300 per player, firms will supply 50 million players.

Supply Schedule

Price (dollars per player)	Quantity (millions of players per month)
$300	50
250	45
200	40
150	35
100	30

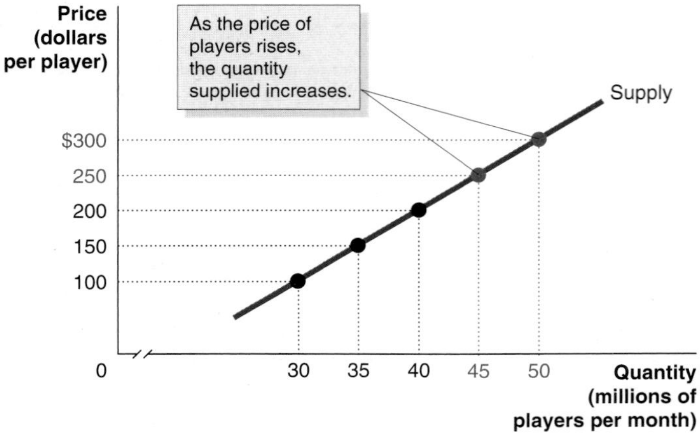

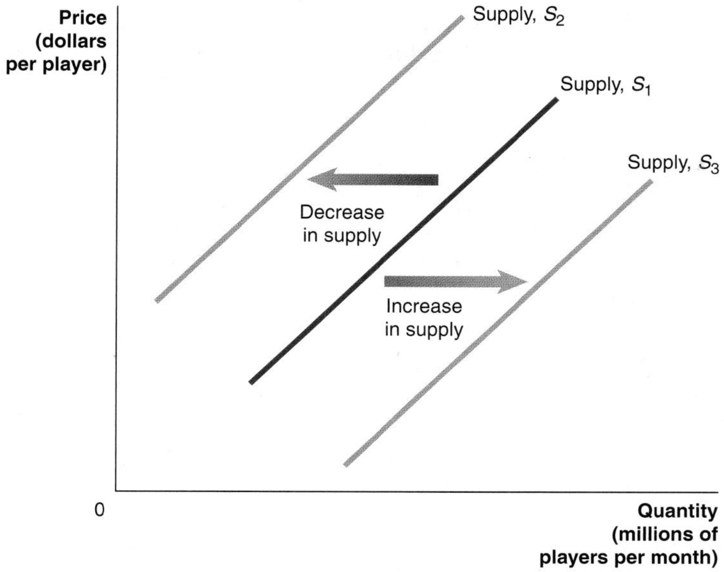

Figure 3-5
Shifting the Supply Curve

When firms increase the quantity of a product they wish to sell at a given price, the supply curve shifts to the right. The shift from S_1 to S_3 represents an *increase in supply*. When firms decrease the quantity of a product they wish to sell at a given price, the supply curve shifts to the left. The shift from S_1 to S_2 represents a *decrease in supply*.

Variables That Shift Supply

The following are the most important variables that shift supply:

- Prices of inputs
- Technological change
- Prices of substitutes in production
- Number of firms in the market
- Expected future prices

We next discuss how each of these variables affects the supply of digital music players.

Prices of Inputs The factor most likely to cause the supply curve for a product to shift is a change in the price of an *input*. An input is anything used in the production of a good or service. For instance, if the price of a component of digital music players, such as the microprocessor, rises, the cost of producing music players will increase, and players will be less profitable at every price. The supply of players will decline, and the market supply curve for players will shift to the left. Similarly, if the price of an input declines, the supply of players will increase, and the supply curve will shift to the right.

Technological Change A second factor that causes a change in supply is *technological change*. **Technological change** is a positive or negative change in the ability of a firm to produce a given level of output with a given quantity of inputs. Positive technological change occurs whenever a firm is able to produce more output using the same amount of inputs. This shift will happen when the *productivity* of workers or machines increases. If a firm can produce more output with the same amount of inputs, its costs will be lower, and the good will be more profitable to produce at any given price. As a result, when positive technological change occurs, the firm will increase the quantity supplied at every price, and its supply curve will shift to the right. Normally, we expect technological change to have a positive impact on a firm's willingness to supply a product. Negative technological change is relatively rare, although it could result from a natural disaster or a war that reduces the ability of a firm to supply as much output with a given amount of inputs. Negative technological change will raise a firm's costs, and the good will be less profitable to produce. Therefore, negative technological change causes a firm's supply curve to shift to the left.

Technological change A positive or negative change in the ability of a firm to produce a given level of output with a given quantity of inputs.

Prices of Substitutes in Production Firms often choose which good or service they will produce. Alternative products that a firm could produce are called *substitutes in production.* To this point, we have considered the market for all types of digital music players. But suppose we now consider separate markets for music players with screens capable of showing videos and for smaller players, without screens, that play only music. If the price of video music players increases, video music players will become more profitable, and Apple, Microsoft, and the other companies making music players will shift some of their productive capacity away from smaller players and toward video players. The companies will offer fewer smaller players for sale at every price, so the supply curve for smaller players will shift to the left.

Number of Firms in the Market A change in the number of firms in the market will change supply. When new firms *enter* a market, the supply curve shifts to the right, and when existing firms leave, or *exit,* a market, the supply curve for digital music players shifts to the left. For instance, when Microsoft introduced the Zune, the market supply curve for digital music players shifted to the right.

Expected Future Prices If a firm expects that the price of its product will be higher in the future than it is today, it has an incentive to decrease supply now and increase it in the future. For instance, if Apple believes that prices for digital music players are temporarily

TABLE 3-2

Variables That Shift Market Supply Curves

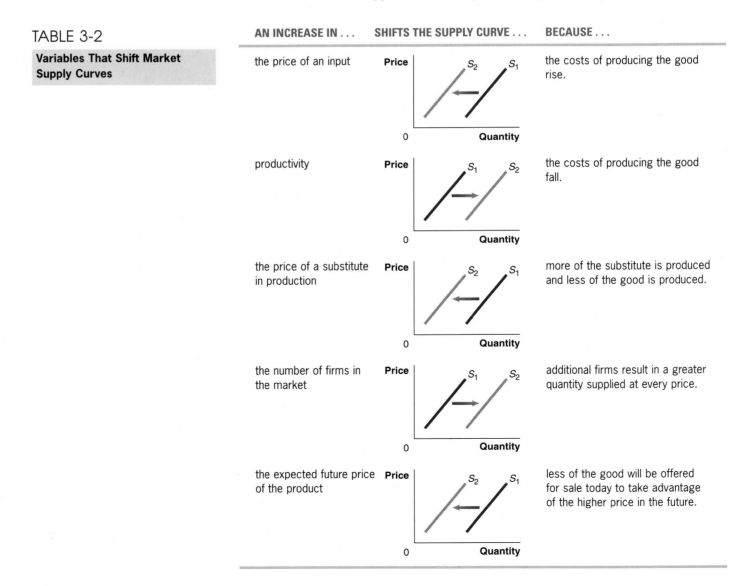

<table>
<tr><th>AN INCREASE IN . . .</th><th>SHIFTS THE SUPPLY CURVE . . .</th><th>BECAUSE . . .</th></tr>
<tr><td>the price of an input</td><td>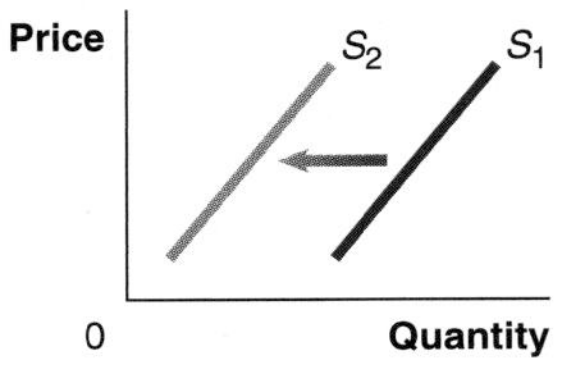</td><td>the costs of producing the good rise.</td></tr>
<tr><td>productivity</td><td>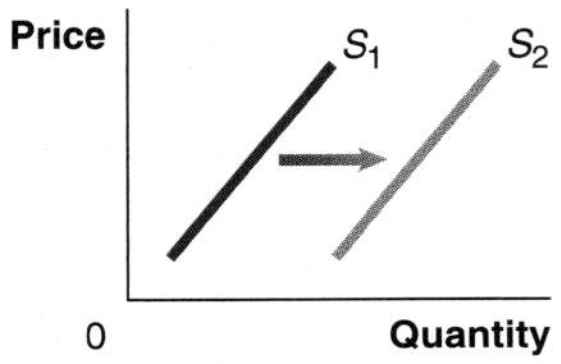</td><td>the costs of producing the good fall.</td></tr>
<tr><td>the price of a substitute in production</td><td>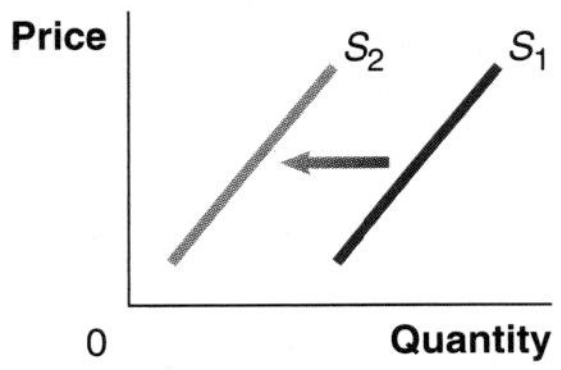</td><td>more of the substitute is produced and less of the good is produced.</td></tr>
<tr><td>the number of firms in the market</td><td>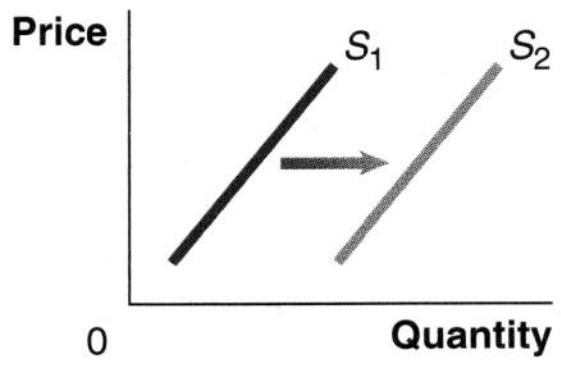</td><td>additional firms result in a greater quantity supplied at every price.</td></tr>
<tr><td>the expected future price of the product</td><td>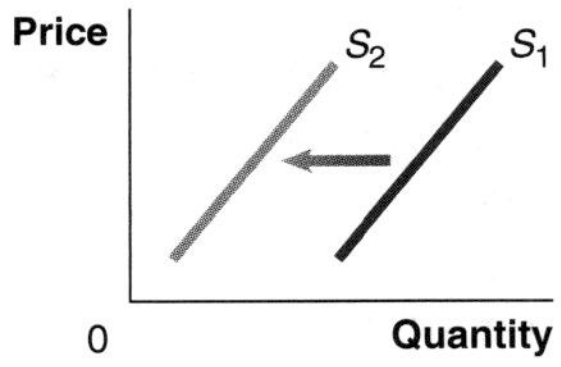</td><td>less of the good will be offered for sale today to take advantage of the higher price in the future.</td></tr>
</table>

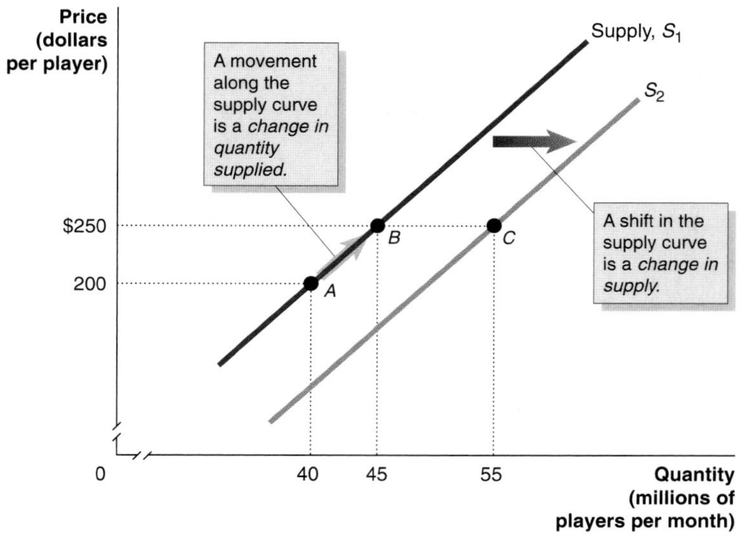

Figure 3-6

A Change in Supply versus a Change in the Quantity Supplied

If the price of digital music players rises from $200 to $250, the result will be a movement up the supply curve from point *A* to point *B*—an increase in quantity supplied by Apple, Microsoft, and Toshiba and the other firms from 40 million to 45 million. If the price of an input decreases or another factor changes that makes sellers supply more of the product at every price, the supply curve will shift to the right—an increase in supply. In this case, the increase in supply from S_1 to S_2 causes the quantity of digital music players supplied at a price of $250 to increase from 45 million at point *B* to 55 million at point *C*.

low—perhaps because of a price war among firms making players—it may store some of its production today to sell tomorrow, when it expects prices will be higher.

Table 3-2 on page 78 summarizes the most important variables that cause market supply curves to shift. You should note that the table shows the shift in the supply curve that results from an *increase* in each of the variables. A *decrease* in these variables would cause the supply curve to shift in the opposite direction.

A Change in Supply versus a Change in Quantity Supplied

We noted earlier the important difference between a change in demand and a change in quantity demanded. There is a similar difference between a *change in supply* and a *change in quantity supplied.* A change in supply refers to a shift of the supply curve. The supply curve will shift when there is a change in one of the variables, *other than the price of the product*, that affects the willingness of suppliers to sell the product. A change in quantity supplied refers to a movement along the supply curve as a result of a change in the product's price. Figure 3-6 illustrates this important distinction. If the price of music players rises from $200 to $250, the result will be a movement up the supply curve from point *A* to point *B*—an increase in quantity supplied from 40 million to 45 million. If the price of an input decreases or another factor makes sellers supply more of the product at every price change, the supply curve will shift to the right—an increase in supply. In this case, the increase in supply from S_1 to S_2 causes the quantity of digital music players supplied at a price of $250 to increase from 45 million at point *B* to 55 million at point *C*.

3.3 LEARNING OBJECTIVE

3.3 | Use a graph to illustrate market equilibrium.

Market Equilibrium: Putting Demand and Supply Together

The purpose of markets is to bring buyers and sellers together. As we saw in Chapter 2, instead of being chaotic and disorderly, the interaction of buyers and sellers in markets ultimately results in firms being led to produce those goods and services consumers desire most. To understand how this process happens, we first need to see how markets work to reconcile the plans of buyers and sellers.

In Figure 3-7, we bring together the market demand curve for digital music players and the market supply curve. Notice that the demand curve crosses the supply curve at

Figure 3-7

Market Equilibrium

Where the demand curve crosses the supply curve determines market equilibrium. In this case, the demand curve for digital music players crosses the supply curve at a price of $200 and a quantity of 40 million. Only at this point is the quantity of players consumers are willing to buy equal to the quantity of players Apple, Microsoft, Toshiba, and the other firms are willing to sell: The quantity demanded is equal to the quantity supplied.

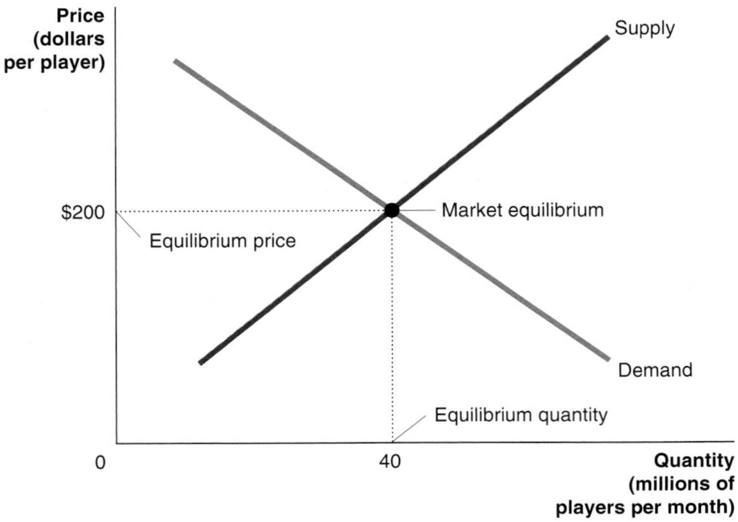

only one point. This point represents a price of $200 and a quantity of 40 million players. Only at this point is the quantity of players consumers are willing to buy equal to the quantity of players firms are willing to sell. This is the point of **market equilibrium**. Only at market equilibrium will the quantity demanded equal the quantity supplied. In this case, the *equilibrium price* is $200, and the *equilibrium quantity* is 40 million. As we noted at the beginning of the chapter, markets that have many buyers and many sellers are competitive markets, and equilibrium in these markets is a **competitive market equilibrium**. In the market for digital music players, there are many buyers but fewer than 20 firms. Whether 20 firms is enough for our model of demand and supply to apply to this market is a matter of judgment. In this chapter, we are assuming that the market for digital music players has enough sellers to be competitive.

Market equilibrium A situation in which quantity demanded equals quantity supplied.

Competitive market equilibrium A market equilibrium with many buyers and many sellers.

How Markets Eliminate Surpluses and Shortages

A market that is not in equilibrium moves toward equilibrium. Once a market is in equilibrium, it remains in equilibrium. To see why, consider what happens if a market is not in equilibrium. For instance, suppose that the price in the market for digital music players was $250, rather than the equilibrium price of $200. As Figure 3-8 shows, at a price of $250, the quantity of players supplied would be 45 million, and the quantity of players demanded would be 35 million. When the quantity supplied is greater than the quantity demanded, there is a **surplus** in the market. In this case, the surplus is equal to 10 million players (45 million − 35 million = 10 million). When there is a surplus, firms have unsold goods piling up, which gives them an incentive to increase their sales by cutting the price. Cutting the price will simultaneously increase the quantity demanded and decrease the quantity supplied. This adjustment will reduce the surplus, but as long as the price is above $200, there will be a surplus, and downward pressure on the price will continue. Only when the price has fallen to $200 will the market be in equilibrium.

Surplus A situation in which the quantity supplied is greater than the quantity demanded.

If, however, the price were $100, the quantity supplied would be 30 million, and the quantity demanded would be 50 million, as shown in Figure 3-8. When the quantity demanded is greater than the quantity supplied, there is a **shortage** in the market. In this case, the shortage is equal to 20 million digital music players (50 million − 30 million = 20 million). When a shortage occurs, some consumers will be unable to buy a digital music player at the current price. In this situation, firms will realize that they can raise the price without losing sales. A higher price will simultaneously increase the quantity supplied and decrease the quantity demanded. This adjustment will reduce the shortage, but as long as the price is below $200, there will be a shortage, and upward pressure on the price will continue. Only when the price has risen to $200 will the market be in equilibrium.

Shortage A situation in which the quantity demanded is greater than the quantity supplied.

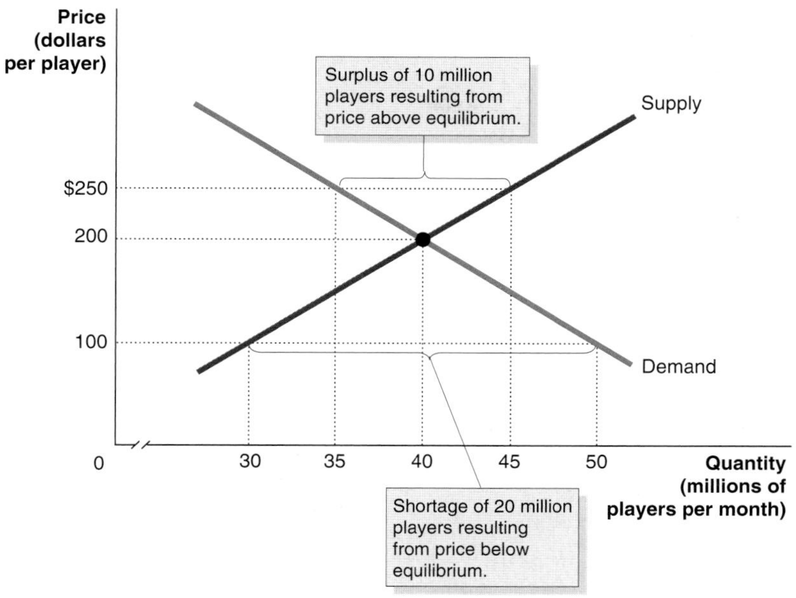

Figure 3-8

The Effect of Surpluses and Shortages on the Market Price

When the market price is above equilibrium, there will be a *surplus*. In the figure, a price of $250 for digital music players results in 45 million being supplied but only 35 million being demanded, or a surplus of 10 million. As Apple, Microsoft, Toshiba, and the other firms cut the price to dispose of the surplus, the price will fall to the equilibrium of $200. When the market price is below equilibrium, there will be a *shortage*. A price of $100 results in 50 million players being demanded but only 30 million being supplied, or a shortage of 20 million. As consumers who are unable to buy a player offer to pay higher prices, the price will rise to the equilibrium of $200.

At a competitive market equilibrium, all consumers willing to pay the market price will be able to buy as much of the product as they want, and all firms willing to accept the market price will be able to sell as much of the product as they want. As a result, there will be no reason for the price to change unless either the demand curve or the supply curve shifts.

Demand and Supply Both Count

Always keep in mind that it is the interaction of demand and supply that determines the equilibrium price. Neither consumers nor firms can dictate what the equilibrium price will be. No firm can sell anything at any price unless it can find a willing buyer, and no consumer can buy anything at any price without finding a willing seller.

Solved Problem | 3-3

Demand and Supply Both Count: A Tale of Two Letters

Which letter is likely to be worth more: one written by Abraham Lincoln or one written by his assassin, John Wilkes Booth? Lincoln is one of the greatest presidents, and many people collect anything written by him. The demand for letters written by Lincoln surely would seem to be much greater than the demand for letters written by Booth. Yet when R. M. Smythe and Co. auctioned off on the same day a letter written by Lincoln and a letter written by Booth, the Booth letter sold for $31,050, and the Lincoln letter sold for only $21,850. Use a demand and supply graph to explain how the Booth letter has a higher market price than the Lincoln letter, even though the demand for letters written by Lincoln is greater than the demand for letters written by Booth.

SOLVING THE PROBLEM:

Step 1: **Review the chapter material.** This problem is about prices being determined at market equilibrium, so you may want to review the section "Market Equilibrium: Putting Demand and Supply Together," which begins on page 79.

Step 2: **Draw demand curves that illustrate the greater demand for Lincoln's letters.** Begin by drawing two demand curves. Label one "Demand for Lincoln's letters" and the other "Demand for Booth's letters." Make sure that the Lincoln demand curve is much farther to the right than the Booth demand curve.

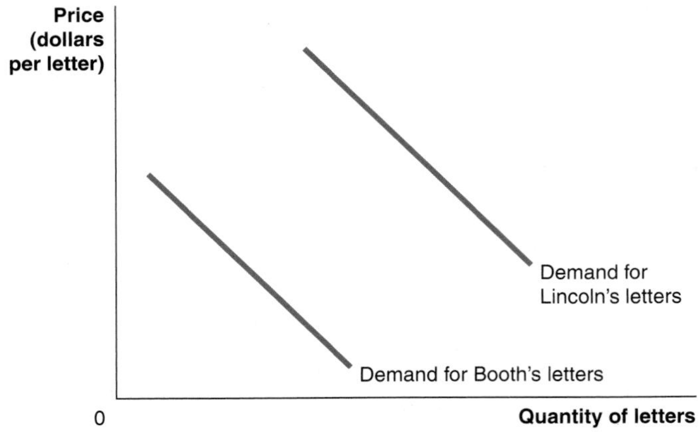

Step 3: **Draw supply curves that illustrate the equilibrium price of Booth's letters being higher than the equilibrium price of Lincoln's letters.** Based on the demand curves you have just drawn, think about how it might be possible for the market price of Lincoln's letters to be lower than the market price of Booth's letters. The only way this can be true is if the supply of Lincoln's letters is much greater than the supply of Booth's letters. Draw on your graph a supply curve for Lincoln's letters and a supply curve for Booth's letters that will result in an equilibrium price of Booth's letters of $31,050 and an equilibrium price of Lincoln's letters of $21,850. You have now solved the problem.

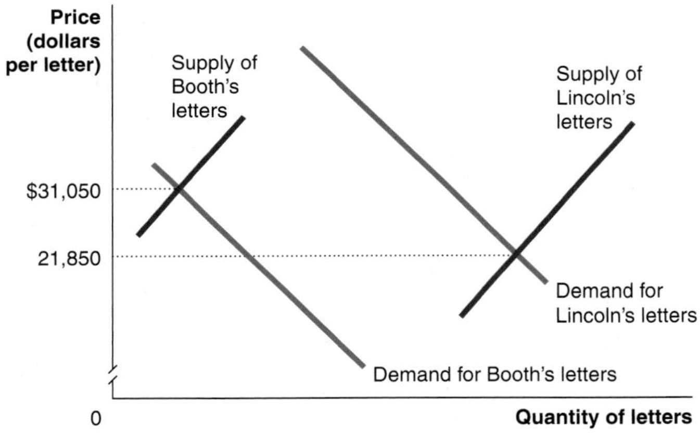

EXTRA CREDIT: The explanation for this puzzle is that both demand and supply count when determining market price. The demand for Lincoln's letters is much greater than the demand for Booth's letters, but the supply of Booth's letters is very small. Historians believe that only eight letters written by Booth exist today. (Note that the supply curves for letters written by Booth and by Lincoln slope up even though only a fixed number of each of these types of letters is available and, obviously, no more can be produced. The upward slope of the supply curves occurs because the higher the price, the larger the quantity of letters that will be offered for sale by people who currently own them.)

>> End Solved Problem 3-3

YOUR TURN: For more practice, do related problem 3.4 on page 94 at the end of this chapter.

3.4 | Use demand and supply graphs to predict changes in prices and quantities.

3.4 LEARNING OBJECTIVE

The Effect of Demand and Supply Shifts on Equilibrium

We have seen that the interaction of demand and supply in markets determines the quantity of a good that is produced and the price at which it sells. We have also seen that several variables cause demand curves to shift, and other variables cause supply curves to shift. As a result, demand and supply curves in most markets are constantly shifting, and the prices and quantities that represent equilibrium are constantly changing. In this section, we see how shifts in demand and supply curves affect equilibrium price and quantity.

The Effect of Shifts in Supply on Equilibrium

When Microsoft decided to start selling the Zune music player, the market supply curve for music players shifted to the right. Figure 3-9 shows the supply curve shifting from S_1 to S_2. When the supply curve shifts to the right, there will be a surplus at the original equilibrium price, P_1. The surplus is eliminated as the equilibrium price falls to P_2, and the equilibrium quantity rises from Q_1 to Q_2. If existing firms exit the market, the supply curve will shift to the left, causing the equilibrium price to rise and the equilibrium quantity to fall.

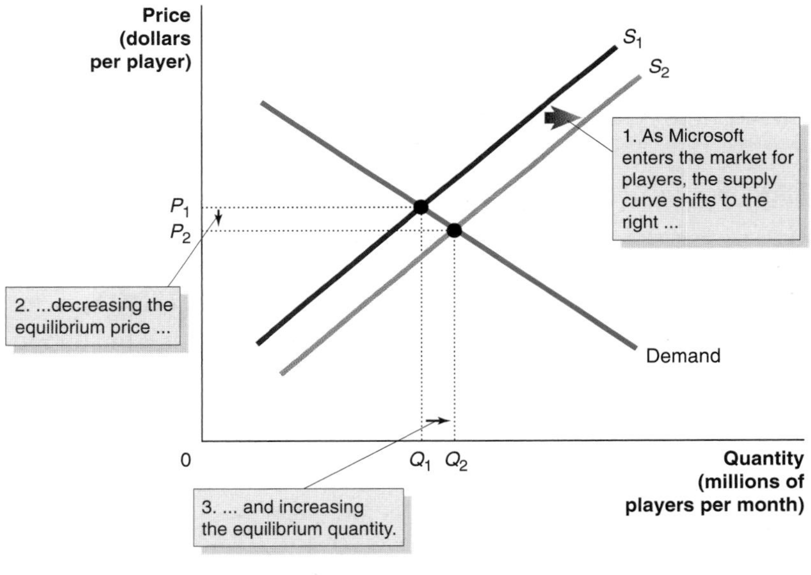

Figure 3-9

The Effect of an Increase in Supply on Equilibrium

If a firm enters a market, as Microsoft entered the market for digital music players when it launched the Zune, the equilibrium price will fall, and the equilibrium quantity will rise.

1. As Microsoft enters the market for digital music players, a larger quantity of players will be supplied at every price, so the market supply curve shifts to the right, from S_1 to S_2, which causes a surplus of players at the original price, P_1.
2. The equilibrium price falls from P_1 to P_2.
3. The equilibrium quantity rises from Q_1 to Q_2.

Making the Connection

The Falling Price of LCD Televisions

Research on flat-screen televisions using liquid crystal displays (LCDs) began in the 1960s. However, it was surprisingly difficult to use this research to produce a television priced low enough for many consumers to purchase. One researcher noted, "In the 1960s, we used to say 'In ten years, we're going to have the TV on the wall.' We said the same thing in the seventies and then in the eighties." A key technical problem in manufacturing LCD televisions was making glass sheets large enough, thin enough, and clean enough to be used as LCD screens. Finally, in 1999, Corning, Inc., developed a process to manufacture glass that was less than 1 millimeter thick and very clean because it was produced without being touched by machinery.

Corning's breakthrough led to what the *Wall Street Journal* described as a "race to build new, better factories." The firms producing the flat screens are all located in Taiwan, South Korea, and Japan. The leading firms are Korea's Samsung Electronics and LG Phillips LCD, Taiwan's AU Optronics, and Japan's Sharp Corporation. In 2004, AU Optronics opened a new factory with 2.4 million square feet of clean room in which the LCD screens are manufactured. This factory is nearly five times as large as the largest factory in which Intel makes computer chips. In all, 10 new factories manufacturing LCD screens came into operation between late 2004 and late 2005. The figure shows that this increase in supply drove the price of a typical large LCD television from $4,000 in the fall of 2004 to $1,600 at the end of 2006, increasing the quantity demanded worldwide from 8 million to 46 million.

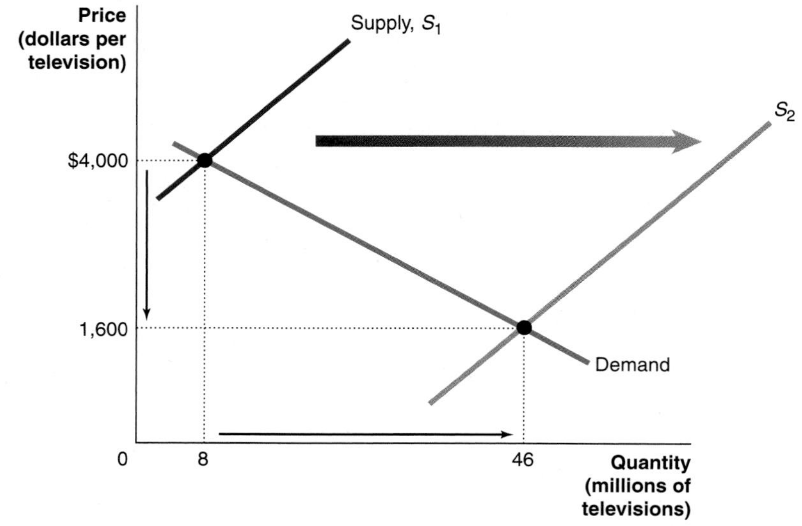

Sources: David Richards, "Sony and Panasonic Flat Screen Kings," Smarthouse.com, February 13, 2007; Evan Ramstad, "Big Display: Once a Footnote, Flat Screens Grow into Huge Industry," *Wall Street Journal*, August 30, 2004, p. A1; and Michael Schuman, "Flat Chance: Prices on Cool TVs Are Dropping as New Factories Come on Line," *Time*, October 18, 2004, pp. 64–66.

YOUR TURN: For more practice, do problem 4.7 on page 95 at the end of this chapter.

The Effect of Shifts in Demand on Equilibrium

When population growth and income growth occur, the market demand for music players shifts to the right. Figure 3-10 shows the effect of a demand curve shifting to the right, from D_1 to D_2. This shift causes a shortage at the original equilibrium price, P_1. To eliminate the shortage, the equilibrium price rises to P_2, and the equilibrium quantity

Figure 3-10

The Effect of an Increase in Demand on Equilibrium

Increases in income and population will cause the equilibrium price and quantity to rise:

1. As population and income grow, the quantity demanded increases at every price, and the market demand curve shifts to the right, from D_1 to D_2, which causes a shortage of digital music players at the original price, P_1.
2. The equilibrium price rises from P_1 to P_2.
3. The equilibrium quantity rises from Q_1 to Q_2.

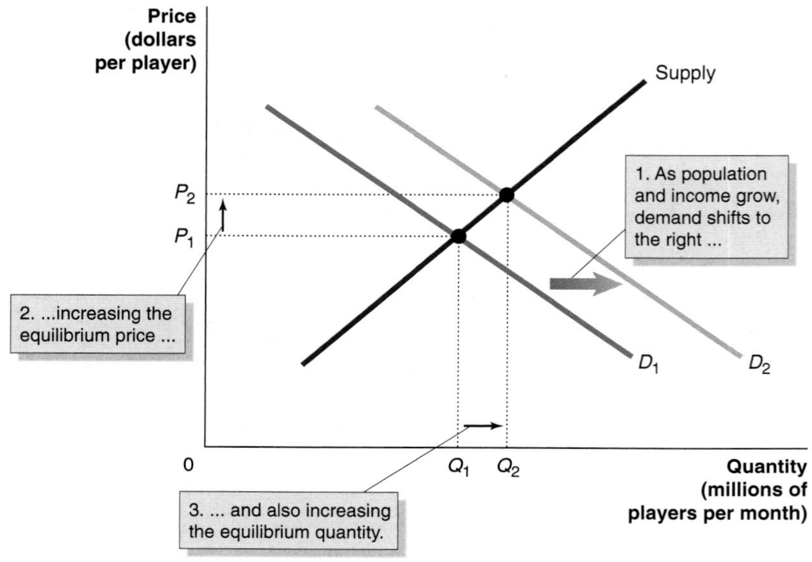

rises from Q_1 to Q_2. By contrast, if the price of a complementary good, such as downloads from music Web sites, were to rise, the demand for music players would decrease. This change would cause the demand curve for players to shift to the left, and the equilibrium price and quantity would both decrease.

The Effect of Shifts in Demand and Supply over Time

Whenever only demand or only supply shifts, we can easily predict the effect on equilibrium price and quantity. But what happens if *both* curves shift? For instance, in many markets, the demand curve shifts to the right over time, as population and income grow. The supply curve also often shifts to the right as new firms enter the market and positive technological change occurs. Whether the equilibrium price in a market rises or falls over time depends on whether demand shifts to the right more than does supply. Panel (a) of Figure 3-11 shows that when demand shifts to the right more than supply, the equilibrium price rises. But, as panel (b) shows, when supply shifts to the right more than demand, the equilibrium price falls.

Table 3-3 on page 86 summarizes all possible combinations of shifts in demand and supply over time and the effects of the shifts on equilibrium price (P) and quantity (Q). For example, the entry in red in the table shows that if the demand curve shifts to the right and the supply curve also shifts to the right, then the equilibrium quantity will increase, while the equilibrium price may increase, decrease, or remain unchanged. To make sure you understand each entry in the table, draw demand and supply graphs to check whether you can reproduce the predicted changes in equilibrium price and quantity. If the entry in the table says the predicted change in equilibrium price or quantity can be either an increase or a decrease, draw two graphs similar to panels (a) and (b) of Figure 3-11, one showing the equilibrium price or quantity increasing and the other showing it decreasing. Note also that in the ambiguous cases where either price or quantity might increase or decrease, it is also possible that price or quantity might remain unchanged. Be sure you understand why this is true.

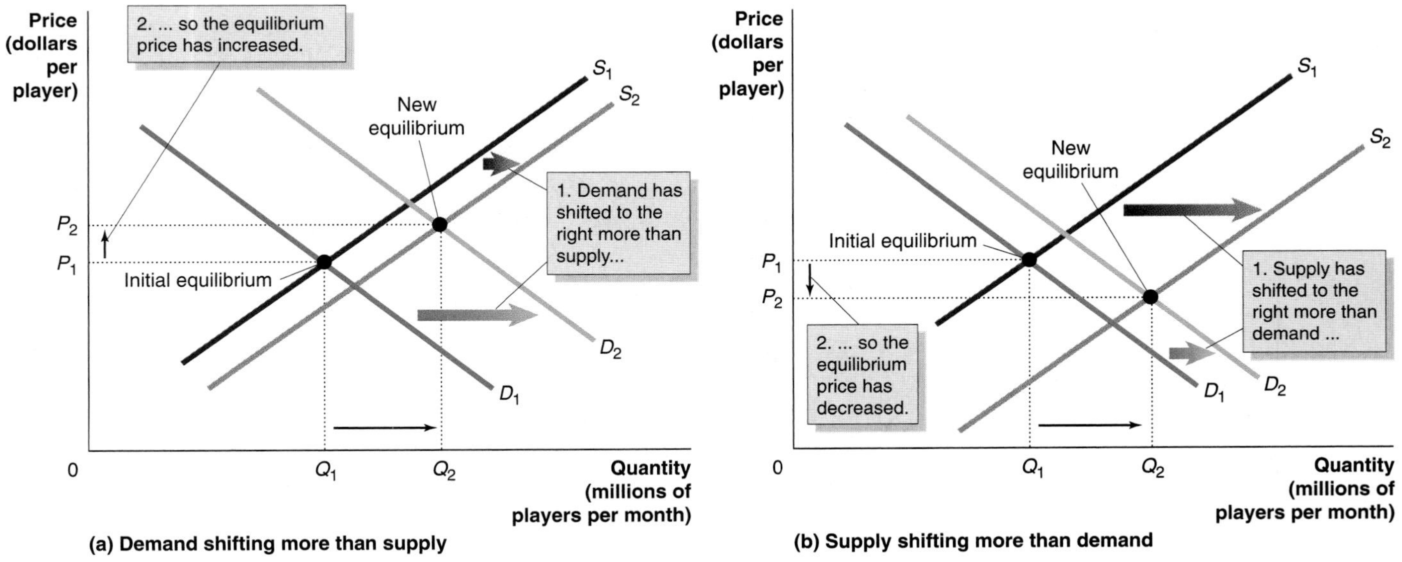

Figure 3-11 | Shifts in Demand and Supply over Time

Whether the price of a product rises or falls over time depends on whether demand shifts to the right more than supply.

In panel (a), demand shifts to the right more than supply, and the equilibrium price rises.

1. Demand shifts to the right more than supply.
2. Equilibrium price rises from P_1 to P_2.

In panel (b), supply shifts to the right more than demand, and the equilibrium price falls.

1. Supply shifts to the right more than demand.
2. Equilibrium price falls from P_1 to P_2.

TABLE 3-3

How Shifts in Demand and Supply Affect Equilibrium Price (*P*) and Quantity (*Q*)

	SUPPLY CURVE UNCHANGED	SUPPLY CURVE SHIFTS TO THE RIGHT	SUPPLY CURVE SHIFTS TO THE LEFT
DEMAND CURVE UNCHANGED	*Q* unchanged *P* unchanged	*Q* increases *P* decreases	*Q* decreases *P* increases
DEMAND CURVE SHIFTS TO THE RIGHT	*Q* increases *P* increases	*Q* increases *P* increases or decreases	*Q* increases or decreases *P* increases
DEMAND CURVE SHIFTS TO THE LEFT	*Q* decreases *P* decreases	*Q* increases or decreases *P* decreases	*Q* decreases *P* decreases or decreases

Solved Problem | 3-4

High Demand and Low Prices in the Lobster Market?

During the spring, when demand for lobster is relatively low, Maine lobstermen are able to sell their lobster catches for about $4.50 per pound. During the summer, when demand for lobster is much higher, Maine lobstermen are able to sell their lobster catches for only about $3.00 per pound. It may seem strange that the market price is higher when demand is low than when demand is high. Can you resolve this paradox with the help of a demand and supply graph?

SOLVING THE PROBLEM:

Step 1: **Review the chapter material.** This problem is about how shifts in demand and supply curves affect the equilibrium price, so you may want to review the section "The Effect of Shifts in Demand and Supply over Time," which begins on page 85.

Step 2: **Draw the demand and supply graph.** Draw a demand and supply graph, showing the market equilibrium in the spring. Label the equilibrium price $4.50. Label both the demand and supply curves "spring."

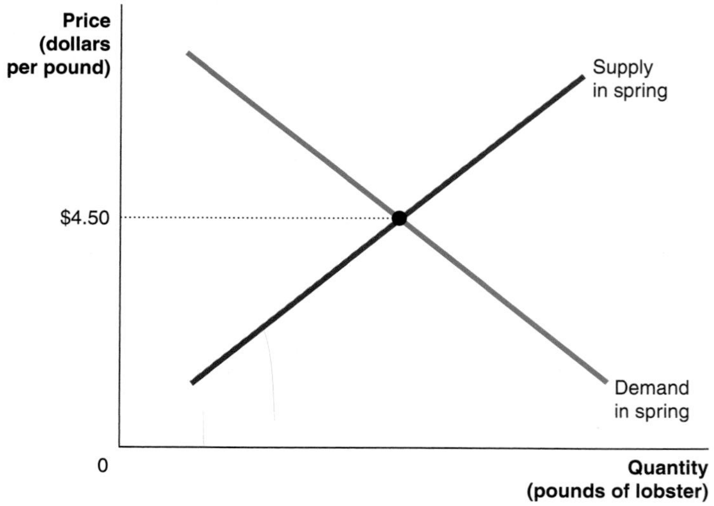

Step 3: Add to your graph a demand curve for summer.

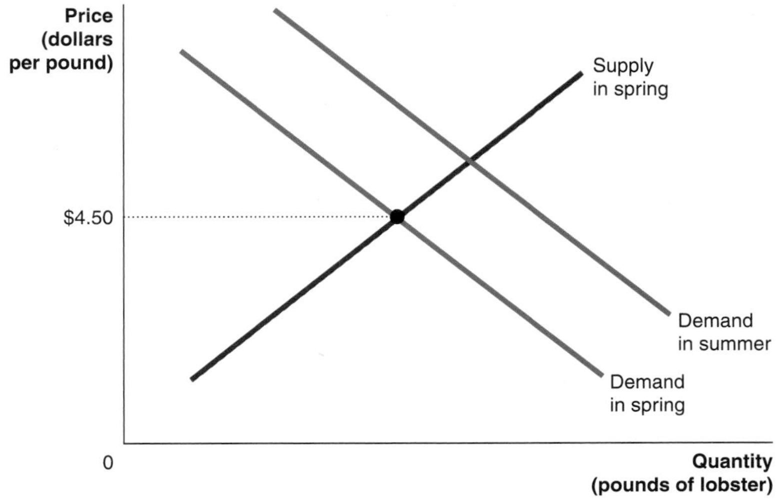

Step 4: Explain the graph. After studying the graph, it is possible to see how the equilibrium price can fall from $4.50 to $3.00, despite the increase in demand: The supply curve must have shifted to the right by enough to cause the equilibrium price to fall to $3.00. Draw the new supply curve, label it "summer," and label the new equilibrium price $3.00. The demand for lobster does increase in summer compared with the spring. But the increase in the supply of lobster between spring and summer is even greater. So, the equilibrium price falls.

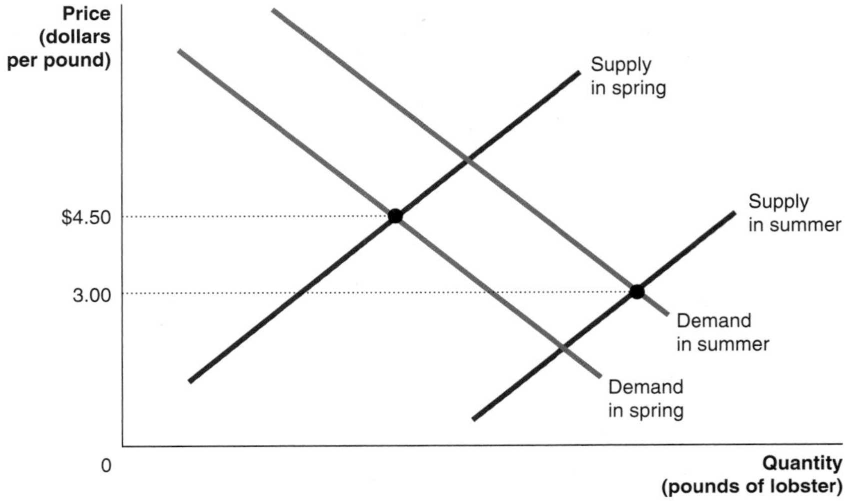

Source: Carey Goldberg, "Down East, the Lobster Hauls Are Up Big," *New York Times*, May 31, 2001.

YOUR TURN: For more practice, do related problem 4.5 on page 95 at the end of this chapter.

>> End Solved Problem 3-4

Shifts in a Curve versus Movements along a Curve

When analyzing markets using demand and supply curves, it is important to remember that *when a shift in a demand or supply curve causes a change in equilibrium price, the change in price does not cause a further shift in demand or supply.* For instance, suppose an increase in supply causes the price of a good to fall, while everything else that affects the willingness of consumers to buy the good is constant. The result will be an increase in the quantity demanded but not an increase in demand. For demand to increase, the whole curve must shift. The point is the same for supply: If the price of the good falls but everything else that affects the willingness of sellers to supply the good is constant, the quantity supplied decreases, but the supply does not. For supply to decrease, the whole curve must shift.

Don't Let This Happen to **YOU!**

Remember: A Change in a Good's Price Does *Not* Cause the Demand or Supply Curve to Shift

Suppose a student is asked to draw a demand and supply graph to illustrate how an increase in the price of oranges would affect the market for apples, other variables being constant. He draws the graph on the left below and explains it as follows: "Because apples and oranges are substitutes, an increase in the price of oranges will cause an initial shift to the right in the demand curve for apples, from D_1 to D_2. However, because this initial shift in the demand curve for apples results in a higher price for apples, P_2, consumers will find apples less desirable, and the demand curve will shift to the left, from D_2 to D_3, resulting in a final equilibrium price of P_3." Do you agree or disagree with the student's analysis?

You should disagree. The student has correctly understood that an increase in the price of oranges will cause the demand curve for apples to shift to the right. But the second demand curve shift the student describes, from D_2 to D_3, will not take place. Changes in the price of a product do not result in shifts in the product's demand curve. Changes in the price of a product result only in movements along a demand curve.

The graph on the right below shows the correct analysis. The increase in the price of oranges causes the demand curve for apples to increase from D_1 to D_2. At the original price, P_1, the increase in demand initially results in a shortage of apples equal to $Q_3 - Q_1$. But, as we have seen, a shortage causes the price to increase until the shortage is eliminated. In this case, the price will rise to P_2, where the quantity demanded and the quantity supplied are both equal to Q_2. Notice that the increase in price causes a decrease in the *quantity demanded* from Q_3 to Q_2, but does *not* cause a decrease in demand.

YOUR TURN: Test your understanding by doing related problems 4.13 and 4.14 on page 96 at the end of this chapter.

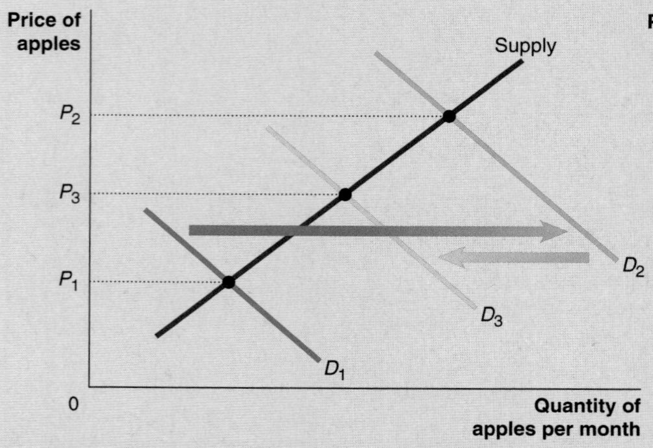

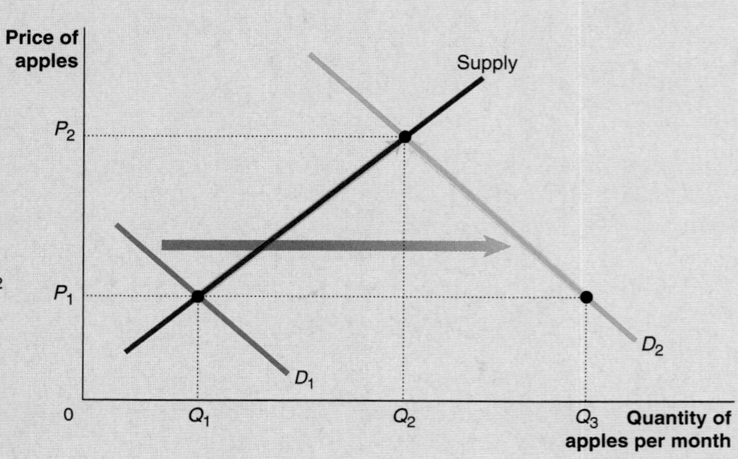

>> Continued from page 67

Economics in YOUR Life!

At the beginning of the chapter, we asked you to consider two questions: Would you choose to buy a Zune if it had a lower price than a comparable iPod? and Would you choose a Zune if the songs sold on Zune Marketplace were cheaper than the songs sold on iTunes? To determine the answers, you have to recognize that iPods and Zunes are substitutes, while Zunes and songs sold on Zune Marketplace are complements. If a Zune had a lower price than an iPod, this would cause consumers to purchase the Zune rather than the iPod, provided that the two players have the same features. If consumers believe that the Zune and the iPod are very close substitutes, a fall in the price of Zunes would cause the demand for iPods to decline, as the quantity of Zunes demanded increased. If Microsoft reduced the price of a song sold on Zune Marketplace so that it was lower than the price of the same song on iTunes, even if iPods and Zunes had the same price, the demand for Zunes would increase, and the demand for iPods would decrease.

Conclusion

The interaction of demand and supply determines market equilibrium. The model of demand and supply provides us with a powerful tool for predicting how changes in the actions of consumers and firms will cause changes in equilibrium prices and quantities. As we have seen in this chapter, the model can often be used to analyze markets that do not meet all the requirements for being perfectly competitive. As long as there is intense competition among sellers, the model of demand and supply can often successfully predict changes in prices and quantities. We will use the model in the next chapter to analyze economic efficiency and the results of government-imposed price floors and price ceilings. Before moving on, read *An Inside Look* on the next page to learn how Apple and AT&T benefit from collaborating on the iPhone.

An Inside **LOOK**

How Does the iPhone Help Apple and AT&T?

WALL STREET JOURNAL, FEBRUARY 17, 2007

Apple Coup: How Steve Jobs Played Hardball in iPhone Birth

During a visit to Las Vegas last December for a rodeo event, Cingular Wireless chief executive Stan Sigman received a welcome guest: Steve Jobs. The Apple Inc. chief stopped by Mr. Sigman's Four Seasons hotel suite to show off the iPhone, a sleek cellphone designed to surf the Web and double as an iPod music player.

The phone had been in development by Apple and Cingular [now AT&T] for two years and was weeks away from being revealed to the world. And yet this was the first time Mr. Sigman got to see it. For three hours, Mr. Jobs played with the device, with its touch-screen that allows users to view contacts, dial numbers and flip through photos with the swipe of a finger. Mr. Sigman looked on in awe, according to a person familiar with the meeting . . .

Mr. Jobs is famous for making a splash with new products that upend industry models. Several years ago, he personally lobbied music industry executives and obtained licenses for songs that gave Apple the flexibility to build its successful iTunes store.

(a) Apple eyed the cellphone market as both an opportunity to expand its iPod business and, if ignored, a potential threat to the company, people familiar with its strategy say. Cellphones are gradually offering more sophisticated capabilities and features, including increased storage capacity and entertainment functions. That stands to make them more competitive with iPods over time. Already, music phones like Samsung Electronics Co.'s BlackJack, Sony Ericsson's Walkman models and LG Electronic Inc.'s Chocolate are edging onto Apple's turf . . .

In early 2005, Mr. Jobs called Mr. Sigman to pitch the initial concept of the iPhone. The two executives later met in New York, and agreed to pursue the idea. Mr. Sigman is a Texan who wears cowboy boots and business suits, while Mr. Jobs is a former hippie who sports black turtlenecks and jeans. Despite their vastly different styles, the two executives found common ground. Over the next year and a half, the two sides negotiated to reach an agreement that would make sense for both of them . . .

(b) While Mr. Jobs considered Cingular a logical choice as a partner to carry the device—its GSM technology is the prevailing standard in much of the world—Apple continued to shop its ideas to other carriers. Mr. Jobs reached out to Verizon Wireless chief executive Denny Strigl in the middle of 2005 and proposed a partnership with the carrier, a joint venture of Verizon Communications Inc. and Vodafone Group PLC. The companies held a few discussions over the next year, but the talks eventually soured.

There were a few sticking points. Verizon balked at the notion of cutting out its big retail partners, like Circuit City, who would not be allowed to sell the phone. And the company's chief marketing officer, John Stratton, was firm that Verizon wouldn't give up its ability to sell content like music and videos through its proprietary V Cast service, people familiar with the discussions say. . . .

In January, Mr. Jobs finally unveiled the phone at Macworld, the conference he has used to launch such key products as the iPod Mini. Since then, the two companies have continued to test the iPhone at an undisclosed facility, a person familiar with the matter said. The handful of Cingular people who have access to the sample phones at the company's headquarters were required to sign confidentiality agreements, a person familiar with the matter says. Meanwhile, competitors already are responding. Samsung and LG both have announced phones in recent weeks with designs that look similar to the iPhone. Apple has said it intends to sell 10 million of the devices by 2008, with price tags for two different versions set steeply at $499 and $599.

(c) Cingular, which has more than 60 million customers, hopes the iPhone will give it a lift when it hits stores in June, at a time when attracting new subscribers is getting more difficult for all operators.

Source: Amol Sharma, Nick Wingfield, and Li Yuan, "Apple Coup: How Steve Jobs Played Hardball in iPhone Birth," Wall Street Journal, *February 17, 2007, p. A1.*

Key Points in the Article

The article discusses Apple's new iPhone, which combines features of the iPod and a cell phone. Apple has teamed up with Cingular, now AT&T, to provide cell phone service for the iPhone. The phone will also function as an iPod that plays music in Apple's proprietary format. The iPhone helps both companies. Apple gains because it now has a digital music player that doubles as a cell phone and competes with the other music phones on the market. AT&T gains a potentially large customer base for its cell phone services.

Analyzing the News

a Apple has viewed the evolution of the cell phone as a threat to the iPod because over time, cell phone manufacturers have added features that are similar to those of the iPod. For example, manufacturers have increased the storage capacity of cell phones so that people can store their music, pictures, and videos. Cell phones can also function as cameras and video recorders. These cell phones are a threat to the iPod because they are substitute goods that offer many of the same features.

If people are forced to choose just one product, then they might choose a cell phone that can play music over an iPod that cannot function as a phone. The figure shows the result. The demand curve for iPods shifts to the left, which reduces the price and quantity sold of iPods. Because the iPod is a critical product for Apple, this would significantly harm the entire company. Introducing the iPhone is a strategy to protect a very lucrative market for Apple.

b Apple could have worked with a number of different cell phone service providers. Ultimately, Apple chose to partner with Cingular for a couple of reasons. First, Cingular uses technology that is the industry standard. Second, Cingular was willing to make concessions that other cell phone service providers were not willing to make. The chapter opener pointed out that one of the key factors in the iPod's success was that Apple both made the iPod and sold music through iTunes. This means that the two products were developed by the same company and worked seamlessly together. One reason that Apple did not end up partnering with Verizon is that Verizon insisted on the right to continue to sell downloads of music and videos. This raised the possibility of compatibility problems with downloads available through iTunes.

c AT&T also benefits from the introduction of the iPhone. The iPhone will work only with AT&T's cellular phone service, so if you want to purchase an iPhone, you have to purchase AT&T's service. That means the iPhone and AT&T's services are complementary goods—and as sales of iPhones increase, the demand for AT&T's services should also increase.

Thinking Critically

1. What effect will the introduction of the iPhone have on sales of the iPod? Are there any reasons why someone might want to own both an iPhone and an iPod? Would it be better to think of the iPhone and the iPod as substitutes or complements? Briefly explain.
2. Apple plans to sell two versions of the iPhone: one for $499 and one for $599, which are significantly higher than the price of the most expensive iPod and much higher than the prices of cell phones. Are most customers likely to see the iPhone as a closer substitute for other cell phones or for other digital music players? Is the high price of the iPhone relevant to your answer? Briefly explain.

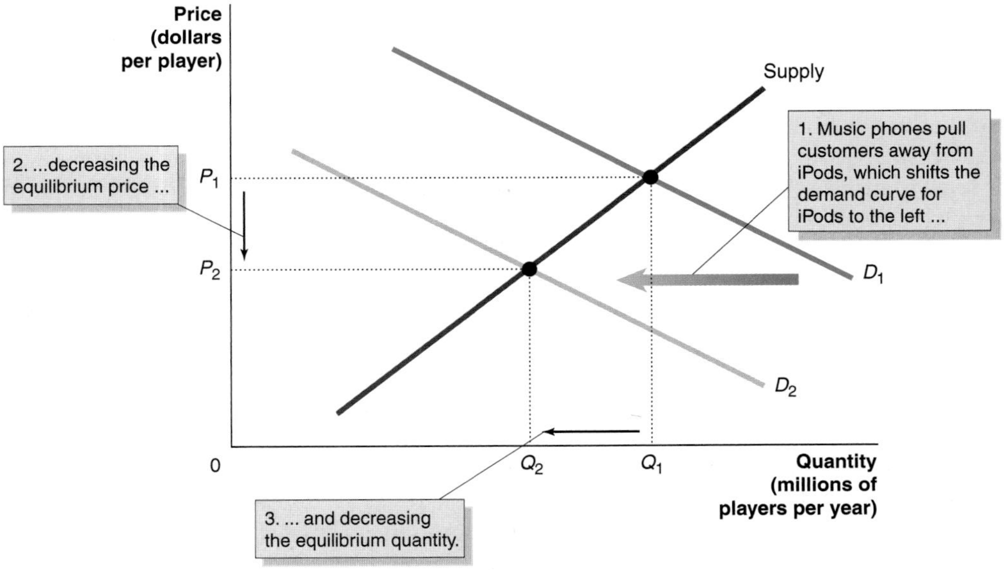

Music phones may cause a decrease in the demand for iPods.

Key Terms

Ceteris paribus ("all else equal"), p. 70
Competitive market equilibrium, p. 80
Complements, p. 71
Demand curve, p. 68
Demand schedule, p. 68
Demographics, p. 72
Income effect, p. 69
Inferior good, p. 71
Law of demand, p. 69
Law of supply, p. 76
Market demand, p. 68
Market equilibrium, p. 80
Normal good, p. 71
Perfectly competitive market, p. 68
Quantity demanded, p. 68
Quantity supplied, p. 75
Shortage, p. 80
Substitutes, p. 71
Substitution effect, p. 69
Supply curve, p. 76
Supply schedule, p. 76
Surplus, p. 80
Technological change, p. 77

3.1 LEARNING OBJECTIVE 3.1 | Discuss the variables that influence demand, **pages 68–75.**

The Demand Side of the Market

Summary

The model of demand and supply is the most powerful in economics. The model applies exactly only to **perfectly competitive markets**, where there are many buyers and sellers, all the products sold are identical, and there are no barriers to new sellers entering the market. But the model can also be useful in analyzing markets that don't meet all of these requirements. The **quantity demanded** is the amount of a good or service that a consumer is willing and able to purchase at a given price. A **demand schedule** is a table that shows the relationship between the price of a product and the quantity of the product demanded. A **demand curve** is a graph that shows the relationship between the price of a good and the quantity of the good consumers are willing and able to buy over a period of time. **Market demand** is the demand by all consumers of a given good or service. The **law of demand** states that ***ceteris paribus***—holding everything else constant—the quantity of a product demanded increases when the price falls and decreases when the price rises. Demand curves slope downward because of the **substitution effect**, which is the change in quantity demanded that results from a price change making one good more or less expensive relative to another good, and the **income effect**, which is the change in quantity demanded of a good that results from the effect of a change in the good's price on consumer purchasing power. Changes in income, the prices of related goods, tastes, population and demographics, and expected future prices all cause the demand curve to shift. **Substitutes** are goods that can be used for the same purpose. **Complements** are goods that are used together. A **normal good** is a good for which demand increases as income increases. An **inferior good** is a good for which demand decreases as income increases. **Demographics** are the characteristics of a population with respect to age, race, and gender. A change in demand refers to a shift of the demand curve. A change in quantity demanded refers to a movement along the demand curve as a result of a change in the product's price.

myeconlab Get Ahead of the Curve Visit www.myeconlab.com to complete these exercises online and get instant feedback.

Review Questions

1.1 What is a demand schedule? What is a demand curve?

1.2 What do economists mean when they use the Latin expression *ceteris paribus*?

1.3 What is the difference between a change in demand and a change in quantity demanded?

1.4 What is the law of demand? What are the main variables that will cause the demand curve to shift? Give an example of each.

Problems and Applications

1.5 (Related to the *Making the Connection* on page 71) For each of the following pairs of products, state which are complements, which are substitutes, and which are unrelated.
   a. Pepsi and Coke
   b. Oscar Mayer hot dogs and Wonder hot dog buns
   c. Jif peanut butter and Smucker's strawberry jam
   d. iPods and Texas Instruments financial calculators

1.6 (Related to the *Chapter Opener* on page 66) Suppose Apple discovers that it is selling relatively few downloads of television programs on iTunes. Are downloads of television programs substitutes or complements for downloads of music? For downloads of movies? How might the answers to these questions affect Apple's decision about whether to continue offering downloads of television programs on iTunes?

1.7 State whether each of the following events will result in a movement along the demand curve for McDonald's Big Mac hamburgers or whether it will cause the curve to shift. If the demand curve shifts, indicate whether it will shift to the left or to the right and draw a graph to illustrate the shift.
   a. The price of Burger King's Whopper hamburger declines.

b. McDonald's distributes coupons for $1.00 off on a purchase of a Big Mac.
c. Because of a shortage of potatoes, the price of French fries increases.
d. Kentucky Fried Chicken raises the price of a bucket of fried chicken.

1.8 **(Related to the *Making the Connection* on page 72)** Name three products whose demand is likely to increase rapidly if the following demographic groups increase at a faster rate than the population as a whole:
a. Teenagers
b. Children under five
c. People over age 65

1.9 Suppose the data in the following table present the price of a base model Ford Explorer sport-utility vehicle (SUV) and the quantity of Explorers sold. Do these data indicate that the demand curve for Explorers is upward sloping? Explain.

YEAR	PRICE	QUANTITY
2006	$27,865	325,265
2007	28,325	330,648
2008	28,765	352,666

1.10 **(Related to the *Making the Connection* on page 75)** In early 2007, Apple forecast that it would sell 10 million iPhones during the product's first year on the market. What factors could affect the accuracy of this forecast? Is the forecast likely to be more or less accurate than Apple's forecast of how many iPods they would sell during the same time period? Briefly explain.

>> End Learning Objective 3.1

3.2 LEARNING OBJECTIVE 3.2 | Discuss the variables that influence supply, **pages 75–79.**

The Supply Side of the Market

Summary

The **quantity supplied** is the amount of a good that a firm is willing and able to supply at a given price. A **supply schedule** is a table that shows the relationship between the price of a product and the quantity of the product supplied. A **supply curve** shows on a graph the relationship between the price of a product and the quantity of the product supplied. When the price of a product rises, producing the product is more profitable, and a greater amount will be supplied. The **law of supply** states that, holding everything else constant, the quantity of a product supplied increases when the price rises and decreases when the price falls. Changes in the prices of inputs, technology, the prices of substitutes in production, expected future prices, and the number of firms in a market all cause the supply curve to shift. **Technological change** is a positive or negative change in the ability of a firm to produce a given level of output with a given quantity of inputs. A change in supply refers to a shift of the supply curve. A change in quantity supplied refers to a movement along the supply curve as a result of a change in the product's price.

myeconlab Get Ahead of the Curve — Visit www.myeconlab.com to complete these exercises online and get instant feedback.

Review Questions

2.1 What is a supply schedule? What is a supply curve?

2.2 What is the law of supply? What are the main variables that will cause a supply curve to shift? Give an example of each.

Problems and Applications

2.3 Briefly explain whether each of the following statements describes a change in supply or a change in the quantity supplied.
a. To take advantage of high prices for snow shovels during a very snowy winter, Alexander Shovels, Inc., decides to increase output.
b. The success of Apple's iPod leads more firms to begin producing digital music players.
c. In the six months following Hurricane Katrina, production of oil in the Gulf of Mexico declined by 25 percent.

2.4 Will each firm in a given industry always supply the same quantity as every other firm at each price? What factors might cause the quantity of digital music players supplied by each firm at each price to be different?

2.5 If the price of a good increases, is the increase in the quantity of the good supplied likely to be smaller or larger, the longer the time period being considered? Briefly explain.

>> End Learning Objective 3.2

3.3 LEARNING OBJECTIVE 3.3 | Use a graph to illustrate market equilibrium, **pages 79–82.**

Market Equilibrium: Putting Demand and Supply Together

Summary

Market equilibrium occurs where the demand curve intersects the supply curve. A **competitive market equilibrium** has a market equilibrium with many buyers and many sellers. Only at this point is the quantity demanded equal to the quantity supplied. Prices above equilibrium result in **surpluses**, with the quantity supplied being greater than the quantity demanded. Surpluses cause the market price to fall. Prices below equilibrium result in **shortages**, with the quantity demanded being greater than the quantity supplied. Shortages cause the market price to rise.

myeconlab Get Ahead of the Curve Visit www.myeconlab.com to complete these exercises online and get instant feedback.

Review Questions

3.1 What do economists mean by market equilibrium?

3.2 What happens in a market if the current price is above the equilibrium price? What happens if the current price is below the equilibrium price?

Problems and Applications

3.3 Briefly explain whether you agree with the following statement: "When there is a shortage of a good, consumers eventually give up trying to buy it, so the demand for the good declines, and the price falls until the market is finally in equilibrium."

3.4 **(Related to *Solved Problem 3-3* on page 81)** In *The Wealth of Nations*, Adam Smith discussed what has come to be known as the "diamond and water paradox":

> Nothing is more useful than water: but it will purchase scarce anything; scarce anything can be had in exchange for it. A diamond, on the contrary, has scarce any value in use; but a very great quantity of other goods may frequently be had in exchange for it.

Graph the market for diamonds and the market for water. Show how it is possible for the price of water to be much lower than the price of diamonds, even though the demand for water is much greater than the demand for diamonds.

3.5 Briefly explain under what conditions zero would be the equilibrium quantity.

3.6 If a market is in equilibrium, is it necessarily true that all buyers and all sellers are satisfied with the market price? Briefly explain.

>> End Learning Objective 3.3

3.4 LEARNING OBJECTIVE 3.4 | Use demand and supply graphs to predict changes in prices and quantities, **pages 83–89.**

The Effect of Demand and Supply Shifts on Equilibrium

Summary

In most markets, demand and supply curves shift frequently, causing changes in equilibrium prices and quantities. Over time, if demand increases more than supply, equilibrium price will rise. If supply increases more than demand, equilibrium price will fall.

myeconlab Get Ahead of the Curve Visit www.myeconlab.com to complete these exercises online and get instant feedback.

Review Questions

4.1 Draw a demand and supply curve to show the effect on the equilibrium price in a market in the following two situations:

a. The demand curve shifts to the right.
b. The supply curve shifts to the left.

4.2 If, over time, the demand curve for a product shifts to the right more than the supply curve does, what will happen to the equilibrium price? What will happen to the equilibrium price if the supply curve shifts to the right more than the demand curve? For each case, draw a demand and supply graph to illustrate your answer.

Problems and Applications

4.3 As oil prices rose during 2006, the demand for alternative fuels increased. Ethanol, one alternative fuel, is made from corn. According to an article in the *Wall Street Journal*, the price of tortillas, which are made from corn, also rose during 2006: "The price spike [in tortillas] is part of a ripple effect from the ethanol boom."

a. Draw a demand and supply graph for the corn market and use it to show the effect on this market of an increase in the demand for ethanol. Be sure to indicate the equilibrium price and quantity before and after the increase in the demand for ethanol.
b. Draw a demand and supply graph for the tortilla market and use it to show the effect on this market of an increase in the price of corn. Once again, be sure to indicate the equilibrium price and quantity before and after the increase in the demand for ethanol.

Source: Mark Gongloff, "Tortilla Soup," *Wall Street Journal*, January 25, 2007.

4.4 A recent study indicated that "stricter college alcohol policies, such as raising the price of alcohol, or banning alcohol on campus, decrease the number of students who use marijuana."
a. On the basis of this information, are alcohol and marijuana substitutes or complements?
b. Suppose that campus authorities reduce the supply of alcohol on campus. Use demand and supply graphs to illustrate the impact on the campus alcohol and marijuana markets.

Source: Jenny Williams, Rosalie Pacula, Frank Chaloupka, and Henry Wechsler, "Alcohol and Marijuana Use Among College Students: Economic Complements or Substitutes?" *Health Economics*, Volume 13, Issue 9, September 2005, pp. 825–843.

4.5 **(Related to *Solved Problem 3-4* on page 86)** The demand for watermelons is highest during summer and lowest during winter. Yet watermelon prices are normally lower in summer than in winter. Use a demand and supply graph to demonstrate how this is possible. Be sure to carefully label the curves in your graph and to clearly indicate the equilibrium summer price and the equilibrium winter price.

4.6 According to an article in the *Wall Street Journal*:

> As occupancy rates at luxury hotels have grown 13% over the last five years, prices have risen by 19%, according to Smith Travel Research. (That comes despite an 18.5% increase in the number of rooms over the same period.)

Use a demand and supply graph to explain how these three things could be true: an increase in the equilibrium quantity of hotel rooms occupied, an increase in the equilibrium price of hotel rooms, and an increase in the number of hotel rooms available.

Source: Nancy Keates, "Cracking Down on Chair Hogs," *Wall Street Journal*, February 23, 2007, p. W1.

4.7 **(Related to the *Making the Connection* on page 83)** The average price of a high-definition plasma or LCD television fell between 2001 and 2006, from more than $8,000 to about $1,500. During that period, Sharp, Matsushita Electric Industrial, and Samsung all began producing plasma or LCD televisions. Use a demand and supply graph to explain what happened to the quantity of plasma and LCD televisions sold during this period.

4.8 According to an article in the *Wall Street Journal*, during 2006, the demand for full-size pickup trucks declined as a result of rising gas prices and a decline in housing construction (construction firms are an important part of the market for full-size pickup trucks). At the same time, Toyota began production of trucks at a new truck factory in Texas.
a. Draw a demand and supply graph illustrating these developments in the market for full-size pickup trucks. Be sure to indicate changes in the equilibrium price and equilibrium quantity.
b. Briefly discuss whether this problem provides enough information to determine whether the equilibrium quantity of trucks increased or decreased.

Source: Neal E. Boudette and Jeffrey C. McCracken, "Detroit's Cash Cow Stumbles," *Wall Street Journal*, August 1, 2006, p. B1.

4.9 Beginning in the late 1990s, many consumers were having their vision problems corrected with laser surgery. An article in the *Wall Street Journal* noted two developments in the market for laser eye surgery. The first involved increasing concerns related to side effects from the surgery, including blurred vision and, occasionally, blindness. The second development was that the companies renting eye-surgery machinery to doctors had reduced their charges. One large company had cut its charge from $250 per patient to $100. Use a demand and supply graph to illustrate the effects of these two developments on the market for laser eye surgery.

Source: Laura Johannes and James Bandler, "Slowing Economy, Safety Concerns Zap Growth in Laser Eye Surgery," *Wall Street Journal*, January 8, 2001, p. B1.

4.10 The market for autographs, including letters or other documents signed by famous people, is subject to frequent large price changes, as are markets for most collectibles. The following table is adapted from one that originally appeared in an article in the *Wall Street Journal*. It gives the 1997 price for an autograph, the 2001 price, and a brief comment by the *Wall Street Journal* reporter. Use the information contained in the Comment column of the table to draw a demand and supply graph for each of the three autographs listed that can account for the change in its market price from 1997 to 2001.

AUTOGRAPH	1997 PRICE	2001 PRICE	COMMENT
The Beatles	$2,500	$7,475	"As boomers get rich, so do prices for pieces . . . signed by the Fab Four."
Princess Diana	14,000	2,000	"Demand rose after her death in 1997, but now the market's full of items like her signed Christmas cards."
Robert E. Lee	200,000	100,000	"The Civil War's out."

Source: Brooks Barnes, "Signature Market: Hard to Read," *Wall Street Journal*, July 13, 2001.

4.11 Historically, the production of many perishable foods, such as dairy products, was highly seasonal. Thus, as the supply of those products fluctuated, prices tended to fluctuate tremendously—typically by 25 to 50 percent or more—over the course of the year. One impact of mechanical refrigeration, which was commercialized on a large scale in the last decade of the nineteenth century, was that suppliers could store perishables from one season to the next. Economists have estimated that as a result of refrigerated storage, wholesale prices rose by roughly 10 percent during peak supply periods, while they fell by almost the same amount during the off season. Use a demand and supply graph for each season to illustrate how refrigeration affected the market for perishable food.

Source: Lee A. Craig, Barry Goodwin, and Thomas Grennes, "The Effect of Mechanical Refrigeration on Nutrition in the U.S.," *Social Science History*, Vol. 28, No. 2 (Summer 2004), pp. 327–328.

4.12 Briefly explain whether each of the following statements is true or false.

a. If the demand and supply for a product both increase, the equilibrium quantity of the product must also increase.

b. If the demand and supply for a product both increase, the equilibrium price of the product must also increase.

c. If the demand for a product decreases and the supply of the product increases, the equilibrium price of the product may increase or decrease, depending on whether supply or demand has shifted more.

4.13 **(Related to the *Don't Let This Happen to You!* on page 88)** A student writes the following: "Increased production leads to a lower price, which in turn increases demand." Do you agree with his reasoning? Briefly explain.

4.14 **(Related to the *Don't Let This Happen To You!* on page 88)** A student was asked to draw a demand and supply graph to illustrate the effect on the laptop computer market of a fall in the price of computer hard drives, *ceteris paribus*. She drew the graph at the top of the next column and explained it as follows:

> Hard drives are an input to laptop computers, so a fall in the price of hard drives will cause the supply curve for personal computers to shift to the right (from S_1 to S_2). Because this shift in the supply curve results in a lower price (P_2), consumers will want to buy more laptops, and the demand curve will shift to the right (from D_1 to D_2). We know that more laptops will be sold, but we can't be sure whether the price of laptops will rise or fall. That depends on whether the supply curve or the demand curve has shifted farther to the right. I assume that the effect on supply is greater than the effect on demand, so I show the final equilibrium price (P_3) as being lower than the initial equilibrium price (P_1).

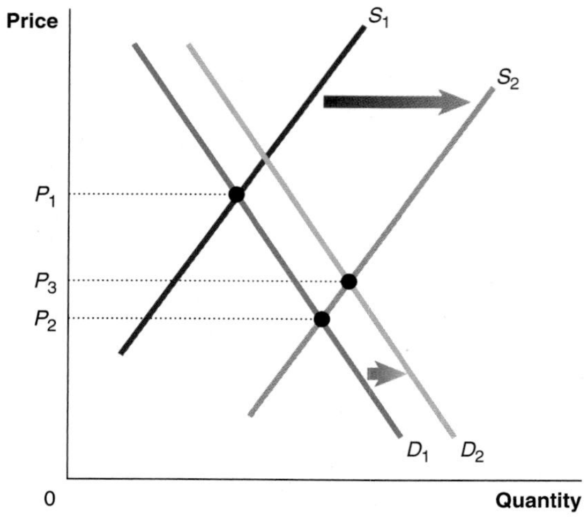

Explain whether you agree or disagree with the student's analysis. Be careful to explain exactly what—if anything—you find wrong with her analysis.

4.15 Following are four graphs and four market scenarios, each of which would cause either a movement along the supply curve for Pepsi or a shift of the supply curve. Match each scenario with the appropriate graph.

1.

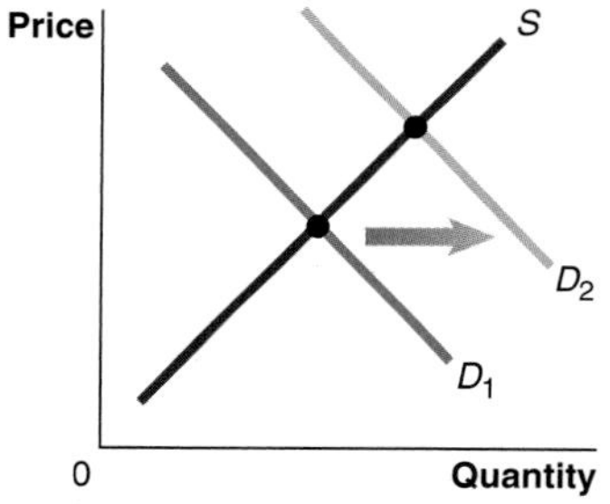

2.

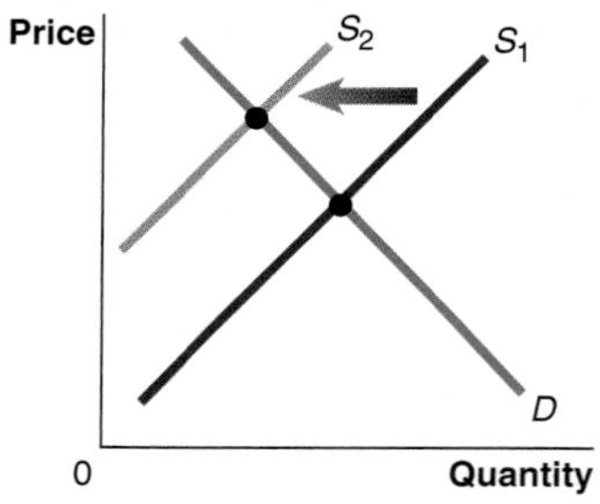

3.

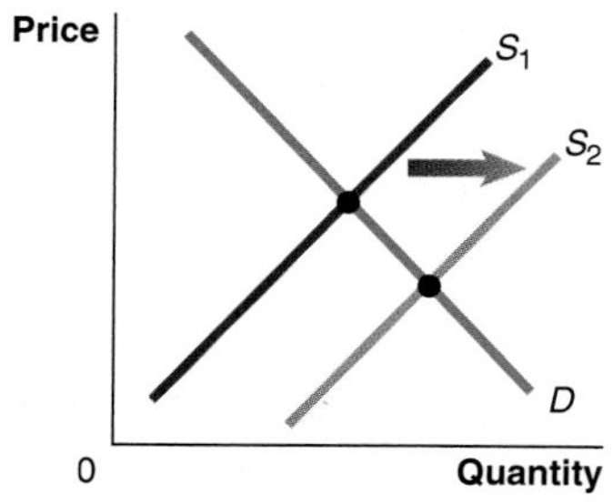

4.

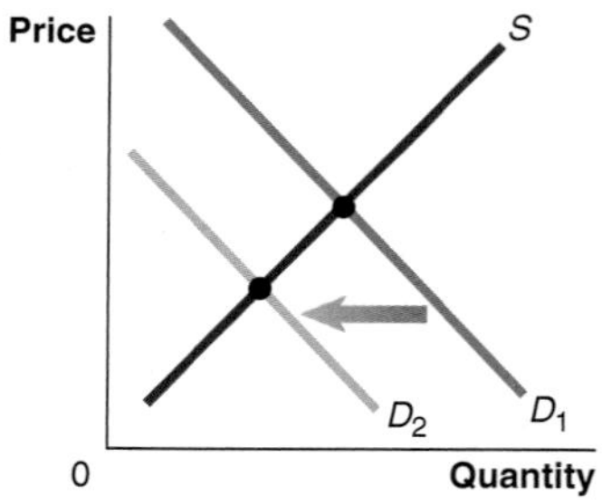

a. A decrease in the supply of Coke

b. A drop in the average household income in the United States from $42,000 to $41,000

c. An improvement in soft-drink bottling technology

d. An increase in the price of sugar

4.16 David Surdam, an economist at Loyola University of Chicago, makes the following observation of the world cotton market at the beginning of the Civil War:

> As the supply of American-grown raw cotton decreased and the price of raw cotton increased, there would be a *movement along* the supply curve of non-American raw cotton suppliers, and the quantity supplied by these producers would increase.

Illustrate this observation with one demand and supply graph for the market for American-grown cotton and another demand and supply graph for the market for non-American cotton. Make sure your graphs clearly show (1) the initial equilibrium before the decrease in the supply of American-grown cotton and (2) the final equilibrium. Also clearly show any shifts in the demand and supply curves for each market.

Source: David G. Surdam, "King Cotton: Monarch or Pretender? The State of the Market for Raw Cotton on the Eve of the American Civil War," *The Economic History Review*, Vol. 51, No. 1 (February 1998), p. 116.

4.17 Proposals have been made to increase government regulation of firms providing childcare services by, for instance, setting education requirements for childcare workers. Suppose that these regulations increase the quality of childcare and cause the demand for childcare services to increase. At the same time, assume that complying with the new government regulations increases the costs of firms providing childcare services. Draw a demand and supply graph to illustrate the effects of these changes in the market for childcare services. Briefly explain whether the total quantity of childcare services purchased will increase or decrease as a result of regulation.

4.18 Below are the supply and demand functions for two markets. One of the markets is for BMW automobiles, and the other is for a cancer-fighting drug, without which lung cancer patients will die. Briefly explain which diagram most likely represents which market.

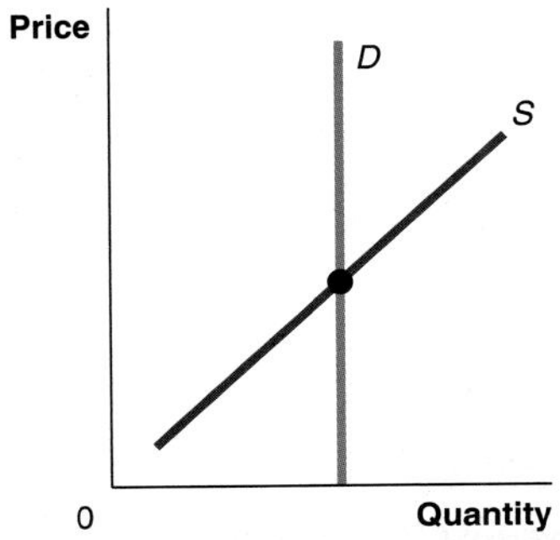

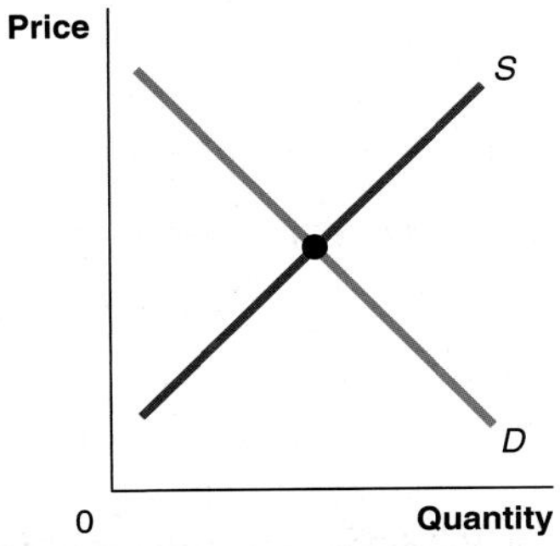

>> End Learning Objective 3.4

Economic Efficiency, Government Price Setting, and Taxes

Should the Government Control Apartment Rents?

Robert F. Moss owns an apartment building in New York City. Unlike most other business owners, he is not free to charge the prices he would like for the service he offers. In New York, San Francisco, Los Angeles, and nearly 200 smaller cities, apartments are subject to rent control by the local government. Rent control puts a legal limit on the rent that landlords can charge for an apartment.

New York City has two million apartments, about one million of which are subject to rent control. The other one million apartments have their rents determined in the market by the demand and supply for apartments. Mr. Moss's building includes apartments that are rent controlled and apartments that are not. The market-determined rents are usually far above the controlled rents. The government regulations that determine what Mr. Moss can charge for a rent-controlled apartment are very complex. The following is Mr. Moss's description:

> When [an apartment] is vacated, state rent laws entitle landlords to raise rents in three primary ways: a vacancy increase of 20 percent for a new tenant's two-year lease (a bit less for a one-year lease); one-fortieth per month of the cost of any improvements, and a "longevity bonus" for longtime residents (calculated at six-tenths of 1 percent times the tenant's last legal rent multiplied by the number of years of residency beyond eight). . . . Apartments renting for $2,000 a month are automatically deregulated if they are vacant. Occupied apartments whose rent reaches that figure can be deregulated if the income of the tenants has been $175,000 or more for two years.

As this description shows, someone earning a living by renting out apartments in New York City has to deal with much more complex government regulation of prices than someone who owns, for instance, a McDonald's restaurant.

Larger companies also struggle with the complexity of rent-control regulations. This was the case for several companies that built multiple apartment buildings in New York during the 1970s. In exchange for renting apartments to moderate- and low-income tenants at controlled rents, the companies were allowed to charge market rents after 20 years. Unfortunately for the companies, when the 20 years were over, attempts to start charging market rents were often met with lawsuits from unhappy tenants. New York Mayor Michael Bloomberg proposed that the law be changed to keep many of these apartment buildings under rent control.

Tenants in rent-controlled apartments in New York are very reluctant to see rent control end because rents for rent-controlled apartments are much lower than rents for apartments that aren't rent controlled. As we will see in this chapter, however rent control can also cause significant problems for renters. **AN INSIDE LOOK AT POLICY** on **page 122** explores the debate over rent control laws in Los Angeles.

Source: Robert F. Moss, "A Landlord's Lot is Sometimes Not an Easy One," *New York Times*, August 3, 2003, Section 11, p. 1.

LEARNING Objectives

After studying this chapter, you should be able to:

4.1 Distinguish between the concepts of **consumer surplus** and **producer surplus**, page 100.

4.2 Understand the concept of **economic efficiency**, page 105.

4.3 Explain the economic effect of government-imposed **price ceilings** and **price floors**, page 107.

4.4 Analyze the economic impact of **taxes**, page 115.

APPENDIX Use **quantitative** demand and supply **analysis**, page 131.

Economics in YOUR Life!

Does Rent Control Make It Easier to Find an Affordable Apartment?

Suppose you have job offers in two cities. One factor in deciding which job to accept is whether you can find an affordable apartment. If one city has rent control, are you more likely to find an affordable apartment in that city, or would you be better off looking for an apartment in a city without rent control? As you read the chapter, see if you can answer this question. You can check your answer against the one we provide at the end of the chapter. » **Continued on page 120**

We saw in Chapter 3 that, in a competitive market, the price adjusts to ensure that the quantity demanded equals the quantity supplied. Stated another way, in equilibrium, every consumer willing to pay the market price is able to buy as much of the product as the consumer wants, and every firm willing to accept the market price can sell as much as it wants. Even so, consumers would naturally prefer to pay a lower price, and sellers would prefer to receive a higher price. Normally, consumers and firms have no choice but to accept the equilibrium price if they wish to participate in the market. Occasionally, however, consumers succeed in having the government impose a **price ceiling**, which is a legally determined maximum price that sellers may charge. Rent control is an example of a price ceiling. Firms also sometimes succeed in having the government impose a **price floor**, which is a legally determined minimum price that sellers may receive. In markets for farm products such as milk, the government has been setting price floors that are above the equilibrium market price since the 1930s.

Price ceiling A legally determined maximum price that sellers may charge.

Price floor A legally determined minimum price that sellers may receive.

Another way in which the government intervenes in markets is by imposing taxes. The government relies on the revenue raised from taxes to finance its operations. As we will see, though, imposing taxes alters the equilibrium in a market.

Unfortunately, whenever the government imposes a price ceiling, a price floor, or a tax, there are predictable negative economic consequences. It is important for government policymakers and voters to understand these negative consequences when evaluating the effects of these policies. Economists have developed the concepts of *consumer surplus, producer surplus*, and *economic surplus*, which we discuss in the next section. In the sections that follow, we use these concepts to analyze the economic effects of price ceilings, price floors, and taxes. (As we will see in later chapters, these concepts are also useful in many other contexts.)

4.1 LEARNING OBJECTIVE

4.1 | Distinguish between the concepts of consumer surplus and producer surplus.

Consumer Surplus and Producer Surplus

Consumer surplus measures the dollar benefit consumers receive from buying goods or services in a particular market. Producer surplus measures the dollar benefit firms receive from selling goods or services in a particular market. Economic surplus in a market is the sum of consumer surplus plus producer surplus. As we will see, *when the government imposes a price ceiling or a price floor, the amount of economic surplus in a market is reduced*—in other words, price ceilings and price floors reduce the total benefit to consumers and firms from buying and selling in a market. To understand why this is true, we need to understand how consumer surplus and producer surplus are determined.

Consumer Surplus

Consumer surplus The difference between the highest price a consumer is willing to pay and the price the consumer actually pays.

Consumer surplus measures the difference between the highest price a consumer is willing to pay and the price the consumer actually pays. For example, suppose you are in Wal-Mart and you see a DVD of *Spider-Man 3* on the rack. No price is indicated on the package, so you bring it over to the register to check the price. As you walk to the register, you think to yourself that $20 is the highest price you would be willing to pay. At the register, you find out that the price is actually $12, so you buy the DVD. Your consumer surplus in this example is $8: the difference between the $20 you were willing to pay and the $8 you actually paid.

Marginal benefit The additional benefit to a consumer from consuming one more unit of a good or service.

We can use the demand curve to measure the total consumer surplus in a market. Demand curves show the willingness of consumers to purchase a product at different prices. Consumers are willing to purchase a product up to the point where the marginal benefit of consuming a product is equal to its price. The **marginal benefit** is the addi-

Consumer	Highest Price Willing to Pay
Theresa	$6
Tom	5
Terri	4
Tim	3

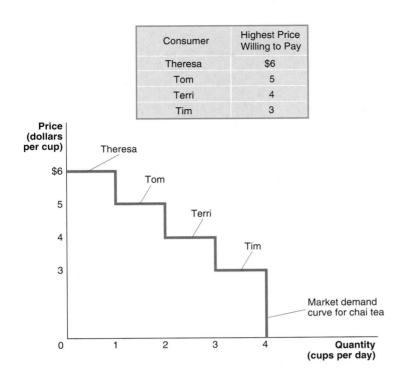

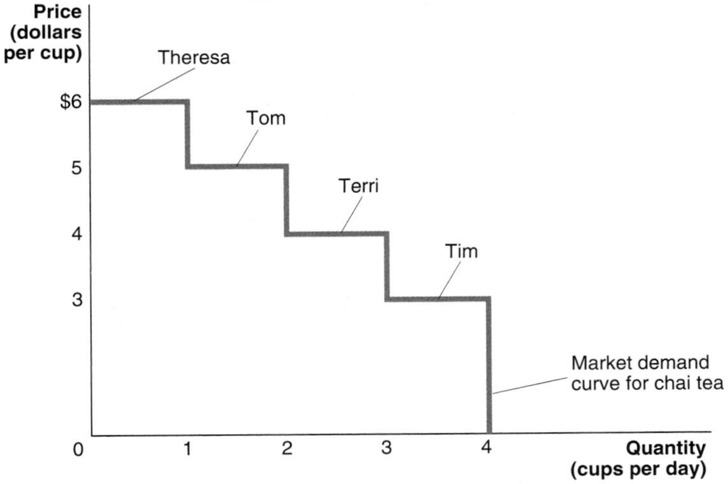

Figure 4-1

Deriving the Demand Curve for Chai Tea

With four consumers in the market for chai tea, the demand curve is determined by the highest price each consumer is willing to pay. For prices above $6, no tea is sold because $6 is the highest price any consumer is willing to pay. For prices of $3 and below, all four consumers are willing to buy a cup of tea.

tional benefit to a consumer from consuming one more unit of a good or service. As a simple example, suppose there are only four consumers in the market for chai tea: Theresa, Tom, Terri, and Tim. Because these four consumers have different tastes for tea and different incomes, the marginal benefit each of them receives from consuming a cup of tea will be different. Therefore, the highest price each is willing to pay for a cup of tea is also different. In Figure 4-1, the information from the table is used to construct a demand curve for chai tea. For prices above $6 per cup, no tea is sold because $6 is the highest price any of the consumers is willing to pay. At a price of $5, both Theresa and Tom are willing to buy, so two cups are sold. At prices of $3 and below, all four consumers are willing to buy, and four cups are sold.

Suppose the market price of tea is $3.50 per cup. As Figure 4-2 on page 102 shows, the demand curve allows us to calculate the total consumer surplus in this market. In panel (a), we can see that the highest price Theresa is willing to pay is $6, but because she pays only $3.50, her consumer surplus is $2.50 (shown by the area of rectangle *A*). Similarly, Tom's consumer surplus is $1.50 (rectangle *B*), and Terri's consumer surplus is $0.50 (rectangle *C*). Tim is unwilling to buy a cup of tea at a price of $3.50, so he doesn't participate in this market and receives no consumer surplus. In this simple example, the total consumer surplus is equal to $2.50 + $1.50 + $0.50 = $4.50 (or the sum of the areas of rectangles *A*, *B*, and *C*). Panel (b) shows that a lower price will increase consumer surplus. If the price of tea drops from $3.50 per cup to $3.00, Theresa, Tom, and Terri each receive $0.50 more in consumer surplus (shown by the shaded areas), so total consumer surplus in the market rises to $6.00. Tim now buys a cup of tea but doesn't receive any consumer surplus because the price is equal to the highest price he is willing to pay. In fact, Tim is indifferent between buying the cup or not—his well-being is the same either way.

The market demand curves shown in Figures 4-1 and 4-2 do not look like the smooth curves we saw in Chapter 3. This is because this example uses a small number of consumers, each consuming a single cup of tea. With many consumers, the market demand curve for chai tea will have the normal smooth shape shown in Figure 4-3. In this figure, the quantity demanded at a price of $2.00 is 15,000 cups per day. We can calculate total consumer surplus in Figure 4-3 the same way we did in Figures 4-1 and

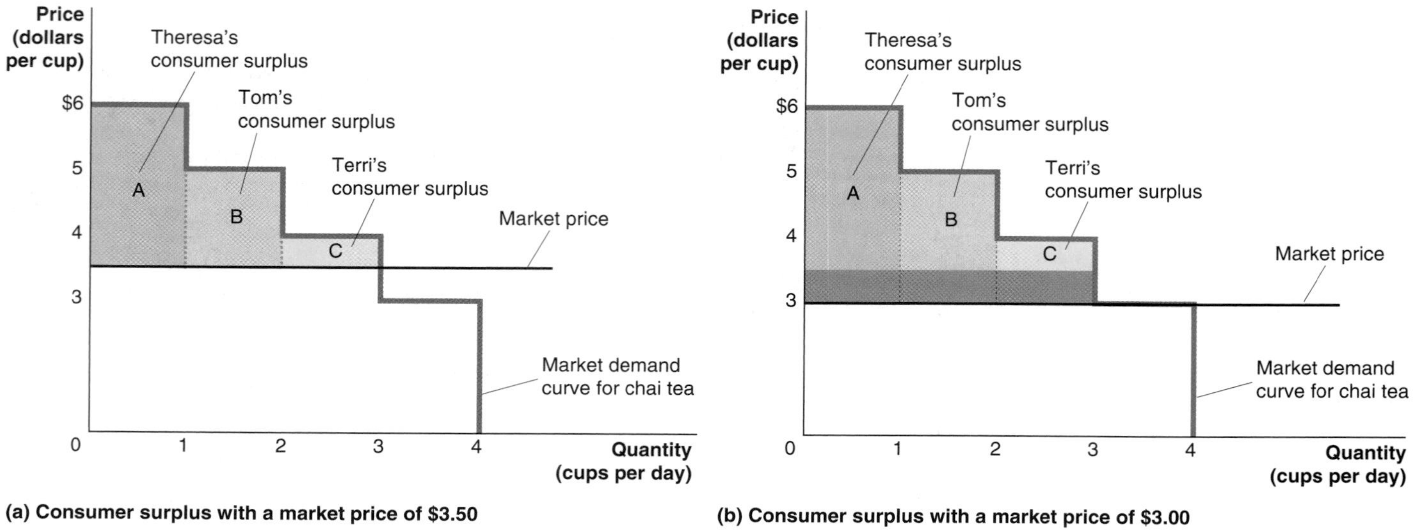

Figure 4-2 | Measuring Consumer Surplus

Panel (a) shows the consumer surplus for Theresa, Tom, and Terri when the price of tea is $3.50 per cup. Theresa's consumer surplus is equal to the area of rectangle *A* and is the difference between the highest price she would pay—$6—and the market price of $3.50. Tom's consumer surplus is equal to the area of rectangle *B*, and Terri's consumer surplus is equal to the area of rectangle *C*. Total consumer surplus in this market is equal to the sum of the areas of rectangles *A*, *B*, and *C*, or the total area below the demand curve and above the market price. In panel (b), consumer surplus increases by the shaded area as the market price declines from $3.50 to $3.00.

4-2: by adding up the consumer surplus received on each unit purchased. Once again, we can draw an important conclusion: *The total amount of consumer surplus in a market is equal to the area below the demand curve and above the market price.* Consumer surplus is shown as the blue area in Figure 4-3 and represents the benefit to consumers in excess of the price they paid to purchase the product—in this case, chai tea.

Figure 4-3

Total Consumer Surplus in the Market for Chai Tea

The demand curve tells us that most buyers of chai tea would have been willing to pay more than the market price of $2.00. For each buyer, consumer surplus is equal to the difference between the highest price he or she is willing to pay and the market price actually paid. Therefore, the total amount of consumer surplus in the market for chai tea is equal to the area below the demand curve and above the market price. Consumer surplus represents the benefit to consumers in excess of the price they paid to purchase the product.

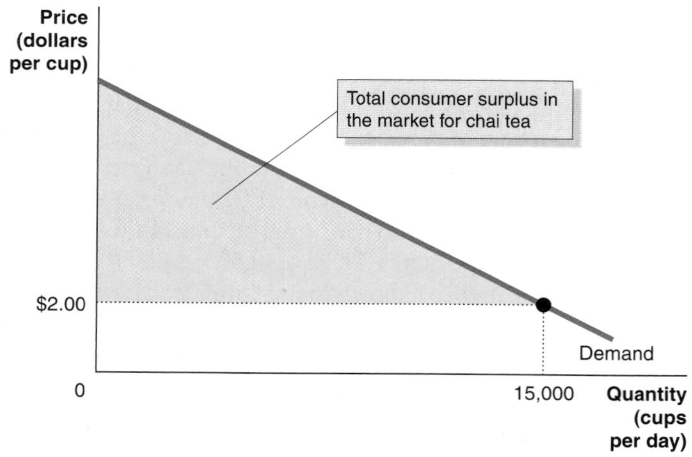

Making the Connection | The Consumer Surplus from Satellite Television

Consumer surplus allows us to measure the benefit consumers receive in excess of the price they paid to purchase a product. Recently, Austan Goolsbee and Amil Petrin, economists at the Graduate

School of Business at the University of Chicago, estimated the consumer surplus that households receive from subscribing to satellite television. To do this, they estimated the demand curve for satellite television and then computed the shaded area shown in the graph.

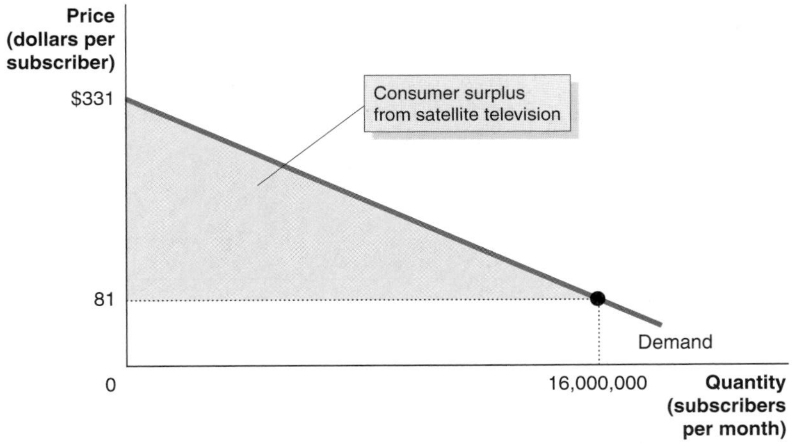

In 2001, the year for which the study was conducted, 16 million consumers paid an average price of $81 per month to subscribe to DIRECTV or DISH Network, the two main providers of satellite television. The demand curve shows that many consumers would have been willing to pay more than $81 rather than do without satellite television. Goolsbee and Petrin calculated that the consumer surplus for households subscribing to satellite television averaged $127 per month, which is the difference between the price they would have paid and the $81 they did pay. The shaded area on the graph represents the total consumer surplus in the market for satellite television. Goolsbee and Petrin estimate that the value of this area is $2 billion. This is one year's benefit to the consumers who subscribe to satellite television.

Source: Austan Goolsbee and Amil Petrin, "The Consumer Gains from Direct Broadcast Satellites and the Competition with Cable TV," *Econometrica*, Vol. 72, No. 2, March 2004, pp. 351–381.

YOUR TURN: Test your understanding by doing related problem 1.8 on page 124 at the end of this chapter.

Producer Surplus

Just as demand curves show the willingness of consumers to buy a product at different prices, supply curves show the willingness of firms to supply a product at different prices. The willingness to supply a product depends on the cost of producing it. Firms will supply an additional unit of a product only if they receive a price equal to the additional cost of producing that unit. **Marginal cost** is the additional cost to a firm of producing one more unit of a good or service. Consider the marginal cost to the firm Heavenly Tea of producing one more cup: In this case, the marginal cost includes the ingredients to make the tea and the wages paid to the worker preparing the tea. Often, the marginal cost of producing a good increases as more of the good is produced during a given period of time. This is the key reason—as we saw in Chapter 3—that supply curves are upward sloping.

Marginal cost The additional cost to a firm of producing one more unit of a good or service.

Panel (a) of Figure 4-4 shows Heavenly Tea's producer surplus. For simplicity, we show Heavenly producing only a small quantity of tea. The figure shows that Heavenly's marginal cost of producing the first cup of tea is $1.00. Its marginal cost of producing

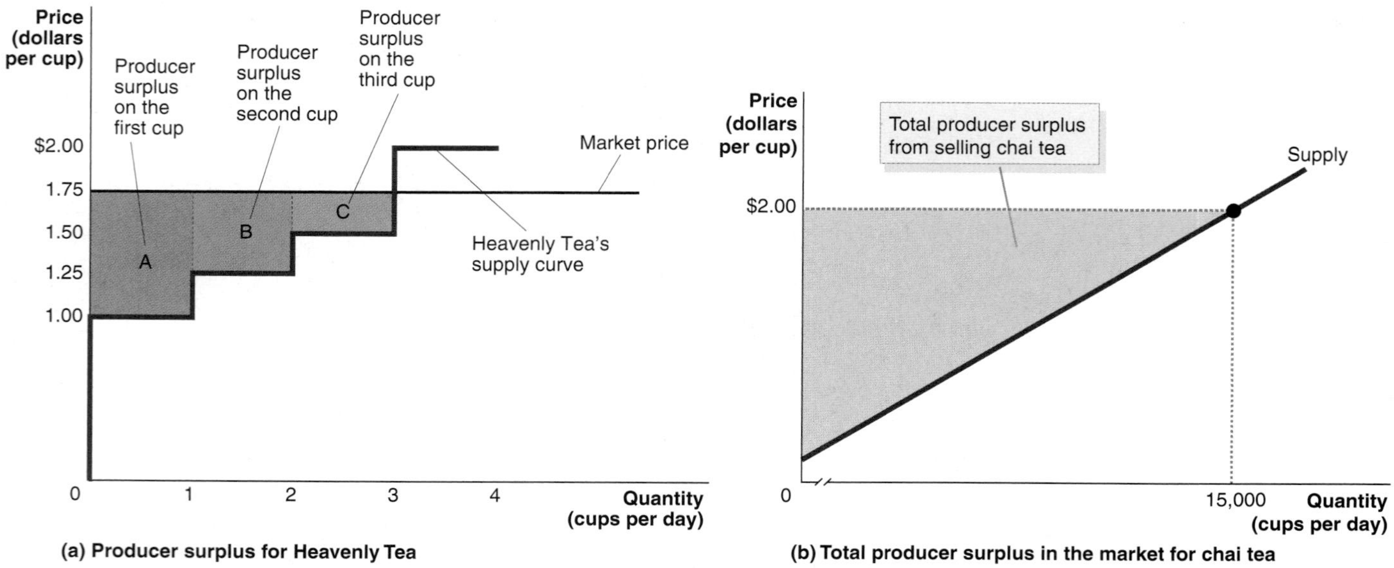

Figure 4-4 | Calculating Producer Surplus

Panel (a) shows Heavenly Tea's producer surplus. Producer surplus is the difference between the lowest price a firm would be willing to accept and the price it actually receives. The lowest price Heavenly Tea is willing to accept to supply a cup of tea is equal to its marginal cost of producing that cup. When the market price of tea is $1.75, Heavenly receives producer surplus of $0.75 on the first cup (the area of rectangle *A*), $0.50 on the second cup (rectangle *B*), and $0.25 on the third cup (rectangle *C*). In panel (b), the total amount of producer surplus tea sellers receive from selling chai tea can be calculated by adding up for the entire market the producer surplus received on each cup sold. In the figure, total producer surplus is equal to the area above the supply curve and below the market price, shown in red.

Producer surplus The difference between the lowest price a firm would be willing to accept and the price it actually receives.

the second cup is $1.25, and so on. The marginal cost of each cup of tea is the lowest price Heavenly is willing to accept to supply that cup. The supply curve, then, is also a marginal cost curve. Suppose the market price of tea is $1.75 per cup. On the first cup of tea, the price is $0.75 higher than the lowest price Heavenly is willing to accept. **Producer surplus** is the difference between the lowest price a firm would be willing to accept and the price it actually receives. Therefore, Heavenly's producer surplus on the first cup is $0.75 (shown by the area of rectangle *A*). Its producer surplus on the second cup is $0.50 (rectangle *B*). Its producer surplus on the third cup is $0.25 (rectangle *C*). Heavenly will not be willing to supply the fourth cup because the marginal cost of producing it is greater than the market price. Heavenly Tea's total producer surplus is equal to $0.75 + $0.50 + $0.25 = $1.50 (or the sum of rectangles *A*, *B*, and *C*). A higher price will increase producer surplus. For example, if the market price of chai tea rises from $1.75 to $2.00, Heavenly Tea's producer surplus will increase from $1.50 to $2.25. (Make sure you understand how the new level of producer surplus was calculated.)

The supply curve shown in panel (a) of Figure 4-4 does not look like the smooth curves we saw in Chapter 3 because this example uses a single firm producing only a small quantity of tea. With many firms, the market supply curve for chai tea will have the normal smooth shape shown in panel (b) of Figure 4-4. In panel (b), the quantity supplied at a price of $2.00 is 15,000 cups per day. We can calculate total producer surplus in panel (b) the same way we did in panel (a): by adding up the producer surplus received on each cup sold. Therefore, *the total amount of producer surplus in a market is equal to the area above the market supply curve and below the market price.* The total producer surplus tea sellers receive from selling chai tea is shown as the red area in panel (b) of Figure 4-4.

What Consumer Surplus and Producer Surplus Measure

We have seen that consumer surplus measures the benefit to consumers from participating in a market, and producer surplus measures the benefit to producers from participating in a market. It is important, however, to be clear what we mean by this. In a sense, consumer surplus measures the *net* benefit to consumers from participating in a market rather than the *total* benefit. That is, if the price of a product were zero, the consumer surplus in a market would be all of the area under the demand curve. When the price is not zero, consumer surplus is the area below the demand curve and above the market price. So, consumer surplus in a market is equal to the total benefit received by consumers minus the total amount they must pay to buy the good.

Similarly, producer surplus measures the *net* benefit received by producers from participating in a market. If producers could supply a good at zero cost, the producer surplus in a market would be all of the area below the market price. When cost is not zero, producer surplus is the area below the market price and above the supply curve. So, producer surplus in a market is equal to the total amount firms receive from consumers minus the cost of producing the good.

4.2 LEARNING OBJECTIVE

4.2 | Understand the concept of economic efficiency.

The Efficiency of Competitive Markets

In Chapter 3, we defined a *competitive market* as a market with many buyers and many sellers. An important advantage of the market system is that it results in efficient economic outcomes. But what do we mean by *economic efficiency*? The concepts we have developed so far in this chapter give us two ways to think about the economic efficiency of competitive markets. We can think in terms of marginal benefit and marginal cost. We can also think in terms of consumer surplus and producer surplus. As we will see, these two approaches lead to the same outcome, but using both can increase our understanding of economic efficiency.

Marginal Benefit Equals Marginal Cost in Competitive Equilibrium

Figure 4-5 again shows the market for chai tea. Recall from our discussion that the demand curve shows the marginal benefit received by consumers, and the supply curve shows the marginal cost of production. To achieve economic efficiency in this market, the marginal

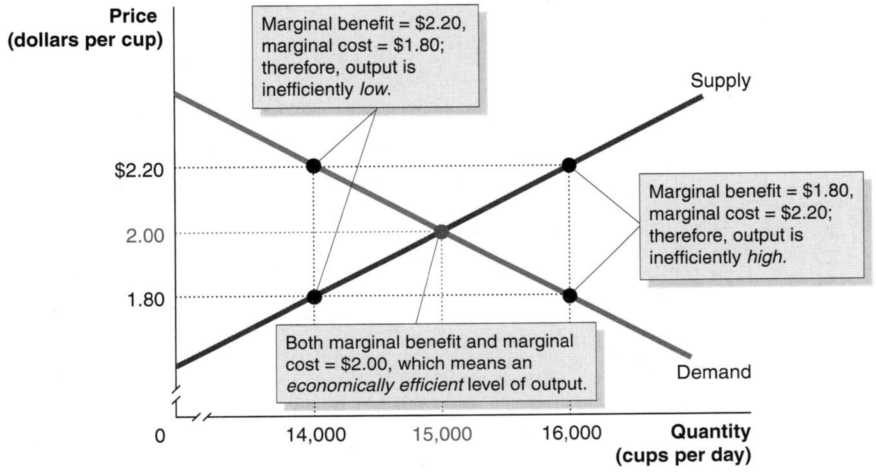

Figure 4-5

Marginal Benefit Equals Marginal Cost Only at Competitive Equilibrium

In a competitive market, equilibrium occurs at a quantity of 15,000 cups and price of $2.00 per cup, where marginal benefit equals marginal cost. This is the economically efficient level of output because every cup has been produced where the marginal benefit to buyers is greater than or equal to the marginal cost to producers.

benefit from the last unit sold should equal the marginal cost of production. The figure shows that this equality occurs at competitive equilibrium where 15,000 cups per day are produced, and marginal benefit and marginal cost are both equal to $2.00. Why is this outcome economically efficient? Because every cup of chai tea has been produced where the marginal benefit to buyers is greater than or equal to the marginal cost to producers.

Another way to see why the level of output at competitive equilibrium is efficient is to consider what would be true if output were at a different level. For instance, suppose that output of chai tea were 14,000 cups per day. Figure 4-5 shows that at this level of output, the marginal benefit from the last cup sold is $2.20, whereas the marginal cost is only $1.80. This level of output is not efficient because 1,000 more cups could be produced for which the additional benefit to consumers would be greater than the additional cost of production. Consumers would willingly purchase those cups, and tea sellers would willingly supply them, making both consumers and sellers better off. Similarly, if the output of chai tea were 16,000 cups per day, the marginal cost of the 16,000th cup is $2.20, whereas the marginal benefit is only $1.80. Tea sellers would only be willing to supply this cup at a price of $2.20, which is $0.40 higher than consumers would be willing to pay. In fact, consumers would not be willing to pay the price tea sellers would need to receive for any cup beyond the 15,000th.

To summarize, we can say this: *Equilibrium in a competitive market results in the economically efficient level of output, where marginal benefit equals marginal cost.*

Economic Surplus

Economic surplus The sum of consumer surplus and producer surplus.

Economic surplus in a market is the sum of consumer surplus and producer surplus. In a competitive market, with many buyers and sellers and no government restrictions, economic surplus is at a maximum when the market is in equilibrium. To see this, let's look one more time at the market for chai tea shown in Figure 4-6. The consumer surplus in this market is the blue area below the demand curve and above the line indicating the equilibrium price of $2.00. The producer surplus is the red area above the supply curve and below the price line.

Deadweight Loss

To show that economic surplus is maximized at equilibrium, consider the situation in which the price of chai tea is *above* the equilibrium price, as shown in Figure 4-7. At a price of $2.20 per cup, the number of cups consumers are willing to buy per day drops from 15,000 to 14,000. At competitive equilibrium, consumer surplus is equal to the sum of areas *A*, *B*, and *C*. At a price of $2.20, fewer cups are sold at a higher price, so consumer surplus declines to just the area of *A*. At competitive equilibrium, producer surplus is equal to the sum of areas *D* and *E*. At the higher price of $2.20, producer surplus changes to be equal to the sum of areas *B* and *D*. The sum of consumer and producer surplus—economic surplus—has been reduced to the sum of areas *A*, *B*, and *D*. Notice that this is less than the original economic surplus by an amount equal to areas *C* and *E*.

Figure 4-6

Economic Surplus Equals the Sum of Consumer Surplus and Producer Surplus

The economic surplus in a market is the sum of the blue area representing consumer surplus and the red area representing producer surplus.

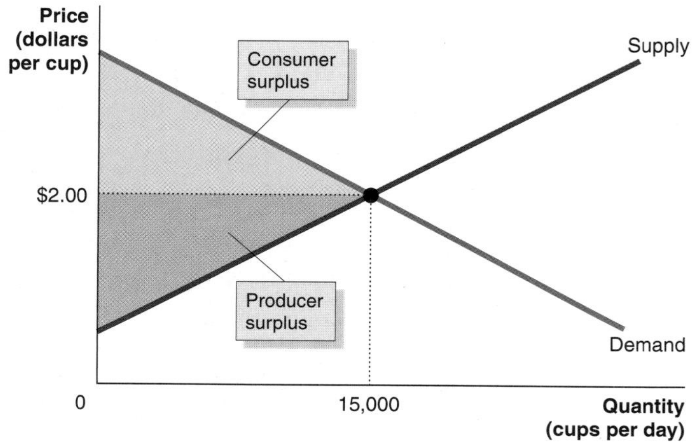

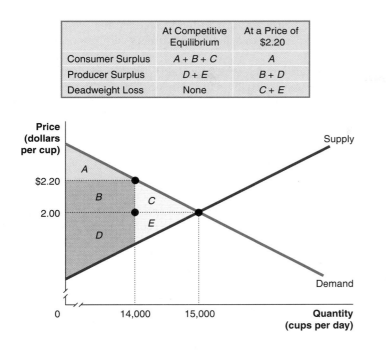

	At Competitive Equilibrium	At a Price of $2.20
Consumer Surplus	*A* + *B* + *C*	*A*
Producer Surplus	*D* + *E*	*B* + *D*
Deadweight Loss	None	*C* + *E*

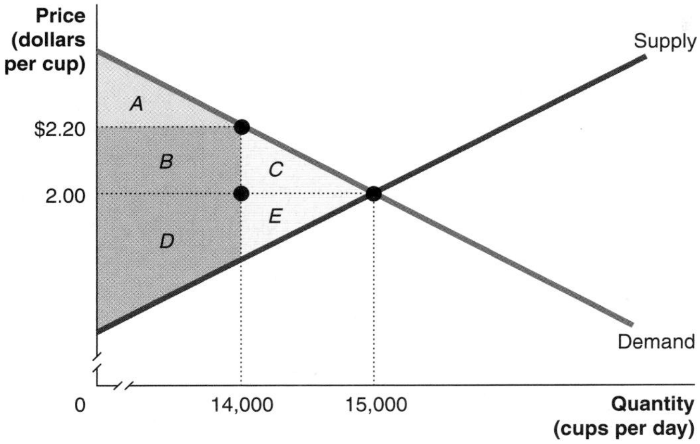

Figure 4-7

When a Market Is Not in Equilibrium, There Is a Deadweight Loss

Economic surplus is maximized when a market is in competitive equilibrium. When a market is not in equilibrium, there is a deadweight loss. When the price of chai tea is $2.20, instead of $2.00, consumer surplus declines from an amount equal to the sum of areas *A*, *B*, and *C* to just area *A*. Producer surplus increases from the sum of areas *D* and *E* to the sum of areas *B* and *D*. At competitive equilibrium, there is no deadweight loss. At a price of $2.20, there is a deadweight loss equal to the sum of areas *C* and *E*.

Economic surplus has declined because at a price of $2.20, all the cups between the 14,000th and the 15,000th, which would have been produced in competitive equilibrium, are not being produced. These "missing" cups are not providing any consumer or producer surplus, so economic surplus has declined. The reduction in economic surplus resulting from a market not being in competitive equilibrium is called the **deadweight loss**. In the figure, it is equal to the sum of areas *C* and *E*.

Deadweight loss The reduction in economic surplus resulting from a market not being in competitive equilibrium.

Economic Surplus and Economic Efficiency

Consumer surplus measures the benefit to consumers from buying a particular product, such as chai tea. Producer surplus measures the benefit to firms from selling a particular product. Therefore, economic surplus—which is the sum of the benefit to firms plus the benefit to consumers—is the best measure we have of the benefit to society from the production of a particular good or service. This gives us a second way of characterizing the economic efficiency of a competitive market: *Equilibrium in a competitive market results in the greatest amount of economic surplus, or total net benefit to society, from the production of a good or service.* Anything that causes the market for a good or service not to be in competitive equilibrium reduces the total benefit to society from the production of that good or service.

Now we can give a more general definition of *economic efficiency* in terms of our two approaches: **Economic efficiency** is a market outcome in which the marginal benefit to consumers of the last unit produced is equal to its marginal cost of production and in which the sum of consumer surplus and producer surplus is at a maximum.

Economic efficiency A market outcome in which the marginal benefit to consumers of the last unit produced is equal to its marginal cost of production and in which the sum of consumer surplus and producer surplus is at a maximum.

4.3 LEARNING OBJECTIVE

4.3 | Explain the economic effect of government-imposed price ceilings and price floors.

Government Intervention in the Market: Price Floors and Price Ceilings

Notice that we have *not* concluded that every *individual* is better off if a market is at competitive equilibrium. We have only concluded that economic surplus, or the *total* net benefit to society, is greatest at competitive equilibrium. Any individual producer would rather charge a higher price, and any individual consumer would rather pay a lower price, but usually producers can sell and consumers can buy only at the competitive equilibrium price.

Producers or consumers who are dissatisfied with the competitive equilibrium price can lobby the government to legally require that a different price be charged. The U.S. government only occasionally overrides the market outcome by setting prices. When the government does intervene, it can either attempt to aid sellers by requiring that a price be above equilibrium—a price floor—or aid buyers by requiring that a price be below equilibrium—a price ceiling. To affect the market outcome, a price floor must be set above the equilibrium price and a price ceiling must be set below the equilibrium price. Otherwise, the price ceiling or price floor will not be *binding* on buyers and sellers. The preceding section demonstrates that moving away from competitive equilibrium will reduce economic efficiency. We can use the concepts of consumer surplus, producer surplus, and deadweight loss to see more clearly the economic inefficiency of binding price floors and price ceilings.

Price Floors: Government Policy in Agricultural Markets

The Great Depression of the 1930s was the greatest economic disaster in U.S. history, affecting every sector of the U.S. economy. Many farmers were unable to sell their products or could sell them only at very low prices. Farmers were able to convince the federal government to intervene to raise prices by setting price floors for many agricultural products. Government intervention in agriculture—often referred to as the "farm program"—has continued ever since. To see how a price floor in an agricultural market works, suppose that the equilibrium price in the wheat market is \$3.00 per bushel but the government decides to set a price floor of \$3.50 per bushel. As Figure 4-8 shows, the price of wheat rises from \$3.00 to \$3.50, and the quantity of wheat sold falls from 2.0 billion bushels per year to 1.8 billion. Initially, suppose that production of wheat also falls to 1.8 billion bushels.

Just as we saw in the earlier example of the market for chai tea (refer to Figure 4-7), the producer surplus received by wheat farmers increases by an amount equal to the area of the red rectangle *A* and falls by an amount equal to the area of the yellow triangle *C*. The area of the red rectangle *A* represents a transfer from consumer surplus to producer surplus. The total fall in consumer surplus is equal to the area of the red rectangle *A* plus the area of the yellow triangle *B*. Wheat farmers benefit from this program, but consumers lose. There is also a deadweight loss equal to the areas of the yellow triangles *B* and *C*, which represents the decline in economic efficiency due to the price floor. There

Figure 4-8

The Economic Effect of a Price Floor in the Wheat Market

If wheat farmers convince the government to impose a price floor of \$3.50 per bushel, the amount of wheat sold will fall from 2.0 billion bushels per year to 1.8 billion. If we assume that farmers produce 1.8 billion bushels, producer surplus then increases by the red rectangle *A*—which is transferred from consumer surplus—and falls by the yellow triangle *C*. Consumer surplus declines by the red rectangle *A* plus the yellow triangle *B*. There is a deadweight loss equal to the yellow triangles *B* and *C*, representing the decline in economic efficiency due to the price floor. In reality, a price floor of \$3.50 per bushel will cause farmers to expand their production from 2.0 billion to 2.2 billion bushels, resulting in a surplus of wheat.

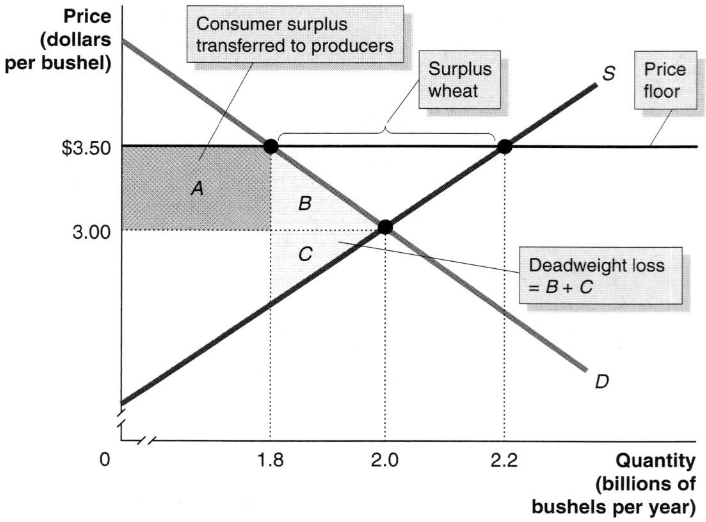

is a deadweight loss because the price floor has reduced the amount of economic surplus in the market for wheat. Or, looked at another way, the price floor has caused the marginal benefit of the last bushel of wheat to be greater than the marginal cost of producing it. We can conclude that a price floor reduces economic efficiency.

The actual federal government farm programs have been more complicated than just legally requiring farmers not to sell their output below a minimum price. We assumed initially that farmers reduce their production of wheat to the amount consumers are willing to buy. In fact, as Figure 4-8 shows, a price floor will cause the quantity of wheat that farmers want to supply to increase from 2.0 billion to 2.2 billion bushels. Because the higher price also reduces the amount of wheat consumers wish to buy, the result is a surplus of 0.4 billion bushels of wheat (the 2.2 billion bushels supplied minus the 1.8 billion demanded).

The federal government's farm programs have often resulted in large surpluses of wheat and other agricultural products. The government has usually either bought the surplus food or paid farmers to restrict supply by taking some land out of cultivation. Because both of these options are expensive, Congress passed the Freedom to Farm Act of 1996. The intent of the act was to phase out price floors and government purchases of surpluses and return to a free market in agriculture. To allow farmers time to adjust, the federal government began paying farmers *subsidies*, or cash payments based on the number of acres planted. Although the subsidies were originally scheduled to be phased out, Congress has continued to pay them.

Making the Connection | Price Floors in Labor Markets: The Debate over Minimum Wage Policy

The minimum wage may be the most controversial "price floor." Supporters see the minimum wage as a way of raising the incomes of low-skilled workers. Opponents argue that it results in fewer jobs and imposes large costs on small businesses.

In summer 2008, the national minimum wage as set by Congress is \$6.55 per hour for most occupations. (The minimum wage is scheduled to increase to \$7.25 per hour in 2009.) It is illegal for an employer to pay less than this wage in those occupations. For most workers, the minimum wage is irrelevant because it is well below the wage employers are voluntarily willing to pay them. But for low-skilled workers—such as workers in fast-food restaurants—the minimum wage is above the wage they would otherwise receive. The following figure shows the effect of the minimum wage on employment in the market for low-skilled labor.

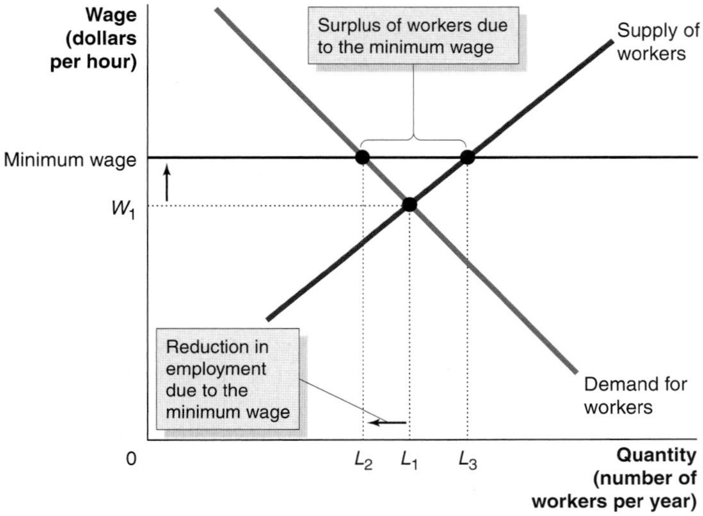

Without a minimum wage, the equilibrium wage would be W_1, and the number of workers hired would be L_1. With a minimum wage set above the equilibrium wage, the quantity of workers demanded by employers declines from L_1 to L_2, and the quantity of labor supplied increases to L_3, leading to a surplus of workers unable to find jobs equal to $L_3 - L_2$. The quantity of labor supplied increases because the higher wage attracts more people to work. For instance, some teenagers may decide that working after school is worthwhile at the minimum wage of \$6.55 per hour but would not be worthwhile at a lower wage.

This analysis is very similar to our analysis of the wheat market in Figure 4-8. Just as a price floor in the wheat market leads to less wheat consumed, a price floor in the labor market should lead to fewer workers hired. Views differ sharply among economists, however, concerning how large a reduction in employment the minimum wage causes. For instance, David Card of the University of California, Berkeley, and Alan Krueger of Princeton University conducted a study of fast-food restaurants in New Jersey and Pennsylvania that indicates that the effect of minimum wage increases on employment is very small. Card and Krueger's study has been very controversial, however. Other economists have examined similar data and have come to the different conclusion that the minimum wage leads to a significant decrease in employment.

Whatever the extent of employment losses from the minimum wage, because it is a price floor, it will cause a deadweight loss, just as a price floor in the wheat market does. Therefore, many economists favor alternative policies for attaining the goal of raising the incomes of low-skilled workers. One policy many economists support is the *earned income tax credit.* The earned income tax credit reduces the amount of tax that low-income wage earners would otherwise pay to the federal government. Workers with very low incomes who do not owe any tax receive a payment from the government. Compared with the minimum wage, the earned income tax credit can increase the incomes of low-skilled workers without reducing employment. The earned income tax credit also places a lesser burden on the small businesses that employ many low-skilled workers, and it might cause a smaller loss of economic efficiency.

Sources: David Card and Alan B. Krueger, *Myth and Measurement: The New Economics of the Minimum Wage*, Princeton, NJ: Princeton University Press, 1995; David Neumark and William Wascher, "Minimum Wages and Employment: A Case Study of the Fast-Food Industry in New Jersey and Pennsylvania: Comment," *American Economic Review*, Vol. 90, No. 5, December 2000, pp. 1362–1396; and David Card and Alan B. Krueger, "Minimum Wages and Employment: A Case Study of the Fast-Food Industry in New Jersey and Pennsylvania: Reply," *American Economic Review*, Vol. 90, No. 5, December 2000, pp. 1397–1420.

YOUR TURN: Test your understanding by doing related problem 3.12 on page 127 at the end of this chapter.

Price Ceilings: Government Rent Control Policy in Housing Markets

Support for governments setting price floors typically comes from sellers, and support for governments setting price ceilings typically comes from consumers. For example, when there is a sharp increase in gasoline prices, there are often proposals for the government to impose a price ceiling on the market for gasoline. As we saw in the opener to this chapter, New York is one of the cities that imposes rent controls, which put a ceiling on the maximum rent that landlords can charge for an apartment. Figure 4-9 shows the market for apartments in a city that has rent controls.

Without rent control, the equilibrium rent would be \$1,500 per month, and 2,000,000 apartments would be rented. With a maximum legal rent of \$1,000 per month, landlords reduce the quantity of apartments supplied to 1,900,000. The fall in the quantity of apartments supplied is the result of some apartments being converted to offices or sold off as condominiums, some small apartment buildings being converted to single-family homes, and, over time, some apartment buildings being abandoned. In New York City, rent control has resulted in whole city blocks being abandoned by land-

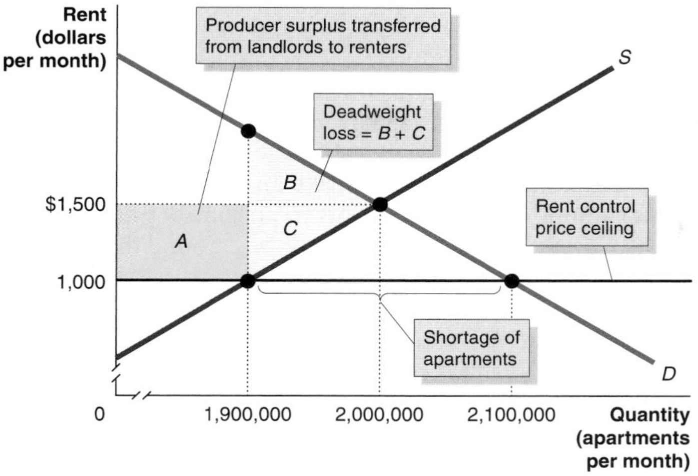

Figure 4-9

The Economic Effect of a Rent Ceiling

Without rent control, the equilibrium rent is $1,500 per month. At that price, 2,000,000 apartments would be rented. If the government imposes a rent ceiling of $1,000, the quantity of apartments supplied falls to 1,900,000, and the quantity of apartments demanded increases to 2,100,000, resulting in a shortage of 200,000 apartments. Producer surplus equal to the area of the blue rectangle *A* is transferred from landlords to renters, and there is a deadweight loss equal to the areas of yellow triangles *B* and *C*.

lords who were unable to cover their costs with the rents they were allowed to charge. In London, when rent controls were applied to rooms and apartments located in a landlord's own home, the quantity of these apartments supplied dropped by 75 percent.

In Figure 4-9, with the rent ceiling of $1,000, the quantity of apartments demanded rises to 2,100,000. There is a shortage of 200,000 apartments. Consumer surplus increases by rectangle *A* and falls by triangle *B*. Rectangle *A* would have been part of producer surplus if rent control were not in place. With rent control, it is part of consumer surplus. Rent control causes the producer surplus received by landlords to fall by rectangle *A* plus triangle *C*. Triangles *B* and *C* represent the deadweight loss. There is a deadweight loss because rent control has reduced the amount of economic surplus in the market for apartments. Rent control has caused the marginal benefit of the last apartment rented to be greater than the marginal cost of supplying it. We can conclude that a price ceiling, such as rent control, reduces economic efficiency. The appendix to this chapter shows how we can make quantitative estimates of the deadweight loss, and it shows the changes in consumer surplus and producer surplus that result from rent control.

Renters as a group benefit from rent controls—total consumer surplus is larger—but landlords lose. Because of the deadweight loss, the total loss to landlords is greater than the gain to renters. Notice also that although renters as a group benefit, the number of renters is reduced, so some renters are made worse off by rent controls because they are unable to find an apartment at the legal rent.

Don't Let This Happen to **YOU!**

Don't Confuse "Scarcity" with a "Shortage"

At first glance, the following statement seems correct: "There is a shortage of every good that is scarce." In everyday conversation, we describe a good as "scarce" if we have trouble finding it. For instance, if you are looking for a present for a child, you might call the latest hot toy "scarce" if you are willing to buy it at its listed price but can't find it online or in any store. But recall from Chapter 2 that economists have a broad definition of *scarce*. In the economic sense, almost everything—except undesirable things like garbage—is scarce. A shortage of a good occurs only if the quantity demanded is greater than the quantity supplied at the current price. Therefore, the preceding statement—"There is a shortage of every good that is scarce"—is incorrect. In fact, there is no shortage of most scarce goods.

YOUR TURN: Test your understanding by doing related problem 3.16 on page 128 at the end of this chapter.

Black Markets

To this point, our analysis of rent controls is incomplete. In practice, renters may be worse off and landlords may be better off than Figure 4-9 makes it seem. We have assumed that renters and landlords actually abide by the price ceiling, but sometimes they don't. Because rent control leads to a shortage of apartments, renters who would otherwise not be able to find apartments have an incentive to offer landlords rents above the legal maximum. When governments try to control prices by setting price ceilings or price floors, buyers and sellers often find a way around the controls. The result is a **black market** where buying and selling take place at prices that violate government price regulations.

Black market A market in which buying and selling take place at prices that violate government price regulations.

In a housing market with rent controls, the total amount of consumer surplus received by renters may be reduced and the total amount of producer surplus received by landlords may be increased if apartments are being rented at prices above the legal price ceiling.

Solved Problem | **4-3**

What's the Economic Effect of a "Black Market" for Apartments?

In many cities with rent controls, the actual rents paid can be much higher than the legal maximum. Because rent controls cause a shortage of apartments, desperate tenants are often willing to pay landlords rents that are higher than the law allows, perhaps by writing a check for the legally allowed rent and paying an additional amount in cash. Look again at Figure 4-9 on page 111. Suppose that competition among tenants results in the black market rent rising to $2,000 per month. At this rent, tenants demand 1,900,000 apartments. Use a graph showing the market for apartments to compare this situation with the one shown in Figure 4-9. Be sure to note any differences in consumer surplus, producer surplus, and deadweight loss.

SOLVING THE PROBLEM:

Step 1: **Review the chapter material.** This problem is about price controls in the market for apartments, so you may want to review the section "Price Ceilings: Government Rent Control Policy in Housing Markets," which begins on page 110.

Step 2: **Draw a graph similar to Figure 4-9, with the addition of the black market price.**

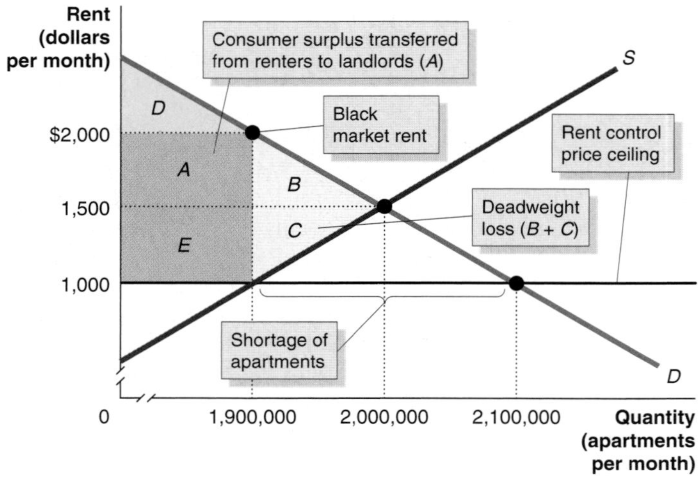

Step 3: **Analyze the changes from Figure 4-9.** Because the black market rent is now \$2,000—even higher than the original competitive equilibrium rent of \$1,500—compared with Figure 4-9, consumer surplus declines by an amount equal to the red rectangle *A* plus the red rectangle *E*. The remaining consumer surplus is the blue triangle *D*. Note that the rectangle *A*, which would have been part of consumer surplus without rent control, represents a transfer from renters to landlords. Compared with the situation shown in Figure 4-9, producer surplus has increased by an amount equal to rectangles *A* and *E*, and consumer surplus has declined by the same amount. Deadweight loss is equal to triangles *B* and *C*, the same as in Figure 4-9.

EXTRA CREDIT: This analysis leads to a surprising result: With an active black market in apartments, rent control may leave renters as a group worse off—with less consumer surplus—than if there were no rent control. There is one more possibility to consider, however. If enough landlords become convinced that they can get away with charging rents above the legal ceiling, the quantity of apartments supplied will increase. Eventually, the market could even end up at the competitive equilibrium, with an equilibrium rent of \$1,500 and equilibrium quantity of 2,000,000 apartments. In that case the rent control price ceiling becomes nonbinding, not because it was set below the equilibrium price but because it was not legally enforced.

YOUR TURN: For more practice, do related problems 3.14 on page 127 and 3.23 on page 129 at the end of this chapter.

>> End Solved Problem 4-3

Rent controls can also lead to an increase in racial and other types of discrimination. With rent controls, more renters are looking for apartments than there are apartments to rent. Landlords can afford to indulge their prejudices by refusing to rent to people they don't like. In cities without rent controls, landlords face more competition, which makes it more difficult to turn down tenants on the basis of irrelevant characteristics, such as race.

Making the Connection

Does Holiday Gift Giving Have a Deadweight Loss?

The deadweight loss that results from rent control occurs, in part, because consumers rent fewer apartments than they would in a competitive equilibrium. Their choices are *constrained* by government. When you receive a gift, you are also constrained because the person who gave the gift has already chosen the product. In many cases, you would have chosen a different gift for yourself. Economist Joel Waldfogel of the University of Pennsylvania points out that gift giving results in a deadweight loss. The amount of the deadweight loss is equal to the difference between the gift's price and the dollar value the recipient places on the gift. Waldfogel surveyed his students, asking them to list every gift they had received for Christmas, to estimate the retail price of each gift, and to state how much they would have been willing to pay for each gift. Waldfogel's students estimated that their families and friends had paid \$438 on average for the students' gifts. The students themselves, however, would have been willing to pay only \$313 to buy the presents. If the deadweight losses experienced by Waldfogel's students were extrapolated to the whole population, the deadweight loss of Christmas gift giving could be as much as \$13 billion.

Gift giving may lead to deadweight loss.

If the gifts had been cash, the people receiving the gifts would not have been constrained by the gift givers' choices, and there would have been no deadweight loss. If your sister had given you cash instead of that sweater you didn't like, you could have bought whatever you wanted. Why then do people continue giving presents rather than cash? One answer is that most people receive more satisfaction from giving or receiving a present than from giving or receiving cash. If we take this satisfaction into account, the deadweight loss from gift giving will be lower than in Waldfogel's calculations. In fact, a later study by economists John List of the University of Maryland and Jason Shogren of the University of Wyoming showed that as much as half the value of a gift to a recipient was its sentimental value. As Professor Shogren concluded, "People get a whole heck of a lot of value out of doing something for others and other people doing something for them. Aunt Helga gave you that ugly scarf, but hey, it's Aunt Helga."

Sources: Mark Whitehouse, "How Christmas Brings Out the Grinch in Economists," *Wall Street Journal*, December 23, 2006, p. A1; Joel Waldfogel, "The Deadweight Loss of Christmas," *American Economic Review*, Vol. 83, No. 4, December 1993, pp. 328–336; and John A. List and Jason F. Shogren, "The Deadweight Loss of Christmas: Comment," *American Economic Review*, Vol. 88, No, 5, 1998, pp. 1350–1355.

YOUR TURN: Test your understanding by doing related problem 3.15 on page 128 at the end of this chapter.

The Results of Government Price Controls: Winners, Losers, and Inefficiency

When the government imposes price floors or price ceilings, three important results occur:

- Some people win.
- Some people lose.
- There is a loss of economic efficiency.

The winners with rent control are the people who are paying less for rent because they live in rent-controlled apartments. Landlords may also gain if they break the law by charging rents above the legal maximum for their rent-controlled apartments, provided that those illegal rents are higher than the competitive equilibrium rents would be. The losers from rent control are the landlords of rent-controlled apartments who abide by the law and renters who are unable to find apartments to rent at the controlled price. Rent control reduces economic efficiency because fewer apartments are rented than would be rented in a competitive market (refer again to Figure 4-9). The resulting deadweight loss measures the decrease in economic efficiency.

Positive and Normative Analysis of Price Ceilings and Price Floors

Are rent controls, government farm programs, and other price ceilings and price floors bad? As we saw in Chapter 1, questions of this type have no right or wrong answers. Economists are generally skeptical of government attempts to interfere with competitive market equilibrium. Economists know the role competitive markets have played in raising the average person's standard of living. They also know that too much government intervention has the potential to reduce the ability of the market system to produce similar increases in living standards in the future.

But recall from Chapter 1 the difference between positive and normative analysis. Positive analysis is concerned with *what is*, and normative analysis is concerned with *what should be*. Our analysis of rent control and of the federal farm programs in this chapter is positive analysis. We discussed the economic results of these programs. Whether these programs are desirable or undesirable is a normative question. Whether the gains to the winners more than make up for the losses to the losers and for the decline in economic efficiency is a matter of judgment and not strictly an economic question. Price ceilings and price floors continue to exist partly because people who understand their downside still believe they are good policies and therefore support them. The policies also persist because many people who support them do not understand the economic analysis in this chapter and so do not understand the drawbacks to these policies.

4.4 | Analyze the economic impact of taxes.

4.4 LEARNING OBJECTIVE

The Economic Impact of Taxes

Supreme Court Justice Oliver Wendell Holmes once remarked, "Taxes are what we pay for a civilized society." When the government taxes a good, however, it affects the market equilibrium for that good. Just as with a price ceiling or price floor, one result of a tax is a decline in economic efficiency. Analyzing taxes is an important part of the field of economics known as *public finance*. In this section, we will use the model of demand and supply and the concepts of consumer surplus, producer surplus, and deadweight loss to analyze the economic impact of taxes.

The Effect of Taxes on Economic Efficiency

Whenever a government taxes a good or service, less of that good or service will be produced and consumed. For example, a tax on cigarettes will raise the cost of smoking and reduce the amount of smoking that takes place. We can use a demand and supply graph to illustrate this point. Figure 4-10 shows the market for cigarettes.

Without the tax, the equilibrium price of cigarettes would be \$4.00 per pack, and 4 billion packs of cigarettes would be sold per year (point *A*). If the federal government requires sellers of cigarettes to pay a \$1.00-per-pack tax, then their cost of selling cigarettes will increase by \$1.00 per pack. This causes the supply curve for cigarettes to

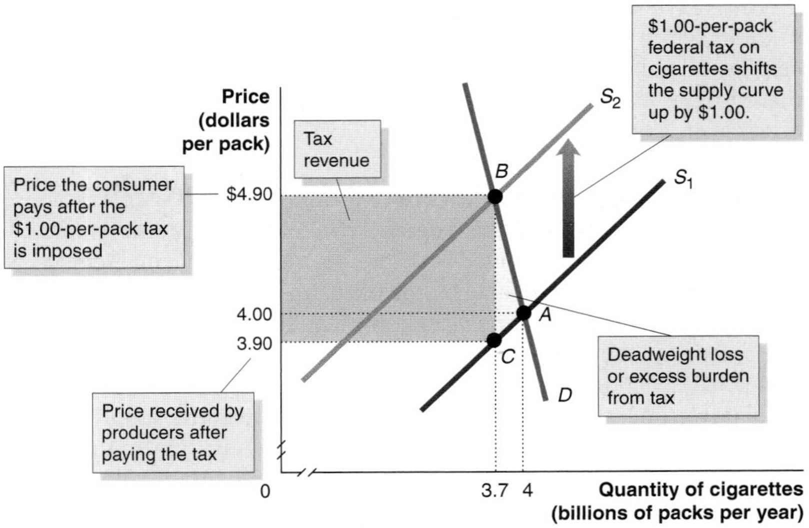

Figure 4-10 | The Effect of a Tax on the Market for Cigarettes

Without the tax, market equilibrium occurs at point *A*. The equilibrium price of cigarettes is \$4.00 per pack, and 4 billion packs of cigarettes are sold per year. A \$1.00-per-pack tax on cigarettes will cause the supply curve for cigarettes to shift up by \$1.00, from S_1 to S_2. The new equilibrium occurs at point *B*. The price of cigarettes will increase by \$0.90, to \$4.90 per pack, and the quantity sold will fall to 3.7 billion packs. The tax on cigarettes has increased the price paid by consumers from \$4.00 to \$4.90 per pack. Producers receive a price of \$4.90 per pack (point *B*), but after paying the \$1.00 tax, they are left with \$3.90 (point *C*). The government will receive tax revenue equal to the green shaded box. Some consumer surplus and some producer surplus will become tax revenue for the government and some will become deadweight loss, shown by the yellow-shaded area.

shift up by $1.00 because sellers will now require a price that is $1.00 greater to supply the same quantity of cigarettes. In Figure 4-10, for example, without the tax, sellers would be willing to supply a quantity of 3.7 billion packs of cigarettes at a price of $3.90 per pack (point *C*). With the tax, they will supply only 3.7 billion packs of cigarettes if the price is $4.90 per pack (point *B*). The shift in the supply curve will result in a new equilibrium price of $4.90 and a new equilibrium quantity of 3.7 billion packs (point *B*).

The federal government will collect tax revenue equal to the tax per pack multiplied by the number of packs sold, or $3.7 billion. The area shaded in green in Figure 4-10 represents the government's tax revenue. Consumers will pay a higher price of $4.90 per pack. Although sellers appear to be receiving a higher price per pack, after they have paid the tax, the price they receive falls from $4.00 per pack to $3.90 per pack. There is a loss of consumer surplus because consumers are paying a higher price. The price producers receive falls, so there is also a loss of producer surplus. Therefore, the tax on cigarettes has reduced *both* consumer surplus and producer surplus. Some of the reduction in consumer and producer surplus becomes tax revenue for the government. The rest of the reduction in consumer and producer surplus is equal to the deadweight loss from the tax, shown by the yellow-shaded triangle in the figure.

We can conclude that the true burden of a tax is not just the amount paid to government by consumers and producers but also includes the deadweight loss. The deadweight loss from a tax is referred to as the *excess burden* of the tax. *A tax is efficient if it imposes a small excess burden relative to the tax revenue it raises.* One contribution economists make to government tax policy is to provide advice to policymakers on which taxes are most efficient.

Tax Incidence: Who Actually Pays a Tax?

Tax incidence The actual division of the burden of a tax between buyers and sellers in a market.

The answer to the question "Who pays a tax?" seems obvious: Whoever is legally required to send a tax payment to the government pays the tax. But there can be an important difference between who is legally required to pay the tax and who actually *bears the burden* of the tax. The actual division of the burden of a tax is referred to as **tax incidence**. The federal government currently levies an excise tax of 18.4 cents per gallon of gasoline sold. Gas station owners collect this tax and forward it to the federal government, but who actually bears the burden of the tax?

Determining Tax Incidence on a Demand and Supply Graph Suppose that the retail price of gasoline—including the federal excise tax—is $3.08 per gallon, 140 billion gallons of gasoline are sold in the United States per year, and the federal excise tax is 10 cents per gallon. Figure 4-11 allows us to analyze the incidence of the tax.

Consider the market for gasoline if there were no federal excise tax on gasoline. This equilibrium occurs at the intersection of the demand curve and supply curve, S_1. The equilibrium price is $3.00 per gallon, and the equilibrium quantity is 144 billion gallons. If the federal government imposes a 10-cents-per-gallon tax, the supply curve for gasoline will shift up by 10 cents per gallon. At the new equilibrium, where the demand curve intersects the supply curve, S_2, the price has risen by 8 cents per gallon, from $3.00 to $3.08. Notice that only in the extremely unlikely case that demand is a vertical line will the market price rise by the full amount of the tax. Consumers are paying 8 cents more per gallon. Sellers of gasoline receive a new higher price of $3.08 per gallon, but after paying the 10-cents-per-gallon tax, they are left with $2.98 per gallon, or 2 cents less than they had been receiving in the old equilibrium.

Although the sellers of gasoline are responsible for collecting the tax and sending the tax receipts to the government, they do not bear most of the burden of the tax. In this case, consumers pay 8 cents of the tax because the market price has risen by 8 cents, and sellers pay 2 cents of the tax because after sending the tax to the government, they are receiving 2 cents less per gallon of gasoline sold. Expressed in percentage terms, consumers pay 80 percent of the tax, and sellers pay 20 percent of the tax.

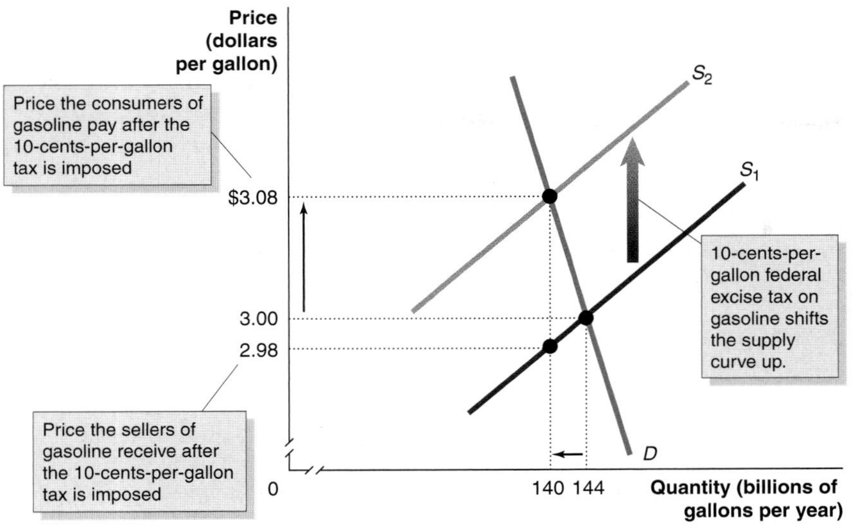

Figure 4-11

The Incidence of a Tax on Gasoline

With no tax on gasoline, the price would be \$3.00 per gallon, and 144 billion gallons of gasoline would be sold each year. A 10-cents-per-gallon excise tax shifts up the supply curve from S_1 to S_2, raises the price consumers pay from \$3.00 to \$3.08, and lowers the price producers receive from \$3.00 to \$2.98. Therefore, consumers pay 8 cents of the 10-cents-per-gallon tax on gasoline, and producers pay 2 cents.

Solved Problem | 4-4

When Do Consumers Pay All of a Sales Tax Increase?

Briefly explain whether you agree with the following statement: "If the federal government raises the sales tax on gasoline by \$0.25, then the price of gasoline will rise by \$0.25. Consumers can't get by without gasoline, so they have to pay the whole amount of any increase in the sales tax." Illustrate your answer with a graph.

SOLVING THE PROBLEM:

Step 1: **Review the chapter material.** This problem is about tax incidence, so you may want to review the section "Tax Incidence: Who Actually Pays a Tax?" which begins on page 116.

Step 2: **Draw a graph like Figure 4-11 to illustrate the circumstances when consumers will pay all of an increase in a sales tax.**

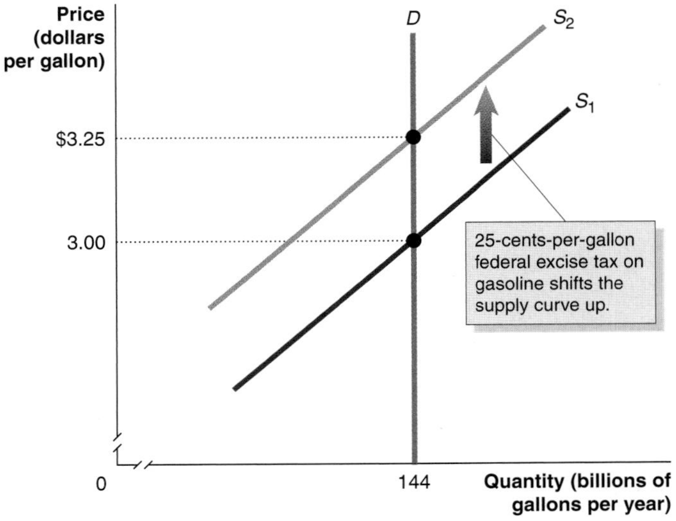

Step 3: Use the graph to evaluate the statement. The graph shows that consumers will pay all of an increase in a sales tax only if the demand curve is a vertical line. It is very unlikely that the demand for gasoline looks like this because we expect that for every good, an increase in price will cause a decrease in the quantity demanded. Because the demand curve for gasoline is not a vertical line, the statement is incorrect.

>> End Solved Problem 4-4

YOUR TURN: For more practice, do related problem 4.5 on page 130 at the end of the chapter.

Does It Matter Whether the Tax Is on Buyers or Sellers? We have already seen the important distinction between the true burden of a tax and whether buyers or sellers are legally required to pay a tax. We can reinforce this point by noting explicitly that the incidence of a tax does *not* depend on whether a tax is collected from the buyers of a good or from the sellers. Figure 4-12 illustrates this point by showing the effect on equilibrium in the market for gasoline if a 10-cents-per-gallon tax is imposed on buyers rather than on sellers. That is, we are now assuming that instead of sellers having to collect the 10-cents-per-gallon tax at the pump, buyers are responsible for keeping track of how many gallons of gasoline they purchase and sending the tax to the government. (Of course, it would be very difficult for buyers to keep track of their purchases or for the government to check whether they were paying all of the tax they owed. That is why the government collects the tax on gasoline from sellers.)

Figure 4-12 is similar to Figure 4-11 except that it shows the gasoline tax being imposed on buyers rather than sellers. In Figure 4-12, the supply curve does not shift because nothing has happened to change the willingness of sellers to change the quantity of gasoline they supply. The demand curve has shifted, however, because consumers now have to pay a 10-cent tax on every gallon of gasoline they buy. Therefore, at every quantity, they are willing to pay a price 10 cents less than they would have without the tax. We indicate this in the figure by shifting the demand curve down by 10 cents, from D_1 to D_2. Once the tax has been imposed and the demand curve has shifted down, the new equilibrium quantity of gasoline is 140 billion gallons, which is exactly the same as in Figure 4-11.

The new equilibrium price after the tax is imposed appears to be different in Figure 4-12 than in Figure 4-11, but if we include the tax, buyers will pay and sellers will receive the same price in both figures. To see this, notice that in Figure 4-11, buyers paid sellers a price of $3.08 per gallon. In Figure 4-12, they pay sellers only $2.98, but they must also pay the government a tax of 10 cents per gallon. So, the total price buyers pay remains

Figure 4-12

The Incidence of a Tax on Gasoline Paid by Buyers

With no tax on gasoline, the demand curve is D_1. If a 10-cents-per-gallon tax is imposed that consumers are responsible for paying, the demand curve shifts down by the amount of the tax, from D_1 to D_2. In the new equilibrium, consumers pay a price of $3.08 per gallon, including the tax. Producers receive $2.98 per gallon. This is the same result we saw when producers were responsible for paying the tax.

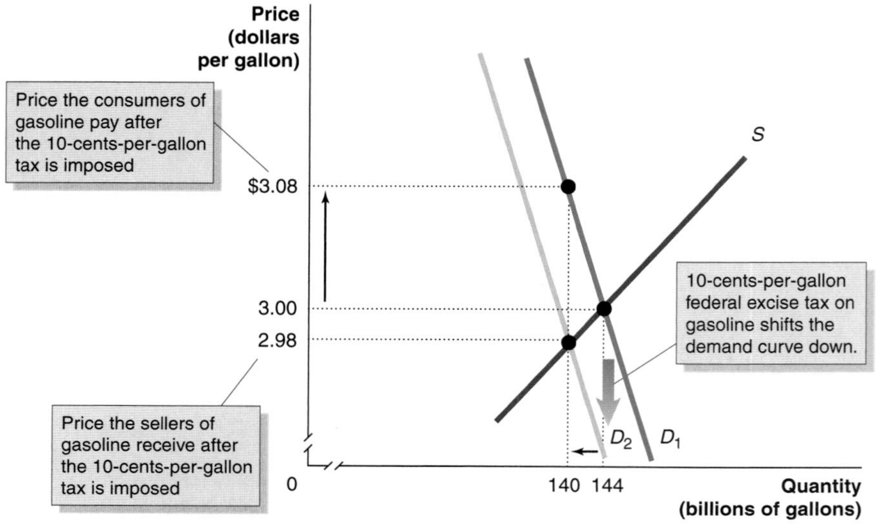

$3.08 per gallon. In Figure 4-11, sellers receive $3.08 per gallon from buyers, but after they pay the tax of 10 cents per gallon, they are left with $2.98, which is the same amount they receive in Figure 4-12.

Making the Connection | Is the Burden of the Social Security Tax Really Shared Equally between Workers and Firms?

Everyone who receives a paycheck has several different taxes withheld from it by their employers, who forward these taxes directly to the government. In fact, many people are shocked after getting their first job, when they discover the gap between their gross pay and their net pay after taxes have been deducted. The largest tax many people of low or moderate income pay is the FICA, which stands for the Federal Insurance Contributions Act. The FICA funds the Social Security and Medicare programs, which provide income and health care to the elderly and disabled. The FICA is sometimes referred to as the *payroll tax*. When Congress passed the FICA, it wanted employers and workers to equally share the burden of the tax. Currently, the FICA is 15.3 percent of wages, with 7.65 percent paid by workers by being withheld from their paychecks and the other 7.65 percent paid by employers.

How much FICA do you think this employee pays?

But does requiring workers and employers to each pay half the tax mean that the burden of the tax is also shared equally? Our discussion in this chapter shows us that the answer is no. In the labor market, employers are buyers, and workers are sellers. As we saw in the example of federal taxes on gasoline, whether the tax is collected from buyers or from sellers does not affect the incidence of the tax. Most economists believe, in fact, that the burden of the FICA falls almost entirely on workers. The following figure, which shows the market for labor, illustrates why.

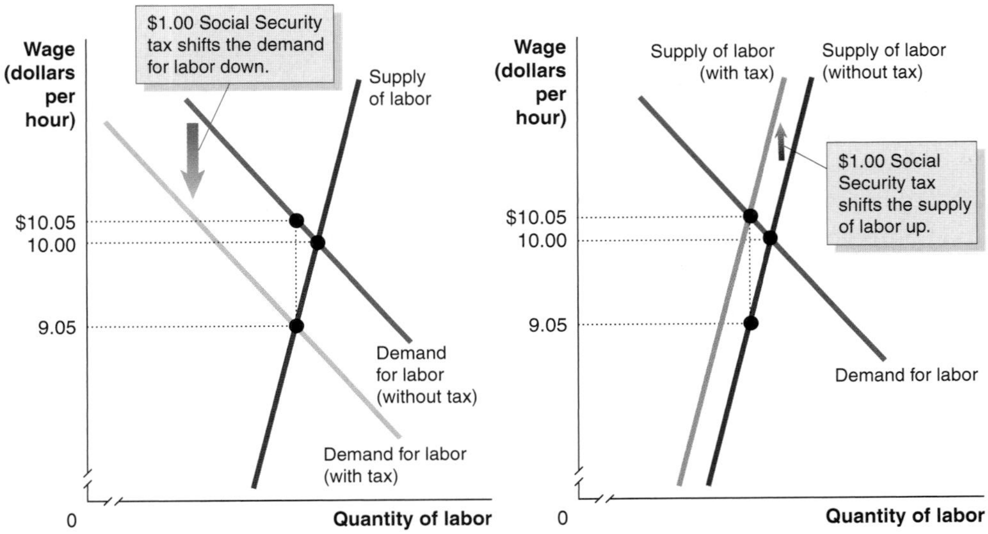

(a) The Social Security tax paid by employers **(b) The Social Security tax paid by workers**

In the market for labor, the demand curve reflects the quantity of labor demanded by employers at various wages, and the supply curve reflects the quantity of labor supplied by workers at various wages. The intersection of the demand curve and the supply curve determines the equilibrium wage. In both panels, the equilibrium wage without a Social Security payroll tax is $10 per hour. For simplicity, let's assume that the payroll tax equals $1 per hour of work. In panel (a), we assume that employers must pay the tax. The tax causes the demand for labor curve to shift down by $1 at every quantity of labor because firms now must pay a $1 tax for every hour of labor they hire. We have drawn the supply curve for labor as being very steep because most economists believe the quantity of labor supplied by workers does not change much as the wage rate changes. Workers pay $0.95 of the tax because their wages fall from $10 before the tax to $9.05 after the tax. Firms pay only $0.05 of the tax because the amount they pay for an hour of labor increases from $10 before the tax to $10.05 after the tax. In panel (a), after the tax is imposed, the equilibrium wage declines from $10 per hour to $9.05 per hour. Firms are now paying a total of $10.05 for every hour of work they hire: $9.05 in wages to workers and $1 in tax to the government. In other words, workers have paid $0.95 of the $1 tax, and firms have paid only $0.05.

Panel (b) shows that this result is exactly the same if the tax is imposed on workers rather than on firms. In this case, the tax causes the supply curve for labor to shift up by $1 at every quantity of labor because workers must now pay a tax of $1 for every hour they work. After the tax is imposed, the equilibrium wage increases to $10.05 per hour. But workers receive only $9.05 after they have paid the $1.00 tax. Once again, workers have paid $0.95 of the $1 tax, and firms have paid only $0.05.

Although the figure presents a simplified analysis, it reflects the conclusion of most economists who have studied the incidence of the FICA: Even though Congress requires half the tax to be paid by employers and the other half to be paid by workers, in fact, the burden of the tax falls almost entirely on workers. This conclusion would not be changed even if Congress revised the law to require either employers or workers to pay all of the tax. The forces of demand and supply working in the labor market, and not Congress, determine the incidence of the tax.

YOUR TURN: Test your understanding by doing related problem 4.6 on page 130 at the end of this chapter.

» Continued from page 99

Economics in YOUR Life!

At the beginning of the chapter, we posed the following question: If you have two job offers in different cities, one with rent control and one without, will you be more likely to find an affordable apartment in the city with rent control? In answering the question, this chapter has shown that although rent control can keep rents lower than they might otherwise be, it can also lead to a permanent shortage of apartments. You may have to search for a long time to find a suitable apartment, and landlords may even ask you to give them payments "under the table," which would make your actual rent higher than the controlled rent. Finding an apartment in a city without rent control should be much easier, although the rent may be higher.

Conclusion

The model of demand and supply introduced in Chapter 3 showed that markets free from government intervention eliminate surpluses and shortages and do a good job of responding to the wants of consumers. We have seen in this chapter that both consumers and firms sometimes try to use the government to change market outcomes in their favor. The concepts of consumer and producer surplus and deadweight loss allow us to measure the benefits consumers and producers receive from competitive market equilibrium. They also allow us to measure the effects of government price floors and price ceilings and the economic impact of taxes.

Read *An Inside Look at Policy* on page 122 for a discussion of the debate over rent control in Los Angeles.

Is Rent Control a Lifeline or Stranglehold?

LOS ANGELES TIMES, JANUARY 14, 2007

The Landlords: Two Sides of a Coin

With apologies to David Letterman, the Top Five reasons why landlords hate rent control are:

No. 1. As private citizens, they believe they shouldn't be forced to do the government's job of providing low-cost housing.

No. 2. In few sectors of private enterprise does a city tell a business how much it may charge.

No. 3. Rent-control buildings sell for less, even in high-rolling realty days.

No. 4. Capping what they may collect in rents translates to capping what they can spend on maintenance and repair—and then they get dinged for lousy upkeep.

No. 5: It's virtually impossible to evict undesirable tenants from a rent-controlled building; owners of buildings not under rent control can boot them out for nearly any reason. . . .

(a) Some Westside owners [in Los Angeles], in particular, complain that longtime renters get a lifetime break, even when they easily can afford market rates. Rent-control laws do not require financial-means testing, so professionals, for example, could still be living in rent-controlled units they secured when they were struggling students. Also, some renters secretly sublet their cheap units for market rate, flouting the terms of their contracts, landlords say. . . .

In an identical unit in the building, a recent tenant was paying about $900 a month while charging $1,000 for one of the bedrooms she rented out on the side, Lambert [a Santa Monica landlord of a rent-controlled building] said.

Selling rent-controlled buildings is no cakewalk, either, said Bruce Bernard, who has bought and sold scores of such buildings in Los Angeles. He recently got his asking price of $6.5 million for a 42-unit building in Hollywood that was not under rent control. One mile away, he also recently sold a 20-unit rent-controlled building with similar amenities for $2.3 million, which was $1.1 million less than his listing price.

(b) More dramatically, Lambert got zero offers on his 15-unit rent-controlled building listed for $890,000 just before the 1994 Northridge earthquake. The temblor shoved the building off the foundation, resulting in all of the tenants vacating the red-tagged structure. Despite $500,000 in needed repairs and not a penny of rent coming in, Lambert quickly sold the building after it was legally rent decontrolled—for $950,000. "It was worth more with all that damage and no rent control than the day before the quake, when it had paying tenants. What does that tell you?"

Hard as it is to sell rent-controlled units for a market-rate profit, owners of those buildings face more urgent daily concerns: covering rising insurance, taxes, upkeep, water, plumbing, landscaping and other costs with 3% or 4% annual rent increases. The result often is that repairs are not made in a timely fashion. . . .

(c) The Rent Stabilization Ordinance allows owners to "pass through" half of the costs of capital improvements to tenants. For example, when an owner replaces a roof for $20,000, he or she may divide half of that cost by the number of units in the building and charge the tenants of each unit up to $55 per month—spread out over multiple years—to cover the cost of the repair.

Even so, Stephens [a landlord near the Hollywood Bowl] said, "sometimes you get killed" economically. Landlords complain that some renters, hip to the strict Rent Escrow Account Program—which allows them to pay the city up to 50% of their rent and landlords nothing while units with health or safety violations are being brought up to code—deliberately ruin buildings to avoid paying full rent.

Attorney Harold Greenberg, who owns buildings and represents landlords, recalled a tenant who took a sledgehammer to the walls of his apartment, then reported the damage to the city, getting a rent discount while repairs were underway.

Bennett said he fixed a broken pole in the parking lot of one of his buildings and tenants subsequently rammed their cars into it five more times. Bennett finally closed the lot.

"We pay for repairs and pay for the inspections," said Jim Clarke, manager of government relations for the Apartment Assn. of Greater Los Angeles. "We've become the housing department's cash cow." . . .

Source: Diane Wedner, "The Landlords: Two Sides of a Coin," Los Angeles Times, *January 14, 2007, p. K1.*

Key Points in the Article

The article discusses the effects of rent-control laws in the Los Angeles market. Los Angeles, like New York City, which we discussed in the chapter opener, places limits on the rents that landlords can charge some tenants. The purpose of rent-control laws is to ensure that low-income people can find affordable housing. As the article and the chapter explain, rent controls impose substantial costs on landlords, which, in turn, may also harm renters.

Analyzing the News

a The law in Los Angeles does not require that tenants in rent-controlled apartments prove they have low incomes, so some rent-controlled apartments are rented to people with high incomes. In other words, there is nothing in the law to guarantee that rent-controlled apartments go to the intended beneficiaries of the law. A rent-control law may actually increase the rent some tenants pay. The figure in Solved Problem 4-3 on page 112 shows that the rent-control laws create a shortage of apartments and that the resulting black market rent is often higher than the rent without rent-control laws. That is why the Santa Monica tenant in the article was able to charge $1,000 to rent a single room of her rent-controlled apartment when she paid just $900 to rent the entire apartment.

b Not surprisingly, rent-control laws reduce the price for which a landlord can sell a rent-controlled apartment complex. Clearly, this hurts the landlord, but it can also harm renters. The lower selling price for rent-controlled apartment complexes makes building those complexes less profitable. If developers can't make a profit building rent-controlled apartment complexes, then they won't build them. Over time, the number of rent-controlled complexes should decrease as old complexes become run down and developers lack the incentive to build new ones. The supply of rent-controlled apartments should decrease, making the apartment shortage worse. The figure below shows the effect of the decrease in rent-controlled apartment complexes as a shift of the supply curve to the left, from S_1 to S_2. This shift causes the shortage of apartments to increase from $(Q_1 - Q_2)$ to $(Q_1 - Q_3)$. In addition, the black market rent also increases from Black Market$_1$ to Black Market$_2$.

c Rent-control laws also limit the ability of landlords to raise rents to pay for repairs. Indeed, as the article indicates, some of the laws are written in a way that actually gives tenants an incentive to purposely damage the apartment complex. Both the limit on recovering repair costs and the incentives for tenants to damage the property increase the costs of running rent-controlled apartment complexes. These costs can cause the supply curve in this market to shift even further to the left and make the effects we described in part *b* even larger.

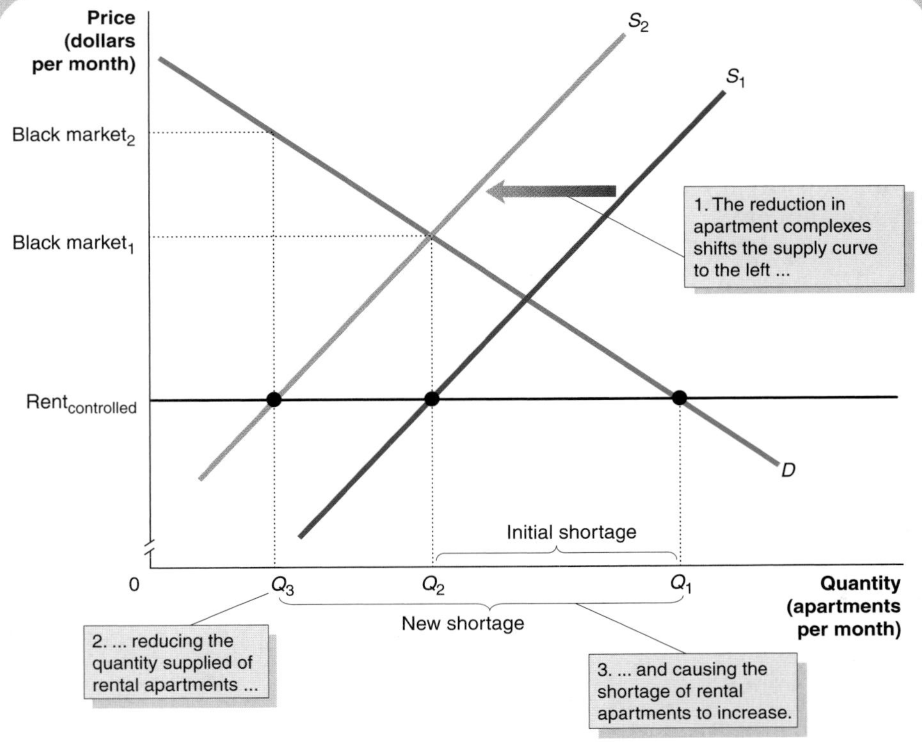

The effect of rent-control laws over time.

Thinking Critically About Policy

1. The article describes the significant costs associated with rent-control laws. Despite these costs, rent-control laws are very popular with tenants and local politicians. Why would some tenants support rent-control laws? Do all tenants in the market gain from rent-control laws?
2. Economists are critical of rent-control laws for several reasons. One reason is that the laws create a deadweight loss. The magnitude of this deadweight loss depends on the slopes of the demand and supply curves. Look at the figure for Solved Problem 4-3 on page 112. The deadweight loss equals $B + C$, which is the yellow area. What causes the deadweight loss? What would the supply curve have to look like for the deadweight loss to equal zero?

Key Terms

4.1 LEARNING OBJECTIVE 4.1 | Distinguish between the concepts of consumer surplus and producer surplus, **pages 100–105.**

Consumer Surplus and Producer Surplus

Summary

Although most prices are determined by demand and supply in markets, the government sometimes imposes *price ceilings* and *price floors*. A **price ceiling** is a legally determined maximum price that sellers may charge. A **price floor** is a legally determined minimum price that sellers may receive. Economists analyze the effects of price ceilings and price floors using *consumer surplus* and *producer surplus*. **Marginal benefit** is the additional benefit to a consumer from consuming one more unit of a good or service. The demand curve is also a marginal benefit curve. **Consumer surplus** is the difference between the highest price a consumer is willing to pay for a product and the price the consumer actually pays. The total amount of consumer surplus in a market is equal to the area below the demand curve and above the market price. **Marginal cost** is the additional cost to a firm of producing one more unit of a good or service. The supply curve is also a marginal cost curve. **Producer surplus** is the difference between the lowest price a firm is willing to accept and the price it actually receives. The total amount of producer surplus in a market is equal to the area above the supply curve and below the market price.

myeconlab Get Ahead of the Curve Visit www.myeconlab.com to complete these exercises online and get instant feedback.

Review Questions

1.1 What is marginal benefit? Why is the demand curve referred to as a marginal benefit curve?

1.2 What is marginal cost? Why is the supply curve referred to as a marginal cost curve?

1.3 What is consumer surplus? How does consumer surplus change as the equilibrium price of a good rises or falls?

1.4 What is producer surplus? How does producer surplus change as the equilibrium price of a good rises or falls?

Problems and Applications

1.5 Suppose that a frost in Florida reduces the size of the orange crop, which causes the supply curve for oranges to shift to the left. Briefly explain whether each of the following will increase or decrease. Use demand and supply to illustrate your answers.
   a. Consumer surplus
   b. Producer surplus

1.6 A student makes the following argument: "When a market is in equilibrium, there is no consumer surplus. We know this because in equilibrium, the market price is equal to the price consumers are willing to pay for the good." Briefly explain whether you agree with the student's argument.

1.7 The following graph illustrates the market for a breast cancer–fighting drug, without which breast cancer patients cannot survive. What is the consumer surplus in this market? How does it differ from the consumer surplus in the markets you have studied up to this point?

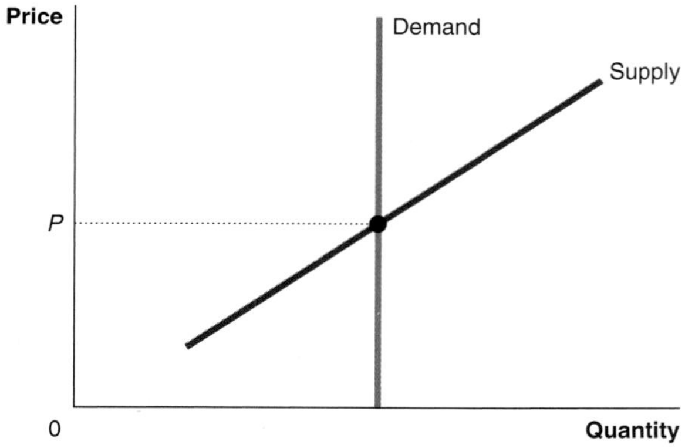

1.8 **(Related to the *Making the Connection* on page 102)** The *Making the Connection* states that the value of the area representing consumer surplus from satellite television is $2 billion. Use the information from the graph in the *Making the Connection* to show how this value was calculated. (For a review of how to calculate the area of a triangle, see the appendix to Chapter 1.)

1.9 The graph in the next column shows the market for tickets to a concert that will be held in a local arena that seats 15,000 people. What is the producer surplus in this market? How does it differ from the producer surplus in the markets you have studied up to this point?

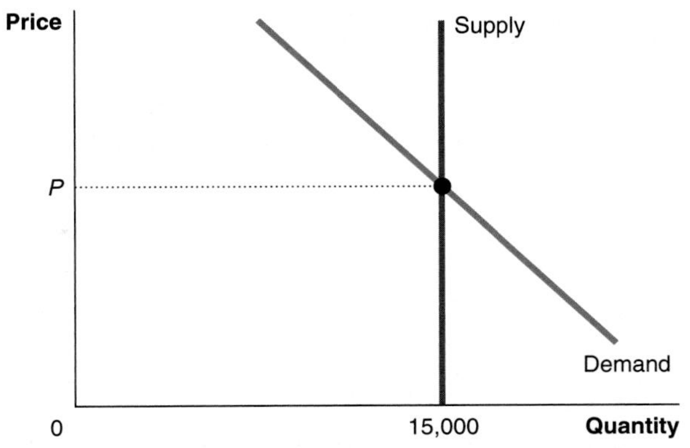

>> End Learning Objective 4.1

4.2 LEARNING OBJECTIVE 4.2 | Understand the concept of economic efficiency, **pages 105–107.**

The Efficiency of Competitive Markets

Summary

Equilibrium in a competitive market is **economically efficient. Economic surplus** is the sum of consumer surplus and producer surplus. Economic efficiency is a market outcome in which the marginal benefit to consumers from the last unit produced is equal to the marginal cost of production and where the sum of consumer surplus and producer surplus is at a maximum. When the market price is above or below the equilibrium price, there is a reduction in economic surplus. The reduction in economic surplus resulting from a market not being in competitive equilibrium is called the **deadweight loss.**

myeconlab Get Ahead of the Curve Visit www.myeconlab.com to complete these exercises online and get instant feedback.

Review Questions

2.1 Define economic surplus and deadweight loss?

2.2 What is economic efficiency? Why do economists define efficiency in this way?

Problems and Applications

2.3 Suppose you were assigned the task of coming up with a single number that would allow someone to compare the economic activity in one country to that in another country. How might such a number be related to economic efficiency and consumer and producer surplus?

2.4 Briefly explain whether you agree with the following statement: "If at the current quantity marginal benefit is greater than marginal cost, there will be a deadweight loss in the market. However, there is no deadweight loss when marginal cost is greater than marginal benefit."

2.5 Briefly explain whether you agree with the following statement: "If consumer surplus in a market increases, producer surplus must decrease."

2.6 Does an increase in economic surplus in a market always mean that economic efficiency in the market has increased? Briefly explain.

2.7 Using the graph below, explain why economic surplus would be smaller if Q_1 or Q_3 were the quantity produced than if Q_2 is the quantity produced.

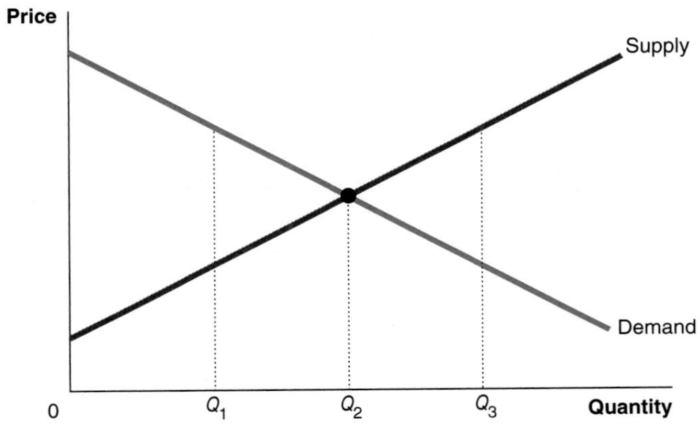

>> End Learning Objective 4.2

4.3 LEARNING OBJECTIVE 4.3 | Explain the economic effect of government-imposed price ceilings and price floors, **pages 107–115.**

Government Intervention in the Market: Price Floors and Price Ceilings

Summary

Producers or consumers who are dissatisfied with the market outcome can attempt to convince the government to impose price floors or price ceilings. Price floors usually increase producer surplus, decrease consumer surplus, and cause a deadweight loss. Price ceilings usually increase consumer surplus, reduce producer surplus, and cause a deadweight loss. The results of the government imposing price ceilings and price floors are that some people win, some people lose, and a loss of economic efficiency occurs. Price ceilings and price floors can lead to a **black market**, where buying and selling takes place at prices that violate government price regulations. Positive analysis is concerned with what is, and normative analysis is concerned with what should be. Positive analysis shows that price ceilings and price floors cause deadweight losses. Whether these policies are desirable or undesirable, though, is a normative question.

Review Questions

3.1 Why do some consumers tend to favor price controls while others tend to oppose them?

3.2 Do producers tend to favor price floors or price ceilings? Why?

3.3 What is a black market? Under what circumstances do black markets arise?

3.4 Can economic analysis provide a final answer to the question of whether the government should intervene in markets by imposing price ceilings and price floors? Why or why not?

Problems and Applications

3.5 The graph in the next column shows the market for apples. Assume the government has imposed a price floor of $10 per crate.

a. How many crates of apples will be sold after the price floor has been imposed?
b. Will there be a shortage or a surplus? If there is a shortage or a surplus, how large will it be?
c. Will apple producers benefit from the price floor? If so, explain how they will benefit.

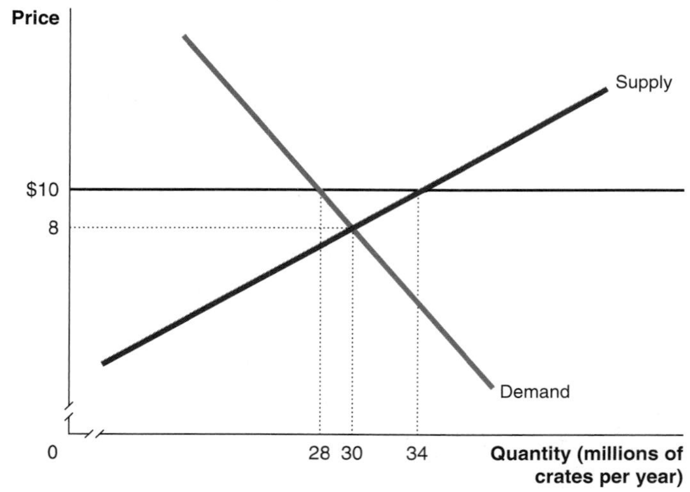

3.6 Use the information on the kumquat market in the table to answer the following questions.

PRICE (PER CRATE)	QUANTITY DEMANDED (MILLIONS OF CRATES PER YEAR)	QUANTITY SUPPLIED (MILLIONS OF CRATES PER YEAR)
$10	120	20
15	110	60
20	100	100
25	90	140
30	80	180
35	70	220

a. What are the equilibrium price and quantity? How much revenue do kumquat producers receive when the market is in equilibrium? Draw a graph showing the market equilibrium and the area representing the revenue received by kumquat producers.
b. Suppose the federal government decides to impose a price floor of $30 per crate. Now how many crates of kumquats will consumers purchase? How much revenue will kumquat producers receive? Assume that the government does not purchase any surplus kumquats. On your graph from question (a), show the price floor, the change in the quantity of kumquats purchased, and the revenue received by kumquat producers after the price floor is imposed.
c. Suppose the government imposes a price floor of $30 per crate and purchases any surplus kumquats from producers. Now how much revenue will kumquat producers receive? How much will the

government spend purchasing surplus kumquats? On your graph from question (a), show the area representing the amount the government spends to purchase the surplus kumquats.

3.7 Suppose that the government sets a price floor for milk that is above the competitive equilibrium price.

a. Draw a graph showing this situation. Be sure your graph shows the competitive equilibrium price, the price floor, the quantity that would be sold in competitive equilibrium, and the quantity that is sold with the price floor.

b. Compare the economic surplus in this market when there is a price floor and when there is no price floor.

3.8 During 2007, the Venezuelan government allowed consumers to buy only a limited quantity of sugar. The government also imposed a ceiling on the price of sugar. As a result, both the quantity of sugar consumed and the market price of sugar were below the competitive equilibrium price and quantity. Draw a graph to illustrate this situation. On your graph, be sure to indicate the areas representing consumer surplus, producer surplus, and deadweight loss.

3.9 Refer again to question 3.8. An article in the *New York Times* contained the following (Hugo Chávez is the president of Venezuela):

> José Vielma Mora, the chief of Seniat, the government's tax agency, oversaw a raid this month on a warehouse here where officials seized about 165 tons of sugar. Mr. Vielma said the raid exposed hoarding by vendors who were unwilling to sell the sugar at official prices. He and other officials in Mr. Chávez's government have repeatedly blamed the shortages on producers, intermediaries and grocers.

Do you agree that the shortages in the Venezuelan sugar market are the fault of "producers, intermediaries and grocers"? Briefly explain.

Source: Simon Romero, "Chavez Threatens to Jail Price Control Violators," *New York Times*, February 17, 2007.

3.10 To drive a taxi legally in New York City, you must have a medallion issued by the city government. City officials have issued only 12,187 medallions. Let's assume this puts an absolute limit on the number of taxi rides that can be supplied in New York City on any day because no one breaks the law by driving a taxi without a medallion. Let's also assume that each taxi can provide 6 trips per day. In that case, the supply of taxi rides is fixed at 73,122 (or 6 rides per taxi × 12,187 taxis). We show this in the following graph, with a vertical line at this quantity. *Assume that there are no government controls on the prices that drivers can charge for rides.* Use the graph to answer the following questions.

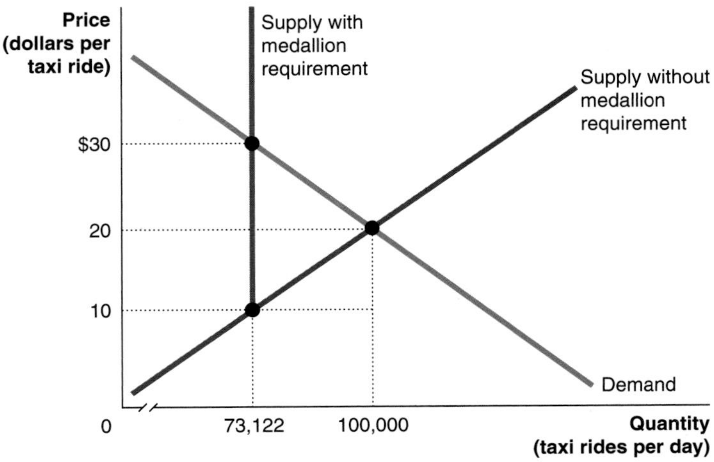

a. What would the equilibrium price and quantity be in this market if there were no medallion requirement?

b. What are the price and quantity with the medallion requirement?

c. Indicate on the graph the areas representing consumer surplus and producer surplus if there were no medallion requirement.

d. Indicate on the graph the areas representing consumer surplus, producer surplus, and deadweight loss with the medallion requirement.

3.11 If the goal of the federal government's farm program is to raise the incomes of poor family farmers, is the current system of price floors and subsidy payments based on the number of acres farmed a good way to reach the goal? Briefly explain. What other ways might the federal government attempt to reach its goals?

3.12 **(Related to the *Making the Connection* on page 109)** Some economists studying the effects of the minimum wage law have found that it tends to reduce the employment of black teenagers relative to white teenagers. Does the graph in the *Making the Connection* on page 109 help you understand why black teenagers may have been disproportionately affected by the minimum wage? Briefly explain.

3.13 **(Related to the *Chapter Opener* on page 98)** Suppose the competitive equilibrium rent for a standard two-bedroom apartment in Lawrence is \$600. Now suppose the city council passes a rent-control law imposing a price ceiling of \$500. Use a demand and supply graph to illustrate the impact of the rent-control law. Suppose that shortly after the law is passed, a large employer in the area announces that it will close a plant in Lawrence and lay off 5,000 workers. Show on your graph how this will affect the market for rental property in Lawrence.

3.14 **(Related to *Solved Problem 4-3* on page 112)** Use the information on the market for apartments in Bay City in the table on the next page to answer the following questions.

RENT	QUANTITY DEMANDED	QUANTITY SUPPLIED
$500	375,000	225,000
600	350,000	250,000
700	325,000	275,000
800	300,000	300,000
900	275,000	325,000
1,000	250,000	350,000

a. In the absence of rent control, what is the equilibrium rent and what is the equilibrium quantity of apartments rented? Draw a demand and supply graph of the market for apartments to illustrate your answer. In equilibrium, will there be any renters who are unable to find an apartment to rent or any landlords who are unable to find a renter for an apartment?
b. Suppose the government sets a ceiling on rents of $600 per month. What is the quantity of apartments demanded, and what is the quantity of apartments supplied?
c. Assume that all landlords abide by the law. Use a demand and supply graph to illustrate the impact of this price ceiling on the market for apartments. Be sure to indicate on your graph each of the following: (i) the area representing consumer surplus after the price ceiling has been imposed, (ii) the area representing producer surplus after the price ceiling has been imposed, and (iii) the area representing the deadweight loss after the ceiling has been imposed.
d. Assume that the quantity of apartments supplied is the same as you determined in (b). But now assume that landlords ignore the law and rent this quantity of apartments for the highest rent they can get. Briefly explain what this rent will be.

3.15 **(Related to the *Making the Connection* on page 113)** Joel Waldfogel argues that there may be a deadweight loss to holiday gift giving. An article in the *Wall Street Journal* suggests that retail stores might be better off if the tradition of holiday gift giving ended: "In theory, smoother sales throughout the year would be better for retailers, enabling them to avoid the extra costs of planning and stocking up for the holidays." Owners of many stores disagree, however. The owner of a store in New York City was quoted in the article as arguing: "Christmas is the lifeblood of the retail business. It's a time of year when people don't have a choice. They *have* to spend." Do you believe the efficiency of the economy would be improved if the tradition of holiday gift giving ended? Briefly explain your reasoning.

Source: Mark Whitehouse, "How Christmas Brings Out the Grinch in Economists," *Wall Street Journal*, December 23, 2006, p. A1.

3.16 **(Related to the *Don't Let This Happen to You!* on page 111)** Briefly explain whether you agree or disagree with the following statement: "If there is a shortage of a good, it must be scarce, but there is not a shortage of every scarce good."

3.17 A student makes the following argument:

> A price floor reduces the amount of a product that consumers buy because it keeps the price above the competitive market equilibrium. A price ceiling, on the other hand, increases the amount of a product that consumers buy because it keeps the price below the competitive market equilibrium.

Do you agree with the student's reasoning? Use a demand and supply graph to illustrate your answer.

3.18 An advocate of medical care system reform makes the following argument:

> The 15,000 kidneys that are transplanted in the United States each year are received free from organ donors. Despite this, because of hospital and doctor's fees, the average price of a kidney transplant is $250,000. As a result, only rich people or people with very good health insurance can afford these transplants. The government should put a ceiling of $100,000 on the price of kidney transplants. That way, middle-income people will be able to afford them, the demand for kidney transplants will increase, and more kidney transplants will take place.

Do you agree with the advocate's reasoning? Use a demand and supply graph to illustrate your answer.

3.19 **(Related to the *Chapter Opener* on page 98)** The cities of Peabody and Woburn are five miles apart. Woburn enacts a rent-control law that puts a ceiling on rents well below their competitive market value. Predict the impact of this law on the competitive equilibrium rent in Peabody, which does not have a rent-control law. Illustrate your answer with a demand and supply graph.

3.20 **(Related to the *Chapter Opener* on page 98)** Rent controls were first imposed in New York City in the early 1940s, during a housing shortage brought on by World War II. Why do you think that, once established, rent controls continued in New York City for many decades?

3.21 **(Related to the *Chapter Opener* on page 98)** The competitive equilibrium rent in the city of Lowell is currently $1,000 per month. The government decides to enact rent control and to establish a price ceiling for apartments of $750 per month. Briefly explain whether rent control is likely to make each of the following people better or worse off.

a. Someone currently renting an apartment in Lowell

b. Someone who will be moving to Lowell next year and who intends to rent an apartment
c. A landlord who intends to abide by the rent-control law
d. A landlord who intends to ignore the law and illegally charge the highest rent possible for his apartments

3.22 **(Related to the *Chapter Opener* on page 98)** The following is from an article in the *New York Times*:

> Imagine finding the perfect apartment, only to learn that the landlord is denying you the place because you are on a blacklist of supposedly high-risk renters. Nothing is wrong with your credit rating, but your name showed up on the list because a private screening service found it in housing court records about a dispute you had with a previous landlord—a dispute that was resolved in your favor.

Is it more likely that a "blacklist" of "high-risk" tenants will exist in a city with rent control or one without rent control? Briefly explain.

Source: Motoko Rich, "A Blacklist of Renters," *New York Times*, April 8, 2004.

3.23 **(Related to *Solved Problem 4-3* on page 112)** Suppose that initially the gasoline market is in equilibrium, at a price of \$3.00 per gallon and a quantity of 45 million gallons per month. Then a war in the Middle East disrupts imports of oil into the United States, shifting the supply curve for gasoline from S_1 to S_2. The price of gasoline begins to rise, and consumers protest. The federal government responds by setting a price ceiling of \$3.00 per gallon. Use the graph to answer the following questions.

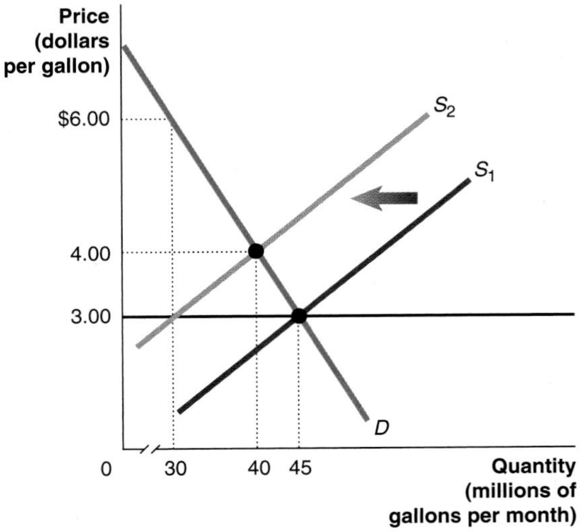

a. If there were no price ceiling, what would be the equilibrium price of gasoline, the quantity of gasoline demanded, and the quantity of gasoline supplied? Now assume that the price ceiling is imposed and that there is no black market in gasoline. What are the price of gasoline, the quantity of gasoline demanded, and the quantity of gasoline supplied? How large is the shortage of gasoline?
b. Assume that the price ceiling is imposed and there is no black market in gasoline. Show on the graph the areas representing consumer surplus, producer surplus, and deadweight loss.
c. Now assume that there is a black market and the price of gasoline rises to the maximum that consumers are willing to pay for the amount supplied by producers at \$3.00 per gallon. Show on the graph the areas representing producer surplus, consumer surplus, and deadweight loss.
d. Are consumers made better off with the price ceiling than without it? Briefly explain.

3.24 In the United States, Amazon.com, BarnesandNoble.com, and many other retailers sell books, DVDs, and music CDs for less than the price marked on the package. In Japan, retailers are not allowed to discount prices in this way. Who benefits and who loses from this Japanese law?

3.25 An editorial in *Economist* discusses the fact that in most countries—including the United States—it is illegal for individuals to buy or sell body parts, such as kidneys.

a. Draw a demand and supply graph for the market for kidneys. Show on your graph the legal maximum price of zero and indicate the quantity of kidneys supplied at this price. (Hint: Because we know that some kidneys are donated, the quantity supplied will not be zero.)
b. The editorial argues that buying and selling kidneys should be legalized:

> With proper regulation, a kidney market would be a big improvement over the current sorry state of affairs. Sellers could be checked for disease and drug use, and cared for after operations. . . . Buyers would get better kidneys, faster. Both sellers and buyers would do better than in the illegal market, where much of the money goes to middlemen.

Do you agree with this argument? Should the government treat kidneys like other goods and allow the market to determine the price?

Source: "Psst, Wanna Buy a Kidney?" *Economist*, November 18, 2006, p. 15.

>> End Learning Objective 4.3

4.4 LEARNING OBJECTIVE 4.4 | Analyze the economic impact of taxes, **pages 115–120.**

The Economic Impact of Taxes

Summary

Most taxes result in a loss of consumer surplus, a loss of producer surplus, and a deadweight loss. The true burden of a tax is not just the amount paid to government by consumers and producers but also includes the deadweight loss. The deadweight loss from a tax is the excess burden of the tax. **Tax incidence** is the actual division of the burden of a tax. In most cases, consumers and firms share the burden of a tax levied on a good or service.

Review Questions

4.1 What is meant by tax incidence?

4.2 Does it matter whether buyers or sellers are legally responsible for paying a tax? Briefly explain.

Problems and Applications

4.3 Suppose the current equilibrium price of cheese pizzas is $10, and 10 million pizzas are sold per month. After the federal government imposes a $0.50 per pizza tax, the equilibrium price of pizzas rises to $10.40, and the equilibrium quantity falls to 9 million. Illustrate this situation with a demand and supply graph. Be sure your graph shows the equilibrium price before and after the tax, the equilibrium quantity before and after the tax, and the areas representing consumer surplus after the tax, producer surplus after the tax, tax revenue collected by the government, and deadweight loss.

4.4 Use the graph of the market for cigarettes in the next column to answer the following questions.

a. According to the graph, how much is the government tax on cigarettes?

b. What price do producers receive after paying the tax?

c. How much tax revenue does the government collect?

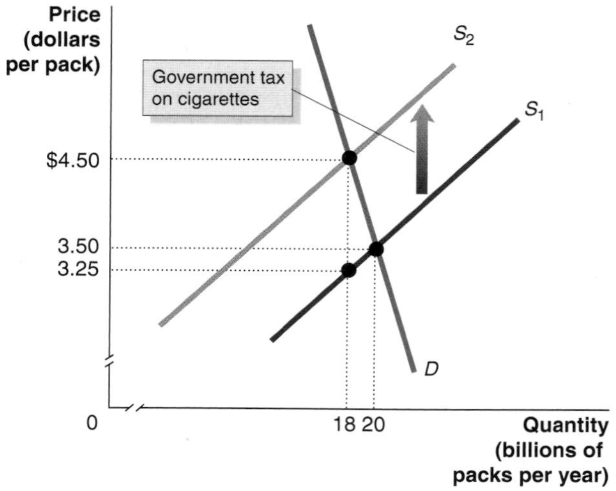

4.5 **(Related to *Solved Problem 4-4* on page 117)** Suppose the federal government decides to levy a sales tax on pizza of $1.00 per pie. Briefly explain whether you agree with the following statement by a representative of the pizza industry:

> The pizza industry is very competitive. As a result, pizza sellers will have to pay the whole tax because they are unable to pass any of it on to consumers in the form of higher prices. Therefore, a sales tax of $1.00 per pie will result in pizza sellers receiving $1.00 less on each pie sold, after paying the tax.

Illustrate your answer with a graph.

4.6 **(Related to the *Making the Connection* on page 119)** If the price consumers pay and the price sellers receive are not affected by whether consumers or sellers collect a tax on a good or service, why does the government usually require sellers and not consumers to collect a tax?

>> End Learning Objective 4.4

Appendix

Quantitative Demand and Supply Analysis

Graphs help us understand economic change *qualitatively*. For instance, a demand and supply graph can tell us that if household incomes rise, the demand curve for a normal good will shift to the right, and its price will rise. Often, though, economists, business managers, and policymakers want to know more than the qualitative direction of change; they want a *quantitative estimate* of the size of the change.

In Chapter 4, we carried out a qualitative analysis of rent controls. We saw that imposing rent controls involves a trade-off: Renters as a group gain, but landlords lose, and the market for apartments becomes less efficient, as shown by the deadweight loss. To better evaluate rent controls, we need to know more than just that these gains and losses exist; we need to know how large they are. A quantitative analysis of rent controls will tell us how large the gains and losses are.

LEARNING OBJECTIVE

Use **quantitative** demand and supply **analysis**.

Demand and Supply Equations

The first step in a quantitative analysis is to supplement our use of demand and supply curves with demand and supply *equations*. We noted briefly in Chapter 3 that economists often statistically estimate equations for demand curves. Supply curves can also be statistically estimated. For example, suppose that economists have estimated that the demand for apartments in New York City is:

$$Q^D = 3{,}000{,}000 - 1{,}000P,$$

and the supply of apartments is:

$$Q^S = -450{,}000 + 1{,}300P.$$

We have used Q^D for the quantity of apartments demanded per month, Q^S for the quantity of apartments supplied per month, and P for the apartment rent in dollars per month. In reality, both the quantity of apartments demanded and the quantity of apartments supplied will depend on more than just the rental price of apartments in New York City. For instance, the demand for apartments in New York City will also depend on the average incomes of families in the New York area and on the rents of apartments in surrounding cities. For simplicity, we will ignore these other factors.

With no government intervention, we know that at competitive market equilibrium, the quantity demanded must equal the quantity supplied, or:

$$Q^D = Q^S.$$

We can use this equation, which is called an *equilibrium condition*, to solve for the equilibrium monthly apartment rent by setting the demand equation equal to the supply equation:

$$3{,}000{,}000 - 1{,}000P = -450{,}000 + 1{,}300P$$

$$3{,}450{,}000 = 2{,}300P$$

$$P = \frac{3{,}450{,}000}{2{,}300} = \$1{,}500.$$

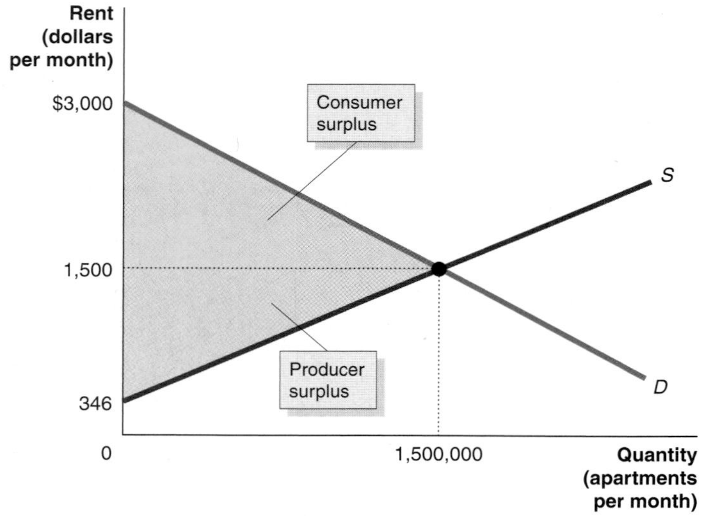

Figure 4A-1

Graphing Supply and Demand Equations

After statistically estimating supply and demand equations, we can use the equations to draw supply and demand curves. In this case, the equilibrium rent for apartments is \$1,500 per month, and the equilibrium quantity of apartments rented is 1,500,000. The supply equation tells us that at a rent of \$346, the quantity of apartments supplied will be zero. The demand equation tells us that at a rent of \$3,000, the quantity of apartments demanded will be zero. The areas representing consumer surplus and producer surplus are also indicated on the graph.

We can then substitute this price back into either the supply equation or the demand equation to find the equilibrium quantity of apartments rented:

$$Q^D = 3{,}000{,}000 - 1{,}000P = 3{,}000{,}000 - 1{,}000(1{,}500) = 1{,}500{,}000$$

$$Q^S = -450{,}000 + 1{,}300P = -450{,}000 + 1{,}300(1{,}500) = 1{,}500{,}000.$$

Figure 4A-1 illustrates the information from these equations in a graph. The figure shows the values for rent when the quantity supplied is zero and when the quantity demanded is zero. These values can be calculated from the demand equation and the supply equation by setting Q^D and Q^S equal to zero and solving for price:

$$Q^D = 0 = 3{,}000{,}000 - 1{,}000P$$

$$P = \frac{3{,}000{,}000}{1{,}000} = \$3{,}000$$

and:

$$Q^S = 0 = -450{,}000 + 1{,}300P$$

$$P = \frac{-450{,}000}{-1{,}300} = \$346.15.$$

Calculating Consumer Surplus and Producer Surplus

Figure 4A-1 shows consumer surplus and producer surplus in this market. Recall that the sum of consumer surplus and producer surplus equals the net benefit that renters and landlords receive from participating in the market for apartments. We can use the values from the demand and supply equations to calculate the value of consumer surplus and producer surplus. Remember that consumer surplus is the area below the demand curve and above the line representing market price. Notice that this area forms a right triangle because the demand curve is a straight line—it is *linear*. As we noted in the appendix to Chapter 1, the area of a triangle is equal to ½ multiplied by the base of the triangle multiplied by the height of the triangle. In this case, the area is:

$$\tfrac{1}{2} \times (1{,}500{,}000) \times (3{,}000 - 1{,}500) = \$1{,}125{,}000{,}000.$$

So, this calculation tells us that the consumer surplus in the market for rental apartments in New York City would be about \$1.125 billion.

We can calculate producer surplus in a similar way. Remember that producer surplus is the area above the supply curve and below the line representing market price. Because our supply curve is also a straight line, producer surplus on the figure is equal to the area of the right triangle:

$$\tfrac{1}{2} \times 1{,}500{,}000 \times (1{,}500 - 346) = \$865{,}500{,}000.$$

This calculation tells us that the producer surplus in the market for rental apartments in New York City is about \$865 million.

We can use this same type of analysis to measure the impact of rent control on consumer surplus, producer surplus, and economic efficiency. For instance, suppose the city imposes a rent ceiling of \$1,000 per month. Figure 4A-2 can help guide us as we measure the impact.

First, we can calculate the quantity of apartments that will actually be rented by substituting the rent ceiling of \$1,000 into the supply equation:

$$Q^S = -450{,}000 + (1{,}300 \times 1{,}000) = 850{,}000.$$

We also need to know the price on the demand curve when the quantity of apartments is 850,000. We can do this by substituting 850,000 for quantity in the demand equation and solving for price:

$$850{,}000 = 3{,}000{,}000 - 1{,}000P$$

$$P = \frac{-2{,}150{,}000}{-1{,}000} = \$2{,}150.$$

Compared with its value in competitive equilibrium, consumer surplus has been reduced by a value equal to the area of the yellow triangle *B* but increased by a value equal to the area of the blue rectangle *A*. The area of the yellow triangle *B* is:

$$\tfrac{1}{2} \times (1{,}500{,}000 - 850{,}000) \times (2{,}150 - 1{,}500) = \$211{,}250{,}000,$$

and the area of the blue rectangle *A* is base multiplied by height, or:

$$(\$1{,}500 - \$1{,}000) \times (850{,}000) = \$425{,}000{,}000.$$

The value of consumer surplus in competitive equilibrium was \$1,125,000,000. As a result of the rent ceiling, it will be increased to:

$$(\$1{,}125{,}000{,}000 + \$425{,}000{,}000) - \$211{,}250{,}000 = \$1{,}338{,}750{,}000.$$

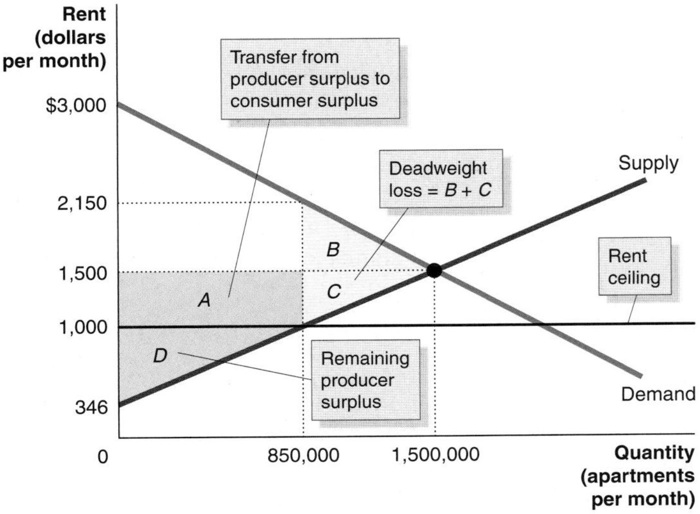

Figure 4A-2

Calculating the Economic Effect of Rent Controls

Once we have estimated equations for the demand and supply of rental housing, a diagram can guide our numeric estimates of the economic effects of rent control. Consumer surplus falls by an amount equal to the area of the yellow triangle *B* and increases by an amount equal to the area of the blue rectangle *A*. The difference between the values of these two areas is \$213,750,000. Producer surplus falls by an amount equal to the area of the blue rectangle *A* plus the area of the yellow triangle *C*. The value of these two areas is \$587,500,000. The remaining producer surplus is equal to the area of triangle *D*, or \$278,000,000. Deadweight loss is equal to the area of triangle *B* plus the area of triangle *C*, or \$373,750,000.

Compared with its value in competitive equilibrium, producer surplus has been reduced by a value equal to the area of the yellow triangle *C* plus a value equal to the area of the blue rectangle. The area of the yellow triangle *C* is:

$$\frac{1}{2} \times 1{,}500{,}000 - 850{,}000) \times (1{,}500 - 1{,}000) = \$162{,}500{,}000.$$

We have already calculated the area of the blue rectangle *A* as $425,000,000. The value of producer surplus in competitive equilibrium was $865,500,000. As a result of the rent ceiling, it will be reduced to:

$$\$865{,}500{,}000 - \$162{,}500{,}000 - \$425{,}000{,}000 = \$278{,}000{,}000.$$

The loss of economic efficiency, as measured by the deadweight loss, is equal to the value represented by the areas of the yellow triangles *B* and *C*, or:

$$\$211{,}250{,}000 + \$162{,}500{,}000 = \$373{,}750{,}000.$$

The following table summarizes the results of the analysis (the values are in millions of dollars).

CONSUMER SURPLUS		PRODUCER SURPLUS		DEADWEIGHT LOSS	
COMPETITIVE EQUILIBRIUM	RENT CONTROL	COMPETITIVE EQUILIBRIUM	RENT CONTROL	COMPETITIVE EQUILIBRIUM	RENT CONTROL
$1,125	$1,338.75	$865.50	$278	$0	$373.75

Qualitatively, we know that imposing rent controls will make consumers better off, make landlords worse off, and decrease economic efficiency. The advantage of the analysis we have just gone through is that it puts dollar values on the qualitative results. We can now see how much consumers have gained, how much landlords have lost, and how great the decline in economic efficiency has been. Sometimes the quantitative results can be surprising. Notice, for instance, that after the imposition of rent control, the deadweight loss is actually greater than the remaining producer surplus.

Economists often study issues where the qualitative results of actions are apparent, even to non-economists. You don't have to be an economist to understand who wins and loses from rent control or that if a company cuts the price of its product, its sales will increase. Business managers, policymakers, and the general public do, however, need economists to measure quantitatively the effects of different actions—including policies such as rent control—so that they can better assess the results of these actions.

LEARNING OBJECTIVE Use Quantitative Demand and Supply Analysis, **pages 131–134.**

myeconlab Get Ahead of the Curve Visit www.myeconlab.com to complete these exercises online and get instant feedback.

Review Questions

4A.1 In a linear demand equation, what economic information is conveyed by the intercept on the price axis?

4A.2 Suppose you were assigned the task of choosing a price that maximized economic surplus in a market. What price would you choose? Why?

4A.3 Consumer surplus is used as a measure of a consumer's net benefit from purchasing a good or service. Explain why consumer surplus is a measure of net benefit.

4A.4 Why would economists use the term *deadweight loss* to describe the impact on consumer and producer surplus from a price control?

Problems and Applications

4A.5 Suppose that you have been hired to analyze the impact on employment from the imposition of a minimum wage in the labor market. Further suppose that you estimate the supply and demand functions for labor, where *L* stands for the quantity of labor (measured in thousands of workers) and *W* stands for the wage rate (measured in dollars per hour):

Demand: $L^D = 100 - 4W$
Supply: $L^S = 6W$

First, calculate the free-market equilibrium wage and quantity of labor. Now suppose the proposed minimum wage is $12. How large will the surplus of labor in this market be?

4A.6 The following graphs illustrate the markets for two different types of labor. Suppose an identical minimum wage is imposed in both markets. In which market will the minimum wage have the largest impact on employment? Why?

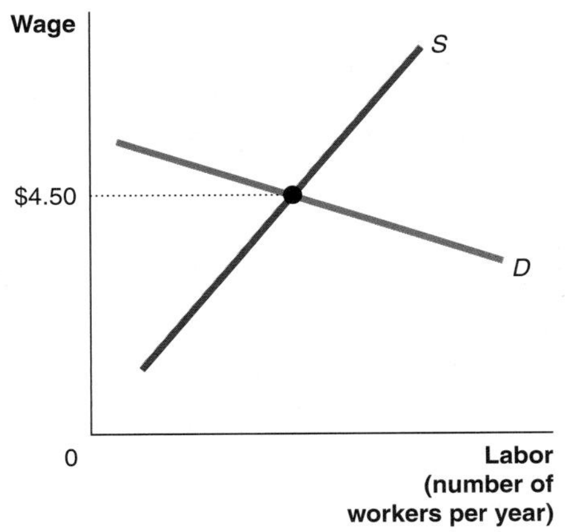

4A.7 Suppose that you are the vice president of operations of a manufacturing firm that sells an industrial lubricant in a competitive market. Further suppose that your economist gives you the following supply and demand functions:

Demand: $Q^D = 45 - 2P$
Supply: $Q^S = -15 + P$

What is the consumer surplus in this market? What is the producer surplus?

4A.8 The following graph shows a market in which a price floor of $3.00 per unit has been imposed. Calculate the values of each of the following.

a. The deadweight loss
b. The transfer of producer surplus to consumers or the transfer of consumer surplus to producers
c. Producer surplus after the price floor is imposed
d. Consumer surplus after the price floor is imposed

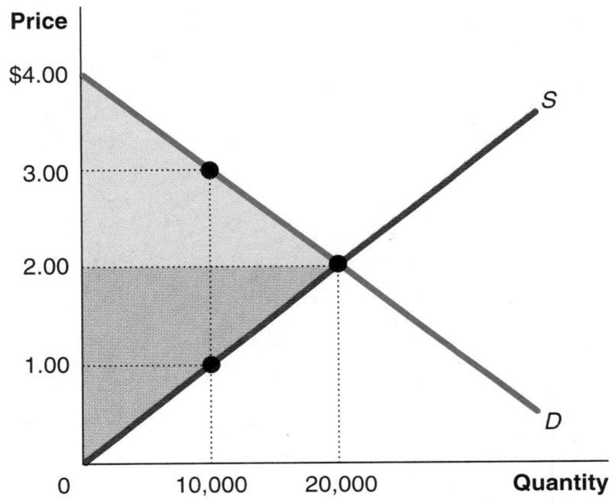

4A.9 Construct a table like the one in this appendix on page 134, but assume that the rent ceiling is $1,200 rather than $1,000.

>> End Appendix Learning Objective

Chapter 5

Firms, the Stock Market, and Corporate Governance

Google: From Dorm Room to Wall Street

There could be no question that Google was cool. The world's most widely used Internet search engine, Google had become the essence of cool as a way to research information stored on Web sites. Founded in 1998 by Larry Page and Sergey Brin, Google grew quickly. By 2006, Google employed 10,000 people and earned $10.6 billion in revenue. Google's founders had transformed the Internet search engine and brought value to users through a combination of intellect, technology, and the talents of many employees. Google's key advantage over competitors such as A9 and Ask Jeeves was its search algorithms that allowed users to easily find the Web sites most relevant to a subject. Google had other advantages as well, such as its automatic foreign-language translation. Google had become so dominant that other major Web sites, such as AOL and Yahoo, were using it as their search engine. Google has also succeeded in expanding into foreign markets. In China, Google has been successful even though it remains in a struggle for market share with the local Chinese firm Baidu.com.

And Google was hot. In 2004, Google sold part of the firm to outside investors by offering stock—and partial ownership—to the public. This stock offering vaulted Larry Page and Sergey Brin to the ranks of the super-rich. Google's stock offering also gained significant press attention, as the firm bypassed conventional financial practice and used an automated online auction to help set the share price and determine who should receive stock. The offering's size grabbed attention, too: It was the most anticipated stock sale since the 1995 launch of Netscape, a deal that sparked the late-1990s Internet gold rush on Wall Street.

As Google grew larger, it was less the informal organization put together by the founders and more a complex organization with greater need for management and funds to grow. Indeed, Google's offering of stock to outside investors provided the firm with a major inflow of funds for growth.

Once a firm grows very large, its owners often do not continue to manage it. Large corporations are owned by millions of individual investors who have purchased the firms' stock. With ownership so dispersed, the top managers who actually run a firm have the opportunity to make decisions that are in the managers' best interests but that may not be in the best interests of the stockholders who own the firm.

Against this backdrop, Google faced significant costs associated with selling stock to the public. High-profile corporate accounting scandals in 2001 and 2002 at major U.S. firms, such as Enron, WorldCom, and Tyco, led to the passage of stronger—and more costly—securities regulation under the Sarbanes-Oxley Act, enacted by Congress in 2002. Google's growth prospects and the health of the financial system were intertwined. **AN INSIDE LOOK** on **page 154** discusses the compensation Google pays its top executives.

LEARNING Objectives

After studying this chapter, you should be able to:

5.1 Categorize the major **types of firms** in the United States, page 138.

5.2 Describe the typical **management structure** of corporations and understand the concepts of **separation of ownership from control** and the **principal–agent problem**, page 140.

5.3 Explain how firms obtain the **funds** they need to **operate** and **expand**, page 142.

5.4 Understand the information provided in corporations' **financial statements**, page 147.

5.5 Understand the role of government in **corporate governance**, page 149.

APPENDIX Understand the concept of **present value** and the information contained on a firm's **income statement** and **balance sheet**, page 161.

Economics in YOUR Life!

Is It Risky to Own Stock?

Although stockholders legally own corporations, managers often have a great deal of freedom in deciding how corporations are run. As a result, managers can make decisions, such as spending money on large corporate headquarters or decorating their offices with expensive paintings, that are in their interests but not in the interests of the shareholders. If managers make decisions that waste money and lower the profits of a firm, the price of the firm's stock will fall, which hurts the investors who own the stock. Suppose you own stock in a corporation, such as Google. Why is it difficult to get the managers to act in your interest rather than in their own? Given this problem, should you ever take on the risk of buying stock? As you read the chapter, see if you can answer these questions. You can check your answers against those we provide at the end of the chapter.

» **Continued on page 153**

In this chapter, we look at the firm: how it is organized, how it raises funds, and the information it provides to investors. As we have already discussed, firms in a market system are responsible for organizing the factors of production to produce goods and services. Firms are the vehicles entrepreneurs use to earn profits. To succeed, entrepreneurs must meet consumer wants by producing new or better goods and services or by finding ways of producing existing goods and services at a lower cost so they can be sold at a lower price. Entrepreneurs also need access to sufficient funds, and they must be able to efficiently organize production. As the typical firm in many industries has become larger during the past 100 years, the task of efficiently organizing production has become more difficult. Toward the end of this chapter, we look at why a series of corporate scandals occurred beginning in 2002 and at the steps firms and the government have taken to avoid similar problems in the future.

5.1 LEARNING OBJECTIVE

5.1 | Categorize the major types of firms in the United States.

Types of Firms

Sole proprietorship A firm owned by a single individual and not organized as a corporation.

Partnership A firm owned jointly by two or more persons and not organized as a corporation.

Corporation A legal form of business that provides the owners with limited liability.

In studying a market economy, it is important to understand the basics of how firms operate. In the United States, there are three legal categories of firms: *sole proprietorships*, *partnerships*, and *corporations*. A **sole proprietorship** is a firm owned by a single individual. Although most sole proprietorships are small, some are quite large in terms of sales, number of persons employed, and profits earned. **Partnerships** are firms owned jointly by two or more—sometimes many—persons. Most law and accounting firms are partnerships. The famous Lloyd's of London insurance company is a partnership. Although some partnerships, such as Lloyd's, can be quite large, most large firms are organized as *corporations*. A **corporation** is a legal form of business that provides the owners with limited liability.

Who Is Liable? Limited and Unlimited Liability

Asset Anything of value owned by a person or a firm.

A key distinction among the three types of firms is that the owners of sole proprietorships and partnerships have unlimited liability. Unlimited liability means there is no legal distinction between the personal assets of the owners of the firm and the assets of the firm. An **asset** is anything of value owned by a person or a firm. If a sole proprietorship or a partnership owes a lot of money to the firm's suppliers or employees, the suppliers and employees have a legal right to sue the firm for payment, even if this requires the firm's owners to sell some of their personal assets, such as stocks or bonds. In other words, with sole proprietorships and partnerships, the owners are not legally distinct from the firms they own.

It may seem only fair that the owners of a firm be responsible for a firm's debts. But early in the nineteenth century, it became clear to many state legislatures in the United States that unlimited liability was a significant problem for any firm that was attempting to raise funds from large numbers of investors. An investor might be interested in making a relatively small investment in a firm but be unwilling to become a partner in the firm for fear of placing at risk all of his or her personal assets if the firm were to fail. To get around this problem, state legislatures began to pass *general incorporation laws*, which allowed firms to be organized as corporations. Under the corporate form of business, the owners of a firm have **limited liability**, which means that if the firm fails, the owners can never lose more than the amount they had invested in the firm. The personal assets of the owners of the firm are not affected by the failure of the firm. In fact, in the eyes of the law, a corporation is a legal "person" separate from its owners. Limited

Limited liability The legal provision that shields owners of a corporation from losing more than they have invested in the firm.

TABLE 5-1

Differences among Business Organizations

	SOLE PROPRIETORSHIP	PARTNERSHIP	CORPORATION
ADVANTAGES	• Control by owner • No layers of management	• Ability to share work • Ability to share risks	• Limited personal liability • Greater ability to raise funds
DISADVANTAGES	• Unlimited personal liability • Limited ability to raise funds	• Unlimited personal liability • Limited ability to raise funds	• Costly to organize • Possible double taxation of income

liability has made it possible for corporations to raise funds by issuing shares of stock to large numbers of investors. For example, if you buy a share of Google stock, you are a part owner of the firm, but even if Google were to go bankrupt, you would not be personally responsible for any of Google's debts. Therefore, you could not lose more than the amount you paid for the stock.

Corporate organizations also have some disadvantages. In the United States, corporate profits are taxed twice—once at the corporate level and again when investors receive a share of corporate profits. Corporations generally are larger than sole proprietorships and partnerships and therefore more difficult to organize and run. Table 5-1 reviews the advantages and disadvantages of different forms of business organization.

Making the Connection | What's in a "Name"? Lloyd's of London Learns about Unlimited Liability the Hard Way

The world-famous insurance company Lloyd's of London got its start in Edward Lloyd's coffeehouse in London in the late 1600s. Ship owners would come to the coffeehouse looking for someone to insure (or "underwrite") their ships and cargos in exchange for a flat fee (or "premium"). The customers of the coffeehouse, themselves merchants or ship owners, who agreed to insure ships or cargos would have to make payment from their personal funds if an insured ship was lost at sea. By the late 1700s, the system had become more formal: Each underwriter would recruit investors, known as "Names," and use the funds raised to back insurance policies sold to a wide variety of clients. In the twentieth century, Lloyd's became famous for some of its unusual insurance policies. It issued a policy insuring the legs of Betty Grable, a 1940s movie star. One man bought an insurance policy against seeing a ghost.

Investors in Lloyd's of London lost billions of dollars during the 1980s and 1990s.

By the late 1980s, 34,000 persons around the world had invested in Lloyd's as Names. A series of disasters in the late 1980s and early 1990s—including the *Exxon Valdez* oil spill in Alaska, Hurricane Hugo in South Carolina, and an earthquake in San Francisco—resulted in huge payments on insurance policies written by Lloyd's. In 1989, Lloyd's lost $3.85 billion. In 1990, it lost an additional $4.4 billion. It then became clear to many of the Names that Lloyd's was not a corporation and that the Names did not have the limited liability enjoyed by corporate shareholders. On the contrary, the Names were personally responsible for paying the losses on the insurance policies. Many Names lost far more than they had invested. Some investors, such as Charles Schwab, the discount stockbroker, were wealthy enough to sustain their losses, but others were less fortunate. One California investor ended up living in poverty after having to sell his $1 million house to pay his share of the losses. Another Name, Sir Richard Fitch, a British admiral, committed suicide after most of his wealth was wiped out. As many as 30 Names may have committed suicide as a result of their losses.

By 2007, only 1,100 Names—undoubtedly sadder but wiser—remained as investors in Lloyd's. New rules have allowed insurance companies to underwrite

Lloyd's policies for the first time. Today, Names provide only about 20 percent of Lloyd's funds.

Sources: "The Rip van Winkle of Risk," *Economist*, January 4, 2007; Charles Fleming, "The Master of Disaster Is Trying to Avoid One," *Wall Street Journal*, November 17, 2003; and "Lloyd's of London: Insuring for the Future," *Economist*, September 16, 2004.

YOUR TURN: Test your understanding by doing related problem 1.4 and 1.5 on page 156 at the end of this chapter.

Corporations Earn the Majority of Revenue and Profits

Figure 5-1 gives basic statistics on the three types of business organizations. Panel (a) shows that almost three-quarters of all firms are sole proprietorships. Panels (b) and (c) show that although only 20 percent of all firms are corporations, corporations account for the majority of revenue and profits earned by all firms. *Profit* is the difference between revenue and the total cost to a firm of producing the goods and services it offers for sale.

There are more than 5 million corporations in the United States, but only 26,000 have annual revenues of more than $50 million. We can think of these 26,000 firms—including Microsoft, General Electric, and Google—as representing "big business." These large firms earn almost 85 percent of the total profits of all corporations in the United States.

5.2 LEARNING OBJECTIVE

5.2 | Describe the typical management structure of corporations and understand the concepts of separation of ownership from control and the principal-agent problem.

The Structure of Corporations and the Principal-Agent Problem

Corporate governance The way in which a corporation is structured and the effect a corporation's structure has on the firm's behavior.

Because large corporations account for most sales and profits in the economy, it is important to know how they are managed. Most large corporations have a similar management structure. The way in which a corporation is structured and the effect a corporation's structure has on the firm's behavior is referred to as **corporate governance**.

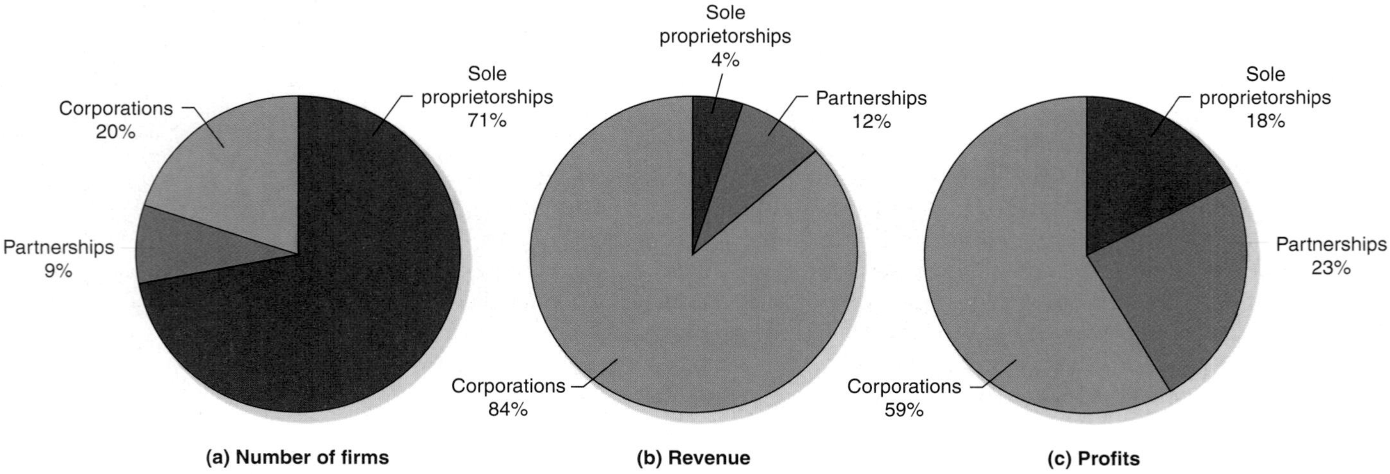

Figure 5-1 | Business Organizations: Sole Proprietorships, Partnerships, and Corporations

The three types of firms in the United States are sole proprietorships, partnerships, and corporations. Panel (a) shows that only 20 percent of all firms are corporations. Yet, as panels (b) and (c) show, corporations account for a majority of the total revenue and profits earned by all firms.

Source: U.S. Census Bureau, *The 2007 Statistical Abstract of the United States.*

Corporate Structure and Corporate Governance

Corporations are legally owned by their *shareholders*, the owners of the corporation's stock. Unlike family businesses, a corporation's shareholders, although they are the firm's owners, do not manage the firm directly. Instead, they elect a *board of directors* to represent their interests. The board of directors appoints a *chief executive officer* (CEO) to run the day-to-day operations of the corporation. Sometimes the board of directors also appoints other members of *top management*, such as the *chief financial officer* (CFO). At other times, the CEO appoints other members of top management. Members of top management, including the CEO and CFO, often serve on the board of directors. Members of management serving on the board of directors are referred to as *inside directors*. Members of the board of directors who do not have a direct management role in the firm are referred to as *outside directors*. The outside directors are intended to act as checks on the decisions of top managers, but the distinction between an outside director and an inside director is not always clear. For example, the CEO of a firm that sells a good or service to a large corporation may sit on the board of directors of that corporation. Although an outside director, this person may be reluctant to displease the top managers because the top managers have the power to stop purchasing from his firm. In some instances, top managers have effectively controlled their firms' boards of directors.

Unlike founder-dominated businesses, the top management of large corporations does not generally own a large share of the firm's stock, so large corporations have a **separation of ownership from control**. Although the shareholders actually own the firm, top management controls the day-to-day operations of the firm. Because top managers do not own the entire firm, they may have an incentive to decrease the firm's profits by spending money to purchase private jets or schedule management meetings at luxurious resorts. Economists refer to the conflict between the interests of shareholders and the interests of top management as a **principal–agent problem**. This problem occurs when agents—in this case, a firm's top management—pursue their own interests rather than the interests of the principal who hired them—in this case, the shareholders of the corporation. To reduce the impact of the principal–agent problem, many boards of directors in the 1990s began to tie the salaries of top managers to the profits of the firm or to the price of the firm's stock. They hoped this would give top managers an incentive to make the firm as profitable as possible, thereby benefiting its shareholders.

Separation of ownership from control A situation in a corporation in which the top management, rather than the shareholders, control day-to-day operations.

Principal–agent problem A problem caused by an agent pursuing his own interests rather than the interests of the principal who hired him.

Solved Problem | 5-2

Does the Principal–Agent Problem Apply to the Relationship between Managers and Workers?

Briefly explain whether you agree or disagree with the following argument:

> The principal–agent problem applies not just to the relationship between shareholders and top managers. It also applies to the relationship between managers and workers. Just as shareholders have trouble monitoring whether top managers are earning as much profit as possible, managers have trouble monitoring whether workers are working as hard as possible.

SOLVING THE PROBLEM:

Step 1: **Review the chapter material.** This problem concerns the principal–agent problem, so you may want to review the section "Corporate Structure and Corporate Governance," which is on this page.

Step 2: **Evaluate the argument.** You should agree with the argument. A corporation's shareholders have difficulty monitoring the activities of top managers. In practice, they attempt to do so indirectly through the corporation's board of directors. But the firm's top managers may influence—or even control—the firm's board of directors. Even if top managers do not control a board of directors, it may be difficult for the board to know whether actions managers take—say, opening a branch office in Paris—will increase the profitability of the firm or just increase the enjoyment of the top managers.

To answer the problem, we must extend this analysis to the relationship between managers and workers: Managers would like workers to work as hard as possible. Workers would often rather not work hard, particularly if they do not see a direct financial reward for doing so. Managers can have trouble monitoring whether workers are working hard or goofing off. Is that worker in his cubicle diligently staring at a computer screen because he is hard at work on a report or because he is surfing the Web for sports scores or writing a long e-mail to his girlfriend? So, the principal–agent problem does apply to the relationship between managers and workers.

EXTRA CREDIT: Boards of directors try to reduce the principal–agent problem by designing compensation policies for top managers that give them financial incentives to increase profits. Similarly, managers try to reduce the principal–agent problem by designing compensation policies that give workers an incentive to work harder. For example, some manufacturers pay factory workers on the basis of how much they produce rather than on the basis of how many hours they work.

YOUR TURN: For more practice, do related problems 2.4 and 2.5 on page 157 at the end of this chapter.

>> End Solved Problem 5-2

5.3 LEARNING OBJECTIVE

5.3 | Explain how firms obtain the funds they need to operate and expand.

How Firms Raise Funds

Owners and managers of firms try to earn a profit. To earn a profit, a firm must raise funds to pay for its operations, including paying its employees and buying machines. Indeed, a central challenge for anyone running a firm, whether that person is a sole proprietor or a top manager of a large corporation, is raising the funds needed to operate and expand the business. Suppose you decide to open an online trading service using $100,000 you have saved in a bank. You use the $100,000 to rent a building for your firm, to buy computers, and to pay other start-up expenses. Your firm is a great success, and you decide to expand by moving to a larger building and buying more computers. As the owner of a small business, you can obtain the funds for this expansion in three ways:

1. If you are making a profit, you could reinvest the profits back into your firm. Profits that are reinvested in a firm rather than taken out of a firm and paid to the firm's owners are *retained earnings.*
2. You could obtain funds by taking on one or more partners who invest in the firm. This arrangement would increase the firm's *financial capital.*
3. Finally, you could borrow the funds from relatives, friends, or a bank.

The managers of a large firm have some additional ways to raise funds, as we will see in the next section.

Sources of External Funds

Unless firms rely on retained earnings, they have to obtain the *external funds* they need from others who have funds available to invest. It is the role of an economy's *financial system* to transfer funds from savers to borrowers—directly through financial markets or indirectly through financial intermediaries such as banks.

Firms can raise external funds in two ways. The first relies on financial intermediaries such as banks and is called **indirect finance**. If you put $1,000 in a checking account or a savings account, or if you buy a $1,000 certificate of deposit (CD), the bank will loan most of those funds to borrowers. The bank will combine your funds with those of other depositors and, for example, make a $100,000 loan to a local business. Small businesses rely heavily on bank loans as their primary source of external funds.

Indirect finance A flow of funds from savers to borrowers through financial intermediaries such as banks. Intermediaries raise funds from savers to lend to firms (and other borrowers).

The second way for firms to acquire external funds is through *financial markets.* Raising funds in these markets, such as the New York Stock Exchange on Wall Street in New York, is called **direct finance**. Direct finance usually takes the form of the borrower selling the lender a *financial security.* A financial security is a document—sometimes in electronic form—that states the terms under which the funds have passed from the buyer of the security—who is lending funds—to the borrower. *Bonds* and *stocks* are the two main types of financial securities. Typically, only large corporations are able to sell bonds and stocks on financial markets. Investors are generally unwilling to buy securities issued by small and medium-sized firms because the investors lack sufficient information on the financial health of smaller firms.

Direct finance A flow of funds from savers to firms through financial markets, such as the New York Stock Exchange.

Bonds **Bonds** are financial securities that represent promises to repay a fixed amount of funds. When General Electric (GE) sells a bond to raise funds, it promises to pay the purchaser of the bond an interest payment each year for the term of the bond, as well as a final payment of the amount of the loan, or the *principal,* at the end of the term. GE may need to raise many millions of dollars to build a factory, but each individual bond has a principal, or *face value,* of $1,000, which is the amount each bond purchaser is lending GE. So, GE must sell many bonds to raise all the funds it needs. Suppose GE promises it will pay interest of $60 per year to anyone who will buy one of its bonds. The interest payments on a bond are referred to as **coupon payments**. The **interest rate** is the cost of borrowing funds, usually expressed as a percentage of the amount borrowed. If we express the coupon as a percentage of the face value of the bond, we find the interest rate on the bond, called the *coupon rate.* In this case, the interest rate is:

Bond A financial security that represents a promise to repay a fixed amount of funds.

Coupon payment An interest payment on a bond.

Interest rate The cost of borrowing funds, usually expressed as a percentage of the amount borrowed.

$$\frac{\$60}{\$1{,}000} = 0.06, \text{ or } 6\%.$$

Many bonds that corporations issue have terms, or *maturities,* of 30 years. For example, if you bought a bond from GE, GE would pay you $60 per year for 30 years, and at the end of the thirtieth year, GE would pay you back the $1,000 principal.

Stocks When you buy a newly issued bond from a firm, you are lending funds to that firm. When you buy **stock** issued by a firm, you are actually buying part ownership of the firm. When a corporation sells stock, it is doing the same thing the owner of a small business does when she takes on a partner: The firm is increasing its financial capital by bringing additional owners into the firm. Any individual shareholder usually owns only a small fraction of the total shares of stock issued by a corporation.

Stock A financial security that represents partial ownership of a firm.

A shareholder is entitled to a share of the corporation's profits, if there are any. Corporations generally keep some of their profits—known as retained earnings—to finance future expansion. The remaining profits are paid to shareholders as **dividends.** If investors expect the firm to earn economic profits on its retained earnings, the firm's share price will rise, providing a *capital gain* for investors. If a corporation is unable to

Dividends Payments by a corporation to its shareholders.

make a profit, it usually does not pay a dividend. Under the law, corporations must make payments on any debt they have before making payments to their owners. That is, a corporation must make promised payments to bondholders before it may make any dividend payments to shareholders. In addition, when firms sell stock, they acquire from investors an open-ended commitment of funds to the firm. Therefore, unlike bonds, stocks do not have a maturity date, so the firm is not obliged to return the investor's funds at any particular date.

Stock and Bond Markets Provide Capital—and Information

The original purchasers of stocks and bonds may resell them to other investors. In fact, most of the buying and selling of stocks and bonds that takes place each day is investors reselling existing stocks and bonds to each other rather than corporations selling new stocks and bonds to investors. The buyers and sellers of stocks and bonds together make up the *stock and bond markets*. There is no single place where stocks and bonds are bought and sold. Some trading of stocks and bonds takes place in buildings known as *exchanges*, such as the New York Stock Exchange or Tokyo Stock Exchange. In the United States, the stocks and bonds of the largest corporations are traded on the New York Stock Exchange. The development of computer technology has spread the trading of stocks and bonds outside exchanges to *securities dealers* linked by computers. These dealers comprise the *over-the-counter market*. The stocks of many computer and other high-technology firms—including Apple, Google, and Microsoft—are traded in the most important of the over-the-counter markets, the *National Association of Securities Dealers Automated Quotation* system, which is referred to by its acronym, Nasdaq.

Don't Let This Happen to **YOU!**

When Google Shares Change Hands, Google Doesn't Get the Money

Google is a popular investment, with investors buying and selling shares often as their views about the firm's valuation shift. That's great for Google, right? Think of all that money flowing into Google's coffers as shares change hands and the stock price goes up. *Wrong*. Google raises funds in a primary market, but shares change hands in a secondary market. Those trades don't put money into Google's hands, but they do give important information to the firm's managers. Let's see why.

Primary markets are those in which newly issued claims are sold to initial buyers by the issuer. Businesses can raise funds in a primary financial market in two ways—by borrowing (selling bonds) or by selling shares of stock—which result in different types of claims on the borrowing firm's future income. Although you hear about the stock market fluctuations each night on the evening news, bonds actually account for more of the funds raised by borrowers. In mid-2007, the value of bonds in the United States was about $27 trillion compared to $15 trillion for stocks, or equities.

In *secondary markets*, stocks and bonds that have already been issued are sold by one investor to another. If Google sells shares to the public, it is turning to a primary market for new funds. Once Google shares are issued, investors trade the shares in the secondary market. The founders of Google do not receive any new funds when Google shares are traded on secondary markets. The initial seller of a stock or bond raises funds from a lender only in the primary market. Secondary markets convey information to firms' managers and to investors by determining the price of financial instruments. For example, a major increase in Google's stock price conveys the market's good feelings about the firm, and the firm may decide to raise funds to expand. Hence, secondary markets are valuable sources of information for corporations that are considering raising funds.

Primary and secondary markets are both important, but they play different roles. As an investor, you principally trade stocks and bonds in a secondary market. As a corporate manager, you may help decide how to raise new funds to expand the firm where you work.

YOUR TURN: Test your understanding by doing related problem 3.10 on page 158 at the end of this chapter.

Shares of stock represent claims on the profits of the firms that issue them. Therefore, as the fortunes of the firms change and they earn more or less profit, the prices of the stock the firms have issued should also change. Similarly, bonds represent claims to receive coupon payments and one final payment of principal. Therefore, a particular bond that was issued in the past may have its price go up or down, depending on whether the coupon payments being offered on newly issued bonds are higher or lower than on existing bonds. If you hold a bond with a coupon of $80 per year, and newly issued bonds have coupons of $100 per year, the price of your bond will fall because it is less attractive to investors. The price of a bond will be affected by changes in investors' perceptions of the issuing firm's ability to make the coupon payments. For example, if investors begin to believe that a firm may soon go out of business and stop making coupon payments to its bondholders, the price of the firm's bonds will fall to very low levels.

Changes in the value of a firm's stocks and bonds offer important information for a firm's managers, as well as for investors. An increase in the stock price means that investors are more optimistic about the firm's profit prospects, and the firm's managers may wish to expand the firm's operations as a result. By contrast, a decrease in the firm's stock price indicates that investors are less optimistic about the firms' profit prospects, so management may want to shrink the firm's operations. Likewise, changes in the value of the firm's bonds imply changes in the cost of external funds to finance the firm's investment in research and development or in new factories. A higher bond price indicates a lower cost of new external funds, while a lower bond price indicates a higher cost of new external funds.

Making the Connection

Following Abercrombie & Fitch's Stock Price in the Financial Pages

If you read the stock listings in your local paper or the *Wall Street Journal*, you will notice that newspapers manage to pack into a small space a lot of information about what happened to stocks during the previous day's trading. The figure on the next page reproduces a small portion of the listings from the *Wall Street Journal* from March 6, 2007, for stocks listed on the New York Stock Exchange. The listings provide information on the buying and selling of the stock of five firms during the previous day. Let's focus on the highlighted listing for Abercrombie & Fitch, the clothing store, and examine the information in each column:

- The first column gives the name of the company.
- The second column gives the firm's "ticker" symbol (ANF), which you may have seen scrolling along the bottom of the screen on cable financial news channels.
- The third column (Open) gives the price (in dollars) of the stock at the time that trading began, which is 9:30 A.M. on the New York Stock Exchange. Abercrombie & Fitch had opened for trading the previous day at a price of $74.54.
- The fourth column (High) and the fifth column (Low) give the highest price and the lowest price the stock sold for during the previous day.
- The sixth column (Close) gives the price the stock sold for the last time it was traded before the close of trading on the previous day (4:30 P.M.), which in this case was $73.42.
- The seventh column (Net Chg) gives the amount by which the closing price changed from the closing price the day before. In this case, the price of Abercrombie

& Fitch's stock had fallen by $1.52 per share from its closing price the day before. Changes in Abercrombie & Fitch's stock price give the firm's managers a signal that they may want to expand or contract the firm's operations.

- The eighth column (% Chg) gives the change in the price in percentage terms rather than in dollar terms.

- The ninth column (Vol) gives the number of shares of stock traded on the previous day.

- The tenth column (52 Week High) and the eleventh column (52 Week Low) give the highest price the stock has sold for and the lowest price the stock has sold for during the previous year. These numbers tell how *volatile* the stock price is—that is, how much it fluctuates over the course of the year.

- The twelfth column (Div) gives the dividend expressed in dollars. In this case, .70 means that Abercrombie paid a dividend of $0.70 per share.

- The thirteenth column (Yield) gives the *dividend yield*, which is calculated by dividing the dividend by the *closing price* of the stock—that is, the price at which Abercrombie's stock last sold before the close of trading on the previous day.

- The fourteenth column (PE) gives the *P-E ratio* (or *price-earnings ratio*), which is calculated by dividing the price of the firm's stock by its earnings per share. (Remember that because firms retain some earnings, earnings per share is not necessarily the same as dividends per share.) Abercrombie's P-E ratio was 16, meaning that its price per share was 16 times its earnings per share. You would have to pay $16 to buy $1 of Abercrombie & Fitch's earnings.

- The final column (Year-To-Date % Chg) gives the percentage change in the price of the stock from the beginning of the year to the previous day. In this case, the price of Abercrombie's stock had increased by 5.4 percent since the beginning of 2007.

	Symbol	Open	High	Low	Close	Net Chg	%Chg	Vol	52 Week High	52 Week Low	Div	Yield	PE	Year-To-Date %Chg
ABB LTD ADS	ABB	15.95	16.21	15.94	15.96	-0.56	-3.39	4,478,028	19.3	10.1	0.1	0.6	25	-11.2
ABBOTT LABORATORIES	ABT	52.80	53.59	52.72	52.75	-0.26	-0.49	6,910,610	55.1	40.6	1.30	2.5	48	8.3
ABERCROMBIE & FITCH CO.	ANF	74.54	75.07	73.37	73.42	-1.52	-2.03	1,580,908	83.8	50	0.7	1.0	16	5.4
ABITIBI-CONSOLIDATED INC.	ABY	2.72	2.74	2.70	2.70	-0.03	-1.1	965,400	4.53	2.23	...	...	...	5.5
ACADIA REALTY TRUST SBI	AKR	26.65	26.77	26.30	26.36	-0.49	-1.82	429,604	28.1	19.5	.80	3.0	22	5.4

Source: Wall Street Journal Eastern Edition [Staff produced copy only] by *Wall Street Journal*. Copyright 2007 by Dow Jones & Co Inc. Reproduced with permission of Dow Jones & Co. Inc. in the format Textbook via Copyright Clearance Center.

YOUR TURN: Test your understanding by doing related problem 3.11 on page 158 at the end of this chapter.

5.4 | Understand the information provided in corporations' financial statements.

5.4 LEARNING OBJECTIVE

Using Financial Statements to Evaluate a Corporation

To raise funds, a firm's managers must persuade financial intermediaries or buyers of its bonds or stock that it will be profitable. Before a firm can sell new issues of stock or bonds, it must first provide investors and financial regulators with information about its finances. To borrow from a bank or another financial intermediary, the firm must disclose financial information to the lender as well.

In most high-income countries, government agencies require firms that want to sell securities in financial markets to disclose specific financial information to the public. In the United States, the Securities and Exchange Commission requires publicly owned firms to report their performance in financial statements prepared using standard accounting methods, often referred to as *generally accepted accounting principles.* Such disclosure reduces information costs, but it doesn't eliminate them—for two reasons. First, some firms may be too young to have much information for potential investors to evaluate. Second, managers may try to present the required information in the best possible light so that investors will overvalue their securities.

Private firms also collect information on business borrowers and sell the information to lenders and investors. As long as the information-gathering firm does a good job, lenders and investors purchasing the information will be better able to judge the quality of borrowing firms. Firms specializing in information—including Moody's Investors Service, Standard & Poor's Corporation, Value Line, and Dun & Bradstreet—collect information from businesses and sell it to subscribers. Buyers include individual investors, libraries, and financial intermediaries. You can find some of these publications in your college library or through online information services.

Making the Connection

A Bull in China's Financial Shop

Prospects for Sichuan Changhong Electric Co., manufacturer of plasma televisions and liquid crystal displays, looked excellent in 2007, with rapidly growing output, employment, and profits earned from trade in the world economy. And Changhong was not alone. In the 2000s, the Chinese economy was sizzling. China's output grew by 10.7 percent during 2006, dominated by an astonishing 24 percent growth in investment in plant and equipment. The Chinese economic juggernaut caught the attention of the global business community—and charged onto the U.S. political stage, as China's growth fueled concerns about job losses in the United States.

Will China's weak financial system derail economic growth?

Yet at the same time, many economists and financial commentators worried that the Chinese expansion—which was fueling rising living standards in a rapidly developing economy with 1.3 billion people—would come to an end. Indeed, the debate seemed to be over whether China's boom would have a "soft landing" (with gradually declining growth) or a "hard landing" (possibly leading to an economic financial crisis).

Why the debate? Although China's saving rate was estimated to be a very high 40 percent of gross domestic product (GDP)—double or triple the rate in most other countries—the financial system was doing a poor job of allocating capital. Excessive expansion in office construction and factories was fueled less by careful financial analysis than by the directions of national and local government officials trying to encourage growth. With nonperforming loans—where the borrower cannot make promised payments to lenders—at unheard-of levels, China's banks were in financial trouble. Worse still, they continued to lend to weak, politically connected borrowers.

China's prospects for long-term economic growth depend importantly on a better-developed financial system to generate information for borrowers and lenders. Many economists have urged Chinese officials to improve accounting transparency and information disclosure so that stock and bond markets can flourish. In the absence of well-functioning financial markets, banks are crucial allocators of capital. There, too, information disclosure and less government direction of lending will help oil the Chinese growth machine in the long run.

Chinese firms, like Changhong, may well play a major role on the world's economic stage. But China's creaky financial system needs repair if Chinese firms are to grow rapidly enough to raise the standard of living for Chinese workers over the long run.

YOUR TURN: Test your understanding by doing related problem 4.7 on page 159 at the end of this chapter.

Liability Anything owed by a person or a firm.

What kind of information do investors and firm managers need? A firm must answer three basic questions: What to produce? How to produce it? and What price to charge? To answer these questions, a firm's managers need two pieces of information: The first is the firm's revenues and costs, and the second is the value of the property and other assets the firm owns and the firm's debts, or other **liabilities**, that it owes to other persons and firms. Potential investors in the firm also need this information to decide whether to buy the firm's stocks or bonds. Managers and investors find this information in the firm's *financial statements*, principally its income statement and balance sheet, which we discuss next.

The Income Statement

Income statement A financial statement that sums up a firm's revenues, costs, and profit over a period of time.

A firm's **income statement** sums up its revenues, costs, and profit over a period of time. Corporations issue annual income statements, although the 12-month *fiscal year* covered may be different from the calendar year to represent the seasonal pattern of the business better. We explore income statements in greater detail in the appendix to this chapter.

Accounting profit A firm's net income measured by revenue minus operating expenses and taxes paid.

Getting to Accounting Profit An income statement shows a firm's revenue, costs, and profit for the firm's fiscal year. To determine profitability, the income statement starts with the firm's revenue and subtracts its operating expenses and taxes paid. The remainder, *net income*, is the **accounting profit** of the firm.

Opportunity cost The highest-valued alternative that must be given up to engage in an activity.

Explicit cost A cost that involves spending money.

Implicit cost A nonmonetary opportunity cost.

. . . And Economic Profit Accounting profit provides information on a firm's current net income measured according to accepted accounting standards. Accounting profit is not, however, the ideal measure of a firm's profits because it neglects some of the firm's costs. By taking into account all costs, *economic profit* provides a better indication than accounting profit of how successful a firm is. Firms making an economic profit will remain in business and may even expand. Firms making an *economic loss* are unlikely to remain in business in the long run. To understand how economic profit is calculated, remember that economists always measure cost as *opportunity cost.* The **opportunity cost** of any activity is the highest-valued alternative that must be given up to engage in that activity. Costs are either *explicit* or *implicit.* When a firm spends money, an **explicit cost** results. If a firm incurs an opportunity cost but does not spend money, an **implicit cost** results. For example, firms incur an explicit labor cost when they pay wages to employees. Firms have many other explicit costs as well, such as the cost of the electricity used to light their buildings or the costs of advertising or insurance.

Some costs are implicit, however. The most important of these is the opportunity cost to investors of the funds they have invested in the firm. Economists refer to the minimum amount that investors must earn on the funds they invest in a firm, expressed as a percentage of the amount invested, as a *normal rate of return*. If a firm fails to provide investors with at least a normal rate of return, it will not be able to remain in business over the long run because investors will not continue to invest their funds in the firm. For example, Bethlehem Steel was once the second-leading producer of steel in the United States and a very profitable firm with stock that sold for more than $50 per share. By 2002, investors became convinced that the firm's uncompetitive labor costs in world markets meant that the firm would never be able to provide investors with a normal rate of return. Many investors expected that the firm would eventually have to declare bankruptcy, and as a result, the price of Bethlehem Steel's stock plummeted to $1 per share. Shortly thereafter, the firm declared bankruptcy, and its remaining assets were sold off to a competing steel firm. The return (in dollars) that investors require to continue investing in a firm is a true cost to the firm and should be subtracted from the firm's revenues to calculate its profits.

The necessary rate of return that investors must receive to continue investing in a firm varies from firm to firm. If the investment is risky—as would be the case with a biotechnology start-up—investors may require a high rate of return to compensate them for the risk. Investors in firms in more established industries, such as electric utilities, may require lower rates of return. The exact rate of return investors require to invest in any particular firm is difficult to calculate, which also makes it difficult for an accountant to include the return as a cost on an income statement. Firms have other implicit costs besides the return investors require that can also be difficult to calculate. As a result, the rules of accounting generally require that accounts include only explicit costs in the firm's financial records. *Economic costs* include both explicit costs *and* implicit costs. **Economic profit** is equal to a firm's revenues minus all of its costs, implicit and explicit. Because accounting profit excludes some implicit costs, it is larger than economic profit.

Economic profit A firm's revenues minus all of its implicit and explicit costs.

The Balance Sheet

A firm's **balance sheet** sums up its financial position on a particular day, usually the end of a quarter or year. Recall that an asset is anything of value that a firm owns, and a liability is a debt or obligation owed by a firm. Subtracting the value of a firm's liabilities from the value of its assets leaves its *net worth*. We can think of the net worth as what the firm's owners would be left with if the firm were closed, its assets were sold, and its liabilities were paid off. Investors can determine a firm's net worth by inspecting its balance sheet. We analyze a balance sheet in detail in the appendix to this chapter, which begins on page 161.

Balance sheet A financial statement that sums up a firm's financial position on a particular day, usually the end of a quarter or year.

5.5 LEARNING OBJECTIVE

5.5 | Understand the role of government in corporate governance.

Corporate Governance Policy

A firm's financial statements provide important information on the firm's ability to add value for investors and the economy. Accurate and easy-to-understand financial statements are inputs for decisions by the firm's managers and investors. Indeed, the information in accounting statements helps guide resource allocation in the economy.

Firms disclose financial statements in periodic filings to the federal government and in *annual reports* to shareholders. An investor is more likely to buy a firm's stock if the firm's income statement shows a large after-tax profit and if its balance sheet shows a large net worth. The top management of a firm has at least two reasons to attract investors and keep the firm's stock price high. First, a higher stock price increases the funds the firm can raise when it sells a given amount of stock. Second, to reduce the principal–agent problem, boards of directors often tie the salaries of top managers to the firm's stock price or to the profitability of the firm.

Top managers clearly have an incentive to maximize the profits reported on the income statement and the net worth reported on the balance sheet. If top managers make good decisions, the firm's profits will be high, and the firm's assets will be large relative to its liabilities. The business scandals that came to light in 2002 revealed, however, that some top managers have inflated profits and hidden liabilities that should have been listed on their balance sheets.

At Enron, an energy trading firm, CFO Andrew Fastow was accused of creating partnerships that were supposedly independent of Enron but in fact were owned by the firm. He was accused of transferring large amounts of Enron's debts to these partnerships, which reduced the liabilities on Enron's balance sheet, thereby increasing the firm's net worth. Fastow's deception made Enron more attractive to investors, increasing its stock price—and Fastow's compensation. In 2001, however, Enron was forced into bankruptcy. The firm's shareholders lost billions of dollars, and many employees lost their jobs. In 2004, Fastow pleaded guilty to conspiracy and was sentenced to 10 years in federal prison. Enron's CEO, Kenneth Lay, was found guilty of securities fraud in 2006 but died prior to being sentenced.

At WorldCom, a telecommunications firm, David Myers, the firm's controller, pleaded guilty to falsifying "WorldCom's books, to reduce WorldCom's reported actual costs and therefore increase WorldCom's reported earnings." Myers's actions caused WorldCom's income statement to overstate the firm's profits by more than $10 billion. WorldCom CEO Bernard Ebbers is serving a 25-year prison sentence for fraud. The scandals at Enron and WorldCom were the largest cases of corporate fraud in U.S. history.

How was it possible for corporations such as Enron and WorldCom to falsify their financial statements? The federal government regulates how financial statements are prepared, but this regulation cannot by itself guarantee the accuracy of the statements. All firms that issue stock to the public have certified public accountants *audit* their financial statements. The accountants are employees of accounting firms, *not* of the firms being audited. The audits are intended to provide investors with an independent opinion as to whether a firm's financial statements fairly represent the true financial condition of the firm. Unfortunately, as the Enron and WorldCom scandals revealed, top managers who are determined to deceive investors about the true financial condition of their firms can also deceive outside auditors.

The private sector's response to the corporate scandals was almost immediate. In addition to the reexamination of corporate governance practices at many corporations, the New York Stock Exchange and the Nasdaq put forth initiatives to ensure the accuracy and accessibility of information.

To guard against future scandals, new federal legislation was enacted in 2002. The landmark *Sarbanes-Oxley Act of 2002* requires that corporate directors have a certain level of expertise with financial information and mandates that CEOs personally certify the accuracy of financial statements. The Sarbanes-Oxley Act also requires that financial analysts and auditors disclose whether any conflicts of interest might exist that would limit their independence in evaluating a firm's financial condition. The purpose of this provision is to ensure that analysts and auditors are acting in the best interests of shareholders. The act promotes management accountability by specifying the responsibilities of corporate officers and by increasing penalties, including long jail sentences, for managers who do not meet their responsibilities.

Perhaps the most noticeable corporate governance reform under the Sarbanes-Oxley Act is the creation of the Public Company Accounting Oversight Board, a national board that oversees the auditing of public companies' financial reports. The board's mission is to promote the independence of auditors to ensure that they disclose accurate information. On balance, most observers acknowledge that the Sarbanes-Oxley Act brought back confidence in the U.S. corporate governance system, though questions remain for the future about whether the act may chill legitimate business risk-taking by diverting management attention from the core business toward regulatory compliance. And the high accounting costs of implementing Sarbanes-Oxley are borne by all shareholders.

By 2007, it had become clear that Sarbanes-Oxley had raised the costs to firms of issuing stocks and bonds in the United States. Section 404 of Sarbanes-Oxley is intended to reassure investors that accounting "errors"—whether from fraud, mistakes, or omissions—will be minimized by requiring firms to maintain effective controls over financial reporting. Many economists believe, though, that the rules for implementing Section 404 set forth by the Securities and Exchange Commission and the Public Company Accounting Oversight Board have turned out to be much more costly to firms than anticipated and that these costs may exceed the benefits of the regulations. As a result, the share of new issues of stocks and bonds being listed on the New York Stock Exchange or Nasdaq has declined relative to listings on foreign stock markets, such as the London Stock Exchange. Some economists, though, are skeptical that the decline in the share of new listings on the New York Stock Exchange and Nasdaq is due to the effects of Sarbanes-Oxley. These economists argue that as other global exchanges become more mature, they are naturally able to attract new listings from local firms. Therefore, in this view, the declining fraction of foreign firms willing to list new issues on the New York Stock Exchange or Nasdaq is not an indication that the burden of U.S. regulations is too heavy.

Outside the United States, the European Commission and Japan have also tightened corporate governance rules. The challenge of ensuring the accurate reporting of firms' economic profits without excessively raising firms' costs is a global one.

Solved Problem | 5-5

What Makes a Good Board of Directors?

Western Digital Corporation makes computer hard drives. *BusinessWeek* magazine published the following analysis by Standard & Poor's Equity Research Services of Western Digital's corporate governance:

> Overall, we view Western Digital's corporate-governance policies favorably and believe the company compares well in this regard relative to peers. We see the following factors as positives: the board is controlled by a supermajority (greater than 67%) of independent outsiders; the nominating and compensation committees are comprised solely of independent outside directors; all directors with more than one year of service own stock. . . .

a. What is an "independent outsider" on a board of directors?

b. Why is it good for a firm to have a large majority of independent outsiders on the board of directors?

c. Why would it be good for a firm to have the auditing and compensation committees composed of outsiders?

d. Why would it be good for a firm if its directors own the firm's stock?

Source: Jawahar Hingorani, "Western Digital: A Drive Buy," *BusinessWeek*, January 9, 2007.

SOLVING THE PROBLEM:

Step 1: **Review the chapter material.** The context of this problem is the business scandals of 2002 and the underlying principal–agent problem that arises because of the separation of ownership from control in large corporations, so you may want to review the section "Corporate Governance Policy," which begins on page 149.

Step 2: **Answer question (a) by defining "independent outsiders."** *Insiders* are members of top management who also serve on the board of directors. *Outsiders* are members of the board of directors who are not otherwise employed by the firm. *Independent outsiders* are outsiders who have no business connections with the firm.

Step 3: **Answer question (b) by explaining why it is good for a firm to have a large majority of independent outsiders on the board of directors.** Having members of top management on the board of directors provides the board with information about the firm that only top managers possess. Having too many insiders on a board, however, means that top managers may end up controlling the board rather than the other way around. A corporation's board of directors is supposed to provide the monitoring and control of top managers that shareholders cannot provide directly. This is most likely to happen when a larger majority of the board of directors consists of independent outsiders.

Step 4: **Answer question (c) by explaining why it may be good for a firm to have the auditing and compensation committees composed of outsiders.** The auditing committee is responsible for ensuring that the firm's financial statements are accurate, and the compensation committee is responsible for setting the pay of top management. It is of vital importance to a firm that these activities be carried out in an honest and impartial way. Having these two important committees composed exclusively of independent outside members increases the chances that the committees will act in the best interests of the shareholders rather than in the best interests of top management.

Step 5: **Answer question (d) by explaining why it may be good for a firm to have directors owning the firm's stock.** When directors own the firm's stock, they will then share with other stockholders the desire to see the firm maximize profits. The directors will be more likely to insist that top managers take actions to increase profits rather than to pursue other objectives that may be in the interests of the managers but not the stockholders. Of course, when directors own the firm's stock the directors may be tempted not to object if top managers take steps to improperly inflate the firm's profits, as happened during the business scandals of 2002. On balance, though, most economists believe that it improves corporate governance when a firm's directors own the firms' stock.

YOUR TURN: For more practice, do related problems 5.3 and 5.4 on page 160 at the end of this chapter.

>> End Solved Problem 5-5

>> Continued from page 137

Economics in YOUR Life!

At the beginning of the chapter, we asked you to consider two questions: Why is it difficult to get the managers of a firm to act in your interest rather than in their own? and Given this problem, should you ever take on the risk of buying stock? The reason managers may not act in shareholders' interest is that in large corporations, there is separation of ownership from control: The shareholders own the firm, but the top managers actually control it. This results in the principal–agent problem discussed in the chapter. The principal–agent problem clearly adds to the risk you would face by buying stock rather than doing something safe with your money, such as putting it in the bank. But the rewards to owning stock can also be substantial, potentially earning you far more over the long run than a bank account will. Buying the stock of well-known firms, such as Google, that are closely followed by Wall Street investment analysts helps to reduce the principal–agent problem. It is less likely that the managers of these firms will take actions that are clearly not in the best interests of shareholders because the managers' actions are difficult to conceal. Buying the stock of large, well-known firms certainly does not completely eliminate the risk from principal–agent problems, however. Enron, WorldCom, and some of the other firms that were involved in the scandals discussed in this chapter were all well known and closely followed by Wall Street analysts, but the misbehavior of their managers went undetected, at least for awhile.

Conclusion

In a market system, firms make independent decisions about which goods and services to produce, how to produce them, and what prices to charge. In modern high-income countries, such as the United States, large corporations account for a majority of the sales and profits earned by firms. Generally, the managers of these corporations do a good job of representing the interests of stockholders, while providing the goods and services demanded by consumers. As the business scandals of 2002 showed, however, some top managers enriched themselves at the expense of stockholders and consumers by manipulating financial statements. Passage of the Sarbanes-Oxley Act of 2002 and other new government regulations have helped restore investor and management confidence in firms' financial statements. However, economists debate whether the benefits from these regulations are greater than their costs.

An Inside Look on the next page discusses the compensation Google pays its top executives.

An Inside **LOOK**

Executive Compensation at Google

ASSOCIATED PRESS, APRIL 4, 2007

Google CEO, Co-Founders Get $1 Salary

The trio of billionaires who run Google Inc. collected less than $600,000 in combined compensation last year while they raked in big jackpots by selling some of their holdings in the online search leader.

a The total amount that Google paid its chief executive, Eric Schmidt, and co-founders Larry Page and Sergey Brin during 2006 would have been less than $5,200 if not for personal security and transportation costs, according to documents filed Wednesday with the Securities and Exchange Commission.

Schmidt's package totaled $557,466, including $532,755 for personal security. Page's pay totaled $38,519, with most of the money covering personal transportation, logistics and security. Brin's 2006 pay consisted solely of a $1 salary and $1,723 bonus. Google paid the same salary and holiday bonus to Schmidt and Page.

The Associated Press bases its executive pay totals on salary, bonus, incentives, perks, above-market returns on deferred compensation and the estimated value of stock options and awards granted during the year.

Schmidt, Page and Brin have refused to take anything more than a token paycheck for the past three years to promote the egalitarian spirit championed by the Mountain View-based company.

b It's a sacrifice that the three executives can afford to make because Google's high-flying stock has elevated them into the ranks of the world's richest people. Meanwhile, hundreds of Google's early employees have become millionaires.

As of March 1, Page, 34, owned 29.2 million Google shares currently worth $13.8 billion while Brin, 33, held 28.6 million shares worth about $13.5 billion. Schmidt, 51, owns 10.7 million shares currently worth $5 billion. The three men have been converting some of their holdings into cash by regularly selling some of their stockholdings since the company went public in August 2004.

Last year, Brin, Page and Schmidt made more than $2 billion combined from their Google stock sales, according to data compiled from SEC filings by Thomson Financial. Brin sold 1.99 million shares for a total windfall of $788 million last year while Page pocketed $666 million by selling 1.72 million shares. Schmidt cashed out 1.39 million shares during 2006 for a total $580 million.

Google's stock price rose by 11 percent last year, a gain that lagged the Standard & Poor's 500 index—a blue-chip bellwether that the company joined during 2006. The S&P 500 rose by 13.6 percent last year.

Since its IPO, Google shares have surged to a more than fivefold increase, a meteoric performance that has created more than $120 billion in shareholder wealth. Google shares fell $1.58 Wednesday to close at $471.02 the Nasdaq Stock Market.

The rapid run-up in Google's stock has been driven by its search engine, which has become synonymous with looking things up on the Internet. The search engine also propels a lucrative online advertising network that enabled Google to turn a 2006 profit of $3.1 billion, more than doubling its earnings from the previous year. The robust growth has enabled Google to add more than 8,000 workers during the past three years. At the end of 2006, Google had 10,674 employees—all of whom were eligible for the same holiday bonus paid to Schmidt, Page and Brin.

Google's brain trust has already agreed to settle for a $1 salary again this year, rejecting an opportunity for a raise, according to the SEC filing.

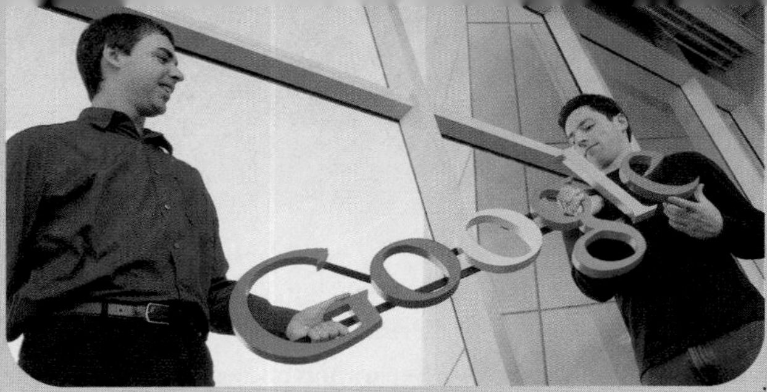

Key Points in the Article

The article discusses how Google CEO Eric Schmidt and the firm's co-founders Sergey Brin and Larry Page are compensated. Google is different from most large corporations in that most of the compensation for the CEO comes in the form of stock. The figure tracks the performance of Google's stock. Prior to August 2004, when Google had its initial public offering (IPO), Eric Schmidt and the co-founders agreed to cut their salaries to $1 a year plus some fringe benefits and stock in the company. Essentially, they bet that the price of the stock would rise. This turned out to be a good bet. Google's IPO was in August 2004. The price opened at $100 per share and closed at $104.06 that day. Google's stock has performed very well since the initial offering, and on April 4, 2007 (the date of the article) the price closed at $471.02 per share. As a result, the CEO and co-founders of Google have become billionaires.

The chapter discusses the principal–agent problem facing modern corporations. In large corporations, the executives of a firm are not usually the owners of the firm. In this situation, executives (especially the CEO) can take actions that are in their own interests rather than the interests of the shareholders. For example, the executives could use their influence to obtain large base salaries that are not sensitive to the firm's stock price. This reduces the executives' incentive to perform well. After all, the executives have large salaries, regardless of whether the firm does well.

Analyzing the News

a At Google, the CEO actually has a low base salary. Eric Schmidt earns a salary of $1 per year. He receives other compensation in the form of bonuses and compensation for security. Schmidt's combined compensation package was only $557,466, which is much less than those of most executives at similar firms.

b Instead of having a large base salary, most of Eric Schmidt's income comes from the sale of Google stock that he owned at the time Google went public or has received since then. He owns 10.7 million shares of Google stocks, making him a major shareholder in the firm. For each $1 increase in the stock price, Schmidt's wealth increases by $10.7 million. This is a strong incentive for him to take actions that will increase the stock price. This is good news to other Google shareholders, because Schmidt's income is tied to increases in the value of Google's stock. It seems Google has significantly reduced the principal–agent problem.

Thinking Critically

1. Compensating executives with stock, or equity, is a way to solve the principal–agent problem, but the practice is not without flaws. Critics of equity compensation point out that it can create incentives for executives to take actions not in the best interests of other shareholders and may have contributed to the corporate scandals discussed in the chapter. How could equity compensation contribute to these scandals?
2. An executive at Google who knew that Google was about to announce a larger than expected profit could have earned a bundle quickly by buying Google stock at $470 per share and then selling it at a higher price a day or so later. Such insider trading is illegal, however. Do you think that insider trading should be illegal? Are there benefits to other investors or to the economy as a whole associated with such trading? Are there problems associated with such trading?

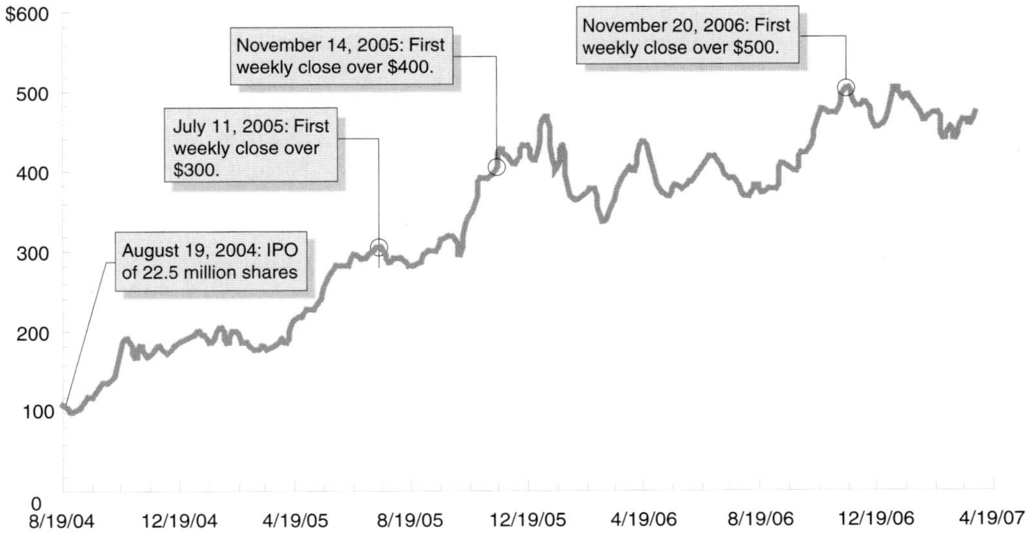

Movements in Google's stock price, August 2004 to April 2007.

Key Terms

Accounting profit, p. 148
Asset, p. 138
Balance sheet, p. 149
Bond, p. 143
Corporate governance, p. 140
Corporation, p. 138
Coupon payment, p. 143
Direct finance, p. 143
Dividends, p. 143
Economic profit, p. 149
Explicit cost, p. 148
Implicit cost, p. 148
Income statement, p. 148
Indirect finance, p. 143
Interest rate, p. 143
Liability, p. 148
Limited liability, p. 138
Opportunity cost, p. 148
Partnership, p. 138
Principal–agent problem, p. 141
Separation of ownership from control, p. 141
Sole proprietorship, p. 138
Stock, p. 143

5.1 LEARNING OBJECTIVE 5.1 | Categorize the major types of firms in the United States, **pages 138–140.**

Types of Firms

Summary

There are three types of firms: A **sole proprietorship** is a firm owned by a single individual and not organized as a corporation. A **partnership** is a firm owned jointly by two or more persons and not organized as a corporation. A **Corporation** is a legal form of business that provides the owners with limited liability. An **asset** is anything of value owned by a person or a firm. The owners of sole proprietorships and partners have unlimited liability, which means there is no legal distinction between the personal assets of the owners of the business and the assets of the business. The owners of corporations have **limited liability**, which means they can never lose more than their investment in the firm. Although only 20 percent of firms are corporations, they account for the majority of revenue and profit earned by all firms.

myeconlab Get Ahead of the Curve — Visit www.myeconlab.com to complete these exercises online and get instant feedback.

Review Questions

1.1 What are the three major types of firms in the United States? Briefly discuss the most important characteristics of each type.

1.2 What is limited liability? Why does the government grant limited liability to the owners of corporations?

Problems and Applications

1.3 Suppose that shortly after graduating from college, you decide to start your own business. Will you be likely to organize the business as a sole proprietorship, a partnership, or a corporation? Explain your reasoning.

1.4 **(Related to the *Making the Connection* on page 139)** Evaluate the following argument:

> I would like to invest in the stock market, but I think that buying shares of stock in a corporation is too risky. Suppose I buy $10,000 of General Motors stock, and the company ends up going bankrupt. Because as a stockholder, I'm part owner of the company, I might be responsible for paying hundreds of thousands of dollars of the company's debts.

1.5 **(Related to the *Making the Connection* on page 139)** In an article in the *New York Times*, sociologist Dalton Conley proposed the *elimination* of limited liability for corporate shareholders. Do you think that corporations should be granted limited liability? What are the benefits of limited liability? What is its downside? Would you be more willing to buy bonds from a corporation with limited liability? Would you be more willing to buy the stock of a corporation with limited liability?

Source: Dalton Conley, "Reward but No Risk," *New York Times*, May 10, 2003.

>> End Learning Objective 5.1

5.2 LEARNING OBJECTIVE 5.2 | Describe the typical management structure of corporations and understand the concepts of separation of ownership from control and the principal–agent problem, **pages 140–142.**

The Structure of Corporations and the Principal–Agent Problem

Summary

Corporate governance refers to the way in which a corporation is structured and the impact a corporation's structure has on the firm's behavior. Most corporations have a similar management structure: The shareholders elect a board of directors that appoints the corporation's top managers, such as the chief executive officer (CEO). Because the top management often does not own a large fraction of the stock in the corporation, large corporations have a **separation of ownership from control**. Because top managers have less incentive to increase the corporation's profits than to increase their own salaries and their own enjoyment, corporations can suffer from a **principal–agent problem.** A principal–agent problem exists when the principals—in this case, the shareholders of the corporation—have difficulty in getting the agent—the corporation's top management—to carry out their wishes.

myeconlab Get Ahead of the Curve — Visit www.myeconlab.com to complete these exercises online and get instant feedback.

Review Questions

2.1 What do we mean by the separation of ownership from control in large corporations?

2.2 How is the separation of ownership from control related to the principal–agent problem?

Problems and Applications

2.3 The principal–agent problem arises almost everywhere in the business world—but it also crops up even closer to home. Discuss the principal–agent problem that exists in the college classroom. Who is the principal? Who is the agent? What is the problem between this principal and this agent?

2.4 **(Related to *Solved Problem 5-2* on page 141)** Briefly explain whether you agree or disagree with the following argument: "The separation of ownership from control in large corporations and the principal–agent problem means that top managers can work short days, take long vacations, and otherwise slack off."

2.5 **(Related to *Solved Problem 5-2* on page 141)** An economic consultant gives the board of directors of a firm the following advice:

> You can increase the profitability of the firm if you change your method of compensating top management. Instead of paying your top management a straight salary, you should pay them a salary plus give them the right to buy the firm's stock in the future at a price above the stock's current market price.

Explain the consultant's reasoning. To what difficulties might this compensation scheme lead?

2.6 The following is from an article in the *New York Times*: "In theory, boards [of directors] design pay packages to attract and inspire good chief executives and to align their interests with those of shareholders. . . . But what kind of pay packages are appropriate at companies still run by the founding family?" The article quotes one expert as arguing: "There is little or no justification for treating an owner-manager in exactly the same way as a standard CEO." What does the article mean by saying that pay packages should "align [chief executives'] interests with those of shareholders"? What kind of pay packages would achieve this objective? Do you agree that an "owner-manager" should have a pay package different from that of a CEO who is not a member of the family that started the firm? Briefly explain.

Source: Diana B. Henriques, "What's Fair Pay for Running the Family Store?" *New York Times*, January 12, 2003.

>> End Learning Objective 5.2

5.3 LEARNING OBJECTIVE 5.3 | Explain how firms obtain the funds they need to operate and expand, **pages 142–146.**

How Firms Raise Funds

Summary

Firms rely on retained earnings—which are profits retained by the firm and not paid out to the firm's owners—or on using the savings of households for the funds they need to operate and expand. With **direct finance**, the savings of households flow directly to businesses when investors buy **stocks** and **bonds** in financial markets. With **indirect finance**, savings flow indirectly to businesses when households deposit money in saving and checking accounts in banks and the banks lend these funds to businesses. Federal, state, and local governments also sell bonds in financial markets and households also borrow funds from banks. When a firm sells a bond, it is borrowing money from the buyer of the bond. The firm makes a **coupon payment** to the buyer of the bond. The **interest rate** is the cost of borrowing funds, usually expressed as a percentage of the amount borrowed. When a firm sells stock, it is selling part ownership of the firm to the buyer of the stock. **Dividends** are payments by a corporation to its shareholders. The original purchasers of stocks and bonds may resell them in stock and bond markets, such as the New York Stock Exchange.

Review Questions

3.1 What is the difference between direct finance and indirect finance? If you borrow money from a bank to buy a new car, are you using direct finance or indirect finance?

3.2 Why is a bond considered to be a loan but a share of stock is not? Why do corporations issue both bonds and shares of stock?

3.3 How do the stock and bond markets provide information to businesses? Why do stock and bond prices change over time?

Problems and Applications

3.4 Suppose that a firm in which you have invested is losing money. Would you rather own the firm's stock or the firm's bonds? Explain.

3.5 Suppose you originally invested in a firm when it was small and unprofitable. Now the firm has grown considerably and is large and profitable. Would you be better off if you had bought the firm's stock or the firm's bonds? Explain.

3.6 If you deposit $20,000 in a savings account at a bank, you might earn 3 percent interest per year. Someone who borrows $20,000 from a bank to buy a new car might have to pay an interest rate of 8 percent per year on the loan. Knowing this, why don't you just lend your money directly to the car buyer, cutting out the bank?

3.7 **(Related to the *Chapter Opener* on page 136)** When Google's owners wanted to raise funds for expansion in 2004, they decided to sell stock in their company rather than borrow the money. Why do some companies fund their expansion by borrowing, while others fund expansion by issuing new stock?

3.8 **(Related to the *Chapter Opener* on page 136)** What impact would the following events be likely to have on the price of Google's stock?

a. A competitor launches a search engine that's just as good as Google's.
b. The corporate income tax is abolished.
c. Google's board of directors becomes dominated by close friends and relatives of its top management.
d. The price of wireless Internet connections unexpectedly drops, so more and more people use the Internet.
e. Google announces a huge profit of $1 billion, but everybody anticipated that Google would earn a huge profit of $1 billion.

3.9 In 2005, the French government began issuing bonds with 50-year maturities. Would this bond be purchased only by very young investors who expect to still be alive when the bond matures? Briefly explain.

3.10 **(Related to the *Don't Let This Happen to You!* on page 144)** Briefly explain whether you agree or disagree with the following statement: "The total value of the shares of Microsoft stock traded on the Nasdaq last week was $250 million, so the firm actually received more revenue from stock sales than from selling software."

3.11 **(Related to the *Making the Connection* on page 145)** Loans from banks are the most important external source of funds to businesses because most businesses are too small to borrow in financial markets by issuing stocks or bonds. Most investors are reluctant to buy the stocks or bonds of small businesses because of the difficulty of gathering accurate information on the financial strength and profitability of the businesses. Nevertheless, news about the stock market is included in nearly every network news program and is often the lead story in the business section of most newspapers. Is there a contradiction here? Why is the average viewer of TV news or the average reader of a newspaper interested in the fluctuations in prices in the stock market?

>> End Learning Objective 5.3

5.4 LEARNING OBJECTIVE 5.4 | Understand the information provided in corporations' financial statements, **pages 147–149.**

Using Financial Statements to Evaluate a Corporation

Summary

A firm's **income statement** sums up its revenues, costs, and profit over a period of time. A firm's **balance sheet** sums up its financial position on a particular day, usually the end of a quarter or year. A balance sheet records a firms assets and liabilities. A **liability** is anything owed by a person or a firm. Firms report their **accounting profit** on their income statements. Accounting profit does not always include all of a firm's **opportunity cost. Explicit cost** is a cost that involves spending money. **Implicit cost** is a nonmonetary opportunity cost. Because accounting profit excludes some implicit costs, it is larger than **economic profit**.

myeconlab Get Ahead of the Curve — Visit www.myeconlab.com to complete these exercises online and get instant feedback.

Review Questions

4.1 What is the difference between a firm's assets and its liabilities? Give an example of an asset and an example of a liability.

4.2 What is the difference between a firm's balance sheet and a firm's income statement?

Problems and Applications

4.3 Paolo currently has $100,000 invested in bonds that earn him 10 percent interest per year. He wants to open a pizza restaurant and is considering either selling the bonds and using the $100,000 to start his restaurant or borrowing the $100,000 from a bank, which would charge him an annual interest rate of 7 percent. He finally decides to sell the bonds and not take out the bank loan. He reasons, "Because I already have the $100,000 invested in the bonds, I don't have to pay anything to use the money. If I take out the bank loan, I have to pay interest, so my costs of producing pizza will be higher if I take out the loan than if I sell the bonds." What do you think of Paolo's reasoning?

4.4 Paolo and Alfredo are twins who both want to open pizza restaurants. Because their parents always liked Alfredo best, they buy two pizza ovens and give both to him. Unfortunately, Paolo must buy his own pizza ovens. Does Alfredo have lower cost of producing pizza than Paolo does because Alfredo received his pizza ovens as a gift while Paolo had to pay for his? Briefly explain.

4.5 Dane decides to give up a job earning $100,000 per year as a corporate lawyer and converts the duplex that he owns into a UFO museum. (He had been renting out the duplex for $20,000 a year.) His direct expenses include $50,000 per year paid to his assistants and $10,000 per year for utilities. Fans flock to the museum to see his collection of extraterrestrial paraphernalia, which he could easily sell on eBay for $1,000,000. Over the course of the year, the museum brings in revenues of $100,000.

a. How much is Dane's accounting profit for the year?
b. Is Dane earning an economic profit? Explain.

4.6 The Securities and Exchange Commission requires that every firm that wishes to issue stock and bonds to the public make available its balance sheet and income statement. Briefly explain how information useful to investors can be found in these financial statements.

4.7 **(Related to the *Making the Connection* on page 147)** The Making the Connection on China argues that "In the absence of well-functioning financial markets, banks are crucial allocators of capital." What is the difference between a financial market and a bank? What is an "allocator of capital"? How do banks allocate capital?

>> End Learning Objective 5.4

5.5 LEARNING OBJECTIVE 5.5 | Understand the role of government in corporate governance, **pages 149–153.**

Corporate Governance Policy

Summary

Because their compensation often rises with the profitability of the corporation, top managers have an incentive to overstate the profits reported on their firm's income statements. During 2002, it became clear that the top managers of several large corporations had done this, even though intentionally falsifying financial statements is illegal. The *Sarbanes-Oxley Act* of 2002 and greater scrutiny of financial statements have helped to restore investor and management confidence in firms' financial statements.

Review Questions

5.1 What is the Sarbanes-Oxley Act? Why was it passed?

5.2 Why are some policymakers and business owners concerned about the Sarbanes-Oxley Act?

Problems and Applications

5.3 **(Related to *Solved Problem 5-5* on page 151)** When Buford Yates, director of accounting at WorldCom, pleaded guilty to fraud, he stated in federal court that top managers at WorldCom ordered him to make certain adjustments to the firm's financial statements:

> I came to believe that the adjustments I was being directed to make in WorldCom's financial statements had no justification and contravened generally accepted accounting principles. I concluded that the purpose of these adjustments was to incorrectly inflate WorldCom's reported earnings.

What are "generally accepted accounting principles"? How would the "adjustments" Yates was ordered to make benefit top managers at WorldCom? Would these adjustments also benefit WorldCom's stockholders? Briefly explain.

Source: Devlin Barrett, "Ex-WorldCom Exec Pleads Guilty," Associated Press, October 8, 2002.

5.4 **(Related to *Solved Problem 5-5* on page 151)** In 2002, *BusinessWeek* listed Apple Computer as having one of the worst boards of directors:

> Founder Steve Jobs owns just two shares in the company. . . . The CEO of Micro Warehouse, which accounted for nearly 2.9% of Apple's net sales in 2001, sits on the compensation committee. . . . There is an interlocking directorship—with Gap CEO Mickey Drexler and Jobs sitting on each other's boards.

Why might investors be concerned that a top manager like Steve Jobs owns only two shares in the firm? Why might investors be concerned if a member of the board of directors also has a business relationship with the firm? What is an "interlocking directorship"? Why is it a bad thing?

Source: "The Best Boards and the Worst Boards," *BusinessWeek*, October 7, 2002, p. 107.

5.5 The following is from a *BusinessWeek* editorial:

> Welcome to the revolution. After years of paying lip service to reform, Enron Corp. and the ensuing wave of business scandal has finally produced a dramatic change in corporate governance. . . . Investors are rewarding companies with good governance and punishing those without it.

How are investors able to reward or punish firms? What impact will these rewards and punishments have on boards of directors and top managers?

Source: "Boardrooms Are Starting to Wake Up," *BusinessWeek*, October 7, 2002, p. 107.

5.6 An article in *BusinessWeek* stated that the Allstate Corporation, a large insurance company, would now require a simple majority vote, rather than a two-thirds majority vote, to elect members to its board of directors and to remove directors in between annual meetings when elections are held. The article also stated that the price of Allstate's stock rose following the announcement. Briefly discuss whether there may have been a possible connection between these changes in Allstate's corporate governance and the increase in the firm's stock price.

Source: "Allstate Announces Changes to Governance," *BusinessWeek*, February 20, 2007.

5.7 According to a survey in 2007, 78 percent of corporate executives responding believed that the costs of complying with the Sarbanes-Oxley Act outweighed the benefits. The total costs of compliance were about $2.92 million dollars per company. Is it possible to put a dollar value on the benefits to complying with Sarbanes-Oxley? Which groups are likely to receive the most benefits from Sarbanes-Oxley: investors, corporations, or some other group?

Source: Kara Scannell, "Costs to Comply with Sarbanes-Oxley Decline Again," *Wall Street Journal*, May 16, 2007, p. C7.

>> End Learning Objective 5.5

Appendix

Tools to Analyze Firms' Financial Information

LEARNING OBJECTIVE

Understand the concept of present value and the information contained on a firm's income statement and balance sheet.

As we saw in the chapter, modern business organizations are not just "black boxes" transforming inputs into output. Most business revenues and profits are earned by large corporations. Unlike founder-dominated firms, the typical large corporation is run by managers who generally do not own a controlling interest in the firm. Large firms raise funds from outside investors, and outside investors seek information on firms and the assurance that the managers of firms will act in the interests of the investors.

This chapter showed how corporations raise funds by issuing stocks and bonds. This appendix provides more detail to support that discussion. We begin by analyzing *present value* as a key concept in determining the prices of financial securities. We then provide greater information on *financial statements* issued by corporations, using Google as an example.

Using Present Value to Make Investment Decisions

Firms raise funds by selling equity (stock) and debt (bonds and loans) to investors and lenders. If you own shares of stock or a bond, you will receive payments in the form of dividends or coupons over a number of years. Most people value funds they already have more highly than funds they will not receive until some time in the future. For example, you would probably not trade $1,000 you already have for $1,000 you will not receive for one year. The longer you have to wait to receive a payment, the less value it will have for you. One thousand dollars you will not receive for two years is worth less to you than $1,000 you will receive after one year. The value you give today to money you will receive in the future is called the future payment's **present value**. The present value of $1,000 you will receive in one year will be less than $1,000.

Present value The value in today's dollars of funds to be paid or received in the future.

Why is this true? Why is the $1,000 you will not receive for one year less valuable to you than the $1,000 you already have? The most important reason is that if you have $1,000 today, you can use that $1,000 today. You can buy goods and services with the money and receive enjoyment from them. The $1,000 you receive in one year does not have direct use to you now.

Also, prices will likely rise during the year you are waiting to receive your $1,000. So, when you finally do receive the $1,000 in one year, you will not be able to buy as much with it as you could with $1,000 today. Finally, there is some risk that you will not receive the $1,000 in one year. The risk may be very great if an unreliable friend borrows $1,000 from you and vaguely promises to pay you back in one year. The risk may be very small if you lend money to the federal government by buying a United States Treasury bond. In either case, though, there is at least some risk that you will not receive the funds promised.

When someone lends money, the lender expects to be paid back both the amount of the loan and some additional interest. Say that you decide that you are willing to lend your $1,000 today if you are paid back $1,100 one year from now. In this case, you are charging $100/$1,000 = 0.10, or 10 percent interest on the funds you have loaned. Economists would say that you value $1,000 today as equivalent to the $1,100 to be received one year in the future.

Notice that \$1,100 can be written as \$1,000 (1 + 0.10). That is, the value of money received in the future is equal to the value of money in the present multiplied by 1 plus the interest rate, with the interest rate expressed as a decimal. Or:

$$\$1{,}100 = 1{,}000\ (1 + 0.10).$$

Notice, also, that if we divide both sides by (1 + 0.10), we can rewrite this formula as:

$$\$1{,}000 = \frac{\$1{,}100}{(1 + 0.10)}.$$

The rewritten formula states that the present value is equal to the future value to be received in one year divided by one plus the interest rate. This formula is important because you can use it to convert any amount to be received in one year into its present value. Writing the formula generally, we have:

$$\text{Present Value} = \frac{\text{Future Value}_1}{(1 + i)}.$$

The present value of funds to be received in one year—Future Value_1—can be calculated by dividing the amount of those funds to be received by 1 plus the interest rate. With an interest rate of 10 percent, the present value of \$1,000,000 to be received one year from now is:

$$\frac{\$1{,}000{,}000}{(1 + 0.10)} = \$909{,}090.91.$$

This method is a very useful way of calculating the value today of funds that won't be received for one year. But financial securities such as stocks and bonds involve promises to pay funds over many years. Therefore, it would be even more useful if we could expand this formula to calculate the present value of funds to be received more than one year in the future.

This expansion is easy to do. Go back to the original example where we assumed you were willing to loan out your \$1,000 for one year, provided that you received 10 percent interest. Suppose you are asked to lend the funds for two years and that you are promised 10 percent interest per year for each year of the loan. That is, you are lending \$1,000, which at 10 percent interest will grow to \$1,100 after one year, and you are agreeing to loan that \$1,100 out for a second year at 10 percent interest. So, after two years, you will be paid back \$1,100 (1 + 0.10), or \$1,210. Or:

$$\$1{,}210 = \$1{,}000\ (1 + 0.10)(1 + 0.10),$$

or:

$$\$1{,}210 = \$1{,}000\ (1 + 0.10)^2.$$

This formula can also be rewritten as:

$$\$1{,}000 = \frac{\$1{,}210}{(1 + 0.10)^2}.$$

To put this formula in words, the \$1,210 you receive two years from now has a present value equal to \$1,210 divided by the quantity 1 plus the interest rate squared. If you were to agree to lend out your \$1,000 for three years at 10 percent interest, you would receive:

$$\$1{,}331 = \$1{,}000\ (1 + 0.10)^3.$$

Notice, again, that:

$$\$1{,}000 = \frac{\$1{,}331}{(1 + 0.10)^3}.$$

You can probably see a pattern here. We can generalize the concept to say that the present value of funds to be received *n* years in the future—whether *n* is 1, 20, or 85 does not matter—equals the amount of the funds to be received divided by the quantity 1 plus the interest rate raised to the *n*th power. For instance, with an interest rate of 10 percent, the value of $1,000,000 to be received 25 years in the future is:

$$\text{Present Value} = \frac{\$1{,}000{,}000}{(1 + 0.10)^{25}} = \$92{,}296.$$

Or, more generally:

$$\text{Present Value} = \frac{\text{Future Value}_n}{(1 + i)^n},$$

where Future Value_n represents funds that will be received in n years.

Solved Problem | 5A-1

How to Receive Your Contest Winnings

Suppose you win a contest and are given the choice of the following prizes:

> ***Prize 1:*** $50,000 to be received right away, with four additional payments of $50,000 to be received each year for the next four years

> ***Prize 2:*** $175,000 to be received right away

Explain which prize you would choose and the basis for your decision.

SOLVING THE PROBLEM:

Step 1: **Review the material.** This problem involves applying the concept of present value, so you may want to review the section "Using Present Value to Make Investment Decisions," which begins on page 161.

Step 2: **Explain the basis for choosing the prize.** Unless you need immediate cash, you should choose the prize with the highest present value.

Step 3: **Calculate the present value of each prize.** Prize 2 consists of one payment of $175,000 received right away, so its present value is $175,000. Prize 1 consists of five payments spread out over time. To find the present value of the prize, we must find the present value of each of these payments and add them together. To calculate present value, we must use an interest rate. Let's assume an interest rate of 10 percent. In that case, the present value of Prize 1 is:

$$\$50{,}000 + \frac{\$50{,}000}{(1 + 0.10)} + \frac{\$50{,}000}{(1 + 0.10)^2} + \frac{\$50{,}000}{(1 + 0.10)^3} + \frac{\$50{,}000}{(1 + 0.10)^4} =$$

$$\$50{,}000 + \$45{,}454.55 + \$41{,}322.31 + \$37{,}565.74 + \$34{,}150.67 = \$208{,}493.$$

Step 4: **State your conclusion.** Prize 1 has the greater present value, so you should choose it rather than Prize 2.

YOUR TURN: For more practice, do related problems 5A.6, 5A.8, 5A.9, and 5A.10 on pages 168 and 169 at the end of this appendix.

>> End Solved Problem 5A-1

Using Present Value to Calculate Bond Prices

Anyone who buys a financial asset, such as shares of stock or a bond, is really buying a promise to receive certain payments—dividends in the case of shares of stock or coupons in the case of a bond. The price investors are willing to pay for a financial asset should be equal to the value of the payments they will receive as a result of owning the asset. Because most of the coupon or dividend payments will be received in the future, it is their present value that matters. Put another way, we have the following important idea: *The price of a financial asset should be equal to the present value of the payments to be received from owning that asset.*

Let's consider an example. Suppose that in 1980, General Electric issued a bond with an $80 coupon that will mature in 2010. It is now 2008, and that bond has been bought and sold by investors many times. You are considering buying it. If you buy the bond, you will receive two years of coupon payments plus a final payment of the bond's principal or face value of $1,000. Suppose, once again, that you need an interest rate of 10 percent to invest your funds. If the bond has a coupon of $80, the present value of the payments you receive from owning the bond—and, therefore, the present value of the bond—will be:

$$\text{Present Value} = \frac{\$80}{(1 + 0.10)} + \frac{\$80}{(1 + 0.10)^2} + \frac{\$1{,}000}{(1 + 0.10)^2} = \$965.29.$$

That is, the present value of the bond will equal the present value of the three payments you will receive during the two years you own the bond. You should, therefore, be willing to pay $965.29 to own this bond and have the right to receive these payments from GE. This process of calculating present values of future payments is used to determine bond prices, with one qualification. The relevant interest rate used by investors in the bond market to calculate the present value and, therefore, the price of an existing bond is usually the coupon rate on comparable newly issued bonds. Therefore, the general formula for the price of a bond is:

$$\text{Bond Price} = \frac{\text{Coupon}_1}{(1 + i)} + \frac{\text{Coupon}_2}{(1 + i)^2} + \cdots + \frac{\text{Coupon}_n}{(1 + i)^n} + \frac{\text{Face Value}}{(1 + i)^n},$$

where Coupon_1 is the coupon payment to be received after one year, Coupon_2 is the coupon payment to be received after two years, up to Coupon_n, which is the coupon payment received in the year the bond matures. The ellipsis takes the place of the coupon payments—if any—received between the second year and the year the bond matures. Face Value is the face value of the bond, to be received when the bond matures. The interest rate on comparable newly issued bonds is i.

Using Present Value to Calculate Stock Prices

When you own a firm's stock, you are legally entitled to your share of the firm's profits. Remember that the profits a firm pays out to its shareholders are referred to as dividends. The price of a share of stock should be equal to the present value of the dividends investors expect to receive as a result of owning that stock. Therefore, the general formula for the price of a stock is:

$$\text{Stock Price} = \frac{\text{Dividend}_1}{(1 + i)} + \frac{\text{Dividend}_2}{(1 + i)^2} + \ldots$$

Notice that this formula looks very similar to the one we used to calculate the price of a bond, with a couple of important differences. First, unlike a bond, stock has no maturity date, so we have to calculate the present value of an infinite number of dividend payments. At first, it may seem that the stock's price must be infinite as well, but remember that dollars you don't receive for many years are worth very little today. For instance, a dividend payment of $10 that will be received 40 years in the future is worth only a little more than $0.20 today at a 10 percent interest rate. The second difference between the stock price formula and the bond price formula is that whereas the coupon payments you receive from owning the bond are known with certainty—they are written on the bond and cannot be changed—you don't know for sure what the dividend payments from owning a stock will be. How large a dividend payment you will receive depends on how profitable the company will be in the future.

Although it is possible to forecast the future profitability of a company, this cannot be done with perfect accuracy. To emphasize this point, some economists rewrite the basic stock price formula by adding a superscript e to each Dividend term to emphasize that these are *expected* dividend payments. Because the future profitability of companies is often very difficult to forecast, it is not surprising that differences of opinion exist over what the price of a particular stock should be. Some investors will be very optimistic about the future profitability of a company and will, therefore, believe that the company's stock should have a high price. Other investors might be very pessimistic and believe that the company's stock should have a low price.

A Simple Formula for Calculating Stock Prices

It is possible to simplify the formula for determining the price of a stock, if we assume that dividends will grow at a constant rate:

$$\text{Stock Price} = \frac{\text{Dividend}}{(i - \text{Growth Rate})}.$$

In this equation, Dividend is the dividend expected to be received one year from now, and Growth Rate is the rate at which those dividends are expected to grow. If a company pays a dividend of \$1 per share to be received one year from now and Growth Rate is 10 percent, the company is expected to pay a dividend of \$1.10 the following year, \$1.21 the year after that, and so on.

Now suppose that IBM pays a dividend of \$5 per share, the consensus of investors is that these dividends will increase at a rate of 5 percent per year for the indefinite future, and the interest rate is 10 percent. Then the price of IBM's stock should be:

$$\text{Stock Price} = \frac{\$5.00}{(0.10 - 0.05)} = \$100.00.$$

Particularly during the years 1999 and 2000, there was much discussion of whether the high prices of many Internet stocks—such as the stock of Amazon.com—were justified, given that many of these companies had not made any profit yet and so had not paid any dividends. Is there any way that a rational investor would pay a high price for the stock of a company currently not earning profits? The formula for determining stock prices shows that it is possible, provided that the investor's assumptions are optimistic enough! For example, during 1999, one stock analyst predicted that Amazon.com would soon be earning \$10 per share of stock. That is, Amazon.com's total earnings divided by the number of shares of its stock outstanding would be \$10. Suppose Amazon.com pays out that \$10 in dividends and that the \$10 will grow rapidly over the years, by, say, 7 percent per year. Then our formula indicates that the price of Amazon.com stock should be:

$$\text{Stock Price} = \frac{\$10.00}{(\$0.10 - 0.07)} = \$333.33.$$

If you are sufficiently optimistic about the future prospects of a company, a high stock price can be justified even if the company is not currently earning a profit. But investors in growth stocks must be careful. Suppose investors believe that growth prospects for Amazon are only 4 percent per year instead of 7 percent because the firm turns out not to be as profitable as initially believed. Then our formula indicates that the price of Amazon.com stock should be:

$$\text{Stock Price} = \frac{\$10.00}{(\$0.10 - 0.04)} = \$166.67,$$

This price is only half the price assuming a more optimistic growth rate. Hence investors use information about a firm's profitability and growth prospects to determine what the firm is worth.

Going Deeper into Financial Statements

Corporations disclose substantial information about their business operations and financial position to actual and potential investors. Some of this information meets the demands of participants in financial markets and of information-collection agencies, such as Moody's Investors Service, which develops credit ratings that help investors judge how risky corporate bonds are. Other information meets the requirements of the U.S. Securities and Exchange Commission.

Key sources of information about a corporation's profitability and financial position are its principal financial statements—the *income statement* and the *balance sheet.* These important information sources were first introduced in the chapter. Here we go into more detail, using recent data for Google as an example.

Analyzing Income Statements

As discussed in the chapter, a firm's income statement summarizes its revenues, costs, and profit over a period of time. Figure 5A-1 shows Google's income statement for 2006.

Google's income statement presents the results of the company's operations during the year. Listed first are the revenues it earned, largely from selling advertising on its Web site, from January 1, 2006, to December 31, 2006: $10,605 million. Listed next are Google's operating expenses, the most important of which is its *cost of revenue*—which is commonly known as *cost of sales* or *cost of goods sold*: $4,225 million. Cost of revenue is the direct cost of producing the products sold, including in this case the salaries of the computer programmers Google hires to write the software for its Web site. Google also has substantial costs for researching and developing its products ($1,229 million) and for advertising and marketing them ($850 million). General and administrative expenses ($850 million) include costs such as the salaries of top managers.

The difference between a firm's revenue and its costs is its profit. "Profit" shows up in several forms on an income statement. A firm's *operating income* is the difference between its revenue and its operating expenses. Most corporations, including Google, also have investments, such as government and corporate bonds, that normally generate some income for them. In this case, Google earned $461 million on its investments, which increased its *income before taxes* to $4,011 million. The federal government taxes the profits of corporations. During 2006, Google paid $934 million—or about 23 percent

Revenue		$10,605	Revenue from sales
Operating expenses			
	Cost of revenues	4,225	Categories of costs
	Research and development	1,229	
	Sales and marketing	850	
	General and administrative	752	
Total operating expenses		7,056	Total cost
Operating income		3,549	Operating income = revenue − operating expenses
Investment income		461	
Income before income taxes		4,010	Before-tax accounting profit
Income taxes		(934)	
Net income (accounting profit)		3,076	After-tax accounting profit

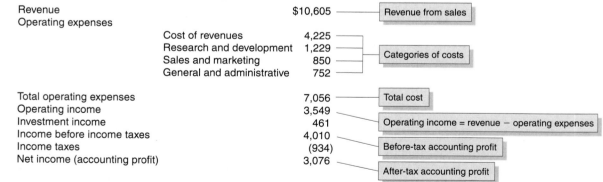

Note: All numbers are in millions of dollars.

Figure 5A-1 | Google's Income Statement for 2006

Google's income statement shows the company's revenue, costs, and profit for 2006. The difference between its revenue ($10,605 million) and its operating expenses ($7,055 million) is its operating income ($3,550 million). Most corporations also have investments, such as government or corporate bonds, that generate some income for them. In this case, Google earned $461 million, giving the firm an income before taxes of $4,011 million. After paying taxes of $934 million, Google was left with a net income, or accounting profit, of $3,076 million for the year.

Source: Google's Income Statement for 2006. Google Inc., "Consolidated Statements of Income," February 1, 2007. Used with permission of Google, Inc.

of its profits—in taxes. *Net income* after taxes was $3,077 million. The net income that firms report on their income statements is referred to as their after-tax *accounting profit.*

Analyzing Balance Sheets

As discussed in the chapter, whereas a firm's income statement reports a firm's activities for a period of time, a firm's balance sheet summarizes its financial position on a particular day, usually the end of a quarter or year. To understand how a balance sheet is organized, first recall that an asset is anything of value that the firm owns, and a liability is a debt or an obligation that the firm owes. Subtracting the value of a firm's liabilities from the value of its assets leaves its *net worth.* Because a corporation's stockholders are its owners, net worth is often listed as **stockholders' equity** on a balance sheet. Using these definitions, we can state the balance sheet equation (also called the basic accounting equation) as follows:

Stockholders' equity The difference between the value of a corporation's assets and the value of its liabilities; also known as net worth.

$$\text{Assets} - \text{Liabilities} = \text{Stockholders' Equity},$$

or:

$$\text{Assets} = \text{Liabilities} + \text{Stockholders' Equity}.$$

This formula tells us that the value of a firm's assets must equal the value of its liabilities plus the value of stockholders' equity. An important accounting rule dating back to the beginning of modern bookkeeping in fifteenth-century Italy holds that balance sheets should list assets on the left side and liabilities and net worth, or stockholders' equity, on the right side. Notice that this means that *the value of the left side of the balance sheet must always equal the value of the right side.* Figure 5A-2 shows Google's balance sheet as of December 31, 2006.

A couple of the entries on the asset side of the balance sheet may be unfamiliar: *Current assets* are assets that the firm could convert into cash quickly, such as the balance in its checking account or its accounts receivable, which is money currently owed to the firm for products that have been delivered but not yet paid for. *Goodwill* represents the difference between the purchase price of a company and the market value of its assets. It represents the ability of a business to earn an economic profit from its assets. For example, if you buy a restaurant that is located on a busy intersection and you employ a chef with a reputation for preparing delicious food, you may pay more than the market value of the tables, chairs, ovens, and other assets. This additional amount you pay will be entered on the asset side of your balance sheet as goodwill.

Current liabilities are short-term debts such as accounts payable, which is money owed to suppliers for goods received but not yet paid for, or bank loans that will be paid back in less than one year. Long-term bank loans and the value of outstanding corporate bonds are *long-term liabilities.*

ASSETS		LIABILITIES AND STOCKHOLDERS' EQUITY	
Current Assets	$13,040	Current Liabilities	$1,305
Property and Equipment	2,395	Long-term liabilities	129
Investments	1,032	Total Liabilities	1,434
Goodwill	1,545	Stockholders' Equity	17,040
Other long-term assets	461		
Total Assets	18,473	Total liabilites and stockholders' equity	18,473

Figure 5A-2 | Google's Balance Sheet as of December 31, 2006

Corporations list their assets on the left of their balance sheets and their liabilities on the right. The difference between the value of the firm's assets and the value of its liabilities equals the net worth of the firm, or stockholders' equity. Stockholders' equity is listed on the right side of the balance sheet. Therefore, the value of the left side of the balance sheet must always equal the value of the right side.

Note: All numbers are in millions of dollars.

Source: Google's Balance Sheet as of December 31, 2006, Google, Inc., "Consolidated Balance Sheets," February 1, 2007. Used with permission of Google, Inc.

Key Terms

Present value, p. 161

Stockholders' equity, p. 167

LEARNING OBJECTIVE Understand the concept of present value and the information contained on a firm's income statement and balance sheet, **pages 161–167.**

Review Questions

5A.1 Why is money you receive at some future date worth less than money you receive today? If the interest rate rises, what effect does this have on the present value of payments you receive in the future?

5A.2 Give the formula for calculating the present value of a bond that will pay a coupon of $100 per year for 10 years and that has a face value of $1,000.

5A.3 Compare the formula for calculating the present value of the payments you will receive from owning a bond to the formula for calculating the present value of the payments you will receive from owning a stock. What are the key similarities? What are the key differences?

5A.4 How is operating income calculated? How does operating income differ from net income? How does net income differ from accounting profit?

5A.5 What's the key difference between a firm's income statement and its balance sheet? What is listed on the left side of a balance sheet? What is listed on the right side?

Problems and Applications

5A.6 **(Related to *Solved Problem 5A-1* on page 163)** If the interest rate is 10 percent, what is the present value of a bond that matures in two years, pays $85 one year from now, and pays $1,085 two years from now?

5A.7 The following is from an Associated Press story on the contract of baseball star Carlos Beltran:

> Beltran's contract calls for his $11 million signing bonus to be paid in four installments: $5 million upon approval and $2 million each this June 15, 2005, and on Jan. 15, 2006, and Jan. 15, 2007. He gets a $10 million salary this year, $12 million in each of the following two seasons and $18.5 million in each of the final four seasons, with $8.5 million deferred annually from 2008–11. The players' association calculated the present day value of the contract at $115,726,946, using a 6 percent discount rate (the prime rate [which is the interest rate banks charge on loans to their best customers] plus 1 percent, rounded to the nearest whole number). For purposes of baseball's luxury tax, which currently uses a 3.62 percent discount rate, the contract is valued at $116,695,898.

Briefly explain why the present value of Beltran's contract is lower if a higher interest is used to make the calculation than if a lower interest rate is used.

Source: "Like Pedro, Beltran Gets Suite on Road," Associated Press, January 18, 2005.

5A.8 **(Related to *Solved Problem 5A-1* on page 163)** Before the 2007 season, the Seattle Mariners baseball team signed catcher Kenji Johjima to a contract that would pay him the following amounts: an immediate $1 million signing bonus, $5.1 million for the 2007 season, $5.2 million for the 2008 season, and $5.2 million for the 2009 season. Assume that he receives each of his three seasonal salaries as a lump sum payment at the end of the season and that he receives his 2007 salary one year after he signed the contract.

a. Some newspaper reports described Johjima as having signed a "$16.5 million contract" with the Mariners. Do you agree that $16.5 million was the value of this contract? Briefly explain.
b. What was the present value of Johjima's contract at the time he signed it (assuming an interest rate of 10 percent)?
c. If you use an interest rate of 5 percent, what was the present value of Johjima's contract?

5A.9 **(Related to *Solved Problem 5A-1* on page 163)** A winner of the Pennsylvania Lottery was given the choice of receiving $18 million at once or $1,440,000 per year for 25 years.

a. If the winner had opted for the 25 annual payments, how much in total would she have received?

b. At an interest rate of 10 percent, what would be the present value of the 25 payments?

c. At an interest rate of 5 percent, what would be the present value of the 25 payments?

d. What interest rate would make the present value of the 25 payments equal to the one payment of $18 million? (This question is difficult and requires the use of a financial calculator or a spreadsheet. *Hint:* If you are familiar with the Excel spreadsheet program, use the RATE function. Questions (b) and (c) can be answered by using the Excel NPV—Net Present Value—function.)

5A.10 **(Related to *Solved Problem 5A-1* on page 163)** Before the start of the 2000 baseball season, the New York Mets decided they didn't want Bobby Bonilla playing for them any longer. But Bonilla had a contract with the Mets for the 2000 season that would have obliged the Mets to pay him $5.9 million. When the Mets released Bonilla, he agreed to take the following payments in lieu of the $5.9 million the Mets would have paid him in the year 2000: He will receive 25 equal payments of $1,193,248.20 each July 1 from 2011 to 2035. If you were Bobby Bonilla, which would you rather have had, the lump sum $5.9 million or the 25 payments beginning in 2011? Explain the basis for your decision.

5A.11 Suppose that eLake, an online auction site, is paying a dividend of $2 per share. You expect this dividend to grow 2 percent per year, and the interest rate is 10 percent. What is the most you would be willing to pay for a share of stock in eLake? If the interest rate is 5 percent, what is the most you would be willing to pay? When interest rates in the economy decline, would you expect stock prices in general to rise or fall? Explain.

5A.12 Suppose you buy the bond of a large corporation at a time when the inflation rate is very low. If the inflation rate increases during the time you hold the bond, what is likely to happen to the price of the bond?

5A.13 Use the information in the following table for calendar year 2006 to prepare the McDonald's Corporation's income statement. Be sure to include entries for operating income and net income.

Revenue from company restaurants	$16,083 million
Revenue from franchised restaurants	5,503 million
Cost of operating company-owned restaurants	13,542 million
Income taxes	1,293 million
Interest expense	402 million
General and administrative cost	2,338 million
Cost of restaurant leases	1,060 million
Other operating costs	67 million

Source: McDonald's Corporation, *Annual Report, 2006*, February 26, 2007.

5A.14 Use the information in the following table on the financial situation of Starbucks Corporation as of December 31, 2006, to prepare the firm's balance sheet. Be sure to include an entry for stockholders' equity.

Current assets	$1,530 million
Current liabilities	1,936 million
Property and equipment	2,288 million
Long-term liabilities	50 million
Goodwill	161 million
Other assets	187 million

Source: Starbucks Corporation, *Annual Report*, 2006.

5A.15 The *current ratio* is equal to a firm's current assets divided by its current liabilities. Use the information in Figure 5A-2 on page 167 to calculate Google's current ratio on December 31, 2006. Investors generally prefer that a firm's current ratio be greater than 1.5. What problems might a firm encounter if the value of its current assets is low relative to the value of its current liabilities?

>> End Appendix Learning Objective

Chapter 6

Comparative Advantage and the Gains from International Trade

Is Using Trade Policy to Help U.S. Industries a Good Idea?

Trade is, simply, the act of buying or selling. Is there a difference between trade that takes place within a country and international trade? Within the United States, domestic trade makes it possible for consumers in Ohio to eat salmon caught in Alaska or for consumers in Montana to drive cars built in Michigan or Kentucky. Similarly, international trade makes it possible for consumers in the United States to drink wine from France or use HD-DVD players from Japan. But one significant difference between domestic trade and international trade is that international trade is more controversial. At one time, nearly all the televisions, shoes, clothing, and toys consumed in the United States were also produced in the United States. Today, these goods are produced mainly by firms in other countries. This shift has benefited U.S. consumers because foreign-made goods have lower prices than the U.S.-made goods they have replaced. But at the same time, many U.S. firms that produced these goods have gone out of business, and their workers have had to find other jobs. Not surprisingly, opinion polls show that many Americans favor reducing international trade because they believe doing so would preserve jobs in the United States.

But do restrictions on trade actually preserve jobs? In fact, restrictions on trade may preserve jobs in particular industries, but only at the cost of reducing jobs in other industries. Consider, for example, U.S. policy on imports of sugar and imports of sugar-based ethanol. Ethanol is made from corn or sugar and can be used as a substitute for gasoline as a fuel in automobiles. Sugar is a better base for ethanol than corn because it ferments more quickly and is therefore cheaper to produce. In Brazil, ethanol is made from sugar, but in the United States, ethanol is made from corn. As a result, Brazilian ethanol costs just 80 cents a gallon, about half the cost of ethanol produced in the United States using corn. The Brazilian makers of ethanol would like to ship this cheap fuel to the United States, but the U.S. government has imposed a 54-cent-per-gallon tariff on imported ethanol. The tariff, combined with the cost of transporting the ethanol to the United States, effectively prices Brazilian ethanol out of the market.

The tariff helps U.S. firms that produce corn-based ethanol and U.S. farmers who grown corn, but it effectively increases fuel costs for many U.S. firms. The higher fuel costs make the products these firms produce more expensive, reducing sales and employment in the industries affected.

In addition to the tariff on sugar-based ethanol, Congress has also enacted a sugar quota, which limits the quantity of raw sugar allowed into the United States. Several countries around the world can produce sugar at lower costs than can U.S. sugar producers. As a result, the *world price* of sugar, which is the price at which sugar can be bought on the world market, is too low for U.S. sugar companies to cover their costs. The sugar quota allows U.S. companies to sell sugar domestically for a price that is about three times as high as the world price. Without the sugar quota, competition from foreign sugar producers would drive many U.S. producers out of business. But the United States also has a large candy industry, which uses many tons of sugar. The high price of sugar has led many U.S. candy firms to relocate their operations to other countries where the price of sugar is much lower. Life Savers, Star Brite mints, and Cherry Balls are a few of the candies no longer manufactured in the United States.

Should the United States have a tariff on imports of sugar-based ethanol and a quota on imports of raw sugar? The tariff and the quota create winners—U.S. producers of corn-based ethanol, U.S. sugar companies, and U.S. corn farmers—and losers—U.S. companies that use sugar, their employees, and U.S. consumers who must pay higher prices for goods that contain sugar and who are not able to buy low-priced sugar-based ethanol as an alternative to gasoline. In this chapter, we will explore who wins and who loses from international trade and review the political debate over whether international trade should be restricted. **AN INSIDE LOOK AT POLICY** on **page 196** discusses a recent trade agreement between the United States and South Korea.

LEARNING Objectives

After studying this chapter, you should be able to:

6.1 Discuss the role of **international trade** in the **U.S. economy**, page 172.

6.2 Understand the difference between **comparative advantage** and **absolute advantage** in international trade, page 175.

6.3 Explain **how countries gain** from international trade, page 177.

6.4 Analyze the economic effects of **government policies** that restrict international **trade**, page 183.

6.5 Evaluate the arguments over **trade policy** and **globalization**, page 190.

APPENDIX Understand **why firms operate in more than one country**, page 205.

Economics in YOUR Life!

Why Haven't You Heard of the Sugar Quota?

Politicians often support restrictions on trade to convince people to vote for them. The workers in the industries protected by tariffs and quotas are likely to vote for these politicians because the workers think trade restrictions will protect their jobs. But most people are not workers in industries protected from foreign competition by trade restrictions. We have seen that the sugar quota protects U.S. sugar companies and the people who work for them, but this amounts to only a few thousand people. Millions of consumers, though, have to pay higher prices for soft drinks, bakery goods, and candy because of the sugar quota. How, then, have sugar companies convinced Congress to enact the sugar quota and why have very few people even heard of the quota? As you read the chapter, see if can answer this question. You can check your answers against those we provide at the end of the chapter. » **Continued on page 195**

Markets for internationally traded goods and services can be analyzed using the tools of demand and supply that we developed in Chapter 3. We saw in Chapter 2 that trade in general—whether within a country or between countries—is based on the principle of comparative advantage. In this chapter, we look more closely at the role of comparative advantage in international trade. We also use the concepts of consumer surplus, producer surplus, and deadweight loss from Chapter 4 to analyze government policies, such as the sugar quota, that interfere with trade. With this background, we can return to the political debate over whether the United States benefits from international trade. We begin by looking at how large a role international trade plays in the U.S. economy.

6.1 LEARNING OBJECTIVE

6.1 | Discuss the role of international trade in the U.S. economy.

The United States in the International Economy

International trade has grown tremendously over the past 50 years. The increase in trade is the result of the falling costs of shipping products around the world, the spread of inexpensive and reliable communications, and changes in government policies. Firms can use large container ships to send their products across the oceans at low cost. Businesspeople today can travel to Europe or Asia using fast, inexpensive, and reliable air transportation. The Internet allows managers to communicate instantaneously and at a very low cost with customers and suppliers around the world. These and other improvements in transportation and communication have created a global marketplace that earlier generations of businesspeople could only dream of.

In addition, over the past 50 years, many governments have changed policies to facilitate international trade. For example, tariff rates have fallen. A **tariff** is a tax imposed by a government on *imports* of a good into a country. **Imports** are goods and services bought domestically but produced in other countries. In the 1930s, the United States charged an average tariff rate above 50 percent. Today, the rate is less than 2 percent. In North America, most tariffs between Canada, Mexico, and the United States were eliminated following the passage of the North American Free Trade Agreement (NAFTA) in 1994. Twenty-seven countries in Europe have formed the European Union, which has eliminated all tariffs among member countries, greatly increasing both imports and **exports**, which are goods and services produced domestically but sold to other countries.

Tariff A tax imposed by a government on imports.

Imports Goods and services bought domestically but produced in other countries.

Exports Goods and services produced domestically but sold to other countries.

The Importance of Trade to the U.S. Economy

U.S. consumers buy increasing quantities of goods and services produced in other countries. At the same time, U.S. businesses sell increasing quantities of goods and services to consumers in other countries. Figure 6-1 shows that since 1950, both exports and imports have been steadily increasing as a fraction of U.S. gross domestic product (GDP). Recall that GDP is the value of all the goods and services produced in a country during a year. In 1950, exports and imports were both about 4 percent of GDP. In 2006, exports were about 11 percent of GDP, and imports were about 17 percent.

Not all sectors of the U.S. economy are affected equally by international trade. For example, although it's difficult to import or export some services, such as haircuts or appendectomies, a large percentage of U.S. agricultural production is exported. Each year, the United States exports about 50 percent of the wheat crop, 40 percent of the rice crop, and 20 percent of the corn crop.

Many U.S. manufacturing industries also depend on trade. About 20 percent of U.S. manufacturing jobs depend directly or indirectly on exports. In some industries, such as computers, the products these workers make are directly exported. In other industries, such as steel, the products are used to make other products, such as bulldozers or

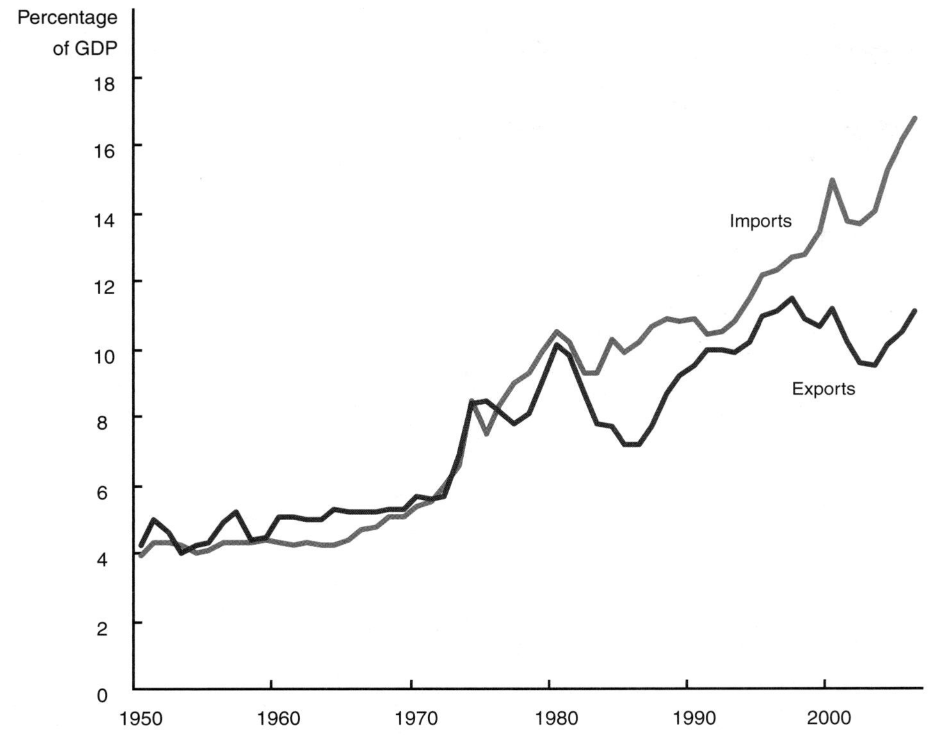

Figure 6-1

International Trade Is of Increasing Importance to the United States

Exports and imports of goods and services as a percentage of total production—measured by GDP—show the importance of international trade to an economy. Since 1950, both imports and exports have been steadily rising as a fraction of the U.S. GDP.

Source: U.S. Department of Commerce, Bureau of Economic Analysis.

machine tools, that are then exported. In all, about two-thirds of U.S. manufacturing industries depend on exports for at least 10 percent of jobs.

U.S. International Trade in a World Context

The United States is the largest exporter in the world, as Figure 6-2 illustrates. Six of the other seven leading exporting countries are also large, high-income countries. Although China is still a relatively low-income country, the rapid growth of the Chinese economy over the past 20 years has resulted in its becoming the third largest exporter.

International trade remains less important to the United States than it is to most other countries. Figure 6-3 shows that imports and exports remain smaller fractions of GDP in the United States than in other countries. In some smaller countries, like Belgium, imports and exports make up more than half of GDP. Japan is the only high-income country that is less dependent on international trade than is the United States.

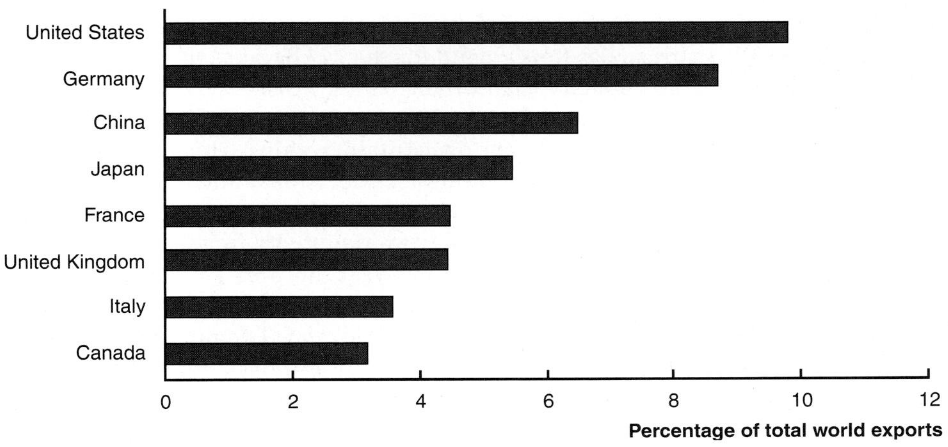

Figure 6-2

The Eight Leading Exporting Countries

The United States is the leading exporting country, accounting for about 10 percent of total world exports. The values are the shares of total world exports of merchandise and commercial services.

Source: World Trade Organization, *International Trade Statistics*, 2006. Reprinted by permission of WTO.

Figure 6-3

International Trade as a Percentage of GDP

International trade is still less important to the United States than to most other countries, with the exception of Japan.

Source: International Monetary Fund, *International Financial Statistics Yearbook*, 2006.

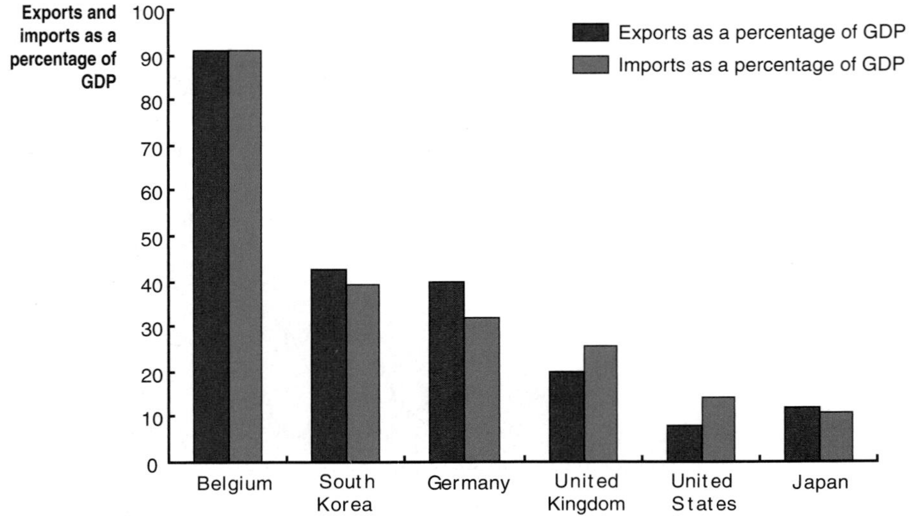

Making the Connection

How Expanding International Trade Has Helped Boeing

The Boeing 747 jumbo jet was a wonder of modern technology when it was introduced in 1970. With a much wider body than existing passenger planes, the 747 had two aisles, with as many as 10 seats per row, and could carry more than 500 passengers. Many early models had a second level with a passenger lounge, complete with a piano. Its range of more than 5,000 miles made it a truly intercontinental plane.

By the late 1990s, however, Boeing, which is based in Chicago and assembles the 747 outside of Seattle, Washington, was experiencing declining sales for the plane. Planes with newer technology were being introduced, and rising prices for jet fuel led some airlines to conclude that jumbo jets were too costly to operate. The decline in passenger travel after September 11, 2001, appeared to be the last nail in the 747's coffin. An executive for Airbus, a European firm that is Boeing's main competitor, boasted, "The 747 is on its last legs. It doesn't have any legs to stand on. Boeing is trying to breathe life into a 1960s-era design. There is only so much you can do with a plane." But in the past few years, the 747 has gone through an unexpected revival, spurred largely by recent growth in international trade. In the 1960s, Boeing's managers made the important decision that the 747 be designed to serve as both a cargo plane and a passenger plane. For example, the nose cone was designed to open to make loading cargo easier.

Rapid growth of international trade has spurred demand for the 747 because it has larger cargo capacity than other planes.

As international trade has grown rapidly in the past few years, so has the demand for the 747 because the plane has larger cargo capacity than other planes. Most low-value goods being shipped long distances—for instance, from China to Europe—are still sent by sea on container ships. However, high-value goods—such as computers, televisions, and some food products—are increasingly likely to be sent by plane, which is a much faster and safer method of shipping. Air freight shipments have been growing at the rapid rate of 6 percent per year. Because of its large carrying capacity, currently about 60 percent of all air freight worldwide is carried on 747s. The latest model, the 747-400, has new, technologically advanced engines and redesigned wings. It has a maximum speed of 675 miles per hour and has a range of more than 7,500 miles—enough to fly nonstop from Los Angeles to Melbourne, Australia. The increased fuel efficiency of the new engines has reduced operating costs. In 2006,

Boeing received orders for 67 airplanes worth $16.75 billion. That's good news for Boeing's 120,000 employees in the United States.

Sources: Leslie Wayne, "Boeing Not Afraid to Say 'Sold Out,'" *New York Times*, November 28, 2006; Leslie Wayne, "Far from Extinct," *New York Times*, December 7, 2006; and Leslie Wayne, "Still Flying High," *New York Times*, December 25, 2006.

YOUR TURN: Test your understanding by doing related problem 1.4 on page 198 at the end of this chapter.

6.2 LEARNING OBJECTIVE

6.2 | Understand the difference between comparative advantage and absolute advantage in international trade.

Comparative Advantage in International Trade

Why have businesses around the world increasingly looked for markets in other countries? Why have consumers increasingly purchased goods and services made in other countries? People trade for one reason: Trade makes them better off. Whenever a buyer and seller agree to a sale, they must both believe they are better off; otherwise, there would be no sale. This outcome must hold whether the buyer and seller live in the same city or in different countries. As we will see, governments are more likely to interfere with international trade than they are with domestic trade, but the reasons for the interference are more political than economic.

A Brief Review of Comparative Advantage

In Chapter 2, we discussed the key economic concept of *comparative advantage*. **Comparative advantage** is the ability of an individual, a firm, or a country to produce a good or service at a lower opportunity cost than competitors. Recall that **opportunity cost** is the highest-valued alternative that must be given up to engage in an activity. People, firms, and countries specialize in economic activities in which they have a comparative advantage. In trading, we benefit from the comparative advantage of other people (or firms or countries), and others benefit from our comparative advantage.

Comparative advantage The ability of an individual, a firm, or a country to produce a good or service at a lower opportunity cost than competitors.

Opportunity Cost The highest-valued alternative that must be given up to engage in an activity.

A good way to think of comparative advantage is to recall the example in Chapter 2 of you and your neighbor picking fruit. Your neighbor is better at picking both apples and cherries than you are. Why, then, doesn't your neighbor pick both types of fruit? Because the opportunity cost to your neighbor of picking her own apples is very high: She is a particularly skilled cherry picker, and every hour spent picking apples is an hour taken away from picking cherries. You can pick apples at a much lower opportunity cost than your neighbor, so you have a comparative advantage in picking apples. Your neighbor can pick cherries at a much lower opportunity cost than you can, so she has a comparative advantage in picking cherries. Your neighbor is better off specializing in picking cherries, and you are better off specializing in picking apples. You can then trade some of your apples for some of your neighbor's cherries, and both of you will end up with more of each fruit.

Comparative Advantage in International Trade

The principle of comparative advantage can explain why people pursue different occupations. It can also explain why countries produce different goods and services. International trade involves many countries importing and exporting many different goods and services. Countries are better off if they specialize in producing the goods for which they have a comparative advantage. They can then trade for the goods for which other countries have a comparative advantage.

We can illustrate why specializing on the basis of comparative advantage makes countries better off with a simple example involving just two countries and two products.

TABLE 6-1

An Example of Japanese Workers Being More Productive Than American Workers

	OUTPUT PER HOUR OF WORK	
	CELL PHONES	DIGITAL MUSIC PLAYERS
JAPAN	12	6
UNITED STATES	2	4

Suppose the United States and Japan produce only cell phones and digital music players, like Apple's iPod. Assume that each country uses only labor to produce each good, and that Japanese and U.S. cell phones and digital music players are exactly the same. Table 6-1 shows how much each country can produce of each good with one hour of labor.

Absolute advantage The ability to produce more of a good or service than competitors when using the same amount of resources.

Notice that Japanese workers are more productive than U.S. workers in making both goods. In one hour of work, Japanese workers can make six times as many cell phones and one and one-half times as many digital music players as U.S. workers. Japan has an *absolute advantage* over the United States in producing both goods. **Absolute advantage** is the ability to produce more of a good or service than competitors when using the same amount of resources. In this case, Japan can produce more of both goods using the same amount of labor as the United States.

It might seem at first that Japan has nothing to gain from trading with the United States because it has an absolute advantage in producing both goods. However, Japan should specialize and produce only cell phones and obtain the digital music players it needs by exporting cell phones to the United States in exchange for digital music players. The reason that Japan benefits from trade is that although it has an *absolute advantage* in the production of both goods, it has a *comparative advantage* only in the production of cell phones. The United States has a comparative advantage in the production of digital music players.

If it seems contrary to common sense that Japan should import digital music players from the United States even though Japan can produce more players per hour of work, think about the opportunity cost to each country of producing each good. If Japan wants to produce more digital music players, it has to switch labor away from cell phone production. Every hour of labor switched from producing cell phones to producing digital music players increases digital music player production by 6 and reduces cell phone production by 12. Japan has to give up 12 cell phones for every 6 digital music players it produces. Therefore, the opportunity cost to Japan of producing one more digital music player is 12/6, or 2 cell phones.

If the United States switches one hour of labor from cell phones to digital music players, production of cell phones falls by 2, and production of digital music players rises by 4. Therefore, the opportunity cost to the United States of producing one more digital music player is 2/4, or 0.5 cell phone. The United States has a lower opportunity cost of producing digital music players and, therefore, has a comparative advantage in making this product. By similar reasoning, we can see that Japan has a comparative advantage in producing cell phones. Table 6-2 summarizes the opportunity each country faces in producing these goods.

TABLE 6-2 | The Opportunity Costs of Producing Cell Phones and Digital Music Players

The table shows the opportunity cost each country faces in producing cell phones and digital music players. For example, the entry in the first row and second column shows that Japan must give up 2 cell phones for every digital music player it produces.

	OPPORTUNITY COSTS	
	CELL PHONES	DIGITAL MUSIC PLAYERS
JAPAN	0.5 digital music player	2 cell phones
UNITED STATES	2 digital music players	0.5 cell phone

6.3 | Explain how countries gain from international trade.

6.3 LEARNING OBJECTIVE

How Countries Gain from International Trade

Can Japan really gain from producing only cell phones and trading with the United States for digital music players? To see that it can, assume at first that Japan and the United States do not trade with each other. A situation in which a country does not trade with other countries is called **autarky**. Assume that in autarky each country has 1,000 hours of labor available to produce the two goods, and each country produces the quantities of the two goods shown in Table 6-3. Because there is no trade, these quantities also represent consumption of the two goods in each country.

Autarky A situation in which a country does not trade with other countries.

Increasing Consumption through Trade

Suppose now that Japan and the United States begin to trade with each other. The **terms of trade** is the ratio at which a country can trade its exports for imports from other countries. For simplicity, let's assume that the terms of trade end up with Japan and the United States being willing to trade one cell phone for one digital music player.

Terms of trade The ratio at which a country can trade its exports for imports from other countries.

Once trade has begun, the United States and Japan can exchange digital music players for cell phones or cell phones for digital music players. For example, if Japan specializes by using all 1,000 available hours of labor to produce cell phones, it will be able to produce 12,000. It then could export 1,500 cell phones to the United States in exchange for 1,500 digital music players. (Remember: We are assuming that the terms of trade are one cell phone for one digital music player.) Japan ends up with 10,500 cell phones and 1,500 digital music players. Compared with the situation before trade, Japan has the same number of digital music players but 1,500 more cell phones. If the United States specializes in producing digital music players, it will be able to produce 4,000. It could then export 1,500 digital music players to Japan in exchange for 1,500 cell phones. The United States ends up with 2,500 digital music players and 1,500 cell phones. Compared with the situation before trade, the United States has the same number of cell phones but 1,500 more digital music players. Trade has allowed both countries to increase the quantities of goods consumed. Table 6-4 summarizes the gains from trade for the United States and Japan.

By trading, Japan and the United States are able to consume more than they could without trade. This outcome is possible because world production of both goods increases after trade. (Remember that, in this example, our "world" consists of just the United States and Japan.)

Why does total production of cell phones and digital music players increase when the United States specializes in producing digital music players and Japan specializes in producing cell phones? A domestic analogy helps to answer this question: If a company shifts production from an old factory to a more efficient modern factory, its output will increase. In effect, the same thing happens in our example. Producing digital music players in Japan and cell phones in the United States is inefficient. Shifting production to the more efficient country—the one with the comparative advantage—increases total production. The key point is this: *Countries gain from specializing in producing goods in which they have a comparative advantage and trading for goods in which other countries have a comparative advantage.*

TABLE 6-3

Production without Trade

	PRODUCTION AND CONSUMPTION	
	CELL PHONES	DIGITAL MUSIC PLAYERS
JAPAN	9,000	1,500
UNITED STATES	1,500	1,000

TABLE 6-4

The Gains from Trade for Japan and the United States

WITHOUT TRADE

	Production and Consumption	
	CELL PHONES	MP3 PLAYERS
Japan	9,000	1,500
United States	1,500	1,000

WITH TRADE

	Production with Trade		Trade		Consumption with Trade	
	CELL PHONES	MP3 PLAYERS	CELL PHONES	MP3 PLAYERS	CELL PHONES	MP3 PLAYERS
Japan	12,000	0	Export 1,500	Import 1,500	10,500	1,500
United States	0	4,000	Import 1,500	Export 1,500	1,500	2,500

With trade, the United States and Japan specialize in the good they have a comparative advantage in producing . . .

. . . and export some of that good in exchange for the good the other country has a comparative advantage in producing.

GAINS FROM TRADE

	Increased Consumption
Japan	1,500 Cell Phones
United States	1,500 MP3 Players

The increased consumption made possible by trade represents the gains from trade.

Solved Problem | 6-3

The Gains from Trade

The first discussion of comparative advantage appears in *On the Principles of Political Economy and Taxation,* a book written by David Ricardo in 1817. Ricardo provided a famous example of the gains from trade, using wine and cloth production in Portugal and England. The following table is adapted from Ricardo's example, with cloth measured in sheets and wine measured in kegs.

OUTPUT PER YEAR OF LABOR

	CLOTH	WINE
PORTUGAL	100	150
ENGLAND	90	60

a. Explain which country has an absolute advantage in the production of each good.

b. Explain which country has a comparative advantage in the production of each good.

c. Suppose that Portugal and England currently do not trade with each other. Each country has 1,000 workers, so each has 1,000 years of labor time to use producing cloth and wine, and the countries are currently producing the amounts of each good shown in the table:

	CLOTH	WINE
PORTUGAL	18,000	123,000
ENGLAND	63,000	18,000

Show that Portugal and England can both gain from trade. Assume that the terms of trade are that one sheet of cloth can be traded for one keg of wine.

SOLVING THE PROBLEM:

Step 1: **Review the chapter material.** This problem is about absolute and comparative advantage and the gains from trade, so you may want to review the section "Comparative Advantage in International Trade," which begins on page 175, and the section "How Countries Gain from International Trade," which begins on page 177.

Step 2: **Answer question (a) by determining which country has an absolute advantage.** Remember that a country has an absolute advantage over another country when it can produce more of a good using the same resources. The first table in the problem shows that Portugal can produce more cloth *and* more wine with one year's worth of labor than can England. Thus, Portugal has an absolute advantage in the production of both goods and, therefore, England does not have an absolute advantage in the production of either good.

Step 3: **Answer question (b) by determining which country has a comparative advantage.** A country has a comparative advantage when it can produce a good at a lower opportunity cost. To produce 100 sheets of cloth, Portugal must give up 150 kegs of wine. Therefore, the opportunity cost to Portugal of producing one sheet of cloth is 150/100, or 1.5 kegs of wine. England has to give up 60 kegs of wine to produce 90 sheets of cloth, so its opportunity cost of producing one sheet of cloth is 60/90, or 0.67 keg of wine. The opportunity costs of producing wine can be calculated in the same way. The following table shows the opportunity cost to Portugal and England of producing each good.

OPPORTUNITY COSTS

	CLOTH	WINE
PORTUGAL	1.5 kegs of wine	0.67 sheets of cloth
ENGLAND	0.67 keg of wine	1.5 sheets of cloth

Portugal has a comparative advantage in wine because its opportunity cost is lower. England has a comparative advantage in cloth because its opportunity cost is lower.

Step 4: **Answer question (c) by showing that both countries can benefit from trade.** By now it should be clear that both countries will be better off if they specialize where they have a comparative advantage and trade for the other product. The following table is very similar to Table 6-4 and shows one example of trade making both countries better off. (To test your understanding, construct another example.)

WITHOUT TRADE

	PRODUCTION AND CONSUMPTION	
	CLOTH	WINE
PORTUGAL	18,000	123,000
ENGLAND	63,000	18,000

WITH TRADE

	PRODUCTION WITH TRADE		TRADE		CONSUMPTION WITH TRADE	
	CLOTH	WINE	CLOTH	WINE	CLOTH	WINE
PORTUGAL	0	150,000	Import 18,000	Export 18,000	18,000	132,000
ENGLAND	90,000	0	Export 18,000	Import 18,000	72,000	18,000

GAINS FROM TRADE

	INCREASED CONSUMPTION
PORTUGAL	9,000 wine
ENGLAND	9,000 cloth

YOUR TURN: For more practice, do related problems 3.4 and 3.5 on page 200 at the end of this chapter.

>> End Solved Problem 6-3

Why Don't We See Complete Specialization?

In our example of two countries producing only two products, each country specializes in producing one of the goods. In the real world, many goods and services are produced in more than one country. For example, the United States and Japan both produce automobiles. We do not see complete specialization in the real world for three main reasons:

- ***Not all goods and services are traded internationally.*** Even if, for example, Japan had a comparative advantage in the production of medical services, it would be difficult for Japan to specialize in producing medical services and then export them. There is no easy way for U.S. patients who need appendectomies to receive them from surgeons in Japan.
- ***Production of most goods involves increasing opportunity costs.*** Recall from Chapter 2 that production of most goods involves increasing opportunity costs. As a result, when the United States devotes more workers to producing digital music players, the opportunity cost of producing more digital music players will increase. At some point, the opportunity cost of producing digital music players in the United States may rise to the level of the opportunity cost of producing digital music players in Japan. When that happens, international trade will no longer push the United States further toward complete specialization. The same will be true of Japan: Increasing opportunity cost will cause Japan to stop short of complete specialization in producing cell phones.
- ***Tastes for products differ.*** Most products are *differentiated.* Cell phones, digital music players, cars, and televisions—to name just a few products—come with a wide variety of features. When buying automobiles, some people look for reliability and good gasoline mileage, others look for room to carry seven passengers, and still others want styling and high performance. So, some car buyers prefer Toyota Prius hybrids, some prefer Chevy Suburbans, and others prefer BMWs. As a result, Japan, the United States, and Germany may each have a comparative advantage in producing different types of automobiles.

Does Anyone Lose as a Result of International Trade?

In our cell phone and digital music player example, consumption increases in both the United States and Japan as a result of trade. Everyone gains, and no one loses. Or do they? In our example, we referred repeatedly to "Japan" or the "United States" producing cell phones or digital music players. But countries do not produce goods—firms do. In a

Don't Let This Happen to **YOU!**

Remember That Trade Creates Both Winners and Losers

The following statement is from a Federal Reserve publication: "Trade is a win–win situation for all countries that participate." Statements like this are sometimes taken to mean that there are no losers from international trade. But notice that the statement refers to *countries,* not individuals. When countries participate in trade, they make their consumers better off by increasing the quantity of goods and services available to them. As we have seen, however, expanding trade eliminates the jobs of workers employed at companies that are less efficient than foreign companies. Trade also creates new jobs at companies that export to foreign markets. It may be difficult, though, for workers who lose their jobs because of trade to easily find others. That is why in the United States, the federal government uses the Trade Adjustment Assistance program to provide funds for workers who have lost their jobs due to international trade. These funds can be used for retraining, for searching for new jobs, or for relocating to areas where new jobs are available. This program—and similar programs in other countries—recognizes that there are losers from international trade as well as winners.

Source: Quote from Federal Reserve Bank of Dallas Web site, *International Trade and the Economy*, www.dallasfed.org/educate/everyday/ev7.html.

YOUR TURN: Test your understanding by doing related problem 3.12 on page 200 at the end of this chapter.

world without trade, there would be cell phone and digital music player firms in both Japan and the United States. In a world with trade, there would only be Japanese cell phone firms and U.S. digital music player firms. Japanese digital music player firms and U.S. cell phone firms would close. Overall, total employment will not change and production will increase as a result of trade. Nevertheless, the owners of Japanese digital music player firms, the owners of U.S. cell phone firms, and the people who work for them are worse off as a result of trade. The losers from trade are likely to do their best to convince the Japanese and U.S. governments to interfere with trade by barring imports of the competing products from the other country or by imposing high tariffs on them.

Where Does Comparative Advantage Come From?

Among the main sources of comparative advantage are the following:

- ***Climate and natural resources.*** This source of comparative advantage is the most obvious. Because of geology, Saudi Arabia has a comparative advantage in the production of oil. Because of climate and soil conditions, Costa Rica has a comparative advantage in the production of bananas, and the United States has a comparative advantage in the production of wheat.
- ***Relative abundance of labor and capital.*** Some countries, such as the United States, have many highly skilled workers and a great deal of machinery. Other countries, such as China, have many unskilled workers and relatively little machinery. As a result, the United States has a comparative advantage in the production of goods that require highly skilled workers or sophisticated machinery to manufacture, such as aircraft, semiconductors, and computer software. China has a comparative advantage in the production of goods that require unskilled workers and small amounts of simple machinery, such as children's toys.
- ***Technology.*** Broadly defined, *technology* is the process firms use to turn inputs into goods and services. At any given time, firms in different countries do not all have access to the same technologies. In part, this difference is the result of past investments countries have made in supporting higher education or in providing support for research and development. Some countries are strong in *product technologies*, which involve the ability to develop new products. For example, firms in the United States have pioneered the development of such products as televisions, digital computers, airliners, and many prescription drugs. Other countries are strong in *process technologies*, which involve the ability to improve the processes used to make existing products. For example, firms in Japan, such as Toyota and Nissan, have succeeded by greatly improving the processes for designing and manufacturing automobiles.
- ***External economies.*** It is difficult to explain the location of some industries on the basis of climate, natural resources, the relative abundance of labor and capital, or technology. For example, why does Southern California have a comparative advantage in making movies or Switzerland in making watches or New York in providing financial services? The answer is that once an industry becomes established in an area, firms that locate in that area gain advantages over firms located elsewhere. The advantages include the availability of skilled workers, the opportunity to interact with other firms in the same industry, and being close to suppliers. These advantages result in lower costs to firms located in the area. Because these lower costs result from increases in the size of the industry in an area, economists refer to them as **external economies**.

External economies Reductions in a firm's costs that result from an increase in the size of an industry.

Making the Connection

Why Is Dalton, Georgia, the Carpet-Making Capital of the World?

Factories within a 65-mile radius of Dalton, Georgia, account for 80 percent of U.S. carpet production and more than half of world carpet production. Carpet production is highly automated and relies primarily on synthetic fibers. Dalton, a small city located in rural northwest Georgia, would not seem to have any advantages in carpet production. In fact, the location of the carpet industry in Dalton was a historical accident.

In the early 1900s, Catherine Evans Whitener started making bedspreads using a method called "tufting," in which she sewed cotton yarn through the fabric and then cut the ends of the yarn so it would fluff up. These bedspreads became very popular. By the 1930s, the process was mechanized and was then applied to carpets. In the early years, the industry used cotton grown in Georgia, but today synthetic fibers, such as nylon and olefin, have largely replaced cotton and wool in carpet manufacturing.

More than 170 carpet factories are now located in the Dalton area. Supporting the carpet industry are local yarn manufacturers, machinery suppliers, and maintenance firms. Dye plants have opened solely to supply the carpet industry. Printing shops have opened, solely to print tags and labels for carpets. Box factories have opened to produce cartons designed specifically for shipping carpets. The local workforce has developed highly specialized skills for running and maintaining the carpet-making machinery.

Because Catherine Evans Whitener started making bedspreads by hand in Dalton, Georgia, 100 years ago, a multibillion-dollar carpet industry is now located there.

A company establishing a carpet factory outside the Dalton area is unable to use the suppliers or the skilled workers available to factories in Dalton. As a result, carpet factories located outside Dalton may have higher costs than factories located in Dalton. Although there is no particular reason why the carpet industry should have originally located in Dalton, external economies gave the area a comparative advantage in carpet making once it began to grow there.

YOUR TURN: Test your understanding by doing related problem 3.13 on page 200 at the end of this chapter.

Comparative Advantage Over Time: The Rise and Fall—and Rise—of the U.S. Consumer Electronics Industry

A country may develop a comparative advantage in the production of a good, and then, as time passes and circumstances change, the country may lose its comparative advantage in producing that good and develop a comparative advantage in producing other goods. For several decades, the United States had a comparative advantage in the production of consumer electronic goods, such as televisions, radios, and stereos. The comparative advantage of the United States in these products was based on having developed most of the underlying technology, having the most modern factories, and having a skilled and experienced workforce. Gradually, however, other countries, particularly Japan, gained access to the technology, built modern factories, and developed skilled workforces. As mentioned earlier, Japanese firms have excelled in process technologies, which involve the ability to improve the processes used to make existing products. By the 1970s and 1980s, Japanese firms were able to produce many consumer electronic goods more cheaply and with higher quality than could U.S. firms. Japanese firms Sony, Panasonic, and Pioneer replaced U.S. firms Magnavox, Zenith, and RCA as world leaders in consumer electronics.

By 2007, however, as the technology underlying consumer electronics evolved, comparative advantage had shifted again, and several U.S. firms surged ahead of their Japanese competitors. For example, Apple Computer had developed the iPod and iPhone; Linksys, a division of Cisco Systems, took the lead in home wireless networking technology; and Kodak developed digital cameras with EasyShare software that made it easy to organize, enhance, and share digital pictures. As pictures and music converted to digital data, process technologies became less important than the ability to design and develop new products. These new consumer electronics products required skills similar to those in computer design and software writing, where the United States had long maintained a comparative advantage.

Once a country has lost its comparative advantage in producing a good, its income will be higher and its economy will be more efficient if it switches from producing the good to importing it, as the United States did when it switched from producing televisions to importing them. As we will see in the next section, however, there is often political pressure on governments to attempt to preserve industries that have lost their comparative advantage.

6.4 LEARNING OBJECTIVE

6.4 | Analyze the economic effects of government policies that restrict international trade.

Government Policies That Restrict International Trade

Free trade, or trade between countries that is without government restrictions, makes consumers better off. We can expand on this idea by using the concepts of consumer surplus and producer surplus from Chapter 4. Figure 6-4 shows the market for the biofuel ethanol in the United States, assuming autarky, where the United States does not trade with other countries. The equilibrium price of ethanol is $2.00 per gallon, and the equilibrium quantity is 6.0 billion gallons per year. The blue area represents consumer surplus, and the red area represents producer surplus.

Free trade Trade between countries that is without government restrictions.

Now suppose that the United States begins importing ethanol from Brazil and other countries that produce lower-priced sugar-based ethanol and that ethanol is selling in those countries for $1.00 per gallon. Because the world market for ethanol is large, we will assume that the United States can buy as much ethanol as it wants without causing the *world price* of $1.00 per gallon to rise. Therefore, once imports of ethanol are permitted

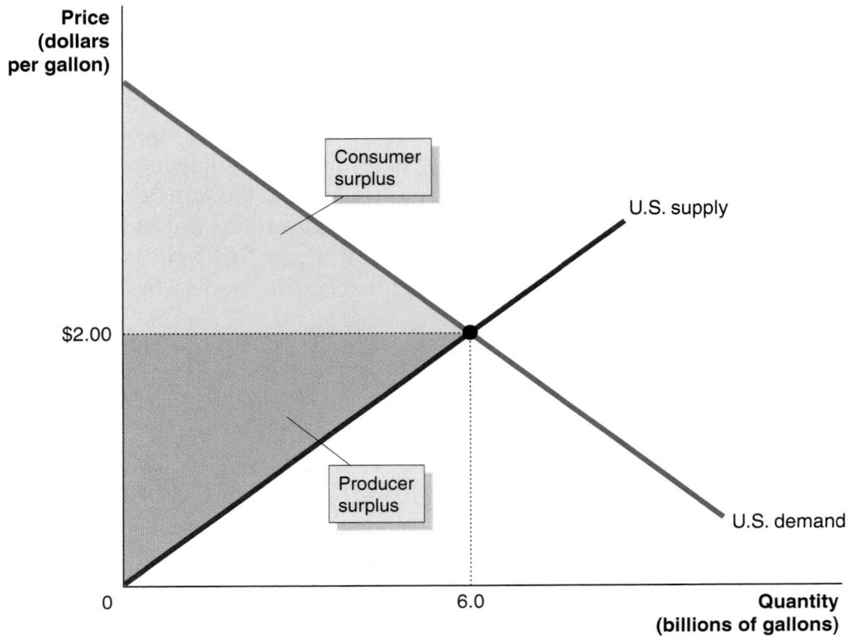

Figure 6-4

The U.S. Market for Ethanol under Autarky

This figure shows the market for ethanol in the United States, assuming autarky, where the United States does not trade with other countries. The equilibrium price of ethanol is $2.00 per gallon, and the equilibrium quantity is 6.0 billion gallons per year. The blue area represents consumer surplus, and the red area represents producer surplus.

Figure 6-5

The Effect of Imports on the U.S. Ethanol Market

When imports are allowed into the United States, the price of ethanol falls from \$2.00 to \$1.00. U.S. consumers increase their purchases from 6.0 billion gallons to 9.0 billion gallons. Equilibrium moves from point *F* to point *G*. U.S. producers reduce the quantity of ethanol they supply from 6.0 billion gallons to 3.0 billion gallons. Imports equal 6.0 billion gallons, which is the difference between U.S. consumption and U.S. production. Consumer surplus equals the areas *A*, *B*, *C*, and *D*. Producer surplus equals the area *E*.

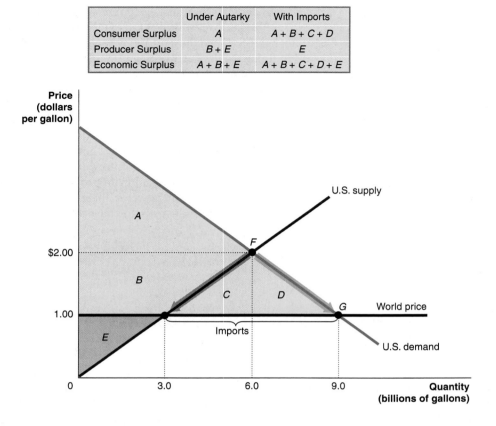

	Under Autarky	With Imports
Consumer Surplus	*A*	*A* + *B* + *C* + *D*
Producer Surplus	*B* + *E*	*E*
Economic Surplus	*A* + *B* + *E*	*A* + *B* + *C* + *D* + *E*

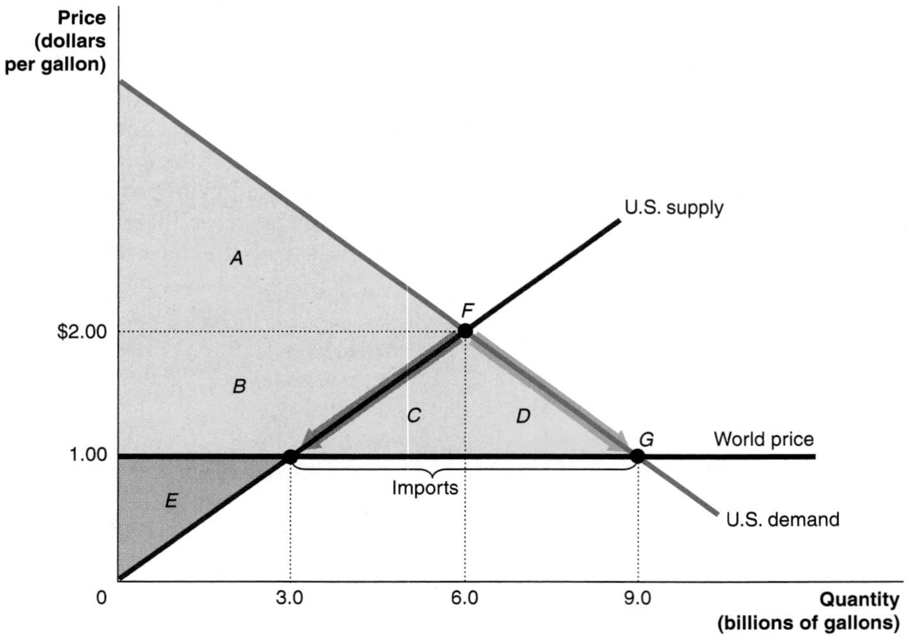

into the United States, U.S. firms will not be able to sell ethanol at prices higher than the world price of \$1.00, and the U.S. price will become equal to the world price.

Figure 6-5 shows the result of allowing imports of ethanol into the United States. With the price lowered from \$2.00 to \$1.00, U.S. consumers increase their purchases from 6.0 billion gallons to 9.0 billion gallons. Equilibrium moves from point *F* to point *G*. In the new equilibrium, U.S. producers have reduced the quantity of ethanol they supply from 6.0 billion gallons to 3.0 billion gallons. Imports will equal 6.0 billion gallons, which is the difference between U.S. consumption and U.S. production.

Under autarky, consumer surplus would be area *A* in Figure 6-5. With imports, the reduction in price increases consumer surplus, so it is now equal to the sum of areas *A*, *B*, *C*, and *D*. Although the lower price increases consumer surplus, it reduces producer surplus. Under autarky, producer surplus was equal to the sum of the areas *B* and *E*. With imports, producer surplus is equal to only area *E*. Recall that economic surplus equals the sum of consumer surplus and producer surplus. Moving from autarky to allowing imports increases economic surplus in the United States by an amount equal to the sum of areas *C* and *D*.

We can conclude that international trade helps consumers but hurts firms that are less efficient than foreign competitors. As a result, these firms and their workers are often strong supporters of government policies that restrict trade. These policies usually take one of two forms:

- Tariffs
- Quotas and voluntary export restraints

Tariffs

The most common interferences with trade are *tariffs*, which are taxes imposed by a government on goods imported into a country. Like any other tax, a tariff increases the cost of selling a good. Figure 6-6 shows the impact of a tariff of \$0.50 per gallon on ethanol

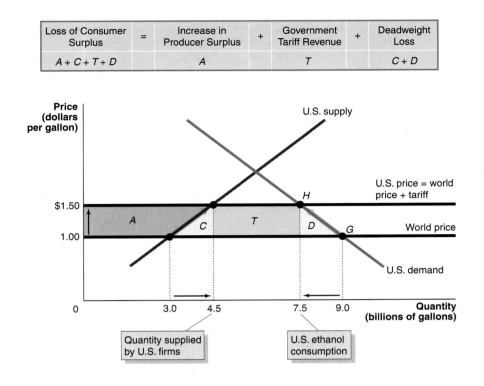

Loss of Consumer Surplus	=	Increase in Producer Surplus	+	Government Tariff Revenue	+	Deadweight Loss
$A + C + T + D$		A		T		$C + D$

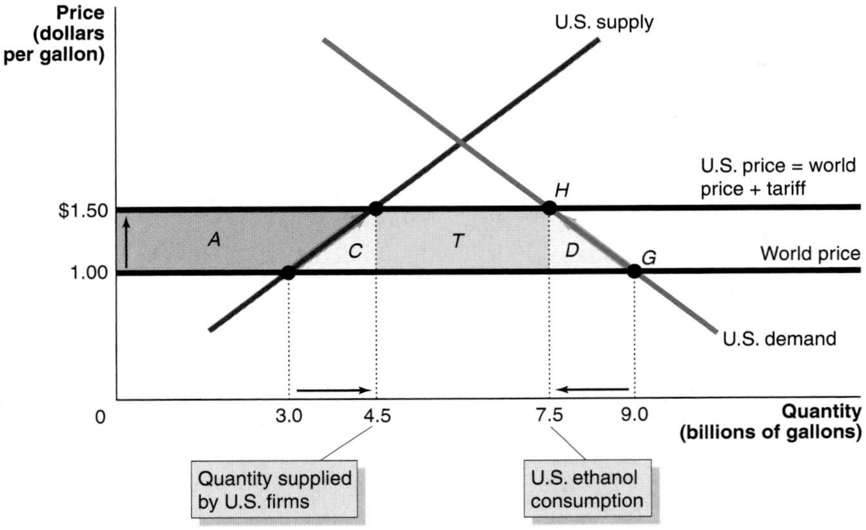

Figure 6-6

The Effects of a Tariff on Ethanol

Without a tariff on ethanol, U.S. producers will sell 3.0 billion gallons of ethanol, U.S. consumers will purchase 9.0 billion gallons, and imports will be 6.0 billion gallons. The U.S. price will equal the world price of $1.00 per gallon. The $0.50-per-gallon tariff raises the price of ethanol in the United States to $1.50 per gallon, and U.S. producers increase the quantity they supply to 4.5 billion gallons. U.S. consumers reduce their purchases to 7.5 billion gallons. Equilibrium moves from point *G* to point *H*. The ethanol tariff causes a loss of consumer surplus equal to the area $A + C + T + D$. The area *A* is the increase in producer surplus due to the higher price. The area *T* is the government's tariff revenue. The areas *C* and *D* represent deadweight loss.

imports into the United States. The $0.50 tariff raises the price of ethanol in the United States from the world price of $1.00 per gallon to $1.50 per gallon. At this higher price, U.S. ethanol producers increase the quantity they supply from 3.0 billion gallons to 4.5 billion gallons. U.S. consumers, though, cut back their purchases of ethanol from 9.0 billion gallons to 7.5 billion gallons. Imports decline from 6.0 billion gallons (9 billion – 6 billion) to 3.0 billion (7.5 billion – 4.5 billion). Equilibrium moves from point *G* to point *H*.

By raising the price of ethanol from $1.00 to $1.50, the tariff reduces consumer surplus by the sum of areas *A*, *T*, *C*, and *D*. Area *A* is the increase in producer surplus from the higher price. The government collects tariff revenue equal to the tariff of $0.50 per gallon multiplied by the 3.0 billion gallons imported. Area *T* represents the government's tariff revenue. Areas *C* and *D* represent losses to U.S. consumers that are not captured by anyone. They are deadweight loss and represent the decline in economic efficiency resulting from the ethanol tariff. Area *C* shows the effect on U.S. consumers of being forced to buy from U.S. producers who are less efficient than foreign producers, and area *D* shows the effect of U.S. consumers buying less ethanol than they would have at the world price. As a result of the tariff, economic surplus has been reduced by the sum of areas *C* and *D*. Recall from Chapter 4 that deadweight loss represents a loss of economic efficiency.

We can conclude that the tariff succeeds in helping U.S. ethanol producers but hurts U.S. consumers and the efficiency of the U.S. economy.

Quotas and Voluntary Export Restraints

A **quota** is a numeric limit on the quantity of a good that can be imported, and it has an effect similar to a tariff. A quota is imposed by the government of the importing country. A **voluntary export restraint (VER)** is an agreement negotiated between two countries that places a numeric limit on the quantity of a good that can be imported by one country from the other country. In the early 1980s, the United States and Japan negotiated a VER that limited the quantity of automobiles the United States would import from Japan. The Japanese government agreed to the VER primarily because it was afraid

Quota A numeric limit imposed by a government on the quantity of a good that can be imported into the country.

Voluntary export restraint (VER) An agreement negotiated between two countries that places a numeric limit on the quantity of a good that can be imported by one country from the other country.

that if it did not, the United States would impose a tariff or quota on imports of Japanese automobiles. Quotas and VERs have similar economic effects.

The main purpose of most tariffs and quotas is to reduce the foreign competition that domestic firms face. We saw an example of this at the beginning of this chapter when we discussed the sugar quota, which Congress imposed to protect U.S. sugar producers. Figure 6-7 shows the actual statistics for the U.S. sugar market in 2006. The effect of a quota is very similar to the effect of a tariff. By limiting imports, a quota forces the domestic price of a good above the world price. In this case, the sugar quota limits sugar imports to 3.5 billion pounds (shown by the bracket in Figure 6-7), forcing the U.S. price of sugar up to $0.22 per pound, or $0.10 higher than the world price. The U.S. price is above the world price because the quota keeps foreign sugar producers from selling the additional sugar in the United States that would drive the price down to the world price. At a price of $0.22 cents per pound, U.S. producers increased the quantity of sugar they supply from 5.9 billion pounds to 18.0 billion pounds, and U.S. consumers cut back their purchases of sugar from 23.1 billion pounds to 21.5 billion pounds. Equilibrium moves from point *E* to point *F*.

Measuring the Economic Effect of the Sugar Quota

Once again, we can use the concepts of consumer surplus, producer surplus, and deadweight loss to measure the economic impact of the sugar quota. Without a sugar quota, the world price of $0.12 per pound would also be the U.S. price. In Figure 6-7, consumer surplus equals the area above the $0.12 price line and below the demand curve. The sugar quota causes the U.S. price to rise to $0.22 cents and reduces consumer surplus by the area *A* + *B* + *C* + *D*. Without a sugar quota, producer surplus received by U.S. sugar producers would be equal to the area below the $0.12 price line and above the supply

Figure 6-7

The Economic Effect of the U.S. Sugar Quota

Without a sugar quota, U.S. sugar producers would have sold 5.9 billion pounds of sugar, U.S. consumers would have purchased 23.1 billion pounds of sugar, and imports would have been 17.2 billion pounds. The U.S. price would have equaled the world price of $0.12 per pound. Because the sugar quota limits imports to 3.5 billion pounds (the bracket in the graph), the price of sugar in the United States rises to $0.22 per pound, and U.S. producers increase the quantity of sugar they supply to 18.0 billion pounds. U.S. consumers reduce their sugar purchases to 21.5 billion pounds. Equilibrium moves from point *E* to point *F*. The sugar quota causes a loss of consumer surplus equal to the area *A* + *B* + *C* + *D*. The area *A* is the gain to U.S. sugar producers. The area *B* is the gain to foreign sugar producers. The areas *C* and *D* represent deadweight loss. The total loss to U.S. consumers in 2006 was $2.24 billion.

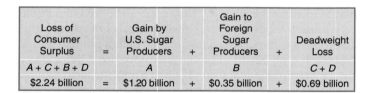

Loss of Consumer Surplus	=	Gain by U.S. Sugar Producers	+	Gain to Foreign Sugar Producers	+	Deadweight Loss
A + *C* + *B* + *D*		*A*		*B*		*C* + *D*
$2.24 billion	=	$1.20 billion	+	$0.35 billion	+	$0.69 billion

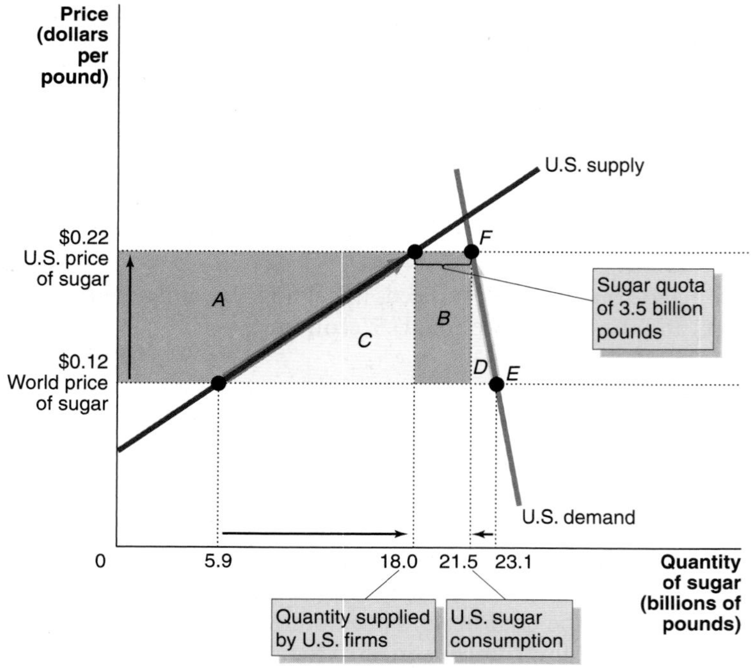

curve. The higher U.S. price resulting from the sugar quota increases the producer surplus of U.S. sugar producers by an amount equal to area *A*.

A foreign producer must have a license from the U.S. government to import sugar under the quota system. Therefore, a foreign sugar producer that is lucky enough to have an import license also benefits from the quota because it is able to sell sugar on the U.S. market at $0.22 per pound instead of $0.12 per pound. The gain to foreign sugar producers is area *B*. Areas *A* and *B* represent transfers from U.S. consumers of sugar to U.S. and foreign producers of sugar. Areas *C* and *D* represent losses to U.S. consumers that are not captured by anyone. They are deadweight losses and represent the decline in economic efficiency resulting from the sugar quota. Area *C* shows the effect of U.S. consumers being forced to buy from U.S. producers that are less efficient than foreign producers, and area *D* shows the effect of U.S. consumers buying less sugar than they would have at the world price.

Figure 6-7 provides enough information to calculate the dollar value of each of the four areas. The results of these calculations are shown in the table in the figure. The total loss to consumers from the sugar quota was $2.24 billion in 2006. About 53 percent of the loss to consumers, or $1.20 billion, was gained by U.S. sugar producers as increased producer surplus. About 16 percent, or $0.35 billion, was gained by foreign sugar producers as increased producer surplus, and about 31 percent, or $0.69 billion, was a deadweight loss to the U.S. economy. The U.S. International Trade Commission estimates that eliminating the sugar quota would result in the loss of about 3,000 jobs in the U.S. sugar industry. The cost to U.S. consumers of saving these jobs is equal to $2.24 billion/3,000, or about $750,000 per job. In fact, this cost is an underestimate because eliminating the sugar quota would result in new jobs being created, particularly in the candy industry. As we saw at the beginning of this chapter, U.S. candy companies have been moving factories to other countries to escape the impact of the sugar quota.

Solved Problem | **6-4**

Measuring the Economic Effect of a Quota

Suppose that the United States currently both produces and imports apples. The U.S. government then decides to restrict international trade in apples by imposing a quota that allows imports of only 4 million boxes of apples into the United States each year. The figure shows the results of imposing the quota.

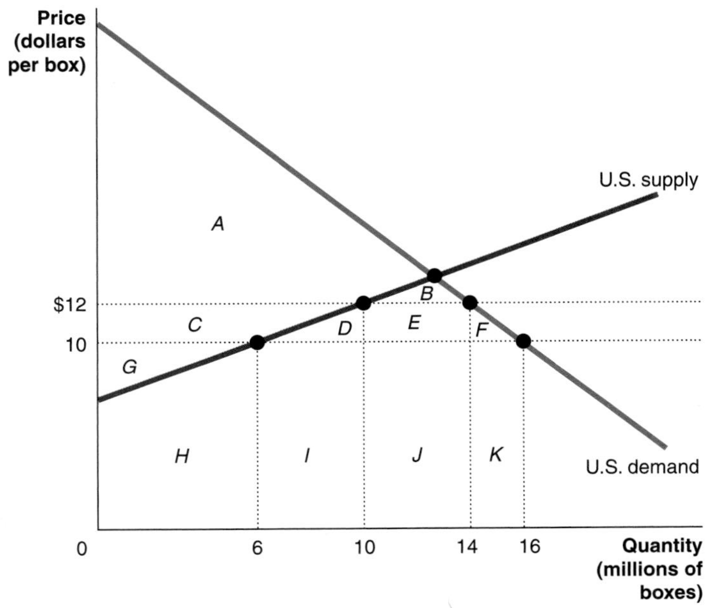

Fill in the following table, using the prices, quantities, and letters in the figure:

	WITHOUT QUOTA	WITH QUOTA
World price of apples	________	________
U.S. price of apples	________	________
Quantity supplied by U.S. firms	________	________
Quantity demanded by U.S. consumers	________	________
Quantity imported	________	________
Area of consumer surplus	________	________
Area of producer surplus	________	________
Area of deadweight loss	________	________

SOLVING THE PROBLEM:

Step 1: **Review the chapter material.** This problem is about measuring the economic effects of a quota, so you may want to review the section "Quotas and Voluntary Export Restraints," which begins on page 185, and "Measuring the Economic Effect of the Sugar Quota," which begins on page 186.

Step 2: **Fill in the table.** After studying Figure 6-7, you should be able to fill in the table. Remember that consumer surplus is the area below the demand curve and above the market price.

	WITHOUT QUOTA	WITH QUOTA
World price of apples	$10	$10
U.S. price of apples	$10	$12
Quantity supplied by U.S. firms	6 million boxes	10 million boxes
Quantity demanded by U.S. consumers	16 million boxes	14 million boxes
Quantity imported	10 millions boxes	4 million boxes
Area of consumer surplus	$A + B + C + D + E + F$	$A + B$
Area of domestic producer surplus	G	$G + C$
Area of deadweight loss	No deadweight loss	$D + F$

>> End Solved Problem 6-4

YOUR TURN: For more practice, do related problem 4.14 on page 202 at the end of this chapter.

The High Cost of Preserving Jobs with Tariffs and Quotas

The sugar quota is not alone in imposing a high cost on U.S. consumers to save jobs at U.S. firms. Table 6-5 shows, for several industries, the cost tariffs and quotas impose on U.S. consumers per year for each job saved.

Many countries besides the United States also use tariffs and quotas to try to protect jobs. Table 6-6 shows the cost to Japanese consumers per year for each job saved as a result of tariffs and quotas in the listed industries. Note the staggering cost of $51 million for each job saved that is imposed on Japanese consumers by the Japanese government's restrictions on imports of rice.

Just as the sugar quota costs jobs in the candy industry, other tariffs and quotas cost jobs outside the industries immediately affected. For example, in 1991, the United States imposed tariffs on flat-panel displays used in laptop computers. This was good news for U.S. producers of these displays but bad news for companies producing laptop computers. Toshiba, Sharp, and Apple all closed their U.S. laptop production facilities and moved production overseas. In fact, whenever one industry receives tariff or quota protection, jobs are lost in other domestic industries.

TABLE 6-5

Preserving U.S. Jobs with Tariffs and Quotas Is Expensive

PRODUCT	NUMBER OF JOBS SAVED	COST TO CONSUMERS PER YEAR FOR EACH JOB SAVED
Benzenoid chemicals	216	$1,376,435
Luggage	226	1,285,078
Softwood lumber	605	1,044,271
Dairy products	2,378	685,323
Frozen orange juice	609	635,103
Ball bearings	146	603,368
Machine tools	1,556	479,452
Women's handbags	773	263,535
Canned tuna	390	257,640

Source: Federal Reserve Bank of Dallas, *2002 Annual Report*, Exhibit 11.

Gains from Unilateral Elimination of Tariffs and Quotas

Some politicians argue that eliminating U.S. tariffs and quotas would help the U.S. economy only if other countries eliminated their tariffs and quotas in exchange. It is easier to gain political support for reducing or eliminating tariffs or quotas if it is done as part of an agreement with other countries that involves their eliminating some of their tariffs or quotas. But as the example of the sugar quota shows, *the U.S. economy would gain from the elimination of tariffs and quotas even if other countries do not reduce their tariffs and quotas.*

Other Barriers to Trade

In addition to tariffs and quotas, governments sometimes erect other barriers to trade. For example, all governments require that imports meet certain health and safety requirements. Sometimes, however, governments use these requirements to shield domestic firms from foreign competition. This can be true when a government imposes stricter health and safety requirements on imported goods than on goods produced by domestic firms.

TABLE 6-6

Preserving Japanese Jobs with Tariffs and Quotas Is Also Expensive

PRODUCT	COST TO CONSUMERS PER YEAR FOR EACH JOB SAVED
Rice	$51,233,000
Natural gas	27,987,000
Gasoline	6,329,000
Paper	3,813,000
Beef, pork, and poultry	1,933,000
Cosmetics	1,778,000
Radio and television sets	915,000

Source: Yoko Sazabami, Shujiro Urata, and Hiroki Kawai, *Measuring the Cost of Protection in Japan*, Washington, DC: Institute for International Economics, 1995. Used with permission.

Many governments also restrict imports of certain products on national security grounds. The argument is that in time of war, a country should not be dependent on imports of critical war materials. Once again, these restrictions are sometimes used more to protect domestic companies from competition than to protect national security. For example, for years, the U.S. government would buy military uniforms only from U.S. manufacturers, even though uniforms are not a critical war material.

6.5 LEARNING OBJECTIVE

6.5 | Evaluate the arguments over trade policy and globalization.

The Argument over Trade Policies and Globalization

The argument over whether the U.S. government should regulate international trade dates back to the early days of the country. One particularly controversial attempt to restrict trade took place during the Great Depression of the 1930s. At that time, the United States and other countries attempted to help domestic firms by raising tariffs on foreign imports. The United States started the process by passing the Smoot-Hawley Tariff in 1930, which raised average tariff rates to more than 50 percent. As other countries retaliated by raising their tariffs, international trade collapsed.

By the end of World War II in 1945, government officials in the United States and Europe were looking for a way to reduce tariffs and revive international trade. To help achieve this goal, they set up the General Agreement on Tariffs and Trade (GATT) in 1948. Countries that joined GATT agreed not to impose new tariffs or import quotas. In addition, a series of *multilateral negotiations*, called *trade rounds*, took place, in which countries agreed to reduce tariffs from the very high levels of the 1930s.

In the 1940s, most international trade was in goods, and the GATT agreement covered only goods. In the following decades, trade in services and in products incorporating *intellectual property*, such as software programs and movies, grew in importance. Many GATT members pressed for a new agreement that would cover services and intellectual property, as well as goods. A new agreement was negotiated, and in January 1995, GATT was replaced by the **World Trade Organization (WTO)**, headquartered in Geneva, Switzerland. More than 130 countries are currently members of the WTO.

World Trade Organization (WTO) An international organization that oversees international trade agreements.

Why Do Some People Oppose the World Trade Organization?

During the years immediately after World War II, many low-income, or developing, countries erected high tariffs and restricted investment by foreign companies. When these policies failed to produce much economic growth, many of these countries decided during the 1980s to become more open to foreign trade and investment. This process became known as **globalization**. Most developing countries joined the WTO and began to follow its policies.

Globalization The process of countries becoming more open to foreign trade and investment.

During the 1990s, opposition to globalization began to increase. In 1999, this opposition took a violent turn at a meeting of the WTO in Seattle, Washington. The purpose of the meeting was to plan a new round of negotiations aimed at further reductions in trade barriers. A large number of protestors assembled in Seattle to meet the WTO delegates. Protests started peacefully but quickly became violent. Protesters looted stores and burned cars, and many delegates were unable to leave their hotel rooms.

Why would attempts to reduce trade barriers with the objective of increasing income around the world cause such a furious reaction? The opposition to the WTO comes from three sources. First, some opponents are specifically against the globalization process that began in the 1980s and became widespread in the 1990s. Second, other opponents have the same motivation as the supporters of tariffs in the 1930s—to erect trade barriers to protect domestic firms from foreign competition. Third, some critics of the WTO support globalization in principle but believe that the WTO favors the interests of the high-income countries at the expense of the low-income countries. Let's look more closely at the sources of opposition to the WTO.

Anti-Globalization Many of the protestors in Seattle distrust globalization. Some believe that free trade and foreign investment destroy the distinctive cultures of many countries. As developing countries began to open their economies to imports from the United States and other high-income countries, these imports of food, clothing, movies, and other goods began to replace the equivalent local products. So, a teenager in Thailand might be sitting in a McDonald's restaurant, wearing Levi's jeans and a Ralph Lauren shirt, listening to a recording by U2 on his iPod, before going to the local movie theater to watch *Spider-Man 3*. Globalization has increased the variety of products available to consumers in developing countries, but some people argue that this is too high a price to pay for what they see as damage to local cultures.

Globalization has also allowed multinational corporations to relocate factories from high-income countries to low-income countries. These new factories in Indonesia, Malaysia, Pakistan, and other countries pay much lower wages than are paid in the United States, Europe, and Japan and often do not meet the environmental or safety regulations that are imposed in high-income countries. Some factories use child labor, which is illegal in high-income countries. Some people have argued that firms with factories in developing countries should pay workers wages as high as those paid in the high-income countries. They also believe these firms should follow the health, safety, and environmental regulations that exist in the high-income countries.

The governments of most developing countries have resisted these proposals. They argue that when the currently rich countries were poor, they also lacked environmental or safety standards, and their workers were paid low wages. They argue that it is easier for rich countries to afford high wages and environmental and safety regulations than it is for poor countries. They also point out that many jobs that seem very poorly paid by high-income country standards are often better than the alternatives available to workers in low-income countries.

Making the Connection | The Unintended Consequences of Banning Goods Made with Child Labor

In many developing countries, such as Indonesia, Thailand, and Peru, children as young as seven or eight work 10 or more hours a day. Reports of very young workers laboring long hours, producing goods for export, have upset many people in high-income countries. In the United States, boycotts have been organized against stores that stock goods made in developing countries with child labor. Many people assume that if child workers in developing countries weren't working in factories making clothing, toys, and other products, they would be in school, as are children in high-income countries.

Would eliminating child labor in developing countries be a good thing?

In fact, children in developing countries usually have few good alternatives to work. Schooling is frequently available for only a few months each year, and even children who attend school rarely do so for more than a few years. Poor families are often unable to afford even the small costs of sending their children to school. Families may even rely on the earnings of very young children to survive, as poor families once did in the United States, Europe, and Japan. There is substantial evidence that as incomes begin to rise in poor countries, families rely less on child labor. The United States eventually outlawed child labor, but not until 1938. In developing countries where child labor is common today, jobs producing export goods are usually better paying and less hazardous than the alternatives.

As preparations began in France for the 1998 World Cup, there were protests that Baden Sports—the main supplier of soccer balls—was purchasing the balls from suppliers in Pakistan that used child workers. France decided to ban all use of soccer balls made by child workers. Bowing to this pressure, Baden Sports moved production from Pakistan, where the balls were hand-stitched by child workers, to China, where the balls were machine-stitched by adult workers in factories. There was some criticism of the boycott of hand-stitched soccer balls at the time. In a broad study of child labor, three economists argued:

> Of the array of possible employment in which impoverished children might engage, soccer ball stitching is probably one of the most benign. . . . [In Pakistan] children generally work alongside other family members in the home or in small workshops. . . . Nor are the children exposed to toxic chemicals, hazardous tools or brutal working conditions. Rather, the only serious criticism concerns the length of the typical child stitcher's work-day and the impact on formal education.

In fact, the alternatives to soccer ball stitching for child workers in Pakistan turned out to be extremely grim. According to Keith Maskus, an economist at the University of Colorado and the World Bank, a "large proportion" of the children who lost their jobs stitching soccer balls ended up begging or in prostitution.

Sources: Drusilla K. Brown, Alan V. Deardorff, and Robert M. Stern, "U.S. Trade and Other Policy Options to Deter Foreign Exploitation of Child Labor," in Magnus Blomstrom and Linda S. Goldberg, eds., *Topics in Empirical International Economics: A Festschrift in Honor of Bob Lipsey*, Chicago: University of Chicago Press, 2001; Tomas Larsson, *The Race to the Top: The Real Story of Globalization*, Washington, DC: Cato Institute, 2001, p. 48; and Eric V. Edmonds and Nina Pavcnik, "Child Labor in the Global Economy," *Journal of Economic Perspectives*, Vol. 19, No. 1, Winter 2005, pp. 199–220.

YOUR TURN: Test your understanding by doing related problem 5.5 on page 203 at the end of this chapter.

Protectionism The use of trade barriers to shield domestic firms from foreign competition.

"Old-Fashioned" Protectionism The anti-globalization argument against free trade and the WTO is relatively new. Another argument against free trade, called *protectionism*, has been around for centuries. **Protectionism** is the use of trade barriers to shield domestic firms from foreign competition. For as long as international trade has existed, governments have attempted to restrict it to protect domestic firms. As we saw with the analysis of the sugar quota, protectionism causes losses to consumers and eliminates jobs in the domestic industries that use the protected product. In addition, by reducing the ability of countries to produce according to comparative advantage, protectionism reduces incomes.

Why, then, does protectionism attract support? Protectionism is usually justified on the basis of one of the following arguments:

- ***Saving jobs.*** Supporters of protectionism argue that free trade reduces employment by driving domestic firms out of business. It is true that when more-efficient foreign firms drive less-efficient domestic firms out of business, jobs are lost, but jobs are also lost when more-efficient domestic firms drive less-efficient domestic firms out of business. These job losses are rarely permanent. In the U.S. economy, jobs are lost and new jobs are created continually. No economic study has ever found a long-term connection between the total number of jobs available and the level of tariff protection for domestic industries. In addition, trade restrictions destroy jobs in some industries at the same time that they preserve jobs in others. The U.S. sugar quota may have saved jobs in the U.S. sugar industry, but, as we saw at the beginning of this chapter, it also has destroyed jobs in the U.S. candy industry.
- ***Protecting high wages.*** Some people worry that firms in high-income countries will have to start paying much lower wages to compete with firms in developing countries.

This fear is misplaced, however, because free trade actually raises living standards by increasing economic efficiency. When a country practices protectionism and produces goods and services it could obtain more inexpensively from other countries, it reduces its standard of living. The United States could ban imports of coffee and begin growing it domestically. But this would entail a very high opportunity cost because coffee could only be grown in the continental United States in greenhouses and would require large amounts of labor and equipment. The coffee would have to sell for a very high price to cover these costs. Suppose the United States did ban coffee imports: Eliminating the ban at some future time would eliminate the jobs of U.S. coffee workers, but the standard of living in the United States would rise as coffee prices declined and labor, machinery, and other resources moved out of coffee production and into production of goods and services for which the United States has a comparative advantage.

- ***Protecting infant industries.*** It is possible that firms in a country may have a comparative advantage in producing a good, but because the country begins production of the good later than other countries, its firms initially have higher costs. In producing some goods and services, substantial "learning by doing" occurs. As workers and firms produce more of the good or service, they gain experience and become more productive. Over time, costs and prices will fall. As the firms in the "infant industry" gain experience, their costs will fall, and they will be able to compete successfully with foreign producers. Under free trade, however, they may not get the chance. The established foreign producers can sell the product at a lower price and drive domestic producers out of business before they gain enough experience to compete. To economists, this is the most persuasive of the protectionist arguments. It has a significant drawback, however. Tariffs used to protect an infant industry eliminate the need for the firms in the industry to become productive enough to compete with foreign firms. After World War II, the governments of many developing countries used the "infant industry" argument to justify high tariff rates. Unfortunately, most of their infant industries never grew up, and they continued for years as inefficient drains on their economies.
- ***Protecting national security.*** As already discussed, a country should not rely on other countries for goods that are critical to its military defense. For example, the United States would probably not want to import all its jet fighter engines from China. The definition of which goods are critical to military defense is a slippery one, however. In fact, it is rare for an industry to ask for protection without raising the issue of national security, even if its products have mainly nonmilitary uses.

Making the Connection | Has NAFTA Helped or Hurt the U.S. Economy?

The North American Free Trade Agreement (NAFTA) was very controversial when it was being negotiated in the early 1990s. During the 1992 presidential campaign, independent candidate Ross Perot claimed to hear a "giant sucking sound" as jobs were pulled out of the United States and into Mexico. NAFTA, which went into effect in 1994, eliminated most tariffs on products shipped between the United States, Canada, and Mexico. This policy change made it possible for each of these countries to better pursue its comparative advantage. For example, before NAFTA, the Mexican government had used tariffs to protect its domestic automobile industry, but that industry was much less efficient than the U.S. automobile industry. When tariffs were removed, Mexican consumers could take advantage of the efficiency of the U.S. industry, and U.S. exports of motor vehicles to Mexico soared. Similarly, Canadian consumers could take advantage of lower-priced U.S. beef, and U.S. consumers could take advantage of lower-priced Canadian lumber. As we would expect, expanding trade increased consumption in all three countries. In the United States, consumption increased about $400 per year for a family of four as a result of NAFTA.

Despite resistance to NAFTA, time proved that the U.S. economy gained jobs.

Contrary to Ross Perot's prediction, NAFTA did not lead to a loss of jobs in the United States. Between 1994, when NAFTA went into effect, and 2007, the number of jobs in the United States increased by more than 21 million. Some commentators argued that jobs in the United States could be preserved with NAFTA, but only if wages for U.S. workers declined to the much lower levels being paid Mexican workers. In fact, a study by Gordon Hanson of the University of California, San Diego, showed that the opposite occurred: Wages for both U.S. and Mexican workers increased following NAFTA. In addition, the gap between U.S. wages and Mexican wages did not close.

There were, of course, people in all three countries who were made worse off by NAFTA. Some firms in each country were no longer competitive after tariffs were lowered. In the United States, government assistance helped workers who lost their jobs to retrain or relocate. Overall, most economists have concluded that NAFTA helped the U.S. economy become more efficient, thereby expanding the consumption of U.S. households.

Source: Gordon H. Hanson, "What Has Happened to Wages in Mexico Since NAFTA? Implications for Hemispheric Free Trade," in Toni Estevadeordal, Dani Rodrick, Alan Taylor and Andres Velasco, eds., *FTAA and Beyond: Prospects for Integration in the Americas*, Cambridge, MA: Harvard University Press, 2004.

YOUR TURN: Test your understanding by doing related problem 5.7 on page 204 at the end of this chapter.

Dumping

Dumping Selling a product for a price below its cost of production.

In recent years, the United States has extended protection to some domestic industries by using a provision in the WTO agreement that allows governments to impose tariffs in the case of *dumping*. **Dumping** is selling a product for a price below its cost of production. Although allowable under the WTO agreement, using tariffs to offset the effects of dumping is very controversial.

In practice, it is difficult to determine whether foreign companies are dumping goods because the true production costs of a good are not easy for foreign governments to calculate. As a result, the WTO allows countries to determine that dumping has occurred if a product is exported for a lower price than it sells for on the home market. There is a problem with this approach, however. Often there are good business reasons for a firm to sell a product for different prices to different consumers. For example, the airlines charge business travelers higher ticket prices than leisure travelers. Firms also use "loss leaders"—products that are sold below cost, or even given away free—when introducing a new product or, in the case of retailing, to attract customers who will also buy full-price products. For example, when Sun Microsystems attempted to establish StarOffice as a competitor to Microsoft Office, Sun gave the software away free on its Web site. During the Christmas season, Wal-Mart sometimes offers toys at prices below what they pay to buy them from manufacturers. It's unclear why these normal business practices should be unacceptable when used in international trade.

Positive versus Normative Analysis (Once Again)

Economists emphasize the burden on the economy imposed by tariffs, quotas, and other government restrictions on free trade. Does it follow that these interferences are bad? Remember from Chapter 1 the distinction between *positive analysis* and *normative analysis.* Positive analysis concerns what *is.* Normative analysis concerns what *ought to be.* Measuring the impact of the sugar quota on the U.S. economy is an example of positive analysis. Asserting that the sugar quota is bad public policy and should be eliminated is normative analysis. The sugar quota—like all other interferences with trade—makes some people better off and some people worse off, and it reduces total income and consumption. Whether increasing the profits of U.S. sugar companies and the number of workers they employ justifies the costs imposed on consumers and the reduction in economic efficiency is a normative question.

Most economists do not support interferences with trade, such as the sugar quota. Few people become economists if they don't believe that markets should usually be as free as possible. But the opposite view is certainly intellectually respectable. It is possible for someone to understand the costs of tariffs and quotas but still believe that tariffs and quotas are a good idea, perhaps because they believe unrestricted free trade would cause too much disruption to the economy.

The success of industries in getting the government to erect barriers to foreign competition depends partly on some members of the public knowing full well the costs of trade barriers but supporting them anyway. However, two other factors are also at work:

1. The costs tariffs and quotas impose on consumers are large in total but relatively small per person. For example, the sugar quota imposes a total burden of about $2.24 billion per year on consumers. Spread across 300 million Americans, the burden is only about $7.50 per person: too little for most people to worry about, even if they know the burden exists.
2. The jobs lost to foreign competition are easy to identify, but the jobs created by foreign trade are less easy to identify.

In other words, the industries that benefit from tariffs and quotas benefit a lot—the sugar quota increases the profits of U.S. sugar producers by more than $1 billion—whereas each consumer loses relatively little. This concentration of benefits and widely spread burdens makes it easy to understand why members of Congress receive strong pressure from some industries to enact tariffs and quotas and relatively little pressure from the general public to reduce them.

>> Continued from page 171

Economics in YOUR Life!

At the beginning of the chapter, we asked you to consider how sugar companies have convinced Congress to enact the sugar quota and why relatively few people have heard of this quota. In the chapter, we saw that the sugar quota costs U.S. consumers more than $2 billion per year as a result of higher sugar prices and has led several U.S. candy makers to eliminate domestic jobs and move their facilities to other countries. This might seem to increase the mystery of why Congress has enacted the sugar quota, especially because it saves relatively few jobs in the U.S. sugar industry. We have also seen, though, that *per person*, the burden of the sugar quota is small—only about $7.50 per person per year. Not many people will take the trouble of writing a letter to their member of Congress or otherwise make their views known in the hope of saving $7.50 per year. In fact, few people will even spend the time to become aware that the quota exists. So, if before you read this chapter you had never heard of the sugar quota, you are certainly not alone.

Conclusion

There are few issues economists agree upon more than the economic benefits of free trade. However, there are few political issues as controversial as government policy toward trade. Many people who would be reluctant to see the government interfere with domestic trade are quite willing to see it interfere with international trade. The damage high tariffs inflicted on the world economy during the 1930s shows what can happen when governments around the world abandon free trade. Whether future episodes of that type can be avoided is by no means certain.

Read *An Inside Look at Policy* on the next page for a discussion of how eliminating tariffs on cars and other goods benefits the United States and South Korea.

The United States and South Korea Reach a Trade Deal

NEW YORK TIMES, APRIL 3, 2007

U.S. and South Korea Agree to Sweeping Trade Deal

United States and South Korean negotiators struck the world's largest bilateral free trade agreement on Monday, giving the United States a badly needed lift to its trade policy at home and South Korea a chance to reinvigorate its export economy. . . .

If ratified, the trade deal would eliminate tariffs on more than 90 percent of the product categories traded between the countries. South Korea agreed to lift trade barriers to important American products like cars and beef, while the United States agreed to allow Seoul to continue to subsidize South Korean rice. . . .

As South Korean workers and farmers protested in the streets—on Sunday, one man even set himself on fire—negotiators haggled to the end early Monday.

a The breakthrough came when both sides compromised on the most delicate deal-breaking issues. Washington dropped its demand that the South Korean government stop protecting its politically powerful rice farmers, and Seoul agreed to resume imports of American beef, halted three years ago over fears of mad cow disease, if, as expected, the World Organization on Animal Health declares United States meat safe in a ruling next month.

South Korea also agreed to phase out the 40 percent tariff on American beef over 15 years. It will remove an 8 percent duty on cars and revise a domestic vehicle tax system that United States officials say discriminates against American cars with bigger engines.

The United States will eliminate the 2.5 percent tariff on South Korean cars with engines smaller than 3,000 cubic centimeters; phase out the 25 percent duty on trucks over the course of 10 years; and remove tariffs, which average 8.9 percent, on 61 percent of South Korean textiles. . . .

The deal is the biggest of its kind for the United States since the North American Free Trade Agreement in 1994 with Canada and Mexico. It is Washington's first bilateral trade pact with a major Asian economy.

b Studies have estimated that the accord would add $20 billion to bilateral trade, estimated last year at $78 billion. Potential gains to the United States economy range from $17 billion to $43 billion, according to Usha C. H. Haley, director of the Global Business Center at the University of New Haven. South Korea's exports to the United States are expected to rise in the first year by 12 percent.

Analysts doubt that the deal will provide an immediate lift to American car manufacturers. Only 5,000 American cars were sold here last year, while South Korean automakers sold 800,000 vehicles in the United States. The gap accounted for 80 percent of the $13 billion United States trade deficit with South Korea last year.

American officials hope that the deal will placate American cattle farmers, who are struggling to recapture global market share after an outbreak of mad cow disease in late 2003. Before the import ban, South Korea was the world's third-largest consumer of American beef, importing $800 million a year.

Consumers in both countries are the deal's biggest winners. Hyundai cars and Samsung flat-panel TV sets, as well as Korean-made clothing, will become significantly cheaper in the United States.

American beef and oranges, as well as Ford cars and Toyota vehicles built in the United States, will be more affordable in South Korea. South Korean TV networks will be able to broadcast more American movies and TV series like "CSI," which already command a huge following here, after Seoul eases a cap on foreign content to 80 percent of total airtime from 75 percent.

c The deal entails heavy political costs for South Korea, which can expect the loss of tens of thousands of farming jobs. Up to 2 trillion won ($2.2 billion) in agricultural revenue will be lost as cheap American corn, soybeans and processed foods come in, according to studies by South Korean economists. . . .

Source: Choe Sang-Hun, "U.S. and South Korea Agree to Sweeping Trade Deal," New York Times, *April 3, 2007, p. C1.*

Key Points in the Article

The article discusses a recent trade agreement negotiated between the United States and South Korea that will reduce restrictions on trade between the two countries. Agreements such as this one to expand trade between two countries are known as *bilateral agreements*. The trade agreements worked out by the World Trade Organization are *multilateral agreements*. Neither Congress nor the South Korean National Assembly has yet ratified the agreement. However, if the legislatures do ratify the agreement, a free-trade zone covering the world's largest and eleventh-largest economies would be created.

Analyzing the News

a In this chapter, we have seen that expanding trade raises living standards by increasing consumption and economic efficiency. Reducing tariffs on trade between South Korea and the United States will aid consumers in both countries. The figure shows the U.S. market following the elimination of the tariff on South Korean cars. (For simplicity, we assume that there are no remaining U.S. tariffs on cars.) The price of cars in the United States falls from P_1 to P_2, and equilibrium in the U.S. car market moves from point *E* to point *F*. U.S. consumption of cars increases from Q_3 to Q_4, the quantity of cars supplied by U.S. car makers declines from Q_2 to Q_1, and imports increase from $Q_3 - Q_2$ to $Q_4 - Q_1$. Consumer surplus increases by the sum of areas *A*, *B*, *C*, and *D*. Area *A* represents a transfer from producer surplus under the tariff to consumer surplus. Areas *C* and *D* represent the conversion of deadweight loss to consumer surplus. Area *B* represents a conversion of government tariff revenue to consumer surplus. Eliminating the tariff reduces the cost to South Korean car producers of selling their product in the United States. U.S. consumers purchase a larger quantity of South Korean cars at a lower price.

b The figure shows that eliminating the tariff on cars also eliminates the revenue the U.S. government had been collecting from this tariff. In high-income countries, such as the United States, governments receive most of their revenue from taxes on personal and corporate income. For example, tariff revenue in the United States for 2006 amounted to only about 1 percent of all revenue received by the federal government, but governments in low-income countries often have difficulty collecting income taxes, so they rely heavily on tariffs for revenue. In these countries, the government's need for revenue can pose a serious barrier to expanding international trade by reducing tariffs because governments have difficulty replacing the revenues lost from tariff reductions. This was also true in the United States early in its history. In 1800, tariffs brought in 90 percent of all federal government revenue. As late as the 1950s, tariffs accounted for 14 percent of federal revenues.

c Trade benefits the entire economy but can create losses for certain groups in the economy. While South Korean consumers will gain from less expensive food, agricultural interests in South Korea will be hurt. These interests are likely to lobby against ratification of the agreement.

Increase in Consumer Surplus	=	Decrease in Producer Surplus	+	Decrease in Government Tariff Revenue	+	Decrease in Deadweight Loss
A + *C* + *B* + *D*		*A*		*B*		*C* + *D*

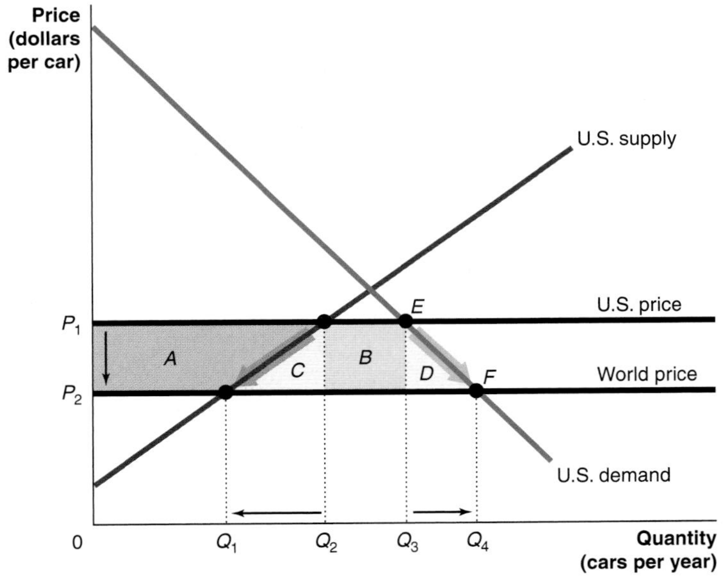

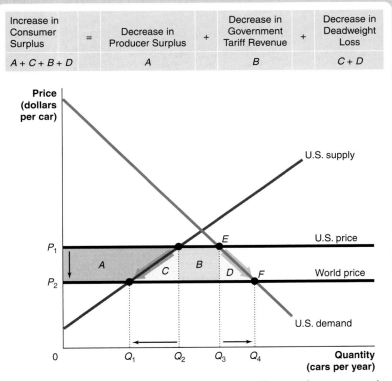

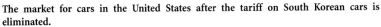

The market for cars in the United States after the tariff on South Korean cars is eliminated.

Thinking Critically About Policy

1. Tariffs on South Korean car and textile imports save jobs for Americans working in those industries. Do you support these tariffs? Why or why not?
2. In which goods mentioned in the article does the United States have a comparative advantage? In which does South Korea have a comparative advantage? Explain your reasoning.

Key Terms

Absolute advantage, p. 176
Autarky, p. 177
Comparative advantage, p. 175
Dumping, p. 194
Exports, p. 172
External economies, p. 181
Free trade, p. 183
Globalization, p. 190
Imports, p. 172
Opportunity cost, p. 175
Protectionism, p. 192
Quota, p. 185
Tariff, p. 172
Terms of trade, p. 177
Voluntary export restraint (VER), p. 185
World Trade Organization (WTO), p. 190

6.1 LEARNING OBJECTIVE 6.1 | Discuss the role of international trade in the U.S. economy, **pages 172–175.**

The United States in the International Economy

Summary

International trade has been increasing in recent decades, in part because of reductions in *tariffs* and other barriers to trade. A **tariff** is a tax imposed by a government on imports. The quantity of goods and services the United States imports and exports has been continually increasing. **Imports** are goods and services bought domestically but produced in other countries. **Exports** are goods and services produced domestically but sold to other countries. Today, the United States is the leading exporting country in the world, and about 20 percent of U.S. manufacturing jobs depend on exports.

myeconlab Get Ahead of the Curve Visit www.myeconlab.com to complete these exercises online and get instant feedback.

Review Questions

1.1 Briefly explain whether you agree or disagree with the following statement: "International trade is more important to the U.S. economy than to most other economies."

Problems and Applications

1.2 If the United States were to stop trading goods and services with other countries, which U.S. industries would be likely to see their sales decline the most? Briefly explain.

1.3 Briefly explain whether you agree with the following statement: "Japan has always been much more heavily involved in international trade than are most other nations. In fact, today Japan exports a larger fraction of its GDP than do Germany, Great Britain, or the United States."

1.4 **(Related to the *Making the Connection* on page 174)** Some politicians in the United States believe that European governments unfairly help Airbus, Boeing's main competitor, by subsidizing, or making payments, to Airbus. Suppose that the U.S. Congress passes legislation forbidding U.S. airlines from buying planes from Airbus or any other non-U.S. aircraft firm. Would this legislation be likely to actually help Boeing? Briefly explain.

>> End Learning Objective 6.1

6.2 LEARNING OBJECTIVE 6.2 | Understand the difference between comparative advantage and absolute advantage in international trade, **pages 175–176.**

Comparative Advantage in International Trade

Summary

Comparative advantage is the ability of an individual, a business, or a country to produce a good or service at the lowest **opportunity cost. Absolute advantage** is the ability to produce more of a good or service than competitors when using the same amount of resources. Countries trade on the basis of comparative advantage, not on the basis of absolute advantage.

myeconlab Get Ahead of the Curve Visit www.myeconlab.com to complete these exercises online and get instant feedback.

Review Questions

2.1 A World Trade Organization publication calls comparative advantage "arguably the single most powerful insight in economics." What is comparative advantage? What makes it such a powerful insight?

Source: World Trade Organization, *Trading into the Future,* April 1999.

2.2 What is the difference between absolute advantage and comparative advantage? Will a country always be an exporter of a good where it has an absolute advantage in production?

Problems and Applications

2.3 Why do the goods that countries import and export change over time? Use the concept of comparative advantage in your answer.

2.4 Briefly explain whether you agree with the following argument: "Unfortunately, Bolivia does not have a comparative advantage with respect to the United States in the production of any good or service." (*Hint:* You do not need any specific information about the economies of Bolivia or the United States to be able to answer this question.)

2.5 In 1987, an economic study showed that, on average, workers in the Japanese consumer electronics industry produced less output per hour than did U.S. workers producing the same goods. Despite this fact, Japan exported large quantities of consumer electronics to the United States. Briefly explain how this is possible.

Source: Study cited in Douglas A. Irwin, *Free Trade under Fire*, Princeton, NJ: Princeton University Press, 2002, p. 27.

2.6 Patrick J. Buchanan, a former presidential candidate, argues in his book on the global economy that there is a flaw in David Ricardo's theory of comparative advantage:

> Classical free trade theory fails the test of common sense. According to Ricardo's law of comparative advantage . . . if America makes better computers and textiles than China does, but our advantage in computers is greater than our advantage in textiles, we should (1) focus on computers, (2) let China make textiles, and (3) trade U.S. computers for Chinese textiles. . . .
>
> The doctrine begs a question. If Americans are more efficient than Chinese in making clothes . . . why surrender the more efficient American industry? Why shift to a reliance on a Chinese textile industry that will take years to catch up to where American factories are today?

Do you agree with Buchanan's argument? Briefly explain.

Source: Patrick J. Buchanan, *The Great Betrayal: How American Sovereignty and Social Justice Are Being Sacrificed to the Gods of the Global Economy*, Boston: Little, Brown, 1998, p. 66.

>> End Learning Objective 6.2

6.3 LEARNING OBJECTIVE 6.3 | Explain how countries gain from international trade, **pages 177–183.**

How Countries Gain from International Trade

Summary

Autarky is a situation in which a country does not trade with other countries. The **terms of trade** is the ratio at which a country can trade its exports for imports from other countries. When a country specializes in producing goods where it has a comparative advantage and trades for the other goods it needs, the country will have a higher level of income and consumption. We do not see complete specialization in production for three reasons: Not all goods and services are traded internationally, production of most goods involves increasing opportunity costs, and tastes for products differ across countries. Although the population of a country as a whole benefits from trade, companies—and their workers—that are unable to compete with lower-cost foreign producers lose. Among the main sources of comparative advantage are climate and natural resources, relative abundance of labor and capital, technology, and *external economies*. **External economies** are reductions in a firm's cost that result from an increase in the size of an industry. A country may develop a comparative advantage in the production of a good, and then as time passes and circumstances change, the country may lose its comparative advantage in producing that good and develop a comparative advantage in producing other goods.

myeconlab Get Ahead of the Curve Visit www.myeconlab.com to complete these exercises online and get instant feedback.

Review Questions

3.1 Briefly explain how international trade increases a country's consumption.

3.2 What is meant by a country specializing in the production of a good? Is it typical for countries to be completely specialized? Briefly explain.

3.3 What are the main sources of comparative advantage?

Problems and Applications

3.4 **(Related to *Solved Problem 6-3* on page 178)** The following table shows the hourly output per worker in two industries in Chile and Argentina.

	OUTPUT PER HOUR OF WORK	
	HATS	BEER
CHILE	8	6
ARGENTINA	1	2

a. Explain which country has an absolute advantage in the production of hats and which country has an absolute advantage in the production of beer.

b. Explain which country has a comparative advantage in the production of hats and which country has a comparative advantage in the production of beer.

c. Suppose that Chile and Argentina currently do not trade with each other. Each has 1,000 hours of labor to use producing hats and beer, and the countries are currently producing the amounts of each good shown in the following table.

	HATS	BEER
CHILE	7,200	600
ARGENTINA	600	800

Using this information, give a numeric example of how Chile and Argentina can both gain from trade. Assume that after trading begins, one hat can be exchanged for one barrel of beer.

3.5 **(Related to *Solved Problem 6-3* on page 178)** A political commentator makes the following statement:

> The idea that international trade should be based on the comparative advantage of each country is fine for rich countries like the United States and Japan. Rich countries have educated workers and large quantities of machinery and equipment. These advantages allow them to produce every product more efficiently than poor countries can. Poor countries like Kenya and Bolivia have nothing to gain from international trade based on comparative advantage.

Do you agree with this argument? Briefly explain.

3.6 Demonstrate how the opportunity costs of producing cell phones and digital music players in Japan and the United States were calculated in Table 6-2 on page 176.

3.7 Briefly explain whether you agree or disagree with the following statement: "Most countries exhaust their comparative advantage in producing a good or service before they reach complete specialization."

3.8 Is free trade likely to benefit a large, populous country more than a small country with fewer people? Briefly explain.

3.9 A Federal Reserve publication offers the following observation: "Too many U.S. citizens associate free trade with job losses rather than opportunities and a higher standard of living." Do you agree? Briefly explain.

Source: Surya Sen and Dan Wassmann, *The Great Trade Debate: From Rhetoric to Reality*, Federal Reserve Bank of Chicago, January 1999.

3.10 Hal Varian, an economist at the University of California, Berkeley, has made two observations about international trade:

a. Trade allows a country "to produce more with less."

b. There is little doubt who wins [from trade] in the long run: consumers.

Briefly explain whether you agree with either or both of these observations.

Source: Hal R. Varian, "The Mixed Bag of Productivity," *New York Times*, October 23, 2003.

3.11 In a recent public opinion poll, 41 percent of people responding believed that free trade hurts the U.S. economy, while only 28 percent believed that it helps the economy. (The remaining people were uncertain of the effects of free trade.) What is "free trade"? Do you believe it helps or hurts the economy? (Be sure to define what you mean by "helps" or "hurts.") Why do you think that more Americans appear to believe that free trade hurts the economy than believe that it helps the economy?

Source: Matthew Benjamin, "Americans Souring on Free Trade Amid Optimism About Economy," *Bloomberg News*, January 19, 2007.

3.12 **(Related to the *Don't Let This Happen to You!* on page 180)** Briefly explain whether you agree or disagree with the following statement: "I can't believe that anyone opposes expanding international trade. After all, when international trade expands, everyone wins."

3.13 **(Related to the *Making the Connection* on page 181)** Explain why there are advantages to a movie studio operating in southern California, rather than in, say, Florida.

>> End Learning Objective 6.3

6.4 LEARNING OBJECTIVE 6.4 | Analyze the economic effects of government policies that restrict international trade, **pages 183–190.**

Government Policies That Restrict International Trade

Summary

Free trade is trade between countries without government restrictions. Government policies that interfere with trade usually take the form of: *tariffs*, *quotas*, or *voluntary export restraints* (VERs). A **tariff** is a tax imposed by a government on imports. A **quota** is a numeric limit imposed by a government on the quantity of a good that can be imported into the country. A **voluntary export restraint (VER)** is an agreement negotiated between two countries that places a numeric limit on the quantity of a good that can be imported by one country from the other country. The federal government's sugar quota costs U.S. consumers $2.24 billion per year, or about $750,000 per year for each job saved in the sugar industry. Saving jobs by using tariffs and quotas is often very expensive.

Review Questions

4.1 What is a tariff? What is a quota? Give an example of a non-tariff barrier to trade.

4.2 Who gains and who loses when a country imposes a tariff or a quota on imports of a good?

Problems and Applications

4.3 An editorial in *BusinessWeek* argued the following:

> [President] Bush needs to send a pure and clear signal that the U.S. supports free trade on its merits. . . . That means resisting any further protectionist demands by lawmakers. It could even mean unilaterally reducing tariffs or taking down trade barriers rather than erecting new ones. Such moves would benefit U.S. consumers while giving a needed boost to struggling economies overseas.

What does the editorial mean by "protectionist demands"? How would the unilateral elimination of U.S. trade barriers benefit both U.S. consumers and economies overseas?

Source: "The Threat of Protectionism," *BusinessWeek*, June 3, 2002.

4.4 Political commentator B. Bruce-Biggs once wrote the following in the *Wall Street Journal*: "This is not to say that the case for international free trade is invalid; it is just irrelevant. It is an 'if only everybody . . .' argument. . . . In the real world almost everybody sees benefits in economic nationalism." What do you think he means by "economic nationalism"? Do you agree that a country benefits from free trade only if every other country also practices free trade? Briefly explain.

Source: B. Bruce-Biggs, "The Coming Overthrow of Free Trade," *Wall Street Journal*, February 24, 1983, p. 28.

4.5 Two U.S. senators make the following argument against allowing free trade: "Fewer and fewer Americans support our government's trade policy. They see a shrinking middle class, lost jobs and exploding trade deficits. Yet supporters of free trade continue to push for more of the same—more job-killing trade agreements. . . . " Do you agree with these senators that reducing barriers to trade reduces the number of jobs available to workers in the United States? Briefly explain.

Source: Byron Dorgan and Sherrod Brown, "How Free Trade Hurts," *Washington Post*, December 23, 2006, p. A21.

4.6 The United States produces beef and also imports beef from other countries.

a. Draw a graph showing the supply and demand for beef in the United States. Assume that the United States can import as much as it wants at the world price of beef without causing the world price of beef to increase. Be sure to indicate on the graph the quantity of beef imported.

b. Now show on your graph the effect of the United States imposing a tariff on beef. Be sure to indicate on your graph the quantity of beef sold by U.S. producers before and after the tariff is imposed, the quantity of beef imported before and after the tariff, and the price of beef in the United States before and after the tariff.

c. Discuss who benefits and who loses when the United States imposes a tariff on beef.

4.7 **(Related to the *Chapter Opener* on page 170)** Which industries are affected unfavorably by the sugar quota and by the tariff on imports of sugar-based ethanol? Are any industries (other than the sugar industry) affected favorably by the sugar quota and the tariff on imports of sugar-based ethanol? (*Hint:* Think about what sugar is used for and whether substitutes exist for these uses and what the substitutes are for sugar-based ethanol.)

4.8 When Congress was considering a bill to impose quotas on imports of textiles, shoes, and other products, Milton Friedman, a Nobel Prize–winning economist, made the following comment: "The consumer will be forced to spend several extra dollars to subsidize the producers [of these goods] by one dollar. A straight handout would be far cheaper." Why would a quota result in consumers paying much more than domestic producers receive? Where do the other dollars go? What does Friedman mean by a "straight handout"? Why would this be cheaper than a quota?

Source: Milton Friedman, "Free Trade," *Newsweek*, August 27, 1970.

4.9 The United States has about 9,000 rice farmers. In 2006, these rice farmers received $780 million in subsidy payments from the U.S. government (or nearly $87,000 per farmer). These payments result in U.S. farmers producing much more rice than they otherwise would, a substantial amount of which is exported. According to an article in the *Wall Street Journal*, Kpalagim Mome, a farmer in the African country of Ghana, can no longer find buyers in Ghana for his rice:

> "We can't sell our rice anymore. It gets worse every year," Mr. Mome says. . . . Years of economic hardship have driven three of his brothers to walk and hitch-hike 2,000 miles across the Sahara to reach the Mediterranean and Europe. His sister plans to leave next year. Mr. Mome's plight is repeated throughout farm communities in Africa and elsewhere in the developing world.

Why would subsidies paid by the U.S. government to U.S. rice farmers reduce the incomes of rice farmers in Africa?

Source: Juliane von Reppert-Bismarck, "How Trade Barriers Keep Africans Adrift," *Wall Street Journal*, December 27, 2006.

4.10 An economic analysis of a proposal to impose a quota on steel imports into the United States indicated that the quota would save 3,700 jobs in the steel industry but cost about 35,000 jobs in other U.S. industries. Why would a quota on steel imports cause employment to fall in other industries? Which other industries are likely to be most affected?

Source: Study cited in Douglas A. Irwin, *Free Trade Under Fire*, Princeton, NJ: Princeton University Press, 2002, p. 82.

4.11 A student makes the following argument:

> Tariffs on imports of foreign goods into the United States will cause the foreign companies to add the amount of the tariff to the prices they charge in the United States for those goods. Instead of putting a tariff on imported goods, we should ban importing them. Banning imported goods is better than putting tariffs on them because U.S. producers benefit from the reduced competition and U.S. consumers don't have to pay the higher prices caused by tariffs.

Briefly explain whether you agree with the student's reasoning.

4.12 Suppose China decides to pay large subsidies to any Chinese company that exports goods or services to the United States. As a result, these companies are able to sell products in the United States at far below their cost of production. In addition, China decides to bar all imports from the United States. The dollars that the United States pays to import Chinese goods are left in banks in China. Will this strategy raise or lower the standard of living in China? Will it raise or lower the standard of living in the United States? Briefly explain. Be sure to provide a definition of "standard of living" in your answer.

4.13 **(Related to the *Chapter Opener* on page 170)** According to an editorial in the *New York Times*, because of the sugar quota, "Sugar growers in this country, long protected from global competition, have had a great run at the expense of just about everyone else—refineries, candy manufacturers, other food companies, individual consumers and farmers in the developing world." Briefly explain how each group mentioned in this editorial is affected by the sugar quota.

Source: "America's Sugar Daddies," *New York Times*, November 29, 2003.

4.14 **(Related to *Solved Problem 6-4* on page 187)** Suppose that the United States currently both produces kumquats and imports them. The U.S. government then decides to restrict international trade in kumquats by imposing a quota that allows imports of only six million pounds of kumquats into the United States each year. The figure shows the results of imposing the quota.

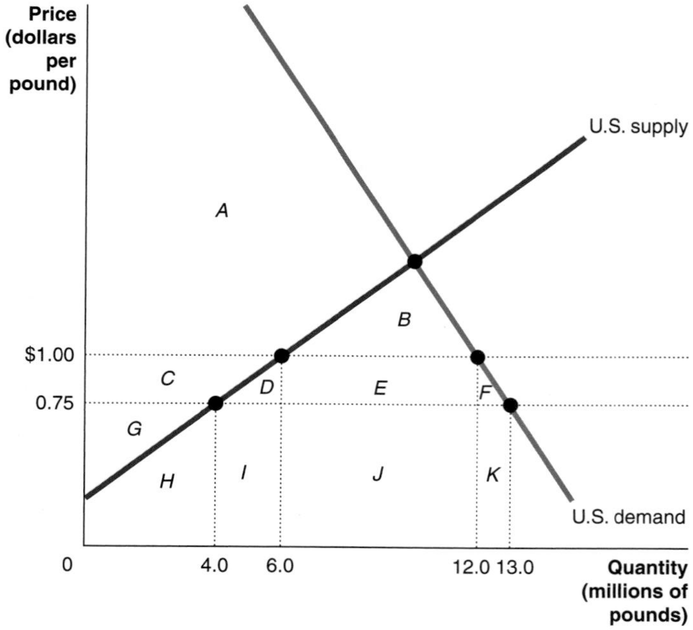

Fill in the table on the following page using the letters in the figure:

	WITHOUT QUOTA	WITH QUOTA
World price of kumquats	______	______
U.S. price of kumquats	______	______
Quantity supplied by U.S. firms	______	______
Quantity demanded	______	______
Quantity imported	______	______
Area of consumer surplus	______	______
Area of domestic producer surplus	______	______
Area of deadweight loss	______	______

>> End Learning Objective 6.4

6.5 LEARNING OBJECTIVE 6.5 | Evaluate the arguments over trade policy and globalization, **pages 190–195.**

The Argument over Trade Policies and Globalization

Summary

The **World Trade Organization (WTO)** is an international organization that enforces international trade agreements. The WTO has promoted **globalization**, the process of countries becoming more open to foreign trade and investment. Some critics of the WTO argue that globalization has damaged local cultures around the world. Other critics oppose the WTO because they believe in **protectionism**, which is the use of trade barriers to shield domestic firms from foreign competition. The WTO allows countries to use tariffs in cases of **dumping**, when an imported product is sold for a price below its cost of production. Economists can point out the burden imposed on the economy by tariffs, quotas, and other government interferences with free trade. But whether these policies should be used is a normative decision.

myeconlab Get Ahead of the Curve Visit www.myeconlab.com to complete these exercises online and get instant feedback.

Review Questions

5.1 What events led to the General Agreement on Tariffs and Trade? Why did the World Trade Organization eventually replace GATT?

5.2 What is globalization? Why are some people opposed to globalization?

5.3 What is protectionism? Who benefits and who loses from protectionist policies? What are the main arguments people use to justify protectionism?

5.4 What is dumping? Who benefits and who loses from dumping? What problems arise when implementing anti-dumping laws?

Problems and Applications

5.5 (Related to the *Making the Connection* on page 191) The following excerpt is from a newspaper story on President Bill Clinton's proposals for changes in the World Trade Organization. The story was published just before the 1999 World Trade Organization meeting in Seattle that ended in rioting:

> [President Clinton] suggested that a working group on labor be created within the WTO to develop core labor standards that would become "part of every trade agreement. And ultimately I would favor a system in which sanctions would come for violating any provision of a trade agreement. . . . " But the new U.S. stand is sure to meet massive resistance from developing countries, which make up more than 100 of the 135 countries in the WTO. They are not interested in adopting tougher U.S. labor standards.

What did President Clinton mean by "core labor standards"? Why would developing countries resist adopting these standards?

5.6 Steven Landsburg, an economist at the University of Rochester, wrote the following in an article in the *New York Times*:

> Free trade is not only about the right of American consumers to buy at the cheapest possible price; it's also about the right of foreign producers to earn a living. Steelworkers in West Virginia struggle hard to make ends meet. So do steelworkers in South Korea. To protect one at the expense of the other, solely because of where they happened to be born, is a moral outrage.

How does the U.S. government protect steelworkers in West Virginia at the expense of steelworkers in South Korea? Is Landsburg making a positive or a normative statement? A few days later, Tom Redburn published an article disagreeing with Landsburg:

> It is not some evil character flaw to care more about the welfare of people nearby

> than about that of those far away—it's human nature. And it is morally—and economically—defensible. . . . A society that ignores the consequences of economic disruption on those among its citizens who come out at the short end of the stick is not only heartless, it also undermines its own cohesion and adaptability.

Which of the two arguments do you find most convincing?

Sources: Steven E. Landsburg, "Who Cares if the Playing Field Is Level?" *New York Times*, June 13, 2001; and Tom Redburn, "Economic View: Of Politics, Free Markets, and Tending to Society," *New York Times*, June 17, 2001.

5.7 **(Related to the *Making the Connection* on page 193)** An editorial in the *New York Times* contained the following observation:

> Globalization is tough to sell to average people. Economists can promote the very real benefits of a robustly growing world: when they sell more overseas, American businesses can employ more people. But what sticks in our minds is the television image of the father of three laid off when his factory moves offshore.

Do you agree that the negative effects of international trade are more visible than the positive effects? Briefly explain.

Source: "Still Flying High," *New York Times*, December 25, 2006.

5.8 The following appeared in an article in *BusinessWeek* that argued against free trade: "The U.S. is currently in a precarious position. In addition to geopolitical threats, we face a severe economic shock. We have already lost trillions of dollars and millions of jobs to foreigners." If a country engages in free trade, is the total number of jobs in the country likely to decline? Briefly explain.

Source: Vladimir Masch, "A Radical Plan to Manage Globalization," *BusinessWeek*, February 14, 2007.

>> End Learning Objective 6.5

Appendix

Multinational Firms

LEARNING OBJECTIVE

Understand why firms operate in more than one country.

Most large corporations are multinational. **Multinational enterprises** are firms that conduct operations in more than one country—as opposed to simply trading with other countries. For example, the U.S. firm General Electric employs more than 300,000 people in more than 100 countries. Toyota Motor Corporation of Japan has invested more than $10 billion in factories and other facilities in the United States and assembles more than a million cars and trucks in North American factories. (Almost two-thirds of the cars and trucks Toyota sells in the United States are assembled in North American factories.) The Nestlé Company is headquartered in the small city of Vevey, Switzerland, but it produces and sells food products in practically every country in the world. It has more than 500 factories worldwide, employing about 260,000 people.

Multinational enterprise A firm that conducts operations in more than one country.

Table 6A-1 shows the top 25 multinational corporations, ranked by the value of their revenues in 2006. Large corporations based in the United States generally established multinational operations earlier than did firms based in other countries. Today, 5 of the 10 largest multinational corporations in the world are based in the United States. The table shows that large corporations in the motor vehicle, banking, insurance, and petroleum refining industries are most likely to have extensive multinational operations.

A Brief History of Multinational Enterprises

From at least 2500 B.C., companies have traded over long distances. Well-developed systems of long-distance trade existed in the eastern Mediterranean by 1500 B.C. By the Middle Ages, a number of multinational firms had been established in Europe. For example, the Medici bank was based in Florence, Italy, but had branches in France, Switzerland, and England. Some multinational companies founded during these years still exist. The Austrian freight forwarding firm Gebrueder Weiss, which had offices in several countries in the fourteenth century, continues to operate today. Before the twentieth century, multinational firms were still relatively rare, however.

In the late nineteenth and early twentieth centuries, a few large U.S. corporations began to expand their operations beyond the domestic market. Two key technological innovations made it possible for these firms to coordinate operations on several continents. The first innovation was the successful completion of the transatlantic cable in 1866, which made possible instant communication by telegraph between the United States and Europe. The second innovation was the development of more efficient steam engines, which reduced the cost and increased the speed of long ocean voyages. U.S. firms such as Standard Oil, the Singer Sewing Machine Company, and the American Tobacco Company took advantage of these innovations to establish factories and distribution networks around the world. When firms build or buy facilities in foreign countries, they are engaging in **foreign direct investment**. When individuals or firms buy stocks or bonds issued in another country, they are engaging in **foreign portfolio investment**. In the early twentieth century, most U.S. firms expanded abroad through foreign direct investment because the stock and bond markets in other countries were often too poorly developed to make foreign portfolio investment practical.

Foreign direct investment The purchase or building by a domestic firm of a facility in a foreign country.

Foreign portfolio investment The purchase by an individual or a firm of stocks or bonds issued in another country.

TABLE 6A-1

Top 25 Multinational Corporations, 2007

RANK	CORPORATION	HOME COUNTRY	INDUSTRY
1	Wal-Mart Stores	United States	Retailing
2	Exxon Mobil	United States	Petroleum refining
3	Royal Dutch Shell	The Netherlands/ United Kingdom	Petroleum refining
4	BP	Great Britain	Petroleum refining
5	General Motors	United States	Motor vehicles
6	Toyota Motor	Japan	Motor vehicles
7	Chevron	United States	Petroleum refining
8	DaimlerChrysler	Germany	Motor vehicles
9	ConocoPhillips	United States	Petroleum refining
10	Total	France	Petroleum refining
11	General Electric	United States	Diversified Financials
12	Ford Motor	United States	Motor vehicles
13	ING Group	The Netherlands	Insurance
14	Citigroup	United States	Banking
15	AXA	France	Insurance
16	Volkswagen	Germany	Motor vehicles
17	Sinopec	China	Petroleum refining
18	Crédit Agricole	France	Banking
19	Allianz	Germany	Insurance
20	Fortis	Belgium	Banking
21	Bank of America Corp.	United States	Banking
22	HSBC Holdings	Great Britain	Banking
23	American International Group	United States	Insurance
24	China National Petroleum	China	Petroleum refining
25	BNP Paribas	France	Banking

Note: Corporations are ranked by their revenue.

Source: "Fortune Global 500," *Fortune*, July 23, 2007.

Strategic Factors in Moving from Domestic to Foreign Markets

Today, most large U.S. corporations have established factories and other facilities overseas. Corporations expand their operations outside the United States when they expect to increase their profitability by doing so. Firms might expect to increase their profits through overseas operations for five main reasons:

- ***To avoid tariffs or the threat of tariffs.*** As we saw in this chapter, tariffs are taxes imposed by countries on imports from other countries. Sometimes firms establish factories in other countries to avoid having to pay tariffs. At other times, a firm establishes a factory in a country to which it is exporting because it fears the other country's government will impose a tariff or some other restriction on its product. Governments often are less concerned about domestic production by foreign-owned companies than they are about imports. As we also saw in this chapter, government restrictions on imports frequently result from a fear that imports will cause job losses in domestic industries. For example, in the 1970s and 1980s, many Americans feared that imports of Japanese automobiles would reduce employment in the U.S. automobile industry. Members of Congress threatened to increase tariffs or impose quotas on imports of Japanese automobiles. In fact, beginning in 1981, a voluntary export restraint reduced imports of Japanese automobiles. In response to this political pressure, the Japanese automobile companies established assembly plants in the United States. Now that a majority of Japanese automobiles sold in the United States are also assembled in the United States by U.S. workers, the Japanese share of the U.S. automobile market is a less heated political issue than it was during the 1970s and 1980s.

- ***To gain access to raw materials.*** Some U.S. firms have expanded abroad to secure supplies of raw materials. U.S. oil firms—beginning with Standard Oil in the late nineteenth century—have had extensive overseas operations aimed at discovering, recovering, and refining crude oil. In early 2001, one of Standard Oil's successor firms, ChevronTexaco, headquartered in San Francisco, opened its largest oil field in Kazakstan, in the former Soviet Union. ChevronTexaco also constructed a 990-mile pipeline to bring the oil from this field on the Caspian Sea across Russia to a port on the Black Sea.
- ***To gain access to low-cost labor.*** In the past 20 years, some U.S. firms have located factories or other facilities in countries such as China, India, Malaysia, and El Salvador to take advantage of the lower wages paid to workers in those countries. Most economists believe that this *outsourcing* ultimately improves the efficiency of the economy and raises the consumption of U.S. households, but it can also disrupt the lives of U.S. workers who lose their jobs. For this reason, outsourcing has caused political controversy.
- ***To minimize exchange-rate risk.*** The exchange rate tells us how many units of foreign currency are received in exchange for a unit of domestic currency. Fluctuations in exchange rates can reduce the profits of a firm that exports goods to other countries. The J. M. Smucker Company, headquartered in Orrville, Ohio, ships jams, ice cream toppings, peanut butter, and other products to more than 70 other countries. Suppose Smucker's has contracted to sell 200,000 cases of jam to a British importer. The British importer will be paying for the shipment in British currency, the pound (the symbol for the pound is £). The importer will pay Smucker's £21 million in 60 days. It is currently possible to exchange $1 for £0.7, so Smucker's expects to receive $30 million (£21 million/£0.70 per dollar) in 60 days. But if the value of the pound falls against the dollar during the next 60 days, the amount Smucker's receives in dollars could be significantly reduced. For example, if the value of the pound falls to £0.80 per $1, then Smucker's will receive only $26.25 million (£21 million/£0.80 per dollar).

  Firms like Smucker's that have extensive international operations are exposed to significant risk to their profits from fluctuations in the values of international currencies. This risk is known as *exchange-rate risk.* If Smucker's began producing jam in Britain, it would reduce its exposure to exchange-rate risk.
- ***To respond to industry competition.*** In some instances, companies expand overseas as a competitive response to an industry rival. The worldwide competition for markets between Pepsi and Coke is an example of this kind of expansion. Coke began expanding overseas before World War II, and by the 1970s it was earning more from its foreign sales than from its sales in the United States. It became clear to Pepsi's management that the firm needed to compete with Coke in foreign as well as domestic markets. In 1972, Pepsi had a major success when it signed an agreement

with the Soviet Union to become the first foreign product sold in that country. Coke and Pepsi continue to compete vigorously in many countries, with their shares of the market often fluctuating significantly.

Many U.S. jobs require technical training and pay higher wages.

Making the Connection

Have Multinational Corporations Reduced Employment and Lowered Wages in the United States?

During the 1990s, some U.S. corporations responded to the greater economic openness of many poorer countries by relocating manufacturing operations to those countries. For example, most U.S. toy firms, such as Mattel, now produce nearly all their toys in factories in China. Most U.S. clothing manufacturers now produce the bulk of their goods in factories in Central America or Asia. These firms have reduced their production costs by paying much lower wages in their overseas factories than they were paying in the United States. The workers who lost their jobs in U.S. factories have often experienced periods of unemployment and have sometimes had to accept lower wages when they find new jobs. Towns and cities where factories closed have also been hurt by losses of tax revenues to support schools and other local services.

Most economists, however, do not believe that relocating jobs abroad has reduced either total employment in the United States or the average wage paid to U.S. workers. The overall level of employment in the United States in the long run is not affected by job losses in particular industries, however painful the losses may be to those experiencing them. The U.S. economy creates more than 2 million additional new jobs during a typical year. Nearly all workers who lose jobs at one firm eventually find new ones at other firms.

Competition from low-wage foreign workers has not reduced the average wages of U.S. workers. Wages are determined by the ability of workers to produce goods and services. This ability depends in part on the workers' education and training and in part on the machinery and equipment available to them. American workers have high wages because, on average, they are well trained and because of the quantity and quality of the machinery and equipment they work with. Low-wage foreign workers are generally less well trained and work with smaller amounts of machinery and equipment than do American workers.

Beginning in the 1990s and continuing through the 2000s, the gap in the United States between the wages of skilled workers and the wages of unskilled workers increased. It has been suggested that competition from low-wage foreign workers forced unskilled U.S. workers to accept lower wages to keep their jobs. To a small extent, the increase in the wage gap in the United States may have been due to this cause. But careful economic studies have shown that most of the increase in the wage gap is due to developments within the U.S. economy—such as the increasing number of jobs that require technical training—that have resulted in higher pay to skilled workers rather than to competition from low-wage foreign workers.

YOUR TURN: Test your understanding by doing related problem 6A.12 on page 210 at the end of this appendix.

Most U.S. firms have followed similar steps in expanding their operations overseas: Newly established firms usually begin by selling only within the United States. If successful in the domestic market, they begin to export. They initially use foreign firms to market and distribute their products. If sales are good in these foreign markets, U.S. firms establish their own overseas marketing and distribution networks. Finally, firms establish their own production facilities in these foreign countries. Since World War II, many U.S. firms have switched from building their own production facilities to a strategy of acquiring local firms that were already producing the good. Some firms have first licensed production to local firms, later acquiring the firms. U.S.-based Colgate-Palmolive, for example, typically has entered a foreign market first by licensing a foreign soap manufacturer to produce its brands, while keeping control over marketing and distribution. Typically, Colgate-Palmolive has eventually acquired ownership of the foreign firm.

Challenges to U.S. Firms in Foreign Markets

It seems obvious that any successful firm will want to expand into foreign markets. After all, it is always better to have more customers than fewer customers. In fact, however, expanding into foreign markets can often be quite difficult, and the additional costs incurred may end up being greater than the additional revenue gained. One problem encountered by U.S. firms is differences in tastes between U.S. and foreign consumers. Although products like Coke seem to appeal to consumers everywhere in the world, other products run into problems because of cultural differences among countries. For example, Singapore banned Janet Jackson's album *All for You* because, according to a government spokesman, its "sexually explicit lyrics" were "not acceptable to our society." In 2002, eBay closed its online auction site in Japan. Although eBay is successful selling collectibles in the United States, many Japanese consumers do not like to buy used goods. In 2006, Wal-Mart announced it would sell its 85 stores in Germany, taking a loss of $1 billion. German consumers were not as receptive as U.S. consumers are to buying groceries, clothes, consumer electronics, and other products in one very large store.

Some U.S. companies have had difficulty adapting their employment practices to deal with the differences between U.S. and foreign labor markets. Many countries have much stronger labor unions than does the United States, and many foreign governments regulate labor markets much more than does the U.S. government. For example, government regulations in most European countries make it much more difficult than it is in the United States to lay off workers.

Competitive Advantages of U.S. Firms

Some U.S. firms have successful foreign operations because of the strength of their brand names. Many producers of soft drinks and many fast food restaurants can be found in nearly every foreign country, but Coca-Cola and McDonald's have such strong name recognition that their appeal extends around the world. Other firms have developed a significant technological edge over foreign rivals. Microsoft, the software giant, and Hewlett-Packard, the computer and printer firm, are examples. Some U.S. firms, such as Dell Computer and Boeing, have advantages over foreign manufacturers based on having developed the most efficient and low-cost way of producing a good.

A U.S. firm's global competitive advantage changes over time. This change is illustrated dramatically by the experience of U.S. semiconductor firms. The semiconductor industry originated in the United States, with the invention of the transistor at Bell Telephone Laboratories in 1947. U.S. predominance in the industry was enhanced further in 1959, with the invention of the integrated circuit, which contains multiple transistors on a single silicon chip. Through 1980, U.S. firms held between 60 and 80 percent of the global market for semiconductors. Beginning in the 1970s, the Japanese government moved to establish a strong domestic semiconductor industry by subsidizing domestic firms and by limiting imports of semiconductors from the United States. The Japanese policy was very successful with respect to DRAM—dynamic random access memory—the most basic chip. By the mid-1980s, Japanese firms dominated the global market, and nearly all U.S. chipmakers had abandoned DRAM manufacture. Many observers predicted the collapse of the U.S. semiconductor industry. Even Intel Corporation, the most successful U.S. semiconductor firm, appeared to be close to bankruptcy.

From this low point, U.S. semiconductor firms rebounded to regain global predominance by the 1990s. The key to the rebound of U.S. firms was the decreasing demand for simple memory chips and the increasing demand for two products: microprocessors—such as Intel's Pentium 4 chip used in personal computers—and ASICs—application-specific integrated circuits—which are used in many electronic products. In manufacturing microprocessors and ASICs, a firm's ability to rapidly design and develop new products is more important than using low-cost production processes. U.S. firms, such as Intel, have proven to be much better at designing and rapidly bringing to market advanced microprocessors and ASICs than have competing firms in Japan, South Korea, and elsewhere.

Key Terms

Foreign direct investment, p. 205

Foreign portfolio investment, p. 205

Multinational enterprise, p. 205

LEARNING OBJECTIVE Understand the reasons why firms operate in more than one country, **pages 205–209.**

myeconlab Get Ahead of the Curve Visit www.myeconlab.com to complete these exercises online and get instant feedback.

Review Questions

6A.1 When did large U.S. corporations first begin to operate internationally? What key technological changes made it easier for U.S. corporations to operate overseas?

6A.2 What is the difference between foreign direct investment and foreign portfolio investment? Is the Camry assembly plant that Toyota operates in Kentucky an example of foreign direct investment or foreign portfolio investment?

6A.3 What are the five main reasons firms expand their operations overseas? Which of these reasons explains why U.S.-based oil companies have extensive overseas operations?

6A.4 What are the main reasons U.S. firms succeed overseas?

Problems and Applications

6A.5 Suppose it is 1850 and you are operating a large factory manufacturing cotton cloth. You are considering expanding your operations overseas. What technical problems are you likely to encounter in coordinating your overseas and domestic operations?

6A.6 The Ford Motor Company and the International Harvester Company were two of the first U.S. firms to establish extensive manufacturing operations overseas. Why might a producer of automobiles and a producer of farm machinery find it particularly advantageous to manufacture their products in countries in which they have substantial sales?

6A.7 Why might many U.S. firms that were expanding their operations overseas after World War II have been more likely to acquire an existing firm in the market they were entering rather than build new facilities there?

6A.8 Would a firm based in the United States ever produce a good in another country if it cost less to produce it in the United States and ship it to the other country? Explain.

6A.9 Is expanding a firm's operations internationally really any different than expanding within a nation? For example, if a firm is based in Texas, what's the difference between it expanding operations to Mexico, Canada, Singapore, or Germany rather than to North Carolina or Pennsylvania?

6A.10 Is expanding a firm's operations internationally really any different than expanding into a new product market? For example, is Whirlpool's expanding into Europe different than Whirlpool's expanding by making a new line of appliances, such as humidifiers?

6A.11 If you ran a successful U.S. firm like Wal-Mart, IBM, or Hershey's, into which countries would you first expand? Why?

6A.12 **(Related to the *Making the Connection* on page 208)** Suppose that the U.S. government wanted to help those textile workers who have lost their jobs as U.S. clothing manufacturers have moved to Central America and Asia. To do this, the government imposes a tariff on imported textiles. What would be the effects of this policy on employment in the U.S. textile industry? Would the policy increase total employment in the United States? What would happen to employment in U.S. industries other than the textile industry?

» End Appendix Learning Objective

GDP: Measuring Total Production and Income

Increases in GDP Help Revive American Airlines

American Airlines has the largest fleet of planes and flies more passengers than any other airline in the world. So, it was good news for the struggling U.S. airline industry when American announced in spring 2007 that it had earned a profit during the first three months of that year for the first time since 2001. Its profits for all of 2006 were $231 million—a sharp contrast with losses of $857 million during 2005. American felt confident enough of its financial health to place an order with Boeing for 47 new 737 jetliners. With the jets having a price of about $71 million each, this was a major expenditure. American's 80,000 employees also hoped to benefit from the firm's rising prosperity. Both the flight attendants' union and the pilots' union pressed American for pay increases.

What caused American's rising profits and purchases of new jets during 2007? American had experienced a substantial increase in demand for tickets. This increase in demand had little to do with American improving the quality of its service or starting an effective new marketing campaign. Instead, American was experiencing the effects of the *business cycle*, which refers to the alternating periods of economic expansion and recession that occur in the United States and other industrial economies. Production and employment increase during expansions and fall during recessions.

In 2007, American was benefiting from the effects of an economic expansion, but just a few years earlier, it had suffered from the effects of an economic recession. Airlines are typically hit hard during recessions, as falling incomes cause some leisure travelers to cancel pleasure trips and some firms to cut back on business travel. The recession that began in 2001 was particularly difficult for airlines because the terrorist attacks of September 11, 2001, made some passengers afraid to travel by air. Increased airport security increased the inconveniences of air travel. Rising prices for jet fuel added to the difficulties airlines encountered in recovering from the 2001 recession. So, although the business cycle expansion had begun to increase sales and profits for many firms by 2003, the airlines did not experience a significant revival until 2006.

Whether the general level of economic activity is increasing is not just important to firms like American, as they decide whether to expand their operations. It is also important to workers hoping for pay increases and to consumers wondering how rapidly prices will be increasing. College students are also affected by the state of the economy at the time they graduate. One recent study found that college students who graduate during a recession have to search longer to find a job and end up accepting jobs that, on average, pay 9 percent less than the jobs accepted by students who graduate during expansions. What's more, students who graduate during recessions will continue to earn less for 8 to 10 years after they graduate. The overall state of the economy is clearly important!

AN INSIDE LOOK on **page 232** discusses the fact that the business cycle does not affect all industries in the same way. For example, some trucking firms experienced slow sales during 2006 while airlines were prospering.

Sources: Melanie Trottman, "American Accelerates Orders for Fuel-Efficient 737s," *Wall Street Journal*, March 29, 2007; Melanie Trottman, "American Air Pilots Seek Raise, Signing Bonuses," *Wall Street Journal*, May 3, 2007; Philip Oreopoulos, Till von Wachter, and Andrew Heisz, "The Short-and-Long-Term Career Effects of Graduating in a Recession," National Bureau of Economic Research Paper 12159, April 2006.

LEARNING Objectives

After studying this chapter, you should be able to:

7.1 Explain how **total production** is measured, page 215.

7.2 Discuss whether **GDP** is a good **measure** of **well-being**, page 222.

7.3 Discuss the difference between **real GDP** and **nominal GDP**, page 225.

7.4 Become familiar with **other measures** of **total production** and **total income**, page 228.

Economics in YOUR Life!

What's the Best Country for You to Work In?

Suppose that an airline offers you a job after graduation. Because the firm has offices in Canada and China, and because you are fluent in English and Mandarin, you get to choose the country in which you will work and live. Because gross domestic product (GDP) is a measure of an economy's total production of goods and services, one factor in your decision is likely to be the growth rate of GDP in each country. In 2006, the growth rate of GDP was 2.6 percent in Canada and 10.5 percent in China. What effect do these two very different growth rates have on your decision to work and live in one country or the other? If China's much larger growth rate does not necessarily lead you to decide to work and live in China, why not? As you read this chapter, see if you can answer these questions. You can check your answers against those we provide at the end of the chapter.

» **Continued on page 231**

Microeconomics The study of how households and firms make choices, how they interact in markets, and how the government attempts to influence their choices.

Macroeconomics The study of the economy as a whole, including topics such as inflation, unemployment, and economic growth.

Business cycle Alternating periods of economic expansion and economic recession.

Expansion The period of a business cycle during which total production and total employment are increasing.

Recession The period of a business cycle during which total production and total employment are decreasing.

Economic growth The ability of an economy to produce increasing quantities of goods and services.

Inflation rate The percentage increase in the price level from one year to the next.

As we saw in Chapter 1, we can divide economics into the subfields of microeconomics and macroeconomics. **Microeconomics** is the study of how households and firms make choices, how they interact in markets, and how the government attempts to influence their choices. **Macroeconomics** is the study of the economy as a whole, including topics such as inflation, unemployment, and economic growth. In microeconomic analysis, economists generally study individual markets, such as the market for personal computers. In macroeconomic analysis, economists study factors that affect many markets at the same time. As we saw in the chapter opener, one important macroeconomic issue is the business cycle. The **business cycle** refers to the alternating periods of expansion and recession that the U.S. economy has experienced since at least the early nineteenth century. A business cycle **expansion** is a period during which total production and total employment are increasing. A business cycle **recession** is a period during which total production and total employment are decreasing. In the following chapters, we will discuss the causes of the business cycle and policies the government may use to reduce its effects.

Another important macroeconomic topic is **economic growth**, which refers to the ability of an economy to produce increasing quantities of goods and services. Economic growth is important because an economy that grows too slowly fails to raise living standards. In many countries in Africa, very little economic growth has occurred in the past 50 years, and many people remain in severe poverty. Macroeconomics analyzes both what determines the rate of economic growth within a country and the reasons growth rates differ so greatly across countries.

Macroeconomics also analyzes what determines the total level of employment in an economy. As we will see, the level of employment is affected significantly by the business cycle, but other factors also help determine the level of employment in the long run. A related issue is why some economies are more successful than others in maintaining high levels of employment over time. Another important macroeconomic issue is what determines the **inflation rate**, or the percentage increase in the average level of prices from one year to the next. As with employment, inflation is affected both by the business cycle and by other long-run factors. Finally, macroeconomics is concerned with the linkages among economies: international trade and international finance.

Macroeconomic analysis provides information that consumers and firms need in order to understand current economic conditions and to help predict future conditions. A family may be reluctant to buy a house if employment in the economy is declining because some family members may be at risk of losing their jobs. Similarly, firms may be reluctant to invest in building new factories or to undertake major new expenditures on information technology if they expect that future sales may be weak. For example, in early 2003, DaimlerChrysler canceled plans to spend $1.2 billion to build a new factory in Windsor, Ontario, to manufacture Dodge pickup trucks. The decision was made because macroeconomic forecasts indicated that consumer demand for trucks and automobiles would be weak. Macroeconomic analysis can also aid the federal government in designing policies that help the U.S. economy perform more efficiently.

In this chapter and Chapter 8, we begin our study of macroeconomics by considering how best to measure key macroeconomic variables. As we will see, there are important issues involved in measuring macroeconomic variables. We start by considering measures of total production and total income in an economy.

7.1 | Explain how total production is measured.

7.1 LEARNING OBJECTIVE

Gross Domestic Product Measures Total Production

"Fourth-Quarter [U.S.] GDP Revised Up"

"India Expects GDP to Grow 9.2%"

"Indonesian GDP Contracts 1.9%"

"Japan's GDP Grows 1.3% in Fourth Quarter"

"Malaysian GDP Expands 5.7%"

These headlines are from articles that appeared in the *Wall Street Journal* in early 2007. Why is GDP so often the focus of news stories? In this section, we explore what GDP is and how it is measured. We also explore why knowledge of GDP is important to consumers, firms, and government policymakers.

Measuring Total Production: Gross Domestic Product

Economists measure total production by **gross domestic product (GDP)**. GDP is the market *value* of all *final* goods and services produced in a country during a period of time, typically one year. In the United States, the Bureau of Economic Analysis (BEA) in the Department of Commerce compiles the data needed to calculate GDP. The BEA issues reports on the GDP every three months. GDP is a central concept in macroeconomics, so we need to consider its definition carefully.

Gross domestic product (GDP) The market value of all final goods and services produced in a country during a period of time, typically one year.

GDP Is Measured Using Market Values, Not Quantities The word *value* is important in the definition of GDP. In microeconomics, we measure production in quantity terms: the number of iPods Apple produces, the tons of wheat U.S. farmers grow, or the number of passengers flown by American Airlines. When we measure total production in the economy, we can't just add together the quantities of every good and service because the result would be a meaningless jumble. Tons of wheat would be added to gallons of milk, numbers of plane flights, and so on. Instead, we measure production by taking the *value*, in dollar terms, of all the goods and services produced.

GDP Includes Only the Market Value of Final Goods In measuring GDP, we include only the value of *final goods and services.* A **final good or service** is one that is purchased by its final user and is not included in the production of any other good or service. Examples of final goods are a hamburger purchased by a consumer and a computer purchased by a business. Some goods and services, though, are used in the production of other goods and services. For example, General Motors does not produce tires for its cars and trucks; it buys them from tire companies, such as Goodyear and Michelin. The tires are an **intermediate good**, while a General Motors truck is a final good. In calculating GDP, we include the value of the General Motors truck but not the value of the tire. If we included the value of the tire, we would be *double counting*: The value of the tire would be counted once when the tire company sold it to General Motors, and a second time when General Motors sold the truck, with the tire installed, to a consumer.

Final good or service A good or service purchased by a final user.

Intermediate good or service A good or service that is an input into another good or service, such as a tire on a truck.

GDP Includes Only Current Production GDP includes only production that takes place during the indicated time period. For example, GDP in 2006 includes only the goods and services produced during that year. In particular, GDP does *not* include the value of used goods. If you buy a DVD of *Spider-Man 3* from Amazon.com, the purchase is included in GDP. If six months later you resell that DVD on eBay, that transaction is not included in GDP.

Solved Problem | 7-1

Calculating GDP

Suppose that a very simple economy produces only four goods and services: eye examinations, pizzas, textbooks, and paper. Assume that all the paper in this economy is used in the production of textbooks. Use the information in the following table to compute GDP for the year 2009.

PRODUCTION AND PRICE STATISTICS FOR 2009

(1) PRODUCT	(2) QUANTITY	(3) PRICE PER UNIT
Eye examinations	100	$50.00
Pizzas	80	10.00
Textbooks	20	100.00
Paper	2,000	0.10

SOLVING THE PROBLEM:

Step 1: **Review the chapter material.** This problem is about gross domestic product, so you may want to review the section "Measuring Total Production: Gross Domestic Product," which begins on page 215.

Step 2: **Determine which goods and services listed in the table should be included in the calculation of GDP.** GDP is the value of all final goods and services. Therefore, we need to calculate the value of the final goods and services listed in the table. Eye examinations, pizzas, and textbooks are final goods. Paper would also be a final good if, for instance, a consumer bought it to use in a printer. However, here we are assuming that publishers purchase all the paper to use in manufacturing textbooks, so the paper is an intermediate good, and its value is not included in GDP.

Step 3: **Calculate the value of the three final goods and services listed in the table.** Value is equal to the quantity produced multiplied by the price per unit, so we multiply the numbers in column (1) by the numbers in column (2).

PRODUCT	(1) QUANTITY	(2) PRICE PER UNIT	(3) VALUE
Eye examinations	100	$50	$5,000
Pizzas	80	10	800
Textbooks	20	100	2,000

Step 4: **Add the value for each of the three final goods and services to find GDP.** GDP = Value of eye examinations produced + Value of pizzas produced + Value of textbooks produced = $5,000 + $800 + $2,000 = $7,800.

YOUR TURN: For more practice, do related problem 1.12 on page 235 at the end of this chapter.

>> End Solved Problem 7-1

Production, Income, and the Circular-Flow Diagram

When we measure the value of total production in the economy by calculating GDP, we are simultaneously measuring the value of total income. To see why the value of total production is equal to the value of total income, consider what happens to the money you spend on a single product. Suppose you buy an Apple iPod for $250 at a Best Buy store. *All* of that $250 must end up as someone's income. Apple and Best Buy will receive some of the $250 as profits, workers at Apple will receive some as wages, the salesperson who sold you the iPod will receive some as salary, the firms that sell parts to Apple will receive some as profits, the workers for these firms will receive some as wages, and so on: Every penny must end up as someone's income. (Note, though, that any sales tax on the iPod will be collected by the store and sent to the government without ending up as anyone's income.) Therefore, if we add up the value of every good and service sold in the economy, we must get a total that is exactly equal to the value of all of the income in the economy.

The circular-flow diagram in Figure 7-1 was introduced in Chapter 2 to illustrate the interaction of firms and households in markets. We use it here to illustrate the flow of spending and money in the economy. Firms sell goods and services to three groups: domestic households, foreign firms and households, and the government. Expenditures

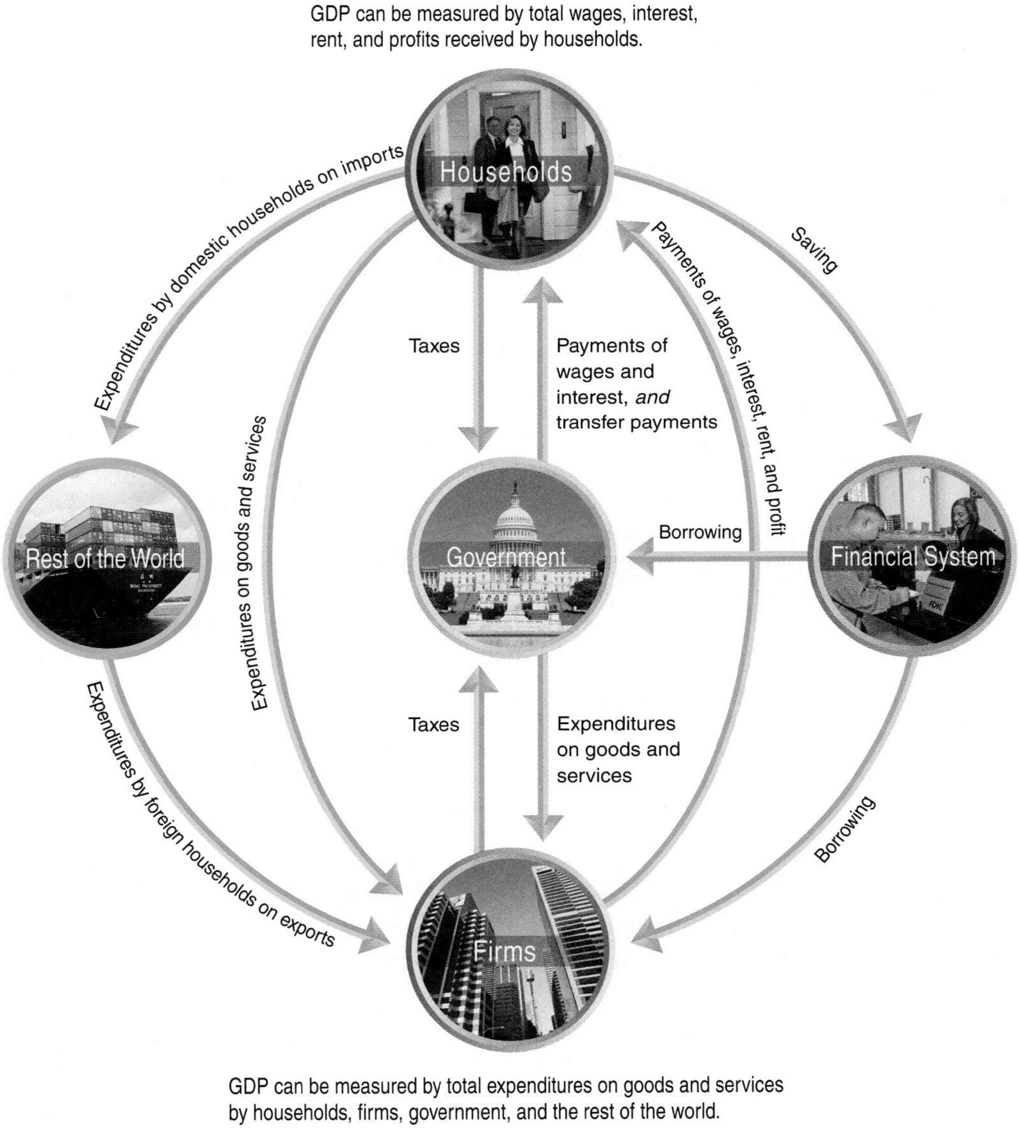

Figure 7-1 | The Circular Flow and the Measurement of GDP

The circular-flow diagram illustrates the flow of spending and money in the economy. Firms sell goods and services to three groups: domestic households, foreign firms and households, and the government. To produce goods and services, firms use factors of production: labor, capital, natural resources, and entrepreneurship. Households supply the factors of production to firms in exchange for income in the form of wages, interest, profit, and rent. Firms make payments of wages and interest to households in exchange for hiring workers and other factors of production. The sum of wages, interest, rent, and profit is total income in the economy. We can measure GDP as the total income received by households. The diagram also shows that households use their income to purchase goods and services, pay taxes, and save. Firms and the government borrow the funds that flow from households into the financial system. We can measure GDP either by calculating the total value of expenditures on final goods and services or by calculating the value of total income.

by foreign firms and households (shown as the "Rest of the World" in the diagram) on domestically produced goods and services are called *exports*. For example, American Airlines sells many tickets to passengers in Europe and Asia. As we note at the bottom of Figure 7-1, we can measure GDP by adding up the total expenditures of these three groups on goods and services.

Firms use the *factors of production*—labor, capital, natural resources, and entrepreneurship—to produce goods and services. Households supply the factors of production to firms in exchange for income. We divide income into four categories: wages, interest, rent, and profit. Firms pay wages to households in exchange for labor services, interest for the use of capital, and rent for natural resources such as land. Profit is the income that remains after a firm has paid wages, interest, and rent. Profit is the return to entrepreneurs for organizing the other factors of production and for bearing the risk of producing and selling goods and services. As Figure 7-1 shows, federal, state, and local governments make payments of wages and interest to households in exchange for hiring workers and other factors of production. Governments also make *transfer payments* to households. **Transfer payments** include Social Security payments to retired and disabled people and unemployment insurance payments to unemployed workers. These payments are not included in GDP because they are not received in exchange for production of a new good or service. The sum of wages, interest, rent, and profit is total income in the economy. As we note at the top of Figure 7-1, we can measure GDP as the total income received by households.

Transfer payments Payments by the government to individuals for which the government does not receive a new good or service in return.

The diagram also allows us to trace the ways that households use their income. Households spend some of their income on goods and services. Some of this spending is on domestically produced goods and services, and some is on foreign-produced goods and services. Spending on foreign-produced goods and services is known as *imports*. Households also use some of their income to pay taxes to the government. (Note that firms also pay taxes to the government.) Some of the income earned by households is not spent on goods and services or paid in taxes but is deposited in checking or savings accounts in banks or is used to buy stocks or bonds. Banks and stock and bond markets make up the *financial system*. The flow of funds from households into the financial system makes it possible for the government and firms to borrow. As we will see, the health of the financial system is of vital importance to an economy. Without the ability to borrow funds through the financial system, firms will have difficulty expanding and adopting new technologies. In fact, as we will discuss in Chapter 9, no country without a well-developed financial system has been able to sustain high levels of economic growth.

The circular flow diagram shows that we can measure GDP either by calculating the total value of expenditures on final goods and services or by calculating the value of total income. We get the same dollar amount of GDP whichever approach we take.

Components of GDP

The BEA divides its statistics on GDP into four major categories of expenditures. Economists use these categories to understand why GDP fluctuates and to forecast future GDP.

Consumption Spending by households on goods and services, not including spending on new houses.

Personal Consumption Expenditures, or "Consumption" **Consumption** expenditures are made by households and are divided into expenditures on *services*, such as medical care, education, and haircuts; expenditures on *nondurable goods*, such as food and clothing; and expenditures on *durable goods*, such as automobiles and furniture. The spending by households on new houses is not included in consumption. Instead, spending on new houses is included in the investment category, which we discuss next.

Investment Spending by firms on new factories, office buildings, machinery, and additions to inventories, and spending by households on new houses.

Gross Private Domestic Investment, or "Investment" Spending on *gross private domestic investment*, or simply **investment**, is divided into three categories: *Business fixed investment* is spending by firms on new factories, office buildings, and machinery

Don't Let This Happen to **YOU!**

Remember What Economists Mean by *Investment*

Notice that the definition of *investment* in this chapter is narrower than in everyday use. For example, people often say they are investing in the stock market or in rare coins. As we have seen, economists reserve the word *investment* for purchases of machinery, factories, and houses. Economists don't include purchases of stock or rare coins or deposits in savings accounts in the definition of investment because these activities don't result in the production of new goods. For example, a share of Microsoft stock represents part ownership of that company. When you buy a share of Microsoft stock, nothing new is produced—there is just a transfer of that small piece of ownership of Microsoft. Similarly, buying a rare coin or putting $1,000 in a savings account does not result in an increase in production. GDP is not affected by any of these activities, so they are not included in the economic definition of investment.

YOUR TURN: Test your understanding by doing related problem 1.8 on page 234 at the end of this chapter.

used to produce other goods. *Residential investment* is spending by households on new housing. *Changes in business inventories* are also included in investment. Inventories are goods that have been produced but not yet sold. If General Motors has $200 million worth of unsold cars at the beginning of the year and $350 million worth of unsold cars at the end of the year, then the firm has spent $150 million on inventory investment during the year.

Government Consumption and Gross Investment, or "Government Purchases" **Government purchases** are spending by federal, state, and local governments on goods and services, such as teachers' salaries, highways, and aircraft carriers. Again, government spending on transfer payments is not included in government purchases because it does not result in the production of new goods and services.

Government purchases Spending by federal, state, and local governments on goods and services.

Making the Connection

Spending on Homeland Security

The federal government established the Department of Homeland Security after September 11, 2001, to guard against future terrorist attacks within the United States. Spending by this department is intended to increase the security of the nation's borders and transportation system, identify and arrest terrorists within the United States, and gather intelligence on potential terrorist threats.

Although the Department of Homeland Security has overall responsibility for homeland security, other federal agencies also have increased their spending on related programs. For example, the Department of Health and Human Services increased its spending on research to find new ways to combat the use of biological weapons from $300 million in 2001 to more than $4 billion in 2006. Several other federal agencies, such as the Department of Justice, the Department of Agriculture, and the Department of Transportation, have increased their spending as well. In 2006, the total spending on homeland security by the Department of Homeland Security and other federal agencies was about $50 billion—more than double the amount spent on these activities before 2001.

Because the United States has a federal system of government, responsibility for some homeland security activities lies with state or local authorities. For example, spending to provide security for the Golden Gate Bridge is the responsibility of the state of California and the city of San Francisco. The Department of Homeland Security provides grants to help support this state

Government spending on homeland security more than doubled between 2001 and 2006.

and local spending. Of course, governments at all levels have limited budgets, so at some point, spending more on homeland security requires them to spend less on other programs.

Sources: Congressional Budget Office, *Federal Funding for Homeland Security: An Update*, July 20, 2005; and Executive Office of the President, Office of Management and Budget, *Department of Homeland Security*, January 29, 2007.

YOUR TURN: Test your understanding by doing related problem 1.11 on page 235 at the end of this chapter.

Net exports Exports minus imports.

Net Exports of Goods and Services, or "Net Exports" **Net exports** are equal to *exports* minus *imports*. Exports are goods and services produced in the United States but purchased by foreign firms, households, and governments. We add exports to our other categories of expenditures because otherwise we would not be including all spending on new goods and services produced in the United States. For example, if a farmer in South Dakota sells wheat to China, the value of the wheat is included in GDP because it represents production in the United States. Imports are goods and services produced in foreign countries but purchased by U.S. firms, households, and governments. We subtract imports from total expenditures because otherwise we would be including spending that does not result in production of new goods and services in the United States. For example, if U.S. consumers buy $50 billion worth of furniture manufactured in China, that spending is included in consumption expenditures. But the value of those imports is subtracted from GDP because the imports do not represent production in the United States.

An Equation for GDP and Some Actual Values

A simple equation sums up the components of GDP:

$$Y = C + I + G + NX.$$

The equation tells us that GDP (denoted as Y) equals consumption (C) plus investment (I) plus government purchases (G) plus net exports (NX). Figure 7-2 shows the values of the components of GDP for the year 2006. The graph in the figure highlights that

COMPONENTS OF GDP (billions of dollars)		
Consumption		$9,269
Durable goods	$1,070	
Nondurable goods	2,715	
Services	5,484	
Investment		2,213
Business fixed investment	1,396	
Residential construction	767	
Change in business inventories	50	
Government Purchases		2,528
Federal	927	
State and local	1,601	
Net Exports		−763
Exports	1,466	
Imports	2,229	
Total GDP		$13,247

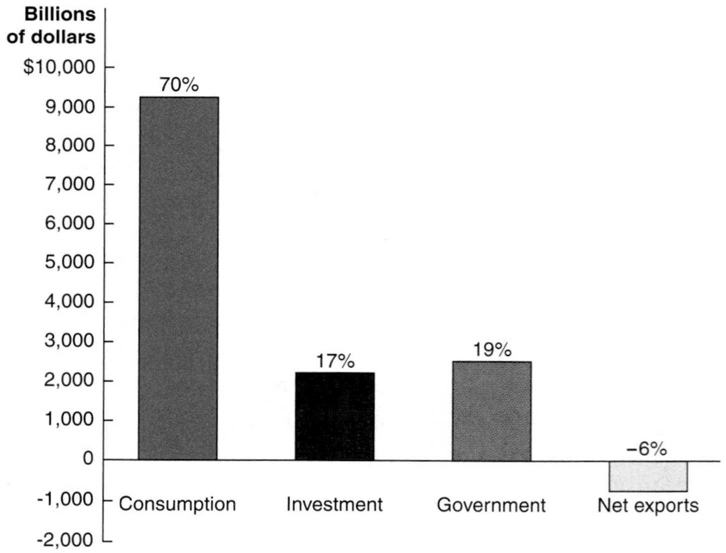

Figure 7-2 | Components of GDP in 2006

Consumption accounts for 70 percent of GDP, far more than any of the other components. In recent years, net exports typically have been negative, which reduces GDP.

consumption is by far the largest component of GDP. The table provides a more detailed breakdown and shows several interesting points:

- Consumer spending on services is greater than the sum of spending on durable and nondurable goods. This greater spending on services reflects the continuing trend in the United States and other high-income countries away from the production of goods and toward the production of services. As the populations of these countries have become, on average, both older and wealthier, their demand for services such as medical care and financial advice has increased faster than their demand for goods.
- Business fixed investment is the largest component of investment. As we will see in later chapters, spending by firms on new factories, computers, and machinery can fluctuate. For example, a decline in business fixed investment played an important role in causing the 2001 recession.
- Purchases made by state and local governments are greater than purchases made by the federal government. Because basic government activities, such as education and law enforcement, occur largely at the state and local levels, state and local government spending is greater than federal government spending.
- Imports are greater than exports, so net exports are negative. We will discuss in Chapter 17 why imports have typically been larger than exports for the U.S. economy.

Measuring GDP by the Value-Added Method

We have seen that GDP can be calculated by adding together all expenditures on final goods and services. An alternative way of calculating GDP is the *value-added method.* **Value added** refers to the additional market value a firm gives to a product and is equal to the difference between the price for which the firm sells a good and the price it paid other firms for intermediate goods. Table 7-1 gives a hypothetical example of the value added by each firm involved in the production of a shirt offered for sale on L.L.Bean's Web site.

Value added The market value a firm adds to a product.

Suppose a cotton farmer sells $1 of raw cotton to a textile mill. If, for simplicity, we ignore any inputs the farmer may have purchased from other firms—such as cottonseed or fertilizer—then the farmer's value added is $1. The textile mill then weaves the raw cotton into cotton fabric, which it sells to a shirt company for $3. The textile mill's value added ($2) is the difference between the price it paid for the raw cotton ($1) and the price for which it can sell the cotton fabric ($3). Similarly, the shirt company's value added is the difference between the price it paid for the cotton fabric ($3) and the price it receives for the shirt from L.L.Bean ($15). L.L.Bean's value added is the difference between the price it pays for the shirt ($15) and the price for which it can sell the shirt on its Web site ($35). Notice that *the price of the shirt on L.L.Bean's Web site is exactly equal to the sum of the value added by each firm involved in the production of the shirt.* We can

Table 7-1
Calculating Value Added

FIRM	VALUE OF PRODUCT	VALUE ADDED	
Cotton farmer	Value of raw cotton = $1	Value added by cotton farmer	= 1
Textile mill	Value of raw cotton woven into cotton fabric = $3	Value added by cotton textile mill = ($3 – $1)	= 2
Shirt company	Value of cotton fabric made into a shirt = $15	Value added by shirt manufacturer = ($15 – $3)	= 12
L.L.Bean	Value of shirt for sale on L.L.Bean's Web site = $35	Value added by L.L.Bean = ($35 – $15)	= 20
	Total value added		= **$35**

calculate GDP by adding up the market value of every final good and service produced during a particular period. Or, we can arrive at the same value for GDP by adding up the value added of every firm involved in producing those final goods and services.

7.2 LEARNING OBJECTIVE

7.2 | Discuss whether GDP is a good measure of well-being.

Does GDP Measure What We Want It to Measure?

Economists use GDP to measure total production in the economy. For that purpose, we would like GDP to be as comprehensive as possible, not overlooking any significant production that takes place in the economy. Most economists believe that GDP does a good—but not flawless—job of measuring production. GDP is also sometimes used as a measure of well-being. Although it is generally true that the more goods and services people have, the better off they are, we will see that GDP provides only a rough measure of well-being.

Shortcomings in GDP as a Measure of Total Production

When the BEA calculates GDP, it does not include two types of production: production in the home and production in the underground economy.

Household Production With only a couple exceptions, the Bureau of Economic Analysis does not attempt to estimate the value of goods and services that are not bought and sold in markets. If a carpenter makes and sells bookcases, the value of those bookcases will be counted in GDP. If the carpenter makes a bookcase for personal use, it will not be counted in GDP. *Household production* refers to goods and services people produce for themselves. The most important type of household production is the services a homemaker provides to the homemaker's family. If a person has been caring for children, cleaning house, and preparing the family meals, the value of such services is not included in GDP. If the person then decides to work outside the home, enrolls the children in daycare, hires a cleaning service, and begins eating family meals in restaurants, the value of GDP will rise by the amount paid for daycare, cleaning services, and restaurant meals, even though production of these services has not actually increased.

The Underground Economy Individuals and firms sometimes conceal the buying and selling of goods and services, in which case their production isn't counted in GDP. Individuals and firms conceal what they buy and sell for three basic reasons: They are dealing in illegal goods and services, such as drugs or prostitution; they want to avoid paying taxes on the income they earn; or they want to avoid government regulations. This concealed buying and selling is referred to as the **underground economy**. Estimates of the size of the underground economy in the United States vary widely, but it may be as much as 10 percent of measured GDP, or more than $1 trillion. The underground economy in some low-income countries, such as Zimbabwe or Peru, may be more than half of measured GDP.

Underground economy Buying and selling of goods and services that is concealed from the government to avoid taxes or regulations or because the goods and services are illegal.

Is not counting household production or production in the underground economy a serious shortcoming of GDP? Most economists would answer "no" because the most important use of GDP is to measure changes in how the economy is performing over short periods of time, such as from one year to the next. For this purpose, omitting household production and production in the underground economy doesn't have much effect because there is not likely to be much change in the amounts of these types of production from one year to the next.

We also use GDP statistics to measure how production of goods and services grows over fairly long periods of a decade or more. For this purpose, omitting household production and production in the underground economy may be more important. For example, beginning in the 1970s, the number of women working outside the home increased dramatically. Some of the goods and services—such as childcare and restaurant meals—produced in the following years were not true additions to total production; rather, they were replacing what had been household production.

Making the Connection

How the Underground Economy Hurts Developing Countries

Although few economists believe the underground economy in the United States amounts to more than 10 percent of measured GDP, the underground economy in some developing countries may be more than 50 percent of measured GDP. In developing countries, the underground economy is often referred to as the *informal sector*, as opposed to the *formal sector* in which output of goods and services is measured. Although it might not seem to matter whether production of goods and services is measured and included in GDP or unmeasured, a large informal sector can be a sign of government policies that are retarding economic growth.

In some developing countries, more than half the workers may be in the underground economy.

Because firms in the informal sector are acting illegally, they tend to be smaller and have less capital than firms acting legally. The entrepreneurs who start firms in the informal sector may be afraid their firms could someday be closed or confiscated by the government. Therefore, the entrepreneurs limit their investments in these firms. As a consequence, workers in these firms have less machinery and equipment to work with and so can produce fewer goods and services. Entrepreneurs in the informal sector also have to pay the costs of avoiding government authorities. For example, construction firms operating in the informal sector in Brazil have to employ lookouts who can warn workers to hide when government inspectors come around. In many countries, firms in the informal sector have to pay substantial bribes to government officials to remain in business. The informal sector is large in some developing economies because taxes are high and government regulations are extensive. For example, firms in Brazil pay 85 percent of all taxes collected, as compared with 41 percent in the United States. Not surprisingly, about half of all Brazilian workers are employed in the informal sector. In Zimbabwe and Peru, the fraction of workers in the informal sector may be as high as 60 or 70 percent.

Many economists believe taxes in developing countries are so high because these countries are attempting to pay for government sectors that are as large relative to their economies as the government sectors of industrial economies. Government spending in Brazil, for example, is 39 percent of measured GDP, compared to 31 percent in the United States. In the early twentieth century, when the United States was much poorer than it is today, government spending was only about 8 percent of GDP, so the tax burden on U.S. firms was much lower. In countries like Brazil, bringing firms into the formal sector from the informal sector may require reductions in government spending and taxes. In many developing countries, however, voters are reluctant to see government services reduced.

Sources: Mary Anastasia O'Grady, "Why Brazil's Underground Economy Grows and Grows," *Wall Street Journal*, September 10, 2004, p. A13; and "In the Shadows," *Economist*, June 17, 2004.

YOUR TURN: Test your understanding by doing related problem 2.6 on page 236 at the end of this chapter.

Shortcomings of GDP as a Measure of Well-Being

The main purpose of GDP is to measure a country's total production. GDP is also frequently used, though, as a measure of well-being. For example, newspaper and magazine articles often include tables that show for different countries the levels of GDP per person, which is usually referred to as *real GDP per capita.* Real GDP per capita is calculated by dividing the value of real GDP for a country by the country's population. These articles imply that people in the countries with higher levels of real GDP per capita are better off. Although increases in GDP often do lead to increases in the well-being of the population, it is important to be aware that GDP is not a perfect measure of well-being for several reasons.

The Value of Leisure Is Not Included in GDP If an economic consultant decides to retire, GDP will decline even though the consultant may value increased leisure more than the income he or she was earning running a consulting firm. The consultant's well-being has increased, but GDP has decreased. In 1890, the typical American worked 60 hours per week. Today, the typical American works fewer than 40 hours per week. If Americans still worked 60-hour weeks, GDP would be much higher than it is, but the well-being of the typical person would be lower because less time would be available for leisure activities.

GDP Is Not Adjusted for Pollution or Other Negative Effects of Production When a dry cleaner cleans and presses clothes, the value of this service is included in GDP. If chemicals the dry cleaner uses pollute the air or water, GDP is not adjusted to compensate for the costs of the pollution. Similarly, the value of cigarettes produced is included in GDP, with no adjustment made for the costs of the lung cancer that some smokers develop.

We should note, though, that increasing GDP often leads countries to devote more resources to pollution reduction. For example, in the United States between 1970 and 2007, as GDP was steadily increasing, emissions of the six main air pollutants declined by more than 50 percent. Developing countries often have higher levels of pollution than high-income countries because the lower GDPs of the developing countries make them more reluctant to spend resources on pollution reduction. Levels of pollution in China are much higher than in the United States, Japan, or the countries of Western Europe. According to the World Health Organization, 7 of the 10 most polluted cities in the world are in China, but as Chinese GDP continues to rise, it is likely to devote more resources to reducing pollution.

GDP Is Not Adjusted for Changes in Crime and Other Social Problems An increase in crime reduces well-being but may actually increase GDP if it leads to greater spending on police, security guards, and alarm systems. GDP is also not adjusted for changes in divorce rates, drug addiction, or other factors that may affect people's well-being.

GDP Measures the Size of the Pie but Not How the Pie Is Divided Up When a country's GDP increases, the country has more goods and services, but those goods and services may be very unequally distributed. Therefore, GDP may not provide good information about the goods and services consumed by the typical person.

To summarize, we can say that a person's well-being depends on many factors that are not taken into account in calculating GDP. Because GDP is designed to measure total production, it should not be surprising that it does an imperfect job of measuring well-being.

Making the Connection

Did World War II Bring Prosperity?

The Great Depression of the 1930s was the worst economic downturn in U.S. history. GDP declined by more than 25 percent between 1929 and 1933 and did not reach its 1929 level again until 1938. The unemployment rate remained at very high levels of 10 percent or more through 1940. Then, in 1941, the United States entered World War II. The following graph shows that GDP rose dramatically during the war years of 1941 to 1945. (The graph shows values for real GDP, which, as we will see in the next section, corrects measures of GDP for changes in the price level.) The unemployment rate also fell to very low levels—below 2 percent.

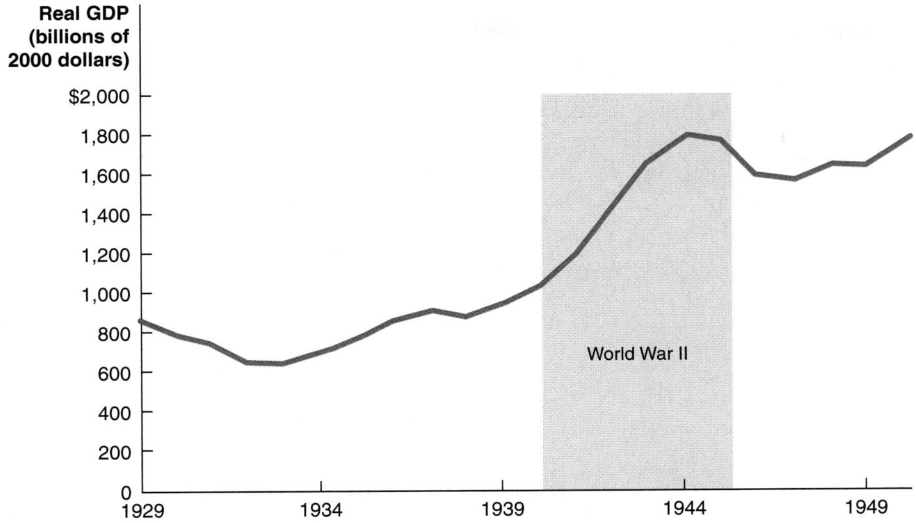

Source: Bureau of Economic Analysis.

Traditionally, historians have argued that World War II brought prosperity back to the U.S. economy. But did it? Economist Robert Higgs argues that if we look at the well-being of the typical person, the World War II years were anything but prosperous. Higgs points out that increased production of tanks, ships, planes, and munitions account for most of the increase in GDP during those years. Between 1943 and 1945, more than 40 percent of the labor force was either in the military or producing war goods. As a result, between 1939 and 1944, production of consumption goods per person increased only about 2 percent, leaving the quantity of consumption goods available to the typical person in 1944 still below what it had been in 1929. With the end of the war, true prosperity did return to the U.S. economy, and by 1946, production of consumption goods per person had risen by more than 25 percent from what it had been in 1929.

World War II was a period of extraordinary sacrifice and achievement by the "greatest generation." But statistics on GDP may give a misleading indication of whether it was also a period of prosperity.

Sources: Robert Higgs, "Wartime Prosperity? A Reassessment of the U.S. Economy in the 1940s," *Journal of Economic History*, Vol. 52, No. 1, March 1992; and Robert Higgs, "From Central Planning to the Market: The American Transition, 1945–1947," *Journal of Economic History*, Vol. 59, No. 3, September 1999.

YOUR TURN: Test your understanding by doing related problem 2.8 on page 236 at the end of this chapter.

7.3 LEARNING OBJECTIVE

7.3 | Discuss the difference between real GDP and nominal GDP.

Real GDP versus Nominal GDP

Because GDP is measured in value terms, we have to be careful about interpreting changes over time. To see why, consider interpreting an increase in the total value of heavy truck production from $40 billion in 2009 to $44 billion in 2010. Can we be sure—because $44 billion is 10 percent greater than $40 billion—that the number of trucks produced in 2010 was 10 percent greater than the number produced in 2009? We can draw this conclusion only if the average price of trucks did not change between 2009 and 2010. In fact, when GDP increases from one year to the next, the increase is due partly to increases in production of goods and services and partly to increases in prices.

Because we are interested mainly in GDP as a measure of production, we need a way of separating the price changes from the quantity changes.

Calculating Real GDP

Real GDP The value of final goods and services evaluated at base-year prices.

Nominal GDP The value of final goods and services evaluated at current-year prices.

The Bureau of Economic Analysis (BEA) separates price changes from quantity changes by calculating a measure of production called *real GDP*. **Nominal GDP** is calculated by summing the current values of final goods and services. **Real GDP** is calculated by designating a particular year as the *base year* and then using the prices of goods and services in the base year to calculate the value of goods and services in all other years. For instance, if the base year is 2000, real GDP for 2009 would be calculated by using prices of goods and services from 2000. By keeping prices constant, we know that changes in real GDP represent changes in the quantity of goods and services produced in the economy.

Solved PROBLEM | 7-3

Calculating Real GDP

Suppose that a very simple economy produces only the following three final goods and services: eye examinations, pizzas, and textbooks. Use the information in the following table to compute real GDP for the year 2009. Assume that the base year is 2000.

	2000		2009	
PRODUCT	QUANTITY	PRICE	QUANTITY	PRICE
Eye examinations	80	$40	100	$50
Pizzas	90	11	80	10
Textbooks	15	90	20	100

SOLVING THE PROBLEM:

Step 1: **Review the chapter material.** This problem is about calculating real GDP, so you may want to review the section "Calculating Real GDP," which begins on this page.

Step 2: **Calculate the value of the three goods and services listed in the table, using the quantities for 2009 and the prices for 2000.** The definition on this page tells us that real GDP is the value of all final goods and services, evaluated at base-year prices. In this case, the base year is 2000, and we are given information on the price of each product in that year.

PRODUCT	2009 QUANTITY	2000 PRICE	VALUE
Eye examinations	100	$40	$4,000
Pizzas	80	11	880
Textbooks	20	90	1,800

Step 3: **Add up the values for the three products to find real GDP.**

Real GDP for 2009 equals the sum of:

Quantity of eye examinations in 2009 × Price of eye exams in 2000 = $4,000

\+ Quantity of pizzas produced in 2009 × Price of pizzas in 2000 = $880

\+ Quantity of textbooks produced in 2009 × Price of textbooks in 2000 = $1,800

or, $6,680

EXTRA CREDIT: Notice that the quantities of each good produced in 2000 were irrelevant for calculating real GDP in 2009. Notice also that the value of $6,680 for real GDP in 2009 is lower than the value of $7,800 for nominal GDP in 2009 calculated in Solved Problem 7-1.

YOUR TURN: For more practice, do related problem 3.3 on page 237 at the end of this chapter.

>> End Solved Problem 7-3

One drawback of calculating real GDP using base-year prices is that, over time, prices may change relative to each other. For example, the price of cell phones may fall relative to the price of milk. Because this change is not reflected in the fixed prices from the base year, the estimate of real GDP is somewhat distorted. The further away the current year is from the base year, the worse the problem becomes. To make the calculation of real GDP more accurate, in 1996, the BEA switched to using *chain-weighted prices*, and it now publishes statistics on real GDP in "chained (2000) dollars."

The details of calculating real GDP using chain-weighted prices are more complicated than we need to discuss here, but the basic idea is straightforward. Starting with the base year, the BEA takes an average of prices in that year and prices in the following year. It then uses this average to calculate real GDP in the year following the base year (currently the year 2000). For the next year—in other words, the year that is two years after the base year—the BEA calculates real GDP by taking an average of prices in that year and the previous year. In this way, prices in each year are "chained" to prices from the previous year, and the distortion from changes in relative prices is minimized.

Holding prices constant means that the *purchasing power* of a dollar remains the same from one year to the next. Ordinarily, the purchasing power of the dollar falls every year, as price increases reduce the amount of goods and services that a dollar can buy.

Comparing Real GDP and Nominal GDP

Real GDP holds prices constant, which makes it a better measure than nominal GDP of changes in the production of goods and services from one year to the next. In fact, growth in the economy is almost always measured as growth in real GDP. If a headline in the *Wall Street Journal* states, "U.S. Economy Grew 4.3% Last Year," the article will report that real GDP increased by 4.3 percent during the previous year.

We describe real GDP as being measured in "base-year dollars." For example, with a base year of 2000, nominal GDP in 2006 was $13,247 billion, and real GDP in 2006 was $11,415 billion in 2000 dollars. Because, on average, prices rise from one year to the next, real GDP is greater than nominal GDP in years before the base year and less than nominal GDP for years after the base year. In the base year, real GDP and nominal GDP are the same because both are calculated for the base year using the same prices and quantities. Figure 7-3 shows movements in nominal GDP and real GDP between 1990 and 2006. In the 1990s, prices were, on average, lower than in 2000, so nominal GDP was lower than real GDP. In 2000, nominal and real GDP were equal. Since 2000, prices have been, on average, higher than in 2000, so nominal GDP is higher than real GDP.

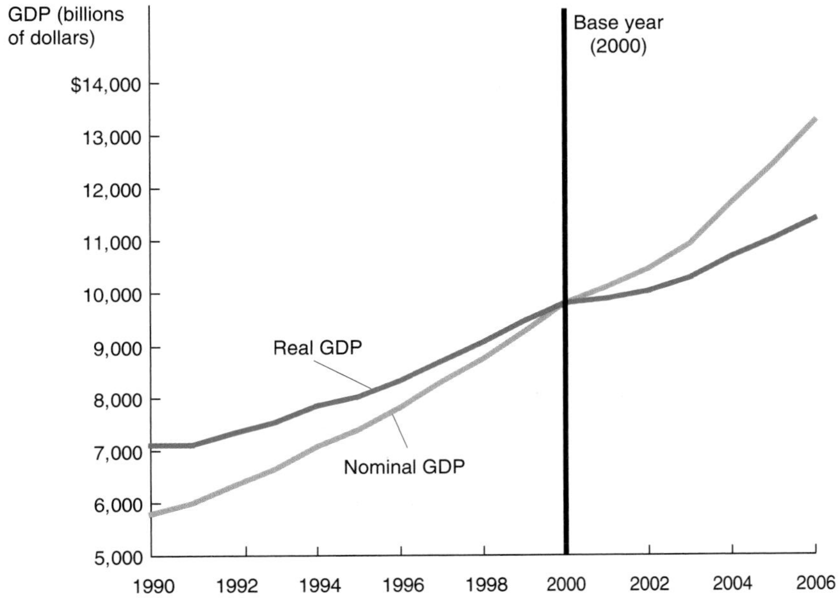

Figure 7-3

Nominal GDP and Real GDP, 1990–2006

Currently, the base year for calculating GDP is 2000. In the 1990s, prices were, on average, lower than in 2000, so nominal GDP was lower than real GDP. In 2000, nominal and real GDP were equal. After 2000, prices have been, on average, higher than in 2000, so nominal GDP is higher than real GDP.

Source: U.S. Bureau of Economic Analysis.

The GDP Deflator

Price level A measure of the average prices of goods and services in the economy.

GDP deflator A measure of the price level, calculated by dividing nominal GDP by real GDP and multiplying by 100.

Economists and policymakers are interested not just in the level of total production, as measured by real GDP, but also in the *price level*. The **price level** measures the average prices of goods and services in the economy. One of the goals of economic policy is a stable price level. We can use values for nominal GDP and real GDP to compute a measure of the price level called the *GDP deflator*. We can calculate the **GDP deflator** using this formula:

$$\text{GDP deflator} = \frac{\text{Nominal GDP}}{\text{Real GDP}} \times 100.$$

To see why the GDP deflator is a measure of the price level, think about what would happen if prices of goods and services rose while production remained the same. In that case, nominal GDP would increase, but real GDP would remain constant, so the GDP deflator would increase. In reality, both prices and production increase each year, but the more prices increase relative to the increase in production, the more nominal GDP increases relative to real GDP, and the higher the value for the GDP deflator. Increases in the GDP deflator allow economists and policymakers to track increases in the price level over time.

Remember that in the base year (currently 2000), nominal GDP is equal to real GDP, so the value of the GDP price deflator will always be 100 in the base year. The following table gives the values for nominal and real GDP for 2005 and 2006.

	2005	2006
NOMINAL GDP	$12,456 billion	$13,247 billion
REAL GDP	$11,049 billion	$11,415 billion

We can use the information from the table to calculate values for the GDP price deflator for 2005 and 2006:

FORMULA	APPLIED TO 2005	APPLIED TO 2006
$\text{GDP Deflator} = \frac{\text{Nominal GDP}}{\text{Real GDP}} \times 100$	$\left(\frac{\$12{,}456 \text{ billion}}{\$11{,}049 \text{ billion}}\right) \times 100 = 113$	$\left(\frac{\$13{,}247 \text{ billion}}{\$11{,}415 \text{ billion}}\right) \times 100 = 116$

From these values for the deflator, we can calculate that the price level increased by 2.7 percent between 2005 and 2006:

$$\frac{116 - 113}{113} = 2.7\%.$$

In Chapter 8, we will see that economists and policymakers also rely on another measure of the price level, known as the consumer price index. In addition, we will discuss the strengths and weaknesses of different measures of the price level.

7.4 LEARNING OBJECTIVE

7.4 | Become familiar with other measures of total production and total income.

Other Measures of Total Production and Total Income

National income accounting refers to the methods the BEA uses to track total production and total income in the economy. The statistical tables containing this information are called the *National Income and Product Accounts (NIPA)*. Every quarter, the BEA releases

NIPA tables containing data on several measures of total production and total income. We have already discussed the most important measure of total production and total income: gross domestic product (GDP). In addition to computing GDP, the BEA computes the following five measures of production and income: gross national product, net national product, national income, personal income, and disposable personal income.

Gross National Product (GNP)

We have seen that GDP is the value of final goods and services produced within the United States. Gross national product (GNP) is the value of final goods and services produced by residents of the United States, even if the production takes place *outside* the United States. U.S. firms have facilities in foreign countries, and foreign firms have facilities in the United States. Ford, for example, has assembly plants in the United Kingdom, and Toyota has assembly plants in the United States. GNP includes foreign production by U.S. firms but excludes U.S. production by foreign firms. For the United States, GNP is almost the same as GDP. For example, in 2006, GDP was $13,247 billion, and GNP was $13,277 billion. This difference is less than one-quarter of 1 percent.

For many years, GNP was the main measure of total production compiled by the federal government and used by economists and policymakers in the United States. However, in many countries other than the United States, a significant percentage of domestic production takes place in foreign-owned facilities. For those countries, GDP is much larger than GNP and is a more accurate measure of the level of production within the country's borders. As a result, many countries and international agencies had long preferred using GDP to using GNP. In 1991, the United States joined those countries in using GDP as its main measure of total production.

Net National Product (NNP)

In producing goods and services, some machinery, equipment, and buildings wear out and have to be replaced. The value of this worn-out machinery, equipment, and buildings is *depreciation*. If we subtract this value from GNP, we are left with net national product (NNP). In the NIPA tables, depreciation is referred to as the *consumption of fixed capital*.

National Income

When a consumer pays sales tax on a product, there is a difference between the amount the consumer has paid for the product and the amount the people who produced the product will receive as income. For instance, suppose you buy a television that is priced at $200. If the sales tax is 6 percent, you will actually pay $212, but the seller will send the $12 in tax directly to the government and it will never show up as anyone's income. Therefore, to calculate the total income actually received by a country's residents, the BEA has to subtract the value of sales taxes from net national product. In the NIPA tables, sales taxes are referred to as *indirect business taxes*. Previously in this chapter, we stressed that the value of total production is equal to the value of total income. This point is not strictly true if by "value of total production" we mean GDP and by "value of total income" we mean national income because national income will always be smaller than GDP. In practice, though, the difference between the value of GDP and value of national income does not matter for most macroeconomic issues.

Personal Income

Personal income is income received by households. To calculate personal income, we subtract the earnings that corporations retain rather than pay to shareholders in the form of dividends. We also add in the payments received by households from the government in the form of *transfer payments* or interest on government bonds.

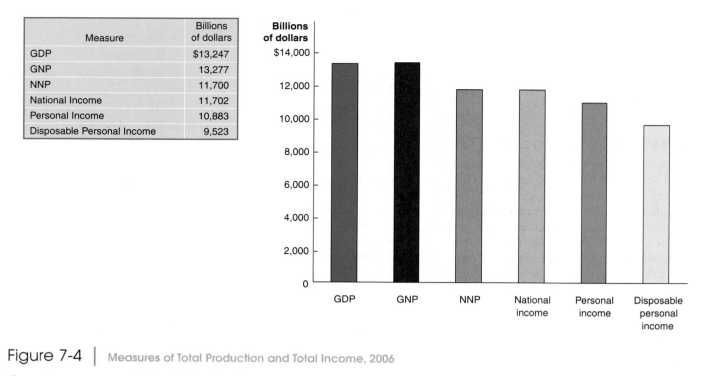

Measure	Billions of dollars
GDP	$13,247
GNP	13,277
NNP	11,700
National Income	11,702
Personal Income	10,883
Disposable Personal Income	9,523

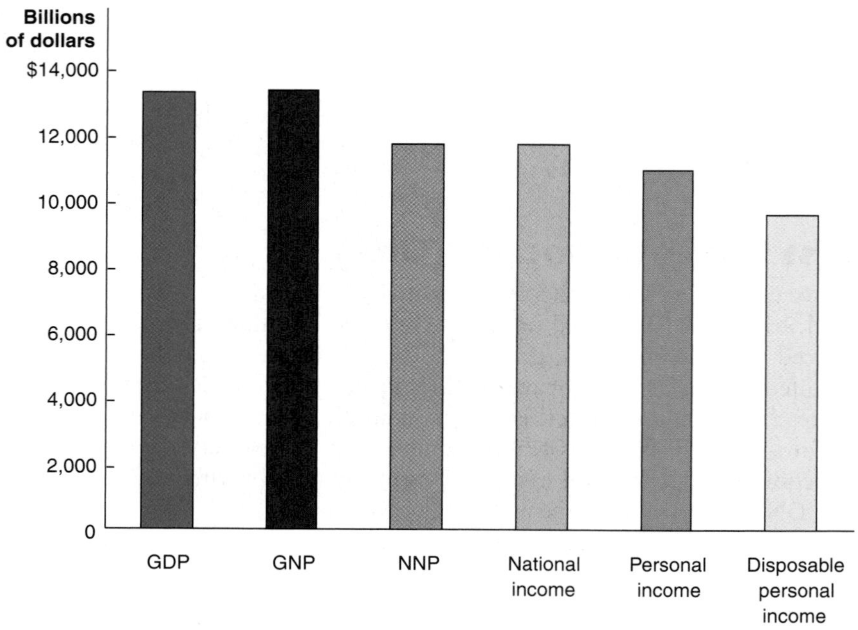

Figure 7-4 | Measures of Total Production and Total Income, 2006

The most important measure of total production and total income is gross domestic product (GDP). As we will see in later chapters, for some purposes, the other measures of total production and total income shown in the figure turn out to be more useful than GDP.

Disposable Personal Income

Disposable personal income is equal to personal income minus personal tax payments, such as the federal personal income tax. It is the best measure of the income households actually have available to spend.

Figure 7-4 shows the values of these measures of total production and total income for the year 2006 in a table and a graph.

The Division of Income

Figure 7-1 on page 217 illustrates the important fact that we can measure GDP in terms of total expenditure or as the total income received by households. GDP calculated as the sum of income payments to households is sometimes referred to as *gross domestic income.* Figure 7-5 shows the division of total income among wages, interest, rent, profit, and certain non-income items. The non-income items are included in gross domestic income because, as we have seen, some of the value of goods and services produced is not directly received by households as income. *Wages* include all compensation received by employees, including fringe benefits such as health insurance. *Interest* is net interest received by households, or the difference between the interest received on savings accounts, government bonds, and other investments and the interest paid on car loans, home mortgages, and other debts. *Rent* is rent received by households. *Profits* include the profits of sole proprietorships, which are usually small businesses, and the profits of corporations. Also included in gross domestic income are indirect business taxes, depreciation, other smaller items, and an allowance for measurement problems called the "statistical discrepancy." The figure shows that the largest component of gross domestic income is wages, which are about three times as large as profits.

		Billions of dollars
Wages		$7,496
Interest		716
Rent		77
Profit		2,387
Profits of sole proprietors	1,015	
Profits of corporations	1,372	
Taxes, depreciation, and statistical discrepancy		2,571
Total		$13,247

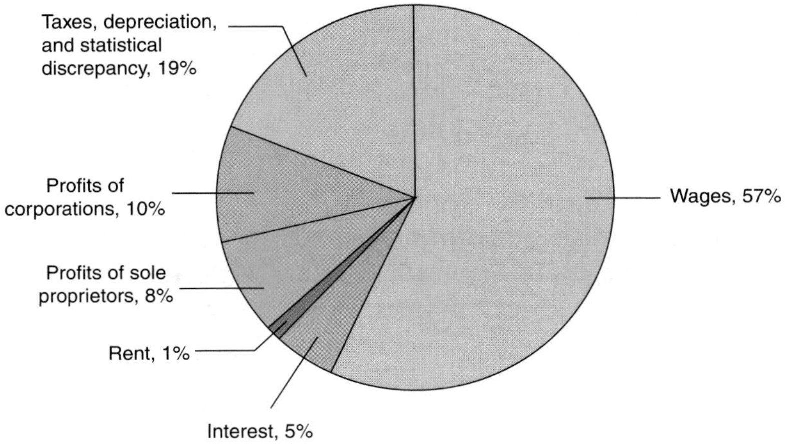

Figure 7-5 | The Division of Income

We can measure GDP in terms of total expenditure or as the total income received by households. The largest component of income received by households is wages, which are about three times as large as the profits received by sole proprietors and the profits received by corporations combined.

Economics in YOUR Life!

>> Continued from page 213

At the beginning of the chapter, we posed two questions: What effect should Canada's and China's two very different growth rates of GDP have on your decision to work and live in one country or the other? And if China's much higher growth rate does not necessarily lead you to decide to work and live in China, why not? This chapter has shown that although it is generally true that the more goods and services people have, the better off they are, GDP provides only a rough measure of well-being. That is to say, GDP does not include the value of leisure; nor is it adjusted for pollution and other negative effects of production or crime and other social problems. So, in deciding where to live and work you would need to balance China's much higher growth rate of GDP against these other considerations. You would also need to take into account that although China's *growth rate* is higher than Canada's, Canada's current *level* of real GDP is higher than China's.

Conclusion

In this chapter, we have begun the study of macroeconomics by examining an important concept—how a nation's total production and income can be measured. Understanding GDP is important for understanding the business cycle and the process of long-run economic growth. In the next chapter, we discuss the issues involved in measuring two other key economic variables: the unemployment rate and the inflation rate.

Read *An Inside Look* on the next page for a discussion of why some trucking firms were experiencing slow sales at the same time that the airlines were prospering.

An Inside **LOOK**

Trucking Industry Depends on the Goods—Not Services—Component of GDP

OMAHA WORLD-HERALD, JANUARY 11, 2007

Economic Slowdown Slams Breaks on Trucking Sector

A sudden, dramatic drop in freight demand has sucked the air out of a trucking sector pumped up by several years of growth.

(a) "For the trucking industry, the first half of this year is likely to be the toughest environment we have seen since the last recession," Bob Costello, chief economist and vice president of the American Trucking Associations [ATA], said in a telephone interview Wednesday. That's bad news for the rest of the economy, for which trucking is considered a bellwether. "Trucking sees slowdowns and recovery first," Costello said. "I do anticipate that we will start to recover before the general economy."

The second half of 2007 looks better for trucking, he said. "The general consensus is that 2008 will be a better time for the economy, and I would expect trucking to improve before that," he said. November was the single worst month for for-hire truck tonnage since the last recession, according to the ATA's index. The ATA reported the truck-tonnage index dropped 3.6 percent in November from October and 8.8 percent compared to the same month a year earlier. . . .

Jim Hill at Omaha-based Merit Transportation Co. said the pace of what he termed one of the slowest fourth quarters he has seen in more than 20 years in the trucking business has continued into January. Although he remains optimistic about Merit's corner of the trucking world—refrigerated transportation—Hill said consumer demand is off. . . . Merit delayed by a year the $6 million purchase of 40 tractors and 40 trailers from fall 2006 when demand suddenly deflated. . . .

(b) The factors behind the slowdown are varied, Costello said. "It's really broad-based." Slowdowns in housing and auto markets are easy targets, "but it's more than that," he said.

The portion of the gross national product made up of goods, rather than services, is projected to grow at a slower 1.6 percent rate than the overall economy's 2.3 percent rate, he said.

"We don't haul services. We get more bang for your buck from the goods side of the economy," he said. A persistent driver shortage kept trucking companies from expanding further during the good times, Costello said. . . . With the driver shortage limiting how much firms can transport, a quick change in demand could quickly eat up any excess capacity. . . .

(c) Tonn Ostergard, president and chief executive of Crete Carrier Corp., said the transportation industry has changed greatly since 2000, when trucking first felt the effects of the last recession. Comparisons are difficult because circumstances are different, he said.

Shippers have changed the way they manage transportation, maintaining thinner inventories and building distribution centers closer to their customers for overnight restocking. "We don't see the cycles that we used to see," he said. "They are much more proactive about managing their supply chain. They continually improve on things—their technology, their distribution patterns." More shippers also are responding to fuel prices by moving freight to intermodal rail, he said. . . .

Lincoln-based Crete Carrier is one of the nation's largest privately held trucking companies. Ostergard declined to release revenue figures. "The first 11 days of the new year aren't particularly rebounding, but January is never going to be as solid as other months. By some comparative measurements, January has been just a little below what we would have expected," he said. The company didn't make major changes in the fourth quarter.

"That's what separates well-managed companies from the rest of the pack," he said. "You work a little harder and manage the business a little better. We're working closer with our customers and doing everything we can to be as efficient as possible."

At Merit, Hill sees opportunity in the refrigerated segment, and the private company is projected to grow again in 2007. The company, which was founded in 1999, limited its growth in 2006. . . .

Source: Stacie Hamel, "Economic Slowdown Slams Breaks on Trucking Sector," Omaha World-Herald, January 11, 2007. Reprinted by permission.

Key Points in the Article

This article discusses a significant decline in the demand for ground-freight transportation in the last quarter of 2006, which many in the trucking industry anticipated would continue during the first two quarters of 2007. Some in the industry feared that this decline might be the worst that they had seen since the recession of 2001. The article cites several causes for the downturn in the demand for trucking, including the slowdowns in the housing and automobile industries, and the long-term trend toward faster growth in services than in goods. The article also notes that the trucking industry is relatively less cyclical now than it was during the recession in 2001. Since the last recession, shippers have learned to manage inventories much more efficiently.

Analyzing the News

a Trucking-industry observers expect that the first two quarters of 2007 will be the worst for the industry since the recession of 2001. The early stages of this slowdown were apparent in November 2006, when the American Trucking Association's (ATA's) truck-tonnage index fell 8.8 percent from a year earlier; this was the worst showing since 2001. As Bob Costello, chief economist and vice president of the ATA explains, this much-anticipated industry slowdown may not bode well for the overall U.S. economy. This is because activity in the trucking industry tends to slow before activity in the overall U.S. economy does.

b The reasons for the slowdown are varied; however, three factors seem to have played a particularly significant role. According to the article, the first two factors are slowdowns in the demand for housing and automobiles. As the demand for new residential construction and automobiles declined, so too did the demand for the ground-freight transportation required to get building materials to job sites and automobiles to dealers' lots. The third has been the slowdown in the growth of the goods portion of U.S. GDP. This is obviously a problem for the trucking industry, which ships goods but not services. In fact, the percentage of U.S. GDP composed of goods has fallen consistently since at least 1980. This pattern is shown in the figure below, which shows that goods have fallen from 41 percent of GDP in 1980 to 31 percent in 2006; during this same period, services have increased from 47 percent of GDP to 58 percent.

c The trucking industry is less cyclical today than it was during the recession of 2001. According to Tonn Ostergard, president and chief executive of Crete Carrier Corp., this is because shippers, who hire trucking companies, have learned to manage more efficiently their inventories and supply chains—networks of resources involved in moving goods to where they are needed. So, the demand for trucking is no longer as sensitive as it once was to general fluctuations in economic activity.

Thinking Critically

1. Both trucking firms and airlines are in the transportation business, yet while 2006 and 2007 were good years for the airlines, they were poor years for trucking firms. Why did macroeconomic conditions in these years affect these two industries differently?
2. In the past 20 years, exports and imports have both increased as a fraction of GDP. Has this trend been good news or bad news for the trucking industry?

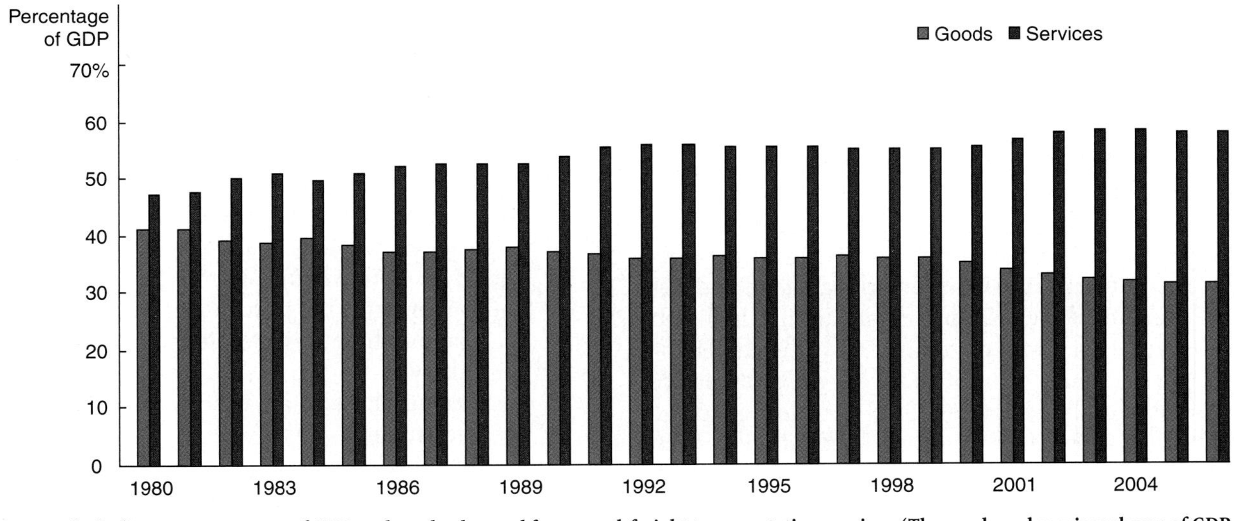

As goods decline as a percentage of GDP, so does the demand for ground-freight transportation services. (The goods and services shares of GDP do not sum to 100 percent because GDP is composed of goods, services, and structures.)

Key Terms

Business cycle, p. 214	Government purchases, p. 219	Investment, p. 218	Real GDP, p. 226
Consumption, p. 218	Gross domestic product (GDP), p. 215	Macroeconomics, p. 214	Recession, p. 214
Economic growth, p. 214	Inflation rate, p. 214	Microeconomics, p. 214	Transfer payments, p. 218
Expansion, p. 214	Intermediate good or service, p. 215	Net exports, p. 220	Underground economy, p. 222
Final good or service, p. 215		Nominal GDP, p. 226	Value added, p. 221
GDP deflator, p. 228		Price level, p. 228	

7.1 LEARNING OBJECTIVE 7.1 | Explain how total production is measured, **pages 215–222.**

Gross Domestic Product Measures Total Production

Summary

Economics is divided into the subfields of **microeconomics**—which studies how households and firms make choices—and **macroeconomics**—which studies the economy as a whole. An important macroeconomic issue is the **business cycle**, which refers to alternating periods of economic expansion and economic recession. An **expansion** is a period during which production and employment are increasing. A **recession** is a period during which production and employment are decreasing. Another important macroeconomic topic is **economic growth**, which refers to the ability of the economy to produce increasing quantities of goods and services. Macroeconomics also studies the **inflation rate**, or the percentage increase in the price level from one year to the next. Economists measure total production by **gross domestic product (GDP)**, which is the value of all *final goods and services* produced in an economy during a period of time. A **final good or service** is purchased by a final user. An **intermediate good or service** is an input into another good or service and is not included in GDP. When we measure the value of total production in the economy by calculating GDP, we are simultaneously measuring the value of total income. GDP is divided into four major categories of expenditures: **consumption, investment, government purchases, and net exports**. Government **transfer payments** are not included in GDP because they are payments to individuals for which the government does not receive a good or service in return. We can also calculate GDP by adding up the **value added** of every firm involved in producing final goods and services.

myeconlab Visit www.myeconlab.com to complete these exercises online and get instant feedback.

Review Questions

1.1 Why in microeconomics can we measure production in terms of quantity, but in macroeconomics we measure production in terms of market value?

1.2 If the U.S. Bureau of Economic Analysis added up the values of every good and service sold during the year, would the total be larger or smaller than GDP?

1.3 In the circular flow of expenditure and income, why must the value of total production in an economy equal the value of total income?

1.4 Describe the four major components of expenditures in GDP and write the equation used to represent the relationship between GDP and the four expenditure components.

1.5 What is the difference between the value of a firm's final product and the value added by the firm to the final product?

Problems and Applications

1.6 Is the value of intermediate goods and services produced during the year included in GDP? For example, are computer chips produced and installed on a new PC included in GDP? (Note that this question does not ask whether the computer chips are directly counted in GDP but rather whether their production is included in GDP.)

1.7 Briefly explain whether each of the following transactions represents the purchase of a final good.
   a. The purchase of wheat from a wheat farmer by a bakery
   b. The purchase of an aircraft carrier by the federal government
   c. The purchase of French wine by a U.S. consumer
   d. The purchase of a new machine tool by the Ford Motor Company

1.8 **(Related to the *Don't Let This Happen to You!* on page 219)** Briefly explain whether you agree or disagree with the following statement: "In years when people buy many shares of stock, investment will be high and, therefore, so will GDP."

1.9 **(Related to the *Chapter Opener* on page 212)** Which component of GDP will be affected by each of the following transactions involving American

Airlines? If you do not believe any component of GDP will be affected by the transactions, briefly explain why.

a. You purchase a ticket on American flight to Seattle to visit your uncle.
b. American purchases a new jetliner from Boeing.
c. American purchases new seats to be installed on a jetliner it already owns.
d. American purchases 100 million gallons of jet fuel.
e. A person in France purchases a ticket to fly on an American flight from Paris to New York.
f. The city of Nashville agrees to spend funds to extend one of the runways at Nashville International Airport so that American will be able to land larger jets.

1.10 Is the value of a house built in 2000 and resold in 2009 included in the GDP of 2009? Why or why not? Would the services of the real estate agent who helped sell (or buy) the house in 2009 be counted in GDP for 2009? Why or why not?

1.11 **(Related to the *Making the Connection* on page 219)** In recent years, the BEA has classified government purchases into consumption expenditures and gross government investment. Would you classify the expenditures for the Department of Homeland Security as government investment or as government consumption? Briefly explain.

1.12 **(Related to *Solved Problem 7-1* on page 216)** Suppose that a simple economy produces only the following four goods and services: textbooks, hamburgers, shirts, and cotton. Assume that all the cotton is used in the production of shirts. Use the information in the following table to calculate nominal GDP for 2009.

PRODUCTION AND PRICE STATISTICS FOR 2009

PRODUCT	QUANTITY	PRICE
Textbooks	100	$60.00
Hamburgers	100	2.00
Shirts	50	25.00
Cotton	8,000	0.60

1.13 For the total value of expenditures on final goods and services to equal the total value of income generated from producing those final goods and services, all the money that a business receives from the sale of its product must be paid out as income to the owners of the factors of production. How can a business make a profit if it pays out as income all the money it receives?

1.14 How does the value added of a business differ from the profits of a business?

1.15 It is reported that some state-owned firms in the former Soviet Union produced goods and services whose value was less than the value of the raw materials the firms used to produce their goods and services. If so, what would have been the value added of these state-owned firms? Would such a firm be able to survive in a free-market economy?

1.16 An artist buys scrap metal from a local steel mill as a raw material for her metal sculptures. Last year, she bought $5,000 worth of the scrap metal. During the year, she produced 10 metal sculptures that she sold for $800 each to the local art store. The local art store sold all of them to local art collectors at an average price of $1,000 each. For the 10 metal sculptures, what was the total value added of the artist and what was the total value added of the local art store?

>> End Learning Objective 7.1

7.2 LEARNING OBJECTIVE 7.2 | Discuss whether GDP is a good measure of well-being, **pages 222–225.**

Does GDP Measure What We Want It to Measure?

Summary

GDP does not include household production, which refers to goods and services people produce for themselves, nor does it include production in the **underground economy**, which consists of concealed buying and selling. The underground economy in some developing countries may be more than half of measured GDP. GDP is not a perfect measure of well-being because it does not include the value of leisure, it is not adjusted for pollution or other negative effects of production, and it is not adjusted for changes in crime and other social problems.

myeconlab Get Ahead of the Curve Visit www.myeconlab.com to complete these exercises online and get instant feedback.

Review Questions

2.1 Why does the size of a country's GDP matter? How does it affect the quality of life of the country's people?

2.2 Why is GDP an imperfect measure of economic well-being? What types of production does GDP not measure? Even if GDP included these types of production, why would it still be an imperfect measure of economic well-being?

Problems and Applications

2.3 Which of the following are likely to increase measured GDP, and which are likely to reduce it?
   a. The fraction of women working outside the home increases.
   b. There is a sharp increase in the crime rate.
   c. Higher tax rates cause some people to hide more of the income they earn.

2.4 What would you expect to happen to household production as unemployment rises during a recession? What would you expect to happen to household production as unemployment falls during an expansion? Would you therefore expect the fluctuation in actual production—GDP plus household production—to be greater or less than the fluctuation in measured GDP?

2.5 Review the definition of real GDP per capita on page 215 before answering the following question. Does the fact that the typical American works less than 40 hours per week today and worked 60 hours per week in 1890 make the difference between the economic well-being of Americans today versus 1890 higher or lower than indicated by the difference in real GDP per capita today versus 1890? Explain.

2.6 **(Related to the *Making the Connection* on page 223)** A report of the World Bank, an international organization devoted to increasing economic growth in developing countries, includes the following statement: "Informal economic activities pose a particular measurement problem [in calculating GDP], especially in developing countries, where much economic activity may go unrecorded." What do they mean by "informal economic activities"? Why would these activities make it harder to measure GDP? Why might they make it harder to evaluate the standard of living in developing countries relative to the standard of living in the United States?

Source: The World Bank, *World Development Indicators*, Washington, DC: The World Bank, 2003, p. 189.

2.7 Each year, the United Nations publishes the Human Development Report, which provides information on the standard of living in nearly every country in the world. The report includes data on real GDP per person and also contains a broader measure of the standard of living called the Human Development Index (HDI). The HDI combines data on real GDP per person with data on life expectancy at birth, adult literacy, and school enrollment. The following table shows values for real GDP per person and the HDI for several countries. Prepare one list that ranks countries from highest real GDP per person to lowest and another list that ranks countries from highest HDI to lowest. Briefly discuss possible reasons for any differences in the rankings of countries in your two lists. (All values in the table are for the year 2004.)

COUNTRY	REAL GDP PER PERSON	HDI
Australia	$30,331	0.957
China	5,896	0.768
Greece	22,205	0.921
Iran	7,525	0.746
Norway	38,454	0.965
Singapore	28,077	0.916
South Korea	20,499	0.912
United Arab Emirates	24,056	0.839
United States	39,676	0.948

Source: United Nations Development Programme, *Human Development Report, 2006*, New York: Palgrave Macmillan, 2006.

2.8 **(Related to the *Making the Connection* on page 224)** Think about the increase in spending for the Department of Homeland Security and the wars in Afghanistan and Iraq. These all represent government expenditures that have increased GDP. Briefly explain whether you think that these increases in GDP have made the typical person better off.

>> End Learning Objective 7.2

7.3 LEARNING OBJECTIVE 7.3 | Discuss the difference between real GDP and nominal GDP, **pages 225–228.**

Real GDP versus Nominal GDP

Summary

Nominal GDP is the value of final goods and services evaluated at current-year prices. **Real GDP** is the value of final goods and services evaluated at *base-year* prices. By keeping prices constant, we know that changes in real GDP represent changes in the quantity of goods and services produced in the economy. When the **price level**, the average prices of goods and services in the economy, is increasing, real GDP is greater than nominal GDP in years before the base year and less than nominal GDP for years after the base year. The **GDP deflator** is a measure of the price level and is calculated by dividing nominal GDP by real GDP and multiplying by 100.

Review Questions

3.1 Why does inflation make nominal GDP a poor measure of the increase in total production from one year to the next? How does the U.S. Bureau of Economic

Analysis deal with the problem inflation causes with nominal GDP?

3.2 What is the GDP deflator, and how is it calculated?

Problems and Applications

3.3 **(Related to *Solved Problem 7-3* on page 226)** Suppose the information in the following table is for a simple economy that produces only the following four goods and services: textbooks, hamburgers, shirts, and cotton. Assume that all the cotton is used in the production of shirts.

	2000 STATISTICS		2009 STATISTICS		2010 STATISTICS	
PRODUCT	QUANTITY	PRICE	QUANTITY	PRICE	QUANTITY	PRICE
Textbooks	90	$50.00	100	$60.00	100	$65.00
Hamburgers	75	2.00	100	2.00	120	2.25
Shirts	50	30.00	50	25.00	65	25.00
Cotton	10,000	0.80	8,000	0.60	12,000	0.70

a. Use the information in the table to calculate real GDP for 2009 and 2010, assuming that the base year is 2000.
b. What is the growth rate of real GDP during 2010?

3.4 Assuming that inflation has occurred over time, what is the relationship between nominal GDP and real GDP in each of the following situations?
a. Years after the base year
b. In the base year
c. Years before the base year

3.5 If the quantity of final goods and services produced decreased, could real GDP increase? Could nominal GDP increase? If so, how?

3.6 Use the data in the following table to calculate the GDP deflator for each year (values are in billions of dollars).

	NOMINAL GDP	REAL GDP
2002	$10,470	$10,049
2003	10,961	10,301
2004	11,713	10,704
2005	12,456	11,049
2006	13,247	11,415

Which year from 2003 to 2006 saw the largest percentage increase in the price level, as measured by changes in the GDP deflator? Briefly explain.

>> End Learning Objective 7.3

7.4 LEARNING OBJECTIVE 7.4 | Become familiar with other measures of total production and total income, **pages 228–231.**

Other Measures of Total Production and Total Income

Summary

The most important measure of total production and total income is gross domestic product (GDP). As we will see in later chapters, for some purposes, the other measures of total production and total income shown in Figure 7-4 are actually more useful than GDP. These measures are gross national product (GNP), net national product (NNP), national income, personal income, and disposable personal income.

Review Questions

4.1 Under what circumstances would GDP be a better measure of total production and total income than GNP?

4.2 What are the differences in national income, personal income, and personal disposable income?

Problems and Applications

4.3 Suppose a country has many of its citizens temporarily working in other countries, and many of its firms have facilities in other countries. Furthermore, relatively few citizens of foreign countries are working in this country, and relatively few foreign firms have facilities in this country. In these circumstances, which would you expect to be larger for this country, GDP or GNP? Briefly explain.

4.4 Suppose the amount the federal government collects in personal income taxes increases, while the level of GDP remains the same. What will happen to the values of national income, personal income, and personal disposable income?

4.5 If you were attempting to forecast the level of consumption spending by households, which measure of total production or total income might be most helpful to you in making your forecast? Briefly explain.

4.6 Briefly discuss the accuracy of the following statement: "Corporate profits are much too high: Most corporations make profits equal to 50 percent of the price of the products they sell."

>> End Learning Objective 7.4

Unemployment and Inflation

Alcatel-Lucent Contributes to Unemployment

When we study macroeconomics, we are looking at the big picture: total production, total employment, and the price level. Of course, the big picture is determined by the decisions of millions of individual consumers and firms. Lucent Technologies has been involved in developing many important innovations, including equipment for long-distance television transmission, the transistor, the Unix computer operating system, and Wi-Fi wireless broadband technology.

When total employment in the United States declined during 2001, Lucent contributed to the decline. In 2000, Lucent employed 175,000 workers. It began laying off large numbers of workers during 2001. By 2005, Lucent employed only 31,500 workers. In December 2006, Lucent merged with the French technology firm Alcatel to form the new firm Alcatel-Lucent. Unfortunately, the new firm continued to have problems. In January 2007, Alcatel-Lucent reported that during the fourth quarter of 2006, its sales had fallen by 16 percent, while its profits were near zero. According to Chief Executive Patricia Russo, the quarter "proved challenging from a market perspective, driven by a shift in spending from some of our large North American customers and heightened competition in the global wireless market." In the face of this growing competition from communications-technology rivals such as Ericsson of Sweden and Huawei of China, the company could not increase revenue, and so its only option was to reduce costs. Less than one month after the company reported its disappointing earnings, Ms. Russo announced the elimination of 12,500 jobs.

Alcatel-Lucent's decision will ultimately leave thousands of people unemployed. In this chapter, we will focus on measuring changes in unemployment and changes in the price level, or *inflation*. Because unemployment and inflation are both important macroeconomic problems, it is important to understand how they are measured. For an example of a newspaper discussion of newly released government statistics on unemployment, read **AN INSIDE LOOK** on **page 266**.

Sources: Carol Matlock, "The Reasons for Alcatel's 'Shocking' Miss," *BusinessWeek Online*, January 24, 2007; and "Unix's Founding Fathers," *Economist*, June 10, 2004.

LEARNING Objectives

After studying this chapter, you should be able to:

8.1 Define **unemployment rate** and **labor force participation rate** and understand how they are computed, page 240.

8.2 Identify the three **types** of **unemployment**, page 248.

8.3 Explain what **factors determine** the **unemployment rate**, page 250.

8.4 Define **price level** and **inflation rate** and understand how they are computed, page 254.

8.5 Use **price indexes** to adjust for the effects of inflation, page 258.

8.6 Distinguish between the **nominal interest rate** and the **real interest rate**, page 260.

8.7 Discuss the **problems** that **inflation** causes, page 262.

Economics in YOUR Life!

Should You Change Your Career Plans if You Graduate During a Recession?

Suppose that you are about to graduate from college with a bachelor's degree in engineering. You plan to seek a job in manufacturing. If the economy is currently in a recession and the unemployment rate is a relatively high 7 percent, should you change your career plans? Should you still try for a job in manufacturing, or should you try to enter another industry or, perhaps, stay in school to get a master's degree? As you read this chapter, see if you can answer these questions. You can check your answers against those we provide at the end of the chapter. » **Continued on page 265**

Unemployment and inflation are the macroeconomic problems that are most often discussed in the media and during political campaigns. For many members of the general public, the state of the economy is summarized in just two measures: the unemployment rate and the inflation rate. In the 1960s, Arthur Okun, who was chairman of the Council of Economic Advisers during President Lyndon Johnson's administration, coined the term *misery index*, which adds together the inflation rate and the unemployment rate to give a rough measure of the state of the economy. As we will see in later chapters, although inflation and unemployment are important problems, the long-run success of an economy is best judged by its ability to generate high levels of real GDP per person. We devote this chapter to discussing how the government measures the unemployment and inflation rates. In particular, we will look closely at the statistics on unemployment and inflation that the federal government issues each month.

8.1 LEARNING OBJECTIVE

8.1 | Define unemployment rate and labor force participation rate and understand how they are computed.

Measuring the Unemployment Rate and the Labor Force Participation Rate

At 8:30 A.M. on a Friday early in each month, the U.S. Department of Labor reports its estimate of the previous month's unemployment rate. If the unemployment rate is higher or lower than expected, investors are likely to change their views on the health of the economy. The result is seen an hour later, when trading begins on the New York Stock Exchange. Good news about unemployment usually causes stock prices to rise, and bad news causes stock prices to fall. The unemployment rate can also have important political implications. In most presidential elections, the incumbent president is reelected if unemployment is falling early in the election year but is defeated if unemployment is rising. This relationship held true in 2004, when the unemployment rate was lower during the first six months of 2004 than it had been during the last six months of 2003, and incumbent George W. Bush was reelected.

The unemployment rate is a key macroeconomic statistic. But how does the Department of Labor prepare its estimates of the unemployment rate, and how accurate are these estimates? We will explore the answers to these questions in this section.

The Household Survey

Each month, the U.S. Bureau of the Census conducts the *Current Population Survey* (often referred to as the *household survey*) to collect data needed to compute the unemployment rate. The bureau interviews adults in a sample of 60,000 households, chosen to represent the U.S. population, about the employment status of everyone in the household 16 years of age and older. The Department of Labor's Bureau of Labor Statistics (BLS) uses these data to calculate the monthly unemployment rate. People are considered *employed* if they worked during the week before the survey or if they were temporarily away from their job because they were ill, on vacation, on strike, or for other reasons. People are considered *unemployed* if they did not work in the previous week but were available for work and had actively looked for work at some time during the previous four weeks. The **labor force** is the sum of the *employed* and the *unemployed*. The **unemployment rate** is the percentage of the labor force that is unemployed.

Labor force The sum of employed and unemployed workers in the economy.

Unemployment rate The percentage of the labor force that is unemployed.

People who do not have a job and who are not actively looking for a job are classified by the BLS as *not in the labor force*. People not in the labor force include retirees, homemakers, full-time students, and people on active military service, in prison, or in mental hospitals. Also not in the labor force are people who are available for work and who have actively looked for a job at some point during the previous 12 months but who have not looked during the previous four weeks. Some people have not actively looked

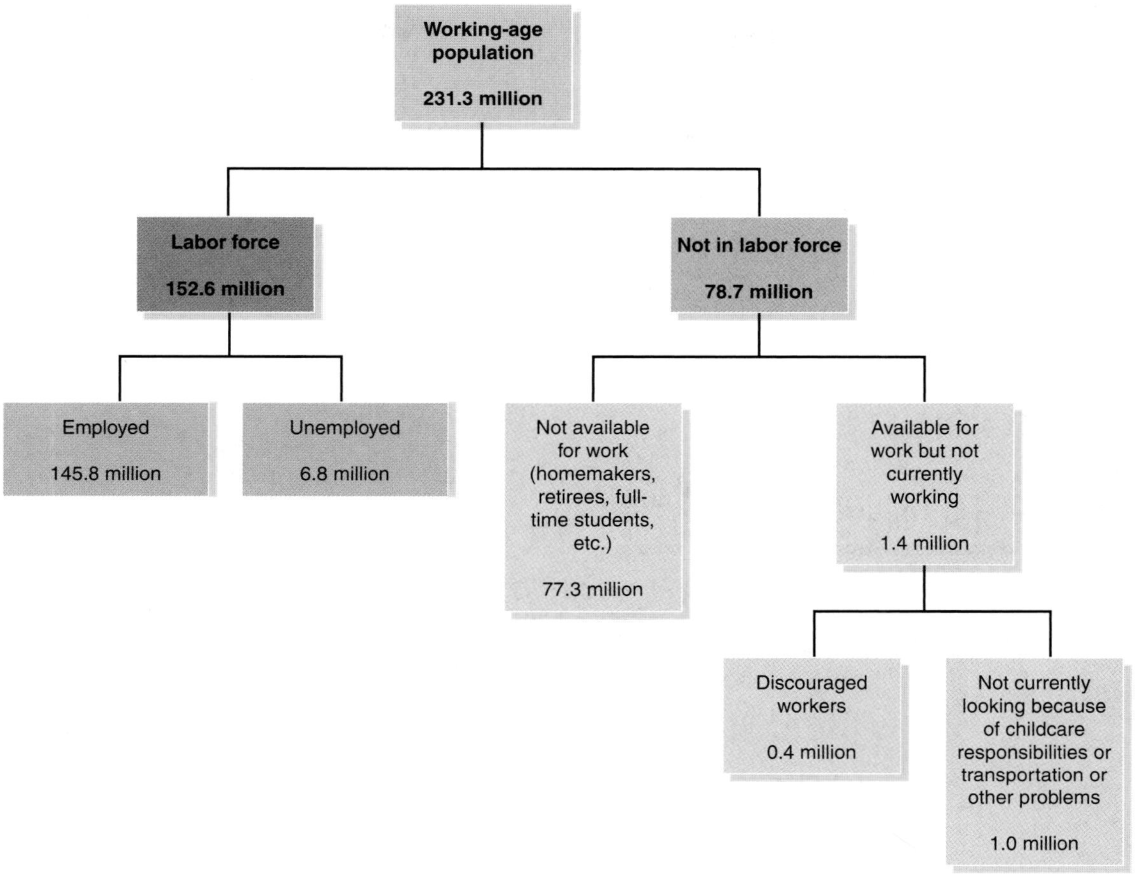

Figure 8-1 | The Employment Status of the Civilian Working-Age Population, April 2007

In April 2007, the working-age population of the United States was 231.3 million. The working-age population is divided into those in the labor force (152.6 million) and those not in the labor force (78.7 million). The labor force is divided into the employed (145.8 million) and the unemployed (6.8 million). Those not in the labor force are divided into those not available for work (77.3 million) and those available for work (1.4 million). Finally, those available for work but not in the labor force are divided into discouraged workers (0.4 million) and those currently not working for other reasons (1.0 million).

Source: U.S. Department of Labor, *Employment Situation Summary*, April 2007.

for work lately for reasons such as transportation difficulties or childcare responsibilities. Other people who have not actively looked for work are called *discouraged workers*. **Discouraged workers** are available for work but have not looked for a job during the previous four weeks because they believe no jobs are available for them.

Discouraged workers People who are available for work but have not looked for a job during the previous four weeks because they believe no jobs are available for them.

Figure 8-1 shows the employment status of the civilian working-age population in April 2007. We can use the information in the figure to calculate two important macroeconomic indicators:

- ***The unemployment rate.*** The unemployment rate measures the percentage of the labor force that is unemployed:

$$\frac{\text{Number of unemployed}}{\text{Labor force}} \times 100 = \text{Unemployment rate.}$$

Using the numbers from Figure 8-1, we can calculate the unemployment rate for April 2007:

$$\frac{6.8\text{ million}}{152.6\text{ million}} \times 100 = 4.5\%.$$

Labor force participation rate The percentage of the working-age population in the labor force.

- ***The labor force participation rate.*** The **labor force participation rate** measures the percentage of the working-age population that is in the labor force:

$$\frac{\text{Labor force}}{\text{Working-age population}} \times 100 = \text{Labor force participation rate.}$$

For April 2007, the labor force participation rate was:

$$\frac{152.6 \text{ million}}{231.3 \text{ million}} \times 100 = 66.0\%.$$

Solved Problem | 8-1

What Happens if You Include the Military?

In the BLS household survey, people on active military service are not included in the totals for employment, the labor force, or the working-age population. Suppose people in the military were included in these categories. How would the unemployment rate and the labor force participation rate change?

SOLVING THE PROBLEM:

Step 1: **Review the chapter material.** This problem is about calculating the unemployment rate and the labor force participation rate, so you may want to review the section "Measuring the Unemployment Rate and the Labor Force Participation Rate," which begins on page 240.

Step 2: **Show that including the military decreases the measured unemployment rate.** The unemployment rate is calculated as:

$$\frac{\text{Number of unemployed}}{\text{Labor force}} \times 100.$$

Including people in the military would increase the number of people counted as being in the labor force but would leave unchanged the number of people counted as unemployed. Therefore, the unemployment rate would decrease.

Step 3: **Show that including the military increases the measured labor force participation rate.** The labor force participation rate is calculated as:

$$\frac{\text{Labor force}}{\text{Working-age population}} \times 100.$$

Including people in the military would increase both the number of people in the labor force and the number of people in the working-age population by the same amount. This change would increase the labor force participation rate because adding the same number to both the numerator and the denominator of a fraction that is less than one increases the value of the fraction.

To see why this is true, consider the following simple example. Suppose that 100,000,000 people are in the working-age population and 50,000,000 are in the labor force, not counting people in the military. Suppose that 1,000,000 people are in the military. Then, the labor force participation rate excluding the military is:

$$\frac{50{,}000{,}000}{100{,}000{,}000} \times 100 = 50\%,$$

and the labor force participation rate including the military is:

$$\frac{51,000,000}{101,000,000} \times 100 = 50.5\%.$$

YOUR TURN: For more practice, do related problem 1.7 on page 268 at the end of this chapter. >> End Solved Problem 8-1

Problems with Measuring the Unemployment Rate

Although the BLS reports the unemployment rate measured to the tenth of a percentage point, it is not a perfect measure of the current state of joblessness in the economy. One problem that the BLS confronts is distinguishing between the unemployed and people who are not in the labor force. During an economic recession, for example, an increase in discouraged workers usually occurs, as people who have had trouble finding a job stop actively looking. Because these workers are not counted as unemployed, the unemployment rate as measured by the BLS may significantly understate the true degree of joblessness in the economy. The BLS also counts people as being employed if they hold part-time jobs even though they would prefer to hold full-time jobs. In a recession, counting as "employed" a part-time worker who wants to work full time tends to understate the degree of joblessness in the economy and make the employment situation appear better than it is.

Not counting discouraged workers as unemployed and counting people as employed who are working part time, although they would prefer to be working full time, has a substantial effect on the measured unemployment rate. For example, in April 2007, if the BLS counted as unemployed all people who were available for work but not actively looking for a job and all people who were in part-time jobs but wanted full-time jobs, the unemployment rate would have increased from 4.5 percent to 8.2 percent.

There are other measurement problems, however, that cause the measured unemployment rate to *overstate* the true extent of joblessness. These problems arise because the Current Population Survey does not verify the responses of people included in the survey. Some people who claim to be unemployed and actively looking for work may not be actively looking. A person might claim to be actively looking for a job to remain eligible for government payments to the unemployed. In this case, a person who is actually not in the labor force is counted as unemployed. Other people might be employed but engaged in illegal activity—such as drug dealing—or might want to conceal a legitimate job to avoid paying taxes. In these cases, individuals who are actually employed are counted as unemployed. These inaccurate responses to the survey bias the unemployment rate as measured by the BLS toward overstating the true extent of joblessness. We can conclude that, although the unemployment rate provides some useful information about the employment situation in the country, it is far from an exact measure of joblessness in the economy.

Trends in Labor Force Participation

The labor force participation rate is important because it determines the amount of labor that will be available to the economy from a given population. The higher the labor force participation rate, the more labor will be available and the higher a country's levels of GDP and GDP per person. Figure 8-2 highlights two important trends in labor force participation rates of adults aged 20 and over in the United States since 1950—the rising labor force participation rate of adult women and the falling labor force participation rate of adult men.

The labor force participation rate of adult males has fallen from 89 percent in 1948 to 76 percent in 2006. Most of this decline is due to older men retiring earlier and younger men remaining in school longer. There has also been a decline in labor force participation among males who are not in school but who are too young to retire.

Figure 8-2

Trends in the Labor Force Participation Rates of Adult Men and Women Since 1948

The labor force participation rate of adult men has declined gradually since 1948, but the labor force participation rate of adult women has increased significantly, leaving the overall labor force participation rate higher today than it was in 1948.

Source: U.S. Bureau of Labor Statistics.

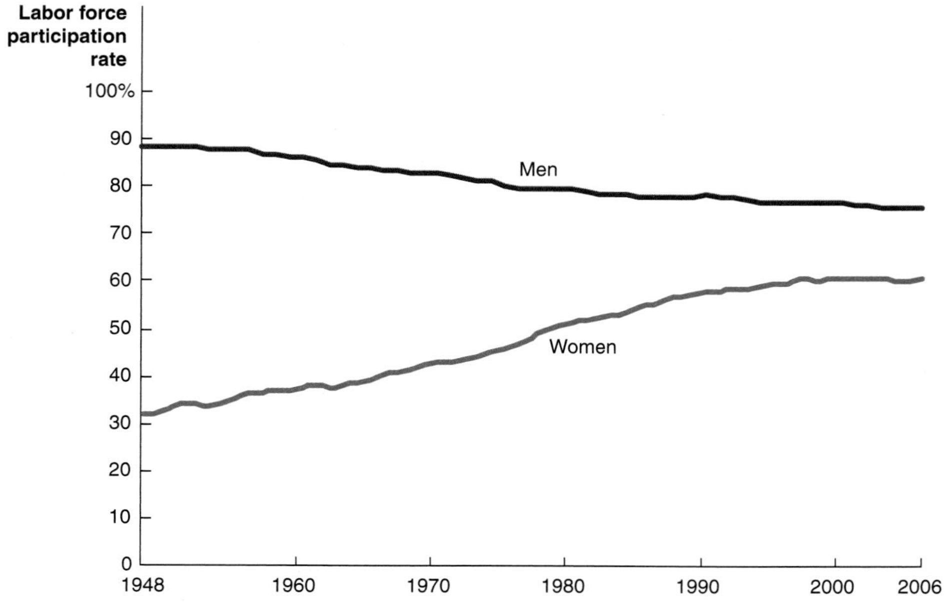

Making the Connection

What Explains the Increase in "Kramers"?

Cosmo Kramer is the name of Jerry Seinfeld's next-door neighbor on the popular television comedy *Seinfeld.* One of the running jokes on the program is Kramer's ability to support himself without apparently ever holding a job. In recent years, there has been an increase in the number of men who seem to be following Kramer's lifestyle. In 1967, only 2.2 percent of men between the ages of 25 and 54 who were not in school did no paid work at all during the year. By 2006, 9.4 percent of men in this age category did not work. The rate of nonworking men is even higher among some groups. For example, about 20 percent of men aged 25 to 54 who lack a high school degree do not have a job and are not looking for one.

Why do more men seem to be adopting Kramer's lifestyle?

More than half of nonworking men receive Social Security Disability Insurance. Under this program, people with disabilities receive cash payments from the federal government and receive medical benefits under the Medicaid program. In 1984, Congress passed legislation that made it easier for people with disabilities that are difficult to verify medically, such as back injuries or mental illnesses, to qualify for disability payments. In addition, the value of disability payments has increased faster than the wages of low-skilled workers. The result is that some men who in the past might have been working or actively looking for work are now being supported by disability payments and are not in the labor force.

An increasing share of nonworking men, however, are not disabled. How do nonworking men who do not receive disability payments support themselves, and how do they spend their time? Most nonworking men live with their parents, wives, or other relatives. Many of these men appear to rely on these other household members for food, clothing, and money. A recent study by Jay Stewart of the Bureau of Labor Statistics shows that most nonworking men are not substituting nonmarket work—such as childcare or housework—for market work. Instead, nonworking men engage in leisure activities, such as sports, watching television, or sleeping during the hours freed up by not working. Stewart concludes that "the average day of a nonworking man looks very much like the average day-off of a man who works full time."

Sources: Alan Krueger, "A Growing Number of Men Are Not Working, So What Are They Doing?" *New York Times*, April 29, 2004, p. C2; and Jay Stewart, "Male Nonworkers: Who Are They and Who Supports Them?" *Demography*, Vol. 43, No. 3, August 2006, pp. 537–552.

YOUR TURN: Test your understanding by doing related problem 1.9 on page 269 at the end of this chapter.

The decline in labor force participation among adult men has been more than offset by a sharp increase in the labor force participation rate for adult women, which rose from 32 percent in 1948 to 61 percent in 2006. As a result, the overall labor force participation rate for adult workers rose from 59 percent in 1948 to 68 percent in 2006. The increase in the labor force participation rate for women has several causes, including changing social attitudes due in part to the women's movement, federal legislation outlawing discrimination, increasing wages for women, and the typical family having fewer children.

Unemployment Rates for Demographic Groups

Different groups in the population can have very different unemployment rates. Figure 8-3 shows unemployment rates for different demographic groups in April 2007, when the unemployment rate for the entire population was 4.5 percent. White adults had an unemployment rate of 3.5 percent. The unemployment rate for black adults was 7.1 percent, or more than twice the rate for white adults. Teenagers have higher unemployment rates than adults. The black teenage unemployment rate of 30.6 percent was the highest for the groups shown.

How Long Are People Usually Unemployed?

The longer a person is unemployed, the greater the hardship. During the Great Depression of the 1930s, some people were unemployed for years at a time. In the modern U.S. economy, the typical unemployed person stays unemployed for a relatively brief period of time. Table 8-1 shows for April 2007 the percentage of the unemployed who had been unemployed for a given period of time. Eighty-two percent of the people

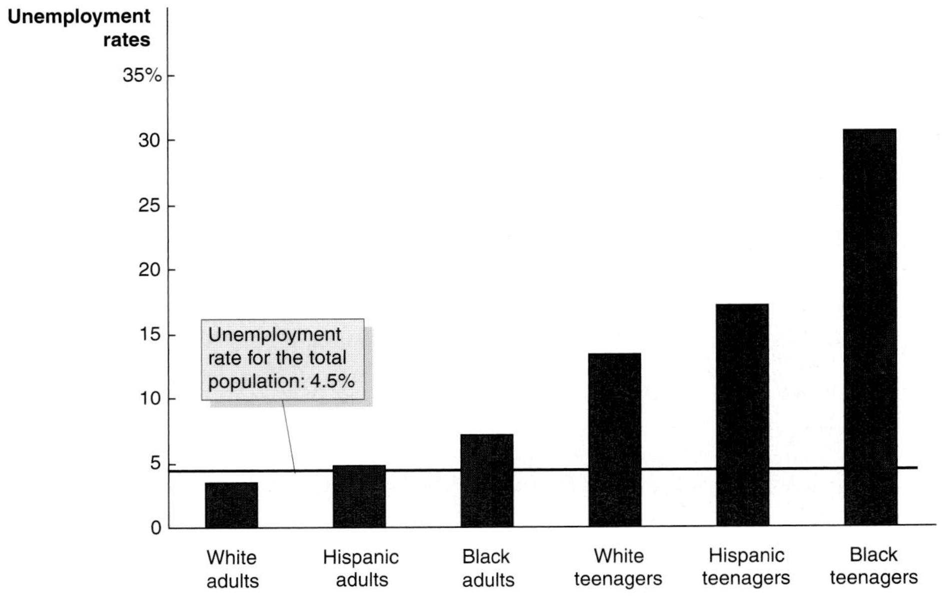

Figure 8-3

Unemployment Rates in the United States by Demographic Group, April 2007

The unemployment rate of black adults is more than twice that of white adults, and the unemployment rate of black teenagers is more than twice that of white teenagers. The adult unemployment rates apply to persons aged 20 and over who are in the labor force. The teenage unemployment rates apply to persons aged 16 to 19 who are in the labor force.
Note: People identified as Hispanic may be of any race.
Source: U.S. Department of Labor, *Employment Situation Summary*, April 2007.

TABLE 8-1

Duration of Unemployment

LENGTH OF TIME UNEMPLOYED	PERCENTAGE OF TOTAL UNEMPLOYED
Less than 5 weeks	35.6%
5 to 14 weeks	31.3
15 to 26 weeks	15.7
27 weeks or more	17.5

Source: U.S. Department of Labor, *Employment Situation Summary*, April 2007.

unemployed in that month had been unemployed for less than six months. Half had been unemployed for nine weeks or less. The important conclusion is that, *except in severe recessions, the typical person who loses a job finds another one or is recalled to a previous job within a few months.*

The Establishment Survey: Another Measure of Employment

In addition to the household survey, the BLS uses the *establishment survey*, sometimes called the *payroll survey*, to measure total employment in the economy. This monthly survey samples about 300,000 business establishments. An establishment is a factory, a store, or an office. A small company typically operates only one establishment, but large companies may operate many establishments. The establishment survey provides information on the total number of persons who are employed *and on a company payroll.* The establishment survey has three drawbacks. First, the survey does not provide information on the number of self-employed persons because they are not on a company payroll. Second, the survey may fail to count some persons employed at newly opened firms that are not included in the survey. Third, the survey provides no information on unemployment. Despite these drawbacks, the establishment survey has the advantage of being determined by actual payrolls rather than by unverified answers, as is the case with the household survey. In recent years, some economists have come to rely more on establishment survey data than on household survey data in analyzing current labor market conditions. Some financial analysts who forecast the future state of the economy to help forecast stock prices have also begun to rely more on establishment survey data than on household survey data.

Table 8-2 shows household survey and establishment survey data for the months of March and April 2007. Notice that the household survey, because it includes the self-

TABLE 8-2 | Household and Establishment Survey Data for March and April 2007

	HOUSEHOLD SURVEY			ESTABLISHMENT SURVEY		
	MARCH	APRIL	CHANGE	MARCH	APRIL	CHANGE
EMPLOYED	146,254,000	145,786,000	–468,000	137,596,000	137,684,000	+88,000
UNEMPLOYED	6,724,000	6,801,000	+77,000			
LABOR FORCE	152,979,000	152,587,000	–392,000			
UNEMPLOYMENT RATE	4.4%	4.5%	+0.1%			

Source: U.S. Department of Labor, *Employment Situation Summary*, April 2007.

Note: The sum of employed and unemployed may not equal the labor force due to rounding.

employed, gives a larger total for employment than does the establishment survey. The household survey provides information on the number of persons unemployed and on the number of persons in the labor force. This information is not available in the establishment survey. In the household survey, employment fell by 468,000 between March and April 2007, while it actually rose by 88,000 in the establishment survey. This discrepancy is partly due to the slightly different groups covered by the two surveys and partly to inaccuracies in the surveys.

Job Creation and Job Destruction Over Time

One important fact about employment is not very well known: The U.S. economy creates and destroys millions of jobs every year. In 2005, for example, about 31.4 million jobs were created, and about 29.4 million jobs were destroyed. This degree of job creation and destruction is not surprising in a vibrant market system where new firms are constantly being started, some existing firms are expanding, some existing firms are contracting, and some firms are going out of business. The creation and destruction of jobs results from changes in consumer tastes, technological progress, and the success and failures of entrepreneurs in responding to the opportunities and challenges of shifting consumer tastes and technological change. The volume of job creation and job destruction helps explain why the typical person who loses a job is unemployed for a relatively brief period of time.

When the BLS announces each month the increases or decreases in the number of persons employed and unemployed, these are net *figures.* That is, the change in the number of persons employed is equal to the total number of jobs created minus the number of jobs eliminated. Take, for example, the months from April to June 2006. During that period, 7,761,000 jobs were created, and 7,295,000 were eliminated, for a net increase of 466,000 jobs. Because the net change is so much smaller than the total job increases and decreases, the net change gives a misleading indication of how dynamic the U.S. job market really is.

The data in Table 8-3 reinforce the idea of how large the volume of job creation and job elimination is over a period as brief as three months. The table shows the number of establishments creating and eliminating jobs during the period from April through June 2006. During these three months, 13 percent of all private sector jobs were either created or destroyed. Fifty-six percent of establishments either eliminated jobs or added new jobs. About 360,000 new establishments opened, creating 1.48 million new jobs, and 341,000 establishments closed, eliminating 1.36 million jobs.

TABLE 8-3

Establishments Creating and Eliminating Jobs, April–June 2006

	NUMBER OF ESTABLISHMENTS	NUMBER OF JOBS
ESTABLISHMENTS CREATING JOBS		
Existing establishments	1,558,000	6,286,000
New establishments	360,000	1,475,000
ESTABLISHMENTS ELIMINATING JOBS		
Existing establishments	1,543,000	5,937,000
Closing establishments	341,000	1,358,000

Source: U.S. Bureau of Labor Statistics, *Business Employment Dynamics: Second Quarter 2006*, February 14, 2007.

8.2 LEARNING OBJECTIVE

8.2 | Identify the three types of unemployment.

Types of Unemployment

Figure 8-4 illustrates that the unemployment rate follows the business cycle, rising during recessions and falling during expansions. Notice, though, that the unemployment rate never falls to zero. To understand why this is true, we need to discuss the three types of unemployment:

- Frictional unemployment
- Structural unemployment
- Cyclical unemployment

Frictional Unemployment and Job Search

Frictional unemployment Short-term unemployment that arises from the process of matching workers with jobs.

Workers have different skills, interests, and abilities, and jobs have different skill requirements, working conditions, and pay levels. As a result, a new worker entering the labor force or a worker who has lost a job probably will not find an acceptable job right away. Most workers spend at least some time engaging in *job search*, just as most firms spend time searching for a new person to fill a job opening. **Frictional unemployment** is short-term unemployment that arises from the process of matching workers with jobs. Some frictional unemployment is unavoidable. As we have seen, the U.S. economy creates and destroys millions of jobs each year. The process of job search takes time, so there will always be some workers who are frictionally unemployed because they are between jobs and in the process of searching for new ones.

Some unemployment is due to seasonal factors, such as weather or fluctuations in demand for some products or services during different times of the year. For example, stores located in beach resort areas reduce their hiring during the winter, and ski resorts reduce their hiring during the summer. Department stores increase their hiring in November and December and reduce their hiring after New Year's Day. In agricultural areas, employment increases during harvest season and declines thereafter. Construction workers experience greater unemployment during the winter than during the summer. *Seasonal unemployment* refers to unemployment due to factors such as weather, variations in tourism, and other calendar-related events. Because seasonal unemployment can make the unemployment rate seem artificially high during some months and artificially low during other months, the BLS reports two unemployment

Figure 8-4

The Annual Unemployment Rate in the United States, 1950–2006

The unemployment rate rises during recessions and falls during expansion. Shaded areas indicate recessions.

Source: U.S. Bureau of Labor Statistics.

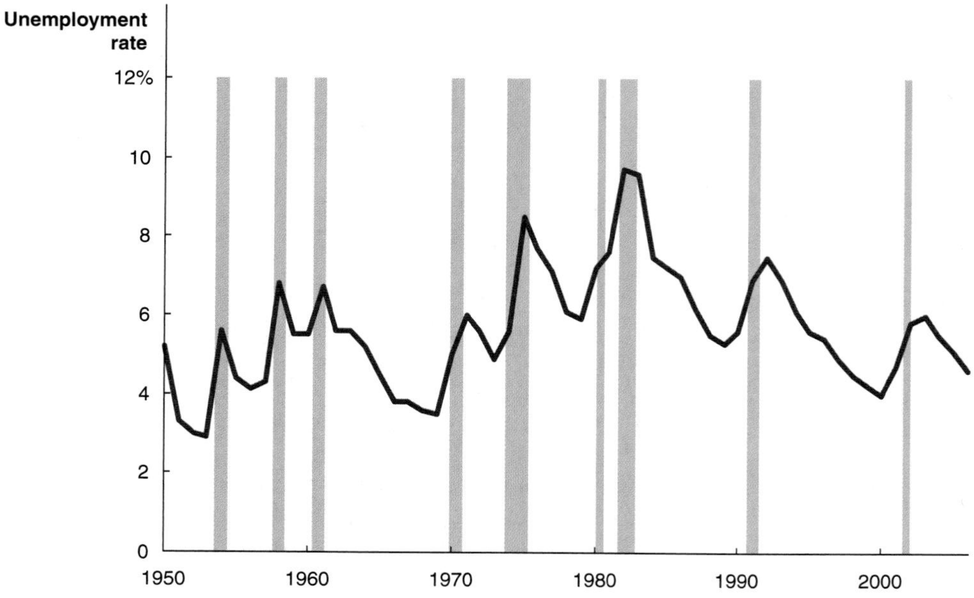

rates each month—one that is *seasonally adjusted* and one that is not seasonally adjusted. The seasonally adjusted data eliminate the effects of seasonal unemployment. Economists and policymakers rely on the seasonally adjusted data as a more accurate measure of the current state of the labor market.

Would eliminating all frictional unemployment be good for the economy? No, because some frictional unemployment actually increases economic efficiency. Frictional unemployment occurs because workers and firms take the time necessary to ensure a good match between the attributes of workers and the characteristics of jobs. By devoting time to job search, workers end up with jobs they find satisfying and in which they can be productive. Of course, having more productive and better-satisfied workers is also in the best interest of firms.

Structural Unemployment

By 2007, computer-generated three-dimensional animation, which was used in movies such as *Shrek* and *Ratatouille*, had become much more popular than traditional hand-drawn two-dimensional animation. Many people who were highly skilled in hand-drawn animation lost their jobs at Walt Disney Pictures, Dreamworks, and other movie studios. To become employed again, many of these people either became skilled in computer-generated animation or found new occupations. In the meantime, they were unemployed. Economists consider these animators *structurally unemployed.* **Structural unemployment** arises from a persistent mismatch between the job skills or attributes of workers and the requirements of jobs. While frictional unemployment is short term, structural unemployment can last for longer periods because workers need time to learn new skills. For example, employment by U.S. steel firms dropped by more than half between the early 1980s and the early 2000s as a result of competition from foreign producers and technological change that substituted machines for workers. Many steel-workers found new jobs in other industries only after lengthy periods of retraining.

Structural unemployment Unemployment arising from a persistent mismatch between the skills and characteristics of workers and the requirements of jobs.

Some workers lack even basic skills, such as literacy, or have addictions to drugs or alcohol that make it difficult for them to perform adequately the duties of almost any job. These workers may remain structurally unemployed for years.

Cyclical Unemployment

When the economy moves into recession, many firms find their sales falling and cut back on production. As production falls, they start laying off workers. Workers who lose their jobs because of a recession are experiencing **cyclical unemployment**. For example, Freightliner, which is the leading manufacturer of trucks and other commercial vehicles in North America, laid off workers from its heavy truck plants during the recession of 2001. As the economy recovered from the recession, Freightliner began rehiring those workers. The Freightliner workers had experienced cyclical unemployment.

Cyclical unemployment Unemployment caused by a business cycle recession.

Full Employment

As the economy moves through the expansion phase of the business cycle, cyclical unemployment will eventually drop to zero. The unemployment rate will not be zero, however, because of frictional and structural unemployment. As Figure 8-4 shows, the unemployment rate in the United States is rarely below 4 percent. When the only remaining unemployment is structural and frictional unemployment, the economy is said to be at *full employment.*

Economists consider frictional and structural unemployment as the normal underlying level of unemployment in the economy. The fluctuations around this normal level of unemployment, which we see in Figure 8-4, are mainly due to the changes in the level of cyclical unemployment. This normal level of unemployment, which is the sum of frictional and structural unemployment, is referred to as the **natural rate of unemployment**. Economists disagree on the exact value of the natural rate of unemployment, and there is good reason to believe it varies over time. Currently, most economists estimate the natural rate to be about 5 percent. The natural rate of unemployment is also sometimes called the *full-employment rate of unemployment.*

Natural rate of unemployment The normal rate of unemployment, consisting of frictional unemployment plus structural unemployment.

Making the Connection

How Should We Categorize the Unemployment at Alcatel-Lucent?

We saw at the beginning of this chapter that the technology firm Alcatel-Lucent has experienced sharp declines in employment over the past few years. Was the unemployment caused by the layoffs at Alcatel-Lucent frictional unemployment, structural unemployment, or cyclical unemployment? In answering this question, we should acknowledge that categorizing unemployment as frictional, structural, or cyclical is useful in understanding the sources of unemployment, but it can be difficult to apply these categories in a particular case. The Bureau of Labor Statistics, for instance, provides estimates of total unemployment but does not classify it as frictional, structural, or cyclical.

The people who lost their jobs at Alcatel-Lucent fit into more than one category of unemployment.

Despite these difficulties, we can roughly categorize the unemployment at Alcatel-Lucent. We begin by considering the three basic reasons the layoffs occurred: the long-lived decline in some of the telecommunications products Alcatel-Lucent sells; the recession of 2001 that reduced the demand for the firm's products; and the failure of the firm's managers to compete successfully against other firms in the industry. Each reason corresponds to a category of unemployment. Because the demand for the telecommunications products Alcatel-Lucent sells—particularly products used with fiber-optic cable networks—declined for a significant period, employment at Lucent and competing firms also declined. Between late 2000 and mid-2002, employment in the telecommunications industry declined by more than 500,000. Certain categories of employees, such as optical engineers, had difficulty finding new jobs. They were structurally unemployed because they were not able to find new jobs without learning new skills. Some of the decline in Alcatel-Lucent's sales was due to the 2001 recession rather than to long-term problems in the telecommunications industry. So, some of the workers who lost their jobs during that period were cyclically unemployed. Finally, in 2006, Alcatel-Lucent had difficulty competing with other communications-technology firms and as a result experienced declining sales, which led to further layoffs. Some workers who lost their jobs at Alcatel-Lucent were able to find new jobs at the firm's competitors after relatively brief job searches. These workers were frictionally unemployed.

YOUR TURN: Test your understanding by doing related problem 2.4 on page 269 at the end of this chapter.

8.3 LEARNING OBJECTIVE

8.3 | Explain what factors determine the unemployment rate.

Explaining Unemployment

We have seen that some unemployment is caused by the business cycle. In later chapters, we will explore the causes of the business cycle, which will help us understand the causes of cyclical unemployment. In this section, we will look at what determines the levels of frictional and structural unemployment.

Government Policies and the Unemployment Rate

Workers search for jobs by sending out resumes, registering with Internet job sites such as Monster.com, and getting job referrals from friends and relatives. Firms fill job openings by advertising in newspapers, participating in job fairs, and recruiting on college campuses. Government policy can aid these private efforts. Governments can help reduce the level of frictional unemployment by pursuing policies that help speed up the process of matching unemployed workers with unfilled jobs. Governments can help reduce structural unemployment through policies that aid the retraining of workers. For example, the federal government's Trade Adjustment Assistance program offers training to workers whose firms laid them off as a result of competition from foreign firms.

Some government policies, however, can add to the level of frictional and structural unemployment. These government policies increase the unemployment rate either by increasing the time workers devote to searching for jobs, by providing disincentives to firms to hire workers, or by keeping wages above their market level.

Unemployment Insurance and Other Payments to the Unemployed Suppose you have been in the labor force for a few years but have just lost your job. You could probably find a low-wage job immediately if you needed to—perhaps at Wal-Mart or McDonald's. But you might decide to search for a better, higher-paying job by sending out resumes and responding to want ads and Internet job postings. Remember from Chapter 1 that the *opportunity cost* of any activity is the highest-valued alternative that you must give up to engage in that activity. In this case, the opportunity cost of continuing to search for a job is the salary you are giving up at the job you could have taken. The longer you search, the greater your chances of finding a better, higher-paying job, but the longer you search, the greater the opportunity cost of the salary you are giving up by not working.

In the United States and most other industrial countries, the unemployed are eligible for *unemployment insurance payments* from the government. In the United States, these payments are equal to about half the average wage. The unemployed spend more time searching for jobs because they receive these payments. This additional time spent searching raises the unemployment rate. Does this mean that the unemployment insurance program is a bad idea? Most economists would say no. Before Congress established the unemployment insurance program at the end of the 1930s, unemployed workers suffered very large declines in their incomes, which led them to greatly reduce their spending. This reduced spending contributed to the severity of recessions. Unemployment insurance helps the unemployed maintain their income and spending, which lessens the personal hardship of being unemployed and also helps reduce the severity of recessions.

International Comparisons In the United States, unemployed workers are typically eligible to receive unemployment insurance payments equal to about half their previous wage for only six months. After that, the opportunity cost of continuing to search for a job rises. In many other high-income countries, such as Canada and most of the countries of Western Europe, workers are eligible to receive unemployment payments for a year or more, and the payments may equal 70 percent to 80 percent of their previous wage. In addition, many of these countries have generous *social insurance programs* that allow unemployed adults to receive some government payments even after their eligibility for unemployment insurance has ended. In the United States, very few government programs make payments to healthy adults, with the exception of the Temporary Assistance for Needy Families program, which allows single parents to receive payments for up to five years. Although there are many reasons unemployment rates may differ across countries, most economists believe that because the opportunity cost of job search is lower in Canada and Western Europe, unemployed workers in those countries search longer for jobs and, therefore, the unemployment rates in those countries tend to be higher than in the United States.

Figure 8-5 shows the average yearly unemployment rate for the 10-year period from 1997 to 2006 for the United States, Canada, Japan, and several Western European countries. The United States and Japan provide unemployment insurance payments for only a short period of time, and their average unemployment rate during these years was lower than for the other countries shown. Many European countries also have laws that make it difficult for companies to fire workers. These laws create a disincentive for firms to hire workers, which also contributes to a higher unemployment rate.

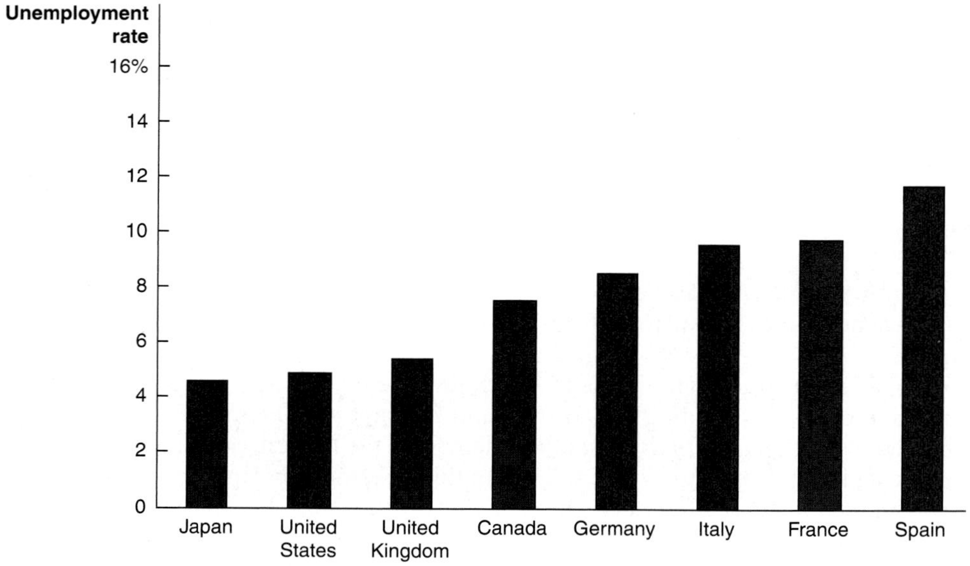

Figure 8-5 | Average Unemployment Rates in the United States, Canada, Japan, and Europe, 1997–2006

The unemployment rate in the United States is usually lower than the unemployment rates in most other high-income countries, partly because the United States has tougher requirements for the unemployed to receive government payments. These requirements raise the costs of searching for a better job and lower the unemployment rate.
Source: Organization for Economic Cooperation and Development.

Minimum Wage Laws In 1938, the federal government enacted a national minimum wage law. At first, the lowest legal wage firms could pay workers was \$0.25 per hour. Over the years, Congress gradually has raised the minimum wage; by 2009, it will reach \$7.25 per hour. Some states and cities also have minimum wage laws. For example, in 2008, California set its minimum wage at \$8.00 per hour, and the minimum wage in San Francisco in 2007 was \$9.14 per hour. If the minimum wage is set above the market wage determined by the demand and supply of labor, the quantity of labor supplied will be greater than the quantity of labor demanded. Some workers will be unemployed who would have been employed if there were no minimum wage. As a result, the unemployment rate will be higher than it would be without a minimum wage. Economists agree that the current minimum wage is above the market wage for some workers, but they disagree on the amount of unemployment that has resulted. Because teenagers generally have relatively few job-related skills, they are the group most likely to receive the minimum wage. Studies estimate that a 10 percent increase in the minimum wage reduces teenage employment by about 2 percent. Because teenagers and others receiving the minimum wage are a relatively small part of the labor force, most economists believe that, at its present level, the effect of the minimum wage on the unemployment rate in the United States is fairly small.

Labor Unions

Labor unions are organizations of workers that bargain with employers for higher wages and better working conditions for their members. In unionized industries, the wage is usually above what otherwise would be the market wage. This above-market wage results in employers in unionized industries hiring fewer workers, but does it also increase the overall unemployment rate in the economy? Most economists would say the answer is "no" because only about 9 percent of workers outside the government sector are unionized. Although unions remain strong in a few industries, such as airlines, automobiles, steel, and telecommunications, most industries in the United States are not unionized. The result is that workers who can't find jobs in unionized industries because the wage is above its market level can find jobs in other industries.

Efficiency Wages

Many firms pay higher-than-market wages, not because the government requires them to or because they are unionized, but because they believe doing so will increase their profits. This link may seem like a paradox. Wages are the largest cost for many employers, so paying higher wages seems like a good way for firms to lower profits rather than to increase them. The key to understanding the paradox is that the level of wages can affect the level of worker productivity. Many studies have shown that workers are motivated to work harder by higher wages. An **efficiency wage** is a higher-than-market wage that a firm pays to motivate workers to be more productive. Can't firms ensure that workers work hard by supervising them? In some cases, they can. For example, a telemarketing firm can monitor workers electronically to ensure that they make the required number of phone calls per hour. In many business situations, however, it is much more difficult to monitor workers. Many firms must rely on workers being motivated enough to work hard. In fact, the following is the key to the efficiency wage: By paying a wage above the market wage, a firm raises the costs to workers of losing their jobs because most alternative jobs will pay only the market wage. The increase in productivity that results from paying the high wage can more than offset the cost of the wage, thereby lowering the firm's costs of production.

Efficiency wage A higher-than-market wage that a firm pays to increase worker productivity.

Because the efficiency wage is above the market wage, it results in the quantity of labor supplied being greater than the quantity of labor demanded, just as do minimum wage laws and unions. So, efficiency wages are another reason economies experience some unemployment even when cyclical unemployment is zero.

Making the Connection

Why Does Costco Pay Its Workers So Much More Than Wal-Mart Does?

The concept of efficiency wages raises the possibility that firms might find it more profitable to pay higher wages even when it is possible to pay lower wages. We might expect that a firm would maximize profits by paying the lowest wages at which it was able to attract the number of workers needed. But if low wages significantly reduce worker productivity, then paying higher wages might actually reduce costs and increase profits. Wal-Mart and Costco are competitors in the discount department store industry, but the two companies have taken different approaches to compensating their workers.

Costco's relatively high wages and health benefits reduce employee turnover and raise morale and productivity.

Wal-Mart employs more than 1.3 million workers in the United States, more than three times as many as McDonald's, which is the second largest employer. Becoming a sales associate at Wal-Mart is one way to begin a career in retailing that may ultimately lead to a high-paying job. About three-quarters of Wal-Mart's store managers started as hourly workers. But Wal-Mart's hourly workers receive relatively low wages. In 2007, Wal-Mart paid its hourly workers on average about \$10.50 per hour. In contrast, the lowest wage that Wal-Mart's rival Costco pays is about \$11 per hour, and the average wage is about \$17 per hour. Costco's benefits also are more generous, with about 90 percent of its employees covered by medical insurance, as opposed to about 50 percent at Wal-Mart.

Why does Costco pay wages so much higher than Wal-Mart pays? Costco's chief executive officer, Jim Sinegal, argues that paying high wages reduces employee turnover and raises morale and productivity: "Paying good wages and keeping your people working for you is very good business. . . . Imagine that you have 120,000 loyal ambassadors out there who are constantly saying good things about Costco. It has to be a significant advantage for you." But it is likely that not all the difference between the wages Costco pays and the wages Wal-Mart pays is due to Costco's employing a strategy of paying efficiency wages. Unlike Wal-Mart, Costco charges a fee of at least $45 per year to shop in its stores. The typical Costco store stocks only about 4,000 items as opposed to the 100,000 items that the average Wal-Mart store stocks. Costco stores also stock more high-priced items, such as jewelry and consumer electronics. As a result, the average income of Costco customers is about $74,000, more than twice as high as the average income of Wal-Mart customers. One observer concludes that Costco pays higher wages than Wal-Mart "because it requires higher-skilled workers to sell higher-end products to its more affluent customers." So, even if Costco were not pursuing a strategy of paying efficiency wages, it is likely it would still have to pay higher wages than Wal-Mart does.

Sources: Alan B. Goldberg and Bill Ritter, "Costco CEO Finds Pro-Worker Means Profitability," ABCNews.com, August 2, 2006; Lori Montgomery, "Maverick CEO Joins Push to Raise Minimum Wage," *Washington Post*, January 30, 2007; and John Tierney, "The Good Goliath," *New York Times*, November 29, 2005.

YOUR TURN: Test your understanding by doing related problem 3.7 on page 270 at the end of this chapter.

8.4 LEARNING OBJECTIVE

8.4 | Define price level and inflation rate and understand how they are computed.

Measuring Inflation

One of the facts of economic life is that the prices of most goods and services rise over time. As a result, the cost of living continually rises. In 1914, Henry Ford began paying his workers a wage of $5 per day, which was more than twice as much as other automobile manufacturers. Ford's $5-a-day wage provided his workers with a middle class income because prices were so low. In 1914, Ford's Model T, the best-selling car in the country, sold for less than $600, the price of a man's suit was $15, the price of a ticket to a movie theater was $0.15, and the price of a box of Kellogg's Corn Flakes was $0.08. In 2009, with the cost of living being much higher than it was in 1914, the minimum wage law will require firms to pay a wage of at least $7.25 per *hour*, more than Ford's highly paid workers earned in a day.

Price level A measure of the average prices of goods and services in the economy.

Inflation rate The percentage increase in the price level from one year to the next.

Knowledge of how the government's employment and unemployment statistics are compiled is important in interpreting them. The same is true of the government's statistics on the cost of living. As we saw in Chapter 7, the **price level** measures the average prices of goods and services in the economy. The **inflation rate** is the percentage increase in the price level from one year to the next. In Chapter 7, we introduced the *GDP deflator* as a measure of the price level. The GDP deflator is the broadest measure we have of the price level because it includes the price of every final good and service. But, for some purposes, it is too broad. For example, if we want to know the impact of inflation on the typical household, the GDP price deflator may be misleading because it includes the prices of products such as large electric generators and machine tools that are included in the investment component of GDP but are not purchased by the typical household. In this chapter, we will focus on measuring the inflation rate by changes in the *consumer price index* because changes in this index come closest to measuring changes in the cost of living as experienced by the typical household. We will also briefly discuss a third measure of inflation: the *producer price index.*

The Consumer Price Index

To obtain prices of a representative group of goods and services, the BLS surveys 30,000 households nationwide on their spending habits. It uses the results of this survey to construct a *market basket* of 211 types of goods and services purchased by the typical urban

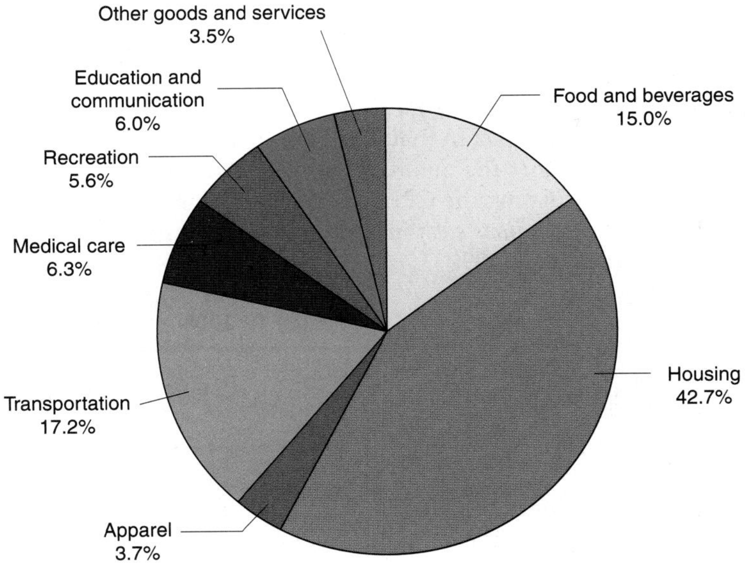

Figure 8-6 | The CPI Market Basket, December 2006

The Bureau of Labor Statistics surveys 30,000 households on their spending habits. The results are used to construct a *market basket* of goods and services purchased by the typical urban family of four. The chart shows these goods and services, grouped into eight broad categories. The percentages represent the expenditure shares of the categories within the market basket. The categories housing, transportation, and food make up about three-quarters of the market basket.
Source: Bureau of Labor Statistics.

family of four. Figure 8-6 shows the goods and services in the market basket, grouped into eight broad categories. Almost three-quarters of the market basket falls into the categories of housing, transportation, and food. Each month, hundreds of BLS employees visit 23,000 stores in 87 cities and record prices of the goods and services in the market basket. Each price in the consumer price index is given a weight equal to the fraction of the typical family's budget spent on that good or service. The **consumer price index (CPI)** is an average of the prices of the goods and services purchased by the typical urban family of four. One year is chosen as the base year, and the value of the CPI is set equal to 100 for that year. In any year other than the base year, the CPI is equal to the ratio of the dollar amount necessary to buy the market basket of goods in that year divided by the dollar amount necessary to buy the market basket of goods in the base year, multiplied by 100. Because the CPI measures the cost to the typical family to buy a representative basket of goods and services, it is sometimes referred to as the *cost-of-living index*.

Consumer price index (CPI) An average of the prices of the goods and services purchased by the typical urban family of four.

A simple example can clarify how the CPI is constructed. For purposes of this example, we assume that the market basket has only three products: eye examinations, pizzas, and books:

	BASE YEAR (1999)			2008		2009	
PRODUCT	QUANTITY	PRICE	EXPENDITURES	PRICE	EXPENDITURES (ON BASE-YEAR QUANTITIES)	PRICE	EXPENDITURES (ON BASE-YEAR QUANTITIES)
Eye examinations	1	$50.00	$50.00	$100.00	$100.00	$85.00	$85.00
Pizzas	20	10.00	200.00	15.00	300.00	14.00	280.00
Books	20	25.00	500.00	25.00	500.00	27.50	550.00
Total			$750.00		$900.00		$915.00

Suppose that during the base year of 1999, a survey determines that each month, the typical family purchases 1 eye examination, 20 pizzas, and 20 books. At 1999 prices, the typical family must spend $750.00 to purchase this market basket of goods and services. The CPI for every year after the base year is determined by dividing the amount necessary to purchase the market basket in that year by the amount required in the base year, multiplied by 100. Notice that the quantities of the products purchased in 2008 and 2009 are irrelevant in calculating the CPI because *we are assuming that households buy the same market basket of products each month.* Using the numbers in the table, we can calculate the CPI for 2008 and 2009:

FORMULA	APPLIED TO 2008	APPLIED TO 2009
$\text{CPI} = \frac{\text{Expenditures in the current year}}{\text{Expenditures in the base year}} \times 100$	$\left(\frac{\$900}{\$750}\right) \times 100 = 120$	$\left(\frac{\$915}{\$750}\right) \times 100 = 122$

How do we interpret values such as 120 and 122? The first thing to recognize is that they are *index numbers*, which means they are not measured in dollars or any other units. *The CPI is intended to measure changes in the price level over time.* We can't use the CPI to tell us in an absolute sense how high the price level is, only how much it has changed over time. We measure the inflation rate as the percentage increase in the CPI from one year to the next. For our simple example, the inflation rate in 2009 would be the percentage change in the CPI from 2008 to 2009:

$$\left(\frac{122 - 120}{120}\right) \times 100 = 1.7\%.$$

Because the CPI is designed to measure the cost of living, we can also say that the cost of living increased by 1.7 percent during 2009.

Is the CPI Accurate?

The CPI is the most widely used measure of inflation. Policymakers use the CPI to track the state of the economy. Businesses use it to help set the prices of their products and the wages and salaries of their employees. Each year, the federal government increases the

Don't Let This Happen to **YOU!**

Don't Miscalculate the Inflation Rate

Suppose you are given the data in the following table and are asked to calculate the inflation rate for 2006.

YEAR	CPI
2005	195
2006	202

It is tempting to avoid any calculations and simply to report that the inflation rate in 2006 was 102 percent because 202 is a 102 percent increase from 100. But 102 percent would be the wrong answer. A value for the CPI of 202 in 2006 tells us that the price level in 2006 was 102 percent higher than in the base year, but the inflation rate is the percentage increase in the price level from the previous year, *not* the percentage increase from the base year. The correct calculation of the inflation rate for 2006 is:

$$\left(\frac{202 - 195}{195}\right) \times 100 = 3.6\%.$$

YOUR TURN: Test your understanding by doing related problem 4.3 on page 271 at the end of this chapter.

Social Security payments made to retired workers by a percentage equal to the increase in the CPI during the previous year. In setting alimony and child support payments in divorce cases, judges often order that the payments increase each year by the inflation rate, as measured by the CPI.

It is important that the CPI be as accurate as possible, but there are four biases that make changes in the CPI overstate the true inflation rate:

- ***Substitution bias.*** In constructing the CPI, the BLS assumes that each month, consumers purchase the same amount of each product in the market basket. In fact, consumers are likely to buy fewer of those products that increase most in price and more of those products that increase least in price (or fall the most in price). For instance, if apple prices rise rapidly during the month while orange prices fall, consumers will reduce their apple purchases and increase their orange purchases. Therefore, the prices of the market basket consumers actually buy will rise less than the prices of the market basket the BLS uses to compute the CPI.
- ***Increase in quality bias.*** Over time, most products included in the CPI improve in quality: Automobiles become more durable and side air bags become standard equipment, computers become faster and have more memory, dishwashers use less water while getting dishes cleaner, and so on. Increases in the prices of these products partly reflect their improved quality and partly are pure inflation. The BLS attempts to make adjustments so that only the pure inflation part of price increases is included in the CPI. These adjustments are difficult to make, so the recorded price increases overstate the pure inflation in some products.
- ***New product bias.*** For many years, the BLS updated the market basket of goods used in computing the CPI only every 10 years. That meant that new products introduced between updates were not included in the market basket. For example, the 1987 update took place before cell phones were introduced. Although millions of American households used cell phones by the mid-1990s, they were not included in the CPI until the 1997 update. The prices of many products, such as cell phones, HD-DVD players, and computers, decrease in the years immediately after they are introduced. If the market basket is not updated frequently, these price decreases are not included in the CPI.
- ***Outlet bias.*** During the mid-1990s, many consumers began to increase their purchases from discount stores such as Sam's Club. By the late 1990s, the Internet began to account for a significant fraction of sales of some products. Because the BLS continued to collect price statistics from traditional full-price retail stores, the CPI was not reflecting the prices some consumers actually paid.

Most economists believe these biases cause changes in the CPI to overstate the true inflation rate by one-half of a percentage point to one percentage point. That is, if the CPI indicates that the inflation rate was 3 percent, it is probably between 2 percent and 2.5 percent. The BLS continues to take steps to reduce the size of the bias. For example, the BLS has reduced the size of the substitution and new product biases by updating the market basket every 2 years rather than every 10 years. The BLS has reduced the size of the outlet bias by conducting a point-of-purchase survey to track where consumers actually make their purchases. Finally, the BLS has used statistical methods to reduce the size of the quality bias. Prior to these changes, the size of the total bias in the CPI was probably greater than 1 percent.

The Producer Price Index

In addition to the GDP deflator and the CPI, the government also computes the **producer price index (PPI)**. Like the CPI, the PPI tracks the prices of a market basket of goods. But, whereas the CPI tracks the prices of goods and services purchased by the typical household, the PPI tracks the prices firms receive for goods and services at all

Producer price index (PPI) An average of the prices received by producers of goods and services at all stages of the production process.

stages of production. The PPI includes the prices of intermediate goods, such as flour, cotton, yarn, steel, and lumber, and raw materials, such as raw cotton, coal, and crude petroleum. If the prices of these goods rise, the cost to firms of producing final goods and services will rise, which may lead firms to increase the prices of goods and services purchased by consumers. Changes in the PPI therefore can give an early warning of future movements in the CPI.

8.5 LEARNING OBJECTIVE

8.5 | Use price indexes to adjust for the effects of inflation.

Using Price Indexes to Adjust for the Effects of Inflation

The typical college student today is likely to receive a much higher salary than the student's parents did 25 or more years ago, but prices 25 years ago were, on average, much lower than prices today. Put another way, the purchasing power of a dollar was much higher 25 years ago because the prices of most goods and services were much lower. Price indexes such as the CPI give us a way of adjusting for the effects of inflation so that we can compare dollar values from different years. For example, suppose your mother received a salary of \$20,000 in 1980. By using the CPI, we can calculate what \$20,000 in 1980 is equivalent to in 2006. The consumer price index is 82 for 1980 and 202 for 2006. Because 202/82 = 2.5, we know that, on average, prices were about 2.5 times as high in 2006 as in 1980. We can use this result to inflate a salary of \$20,000 received in 1980 to its value in current purchasing power:

$$\text{Value in 2006 dollars} = \text{Value in 1980 dollars} \times \left(\frac{\text{CPI in 2006}}{\text{CPI in 1980}}\right)$$

$$= \$20{,}000 \times \left(\frac{202}{82}\right) = \$49{,}268.$$

Our calculation shows that if you are paid a salary of \$49,268 today, you will be able to purchase roughly the same amount of goods and services that your mother could have purchased with a salary of \$20,000 in 1980. Economic variables that are calculated in current-year prices are referred to as *nominal variables.* The calculation we have just made used a price index to adjust a nominal variable—your mother's salary—for the effects of inflation.

For some purposes, we are interested in tracking changes in an economic variable over time rather than in seeing what its value would be in today's dollars. In that case, to correct for the effects of inflation, we can divide the nominal variable by a price index and multiply by 100 to obtain a *real variable.* The real variable will be measured in dollars of the base year for the price index. Currently, the base year for the CPI is the average of prices in the years 1982 to 1984.

Solved Problem | **8-5**

Calculating Real Average Hourly Earnings

In addition to data on employment, the BLS establishment survey gathers data on average hourly earnings of production workers. Production workers are all workers, except for managers and professionals. Average hourly earnings are the wages or salaries earned by these workers per hour. Economists closely follow average hourly earnings because they are a broad measure of the typical worker's income. Use the information in the following table to calculate real average hourly earnings for each year. What was the percentage change in real average hourly earnings between 2005 and 2006?

YEAR	NOMINAL AVERAGE HOURLY EARNINGS	CPI (1982–1984 = 100)
2004	$15.69	188.9
2005	16.13	195.3
2006	16.76	201.6

SOLVING THE PROBLEM:

Step 1: **Review the chapter material.** This problem is about using price indexes to correct for inflation, so you may want to review the section "Using Price Indexes to Adjust for the Effects of Inflation," which begins on page 258.

Step 2: **Calculate real average hourly earnings for each year.** To calculate real average hourly earnings for each year, divide nominal average hourly earnings by the CPI and multiply by 100. For example, real average hourly earnings for 2004 are equal to:

$$\frac{\$15.69}{188.9} \times 100 = \$8.31.$$

These are the results for all the years:

YEAR	NOMINAL AVERAGE HOURLY EARNINGS	CPI (1982–1984 = 100)	REAL AVERAGE HOURLY EARNINGS (1982–1984 DOLLARS)
2004	$15.69	188.9	$8.31
2005	16.13	195.3	8.26
2006	16.76	201.6	8.31

Step 3: **Calculate the percentage change in real average earnings from 2005 to 2006.** This percentage change is equal to:

$$\frac{\$8.31 - \$8.26}{\$8.26} \times 100 = 0.6\%.$$

We can conclude that both nominal average hourly earnings and real average hourly earnings increased between 2005 and 2006.

EXTRA CREDIT: The values we have computed for real average hourly earnings are in 1982–1984 dollars. Because this period is more than 20 years ago, the values are somewhat difficult to interpret. We can convert the earnings to 2006 dollars using the method we used earlier to calculate your mother's salary. But notice that, for purposes of calculating the *change* in the value of real average hourly earnings over time, the base year of the price index doesn't matter. The change from 2005 to 2006 would have still been 0.6 percent, no matter what the base year of the price index. If you don't see that this is true, test it by using the mother's salary method to calculate real average hourly earnings for 2005 and 2006 in 2006 dollars. Then calculate the percentage change. Unless you make an arithmetic error, you should find the answer is still 0.6 percent.

YOUR TURN: For more practice, do related problems 5.3, 5.4, 5.5, and 5.6 on pages 271–272 at the end of this chapter.

>> End Solved Problem 8-5

Falling Real Wages at Alcatel-Lucent

Nominal average hourly earnings are often referred to as the *nominal wage*, and real average hourly earnings are often referred to as the *real wage*. In a multiyear wage contract, a union knows that unless it is able to negotiate increases in nominal wages that are greater than the expected inflation rate, real wages will fall. Before its merger with Alcatel, Lucent Technology and its unionized workers signed a contract that called for nominal wages to increase 16 percent over a period of seven years. If the inflation rate is 3 percent per year over those seven years, the price level will have risen by about 23 percent by the end of the seventh year. With nominal wages rising 16 percent and the price level rising 23 percent, Lucent's workers will have experienced falling real wages.

Both Lucent and its unions realized that the agreement they were signing was likely to lead to falling real wages. The unions accepted the agreement because employment at telecommunications firms had declined sharply. Lucent stated that it might grant further wage increases in the later years of the contract. Lucent probably made this promise because it recognized that if output and employment in the telecommunications industry revived more quickly than expected, the firm would need to pay higher wages to attract and retain good workers.

8.6 LEARNING OBJECTIVE

8.6 | Distinguish between the nominal interest rate and the real interest rate.

Real versus Nominal Interest Rates

The difference between nominal and real values is important when money is being borrowed and lent. As we saw in Chapter 5, the *interest rate* is the cost of borrowing funds, expressed as a percentage of the amount borrowed. If you lend someone $1,000 for one year and charge an interest rate of 6 percent, the borrower will pay back $1,060, or 6 percent more than the amount you lent. But is $1,060 received one year from now really 6 percent more than $1,000 today? If prices rise during the year, you will not be able to buy as much with $1,060 one year from now as you could with that amount today. Your true return from lending the $1,000 is equal to the percentage change in your purchasing power after taking into account the effects of inflation.

Nominal interest rate The stated interest rate on a loan.

Real interest rate The nominal interest rate minus the inflation rate.

The stated interest rate on a loan is the **nominal interest rate**. The **real interest rate** corrects the nominal interest rate for the effect of inflation on purchasing power. As a simple example, suppose that the only good you purchase is DVDs, and at the beginning of the year, the price of DVDs is $10.00. With $1,000, you can purchase 100 DVDs. If you lend the $1,000 out for one year at an interest rate of 6 percent, you will receive $1,060 at the end of the year. Suppose the inflation rate during the year is 2 percent, so that the price of DVDs has risen to $10.20 by the end of the year. How has your purchasing power increased as a result of making the loan? At the beginning of the year, your $1,000 could purchase 100 DVDs. At the end of the year, your $1,060 can purchase $1,060/$10.20 = 103.92 DVDs. In other words, you can purchase almost 4 percent more DVDs. So, in this case the real interest rate you received from lending was a little less than 4 percent (actually, 3.92 percent). For low rates of inflation, a convenient approximation for the real interest rate is:

$$\text{Real interest rate} = \text{Nominal interest rate} - \text{Inflation rate}.$$

In our example, we can calculate the real interest rate by using this formula as 6 percent − 2 percent = 4 percent, which is close to the actual value of 3.92 percent. If the inflation rate during the year was 4 percent, the real interest rate would be only 2 percent. Holding the nominal interest rate constant, the higher the inflation rate, the lower the real interest rate. Notice that if the inflation rate turns out to be higher than expected, borrowers pay and lenders receive a lower real interest rate than either of them expected. For example, if both you and the person to whom you lent the $1,000 expected the inflation rate to be 2 percent, you both expected the real interest rate on the loan to be 4 percent. If inflation actually turns out to be 4 percent, the real interest rate on the loan will be 2 percent: That's bad news for you but good news for your borrower.

For the economy as a whole, we can measure the nominal interest rate as the interest rate on three-month U.S. Treasury bills. U.S. Treasury bills are short-term loans investors make to the federal government. We can use inflation as measured by changes in the CPI to calculate the real interest rate on Treasury bills. Figure 8-7 shows the nominal and real interest rates for the years 1970 to 2006. Notice that when the inflation rate is low, as it was during the 1990s, the gap between the nominal and real interest rates is small. When the inflation rate is high, as it was during the 1970s, the gap between the nominal and real interest rates becomes large. In fact, a particular nominal interest rate can be associated in different periods with very different real interest rates. For example, during late 1975, the nominal interest rate was about 5.5 percent, but because the inflation rate was 7 percent, the real interest rate was –1.5 percent. In early 1987, the nominal interest rate was also 5.5 percent, but because the inflation rate was only 2 percent, the real interest rate was 3.5 percent.

This example shows that it is impossible to know whether a particular nominal interest rate is "high" or "low." It all depends on the inflation rate. *The real interest rate provides a better measure of the true cost of borrowing and the true return from lending than does the nominal interest rate.* When a firm like Alcatel-Lucent is deciding whether

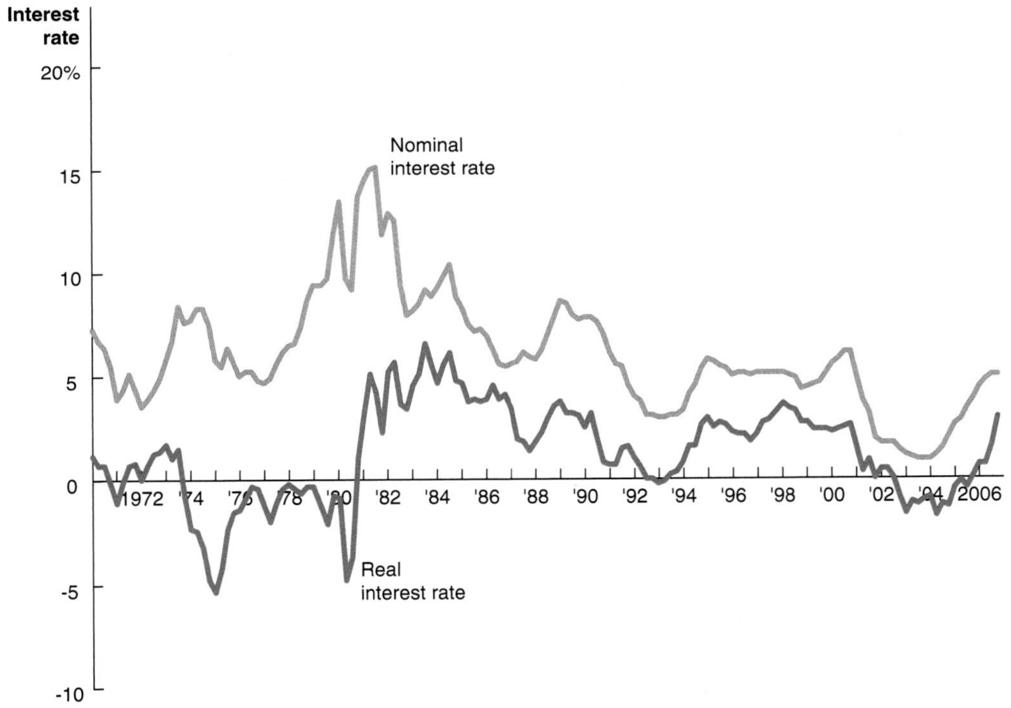

Figure 8-7 | Nominal and Real Interest Rates, 1970–2006

The real interest rate is equal to the nominal interest rate minus the inflation rate. The real interest rate provides a better measure of the true cost of borrowing and the true return on lending than does the nominal interest rate. The nominal interest rate in the figure is the interest rate on three-month U.S. Treasury bills. The inflation rate is measured by changes in the CPI.

Sources: Federal Reserve Bank of St. Louis; and Bureau of Labor Statistics.

to borrow the funds to buy an investment good, such as a new factory, it will look at the real interest rate because the real interest rate measures the true cost to the firm of borrowing.

Is it possible for the nominal interest rate to be less than the real interest rate? Yes, but only when the inflation rate is negative. A negative inflation rate is referred to as **deflation** and occurs on the rare occasions when the price level falls. During the years shown in Figure 8-7, the inflation rate as measured by changes in the CPI was never negative.

Deflation A decline in the price level.

8.7 LEARNING OBJECTIVE

8.7 | Discuss the problems that inflation causes.

Does Inflation Impose Costs on the Economy?

Imagine waking up tomorrow morning and finding that every price in the economy has doubled. The prices of food, gasoline, DVDs, computers, houses, and haircuts have all doubled. But suppose that all wages and salaries have also doubled. Will this doubling of prices and wages matter? Think about walking into Best Buy expecting to find an iPod selling for $250. Instead, you find it selling for $500. Will you turn around and walk out? Probably not because your salary has also increased overnight from $30,000 per year to $60,000 per year. So, the purchasing power of your salary has remained the same, and you are just as likely to buy the iPod today as you were yesterday.

This hypothetical situation makes an important point: Nominal incomes generally increase with inflation. Remember from Chapter 7 that we can think of the $250 price of the iPod as representing either the value of the product or the value of all the income generated in producing the product. The two amounts are the same, whether the iPod sells for $250 or $500. When the price of the iPod rises from $250 to $500, that extra $250 ends up as income that goes to the workers at Apple, the salespeople at Best Buy, or the stockholders of Apple, just as the first $250 did.

It's tempting to think that the problem with inflation is that, as prices rise, consumers can no longer afford to buy as many goods and services, but our example shows that this is a fallacy. An expected inflation rate of 10 percent will raise the average price of goods and services by 10 percent, but it will also raise average incomes by 10 percent. Goods and services will be as affordable to the average consumer as they were before the inflation.

Inflation Affects the Distribution of Income

If inflation will not reduce the affordability of goods and services to the average consumer, why do people dislike inflation? One reason is that the argument in the previous section applies to the *average* person but not to every person. Some people will find their incomes rising faster than the rate of inflation, and so their purchasing power will rise. Other people will find their incomes rising slower than the rate of inflation—or not at all—and their purchasing power will fall. People on fixed incomes are particularly likely to be hurt by inflation. If a retired worker receives a pension fixed at $2,000 per month, over time, inflation will reduce the purchasing power of that payment. In that way, inflation can change the distribution of income in a way that strikes many people as being unfair.

The extent to which inflation redistributes income depends in part on whether the inflation is *anticipated*—in which case consumers, workers, and firms can see it coming and can prepare for it—or *unanticipated*—in which case they do not see it coming and do not prepare for it.

The Problem with Anticipated Inflation

Like many of life's other problems, inflation is easier to manage if you see it coming. Suppose that everyone knows that the inflation rate for the next 10 years will be 10 percent per year. Workers know that unless their wages go up by at least 10 percent per year, the real purchasing power of their wages will fall. Businesses will be willing to increase workers' wages enough to compensate for inflation because they know that the prices of the products they sell will increase. Lenders will realize that the loans they make will be paid back with dollars that are losing 10 percent of their value each year, so they will charge a higher interest rate to compensate for this. Borrowers will be willing to pay these higher interest rates because they also know they are paying back these loans with dollars that are losing value. So far, there don't seem to be costs to anticipated inflation.

Even when inflation is perfectly anticipated, however, some individuals will experience a cost. Inevitably, there will be a redistribution of income, as some people's incomes fall behind even an anticipated level of inflation. In addition, firms and consumers have to hold some paper money to facilitate their buying and selling. Anyone holding paper money will find its purchasing power decreasing each year by the rate of inflation. To avoid this cost, workers and firms will try to hold as little paper money as possible, but they will have to hold some. In addition, firms that print catalogs listing the prices of their products will have to reprint them more frequently. Supermarkets and other stores that mark prices on packages or on store shelves will have to devote more time and labor to changing the marked prices. The costs to firms of changing prices are called **menu costs**. Although at moderate levels of anticipated inflation, menu costs are relatively small, at very high levels of inflation, such as are experienced in some developing countries, menu costs and the costs due to paper money losing value can become substantial. Finally, even anticipated inflation acts to raise the taxes paid by investors and raises the cost of capital for business investment. These effects arise because investors are taxed on the nominal payments they receive rather than on the real payments.

Menu costs The costs to firms of changing prices.

Making the Connection | Why a Lower Inflation Rate Is Like a Tax Cut for Alcatel-Lucent's Bondholders

Borrowers and lenders are interested in the real interest rate rather than the nominal interest rate. Therefore, if expected inflation increases, the nominal interest rate will rise, and if expected inflation decreases, the nominal interest rate will fall. Suppose that Alcatel-Lucent sells bonds to investors to raise funds to purchase investment goods. Suppose also that Alcatel-Lucent is willing to pay, and investors are willing to receive, a real interest rate of 4 percent. If the inflation rate is expected to be 2 percent, the nominal interest rate on Alcatel-Lucent's bonds must be 6 percent for the real interest rate to be 4 percent. If the inflation rate is expected to be 6 percent, the nominal rate on the bond must rise to 10 percent for the real interest rate to be 4 percent. The following table summarizes this information, assuming that the bond has a principal, or face value, of $1,000 (see Chapter 5 for a review of bonds).

PRINCIPAL	REAL INTEREST RATE	INFLATION RATE	NOMINAL INTEREST RATE
$1,000	4%	6%	10%
$1,000	4%	2%	6%

With a nominal interest rate of 6 percent, the interest payment (also known as the *coupon payment*) on newly issued bonds is $60. When the nominal interest rate rises to 10 percent, the interest payment on newly issued bonds is $100. Unfortunately for investors, the government taxes the nominal payment on bonds, with no adjustment for inflation. So, even though in this case, the increase in the interest payment from $60 to $100 represents only compensation for inflation, the whole $100 is subject to the income tax. The following table shows the effect of inflation on an investor's real after-tax interest payment, assuming a tax rate of 25 percent.

INFLATION RATE	NOMINAL INTEREST PAYMENT	TAX PAYMENT	AFTER-TAX INTEREST PAYMENT	ADJUSTMENT FOR INFLATION	REAL AFTER-TAX INTEREST PAYMENT
6%	$100	– $25	= $75	– $60	= $15
2%	$60	– $15	= $45	– $20	= $25

The table shows that reducing the inflation rate from 6 percent to 2 percent will increase the real after-tax payment received by investors who purchase a $1,000 Alcatel-Lucent bond from $15 to $25. By raising the after-tax reward to investors, lower inflation rates will increase the incentive for investors to lend funds to firms. The greater the flow of funds to firms, the greater the amount of investment spending that will occur.

YOUR TURN: Test your understanding by doing related problem 7.7 on page 273 at the end of this chapter.

The Problem with Unanticipated Inflation

In any advanced economy—such as the United States—households, workers, and firms routinely enter into contracts that commit them to make or receive certain payments for years in the future. For example, before it merged with Alcatel, Lucent Technologies in 2004 signed a seven-year wage contract with two of its unions. Once signed, this contract committed Lucent to paying a specified wage for the duration of the contract. When people buy homes, they usually borrow most of the amount they need from a bank. These loans, called *mortgage loans*, commit a borrower to make a fixed monthly payment for the length of the loan. Most mortgage loans are for long periods, often as much as 30 years.

To make these long-term commitments, households, workers, and firms must forecast the rate of inflation. If a firm believes the inflation rate over the next three years will be 6 percent per year, signing a three-year contract with a union that calls for wage increases of 8 percent per year may seem reasonable because the firm may be able to raise its prices by at least the rate of inflation each year. If the firm believes that the inflation rate will be only 2 percent over the next three years, paying wage increases of 8 percent may significantly reduce its profits or even force it out of business.

When people borrow money or banks lend money, they must forecast the inflation rate so they can calculate the real rate of interest on a loan. In 1980, banks were charging interest rates of 18 percent or more on mortgage loans. This rate seems very high compared to the roughly 6 percent charged on such loans in 2007, but the inflation rate in 1980 was more than 13 percent and was expected to remain high. In fact, the inflation rate declined unexpectedly during the early 1980s. By 1983, the inflation rate was only about 3 percent. People who borrowed money for 30 years at the high interest rates of 1980 soon found that the real interest rate on their loans was much higher than they expected.

When the actual inflation rate turns out to be very different from the expected inflation rate, some people gain, and other people lose. This outcome seems unfair to most people because they are either winning or losing only because something unanticipated has happened. This apparently unfair redistribution is a key reason why people dislike unanticipated inflation.

>> Continued from page 239

Economics in YOUR Life!

At the beginning of this chapter, we posed a question: Should you change your career plans if you graduate during a recession when the unemployment rate is high? We have seen in this chapter that the high unemployment rates during a recession, although painful for people who lose their jobs, do not generally last very long. So, on the one hand, if you graduate with an engineering degree and want a job in manufacturing, you may have some difficulty finding one during a recession, but you probably do not need to change your career plans. On the other hand, if you plan at some point to earn a master's degree, you might consider staying in school to ride out the temporary increases in unemployment caused by the recession. You may also want to keep in mind the result of a recent study that college graduates who enter the labor force during a recession typically receive wages that are about 9 percent less than those received by college graduates who enter the labor force during an economic expansion.

Conclusion

Inflation and unemployment are key macroeconomic problems. Presidential elections are often won or lost on the basis of which candidate is able to convince the public that he or she can best deal with these problems. Many economists, however, would argue that, in the long run, maintaining high rates of growth of real GDP per person is the most important macroeconomic concern. Only when real GDP per person is increasing will a country's standard of living increase. We turn in the next chapter to discussing this important issue of economic growth.

Read *An Inside Look* on the next page for an example of a newspaper discussion of newly released government statistics on unemployment.

Making Sense of Employment Data

WALL STREET JOURNAL, FEBRUARY 3, 2007

Jobs Data Signal Growth Is Easing but Still Solid

U.S. employers were more cautious about taking on new workers in January, a hint that economic growth may be easing. But plenty of underlying signs suggest that a strong labor market will continue to lift wages and boost consumer spending in the months ahead.

a The Labor Department Friday said nonfarm payrolls rose by 110,000 jobs last month following December's gain of 206,000 jobs. The smaller increase in January—together with a rise in the unemployment rate to 4.6% from 4.5% in December and a tepid 0.2% gain in the typical employee's pay last month—suggests the economy is slowing somewhat after a strong finish to 2006.

But the tone of the report wasn't entirely soft. Revised data showed that employers brought on 80,000 more workers in November and December than initially thought, which means employers have added an average of 170,000 jobs a month since November. . . .

b In its annual revision, based on a thorough count of unemployment insurance tax records, the Labor Department said the economy created more than 2.2 million jobs last year, 400,000 more than previously estimated.

That helps explain why consumers seemed so resilient last year despite higher interest rates and a sharp reversal in the housing market, and it bodes well for economic growth this year. "One reason the U.S. economy has weathered this downdraft in housing and autos is that it's been generating a lot of income" for consumers, said Robert Gay, a former senior economist at the Federal Reserve. . . .

c White-collar, service-sector workers like Mr. Gay, now a hedge-fund consultant in New York, have been in particular demand. Employment in the category of professional and business services, which includes accountants, consultants and lawyers, grew by 25,000 positions in January. The health-care field added 18,000 workers last month and an average 28,000 positions a month last year.

FairPoint Communications Inc., a Charlotte, N.C., telecommunications company, said it plans to add 600 jobs this year, to "support field operations" and mostly in the accounting, logistics, information-technology and human-resources departments.

Roy Krause, chief executive of Spherion, a staffing firm in Fort Lauderdale, Fla., said, "You're taking out of a lot of companies the 60-year-old middle-management professional that needs to be replaced somehow." He said Spherion's professional placements are running 8% to 10% higher than a year ago, compared with 4% to 5% growth for clerical or industrial placements.

Amid the vigorous labor market, the University of Michigan yesterday said its consumer-sentiment survey rose to 96.9 in January from 91.7 in December, hitting its highest mark in two years. Meanwhile, the Commerce Department said factory orders surged 2.4% in December after a 1.2% gain in November, but underlying trends suggest the manufacturing sector could struggle in the months ahead as it works off stockpiles of unsold goods.

Source: Christopher Conkey, "Jobs Data Signal Growth Is Easing but Still Solid," Wall Street Journal*, February 3, 2007, p. A3.*

Key Points in the Article

This article discusses a jobs report that the U.S. Department of Labor released for January 2007. Although employment increased by 110,000, the unemployment rate increased slightly. The article also shows that U.S. job growth is not distributed proportionately across all sectors of the economy. For example, although these data are not included in this article, during 2006, while the national unemployment rate averaged 4.6 percent, the unemployment rate in the financial sector averaged less than 3 percent, while the unemployment rate in the construction sector topped 6 percent.

Analyzing the News

a On February 2, 2007, the U.S. Department of Labor announced that although the economy added 111,000 new jobs in January, the unemployment rate increased from 4.5 percent to 4.6 percent. This article actually combines information from the establishment survey and the household survey without alerting the reader. The number for the increase in employment is from the establishment survey, while the unemployment rates numbers are from the household survey. Not stated in the article is the fact that employment as measured by the household survey increased by only 31,000. This discrepancy between the measures of changes in employment is not unusual, as we saw in Table 8-2 in the chapter. Because many economists consider the employment numbers in the establishment survey to be more reliable, they are the ones often reported in the media. But because the establishment survey does not measure unemployment and because there is significant public interest in changes in the unemployment rate, the household survey estimate of the unemployment rate is also reported.

b The article also mentions that each year, the Department of Labor revises the initial estimates of changes in employment by using additional sources of information, such as unemployment insurance tax records. Remember that both the establishment survey and the household survey are *surveys* rather than complete counts. It would be impossible for the government to gather information from every household for the household survey or every firm for the establishment survey. Instead, the Labor Department relies on samples of households and samples of firms. After the household survey has been completed each month, the Labor Department does not attempt to gather any more information from households on the labor market status, so the household survey data is never revised. The Labor Department does attempt to gather additional information on the number of workers actually on company payrolls and issues revisions of the payroll survey data as more information becomes available. In the case discussed in the article, the Department of Labor decided that employment had increased by 400,000 more during 2006 than it had originally estimated.

c The jobs that the U.S. economy created between December 2006 and January 2007 were not distributed evenly across all sectors of the economy. In particular, the demand for workers in the information, financial, and education and health sectors was the strongest. This pattern is shown in the figure below, with the unemployment rates in these sectors during 2006 being some of the lowest among all sectors of the economy.

Thinking Critically

1. The figure shows that the unemployment rate in the construction industry in January 2007 was 6.7 percent, which was more than 2 percentage points above the overall unemployment rate. Some economists believed that beginning in 2005, housing construction entered a period of decline that might last for several years. If this assumption was true, how should we characterize unemployment in the construction industry: mainly frictional, mainly structural, mainly cyclical, or some combination of these types?
2. Suppose that you manage a used-book store in a college town. Your employees request a 3 percent wage increase for next year. Meanwhile, you expect inflation to be 4 percent next year. Should you agree to the 3 percent wage increase? Why or why not?

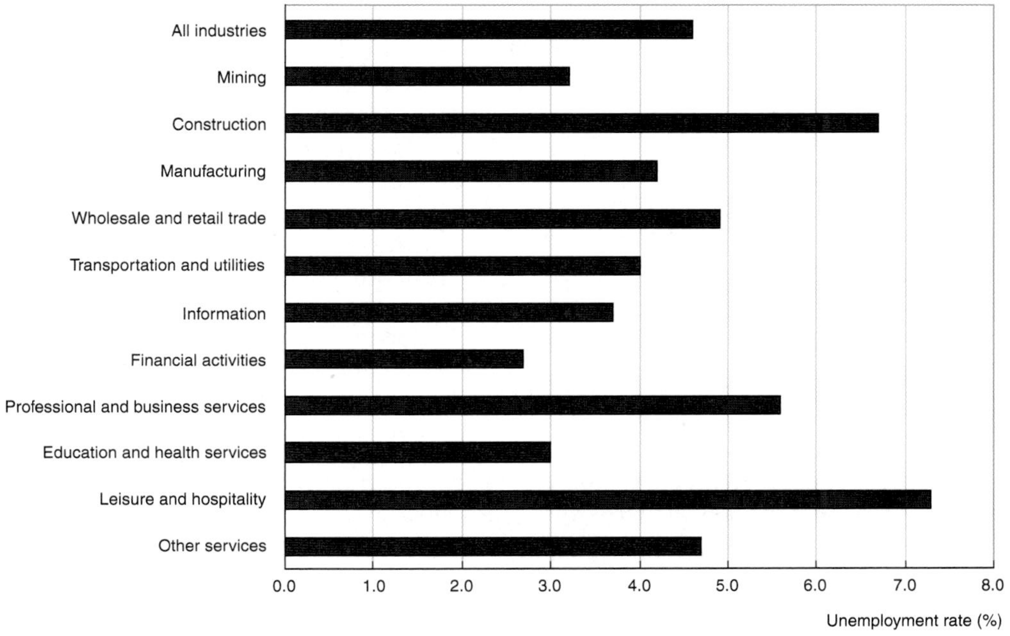

Unemployment rates are different across sectors of the economy.

Key Terms

Consumer price index (CPI), p. 255
Cyclical unemployment, p. 249
Deflation, p. 262
Discouraged workers, p. 241
Efficiency wage, p. 253
Frictional unemployment, p. 248
Inflation rate, p. 254
Labor force, p. 240
Labor force participation rate, p. 242
Menu costs, p. 263
Natural rate of unemployment, p. 249
Nominal interest rate, p. 260
Price level, p. 254
Producer price index (PPI), p. 257
Real interest rate, p. 260
Structural unemployment, p. 249
Unemployment rate, p. 240

8.1 LEARNING OBJECTIVE 8.1 | Define unemployment rate and labor force participation rate and understand how they are computed, **pages 240–247.**

Measuring the Unemployment Rate and the Labor Force Participation Rate

Summary

The U.S. Bureau of Labor Statistics uses the results of the monthly household survey to calculate the *unemployment rate* and the *labor force participation rate*. The **labor force** is the total number of people who have jobs plus the number of people who do not have jobs but are actively looking for them. The **unemployment rate** is the percentage of the labor force that is unemployed. **Discouraged workers** are people who are available for work but who are not actively looking for a job. Discouraged workers are not counted as unemployed. The **labor force participation rate** is the percentage of the working-age population in the labor force. Since 1950, the labor force participation rate of women has been rising, while the labor force participation rate of men has been falling. White men and women have below-average unemployment rates. Teenagers and black men and women have above-average unemployment rates. The typical unemployed person finds a new job or returns to his or her previous job within a few months. Each year, millions of jobs are created and destroyed in the United States.

myeconlab Get Ahead of the Curve Visit www.myeconlab.com to complete these exercises online and get instant feedback.

Review Questions

1.1 How is the unemployment rate calculated? Which groups tend to have above-average unemployment rates, and which groups tend to have below-average unemployment rates?

1.2 How is the labor force participation rate calculated? In the years since 1950, how have the labor force participation rates of men and women changed?

1.3 What is the difference between the household survey and the establishment survey? Which survey do many economists prefer for measuring changes in employment? Why?

Problems and Applications

1.4 Fill in the missing values in the table of data collected in the household survey for the year 2006.

Working-age population	
Employment	151,428,000
Unemployment	
Unemployment rate	4.6%
Labor force	
Labor force participation rate	66.2%

1.5 **(Related to the *Chapter Opener* on page 238)** What would be some general reasons a firm would lay off a substantial number of workers?

1.6 Figure 8-2 on page 244 shows that the rapid increases in the labor force participation rate of women slowed down after 1995. Why might this slowdown have occurred? Discuss whether the labor force participation rate for women eventually might be equal to the rate for men.

1.7 **(Related to *Solved Problem 8-1* on page 242)** Homemakers are not included in the employment or labor force totals compiled in the Bureau of Labor Statistics household survey. They are included in the working-age population totals. Suppose that homemakers were counted as employed and included in the labor force statistics. What would be the impact on the unemployment rate and the labor force participation rate?

1.8 According to the Bureau of Labor Statistics, at the end of April 2007 there were 4.1 million job openings at businesses in the United States. At the same time, there were about 6.8 million people unemployed. Why didn't the unemployed workers accept these job openings, thereby reducing the total number of unemployed by 60 percent?

Source: Sudeep Reddy, "Employment Softening in Housing Sector," *Wall Street Journal*, June 12, 2007.

1.9 **(Related to the *Making the Connection* on page 244)** In recent years, the percentage of men between the ages of 25 and 54 who are not in the labor force has increased. Suppose the federal government enacted a law that required the men between those ages who were not disabled or in school must either be in the labor force or pay a substantial fine. What would happen to measured GDP? What would happen to the measured income of these men? Would these men be better off as a result of this policy?

1.10 Between December 2001 and January 2002, the total number of people employed and the unemployment rate both fell. Briefly explain how this is possible.

1.11 The following appeared in a *BusinessWeek* article:

> [The household survey for January 2002] from the Bureau of Labor Statistics showed that the labor force participation rate—the percentage of people either employed or actively job-hunting—fell by 0.8 percentage points over the past year, to 66.4%. . . . The sharp decline suggests the published unemployment rate understates the damage to the labor market.

Why would a fall in the labor force participation rate indicate that the unemployment rate is not doing a good job reflecting labor market conditions?

Source: "Climbing Out of the Job Pool," *BusinessWeek*, February 25, 2002, p. 32.

1.12 In an article on the conditions in the labor market, two business reporters remarked that the unemployment rate "typically rises months after the economy rebounds." What do they mean by the phrase "the economy rebounds"? Why would the unemployment rate be rising if the economy is rebounding?

Source: Vince Golle and Terry Barrett, "Hiring Picks Up, Factories Expand," *Bloomberg News*, April 1, 2002.

>> End Learning Objective 8.1

8.2 LEARNING OBJECTIVE 8.2 | Identify the three types of unemployment, **pages 248–250.**

Types of Unemployment

Summary

There are three types of unemployment: frictional, structural, and cyclical. **Frictional unemployment** is short-term unemployment that arises from the process of matching workers with jobs. One type of frictional unemployment is *seasonal unemployment*, which refers to unemployment due to factors such as weather, variations in tourism, and other calendar-related events. **Structural unemployment** arises from a persistent mismatch between the job skills or attributes of workers and the requirements of jobs. **Cyclical unemployment** is caused by a business cycle recession. The **natural rate of unemployment** is the normal rate of unemployment, consisting of structural unemployment and frictional unemployment. The natural rate of unemployment is also sometimes called the *full-employment rate of unemployment.*

myeconlab Get Ahead of the Curve Visit www.myeconlab.com to complete these exercises online and get instant feedback.

Review Questions

2.1 What is the relationship between frictional unemployment and job search?

2.2 Why isn't the natural rate of unemployment equal to zero?

Problems and Applications

2.3 Macroeconomic conditions affect the decisions firms and families make. Why, for example, might a college student after graduation enter the job market during an economic expansion but apply for graduate school during a recession?

2.4 **(Related to the *Making the Connection* on page 250)** What advice for finding a job would you give someone who is frictionally unemployed? What advice would you give someone who is structurally unemployed? What advice would you give someone who is cyclically unemployed?

2.5 Recall from Chapter 3 the definitions of normal and inferior goods. During an economic expansion, would you rather be working in an industry that produces a normal good or in an industry that produces an inferior good? Why? During a recession, would you rather be working in an industry that produces a normal good or an inferior good? Why?

2.6 If Congress eliminated the unemployment insurance system, what would be the effect on the level of frictional unemployment? What would be the effect on the level of real GDP? Would well-being in the economy be increased? Briefly explain.

>> End Learning Objective 8.2

8.3 LEARNING OBJECTIVE 8.3 | Explain what factors determine the unemployment rate, **pages 250–254.**

Explaining Unemployment

Summary

Government policies can reduce the level of frictional and structural unemployment by aiding the search for jobs and the retraining of workers. Some government policies, however, can add to the level of frictional and structural unemployment. Unemployment insurance payments can raise the unemployment rate by extending the time that unemployed workers search for jobs. Government policies have caused the unemployment rates in most other industrial countries to be higher than in the United States. Wages above market levels can also increase unemployment. Wages may be above market levels because of the minimum wage, labor unions, and *efficiency wages*. An **efficiency wage** is a higher-than-market wage paid by a firm to increase worker productivity.

myeconlab Get Ahead of the Curve Visit www.myeconlab.com to complete these exercises online and get instant feedback.

Review Questions

3.1 What affect does the payment of government unemployment insurance have on the unemployment rate?

3.2 Discuss the effect of each of the following on the unemployment rate.
- a. The minimum wage law
- b. Labor unions
- c. Efficiency wages

Problems and Applications

3.3 In 2007, Ségolène Royal, who was running unsuccessfully for president of France, proposed that workers who lost their jobs would receive unemployment payments equal to 90 percent of their previous wages during their first year of unemployment. If this proposal were enacted, what would likely be the effect on the unemployment rate in France? Briefly explain.

Source: Alessandra Galloni and David Gauthier-Villars, "France's Royal Introduces Platform Ahead of Election," *Wall Street Journal*, February 12, 2007, p. A.8.

3.4 Discuss the likely impact of each of the following on the unemployment rate.
- a. The length of time workers are eligible to receive unemployment insurance payments doubles.
- b. The minimum wage is abolished.
- c. Most U.S. workers join labor unions.
- d. More companies make information on job openings easily available on Internet job sites.

3.5 Why do you think the minimum wage was set at only $0.25 per hour in 1938? Wouldn't this wage have been well below the equilibrium wage?

3.6 An economic consultant studies the labor policies of a firm where it is difficult to monitor workers and prepares a report in which she recommends that the firm raise employee wages. At a meeting of the firm's managers to discuss the report, one manager makes the following argument: "I think the wages we are paying are fine. As long as enough people are willing to work here at the wages we are currently paying, why should we raise them?" What argument can the economic consultant make to justify her advice that the firm should increase its wages?

3.7 (Related to the *Making the Connection* on page 253) If Wal-Mart adopted Costco's compensation policies, what would likely happen to the number of workers employed by Wal-Mart? Is it likely that consumers would be better off or worse off?

>> End Learning Objective 8.3

8.4 LEARNING OBJECTIVE 8.4 | Define price level and inflation rate and understand how they are computed, **pages 254–258.**

Measuring Inflation

Summary

The **price level** measures the average prices of goods and services. The **inflation rate** is equal to the percentage change in the price level from one year to the next. The federal government compiles statistics on three different measures of the price level: the consumer price index (CPI), the GDP price deflator, and the producer price index (PPI). The **consumer price index (CPI)** is an average of the prices of goods and services purchased by the typical urban family of four. Changes in the CPI are the best measure of changes in the cost of living as experienced by the typical household. Biases in the construction of the CPI cause changes in it to overstate the true inflation rate by one-half of a percentage point to one percentage point. The **producer price index (PPI)** is an average of prices received by producers of goods and services at all stages of production.

myeconlab Get Ahead of the Curve Visit www.myeconlab.com to complete these exercises online and get instant feedback.

Review Questions

4.1 Briefly describe the three major measures of the price level. Which measure is used most frequently?

4.2 What potential biases exist in calculating the consumer price index? What steps has the Bureau of Labor Statistics taken to reduce the size of the biases?

Problems and Applications

4.3 **(Related to the *Don't Let This Happen to You!* on page 256)** Briefly explain whether you agree or disagree with the following statement: "I don't believe the government price statistics. The CPI for 2004 was 189, but I know that the inflation rate couldn't have been as high as 89 percent in 2004."

4.4 Briefly explain whether you agree with the following statement: "If changes in the CPI were a more accurate measure of the inflation rate, the federal government would pay less in Social Security payments each year."

4.5 Consider a simple economy that produces only three products. Use the information in the following table to calculate the inflation rate for 2009 as measured by the consumer price index.

		PRICE		
PRODUCT	QUANTITY	BASE YEAR (1999)	2008	2009
Haircuts	2	$10.00	$11.00	$16.20
Hamburgers	10	2.00	2.45	2.40
DVDs	6	15.00	15.00	14.00

4.6 The *Wall Street Journal* publishes an index of the prices of luxury homes in various cities. The base year for the index is January 2000. Here are the indexes for December 2005 and December 2006.

CITY	DECEMBER 2005	DECEMBER 2006
New York	184.6	193.1
Los Angeles	223.9	226.7
Chicago	153.4	157.1
Seattle	147.4	159.1

a. In which city did the prices of luxury homes increase the most during this year?

b. Can you determine on the basis of these numbers which city had the most expensive luxury homes in December 2006? Briefly explain.

Source: "Luxury Home Index," *Wall Street Journal*, December 29, 2006.

>> End Learning Objective 8.4

8.5 LEARNING OBJECTIVE 8.5 | Use price indexes to adjust for the effects of inflation, **pages 258–260.**

Using Price Indexes to Adjust for the Effects of Inflation

Summary

Price indexes are designed to measure changes in the price level over time, not the absolute level of prices. To correct for the effects of inflation, we can divide a *nominal variable* by a price index and multiply by 100 to obtain a *real variable*. The real variable will be measured in dollars of the base year for the price index.

myeconlab Get Ahead of the Curve Visit www.myeconlab.com to complete these exercises online and get instant feedback.

Review Questions

5.1 What is the difference between a nominal variable and a real variable?

5.2 Briefly explain how you can use data on nominal wages for 2002 to 2008 and data on the consumer price index for the same years to calculate the real wage for these years.

Problems and Applications

5.3 **(Related to *Solved Problem 8-5* on page 258)** In 1914, when Henry Ford paid his workers $5 per day for an eight-hour day, the CPI was 10. In 2006, when the average wage in the automobile industry was about $30 per hour, the CPI was 202. Were auto workers in 1914 or auto workers in 2006 paid more in real terms? Be sure to show your calculation.

5.4 **(Related to *Solved Problem 8-5* on page 258)** Use the information in the following table to determine the percentage changes in the U.S. and French *real* minimum wages between 1956 and 2006.

	UNITED STATES		FRANCE	
YEAR	MINIMUM WAGE (DOLLARS PER HOUR)	CPI	MINIMUM WAGE (EUROS PER HOUR)	CPI
1956	$1.00	27	0.19 euros	10
2006	5.15	202	8.27 euros	113

Does it matter for your answer that you have not been told the base year for the U.S. CPI or the French CPI? Was the percentage increase in the price level greater in the United States or in France during these years?

Sources: John M. Abowd, Francis Kramarz, Thomas Lemieux, and David N. Margolis, "Minimum Wages and Youth Employment in France and the United States," in D. Blanchflower and R. Freeman, eds., *Youth Employment and Joblessness in Advanced Countries*, Chicago: University of Chicago Press, 1999, pp. 427–472 (the value for the minimum wage is given in francs; it was converted to euros at a conversion rate of 1 euro = 6.55957 francs); Insee online data bank, www.insee.fr; U.S. Department of Labor; and U.S. Bureau of Labor Statistics.

5.5 **(Related to *Solved Problem 8-5* on page 258)** The Great Depression was the worst economic disaster in U.S. history in terms of declines in real GDP and increases in the unemployment rate. Use the data in the following table to calculate the percentage decline in real GDP between 1929 and 1933.

YEAR	NOMINAL GDP (BILLIONS OF DOLLARS)	GDP PRICE DEFLATOR (2000 = 100)
1929	103.6	11.9
1933	56.4	8.9

5.6 **(Related to *Solved Problem 8-5* on page 258)** The following table shows the top 10 films of all time through 2006, measured by box office receipts in the United States, as well as several other films farther down the list:

RANK	FILM	TOTAL BOX OFFICE RECEIPTS	YEAR RELEASED	CPI
1	*Titanic*	$600,779,824	1997	161
2	*Star Wars*	460,935,655	1977	61
3	*Shrek 2*	436,471,036	2004	189
4	*E.T. the Extra-Terrestrial*	434,949,459	1982	97
5	*Star Wars: Episode I—The Phantom Menace*	431,065,444	1999	167
6	*Pirates of the Caribbean: Dead Man's Chest*	423,032,628	2006	202
7	*Spider-Man*	403,706,375	2002	180
8	*Star Wars: Episode III—Revenge of the Sith*	380,262,555	2005	195
9	*Lord of the Rings: The Return of the King*	377,019,252	2003	184
10	*Spider-Man 2*	373,377,893	2004	189
34	*Jaws*	260,000,000	1975	54
73	*Gone with the Wind*	198,655,278	1939	14
84	*Snow White and the Seven Dwarfs*	184,208,842	1937	14
124	*The Sound of Music*	163,214,286	1965	32
145	*One Hundred and One Dalmatians*	153,000,000	1961	30

The CPI in 2006 was 202. Use this information and the data in the table to calculate the box office receipts for each film in 2006 dollars. Assume that each film generated all of its box office receipts during the year it was released. Use your results to prepare a new list of the top 10 films based on their earnings in 2006 dollars. (Some of the films, such as the first *Star Wars* film, *Gone with the Wind*, and *Snow White and the Seven Dwarfs*, were re-released several times, so their receipts were actually earned during several different years, but we will ignore that complication.)

Source: IMDb online database, www.imdb.com.

>> End Learning Objective 8.5

8.6 LEARNING OBJECTIVE 8.6 | Distinguish between the nominal interest rate and the real interest rate, **pages 260–262.**

Real versus Nominal Interest Rates

Summary

The stated interest rate on a loan is the **nominal interest rate.** The **real interest rate** is the nominal interest rate minus the inflation rate. Because it is corrected for the effects of inflation, the real interest rate provides a better measure of the true cost of borrowing and the true return from lending than does the nominal interest rate. The nominal interest rate is always greater than the real interest rate unless the economy experiences *deflation.* **Deflation** is a decline in the price level.

myeconlab Get Ahead of the Curve Visit www.myeconlab.com to complete these exercises online and get instant feedback.

Review Questions

6.1 What is the difference between the nominal interest rate and the real interest rate?

6.2 If the inflation is expected to increase, what is likely to happen to the nominal interest rate? Briefly explain.

Problems and Applications

6.3 The following appeared in a newspaper article: "Inflation in the Lehigh Valley during the first quarter of [the year] was less than half the national rate. . . . So, unlike much of the nation, the fear here is deflation—when prices sink so low the CPI drops below zero." Do you agree with the reporter's definition of deflation? Briefly explain.

Source: Dan Shope, "Valley's Inflation Rate Slides." (Allentown, PA) *Morning Call*, July 9, 1996.

6.4 Suppose you were borrowing money to buy a car. Which of these situations would you prefer: The interest rate on your car loan is 20 percent and the inflation rate is 19 percent or the interest rate on your car loan is 5 percent and the inflation rate is 2 percent? Briefly explain.

6.5 Describing the situation in England in 1920, the historian Robert Skidelsky wrote the following: "Who would not borrow at 4 per cent a year, with prices going up 4 per cent a *month*?" What was the real interest rate paid by borrowers in this situation? (*Hint:* What is the annual inflation rate, if the monthly inflation rate is 4 percent?)

Source: Robert Skidelsky, *John Maynard Keynes: Volume 2, The Economist as Saviour, 1920–1937*, New York: The Penguin Press, 1992, p. 39, emphasis in original.

6.6 Suppose that the only good you purchase is hamburgers and that at the beginning of the year, the price of hamburgers is \$2.00. Suppose you lend \$1,000 for one year at an interest rate of 5 percent. At the end of the year, hamburgers cost \$2.08. What was the real rate of interest you earned on your loan?

>> End Learning Objective 8.6

8.7 LEARNING OBJECTIVE 8.7 | Discuss the problems that inflation causes, **pages 262–265.**

Does Inflation Impose Costs on the Economy?

Summary

Inflation does not reduce the affordability of goods and services to the average consumer, but it still imposes costs on the economy. When inflation is anticipated, its main costs are that paper money loses some of its value and firms incur *menu costs.* **Menu costs** include the costs of changing prices on products and printing new catalogs. When inflation is unanticipated, the actual inflation rate can turn out to be different from the expected inflation rate. As a result, income is redistributed as some people gain and some people lose.

myeconlab Get Ahead of the Curve Visit www.myeconlab.com to complete these exercises online and get instant feedback.

Review Questions

7.1 How can inflation affect the distribution of income?

7.2 Which is a greater problem: anticipated inflation or unanticipated inflation? Why?

Problems and Applications

7.3 What are menu costs? What affect has the Internet had on the size of menu costs?

7.4 Suppose that the inflation rate turns out to be much higher than most people expected. In that case, would you rather have been a borrower or a lender? Briefly explain.

7.5 During the late nineteenth century in the United States, many farmers borrowed heavily to buy land. During most of the period between 1870 and the mid-1890s, the United States experienced mild deflation: The price level declined each year. Many farmers engaged in political protests during these years, and deflation was often a subject of their protests. Explain why farmers would have felt burdened by deflation.

7.6 Suppose James and Frank both retire this year. For income from retirement, James will rely on a pension from his company that pays him a fixed \$2,500 per month for as long as he lives. James hasn't saved anything for retirement. Frank has no pension but has saved a considerable amount, which he has invested in certificates of deposit (CDs) at his bank. Currently, Frank's CDs pay him interest of \$2,300 per month.

a. Ten years from now, is James or Frank likely to have a higher real income? In your answer, be sure to define real income.

b. Now suppose that instead of being a constant amount, James's pension increases each year by the same percentage as the CPI. For example, if the CPI increases by 5 percent in the first year after James retires, then his pension in the second year equal \$2,500 + (\$2,500 × .05) = \$2,625. In this case, 10 years from now, is James or Frank likely to have a higher real income?

7.7 **(Related to the *Making the Connection* on page 263)** Suppose that Alcatel-Lucent and the investors buying the firm's bonds both expect a 2 percent inflation rate for the year. Given that expectation, suppose the nominal interest rate on the bonds is 6 percent and the real interest rate is 4 percent. Suppose that a year after the investors have purchased the bonds, the inflation turns out to be 6 percent, rather than the 2 percent that had been expected. Who gains and who loses from the unexpectedly high inflation rate?

>> End Learning Objective 8.7

Economic Growth, the Financial System, and Business Cycles

Growth and the Business Cycle at Boeing

On the morning of December 17, 1903, at Kitty Hawk, North Carolina, the Wright Flyer became the first human-piloted, machine-powered, heavier-than-air craft to fly—for all of 12 seconds and a distance of 120 feet. Roughly a century later, on November 10, 2005, the Boeing 777-200LR became the first commercial aircraft to fly nonstop more than halfway around the world—for 22 hours and 42 minutes across 13,422 miles, from Hong Kong eastbound to London. This tremendous advance in aviation technology has been matched by technological progress in many other areas of the economy. In this chapter, we begin to explore how technological change has affected the standard of living in the United States and around the world.

Boeing was established in 1916, when William Boeing incorporated his twin-float seaplane business, which he later named Boeing Airplane Co. Today, Boeing is one of the world's largest designers and manufacturers of commercial jetliners, military aircraft, satellites, missiles, and defense systems. The company is headquartered in Chicago and employs more than 150,000 people in 70 countries. Boeing's experiences have often mirrored those of the U.S. economy. Two key macroeconomic facts are that in the long run, the U.S. economy has experienced economic growth, and in the short run, the economy has experienced a series of business cycles. Living standards in the United States have increased enormously because, in the long run, growth in the production of goods and services has been faster than growth in population. But the increase in living standards has been interrupted by periods of business cycle recession during which production of goods and services has declined. Boeing has experienced growth over the long run, while also being affected by the business cycle.

Over the past several years, Boeing has experienced an increase in orders as a result of economic growth in the United States, Europe, and several Asian countries. In 2006, the firm experienced a record 1,044 orders for new commercial jets. While benefiting from economic growth, Boeing has been vulnerable to the business cycle. Firms like Boeing that produce expensive durable goods are particularly likely to experience a decline in demand during a business cycle recession. For example, the U.S. economy experienced a recession in 2001, which, together with the terrorist attacks on September 11, caused orders for Boeing's commercial aircraft to decline by 45 percent. In this chapter, we will provide an overview of long-run growth and the business cycle and discuss their importance for individual firms, for consumers, and for the economy as a whole.

For another example of how companies can contribute to, and benefit from, long-run economic growth, read **AN INSIDE LOOK AT POLICY** on **page 302**, where we discuss how China's domestic aviation market, which is the second largest in the world, is struggling because of a shortage of trained workers.

Sources: Lynn Lunsford, "Boeing's Boom Has Wings," *Wall Street Journal*, January 5, 2007, p. A8; Lynn Lunsford, "Ugly in the Air: Boeing's New Plane Gets Gawks and Stares," *Wall Street Journal*, January 8, 2007, p. A1; and James Wallace, "Boeing 777 Stretches Its Wings, Record," *Seattle-Post Intelligencer*, November 11, 2005, p. B2.

LEARNING Objectives

After studying this chapter, you should be able to:

9.1 Discuss the importance of **long-run economic growth**, page 276.

9.2 Discuss the role of the **financial system** in facilitating long-run **economic growth**, page 283.

9.3 Explain what happens during a **business cycle**, page 292.

Economics in YOUR Life!

If You Spend More, Will the Economy Grow More?

Suppose that, after a full day of unsuccessfully shopping for a pair of jeans, you decide to use the money you would have spent to open a savings account instead. When you return home empty handed, your roommate informs you that your decision to save instead of consume will reduce economic growth because consumption expenditures comprise over two-thirds of gross domestic product. How do you respond to your roommate's assertion? As you read this chapter, see if you can answer this question. You can check your answer against the one we provide at the end of the chapter. » **Continued on page 301**

A key measure of the success of any economy is its ability to increase production of goods and services faster than the growth in population. Increasing production faster than population growth is the only way that the standard of living of the average person in a country can increase. Unfortunately, many economies around the world are not growing at all or are growing very slowly. In many countries in sub-Saharan Africa, living standards are barely higher, or in some cases are lower, than they were 50 years ago. Most people in these countries live in the same grinding poverty as their ancestors. In the United States and other developed countries, however, living standards are much higher than they were 50 years ago. An important macroeconomic question is why some countries grow much faster than others.

As we will see, one determinant of economic growth is the ability of firms to expand their operations, buy additional equipment, train workers, and adopt new technologies. To carry out these activities, firms must acquire funds from households, either directly through financial markets—such as the stock and bond markets—or indirectly through financial intermediaries—such as banks. Financial markets and financial intermediaries together comprise the *financial system*. In this chapter, we will present an overview of the financial system and see how funds flow from households to firms through the *market for loanable funds*.

Dating back to at least the early nineteenth century, the U.S. economy has experienced periods of expanding production and employment followed by periods of recession during which production and employment decline. As we noted in Chapter 7, these alternating periods of expansion and recession are called the **business cycle**. The business cycle is not uniform: Each period of expansion is not the same length, nor is each period of recession, but every period of expansion in U.S. history has been followed by a period of recession, and every period of recession has been followed by a period of expansion.

Business cycle Alternating periods of economic expansion and economic recession.

In this chapter, we begin the exploration of two key aspects of macroeconomics—the long-run growth that has steadily raised living standards in the United States and the short-run fluctuations of the business cycle.

9.1 LEARNING OBJECTIVE

9.1 | Discuss the importance of long-run economic growth.

Long-Run Economic Growth

Most people in the United States, Western Europe, Japan, and other advanced countries expect that over time, their standard of living will improve. They expect that year after year, firms will introduce new and improved products, new prescription drugs and better surgical techniques will overcome more diseases, and their ability to afford these goods and services will increase. For most people, these are reasonable expectations.

In 1900, the United States was already enjoying the highest standard of living in the world. Yet in that year, only 3 percent of U.S. homes had electricity, and only 15 percent had indoor flush toilets. Diseases such as smallpox, typhus, dysentery, and cholera were still menacing the health of Americans. In 1900, 5,000 of the 45,000 children born in Chicago died before their first birthday. In 1900, there were, of course, no televisions, radios, computers, air-conditioners, or refrigerators. Many homes were heated in the winter by burning coal, which contributed to the severe pollution that fouled the air of most large cities. There were no modern appliances, so most women worked inside the home at least 80 hours per week. The typical American homemaker in 1900 baked a half ton of bread per year.

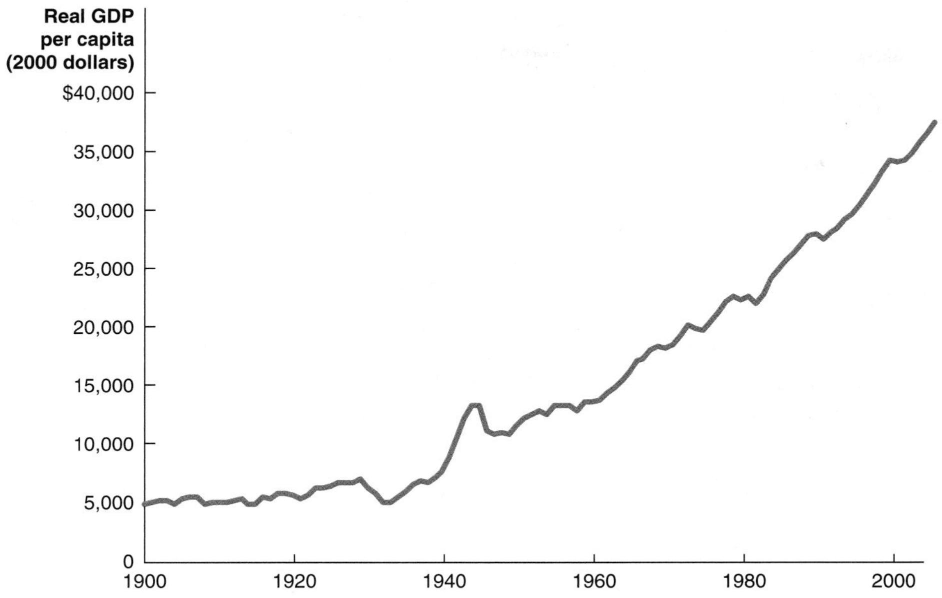

Figure 9-1 | The Growth in Real GDP per Capita, 1900–2006

Measured in 2000 dollars, real GDP per capita in the United States grew from about $4,900 in 1900 to about $38,000 in 2006. The average American in the year 2006 could buy nearly eight times as many goods and services as the average American in the year 1900.

Source: Louis D. Johnston and Samuel H. Williamson, "The Annual Real and Nominal GDP for the United States, 1790–Present," Economic History Services, April 1, 2006, www.eh.net/hmit/gdp; and U.S. Bureau of Economic Analysis.

The process of **long-run economic growth** brought the typical American from the standard of living of 1900 to the standard of living of today. The best measure of the standard of living is real GDP per person, which is usually referred to as *real GDP per capita*. So, we measure long-run economic growth by increases in real GDP per capita over long periods of time, generally decades or more. We use real GDP rather than nominal GDP to adjust for changes in the price level over time. Figure 9-1 shows the growth in real GDP per capita in the United States from 1900 to 2006. The figure shows that although real GDP per capita fluctuates because of the short-run effects of the business cycle, over the long-run, the trend is strongly upward. It is the upward trend in real GDP per capita that we focus on when discussing long-run economic growth.

Long-run economic growth The process by which rising productivity increases the average standard of living.

The values in Figure 9-1 are measured in prices of the year 2000, so they represent constant amounts of purchasing power. In 1900, real GDP per capita was about $4,900. Over a century later, in 2006, it had risen to about $38,000, which means that the average American in 2006 could purchase nearly eight times as many goods and services as the average American in 1900. Large as it is, this increase in real GDP per capita actually understates the true increase in the standard of living of Americans in 2006 compared with 1900. Many of today's goods and services were not available in 1900. For example, if you lived in 1900 and became ill with a serious infection, you would have been unable to purchase antibiotics to treat your illness—no matter how high your income. You might have died from an illness for which even a very poor person in today's society could receive effective medical treatment. Of course, the quantity of goods and services that a person can buy is not a perfect measure of how happy or contented that person may be. The level of pollution, the level of crime, spiritual well-being, and many other factors ignored in calculating GDP contribute to a person's happiness. Nevertheless, economists rely heavily on comparisons of real GDP per capita because it is the best means of comparing the performance of one economy over time or the performance of different economies at any particular time.

Making the Connection | The Connection between Economic Prosperity and Health

We can see the direct impact of economic growth on living standards by looking at improvements in health in the high-income countries over the past 100 years. The research of Robert Fogel, winner of the Nobel Prize in Economics, has highlighted the close connection between economic growth, improvements in technology, and improvements in human physiology. One important measure of health is life expectancy at birth. As the following graph shows, in 1900 life expectancy was less than 50 years in the United States, the United Kingdom, and France. Today, life expectancy is about 80 years. Although life expectancies in the lowest-income countries remain very short, some countries that have begun to experience economic growth have seen dramatic increases in life expectancies. For example, life expectancy in India has more than doubled from 27 years in 1900 to 69 years today.

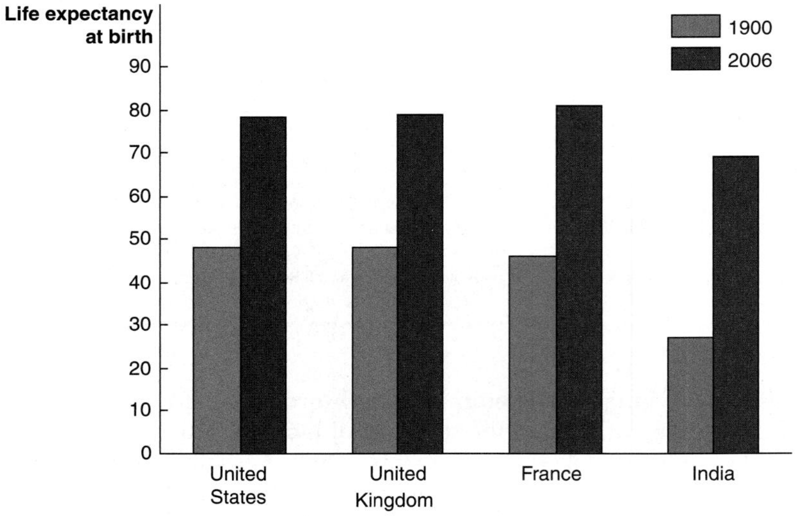

Sources: Robert William Fogel, *The Escape from Hunger and Premature Death, 1700–2100*, New York: Cambridge University Press, 2004, p. 2; and U.S. Central Intelligence Agency, *The World Factbook 2006*, online version.

Many economists believe there is a link between health and economic growth. In the United States and Western Europe during the nineteenth century, improvements in agricultural technology and rising incomes led to dramatic improvements in the nutrition of the average person. The development of the germ theory of disease and technological progress in the purification of water in the late nineteenth century led to sharp declines in sickness due to waterborne diseases. As people became taller, stronger, and less susceptible to disease, they also became more productive. Today, economists studying economic development have put increasing emphasis on the need for low-income countries to reduce disease and increase nutrition if they are to experience economic growth.

Many researchers believe that the state of human physiology will continue to improve as technology advances. In high-income countries, life expectancy at birth is expected to rise from about 80 years today to about 90 years by the middle of the century. Technological advance will continue to reduce the average number of hours worked per day and the number of years the average person spends in the paid workforce. Individuals spend about 10 hours per day sleeping, eating, and bathing. Their remaining "discretionary hours" are divided between paid work and leisure. The following graph is based on estimates by Robert Fogel that contrast how individuals in the United States will divide their time in 2040 compared with 1880 and 1995.

Not only will technology and economic growth allow people in the near future to live longer lives, but a much smaller fraction of those lives will need to be spent at paid work.

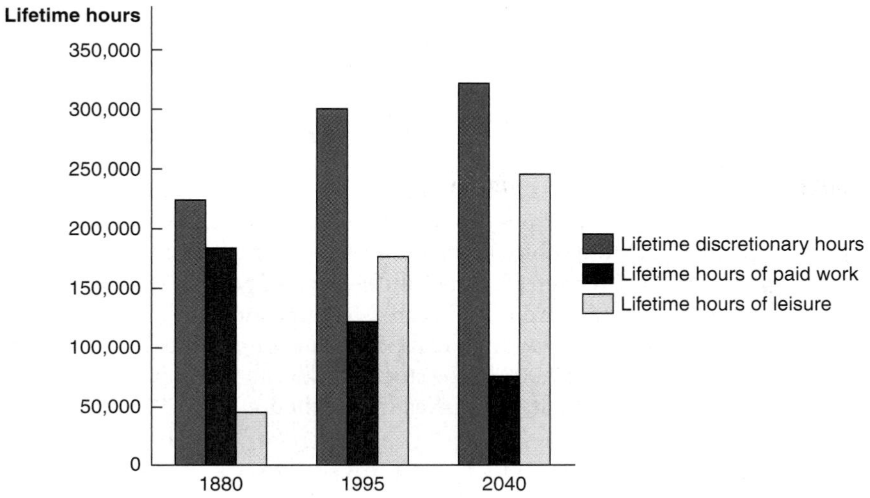

Source: Robert William Fogel, *The Escape from Hunger and Premature Death, 1700–2100*, New York: Cambridge University Press, 2004, p. 71.

YOUR TURN: Test your understanding by doing related problem 1.7 on page 304 at the end of this chapter.

Calculating Growth Rates and the Rule of 70

The growth rate of real GDP or real GDP per capita during a particular year is equal to the percentage change from the previous year. For example, measured in prices of the year 2000, real GDP equaled $11,049 billion in 2005 and rose to $11,415 billion in 2006. We calculate the growth of real GDP in 2006 as:

$$\left(\frac{\$11{,}415 \text{ billion} - \$11{,}049 \text{ billion}}{\$11{,}049 \text{ billion}}\right) \times 100 = 3.3\%.$$

For longer periods of time, we can use the *average annual growth rate*. For example, real GDP in the United States was $1,777 billion in 1950 and $11,415 billion in 2006. To find the average annual growth rate during this 56-year period, we compute the annual growth rate that would result in $1,777 billion increasing to $11,415 billion over 56 years. In this case, the growth rate is 3.4 percent. That is, if $1,777 billion grows at an average rate of 3.4 percent per year, after 56 years it will have grown to $11,415 billion.

For shorter periods of time, we get approximately the same answer by averaging the growth rate for each year. For example, real GDP in the United States grew by 3.9 percent in 2004, 3.2 percent in 2005, and 3.3 percent in 2006. So, the average annual growth rate of real GDP for the period 2004–2006 was 3.5 percent, which is the average of the three annual growth rates:

$$\frac{3.9\% + 3.2\% + 3.3\%}{3} = 3.5\%.$$

When discussing long-run economic growth, we usually shorten "average annual growth rate" to "growth rate."

We can judge how rapidly an economic variable is growing by calculating the number of years it would take to double. For example, if real GDP per capita in a country doubles, say, every 20 years, most people in the country will experience significant increases in their standard of living over the course of their lives. If real GDP per capita doubles only every 100 years, increases in the standard of living will be too slow to notice. One easy way to calculate approximately how many years it will take real GDP per capita to double is to use the *rule of 70*. The formula for the rule of 70 is as follows:

$$\text{Number of years to double} = \frac{70}{\text{Growth rate}}.$$

For example, if real GDP per capita is growing at a rate of 5 percent per year, it will double in 70/5 = 14 years. If real GDP per capita is growing at the rate of 2 percent per year, it will take 70/2 = 35 years to double. These examples illustrate an important point that we will discuss further in Chapter 10: Small differences in growth rates can have large effects on how rapidly the standard of living in a country increases. Finally, notice that the rule of 70 applies not just to growth in real GDP per capita but to growth in any variable. For example, if you invest $1,000 in the stock market, and your investment grows at an average annual rate of 7 percent, your investment will double to $2,000 in 10 years.

What Determines the Rate of Long-Run Growth?

Labor productivity The quantity of goods and services that can be produced by one worker or by one hour of work.

In Chapter 10, we will explore the sources of economic growth in more detail and discuss why growth in the United States and other high-income countries has been so much faster than growth in poorer countries. For now, we will focus on the basic point that *increases in real GDP per capita depend on increases in labor productivity*. **Labor productivity** is the quantity of goods and services that can be produced by one worker or by one hour of work. In analyzing long-run growth, economists usually measure labor productivity as output per hour of work to avoid the effects of fluctuations in the length of the workday and in the fraction of the population employed. If the quantity of goods and services consumed by the average person is to increase, the quantity of goods and services produced per hour of work must also increase. Why in 2006 was the average American able to consume almost eight times as many goods and services as the average American in 1900? Because the average American worker in 2006 was eight times as productive as the average American worker in 1900.

If increases in labor productivity are the key to long-run economic growth, what causes labor productivity to increase? Economists believe two key factors determine labor productivity: the quantity of capital per hour worked and the level of technology. Therefore, economic growth occurs if the quantity of capital per hour worked increases and if technological change occurs.

Capital Manufactured goods that are used to produce other goods and services.

Increases in Capital per Hour Worked Workers today in high-income countries such as the United States have more physical capital available than workers in low-income countries or workers in the high-income countries of 100 years ago. Recall that **capital** refers to manufactured goods that are used to produce other goods and services. Examples of capital are computers, factory buildings, machine tools, warehouses, and trucks. The total amount of physical capital available in a country is known as the country's *capital stock*.

As the capital stock per hour worked increases, worker productivity increases. A secretary with a personal computer can produce more documents per day than a secretary who has only a typewriter. A worker with a backhoe can excavate more earth than a worker who has only a shovel.

Human capital refers to the accumulated knowledge and skills workers acquire from education and training or from their life experiences. For example, workers with a college education generally have more skills and are more productive than workers who have only a high school degree. Increases in human capital are particularly important in stimulating economic growth.

Technological Change Economic growth depends more on *technological change* than on increases in capital per hour worked. Technology refers to the processes a firm uses to turn inputs into outputs of goods and services. Technological change is an increase in the quantity of output firms can produce using a given quantity of inputs. Technological change can come from many sources. For example, a firm's managers may rearrange a factory floor or the layout of a retail store to increase production and sales. Most technological change, however, is embodied in new machinery, equipment, or software.

A very important point is that just accumulating more inputs—such as labor, capital, and natural resources—will not ensure that an economy experiences economic growth unless technological change also occurs. For example, the Soviet Union failed to maintain a high rate of economic growth, even though it continued to increase the quantity of capital available per hour worked, because it experienced relatively little technological change.

In implementing technological change, *entrepreneurs* are of crucial importance. Recall from Chapter 2 that an entrepreneur is someone who operates a business, bringing together the factors of production—labor, capital, and natural resources—to produce goods and services. In a market economy, entrepreneurs make the crucial decisions about whether to introduce new technology to produce better or lower-cost products. Entrepreneurs also decide whether to allocate the firm's resources to research and development that can result in new technologies. One of the difficulties centrally planned economies have in sustaining economic growth is that managers employed by the government are usually much slower to develop and adopt new technologies than entrepreneurs in a market system.

Solved Problem | 9-1

The Role of Technological Change in Growth

Between 1960 and 1995, real GDP per capita in Singapore grew at an average annual rate of 6.2 percent. This very rapid growth rate results in the level of real GDP per capita doubling about every 11.5 years. In 1995, Alywn Young of the University of Chicago published an article in which he argued that Singapore's growth depended more on increases in capital per hour worked, increases in the labor force participation rate, and the transfer of workers from agricultural to nonagricultural jobs than on technological change. If Young's analysis was correct, predict what was likely to happen to Singapore's growth rate in the years after 1995.

SOLVING THE PROBLEM:

Step 1: **Review the chapter material.** This problem is about what determines the rate of long-run growth, so you may want to review the section "What Determines the Rate of Long-Run Growth?" which begins on page 280.

Step 2: **Predict what happened to the growth rate in Singapore after 1995.** As countries begin to develop, they often experience an increase in the labor force participation rate, as workers who are not part of the paid labor force respond to rising wage rates. Many workers also leave the agricultural sector—where output per hour worked is often low—for the nonagricultural sector. These changes increase real GDP per capita, but they are "one-shot" changes that eventually come to an end, as the labor force participation rate and the fraction of the labor force outside agriculture both approach the levels found in high-income countries. Similarly, as we already noted, increases in capital per hour worked cannot sustain high rates of economic growth unless they are accompanied by technological change.

We can conclude that Singapore was unlikely to sustain its high growth rates in the years after 1995. In fact, from 1996 to 2006, the growth of real GDP per capita slowed to an average rate of 2.5 percent per year. Although this growth rate is comparable to those experienced in high-income countries, such as the United States, it leads to a doubling of real GDP per capita only every 28 years rather than every 11.5 years.

Source: Alwyn Young, "The Tyranny of Numbers: Confronting the Statistical Realities of the East Asian Growth Experience," *Quarterly Journal of Economics*, Vol. 110, No. 3, August 1995, pp. 641–680.

YOUR TURN: For more practice, do related problem 1.12 on page 305 at the end of this chapter.

>> End Solved Problem 9-1

Finally, an additional requirement for economic growth is that the government provides secure rights to private property. As we saw in Chapter 2, a market system cannot function unless rights to private property are secure. In addition, the government can help the market work and aid economic growth by establishing an independent court system that enforces contracts between private individuals. Many economists would also say the government has a role in facilitating the development of an efficient financial system, as well as systems of education, transportation, and communication. Economist Richard Sylla of New York University has argued that every country that has experienced economic growth first experienced a "financial revolution." For example, before the United States was able to experience significant economic growth in the early nineteenth century, the country's banking and monetary systems were reformed under the guidance of Alexander Hamilton, the first secretary of the treasury. Without supportive government policies, long-run economic growth is unlikely.

Making the Connection

What Explains Rapid Economic Growth in Botswana?

Economic growth in much of sub-Saharan Africa has been very slow. As desperately poor as most of these countries were in 1960, some are even poorer today. The growth rate in one country in this region stands out, however, as being exceptionally rapid. The following graph shows the average annual growth rate in real GDP per capita between 1960 and 2004 for Botswana and the six most populous sub-Saharan countries. Botswana's average annual growth rate over this 44-year period was four times as great as that of Tanzania and South Africa, which were the second-fastest-growing countries in the group. Botswana may seem an unlikely country to experience rapid growth because it has been hard hit by the HIV epidemic. Despite the disruptive effects of the epidemic, growth in real per capita GDP slowed only moderately to 4.7 percent in 2006.

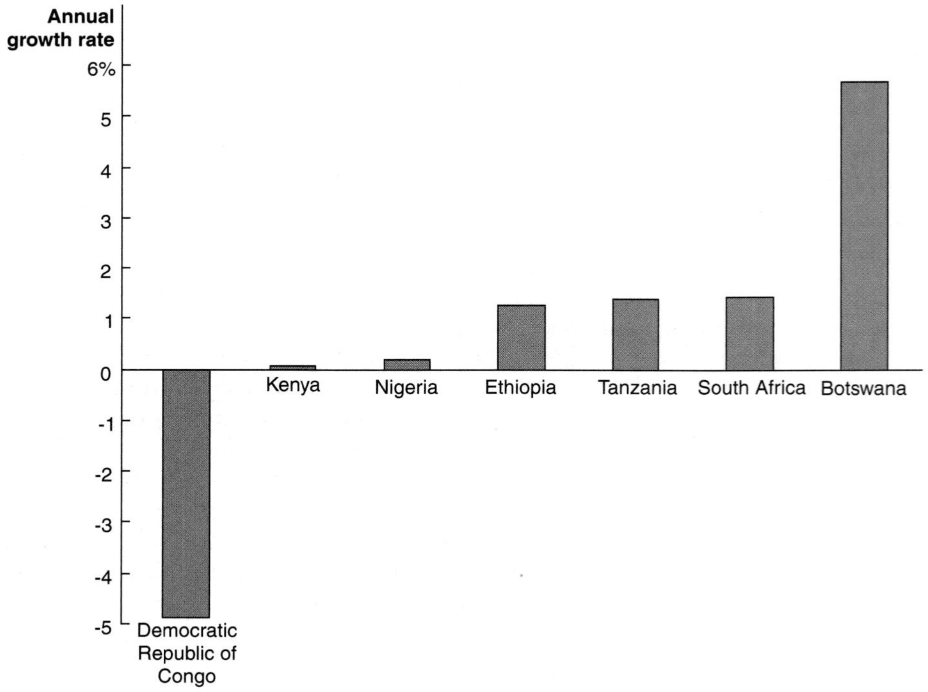

Note: Data for Democratic Republic of Congo are for 1970–2004.

Source: Authors' calculations from data in Alan Heston, Robert Summers, and Bettina Aten, *Penn World Table Version 6.2*, Center for International Comparisons of Production, Income and Prices at the University of Pennsylvania, September 2006.

What explains Botswana's rapid growth rate? Several factors have been important. Botswana avoided the civil wars that plagued other African countries during these years. The country also benefited from earnings from diamond exports. But many economists believe the pro-growth policies of its government are the most important reason for the country's success. Economists Shantayanan Devarajan of the World Bank, William Easterly of New York University, and Howard Pack of the University of Pennsylvania have summarized these policies:

> The government [of Botswana] made it clear it would protect private property rights. It was a "government of cattlemen" who were attuned to commercial interests. . . . The relative political stability and relatively low corruption also made Botswana a favorable location for investment. Botswana's relatively high level of press freedom and democracy (continuing a pre-colonial tradition that held chiefs responsible to tribal members) held the government responsible for any economic policy mistakes.

These policies—protecting private property, avoiding political instability and corruption, and allowing press freedom and democracy—may seem a straightforward recipe for providing an environment in which economic growth can occur. As we will see in Chapter 10, however, in practice, these are policies many countries have difficulty implementing successfully.

Source: Shantayanan Devarajan, William Easterly, and Howard Pack, "Low Investment Is Not the Constraint on African Development," *Economic Development and Cultural Change*, Vol. 51, No. 3, April 2003, pp. 547–571.

YOUR TURN: Test your understanding by doing related problem 1.14 on page 305 at the end of this chapter.

Potential Real GDP

Because economists take a long-run perspective in discussing economic growth, the concept of *potential GDP* is useful. **Potential GDP** is the level of GDP attained when all firms are producing at capacity. The capacity of a firm is *not* the maximum output the firm is capable of producing. A Boeing assembly plant could operate 24 hours per day for 52 weeks per year and would be at its maximum production level. The plant's capacity, however, is measured by its production when operating on normal hours, using a normal workforce. If all firms in the economy were operating at capacity, the level of total production of final goods and services would equal potential GDP. Potential GDP will increase over time as the labor force grows over time, new factories and office buildings are built, new machinery and equipment are installed, and technological change takes place.

Potential GDP The level of GDP attained when all firms are producing at capacity.

Growth in potential real GDP in the United States is estimated to be about 3.5 percent per year. In other words, each year, the capacity of the economy to produce final goods and services expands by 3.5 percent. The *actual* level of GDP may increase by more or less than 3.5 percent as the economy moves through the business cycle. Figure 9-2 on page 284 shows movements in actual and potential real GDP for the years since 1950. The smooth light blue line represents potential real GDP, and the dark blue line represents actual real GDP.

9.2 LEARNING OBJECTIVE

9.2 | Discuss the role of the financial system in facilitating long-run economic growth.

Saving, Investment, and the Financial System

The process of economic growth depends on the ability of firms to expand their operations, buy additional equipment, train workers, and adopt new technologies. Firms can finance some of these activities from *retained earnings*, which are profits that are

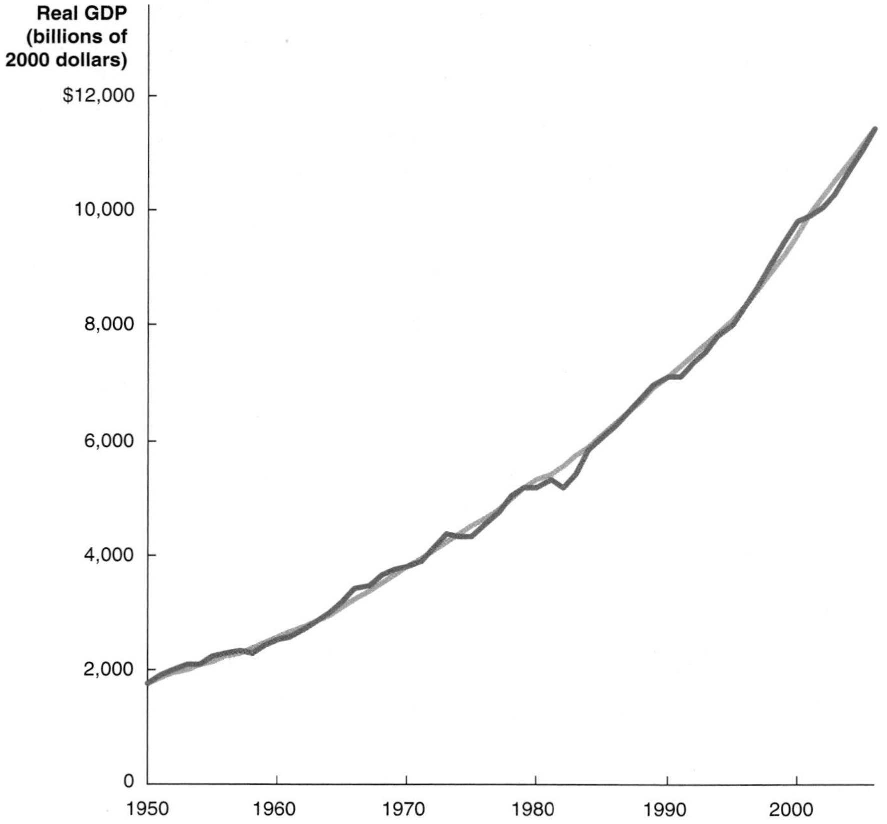

Figure 9-2 | Actual and Potential Real GDP

Potential real GDP increases every year as the labor force and the capital stock grow and technological change occurs. The smooth light blue line represents potential real GDP, and the dark blue line represents actual real GDP. Because of the business cycle, actual real GDP has sometimes been greater than potential real GDP and sometimes less.

Sources: Congressional Budget Office, *Spreadsheets for Selected Estimates and Projections*, January 2007; and Bureau of Economic Analysis.

reinvested in the firm rather than paid to the firm's owners. For many firms, retained earnings are not sufficient to finance the rapid expansion required in economies experiencing high rates of economic growth. Firms acquire funds from households, either directly through financial markets—such as the stock and bond markets—or indirectly through financial intermediaries—such as banks. Financial markets and financial intermediaries together comprise the **financial system**. Without a well-functioning financial system, economic growth is impossible because firms will be unable to expand and adopt new technologies. As we noted earlier, no country without a well-developed financial system has been able to sustain high levels of economic growth.

Financial system The system of financial markets and financial intermediaries through which firms acquire funds from households.

An Overview of the Financial System

The financial system channels funds from savers to borrowers and channels returns on the borrowed funds back to savers. Recall from Chapter 5 that in **financial markets**, such as the stock market or the bond market, firms raise funds by selling financial securities directly to savers. A financial security is a document—sometimes in electronic form—that states the terms under which funds pass from the buyer of the security—who is lending funds—to the seller. *Stocks* are financial securities that represent partial ownership of a firm. If you buy one share of stock in General Electric, you become one

Financial markets Markets where financial securities, such as stocks and bonds, are bought and sold.

of millions of owners of that firm. *Bonds* are financial securities that represent promises to repay a fixed amount of funds. When General Electric sells a bond, the firm promises to pay the purchaser of the bond an interest payment each year for the term of the bond, as well as a final payment of the amount of the loan.

Financial intermediaries Firms, such as banks, mutual funds, pension funds, and insurance companies, that borrow funds from savers and lend them to borrowers.

Financial intermediaries, such as banks, mutual funds, pension funds, and insurance companies, act as go-betweens for borrowers and lenders. In effect, financial intermediaries borrow funds from savers and lend them to borrowers. When you deposit funds in your checking account, you are lending your funds to the bank. The bank may lend your funds (together with the funds of other savers) to an entrepreneur who wants to start a business. Suppose Lena wants to open a laundry. Rather than you lending money directly to Lena's Laundry, the bank acts as a go-between for you and Lena. Intermediaries pool the funds of many small savers to lend to many individual borrowers. The intermediaries pay interest to savers in exchange for the use of savers' funds and earn a profit by lending money to borrowers and charging borrowers a higher rate of interest on the loans. For example, a bank might pay you as a depositor a 3 percent rate of interest, while it lends the money to Lena's Laundry at a 6 percent rate of interest.

Banks, mutual funds, pension funds, and insurance companies also make investments in stocks and bonds on behalf of savers. For example, *mutual funds* sell shares to savers and then use the funds to buy a portfolio of stocks, bonds, mortgages, and other financial securities. Mutual funds are either closed-end or open-end funds. In closed-end mutual funds, the mutual fund company issues shares that investors may buy and sell in financial markets, like shares of stock issued by corporations. More common are open-end mutual funds, which issue shares that the mutual fund company will buy back—or redeem—at a price that represents the underlying value of the financial securities owned by the fund. Large mutual fund companies, such as Fidelity, Vanguard, and Dreyfus, offer many alternative stock and bond funds. Some funds hold a wide range of stocks or bonds; others specialize in securities issued by a particular industry or sector, such as technology; and others invest as an index fund in a fixed market basket of securities such as shares of the Standard & Poor's 500 firms. Over the past 30 years, the role of mutual funds in the financial system has increased dramatically. By 2007, competition among hundreds of mutual fund firms gave investors thousands of funds from which to choose.

In addition to matching households that have excess funds with firms that want to borrow funds, the financial system provides three key services for savers and borrowers: risk sharing, liquidity, and information. *Risk* is the chance that the value of a financial security will change relative to what you expect. For example, you may buy a share of stock in Google at a price of $450, only to have the price fall to $100. Most individual savers are not gamblers and seek a steady return on their savings rather than erratic swings between high and low earnings. The financial system provides risk sharing by allowing savers to spread their money among many financial investments. For example, you can divide your money among a bank certificate of deposit, individual bonds, and a mutual fund.

Liquidity is the ease with which a financial security can be exchanged for money. The financial system provides the service of liquidity by providing savers with markets in which they can sell their holdings of financial securities. For example, savers can easily sell their holdings of the stocks and bonds issued by large corporations on the major stock and bond markets.

A third service that the financial system provides savers is the collection and communication of *information*, or facts about borrowers and expectations about returns on financial securities. For example, Lena's Laundry may want to borrow $10,000 from you. Finding out what Lena intends to do with the funds and how likely she is to pay you back may be costly and time-consuming. By depositing $10,000 in the bank, you are, in effect, allowing the bank to gather this information for you. Because banks specialize in gathering information on borrowers, they are able to do it faster and at a lower cost than can individual savers. The financial system plays an important role in communicating information. If you read a newspaper headline announcing that an automobile firm has invented a car with an engine that runs on water, how would you determine the effect of this discovery on the firm's profits? Financial markets do that job for you by incorporating information into the prices of stocks, bonds, and other financial securities. In this example, the expectation of higher future profits would boost the prices of the automobile firm's stock and bonds.

The Macroeconomics of Saving and Investment

As we have seen, the funds available to firms through the financial system come from saving. When firms use funds to purchase machinery, factories, and office buildings, they are engaging in investment. In this section, we explore the macroeconomics of saving and investment. A key point we will develop is that *the total value of saving in the economy must equal the total value of investment.* We saw in Chapter 7 that *national income accounting* refers to the methods the Bureau of Economic Analysis uses to keep track of total production and total income in the economy. We can use some relationships from national income accounting to understand why total saving must equal total investment.

We begin with the relationship between GDP (Y) and its components, consumption (C), investment (I), government purchases (G), and net exports (NX):

$$Y = C + I + G + NX.$$

Remember that GDP is a measure of both total production in the economy and total income.

In an *open economy*, there is interaction with other economies in terms of both trading of goods and services and borrowing and lending. All economies today are open economies, although they vary significantly in the extent of their openness. In a *closed economy*, there is no trading or borrowing and lending with other economies. For simplicity, we will develop the relationship between saving and investment for a closed economy. This allows us to focus on the most important points in a simpler framework. We will consider the case of an open economy in Chapter 17.

In a closed economy, net exports are zero, so we can rewrite the relationship between GDP and its components as:

$$Y = C + I + G.$$

If we rearrange this relationship, we have an expression for investment in terms of the other variables:

$$I = Y - C - G.$$

This expression tells us that in a closed economy, investment spending is equal to total income minus consumption spending and minus government purchases.

We can also derive an expression for total saving. *Private saving* is equal to what households retain of their income after purchasing goods and services (C) and paying taxes (T). Households receive income for supplying the factors of production to firms. This portion of household income is equal to Y. Households also receive income from government in the form of *transfer payments* (TR). Recall that transfer payments include Social Security payments and unemployment insurance payments. We can write an expression for private saving (S_{private}):

$$S_{\text{private}} = Y + TR - C - T.$$

The government also engages in saving. *Public saving* (S_{public}) equals the amount of tax revenue the government retains after paying for government purchases and making transfer payments to households:

$$S_{\text{public}} = T - G - TR.$$

So, total saving in the economy (S) is equal to the sum of private saving and public saving:

$$S = S_{\text{private}} + S_{\text{public}},$$

or:

$$S = (Y + TR - C - T) + (T - G - TR),$$

or:

$$S = Y - C - G.$$

The right-hand side of this expression is identical to the expression we derived earlier for investment spending. So, we can conclude that total saving must equal total investment:

$$S = I.$$

When the government spends the same amount that it collects in taxes, there is a *balanced budget*. When the government spends more than it collects in taxes, there is a *budget deficit*. In the case of a deficit, T is less than $G + TR$, which means that public saving is negative. Negative saving is also known as *dissaving*. How can public saving be negative? When the federal government runs a budget deficit, the U.S. Department of the Treasury sells Treasury bonds to borrow the money necessary to fund the gap between taxes and spending. In this case, rather than adding to the total amount of saving available to be borrowed for investment spending, the government is subtracting from it. (Notice that if households borrow more than they save, the total amount of saving will also fall.) With less saving, investment must also be lower. We can conclude that, holding constant all other factors, there is a lower level of investment spending in the economy when there is a budget deficit than when there is a balanced budget.

When the government spends less than it collects in taxes, there is a *budget surplus*. A budget surplus increases public saving and the total level of saving in the economy. A higher level of saving results in a higher level of investment spending. Therefore, holding constant all other factors, there is a higher level of investment spending in the economy when there is a budget surplus than when there is a balanced budget.

The U.S. federal government has experienced dramatic swings in the state of its budget over the past 15 years. In 1992, the federal budget deficit was $297.4 billion. This figure changed to a surplus of $189.5 billion in 2000 and was back to a deficit of $153.6 billion in 2006.

The Market for Loanable Funds

We have seen that the value of total saving must equal the value of total investment, but we have not yet discussed how this equality actually is brought about in the financial system. We can think of the financial system as being composed of many markets through which funds flow from lenders to borrowers: the market for certificates of deposit at banks, the market for stocks, the market for bonds, the market for mutual fund shares, and so on. For simplicity, we can combine these markets into a single market for *loanable funds*. In the model of the **market for loanable funds**, the interaction of borrowers and lenders determines the market interest rate and the quantity of loanable funds exchanged. As we will discuss in Chapter 17, firms can also borrow from savers in other countries. For the remainder of this chapter, we will assume that there are no interactions between households and firms in the United States and those in other countries.

Market for loanable funds The interaction of borrowers and lenders that determines the market interest rate and the quantity of loanable funds exchanged.

Demand and Supply in the Loanable Funds Market The demand for loanable funds is determined by the willingness of firms to borrow money to engage in new investment projects, such as building new factories or carrying out research and

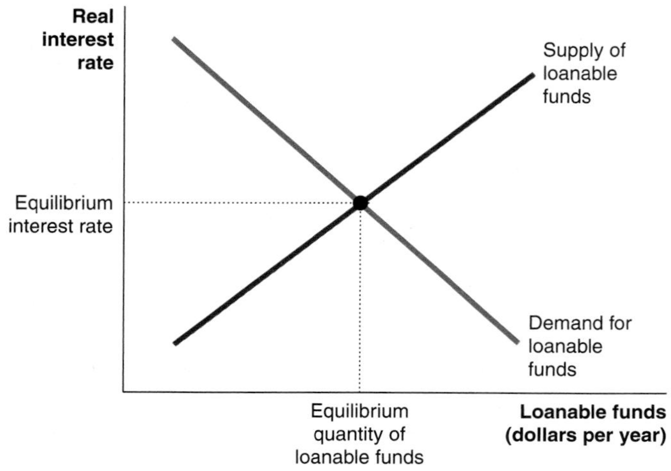

Figure 9-3 | The Market for Loanable Funds

The demand for loanable funds is determined by the willingness of firms to borrow money to engage in new investment projects. The supply of loanable funds is determined by the willingness of households to save and by the extent of government saving or dissaving. Equilibrium in the market for loanable funds determines the real interest rate and the quantity of loanable funds exchanged.

development of new products. In determining whether to borrow funds, firms compare the return they expect to make on an investment with the interest rate they must pay to borrow the necessary funds. For example, if Home Depot is considering opening several new stores and expects to earn a return of 15 percent on its investment, the investment will be profitable if it can borrow the funds at an interest rate of 10 percent but will not be profitable if the interest rate is 20 percent. In Figure 9-3, the demand for loanable funds is downward sloping because the lower the interest rate, the more investment projects firms can profitably undertake, and the greater the quantity of loanable funds they will demand.

The supply of loanable funds is determined by the willingness of households to save and by the extent of government saving or dissaving. When households save, they reduce the amount of goods and services they can consume and enjoy today. The willingness of households to save rather than consume their incomes today will be determined in part by the interest rate they receive when they lend their savings. The higher the interest rate, the greater the reward to saving and the larger the amount of funds households will save. Therefore, the supply curve for loanable funds in Figure 9-3 is upward sloping because the higher the interest rate, the greater the quantity of saving supplied.

In Chapter 8, we discussed the distinction between the *nominal interest rate* and the *real interest rate.* The nominal interest rate is the stated interest rate on a loan. The real interest rate corrects the nominal interest rate for the impact of inflation and is equal to the nominal interest rate minus the inflation rate. Because both borrowers and lenders are interested in the real interest rate they will receive or pay, equilibrium in the market for loanable funds determines the real interest rate rather than the nominal interest rate.

Making the Connection

Ebenezer Scrooge: Accidental Promoter of Economic Growth?

Ebenezer Scrooge's name has become synonymous with miserliness. Before his reform at the end of Charles Dickens's *A Christmas Carol*, Scrooge is extraordinarily reluctant to spend money. Although he earns a substantial income, he lives in a cold, dark house that he refuses to heat or light properly, and he eats a meager diet of gruel because he refuses to buy more expensive food. Throughout most of the book, Dickens portrays Scrooge's behavior in an unfavorable way. Only at the end of the book, when the reformed Scrooge begins to spend lavishly on himself and others, does Dickens praise his behavior.

As economist Steven Landsburg of the University of Rochester points out, however, economically speaking, it may be the pre-reform Scrooge who is more worthy of praise:

> In this whole world, there is nobody more generous than the miser—the man who *could* deplete the world's resources but chooses not to. The only difference between miserliness and philanthropy is that the philanthropist serves a favored few while the miser spreads his largess far and wide.

Who was better for economic growth: Scrooge the saver or Scrooge the spender?

We can extend Landsburg's discussion to consider whether the actions of the pre-reform Scrooge or the actions of the post-reform Scrooge were more helpful to economic growth. Pre-reform Scrooge spends very little, investing most of his income in the financial markets. These funds became available for firms to borrow to build new factories and to carry out research and development. Post-reform Scrooge spends much more—and saves much less. Funds that he had previously saved are now spent on food for Bob Cratchit's family and on "making merry" at Christmas. In other words, the actions of post-reform Scrooge contributed to more consumption goods being produced and fewer investment goods. We can conclude that Scrooge's reform caused economic growth to slow down—if only by a little. The larger point is, of course, that savers provide the funds that are indispensable for the investment spending that economic growth requires, and the only way to save is to not consume.

Source: Steven E. Landsburg, "What I Like About Scrooge," *Slate*, December 9, 2004.

YOUR TURN: Test your understanding by doing related problem 2.17 on page 307 at the end of this chapter.

Explaining Movements in Saving, Investment, and Interest Rates Equilibrium in the market for loanable funds determines the quantity of loanable funds that will flow from lenders to borrowers each period. It also determines the real interest rate that lenders will receive and that borrowers must pay. We draw the demand curve for loanable funds by holding constant all factors, other than the interest rate, that affect the willingness of borrowers to demand funds. We draw the supply curve by holding constant all factors, other than the interest rate, that affect the willingness of lenders to supply funds. A shift in either the demand curve or the supply curve will change the equilibrium interest rate and the equilibrium quantity of loanable funds.

Suppose, for example, that the profitability of new investment increases due to technological change. Firms will increase their demand for loanable funds. Figure 9-4 shows the impact of an increase in demand in the market for loanable funds. As in the markets for goods and services we studied in Chapter 3, an increase in demand in the market for loanable funds shifts the demand curve to the right. In the new equilibrium, the interest rate increases from i_1 to i_2, and the equilibrium quantity of loanable funds increases from L_1 to L_2. Notice that an increase in the quantity of loanable funds means that both the quantity of saving by households and the quantity of investment by firms have increased. Increasing investment increases the capital stock and the quantity of capital per hour worked, helping to increase economic growth.

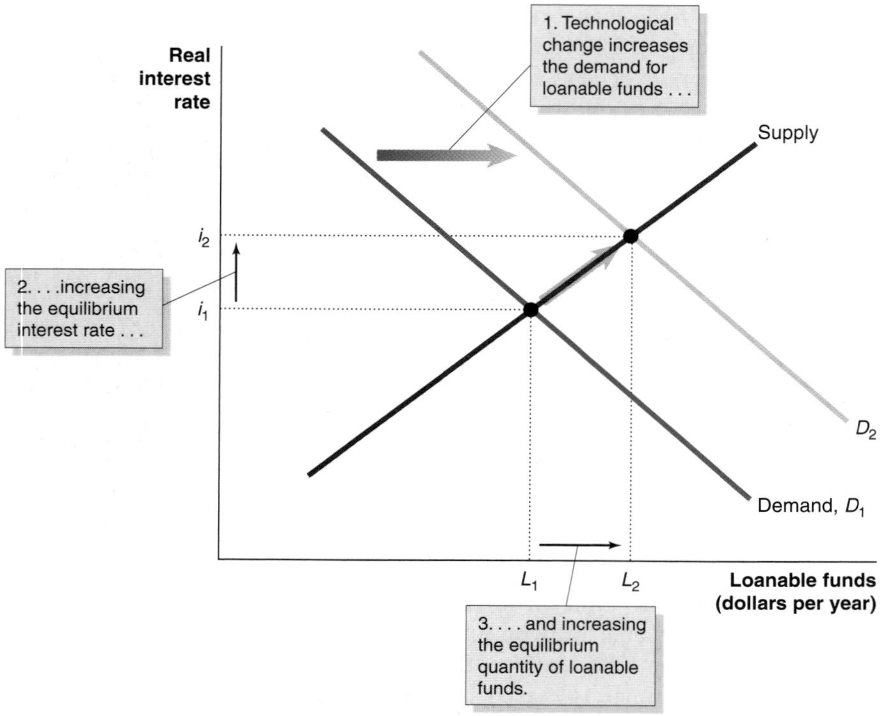

Figure 9-4 | An Increase in the Demand for Loanable Funds

An increase in the demand for loanable funds increases the equilibrium interest rate from i_1 to i_2, and it increases the equilibrium quantity of loanable funds from L_1 to L_2. As a result, saving and investment both increase.

We can also use the market for loanable funds to examine the impact of a government budget deficit. Putting aside the effects of foreign saving—which we will consider in Chapter 17—recall that if the government begins running a budget deficit, it reduces the total amount of saving in the economy. Suppose the government increases spending, which results in a budget deficit. We illustrate the effects of the budget deficit in Figure 9-5 by shifting the supply of loanable funds to the left. In the new equilibrium, the interest rate is higher, and the equilibrium quantity of loanable funds is lower. Running a deficit has reduced the level of total saving in the economy and, by increasing the interest rate, has also reduced the level of investment spending by firms. By borrowing to finance its budget deficit, the government will have *crowded out* some firms that would otherwise have been able to borrow to finance investment. **Crowding out** refers to a decline in investment spending as a result of an increase in government purchases. In Figure 9-5, the decline in investment spending due to crowding out is shown by the movement from L_1 to L_2 on the demand for loanable funds curve. Lower investment spending means that the capital stock and the quantity of capital per hour worked will not increase as much.

Crowding out A decline in private expenditures as a result of an increase in government purchases.

A government budget surplus would have the opposite effect of a deficit. A budget surplus increases the total amount of saving in the economy, shifting the supply of loanable funds to the right. In the new equilibrium, the interest rate will be lower, and the quantity of loanable funds will be higher. We can conclude that a budget surplus increases the level of saving and investment.

In practice, however, the impact of government budget deficits and surpluses on the equilibrium interest rate is relatively small. (This finding reflects in part the importance of global saving in determining the interest rate.) For example, a recent study found that increasing government borrowing by an amount equal to 1 percent of GDP would increase the equilibrium real interest rate by only about three one-

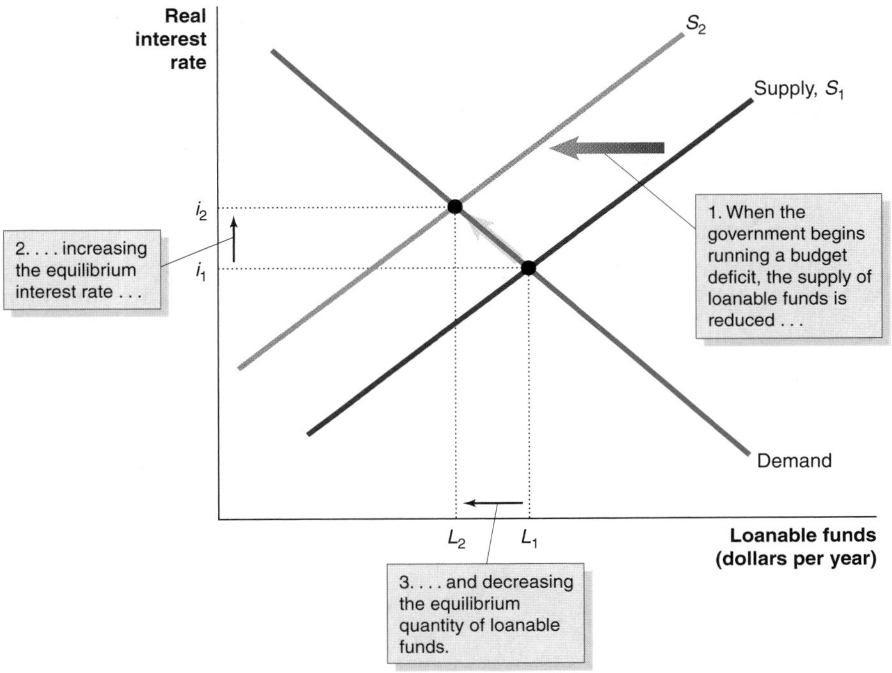

Figure 9-5 | The Effect of a Budget Deficit on the Market for Loanable Funds

When the government begins running a budget deficit, the supply of loanable funds shifts to the left. The equilibrium interest rate increases from i_1 to i_2, and the equilibrium quantity of loanable funds falls from L_1 to L_2. As a result, saving and investment both decline.

hundredths of a percentage point. However, this small effect on interest rates does not imply that we can ignore the effect of deficits on economic growth. Paying off government debt in the future may require higher taxes, which can depress economic growth.

Solved Problem | 9-2

How Would a Consumption Tax Affect Saving, Investment, the Interest Rate, and Economic Growth?

Some economists and policymakers have suggested that the federal government shift from relying on an income tax to relying on a *consumption tax*. Under the income tax, households pay taxes on all income earned. Under a consumption tax, households pay taxes only on the income they spend. Households would pay taxes on saved income only if they spend the money at a later time. Use the market for loanable funds model to analyze the effect on saving, investment, the interest rate, and economic growth of switching from an income tax to a consumption tax.

SOLVING THE PROBLEM:

Step 1: **Review the chapter material.** This problem is about applying the market for loanable funds model, so you may want to review the section "Explaining Movements in Saving, Investment, and Interest Rates," which begins on page 289.

Step 2: Explain the effect of switching from an income tax to a consumption tax. Households are interested in the return they receive from saving after they have paid their taxes. For example, consider someone who puts his savings in a certificate of deposit at an interest rate of 4 percent and whose tax rate is 25 percent. Under an income tax, this person's after-tax return to saving is 3 percent $[4 \times (1 - 0.25)]$. Under a consumption tax, income that is saved is not taxed, so the return rises to 4 percent. We can conclude that moving from an income tax to a consumption tax would increase the return to saving, causing the supply of loanable funds to increase.

Step 3: Draw a graph of the market for loanable funds to illustrate your answer.

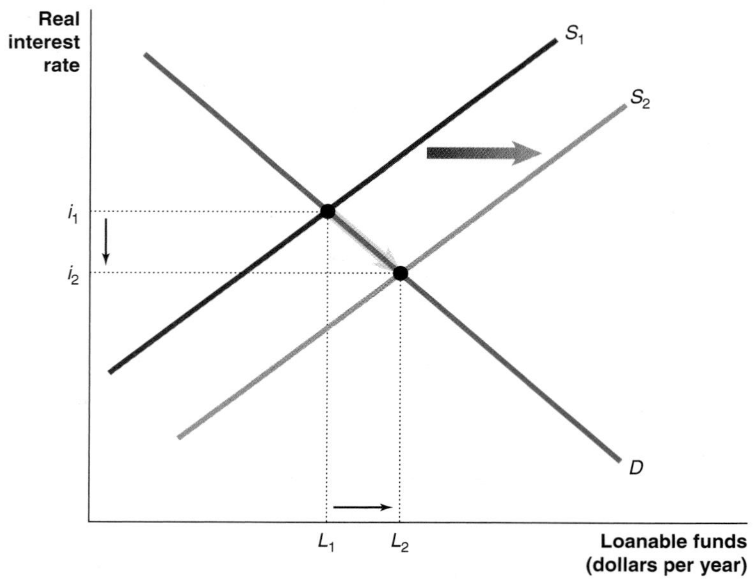

The supply curve for loanable funds will shift to the right as the after-tax return to saving increases under the consumption tax. The equilibrium interest rate will fall, and the levels of saving and investment will both increase. Because investment increases, the capital stock and the quantity of capital per hour worked will grow, and the rate of economic growth should increase. Note that the size of the fall in the interest rate and the increase in loanable funds shown in the graph are larger than the effects that most economists expect would actually result from the replacement of the income tax with a consumption tax.

>> End Solved Problem 9-2

YOUR TURN: For more practice, do related problem 2.16 on page 306 at the end of this chapter.

9.3 LEARNING OBJECTIVE

9.3 | Explain what happens during a business cycle.

The Business Cycle

Figure 9-1 on page 277 shows the tremendous increase during the last century in the standard of living of the average American. But close inspection of the figure reveals that real GDP per capita did not increase every year during this century. For example, during the first half of the 1930s, real GDP per capita *fell* for several years in a row. What accounts for these fluctuations in the long-run upward trend?

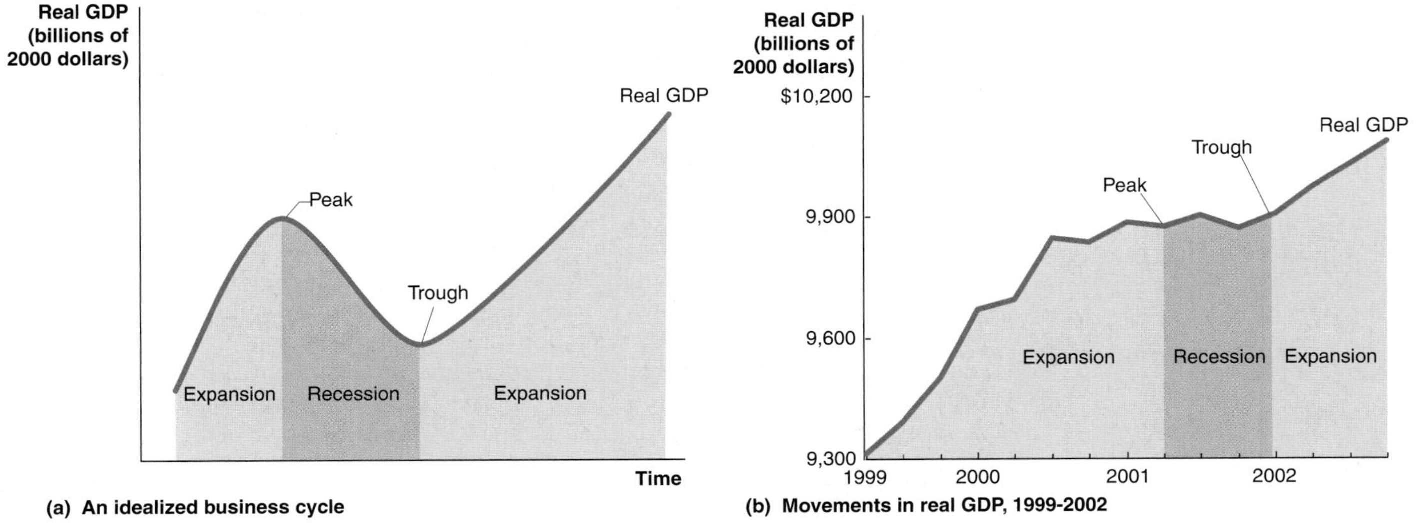

Figure 9-6 | The Business Cycle

Panel (a) shows an idealized business cycle with real GDP increasing smoothly in an expansion to a business cycle peak and then decreasing smoothly in a recession to a business cycle trough, which is followed by another expansion. The periods of expansion are shown in green, and the period of recession is shown in red. In panel (b), the actual movements in real GDP for 1999 to 2002 are shown. Real GDP fluctuates during the period around the business cycle peak of March 2001. The following recession was fairly short, and a business cycle trough was reached in November 2001, when the next expansion began.

Some Basic Business Cycle Definitions

The fluctuations in real GDP per capita shown in Figure 9-1 reflect the underlying fluctuations in real GDP. Dating back at least to the early nineteenth century, the U.S. economy has experienced a business cycle that consists of alternating periods of expanding and contracting economic activity. Because real GDP is our best measure of economic activity, the business cycle is usually illustrated using movements in real GDP.

During the *expansion phase* of the business cycle, production, employment, and income are increasing. The period of expansion ends with a *business cycle peak*. Following the business cycle peak, production, employment, and income decline as the economy enters the *recession phase* of the cycle. The recession comes to an end with a *business cycle trough*, after which another period of expansion begins. Figure 9-6 illustrates the phases of the business cycle. Panel (a) shows an idealized business cycle with real GDP increasing smoothly in an expansion to a business cycle peak and then decreasing smoothly in a recession to a business cycle trough, which is followed by another expansion. Panel (b) shows the somewhat messier reality of an actual business cycle by plotting fluctuations in real GDP during the period from 1999 to 2002. The figure shows that the expansion that began in 1991 continued through the late 1990s, until a business cycle peak was reached in March 2001. The following recession was fairly short, and a business cycle trough was reached in November 2001, when the next expansion began. But notice that real GDP declined in the third quarter of 2000, before rising in the fourth quarter of 2000, declining in the first quarter of 2001, rising in the second quarter of 2001, and then falling again in the third quarter of 2001. Inconsistent movements in real GDP around the business cycle peak can mean that the beginning and ending of a recession may not be clear-cut. In fact, some economists have argued that the recession of 2001 actually began with the fall in real GDP during the third quarter of 2000.

Making the Connection

Who Decides if the Economy Is in a Recession?

The federal government produces many statistics that make it possible to monitor the economy, but the federal government does not officially decide when a recession begins or ends. Instead, most economists accept the decisions of the Business Cycle Dating Committee of the National Bureau of Economic Research (NBER), a private research group located in Cambridge, Massachusetts. Although writers for newspapers and magazines often define a recession as two consecutive quarters of declining real GDP, the NBER has the following broader definition: "A recession is a significant decline in activity spread across the economy, lasting more than a few months, visible in industrial production, employment, real income, and wholesale-retail trade." The Business Cycle Dating Committee decided that the U.S. economy had reached a business cycle peak in March 2001 and a business cycle trough in November 2001, even though real GDP did not decline for two consecutive quarters during this period.

The NBER is fairly slow in announcing business cycle dates because it takes time to gather and analyze economic statistics. Typically, the NBER will announce that the economy is in a recession only well after the recession has begun. For instance, the NBER did not announce that a recession had begun in March 2001 until nearly eight months later, at the end of November. November was the same month that the NBER subsequently decided that the recession had ended, but it did not make this announcement until July 2003. Similarly, the NBER did not announce that a recession had begun in July 1990 until April 1991, one month after the recession had actually ended. Nonetheless, policymakers look to the NBER to chronicle the economy's expansions and contractions.

The following table lists the business cycle peaks and troughs identified by the NBER for the years since 1950. The length of each recession is the number of months from the peak to the following trough:

PEAK	TROUGH	LENGTH OF RECESSION
July 1953	May 1954	10 months
August 1957	April 1958	8 months
April 1960	February 1961	10 months
December 1969	November 1970	11 months
November 1973	March 1975	16 months
January 1980	July 1980	6 months
July 1981	November 1982	16 months
July 1990	March 1991	8 months
March 2001	November 2001	8 months

Sources: *NBER Reporter*, Fall 2001; and NBER Web site (www.nber.org).

YOUR TURN: Test your understanding by doing related problem 3.7 on page 307 at the end of this chapter.

What Happens during a Business Cycle?

Each business cycle is different. The lengths of the expansion and recession phases and which sectors of the economy are most affected are rarely the same in any two cycles. But most business cycles share certain characteristics, which we will discuss in this section. As the economy nears the end of an expansion, interest rates usually are rising, and the wages of workers usually are rising faster than prices. As a result of rising interest rates and rising wages, the profits of firms will be falling. Typically, toward the end of an expansion, both households and firms will have substantially increased their debts. These debts are the result of the borrowing firms and households undertake to help finance their spending during the expansion.

A recession will often begin with a decline in spending by firms on capital goods, such as machinery, equipment, new factories, and new office buildings, or by households on new houses and consumer durables, such as furniture and automobiles. As spending declines, firms selling capital goods and consumer durables will find their sales declining. As sales decline, firms cut back on production and begin to lay off workers. Rising unemployment and falling profits reduce income, which leads to further declines in spending.

As the recession continues, economic conditions gradually begin to improve. The declines in spending eventually come to an end; households and firms begin to reduce their debt, thereby increasing their ability to spend; and interest rates decline, making it more likely that households and firms will borrow to finance new spending. Firms begin to increase their spending on capital goods as they anticipate the need for additional production during the next expansion. Increased spending by households on consumer durables and by businesses on capital goods will finally bring the recession to an end and begin the next expansion.

The Effect of the Business Cycle on Boeing Durables are goods that are expected to last for three or more years. Consumer durables include furniture, appliances, and automobiles, and producer durables include machine tools, electric generators, and commercial airplanes. Durables are affected more by the business cycle than are nondurables—such as food and clothing—or services—such as haircuts and medical care. During a recession, workers reduce spending if they lose their jobs, fear losing their jobs, or suffer wage cuts. Because people can often continue to use their existing furniture, appliances, or automobiles, they are more likely to postpone spending on durables than spending on other goods. Similarly, when firms experience declining sales and profits during a recession, they often cut back on purchases of producer durables.

We mentioned in our discussion of Boeing at the beginning of this chapter that the firm's sales were significantly affected by the business cycle. Panel (a) of Figure 9-7

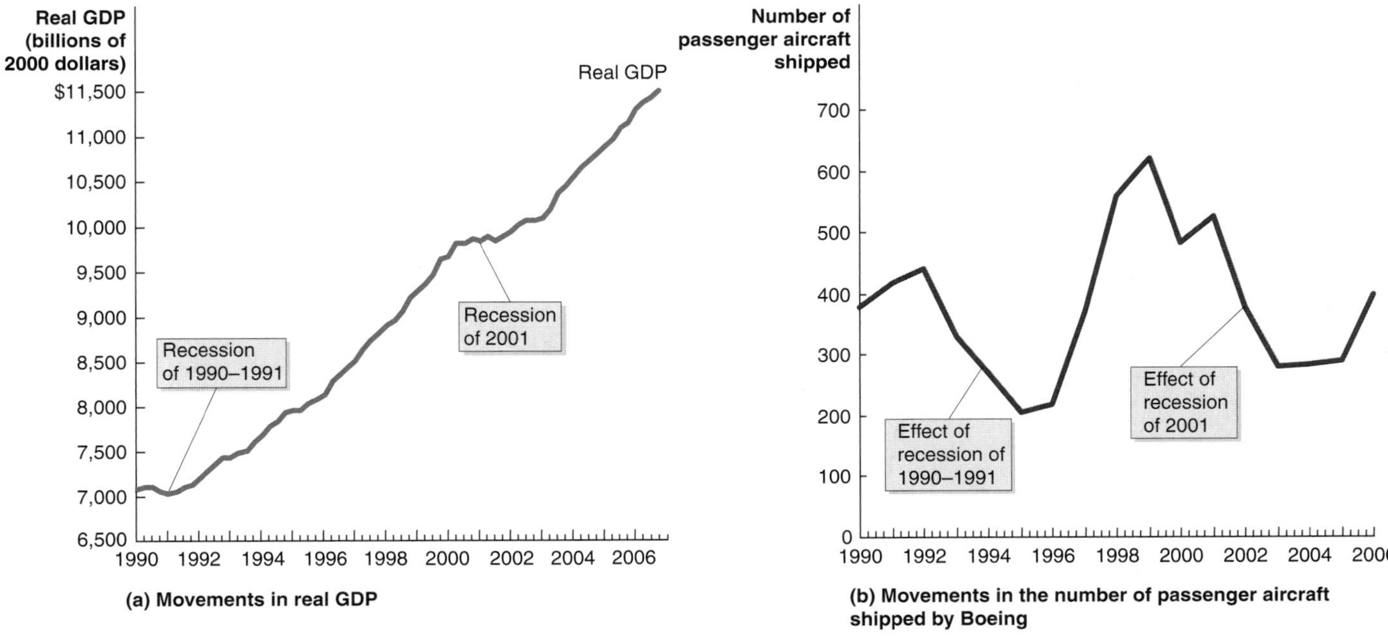

Figure 9-7 | The Effect of the Business Cycle on Boeing

Panel (a) shows movements in real GDP for each quarter from the beginning of 1990 through the end of 2006. Panel (b) shows movements in the number of passenger aircraft shipped by Boeing for the same years. In panel (b), the effects of the recessions on Boeing are more dramatic than the effects on the economy as a whole.

Sources: U.S. Bureau of Economic Analysis; Aerospace Industries Association; and Boeing.

shows movements in real GDP for each quarter from the beginning of 1990 through the end of 2006. We can see both the upward trend in real GDP over time and the effects of the recessions of 1990–1991 and 2001. Panel (b) shows movements in the total number of passenger aircraft shipped by Boeing during the same years. The effects of the recession on Boeing are much more dramatic and long-lived than the effects on the economy as a whole. In each of the two recessions shown, airlines suffered a decline in ticket sales and cut back on purchases of aircraft. As a result, Boeing suffered a sharp decline in sales during each recession.

The Effect of the Business Cycle on the Inflation Rate In Chapter 8, we saw that the *price level* measures the average prices of goods and services in the economy and that the *inflation rate* is the percentage increase in the price level from one year to the next. An important fact about the business cycle is that during economic expansions, the inflation rate usually increases, particularly near the end of the expansion, and during recessions, the inflation rate usually decreases. Figure 9-8 illustrates that this was true of the recession of 2001.

As Figure 9-8 shows, toward the end of the 1991–2001 expansion, the inflation rate rose from about 1.5 percent to about 3.5 percent. The recession that began in March 2001 caused the inflation rate to fall back to below 2 percent. Figure 9-9 shows that

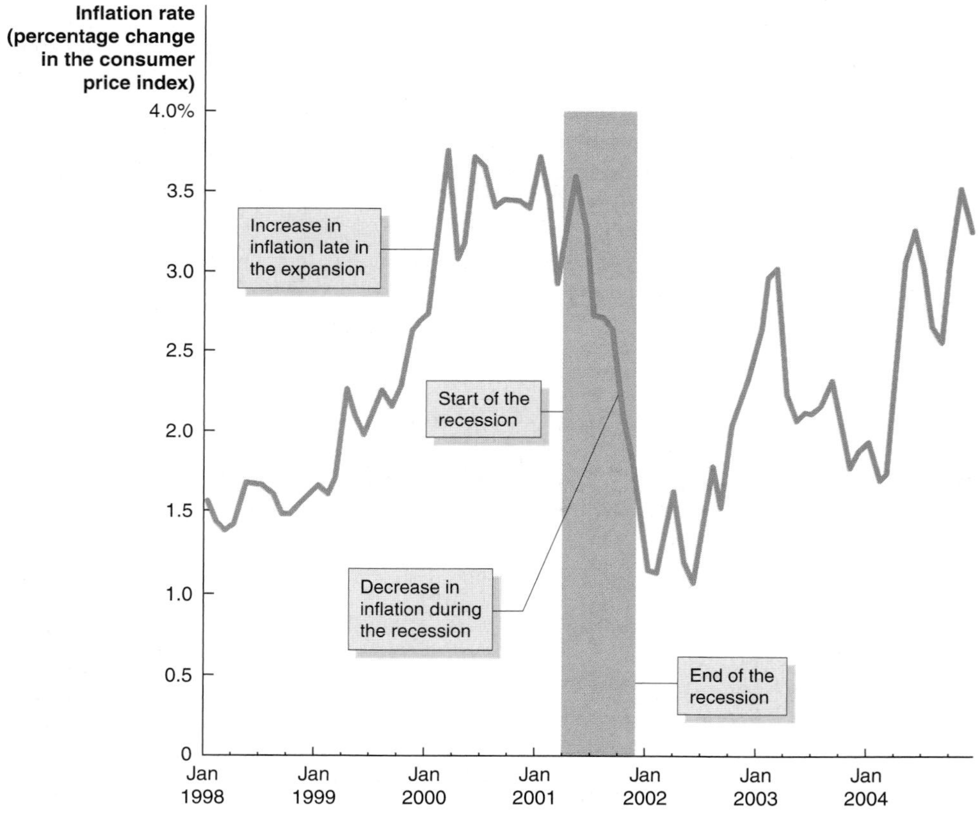

Figure 9-8 | The Effect of the 2001 Recession on the Inflation Rate

Toward the end of the 1991–2001 expansion, the inflation rate began to rise. The recession that began in March 2001, marked by the shaded vertical bar, caused the inflation rate to fall. By the end of the recession in November 2001, the inflation rate was significantly below what it had been at the beginning of the recession.

Note: The points on the figure represent the annual inflation rate measured by the change in the CPI for the year ending in the indicated month.

Source: U.S. Bureau of Labor Statistics.

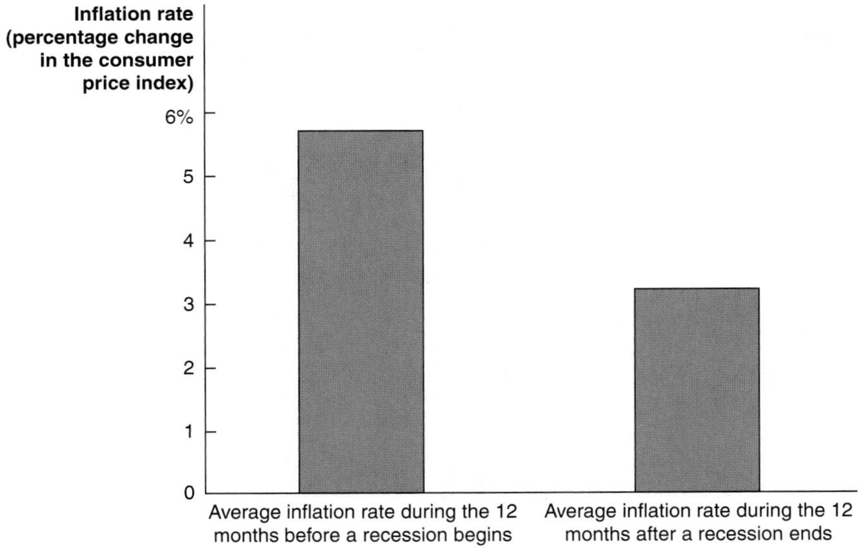

Figure 9-9 | The Impact of Recessions on the Inflation Rate

In every recession since 1950, the inflation rate has been lower during the 12 months after the business cycle trough than it was during the 12 months before the business cycle peak. The average decline in the inflation rate has been 2.5 percentage points.

Source: U.S. Bureau of Labor Statistics.

recessions have consistently had the effect of lowering the inflation rate. In every recession since 1950, the inflation rate has been lower during the 12 months after the recession ends than it was during the 12 months before the recession began. The average decline in the inflation rate has been about 2.5 percentage points. This result is not surprising. During a business cycle expansion, spending by businesses and households is strong, and producers of goods and services find it easier to raise prices. As spending declines during a recession, firms have a more difficult time selling their goods and services and are likely to increase prices less than they otherwise might have.

The Effect of the Business Cycle on the Unemployment Rate Recessions cause the inflation rate to fall, but they cause the unemployment rate to increase. As firms see their sales decline, they begin to reduce production and lay off workers. Figure 9-10 shows the impact of the recession of 2001 on the unemployment rate. As the recession

Don't Let This Happen to **YOU!**

Don't Confuse the Price Level and the Inflation Rate

Do you agree with the following statement: "The consumer price index is a widely used measure of the inflation rate"? This statement may sound plausible, but it is incorrect. As we saw in Chapter 8, the consumer price index is a measure of the *price level,* not of the inflation rate. We can measure the inflation rate as the *percentage change* in the consumer price index from one year to the next. In macroeconomics, it is important not to confuse the level of a variable with the change in the variable. To give another example, real GDP does not measure economic growth. Economic growth is measured by the percentage change in real GDP from one year to the next.

YOUR TURN: Test your understanding by doing related problem 3.6 on page 307 at the end of this chapter.

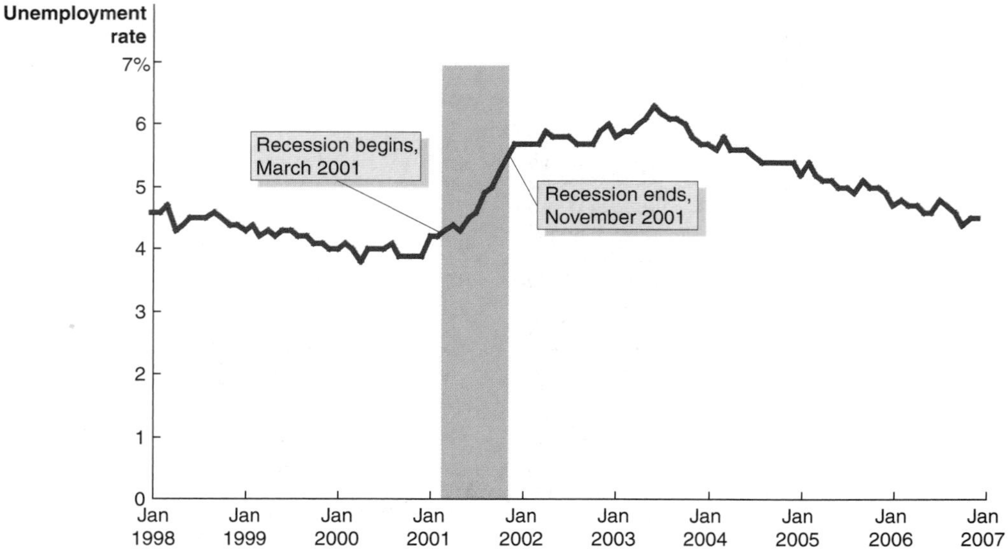

Figure 9-10 | How the Recession of 2001 Affected the Unemployment Rate

The reluctance of firms to hire new employees during the early stages of a recovery means that the unemployment rate usually continues to rise even after the recession has ended.

Source: U.S. Bureau of Labor Statistics.

began in March 2001, the unemployment rate started to rise. The rate continued to rise even after the end of the recession in November 2001. This pattern is typical and is due to two factors. First, during the business cycle, discouraged workers drop out of and then return to the labor force, as we discussed in Chapter 8. When discouraged workers drop out of the labor force during a recession, they keep the measured unemployment rate from increasing as much as it would if these workers were counted as unemployed. When discouraged workers return to the labor force as the recession ends, they increase the measured unemployment rate because they are now counted as being unemployed. Second, firms continue to operate well below their capacity even after a recession has ended and production has begun to increase. As a result, at first, firms may not hire back all the workers they have laid off and may even continue for a while to lay off more workers.

As the U.S. economy began to recover from the 2001 recession, the *Wall Street Journal* published an article giving advice to small firms on their hiring policies during the period after a recession has ended. One piece of advice was "Just because some new orders arrived, don't run out and hire a bunch of new workers." The owner of one small accounting firm suggested that during the early stages of an expansion, companies should use overtime by existing employees to meet sales rather than hire new workers.

Figure 9-11 shows that for the recessions since 1950, the unemployment rate has risen on average by about 1.2 percentage points during the 12 months after a recession has begun. So, on average, more than a million more workers have been unemployed during the 12 months after a recession has begun than during the previous 12 months.

Recessions Have Been Milder and the Economy Has Been More Stable Since 1950 Although today the U.S. economy still experiences business cycles, just as it has for at least the past 175 years, the cycles have become milder. Figure 9-12, which shows the year-to-year percentage changes in real GDP since 1900, illustrates a striking change in

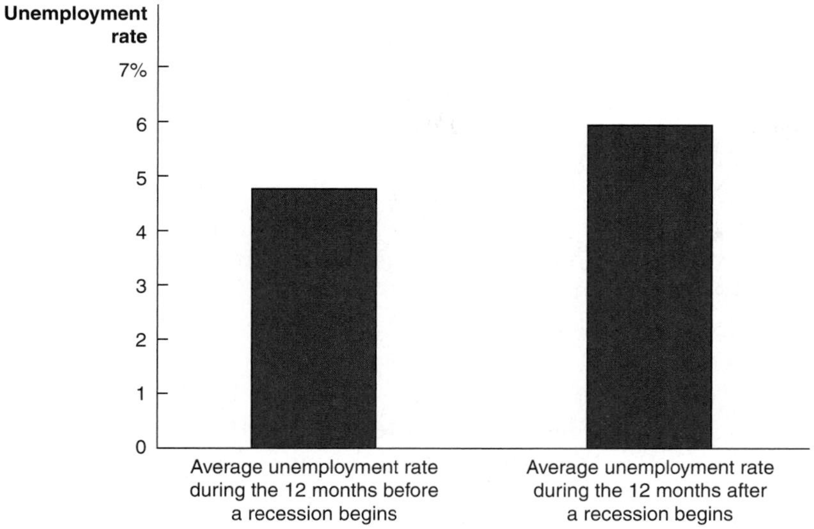

Figure 9-11 | The Impact of Recessions on the Unemployment Rate

Unemployment rises in every recession. For the recessions since 1950, the unemployment rate has risen, on average, by about 1.2 percentage points during the 12 months after a recession has begun.
Source: U.S. Bureau of Labor Statistics.

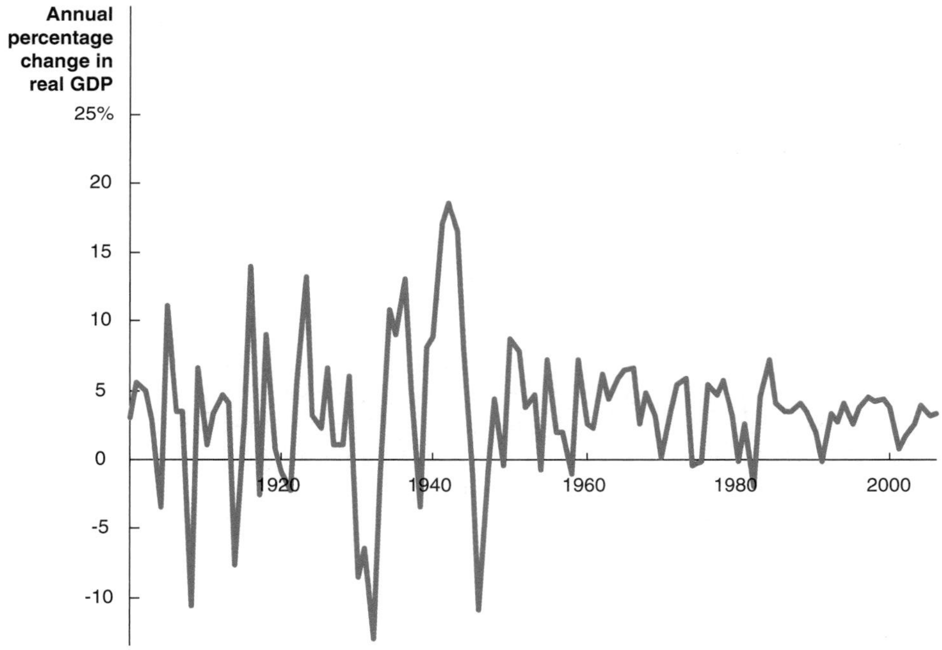

Figure 9-12 | Fluctuations in Real GDP, 1900–2006

In the first half of the twentieth century, real GDP had much more severe swings than in the second half of the twentieth century.
Sources: Louis D. Johnston and Samuel H. Williamson, "The Annual Real and Nominal GDP for the United States, 1790–Present," Economic History Services, April 1, 2006, www.eh.net/hmit/gdp; and U.S. Bureau of Economic Analysis.

TABLE 9-1

The Business Cycle Has Become Milder

PERIOD	AVERAGE LENGTH OF EXPANSIONS	AVERAGE LENGTH OF RECESSIONS
1870–1900	26 months	26 months
1900–1950	25 months	19 months
1950–2001	61 months	9 months

Note: The World War I and World War II periods have been omitted from the computations in the table, as has the expansion that began in November 2001.

Source: National Bureau of Economic Research

fluctuations in real GDP beginning around 1950. Before 1950, real GDP went through much greater year-to-year fluctuations than it has since that time. During the past 50 years, the U.S. economy has not experienced anything similar to the sharp fluctuations in real GDP that occurred during the early 1930s.

Another way to compare changes in the severity of business cycles over time is to look at changes in the lengths of expansions and recessions. Table 9-1 shows that in the late nineteenth century, the average length of recessions was the same as the average length of expansions. During the first half of the twentieth century, the average length of expansions decreased slightly, and the average length of recessions decreased significantly. As a result, expansions were about six months longer than recessions during these years. The most striking change came after 1950, when the length of expansions greatly increased and the length of recessions fell. In the second half of the twentieth century, expansions were more than six times as long as recessions. In other words, in the late nineteenth century, the U.S. economy spent as much time in recession as it did in expansion. During the second half of the twentieth century, the U.S. economy experienced long expansions interrupted by relatively short recessions.

Why Is the Economy More Stable?

Shorter recessions, longer expansions, and less severe fluctuations in real GDP have resulted in a significant improvement in the economic well-being of Americans. Economists have offered three explanations of why the economy has been more stable since 1950:

- ***The increasing importance of services and the declining importance of goods.*** As services, such as medical care or investment advice, have become a much larger fraction of GDP, there has been a corresponding decline in the production of goods. For example, at one time, manufacturing production accounted for about 40 percent of GDP, while today it accounts for only about 12 percent. Manufacturing production, particularly production of durable goods such as automobiles, fluctuates more than the production of services. Because durable goods are more expensive, during a recession, households will cut back more on purchases of them than they will on purchases of services.

- ***The establishment of unemployment insurance and other government transfer programs that provide funds to the unemployed.*** Before the 1930s, programs such as unemployment insurance, which provides government payments to workers who lose their jobs, and Social Security, which provides government payments to retired and disabled workers, did not exist. These and other government programs make it possible for workers who lose their jobs during recessions to have higher incomes and, therefore, to spend more than they would otherwise. This additional spending may have helped to shorten recessions.

- ***Active federal government policies to stabilize the economy.*** Before the Great Depression of the 1930s, the federal government did not attempt to end recessions or prolong expansions. Because the Great Depression was so severe, with the unemployment rate rising to more than 25 percent of the labor force and real GDP declining by almost 30 percent, public opinion began favoring attempts by the government to stabilize the economy. In the Employment Act of 1946, the federal government committed itself to "foster and promote . . . conditions under which there will be afforded useful employment to those able, willing, and seeking to work; and to promote maximum employment, production, and purchasing power." Beginning in the 1930s, economists also began to increase their understanding of why GDP fluctuates. As we will see in later chapters, the models economists developed to understand fluctuations in GDP also made it possible to evaluate the effects government policy would have on the economy. In the years since World War II, the federal government has actively tried to use policy measures to end recessions and prolong expansions. Many economists believe that these government policies have played a key role in stabilizing the economy. Other economists, however, argue that active policy has had little effect. This macroeconomic debate is an important one, so we will consider it further in Chapters 14 and 15 when we discuss the federal government's *monetary* and *fiscal policies.*

Continued from page 275

Economics in YOUR Life!

At the beginning of the chapter, we posed a question: How do you respond to your roommate's assertion that your decision to save instead of consume will reduce economic growth? In answering this question, this chapter has shown that consumption spending promotes the production of more consumption goods and services—such as jeans and haircuts—and fewer investment goods and services—such as physical capital and worker education. This is because saving—and, so, not consuming—is necessary to fund investment expenditure. Because an economy uses investment goods and services to produce other goods and services, your decision to save instead of consume will promote, rather than reduce, economic growth.

Conclusion

The U.S. economy remains a remarkable engine for improving the well-being of Americans. The standard of living of Americans today is much higher than it was 100 years ago. But households and firms are still subject to the ups and downs of the business cycle. In the following chapters, we will continue our analysis of this basic fact of macroeconomics: Ever-increasing long-run prosperity is achieved in the context of short-run instability.

Read *An Inside Look at Policy* on the next page to learn why China's domestic aviation market is struggling and what role the government plays in addressing the problem.

China's Airlines Are Failing to Translate Rapid Growth into Profits

ECONOMIST, FEBRUARY 23, 2006

Chinese Aviation: On a Wing and a Prayer

Despite a rousing flying display from the gigantic new Airbus A380, visitors at this week's Asian Aerospace show, which opened on February 21st, were looking to the north as much as up. After a quarter of a century at Singapore's Changi Exhibition Centre, Asian Aerospace—the world's third biggest air show—will move to Hong Kong from next year. The reason, as so often these days, is the growing pull of China.

Granted, there is excitement about India, Dubai and south-east Asia. But for the aerospace industry, China's combination of rapid growth and huge absolute numbers is the real prize. Chinese airlines carried 138M passengers last year, a number that has doubled in the past five years and already turned the mainland into the second largest aviation market behind America. The Chinese government expects the figure to double again over the next five years. Freight volumes are growing even faster, increasing by 20% last year.

a As a result, China is buying aircraft as never before. In 2005, it accounted for 219 planes, or fully one-fifth of Airbus's global orders in a record year. Boeing's latest analysis forecasts that over the next two decades, China will need 2,600 new planes, worth more than $213 billion.

But while airframe-makers and their suppliers are rubbing their hands, China's airlines are so far experiencing almost profitless growth. True, China has done wonders to mobilise the country, building the infrastructure needed to support the growth of its aviation industry and improving its safety. China now has 130 airports handling more than 1M passengers a year, with another 55 international airports planned by 2020. But despite a big jump in passenger numbers and revenues, the entire sector has reported measly profits of just 10 billion yuan ($1.2 billion) in the past five years.

This year, Air China is the only one of the big three carriers expected to be in the black. China Southern and China Eastern have already warned of sharp losses. . . .

b Part of the airlines' failure to make profits is simply the consequence of rapid expansion. Investing in all those new planes means most Chinese airlines are heavily in debt. A more serious issue, despite limited liberalization over the past few years, is the continued presence of the state's dead hand. Ticket prices, for example, remain more or less regulated, preventing carriers from practising the sophisticated yield management of western peers. . . . Meanwhile, a domestic jet-fuel monopoly means fuel accounts for an average of 40% of costs at Chinese airlines, compared with 24% for airlines worldwide.

c Another issue is rising labour costs due to a lack of qualified staff. In particular, China will need more than 1,000 pilots a year over the next decade, but with only one state flying school, Guanghan near Chengdu in Sichuan province, it can train 600 at most. Air China admitted this month that its planned introduction of 20–30 new aircraft in 2006 depended on it being able to man them. The suppliers are aware of this problem. Airbus has a training centre in Beijing and is setting up simulators elsewhere—as is Boeing. China is also allowing some private training schools to spring up, while China Southern already has its own training centre in Australia. But the shortage is acute and Chinese airlines are now talking of recruiting, reluctantly, pilots from overseas. Not only do they regard this as a blow to national pride; foreign crews also cost more.

Their weak profitability, coupled with ambitious plans to expand capacity, leaves the mainland carriers exposed to even a temporary slowdown in traffic growth. Further consolidation, allowing an attack on their structurally high costs, is one remedy. Another would be to liberalise the market for both fares and fuel. A braver step would be to let in foreign operators to boost competition. . . . Whichever route the government chooses, it needs to act rapidly. After all, the industry has been hit by at least one major shock every three years, from terrorist attacks to the SARS virus. After a couple of good years, the next bad one is due some time soon.

Key Points in the Article

This article discusses the rapidly expanding Chinese airline industry. It explains that China's domestic aviation market has grown dramatically in the past few years. In 2005, China's airlines carried a record 138 million passengers and ordered 219 new Airbus and Boeing airplanes. Today, the Chinese mainland comprises the second-largest airline market in the world; only the U.S. domestic airline market is larger. Nonetheless, Chinese airlines have struggled to earn a profit. According to the article, this struggle has to do with three common factors associated with long-run growth: the Chinese airline industry's recent large investments in new planes; the Chinese government's failure to liberalize markets for air travel; and a shortage of human capital, including pilots. The last problem has become so acute that Airbus and Boeing, both of which stand to gain from China's growth, have established pilot-training centers, complete with flight simulators, throughout China.

Analyzing the News

a To help the Chinese domestic airline industry grow, the Chinese government has sought to improve the country's infrastructure. The government has constructed and modernized 130 airports and invested in the technology necessary to improve air safety. These improvements, along with a large and growing domestic market for air travel, have fostered dramatic growth among China's airlines. This pattern is shown in Figure 1, where China Southern Airlines and China Eastern Airlines—two of China's three largest carriers—ranked among the top 10 airlines in the world in 2005, according to passengers carried on domestic flights. Nonetheless, China's airlines do not lead the industry in profitability. Figure 2 shows that none of China's carriers ranked among the top 10 airlines in the world in 2006 according to profitability; and only Air China—the other of China's three largest carriers—reported a profit, which earned it a rank of fifteenth in the world for profitability.

b One reason China's airlines are struggling to generate profits is their recent large investments in new airplanes. A more important reason China's airlines are struggling has to do with the Chinese government's failure to liberalize markets, including the market for air travel. As you read in this chapter, a requirement for economic growth—and profitability—is that governments facilitate the development of efficient markets. To do so, governments should avoid interfering with markets by setting prices or prohibiting entry into those markets. However, China's government continues to regulate ticket prices, while a government-sanctioned domestic jet-fuel monopoly has effectively raised the cost of operating airlines in China.

c China's airline industry faces a shortage of human capital, especially airline pilots. According to the article, if China's airline industry continues to grow at its current rate, it will need 1,000 additional pilots every year for the next decade; meanwhile, the country's single state-run flying school can produce only 600 pilots a year. This shortage of human capital is a problem for airplane manufacturers Airbus and Boeing, which stand to gain from China's growth. So, with permission from the Chinese government, both companies have established pilot-training centers throughout China.

Thinking Critically About Policy

1. Suppose the Chinese government ceased to regulate airline ticket prices and allowed foreign firms to sell jet fuel to China's domestic air carriers. How might such a change in policy affect the airlines' profitability?
2. Suppose the Chinese government decided to provide low-interest loans to domestic air carriers, regardless of their creditworthiness, in an attempt to foster long-term profitability in the industry. Would such a policy be likely to succeed?

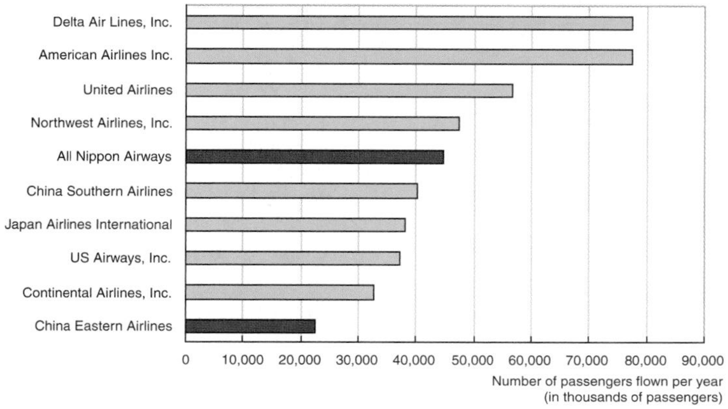

Figure 1. Airlines ranked by passengers carried on domestic flights, 2005.

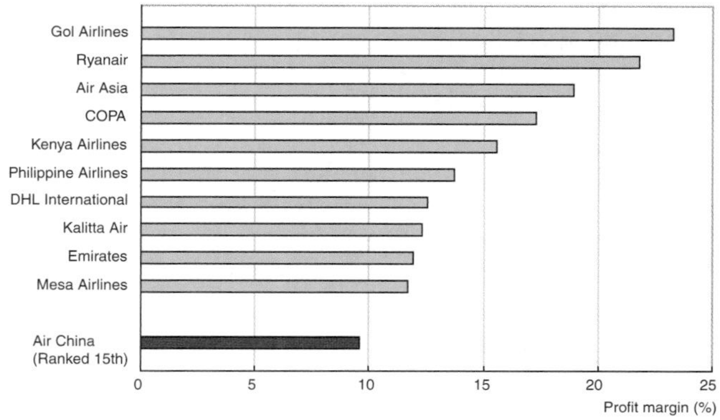

Figure 2. Airlines ranked by operating profit margin, 2005.

Key Terms

Business cycle, p. 276	Financial intermediaries, p. 285	Labor productivity, p. 280	Market for loanable funds, p. 287
Capital, p. 280	Financial markets, p. 284	Long-run economic growth, p. 277	Potential GDP, p. 283
Crowding out, p. 290	Financial system, p. 284		

9.1 LEARNING OBJECTIVE 9.1 | Discuss the importance of long-run economic growth, **pages 276–283.**

Long-Run Economic Growth

Summary

The U.S. economy has experienced both *long-run economic growth* and the *business cycle*. The **business cycle** refers to alternating periods of economic expansion and economic recession. **Long-run economic growth** is the process by which rising productivity increases the standard of living of the typical person. Because of economic growth, the typical American today can buy almost eight times as much as the typical American of 1900. Long-run growth is measured by increases in real GDP per capita. Increases in real GDP per capita depend on increases in labor productivity. **Labor productivity** is the quantity of goods and services that can be produced by one worker or by one hour of work. Economists believe two key factors determine labor productivity—the quantity of capital per hour worked and the level of technology. **Capital** refers to manufactured goods that are used to produce other goods and services. *Human capital* is the accumulated knowledge and skills workers acquire from education, training, or their life experiences. Economic growth occurs if the quantity of capital per hour worked increases and if technological change occurs. Economists often discuss economic growth in terms of growth in **potential GDP**, which is the level of GDP attained when all firms are producing at capacity.

myeconlab Get Ahead of the Curve Visit www.myeconlab.com to complete these exercises online and get instant feedback.

Review Questions

1.1 By how much did real GDP per capita increase in the United States between 1900 and 2006? Discuss whether the increase in real GDP per capita is likely to be greater or smaller than the true increase in living standards.

1.2 What is the most important factor in explaining increases in real GDP per capita in the long run?

1.3 What two key factors cause labor productivity to increase over time?

1.4 What is potential real GDP? Does potential real GDP remain constant over time?

Problems and Applications

1.5 Briefly discuss whether you would rather live in the United States of 1900 with an income of $1,000,000 per year or the United States of 2008 with an income of $50,000 per year. Assume that the incomes for both years are measured in 2000 dollars.

1.6 A question from Chapter 7 asked about the relationship between real GDP and the standard of living in a country. Based on what you read about economic growth in this chapter, elaborate on the importance of growth in GDP, particularly real GDP per capita, to the quality of life of a country's citizens.

1.7 (Related to the *Making the Connection* on page 278) Think about the relationship between economic prosperity and life expectancy. What implications does this relationship have for the size of the health care sector of the economy? In particular, is this sector likely to expand or contract in coming years?

1.8 Use the table to answer the following questions.

YEAR	REAL GDP (BILLIONS OF 2000 DOLLARS)
1990	$7,113
1991	7,101
1992	7,337
1993	7,533
1994	7,836

a. Calculate the growth rate of real GDP for each year from 1991 to 1994.

b. Calculate the average annual growth rate of real GDP for the period from 1991 to 1994.

1.9 Real GDP per capita in the United States, as mentioned in the chapter, grew from about $4,900 in 1900 to about $38,000 in 2006, which represents an annual growth rate of 1.9 percent. If the United States continues to grow at this rate, how many years will it take for real GDP per capita to double?

1.10 The economy of China has boomed since the late 1970s, having periods during which real GDP per capita has grown at rates of 9 percent per year or more. At a 9 percent growth rate in real GDP per capita, how many years will it take to double?

1.11 Labor productivity in the agricultural sector of the United States is more than 31 times higher than in the agricultural sector of China. What factors would cause U.S. labor productivity to be so much higher than Chinese labor productivity?

Source: "China: Awakening Giant," Federal Reserve Bank of Dallas, *Southwest Economy*, September/October 2003, p. 2.

1.12 **(Related to *Solved Problem 9-1* on page 281)** Two reasons for the rapid economic growth of China over the past two to three decades have been the massive movement of workers from agriculture to manufacturing jobs and the transformation of parts of its economy into a market system. In China, labor productivity in manufacturing substantially exceeds labor productivity in agriculture, and as many as 150 million Chinese workers will move from agriculture to manufacturing over the next decade or so. In 1978, China began to transform its economy into a market system, and today, nearly 40 percent of Chinese workers are employed in private firms (up from 0 percent in 1978). In the long run, which of these two factors—movement of workers from agriculture to manufacturing or transforming the economy into a market system—will be more important for China's economic growth? Briefly explain.

Source: "China: Awakening Giant," Federal Reserve Bank of Dallas, *Southwest Economy*, September/October 2003.

1.13 A newspaper story on labor productivity in the United States includes the following observation: "Productivity is the vital element needed to boost living standards." Briefly explain whether you agree. Make clear in your answer what you mean by living standards.

Source: Martin Crutsinger, "Productivity Rebounds in Fourth Quarter," Associated Press, February 8, 2007.

1.14 **(Related to the *Making the Connection* on page 282)** If the keys to Botswana's rapid economic growth seem obvious, why have other countries in the region had so much difficulty following them?

>> End Learning Objective 9.1

9.2 LEARNING OBJECTIVE 9.2 | Discuss the role of the financial system in facilitating long-run economic growth, **pages 283–292.**

Saving, Investment, and the Financial System

Summary

Financial markets and financial intermediaries together comprise the **financial system**. A well-functioning financial system is an important determinant of economic growth. Firms acquire funds from households, either directly through financial markets—such as the stock and bond markets—or indirectly through financial intermediaries—such as banks. The funds available to firms come from *saving*. There are two categories of saving in the economy: *private saving* by households and *public saving* by the government. The value of total saving in the economy is always equal to the value of total investment spending. In the model of the **market for loanable funds**, the interaction of borrowers and lenders determines the market interest rate and the quantity of loanable funds exchanged.

myeconlab Get Ahead of the Curve Visit www.myeconlab.com to complete these exercises online and get instant feedback.

Review Questions

2.1 Why is the financial system of a country important for long-run economic growth? Why is it essential for economic growth that firms have access to adequate sources of funds?

2.2 How does the financial system—either financial markets or financial intermediaries—provide risk sharing, liquidity, and information for savers and borrowers?

2.3 Briefly explain why the total value of saving in the economy must equal the total value of investment.

2.4 What are loanable funds? Why do businesses demand loanable funds? Why do households supply loanable funds?

Problems and Applications

2.5 Suppose you can receive an interest rate of 3 percent on a certificate of deposit at a bank that is charging borrowers 7 percent on new car loans. Why might you be unwilling to loan money directly to someone who wants to borrow from you to buy a new car, even if that person offers to pay you an interest rate higher than 3 percent?

2.6 An article argues that a main barrier to continued rapid economic growth in China is "its fragile banking system." Why might a weak banking system make economic growth difficult?

Source: "The Real Great Leap Forward," *Economist*, September 30, 2004.

2.7 According to an article in the *Wall Street Journal*, the government of Indonesia forecast that its budget deficit would increase from 1.1 percent of GDP in 2007 to 1.8 percent in 2008. Assuming that other factors that affect the demand and supply of loanable funds remain the same, what would be the effect of this larger budget deficit on the equilibrium real interest rate and the quantity of loanable funds? What would be the effect on the equilibrium quantity of saving and investment? Illustrate your answer using a graph showing the market for loanable funds in Indonesia.

Source: "Jakarta Forecasts Growth of as Much as 7% in 2008," *Wall Street Journal*, May 23, 2007.

2.8 Consider the following data for a closed economy:
Y = \$11 trillion
C = \$8 trillion
I = \$2 trillion
TR = \$1 trillion
T = \$3 trillion
Use the data to calculate the following.
a. Private saving
b. Public saving
c. Government purchases
d. The government budget deficit or budget surplus

2.9 Consider the following data for a closed economy:
Y = \$12 trillion
C = \$8 trillion
G = \$2 trillion
S_{public} = −\$0.5 trillion
T = \$2 trillion
Use the data to calculate the following.
a. Private saving
b. Investment spending
c. Transfer payments
d. The government budget deficit or budget surplus

2.10 In problem 2.9, suppose that government purchases increase from \$2 trillion to \$2.5 trillion. If the values for Y and C are unchanged, what must happen to the values of S and I? Briefly explain.

2.11 Use the graph to answer the following questions.

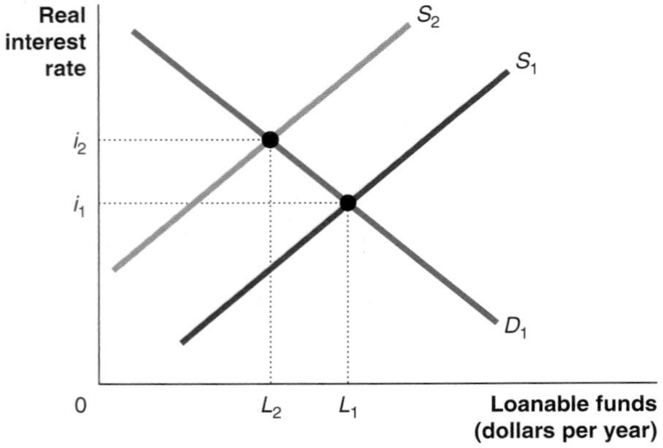

a. Does the shift from S_1 to S_2 represent an increase or a decrease in the supply of loanable funds?
b. With the shift in supply, what happens to the equilibrium quantity of loanable funds?
c. With the change in the equilibrium quantity of loanable funds, what happens to the quantity of saving? What happens to the quantity of investment?

2.12 Use the graph to answer the following questions.

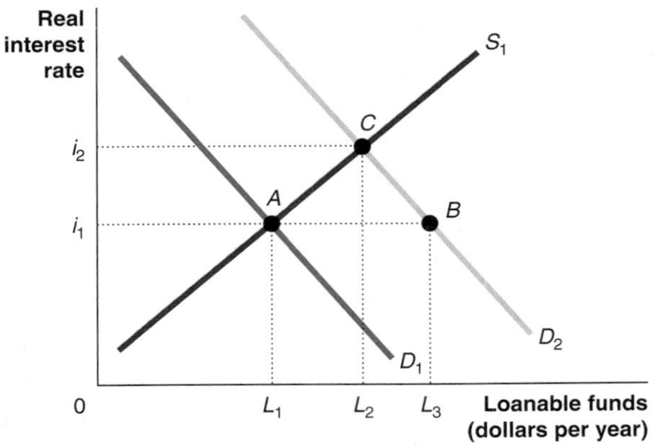

a. With the shift in the demand for loanable funds, what happens to the equilibrium real interest rate and the equilibrium quantity of loanable funds?
b. How can the equilibrium quantity of loanable funds increase when the real interest rate increases? Doesn't the quantity of loanable funds demanded decrease when the interest rate increases?
c. How much would the quantity of loanable funds demanded have increased if the interest rate had remained at i_1?
d. How much does the quantity of loanable funds supplied increase with the increase in the interest rate from i_1 to i_2?

2.13 Suppose that the economy is currently in a recession and that economic forecasts indicate that the economy will soon enter an expansion. What is the likely effect of the expansion on the expected profitability of new investment in plant and equipment? In the market for loanable funds, graph and explain the effect of the forecast of an economic expansion, assuming that borrowers and lenders believe the forecast is accurate. What happens to the equilibrium real interest rate and the quantity of loanable funds? What happens to the quantity of saving and investment?

2.14 Firms care about their after-tax rate of return on investment projects. In the market for loanable funds, graph and explain the effect of an increase in taxes on business profits. (For simplicity, assume no change in the federal budget deficit or budget surplus.) What happens to the equilibrium real interest rate and the quantity of loanable funds? What will be the effect on the quantity of investment by firms and the economy's capital stock in the future?

2.15 Use a market for loanable funds graph to illustrate the effect of the federal budget surpluses of the late 1990s. What happens to the equilibrium real interest rate and the quantity of loanable funds? What happens to the quantity of saving and investment?

2.16 **(Related to *Solved Problem 9-2* on page 291)** As discussed in Chapter 8, savers are taxed on the nominal interest payments they receive rather than the real interest payments. Suppose the government shifted from taxing nominal interest payments to taxing only real interest payments. Use a market for loanable funds graph to analyze the effects of this change in tax policy. What happens to the equilibrium real interest rate and the equilibrium quantity of loanable funds? What happens to the quantity of saving and investment?

2.17 **(Related to the *Making the Connection* on page 288)** The *Making the Connection* claims that Ebenezer Scrooge promoted economic growth more when he was a miser and saved most of his income than when he reformed and began spending freely. Suppose, though, that most of his spending after he reformed involved buying food for the Cratchits and other poor families. Many economists believe there is a close connection between how much very poor people eat and how much they are able to work and how productive they are while working. Does this fact affect the conclusion about whether the pre-reform or post-reform Scrooge had a more positive impact on economic growth? Briefly explain.

>> End Learning Objective 9.2

9.3 LEARNING OBJECTIVE 9.3 | Explain what happens during a business cycle, **pages 292–301.**

The Business Cycle

Summary

During the expansion phase of a business cycle, production, employment, and income are increasing. The period of expansion ends with a business cycle peak. Following the business cycle peak, production, employment, and income decline during the recession phase of the cycle. The recession comes to an end with a business cycle trough, after which another period of expansion begins. The inflation rate usually rises near the end of a business cycle expansion and then falls during a recession. The unemployment rate declines during the later part of an expansion and increases during a recession. The unemployment rate often continues to increase even after an expansion has begun. Economists have not found a method to predict when recessions will begin and end. Recessions are difficult to predict because they have more than one cause. Recessions have been milder and the economy has been more stable since 1950.

Review Questions

3.1 What are the names of the following events in a business cycle?
a. The high point of economic activity
b. The low point of economic activity
c. The period between the high point of economic activity and the following low point
d. The period between the low point of economic activity and the following high point

3.2 Briefly describe the effect of the business cycle on the inflation rate and the unemployment rate.

3.3 Briefly compare the severity of recessions in the first half of the twentieth century with recessions in the second half. Do economists agree on how to explain this difference?

Problems and Applications

3.4 **(Related to the *Chapter Opener* on page 274)** Briefly explain whether production of each of the following goods is likely to fluctuate more or less than real GDP does during the business cycle.
a. Ford F-150 trucks
b. McDonald's Big Macs
c. Kenmore refrigerators
d. Huggies diapers
e. Caterpillar industrial tractors

3.5 The National Bureau of Economic Research, a private group, is responsible for declaring when recessions begin and end. Can you think of reasons why the Bureau of Economic Analysis, part of the federal government, might not want to take on this responsibility?

3.6 **(Related to the *Don't Let This Happen to You!* on page 297)** "Real GDP in 2006 was $11.4 trillion. This value is a large number. Therefore, economic growth must have been high during 2006." Briefly explain whether you agree or disagree with this statement.

3.7 **(Related to the *Making the Connection* on page 294)** During the late 1990s, some people asserted that the business cycle was dead, meaning that we would have no more recessions. Examine the table of business cycle peaks and troughs since 1950 on page 294. How many recessions has the U.S. economy experienced since the end of 1982? Since 1950, have recessions become more or less frequent? From the history of the business cycle, do you think that the U.S. economy will have another recession within the next 20 years?

3.8 Imagine you own a business and that during the next recession you lay off 20 percent of your workforce. When economic activity picks up and your sales begin to increase, why might you not immediately start rehiring workers?

>> End Learning Objective 9.3

Chapter 10

Long-Run Economic Growth: Sources and Policies

MySpace Meets the Chinese Economic Miracle

MySpace.com was founded in 2003 by Tom Anderson and Chris DeWolfe, who intended the site to be a virtual meeting place for (fellow) striving musicians in the Los Angeles area. In July 2005, one month after web traffic on MySpace.com exceeded that on Google, Rupert Murdoch's News Corporation bought MySpace for $580 million. Since then, the company has been aggressively expanding into international markets, including China—home to roughly 135 million Internet users in their twenties and thirties. But to enter the Chinese market, News Corporation must overcome a crucial challenge: a government that regulates the Internet for speech that it deems subversive. To deal with this problem, News Corporation needed to find a Chinese partner who can keep the Chinese version of MySpace from breaking the law. Or, in the words of Fan Bao, chief executive of an investment banking firm in Beijing, "what it takes to be successful in China is a local entrepreneur."

Entrepreneurship is a relatively new resource in China. From the time the Communist Party seized control of China in 1949, until the late 1970s, the government controlled production, and there was little place for private businesses run by entrepreneurs. China moved away from a *centrally planned economy* in 1976, with the death of Communist Party Leader Mao Zedong. Mao's successor, Deng Xiaoping, introduced market-oriented reforms in 1978. Real GDP per capita had grown very slowly between 1949 and 1978. Following Deng's reforms, real GDP per capita grew at a rate of 6.5 percent per year between 1979 and 1995 and at the white-hot rate of more than 9 percent per year between 1996 and 2006. If this growth rate continues, per capita GDP in China will double every eight years. These rapid growth rates have transformed the Chinese economy. Not only is real GDP per capita 10 times higher than it was 50 years ago, but it is now possible for the typical family in China to aspire for the first time to own an automobile, a television set, a refrigerator, an air-conditioner, and other goods that have long been taken for granted by consumers in high-income countries.

Despite its very rapid recent growth, as the experience of MySpace has shown, China is not a democracy, and the Chinese government still intervenes in the economy in sometimes arbitrary ways. China has failed to fully establish the rule of law, particularly with respect to the consistent enforcement of property rights. This is a problem for the long-term prospects of the Chinese economy because entrepreneurs cannot fulfill their role in the market system of bringing together the factors of production—labor, capital, and natural resources—to produce goods and services unless the government establishes the rule of law.

LEARNING Objectives

After studying this chapter, you should be able to:

10.1 Define **economic growth**, calculate economic growth rates, and describe global trends in economic growth, page 310.

10.2 Use the **economic growth model** to explain why growth rates differ across countries, page 315.

10.3 Discuss **fluctuations** in **productivity growth** in the United States, page 322.

10.4 Explain **economic catch-up** and discuss why many poor countries have not experienced rapid economic growth, page 327.

10.5 Discuss **government policies** that foster economic growth, page 334.

For another example of how economic institutions can promote or inhibit entrepreneurship, read **AN INSIDE LOOK** on **page 338**, which discusses why Europe's economy has proven unable to grow at rates similar to those of the United States.

Sources: Patricia Sellers, "MySpace Cowboys," *Fortune*, August 29, 2006; and Geoffrey A. Fowler and Jason Dean, "In China, MySpace May Need to Be 'OurSpace,'" *Wall Street Journal*, February 2, 2007, p. B1.

Economics in YOUR Life!

Would You Be Better Off without China?

Suppose that you could choose to live and work in a world with the Chinese economy growing very rapidly or a world with the Chinese economy like it was before 1978—very poor and growing slowly. Which world would you choose to live in? How does the current high-growth, high-export Chinese economy affect you as a consumer? How does it affect you as someone about to start a career? As you read the chapter, see if you can answer these questions. You can check your answers against those we provide at the end of the chapter. » **Continued on page 337**

Economic growth is not inevitable. For most of human history, no sustained increases in output per capita occurred, and, in the words of the philosopher Thomas Hobbes, the lives of most people were "poor, nasty, brutish, and short." Sustained economic growth first began with the Industrial Revolution in England in the late eighteenth century. From there, economic growth spread to the United States, Canada, and the countries of Western Europe. Following World War II, rapid economic growth also began in Japan, but the economies of most other countries stagnated, leaving their people mired in poverty.

Real GDP per capita is the best measure of a country's standard of living because it represents the ability of the average person to buy goods and services. Economic growth occurs when real GDP per capita increases. Why have countries such as the United States and the United Kingdom, which had high standards of living at the beginning of the twentieth century, continued to grow rapidly? Why have countries such as Argentina, which at one time had relatively high standards of living, failed to keep pace? Why was the Soviet Union unable to sustain the rapid growth rates of its early years? Why are some countries that were very poor at the beginning of the twentieth century still very poor today? And why have some countries, such as South Korea and Japan, that once were very poor now become much richer? What explains China's very rapid recent growth rates? In this chapter, we will develop a *model of economic growth* that helps us answer these important questions.

10.1 LEARNING OBJECTIVE

10.1 | Define economic growth, calculate economic growth rates, and describe global trends in economic growth.

Economic Growth Over Time and Around the World

You live in a world that is very different from the world when your grandparents were young. You can listen to music on a thin iPod. Your grandparents played vinyl records on large stereo systems. You can pick up a cell phone or send an e-mail to someone in another city, state, or country. Your grandparents mailed letters that took days or weeks to arrive. More importantly, you have access to health care and medicines that have prolonged life and improved its quality. In many poorer countries, however, people endure grinding poverty and have only the bare necessities of life, just as their great-grandparents did.

The difference between you and people in poor countries is that you live in a country that has experienced substantial economic growth. With economic growth, an economy produces both increasing quantities of goods and services and better goods and services. It is only through economic growth that living standards can increase, but through most of human history, no economic growth took place. Even today, billions of people are living in countries where economic growth is extremely slow.

Economic Growth from 1,000,000 B.C. to the Present

In 1,000,000 B.C., our ancestors survived by hunting animals and gathering edible plant life. Farming was many years in the future, and production was limited to food, clothing, shelter, and simple tools. Bradford DeLong, an economist at the University of California, Berkeley, estimates that in these primitive circumstances, GDP per capita was about $123 per year in 2006 dollars, which was the bare amount necessary to sustain life. DeLong estimates that real GDP per capita worldwide was still $123 in the year 1300 A.D. In other words, no sustained economic growth occurred between 1,000,000 B.C. and 1300 A.D.

A peasant toiling on a farm in France in the year 1300 was no better off than his ancestors thousands of years before. In fact, for most of human existence, the typical person had the bare minimum of food, clothing, and shelter necessary to sustain life. Few people survived beyond the age of forty, and most people suffered from debilitating illnesses.

Significant economic growth did not begin until the **Industrial Revolution**, which started in England around the year 1750. The production of cotton cloth in factories using machinery powered by steam engines marked the beginning of the Industrial Revolution. Before that time, production of goods had relied almost exclusively on human or animal power. Mechanical power spread to the production of many other goods, greatly increasing the quantity of goods each worker could produce. First England, and then other countries, such as the United States, France, and Germany, experienced *long-run economic growth*, with sustained increases in real GDP per capita that eventually raised living standards in these countries to the high levels of today.

Industrial Revolution The application of mechanical power to the production of goods, beginning in England around 1750.

Making the Connection | Why Did the Industrial Revolution Begin in England?

The Industrial Revolution was a key turning point in human history. Before the Industrial Revolution, economic growth was slow and halting. After the Industrial Revolution, in a number of countries economic growth became rapid and sustained. Although historians and economists agree on the importance of the Industrial Revolution, they have not reached a consensus on why it happened where and when it did. Why the eighteenth century and not the sixteenth century or the twenty-first century? Why England and not China or India or Africa or Japan?

There is always a temptation to read history backward. We know when and where the Industrial Revolution occurred; therefore, it had to happen where it did and when it did. But what was so special about England in the eighteenth century? Nobel laureate Douglass North, of Washington University in St. Louis, has argued that institutions in England differed significantly from those in other countries in ways that greatly aided economic growth. North believes that the Glorious Revolution of 1688 was a key turning point. After that date, the British Parliament, rather than the king, controlled the government. The British court system also became independent of the king. As a result, the British government was able credibly to commit to upholding private property rights, protecting wealth, and eliminating arbitrary increases in taxes. These institutional changes gave entrepreneurs the incentive to make the investments necessary to use the important technological developments of the second half of the eighteenth century—particularly the spinning jenny and the water frame, which were used in the production of cotton textiles, and the steam engine, which was used in mining and in the manufacture of textiles and other products. Without the institutional changes, entrepreneurs would have been reluctant to risk having their property seized or their wealth confiscated by the government.

Although not all economists agree with North's specific argument about the origins of the Industrial Revolution, we will see that most economists accept the idea that economic growth is not likely to occur unless a country's government provides the type of institutional framework North describes.

The British government's guarantee of property rights set the stage for the Industrial Revolution.

Sources: Douglass C. North, *Understanding the Process of Economic Change*, Princeton, NJ: Princeton University Press, 2005; and Douglass C. North and Barry R. Weingast, "Constitutions and Commitment: The Evolution of Institutions Governing Public Choice in Seventeenth-Century England," *Journal of Economic History*, Vol. 49, No. 4, December 1989.

YOUR TURN: Test your understanding by doing related problem 1.3 on page 340 at the end of this chapter.

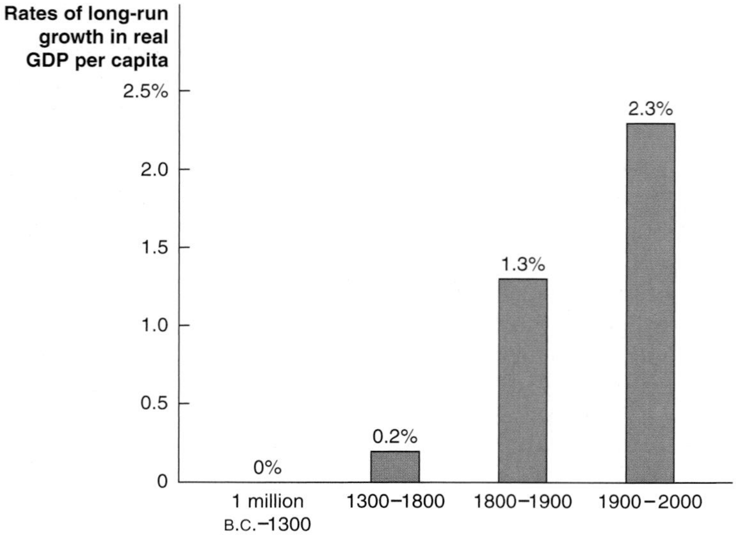

Figure 10-1

Average Annual Growth Rates for the World Economy

World economic growth was essentially zero in the years before 1300, and it was very slow—an average of only 0.2 percent per year—before 1800. The Industrial Revolution made possible the sustained increases in real GDP per capita that have allowed some countries to attain a high standard of living.

Source: J. Bradford DeLong, "Estimating World GDP, One Million B.C.–Present," working paper, University of California, Berkeley.

Figure 10-1 shows how growth rates of real GDP per capita for the entire world have changed over long periods. Prior to 1300 A.D., there were no sustained increases in real GDP per capita. Over the next 500 years, to 1800, there was very slow growth. Significant growth began in the nineteenth century as a result of the Industrial Revolution. A further acceleration in growth occurred during the twentieth century as the average annual growth rate increased from 1.3 percent per year to 2.3 percent per year.

Small Differences in Growth Rates Are Important

The difference between 1.3 percent and 2.3 percent may seem trivial but, over long periods, small differences in growth rates can have a large impact. For example, suppose you have $100 in a savings account earning an interest rate of 1.3 percent, which means you will receive an interest payment of $1.30 this year. If the interest rate on the account is 2.3 percent, you will earn $2.30. The difference of an extra $1.00 interest payment seems insignificant. But if you leave the interest as well as the original $100 in your account for another year, the difference becomes greater because now the higher interest rate is applied to a larger amount—$102.30—and the lower interest rate is applied to a smaller amount—$101.30. This process, known as *compounding*, magnifies even small differences in interest rates over long periods of time. Over a period of 50 years, your $100 would grow to $312 at an interest rate of 2.3 percent but to only $191 at an interest rate of 1.3 percent.

What applies to interest rates also applies to growth rates. For example, in 1950, real GDP per capita in Argentina was $6,942 (measured in 2000 dollars), which was larger than France's real GDP per capita of $5,921. Over the next 54 years, the economic growth rate in France averaged 2.8 percent per year, while in Argentina, it was only 0.8 percent per year. Although this difference in growth rates of two percentage points may seem small, in 2004, real GDP per capita in France had risen to $26,168, while real GDP per capita in Argentina was only $10,939. In other words, because of a relatively small difference in the growth rates of the two economies, the standard of living of the typical person in France went from being below that of the typical person in Argentina to being much higher. The important point to keep in mind is this: *In the long run, small differences in economic growth rates result in big differences in living standards.*

Why Do Growth Rates Matter?

Why should anyone care about growth rates? Growth rates matter because an economy that grows too slowly fails to raise living standards. In some countries in Africa and Asia, very little economic growth has occurred in the past 50 years, so many people remain in

Don't Let This Happen to **YOU!**

Don't Confuse the Average Annual Percentage Change with the Total Percentage Change

When economists talk about growth rates over a period of more than one year, the numbers are always *average annual percentage changes* and *not* total percentage changes. For example, in the United States, real GDP per capita was \$11,752 billion in 1950 and \$38,127 billion in 2006. The percentage change in real GDP per capita between these two years is:

$$\frac{(\$38{,}127 \text{ billion} - \$11{,}752 \text{ billion})}{\$11{,}752 \text{ billion}} \times 100 = 224\%.$$

However, this is *not* the growth rate between the two years. The growth rate between these two years is the rate at which \$11,752 billion in 1950 would have to grow on average *each year* to end up as \$38,127 billion in 2006, which is 2.1 percent.

YOUR TURN: Test your understanding by doing related problem 1.6 on page 341 at the end of this chapter.

severe poverty. In high-income countries, only 4 out of every 1,000 babies die before the age of one. In the poorest countries, more than 100 out of every 1,000 babies die before the age of one, and millions of children die each year from diseases that could be avoided by access to clean water or cured by medicines that cost only a few dollars.

Although their problems are less dramatic, countries that experience slow growth have also missed an opportunity to improve the lives of their citizens. For example, the failure of Argentina to grow as rapidly as the other countries that had similar levels of GDP per capita in 1950 has left many of its people in poverty. Life expectancy in Argentina is several years lower than in the United States and other high-income countries, and more than twice times as many babies in Argentina die before the age of one.

Making the Connection

The Benefits of an Earlier Start: Standards of Living in China and Japan

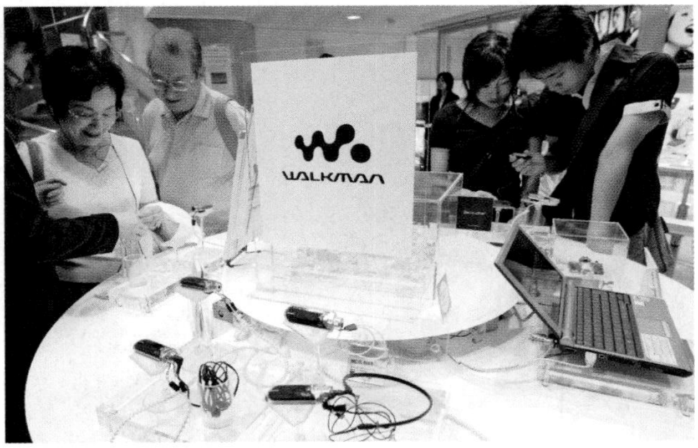

Sustained high rates of economic growth have helped Japan attain high living standards.

We noted at the beginning of this chapter that China has experienced very high growth rates in recent years. Between 1996 and 2006, real GDP per capita in China grew at an average annual rate of 9.1 percent. Japan, in contrast, grew at the much slower rate of 2.1 percent. Between 1950 and 1978, however, China had grown relatively slowly while Japan was growing rapidly. As a result, in 2006, the standard of living in China was still well below that in Japan. For example, GDP per capita measured in U.S. dollars was \$7,600 in China in 2006 but \$33,100—or more than four times higher—in Japan. The following table shows other measures of the standard of living for China and Japan.

	CHINA	JAPAN
Life expectancy at birth	71.9 years	82.2 years
Infant mortality (per 1,000 live births)	23	3
Percentage of the population surviving on less than \$2 per day	47%	0%
Percentage of the population with access to treated water	77%	100%
Percentage of the population with access to improved sanitation	44%	100%
Internet users per 1,000 people	73	587

In each of the measures shown in the preceding table, China continues to lag behind Japan as well as the United States and other high-income countries. If the

Chinese economy can sustain the high growth rates of recent years, it will continue to close the gap with Japan in real GDP per capita and other measures of the standard of living. The moral of the story is that only by sustaining high rates of economic growth over many years will the currently low-income countries be able to attain the high living standards people in Japan, the United States, and other high-income countries enjoy today.

Source: United Nations Development Programme, *Human Development Report, 2006*, New York: Palgrave Macmillan, 2006.

YOUR TURN: Test your understanding by doing related problem 1.7 on page 341 at the end of this chapter.

"The Rich Get Richer and . . . "

We can divide the world's economies into two groups: the *high-income countries*, sometimes also referred to as the industrial countries, and the poorer countries, or *developing countries*. The high-income countries include the countries of Western Europe, Australia, Canada, Japan, New Zealand, and the United States. The developing countries include most of the countries of Africa, Asia, and Latin America. In the 1980s and 1990s, a small group of countries, mostly East Asian countries such as Singapore, South Korea, and Taiwan, experienced high rates of growth and are sometimes referred to as the *newly industrializing countries*. Figure 10-2 shows the levels of GDP per capita around the world in 2006. GDP is measured in U.S. dollars, corrected for differences across countries in the cost of living. In 2006, GDP per capita ranged from a high of $68,800 in Luxembourg to a low of $600 in Somalia. To understand why the gap between rich and poor countries exists, we need to look at what causes economies to grow.

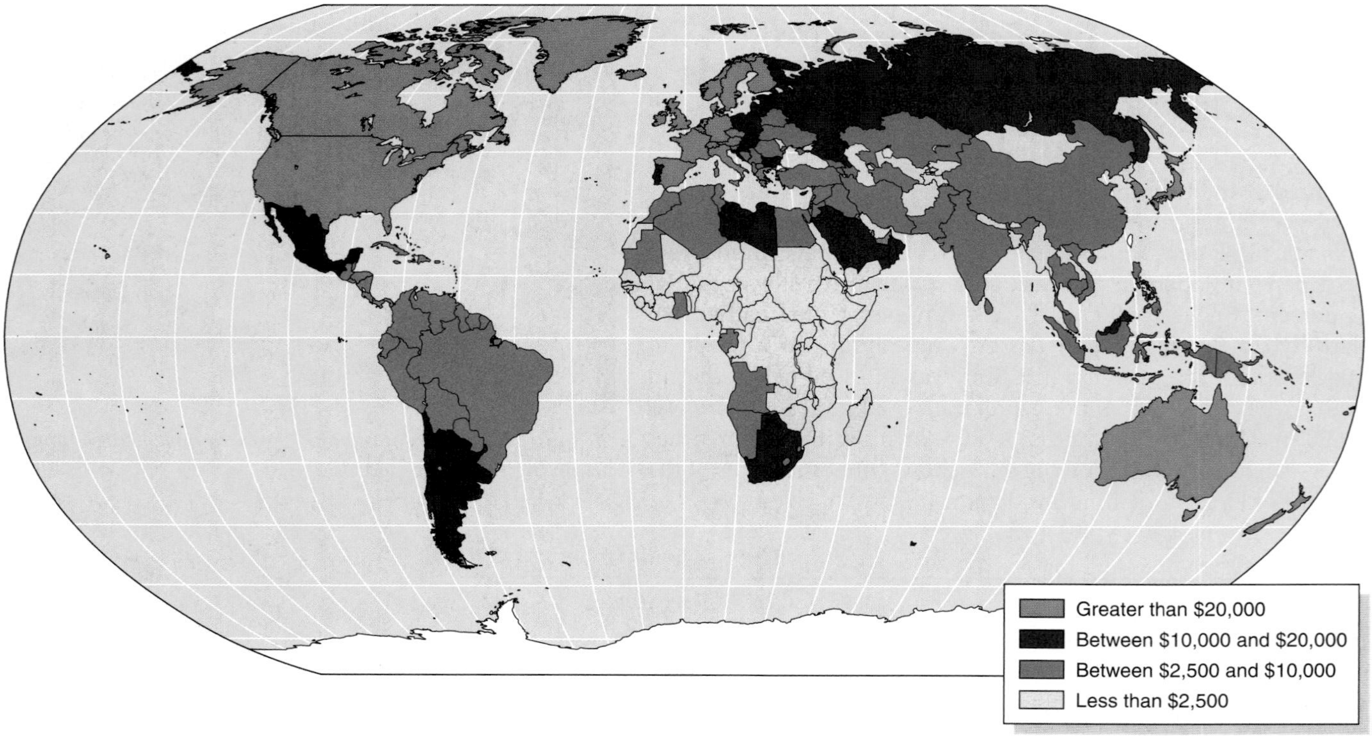

Figure 10-2 | GDP per Capita, 2006

GDP per capita is measured in U.S. dollars corrected for differences across countries in the cost of living.

10.2 LEARNING OBJECTIVE

10.2 | Use the economic growth model to explain why growth rates differ across countries.

What Determines How Fast Economies Grow?

To explain changes in economic growth rates over time within countries and differences in growth rates among countries, we need to develop an *economic growth model*. An **economic growth model** explains growth rates in real GDP per capita over the long run. As we noted in Chapter 9, the average person can buy more goods and services only if the average worker produces more goods and services. Recall that **labor productivity** is the quantity of goods and services that can be produced by one worker or by one hour of work. Because of the importance of labor productivity in explaining economic growth, the economic growth model focuses on the causes of long-run increases in labor productivity.

Economic growth model A model that explains growth rates in real GDP per capita over the long run.

Labor productivity The quantity of goods and services that can be produced by one worker or by one hour of work.

How can a country's workers become more productive? Economists believe two key factors determine labor productivity: the quantity of capital per hour worked and the level of technology. Therefore, the economic growth model focuses on technological change and changes over time in the quantity of capital available to workers in explaining changes in real GDP per capita. Recall that **technological change** is a change in the quantity of output firms can produce using a given quantity of inputs.

Technological change A change in the quantity of output a firm can produce using a given quantity of inputs.

There are three main sources of technological change:

- ***Better machinery and equipment.*** Beginning with the steam engine during the Industrial Revolution, the invention of new machinery has been an important source of rising labor productivity. Today, continuing improvements in computers, factory machine tools, electric generators, and many other machines contribute to increases in labor productivity.
- ***Increases in human capital.*** Capital refers to *physical capital*, including computers, factory buildings, machine tools, warehouses, and trucks. The more physical capital workers have available, the more output they can produce. **Human capital** is the accumulated knowledge and skills that workers acquire from education and training or from their life experiences. As workers increase their human capital through education or on-the-job training, their productivity also increases. The more educated workers are, the greater is their human capital.
- ***Better means of organizing and managing production.*** Labor productivity increases if managers can do a better job of organizing production. For example, the *just-in-time system*, first developed by Toyota Motor Corporation, involves assembling goods from parts that arrive at the factory at the exact time they are needed. With this system, fewer workers are needed to store and keep track of parts in the factory, so the quantity of goods produced per hour worked increases.

Human capital The accumulated knowledge and skills that workers acquire from education and training or from their life experiences.

It is important to note that technological change is *not* the same thing as more physical capital. New capital can embody technological change, as when a new processor is embodied in a new computer. But simply adding more capital of the same kind as existing capital is not technological change. To summarize, we can say that the more capital workers have available on their jobs, the better the capital, the more human capital workers have, and the better job business managers do in organizing production, the higher a country's standard of living will be.

The Per-Worker Production Function

The economic growth model explains increases in real GDP per capita over time as resulting from increases in just two factors: the quantity of physical capital available to workers and technological change. Often when analyzing economic growth, we look at increases in real GDP *per hour worked* and increases in capital *per hour worked*. We use

Figure 10-3

The Per-Worker Production Function

The per-worker production function shows the relationship between capital per hour worked and real GDP per hour worked, holding technology constant. Increases in capital per hour worked increase output per hour worked but at a diminishing rate. For example, an increase in capital per hour worked from \$20,000 to \$30,000 increases real GDP per hour worked from \$200 to \$350. An increase in capital per hour worked from \$30,000 to \$40,000 increases real GDP per hour worked only from \$350 to \$475. Each additional \$10,000 increase in capital per hour worked results in progressively smaller increases in output per work.

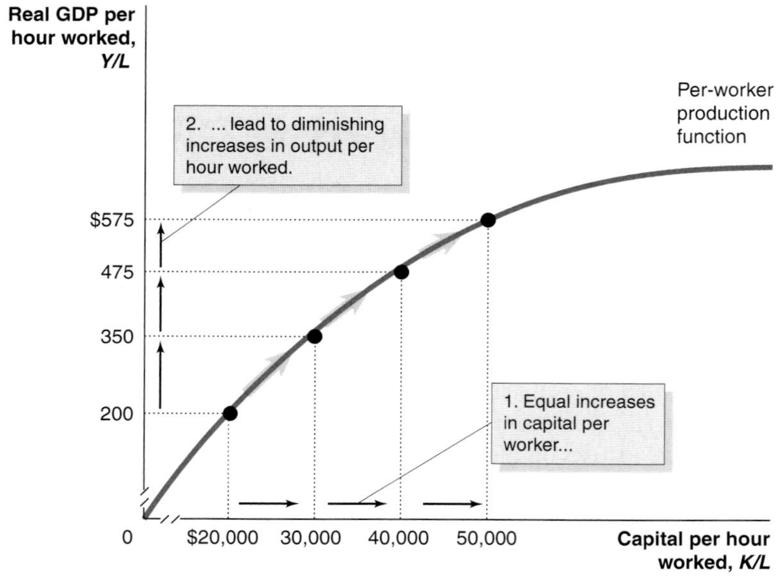

Per-worker production function The relationship between real GDP per hour worked and capital per hour worked, holding the level of technology constant.

measures of GDP and capital per hour rather than per person so we can analyze changes in the underlying ability of an economy to produce more goods with a given amount of labor without having to worry about changes in the fraction of the population working or in the length of the workday. We can illustrate the economic growth model using the **per-worker production function**, which is the relationship between real GDP per hour worked and capital per hour worked, *holding the level of technology constant.* Figure 10-3 shows the per-worker production function as a graph. In the figure, we measure capital per hour worked along the horizontal axis and real GDP per hour worked along the vertical axis. Letting *K* stand for capital, *L* stand for labor, and *Y* stand for real GDP, real GDP per hour worked is *Y/L*, and capital per hour worked is *K/L*. The curve represents the production function. Notice that we do not explicitly show technological change in the figure. We assume that as we move along the production function shown in the figure, the level of technology remains constant. As we will see, we can illustrate technological change using this graph by *shifting up* the curve representing the production function.

The figure shows that increases in the quantity of capital per hour worked result in movements up the per-worker production function, increasing the quantity of output each worker produces. When *holding technology constant,* however, equal increases in the amount of capital per hour worked lead to *diminishing* increases in output per hour worked. For example, increasing capital per hour worked from \$20,000 to \$30,000 increases real GDP per hour worked from \$200 to \$350, an increase of \$150. Another \$10,000 increase in capital per hour worked, from \$30,000 to \$40,000, increases real GDP per hour worked from \$350 to \$475, an increase of only \$125. Each additional \$10,000 increase in capital per hour worked results in progressively smaller increases in real GDP per hour worked. In fact, at very high levels of capital per hour worked, further increases in capital per hour worked will not result in any increase in real GDP per hour worked. This effect results from the *law of diminishing returns,* which states that as we add more of one input—in this case, capital—to a fixed quantity of another input—in this case, labor—output increases by smaller additional amounts.

Why are there diminishing returns to capital? Consider a simple example in which you own a copy store. At first you have 10 employees but only 1 copy machine, so each of your workers is able to produce relatively few copies per day. When you buy a second copy machine, your employees will be able to produce more copies. Adding additional copy machines will continue to increase your output—but by increasingly smaller amounts. For example, adding a twentieth copy machine to the 19 you already have will not increase the copies each worker is able to make by nearly as much as adding a second copy machine did. Eventually, adding additional copying machines will not increase your output at all.

Which Is More Important for Economic Growth: More Capital or Technological Change?

Technological change helps economies avoid diminishing returns to capital. Let's consider a couple of simple examples of the effects of technological change. First, suppose you have 10 copy machines in your copy store. Each of the copy machines can produce 10 copies per minute. You don't believe that adding an eleventh machine identical to the 10 you already have will significantly increase the number of copies your employees can produce in a day. Then you find out that a new copy machine has become available that produces 20 copies per minute. If you replace your existing machines with the new machines, the productivity of your workers will increase. The replacement of existing capital with more productive capital is an example of technological change.

Or suppose you realize that the layout of your store could be improved. Maybe the paper for the machines is on shelves at the back of the store, which requires your workers to waste time walking back and forth whenever the machines run out of paper. By placing the paper closer to the copy machines, you can improve the productivity of your workers. Reorganizing how production takes place so as to increase output is also an example of technological change.

Technological Change: The Key to Sustaining Economic Growth

Figure 10-4 shows the impact of technological change on the per-worker production function. Technological change shifts up the per-worker production function and allows an economy to produce more real GDP per hour worked with the same quantity of capital per hour worked. For example, if the current level of technology puts the economy on Production function$_1$, then when capital per hour worked is \$50,000, real GDP per hour worked is \$575. Technological change that shifts the economy to Production function$_2$ makes it possible to produce \$675 in goods and services per hour worked with the same level of capital per hour worked. Further increases in technology that shift the economy to higher production functions result in further increases in real GDP per

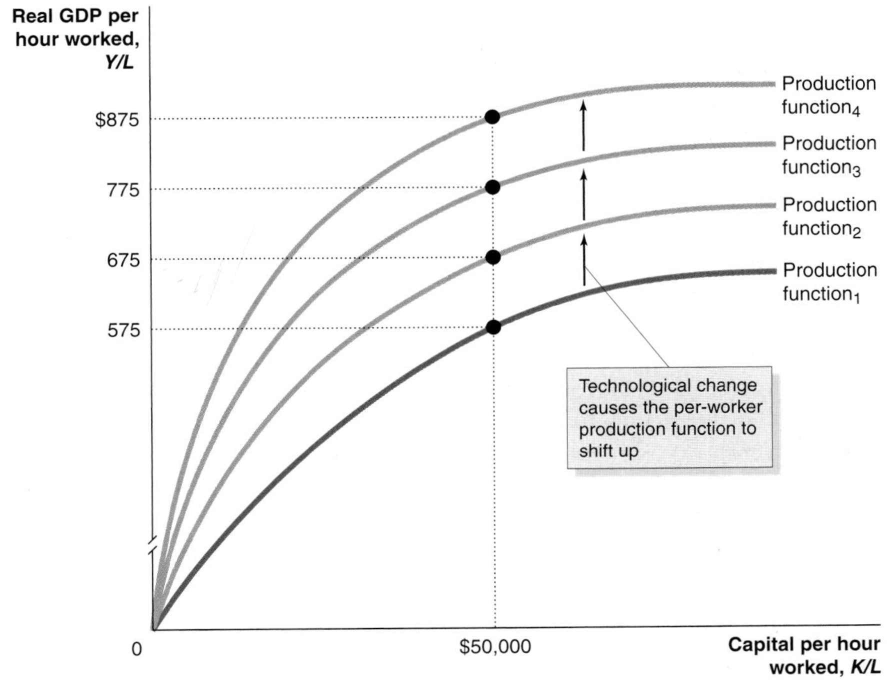

Figure 10-4

Technological Change Increases Output per Hour Worked

Technological change shifts up the production function and allows more output per hour worked with the same amount of capital per hour worked. For example, along Production function$_1$ with \$50,000 in capital per hour worked, the economy can produce \$575 in real GDP per hour worked. However, an increase in technology that shifts the economy to Production function$_2$ makes it possible to produce \$675 in real GDP per hour worked with the same level of capital per hour worked.

hour worked. Because of diminishing returns to capital, continuing increases in real GDP per hour worked can be sustained only if there is technological change. Remember that a country will experience increases in its standard of living only if it experiences increases in real GDP per hour worked. Therefore, we can draw the following important conclusion: *In the long run, a country will experience an increasing standard of living only if it experiences continuing technological change.*

The fall of the Berlin Wall in 1989 symbolized the failure of Communism.

Making the Connection

Why Did the Soviet Union's Economy Fail?

The economic growth model can help explain one of the most striking events of the twentieth century: the economic collapse of the Soviet Union. The Soviet Union was formed from the old Russian Empire following the Communist revolution of 1917. Under Communism, the Soviet Union was a centrally planned economy where the government owned nearly every business and made all production and pricing decisions. In 1960, Nikita Khrushchev, the leader of the Soviet Union, addressed the United Nations in New York City. He declared to the United States and the other democracies, "We will bury you. Your grandchildren will live under Communism."

Many people at the time took Khrushchev's boast seriously. Capital per hour worked grew rapidly in the Soviet Union from 1950 through the 1980s. At first, these increases in capital per hour worked also produced rapid increases in real GDP per hour worked. Rapid increases in real GDP per hour worked during the 1950s caused some economists in the United States to predict incorrectly that the Soviet Union would someday surpass the United States economically. In fact, diminishing returns to capital meant that the additional factories the Soviet Union was building resulted in smaller and smaller increases in real GDP per hour worked.

The Soviet Union did experience some technological change—but at a rate much slower than in the United States and other industrial countries. Why did the Soviet Union fail the crucial requirement for growth: implementing new technologies? The key reason is that in a centrally planned economy, the persons in charge of running most businesses are government employees and not entrepreneurs or independent businesspeople, as is the case in market economies. Soviet managers had little incentive to adopt new ways of doing things. Their pay depended on producing the quantity of output specified in the government's economic plan, not on discovering new, better, and lower-cost ways to produce goods. In addition, these managers did not have to worry about competition from either domestic or foreign firms.

Entrepreneurs and managers of firms in the United States, by contrast, are under intense competitive pressure from other firms. They must constantly search for better ways of producing the goods and services they sell. Developing and using new technologies is an important way to gain a competitive edge and higher profits. The drive for profit provides an incentive for technological change that centrally planned economies are unable to duplicate. In market economies, decisions about which investments to make and which technologies to adopt are made by entrepreneurs and managers who have their own money on the line. In the Soviet system, these decisions were usually made by salaried bureaucrats trying to fulfill a plan formulated in Moscow. Nothing concentrates the mind like having your own funds at risk.

In hindsight, it is clear that a centrally planned economy, such as the Soviet Union's, could not, over the long run, grow faster than a market economy. The Soviet Union collapsed in 1991, and contemporary Russia now has a more market-oriented system, although the government continues to play a much larger role in the economy than does the government in the United States.

YOUR TURN: Test your understanding by doing related problems 2.10 and 2.11 on pages 342–343 at the end of this chapter.

Solved Problem | 10-2

Using the Economic Growth Model to Analyze the Failure of the Soviet Union's Economy

Use the economic growth model and the information in the *Making the Connection* on page 318 to analyze the economic problems the Soviet Union encountered.

SOLVING THE PROBLEM:

Step 1: Review the chapter material. This problem is about using the economic growth model to explain the failure of the Soviet economy, so you may want to review the *Making the Connection* on page 318.

Step 2: Draw a graph like Figure 10-3 to illustrate the economic problems of the Soviet Union. For simplicity, we can assume that the Soviet Union experienced no technological change.

The Soviet Union experienced rapid increases in capital per hour worked from 1950 through the 1980s, but its failure to implement new technology meant that output per hour worked grew at a slower and slower rate.

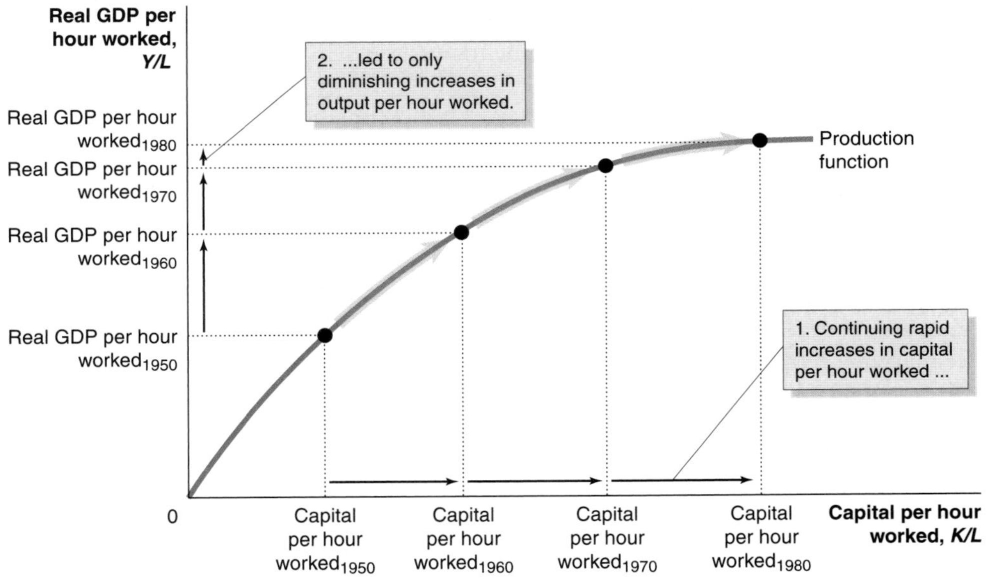

EXTRA CREDIT: The Soviet Union hoped to raise the standard of living of its citizens above that enjoyed in the United States and other high-income countries. Its strategy was to make continuous increases in the quantity of capital available to its workers. The economic growth model helps us understand the flaws in this policy for achieving economic growth.

YOUR TURN: For more practice, do related problems 2.7 and 2.8 on page 342 at the end of this chapter.

>> End Solved Problem 10-2

New Growth Theory

New growth theory A model of long-run economic growth which emphasizes that technological change is influenced by economic incentives and so is determined by the working of the market system.

The economic growth model we have been using was first developed in the 1950s by Nobel laureate Robert Solow, of MIT. According to this model, productivity growth is the key factor in explaining long-run growth in real GDP per capita. In recent years, some economists have become dissatisfied with this model because it does not explain the factors that determine productivity growth. What has become known as the **new growth theory** was developed by Paul Romer, an economist at Stanford University, to provide a better explanation of the sources of productivity change. Romer argues that the rate of technological change is influenced by how individuals and firms respond to economic incentives. Earlier accounts of economic growth left technological change unexplained or attributed it to factors such as chance scientific discoveries.

Romer argues that the accumulation of *knowledge capital* is a key determinant of economic growth. Firms add to an economy's stock of knowledge capital when they engage in research and development or otherwise contribute to technological change. We have seen that accumulation of physical capital is subject to diminishing returns: Increases in capital per hour worked lead to increases in real GDP per hour worked but at a decreasing rate. Romer argues that the same is true of knowledge capital *at the firm level.* As firms add to their stock of knowledge capital, they increase their output but at a decreasing rate. At the level of the economy, however, Romer argues that knowledge capital is subject to *increasing returns.* Increasing returns can exist because knowledge, once discovered, becomes available to everyone. The use of physical capital, such as a computer or machine tool, is *rival* because if one firm uses it other firms cannot, and it is *excludable* because the firm that owns the capital can keep other firms from using it. The use of knowledge capital, such as the chemical formula for a drug that cures cancer, is nonrival, however, because one firm's using that knowledge does not prevent another firm's using it. Knowledge capital is also nonexcludable because once something like a chemical formula becomes known, it becomes widely available for other firms to use (unless, as we discuss shortly, the government gives the firm that invents a new product the legal right to exclusive use of it).

Because knowledge capital is nonrival and nonexcludable, firms can *free ride* on the research and development of other firms. Firms free ride when they benefit from the results of research and development they did not pay for. For example, transistor technology was first developed at Western Electric's Bell Laboratories in the 1950s and served as the basic technology of the information revolution. Bell Laboratories, however, received only a tiny fraction of the immense profits that were eventually made by all the firms that used this technology. Romer points out that firms are unlikely to invest in research and development up to the point where the marginal cost of the research equals the marginal return from the knowledge gained because much of the marginal return will be gained by *other* firms. Therefore, there is likely to be an inefficiently small amount of research and development, slowing the accumulation of knowledge capital and economic growth.

Government policy can help increase the accumulation of knowledge capital in three ways:

Patent The exclusive right to a product for a period of 20 years from the date the product is invented.

- ***Protecting intellectual property with patents and copyrights.*** Governments can increase the incentive to engage in research and development by giving firms the exclusive rights to their discoveries for a period of years. The U.S. government grants patents to companies that develop new products or new ways of making existing products. A **patent** gives a firm the exclusive legal right to a new product for a period of 20 years from the date the product is invented. For example, a pharmaceutical firm that develops a drug that cures cancer can secure a patent on the drug, keeping other firms from manufacturing the drug without permission. The profits earned during the period the patent is in force provide an incentive for undertaking the research and development. The patent system has drawbacks, however. In filing for a patent, a firm must disclose information about the product or process. This information enters the public record and may help competing firms develop products or processes that are similar but that do not infringe on the patent. To avoid this problem, a firm may try to keep the results of its research a *trade secret*, without patenting it. A famous example of a trade secret is the formula for Coca-Cola. Tension also arises between the government's objectives of providing patent protection that gives firms the incentive to engage in research and development and making sure that the knowledge gained through the research is widely disseminated for the greatest impact on the economy. Economists debate the features of an ideal patent system.

Just as a new product or a new method of making a product receives patent protection, books, films, and software receive *copyright* protection. Under U.S. law, the creator of a book, film, or piece of software has the exclusive right to use the creation during the creator's lifetime. The creator's heirs retain this exclusive right for 70 years after the creator's death.

- ***Subsidizing research and development.*** The government can use subsidies to increase the quantity of research and development that takes place. In the United States, the federal government carries out some research directly. For example, the National Institutes of Health conducts medical research. The government also subsidizes research by providing grants to researchers in universities through the National Science Foundation and other agencies. Finally, the government provides tax benefits to firms that invest in research and development.
- ***Subsidizing education.*** People with technical training carry out research and development. If firms are unable to capture all the profits from research and development, the wages and salaries paid to technical workers will be reduced. These lower wages and salaries reduce the incentive to workers to receive this training. If the government subsidizes education, it can increase the number of workers who have technical training. In the United States, the government subsidizes education by directly providing free education from grades kindergarten through 12 and by providing support for public colleges and universities. The government also provides student loans at reduced interest rates.

These government policies can bring the accumulation of knowledge capital closer to the optimal level.

Joseph Schumpeter and Creative Destruction

The new growth theory has revived interest in the ideas of Joseph Schumpeter. Schumpeter was born in Austria in 1883. He served briefly as that country's finance minister, before becoming an economics professor at Harvard in 1932. Schumpeter developed a model of growth that emphasized his view that new products unleash a "gale of creative destruction" in which older products—and, often, the firms that produced them—are driven out of the market. According to Schumpeter, the key to rising living standards is not small changes to existing products but, rather, new products that meet consumer wants in qualitatively better ways. For example, in the early twentieth century, the automobile displaced the horse-drawn carriage by meeting consumer demand for personal transportation in a way that was qualitatively better. In the early twenty-first century, the DVD and the DVD player displaced the VHS tape and the VCR by better meeting consumer demand for watching films at home.

To Schumpeter, the entrepreneur is central to economic growth: "The function of entrepreneurs is to reform or revolutionize the pattern of production by exploiting an invention or, more generally, an untried technological possibility for producing new commodities or producing an old one in a new way."

The profits an entrepreneur hopes to earn provide the incentive for bringing together the factors of production—labor, capital, and natural resources—to start new firms and introduce new goods and services. Successful entrepreneurs can use their profits to finance the development of new products and are better able to attract funds from investors.

10.3 LEARNING OBJECTIVE

10.3 | Discuss fluctuations in productivity growth in the United States.

Economic Growth in the United States

The economic growth model can help us understand the record of growth in the United States. Figure 10-5 shows average annual growth rates in real GDP per hour worked since 1800. As the United States experienced the Industrial Revolution during the nineteenth century, U.S. firms increased the quantities of capital per hour worked. New technologies such as the steam engine, the railroad, and the telegraph also became available. Together, these factors resulted in an average annual growth rate of real GDP per worker of 1.3 percent from 1800 to 1900. Real GDP per capita grew at a slower rate of 1.1 percent during this period. At this growth rate, real GDP per capita would double about every 63 years, which means that living standards were growing steadily, but relatively slowly.

By the twentieth century, technological change had been institutionalized. Many large corporations began to set up research and development facilities to improve the quality of their products and the efficiency with which they produced them. Universities also began to conduct research that had business applications. After World War II, many corporations began to provide significant funds to universities to help pay for research. In 1950, the federal government created the National Science Foundation, whose main goal is to support university researchers. The accelerating rate of technological change led to more rapid growth rates.

Economic Growth in the United States since 1950: Fast, Then Slow, Then Fast Again

Continuing technological change allowed the U.S. economy to avoid the diminishing returns to capital that stifled growth in the Soviet economy. In fact, until the 1970s, the growth rate of the U.S. economy accelerated over time. As Figure 10-5 shows, growth in the first half of the twentieth century was faster than growth during the nineteenth century, and growth from 1950 to 1972 was faster yet. Then the unexpected happened: For more than 20 years, from 1973 to 1994, the growth rate of real GDP per hour worked slowed. The growth rate during these years was more than one percentage point per year lower than during the 1950–1972 period. Measured in 2000 dollars, real GDP per hour worked in the United States was $25,903 in 1972. If it had continued to grow from 1973

Figure 10-5

Average Annual Growth Rates in Real GDP per Hour Worked in the United States

The growth rate in the United States increased from 1800 through the mid-1970s. Then, for more than 20 years, growth slowed before increasing again in the mid-1990s.

Note: The values for 1800–1900 are real GDP per worker. The values for 1900–2006 are real GDP per hour worked and are the authors' calculations, based on data in Neville Francis and Valerie A. Ramey, "The Source of Historical Economic Fluctuations: An Analysis Using Long-Run Restrictions," in Jeffrey Frankel, Richard Clarida, and Francesco Giavazzi, eds., *International Seminar in Macroeconomics*, Chicago: University of Chicago Press, 2005; the authors thank Neville Francis for kindly providing these data.

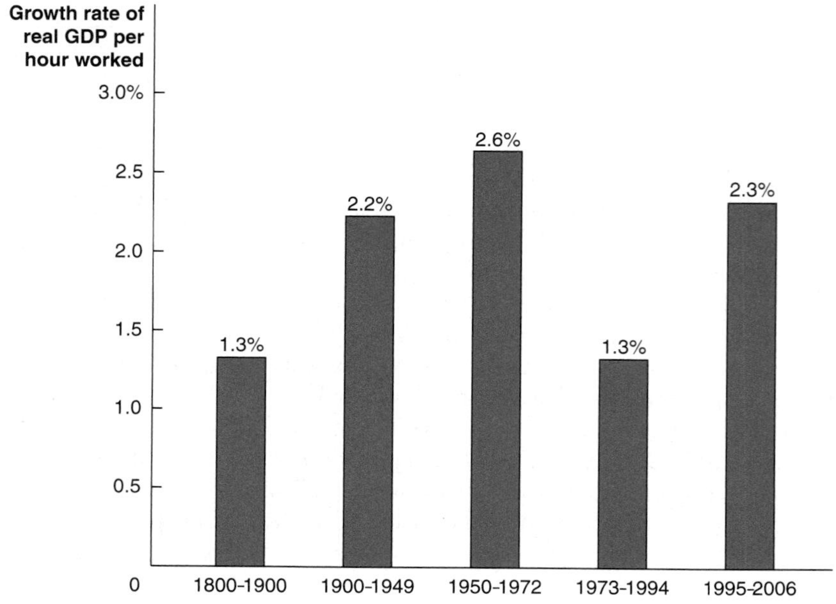

to 1994 at the same rate it had been growing from 1950 to 1972, it would have been about $45,500 in 1994, which is 30 percent higher than it actually was. The United States would today be a significantly richer country if the growth in the productivity of U.S. workers had not slowed down from the mid-1970s to the mid-1990s.

What Caused the Productivity Slowdown of 1973–1994?

Several explanations have been offered for the productivity slowdown of the mid-1970s to mid-1990s, but none is completely satisfying. We can briefly discuss three possible explanations for the slowdown:

- Measurement problems
- High oil prices
- A decline in labor quality

Was It a Measurement Problem? Some economists argue that productivity really didn't slow down from the mid-1970s to mid-1990s. They argue it only *appears* to have slowed down because of problems in measuring productivity accurately. After 1970, services—such as haircuts and financial advice—became a larger fraction of GDP, and goods—such as automobiles and hamburgers—became a smaller fraction. It is more difficult to measure increases in the output of services than to measure increases in the output of goods. Beginning in the 1970s, advances in information technology improved the convenience of some services without actually increasing the quantity of the services offered. For example, before banks began using automated teller machines (ATMs) in the 1980s, to withdraw money, you would have to go to a bank before closing time—which was usually 3:00 P.M. Once ATMs became available, you could withdraw money at any time of the day or night at a variety of locations. This increased convenience from ATMs does not show up in GDP. If it did, measured output per hour worked would have grown more rapidly.

There may also be a measurement problem in accounting for improvements in the environment and in health and safety. The Clean Air Act, passed in 1970, was the first of several federal laws that required firms to significantly reduce pollution. Other laws passed during the 1970s were aimed at promoting health and safety. The Occupational Safety and Health Administration (OSHA) and the Consumer Product Safety Commission were also given the authority to issue guidelines that firms are legally required to obey. As a result, firms had to spend billions of dollars reducing pollution, improving workplace safety, and redesigning products to improve their safety. This spending did not result in additional output that would be included in GDP—although it may have increased overall well-being. If these increases in well-being had been included in GDP, measured output per hour worked would have grown more rapidly.

It is possible that these changes in the economy during the 1970s—increased production of services and increased spending by firms to comply with environmental, safety, and health regulations—account for some of the slowdown in the growth rate of output per hour worked. However, most economists do not believe that the effect of these factors is large enough to be the whole explanation.

Was It the Effect of High Oil Prices? In 1973, the Organization of Petroleum Exporting Countries (OPEC) increased the price of a barrel of oil from less than $3 to more than $10. A second sharp increase in oil prices occurred in the late 1970s, when the price of a barrel of oil rose from about $20 to more than $35. These higher oil prices increased production costs for many firms in the United States. Some firms use oil directly in the production process. Other firms use products, such as plastics, that are made from oil. Some utilities burn oil to generate electricity, so electricity prices rose. Rising oil prices led to rising gasoline prices, which raised transportation costs for many firms. To conserve oil and use less energy, firms reorganized production in ways that reduced output per hour worked.

In the early 1980s, many economists thought the oil price increases explained the productivity slowdown, but the productivity slowdown continued after U.S. firms had fully adjusted to high oil prices. In fact, it continued into the late 1980s and early 1990s, when oil prices declined.

Was It the Declining Quality of Labor? Some economists argue that deterioration in the U.S. educational system may have contributed to the slowdown in growth from the mid-1970s to mid-1990s. Scores on some standardized tests began to decline in the 1970s. This decline may indicate that, on average, workers entering the labor force were less well educated and less productive than in earlier decades. A more subtle argument is that the skills required to perform many jobs increased during the 1970s and 1980s, while the preparation that workers had received in school did not keep pace. It is difficult to quantify the skill requirements of jobs and the skills of workers. So, it is difficult to estimate how much of the growth slowdown may have been due to the failure of worker skills to keep pace with the skill requirements of jobs.

The Productivity Slowdown Affected All Industrial Countries In assessing possible causes of the productivity slowdown, it is important to note that the United States was not alone in experiencing the slowdown in productivity. All the leading industrial countries experienced a growth slowdown between the mid-1970s and the mid-1990s. Therefore, explanations for the slowdown that rely on factors affecting only the United States—such as the deterioration in the quality of education—are not likely to be correct. Because all the industrial economies began producing more services and fewer goods and enacted stricter environmental regulations at about the same time, explanations of the productivity slowdown that emphasize measurement problems become more plausible. In the end, though, economists have not yet reached a consensus on why the productivity slowdown took place.

The Productivity Boom: Are We in a "New Economy"?

The productivity slowdown began abruptly in the mid-1970s and ended just as abruptly in the mid-1990s. As Figure 10-5 shows, productivity growth in the United States between 1995 and 2006 was almost as fast as before the growth slowdown. Some economists argue that the development of a "new economy" based on information technology caused the higher productivity growth that began in the mid-1990s. The spread of ever faster and increasingly less expensive computers has made communication and data processing easier and faster than ever before. Today, a single desktop computer has more computing power than all the mainframe computers NASA used to control the Apollo spacecrafts that landed on the moon in the late 1960s and early 1970s.

Faster data processing has had a major impact on nearly every firm. Business record keeping, once done laboriously by hand, is now done more quickly and accurately by computer. The increase in Internet use during the 1990s brought changes to the ways firms sell to consumers and to each other. Cell phones, laptop computers, and wireless Internet access allow people to work away from the office, whether at home or while traveling. These developments have significantly increased labor productivity.

Many economists are optimistic that the increases in productivity that began in the mid-1990s will continue. The use of computers, as well as information and communications technology in general, increases as prices continue to fall. By 2007, well-equipped desktop computers could be purchased for less than $300. Further innovations in information and communications technology may continue to contribute to strong productivity growth. Some economists are skeptical, however, about the ability of the economy to continue to sustain high rates of productivity growth. These economists argue that in the 1990s, innovations in information and communications technology—such as the development of the World Wide Web, Windows 95, and computerized inventory control systems—raised labor productivity by having a substantial effect on how businesses operated. By the early 2000s, these economists argue, innovations in information and communications technology were having a greater impact on consumer products, such as cell phones, than on the processes internal to firms that would lead to higher productivity. If the rapid increases in output per hour worked that began in the mid-1990s do continue, this trend will be good news for increases in living standards in the United States.

Why Has Productivity Growth Been Faster in the United States than in Other Countries?

One notable aspect of the increase in productivity after 1995 is that, unlike the earlier productivity slowdown, it has not been experienced equally by all of the leading industrial countries. Figure 10-6 shows labor productivity growth during the years from 1996 to 2006 for the leading industrial countries, known collectively as the *Group of Seven*, or the *G-7* countries. Productivity growth was significantly higher in the United States than in the other countries, with the exception of the United Kingdom. Japan, France, Germany, and Italy actually experienced *slower* productivity growth during these years than during the years from 1973 to 1995.

Why has productivity growth in the United States been more rapid than in most other industrial countries? Many economists believe there are two main explanations: the greater flexibility of U.S. labor markets and the greater efficiency of the U.S. financial system. U.S. labor markets are more flexible than labor markets in other countries for several reasons. In many European countries, government regulations make it difficult for firms to fire workers. These regulations make firms reluctant to hire workers. As a result, many younger workers have difficulty finding jobs, and once a job is found, a worker tends to remain in it even if his or her skills and preferences are not a good match for the characteristics of the job. In the United States, by contrast, government regulations are less restrictive, workers have an easier time finding jobs, and workers also change jobs fairly frequently. For example, a typical young worker in the United States will hold seven different jobs during the worker's first 10 years in the labor force. This high rate of job mobility ensures a better match between workers' skills and preferences and the characteristics of jobs, which increases labor productivity. The higher productivity translates into higher wages: One-third of the increase in wages experienced by young workers results from job changes. Workers can also build skills through being exposed to a variety of different jobs. Workers in the United States may acquire as much as half of their skills through job mobility, on-the-job learning, and workplace education.

Many European countries also have restrictive work rules that limit the flexibility of firms to implement new technologies. Some of these work rules are imposed by government regulation, others are negotiated by labor unions. Because these rules restrict the

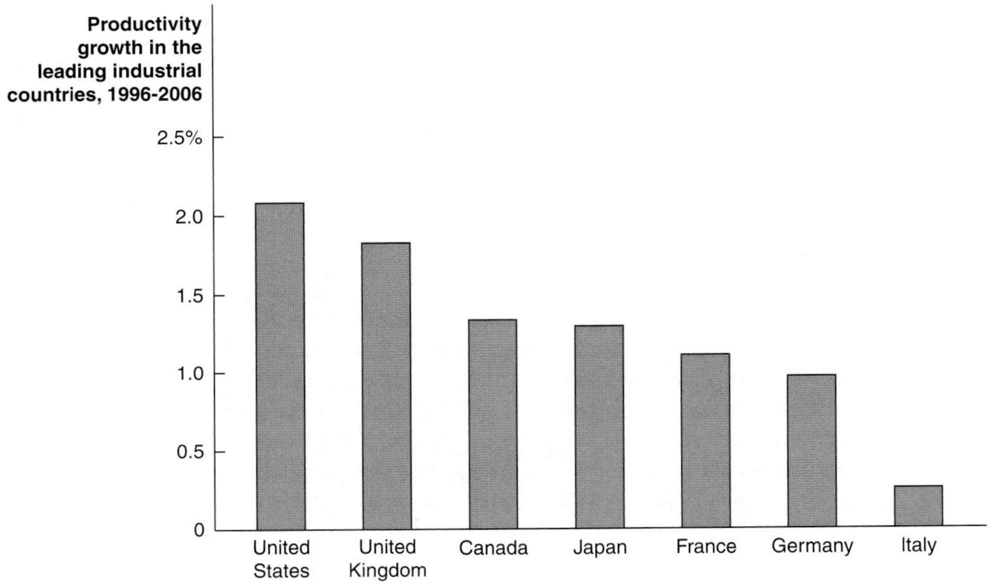

Figure 10-6

Productivity Growth in the Leading Industrial Economies, 1996–2006

Productivity growth as measured by the average annual growth rate of labor productivity was more rapid in the United States than in the other leading industrial countries during the years between 1996 and 2006.

Source: Organization for Economic Cooperation and Development, *Economic Outlook, 2006,* Annex Table 12.

tasks workers can be asked to perform and the hours during the day they can be asked to work, they reduce the ability of firms to use new technologies that may require workers to learn new skills, perform new tasks, or work during the night or early mornings. Firms must often negotiate with workers before introducing new products or relocating facilities. The hours that retail stores may be open are regulated in most European countries. These regulations reduce the revenue firms can generate from implementing new technologies and therefore reduce the incentives that firms have to adopt the technologies.

Workers in the United States tend to enter the labor force earlier, retire later, and experience fewer long spells of unemployment than do workers in Europe. These differences between the labor force experiences of U.S. and European workers, including the greater tendency for U.S. teenagers and college students to work at least part time, can be explained in several ways. One key difference, however, is the design of the systems of government-provided unemployment insurance. As we noted in Chapter 8, unemployed workers in the United States are usually eligible to receive unemployment insurance payments equal to about half their previous wage for only six months. After that time, the opportunity cost of continuing to search for a job rises. In many other high-income countries, such as Canada and most of the countries of Western Europe, workers are eligible to receive unemployment payments for a year or more, and the payments may equal 70 percent to 80 percent of their previous wage. Because the opportunity cost of being unemployed is lower in those countries, the unemployment rate tends to be higher, and the fraction of the labor force that is unemployed for more than one year also tends to be higher. Studies have shown that workers who are employed for longer periods tend to have greater skills, greater productivity, and higher wages. Many economists believe that the design of the U.S. unemployment insurance program has contributed to the greater flexibility of U.S. labor markets and to higher rates of growth in labor productivity.

As we have seen, technological change is essential for rapid productivity growth. To obtain the funds needed to implement new technologies, firms turn to the financial system. It is important that funds for investment be not only available but also allocated efficiently. In the Soviet Union, there was no shortage of funds available for investment, but the funds were directed by the government mainly into building additional factories that employed old technologies rather than being directed by entrepreneurs into funding the innovations that would have raised productivity and living standards. We saw in Chapter 5 that large corporations can raise funds by selling stocks and bonds in financial markets. U.S. corporations benefit from the efficiency of U.S. financial markets. The level of legal protection of investors is relatively high in U.S. financial markets, which encourages both U.S. and foreign investors to buy stocks and bonds issued by U.S. firms. The volume of trading in U.S. financial markets also assures investors that they will be able to quickly sell the stocks and the bonds they buy. This *liquidity* also serves to attract investors to U.S. markets.

Smaller firms that are unable to issue stocks and bonds often obtain funding from banks. However, entrepreneurs founding new firms, particularly firms that are based on new technologies, often cannot rely on banks or on sales of stocks and bonds in financial markets. Investors are usually unwilling to buy the stocks and bonds of a new firm that lacks a track record of profitability. Banks are similarly reluctant to lend money to a firm whose business plan is based on introducing a new product or a new way of producing an existing product. Many firms that are established to bring new technologies to market obtain funds from *venture capital firms*. Venture capital firms raise funds from institutional investors, such as pension funds, and from wealthy individuals, to invest in start-up firms. The owners of venture capital firms closely examine the business plans of start-up firms, looking for those that appear most likely to succeed. In exchange for providing funding, a venture capital firm often becomes part owner of the start-up, placing its representative on the start-up's board of directors and sometimes even playing a role in managing the firm. A successful venture capital firm is able to attract investors who would not otherwise be willing to provide funds to start-up firms because the investors would lack sufficient credible information on any start-up's prospectus. The ability of venture capital firms to finance technology-driven start-up firms may be giving the United States an advantage in bringing new products and new processes to market.

10.4 LEARNING OBJECTIVE

10.4 | Explain economic catch-up and discuss why many poor countries have not experienced rapid economic growth.

Why Isn't the Whole World Rich?

The economic growth model tells us that economies grow when the quantity of capital per hour worked increases and when technological change takes place. This model seems to provide a good blueprint for developing countries to become rich: Increase the quantity of capital per hour worked and use the best available technology. There are economic incentives for both of these things to happen in poor countries. The profitability of using additional capital or better technology is generally greater in a developing country than in a high-income country. For example, replacing an existing computer with a new, faster computer will generally have a relatively small payoff for a firm in the United States. In contrast, installing a new computer in a Zambian firm where records are kept by hand is likely to have an enormous payoff.

This observation leads to the following important conclusion: *The economic growth model predicts that poor countries will grow faster than rich countries.* If this prediction is correct, we should observe poor countries catching up to the rich countries in levels of GDP per capita (or income per capita). Has this **catch-up**—or *convergence*—actually occurred? Here we come to a paradox: The lower-income *industrial* countries have been catching up to the higher-income industrial countries, but the developing countries as a group have not been catching up to the industrial countries as a group.

Catch-up The prediction that the level of GDP per capita (or income per capita) in poor countries will grow faster than in rich countries.

Catch-up: Sometimes, but Not Always

We can construct a graph that makes it easier to see whether catch-up is happening. In Figure 10-7 the horizontal axis shows the initial level of GDP per capita, and the vertical axis shows the rate at which GDP per capita is growing. We can then plot points on the graph for rich and poor countries. Each point represents the combination of a country's initial level of GDP per capita and its growth rate over the following years. Low-income countries should be in the upper-left part of the graph because they would have low initial levels of GDP per capita but fast growth rates. High-income countries should be in the lower-right part of the graph because they would have high initial levels of GDP per capita but slow growth rates.

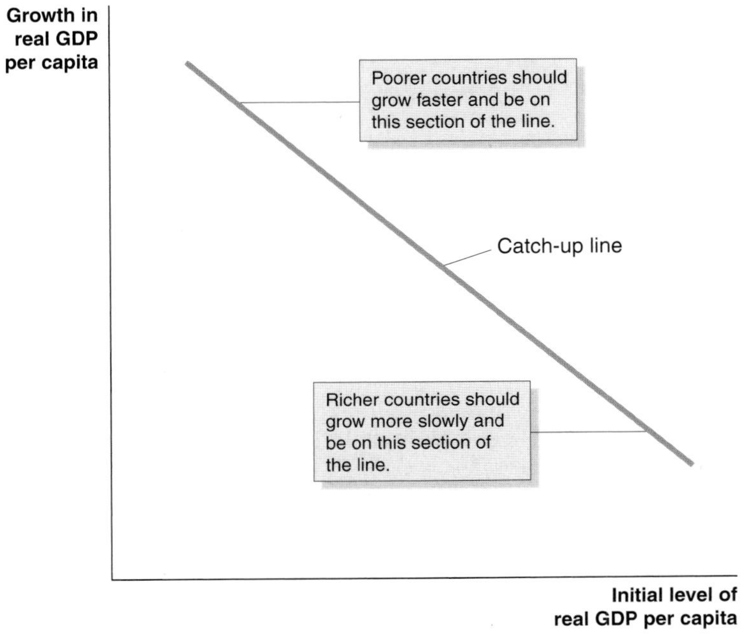
Growth in real GDP per capita
Poorer countries should grow faster and be on this section of the line.
Catch-up line
Richer countries should grow more slowly and be on this section of the line.
Initial level of real GDP per capita

Figure 10-7

The Catch-up Predicted by the Economic Growth Model

According to the economic growth model, countries that start with lower levels of GDP per capita should grow faster (points near the top of the line) than countries that start with higher levels of GDP per capita (points near the bottom of the line).

Figure 10-8

There Has Been Catch-up among Industrial Countries

The industrial countries such as Ireland and Japan that had the lowest incomes in 1960 grew the fastest between 1960 and 2004. Countries like Switzerland and the United States that had the highest incomes in 1960 grew the slowest.

Note: Data are real GDP per capita in 2000 dollars. Each point in the figure represents one industrial country.

Source: Authors' calculations from data in Alan Heston, Robert Summers, and Bettina Aten, *Penn World Table Version 6.2*, Center for International Comparisons of Production, Income and Prices at the University of Pennsylvania, September 2006.

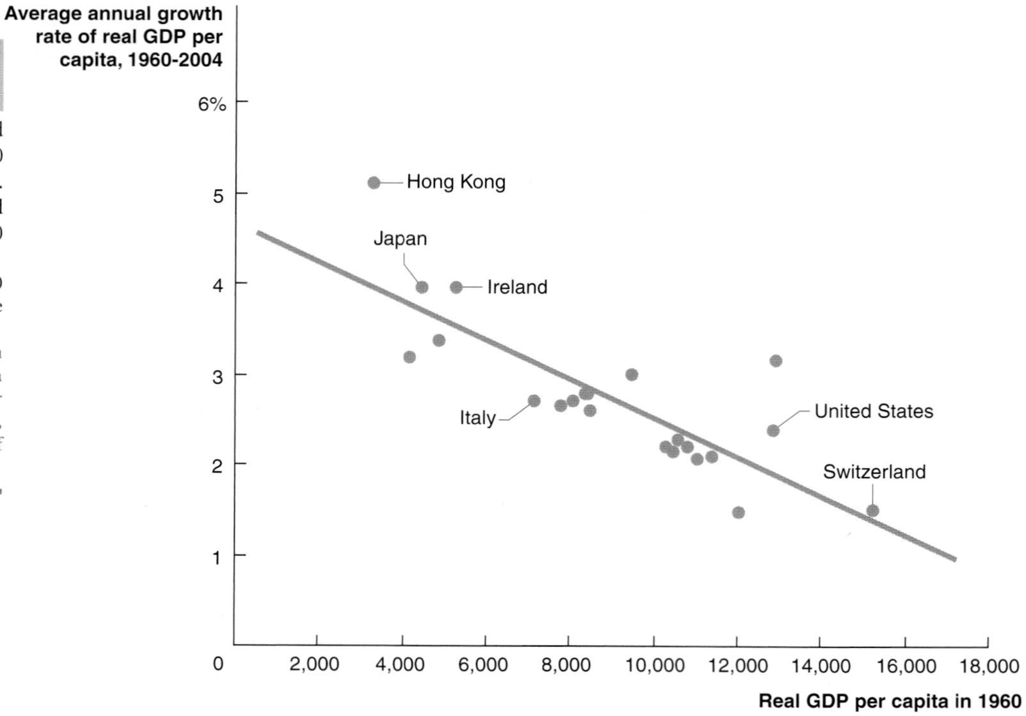

Catch-up Among the Industrial Countries If we look at only the industrial countries, we can see the catch-up predicted by the economic growth model. Figure 10-8 shows that the industrial countries that had the lowest incomes in 1960, such as Ireland and Japan, grew the fastest between 1960 and 2004. Countries that had the highest incomes in 1960, such as Switzerland and the United States, grew the slowest.

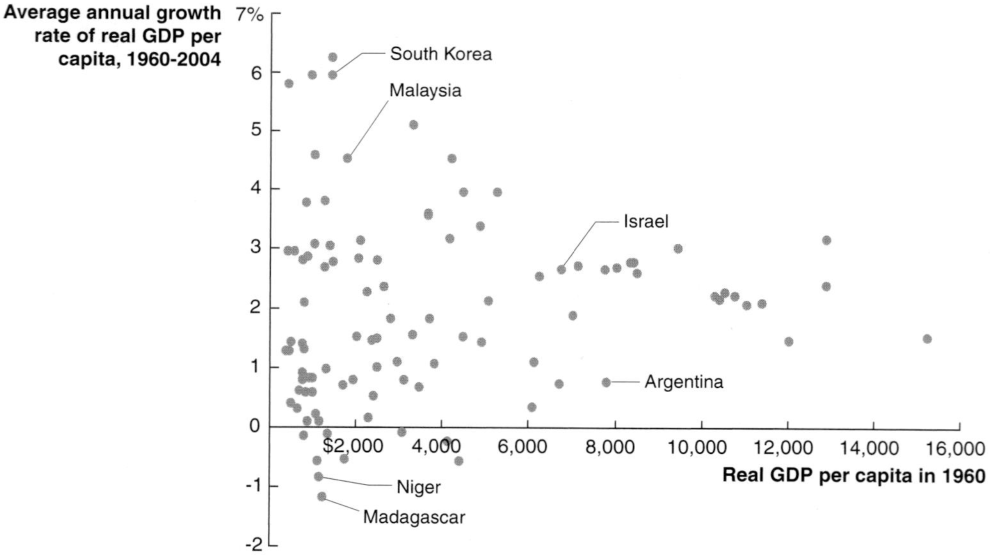

Figure 10-9 | Most of the World Hasn't Been Catching Up

Looking at all countries for which statistics are available does not show the catch-up predicted by the economic growth model. Some countries, such as Niger and Madagascar, that had low levels of real GDP per capita in 1960 actually experienced *negative* economic growth. Other countries, such as Malaysia and South Korea, that started with low levels of real GDP per capita grew rapidly. Some middle-income countries in 1960, such as Argentina, hardly grew between 1960 and 2004, while others, such as Israel, experienced significant growth.

Note: Data are real GDP per capita in 2000 dollars. Each point in the figure represents one country.

Source: Authors' calculations from data in Alan Heston, Robert Summers, and Bettina Aten, *Penn World Table Version 6.2*, Center for International Comparisons of Production, Income and Prices at the University of Pennsylvania, September 2006.

Are the Developing Countries Catching Up to the Industrial Countries? If we expand the analysis to include every country for which statistics are available, it becomes more difficult to find the catch-up predicted by the economic growth model. Figure 10-9 does not show a consistent relationship between the level of real GDP in 1960 and growth from 1960 to 2004. Some countries, such as Niger and Madagascar, that had low levels of real GDP per capita in 1960 actually experienced *negative* economic growth: They had *lower* levels of real GDP per capita in 2004 than in 1960. Other countries, such as Malaysia and South Korea, that started with low levels of real GDP per capita grew rapidly. Some middle-income countries in 1960, such as Argentina, hardly grew between 1960 and 2004, while others, such as Israel, experienced significant growth.

Solved Problem | **10-4**

The Economic Growth Model's Prediction of Catch-up

The economic growth model makes predictions about the relationship between an economy's initial level of real GDP per capita relative to other economies and how fast the economy will grow in the future.

a. Consider the statistics in the following table.

COUNTRY	REAL GDP PER CAPITA IN 1960 (2000 DOLLARS)	ANNUAL GROWTH IN REAL GDP PER CAPITA, 1960–2004
Taiwan	$1,443	6.26%
Tunisia	2,102	3.13
Brazil	2,643	2.36
Algeria	3,843	1.04
Argentina	7,838	0.76

Are these statistics consistent with the economic growth model? Briefly explain.

b. Now consider the statistics in the following table.

COUNTRY	REAL GDP PER CAPITA IN 1960 (2000 DOLLARS)	ANNUAL GROWTH IN REAL GDP PER CAPITA, 1960–2004
Japan	$4,509	3.94%
Italy	7,167	2.70
France	8,531	2.58
United Kingdom	10,323	2.19

Are these statistics consistent with the economic growth model? Briefly explain.

c. Construct a new table that lists all nine countries, from lowest real GDP per capita in 1960 to highest. Are the statistics in your new table consistent with the economic growth model?

SOLVING THE PROBLEM:

Step 1: Review the chapter material. This problem is about catch-up in the economic growth model, so you may want to review the section "Why Isn't the Whole World Rich?" which begins on page 327.

Step 2: Explain whether the statistics in the first table are consistent with the economic growth model. These statistics are consistent with the economic growth model. The countries with the lowest levels of real GDP per capita in 1960 had the fastest growth rates between 1960 and 2004, and the countries with the highest levels of real GDP per capita had the slowest growth rates.

Step 3: Explain whether the statistics in the second table are consistent with the economic growth model. These statistics are also consistent with the economic growth model. Once again, the countries with the lowest levels of real GDP per capita in 1960 had the fastest growth rates between 1960 and 2004, and the countries with the highest levels of real GDP per capita had the slowest growth rates.

Step 4: Construct a table that includes all nine countries from the tables in questions (a) and (b) and discuss the results.

COUNTRY	REAL GDP PER CAPITA IN 1960 (2000 DOLLARS)	ANNUAL GROWTH IN REAL GDP PER CAPITA, 1960–2004
Taiwan	$1,443	6.26%
Tunisia	2,102	3.13
Brazil	2,643	2.36
Algeria	3,843	1.04
Japan	4,509	3.94
Italy	7,167	2.70
Argentina	7,838	0.76
France	8,531	2.58
United Kingdom	10,323	2.19

The statistics in the new table are not consistent with the predictions of the economic growth model. For example, France and the United Kingdom had higher levels of real GDP per capita in 1960 than did Algeria and Argentina. The economic growth model predicts that France and the United Kingdom should, therefore, have grown more slowly than Algeria and Argentina. The data in the table show, however, that they grew faster. Similarly, Italy grew faster than Brazil even though its real GDP per capita was already much higher than Brazil's in 1960.

EXTRA CREDIT: The statistics in these tables confirm what we saw in Figures 10-8 and 10-9: There has been catch-up among the industrial countries, but there has not been catch-up if we include all the countries of the world in the analysis.

>> End Solved Problem 10-4

YOUR TURN: For more practice, do problems 4.4 and 4.5 on page 344 at the end of this chapter.

Why Don't More Low-Income Countries Experience Rapid Growth?

The economic growth model predicts that the countries that were very poor in 1960 should have grown rapidly over the next 40 years. As we have just seen, a few did, but most did not. Why are many low-income countries growing so slowly? There is no single answer, but most economists point to four key factors:

- Failure to enforce the rule of law
- Wars and revolutions
- Poor public education and health
- Low rates of saving and investment

Property rights The rights individuals or firms have to the exclusive use of their property, including the right to buy or sell it.

Failure to Enforce the Rule of Law In the years since 1960, increasing numbers of developing countries, including China, have abandoned centrally planned economies in favor of more market-oriented economies. For entrepreneurs in a market economy to succeed, however, the government must guarantee private **property rights** and enforce contracts. Unless entrepreneurs feel secure in their property, they will not risk starting a business. It is also very difficult for businesses to operate successfully in a market economy unless they can use an independent court system to enforce contracts. The failure of many developing countries to guarantee private property rights and to enforce contracts has hindered their economic growth.

Consider, for example, the production of shoes in a developing country. Suppose the owner of a shoe factory signs a contract with a leather supplier to deliver a specific quantity of leather on a particular date for a particular price. On the basis of this contract, the owner of the shoe factory signs a contract to deliver a specific quantity of shoes to a shoe wholesaler. This contract specifies the quantity of shoes to be delivered, the quality of the shoes, the delivery date, and the price. The owner of the tannery that produces the leather uses the contract with the shoe factory to enter into a contract with cattle ranchers for the delivery of hides. The shoe wholesaler enters into contracts to deliver shoes to retail stores, where they are sold to consumers. For the flow of goods from cattle ranchers to shoe customers to operate efficiently, each business must carry out the terms of the contract it has signed. In developed countries, such as the United States, businesses know that if they fail to carry out a contract, they may be sued in court and forced to compensate the other party for any economic damages.

Many developing countries do not have functioning, independent court systems. Even if a court system does exist, a case may not be heard for many years. In some countries, bribery of judges and political favoritism in court rulings are common. If firms cannot enforce contracts through the court system, they will insist on carrying out only face-to-face cash transactions. For example, the shoe manufacturer will wait until the leather producer brings the hides to the factory and will then buy them for cash. The wholesaler will wait until the shoes have been produced before making plans for sales to retail stores. Production still takes place, but it is carried out more slowly and inefficiently. In these circumstances, firms have difficulty finding investors willing to provide them with the funds they need to expand.

The **rule of law** refers to the ability of a government to enforce the laws of the country, particularly with respect to protecting private property and enforcing contracts. The World Bank is an agency of the United Nations whose role is to provide financial aid and policy advice to low-income countries. Economists at the World Bank have ranked 118 developing countries on the basis of how well their governments enforce the rule of law. Figure 10-10 shows the difference in average annual growth rates between the 20 developing countries that do the best job of enforcing the rule of law, such as the Czech Republic and Israel, and the 20 countries that do the worst job, such as the Congo and

Rule of law The ability of a government to enforce the laws of the country, particularly with respect to protecting private property and enforcing contracts.

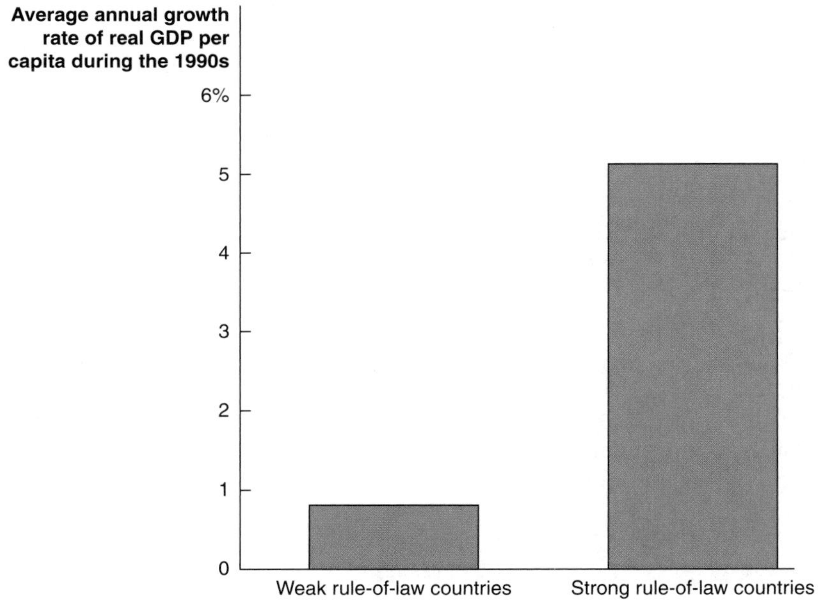

Figure 10-10 | The Rule of Law and Growth

The 20 developing countries that have the strongest rule of law, such as the Czech Republic and Israel, grew more than six times faster during the 1990s than the 20 developing countries that have the weakest rule of law, such as the Congo and Albania.

Source: Authors' calculation from data in David Dollar and Aart Kraay, "Property Rights, Political Rights, and the Development of Poor Countries in the Post-Colonial Period," World Bank Development Research Group working paper, October 2000.

Albania. Real GDP per capita in the 20 countries with the strongest rule of law grew more than six times faster during the 1990s than real GDP per capita in the 20 countries with the weakest rule of law.

Wars and Revolutions Many of the countries that were very poor in 1960 have experienced extended periods of war or violent changes of government during the years since. These wars have made it impossible for countries such as Afghanistan, Angola, Ethiopia, the Central African Republic, and the Congo to accumulate capital or adopt new technologies. In fact, conducting any kind of business has been very difficult. The positive effect on growth of ending war was shown in Mozambique, which suffered through almost two decades of civil war and declining real GDP per capita. With the end of civil war, Mozambique experienced a strong annual growth rate of 4.5 percent in real GDP per capita from 1990 to 2006.

Poor Public Education and Health We have seen that human capital is one of the determinants of labor productivity. Many low-income countries have weak public school systems, so many workers are unable to read and write. Few workers acquire the skills necessary to use the latest technology.

Many low-income countries suffer from diseases that are either nonexistent or treated readily in high-income countries. For example, few people in developed countries suffer from malaria, but more than one million Africans die from it each year. Treatments for AIDS have greatly reduced deaths from this disease in the United States and Europe. But millions of people in low-income countries continue to die from AIDS. Low-income countries often lack the resources, and their governments are often too ineffective, to provide even routine medical care, such as childhood vaccinations.

People who are sick work less and are less productive when they do work. Poor nutrition or exposure to certain diseases in childhood can leave people permanently weakened and can affect their intelligence as adults. Poor health has a significant negative impact on the human capital of workers in developing countries.

Low Rates of Saving and Investment To invest in factories, machinery, and computers, firms need funds. Some of the funds can come from the owners of the firm and from their friends and family, but as we noted in Chapter 9, firms in high-income countries raise most of their funds from bank loans and selling stocks and bonds in financial markets. In most developing countries, stock and bond markets do not exist, and often the banking system is very weak. In high-income countries, the funds that banks lend to businesses come from the savings of households. In high-income countries, many households are able to save a significant fraction of their income. In developing countries, many households barely survive on their incomes and, therefore, have little or no savings.

The low savings rates in developing countries contribute to a *vicious cycle* of poverty. Because households have low incomes, they save very little. Because households save very little, few funds are available for firms to borrow. Lacking funds, firms do not invest in the new factories, machinery, and equipment needed for economic growth. Because the economy does not grow, household incomes remain low, as do their savings, and so on.

The Benefits of Globalization

One way for a developing country to break out of the vicious cycle of low saving and investment and low growth is through foreign investment. **Foreign direct investment (FDI)** occurs when corporations build or purchase facilities in foreign countries. **Foreign portfolio investment** occurs when an individual or a firm buys stock or bonds issued in another country. Foreign direct investment and foreign portfolio investment can give a low-income country access to funds and technology that otherwise would not be available. Until recently, many developing countries were reluctant to take advantage of this opportunity.

Foreign direct investment (FDI) The purchase or building by a corporation of a facility in a foreign country.

Foreign portfolio investment The purchase by an individual or a firm of stock or bonds issued in another country.

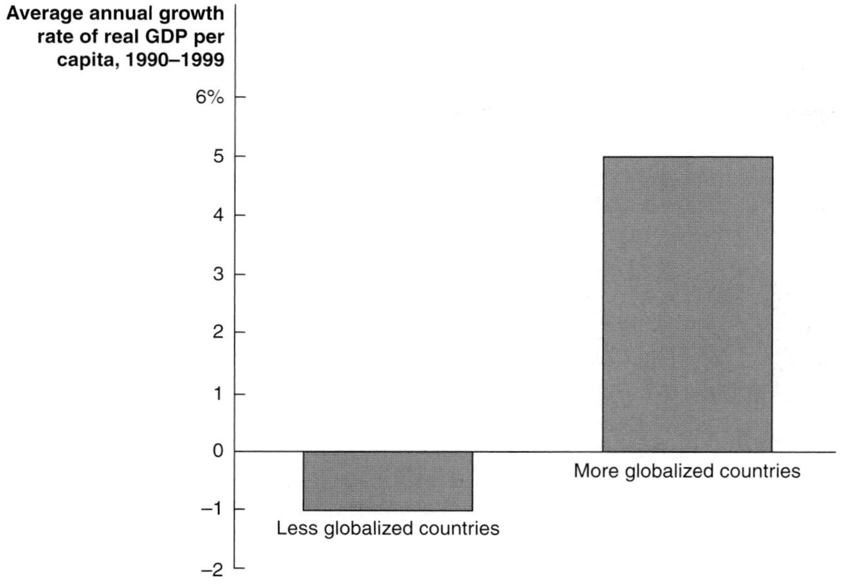

Figure 10-11 | Globalization and Growth

Developing countries that were more open to foreign trade and investment grew much faster during the 1990s than developing countries that were less open.

David Dollar, "Globalization, Inequality, and Poverty since 1980," *World Bank Research Observer*, Vol. 20, No. 2, Fall 2005, pp. 145-175.

From the 1940s through the 1970s, many developing countries sealed themselves off from the global economy. They did this for several reasons. During the 1930s and early 1940s, the global trading and financial system collapsed as a result of the Great Depression and World War II. Developing countries that relied on exporting to the industrial countries were hurt economically. The example of the Soviet Union indicated that it might be possible to achieve rapid growth without participating in the global economy. Also, many countries in Africa and Asia achieved independence from the colonial powers of Europe during the 1950s and 1960s and were afraid of being dominated by them economically. As a result, many developing countries imposed high tariffs on foreign imports and strongly discouraged or even prohibited foreign investment. This made it difficult to break out of the vicious cycle of poverty.

The policies of high tariff barriers and avoiding foreign investment failed to produce much growth, so by the 1980s, many developing countries began to change policies. The result was *globalization*. **Globalization** refers to the process of countries becoming more open to foreign trade and investment.

Globalization The process of countries becoming more open to foreign trade and investment.

If we measure globalization by the fraction of a country's GDP accounted for by exports, we see that globalization and growth are strongly positively associated. Figure 10-11 shows that developing countries that were more globalized grew faster during the 1990s than developing countries that were less globalized. Globalization has benefited developing countries by making it easier for them to get investment funds and technology.

Making the Connection | Globalization and the Spread of Technology in Bangladesh

Today, Bangladesh exports more than $2 billion worth of shirts and other clothing. But the manufacture of clothing in factories only began in Bangladesh in 1980, when a local entrepreneur, Noorul

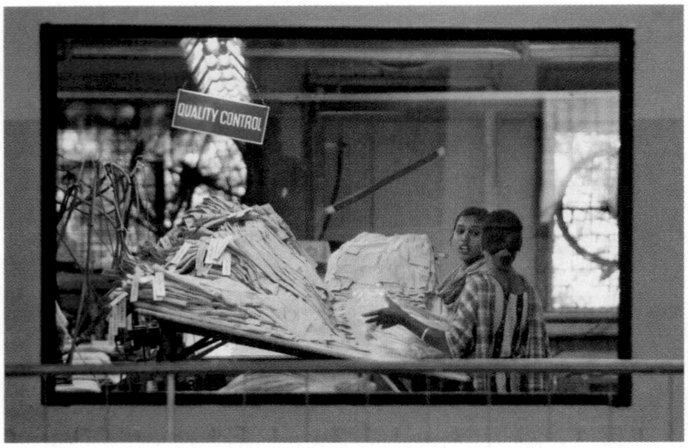

The spread of technology spurred Bangladesh's booming clothing industry.

Quader, started Desh Garments Ltd. This firm had just one shirt factory that employed 40 workers and produced only $55,550 worth of shirts its first year. Initially, Quader relied on an agreement with Daewoo Corporation of South Korea. Daewoo could export only limited numbers of shirts from Korea to the United States and Europe because the U.S. and European governments placed restrictions on clothing imports from Korea in an effort to protect domestic clothing producers. These restrictions did not apply to imports from Bangladesh.

Under the agreement with Daewoo, Quader was responsible for setting up and running the clothing factory. Daewoo would provide the most critical ingredient: training for 130 Desh workers at one of Daewoo's plants in Korea. In return, Quader would pay Daewoo an 8 percent royalty on each shirt sold. The business was a tremendous success for Quader, with production soaring from 43,000 shirts in 1980 to 2.3 million in 1987 and to 9.6 million in 2006. It was an even greater success for Bangladesh. Almost all the 130 Desh workers trained in Korea eventually left Desh to set up their own firms. In addition to making shirts, these new firms began producing coats, pants, and other clothing. The Desh workers, trained by Daewoo in garment-making technology, became the basis of Bangladesh's booming clothing industry.

This story illustrates not only how globalization can aid the spread of technology to the developing world but also the important difference between capital and technology: Although there are diminishing returns to capital, there actually may be increasing returns to technology. The investment Daewoo made in developing the best way to manufacture clothing and export it to high-income countries provided a return not only to Daewoo but also to Desh and then to the other companies in Bangladesh founded by workers who left Desh. Unlike with a piece of machinery, there is no limit to the number of people who can use knowledge about the best way to produce a good. As we discussed previously, the idea that there may be increasing returns to technology has been an important part of recent developments in the theory of economic growth. From this perspective, technological advance is not just a matter of new scientific discoveries but also depends on the incentives given to entrepreneurs to find new and better ways of producing goods and services.

Source: William Easterly, *The Elusive Quest for Growth: Economists' Adventures and Misadventures in the Tropics*, Cambridge, MA: MIT Press, 2001, pp. 146–150.

YOUR TURN: Test your understanding by doing related problems 4.7 and 4.8 on page 344 at the end of this chapter.

10.5 LEARNING OBJECTIVE

10.5 | Discuss government policies that foster economic growth.

Growth Policies

What can governments do to promote long-run economic growth? We have seen that even small differences in growth rates compounded over the years can lead to major differences in standards of living. Therefore, there is potentially a very high payoff to government policies that increase growth rates. We have already discussed some of these policies in this chapter. In this section, we explore additional policies.

Enhancing Property Rights and the Rule of Law

We have seen that a market system cannot work well unless property rights are enforced. Entrepreneurs are unlikely to risk their own funds, and investors are unlikely to lend their funds to entrepreneurs, unless property is safe from being arbitrarily seized. In many developing countries, the rule of law and property rights are undermined by *corruption*. With corruption, government officials may require bribes to carry out their obligations or may steal government property and resources. For example, in some developing countries, it is impossible for an entrepreneur to obtain a permit to start a business without paying bribes, often to several different officials. In some countries, tax revenues and foreign aid also frequently end up in the pockets of government officials. Research has shown that countries where corruption is most widespread grow much more slowly than countries where corruption is less of a problem.

Although today the United States ranks among the least corrupt countries, recent research by economists Edward Glaeser and Claudia Goldin of Harvard University has shown that in the late nineteenth and early twentieth centuries, corruption was a significant problem in the United States. The fact that political reform movements and crusading newspapers helped to reduce corruption in the United States to relatively low levels by the 1920s provides some hope for reform movements that aim to reduce corruption in developing countries today.

Property rights are unlikely to be secure in countries that are afflicted by wars and civil strife. For a number of countries, increased political stability is a necessary prerequisite to economic growth.

Improving Health and Education

Recently, many economists have become convinced that poor health is a major impediment to growth in some countries. As we saw in Chapter 9, the research of Nobel laureate Robert Fogel has emphasized the important interaction between health and economic growth. As people's health improves and they became taller, stronger, and less susceptible to disease, they also became more productive. Recent initiatives in developing countries to increase vaccinations against infectious diseases, to improve access to treated water, and to improve sanitation have begun to reduce rates of illness and death.

We discussed earlier in this chapter Paul Romer's argument that there are increasing returns to knowledge capital. Nobel laureate Robert Lucas, of the University of Chicago, has made a similar argument that there are increasing returns to *human* capital. Lucas argues that productivity increases as the total stock of human capital increases but that these productivity increases are not completely captured by individuals as they decide how much education to purchase. Therefore, the market may produce an inefficiently low level of education and training unless education is supported by the government. Some researchers have been unable to find evidence of increasing returns to human capital, but many economists believe that government subsidies to education have played an important role in promoting economic growth.

The rising incomes that result from economic growth can help developing countries deal with the *brain drain*. The brain drain refers to highly educated and successful individuals leaving developing countries for high-income countries. This migration occurs when successful individuals believe that economic opportunities are very limited in the domestic economy. Rapid economic growth in India and China in recent years has resulted in more entrepreneurs, engineers, and scientists deciding to remain in those countries rather than leave for the United States or other high-income countries.

Policies with Respect to Technology

One of the lessons from the economic growth model is that technological change is more important than increases in capital in explaining long-run growth. Government policies that facilitate access to technology are crucial for low-income countries. The easiest way for developing countries to gain access to technology is through foreign direct investment in which foreign firms are allowed to build new facilities or to buy domestic firms.

Recent economic growth in India has been greatly aided by the Indian government's relaxation of regulations on foreign investment. Relaxing these regulations made it possible for India to have access to the technology of Dell, Microsoft, and other multinational corporations.

In high-income countries, government policies can aid the growth of technology by subsidizing research and development. As we noted previously, in the United States, the federal government conducts some research and development on its own and also provides grants to researchers in universities. Tax breaks to firms undertaking research and development also facilitate technological change.

Policies with Respect to Saving and Investment

We noted in Chapter 9 that firms turn to the loanable funds market to finance expansion and research and development. Policies that increase the incentives to save and invest will increase the equilibrium level of loanable funds and may increase the level of real GDP per capita. As we also discussed in Chapter 9, tax incentives can lead to increased savings. In the United States, many workers are able to save for retirement by placing funds in 401(k) or 403(b) plans or in Individual Retirement Accounts (IRAs). Income placed in these accounts is not taxed until it is withdrawn during retirement. Because the funds are allowed to accumulate tax free, the return is increased, which raises the incentive to save.

Governments also increase incentives for firms to engage in investment in physical capital by using *investment tax credits*. Investment tax credits allow firms to deduct from their taxes some fraction of the funds they have spent on investment. Reductions in the taxes firms pay on their profits also increase the after-tax return on investments.

Is Economic Growth Good or Bad?

Although we didn't state so explicitly, in this chapter, we have assumed that economic growth is desirable and that governments should undertake policies that will increase growth rates. It seems undeniable that increasing the growth rates of very low-income countries would help relieve the daily suffering that many people in those countries must endure. But some people are unconvinced that, at least in the high-income countries, further economic growth is desirable.

The arguments against further economic growth tend to be motivated either by concern about the effects of growth on the environment or by concern about the effects of the globalization process that has accompanied economic growth in recent years. In 1973, the Club of Rome published a controversial book titled *The Limits to Growth*, which predicted that economic growth would likely grind to a halt in the United States and other high-income countries because of increasing pollution and the depletion of natural resources, such as oil. Although these dire predictions have not yet come to pass, many remain concerned that economic growth may be contributing to global warming, deforestation, and other environmental problems.

In Chapter 6, we discussed the opposition to globalization. We noted that some people believe that globalization has undermined the distinctive cultures of many countries, as imports of food, clothing, movies, and other goods displace domestically produced goods. We have seen that allowing foreign direct investment is an important way in which low-income countries can gain access to the latest technology. Some people, however, see multinational firms that locate in low-income countries as paying very low wages and as failing to follow the same safety and environmental regulations they are required to follow in the high-income countries.

As with many other normative questions, economic analysis can contribute to the ongoing political debate over the consequences of economic growth, but it cannot settle the issue.

>> Continued from page 309

Economics in YOUR Life!

At the beginning of the chapter, we posed the question: Suppose that you could choose to live and work in a world with the Chinese economy growing very rapidly or a world with the Chinese economy being very poor and growing slowly. Which world would you choose to live in? It's impossible to walk into stores in the United States without seeing products imported from China. Many of these products were at one time made in the United States. Imports from China replace domestically produced goods when the imports are either less expensive or of higher quality than the domestic goods they replace. Therefore, the rapid economic growth that has enabled Chinese firms to be competitive with firms in the United States has been a benefit to you as a consumer; you have lower-priced goods and better goods available to buy than you would if China had remained very poor. As you begin your career, there are some U.S. industries that, because of competition from Chinese firms, will have fewer jobs to offer. But, as we saw when discussing international trade in Chapter 6, expanding trade changes the types of products each country makes, and, therefore, the types of jobs available, but it does not affect the total number of jobs. So, the economic rise of China will affect the mix of jobs available to you in the United States but will not make finding a job any more difficult.

Conclusion

For much of human history, most people have had to struggle to survive. Even today, two-thirds of the world's population lives in extreme poverty. The differences in living standards among countries today are the result of many decades of sharply different rates of economic growth. According to the economic growth model, increases in the quantity of capital per hour worked and increases in technology determine how rapidly real GDP per hour worked and a country's standard of living will increase. The keys to higher living standards seem straightforward enough: Establish the rule of law, provide basic education and health care for the population, increase the amount of capital per hour worked, adopt the best technology, and participate in the global economy. However, for many countries, these policies have proved very difficult to implement.

Having discussed what determines the growth rate of economies, we will turn in the following chapters to the question of why economies experience short-run fluctuations in output, employment, and inflation. First, read *An Inside Look* on the next page for a discussion of recent economic growth in Europe.

Entrepreneurship and Sustained Economic Growth in Europe

ECONOMIST, FEBRUARY 19, 2007

Feeling Brighter

Competition for the title of "sick man of Europe" has been stiff for the past few years. Contenders included Germany, still feeling the lingering effects of unification. Italy, seemingly unable to keep its manufacturers competitive without devaluing its currency, had a good claim. Their problems were replicated across the continent: how to stay competitive with rigidly regulated labour and services markets. Crafting monetary policy for a currency zone that includes Ireland's boom and Italy's bust was a troublesome affair.

a After the gloom, sunshine now seems to be breaking through all over. Despite high energy prices, tighter money, and economic slowdown in America, the economies of the Europe Union have prospered. Industrial production in Europe rose by 1% in December compared with the month before, and by 4% for the year as a whole, much better than anticipated. Foreign trade rose briskly too. And three of the big economies—Germany, France and Italy—look very strong. Preliminary estimates of fourth quarter GDP released on Tuesday, February 13th show them exceeding expectations, and in the case of Italy and Germany by a wide margin.

The future looks brighter still. On February 16th the European Commission released its interim forecast for 2007. This suggests that the European economy as a whole will grow by 2.7% this year, substantially exceeding its earlier estimate of 2.4%. In 2006 3M new jobs were created, driving the unemployment rate down to 7.5% (in the euro area), and labour markets are expected to remain strong. Inflation should come down too, as energy prices fall further.

Germany is doing particularly well, thanks to a restructuring of its labour markets that has improved competitiveness. Unemployment, though still high, has dropped sharply over the past few years. Germans have also resisted immodest wage increases, unlike faster growers, such as Spain, which have seen their competitive position eroded by soaring labour costs. Even with its newfound strength, however, Europe is barely outstripping America. Ben Bernanke, the chairman of the Federal Reserve, anticipates a slowdown to more sustainable growth rates of 2.5–3% in America's immediate future—roughly the same pace that is exciting Europeans. The question of whether Europe will ever catch up is still much in the news in America.

b Edmund Phelps, winner of the 2006 Nobel prize for economics for his work on savings and labour markets, argues that the structural explanation for Europe's slower growth rates masks deeper problems with dynamism. Countries like France, Germany and Italy display markedly lower rates of commercially successful innovation. There is less churn in the top ranks of companies, and employees are given less latitude to innovate and make decisions. In part he believes that the problem is economic institutions: regulatory barriers to entrepreneurship, a financial system that favours insiders, and a high level of input from labour, which tends to be biased towards the status quo. But he also points to cultural differences that might impede Europe's growth even if those regulatory barriers are swept away: workers in Europe's big economies are less likely to regard the opportunity for innovation, autonomy and interesting work as vital components of a job.

c This is one possible explanation for the difference between Europe's rapid growth in the decades following the second world war, and its current, more lackadaisical pace. Barry Eichengreen, a professor of economics at Berkeley, has just published a book arguing that Europe is very good at "extensive growth"—roughly, producing more of what we already know how to make—and less good at "intensive growth", which involves finding new products and new ways of doing things. Mr Eichengreen argues that Europe's "co-ordinated capitalism" served the first task well (and better than the messily undirected market), but has balked at pushing back new economic frontiers.

Of course, 15 years ago Americans were bombarded with books promising that Germany or Japan was poised to depose them as the world's economic powerhouse. It is always dangerous to extrapolate too much from current trends, especially since idiosyncratic factors (such as Germany's need to absorb an economy left crippled by communism) often come into play. But perhaps optimism should be tempered with at least a smidgen of European caution.

Source: "Feeling Brighter," Economist, *February 19, 2007. Reprinted by permission of* The Economist *via Copyright Clearance Center.*

Key Points in the Article

This article discussed the relatively strong performance of Europe's largest economies in the last couple of years. But the article also discusses what many economists believe to be the reason for Europe's relatively lackluster growth over the longer term: a relative lack of innovation. The article also raises the question of why Europe was unable to sustain the rapid growth that it achieved in the decades immediately following World War II. Finally, the article discusses Barry Eichengreen's argument that this earlier rapid growth occurred with relatively few technological innovations and, hence, was particularly vulnerable to diminishing returns.

Analyzing the News

(a) Europe's economies have prospered in recent years, and growth in three of its largest economies—Germany, France, and Italy—has exceeded economists' expectations. This prosperity is particularly impressive given that it comes at a time of rising energy prices, relatively high interest rates, and a slowing U.S. economy. High energy prices and high interest rates reduce the growth in consumption spending and business investment spending, and a slowing U.S. economy reduces the growth in European exports to the United States.

(b) Despite its strong growth in the last couple of years, the European economy have been growing more slowly than the United States. The 2.7 percent growth that Europe will likely achieve in 2007 is high by European standards, but only moderate by U.S. standards. Europe's relatively low unemployment rate of 7.5 percent is also very high by U.S. standards. According to Edmund Phelps, the European economy lacks the economic institutions necessary to promote entrepreneurship. This is a problem because, as you read in this chapter, many economists believe that the innovation required to sustain strong economic growth is, to a large extent, dependent on economic incentives and the entrepreneurs who respond to those incentives.

(c) Europe's relatively sluggish growth in recent years is particularly curious given that the European economy achieved extremely rapid growth in the decades immediately following World War II. According to Barry Eichengreen, Europe's earlier rapid growth was not sustainable because it was based on goods and services that Europe produced with existing technology. This was a problem because this so-called extensive growth increased output per hour worked but at a decreasing rate due to the law of diminishing returns. This point is illustrated in Figure 1, where, holding technological change constant, an increase in capital per hour worked from $(K/L)_1$ to $(K/L)_2$ leads to an increase in output per hour worked from $(Y/L)_1$ to $(Y/L)_2$. For Europe to sustain strong economic growth, it must produce new goods and services in innovative ways. Intensive growth of this type helps economies avoid the law of diminishing returns. This pattern is shown in Figure 2, where technological change shifts up the production function and allows output per hour worked to increase from $(Y/L)_1$ to $(Y/L)_2$ while the amount of capital per hour worked remains at $(K/L)_1$.

Thinking Critically

1. Suppose European governments remove restrictions on employers' rights to fire workers. What effect would this policy likely have on the extent of European entrepreneurship and, hence, innovation?
2. Because economic growth requires innovation and change, it can lead to structural unemployment. What are some policies that governments can implement in order to relieve the social and economic strains that intensive economic growth can place on an economy's labor force?

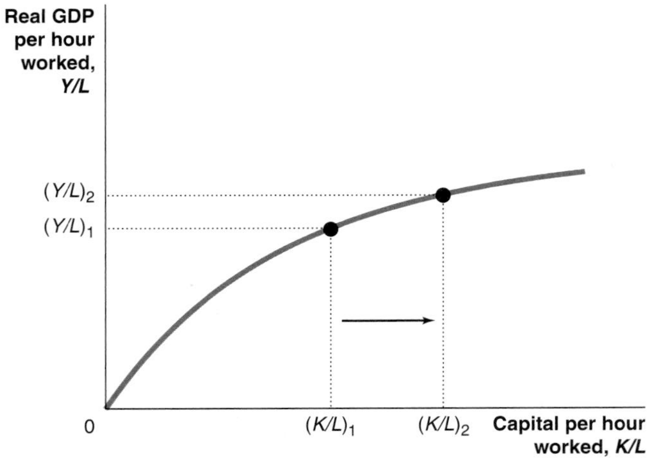

Figure 1. To increase output per worker during the aftermath of World War II, Europe increased capital per worker.

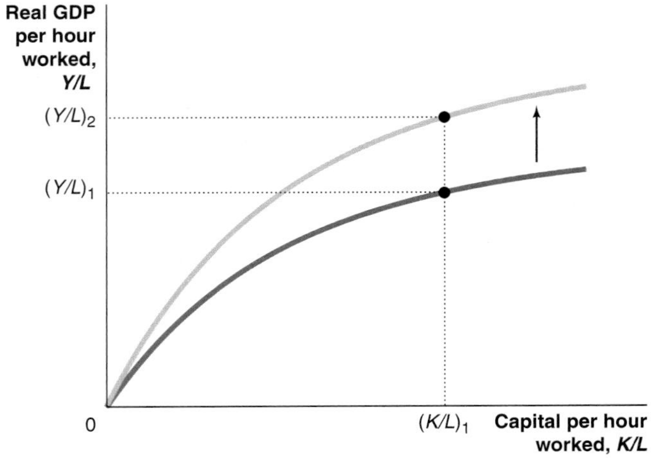

Figure 2. To increase output per worker today, Europe must find new and innovative ways to produce.

Key Terms

Catch-up, p. 327
Economic growth model, p. 315
Foreign direct investment (FDI), p. 332
Foreign portfolio investment, p. 332
Globalization, p. 333
Human capital, p. 315
Industrial Revolution, p. 311
Labor productivity, p. 315
New growth theory, p. 320
Patent, p. 320
Per-worker production function, p. 316
Property rights, p. 330
Rule of law, p. 331
Technological change, p. 315

10.1 LEARNING OBJECTIVE 10.1 | Define economic growth, calculate economic growth rates, and describe global trends in economic growth, **pages 310–314.**

Economic Growth Over Time and Around the World

Summary

Until around the year 1300 A.D., most people survived with barely enough food. Living standards began to rise significantly only after the **Industrial Revolution** began in England in the 1700s with the application of mechanical power to the production of goods. The best measure of a country's standard of living is its level of real GDP per capita. Economic growth occurs when real GDP per capita increases, thereby increasing the country's standard of living.

myeconlab Get Ahead of the Curve Visit www.myeconlab.com to complete these exercises online and get instant feedback.

Review Questions

1.1 Why does a country's rate of economic growth matter?

1.2 Explain the difference between the total percentage increase in real GDP between 1997 and 2007 and the average annual growth rate in real GDP between the same years.

Problems and Applications

1.3 **(Related to the *Making the Connection* on page 311)** Recently, economists Carol Shiue and Wolfgang Keller of the University of Texas at Austin published a study of "market efficiency" in the eighteenth century in England, other European countries, and China. If the markets in a country are efficient, a product should have the same price wherever in the country it is sold, allowing for the effect of transportation costs. If prices are not the same in two areas within a country, it is possible to make profits by buying the product where its price is low and reselling it where its price is high. This trading will drive prices to equality. Trade is most likely to occur, however, if entrepreneurs feel confident that their gains will not be seized by the government and that contracts to buy and sell can be enforced in the courts. Therefore, in the eighteenth century, the more efficient a country's markets, the more its institutions favored long-run growth. Shiue and Keller found that in 1770, the efficiency of markets in England was significantly greater than the efficiency of markets elsewhere in Europe and in China. How does this finding relate to Douglas North's argument concerning why the Industrial Revolution occurred in England?

Source: Carol H. Shiue and Wolfgang Keller, "Markets in China and Europe on the Eve of the Industrial Revolution," forthcoming, *American Economic Review*, 2007.

1.4 Use the data on real GDP in the following table to answer the questions.

COUNTRY	2003	2004	2005	2006
Australia	$445.1	$457.0	$469.8	$481.1
Hungary	54.2	56.9	59.3	61.6
Poland	182.4	192.0	198.3	210.4

Note: All values are in billions of 2000 U.S. dollars.
Source: Organisation for Economic Cooperation and Development (OECD).

a. Which country experienced the highest rate of economic growth during 2004?
b. Which country experienced the highest rate of economic growth during 2005?
c. Which country experienced the highest average annual growth rate between 2004 and 2006?

1.5 Andover Bank and Lowell Bank each sell one-year certificates of deposit (CDs). The interest rates on these CDs are given in the following table for a three-year period.

BANK	2007	2008	2009
Andover Bank	2%	9%	10%
Lowell Bank	7%	7%	7%

Suppose you deposit $1,000 in a CD in each bank at the beginning of 2007. At the end of 2007, you take your $1,000 and any interest earned and invest it in a CD for the following year. You do this again at the end of 2008. At the end of 2009, will you have earned more on your Andover Bank CDs or on your Lowell Bank CDs? Briefly explain.

1.6 **(Related to the *Don't Let This Happen to You!* on page 313)** Use the data for the United States in the table to answer the following questions.

YEAR	REAL GDP PER CAPITA (2000 PRICES)
2002	$34,861
2003	35,385
2004	36,415
2005	37,241
2006	38,154

a. What was the percentage increase in real GDP per capita between 2002 and 2006?

b. What was the average annual growth rate in real GDP per capita between 2002 and 2006? (*Hint:* Remember from the previous chapter that the average annual growth rate for relatively short periods can be approximated by averaging the growth rate for each year.)

1.7 **(Related to the *Making the Connection* on page 313)** Between 1950 and 1978, Japan experienced high rates of economic growth while China was hardly growing. Today, the standard of living in Japan is higher than the standard of living in China. Would you expect this relationship between when a country began to experience economic growth and its relative standard of living today will always be true? That is, will it always be true that if country A first experienced rapid economic growth at an earlier date than country B, then country A will have a higher standard of living today than country B?

>> End Learning Objective 10.1

10.2 LEARNING OBJECTIVE 10.2 | Use the economic growth model to explain why growth rates differ across countries, **pages 315–321.**

What Determines How Fast Economies Grow?

Summary

An **economic growth model** explains changes in real GDP per capita in the long run. **Labor productivity** is the quantity of goods and services that can be produced by one worker or by one hour of work. Economic growth depends on increases in labor productivity. Labor productivity will increase if there is an increase in the amount of *capital* available to each worker or if there is an improvement in *technology*. **Technological change** is a change in the ability of a firm to produce a given level of output with a given quantity of inputs. There are three main sources of technological change: better machinery and equipment, increases in human capital, and better means of organizing and managing production. **Human capital** is the accumulated knowledge and skills that workers acquire from education and training or from their life experiences. To summarize, we can say that an economy will have a higher standard of living the more capital it has per hour worked, the more human capital its workers have, the better its capital, and the better the job its business managers do in organizing production. **The per-worker production function** shows the relationship between capital per hour worked and output per hour worked, holding technology constant. *Diminishing returns to capital* mean that increases in the quantity of capital per hour worked will result in diminishing increases in output per hour worked. Technological change shifts up the per-worker production function, resulting in more output per hour worked at every level of capital per hour worked. The economic growth model stresses the importance of changes in capital per hour worked and technological change in explaining growth in output per hour worked. *New growth theory* is a model of long-run economic growth that emphasizes that technological change is influenced by how individuals and firms respond to economic incentives. One way governments can promote technological change is by granting **patents**, which are exclusive rights to a product for a period of 20 years from the date the product is invented. To Joseph Schumpeter, the entrepreneur is central to the "creative destruction" by which the standard of living increases as qualitatively better products replace existing products.

myeconlab Get Ahead of the Curve Visit www.myeconlab.com to complete these exercises online and get instant feedback.

Review Questions

2.1 Using the per-worker production function graph, show the effect on real GDP per hour worked of an increase in capital per hour worked, holding technology constant. Now, again using the per-worker production function graph, show the effect on real GDP per hour worked of an increase in technology, holding constant the quantity of capital per hour worked.

2.2 What are the consequences for growth of diminishing returns to capital? How are some economies able to maintain high growth rates despite diminishing returns to capital?

2.3 Why did some economists in the 1950s predict that the Soviet Union would continue to grow faster than the United States for decades to come? Why did this prediction turn out to be wrong?

2.4 Why are firms likely to underinvest in research and development, which slows the accumulation of knowledge capital, slowing economic growth? Briefly discuss three ways in which government policy can increase the accumulation of knowledge capital.

Problems and Applications

2.5 According to a study by an economist at the Federal Reserve Bank of Minneapolis, during the middle 1980s, managers at iron mines in Canada and the United States increased output per hour worked by 100 percent through changes in work rules that increased workers' effort per hour worked and increased the efficiency of workers' effort. Briefly explain whether this increase in output per hour worked is an example of an improvement in technology.

Source: James A. Schmitz, Jr., "What Determines Labor Productivity? Lessons from the Dramatic Recovery of the U.S. and Canadian Iron-Ore Industries Following Their Early 1980s Crisis," Federal Reserve Bank of Minneapolis Research Department Staff Report 286, February 2005.

2.6 Which of the following will result in a movement along Japan's per-worker production function, and which will result in a shift of Japan's per-worker production function? Briefly explain.

a. Capital per hour worked increases from ¥5 million per hour worked to ¥6 million per hour worked.
b. The Japanese government doubles its spending on support of university research.
c. A reform of the Japanese school system results in more highly trained Japanese workers.

2.7 **(Related to *Solved Problem 10-2* on page 319)** Use the graph in the next column to answer the questions.

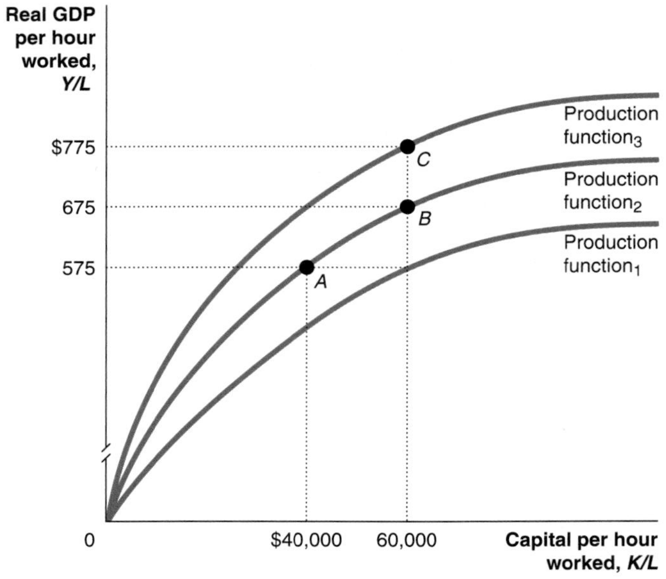

a. True or false: The movement from point *A* to point *B* shows the effects of technological change.
b. True or false: The economy can move from point *B* to point *C* only if there are no diminishing returns to capital.
c. True or false: To move from point *A* to point *C*, the economy must increase the amount of capital per hour worked and experience technological change.

2.8 **(Related to *Solved Problem 10-2* on page 319)** Shortly before the fall of the Soviet Union, the economist Gur Ofer of Hebrew University of Jerusalem, wrote this: "The most outstanding characteristic of Soviet growth strategy is its consistent policy of very high rates of investment, leading to a rapid growth rate of [the] capital stock." Explain why this turned out to be a very poor growth strategy.

Source: Gur Ofer, "Soviet Economic Growth, 1928–1985," *Journal of Economic Literature*, December 1987, p. 1,784.

2.9 Why is the role of the entrepreneur much more important in the new growth theory than in the traditional economic growth model?

2.10 **(Related to the *Making the Connection* on page 318)** The *Making the Connection* on the economy of the Soviet Union argues that a key difference between market economies and centrally planned economies, like that of the former Soviet Union, is:

> In market economies, decisions about which investments to make and which technologies to adopt are made by entrepreneurs and managers with their own money on the line. In the Soviet system, these decisions were usually made by salaried bureaucrats trying to fulfill a plan formulated in Moscow.

But in large corporations, investment decisions are often made by salaried managers who do not, in fact, have their own money on the line. These managers are spending the money of the firm's shareholders, rather than their own money. Why then do the investment decisions of salaried managers in the United States tend to be better for the long-term growth of the economy than were the decisions of salaried bureaucrats in the Soviet Union?

2.11 **(Related to the *Making the Connection* on page 318)** The *Making the Connection* on the economy of the Soviet Union argues that a key problem for the Soviet economy was that "[Soviet managers'] pay depended on producing the quantity of output specified in the government's economic plan, not on discovering new, better, and lower-cost ways to produce goods." How might a centrally planned economy get around the problem of managers lacking incentives to discover and make use of new technologies? What are the main obstacles to solving this problem?

>> End Learning Objective 10.2

10.3 LEARNING OBJECTIVE 10.3 | Discuss fluctuations in productivity growth in the United States, **pages 322–326.**

Economic Growth in the United States

Summary

Productivity in the United States grew rapidly from the end of World War II until the mid-1970s. Growth then slowed down for 20 years before increasing again after 1995. Economists continue to debate the reasons for the growth slowdown of the mid-1970s to mid-1990s. Leading explanations for the productivity slowdown are measurement problems, high oil prices, and a decline in labor quality. Because Western Europe and Japan experienced a productivity slowdown at the same time as the United States, explanations that focus on factors affecting only the United States are unlikely to be correct. Some economists argue that the development of a "new economy" based on information technology caused the higher productivity growth that began in the mid-1990s.

Review Questions

3.1 Describe the record of productivity growth in the United States from 1800 to the present. What explains the slowdown in productivity growth from the mid-1970s to the mid-1990s? Why did productivity growth increase beginning in 1996?

3.2 Compare productivity growth in the United States with productivity growth in Europe in the period between 1996 and the present.

Problems and Applications

3.3 Figure 10-5 on page 322 shows growth rates in real GDP per hour worked in the United States for various periods from 1900 onward. How might the growth rates in the figure be different if they were calculated for real GDP *per capita* instead of per hour worked? (*Hint:* How do you think the number of hours worked per person has changed in the United States since 1900?)

3.4 In early 2007, revised data from the federal government on the performance of the U.S. economy during the fourth quarter of 2006 indicated that real GDP had grown more slowly than previously estimated and that the number of hours worked had grown more rapidly than previously estimated. Keeping these revised data in mind, do you think the Bureau of Labor Statistics increased or decreased its previous estimate of the growth rate in labor productivity during the fourth quarter of 2006? Briefly explain.

3.5 According to an article in the *Wall Street Journal*:

> Henry Harteveldt, travel analyst at tech-consulting firm Forrester Research, says checking in a passenger at such a kiosk costs an airline just 14 cents on average, compared with \$3.02 using an agent. From 2000 to 2005, the share of passengers using such a kiosk at least once leapt from close to zero to 63%. But in 2006, that figure merely crept up to 66%.

Assuming that Hartveldt's data are correct, what would be the implications of his analysis for future increases in labor productivity at the airlines?

Source: Greg Ip, "Productivity Lull Might Signal Growth Is Easing," *Wall Street Journal*, March 31, 2007, p. A1.

3.6 Figure 10-6 on page 325 shows the annual growth rate of labor productivity in the leading industrial economies for 1996 to 2006. Using the rule of 70 from Chapter 9, indicate why the countries of Western Europe, such as Germany, should be concerned about their current growth rates.

>> End Learning Objective 10.3

10.4 LEARNING OBJECTIVE 10.4 | Explain economic catch-up and discuss why many poor countries have not experienced rapid economic growth, **pages 327–334.**

Why Isn't the Whole World Rich?

Summary

The economic growth model predicts that poor countries will grow faster than rich countries, resulting in **catch-up**. In recent decades, some poor countries have grown faster than rich countries, but many have not. Some poor countries do not experience rapid growth for four main reasons: wars and revolutions, poor public education and health, failure to enforce the rule of law, and low rates of saving and investment. The **rule of law** refers to the ability of a government to enforce the laws of the country, particularly with respect to protecting private property and enforcing contracts. **Globalization** has aided countries that have opened their economies to foreign trade and investment. **Foreign direct investment (FDI)** is the purchase or building by a corporation of a facility in a foreign country. **Foreign portfolio investment** is the purchase by an individual or firm of stock or bonds issued in another country.

Review Questions

4.1 Why does the economic growth model predict that poor countries should catch up to rich countries in income per capita? Have poor countries been catching up to rich countries?

4.2 What are the main reasons many poor countries have experienced slow growth?

4.3 What does globalization mean? How have developing countries benefited from globalization?

Problems and Applications

4.4 **(Related to *Solved Problem 10-4* on page 329)** Briefly explain whether the statistics in the following table are consistent with the economic growth model's predictions of catch-up.

COUNTRY	REAL GDP PER CAPITA IN 1960	GROWTH IN REAL GDP PER CAPITA, 1960–2004
Uganda	$873	0.57%
China	448	5.79
Madagascar	1,268	−1.18
Ireland	5,294	3.94
United States	12,892	2.37

4.5 **(Related to *Solved Problem 10-4* on page 329)** In the following figure, each dot represents a country, with its initial real GDP per capita and its growth rate of real GDP per capita.

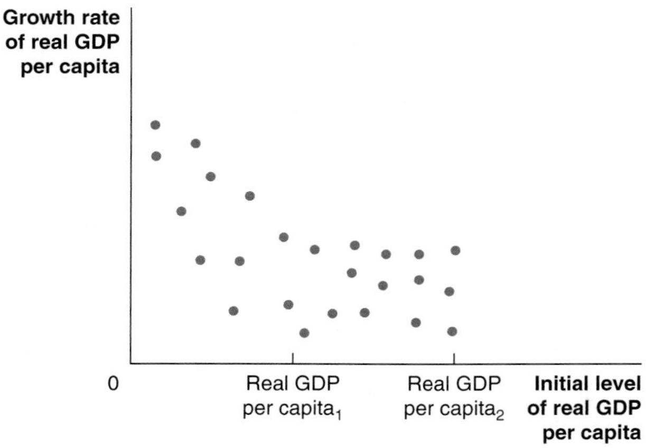

a. For the range of initial GDP per capita from 0 to Real GDP per capita$_2$, does the figure support the economic growth model's prediction of catch-up? Why or why not?
b. For the range of initial GDP per capita from 0 to Real GDP per capita$_1$, does the figure support the catch-up prediction? Why or why not?
c. For the range from initial Real GDP per capita$_1$ to Real GDP per capita$_2$, does the figure support the catch-up prediction? Why or why not?

4.6 An opinion column in the *Economist* argued, "Globalisation, far from being the greatest cause of poverty, is its only feasible cure." What does globalization have to do with reducing poverty?

Source: Clive Crook, "Globalisation and Its Critics," *Economist*, September 27, 2001.

4.7 **(Related to the *Making the Connection* on page 333)** How might multinational corporations that establish facilities in developing countries help break the vicious cycle of poverty in those countries?

4.8 **(Related to the *Making the Connection* on page 333)** What does the experience of Bangladesh suggest about the ability of poor countries to catch-up to the income levels of the rich countries? What policies would make it easier for countries like Bangladesh to catch-up?

4.9 An opinion column by Hernando De Soto in the *New York Times* argues:

> Those who favor the market [have] forgotten that the only way capitalism can

> help the poor prosper is by bringing them into the capitalist system. But that has not happened. . . . The poor in the vast majority of nations cannot yet take advantage of legal structures that are central to the production of wealth.

What does De Soto mean by "legal structures"? Why would they have anything to do with the production of wealth?

Source: Hernando De Soto, "The Constituency of Terror," *New York Times*, October 15, 2001.

4.10 A columnist in the *New York Times* argues that "if you really want to reduce world poverty, you should be cheering on those guys in pinstripe suits at the free-trade negotiations and those investors jetting around the world." What do free-trade negotiations and investors jetting around the world have to do with reducing poverty?

Source: David Brooks, "Good News About Poverty," *New York Times*, November 27, 2004.

4.11 The Roman Empire lasted from 27 B.C. to 476 A.D. The empire was wealthy enough to build such monuments as the Roman Coliseum. Roman engineering skill was at a level high enough that aqueducts built during the empire to carry water long distances remained in use for hundreds of years. Yet the growth rate of real GDP per capita during the empire was very low, perhaps zero. Why didn't the Roman Empire experience sustained economic growth? What would the world be like today if it had? (There are no definite answers to this question; it is intended to get you to think about the preconditions for economic growth.)

>> End Learning Objective 10.4

10.5 LEARNING OBJECTIVE 10.5 | Discuss government policies that foster economic growth, **pages 334–336.**

Growth Policies

Summary

Governments can attempt to increase economic growth through policies that enhance property rights and the rule of law, improve health and education, subsidize research and development, and provide incentives for savings and investment. Whether continued economic growth is desirable is a normative question that cannot be settled by economic analysis.

myeconlab Get Ahead of the Curve — Visit www.myeconlab.com to complete these exercises online and get instant feedback.

Review Questions

5.1 Briefly describe three government policies that can increase economic growth.

5.2 Can economics arrive at the conclusion that economic growth will always improve economic well-being? Briefly explain.

Problems and Applications

5.3 In 2003, then U.S. Secretary of State Colin Powell urged Argentina to take steps to correct "institutional flaws that encourage excess public sector borrowing, corruption, [and] politicized judicial systems." Briefly discuss how each of the three problems cited by Secretary Powell would contribute to reducing Argentina's economic growth rate.

Source: Matt Moffett, "One Tough Mayor Shows Argentina How to Clean House," *Wall Street Journal*, July 1, 2003.

5.4 Is it likely to be easier for the typical developing country to improve the state of public health or to improve the average level of education? Briefly explain.

5.5 Briefly explain which of the following policies are likely to increase the rate of economic growth in the United States.

a. Congress passes an investment tax credit, which reduces a firm's taxes if it installs new machinery and equipment.

b. Congress passes a law that allows taxpayers to reduce their income taxes by the amount of state sales taxes they pay.

c. Congress provides more funds for low-interest loans to college students.

5.6 Economist George Ayittey, in an interview on PBS about economic development in Africa, states that of the 54 African countries, only 8 have a free press. For Africa's economic development, Ayittey argues strongly for the establishment of a free press. Why would a free press be vital for the enhancement of property rights and the rule of law? How could a free press help reduce corruption?

Source: George Ayittey, *Border Jumpers*, Anchor Interview Transcript, WideAngle, PBS.org, July 24, 2005.

5.7 More people in high-income countries than in low-income countries tend to believe that rapid rates of economic growth are not desirable. Recall the concept of a "normal good" from Chapter 3. Does this concept provide insight into why some people in high-income countries might be more concerned with certain consequences of rapid economic growth than are people in low-income countries?

>> End Learning Objective 10.5

Chapter 11

Output and Expenditure in the Short Run

Fluctuating Demand at Cisco Systems

In spring 2001, Cisco Systems, Inc., the leading seller of hardware for computer networks in the world, announced it would cut production, sell off hardware it had already manufactured at deeply discounted prices, and lay off 6,000 of its 44,000 employees. Less than one year earlier, Cisco had rapidly expanded its workforce, purchased large amounts of hardware components, and even loaned $600 million to its suppliers to encourage them to speed up production. What had happened? Cisco had sold much less than it had forecast. As a result, Cisco had hired more people than it needed and produced more computer hardware than it could sell.

Fast forward to spring 2007: Cisco announces record sales and profits, with employment rising to more than 49,000. Why the big swings in Cisco's performance? Because Cisco's main business is selling expensive switches and routers for computer networks, its sales depend on both underlying long-run trends in Internet usage and on the short-run willingness of its business customers to spend on investment goods. During the Internet boom of the late 1990s, many firms spent heavily to establish a presence on the Internet. In addition, telecommunications firms laid more than 39 million miles of fiber-optic cable, anticipating that the volume of high-speed Internet traffic would increase rapidly. Unfortunately for Cisco and other firms, the Internet bubble popped in late 2000. The slower-than-expected growth of the Internet was bad news for Cisco, and its sales in the first three months of 2001 were 30 percent below what they had been during the last three months of 2000.

However, something beyond the Internet bust was happening to the U.S. economy during spring 2001. Firms far removed from the Internet and telecommunications were also experiencing problems. Sales at General Motors and Ford dropped 15 percent from spring 2000 to spring 2001. Delivery of two- and three-day packages at FedEx was down about 10 percent. These firms were all experiencing the effects of a slowdown in the total amount of spending, or *aggregate expenditure*, in the economy. This slowdown caused the U.S. economy to move into recession. In 2007, the explosion in using the Internet to download movies, music, and television programs led firms to expand the capacity of their computer networks. This was good news for Cisco. But Cisco and many other firms also benefited in 2007 from the increase in aggregate expenditures in the economy. In this chapter, we will explore the reasons for changes in aggregate expenditures and how these changes affect the level of total production in the economy.

AN INSIDE LOOK on **page 380** discusses the factors causing U.S. GDP to change during the first quarter of 2007.

Sources: Bobby White, "Cisco Rides Web-Traffic Growth," *Wall Street Journal*, March 7, 2006; and Bobby White and Roger Cheng, "Cisco to Acquire WebEx," *Wall Street Journal*, March 16, 2007.

LEARNING Objectives

After studying this chapter, you should be able to:

11.1 Understand how macroeconomic equilibrium is determined in the **aggregate expenditure model**, page 348.

11.2 Discuss the determinants of the four **components of aggregate expenditure** and define the **marginal propensity to consume** and the **marginal propensity to save**, page 351.

11.3 Use a **45°-line diagram** to illustrate macroeconomic equilibrium, page 363.

11.4 Define the **multiplier effect** and use it to calculate changes in equilibrium GDP, page 371.

11.5 Understand the relationship between the **aggregate demand curve** and aggregate expenditure, page 377.

APPENDIX Apply the **algebra of macroeconomic equilibrium**, page 388.

Economics in YOUR Life!

Consumer Confidence Falls—Is Your Job at Risk?

Suppose that you work part time assembling desktop computers for a large computer company. One morning, you read in the local newspaper that consumer confidence in the economy has fallen and, consequently, many households expect their future income to be dramatically less than their current income. Should you be concerned about losing your job? What factors should you consider in deciding how likely your company is to lay you off? As you read the chapter, see if you can answer these questions. You can check your answers against those we provide at the end of the chapter.

>> **Continued on page 379**

In Chapter 10, we analyzed the determinants of long-run growth in the economy. In the short run, as we saw in Chapter 9, the economy also experiences a business cycle around the long-run upward trend in real GDP. In this chapter, we begin exploring the causes of the business cycle by examining the effect of changes in total spending on real GDP.

Aggregate expenditure (*AE*) The total amount of spending in the economy: the sum of consumption, planned investment, government purchases, and net exports.

During some years, total spending in the economy, or **aggregate expenditure (*AE*)**, increases as much as does the production of goods and services. If this happens, most firms will sell about what they expected to sell, and they probably will not increase or decrease production or the number of workers hired. During other years, total spending in the economy increases more than the production of goods and services. In these years, firms will increase production and hire more workers. But at other times, such as spring 2001, total spending does not increase as much as total production. As a result, firms cut back on production and lay off workers, and the economy moves into a recession. In this chapter, we will explore why changes in total spending play such an important role in the economy.

11.1 LEARNING OBJECTIVE

11.1 | Understand how macroeconomic equilibrium is determined in the aggregate expenditure model.

The Aggregate Expenditure Model

The business cycle involves the interaction of many economic variables. To understand the relationships among some of the most important of these variables, we begin our study of the business cycle in this chapter with a simple model called the *aggregate expenditure model.* Recall from Chapter 7 that GDP is the value of all the final goods and services produced in an economy during a particular year. Real GDP corrects nominal GDP for the effects of inflation. The **aggregate expenditure model** focuses on the short-run relationship between total spending and real GDP. An important assumption of the model is that the price level is constant. In Chapter 12, we will develop a more complete model of the business cycle that relaxes the assumption of constant prices.

Aggregate expenditure model A macroeconomic model that focuses on the relationship between total spending and real GDP, assuming that the price level is constant.

The key idea of the aggregate expenditure model is that *in any particular year, the level of GDP is determined mainly by the level of aggregate expenditure.* To understand the relationship between aggregate expenditure and real GDP, we need to look more closely at the components of aggregate expenditure.

Aggregate Expenditure

Economists first began to study the relationship between changes in aggregate expenditure and changes in GDP during the Great Depression of the 1930s. The United States, the United Kingdom, and other industrial countries suffered declines in real GDP of 25 percent or more during the early 1930s. In 1936, the English economist John Maynard Keynes published a book, *The General Theory of Employment, Interest, and Money*, that systematically analyzed the relationship between changes in aggregate expenditure and changes in GDP. Keynes identified four categories of aggregate expenditure that together equal GDP (these are the same four categories we discussed in Chapter 7):

- ***Consumption (C).*** This is spending by households on goods and services, such as automobiles and haircuts.
- ***Planned Investment (I).*** This is planned spending by firms on capital goods, such as factories, office buildings, and machine tools, and by households on new homes.
- ***Government Purchases (G).*** This is spending by local, state, and federal governments on goods and services, such as aircraft carriers, bridges, and the salaries of FBI agents.
- ***Net Exports (NX).*** This is spending by foreign firms and households on goods and services produced in the United States minus spending by U.S. firms and households on goods and services produced in other countries.

So, we can write:

Aggregate expenditure = Consumption + Planned investment + Government purchases + Net exports,

or:

$$AE = C + I + G + NX.$$

Governments around the world gather statistics on aggregate expenditure on the basis of these four categories. Economists and business analysts usually explain changes in GDP in terms of changes in these four categories of spending.

The Difference between Planned Investment and Actual Investment

Before considering further the relationship between aggregate expenditure and GDP, we need to consider an important distinction: Notice that it is *planned* investment spending, rather than actual investment spending, that is a component of aggregate expenditure. You might wonder how the amount that businesses plan to spend on investment can be different from the amount they actually spend. We can begin resolving this puzzle by remembering that goods that have been produced but have not yet been sold are referred to as **inventories**. Changes in inventories are included as part of investment spending along with spending on machinery, equipment, office buildings, and factories. We assume that the amount businesses plan to spend on machinery and office buildings is equal to the amount they actually spend, but the amount businesses plan to spend on inventories may be different from the amount they actually spend.

Inventories Goods that have been produced but not yet sold.

For example, Doubleday may print 1.5 million copies of the latest John Grisham novel, expecting to sell them all. If Doubleday does sell all 1.5 million, its inventories will be unchanged, but if it sells only 1.2 million, it will have an unplanned increase in inventories. In other words, changes in inventories depend on sales of goods, which firms cannot always forecast with perfect accuracy.

For the economy as a whole, we can say that actual investment spending will be greater than planned investment spending when there is an unplanned increase in inventories. Actual investment spending will be less than planned investment spending when there is an unplanned decrease in inventories. *Therefore, actual investment will equal planned investment only when there is no unplanned change in inventories.* In this chapter, we will use I to represent planned investment. We will also assume that the government data on investment spending compiled by the U.S. Bureau of Economic Analysis represents planned investment spending. This is a simplification, however, because the government collects data on actual investment spending, which equals planned investment spending only when unplanned changes in inventories are zero.

Macroeconomic Equilibrium

Macroeconomic equilibrium is similar to microeconomic equilibrium. In microeconomics, equilibrium in the apple market occurs at the point at which the demand for apples equals the supply of apples. When we have equilibrium in the apple market, the quantity of apples produced and sold will not change unless the demand for apples or the supply of apples changes. For the economy as a whole, macroeconomic equilibrium occurs where total spending, or aggregate expenditure, equals total production, or GDP:

Aggregate expenditure = GDP.

As we saw in Chapter 10, over the long run, real GDP in the United States grows and the standard of living rises. In this chapter, we are interested in understanding why GDP fluctuates in the short run. To simplify the analysis of macroeconomic equilibrium, we assume that the economy is not growing. In the next chapter, we discuss the more realistic case of macroeconomic equilibrium in a growing economy. If we assume that the economy is not growing, then equilibrium GDP will not change unless aggregate expenditure changes.

Adjustments to Macroeconomic Equilibrium

The apple market isn't always in equilibrium because sometimes the quantity of apples demanded is greater than the quantity supplied, and sometimes the quantity supplied is greater than the quantity demanded. The same outcome holds for the economy as a whole. Sometimes the economy is in macroeconomic equilibrium, and sometimes it isn't. When aggregate expenditure is greater than GDP, the total amount of spending in the economy is greater than the total amount of production. With spending being greater than production, many businesses will sell more goods and services than they had expected. For example, the manager of a Home Depot store might like to keep 50 refrigerators in stock to give customers the opportunity to see a variety of different sizes and models. If sales are unexpectedly high, the store may end up with only 20 refrigerators. In that case, the store will have an unplanned decrease in inventories: Its inventory of refrigerators declines by 30.

How will the store manager react when more refrigerators are sold than expected? The manager is likely to order more refrigerators. If other stores selling refrigerators are experiencing similar sales increases and are also increasing their orders, then General Electric, Whirlpool, and other refrigerator manufacturers will significantly increase their production. These manufacturers may also increase the number of workers they hire. If the increase in sales is affecting not just refrigerators but also other appliances, automobiles, furniture, computers, and other goods and services, then GDP and total employment will begin to increase. In summary, *when aggregate expenditure is greater than GDP, inventories will decline, and GDP and total employment will increase.*

Now suppose that aggregate expenditure is less than GDP. With spending being less than production, many businesses will sell fewer goods and services than they had expected, so their inventories will increase. For example, the manager of the Home Depot store who wants 50 refrigerators in stock may find that because of slow sales, the store has 75 refrigerators, so the store manager will cut back on orders for new refrigerators. If other stores also cut back on their orders, General Electric and Whirlpool will reduce production and lay off workers.

If the decrease in sales is affecting not just refrigerators but also many different goods and services, GDP and total employment will begin to decrease. These events happened at many firms during spring 2001. In summary, *when aggregate expenditure is less than GDP, inventories will increase, and GDP and total employment will decrease.*

Only when aggregate expenditure equals GDP will firms sell what they expected to sell. In that case, their inventories will be unchanged, and they will not have an incentive to increase or decrease production. The economy will be in macroeconomic equilibrium. Table 11-1 summarizes the relationship between aggregate expenditure and GDP.

Increases and decreases in aggregate expenditure cause the year-to-year changes in GDP. Economists devote considerable time and energy to forecasting what will happen to each component of aggregate expenditure. If economists forecast that aggregate expenditure will decline in the future, that is equivalent to forecasting that GDP will decline and that the economy will enter a recession. Individuals and firms closely watch these forecasts because changes in GDP can have dramatic consequences. When GDP is increasing, so are wages, profits, and job opportunities. Declining GDP can be bad news for workers, firms, and job seekers.

TABLE 11-1

The Relationship between Aggregate Expenditure and GDP

IF ...	THEN ...	AND ...
Aggregate expenditure is *equal* to GDP	inventories are *unchanged*	the economy is in *macroeconomic equilibrium.*
Aggregate expenditure is *less* than GDP	inventories *rise*	GDP and employment *decrease.*
Aggregate expenditure is *greater* than GDP	inventories *fall*	GDP and employment *increase.*

When economists forecast that aggregate expenditure is likely to decline and that the economy is headed for a recession, the federal government may implement *macroeconomic policies* in an attempt to head off the fall in expenditure and keep the economy from falling into recession. We discuss these macroeconomic polices in Chapters 14 and 15.

11.2 LEARNING OBJECTIVE

11.2 | Discuss the determinants of the four components of aggregate expenditure and define the marginal propensity to consume and the marginal propensity to save.

Determining the Level of Aggregate Expenditure in the Economy

To better understand how macroeconomic equilibrium is determined in the aggregate expenditure model, we look more closely at the components of aggregate expenditure. Table 11-2 lists the four components of aggregate expenditure for the year 2006. Each component is measured in *real* terms, meaning that it is corrected for inflation by being measured in billions of 2000 dollars. Consumption is clearly the largest component of aggregate expenditure. Investment and government purchases are of roughly similar size. Net exports are negative because in 2006, as in most years since the early 1970s, the United States imported more goods and services than it exported. Next, we consider the variables that determine each of the four components of aggregate expenditure.

Consumption

Figure 11-1 shows movements in real consumption for the years 1979 to 2006. Notice that consumption follows a smooth, upward trend. Only during periods of recession does the growth in consumption slow or decline.

The following are the five most important variables that determine the level of consumption:

- Current disposable income
- Household wealth
- Expected future income
- The price level
- The interest rate

We can discuss how changes in each of these variables affect consumption.

Current Disposable Income The most important determinant of consumption is the current disposable income of households. Recall from Chapter 7 that disposable income is the income remaining to households after they have paid the personal income tax and received government *transfer payments*, such as Social Security payments. For most households, the higher their disposable income, the more they spend, and the

TABLE 11-2

Components of Real Aggregate Expenditure, 2006

EXPENDITURE CATEGORY	REAL EXPENDITURE (BILLIONS OF 2000 DOLLARS)
Consumption	$8,091
Investment	1,946
Government	1,998
Net exports	–618

Source: U.S. Bureau of Economic Analysis.

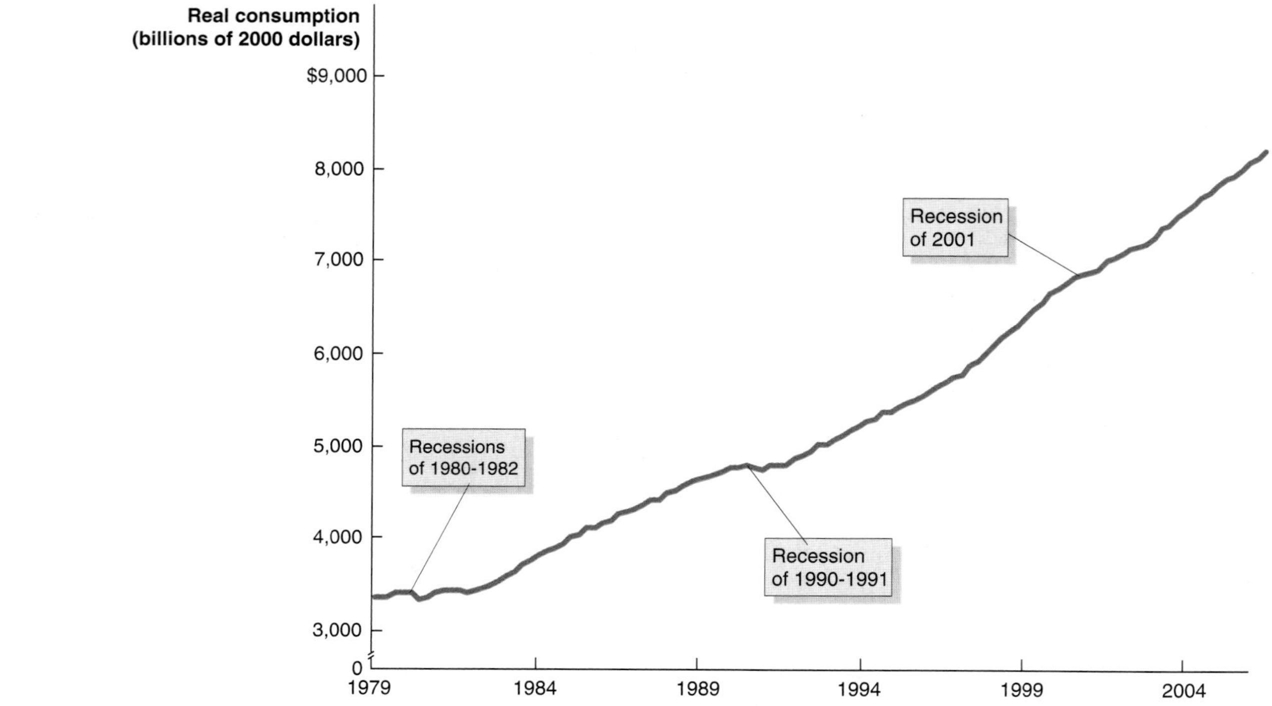

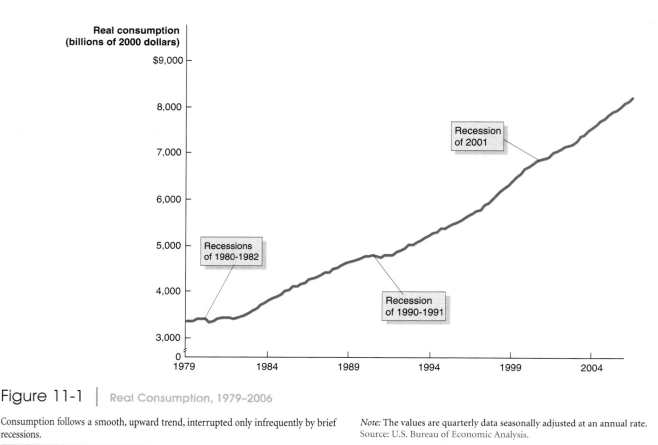

Figure 11-1 | Real Consumption, 1979–2006

Consumption follows a smooth, upward trend, interrupted only infrequently by brief recessions.

Note: The values are quarterly data seasonally adjusted at an annual rate.
Source: U.S. Bureau of Economic Analysis.

lower their income, the less they spend. Macroeconomic consumption is the total of all the consumption of U.S. households. So, we would expect consumption to increase when the current disposable income of households increases and to decrease when the current disposable income of households decreases. As we discussed in Chapter 7, total income in the United States expands during most years. Only during recessions, which happen infrequently, does total income decline. The main reason for the general upward trend in consumption shown in Figure 11-1 is that disposable income has followed a similar upward trend.

Household Wealth Consumption also depends on the wealth of households. A household's *wealth* is the value of its *assets* minus the value of its *liabilities*. Recall from Chapter 5 that an asset is anything of value owned by a person or a firm, and a liability is anything owed by a person or a firm. A household's assets include its home, stock and bond holdings, and bank accounts. A household's liabilities include any loans that it owes. A household with $10 million in wealth is likely to spend more than a household with $10,000 in wealth, even if both households have the same disposable income. Therefore, when the wealth of households increases, consumption should increase, and when the wealth of households decreases, consumption should decrease. Shares of stock are an important category of household wealth. When stock prices increase, household wealth will increase, and so should consumption. For example, a family whose stock holdings increase in value from $50,000 to $100,000 may be willing to spend a larger fraction of its income because it is less concerned with adding to its savings. A decline in stock prices should lead to a decline in consumption. Economists who have studied the determinants of consumption have concluded that permanent increases in wealth have a larger impact than temporary increases. A recent estimate of the effect of changes in wealth on consumption spending indicates that, for every permanent one-dollar increase in household wealth, consumption spending will increase by between four and five cents per year.

Expected Future Income Consumption also depends on expected future income. Most people prefer to keep their consumption fairly stable from year to year, even if their income fluctuates significantly. Real estate brokers, for example, earn most of their income from commissions (fixed percentages of the sale price) on houses they sell. Real estate brokers might have very high incomes some years and much lower incomes in other years. Most brokers keep their consumption steady and do not increase it during good years and then drastically cut back during slower years. If we looked just at a broker's current income, we might have difficulty estimating the broker's current consumption. Instead, we need to take into account the broker's expected future income. We can conclude that current income explains current consumption well *but only when current income is not unusually high or unusually low compared with expected future income.*

The Price Level Recall from Chapter 8 that the *price level* measures the average prices of goods and services in the economy. Consumption is affected by changes in the price level. It is tempting to think that an increase in prices will reduce consumption by making goods and services less affordable. In fact, the effect of an increase in the price of *one* product on the quantity demanded of that product is different from the effect of an increase in the price level on *total* spending by households on goods and services. Changes in the price level affect consumption mainly through their effect on household wealth. An increase in the price level will result in a decrease in the *real* value of household wealth. For example, if you have $2,000 in a checking account, the higher the price level, the fewer goods and services you can buy with your money. If the price level falls, the real value of your $2,000 would increase. Therefore, as the price level rises, the real value of your wealth declines, and so will your consumption, at least a little. Conversely, if the price level falls—which happens very rarely in the United States—your consumption will increase.

The Interest Rate Finally, consumption also depends on the interest rate. When the interest rate is high, the reward to saving is increased, and households are likely to save more and spend less. In Chapter 8, we discussed the distinction between the *nominal interest rate* and the *real interest rate.* The nominal interest rate is the stated interest rate on a loan or a financial investment such as a bond. The real interest rate corrects the nominal interest rate for the impact of inflation and is equal to the nominal interest rate minus the inflation rate. Because households are concerned with the payments they will make or receive after the effects of inflation are taken into account, consumption spending depends on the real interest rate.

We saw in Chapter 7 that consumption spending is divided into three categories: spending on *services*, such as medical care, education, and haircuts; spending on *nondurable goods*, such as food and clothing; and spending on *durable goods*, such as automobiles and furniture. Spending on durable goods is most likely to be affected by changes in the interest rate because a high real interest rate increases the cost of spending financed by borrowing. The monthly payment on a four-year car loan will be higher if the real interest rate on the loan is 4 percent than if the real interest rate is 2 percent.

The Consumption Function Panel (a) in Figure 11-2 illustrates the relationship between consumption and disposable income during the years 1960–2006. In panel (b), we draw a straight line through the points representing consumption and disposable income. The fact that most of the points lie almost on the line shows the close relationship between consumption and disposable income. Because changes in consumption depend on changes in disposable income, we can say that *consumption is a function of disposable income.* The relationship between consumption spending and disposable income illustrated in panel (b) of Figure 11-2 is called the **consumption function.**

Consumption function The relationship between consumption spending and disposable income.

Marginal propensity to consume (*MPC*) The slope of the consumption function: The amount by which consumption spending changes when disposable income changes.

The slope of the consumption function is equal to the change in consumption divided by the change in disposable income and is referred to as the **marginal propensity to consume (*MPC*)**. Using the Greek letter delta, Δ, to represent "change in," C to

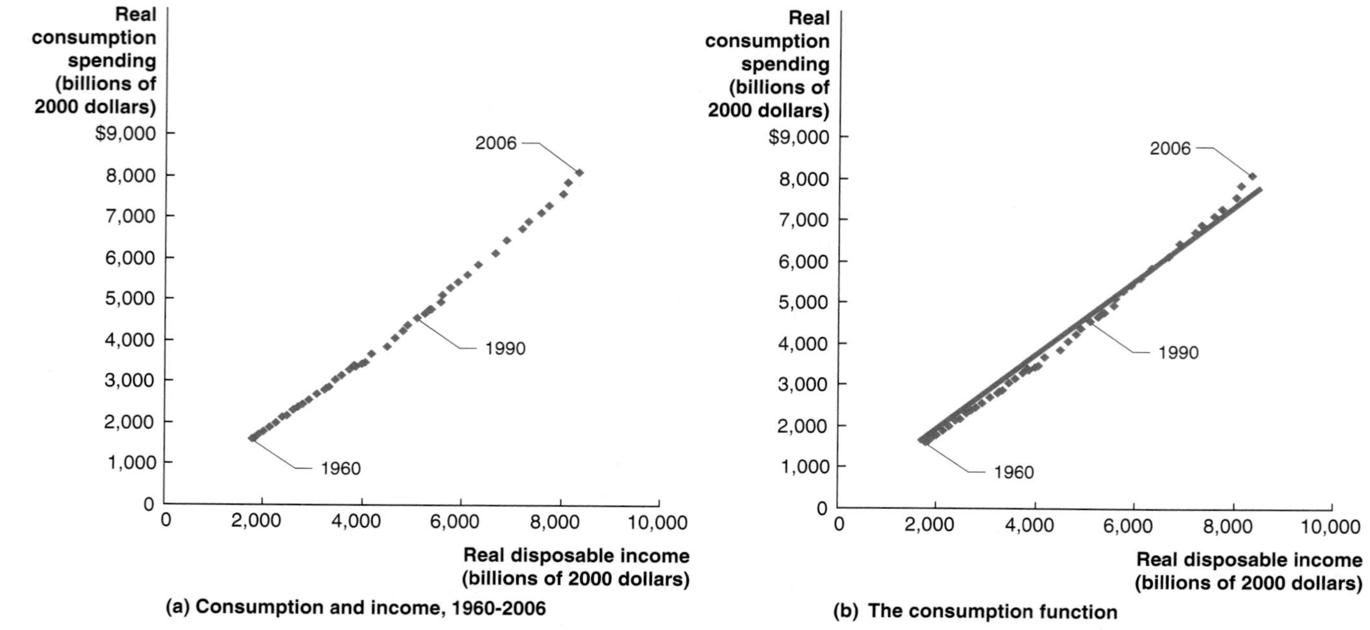

Figure 11-2 | The Relationship between Consumption and Income, 1960–2006

Panel (a) shows the relationship between consumption and income. The points represent combinations of real consumption spending and real disposable income for the years between 1960 and 2006. In panel (b), we draw a straight line through the points from panel (a). The line represents the relationship between consumption and disposable income and is called the *consumption function*. The slope of the consumption function is the marginal propensity to consume.

represent consumption spending, and *YD* to represent disposable income, we can write the expression for the *MPC* as follows:

$$MPC = \frac{\text{Change in consumption}}{\text{Change in disposable income}} = \frac{\Delta C}{\Delta YD}.$$

For example, between 1999 and 2000, consumption spending increased by $301 billion, while disposable income increased by $333 billion. The marginal propensity to consume was, therefore:

$$\frac{\Delta C}{\Delta YD} = \frac{\$301\text{ billion}}{\$333\text{ billion}} = 0.90.$$

The value for the *MPC* tells us that households in 2000 spent 90 percent of the increase in their household income.

We can also use the *MPC* to determine how much consumption will change as income changes. To see this relationship, we rewrite the expression for the *MPC*:

$$MPC = \frac{\text{Change in consumption}}{\text{Change in disposable income}},$$

or:

$$\text{Change in consumption} = \text{Change in disposable income} \times MPC.$$

For example, with an *MPC* of 0.90, a $10 billion increase in disposable income will increase consumption by $10 billion × 0.90, or $9 billion.

The Relationship between Consumption and National Income

We have seen that consumption spending by households depends on disposable income. We now shift our focus slightly to the similar relationship that exists between consumption spending and GDP. We make this shift because we are interested in using the aggregate expenditure model to explain changes in real GDP rather than changes in disposable income. The first step in examining the relationship between consumption and GDP is to recall from Chapter 7 that the differences between GDP and national income are small and can be ignored without affecting our analysis. In fact, in this and the following chapters, we will use the terms *GDP* and *national income* interchangeably. Also recall that disposable income is equal to national income plus government transfer payments minus taxes. Taxes minus government transfer payments are referred to as *net taxes*. So, we can write the following:

Disposable income = National income − Net taxes.

We can rearrange the equation like this:

National income = GDP = Disposable income + Net taxes.

The table in Figure 11-3 shows hypothetical values for national income (or GDP), net taxes, disposable income, and consumption spending. Notice that national income and disposable income differ by a constant amount, which is equal to net taxes of $1,000

National income or GDP (billions of dollars)	Net taxes (billions of dollars)	Disposable income (billions of dollars)	Consumption (billions of dollars)	Change in national income (billions of dollars)	Change in disposable income (billions of dollars)
$1,000	$1,000	$0	$750	—	—
3,000	1,000	2,000	2,250	2,000	2,000
5,000	1,000	4,000	3,750	2,000	2,000
7,000	1,000	6,000	5,250	2,000	2,000
9,000	1,000	8,000	6,750	2,000	2,000
11,000	1,000	10,000	8,250	2,000	2,000
13,000	1,000	12,000	9,750	2,000	2,000

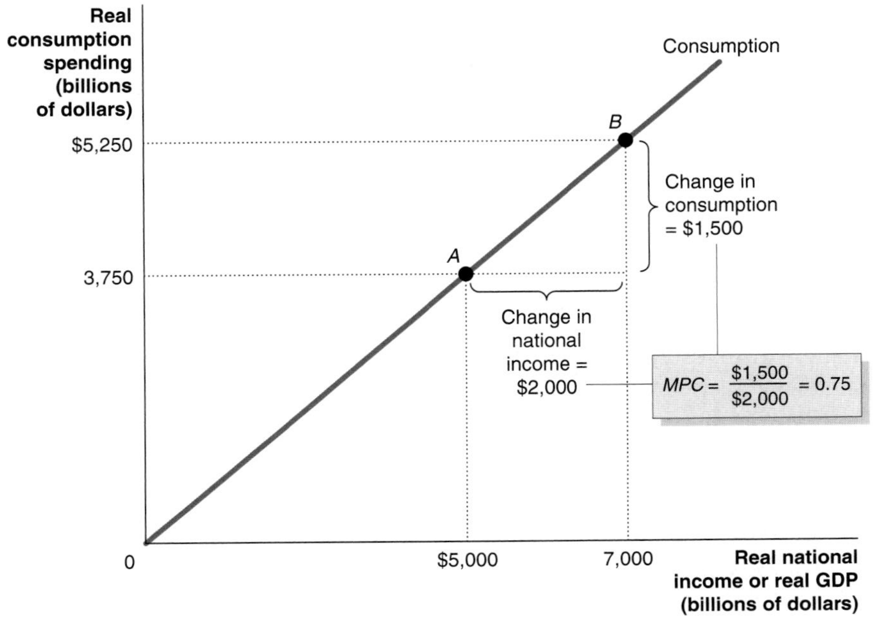

Figure 11-3

The Relationship between Consumption and National Income

Because national income differs from disposable income only by net taxes—which, for simplicity, we assume are constant—we can graph the consumption function using national income rather than disposable income. We can also calculate the *MPC*, which is the slope of the consumption function, using either the change in national income or the change in disposable income and always get the same value. The slope of the consumption function between point *A* and point *B* is equal to the change in consumption—$1,500 billion—divided by the change in national income—$2,000 billion—or 0.75.

billion. In reality, net taxes are not a constant amount because they are affected by changes in income. As income rises, net taxes rise because some taxes, such as the personal income tax, increase and some government transfer payments, such as government payments to unemployed workers, fall. Nothing important is affected in our analysis, however, by our simplifying assumption that net taxes are constant. The graph in Figure 11-3 shows a line representing the relationship between consumption and national income. The line is very similar to the consumption function shown in panel (b) of Figure 11-2. We defined the marginal propensity to consume (*MPC*) as the change in consumption divided by the change in disposable income, which is the slope of the consumption function. In fact, notice that if we calculate the slope of the line in Figure 11-3 between points *A* and *B*, we get a result that will not change whether we use the values for national income or the values for disposable income. Using the values for national income:

$$\frac{\Delta C}{\Delta Y} = \frac{\$5{,}250 \text{ billion} - \$3{,}750 \text{ billion}}{\$7{,}000 \text{ billion} - \$5{,}000 \text{ billion}} = 0.75.$$

Using the corresponding values for disposable income from the table:

$$\frac{\Delta C}{\Delta YD} = \frac{\$5{,}250 \text{ billion} - \$3{,}750 \text{ billion}}{\$6{,}000 \text{ billion} - \$4{,}000 \text{ billion}} = 0.75.$$

It should not be surprising that we get the same result in either case. National income and disposable income differ by a constant amount, so changes in the two numbers always give us the same value, as is shown by the last two columns of the table in Figure 11-3. Therefore, we can graph the consumption function using national income rather than using disposable income. We can also calculate the *MPC* using either the change in national income or the change in disposable income and always get the same value.

Income, Consumption, and Saving

To complete our discussion of consumption, we can look briefly at the relationships among income, consumption, and saving. Households either spend their income, save it, or use it to pay taxes. For the economy as a whole, we can write the following:

National income = Consumption + Saving + Taxes.

When national income increases, there must be some combination of an increase in consumption, an increase in saving, and an increase in taxes:

Change in national income = Change in consumption + Change in saving + Change in taxes.

Using symbols, where *Y* represents national income (and GDP), *C* represents consumption, *S* represents saving, and *T* represents taxes, we can write the following:

$$Y = C + S + T$$

and,

$$\Delta Y = \Delta C + \Delta S + \Delta T.$$

To simplify, we can assume that taxes are always a constant amount, in which case $\Delta T = 0$, so the following is also true:

$$\Delta Y = \Delta C + \Delta S.$$

Marginal propensity to save (*MPS*) The change in saving divided by the change in disposable income.

We have already seen that the marginal propensity to consume equals the change in consumption divided by the change in income. We can define the **marginal propensity to save (*MPS*)** as the amount by which saving increases when disposable income increases and measure the *MPS* as the change in saving divided by the change in disposable income. In calculating the *MPS*, as in calculating the *MPC*, we can safely ignore the difference between national income and disposable income.

If we divide the last equation on the previous page by the change in income, ΔY, we get an equation that shows the relationship between the marginal propensity to consume and the marginal propensity to save:

$$\frac{\Delta Y}{\Delta Y} = \frac{\Delta C}{\Delta Y} + \frac{\Delta S}{\Delta Y}$$

or,

$$1 = MPC + MPS.$$

This last equation tells us that when taxes are constant, the marginal propensity to consume plus the marginal propensity to save must always equal 1. They must add up to 1 because part of any increase in income is consumed, and whatever remains must be saved.

Solved Problem | **11-2**

Calculating the Marginal Propensity to Consume and the Marginal Propensity to Save

Fill in the blanks in the following table. For simplicity, assume that taxes are zero. Show that the *MPC* plus the *MPS* equals 1.

NATIONAL INCOME AND REAL GDP (*Y*)	CONSUMPTION (*C*)	SAVING (*S*)	MARGINAL PROPENSITY TO CONSUME (*MPC*)	MARGINAL PROPENSITY TO SAVE (*MPS*)
$9,000	$8,000		—	—
10,000	8,600			
11,000	9,200			
12,000	9,800			
13,000	10,400			

SOLVING THE PROBLEM:

Step 1: **Review the chapter material.** This problem is about the relationship among income, consumption, and saving, so you may want to review the section "Income, Consumption, and Saving," which begins on page 356.

Step 2: **Fill in the table.** We know that $Y = C + S + T$. With taxes equal to zero, this equation becomes $Y = C + S$. We can use this equation to fill in the "Saving" column. We can use the expressions for the *MPC* and the *MPS* to fill in the other two columns:

$$MPC = \frac{\Delta C}{\Delta Y}$$

$$MPS = \frac{\Delta S}{\Delta Y}$$

For example, to calculate the value of the *MPC* in the second row, we have:

$$MPC = \frac{\Delta C}{\Delta Y} = \frac{\$8{,}600 - \$8{,}000}{\$10{,}000 - \$9{,}000} = \frac{\$600}{\$1{,}000} = 0.6.$$

To calculate the value of the *MPS* in the second row, we have:

$$MPS = \frac{\Delta S}{\Delta Y} = \frac{\$1{,}400 - \$1{,}000}{\$10{,}000 - \$9{,}000} = \frac{\$400}{\$1{,}000} = 0.4.$$

NATIONAL INCOME AND REAL GDP (*Y*)	CONSUMPTION (*C*)	SAVING (*S*)	MARGINAL PROPENSITY TO CONSUME (*MPC*)	MARGINAL PROPENSITY TO SAVE (*MPS*)
$9,000	$8,000	$1,000	—	—
10,000	8,600	1,400	0.6	0.4
11,000	9,200	1,800	0.6	0.4
12,000	9,800	2,200	0.6	0.4
13,000	10,400	2,600	0.6	0.4

Step 3: Show that the *MPC* plus the *MPS* equals 1. At every level of national income, the *MPC* is 0.6 and the *MPS* is 0.4. Therefore, the *MPC* plus the *MPS* is always equal to 1.

YOUR TURN: For more practice, do related problem 2.11 on page 384 at the end of this chapter.

>> End Solved Problem 11-2

Planned Investment

Figure 11-4 shows movements in real investment spending for the years 1979–2006. Notice that, unlike consumption, investment does not follow a smooth, upward trend. Investment declined significantly during the recessions of 1980, 1981–1982, 1990–1991, and 2001. Following the recovery from the 1981–1982 recession, real investment increased only slowly, so that in 1992, it was at about the same level as in 1984. But during the mid- to late 1990s, investment increased very rapidly, led by increases in spending on computers and other information technology, partly as a result of the growth of the Internet. In 2000, real investment spending had risen to nearly twice its 1992 level before declining by 10 percent between 2000 and 2002. Real investment spending increased by more than 25 percent between 2002 and 2006, as the economy recovered from the 2001 recession.

The four most important variables that determine the level of investment are:

- Expectations of future profitability
- The interest rate
- Taxes
- Cash flow

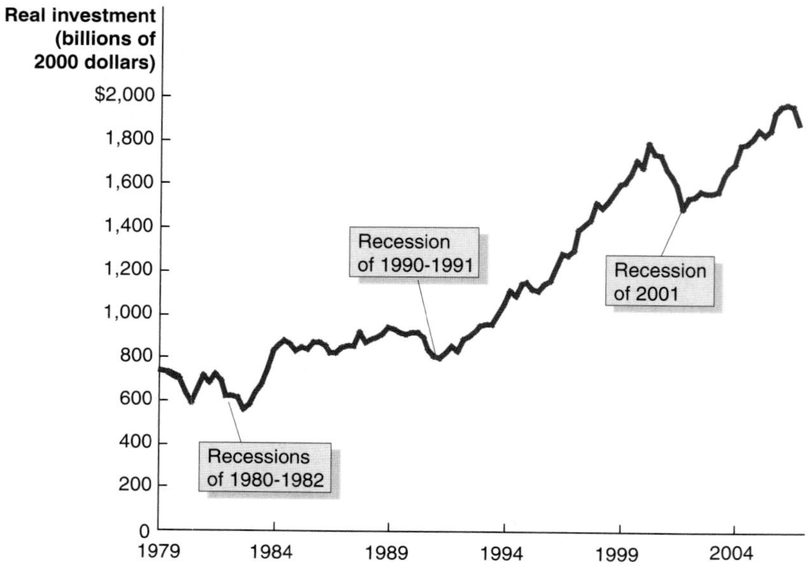

Figure 11-4

Real Investment, 1979–2006

Investment is subject to more changes than is consumption. Investment declined significantly during the recessions of 1980, 1981–1982, 1990–1991, and 2001. Following the recovery from the 1981–1982 recession, investment increased only slowly, so that in 1992, it was at about the same level as in 1984. But during the mid- to late 1990s, investment increased very strongly, partly because the growth of the Internet led firms to increase spending on computers and other information technology. In 2000, real investment had risen to nearly twice its 1992 level before declining by more than 10 percent in 2001.

Note: The values are quarterly data seasonally adjusted at an annual rate

Source: U.S. Bureau of Economic Analysis.

Expectations of Future Profitability Investment goods, such as factories, office buildings, and machinery and equipment, are long lived. A firm is unlikely to build a new factory unless it is optimistic that the demand for its product will remain strong for a period of at least several years. When the economy moves into a recession, many firms postpone buying investment goods even if the demand for their own product is strong because they are afraid that the recession may become worse. The reverse may be true during an expansion. In the late 1990s, many firms increased their investment spending, expecting that capital goods that embodied new information and telecommunication technologies would prove very profitable. The key point is this: *The optimism or pessimism of firms is an important determinant of investment spending.*

The Interest Rate A significant fraction of business investment is financed by borrowing. This borrowing takes the form of issuing corporate bonds or borrowing from banks. Households also borrow to finance most of their spending on new homes. The higher the interest rate, the more expensive it becomes for firms and households to borrow. Because households and firms are interested in the cost of borrowing after taking into account the effects of inflation, investment spending depends on the real interest rate. Therefore, holding the other factors that affect investment spending constant, there is an inverse relationship between the real interest rate and investment spending: *A higher real interest rate results in less investment spending, and a lower real interest rate results in more investment spending.*

Taxes Taxes also affect the level of investment spending. Firms focus on the profits that remain after they have paid taxes. The federal government imposes a *corporate income tax* on the profits corporations earn, including profits from the new buildings, equipment, and other investment goods they purchase. A reduction in the corporate income tax increases the after-tax profitability of investment spending. An increase in the corporate income tax decreases the after-tax profitability of investment spending. *Investment tax incentives* also increase investment spending. An investment tax incentive provides firms with a tax reduction when they spend on new investment goods. For example, in 2002, Congress enacted an investment tax incentive for new investment in equipment and software. This incentive expired at the end of 2004. Partially as a result of this incentive, spending on equipment and software increased from $801 billion at an annual rate in the first quarter of 2002 to $996 billion in the fourth quarter of 2004.

Cash Flow Most firms do not borrow to finance spending on new factories, machinery, and equipment. Instead, they use their own funds. **Cash flow** is the difference between the cash revenues received by a firm and the cash spending by the firm. Noncash receipts or noncash spending would not be included in cash flow. For example, tax laws allow firms to count as a cost an amount for depreciation to replace worn out or obsolete machinery and equipment even if new machinery and equipment have not actually been purchased. Because this is noncash spending, it would not be included when calculating cash flow. The largest contributor to cash flow is profit. The more profitable a firm is, the greater its cash flow and the greater its ability to finance investment. During periods of recession, many firms experience reduced profits, which in turn reduces their ability to finance spending on new factories or machinery and equipment.

Cash flow The difference between the cash revenues received by a firm and the cash spending by the firm.

Making the Connection | Cisco Rides the Roller Coaster of Information Technology Spending

We saw at the beginning of this chapter that Cisco Systems was taken by surprise by the decline in demand for its routers, switches, and other equipment during the first quarter of 2001. In fact, the Internet and telecommunications busts of 2001 were unusual in their severity. The following graph shows that spending on information processing equipment and software followed a fairly smooth, upward trend from the beginning of 1990 to the end of 2000. Measured in 2000 dollars, real spending on information processing equipment and software increased from $101 billion at an annual rate in the first quarter of 1990 to $488 billion in the fourth quarter of 2000. Spending then declined sharply and did not regain the level of the fourth quarter of 2000 until almost three years later, in the third quarter of 2003.

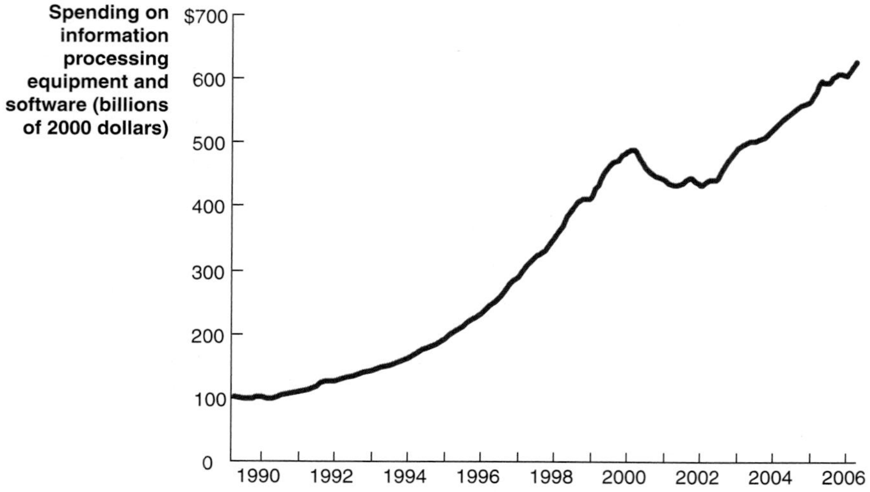

Note: The values are seasonally adjusted at an annual rate.
Source: U.S. Bureau of Economic Analysis.

Cisco benefited greatly from the increased spending on information technology in the 1990s. By the end of 2000, Cisco was second to only Microsoft in the total value of its shares of stock. In early 2000, John Chambers, Cisco's chief executive officer, predicted that by 2004, the firm's annual revenues would rise from $12.2 billion to $50 billion and that the total value of its stock would rise from $454 billion to $1 trillion. Unfortunately, the Internet and telecommunications busts made these goals impossible to attain. Cisco made an accounting profit of $2.1 billion in 2000, but by 2002, that profit had turned into a $1 billion loss as revenues declined. By 2006, Cisco's revenues had risen back to $28 billion, and the firm made a $5.6 billion accounting profit.

What explains Cisco's roller-coaster ride? As we have seen, a key determinant of investment spending is firms' expectations of the future profitability of their purchases of investment goods. In the 1990s, many firms investing in equipment to establish Web sites or to use the fiber-optic cable networks being built overestimated how profitable their investments in this equipment would be. When forecasts of future profitability were adjusted sharply downward in 2001, spending on information technology plummeted. By 2007, however, the spread of high-speed Internet access and the popularity of using the Internet for telephone service and to download movies and television programs led industry analysts to forecast that Internet traffic would be increasing by 70 percent or more per year. Cisco was still selling 70 percent to 85 percent of all network switches and routers, which left the firm well positioned to profit from this future growth.

Sources: Dana Cimilluca, "Thinking the Unthinkable: A Blockbuster Buyout by Cisco," *Wall Street Journal*, May 9, 2007; and "Growing Pains of the Cisco Kid," *Economist*, November 11, 2004.

YOUR TURN: Test your understanding by doing related problem 2.7 on page 383 at the end of this chapter.

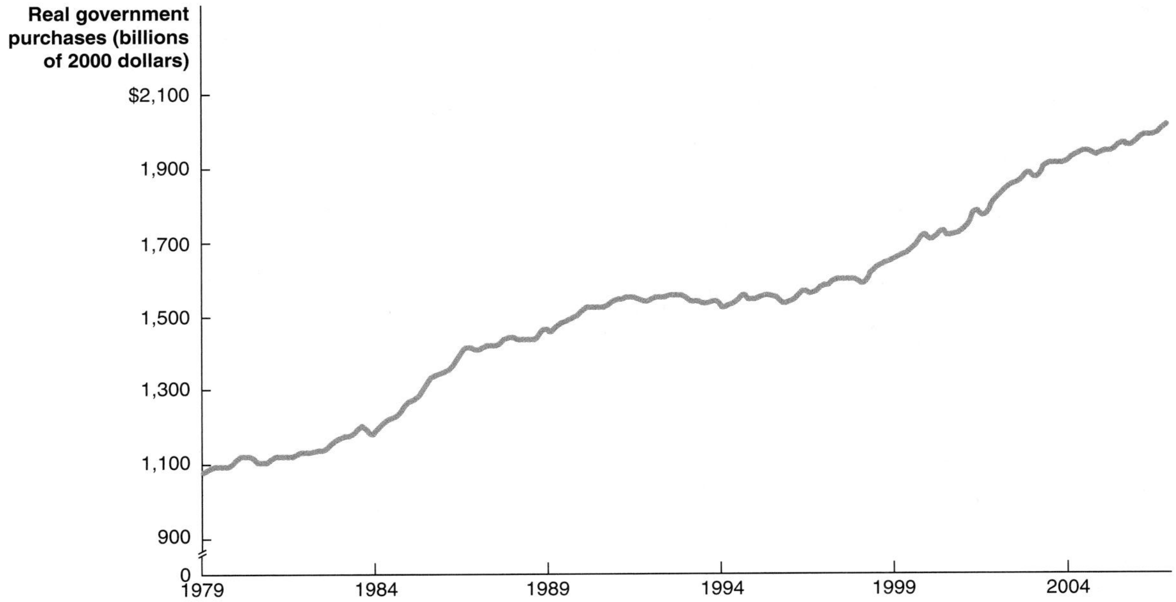

Figure 11-5 | Real Government Purchases, 1979–2006

Government purchases grew steadily for most of the 1979–2006 period, with the exception of the mid-1990s, when concern about the federal budget deficit caused real government purchases to fall for three years, beginning in 1992.

Note: The values are quarterly data seasonally adjusted at an annual rate.
Source: Bureau of Economic Analysis.

Government Purchases

Total government purchases include all spending by federal, local, and state governments for goods and services. Recall from Chapter 7 that government purchases do not include transfer payments, such as Social Security payments by the federal government or pension payments by local governments to retired police officers and firefighters because the government does not receive a good or service in return.

Figure 11-5 shows levels of real government purchases during the years 1979–2006. Government purchases grew steadily for most of this period, with the exception of the mid-1990s, when concern that spending by the federal government was growing much faster than tax receipts led Congress and Presidents George H. W. Bush and Bill Clinton to enact a series of spending reductions. As a result, real government purchases declined for three years, beginning in 1992. Contributing to the slow growth of government purchases during the 1990s was the end of the Cold War between the United States and the Soviet Union in 1989. Real federal government spending on national defense declined from $479 billion in 1990 to $365 billion in 1998 before rising again to $493 billion in 2006 in response to the war on terrorism and the war in Iraq.

Net Exports

Net exports equal exports minus imports. We can calculate net exports by taking the value of spending by foreign firms and households on goods and services produced in the United States and *subtracting* the value of spending by U.S. firms and households on goods and services produced in other countries. Figure 11-6 illustrates movements in real net exports during the years 1979–2006. During nearly all these years, the United States imported more goods and services than it exported, so net exports were negative. Net exports usually increase when the U.S. economy is in recession—although this did not happen during the 2001 recession—and fall when the U.S. economy is expanding. We will explore further the behavior of net exports in Chapter 17.

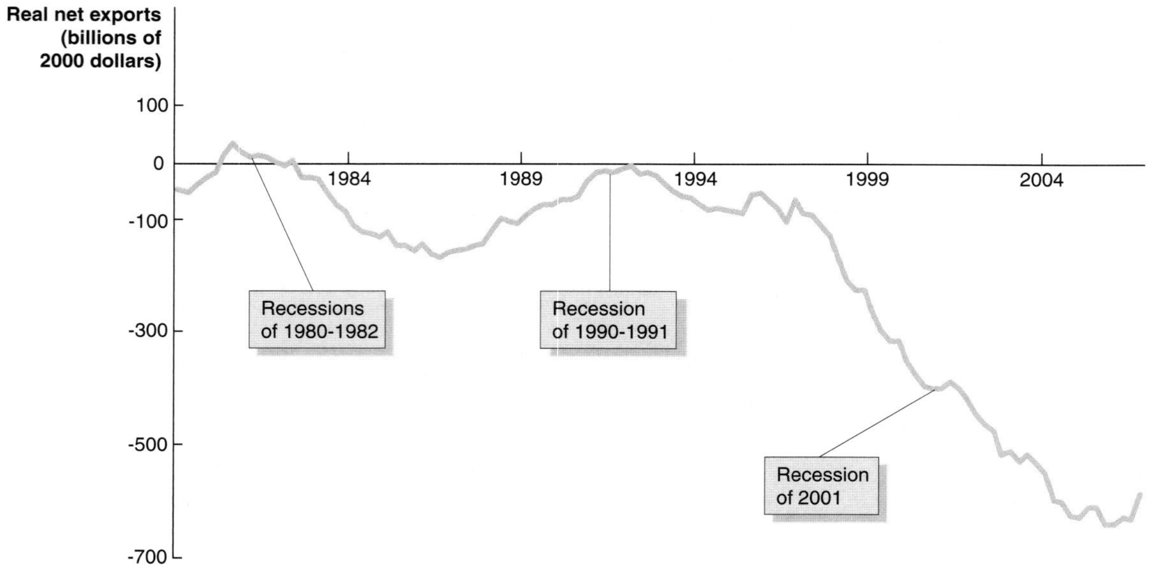

Figure 11-6 | Real Net Exports, 1979–2006

Net exports were negative in most years between 1979 and 2006. Net exports have usually increased when the U.S. economy is in recession and decreased when the U.S. economy is expanding, although they fell during the 2001 recession.

Note: The values are quarterly data seasonally adjusted at an annual rate.
Source: Bureau of Economic Analysis.

The following are the three most important variables that determine the level of net exports:

- The price level in the United States relative to the price levels in other countries
- The growth rate of GDP in the United States relative to the growth rates of GDP in other countries
- The exchange rate between the dollar and other currencies

The Price Level in the United States Relative to the Price Levels in Other Countries If inflation in the United States is lower than inflation in other countries, prices of U.S. products increase more slowly than the prices of products of other countries. This difference in price levels increases the demand for U.S. products relative to the demand for foreign products. So, U.S. exports increase and U.S. imports decrease, which increases net exports. The reverse happens during periods when the inflation rate in the United States is higher than the inflation rates in other countries: U.S. exports decrease and U.S. imports increase, which decreases net exports.

The Growth Rate of GDP in the United States Relative to the Growth Rates of GDP in Other Countries As GDP increases in the United States, the incomes of households rise, leading them to increase their purchases of goods and services. Some of the additional goods and services purchased with rising incomes are produced in the United States, but some are imported. When incomes rise faster in the United States than in other countries, U.S. consumers' purchases of foreign goods and services will increase faster than foreign consumers' purchases of U.S. goods and services. As a result, net exports will fall. When incomes in the United States rise more slowly than incomes in other countries, net exports will rise.

The Exchange Rate Between the Dollar and Other Currencies As the value of the U.S. dollar rises, the foreign currency price of U.S. products sold in other countries rises, and the dollar price of foreign products sold in the United States falls. For example, suppose that the exchange rate between the Japanese yen and the U.S. dollar is 100

Japanese yen for one U.S. dollar, or ¥100 = $1. At this exchange rate, someone in the United States could buy ¥100 for $1, or someone in Japan could buy $1 for ¥100. Leaving aside transportation costs, at this exchange rate, a U.S. product that sells for $1 in the United States will sell for ¥100 in Japan, and a Japanese product that sells for ¥100 in Japan will sell for $1 in the United States. If the exchange rate changes to ¥150 = $1, then the value of the dollar will have risen because it takes more yen to buy $1. At the new exchange rate, the U.S. product that still sells for $1 in the United States will now sell for ¥150 in Japan, reducing the quantity demanded by Japanese consumers. The Japanese product that still sells for ¥100 in Japan will now sell for only $0.67 in the United States, increasing the quantity demanded by U.S. consumers. An increase in the value of the dollar will reduce exports and increase imports, so net exports will fall. A decrease in the value of the dollar will increase exports and reduce imports, so net exports will rise.

11.3 LEARNING OBJECTIVE

11.3 | Use a 45°-line diagram to illustrate macroeconomic equilibrium.

Graphing Macroeconomic Equilibrium

Having examined the components of aggregate expenditure, we can now look more closely at macroeconomic equilibrium. We saw earlier in the chapter that macroeconomic equilibrium occurs when GDP is equal to aggregate expenditure. We can use a graph called the *45°-line diagram* to illustrate macroeconomic equilibrium. (The 45°-line diagram is also sometimes referred to as the *Keynesian cross* because it is based on the analysis of John Maynard Keynes.) To become familiar with this diagram, consider Figure 11-7, which is a 45°-line diagram that shows the relationship between the quantity of Pepsi sold (on the vertical axis) and the quantity of Pepsi produced (on the horizontal axis).

The line on the diagram forms an angle of 45° with the horizontal axis. The line represents all the points that are equal distances from both axes. So, points such as *A* and *B*, where the number of bottles of Pepsi produced equals the number of bottles sold, are on the 45° line. Points such as *C*, where the quantity sold is greater than the quantity produced, lie above the line. Points such as *D*, where the quantity sold is less than the quantity produced, lie below the line.

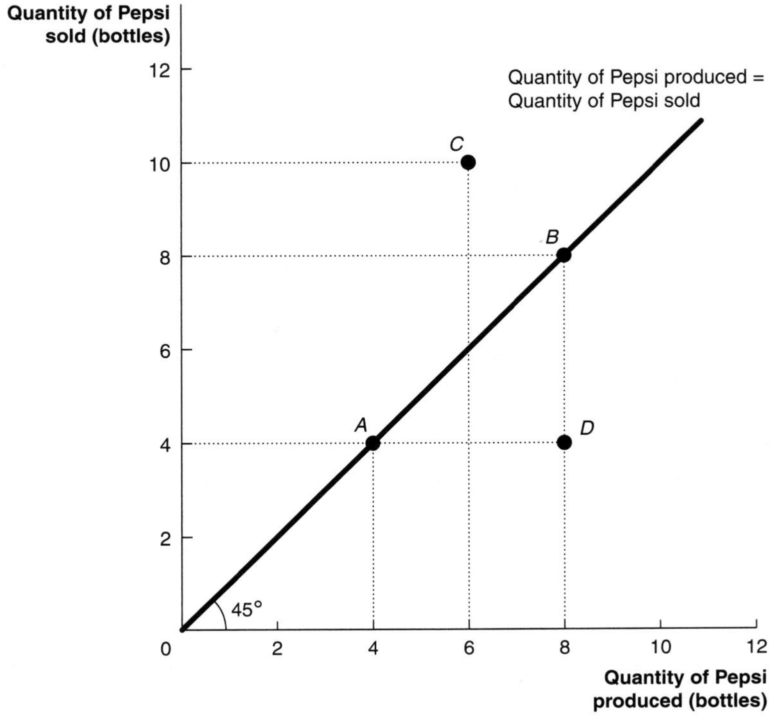

Figure 11-7

An Example of a 45°-Line Diagram

The 45° line shows all the points that are equal distances from both axes. Points such as *A* and *B*, at which the quantity produced equals the quantity sold, are on the 45° line. Points such as *C*, at which the quantity sold is greater than the quantity produced, lie above the line. Points such as *D*, at which the quantity sold is less than the quantity produced, lie below the line.

Figure 11-8

The Relationship between Planned Aggregate Expenditure and GDP on a 45°-Line Diagram

Every point of macroeconomic equilibrium is on the 45° line, where planned aggregate expenditure equals GDP. At points above the line, planned aggregate expenditure is greater than GDP. At points below the line, planned aggregate expenditure is less than GDP.

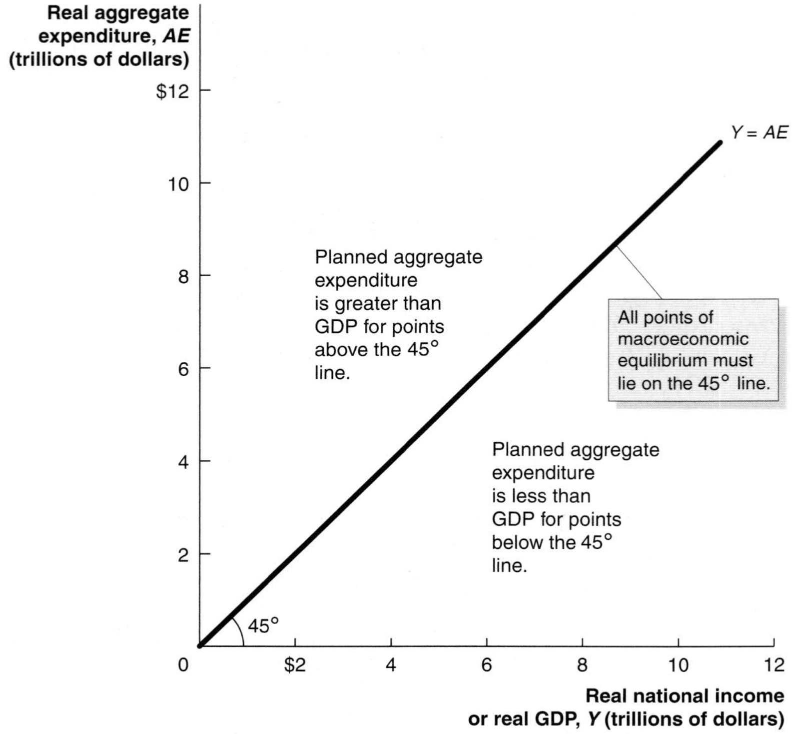

Figure 11-8 is very similar to Figure 11-7, except now we are measuring real national income or real GDP (Y) on the horizontal axis and planned real aggregate expenditure (AE) on the vertical axis. Because macroeconomic equilibrium occurs where planned aggregate expenditure equals GDP, *we know that all points of macroeconomic equilibrium must lie along the 45° line.* For all points above the 45° line, planned aggregate expenditure will be greater than GDP. For all points below the 45° line, planned aggregate expenditure will be less than GDP.

The 45° line shows many potential points of macroeconomic equilibrium. During any particular year, only one of these points will represent the actual level of equilibrium real GDP, given the actual level of planned real expenditure. To determine this point, we need to draw a line on the graph showing the *aggregate expenditure function.* The aggregate expenditure function shows us the amount of planned aggregate expenditure that will occur at every level of national income or GDP.

Changes in GDP have a much greater impact on consumption than on planned investment, government purchases, or net exports. We assume for simplicity that the variables that determine planned investment, government purchases, and net exports all remain constant, as do the variables other than GDP that affect consumption. For example, we assume that a firm's level of planned investment at the beginning of the year will not change during the year, even if the level of GDP changes.

Figure 11-9 shows the aggregate expenditure function on the 45°-line diagram. The lowest upward-sloping line, C, represents the consumption function, as shown in Figure 11-2 on page 354. The quantities of planned investment, government purchases, and net exports are constant because we assumed that the variables they depend on are constant. So, the level of planned aggregate expenditure at any level of GDP is the amount of consumption spending at that level of GDP plus the sum of the constant amounts of planned investment, government purchases, and net exports. In Figure 11-9, we add each component of spending successively to the consumption function line to arrive at the line representing planned aggregate expenditure (AE). The $C + I$ line is higher than the C line by the constant amount of planned investment; the $C + I + G$ line is higher than the $C + I$ line by the constant amount of government purchases; and the $C + I +$

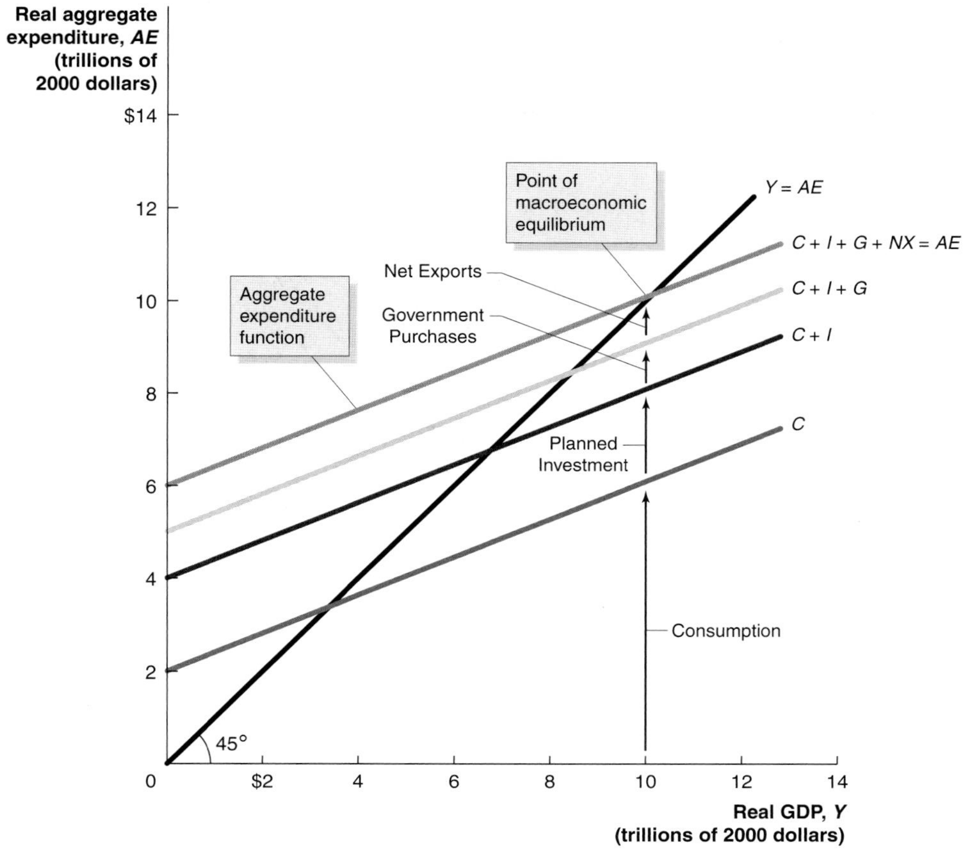

Figure 11-9

Macroeconomic Equilibrium on the 45°-Line Diagram

Macroeconomic equilibrium occurs where the aggregate expenditure line (*AE*) crosses the 45° line. The lowest upward-sloping line, *C*, represents the consumption function. The quantities of planned investment, government purchases, and net exports are constant because we assumed that the variables they depend on are constant. So, the total of planned aggregate expenditure at any level of GDP is just the amount of consumption at that level of GDP plus the sum of the constant amounts of planned investment, government purchases, and net exports. We successively add each component of spending to the consumption function line to arrive at the line representing aggregate expenditure.

$G + NX$ line is higher than the $C + I + G$ line by the constant amount of *NX*. (Notice that in many years, *NX* is negative, which causes the $C + I + G + NX$ line to be *below* the $C + I + G$ line.) The $C + I + G + NX$ line shows all four components of expenditure and is the aggregate expenditure (*AE*) function. At the point where the *AE* line crosses the 45° line, planned aggregate expenditure is equal to GDP, and the economy is in macroeconomic equilibrium.

Figure 11-10 makes the relationship between planned aggregate expenditure and GDP clearer by showing only the 45° line and the *AE* line. The figure shows that the *AE* line intersects the 45° line at a level of real GDP of $10 trillion. Therefore, $10 trillion represents the equilibrium level of real GDP. To see why this is true, consider the situation if real GDP were only $8 trillion. By moving vertically from $8 trillion on the horizontal axis up to the *AE* line, we see that planned aggregate expenditure will be greater than $8 trillion at this level of real GDP. Whenever total spending is greater than total production, firms' inventories will fall. The fall in inventories is equal to the vertical distance between the *AE* line, which shows the level of total spending, and the 45° line, which shows the $8 trillion of total production. Unplanned declines in inventories lead firms to increase their production. As real GDP increases from $8 trillion, so will total income and, therefore, consumption. The economy will move up the *AE* line as consumption increases. The gap between total spending and total production will fall, but as long as the *AE* line is above the 45° line, inventories will continue to decline, and firms will continue to expand production. When real GDP rises to $10 trillion, inventories stop falling, and the economy will be in macroeconomic equilibrium.

As Figure 11-10 shows, if GDP initially is $12 trillion, planned aggregate expenditure will be less than GDP, and firms will experience an unplanned increase in inventories. Rising inventories lead firms to decrease production. As GDP falls from $12 trillion, so will consumption, which causes the economy to move down the *AE* line. The gap between planned aggregate expenditure and GDP will fall, but as long as the *AE* line is

Figure 11-10

Macroeconomic Equilibrium

Macroeconomic equilibrium occurs where the *AE* line crosses the 45° line. In this case, that occurs at GDP of $10 trillion. If GDP is less than $10 trillion, the corresponding point on the *AE* line is above the 45° line, planned aggregate expenditure is greater than total production, firms will experience an unplanned decrease in inventories, and GDP will increase. If GDP is greater than $10 trillion, the corresponding point on the *AE* line is below the 45° line, planned aggregate expenditure is less than total production, firms will experience an unplanned increase in inventories, and GDP will decrease.

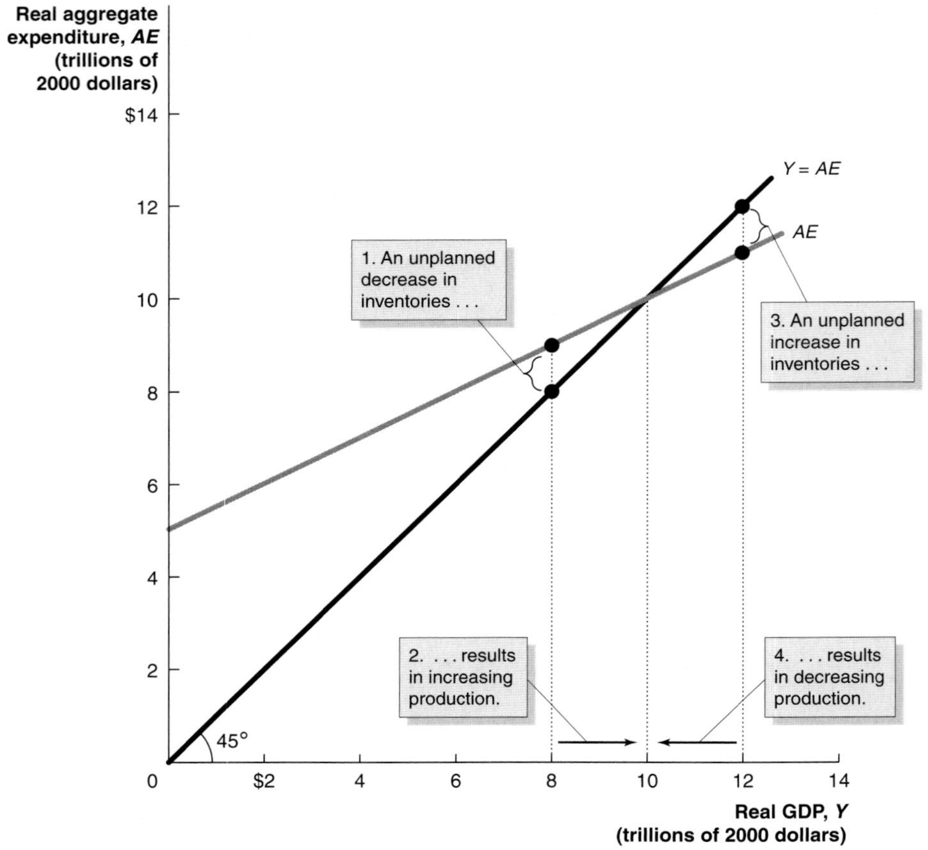

below the 45° line, inventories will continue to rise, and firms will continue to cut production. When GDP falls to $10 trillion, inventories will stop rising, and the economy will be in macroeconomic equilibrium.

Showing a Recession on the 45°-Line Diagram

Notice that *macroeconomic equilibrium can occur at any point on the 45° line.* Ideally, we would like equilibrium to occur at *potential real GDP*. At potential real GDP, firms will be operating at their normal level of capacity, and the economy will be at the *natural rate of unemployment*. As we saw in Chapter 8, at the natural rate of unemployment, the economy will be at *full employment*: Everyone in the labor force who wants a job will have one, except the structurally and frictionally unemployed. However, for equilibrium to occur at the level of potential real GDP, planned aggregate expenditure must be high enough. As Figure 11-11 shows, if there is insufficient total spending, equilibrium will occur at a lower level of real GDP. Many firms will be operating below their normal capacity, and the unemployment rate will be above the natural rate of unemployment.

Suppose that the level of potential real GDP is $10 trillion. As Figure 11-11 shows, when GDP is $10 trillion, planned aggregate expenditure is below $10 trillion, perhaps because business firms have become pessimistic about their future profitability and have reduced their investment spending. The shortfall in planned aggregate expenditure that leads to the recession can be measured as the vertical distance between the *AE* line and the 45° line at the level of potential real GDP. The shortfall in planned aggregate expenditure is exactly equal to the unplanned increase in inventories that would occur if the economy were initially at a level of GDP of $10 trillion. The unplanned increase in inventories measures the amount by which current planned aggregate expenditure is too low for the current level of production to be the equilibrium level. Or, put another way, if any of the four components of aggregate expenditure increased by this amount, the

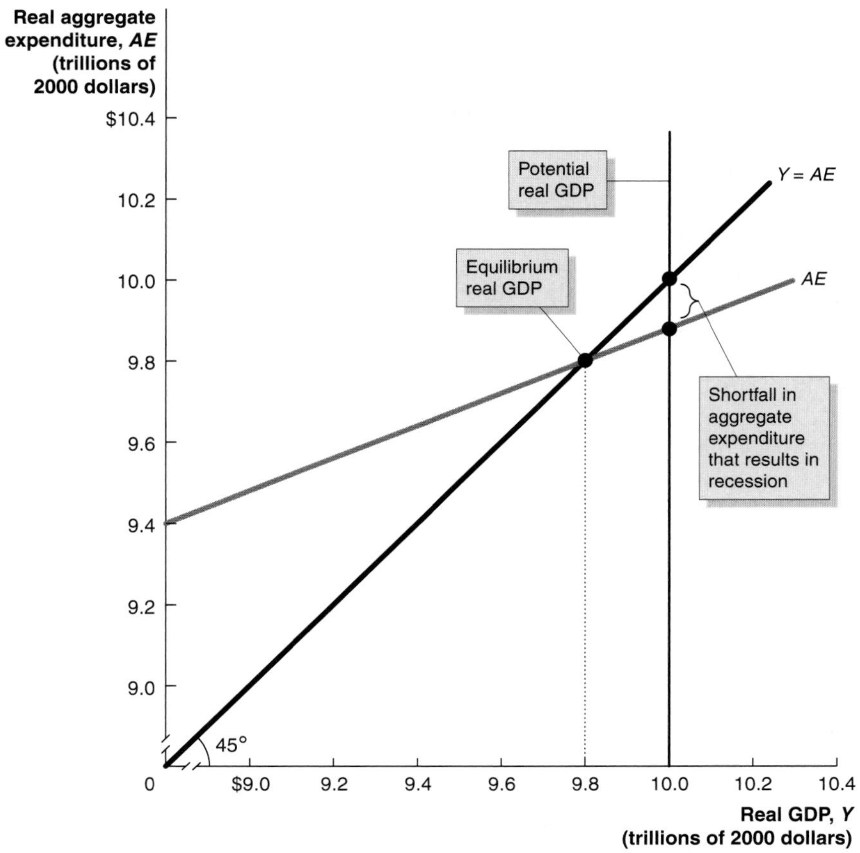

Figure 11-11

Showing a Recession on the 45°-Line Diagram

When the aggregate expenditure line intersects the 45° line at a level of GDP below potential real GDP, the economy is in recession. The figure shows that potential real GDP is $10 trillion, but because planned aggregate expenditure is too low, the equilibrium level of GDP is only $9.8 trillion, where the *AE* line intersects the 45° line. As a result, some firms will be operating below their normal capacity, and unemployment will be above the natural rate of unemployment. We can measure the shortfall in planned aggregate expenditure as the vertical distance between the *AE* line and the 45° line at the level of potential real GDP.

AE line would shift upward and intersect the 45° line at GDP of $10 trillion, and the economy would be in macroeconomic equilibrium at full employment.

Figure 11-11 shows that macroeconomic equilibrium will occur when real GDP is $9.8 trillion. Because this is 2 percent below the potential level of real GDP of $10 trillion, many firms will be operating below their normal capacity, and the unemployment rate will be well above the natural rate of unemployment. The economy will remain at this level of real GDP until there is an increase in one or more of the components of aggregate expenditure.

The Important Role of Inventories

Whenever planned aggregate expenditure is less than real GDP, some firms will experience an unplanned increase in inventories. If firms do not cut back their production promptly when spending declines, they will accumulate inventories. If firms accumulate excess inventories, then even if spending quickly returns to its normal levels, firms will have to sell these excess inventories before they can return to producing at normal levels. The possibility that firms will accumulate excess inventories explains why a brief decline in spending can result in a fairly long recession. In the early twentieth century, the inability of many firms to control their inventories contributed to the length and severity of recessions. By the 1980s and 1990s, many firms used improved systems of inventory control, which helped make recessions shorter and less severe.

Making the Connection

Business Attempts to Control Inventories, Then . . . and Now

A failure to control inventories can cause a firm to suffer losses or even drive it into bankruptcy. For example, early in the twentieth century, excessive accumulation of inventories was a serious problem for the automobile

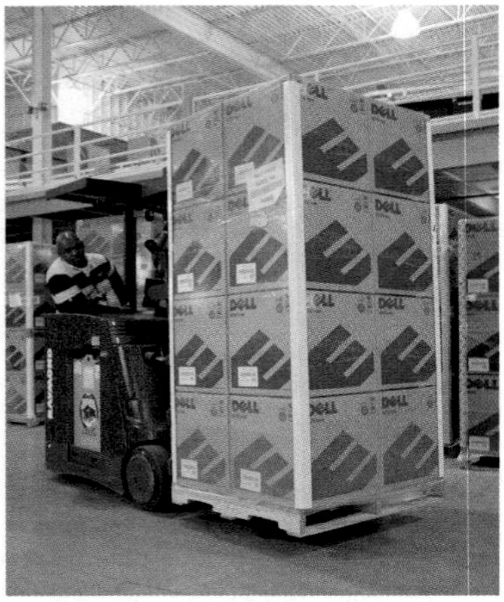

Dell Computer uses supply chain management to keep its inventory low.

industry. In his memoirs, Alfred Sloan, president of General Motors during the 1920s, described checking on inventory by traveling around the country by train and literally counting the number of unsold cars on dealers' lots. Not too surprisingly, this weak method of inventory control caused General Motors to suffer severe financial losses in 1920 and again in 1924. Eventually, automobile firms improved their inventory control methods, although not before a number of firms, including United States Motors, the predecessor of Chrysler Corporation, were driven into bankruptcy.

Modern computer firms, such as Dell and Hewlett-Packard, can also suffer significant losses if they accumulate large inventories of computer components because the prices of the components they buy from their suppliers can decline significantly, even from one week to the next. A firm that has large inventories of components may find that its costs of assembling computers are significantly greater than the costs of competitors who hold smaller inventories.

Dell Computer has pioneered in reducing costs by controlling inventories. Dell does not begin to assemble a new computer until it receives an order from a customer by telephone or over the Internet. As a result, Dell holds no inventories of finished computers. Dell still must hold some inventories of computer components, most of which are purchased from outside suppliers. Dell developed a system of *supply chain management* by which it quickly communicates orders to its suppliers and closely monitors their ability to fill its orders promptly. By the mid-1990s, Dell's suppliers could provide Dell with computer components in only two or three days. Dissatisfied with even this strong performance, in 1999, Dell set up an Internet site for suppliers to monitor Dell's need for components minute by minute and to track the components as they move through Dell's computer assembly process. As a result, the amount of time suppliers take to provide Dell with components has dropped to only six hours. When Dell assembles a computer, suppliers will have manufactured many of the components only a few hours earlier. The inventory control techniques that allow Dell to be a low-cost seller of computers also help the firm to respond quickly to sales declines without a significant buildup of inventories.

At the beginning of this chapter, we discussed Cisco's difficulties during 2001. Unlike Dell, Cisco failed to track demand well or to monitor its supply chain closely. The result was that Cisco was stuck during 2001 with large amounts of unsold inventories and had to trim production and lay off workers.

YOUR TURN: Test your understanding by doing related problem 3.6 on page 384 at the end of this chapter.

A Numerical Example of Macroeconomic Equilibrium

In forecasting real GDP, economists rely on quantitative models of the economy. We can increase our understanding of the causes of changes in real GDP by considering a simple numerical example of macroeconomic equilibrium. Although simplified, this example captures some of the key features contained in the quantitative models used by economic forecasters. Table 11-3 shows several hypothetical combinations of real GDP and planned aggregate expenditure. The first column lists real GDP. The next four columns list levels of the four components of planned aggregate expenditure that occur at the corresponding level of real GDP. We assume that planned investment, government purchases, and net exports do not change as GDP changes. Because consumption depends on GDP, it increases as GDP increases.

In the first row, GDP of $8,000 billion (or $8 trillion) results in consumption of $6,200 billion. Adding consumption, planned investment, government purchases, and net exports across the row gives planned aggregate expenditure of $8,700 billion, which is shown in the sixth column. Because planned aggregate expenditure is greater than GDP, inventories will fall by $700 billion. This unplanned decline in inventories will lead firms to increase production, and GDP will increase. GDP will continue to increase until

TABLE 11-3 | Macroeconomic Equilibrium

REAL GDP (*Y*)	CONSUMPTION (*C*)	PLANNED INVESTMENT (*I*)	GOVERNMENT PURCHASES (*G*)	NET EXPORTS (*NX*)	PLANNED AGGREGATE EXPENDITURE (*AE*)	UNPLANNED CHANGE IN INVENTORIES	REAL GDP WILL . . .
$8,000	$6,200	$1,500	$1,500	–$500	$8,700	–$700	increase
9,000	6,850	1,500	1,500	–500	9,350	–350	increase
10,000	7,500	1,500	1,500	–500	10,000	0	be in equilibrium
11,000	8,150	1,500	1,500	–500	10,650	+350	decrease
12,000	8,800	1,500	1,500	–500	11,300	+700	decrease

Note: The values are in billions of 2000 dollars.

it reaches $10,000 billion. At that level of GDP, planned aggregate expenditure is also $10,000 billion, unplanned changes in inventories are zero, and the economy is in macroeconomic equilibrium.

In the last row of Table 11-3, GDP of $12,000 billion results in consumption of $8,800 billion and planned aggregate expenditure of $11,300 billion. Because planned aggregate expenditure is less than GDP, inventories will increase by $700 billion. This unplanned increase in inventories will lead firms to decrease production, and GDP will decrease. GDP will continue to decrease until it reaches $10,000 billion, unplanned changes in inventories are zero, and the economy is in macroeconomic equilibrium.

Only when real GDP equals $10,000 billion will the economy be in macroeconomic equilibrium. At other levels of real GDP, planned aggregate expenditure will be higher or lower than GDP, and the economy will be expanding or contracting.

Don't Let This Happen to **YOU!**

Don't Confuse Aggregate Expenditure with Consumption Spending

Macroeconomic equilibrium occurs where planned aggregate expenditure equals GDP. But, remember that planned aggregate expenditure equals the sum of consumption spending, planned investment spending, government purchases, and net exports, *not* consumption spending by itself. If GDP were equal to consumption, the economy would not be in equilibrium. Planned investment plus government purchases plus net exports will always be a positive number. Therefore, if consumption were equal to GDP, aggregate expenditure would have to be greater than GDP. In that case, inventories would be decreasing, and GDP would be *increasing*; GDP would not be in equilibrium.

Test your understanding of macroeconomic equilibrium with this problem:

Question: Do you agree with the following argument?

> The chapter says macroeconomic equilibrium occurs where planned aggregate expenditure equals GDP. GDP is equal to national income. So, at equilibrium, planned aggregate expenditure must equal national income. But, we know that consumers do not spend all of their income: They save at least some and use some to pay taxes. Therefore, aggregate expenditure will never equal national income, and the basic macro story is incorrect.

Answer: As was discussed in Chapter 7, national income does equal GDP (disregarding, as we have throughout this chapter, depreciation and indirect business taxes). So, it is correct to say that in macroeconomic equilibrium, planned aggregate expenditure must equal national income. But the last sentence of the argument is incorrect because it assumes that aggregate expenditure is the same as consumption spending. Because of saving and taxes, consumption spending is always much less than national income, but in equilibrium, the sum of consumption spending, planned investment spending, government purchases, and net exports do, in fact, equal GDP and national income. So, the argument is incorrect because it has confused consumption spending with aggregate expenditure.

YOUR TURN: Test your understanding by doing related problem 3.10 on page 385 at the end of this chapter.

Solved Problem | 11-3

Determining Macroeconomic Equilibrium

Fill in the blanks in the following table and determine the equilibrium level of real GDP.

REAL GDP (*Y*)	CONSUMPTION (*C*)	PLANNED INVESTMENT (*I*)	GOVERNMENT PURCHASES (*G*)	NET EXPORTS (*NX*)	PLANNED AGGREGATE EXPENDITURE (*AE*)	UNPLANNED CHANGE IN INVENTORIES
$8,000	$6,200	$1,675	$1,675	–$500		
9,000	6,850	1,675	1,675	–500		
10,000	7,500	1,675	1,675	–500		
11,000	8,150	1,675	1,675	–500		
12,000	8,800	1,675	1,675	–500		

Note: The values are in billions of 2000 dollars.

SOLVING THE PROBLEM:

Step 1: Review the chapter material. This problem is about determining macroeconomic equilibrium, so you may want to review the section "A Numerical Example of Macroeconomic Equilibrium," which begins on page 368.

Step 2: Fill in the missing values in the table. We can calculate the missing values in the last two columns by using two equations:

Planned aggregate expenditure (*AE*) = Consumption (*C*) + Planned investment (*I*) + Government (*G*) + Net exports (*NX*)

and:

Unplanned change in inventories = Real GDP (*Y*) – Planned aggregate expenditure (*AE*).

For example, to fill in the first row, we have *AE* = $6,200 billion + $1,675 billion + $1,675 billion + (–$500 billion) = $9,050 billion; and Unplanned change in inventories = $8,000 billion – $9,050 billion = –$1,050 billion.

REAL GDP (*Y*)	CONSUMPTION (*C*)	PLANNED INVESTMENT (*I*)	GOVERNMENT PURCHASES (*G*)	NET EXPORTS (*NX*)	PLANNED AGGREGATE EXPENDITURE (*AE*)	UNPLANNED CHANGE IN INVENTORIES
$8,000	$6,200	$1,675	$1,675	–$500	$9,050	–$1,050
9,000	6,850	1,675	1,675	–500	9,700	–700
10,000	7,500	1,675	1,675	–500	10,350	–350
11,000	8,150	1,675	1,675	–500	11,000	0
12,000	8,800	1,675	1,675	–500	11,650	350

Step 3: Determine the equilibrium level of real GDP. Once you fill in the table, you should see that equilibrium real GDP must be $11,000 billion because only at that level is real GDP equal to planned aggregate expenditure.

>> End Solved Problem 11-3

YOUR TURN: For more practice, do related problem 3.12 on page 385 at the end of this chapter.

11.4 LEARNING OBJECTIVE

11.4 | Define the multiplier effect and use it to calculate changes in equilibrium GDP.

The Multiplier Effect

To this point, we have seen that aggregate expenditure determines real GDP in the short run and how the economy adjusts if it is not in equilibrium. We have also seen that whenever aggregate expenditure changes, there will be a new level of equilibrium real GDP. In this section, we will look more closely at the effects of a change in aggregate expenditure on equilibrium real GDP. We begin the discussion with Figure 11-12, which illustrates the effects of an increase in planned investment spending. We assume that the economy starts in equilibrium at point *A*, at which real GDP is \$9.6 trillion. Firms then become more optimistic about their future profitability and increase spending on factories, machinery, and equipment by \$100 billion. This increase in investment spending shifts the *AE* line up by \$100 billion, from the dark tan line (AE_1) to the light tan line (AE_2). The new equilibrium occurs at point *B*, at which real GDP is \$10.0 trillion, which equals potential real GDP.

Notice that the initial \$100 billion increase in planned investment spending results in a \$400 billion increase in equilibrium real GDP. The increase in planned investment spending has had a *multiplied effect* on equilibrium real GDP. It is not only investment spending that will have this multiplied effect; any increase in *autonomous expenditure* will shift up the aggregate expenditure function and lead to a multiplied increase in equilibrium GDP. **Autonomous expenditure** does not depend on the level of GDP. In the aggregate expenditure model we have been using, planned investment spending, government spending, and net exports are all autonomous expenditures. Consumption actually has both an autonomous component, which does not depend on the level of GDP, and a nonautonomous—or *induced*—component that does depend on the level of GDP. For example, if households decide to spend more of their incomes—and save less—at every level of income, there will be an autonomous increase in consumption spending, and the aggregate expenditure function will shift up. If, however, real GDP increases and households increase their consumption spending, as indicated by the consumption function, the economy will move up the aggregate expenditure function, and the increase in consumption spending will be nonautonomous.

Autonomous expenditure An expenditure that does not depend on the level of GDP.

The ratio of the increase in equilibrium real GDP to the increase in autonomous expenditure is called the **multiplier**. The series of induced increases in consumption

Multiplier The increase in equilibrium real GDP divided by the increase in autonomous expenditure.

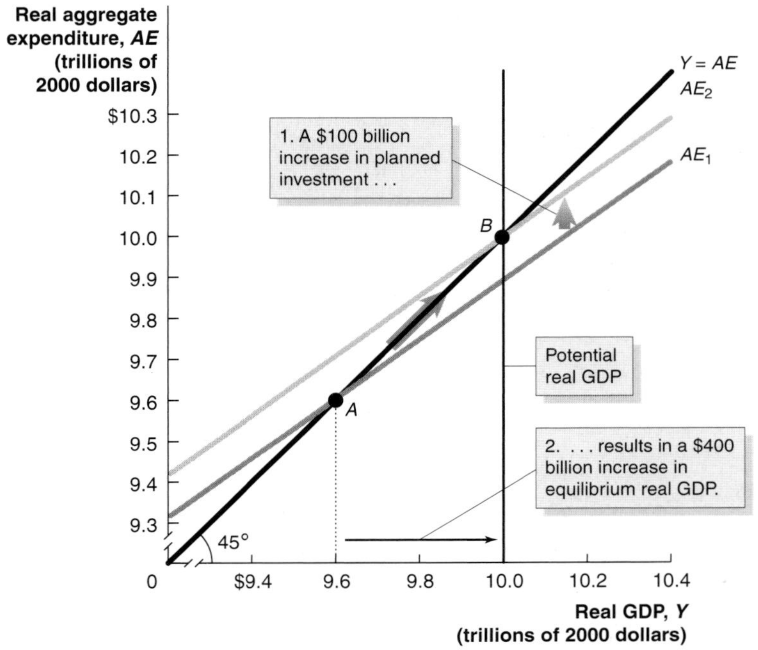

Figure 11-12

The Multiplier Effect

The economy begins at point *A*, at which equilibrium real GDP is \$9.6 trillion. A \$100 billion increase in planned investment shifts up aggregate expenditure from AE_1 to AE_2. The new equilibrium is at point *B*, where real GDP is \$10.0 trillion, which is potential real GDP. Because of the multiplier effect, a \$100 billion increase in investment results in a \$400 billion increase in equilibrium real GDP.

Multiplier effect The process by which an increase in autonomous expenditure leads to a larger increase in real GDP.

spending that results from an initial increase in autonomous expenditure is called the **multiplier effect**. The multiplier effect happens because an initial increase in autonomous expenditure will set off a series of increases in real GDP.

In Figure 11-12, we look more closely at the multiplier effect. Suppose the whole $100 billion increase in investment spending shown in the figure consists of firms buying additional factories and office buildings. Initially, this additional spending will cause the construction of factories and office buildings to increase by $100 billion, so GDP will also increase by $100 billion. Remember that increases in production result in equal increases in national income. So, this increase in real GDP of $100 billion is also an increase in national income of $100 billion. In this example, the income is received as wages and salaries by the employees of the construction firms, as profits by the owners of the firms, and so on. After receiving this additional income, these workers, managers, and owners will increase their consumption of cars, televisions, DVD players, and many other products. If the marginal propensity to consume (*MPC*) is 0.75, we know this increase in consumption spending will be $75 billion. This additional $75 billion in spending will cause the firms making the cars, televisions, and other products to increase production by $75 billion, so GDP will rise by $75 billion. This increase in GDP means national income has also increased by another $75 billion. This increased income will be received by the owners and employees of the firms producing the cars, televisions, and other products. These workers, managers, and owners in turn will increase their consumption spending, and the process of increasing production, income, and consumption will continue.

Eventually, the total increase in consumption will be $300 billion (we will soon show how we know this is true). This $300 billion increase in consumption combined with the initial $100 billion increase in investment spending will result in a total change in equilibrium GDP of $400 billion. Table 11-4 summarizes how changes in GDP and spending

TABLE 11-4

The Multiplier Effect in Action

	ADDITIONAL AUTONOMOUS EXPENDITURE (INVESTMENT)	ADDITIONAL INDUCED EXPENDITURE (CONSUMPTION)	TOTAL ADDITIONAL EXPENDITURE = TOTAL ADDITIONAL GDP
ROUND 1	$100 billion	$0	$100 billion
ROUND 2	0	75 billion	175 billion
ROUND 3	0	56 billion	231 billion
ROUND 4	0	42 billion	273 billion
ROUND 5	0	32 billion	305 billion
⋮	⋮	⋮	⋮
ROUND 10	0	8 billion	377 billion
⋮	⋮	⋮	⋮
ROUND 15	0	2 billion	395 billion
⋮	⋮	⋮	⋮
ROUND 19	0	1 billion	398 billion
⋮	⋮	⋮	⋮
n	0	0	$400 billion

caused by the initial \$100 billion increase in investment will result in equilibrium GDP rising by \$400 billion. We can think of the multiplier effect occurring in rounds of spending. In round 1, there is an increase of \$100 billion in autonomous expenditure—the \$100 billion in planned investment spending in our example—which causes GDP to rise by \$100 billion. In round 2, induced expenditure rises by \$75 billion (which equals the \$100 billion increase in real GDP in round 1 multiplied by the *MPC*). The \$75 billion in induced expenditure in round 2 causes a \$75 billion increase in real GDP, which leads to a \$56 billion increase in induced expenditure in round 3, and so on. The final column sums up the total increases in expenditure, which equal the total increase in GDP. In each round, the additional induced expenditure becomes smaller because the *MPC* is less than 1. By round 10, additional induced expenditure is only \$8 billion, and the total increase in GDP from the beginning of the process is \$377 billion. By round 19, the process is almost complete: Additional induced expenditure is only about \$1 billion, and the total increase in GDP is \$398 billion. Eventually, the process will be finished, although we cannot say precisely how many spending rounds it will take, so we simply label the last round "*n*" rather than give it a specific number.

We can calculate the value of the multiplier in our example by dividing the increase in equilibrium real GDP by the increase in autonomous expenditure:

$$\frac{\Delta Y}{\Delta I} = \frac{\text{Change in real GDP}}{\text{Change in investment spending}} = \frac{\$400 \text{ billion}}{\$100 \text{ billion}} = 4.$$

With a multiplier of 4, each increase in autonomous expenditure of \$1 will result in an increase in equilibrium GDP of \$4.

Making the Connection

The Multiplier in Reverse: The Great Depression of the 1930s

An increase in autonomous expenditure causes an increase in equilibrium real GDP, but the reverse is also true: A decrease in autonomous expenditure causes a decrease in real GDP. Many Americans became aware of this fact in the 1930s when reductions in autonomous expenditure were magnified by the multiplier into the largest decline in real GDP in U.S. history.

The multiplier effect contributed to the very high levels of unemployment during the Great Depression.

In August 1929, the economy reached a business cycle peak, and a downturn in production began. In October, the stock market crashed, destroying billions of dollars of wealth and increasing pessimism among households and firms. Both consumption spending and planned investment spending declined. The passage by the U.S. Congress of the Smoot–Hawley Tariff in June 1930 helped set off a trade war that reduced net exports. A series of banking crises that began in fall 1930 limited the ability of households and firms to finance consumption and investment. As aggregate expenditure declined, many firms experienced declining sales and began to lay off workers. Falling levels of production and income induced further declines in consumption spending, which led to further cutbacks in production and employment, leading to further declines in income, and so on, in a downward spiral. The following table shows the severity of the economic downturn by contrasting the business cycle peak of 1929 with the business cycle trough of 1933.

YEAR	CONSUMPTION	INVESTMENT	NET EXPORTS	REAL GDP	UNEMPLOYMENT RATE
1929	\$661 billion	\$91.3 billion	–\$9.4 billion	\$865 billion	3.2%
1933	\$541 billion	\$17.0 billion	–\$10.2 billion	\$636 billion	24.9%

Note: The values are in 2000 dollars.
Sources: U.S. Bureau of Economic Analysis; and U.S. Bureau of Labor Statistics.

We can use a 45°-line diagram to illustrate the multiplier effect working in reverse during these years. The economy was at potential real GDP in 1929 before the declines in aggregate expenditure began. Declining consumption, planned investment, and net exports shifted the aggregate expenditure function down from AE_{1929} to AE_{1933}, reducing equilibrium real GDP from \$865 billion in 1929 to \$636 billion in 1933. The depth and length of this economic downturn led to its being labeled the Great Depression.

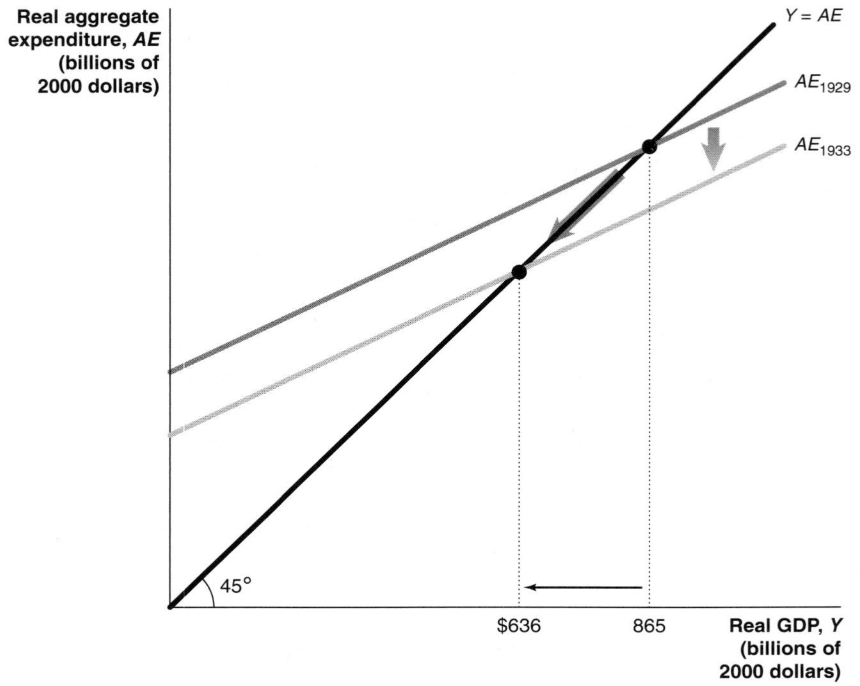

The severity of the Depression meant bankruptcy for thousands of firms. Even firms that survived experienced sharp declines in sales. By 1933, production at U.S. Steel had declined by 90 percent, and production at General Motors had declined by more than 75 percent. High rates of unemployment forced many families into poverty and a daily struggle for survival. Recovery from the business cycle trough in 1933 was slow. Real GDP did not regain its 1929 level until 1936, and a growing labor force meant that the unemployment rate did not fall below 10 percent until the United States entered World War II in 1941.

YOUR TURN: Test your understanding by doing related problem 4.9 on page 386 at the end of this chapter.

A Formula for the Multiplier

Table 11-4 shows that during the multiplier process, each round of increases in consumption is smaller than in the previous round, so eventually, the increases will come to an end, and we will have a new macroeconomic equilibrium. But how do we know that when we add all the increases in GDP, the total will be \$400 billion? We can show this is true by first writing out the total change in equilibrium GDP:

> The total change in equilibrium real GDP equals the initial increase in planned investment spending = \$100 billion
>
> *Plus* the first induced increase in consumption = $MPC \times \$100$ billion
>
> *Plus* the second induced increase in consumption = $MPC \times (MPC \times \$100 \text{ billion}) = MPC^2 \times \$100$ billion
>
> *Plus* the third induced increase in consumption = $MPC \times (MPC^2 \times \$100 \text{ billion}) = MPC^3 \times \$100$ billion

Plus the fourth induced increase in consumption = $MPC \times (MPC^3 \times \$100 \text{ billion}) = MPC^4 \times \$100 \text{ billion}$

And so on . . .

Or:

$$\text{Total change in GDP} = \$100 \text{ billion} + MPC \times \$100 \text{ billion} + MPC^2 \times \$100 \text{ billion} + MPC^3 \times \$100 \text{ billion} + MPC^4 \times \$100 \text{ billion} + \ldots$$

where the ellipsis (. . .) indicates that the expression contains an infinite number of similar terms.

If we factor out the $100 billion from each expression, we have:

$$\text{Total change in GDP} = \$100 \text{ billion} \times (1 + MPC + MPC^2 + MPC^3 + MPC^4 + \ldots)$$

Mathematicians have shown that an expression like the one in the parenthesis sums to:

$$\frac{1}{1 - MPC}.$$

In this case, the *MPC* is equal to 0.75. So, we can now calculate that the change in equilibrium GDP = $1 billion × [1/(1 – 0.75)] = $100 billion × 4 = $400 billion. We have also derived a general formula for the multiplier:

$$\text{Multiplier} = \frac{\text{Change in equilibrium real GDP}}{\text{Change in autonomous expenditure}} = \frac{1}{1 - MPC}.$$

In this case, the multiplier is 1/(1 – 0.75) or 4, which means that for each additional $1 of autonomous spending, equilibrium GDP will increase by $4. A $100 billion increase in planned investment spending results in a $400 billion increase in equilibrium GDP. Notice that the value of the multiplier depends on the value of the *MPC*. In particular, the larger the value of the *MPC*, the larger the value of the multiplier. For example, if the *MPC* were 0.9 instead of 0.75, the value of the multiplier would increase from 4 to 1/(1 – 0.9) = 10.

Summarizing the Multiplier Effect

You should note four key points about the multiplier effect:

1. The multiplier effect occurs both when autonomous expenditure increases and when it decreases. For example, with an *MPC* of 0.75, a *decrease* in planned investment of $100 billion will lead to a *decrease* in equilibrium income of $400 billion.

2. The multiplier effect makes the economy more sensitive to changes in autonomous expenditure than it would otherwise be. When firms decided to cut back their spending on information technology following the Internet and telecommunications busts of 2001, the decision did not only affect firms such as Cisco that made computer and telecommunications equipment. Because the initial decline in investment spending set off a series of declines in production, income, and spending, firms such as automobile dealerships and furniture stores, which are far removed from the computer and telecommunications industries, also experienced sales declines.

3. The larger the *MPC*, the larger the value of the multiplier. With an *MPC* of 0.75, the multiplier is 4, but with an *MPC* of 0.50, the multiplier is only 2. This inverse relationship between the value of the *MPC* and the value of the multiplier holds true because the larger the *MPC*, the more additional consumption takes place after each rise in income during the multiplier process.

4. The formula for the multiplier, 1/(1 – *MPC*), is oversimplified because it ignores some real-world complications, such as the effect that an increasing GDP can have on imports, inflation, and interest rates. These effects combine to cause the simple formula to overstate the true value of the multiplier. Beginning in Chapter 12, we will start to take into account these real-world complications.

Solved Problem | 11-4

Using the Multiplier Formula

Use the information in the table to answer the following questions.

REAL GDP (Y)	CONSUMPTION (C)	PLANNED INVESTMENT (I)	GOVERNMENT PURCHASES (G)	NET EXPORTS (NX)
$8,000	$6,900	$1,000	$1,000	–$500
9,000	7,700	1,000	1,000	–500
10,000	8,500	1,000	1,000	–500
11,000	9,300	1,000	1,000	–500
12,000	10,100	1,000	1,000	–500

Note: The values are in billions of 2000 dollars.

a. What is the equilibrium level of real GDP?

b. What is the *MPC*?

c. Suppose government purchases increase by $200 billion. What will be the new equilibrium level of real GDP? Use the multiplier formula to determine your answer.

SOLVING THE PROBLEM:

Step 1: Review the chapter material. This problem is about the multiplier process, so you may want to review the section "The Multiplier Effect," which begins on page 371.

Step 2: Determine equilibrium real GDP. Just as in Solved Problem 11-2 on page 357, we can find macroeconomic equilibrium by calculating the level of planned aggregate expenditure for each level of real GDP.

REAL GDP (Y)	CONSUMPTION (C)	PLANNED INVESTMENT (I)	GOVERNMENT PURCHASES (G)	NET EXPORTS (NX)	PLANNED AGGREGATE EXPENDITURE (AE)
$8,000	$6,900	$1,000	$1,000	–$500	$8,400
9,000	7,700	1,000	1,000	–500	9,200
10,000	8,500	1,000	1,000	–500	10,000
11,000	9,300	1,000	1,000	–500	10,800
12,000	10,100	1,000	1,000	–500	11,600

We can see that macroeconomic equilibrium will occur when real GDP equals $10,000 billion.

Step 3: Calculate *MPC*.

$$MPC = \frac{\Delta C}{\Delta Y}.$$

In this case,

$$MPC = \frac{\$800 \text{ billion}}{\$1{,}000 \text{ billion}} = 0.8.$$

Step 4: Use the multiplier formula to calculate the new equilibrium level of real GDP. We could find the new level of equilibrium real GDP by constructing a new table with government purchases increased from $1,000 to $1,200. But the multiplier allows us to calculate the answer directly. In this case:

$$\text{Multiplier} = \frac{1}{1 - MPC} = \frac{1}{1 - 0.8} = 5.$$

So:

Change in equilibrium real GDP = Change in autonomous expenditure × 5.

Or:

Change in equilibrium real GDP = \$200 billion × 5 = \$1,000 billion.

Therefore:

The new level of equilibrium GDP = \$10,000 billion + \$1,000 billion = \$11,000 billion.

YOUR TURN: For more practice, do related problem 4.3 on page 386 at the end of this chapter.

>> End Solved Problem 11-4

11.5 LEARNING OBJECTIVE

11.5 | Understand the relationship between the aggregate demand curve and aggregate expenditure.

The Aggregate Demand Curve

When demand for a product increases, firms usually respond by increasing production, but they are also likely to increase prices. Similarly, when demand falls, production falls, but often, prices also fall. We would expect, then, that an increase or a decrease in aggregate expenditure would affect not just real GDP but also the *price level.* So far, we haven't taken into account the effect of changes in the price level on the components of aggregate expenditure. In fact, as we will see, increases in the price level cause aggregate expenditure to fall, and decreases in the price level cause aggregate expenditure to rise. There are three main reasons for this inverse relationship between changes in the price level and changes in aggregate expenditure. We discussed the first two reasons earlier in this chapter when considering the factors that determine consumption and net exports:

- A rising price level decreases consumption by decreasing the real value of household wealth; a falling price level has the reverse effect.
- If the price level in the United States rises relative to the price levels in other countries, U.S. exports will become relatively more expensive, and foreign imports will become relatively less expensive, causing net exports to fall. A falling price level in the United States has the reverse effect.
- When prices rise, firms and households need more money to finance buying and selling. If the central bank (the Federal Reserve in the United States) does not increase the money supply, the result will be an increase in the interest rate. We will analyze in more detail why this happens in Chapter 13. As we discussed earlier in this chapter, at a higher interest rate, investment spending falls as firms borrow less money to build new factories or to install new machinery and equipment, and households borrow less money to buy new houses. A falling price level has the reverse effect. Other things equal, interest rates will fall and investment spending will rise.

We can now incorporate the effect of a change in the price level into the basic aggregate expenditure model in which equilibrium real GDP is determined by the intersection of the aggregate expenditure (*AE*) line and the 45° line. Remember that we measure the price level as an index number with a value of 100 in the base year. If the price level rises from, say, 100 to 103, consumption, planned investment, and net exports will all fall, causing the *AE* line to shift down on the 45°-line diagram. The *AE* line shifts down because with higher prices, less spending will occur in the economy at every level of GDP. Panel (a) of Figure 11-13 shows that the downward shift of the *AE* line results in a lower level of equilibrium real GDP.

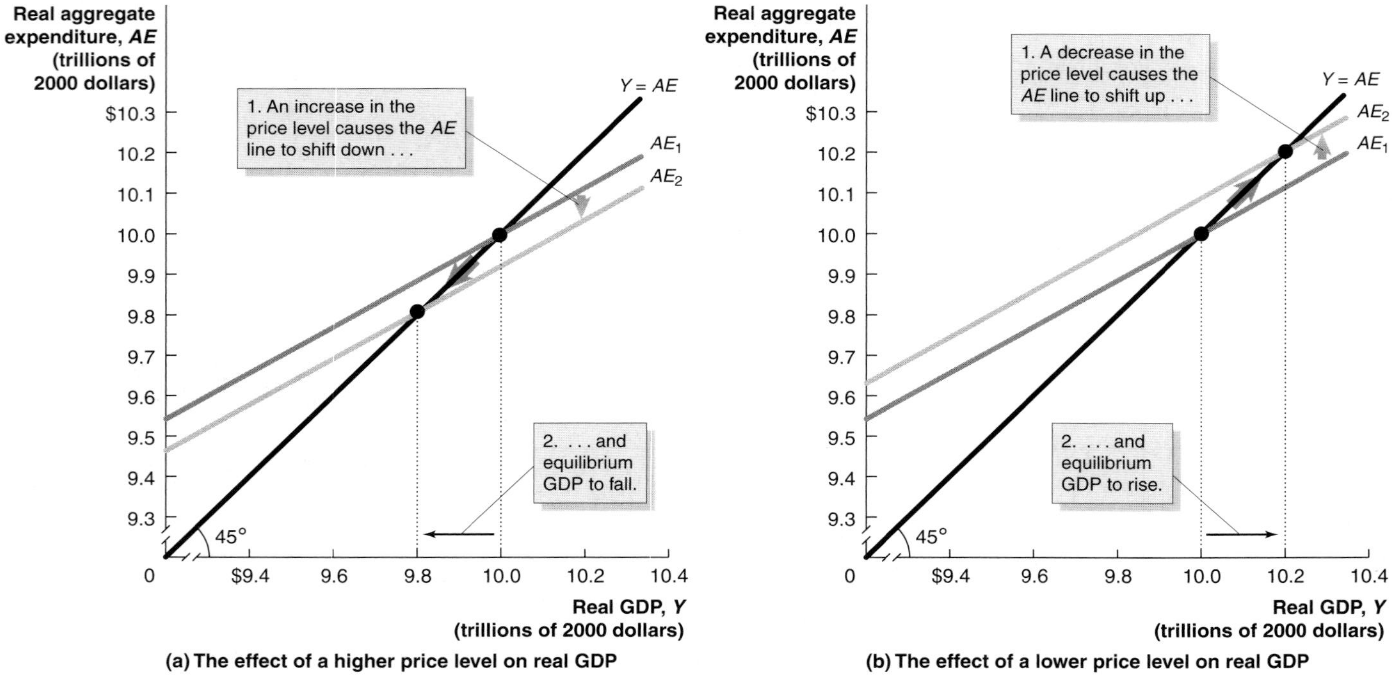

Figure 11-13 | The Effect of a Change in the Price Level on Real GDP

In panel (a), an increase in the price level results in declining consumption, planned investment, and net exports and causes the aggregate expenditure line to shift down from AE_1 to AE_2. As a result, equilibrium real GDP declines from $10.0 trillion to $9.8 trillion. In panel (b), a decrease in the price level results in rising consumption, planned investment, and net exports and causes the aggregate expenditure line to shift up from AE_1 to AE_2. As a result, equilibrium real GDP increases from $10.0 trillion to $10.2 trillion.

If the price level falls from, say, 100 to 97, then investment, consumption, and net exports would all rise. As panel (b) of Figure 11-13 shows, the *AE* line would shift up, which would cause equilibrium real GDP to increase.

Aggregate demand curve A curve that shows the relationship between the price level and the level of planned aggregate expenditure in the economy, holding constant all other factors that affect aggregate expenditure.

Figure 11-14 summarizes the effect of changes in the price level on real GDP. The table shows the combinations of price level and real GDP from Figure 11-13. The figure plots the numbers from the table. In the figure, the price level is measured on the vertical axis, and real GDP is measured on the horizontal axis. The relationship shown in Figure 11-14 between the price level and the level of planned aggregate expenditure is known as the **aggregate demand curve**, or *AD* curve.

Figure 11-14

The Aggregate Demand Curve

The aggregate demand curve, labeled *AD*, shows the relationship between the price level and the level of planned aggregate expenditure in the economy. When the price level is 97, real GDP is $10.2 trillion. An increase in the price level to 100 causes consumption, investment, and net exports to fall, which reduces real GDP to $10.0 trillion.

Price level	Equilibrium real GDP
97	$10.2 trillion
100	10.0 trillion
103	9.8 trillion

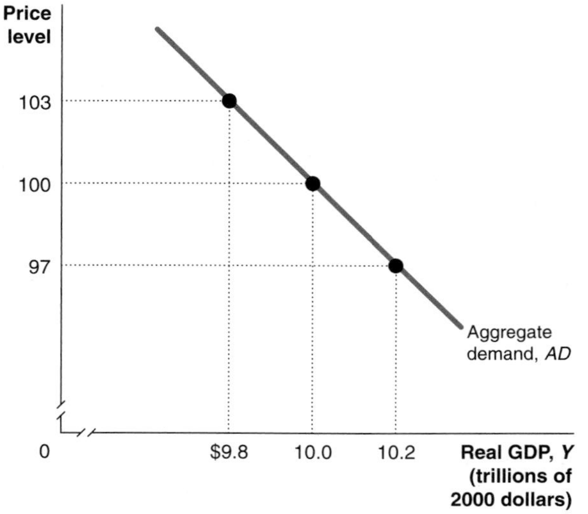

Continued from page 347

Economics in YOUR Life!

At the beginning of this chapter, we asked you to suppose that you work part time assembling desktop computers for a large computer company. You have learned that consumer confidence in the economy has fallen and that many households expect their future income to be dramatically less than their current income. Should you be concerned about losing your job? We have seen in this chapter that if consumers expect their future incomes to decline, they will cut their consumption spending, and consumption spending is about 70 percent of aggregate expenditure. So, there is some chance that consumption spending will fall, which would reduce aggregate expenditures and GDP. If the economy does move into a recession, spending on computers by households and firms may slow down, which could reduce your firm's sales and possibly cost you a job. Before you panic, though, keep in mind that surveys of consumer confidence do not have a good track record in predicting recessions, so you may not have to move back in with your parents after all.

Conclusion

In this chapter, we learned a key macroeconomic idea: In the short run, the level of GDP is determined mainly by the level of aggregate expenditure. When economists forecast changes in GDP, they do so by forecasting changes in the four components of aggregate expenditure. We constructed an aggregate demand curve by taking into account the effect on aggregate expenditure of changes in the price level.

But our story is incomplete. In the next chapter, we will analyze the *aggregate supply curve.* Then, we will use the aggregate demand curve and the aggregate supply curve to show how equilibrium real GDP *and* the equilibrium price level are simultaneously determined.

We also need to discuss the role the financial system and government policy play in determining real GDP and the price level in the short run. We will cover these important topics in the next three chapters. Before moving on, read *An Inside Look* on the next page, which discusses the factors causing U.S. GDP to change during the first quarter of 2007.

An Inside LOOK

Consumer Spending and Business Inventories Send Positive Signals about GDP

WALL STREET JOURNAL, APRIL 28, 2007

Economy Slows but May Hold Seeds of Growth

The U.S. economy started 2007 with its weakest growth in four years, as a housing slump continued to hobble expansion. But consumers spent freely and business investment picked up. . . .

The Commerce Department reported that real gross domestic product, the broadest measure of economic activity adjusted for inflation, grew at a seasonally adjusted annual rate of 1.3% in the first three months of the year. That was down sharply from growth of 2.5% in the fourth quarter of 2006 . . . Residential investment, a proxy for the housing market, was the biggest drag on first-quarter growth, falling at an annualized rate of 17% and slashing one percentage point off GDP. . . .

a Among the more encouraging signs, the GDP report found consumer spending, which accounts for about 70% of economic activity, grew at a 3.8% annual rate in the first quarter. That is down from a 4.2% rate in the prior quarter, but higher than the 3.2% rate for all of 2006. The rise in business investment—up 2.0% compared with a decline of 3.1% last quarter—was a surprise given recent reports that suggested businesses are taking a more cautious outlook and cutting back investments accordingly. Another positive sign: Businesses continued to slow the rate of inventory accumulation, which could foretell an increase in production down the line.

That view was bolstered by news that the dollar declined again Friday on foreign-exchange markets, a trend that should give U.S. exports an edge and thus help lift factory production. . . .

The first-quarter GDP report was "probably the low point in the cycle," said Nariman Behravesh, chief economist at consulting firm Global Insight. "It suggests that in fact we may be setting the stage for a very slight rebound this quarter." Mr. Behravesh believes the economy will be growing at a rate of close to 3% by the end of the year.

Still, the economy faces plenty of lingering challenges. Housing continues to be a significant drag, with residential investment falling for six consecutive quarters. And falling house prices could eventually affect consumers' willingness and ability to spend. . . .

Also, many economists expect some slowdown in the buoyant job market, which has helped consumers by pushing up wages. Sharp declines in residential investment, for example, should ultimately translate into more job losses in housing construction.

There are some signs consumers are losing steam. In a separate report yesterday, the Reuters/University of Michigan consumer sentiment index fell 1.3 points to 87.1 in April, the third-consecutive monthly decline and the lowest level in seven months. High gasoline prices and the housing troubles weighed on consumers, the survey reported, even as some felt optimistic about rising wages and the stock market's recent rally. . . .

b One puzzling aspect of yesterday's report was exports, which declined 1.2% in the first three months of the year, compared with a rise of 10.6% in the fourth quarter of last year. Exports have been a driver of the U.S. economy in recent months, thanks to a weakened dollar and growth throughout Europe and Asia. Many economists viewed yesterday's exports decline as a fluke, which will either be revised upward or bounce back next quarter. Compared with the first quarter of last year, exports were up 5.5%. "The important thing is to have continued growth around the world," said U.S. Commerce Secretary Carlos M. Gutierrez. "We've got a good thing going with exports, and we want to keep it going."

The strong global economy is one reason economists are especially upbeat about the prospect for corporate profits. U.S. companies in recent weeks have reported stronger-than-expected first-quarter earnings, often because of growing overseas operations that made up for sluggishness at home. . . .

Stronger growth in places such as Europe, Japan and China does more than just add to U.S. companies' foreign sales. The change in relative growth rates has also pushed up the value of currencies such as the euro, as investors attracted by improved prospects outside the U.S. put more money into foreign securities. That provides U.S. companies with an added boost when they convert their foreign sales into dollars. Relative to the currencies of U.S. trading partners, the dollar is down about 3% from a year earlier. . . .

Separately, the Labor Department reported Friday that its employment-cost index increased 0.8% in the first three months of the year, compared with gains of 0.9% in the previous three quarters. This was due mostly to a tiny increase in benefits costs as rising stock prices enabled firms to make smaller contributions to defined-benefit pension plans. Wages and salaries still rose briskly.

c Economists also have been watching how much businesses boost inventories. Businesses continued to slow the rate of inventory accumulation for the second straight quarter, trimming 0.3 percentage points from growth, after knocking 1.16 points off growth in the fourth quarter. That could actually bode well for future GDP: By keeping a tight rein on inventories, firms are less likely to respond to a sales shortfall with big cuts in production and employment. And if sales accelerate, they are more likely to boost output.

Source: Connor Dougherty and Mark Whitehouse, "Economy Slows but May Hold Seeds of Growth," Wall Street Journal, *April 28, 2007, p. A1.*

Key Points in the Article

This article discusses a Department of Commerce report on real GDP growth in the United States during the first quarter of 2007. The report indicated that real GDP grew just 1.3 percent in that quarter—far less than economists had expected and far less than the 2.5 percent growth that the U.S. economy had achieved in the fourth quarter of 2006. Economists attributed the disappointing report to a 17 percent drop in residential construction due to a slowdown in the U.S. housing market. Nonetheless, economists were encouraged by strong consumer and business investment spending, which together comprise over 85 percent of aggregate expenditures in the U.S. economy. The article also discusses a surprise in the report: a decline in exports despite a fall in the foreign exchange value of the U.S. dollar. Finally, the article explains that economists were encouraged by the slow growth in business inventories.

Analyzing the News

a The Commerce Department report indicated that consumer expenditure grew by a respectable 3.8 percent annual rate in the first quarter of 2007. This is important for overall growth in the U.S. economy because consumption expenditure comprises over 70 percent of aggregate expenditure. So, even small changes in consumption can have a significant effect on real GDP. The report also indicated that business investment expenditure rose at an unexpectedly high 2.0 percent annual rate. This is important for overall growth in the U.S. economy because, although business investment expenditure comprises only about 16 percent of aggregate expenditure, it is typically volatile from quarter to quarter. Moreover, changes in business investment expenditure often lead to additional changes in consumer expenditure, income, and employment.

b U.S. exports fell by 1.2 percent in the first quarter of 2007. This fact puzzled economists because the foreign exchange value of the U.S. dollar had fallen in recent months, and a relatively cheaper U.S. dollar lowers the prices U.S. goods sell for overseas. So, U.S. exports should have risen, as in the previous quarter when they rose by 10.6 percent. Nonetheless, most economists remain confident that exports will increase in future quarters, as the economies of the major trading partners of the United States continue to grow. This is because when the growth rate of GDP in foreign countries exceeds that of the United States, U.S. exports and, therefore, aggregate expenditure tend to rise.

c Economists were encouraged by the slow growth of business inventories. This is because, as you read in this chapter, when firms' sales drop unexpectedly, they accumulate (unplanned) inventories. In response, they typically reduce production, which causes income and employment to fall. All else equal, unplanned increases in inventories are followed by slower growth in real GDP in the short run. This relationship is shown in the figure, where the economy begins in equilibrium at point *E*, and then aggregate expenditure falls from AE_1 to AE_2. Because planned aggregate expenditure is now less than Y_1, unplanned inventories increase. In response, firms decrease production, income, and employment until the economy reaches equilibrium at Y_2. (point *A*). Therefore, the fact that in the first quarter of 2007, firms slowed the rate at which they accumulated inventories was good news.

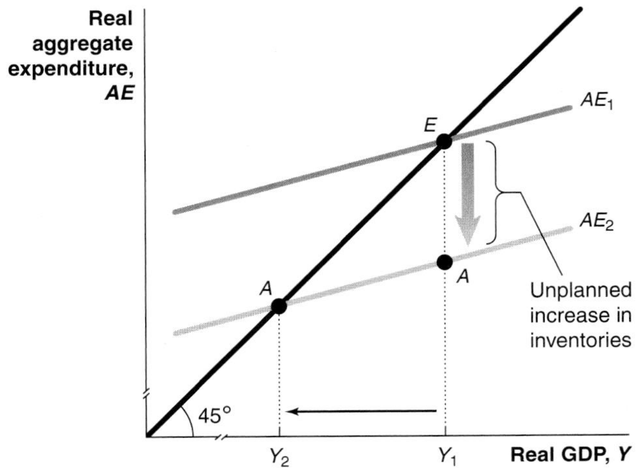

A decrease in aggregate expenditure causes an unplanned increase in inventories and a decrease in real GDP.

Thinking Critically

1. Suppose the U.S. government mailed every taxpayer in the United States a check for $500, which taxpayers did not have to repay. What effect would this tax policy have on U.S. aggregate expenditure?
2. Suppose that Congress enacts a law prohibiting imports from China. What will be the effect of this law on aggregate expenditure and equilibrium real GDP? Does your answer depend on how the governments of other countries react to the law? Briefly explain.

Key Terms

Aggregate demand curve, p. 378
Aggregate expenditure (*AE*), p. 348
Aggregate expenditure model, p. 348
Autonomous expenditure, p. 371
Cash flow, p. 359
Consumption function, p. 353
Inventories, p. 349
Marginal propensity to consume (*MPC*), p. 353
Marginal propensity to save (*MPS*), p. 356
Multiplier, p. 371
Multiplier effect, p. 372

11.1 LEARNING OBJECTIVE 11.1 | Understand how macroeconomic equilibrium is determined in the aggregate expenditure model, **pages 348–351.**

The Aggregate Expenditure Model

Summary

Aggregate expenditure (*AE*) is the total amount of spending in the economy. The **aggregate expenditure model** focuses on the relationship between total spending and real GDP in the short run, assuming that the price level is constant. In any particular year, the level of GDP is determined by the level of total spending, or aggregate expenditure, in the economy. The four components of aggregate expenditure are consumption (*C*), planned investment (*I*), government purchases (*G*), and net exports (*NX*). When aggregate expenditure is greater than GDP, there is an unplanned decrease in **inventories**, which are goods that have been produced but not yet sold, and GDP and total employment will increase. When aggregate expenditure is less than GDP, there is an unplanned increase in inventories, and GDP and total employment will decline. When aggregate expenditure is equal to GDP, firms will sell what they expected to sell, production and employment will be unchanged, and the economy will be in macroeconomic equilibrium.

myeconlab Get Ahead of the Curve Visit www.myeconlab.com to complete these exercises online and get instant feedback.

Review Questions

1.1 What is the main reason for changes in GDP in the short run?

1.2 What are inventories? What usually happens to inventories at the beginning of a recession? At the beginning of an expansion?

Problems and Applications

1.3 Into which category of aggregate expenditures would each of the following transactions fall?
   a. The Jones family buys a new car.
   b. The San Diego Unified School District buys 12 new school busses.
   c. The Jones family buys a new house.
   d. A consumer in Japan orders a computer online from Dell.
   e. Prudential Insurance Company purchases 250 new computers from Dell.

1.4 Suppose Apple plans to produce 16.2 million iPods this year. It expects to sell 16.1 million and add 100,000 to the inventories in its stores.
   a. Suppose that at the end of the year, Apple has sold 15.9 million iPods. What was Apple's planned investment spending? What was Apple's actual investment spending?
   b. Now suppose that at the end of the year, Apple has sold 16.3 million iPods. What was Apple's planned investment spending? What was Apple's actual investment spending?

1.5 In the second quarter of 2005, business inventories declined by $10 billion. What does this information tell us about the relationship between aggregate expenditure and GDP during the second quarter of 2005?

1.6 Suppose you read that business inventories increased dramatically last month. What does this tell you about the state of the economy? Would your answer be affected by whether the increase in inventories was taking place at the end of a recession or the end of an expansion? Briefly explain.

>> End Learning Objective 11.1

11.2 LEARNING OBJECTIVE 11.2 | Discuss the determinants of the four components of aggregate expenditure and define the marginal propensity to consume and the marginal propensity to save, **pages 351–363.**

Determining the Level of Aggregate Expenditure in the Economy

Summary

The five determinants of consumption are current disposable income, household wealth, expected future income, the price level, and the interest rate. The **consumption function** is the relationship between consumption and disposable income. The **marginal propensity to consume (*MPC*)** is the change in consumption divided by the change in disposable income. The **marginal propensity to save (*MPS*)** is the change in saving divided by the change in disposable income. The determinants of planned investment are expectations of future profitability, the real interest rate, taxes, and **cash flow**, which is the difference between the cash revenues received by a firm and the cash spending by the firm. Government purchases include spending by the federal government and by local and state governments for goods and services. Government purchases do not include *transfer payments*, such as Social Security payments by the federal government or pension payments by local governments to retired police officers and firefighters. The three determinants of net exports are the price level in the United States relative to the price levels in other countries, the growth rate of GDP in the United States relative to the growth rates of GDP in other countries, and the exchange rate between the dollar and other currencies.

myeconlab Get Ahead of the Curve Visit www.myeconlab.com to complete these exercises online and get instant feedback.

Review Questions

2.1 What are the four categories of aggregate expenditure? Give an example of each.

2.2 What are the five main determinants of consumption spending? Which of these is the most important?

2.3 Compare what happened to real investment between 1979 and 2006 with what happened to real consumption.

Problems and Applications

2.4 **(Related to the *Chapter Opener* on page 346)** Suppose a major U.S. furniture manufacturer is forecasting demand for its products during the next year. How will the forecast be affected by each of the following?

a. A decrease in consumer spending in the economy
b. An increase in real interest rates
c. An increase in the exchange rate value of the U.S. dollar
d. A decrease in planned investment spending in the economy

2.5 Many people have difficulty borrowing as much money as they would like, even if they are confident that their incomes in the future will be high enough to pay it back easily. For example, many students in medical school will earn high incomes after they graduate and become physicians. If they could, they would probably borrow now in order to live more comfortably while in medical school and pay the loans back out of their higher future income. Unfortunately, banks are usually reluctant to make loans to people who currently have low incomes, even if there is a good chance their incomes will be much higher in the future. If people could always borrow as much as they would like, would you expect consumption to become more or less sensitive to current income? Why?

2.6 An economics student raises the following objection: "The textbook said that a higher interest rate lowers investment, but this doesn't make sense. I know that if I can get a higher interest rate, I am certainly going to invest more in my savings account." Do you agree with this reasoning?

2.7 **(Related to the *Making the Connection* on page 359)** We can use Figure 11-4 on page 358 and the graph in the *Making the Connection* on page 359 to compare movements in real investment between 1990 and 2006 with movements in spending on information processing equipment and software. In 1990, spending on information processing equipment and software was roughly what fraction of real investment? How had this fraction changed by 2006? Compare movements in real investment with movements in spending on information processing equipment and software during the recessions of 1990–1991 and 2001.

2.8 Unemployed workers receive unemployment insurance payments from the government. Does the existence of unemployment insurance make it likely that consumption will fluctuate more or fluctuate less over the business cycle than it would in the absence of unemployment insurance? Briefly explain.

2.9 Explain whether you agree or disagree with the following argument: "Transfer payments should be counted as part of government purchases when we calculate aggregate expenditure. After all, spending is spending. Why does it matter whether the spending is for an aircraft carrier or for a Social Security payment to a retired person?"

2.10 Suppose we drop the assumption that net exports do not depend on real GDP. Draw a graph with the value of net exports on the vertical axis and the value of real GDP on the horizontal axis. Now, add a line representing the relationship between net exports and real GDP. Briefly explain why you drew the graph the way you did.

2.11 **(Related to *Solved Problem 11-2* on page 357)** Fill in the blanks in the table in the next column. Assume for simplicity that taxes are zero.

NATIONAL INCOME AND REAL GDP (*Y*)	CONSUMPTION (*C*)	SAVING (*S*)	MARGINAL PROPENSITY TO CONSUME (*MPC*)	MARGINAL PROPENSITY TO SAVE (*MPS*)
$9,000	$8,000		—	—
10,000	8,750			
11,000	9,500			
12,000	10,250			
13,000	11,000			

>> End Learning Objective 11.2

11.3 LEARNING OBJECTIVE 11.3 | Use a 45°-line diagram to illustrate macroeconomic equilibrium, **pages 363–370.**

Graphing Macroeconomic Equilibrium

Summary

The 45°-line diagram shows all the points where aggregate expenditure equals real GDP. On the 45°-line diagram, macroeconomic equilibrium occurs where the line representing the aggregate expenditure function crosses the 45° line. The economy is in recession when the aggregate expenditure line intersects the 45° line at a level of GDP that is below potential GDP. Numerically, macroeconomic equilibrium occurs when:

Consumption + Planned investment +
Government purchases + Net exports = GDP.

Review Questions

3.1 Use a 45°-line diagram to illustrate macroeconomic equilibrium. Make sure your diagram shows the aggregate expenditure function and the level of equilibrium real GDP and that your axes are properly labeled.

3.2 What is the macroeconomic consequence if firms accumulate large amounts of unplanned inventory at the beginning of a recession?

3.3 What is the difference between aggregate expenditure and consumption spending?

Problems and Applications

3.4 At point *A* in the following graph, is planned aggregate expenditure greater than, equal to, or less than GDP? What about at point *B*? At point *C*? For points *A* and *C*, indicate the vertical distance that measures the unintended change in inventories.

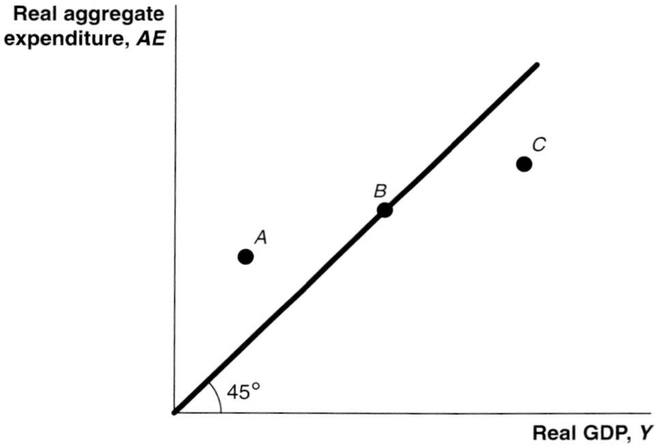

3.5 Is it possible for the economy to be in macroeconomic equilibrium at a level of real GDP that is greater than the potential level of real GDP? Illustrate using a 45°-line diagram.

3.6 **(Related to the *Making the Connection* on page 367)** In a Federal Reserve Board publication, the following observation was made: "The impact of inventory increases on the business cycle depends upon whether they are planned or unplanned." Do you agree? Briefly explain.

3.7 An article in *BusinessWeek* observes the following: "A further ebbing in the inventory drawdown is probably adding to GDP growth this quarter." What does the article mean by "inventory drawdown"? What component of aggregate expenditure would be affected by an inventory drawdown? Why would this add to GDP growth?

Source: James C. Cooper and Kathleen Madigan, "Forward Spin from a Backward Glance at GDP," *BusinessWeek*, April 29, 2002.

3.8 In each of the following situations, indicate what happens to the firm's inventories and whether the firm will be likely to increase or decrease its production in the future.
  a. General Electric expected to sell 120,000 microwaves during the current month but actually sold 100,000.
  b. Ford expected to sell 80,000 Explorers during the current month but actually sold 90,000.

3.9 In November 2006, U.S. exports increased to $124.76 billion from $123.67 billion in October. U.S. imports increased to $183 billion from $182.47 billion in October. An article in the *Wall Street Journal* argued that these statistics "could mean a boost for the economy." Briefly explain the author's reasoning.

Source: Jeff Bater, "U.S. Trade Gap Narrowed to $58.2 Billion in November," *Wall Street Journal*, January 10, 2007.

3.10 **(Related to the *Don't Let This Happen to You!* on page 369)** Briefly explain whether you agree with the following argument: "The equilibrium level of GDP is determined by the level of aggregate expenditure. Therefore, GDP will decline only if households decide to spend less on goods and services."

3.11 An article in the *New York Times* makes the following observation:

> Business spending is a powerful force. It can lift an economy when companies invest in machinery, software, office buildings, factories, trucks, aircraft and all the other tools used in the production of goods and services—or sink an economy when companies cut back.

What does the article mean by "business spending"? How can business spending "lift an economy" or "sink" it? Use a 45°-line diagram to illustrate your answer.

Source: Louis Uchitelle and Jennifer Bayot, "Business Spending Helps to Offset Lag in Refinancing," *New York Times*, August 9, 2003.

3.12 **(Related to *Solved Problem 11-3* on page 370)** Fill in the missing values in the following table. Assume that the value of the *MPC* does not change as real GDP changes.

REAL GDP (*Y*)	CONSUMPTION (*C*)	PLANNED INVESTMENT (*I*)	GOVERNMENT PURCHASES (*G*)	NET EXPORTS (*NX*)	PLANNED AGGREGATE EXPENDITURE (*AE*)	UNPLANNED CHANGE IN INVENTORIES
$9,000	$7,600	$1,200	$1,200	–$400		
10,000	8,400	1,200	1,200	–400		
11,000		1,200	1,200	–400		
12,000		1,200	1,200	–400		
13,000		1,200	1,200	–400		

  a. What is the value of the *MPC*?
  b. What is the value of equilibrium real GDP?

>> End Learning Objective 11.3

11.4 LEARNING OBJECTIVE 11.4 | Define the multiplier effect and use it to calculate changes in equilibrium GDP, **pages 371–377.**

The Multiplier Effect

Summary

Autonomous expenditure is expenditure that does not depend on the level of GDP. An autonomous change is a change in expenditure not caused by a change in income. An *induced change* is a change in aggregate expenditure caused by a change in income. An autonomous change in expenditure will cause rounds of induced changes in expenditure. Therefore, an autonomous change in expenditure will have a *multiplier effect* on equilibrium GDP. The **multiplier effect** is the process by which an increase in autonomous expenditure leads to a larger increase in real GDP. The **multiplier** is the ratio of the change in equilibrium GDP to the change in autonomous expenditure. The formula for the multiplier is:

$$\frac{1}{1 - MPC}.$$

myeconlab Get Ahead of the Curve Visit www.myeconlab.com to complete these exercises online and get instant feedback.

Review Questions

4.1 What is the multiplier effect? Use a 45°-line diagram to illustrate the multiplier effect of a decrease in government purchases.

4.2 What is the formula for the multiplier? Explain why this formula is considered to be too simple.

Problems and Applications

4.3 **(Related to *Solved Problem 11-4* on page 376)** Use the information in the following table to answer the following questions.

REAL GDP (*Y*)	CONSUMPTION (*C*)	PLANNED INVESTMENT (*I*)	GOVERNMENT PURCHASES (*G*)	NET EXPORTS (*NX*)
$8,000	$7,300	$1,000	$1,000	–$500
9,000	7,900	1,000	1,000	–500
10,000	8,500	1,000	1,000	–500
11,000	9,100	1,000	1,000	–500
12,000	9,700	1,000	1,000	–500

a. What is the equilibrium level of real GDP?
b. What is the *MPC?*
c. Suppose net exports increase by $400 billion. What will be the new equilibrium level of real GDP? Use the multiplier formula to determine your answer.

4.4 The following is from a letter to the *Economist* magazine:

> The arithmetic contribution of net exports to Asia's growth may have been only one percentage point, or two points in the case of China, but including multiplier effects the total growth impact has been two to three times higher.

What does this writer mean by "multiplier effects"? What does he mean by "total growth impact"? Why would the multiplier effect increase the impact of exports on economic growth in China and other Asian countries?

Source: "On China's Economy, the Meaning of Africa, Iraq, New York, Cheesesteaks," *Economist*, November 9, 2006.

4.5 Explain whether you agree or disagree with the following statement:

> Many economists claim that the recession of 2001 was caused by a decline in investment. This can't be true. If there had just been a decline in investment, the only firms hurt would have been construction firms, computer firms, and other firms selling investment goods. In fact, many firms experienced falling sales during that recession, including automobile firms and furniture firms.

4.6 Suppose a booming economy in Europe causes net exports to rise by $75 billion in the United States. If the *MPC* is 0.8, what will be the change in equilibrium GDP?

4.7 Would a larger multiplier lead to longer and more severe recessions or shorter and less severe recessions? Briefly explain.

4.8 Use the following graph to answer the questions.

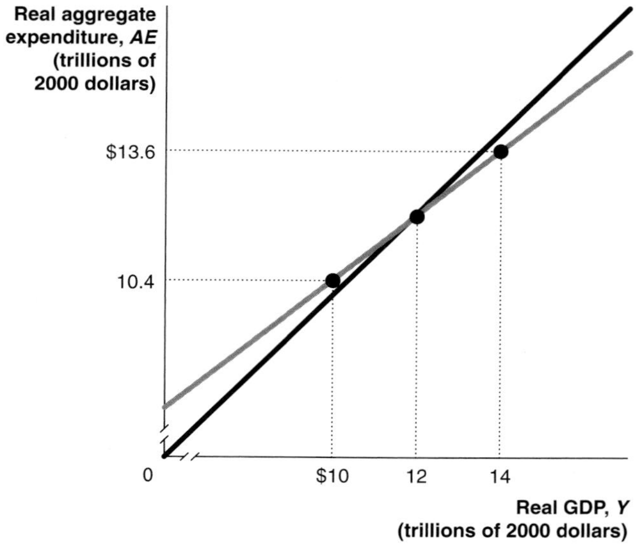

a. What is the value of equilibrium real GDP?
b. What is the value of the *MPC*?
c. What is the value of the multiplier?
d. What is the value of unplanned changes in inventories when real GDP has each of the following values?
   - $10 trillion
   - $12 trillion
   - $14 trillion

4.9 **(Related to the *Making the Connection* on page 373)** If the multiplier had a value of 4 in 1929, how large must the change in autonomous expenditure have been to cause the decline in real GDP between 1929 and 1933 shown in the table on page 373? If the multiplier had a value of 2, how large must the change in autonomous expenditure have been?

4.10 In an article on Microsoft expanding the number of buildings and employees at its Redmond, Washington headquarters, Bill McSherry, director of economic development at the Puget Sound Regional Council in Seattle, was quoted as saying: "The real reason you want these jobs is for the multiplier effect." How is the multiplier effect McSherry is referring to related to the multiplier effect discussed in this chapter?

Source: Kristina Shevory, "Microsoft Is Looking for More Elbow Room, *New York Times*, July 5, 2006.

>> End Learning Objective 11.4

11.5 LEARNING OBJECTIVE 11.5 | Understand the relationship between the aggregate demand curve and aggregate expenditure, **pages 377–379.**

The Aggregate Demand Curve

Summary

Increases in the price level cause a reduction in consumption, investment, and net exports. This causes the aggregate expenditure function to shift down on the 45°-line diagram, leading to a lower equilibrium real GDP. A decrease in the price level leads to a higher equilibrium real GDP. The **aggregate demand curve** shows the relationship between the price level and the level of aggregate expenditure, holding constant all factors that affect aggregate expenditure other than the price level.

Review Questions

5.1 Briefly explain the difference between aggregate expenditure and aggregate demand.

5.2 Briefly explain which components of aggregate expenditure are affected by a change in the price level.

Problems and Applications

5.3 Briefly explain why the aggregate expenditure line is upward sloping, while the aggregate demand curve is downward sloping.

5.4 Briefly explain whether you agree with the following statement: "The reason that the aggregate demand curve slopes downward is that when the price level is higher, people cannot afford to buy as many goods and services."

5.5 Suppose that exports become more sensitive to changes in the price level in the United States. That is, when the price level in the United States rises, exports decline by more than they previously did. Will this change make the aggregate demand curve steeper or less steep? Briefly explain.

>> End Learning Objective 11.5

Appendix

The Algebra of Macroeconomic Equilibrium

LEARNING OBJECTIVE

Apply the algebra of macroeconomic equilibrium.

In this chapter, we relied primarily on graphs and tables to illustrate the aggregate expenditure model of short-run real GDP. Graphs help us understand economic change *qualitatively*. When we write down an economic model using equations, we make it easier to make *quantitative estimates*. When economists forecast future movements in GDP, they often rely on *econometric models*. An econometric model is an economic model written in the form of equations, where each equation has been statistically estimated, using methods similar to the methods used in estimating demand curves that we briefly described in Chapter 3. We can use equations to represent the aggregate expenditure model described in this chapter.

The following equations are based on the example shown in Table 11-3 on page 369. Y stands for real GDP, and the numbers (with the exception of the *MPC*) represent billions of dollars.

1	$C = 1{,}000 + 0.65\,Y$	Consumption function
2	$I = 1{,}500$	Planned investment function
3	$G = 1{,}500$	Government spending function
4	$NX = -500$	Net export function
5	$Y = C + I + G + NX$	Equilibrium condition

The first equation is the consumption function. The *MPC* is 0.65, and 1,000 is autonomous consumption, which is the level of consumption that does not depend on income. If we think of the consumption function as a line on the 45°-line diagram, 1,000 would be the intercept, and 0.65 would be the slope. The "functions" for the other three components of planned aggregate expenditure are very simple because we have assumed that these components are not affected by GDP and, therefore, are constant. Economists who use this type of model to forecast GDP would, of course, use more realistic investment, government, and net export functions. The *parameters* of the functions—such as the value of autonomous consumption and the value of the *MPC* in the consumption function—would be estimated statistically using data on the values of each variable over a period of years.

In this model, equilibrium GDP occurs where GDP is equal to planned aggregate expenditure. Equation 5—the equilibrium condition—shows us how to calculate equilibrium in the model: To calculate equilibrium, we substitute equations 1 through 4 into equation 5. This gives us the following:

$$Y = 1{,}000 + 0.65Y + 1{,}500 + 1{,}500 - 500.$$

We need to solve this expression for Y to find equilibrium GDP. The first step is to subtract $0.65Y$ from both sides of the equation:

$$Y - 0.65Y = 1{,}000 + 1{,}500 + 1{,}500 - 500.$$

Then, we solve for Y:

$$0.35Y = 3{,}500.$$

Or:

$$Y = \frac{3{,}500}{0.35} = 10{,}000.$$

To make this result more general, we can replace particular values with general values represented by letters:

1	$C = \overline{C} + MPC(Y)$	Consumption function
2	$I = \overline{I}$	Planned investment function
3	$G = \overline{G}$	Government spending function
4	$NX = \overline{NX}$	Net export function
5	$Y = C + I + G + NX$	Equilibrium condition

The letters with bars over them represent fixed, or autonomous, values. So, $\overline{C}$ represents autonomous consumption, which had a value of 1,000 in our original example. Now, solving for equilibrium, we get:

$$Y = \overline{C} + MPC(Y) + \overline{I} + \overline{G} + \overline{NX},$$

or:

$$Y - MPC(Y) = \overline{C} + \overline{I} + \overline{G} + \overline{NX},$$

or:

$$Y(1 - MPC) = \overline{C} + \overline{I} + \overline{G} + \overline{NX},$$

or:

$$Y = \frac{\overline{C} + \overline{I} + \overline{GX} + \overline{NX}}{1 - MPC}.$$

Remember that $1/(1-MPC)$ is the multiplier, and all four variables in the numerator of the equation represent autonomous expenditure. Therefore an alternative expression for equilibrium GDP is:

Equilibrium GDP = Autonomous expenditure × Multiplier.

LEARNING OBJECTIVE Apply the algebra of macroeconomic equilibrium, **pages 388–389.**

myeconlab Get Ahead of the Curve — Visit www.myeconlab.com to complete these exercises online and get instant feedback.

Problems and Applications

11A.1 Write a general expression for the aggregate expenditure function. If you think of the aggregate expenditure function as a line on the 45°-line diagram, what would be the intercept and what would be the slope, using the general values represented by letters?

11A.2 Find equilibrium GDP using the following macroeconomic model (the numbers, with the exception of the *MPC*, represent billions of dollars).

a. $C = 1{,}500 + 0.75\,Y$	Consumption function
b. $I = 1{,}250$	Planned investment function
c. $G = 1{,}250$	Government spending function
d. $NX = -500$	Net export function
e. $Y = C + I + G + NX$	Equilibrium condition

11A.3 For the macroeconomic model in problem 11.2A, write the aggregate expenditure function. For GDP of \$16,000, what is the value of aggregate expenditure, and what is the value of the unintended change in inventories? For GDP of \$12,000, what is the value of aggregate expenditure, and what is the value of the unintended change in inventories?

11A.4 Suppose that autonomous consumption is 500, government purchases are 1,000, planned investment spending is 1,250, net exports is −250, and the *MPC* is 0.8. What is equilibrium GDP?

>> End Appendix Learning Objective

Aggregate Demand and Aggregate Supply Analysis

The Fortunes of FedEx Follow the Business Cycle

When Alan Greenspan was chairman of the Federal Reserve, he spoke regularly with Fred Smith, the chairman of Federal Express. Greenspan believed that changes in the number of packages FedEx shipped gave a good indication of the overall state of the economy. FedEx plays such a large role in moving packages around the country that most economists agree with Greenspan that there is a close relationship between fluctuations in FedEx's business and fluctuations in GDP. Some Wall Street analysts refer to this relationship as the "FedEx Indicator" of how the economy is doing.

Like many successful businesses, FedEx began with a single bright idea by a young entrepreneur. In 1965, as an undergraduate, Fred Smith was assigned to write a term paper for an economics course. In the paper, Smith argued that the system for shipping freight by air in the United States was inefficient. At that time, nearly all air freight was shipped on regular passenger planes. This made freight dependent on airline schedules and meant that if airlines cut back on flights to an area, firms in that area were left with reduced freight service. Smith proposed an entirely new system: One firm would control shipping freight from pickup to delivery. The firm would operate its own planes on a "hub-and-spoke" system: Packages would be collected and flown to a central hub, where they would be sorted and then flown to their destination for final delivery by truck. Moreover, by breaking free of airline schedules, the new firm could promise overnight delivery, which most freight companies in the 1960s couldn't do. Smith can't quite remember the grade he received (he has been quoted as saying it may have been a C), but the system he outlined in that term paper became the basis for the FedEx company of today.

Headquartered in Memphis, Tennessee, FedEx earns over $30 billion in annual revenues and has more than 240,000 employees in 220 countries and territories. Despite FedEx's tremendous success over the past 30 years, as Greenspan knew, the business cycle has always affected the company. For example, during the U.S. recession of 2001, the company's profits fell 38 percent in six months as businesses and individuals cut back on shipping packages. When the annual growth rate of real GDP slowed to 2.25 percent in the second half of 2006, FedEx cautioned shareholders that 2007 could be one of its worst years for profit growth in a decade.

To understand why FedEx and other firms are affected by the business cycle, we need to explore the effects that recessions and expansions have on production, employment, and prices. As you will read in this chapter, although no two business cycles are identical, economists use the aggregate demand and aggregate supply model to explain their general features. In later chapters, we use aggregate demand and aggregate supply to understand how the federal government can employ fiscal policy and monetary policy to reduce the severity of business cycles.

AN INSIDE LOOK on **page 418** discusses how a decline in the growth of real GDP affected UPS, one of FedEx's competitors.

Sources: David Gaffen, "The FedEx Indicator," *Wall Street Journal*, February 20, 2007; Roger Frock, *Changing How the World Does Business*, San Francisco: Berrett-Koehler Publishers, 2006; and Corey Dade, "FedEx Says Profit Gains May Be Sluggish," *Wall Street Journal*, March 22, 2007, p. A11.

LEARNING Objectives

After studying this chapter, you should be able to:

12.1 Identify the determinants of **aggregate demand** and distinguish between a **movement** along the aggregate demand curve and a **shift** of the curve, page 392.

12.2 Identify the determinants of **aggregate supply** and distinguish between a **movement** along the short-run aggregate supply curve and a **shift** of the curve, page 399.

12.3 Use the aggregate demand and aggregate supply model to illustrate the difference between **short-run** and **long-run macroeconomic equilibrium**, page 404.

12.4 Use the **dynamic aggregate demand and aggregate supply model** to analyze macroeconomic conditions, page 408.

APPENDIX Understand **macroeconomic schools of thought**, page 426.

Economics in YOUR Life!

Is an Employer Likely to Cut Your Pay During a Recession?
Suppose that you have worked as a barista for a local coffeehouse for two years. From on-the-job training and experience, you have honed your coffee-making skills and mastered the perfect latte. Suddenly, the economy moves into a recession, and sales at the coffeehouse decline. Is the owner of the coffeehouse likely to cut the prices of lattes and other drinks? Suppose the owner asks to meet with you to discuss your wages for next year. Is the owner likely to cut your pay? As you read the chapter, see if you can answer these questions. You can check your answers against those we provide at the end of the chapter. » **Continued on page 417**

We saw in Chapter 9 that the U.S. economy has experienced a long-run upward trend in real gross domestic product (GDP). This upward trend has resulted in the standard of living in the United States being much higher today than it was 50 years ago. In the short run, however, real GDP fluctuates around this long-run upward trend because of the business cycle. Fluctuations in GDP lead to fluctuations in employment. These fluctuations in real GDP and employment are the most visible and dramatic part of the business cycle. During recessions, for example, we are more likely to see factories close, small businesses declare bankruptcy, and workers lose their jobs. During expansions, we are more likely to see new businesses open and new jobs created. In addition to these changes in output and employment, the business cycle causes changes in wages and prices. Some firms react to a decline in sales by cutting back on production, but they may also cut the prices they charge and the wages they pay. Even more firms respond to a recession by raising prices and workers' wages by less than they would have otherwise.

In this chapter, we expand our story of the business cycle by developing the aggregate demand and aggregate supply model. This model will help us analyze the effects of recessions and expansions on production, employment, and prices.

12.1 LEARNING OBJECTIVE

12.1 | Identify the determinants of aggregate demand and distinguish between a movement along the aggregate demand curve and a shift of the curve.

Aggregate Demand

Aggregate demand and aggregate supply model A model that explains short-run fluctuations in real GDP and the price level.

Aggregate demand curve A curve that shows the relationship between the price level and the quantity of real GDP demanded by households, firms, and the government.

To understand what happens during the business cycle, we need an explanation of why real GDP, the unemployment rate, and the inflation rate fluctuate. We have already seen that fluctuations in the unemployment rate are caused mainly by fluctuations in real GDP. In this chapter, we use the **aggregate demand and aggregate supply model** to explain fluctuations in real GDP and the price level. As Figure 12-1 shows, real GDP and the price level in this model are determined in the short run by the intersection of the *aggregate demand curve* and the *aggregate supply curve*. Fluctuations in real GDP and the price level are caused by shifts in the aggregate demand curve or in the aggregate supply curve.

The **aggregate demand curve**, labeled *AD*, shows the relationship between the price level and the quantity of real GDP demanded by households, firms, and the govern-

Figure 12-1

Aggregate Demand and Aggregate Supply

In the short run, real GDP and the price level are determined by the intersection of the aggregate demand curve and the short-run aggregate supply curve. In the figure, real GDP is measured on the horizontal axis, and the price level is measured on the vertical axis by the GDP deflator. In this example, the equilibrium real GDP is $10.0 trillion, and the equilibrium price level is 100.

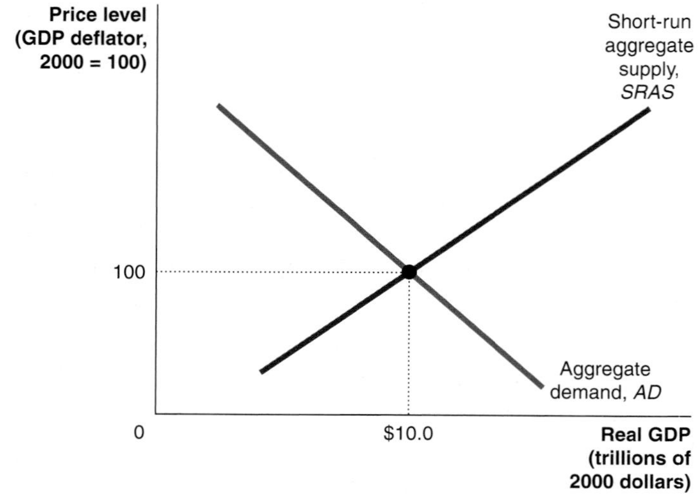

ment. The **short-run aggregate supply curve**, labeled *SRAS*, shows the relationship in the short run between the price level and the quantity of real GDP supplied by firms. The aggregate demand and short-run aggregate supply curves in Figure 12-1 look similar to the individual market demand and supply curves we studied in Chapter 3. However, because these curves apply to the whole economy, rather than to just a single market, the aggregate demand and aggregate supply model is very different from the model of demand and supply in individual markets. Because we are dealing with the economy as a whole, we need *macroeconomic* explanations of why the aggregate demand curve is downward sloping, why the short-run aggregate supply curve is upward sloping, and why the curves shift. We begin by explaining why the aggregate demand curve is downward sloping.

Short-run aggregate supply curve A curve that shows the relationship in the short run between the price level and the quantity of real GDP supplied by firms.

Why Is the Aggregate Demand Curve Downward Sloping?

We saw in Chapter 7 that GDP has four components: consumption (C), investment (I), government purchases (G), and net exports (NX). If we let Y stand for GDP, we can write the following:

$$Y = C + I + G + NX.$$

The aggregate demand curve is downward sloping because a fall in the price level increases the quantity of real GDP demanded. To understand why this is true, we need to look at how changes in the price level affect each of the components of aggregate demand. We begin with the assumption that government purchases are determined by the policy decisions of lawmakers and are not affected by changes in the price level. We can then consider the effect of changes in the price level on each of the other three components: consumption, investment, and net exports.

The Wealth Effect: How a Change in the Price Level Affects Consumption

Current income is the most important variable determining the consumption of households. As income rises, consumption will rise, and as income falls, consumption will fall. But consumption also depends on household wealth. A household's wealth is the difference between the value of its assets and the value of its debts. Consider two households, both with incomes of \$80,000 per year. The first household has wealth of \$5 million, whereas the second household has wealth of \$50,000. The first household is likely to spend more of its income than the second household. So, as total household wealth rises, consumption will rise. Some household wealth is held in cash or other *nominal assets* that lose value as the price level rises and gain value as the price level falls. For instance, if you have \$10,000 in cash, a 10 percent increase in the price level will reduce the purchasing power of that cash by 10 percent. When the price level rises, the *real value* of household wealth declines, and so will consumption. When the price level falls, the real value of household wealth rises, and so will consumption. This impact of the price level on consumption is called the *wealth effect.*

The Interest-Rate Effect: How a Change in the Price Level Affects Investment

When prices rise, households and firms need more money to finance buying and selling. Therefore, when the price level rises, households and firms will try to increase the amount of money they hold by withdrawing funds from banks, borrowing from banks, or selling financial assets, such as bonds. These actions tend to drive up the interest rate charged on bank loans and the interest rate on bonds. (In Chapter 14, we analyze in more detail the relationship between money and interest rates.) A higher interest rate raises the cost of borrowing for firms and households. As a result, firms will borrow less to build new factories or to install new machinery and equipment, and households will borrow less to buy new houses. To a smaller extent, households will also borrow less to finance spending on automobiles, furniture, and other durable goods. Consumption will therefore be reduced.

A lower price level will have the reverse effect, leading to an increase in investment and—to a lesser extent—consumption. This impact of the price level on investment is known as the *interest-rate effect.*

The International-Trade Effect: How a Change in the Price Level Affects Net Exports *Net exports* equal spending by foreign households and firms on goods and services produced in the United States minus spending by U.S. households and firms on goods and services produced in other countries. If the price level in the United States rises relative to the price levels in other countries, U.S. exports will become relatively more expensive, and foreign imports will become relatively less expensive. Some consumers in foreign countries will shift from buying U.S. products to buying domestic products, and some U.S. consumers will also shift from buying U.S. products to buying imported products. U.S. exports will fall, and U.S. imports will rise, causing net exports to fall. A lower price level in the United States has the reverse effect, causing net exports to rise. This impact of the price level on net exports is known as the *international-trade effect.*

Shifts of the Aggregate Demand Curve versus Movements Along It

An important point to remember is that the aggregate demand curve tells us the relationship between the price level and the quantity of real GDP demanded, *holding everything else constant.* If the price level changes but other variables that affect the willingness of households, firms, and the government to spend are unchanged, the economy will move up or down a stationary aggregate demand curve. If any variable changes other than the price level, the aggregate demand curve will shift. For example, if government purchases increase and the price level remains unchanged, the aggregate demand curve will shift to the right at every price level. Or, if firms become pessimistic about the future profitability of investment and cut back spending on factories and machinery, the aggregate demand curve will shift to the left.

The Variables That Shift the Aggregate Demand Curve

The variables that cause the aggregate demand curve to shift fall into three categories:

- Changes in government policies
- Changes in the expectations of households and firms
- Changes in foreign variables

Don't Let This Happen to **YOU!**

Be Clear Why the Aggregate Demand Curve Is Downward Sloping

The aggregate demand curve and the demand curve for a single product are both downward sloping—but for different reasons. When we draw a demand curve for a single product, such as apples, we know that it will slope downward because as the price of apples rises, apples become more expensive relative to other products—like oranges—and consumers buy fewer apples and more of the other products. In other words, consumers substitute other products for apples. When the overall price level rises, the prices of all domestically produced goods and services are rising, so consumers have no other domestic products to which they can switch. The aggregate demand curve slopes downward for the reasons given on pages 393–394: A lower price level raises the real value of household wealth (which increases consumption), lowers interest rates (which increases investment and consumption), and makes U.S. exports less expensive and foreign imports more expensive (which increases net exports).

YOUR TURN: Test your understanding by doing related problem 1.5 on page 420 at the end of this chapter.

Changes in Government Policies As we will discuss further in Chapters 14 and 15, the federal government uses monetary policy and fiscal policy to shift the aggregate demand curve. **Monetary policy** involves the actions the Federal Reserve—the nation's central bank—takes to manage the money supply and interest rates to pursue macroeconomic policy objectives. When the Federal Reserve takes actions to reduce interest rates, it lowers the cost to firms and households of borrowing. Lower borrowing costs increase consumption and investment spending, which shifts the aggregate demand curve to the right. Higher interest rates shift the aggregate demand curve to the left. **Fiscal policy** involves changes in federal taxes and purchases that are intended to achieve macroeconomic policy objectives, such as high employment, price stability, and high rates of economic growth. Because government purchases are one component of aggregate demand, an increase in government purchases shifts the aggregate demand curve to the right, and a decrease in government purchases shifts the aggregate demand curve to the left. An increase in personal income taxes reduces the amount of spendable income available to households. Higher personal income taxes reduce consumption spending and shift the aggregate demand curve to the left. Lower personal income taxes shift the aggregate demand curve to the right. Increases in business taxes reduce the profitability of investment spending and shift the aggregate demand curve to the left. Decreases in business taxes shift the aggregate demand curve to the right.

Monetary policy The actions the Federal Reserve takes to manage the money supply and interest rates to pursue macroeconomic policy objectives.

Fiscal policy Changes in federal taxes and purchases that are intended to achieve macroeconomic policy objectives, such as high employment, price stability, and high rates of economic growth.

Changes in the Expectations of Households and Firms If households become more optimistic about their future incomes, they are likely to increase their current consumption. This increased consumption will shift the aggregate demand curve to the right. If households become more pessimistic about their future incomes, the aggregate demand curve will shift to the left. Similarly, if firms become more optimistic about the future profitability of investment spending, the aggregate demand curve will shift to the right. If firms become more pessimistic, the aggregate demand curve will shift to the left.

Changes in Foreign Variables If firms and households in other countries buy fewer U.S. goods or if firms and households in the United States buy more foreign goods, net exports will fall, and the aggregate demand curve will shift to the left. As we saw in Chapter 7, when real GDP increases, so does the income available for consumers to spend. If real GDP in the United States increases faster than real GDP in other countries, U.S. imports will increase faster than U.S. exports, and net exports will fall, which is what happened during the late 1990s through the mid-2000s. Net exports will also fall if the *exchange rate* between the dollar and foreign currencies rises because the price in foreign currency of U.S. products sold in other countries will rise, and the dollar price of foreign products sold in the United States will fall. For example, if the current exchange rate is $1 = €1, then a $300 iPod exported from the United States to France will cost €300 in France, and a €50 bottle of French wine will cost $50 in the United States. But if the exchange rises to $1 = €1.50, then the iPod's price will rise to €450 in France, causing its sales to decline, and the price of the French wine will fall to $33.33 per bottle in the United States, causing its sales to increase. U.S. exports will fall, U.S. imports will rise, and the aggregate demand curve will shift to the left.

An increase in net exports at every price level will shift the aggregate demand curve to the right. Net exports will increase if real GDP grows more slowly in the United States than in other countries or if the value of the dollar falls against other currencies. A change in net exports that results from a change in the price level in the United States will *not* cause the aggregate demand curve to shift.

Making the Connection | In a Global Economy, How Can You Tell the Imports from the Domestic Goods?

Some U.S. firms appeal to the patriotism of U.S. consumers by urging them to buy products made in the United States. For example, an executive vice president of Ford Motor Company was quoted as saying, "Americans really do want to

Is the Toyota Sienna as American as apple pie?

buy American brands. We will compete vigorously to be America's car company." What could be more All-American than the famous Ford Mustang sports car? And what is more obviously an import than the Toyota Sienna minivan? After all, Toyota's headquarters is in Japan, and competition from cars made by Toyota, Honda, and Nissan has helped cause plummeting employment and production at Ford and the other U.S. "Big Three" automakers. But things are not so simple in the modern global economy. While the Mustang is assembled in Flat Rock, Michigan, the Sienna is not assembled in Japan but in Princeton, Indiana. What is more, most firms that sell products, such as automobiles, that have many parts, purchase those parts from suppliers who may be located anywhere in the world. In fact, according to the U.S. National Highway Traffic Safety Administration, only 65 percent of the content of the Ford Mustang was produced by Ford itself or by firms located in the United States or Canada. The other 35 percent of the content was imported from firms located in other countries. By contrast, 90 percent of the content of the Toyota Sienna is produced in the United States or Canada, and only 10 percent is imported from firms located in other countries. So, a consumer in the United States who buys a Toyota Sienna actually contributes more to increasing U.S. aggregate demand than does a consumer purchasing a Ford Mustang.

The U.S. Bureau of Economic Analysis (BEA), which is in charge of gathering data on imports, as well as the other components of aggregate demand, is well aware of this complication. The BEA is careful to include in the category of imports the parts purchased by U.S.-based firms from foreign suppliers even when the final product being sold is mainly composed of U.S.-made parts.

Source: Jathon Sapsford and Norihiko Shirouzu, "Mom, Apple Pie and . . . Toyota?" *Wall Street Journal*, May 11, 2006, p. B1.

YOUR TURN: Test your understanding by doingrelated problem 1.8 on page 421 at the end of this chapter.

Solved Problem | **12-1**

Movements along the Aggregate Demand Curve versus Shifts of the Aggregate Demand Curve

Suppose the current price level is 120, and the current level of real GDP is $12.2 trillion. Illustrate each of the following situations on a graph.

a. The price level rises to 125, while all other variables remain constant.

b. Firms become pessimistic and reduce their investment. Assume that the price level remains constant.

SOLVING THE PROBLEM:

Step 1: **Review the chapter material.** This problem is about understanding the difference between movements along an aggregate demand curve and shifts of an aggregate demand curve, so you may want to review the section "Shifts of the Aggregate Demand Curve versus Movements Along It," which begins on page 394.

Step 2: **To answer question (a), draw a graph that shows a movement along the aggregate demand curve.** Because there will be a movement along the aggregate demand curve but no shift of the aggregate demand curve, your graph should look like this:

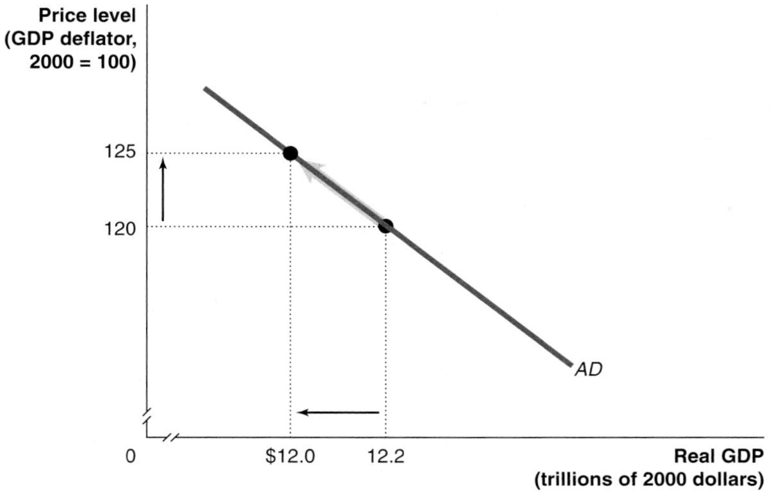

We don't have enough information to be certain what the new level of real GDP will be. We only know that it will be less than the initial level of $12.2 trillion; the graph shows the value as $12.0 trillion.

Step 3: **To answer question (b), draw a graph that shows a shift of the aggregate demand curve.** We know that the aggregate demand curve will shift to the left, but we don't have enough information to know how far to the left it will shift. Let's assume that the shift is $300 billion (or $0.3 trillion). In that case, your graph should look like this:

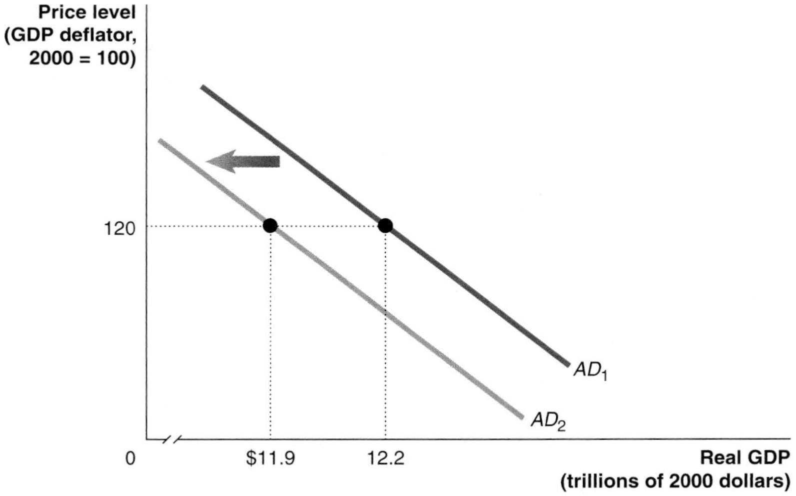

The graph shows a parallel shift in the aggregate demand curve so that at every price level, the quantity of real GDP demanded declines by $300 billion. For example, at a price level of 120, the quantity of real GDP demanded declines from $12.2 trillion to $11.9 trillion.

YOUR TURN: For more practice, do related problem 1.6 on page 421 at the end of this chapter.

>> End Solved Problem 12-1

Table 12-1 summarizes the most important variables that cause the aggregate demand curve to shift. It is important to notice that the table shows the shift in the aggregate demand curve that results from an increase in each of the variables. A *decrease* in these variables would cause the aggregate demand curve to shift in the opposite direction.

TABLE 12-1

Variables That Shift the Aggregate Demand Curve

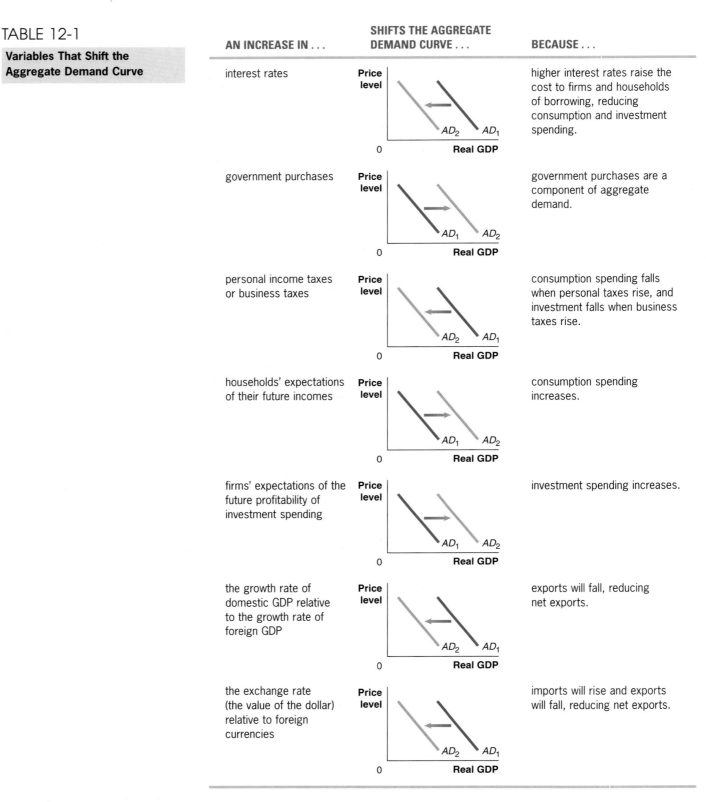

<table>
<tr><th>AN INCREASE IN . . .</th><th>SHIFTS THE AGGREGATE DEMAND CURVE . . .</th><th>BECAUSE . . .</th></tr>
<tr><td>interest rates</td><td>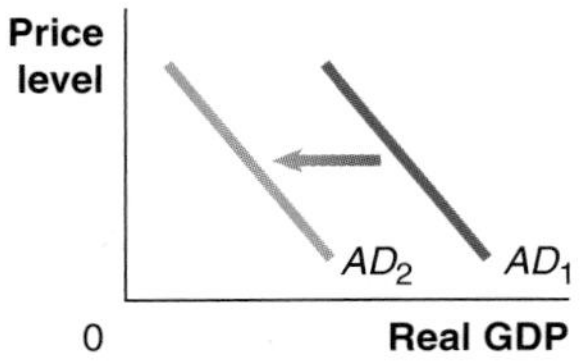</td><td>higher interest rates raise the cost to firms and households of borrowing, reducing consumption and investment spending.</td></tr>
<tr><td>government purchases</td><td>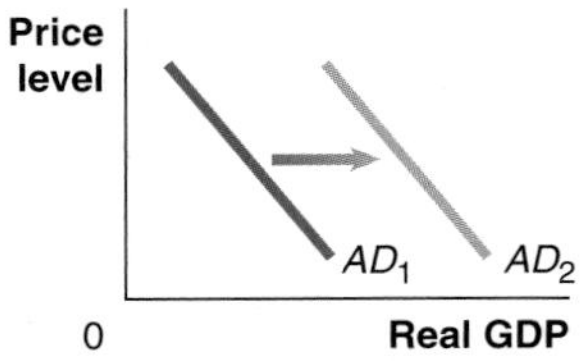</td><td>government purchases are a component of aggregate demand.</td></tr>
<tr><td>personal income taxes or business taxes</td><td>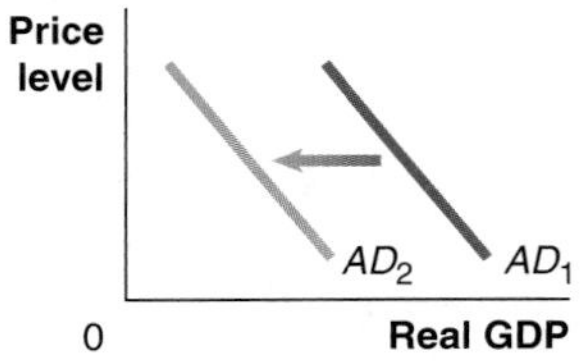</td><td>consumption spending falls when personal taxes rise, and investment falls when business taxes rise.</td></tr>
<tr><td>households' expectations of their future incomes</td><td>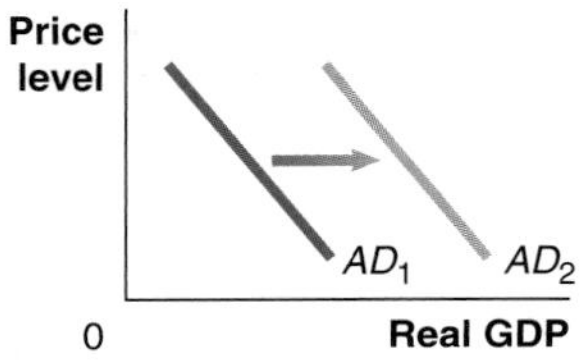</td><td>consumption spending increases.</td></tr>
<tr><td>firms' expectations of the future profitability of investment spending</td><td>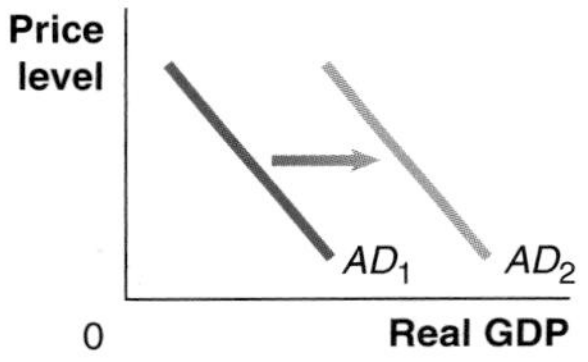</td><td>investment spending increases.</td></tr>
<tr><td>the growth rate of domestic GDP relative to the growth rate of foreign GDP</td><td>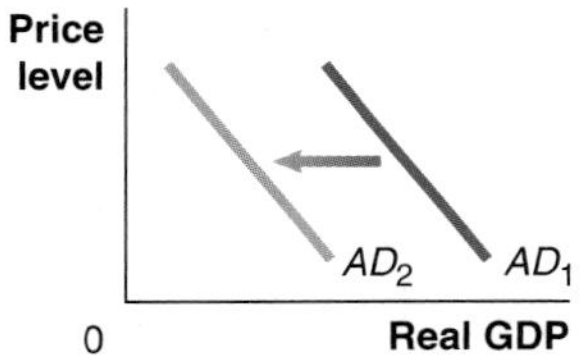</td><td>exports will fall, reducing net exports.</td></tr>
<tr><td>the exchange rate (the value of the dollar) relative to foreign currencies</td><td>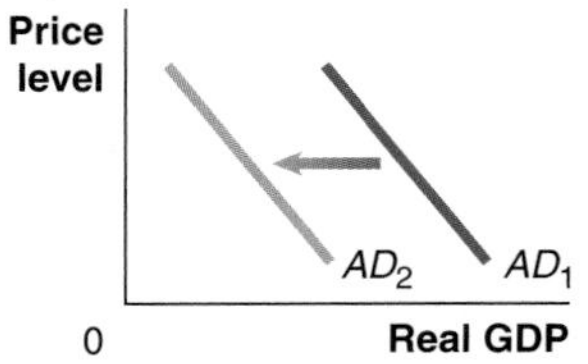</td><td>imports will rise and exports will fall, reducing net exports.</td></tr>
</table>

12.2 LEARNING OBJECTIVE

12.2 | Identify the determinants of aggregate supply and distinguish between a movement along the short-run aggregate supply curve and a shift of the curve.

Aggregate Supply

We just discussed the aggregate demand curve, which is one component of the aggregate demand and aggregate supply model. Now we turn to aggregate supply, which shows the effect of changes in the price level on the quantity of goods and services that firms are willing and able to supply. Because the effect of changes in the price level on aggregate supply is very different in the short run than in the long run, we use two aggregate supply curves: one for the short run and one for the long run. We start by considering the *long-run aggregate supply curve.*

The Long-Run Aggregate Supply Curve

In Chapter 10, we saw that in the long run, the level of real GDP is determined by the number of workers, the *capital stock*—including factories, office buildings, and machinery and equipment—and the available technology. Because changes in the price level do not affect the number of workers, the capital stock, or technology, *in the long run, changes in the price level do not affect the level of real GDP.* Remember that the level of real GDP in the long run is called *potential GDP* or *full-employment GDP.* At potential GDP, firms will operate at their normal level of capacity, and everyone who wants a job will have one, except the structurally and frictionally unemployed. There is no reason for this normal level of capacity to change just because the price level has changed. The **long-run aggregate supply curve** is a curve, labeled *LRAS,* that shows the relationship in the long run between the price level and the quantity of real GDP supplied. As Figure 12-2 shows, the price level was 116 in 2006, and potential real GDP was $11.4 trillion. If the price level had been 106, or if it had been 126, long-run aggregate supply would still have been a constant $11.5 trillion. Therefore, the *LRAS* curve is a vertical line.

Long-run aggregate supply curve A curve that shows the relationship in the long run between the price level and the quantity of real GDP supplied.

Figure 12-2 also shows that the long-run aggregate supply curve shifts to the right every year. This shift occurs because potential real GDP increases each year, as the number of workers in the economy increases, the economy accumulates more machinery and equipment, and technological change occurs. As Figure 12-2 shows, potential real GDP increased from $11.5 trillion in 2006 to $11.8 trillion in 2007 and to $12.1 trillion in 2008.

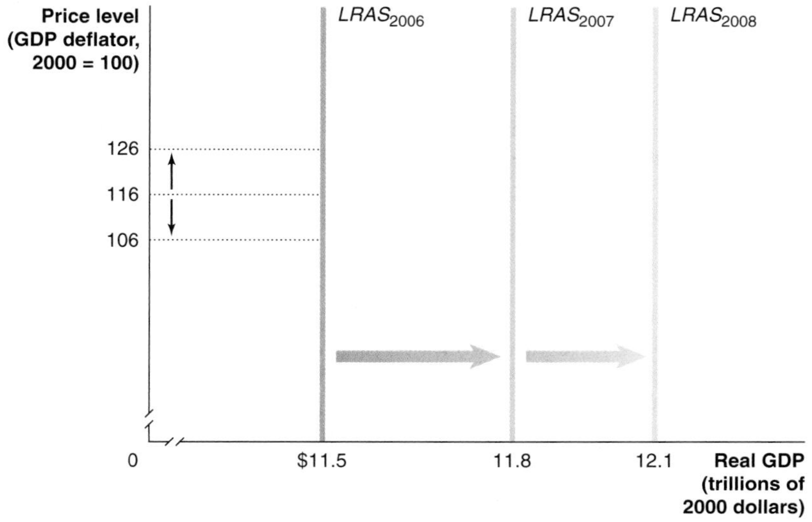

Figure 12-2

The Long-Run Aggregate Supply Curve

Changes in the price level do not affect the level of aggregate supply in the long run. Therefore, the long-run aggregate supply curve, labeled *LRAS,* is a vertical line at the potential level of real GDP. For instance, the price level was 116 in 2006, and potential real GDP was $11.5 trillion. If the price level had been 106, or if it had been 126, long-run aggregate supply would still have been a constant $11.5 trillion. Each year, the long-run aggregate supply curve shifts to the right as the number of workers in the economy increases, more machinery and equipment are accumulated, and technological change occurs.

The Short-Run Aggregate Supply Curve

Although the *LRAS* curve is vertical, the short-run aggregate supply curve, or *SRAS curve*, is upward sloping. The *SRAS* curve is upward sloping because, over the short run, as the price level increases, the quantity of goods and services firms are willing to supply will increase. The main reason firms behave this way is that, *as prices of final goods and services rise, prices of inputs—such as the wages of workers or the price of natural resources—rise more slowly.* Profits rise when the prices of the goods and services firms sell rise more rapidly than the prices they pay for inputs. Therefore, a higher price level leads to higher profits and increases the willingness of firms to supply more goods and services. A secondary reason the *SRAS* curve slopes upward is that, as the price level rises or falls, some firms are slow to adjust their prices. A firm that is slow to raise its prices when the price level is increasing may find its sales increasing and, therefore, will increase production. A firm that is slow to reduce its prices when the price level is decreasing may find its sales falling and, therefore, will decrease production.

Why do some firms adjust prices more slowly than others, and why might the wages of workers and the prices of other inputs change more slowly than the prices of final goods and services? Most economists believe the explanation is that *some firms and workers fail to predict accurately changes in the price level.* If firms and workers could predict the future price level exactly, the short-run aggregate supply curve would be the same as the long-run aggregate supply curve.

But how does the failure of workers and firms to predict the price level accurately result in an upward-sloping *SRAS* curve? Economists are not in complete agreement on this point, but we can briefly discuss the three most common explanations:

1. Contracts make some wages and prices "sticky."
2. Firms are often slow to adjust wages.
3. Menu costs make some prices sticky.

Contracts Make Some Wages and Prices "Sticky" Prices or wages are said to be "sticky" when they do not respond quickly to changes in demand or supply. Contracts can make wages or prices sticky. For example, suppose General Motors negotiates a three-year contract with the United Automobile Workers union at a time when demand for cars is increasing slowly. Suppose that after the contract is signed, the demand for cars starts to increase rapidly, and prices of cars rise. General Motors will find that producing more cars will be profitable because it can increase car prices, while the wages it pays its workers are fixed by contract. Or a steel mill might have signed a multiyear contract to buy coal, which is used in making steel, at a time when the demand for steel was stagnant. If steel demand and steel prices begin to rise rapidly, producing additional steel will be profitable because coal prices will remain fixed by contract. In both of these cases, rising prices lead to higher output. If these examples are representative of enough firms in the economy, a rising price level should lead to a greater quantity of goods and services supplied. In other words, the short-run aggregate supply curve will be upward sloping.

Notice, though, that if the workers at General Motors or the managers of the coal companies had accurately predicted what would happen to prices, this prediction would have been reflected in the contracts, and General Motors and the steel mill would not have earned greater profits when prices rose. In that case, rising prices would not have led to higher output.

Firms Are Often Slow to Adjust Wages We just noted that the wages of many union workers remain fixed by contract for several years. Many nonunion workers also have their wages or salaries adjusted only once a year. For instance, suppose you accept a job at a management consulting firm in June at a salary of $45,000 per year. The firm probably will not adjust your salary until the following June, even if the prices it can charge for its services later in the year are higher or lower than the firm had expected them to be when you were first hired. If firms are slow to adjust wages, a rise in the price level will increase the profitability of hiring more workers and producing more output. A fall in the price level will decrease the profitability of hiring more workers and producing more output. Once again, we have an explanation for why the short-run aggregate supply curve slopes upward.

It is worth noting that firms are often slower to *cut* wages than to increase them. Cutting wages can have a negative effect on the morale and productivity of workers and can also cause some of a firm's best workers to quit and look for jobs elsewhere.

Menu Costs Make Some Prices Sticky Firms base their prices today partly on what they expect future prices to be. For instance, a restaurant has to decide ahead of time the prices it will charge for meals before printing menus. Many firms print catalogs that list the prices of their products. If demand for their products is higher or lower than the firms had expected, they may want to charge prices that are different from the ones printed in their menus or catalogs. Changing prices would be costly, however, because it would involve printing new menus or catalogs. The costs to firms of changing prices are called **menu costs**. To see why menu costs can lead to an upward-sloping short-run aggregate supply curve, consider the effect of an unexpected increase in the price level. In this case, firms will want to increase the prices they charge. Some firms, however, may not be willing to increase prices because of menu costs. Because of their relatively low prices, these firms will find their sales increasing, which will cause them to increase output. Once again, we have an explanation for a higher price level leading to a larger quantity of goods and services supplied.

Menu costs The costs to firms of changing prices.

Shifts of the Short-Run Aggregate Supply Curve versus Movements Along It

It is important to remember the difference between a shift in a curve and a movement along a curve. The short-run aggregate supply curve tells us the short-run relationship between the price level and the quantity of goods and services firms are willing to supply, *holding constant all other variables that affect the willingness of firms to supply goods and services.* If the price level changes but other variables are unchanged, the economy will move up or down a stationary aggregate supply curve. If any variable other than the price level changes, the aggregate supply curve will shift.

Variables That Shift the Short-Run Aggregate Supply Curve

We now briefly discuss the five most important variables that cause the short-run aggregate supply curve to shift.

Increases in the Labor Force and in the Capital Stock A firm will supply more output at every price if it has more workers and more physical capital. The same is true of the economy as a whole. So, as the labor force and the capital stock grow, firms will supply more output at every price level, and the short-run aggregate supply curve will shift to the right. In Japan, the population is aging, and the labor force is decreasing. Holding other variables constant, this decrease in the labor force causes the short-run aggregate supply curve in Japan to shift to the left.

Technological Change As technological change takes place, the productivity of workers and machinery increases, which means firms can produce more goods and services with the same amount of labor and machinery. This improvement reduces the firms' costs of production and, therefore, allows them to produce more output at every price level. As a result, the short-run aggregate supply curve shifts to the right.

Expected Changes in the Future Price Level If workers and firms believe that the price level is going to increase by 3 percent during the next year, they will try to adjust their wages and prices accordingly. For instance, if a labor union believes there will be

Figure 12-3

How Expectations of the Future Price Level Affect the Short-Run Aggregate Supply

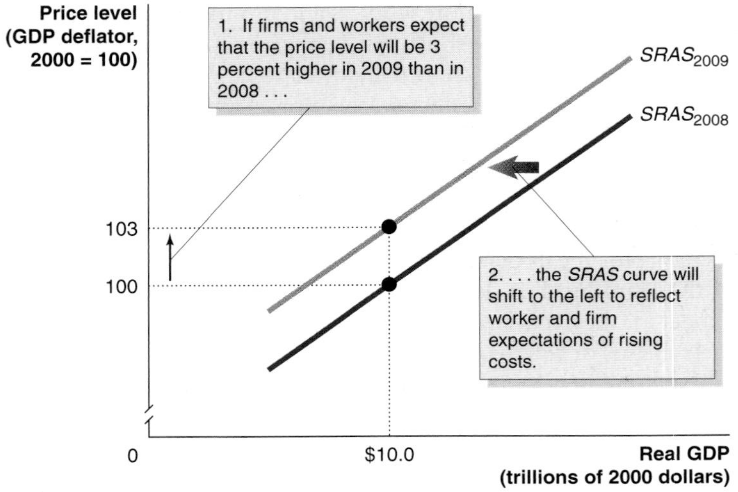

The *SRAS* curve shifts to reflect worker and firm expectations of future prices.

1. If workers and firms expect that the price level will rise by 3 percent, from 100 to 103, they will adjust their wages and prices by that amount.
2. Holding constant all other variables that affect aggregate supply, the short-run aggregate supply curve will shift to the left.

If workers and firms expect that the price level will be lower in the future, the short-run aggregate supply curve will shift to the right.

3 percent inflation next year, it knows that wages must rise 3 percent to preserve the purchasing power of those wages. Similar adjustments by other workers and firms will result in costs increasing throughout the economy by 3 percent. The result, shown in Figure 12-3, is that the short-run aggregate supply curve will shift to the left, so that any level of real GDP is now associated with a price level that is 3 percent higher. In general, *if workers and firms expect the price level to increase by a certain percentage, the* SRAS *curve will shift by an equivalent amount*, holding constant all other variables that affect the *SRAS* curve.

Adjustments of Workers and Firms to Errors in Past Expectations about the Price Level Workers and firms sometimes make wrong predictions about the price level. As time passes, they will attempt to compensate for these errors. Suppose, for example, that the United Automobile Workers signs a contract with General Motors that contains only small wage increases because the company and the union expect only small increases in the price level. If increases in the price level turn out to be unexpectedly large, the union will take this into account when negotiating the next contract. The higher wages General Motors' workers receive under the new contract will increase General Motors' costs and result in General Motors needing to receive higher prices to produce the same level of output. If workers and firms across the economy are adjusting to the price level being higher than expected, the *SRAS* curve will shift to the left. If they are adjusting to the price level being lower than expected, the *SRAS* curve will shift to the right.

Unexpected Changes in the Price of an Important Natural Resource An unexpected increase or decrease in the price of an important natural resource can cause firms' costs to be different from what they had expected. Oil prices can be particularly volatile. Some firms use oil in the production process. Other firms use products, such as plastics, that are made from oil. If oil prices rise unexpectedly, the costs of production will rise for these firms. Some utilities also burn oil to generate electricity, so electricity prices will rise. Rising oil prices lead to rising gasoline prices, which raise transportation costs for many firms. Because firms face rising costs, they will only supply the same level of output at higher prices, and the short-run aggregate supply curve will shift to the left. An unexpected event that causes the short-run aggregate supply curve to shift is known as a **supply shock**. Supply shocks are often caused by an unexpected increase or decrease in the price of an important natural resource. In September 2005, the U.S. economy was hit with a different type of supply shock when hurricane Katrina slammed into the Gulf Coast region. Many people were killed, the city of New Orleans had to be evacuated, and

Supply shock An unexpected event that causes the short-run aggregate supply curve to shift.

as many as one million people in the region were forced to relocate. The Congressional Budget Office estimated that up to 400,000 jobs were temporarily lost because of the hurricane. About one-quarter of U.S. oil and natural gas output comes from the Gulf Coast, and Katrina disrupted about half of this output. The fall in oil production caused prices to soar, with the price of gasoline rising above $3 per gallon.

Because the U.S. economy has experienced inflation every year since the 1930s, workers and firms always expect next year's price level to be higher than this year's price level. Holding everything else constant, expectations of a higher price level will cause the *SRAS* curve to shift to the left. But everything else is not constant because every year the U.S. labor force and the U.S. capital stock expand and changes in technology occur, which cause the *SRAS* curve to shift to the right. Whether in any particular year the *SRAS* curve shifts to the left or to the right depends on which of these variables has the largest impact during that year.

Table 12-2 summarizes the most important variables that cause the *SRAS* curve to shift. It is important to notice that the table shows the shift in the *SRAS* curve that results from an *increase* in each of the variables. A *decrease* in these variables would cause the *SRAS* curve to shift in the opposite direction.

TABLE 12-2

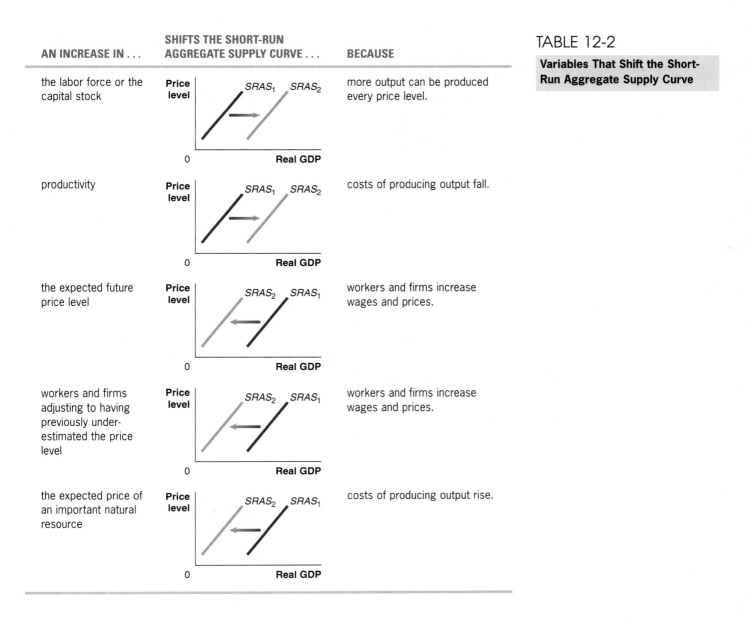

Variables That Shift the Short-Run Aggregate Supply Curve

AN INCREASE IN . . .	SHIFTS THE SHORT-RUN AGGREGATE SUPPLY CURVE . . .	BECAUSE
the labor force or the capital stock	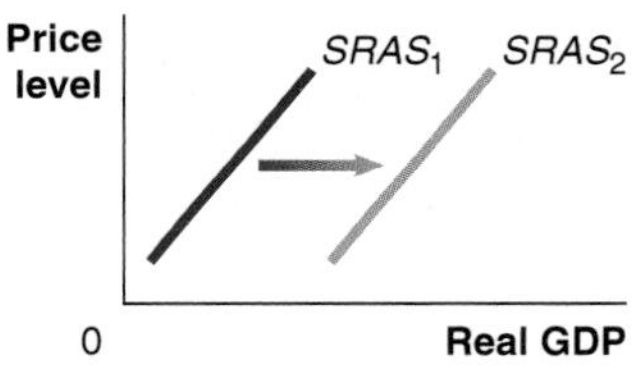	more output can be produced every price level.
productivity	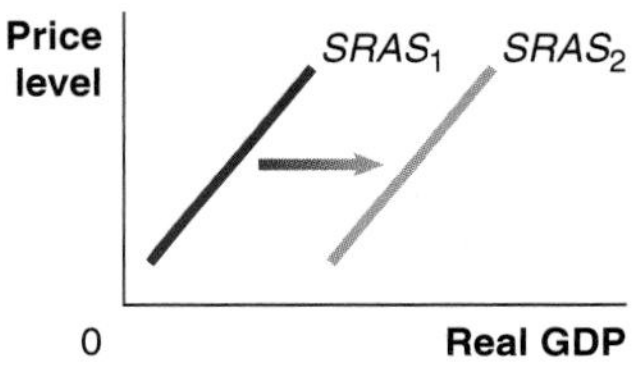	costs of producing output fall.
the expected future price level	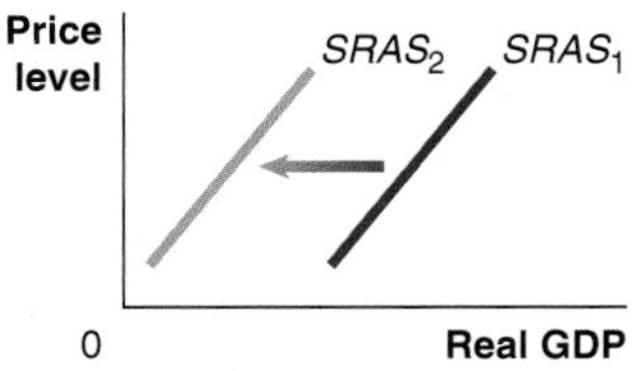	workers and firms increase wages and prices.
workers and firms adjusting to having previously under-estimated the price level	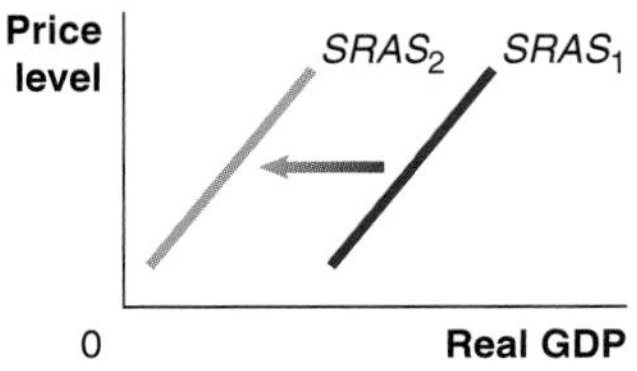	workers and firms increase wages and prices.
the expected price of an important natural resource	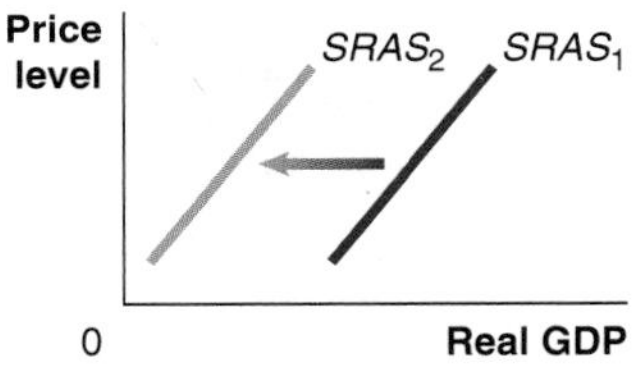	costs of producing output rise.

12.3 LEARNING OBJECTIVE

12.3 | Use the aggregate demand and aggregate supply model to illustrate the difference between short-run and long-run macroeconomic equilibrium.

Macroeconomic Equilibrium in the Long Run and the Short Run

Now that we have discussed the components of the aggregate demand and aggregate supply model, we can use it to analyze changes in real GDP and the price level. In Figure 12-4, we bring the aggregate demand curve, the short-run aggregate supply curve, and the long-run aggregate supply curve together in one graph, to show the *long-run macroeconomic equilibrium* for the economy. In the figure, equilibrium occurs at real GDP of $10.0 trillion and a price level of 100. Notice that in long-run equilibrium, the short-run aggregate supply curve and the aggregate demand curve intersect at a point on the long-run aggregate supply curve. Because equilibrium occurs at a point along the long-run aggregate supply curve, we know the economy is at potential real GDP: Firms will be operating at their normal level of capacity, and everyone who wants a job will have one, except the structurally and frictionally unemployed. We know, however, that the economy is often not in long-run macroeconomic equilibrium. In the following section, we discuss the economic forces that can push the economy away from long-run equilibrium.

Recessions, Expansions, and Supply Shocks

Because the full analysis of the aggregate demand and aggregate supply model can be complicated, we begin with a simplified case, using two assumptions:

1. The economy has not been experiencing any inflation. The price level is currently 100, and workers and firms expect it to remain at 100 in the future.
2. The economy is not experiencing any long-run growth. Potential real GDP is $10.0 trillion and will remain at that level in the future.

These assumptions are simplifications because in reality, the U.S. economy has experienced at least some inflation every year since the 1930s, and the potential real GDP also increases every year. However, the assumptions allow us to understand more easily the key ideas of the aggregate demand and aggregate supply model. In this section, we examine the short-run and long-run effects of recessions, expansions, and supply shocks.

Figure 12-4

Long-Run Macroeconomic Equilibrium

In long-run macroeconomic equilibrium, the *AD* and *SRAS* curves intersect at a point on the *LRAS* curve. In this case, equilibrium occurs at real GDP of $10.0 trillion and a price level of 100.

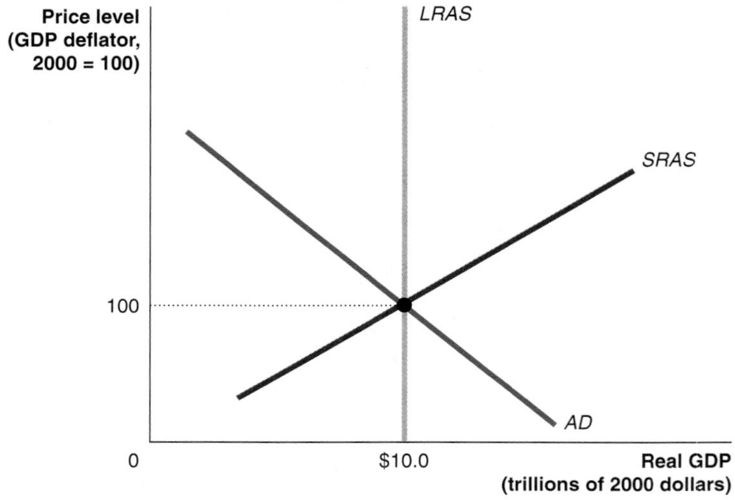

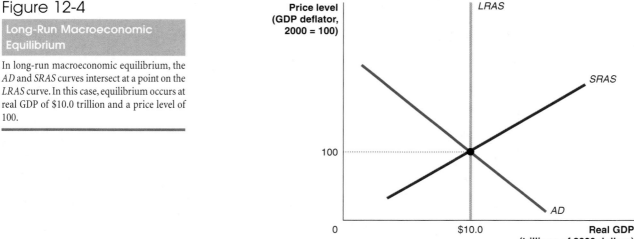

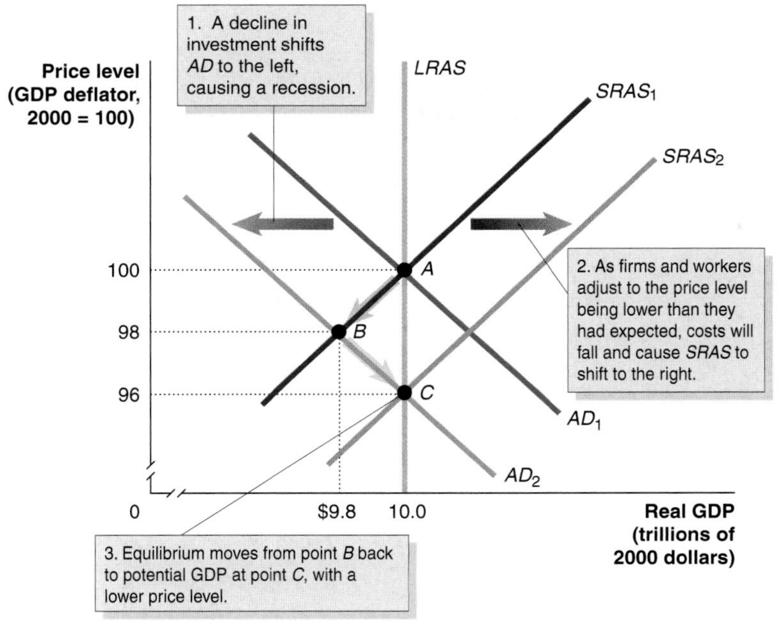

Figure 12-5

The Short-Run and Long-Run Effects of a Decrease in Aggregate Demand

In the short run, a decrease in aggregate demand causes a recession. In the long run, it causes only a decrease in the price level.

Recession

The short-run effect of a decline in aggregate demand. Suppose that an outbreak of fighting in the Middle East causes firms to become pessimistic about the future profitability of new spending on factories and equipment. The decline in investment that results will shift the aggregate demand curve to the left, from AD_1 to AD_2, as shown in Figure 12-5. The economy moves from point *A* to a new *short-run macroeconomic equilibrium,* where the AD_2 curve intersects the *SRAS* curve at point *B*. In the new short-run equilibrium, real GDP has declined from $10.0 trillion to $9.8 trillion and is below its potential level. This lower level of GDP will result in declining profitability for many firms and layoffs for some workers: The economy will be in recession.

Adjustment back to potential GDP in the long run. We know that the recession will eventually end because there are forces at work that push the economy back to potential GDP in the long run. Figure 12-5 also shows how the economy moves from recession back to potential GDP. The shift from AD_1 to AD_2 initially leads to a short-run equilibrium with the price level having fallen from 100 to 98 (point *B*). Workers and firms will begin to adjust to the price level being lower than they had expected it to be. Workers will be willing to accept lower wages—because each dollar of wages is able to buy more goods and services—and firms will be willing to accept lower prices. In addition, the unemployment resulting from the recession will make workers more willing to accept lower wages, and the decline in demand will make firms more willing to accept lower prices. As a result, the *SRAS* curve will shift to the right, from $SRAS_1$ to $SRAS_2$. At this point, the economy will be back in long-run equilibrium (point *C*). The shift from $SRAS_1$ to $SRAS_2$ will not happen instantly. It may take the economy several years to return to potential GDP. The important conclusion is that a decline in aggregate demand causes a recession in the short run, but in the long run, it causes only a decline in the price level.

Economists refer to the process of adjustment back to potential GDP just described as an *automatic mechanism* because it occurs without any actions by the government. An alternative to waiting for the automatic mechanism to end the recession is for the government to use monetary and fiscal policy to shift the *AD* curve to the right and restore potential GDP more quickly. We will discuss monetary and fiscal policy in Chapters 14 and 15. Economists debate whether it is better to wait for the automatic mechanism to end recessions or whether it is better to use monetary and fiscal policy.

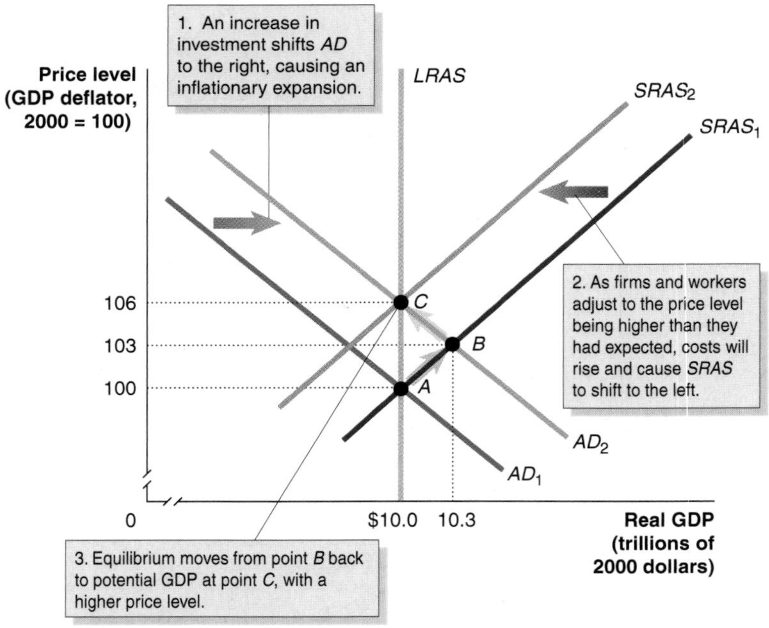

Figure 12-6 | The Short-Run and Long-Run Effects of an Increase in Aggregate Demand

In the short run, an increase in aggregate demand causes an increase in real GDP. In the long run, it causes only an increase in the price level.

Expansion

The short-run effect of an increase in aggregate demand. Suppose that instead of becoming pessimistic, many firms become optimistic about the future profitability of new investment, as happened during the information technology and telecommunications booms of the late 1990s. The resulting increase in investment will shift the *AD* curve to the right, as shown in Figure 12-6. Equilibrium moves from point *A* to point *B*. Real GDP rises from $10.0 trillion to $10.3 trillion, and the price level rises from 100 to 103. The economy will be above potential real GDP: Firms are operating beyond their normal level of capacity, and some workers are employed who ordinarily would be structurally or frictionally unemployed or who would not be in the labor force.

Adjustment back to potential GDP in the long run. Just as an automatic mechanism brings the economy back to potential GDP from a recession, an automatic mechanism brings the economy back from a short-run equilibrium beyond potential GDP. Figure 12-6 illustrates this mechanism. The shift from AD_1 to AD_2 initially leads to a short-run equilibrium, with the price level rising from 100 to 103 (point *B*). Workers and firms will begin to adjust to the price level being higher than they had expected. Workers will push for higher wages—because each dollar of wages is able to buy fewer goods and services—and firms will charge higher prices. In addition, the low levels of unemployment resulting from the expansion will make it easier for workers to negotiate for higher wages, and the increase in demand will make it easier for firms to receive higher prices. As a result, the *SRAS* curve will shift to the left, from $SRAS_1$ to $SRAS_2$. At this point, the economy will be back in long-run equilibrium. Once again, the shift from

SRAS$_1$ to *SRAS*$_2$ will not happen instantly. The process of returning to potential GDP may stretch out for more than a year.

Supply Shock

The short-run effect of a supply shock. Suppose oil prices increase substantially. This supply shock will increase many firms' costs and cause the *SRAS* curve to shift to the left, as shown in panel (a) of Figure 12-7. Notice that the price level is higher in the new short-run equilibrium (102 rather than 100), but real GDP is lower ($9.7 trillion rather than $10 trillion). This unpleasant combination of inflation and recession is called **stagflation.**

Stagflation A combination of inflation and recession, usually resulting from a supply shock.

Adjustment back to potential GDP in the long run. The recession caused by a supply shock increases unemployment and reduces output. This eventually results in workers being willing to accept lower wages and firms being willing to accept lower prices. In panel (b) of Figure 12-7, the short-run aggregate supply curve shifts from *SRAS*$_2$ to *SRAS*$_1$, moving the economy from point *B* back to point *A*. Potential GDP is regained at the original price level. It may take several years for this process to be completed. An alternative would be to use monetary and fiscal policy to shift the aggregate demand to the right. Using policy in this way would bring the economy back to potential GDP more quickly but would result in a permanently higher price level.

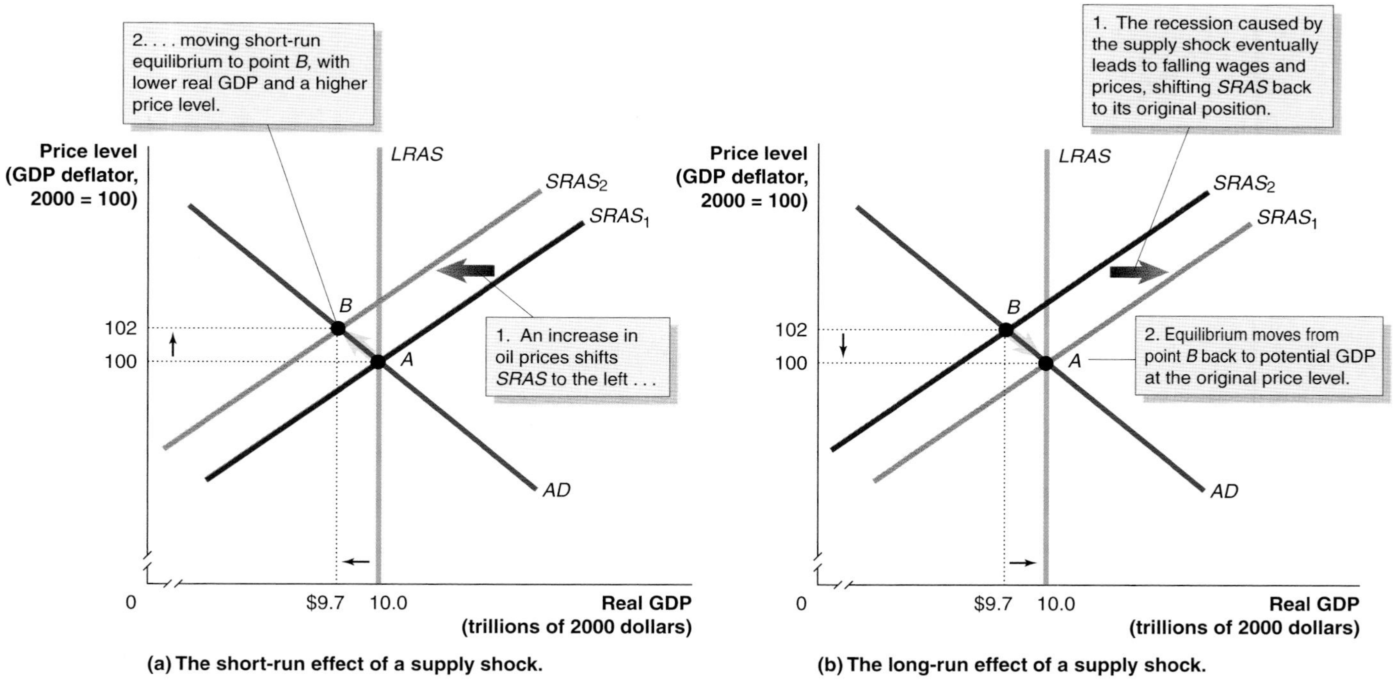

Figure 12-7 | The Short-Run and Long-Run Effects of a Supply Shock

Panel (a) shows that a supply shock, such as a large increase in oil prices, will cause a recession and a higher price level in the short run. The recession caused by the supply shock increases unemployment and reduces output. In panel (b), rising unemployment and falling output result in workers being willing to accept lower wages and firms being willing to accept lower prices. The short-run aggregate supply curve shifts from *SRAS*$_2$ to *SRAS*$_1$. Equilibrium moves from point *B* back to potential GDP and the original price level at point *A*.

12.4 LEARNING OBJECTIVE

12.4 | Use the dynamic aggregate demand and aggregate supply model to analyze macroeconomic conditions.

A Dynamic Aggregate Demand and Aggregate Supply Model

The basic aggregate demand and aggregate supply model used so far in this chapter gives us important insights into how short-run macroeconomic equilibrium is determined. Unfortunately, the model also gives us some misleading results. For instance, it incorrectly predicts that a recession caused by the aggregate demand curve shifting to the left will cause the price level to fall, which has not happened for an entire year since the 1930s. The difficulty with the basic model arises from the following two assumptions we made: (1) that the economy does not experience continuing inflation and (2) that the economy does not experience long-run growth. We can develop a more useful aggregate demand and aggregate supply model by dropping these assumptions. The result will be a model that takes into account that the economy is not *static*, with an unchanging level of potential real GDP and no continuing inflation, but *dynamic*, with potential real GDP that grows over time and inflation that continues every year. We can create a *dynamic aggregate demand and aggregate supply model* by making three changes to the basic model.

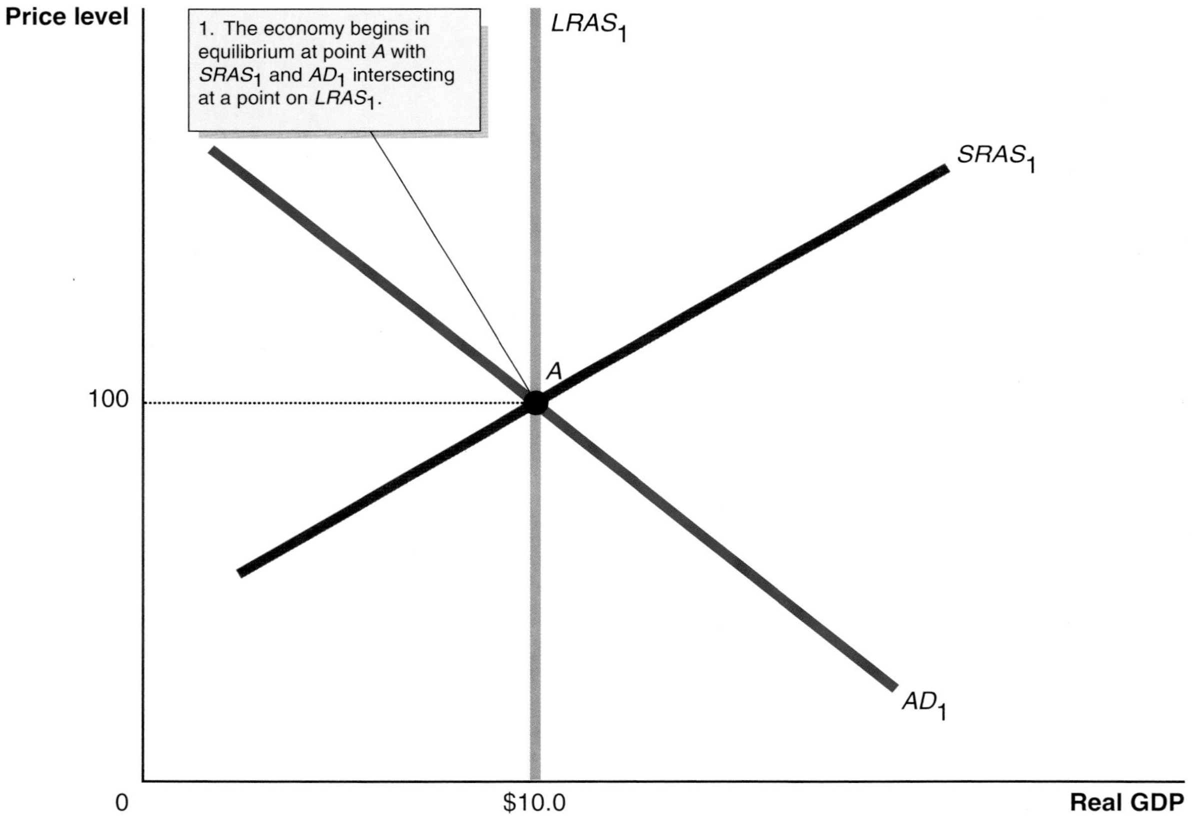

Figure 12-8 | A Dynamic Aggregate Demand and Aggregate Supply Model

We start with the basic aggregate demand and aggregate supply model.

These changes recognize the following important macroeconomic facts:

- Potential real GDP increases continually, shifting the long-run aggregate supply curve to the right.
- During most years, the aggregate demand curve will be shifting to the right.
- Except during periods when workers and firms expect high rates of inflation, the short-run aggregate supply curve will be shifting to the right.

Figure 12-8 incorporates these three changes to the basic aggregate demand and aggregate supply model. We start with $SRAS_1$ and AD_1 intersecting at point *A* at a price level of 100 and real GDP of $10.0 trillion. Because this intersection occurs at a point on $LRAS_1$, we know the economy is in long-run equilibrium. The long-run aggregate supply curve shifts to the right from $LRAS_1$ to $LRAS_2$. This shift occurs because during the year potential real GDP increases as the U.S. labor force and the U.S. capital stock increase and technological progress occurs. The short-run aggregate supply curve shifts from $SRAS_1$ to $SRAS_2$. This shift occurs because the same variables that cause the long-run aggregate supply to shift to the right will also increase the quantity of goods and services that firms are willing to supply in the short run. Finally, the aggregate demand curve shifts to the right from AD_1 to AD_2. The aggregate demand curve shifts for several reasons: As population grows and incomes rise, consumption will increase over time. As the economy grows, firms will expand capacity, and new firms will be formed, increasing investment. An expanding population and an expanding economy require increased government services, such as more police officers and teachers, so government purchases will increase.

The new equilibrium in Figure 12-8 occurs at point *B*, where AD_2 intersects $SRAS_2$ on $LRAS_2$. In the new equilibrium, the price level remains at 100, while real GDP increases to $10.5 trillion. Notice that there has been no inflation because the price level is unchanged at 100. There was no inflation because aggregate demand and aggregate supply shifted to the right by exactly as much as long-run aggregate supply. We would not expect this to be the typical situation for two reasons: First, the *SRAS* curve is also affected by workers' and firms' expectations of future changes in the price level and by supply shocks. These variables can partially, or completely, offset the normal tendency of the *SRAS* curve to shift to the right over the course of a year. Second, we know that sometimes consumers, firms, and the government may cut back expenditures. This reduced spending will result in the aggregate demand curve shifting to the right less than it normally would or, possibly, shifting to the left. In fact, as we will see shortly, *changes in the price level and in real GDP in the short run are determined by the shifts in the* SRAS *and* AD *curves.*

What Is the Usual Cause of Inflation?

The dynamic aggregate demand and aggregate supply model provides a more accurate explanation than the basic model of the source of most inflation. If total spending in the economy grows faster than total production, prices rise. Figure 12-9 illustrates this point by showing that if the *AD* curve shifts to the right by more than the *LRAS* curve, inflation results because equilibrium occurs at a higher price level, point *B*. In the new equilibrium, point *B*, the *SRAS* curve has shifted to the right by less than the *LRAS* curve because the anticipated increase in prices offsets some of the technological change and increases in the labor force and capital stock that occur during the year. Although inflation is generally the result of total spending growing faster than total production, a shift to the left of the short-run aggregate supply curve can also cause an increase in the price level, as we saw earlier in the discussion of supply shocks.

As we saw in Figure 12-8, if aggregate demand increases by the same amount as short-run and long-run aggregate supply, the price level will not change. In this case, the economy experiences economic growth without inflation.

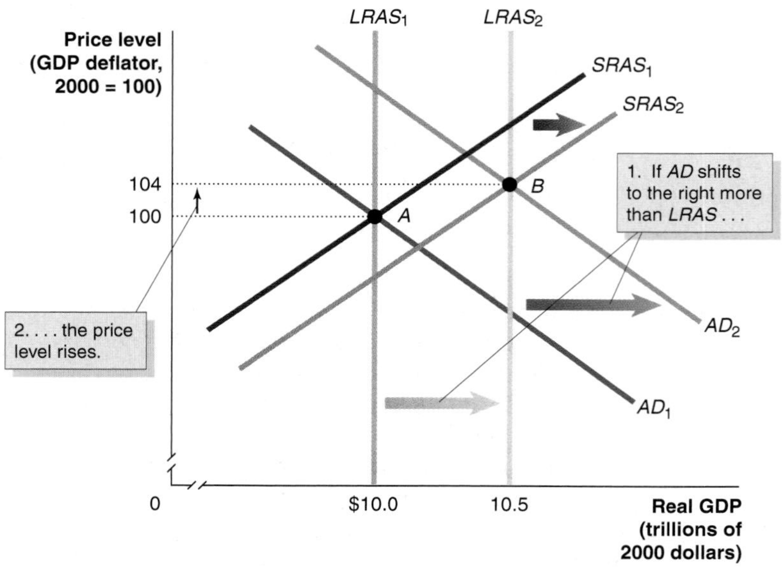

Figure 12-9 | Using Dynamic Aggregate Demand and Aggregate Supply to Understand Inflation

The most common cause of inflation is total spending increasing faster than total production.

1. The economy begins at point *A*, with real GDP of \$10.0 trillion and a price level of 100. An increase in full-employment real GDP from \$10.0 trillion to \$10.5 trillion causes long-run aggregate supply to shift from $LRAS_1$ to $LRAS_2$. Aggregate demand shifts from AD_1 to AD_2.
2. Because *AD* shifts to the right by more than the *LRAS* curve, the price level in the new equilibrium rises from 100 to 104.

The Slow Recovery from the Recession of 2001

We can use the dynamic aggregate demand and aggregate supply model to analyze the slow recovery from the recession of 2001. The recession began in March 2001, as the long economic expansion of the 1990s ended. The recession was caused by a decline in aggregate demand. Several factors contributed to this decline:

- ***The end of the stock market "bubble."*** In the late 1990s, stock prices increased rapidly. Higher stock prices partly resulted from higher corporate profits, but as we saw in Chapter 1, they were also due to the excessive optimism of investors about the future of dot-com companies. The increase in stock prices between 1995 and 2000 increased the wealth of U.S. households by \$9 trillion. Stock prices began to fall in spring 2000 and eventually fell almost as far as they had risen. By 2002, the total value of stocks had declined by \$7 trillion from their peak of two years before. The fall in stock prices reduced spending by households and firms. Firms that had financed investment spending by issuing new stock now had a more difficult time raising funds.

- ***Excessive investment in information technology.*** During the late 1990s, many firms overestimated the future profitability of investment in information technology. For example, telecommunications firms laid many more miles of fiber-optic cable than there was demand in the short run. Some firms also invested in computers and software in anticipation of the year 2000 (Y2K) problem. This problem arose from the technical difficulty many older computers had in correctly interpreting dates in years after 1999. Once older software and computers had been replaced, spending declined. Similarly, many firms had invested heavily to establish a presence on the Internet. When their Internet sales proved disappointing, the companies had more computers than they needed. For these reasons, by spring 2001, many companies had sharply cut back on their investment spending.

- ***The terrorist attacks of September 11, 2001.*** The terrorist attacks on New York and Washington, DC, increased the level of uncertainty in the economy. Many feared further attacks would occur, and they were uncertain how the economy would respond. When firms and households face uncertainty, they often postpone spending until the uncertainty is resolved.

- ***The corporate accounting scandals.*** As we saw in Chapter 5, the top managers of some corporations, such as WorldCom, Tyco, and Enron, manipulated their financial statements during the stock market boom to make their corporations appear more profitable than they actually were. When these accounting manipulations were finally brought to light, some investors lost faith in the accuracy of corporate financial statements, which helped depress stock prices and added to the uncertainty in the economy.

Few economists were surprised that the long expansion of the 1990s eventually ended in recession. Although forecasting the exact date the recession would begin was very difficult, it was inevitable that the expansion would end, just as all previous expansions had. Some economists were surprised, however, at the weakness of the expansion that began when the recession ended in November 2001. Figure 12-10 illustrates the changes in the economy from 2001 to 2002 and shows that the economy remained well below potential GDP during 2002.

In Figure 12-10, the *AD* curve shifts to the right much less than does the *LRAS* curve. As a result, the price level increases only from 102.4 in 2001 to 104.2 in 2002, for a very low inflation rate of 1.8 percent. Real GDP increases only from \$9.9 trillion to \$10.1 trillion,

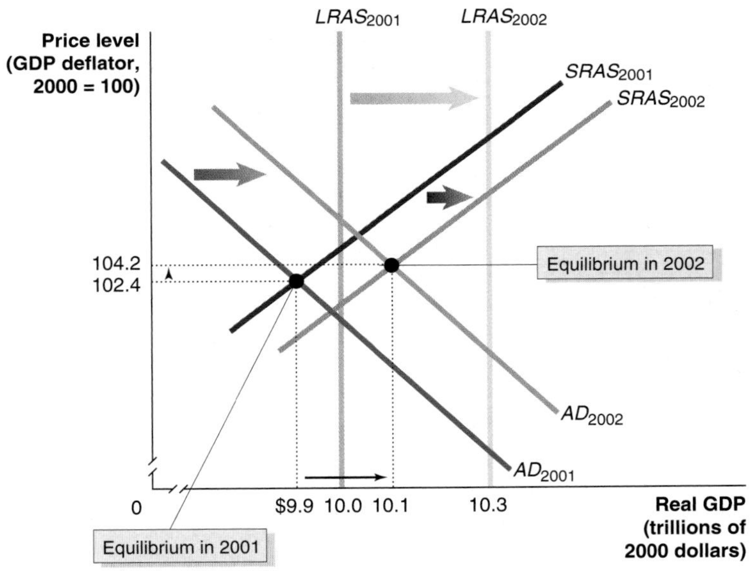

Figure 12-10 | Using Dynamic Aggregate Demand and Aggregate Supply to Understand the Recovery from the 2001 Recession

Between 2001 and 2002, *AD* shifted to the right but not by nearly enough to offset the shift to the right of *LRAS*, which represented the increase in potential real GDP from \$10.0 trillion to \$10.3 trillion. Although real GDP increased from \$9.9 trillion in 2001 to \$10.1 trillion in 2002, this was still far below the potential real GDP, shown by $LRAS_{2002}$. As a result, the unemployment rate rose from 4.7 percent in 2001 to 5.8 percent in 2002. Because the increase in aggregate demand was small, the price level increased only from 102.4 in 2001 to 104.2 in 2002, so the inflation rate for 2002 was only 1.8 percent.

which is below the potential level of $10.3 trillion, shown by $LRAS_{2002}$. Not surprisingly, the unemployment rate actually rose from 4.7 percent in 2001 to 5.8 percent in 2002.

The increase in aggregate demand during 2002 was weak because the factors that had caused the recession continued to weigh on the economy. Stock prices did not begin to rise significantly until 2003. Many firms still did not feel the need to increase investment spending, particularly on information technology, on which they had spent heavily during the late 1990s. Uncertainty remained high as the federal government continued the war on terrorism and prepared for the invasion of Iraq. Finally, each week during 2002 seemed to bring the revelation of a new corporate accounting scandal.

Making the Connection | Does Rising Productivity Growth Reduce Employment?

We saw in Chapter 10 that growth in output per worker—labor productivity—is the key to rising living standards over the long run. But if firms can produce more output with the same number of workers, are they less likely to hire additional workers? Some observers argued that this was happening during 2002 and 2003, as productivity and real GDP rose yet employment grew very little. The following two graphs show that productivity—measured as total output of all nonfarm businesses produced per hour worked—did in fact grow very rapidly during 2002 and 2003 and that employment, as measured by the Bureau of Labor Statistics establishment survey, declined.

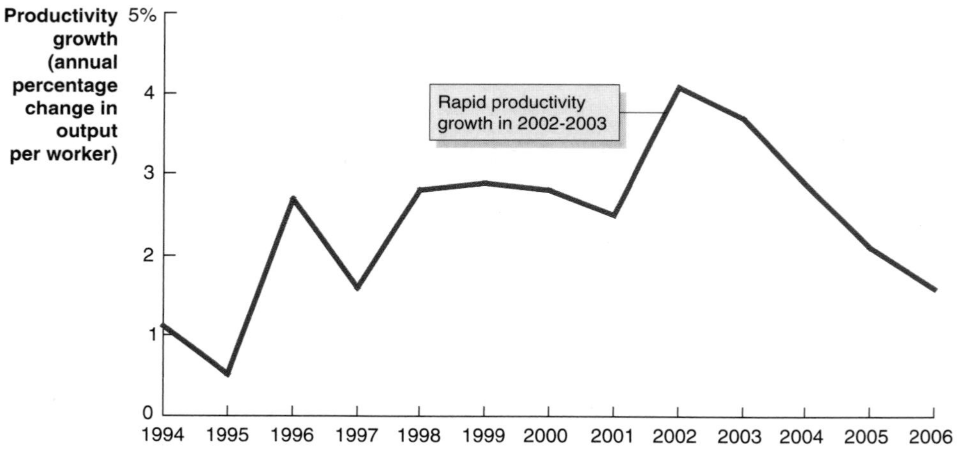

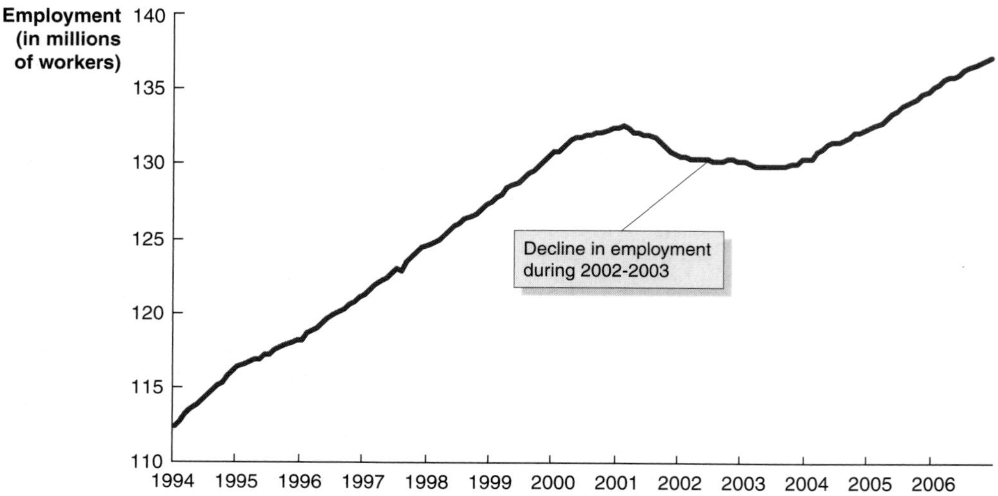

In the dynamic aggregate demand and aggregate supply model, the higher the growth of productivity during a year, the further to the right the *LRAS* and *SRAS* curves will shift. But rising productivity also leads to rising incomes, in part because rising output per worker makes it possible for firms to pay higher wages. These rising incomes raise consumption spending and allow the *AD* curve to shift to the right by enough to maintain GDP at its potential level. In 2002–2003, however, the economy was still operating below potential GDP, and many firms appeared reluctant to expand employment as rapidly as typically happens during an economic recovery. In these circumstances, rising productivity made it possible for at least some firms to expand output without expanding employment. Most economists agree that rapid productivity growth probably played some role in the slow employment growth of 2002 and 2003, but the effect was only temporary. We know that over the long run, the level of employment is determined by population growth and by factors—such as the level of retirement benefits and government unemployment insurance payments—that affect the fraction of the population in the labor force. The level of employment is not determined in the long run by the rate of productivity growth. In fact, between 1994 and 2006, the level of productivity in the U.S. economy increased by 35 percent, while during the same period, the number of people employed increased by almost 25 million. If we look at the two graphs for the whole period, we can see that productivity growth only affects employment in the short run. Productivity has fluctuated considerably over these 12 years, while except for a few years after the 2001 recession, employment has followed a steady upward trend.

YOUR TURN: Test your understanding by doingrelated problem 4.6 on page 424 at the end of this chapter.

The More Rapid Recovery of 2003-2004

The recovery from the recession of 2001 accelerated in the second half of 2003 and through 2004. For several reasons, aggregate demand increased more rapidly than it had during 2002 and early 2003. Low interest rates spurred spending on new houses and helped increase investment spending by firms. Tax cuts increased both consumption and investment spending. Rising stock prices contributed to increased consumption and investment spending. Finally, the value of the dollar declined against most foreign currencies, which helped exports.

Figure 12-11 shows the results of the more rapid increase in aggregate demand during 2004. In 2003, real GDP was 3.7 percent below its potential level, while the unemployment rate was 6.0 percent. The figure shows that the large shift in aggregate demand during 2004 led to an increase in real GDP from \$10.3 trillion to \$10.8 trillion. This level was still below potential real GDP of \$11.0 trillion, but the gap had narrowed to 1.8 percent. As a result, the unemployment rate fell from 6.0 percent to 5.2 percent. The rapid increase in aggregate demand caused a rise in the inflation rate. The price level increased from 106.3 in 2003 to 109.1 in 2004, for an inflation rate of 2.6 percent. This was higher than the inflation rate of 2.0 percent during 2003.

The Economy in 2007: Continuing Expansion or Looming Recession?

The business cycle expansion that began with the end of the 2001 recession continued through late 2007. By that time, the expansion had lasted longer than the average expansion during the period since 1950. Economic growth was somewhat erratic, though, with real GDP increasing at an annual rate of only 0.6 percent during the first quarter of 2007, before bouncing back to increase 4.0 percent during the second quarter. Inflation was running at the relatively high rate of 3.5 percent during the first half of 2007, up from 3.2 percent during 2006. Rising inflation was largely due to the effects of rising oil prices. The price of a barrel of oil had been below \$30 in early 2004 but was above \$70 in

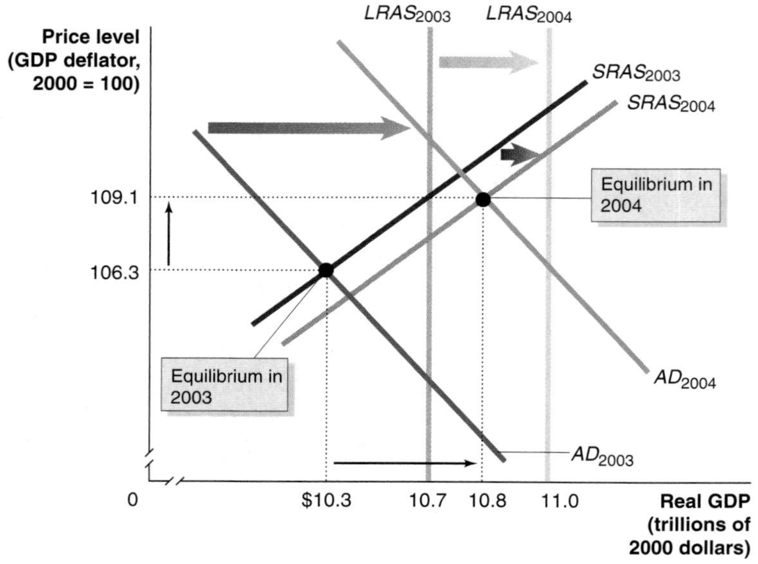

Figure 12-11 | Using Dynamic Aggregate Demand and Aggregate Supply to Understand the More Rapid Recovery of 2003–2004

The figure shows that the large shift in aggregate demand during 2004 led to an increase in real GDP from $10.3 trillion to $10.8 trillion. This was still below the potential real GDP of $11.0 trillion, but the gap had narrowed to 1.8 percent. As a result, the unemployment rate fell from 6.0 percent to 5.2 percent. The rapid increase in aggregate demand caused a rise in the inflation rate. The price level increased from 106.3 in 2003 to 109.1 in 2004, for an inflation rate of 2.6 percent.

mid-2007. Gasoline prices rose from $1.50 per gallon in early 2004 to more than $3.00 per gallon in mid-2007. Rising oil prices resulted in the *SRAS* being to the left of where it would have been, which increased inflation and deceased real GDP growth. Many economists believe that rising gasoline prices also reduced the growth in aggregate demand by reducing spending on other goods and services. Managers at Wal-Mart believed that the slow increase in sales at many of their stores was due to consumers having less income left to spend after filling up their cars.

The economy in 2007 was also feeling the effects of hard times in the housing market. When the economy began to fall into recession during 2001, the Federal Reserve had taken actions to lower interest rates. As the interest rates on mortgage loans declined, more consumers began to buy new homes. New home sales rose 46 percent, from 877,000 in 2000 to 1,283,000 in 2005. This increase in new home sales helped reduce the severity of the 2001 recession and sustain the following expansion. But by 2005, it had become clear that some new construction and some part of the rapidly rising prices for new and existing homes was due to a speculative "bubble." A bubble occurs when people become less concerned with the underlying value of an asset—either a physical asset, such as a house, or a financial asset, such as a stock—and focus instead on expectations of the price of the asset increasing. In some areas of the country, many houses were being purchased by investors who intended to resell them for higher prices than they paid for them and did not intend to live in them. Speculative bubbles eventually come to an end, and the housing bubble began to deflate in 2006. By early 2007, new home sales were running at an annual rate of less than 900,000, down more than 40 percent from the peak in mid-2005. Housing prices were declining as well. The decline in the housing market slowed the growth of aggregate demand as spending on residential construction—a component of investment spending—declined. In addition, with home prices falling, consumption spending on furniture, appliances, and home improvements declined, as many households found it more difficult to borrow against the value of their homes.

In late 2007, economists were divided over whether the twin blows of higher oil prices and a declining housing sector would be sufficient to push the economy into a recession. The majority of economists forecast that growth in real GDP would slow but that the economy would not tip into recession.

Solved Problem | 12-4

Showing the Oil Shock of 1974–1975 on a Dynamic Aggregate Demand and Aggregate Supply Graph

The 1974–1975 recession clearly illustrates how a supply shock affects the economy. Following the Arab–Israeli War of 1973, the Organization of Petroleum Exporting Countries (OPEC) increased the price of a barrel of oil from less than \$3 to more than \$10. Use this information and the statistics in the following table to draw a dynamic aggregate demand and aggregate supply graph showing macroeconomic equilibrium for 1974 and 1975. Assume that the aggregate demand curve did not shift between 1974 and 1975. Provide a brief explanation of your graph.

	ACTUAL REAL GDP	POTENTIAL REAL GDP	PRICE LEVEL
1974	\$4.32 trillion	\$4.35 trillion	34.7
1975	\$4.31 trillion	\$4.50 trillion	38.0

Source: U.S. Bureau of Economic Analysis.

SOLVING THE PROBLEM:

Step 1: **Review the chapter material.** This problem is about using the dynamic aggregate demand and aggregate supply model, so you may want to review the section "A Dynamic Aggregate Demand and Aggregate Supply Model," which begins on page 408.

Step 2: **Use the information in the table to draw the graph.** You need to draw five curves: *SRAS* and *LRAS* for both 1974 and 1975 and *AD*, which is the same for both years. You know that the two *LRAS* curves will be vertical lines at the values given for potential GDP in the table. Because of the large supply shock, you know that the *SRAS* curve shifted to the left. You are instructed to assume that the *AD* curve did not shift. Your graph should look like this:

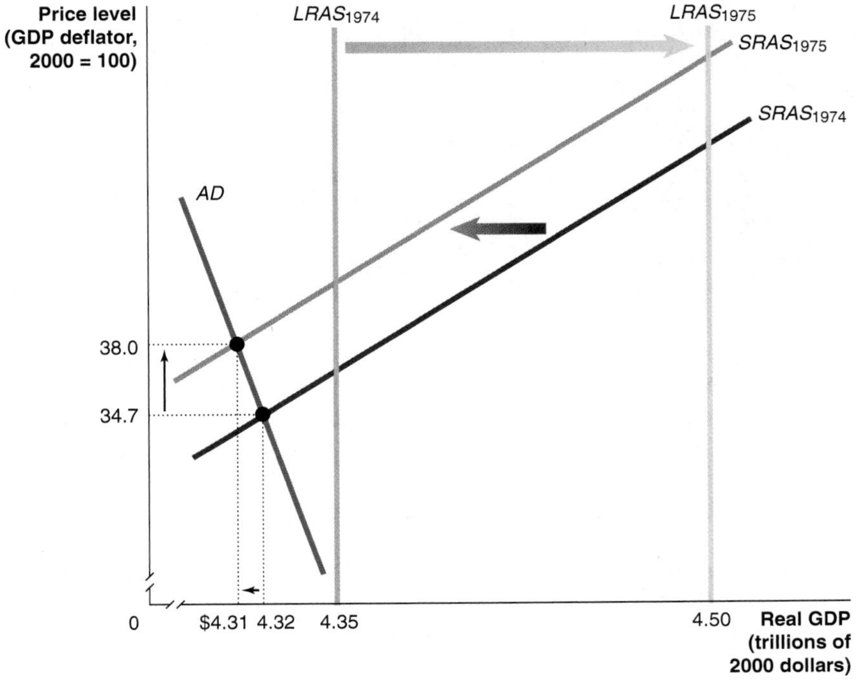

Step 3: Explain your graph. $LRAS_{1974}$ and $LRAS_{1975}$ are at the levels of potential real GDP for each year. Macroeconomic equilibrium for 1974 occurs where the *AD* curve intersects the $SRAS_{1974}$ curve, with real GDP of $4.32 trillion and a price level of 34.7. Macroeconomic equilibrium for 1975 occurs where the *AD* curve intersects the $SRAS_{1975}$ curve, with real GDP of $4.31 trillion and a price level of 38.0.

EXTRA CREDIT: As a result of the supply shock, the economy moved from an equilibrium output just below potential GDP in 1974 (the recession actually began right at the end of 1973) to an equilibrium well below potential GDP in 1975. With real GDP in 1975 about 4.2 percent below its potential level, the unemployment rate soared from 5.6 percent in 1974 to 8.5 percent in 1975.

YOUR TURN: For more practice, do related problems 4.4 and 4.5 on page 424 at the end of this chapter.

>> End Solved Problem 12-4

Making the Connection | Do Oil Shocks Still Cause Recessions?

FedEx burns a lot of gasoline and jet fuel to power its 70,000 trucks and 672 aircraft worldwide. An increase in oil prices causes FedEx to raise the prices it charges its customers, which reduces the quantity of packages those customers ship. If rising oil prices affect enough firms, the short-run aggregate supply curve will shift to the left, potentially pushing the economy into recession. This outcome occurred when oil prices rose from $3 per barrel to $10 per barrel in the early 1970s, pushing the U.S. economy into recession during 1974 and 1975. During those years, real GDP declined, and the unemployment rate rose to 9 percent.

FedEx's trucks and jets have become more fuel efficient.

The effects on the economy of earlier "oil shocks" led some economists during the mid-2000s to predict that the United States would experience a recession as oil prices rose from an average of $33.75 per barrel in 2004 to $47.60 in 2005 and $57.10 in 2006. In fact, though, the economy continued to grow, and at least through 2007, a recession was avoided. Had the economy become less vulnerable to rising oil prices? Some economists argued that, in fact, this was the case. Because of earlier increases in the price of oil, by the mid-2000s, many firms had switched to less-oil-dependent production processes. For example, FedEx and other firms used more fuel efficient jets and trucks. As a result, the U.S. economy was consuming almost 60 percent less oil per dollar of GDP than it had in the mid-1970s. Today, oil price increases do not shift the short-run aggregate supply curve as far to the left as similar increases did 30 years ago.

In addition, the oil price increases of the mid-2000s occurred gradually, which gave individuals and firms time to adjust. Earlier increases in the price of oil had occurred more abruptly—usually as a result of conflict in the Middle East, where at the time more than half of world oil production took place. Finally, the oil price increases of the mid-2000s took place at a time when the U.S. economy was growing, so it was easier to absorb the adverse effects of higher oil prices. Economist Keith Sill of the Federal Reserve Bank of Philadelphia has estimated that a 10 percent increase in oil prices will result in a temporary reduction in the annual growth of real GDP of about 0.5 percent. So, higher oil prices reduced the increases in real GDP during the mid-2000s but did not tip the economy into recession.

Sources: Nick Timiraos, "'Goldilocks' Economy: Can It Last?" *Wall Street Journal*, February 3, 2007, p. A9; and Keith Sill, "The Macroeconomics of Oil Shocks," *Business Review*, First Quarter 2007, pp. 21–31.

YOUR TURN: Test your understanding by doingrelated problem 4.13 on page 425 at the end of this chapter.

Continued from page 391

Economics in YOUR Life!

At the beginning of this chapter, we asked you to consider whether during a recession your employer is likely to reduce your pay and cut the prices of the products he or she sells. In this chapter, the dynamic aggregate demand and aggregate supply model showed that even during a recession, the price level rarely falls. In fact, the price level in the United States has not fallen from one year to the next since the 1930s. A typical firm is therefore unlikely to cut its prices during a recession. So, the owner of the coffeehouse you work in will probably not cut the price of lattes unless sales have declined drastically. We also saw that most firms are more reluctant to cut wages than to increase them because wage cuts can have a negative effect on worker morale and productivity. Given that you are a highly skilled barista, your employer is particularly unlikely to cut your wages for fear that you might quit and work for a competitor.

Conclusion

Chapter 3 demonstrated the power of the microeconomic model of demand and supply in explaining how the prices and quantities of individual products are determined. This chapter showed that we need a different model to explain the behavior of the whole economy. We saw that the macroeconomic model of aggregate demand and aggregate supply explains fluctuations in real GDP and the price level.

One of the great disagreements among economists and political leaders is whether the federal government should intervene to try to reduce fluctuations in real GDP and keep the unemployment and inflation rates low. We explore this important issue in Chapters 14 and 15, but first, in Chapter 13, we consider the role money plays in the economy.

Read *An Inside Look* on the next page to learn how a decline in the growth rate of real GDP affected UPS.

An Inside **LOOK**

Profits at UPS Signal Slow Growth in the U.S. Economy

WALL STREET JOURNAL, APRIL 26, 2007

Freight Carrier Weakness Shows Retailer Uncertainty

a Profit declines and lackluster outlooks from three freight-transportation giants, led by United Parcel Service Inc., indicate rising uncertainty about the economy among retailers and other big customers ahead of the important holiday-shipping season.

Preparations for the holiday-freight rush—when goods from Asia and other overseas suppliers fill ships, trains, planes and trucks—gear up months before the surge later in the year. Slowness now casts growing doubt on a turnaround in shipping volumes that had been predicted for this summer and fall.

"The boom in cargo imports has buoyed the whole shipping system for the last three years, but we can't count on that again this year," said Paul Bingham, a principal at Global Insight Inc., a consulting firm in Waltham, Mass., that expects U.S. containerized imports to rise 6% this year, down from its previous forecast of 7% growth.

b Major freight carriers, such as UPS, which posted its first quarterly decline in net income in more than three years, are deep in discussions with their largest customers about how to handle their holiday-season cargo. Early indications aren't encouraging, with some customers waiting longer than usual to order inventory and line up shipping capacity because of uncertainty about the economy, according to some freight-industry analysts and company executives.

"In talking to our customer base, today they are not real optimistic" about the peak season, Scott Davis, UPS vice chairman and chief financial officer, said in an interview. "They are concerned with where their customers are."

In the first quarter, package-delivery volume at Atlanta-based UPS rose 0.4% from the year earlier to an average of 15.1 million packages a day. That was the slowest growth rate in two years. U.S. deliveries, generating nearly 90% of the company's volume, posted their first decline in four years. Mr. Davis said the economy has slowed "more than we anticipated," adding that UPS is considering "hundreds of initiatives" to trim expenses amid the slump.

In addition to UPS's profit decline of 14%, railroad operator Norfolk Southern Corp. said its first-quarter profit fell 6.6%, hurt by continued weakness in the automotive and housing sectors. Trucking carrier Arkansas Best Corp., Fort Smith, Ark., saw its profit shrink by 22%, but said a cost-cutting program begun last fall helped it offset weakened freight demand.

c The stubbornly persistent freight slowdown that began last year has been particularly tough on trucking companies, which are facing overcapacity and pressure to cut prices because they increased truck purchases before stricter engine-emission standards took effect. Railroad shipments fell nearly 5% in the first quarter, but tight capacity has helped railroad operators maintain their pricing power so far. Norfolk Southern, of Norfolk, Va., said pricing remained strong in the first quarter.

Norfolk Southern didn't indicate when it anticipates a rebound in freight volume. But railroad Burlington Northern Santa Fe Corp. warned earlier this week that it is concerned traffic levels could remain soft for the rest of the year.

For the past two years, retailers and importers were placing orders by now with non-U.S. suppliers for merchandise to sell in the second half, including Christmas, said Mr. Bingham, the freight-industry consultant. Ordering early helped reduce the risk of delay or lost sales if ports and rail lines became congested. This year, though, many importers are less confident of growth prospects and less worried about logistical snags, so ocean-shipping lines are seeing lower booking levels for the holiday-shipping season. . . .

Source: Daniel Machalaba and Corey Dade, "Freight Carrier Weakness Shows Retailer Uncertainty," Wall Street Journal, April 26, 2007, p. A4.

Key Points in the Article

This article discusses why UPS and other freight-transportation companies reported weak earnings for the first quarter of 2007 and indicates that this weakness might persist for much of the year. The article explains that UPS attributed its weak earnings to the slowing growth rate of the U.S. economy. Freight-transportation companies' earnings are dependent on the volume of shipments to retailers; in a slowing economy, retailers typically reduce their orders from manufacturers as they carry smaller planned inventories than usual. Finally, the article mentions that this slowdown in freight transportation has been particularly hard on trucking companies, which find themselves with excess capacity—too many trucks—thanks to the combination of a fall in ground-freight transportation volume and a 2007 environmental regulation that introduced a new—and relatively untested—heavy-truck engine technology. To reduce their dependence on higher-priced trucks with the new engine technology, many trucking firms increased their purchases of trucks during 2006.

Analyzing the News

a UPS, together with railroad-operator Norfolk Southern and truck-carrier Arkansas Best, warned investors of weak profit growth for 2007. Meanwhile, the Department of Commerce announced that the growth in U.S. real GDP slowed to 0.6 percent in the first quarter of the year, and some economists forecast that the U.S. economy would continue to grow slowly through much of 2007. UPS attributed its falling profits to the slow growth of the U.S. economy. During the second and third quarters of each year, transportation companies such as UPS typically generate a large portion of their annual profits by shipping goods to retailers, which accumulate planned inventories as they prepare for the holiday shopping season in the fourth quarter of the year. However, in a slowing economy, retailers typically carry relatively smaller planned inventories and, hence, have relatively less need for the freight-transportation services of companies such as UPS.

b Although the volume of goods that UPS shipped in the first quarter of 2007 grew from a year earlier, the growth was just 0.4 percent, reflecting the weak growth of the U.S. economy over the same period. Put differently, earnings at UPS did not suffer because U.S. aggregate demand fell, rather, earnings suffered because the short-run increase in real GDP was less than the increase in potential real GDP. We can use the dynamic aggregate demand and aggregate supply model that you learned about in this chapter to analyze what happened to the U.S. economy from the first quarter of 2006 to the first quarter of 2007. The figure shows that in the first quarter of 2006, the U.S. economy was in a short-run macroeconomic equilibrium with real GDP of $11.2 trillion and a price level—as measured by the GDP implicit price deflator—of 115.4. During the remainder of 2006 and the early part of 2007, aggregate demand, short-run aggregate supply, and long-run aggregate supply all shifted to the right. Consequently, short-run real GDP rose to $11.4 trillion, and the price level rose to 118.8. So, from the first quarter of 2006 to the first quarter of 2007, the U.S. economy experienced growth in real GDP of only 1.8 percent, while the inflation rate was 2.9 percent.

c As of the first quarter of 2007, the slowdown in ground-freight transportation had been particularly hard on trucking companies, which had too much capacity thanks to a combination of a fall in ground-freight transportation volume and large truck purchases during 2006. Many ground-freight transportation firms rushed to purchase heavy trucks in 2006, before new environmental regulations—with resulting higher prices—took effect. These firms therefore found themselves with too few goods to ship volume and too many trucks in early 2007.

Thinking Critically

1. Between the first quarter of 2006 and the first quarter of 2007, when U.S. real GDP growth slowed to 0.6 percent, the foreign exchange value of the U.S. dollar fell against most of its major trading partners' currencies. What effect, if any, did this fall in the value of the U.S. dollar have on the magnitude of the rightward shift of *AD* shown in the figure on this page?
2. Freight-transportation companies such as UPS provide domestic shipping services in many countries. How, if at all, might this geographic diversification alter how UPS's earnings would otherwise respond to a slowing U.S. economy?

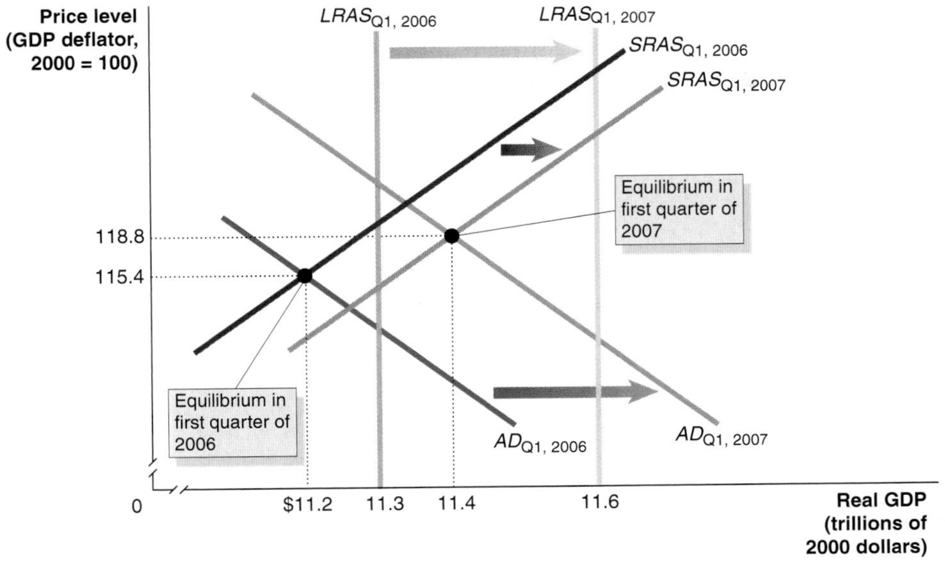

The U.S. economic expansion from the first quarter of 2006 to the first quarter of 2007.

Source: U.S. Bureau of Economic Analysis.

Key Terms

Aggregate demand and aggregate supply model, p. 392

Aggregate demand curve, p. 392

Fiscal policy, p. 395

Long-run aggregate supply curve, p. 399

Menu costs, p. 401

Monetary policy, p. 395

Short-run aggregate supply curve, p. 393

Stagflation, p. 407

Supply shock, p. 402

12.1 LEARNING OBJECTIVE 12.1 | Identify the determinants of aggregate demand and distinguish between a movement along the aggregate demand curve and a shift of the curve, **pages 392–398.**

Aggregate Demand

Summary

The **aggregate demand and aggregate supply model** enables us to explain short-run fluctuations in real GDP and price level. The **aggregate demand curve** shows the relationship between the price level and the level of planned aggregate expenditures by households, firms, and the government. The **short-run aggregate supply curve** shows the relationship in the short run between the price level and the quantity of real GDP supplied by firms. The **long-run aggregate supply curve** shows the relationship in the long run between the price level and the quantity of real GDP supplied. The four components of aggregate demand are consumption (*C*), investment (*I*), government purchases (*G*), and net exports (*NX*). The aggregate demand curve is downward sloping because a decline in the price level causes consumption, investment, and net exports to increase. If the price level changes but all else remains constant, the economy will move up or down a stationary aggregate demand curve. If any variable other than the price level changes, the aggregate demand curve will shift. The variables that cause the aggregate demand curve to shift are divided into three categories: changes in government policies, changes in the expectations of households and firms, and changes in foreign variables. For example, **monetary policy** involves the actions the Federal Reserve takes to manage the money supply and interest rates to pursue macroeconomic policy objectives. When the Federal Reserve takes actions to change interest rates, consumption and investment spending will change, shifting the aggregate demand curve. **Fiscal policy** involves changes in federal taxes and purchases that are intended to achieve macroeconomic policy objectives. Changes in federal taxes and purchases shift the aggregate demand curve.

myeconlab Get Ahead of the Curve — Visit www.myeconlab.com to complete these exercises online and get instant feedback.

Review Questions

1.1 Explain the three reasons the aggregate demand curve slopes downward.

1.2 What are the differences between the *AD* curve and the demand curve for an individual product, such as apples?

1.3 What are the variables that cause the *AD* curve to shift? For each variable, identify whether an increase in that variable will cause the *AD* curve to shift to the right or to the left.

Problems and Applications

1.4 Explain how each of the following events would affect the aggregate demand curve.
   a. An increase in the price level
   b. An increase in government purchases
   c. Higher state income taxes
   d. Higher interest rates
   e. Faster income growth in other countries

1.5 *(Related to the* ***Don't Let This Happen to You!*** *on page 394)* A student was asked to draw an aggregate demand and aggregate supply graph to illustrate the effect of an increase in aggregate supply. The student drew the following graph:
The student explained the graph as follows:

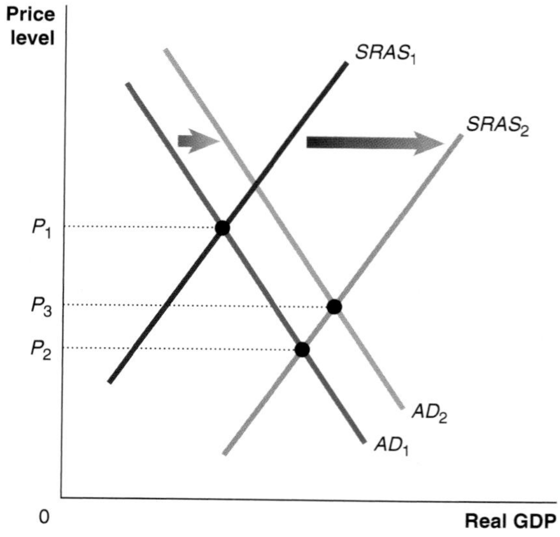

An increase in aggregate supply causes a shift from $SRAS_1$ to $SRAS_2$. Because this shift in the aggregate supply curve results in a lower price level, consumption, investment, and net exports will increase. This change causes the aggregate demand curve to shift to the right, from AD_1 to AD_2. We know that real GDP will increase, but we can't be sure whether the price level will rise or fall because that depends on whether the aggregate supply curve or the aggregate demand curve has shifted farther to the right. I assume that aggregate supply shifts out farther than aggregate demand, so I show the final price level, P_3, as being lower than the initial price level, P_1.

Explain whether you agree or disagree with the student's analysis. Be careful to explain exactly what—if anything—you find wrong with this analysis.

1.6 **(Related to *Solved Problem 12-1* on page 396)** Explain whether each of the following will cause a shift of the *AD* curve or a movement along the *AD* curve.
   a. Firms become more optimistic and increase their spending on machinery and equipment.
   b. The federal government increases taxes in an attempt to reduce a budget deficit.
   c. The U.S. economy experiences 4 percent inflation.

1.7 According to an article published in *BusinessWeek* in October 2002, "The stock market plunge is weighing heavily on both businesses and consumers." Why would a decline in stock prices "weigh heavily" on businesses and consumers? What were the consequences of this for the economy?

Source: James C. Cooper and Kathleen Madigan, "Consumers: Still Some Pluses among the Minuses," *BusinessWeek*, October 21, 2002.

1.8 **(Related to the *Making the Connection* on page 395)** Suppose that a consumer in Germany buys a Ford Mustang for a price of $30,000. Do U.S. exports increase by $30,000? Briefly explain.

>> End Learning Objective 12.1

12.2 LEARNING OBJECTIVE 12.2 | Identify the determinants of aggregate supply and distinguish between a movement along the short-run aggregate supply curve and a shift of the curve, **pages 399–403.**

Aggregate Supply

Summary

The **long-run aggregate supply curve** is a vertical line because in the long run, real GDP is always at its potential level and is unaffected by the price level. The short-run aggregate supply curve slopes upward because workers and firms fail to predict accurately the future price level. The three main explanations of why this failure results in an upward-sloping aggregate supply curve are that (1) contracts make wages and prices "sticky," (2) businesses often adjust wages slowly, and (3) menu costs make some prices sticky. **Menu costs** are the costs to firms of changing prices on menus or catalogs. If the price level changes but all else remains constant, the economy will move up or down a stationary aggregate supply curve. If any variable other than the price level changes, the aggregate supply curve will shift. The aggregate supply curve shifts as a result of increases in the labor force and capital stock, technological change, expected increases or decreases in the future price level, adjustments of workers and firms to errors in past expectations about the price level, and unexpected increases or decreases in the price of an important raw material. A **supply shock** is an unexpected event that causes the short-run aggregate supply curve to shift.

myeconlab Get Ahead of the Curve Visit www.myeconlab.com to complete these exercises online and get instant feedback.

Review Questions

2.1 Explain why the long-run aggregate supply curve is vertical.

2.2 What variables cause the long-run aggregate supply curve to shift? For each variable, identify whether an increase in that variable will cause the long-run aggregate supply curve to shift to the right or to the left.

2.3 Why does the short-run aggregate supply curve slope upward?

2.4 What variables cause the short-run aggregate supply curve to shift? For each variable, identify whether an increase in that variable will cause the short-run aggregate supply curve to shift to the right or to the left.

Problems and Applications

2.5 Explain how each of the following events would affect the long-run aggregate supply curve.
   a. A higher price level
   b. An increase in the labor force

c. An increase in the quantity of capital goods
d. Technological change

2.6 Explain how each of the following events would affect the short-run aggregate supply curve.
a. An increase in the price level
b. An increase in what the price level is expected to be in the future
c. A price level that is currently higher than expected
d. An unexpected increase in the price of an important raw material
e. An increase in the labor force

2.7 Suppose that workers and firms could always predict next year's price level with perfect accuracy. Briefly explain whether in these circumstances the *SRAS* curve still slopes upward.

2.8 Workers and firms often enter into contracts that fix prices or wages, sometimes for years at a time. If the price level turns out to be higher or lower than was expected when the contract was signed, one party to the contract will lose out. Briefly explain why, despite knowing this, workers and firms still sign long-term contracts.

2.9 A newspaper article noted, "About 50 percent of U.S. Steel's domestic production is tied up right now in long-term contracts pegged below market value price."
a. Why would U.S. Steel have entered into contracts to sell steel below the market price? (*Hint:* Is it likely that these contracts were negotiated before 2004?)
b. What impact is U.S. Steel selling steel below the current market price likely to have on its production and on the production of companies that buy its steel?

Source: Charles Sheehan, "Happy Days Are Here Again for U.S. Steel Corp.," (Allentown, Pennsylvania) *Morning Call*, November 28, 2004.

2.10 What are menu costs? How has the widespread use of computers and the Internet affected menu costs? If menu costs were eliminated, would the short-run aggregate supply curve be a vertical line? Briefly explain.

» End Learning Objective 12.2

12.3 LEARNING OBJECTIVE 12.3 | Use the aggregate demand and aggregate supply model to illustrate the difference between short-run and long-run macroeconomic equilibrium, **pages 404–407.**

Macroeconomic Equilibrium in the Long Run and the Short Run

Summary

In long-run macroeconomic equilibrium, the aggregate demand and short-run aggregate supply curves intersect at a point *on* the long-run aggregate supply curve. In short-run macroeconomic equilibrium, the aggregate demand and short-run aggregate supply curves often intersect at a point *off* the long-run aggregate supply curve. An automatic mechanism drives the economy to long-run equilibrium. If short-run equilibrium occurs at a point below potential real GDP, wages and prices will fall, and the short-run aggregate supply curve will shift to the right until potential GDP is restored. If short-run equilibrium occurs at a point beyond potential real GDP, wages and prices will rise, and the short-run aggregate supply curve will shift to the left until potential GDP is restored. Real GDP can be temporarily above or below its potential level, either because of shifts in the aggregate demand curve or because supply shocks lead to shifts in the aggregate supply curve. **Stagflation** is a combination of inflation and recession, usually resulting from a supply shock.

myeconlab Get Ahead of the Curve Visit www.myeconlab.com to complete these exercises online and get instant feedback.

Review Questions

3.1 What is the relationship among the *AD*, *SRAS*, and *LRAS* curves when the economy is in macroeconomic equilibrium?

3.2 What is a supply shock? Why might a supply shock lead to stagflation?

3.3 Why are the long-run effects of an increase in aggregate demand on price and output different from the short-run effects?

Problems and Applications

3.4 Draw a basic aggregate demand and aggregate supply graph (with *LRAS* constant) that shows the economy in long-run equilibrium.
a. Now assume that there is an increase in aggregate demand. Show the resulting short-run equilibrium on your graph. Explain how the economy adjusts back to long-run equilibrium.
b. Now assume that there is an unexpected increase in the price of an important raw material. Show the resulting short-run equilibrium on your graph. Explain how the economy adjusts back to long-run equilibrium.

3.5 Many economists believe that some wages and prices are "sticky downward," meaning that these wages and prices increase quickly when demand is increasing but decrease slowly, if at all, when demand is decreasing. Discuss the consequences of this for the automatic mechanism that brings the economy back to potential GDP after an increase in aggregate demand. Would your answer change if aggregate demand decreased rather than increased? Explain.

3.6 Consider the data in the following table for the years 1969 and 1970 (the values for real GDP are in 2000 dollars).

YEAR	ACTUAL REAL GDP	POTENTIAL REAL GDP	UNEMPLOYMENT RATE
1969	$3.77 trillion	$3.67 trillion	3.5%
1970	$3.77 trillion	$3.80 trillion	4.9%

Sources: U.S. Department of Commerce; and Bureau of Economic Analysis.

a. In 1969, actual real GDP was greater than potential real GDP. Explain how this is possible.
b. Even though real GDP in 1970 was the same as real GDP in 1969, the unemployment rate increased substantially from 1969 to 1970. Why did this increase in unemployment occur?
c. Was the inflation rate in 1970 likely to have been higher or lower than the inflation rate in 1969? Does your answer depend on whether the recession was caused by a change in a component of aggregate demand or by a supply shock?

3.7 Use the following graph to answer the questions.

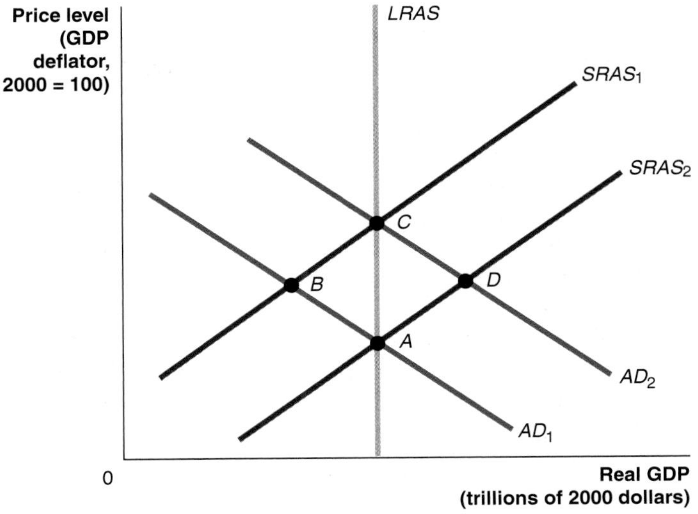

a. Which of the points *A*, *B*, *C*, or *D* can represent a long-run equilibrium?
b. Suppose that initially the economy is at point *A*. If aggregate demand increases from AD_1 to AD_2, which point represents the economy's short-run equilibrium? Which point represents the eventual long-run equilibrium? Briefly explain how the economy adjusts from the short-run equilibrium to the long-run equilibrium.

>> End Learning Objective 12.3

12.4 LEARNING OBJECTIVE 12.4 | Use the dynamic aggregate demand and aggregate supply model to analyze macroeconomic conditions, **pages 408–417.**

A Dynamic Aggregate Demand and Aggregate Supply Model

Summary

To make the aggregate demand and aggregate supply model more realistic, we need to make it *dynamic* by incorporating three facts that were left out of the basic model: (1) Potential real GDP increases continually, shifting the long-run aggregate supply curve to the right; (2) during most years, aggregate demand will be shifting to the right; and (3) except during periods when workers and firms expect high rates of inflation, the aggregate supply curve will be shifting to the right. The dynamic aggregate demand and aggregate supply model allows us to analyze macroeconomic conditions, including the recovery from the 2001 recession.

myeconlab Get Ahead of the Curve Visit www.myeconlab.com to complete these exercises online and get instant feedback.

Review Questions

4.1 What are the key differences between the basic aggregate demand and aggregate supply model and the dynamic aggregate demand and aggregate supply model?

4.2 In the dynamic aggregate demand and aggregate supply model, what is the result of aggregate demand increasing faster than potential real GDP? What is the result of aggregate demand increasing slower than potential real GDP?

Problems and Applications

4.3 Draw a dynamic aggregate demand and aggregate supply graph showing the economy moving from potential GDP in 2006 to potential GDP in 2007, with no inflation. Your graph should contain the *AD*, *SRAS*, and *LRAS* curves for both 2006 and 2007 and should indicate the short-run macroeconomic equilibrium for each year and the directions in which the curves have shifted. Identify what must happen to have growth during 2007 without inflation.

4.4 **(Related to *Solved Problem 12-4* on page 415)** Consider the information in the following table for the first two years of the Great Depression (the values for real GDP are in 2000 dollars).

YEAR	ACTUAL REAL GDP	POTENTIAL REAL GDP	PRICE LEVEL
1929	$865.2 billion	$865.2 billion	12.0
1930	$790.7 billion	$895.7 billion	11.5

Sources: U.S. Department of Commerce; and Bureau of Economic Analysis.

a. What information in the table is different from what we would expect to have had happen during a recession in the past 50 years?

b. Draw a dynamic aggregate demand and aggregate supply graph to illustrate what happened during these years. Your graph should contain the *AD*, *SRAS*, and *LRAS* curves for both 1929 and 1930 and should indicate the short-run macroeconomic equilibrium for each year and the directions in which the curves have shifted.

4.5 **(Related to *Solved Problem 12-4* on page 415)** Look again at Solved Problem 12-4 on the supply shock of 1974–1975. In the table, the price level for 1974 is given as 34.7, and the price level for 1975 is given as 38.0. The values for the price level are well below 100. Does this indicate that inflation must have been low during these years? Briefly explain.

4.6 **(Related to the *Making the Connection* on page 412)** Briefly explain whether you agree or disagree with the following argument: "Whenever productivity increases, it is possible to produce the same amount of goods and services with fewer workers. Therefore, over the long run, as productivity increases, total employment should fall."

4.7 In the graph in the next column, suppose that the economy moves from point *A* in year 1 to point *B* in year 2. Using the graph, briefly explain your answers to each of the questions.

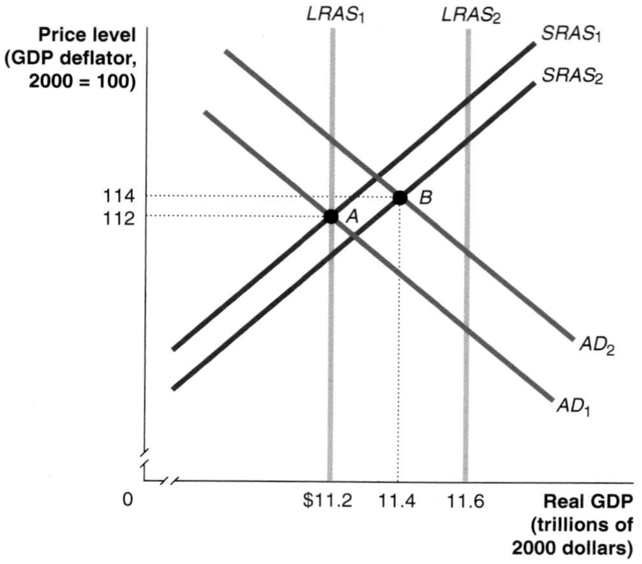

a. What is the growth rate in potential real GDP from year 1 to year 2?

b. Is the unemployment rate in year 2 higher or lower than in year 1?

c. What is the inflation rate in year 2?

d. What is the growth rate of real GDP in year 2?

4.8 Explain whether you agree or disagree with the following statement:

> The dynamic aggregate demand and aggregate supply model predicts that a recession caused by a decline in *AD* will cause the inflation rate to fall. I know that the 2001 recession was caused by a fall in *AD*, but the inflation rate was not lower after the recession. The prices of most products were definitely higher in 2002 than they were in 2001, so the inflation rate could not have fallen.

4.9 An economist at the Federal Reserve Bank of St. Louis wrote the following about the recovery from the 2001 recession:

> [Since the end of the recession,] real business fixed investment (BFI)—expenditures on structures, equipment and software—has declined at a 2.2 percent annual rate. By contrast, in the first four quarters of the typical recovery, real BFI *increases* a little more than 8 percent.

Why didn't investment spending increase after the 2001 recession as much as it normally does in the year following the end of a recession?

Source: Kevin L. Kliesen, "Waiting for the Investment Boom? It Might Be a While," *National Economic Trends*, May 2003.

4.10 An article in the *New York Times* in August 2003 stated the following: "A cutback in business spending when the Internet and stock market bubbles burst brought on the recession of 2001 and the prolonged weakness that has existed since then."

a. What does the article mean by "business spending"?
b. What does it mean by the "Internet and stock market bubbles"?
c. Why would the bursting of these bubbles affect business spending?

Source: Louis Uchitelle and Jennifer Bayot, "Business Spending Helps to Offset Lag in Refinancing," *New York Times*, August 9, 2003.

4.11 The following excerpt is from an article in the *New York Times*: "The number of Americans living below the poverty line increased by more than 1.3 million [during 2002], even though the economy technically edged out of recession during the same period." Briefly discuss why poverty increased during 2002 even though the economy was in the expansion phase of the business cycle.

Source: Lynette Clemetson, "Census Shows Ranks of Poor Rose by 1.3 Million," *New York Times*, September 3, 2003.

4.12 **(Related to the *Chapter Opener* on page 390)** In the chapter opener, we mentioned that former Federal Reserve Chairman Alan Greenspan used to meet regularly with FedEx Chairman Fred Smith because Greenspan believed that changes in the volume of packages being shipped by FedEx was a good indicator of how the general economy was doing. Briefly compare how sensitive FedEx's sales are to changes in the business cycle to how sensitive the following firms' sales are to changes in the business cycle: Ford Motor Company, Starbucks, Toll Brothers (home builders), and Paramount Pictures (movies). In other words, do FedEx's sales fluctuate more or less than the sales of each of these other firms as the economy moves from recession to expansion and back to recession?

4.13 **(Related to the *Making the Connection* on page 416)** Suppose the price of a barrel of oil increases from \$50 to \$70. Use a basic aggregate demand and aggregate supply graph to show the short-run and long-run effects on the economy.

>> End Learning Objective 12.4

Appendix

Macroeconomic Schools of Thought

LEARNING OBJECTIVE

Understand macroeconomic schools of thought.

Macroeconomics as a separate field of economics began with the publication in 1936 of John Maynard Keynes's book *The General Theory of Employment, Interest, and Money*. Keynes, an economist at the University of Cambridge in England, was attempting to explain the devastating Great Depression of the 1930s. As we discussed in Chapter 11, real GDP in the United States declined by more than 25 percent between 1929 and 1933 and did not return to its potential level until the United States entered World War II in 1941. The unemployment rate soared to 25 percent by 1933 and did not return to its 1929 level until 1942. Keynes developed a version of the aggregate demand and aggregate supply model to explain these facts. The widespread acceptance during the 1930s and 1940s of Keynes's model became known as the **Keynesian revolution**.

Keynesian revolution The name given to the widespread acceptance during the 1930s and 1940s of John Maynard Keynes's macroeconomic model.

In fact, the aggregate demand and aggregate supply model remains the most widely accepted approach to analyzing macroeconomic issues. Because the model has been modified significantly from Keynes's day, many economists who use the model today refer to themselves as *new Keynesians*. The new Keynesians emphasize the importance of the stickiness of wages and prices in explaining fluctuations in real GDP. A significant number of economists, however, dispute whether the aggregate demand and aggregate supply model, as we have discussed it in this chapter, is the best way to analyze macroeconomic issues. These alternative *schools of thought* use models that differ significantly from the standard aggregate demand and aggregate supply model. We can briefly consider each of the three major alternative models:

1. The monetarist model
2. The new classical model
3. The real business cycle model

The Monetarist Model

The monetarist model—also known as the neo-Quantity Theory of Money model—was developed beginning in the 1940s by Milton Friedman, an economist at the University of Chicago who was awarded the Nobel Prize in Economics in 1976. Friedman argued that the Keynesian approach overstates the amount of macroeconomic instability in the economy. In particular, he argued that the economy will ordinarily be at potential real GDP. In the book *A Monetary History of the United States: 1867–1960*, written with Anna Jacobson Schwartz, Friedman argued that most fluctuations in real output were caused by fluctuations in the money supply rather than by fluctuations in consumption spending or investment spending. Friedman and Schwartz argued that the severity of the Great Depression was caused by the Federal Reserve's allowing the quantity of money in the economy to fall by more than 25 percent between 1929 and 1933.

In the United States, the Federal Reserve is responsible for managing the quantity of money. As we will discuss further in Chapter 14, the Federal Reserve has typically focused more on controlling interest rates than on controlling the money supply. Friedman has argued that the Federal Reserve should change its practices and adopt a **monetary growth rule**, which is a plan for increasing the quantity of money at a fixed rate. Friedman believed that adopting a monetary growth rule would reduce fluctuations in real GDP, employment, and inflation.

Monetary growth rule A plan for increasing the quantity of money at a fixed rate that does not respond to changes in economic conditions.

Friedman's ideas, which are referred to as **monetarism**, attracted significant support during the 1970s and early 1980s, when the economy experienced high rates of unemployment and inflation. The support for monetarism declined during the late 1980s and 1990s, when the unemployment and inflation rates were relatively low. In Chapter 13, we will discuss the *quantity theory of money*, which underlies the monetarist model.

Monetarism The macroeconomic theories of Milton Friedman and his followers; particularly the idea that the quantity of money should be increased at a constant rate.

The New Classical Model

The new classical model was developed in the mid-1970s by a group of economists including Nobel laureate Robert Lucas of the University of Chicago, Thomas Sargent of New York University, and Robert Barro of Harvard University. Some of the views held by the new classical macroeconomists are similar to those held by economists before the Great Depression. Keynes referred to the economists before the Great Depression as "classical economists." Like the classical economists, the new classical macroeconomists believe that the economy normally will be at potential real GDP. They also believe that wages and prices adjust quickly to changes in demand and supply. Put another way, they believe the stickiness in wages and prices emphasized by the new Keynesians is unimportant.

Lucas argued that workers and firms have *rational expectations*, meaning that they form their expectations of the future values of economic variables, such as the inflation rate, by making use of all available information, including information on variables—such as changes in the quantity of money—that might affect aggregate demand. If the actual inflation rate is lower than the expected inflation rate, the actual real wage will be higher than the expected real wage. These higher real wages will lead to a recession because they will cause firms to hire fewer workers and cut back on production. As workers and firms adjust their expectations to the lower inflation rate, the real wage will decline, and employment and production will expand, bringing the economy out of recession. The ideas of Lucas and his followers are referred to as the **new classical macroeconomics**. Supporters of the new classical model agree with supporters of the monetarist model that the Federal Reserve should adopt a monetary growth rule. They argue that a monetary growth rule will make it easier for workers and firms to accurately forecast the price level, thereby reducing fluctuations in real GDP.

New classical macroeconomics The macroeconomic theories of Robert Lucas and others, particularly the idea that workers and firms have rational expectations.

The Real Business Cycle Model

Beginning in the 1980s, some economists, including Nobel laureates Finn Kydland of Carnegie Mellon University and Edward Prescott of Arizona State University, argued that Lucas was correct in assuming that workers and firms formed their expectations rationally and that wages and prices adjust quickly to supply and demand but wrong about the source of fluctuations in real GDP. They argued that fluctuations in real GDP are caused by temporary shocks to productivity. These shocks can be negative, such as a decline in the availability of oil or other raw materials, or positive, such as technological change that makes it possible to produce more output with the same quantity of inputs.

According to this school of thought, shifts in the aggregate demand curve have no impact on real GDP because the short-run aggregate supply curve is vertical. Other schools of thought all believe that the short-run aggregate supply curve is upward sloping and that only the *long-run* aggregate supply curve is vertical. Fluctuations in real GDP occur when a negative productivity shock causes the short-run aggregate supply curve to shift to the left—reducing real GDP—or a positive productivity shock causes the short-run aggregate supply curve to shift to the right—increasing real GDP. Because this model focuses on "real" factors—productivity shocks—rather than changes in the quantity of money to explain fluctuations in real GDP, it is known as the **real business cycle model**.

Real business cycle model A macroeconomic model that focuses on real, rather than monetary, causes of the business cycle.

Karl Marx predicted that a final economic crisis would lead to the collapse of the market system.

Making the Connection

Karl Marx: Capitalism's Severest Critic

The schools of macroeconomic thought we have discussed in this appendix are considered part of mainstream economic theory because of their acceptance of the market system as the best means of raising living standards in the long run. One quite influential critic of mainstream economic theory was Karl Marx. Marx was born in Trier, Germany, in 1818. After graduating from the University of Berlin in 1841, he began a career as a political journalist and agitator. His political activities caused him to be expelled first from Germany and then from France and Belgium. In 1849, he moved to London, where he spent the remainder of his life.

In 1867, he published the first volume of his greatest work, *Das Kapital.* Marx read closely the most prominent mainstream economists, including Adam Smith, David Ricardo, and John Stuart Mill. But Marx believed that he understood how market systems would evolve in the long run much better than those earlier authors. Marx argued that the market system would eventually be replaced by a Communist economy in which the workers would control production. He believed in the *labor theory of value,* which attributed all of the value of a good or service to the labor that was embodied in it. According to Marx, the owners of businesses—capitalists—did not earn profits by contributing anything of value to the production of goods or services. Instead, capitalists earned profits because their "monopoly of the means of production"—their ownership of factories and machinery—allowed them to exploit workers by paying them wages that were much less than the value of workers' contribution to production.

Marx argued that wages of workers would be driven to levels that allowed only bare survival. He also argued that small firms would eventually be driven out of business by larger firms, forcing owners of small firms into the working class. Control of production would ultimately be concentrated in the hands of a few firms. These few remaining firms would have difficulty selling the goods they produced to the impoverished masses. A final economic crisis would lead the working classes to rise up, seize control of the economy, and establish Communism. Marx died in 1883 without providing a detailed explanation of how the Communist economy would operate.

Marx had relatively little influence on mainstream thinking in the United States, but several political parties in Europe were guided by his ideas. In 1917, the Bolshevik party seized control of Russia and established the Soviet Union, the first Communist state. Although the Soviet Union was a vicious dictatorship under Vladimir Lenin and his successor, Joseph Stalin, its prestige rose when it avoided the macroeconomic difficulties that plagued the market economies during the 1930s. By the late 1940s, Communist parties had also come to power in China and the countries of Eastern Europe. Poor economic performance contributed to the eventual collapse of the Soviet Union and its replacement by a market system, although one in which government intervention is still widespread. The Communist Party remains in power in China, but the economy is evolving toward a market system. Today, only North Korea and Cuba have economies that claim to be based on the ideas of Karl Marx.

Key Terms

Chapter 13

Money, Banks, and the Federal Reserve System

McDonald's Money Problems in Argentina

The McDonald's Big Mac is one of the most widely available products in the world. McDonald's 30,000 restaurants in 119 countries serve 50 million customers per day. Although some McDonald's restaurants are owned by the firm, many are franchises. A *franchise* is a business with the legal right to sell a good or service in a particular area. When a firm uses franchises, local entrepreneurs are able to buy and run the stores in their area. As McDonald's began expanding to other countries in the late 1960s, it relied on the franchise system. Franchisees in other countries were able to adapt the restaurants to the tastes of local customers. For example, although all 200 McDonald's restaurants in Argentina offer Big Macs and French fries, they also offer gourmet coffees and other foods not available in McDonald's restaurants in the United States.

In 2001, McDonald's restaurants in Argentina began to suffer from the macroeconomic problems plaguing that country. Argentina's woes centered on "money." Households and firms had begun to lose faith in the Argentine peso, the country's official money. They believed that the peso would rapidly lose its value, reducing their ability to buy goods and services. Many people converged on banks and tried to withdraw their money so they could either immediately buy goods and services or exchange Argentine pesos for U.S. dollars. To stop the outflow of money from the banking system, the government limited the amount of Argentine currency that could be withdrawn to $1,000 per account per month. This action further weakened the economy by reducing the funds households and firms had available to spend. In addition, banks became cautious about making loans, which in turn led to additional reductions in spending. An Argentine doctor was quoted as saying, "Now there's a lack of cash. . . . None of my patients can pay." Another person observed, "The chain of payments has been broken. There are millions of people forced to resort to bartering—an old sweater, anything, for goods just to survive." A cell phone dealer said, "These days, if customers want to pay us in tomatoes, I'll consider making a deal."

During the currency crisis, one Argentine province decided to issue its own currency, which it called the *patacone*. Because the patacone was not part of Argentina's official currency, there were doubts that local firms would accept it. McDonald's restaurants in the province decided to accept the new currency as payment for a meal they labeled the "Patacombo": two cheeseburgers, an order of French fries, and a soft drink.

Although the crisis in Argentina eventually passed, confidence in money remains vitally important. When you buy a DVD from a store, you get something of value. You give the store clerk dollar bills, or you might write a check with your name and the name of a bank on it or use a debit card linked to your checking account. Dollar bills and checks are pieces of paper that have no value in and of themselves. You and the store owner consider them valuable because others consider them valuable. This confidence and trust are hallmarks of money.

Confidence and trust cannot be taken for granted. As this example from Argentina shows, households and firms losing faith in an official money can harm trade and economic activity in an economy. **AN INSIDE LOOK AT POLICY** on **page 458** discusses how China's central bank is trying to control the money supply by slowing bank lending.

Sources: Tony Smith, "Freeze Has Argentines Crying All the Way to the Bank," Associated Press, December 11, 2001; and Matt Moffett, "Unfunny Money," *Wall Street Journal*, August 21, 2001.

LEARNING Objectives

After studying this chapter, you should be able to:

13.1 Define **money** and discuss its four functions, page 432.

13.2 Discuss the **definitions** of the **money supply** used in the United States today, page 436.

13.3 Explain how **banks create money**, page 440.

13.4 Discuss the three **policy tools** the **Federal Reserve** uses to manage the money supply, page 448.

13.5 Explain the **quantity theory of money** and use it to explain how high rates of inflation occur, page 452.

Economics in YOUR Life!

What if Money Became Increasingly Valuable?

Most people are used to the fact that as prices rise each year, the purchasing power of money falls. You will be able to buy fewer goods and services with $1,000 one year from now than you can today and even fewer goods and services the year after that. In fact, with an inflation rate of just 3 percent, in 25 years, $1,000 will buy only what $475 can buy today. Suppose, though, that you could live in an economy where the purchasing power of money rose each year? What would be the advantages and disadvantages of living in such an economy? As you read the chapter, see if you can answer these questions. You can check your answers against those we provide at the end of the chapter. **Continued on page 457**

In this chapter, we will explore the role of money in the economy. We will see how the banking system creates money and what policy tools the Federal Reserve uses to manage the quantity of money. At the end of the chapter, we will explore the link between changes in the quantity of money and changes in the price level. What you learn in this chapter will serve as an important foundation for understanding monetary policy and fiscal policy, which we study in the next three chapters.

13.1 LEARNING OBJECTIVE

13.1 | Define money and discuss its four functions.

What Is Money and Why Do We Need It?

Could an economy function without money? We know the answer to this is "yes" because there are many historical examples of economies where people traded goods for other goods rather than using money. For example, a farmer on the American frontier during colonial times might have traded a cow for a plow. Most economies, though, use money. What is money? The economic definition of **money** is any asset that people are generally willing to accept in exchange for goods and services or for payment of debts. Recall from Chapter 5 that an **asset** is anything of value owned by a person or a firm. There are many possible kinds of money: In West Africa, at one time, cowrie shells served as money. During World War II, prisoners of war used cigarettes as money.

Money Assets that people are generally willing to accept in exchange for goods and services or for payment of debts.

Asset Anything of value owned by a person or a firm.

Barter and the Invention of Money

To understand the importance of money, let's consider further the situation in economies that do not use money. These economies, where goods and services are traded directly for other goods and services, are called *barter economies*. Barter economies have a major shortcoming. To illustrate this shortcoming, consider a farmer on the American frontier in colonial days. Suppose the farmer needed another cow and proposed trading a spare plow to a neighbor for one of the neighbor's cows. If the neighbor did not want the plow, the trade would not happen. For a barter trade to take place between two people, each person must want what the other one has. Economists refer to this requirement as a *double coincidence of wants*. The farmer who wants the cow might eventually be able to obtain one if he first trades with some other neighbor for something the neighbor with the cow wants. However, it may take several trades before the farmer is ultimately able to trade for what the neighbor with the cow wants. Locating several trading partners and making several intermediate trades can take considerable time and energy.

The problems with barter provide an incentive to identify a product that most people will accept in exchange for what they have to trade. For example, in colonial times, animal skins were very useful in making clothing. The first governor of Tennessee actually received a salary of 1,000 deerskins per year, and the secretary of the treasury received 450 otter skins per year. A good used as money that also has value independent of its use as money is called a **commodity money**. Historically, once a good became widely accepted as money, people who did not have an immediate use for it would be willing to accept it. A colonial farmer—or the governor of Tennessee—might not want a deerskin, but as long as he knew he could use the deerskin to buy other goods and services, he would be willing to accept it in exchange for what he had to sell.

Commodity money A good used as money that also has value independent of its use as money.

Trading goods and services is much easier when money becomes available. People only need to sell what they have for money and then use the money to buy what they want. If the colonial family could find someone to buy their plow, they could use the money to buy the cow they wanted. The family with the cow would accept the money because they knew they could use it to buy what they wanted. When money is available, families are less likely to produce everything or nearly everything they need themselves and more likely to specialize.

Most people in modern economies are highly specialized. They do only one thing—work as a nurse, an accountant, or an engineer—and use the money they earn to buy everything else they need. As we discussed in Chapter 2, people become much more productive by specializing because they can pursue their *comparative advantage*. The high income levels in modern economies are based on the specialization that money makes possible. We can now answer the question, "Why do we need money?" *By making exchange easier, money allows for specialization and higher productivity.*

The Functions of Money

Anything used as money—whether a deerskin, a cowrie seashell, cigarettes, or a dollar bill—should fulfill the following four functions:

- Medium of exchange
- Unit of account
- Store of value
- Standard of deferred payment

Medium of Exchange Money serves as a medium of exchange when sellers are willing to accept it in exchange for goods or services. When the local supermarket accepts your $5 bill in exchange for bread and milk, the $5 bill is serving as a medium of exchange. To go back to our earlier example, with a medium of exchange, the farmer with the extra plow does not have to want a cow, and the farmer with the extra cow does not have to want a plow. Both can exchange their products for money and use the money to buy what they want. An economy is more efficient when a single good is recognized as a medium of exchange.

Unit of Account In a barter system, each good has many prices. A cow may be worth two plows, 20 bushels of wheat, or six axes. Using a good as a medium of exchange confers another benefit: It reduces the need to quote many different prices in trade. Instead of having to quote the price of a single good in terms of many other goods, each good has a single price quoted in terms of the medium of exchange. This function of money gives buyers and sellers a *unit of account*, a way of measuring value in the economy in terms of money. Because the U.S. economy uses dollars as money, each good has a price in terms of dollars.

Store of Value Money allows value to be stored easily: If you do not use all your accumulated dollars to buy goods and services today, you can hold the rest to use in the future. In fact, a fisherman and a farmer would be better off holding money rather than inventories of their perishable goods. The acceptability of money in future transactions depends on its not losing value over time. Money is not the only store of value. Any asset—shares of Google stock, Treasury bonds, real estate, or Renoir paintings, for example—represents a store of value. Indeed, financial assets offer an important benefit relative to holding money because they generally pay a higher rate of interest or offer the prospect of gains in value. Other assets also have advantages relative to money because they provide services. A house, for example, offers you a place to sleep.

Why, then, would you bother to hold any money? The answer has to do with *liquidity*, or the ease with which a given asset can be converted into the medium of exchange. When money is the medium of exchange, it is the most liquid asset. You incur costs when you exchange other assets for money. When you sell bonds or shares of stock to buy a car, for example, you pay a commission to your broker. If you have to sell your house on short notice to finance an unexpected major medical expense, you pay a commission to a real estate agent and probably have to accept a lower price to exchange the house for money quickly. To avoid such costs, people are willing to hold some of their wealth in the form of money, even though other assets offer a greater return as a store of value.

Standard of Deferred Payment Money is useful because it can serve as a standard of deferred payment in borrowing and lending. Money can facilitate exchange at a *given point in time* by providing a medium of exchange and unit of account. It can facilitate exchange *over time* by providing a store of value and a standard of deferred payment. For example, a furniture maker may be willing to sell you a chair today in exchange for money in the future.

How important is it that money be a reliable store of value and standard of deferred payment? People care about how much food, clothing, and other goods and services their dollars will buy. The value of money depends on its purchasing power, which refers to its ability to buy goods and services. Inflation causes a decline in purchasing power because rising prices cause a given amount of money to purchase fewer goods and services. With deflation, the value of money increases because prices are falling.

You have probably heard relatives or friends exclaim, "A dollar doesn't buy what it used to!" They really mean that the purchasing power of a dollar has fallen, that a given amount of money will buy a smaller quantity of the same goods and services than it once did.

What Can Serve as Money?

Having a medium of exchange helps to make transactions easier, allowing the economy to work more smoothly. The next logical question is this: What can serve as money? That is, which assets should be used as the medium of exchange? We saw earlier that an asset must, at a minimum, be generally accepted as payment to serve as money. In practical terms, however, it must be even more.

Five criteria make a good suitable to use as a medium of exchange:

1. The good must be *acceptable* to (that is, usable by) most people.
2. It should be of *standardized quality* so that any two units are identical.
3. It should be *durable* so that value is not lost by spoilage.
4. It should be *valuable* relative to its weight so that amounts large enough to be useful in trade can be easily transported.
5. The medium of exchange should be *divisible* because different goods are valued differently.

Dollar bills meet all these criteria. What determines the acceptability of dollar bills as a medium of exchange? Basically, it is through self-fulfilling expectations: You value something as money only if you believe that others will accept it from you as payment. A society's willingness to use green paper dollars as money makes them an acceptable medium of exchange. This property of acceptability is not unique to money. Your personal computer has the same keyboard organization of letters as other computer keyboards because manufacturers agreed on a standard layout. You learned to speak English because it is probably the language that most people around you speak.

Commodity Money Commodity money meets the criteria for a medium of exchange. Gold, for example, was a common form of money in the nineteenth century because it was a medium of exchange, a unit of account, a store of value, and a standard of deferred payment. But commodity money has a significant problem: Its value depends on its purity. Therefore, someone who wanted to cheat could mix impure metals with a precious metal. Unless traders trusted each other completely, they needed to check the weight and purity of the metal at each trade. In the Middle Ages, respected merchants, who were the predecessors of modern bankers, solved this problem by assaying metals and stamping them with a mark certifying weight and purity and earned a commission in the process. Unstamped (uncertified) commodity money was acceptable only at a discount. Another problem with using gold as money was that the money supply was difficult to control because it depended partly on unpredictable discoveries of new gold fields.

Fiat Money It can be inefficient for an economy to rely on only gold or other precious metals for its money supply. What if you had to transport bars of gold to settle your transactions? Not only would doing so be difficult and costly, but you would also run the risk of being robbed. To get around this problem, private institutions or governments began to store gold and issue paper certificates that could be redeemed for gold. In modern economies, paper currency is generally issued by a *central bank*, which is an agency of the government that regulates the money supply. The **Federal Reserve System** is the central bank of the United States. Today, no government in the world issues paper currency that can be redeemed for gold. Paper currency has no value unless it is used as money and is therefore not a commodity money. Instead, paper currency is a **fiat money**, which has no value except as money. If paper currency has no value except as money, why do consumers and firms use it?

Federal Reserve System The central bank of the United States.

Fiat money Money, such as paper currency, that is authorized by a central bank or governmental body and that does not have to be exchanged by the central bank for gold or some other commodity money.

If you look at the top of a U.S. dollar bill, you will see that it is actually a *Federal Reserve Note*, issued by the Federal Reserve. Because U.S. dollars are fiat money, the Federal Reserve is not required to give you gold or silver for your dollar bills. Federal Reserve currency is *legal tender* in the United States, which means the federal government requires that it be accepted in payment of debts and requires that cash or checks denominated in dollars be used in payment of taxes. Despite being legal tender, without everyone's acceptance, dollar bills would not be a good medium of exchange and could not serve as money. In practice, you, along with everyone else, agree to accept Federal Reserve currency as money. The key to this acceptance is that *households and firms have confidence that if they accept paper dollars in exchange for goods and services, the dollars will not lose much value during the time they hold them.* Without this confidence, dollar bills would not serve as a medium of exchange.

Making the Connection

Money without a Government? The Strange Case of the Iraqi Dinar

The value of the Iraqi dinar was rising against the U.S. dollar. This result may not seem surprising. We saw in Chapter 12 that the exchange rate, or the value of one currency in exchange for another currency, fluctuates—but this was May 2003. The Iraqi government of Saddam Hussein had collapsed the month before, following an invasion by U.S. and British forces. No new Iraqi government had been formed yet, but people continued to use Iraqi paper currency with pictures of Saddam for buying and selling.

U.S. officials in Iraq had expected that as soon as the war was over and Saddam had been forced from power, the currency with his picture on it would lose all its value. This result had seemed inevitable once the United States had begun paying Iraqi officials in U.S. dollars. However, many Iraqis continued to use the dinar because they were familiar with that currency. As one Iraqi put it, "People trust the dinar more than the dollar. It's Iraqi." In fact, for some weeks after the invasion, increasing demand for the dinar caused its value to rise against the dollar. In early April, when U.S. troops first entered Baghdad, it took about 4,000 dinar to buy 1 U.S. dollar. Six weeks later, in mid-May, it took only 1,500 dinar.

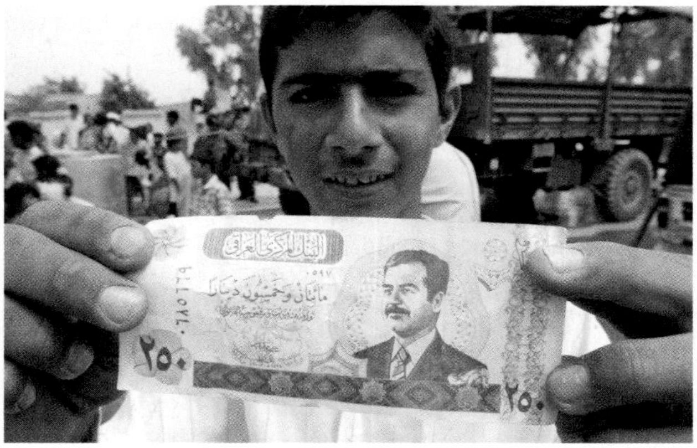

Many Iraqis continued to use currency with Saddam's picture on it, even after he was forced from power.

Eventually, a new Iraqi government was formed, and the government ordered that dinars with Saddam's picture be replaced by a new dinar. The new dinar was printed in factories around the world, and 27 Boeing 747s filled with paper dinars were flown to Baghdad. By January 2004, 2 billion paper dinars in varying denominations had been distributed to banks throughout Iraq, and the old Saddam dinars disappeared from circulation. That dinars issued by Saddam's government actually increased in value for a period after his government had collapsed illustrates an important fact about money: *Anything can be used as money as long as people are willing to accept it in exchange for goods and services*, even paper currency issued by a government that no longer exists.

Sources: Edmund L. Andrews, "His Face Still Gives Fits as Saddam Dinar Soars," *New York Times*, May 18, 2003; Yaroslav Trofimov, "Saddam Hussein Is Scarce, but Not the Saddam Dinar," *Wall Street Journal*, April 24, 2003; and "A Tricky Operation," *Economist*, June 24, 2004.

YOUR TURN: Test your understanding by doing related problem 1.8 on page 461 at the end of this chapter.

13.2 LEARNING OBJECTIVE

13.2 | Discuss the definitions of the money supply used in the United States today.

How Is Money Measured in the United States Today?

The definition of money as a medium of exchange depends on beliefs about whether others will use the medium in trade now and in the future. This definition offers guidance for measuring money in an economy. Interpreted literally, this definition says that money should include only those assets that obviously function as a medium of exchange: currency, checking account deposits, and traveler's checks. These assets can easily be used to buy goods and services and thus act as a medium of exchange.

This strict interpretation is too narrow, however, as a measure of the money supply in the real world. Many other assets can be used as a medium of exchange, but they are not as liquid as a checking account deposit or cash. For example, you can convert your savings account at a bank to cash. Likewise, if you have an account at a brokerage firm, you can write checks against the value of the stocks and bonds the firm holds for you. Although these assets have restrictions on their use and there may be costs to converting them into cash, they can be considered part of the medium of exchange.

In the United States, the Federal Reserve has conducted several studies of the appropriate definition of money. The job of defining the money supply has become more difficult during the past two decades as innovation in financial markets and institutions has created new substitutes for the traditional measures of the medium of exchange. During the 1980s, the Fed changed its definitions of money in response to financial innovation. Outside the United States, other central banks use similar measures. Next we will look more closely at the Fed's definitions of the money supply.

M1: The Narrowest Definition of the Money Supply

M1 The narrowest definition of the money supply: The sum of currency in circulation, checking account deposits in banks, and holdings of traveler's checks.

Figure 13-1 illustrates the definitions of the money supply. The narrowest definition of the money supply is called **M1**. It includes:

1. *Currency*, which is all the paper money and coins that are in circulation, where "in circulation" means not held by banks or the government
2. The value of all checking account deposits at banks
3. The value of traveler's checks (although this last category is so small—less than $7 billion in May 2007—we will ignore it in our discussion of the money supply)

Although currency has a larger value than checking account deposits, checking account deposits are used much more often than currency to make payments. More than 80 percent of all expenditures on goods and services are made with checks rather than with currency. In fact, the total amount of currency in circulation—$756 billion in May 2007—is a misleading number. This amount is more than $2,500 for every man, woman, and child in the United States. If this sounds like an unrealistically large amount of currency to be held per person, it is. Economists estimate that about 60 percent of U.S. currency is actually outside the borders of the United States.

Who holds these dollars outside the United States? Foreign banks and foreign governments hold some dollars, but most are held by households and firms in countries where there is not much confidence in the local currency. When inflation rates are very high, many households and firms do not want to hold their domestic currency because it is losing its value too rapidly. The value of the U.S. dollar will be much more stable. If enough people are willing to accept dollars as well as—or instead of—domestic currency, then dollars become a second currency for the country. In some countries, such as Russia and many Latin American countries, large numbers of U.S. dollars are in circulation.

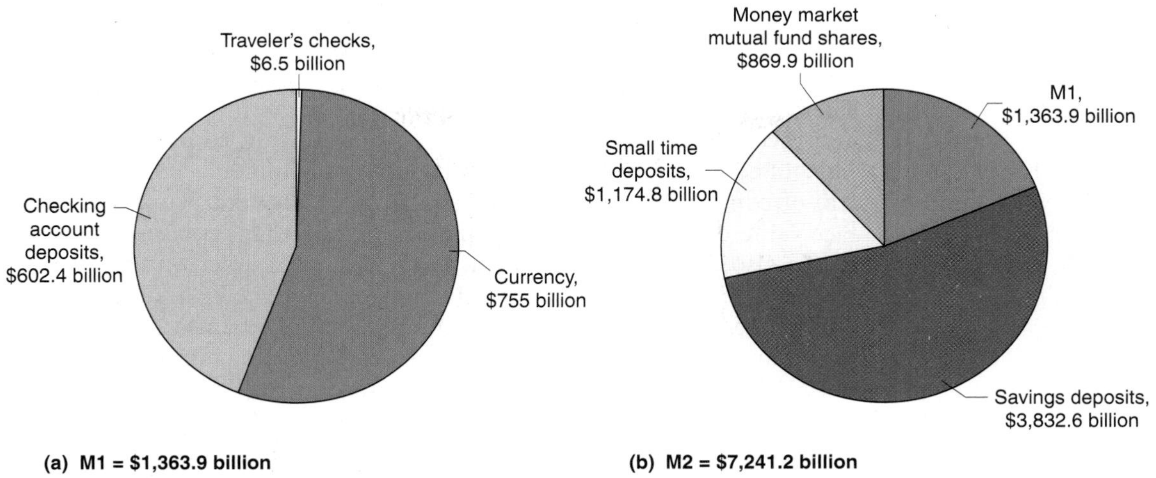

Figure 13-1 | Measuring the Money Supply, May 2007

The Federal Reserve uses two different measures of the money supply: M1 and M2. M2 includes all the assets in M1, as well as additional assets.
Source: Board of Governors of the Federal Reserve System, *Federal Reserve Statistical Release, H6*, May 24, 2007.

Making the Connection

Do We Still Need the Penny?

We have seen that fiat money has no value except as money. Governments actually make a profit from issuing fiat money because fiat money is usually produced using paper or low-value metals that cost far less than the face value of the money. For example, it only costs about four cents for the federal Bureau of Engraving and Printing to manufacture a $20 bill. The government's profit from issuing fiat money—which is equal to the difference between the face value of the money and its production cost—is called *seigniorage.*

With small-denomination coins—like pennies or nickels—there is always the possibility that the coins will cost more to produce than their face value. This was true in the early 1980s when the rising price of copper meant the federal government was spending more than one cent to produce a penny. That led the government to switch from making pennies from copper to making them from zinc. Unfortunately, by 2007, the rising price of zinc meant that once again, the penny cost more than one cent to produce. Many economists began to ask whether the penny should simply be abolished. Not only does it cost more to produce than it is worth, but inflation has eroded its purchasing power to such an extent that some people just find the penny to be a nuisance. Seeing a penny on the sidewalk, many people will walk on by, not bothering to pick it up. In fact, several other countries, including Great Britain, Canada, Australia, and the European countries that use the euro, have eliminated their lowest-denomination coins.

Unfortunately, these cost the government more than a penny to produce.

Some economists, though, have argued that eliminating the penny would subject consumers to a "rounding tax." For example, a good that had been priced at $2.99 will cost $3.00 if the penny is eliminated. Some estimates have put the cost to consumers of the rounding tax as high as $600 million. But Robert Whaples, an economist at Wake Forest University, after analyzing almost 200,000 transactions from a convenience store chain, concluded that "the 'rounding tax' is a myth. In reality, the number of times consumers' bills would be rounded upward is almost exactly equal to the number of times they would be rounded downward."

François Velde, an economist at the Federal Reserve Bank of Chicago, has come up with perhaps the most ingenious solution to the problem of the penny: The federal government would simply declare that Lincoln pennies are now worth five cents. There would then be two five-cent coins in circulation—the current Jefferson nickels and the current Lincoln pennies—and no one-cent coins. In the future, only the Lincoln coins—now worth five cents—would be minted. This would solve the problem of consumers and retail stores having to deal with pennies, it would make the face value of the Lincoln five-cent coin greater than its cost of production, and it would also deal with the problem that the current Jefferson nickel costs more than five cents to produce. But would Lincoln pennies actually be accepted as being worth five cents simply because the government says so? The answer is "yes" because as long as the government was willing to exchange 20 Lincoln coins for a paper dollar, everyone else would be willing to do so as well. Of course, if this plan was adopted, anyone with a hoard of pennies would find their money would be worth five times as much overnight!

Whether or not turning pennies into nickels ends up happening, it seems very likely that one way or another, the penny will eventually disappear from the U.S. money supply.

Sources: Robert Whaples, "Why Keeping the Penny No Longer Makes Sense," *USA Today*, July 12, 2006; Austan Goolsbee, "Now That a Penny Isn't Worth Much, It's Time to Make It Worth 5 Cents," *New York Times*, February 1, 2007; and François Velde, "What's a Penny (or a Nickel) Really Worth?" Federal Reserve Bank of Chicago, *Chicago Fed Letter*, Number 235a, February 2007.

YOUR TURN: Test your understanding by doing related problem 2.8 on page 462 at the end of this chapter.

M2: A Broader Definition of Money

Before 1980, U.S. law prohibited banks from paying interest on checking account deposits. Households and firms held checking account deposits primarily to buy goods and services. M1 was, therefore, very close to the function of money as a medium of exchange. Almost all currency, checking account deposits, and traveler's checks were held with the intention of buying and selling, not to store value. People could store value and receive interest by placing funds in savings accounts in banks or by buying other financial assets, such as stocks and bonds. In 1980, the law was changed to allow banks to pay interest on certain types of checking accounts. This change reduced the difference between checking accounts and savings accounts, although people are still not allowed to write checks against their savings account balances.

M2 A broader definition of the money supply: M1 plus savings account balances, small-denomination time deposits, balances in money market deposit accounts in banks, and noninstitutional money market fund shares.

After 1980, economists began to pay closer attention to a broader definition of the money supply, **M2**. M2 includes everything that is in M1, plus savings account deposits, small-denomination time deposits, such as certificates of deposit (CDs), balances in money market deposit accounts in banks, and noninstitutional money market fund shares. Small-denomination time deposits are similar to savings accounts, but the deposits are for a fixed period of time—usually from six months to several years—and withdrawals before that time are subject to a penalty. Mutual fund companies sell shares to investors and use the funds raised to buy financial assets such as stocks and bonds. Some of these mutual funds, such as Vanguard's Treasury Money Market Fund or Fidelity's Cash Reserves Fund, are called *money market mutual funds* because they invest in very short-term bonds, such as U.S. Treasury bills. The balances in these funds are included in M2. Each week, the Federal Reserve publishes statistics on M1 and M2. In the discussion that follows, we will use the M1 definition of the money supply because it corresponds most closely to money as a medium of exchange.

Don't Let This Happen to **YOU!**

Don't Confuse Money with Income or Wealth

According to *Forbes* magazine, Bill Gates's wealth of more than $55 billion makes him the richest person in the world. He also has a very large income, but how much money does he have? A person's *wealth* is equal to the value of his assets minus the value of any debts he has. A person's *income* is equal to his earnings during the year. Bill Gates's earnings as chairman of Microsoft and from his investments are very large. But his *money* is just equal to what he has in currency and in checking accounts. Only a small proportion of Gates's more than $50 billion in wealth is likely to be in currency or checking accounts. Most of his wealth is invested in stocks and bonds and other financial assets that are not included in the definition of money.

In everyday conversation, we often describe someone who is wealthy or who has a high income as "having a lot of money." But when economists use the word *money*, they are usually referring to currency plus checking account deposits. It is important to keep straight the differences between wealth, income, and money.

Just as money and income are not the same for a person, they are not the same for the whole economy. National income in the United States was equal to $11.7 trillion in 2006. The money supply in 2006 was $1.4 trillion (using the M1 measure). There is no reason national income in a country should be equal to the country's money supply, nor will an increase in a country's money supply necessarily increase the country's national income.

YOUR TURN: Test your understanding by doing related problem 2.6 on page 462 at the end of this chapter.

There are two key points about the money supply to keep in mind:

1. The money supply consists of *both* currency and checking account deposits.
2. Because balances in checking account deposits are included in the money supply, banks play an important role in the process by which the money supply increases and decreases. We will discuss this second point further in the next section.

Solved Problem | **13-2**

The Definitions of M1 and M2

Suppose you decide to withdraw $2,000 from your checking account and use the money to buy a bank certificate of deposit (CD). Briefly explain how this will affect M1 and M2.

SOLVING THE PROBLEM:

Step 1: Review the chapter material. This problem is about the definitions of the money supply, so you may want to review the section "How Is Money Measured in the United States Today?" which begins on page 436.

Step 2: Use the definitions of M1 and M2 to answer the problem. Funds in checking accounts are included in both M1 and M2. Funds in certificates of deposit are included in only M2. It is tempting to answer this problem by saying that shifting $2,000 from a checking account to a certificate of deposit reduces M1 by $2,000 and increases M2 by $2,000, but the $2,000 in your checking account was already counted in M2. So, the correct answer is that your action reduces M1 by $2,000 but leaves M2 unchanged.

YOUR TURN: For more practice, do related problems 2.4 and 2.5 on pages 461–462 at the end of this chapter.

>> End Solved Problem 13-2

What about Credit Cards and Debit Cards?

Many people buy goods and services with credit cards, yet credit cards are not included in definitions of the money supply. The reason is that when you buy something with a credit card, you are in effect taking out a loan from the bank that issued the credit card. Only when you pay your credit card bill at the end of the month—often with a check or an electronic transfer from your checking account—is the transaction complete. In contrast, with a debit card, the funds to make the purchase are taken directly from your checking account. In either case, the cards themselves do not represent money.

13.3 LEARNING OBJECTIVE

13.3 | Explain how banks create money.

How Do Banks Create Money?

We have seen that the most important component of the money supply is checking accounts in banks. To understand the role money plays in the economy, we need to look more closely at how banks operate. Banks are profit-making private businesses, just like bookstores and supermarkets. Some banks are quite small, with just a few branches, and they do business in a limited area. Others are among the largest corporations in the United States, with hundreds of branches spread across many states. The key role that banks play in the economy is to accept deposits and make loans. By doing this, they create checking account deposits.

Bank Balance Sheets

To understand how banks create money, we need to briefly examine a typical bank balance sheet. Recall from Chapter 5 that on a balance sheet, a firm's assets are listed on the left and its liabilities and stockholders' equity are listed on the right. Assets are the value of anything owned by the firm, liabilities are the value of anything the firm owes, and stockholders' equity is the difference between the total value of assets and the total value of liabilities. Stockholders' equity represents the value of the firm if it had to be closed, all its assets were sold, and all its liabilities were paid off. A corporation's stockholders' equity is also referred to as its *net worth*.

ASSETS (IN MILLIONS)		LIABILITIES AND STOCKHOLDERS' EQUITY (IN MILLIONS)	
Reserves	$32,749	Deposits	$407,458
Loans	416,798	Short-term borrowing	50,020
Deposits with other banks	2,167	Long-term debt	138,594
Securities	108,619	Other liabilities	41,333
Buildings and equipment	6,141	Total liabilities	$637,405
Other assets	140,647		
		Stockholders' equity	69,716
Total assets	$707,121	Total Liabilities and stockholders' equity	$707,121

Figure 13-2 | Balance Sheet for Wachovia Bank, December 31, 2006

The items on a bank's balance sheet of greatest economic importance are its reserves, loans, and deposits. Notice that the difference between the value of Wachovia's total assets and its total liabilities is equal to its stockholders' equity. As a consequence, the left side of the balance sheet always equals the right side.

Note: Some entries have been combined to simplify the balance sheet.

Source: Wachovia Corporation and Subsidiaries Consolidated Balance Sheets from Wachovia Corporation, *Annual Report*, 2006.

Don't Let This Happen to YOU!

Know When a Checking Account Is an Asset and When It Is a Liability

Consider the following reasoning: "How can checking account deposits be a liability to a bank? After all, they are something of value that is in the bank. Therefore, checking account deposits should be counted as a bank *asset* rather than as a bank liability."

This statement is incorrect. The balance in a checking account represents something the bank *owes* to the owner of the account. Therefore, it is a liability to the bank, although it is an asset to the owner of the account. Similarly, your car loan is a liability to you—because it is a debt you owe to the bank—but it is an asset to the bank.

YOUR TURN: Test your understanding by doing related problem 3.11 on page 463 at the end of this chapter.

Figure 13-2 shows the balance sheet of Wachovia Bank, which is based in Charlotte, North Carolina, and in 2007 had branches in 21 states. The key assets on a bank's balance sheet are its *reserves*, loans, and holdings of securities, such as U.S. Treasury bills. **Reserves** are deposits that a bank has retained, rather than loaned out or invested by, for instance, buying U.S. Treasury bills. Banks keep reserves either physically within the bank, as *vault cash*, or on deposit with the Federal Reserve. Banks are required by law to keep as reserves 10 percent of their checking account deposits above a threshold level, which in 2007 was $45.8 million. (In 2007, the required reserve ratio was zero on a bank's first $8.5 million in checking account deposits, 3 percent on deposits between $8.5 million and $45.8 million, and 10 percent on deposits above $45.8 million. For simplicity, we will assume that banks are required to keep 10 percent of all reserves.) These reserves are called **required reserves**. The minimum fraction of deposits that banks are required to keep as reserves is called the **required reserve ratio**. We can abbreviate the required reserve ratio as *RR*. Any reserves banks hold over and above the legal requirement are called **excess reserves**. The balance sheet in Figure 13-2 shows that loans are Wachovia's largest asset, which is true of most banks.

Reserves Deposits that a bank keeps as cash in its vault or on deposit with the Federal Reserve.

Required reserves Reserves that a bank is legally required to hold, based on its checking account deposits.

Required reserve ratio The minimum fraction of deposits banks are required by law to keep as reserves.

Excess reserves Reserves that banks hold over and above the legal requirement.

Banks make *consumer loans* to households and *commercial loans* to businesses. A loan is an asset to a bank because it represents a promise by the person taking out the loan to make certain specified payments to the bank. A bank's reserves and its holdings of securities are also assets because they are things of value owned by the bank.

As with most banks, Wachovia's largest liability is its deposits. Deposits include checking accounts, savings accounts, and certificates of deposit. Deposits are liabilities to banks because they are owed to the households or firms that have deposited the funds. If you deposit $100 in your checking account, the bank owes you the $100, and you can ask for it back at any time.

Using T-Accounts to Show How a Bank Can Create Money

It is easier to show how banks create money by using a T-account rather than a balance sheet. A T-account is a stripped-down version of a balance sheet that shows only how a transaction *changes* a bank's balance sheet. For example, suppose you deposit $1,000 in currency into an account at Wachovia Bank. This transaction raises the total deposits at Wachovia by $1,000 and also raises Wachovia's reserves by $1,000. We can show this on the following T-account:

Assets		Liabilities	
Reserves	+$1,000	Deposits	+$1,000

Your deposit of $1,000 into your checking account increases Wachovia's assets and liabilities by the same amount.

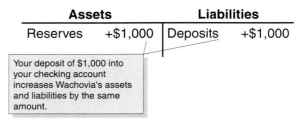

Remember that because the total value of all the entries on the right side of a balance sheet must always be equal to the total value of all the entries on the left side of a balance sheet, any transaction that increases (or decreases) one side of the balance sheet must also increase (or decrease) the other side of the balance sheet. In this case, the T-account shows that we increased both sides of the balance sheet by $1,000.

Initially, this transaction does not increase the money supply. The currency component of the money supply declines by $1,000 because the $1,000 you deposited is no longer in circulation and, therefore, is not counted in the money supply. But the decrease in currency is offset by a $1,000 increase in the checking account deposit component of the money supply.

This initial change is not the end of the story, however. Banks are required to keep 10 percent of deposits as reserves. Because banks do not earn interest on reserves, they have an incentive to loan out or buy securities with the other 90 percent. In this case, Wachovia can keep $100 as required reserves and loan out the other $900, which represents excess reserves. Suppose Wachovia loans out the $900 to someone to buy a very inexpensive used car. Wachovia could give the $900 to the borrower in currency, but usually banks make loans by increasing the borrower's checking account. We can show this with another T-account:

Assets		Liabilities	
Reserves	+$1,000	Deposits	+$1,000
Loans	+$900	Deposits	+$900

1. By loaning out $900 in excess reserves . . .

2. . . . Wachovia has increased the money supply by $900.

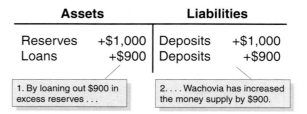

A key point to recognize is that *by making this $900 loan, Wachovia has increased the money supply by $900.* The initial $1,000 in currency you deposited into your checking account has been turned into $1,900 in checking account deposits—a net increase in the money supply of $900.

But the story does not end here. The person who took out the $900 loan did so to buy a used car. To keep things simple, let's suppose he buys the car for exactly $900 and pays by writing a check on his account at Wachovia. The owner of the used car will now deposit the check in her bank. That bank may also be a branch of Wachovia, but in most cities, there are many banks, so let's assume that the seller of the car has her account at a branch of PNC Bank. Once she deposits the check, PNC Bank will send it to Wachovia Bank to *clear* the check and collect the $900. We can show the result using T-accounts:

Wachovia

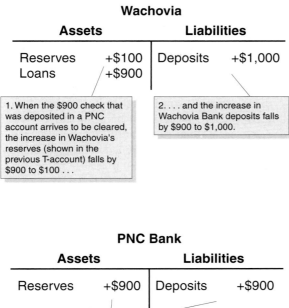

Assets		Liabilities	
Reserves	+$100	Deposits	+$1,000
Loans	+$900		

1. When the $900 check that was deposited in a PNC account arrives to be cleared, the increase in Wachovia's reserves (shown in the previous T-account) falls by $900 to $100 . . .

2. . . . and the increase in Wachovia Bank deposits falls by $900 to $1,000.

PNC Bank

Assets		Liabilities	
Reserves	+$900	Deposits	+$900

1. After the check drawn on the account at Wachovia clears, PNC's reserves and deposits both increase by $900.

Once the car buyer's check has cleared, Wachovia has lost $900 in deposits—the amount loaned to the car buyer—and $900 in reserves—the amount it had to pay PNC when PNC sent Wachovia the car buyer's check. PNC has an increase in checking account deposits of $900—the deposit of the car seller—and an increase in reserves of $900—the amount it received from Wachovia.

PNC has 100 percent reserves against this new $900 deposit, when it only needs 10 percent reserves. The bank has an incentive to keep $90 as reserves and to loan out the other $810, which are excess reserves. If PNC does this, we can show the change in its balance sheet using another T-account:

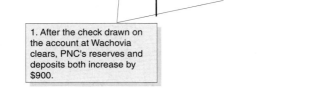

PNC Bank

Assets		Liabilities	
Reserves	+$900	Deposits	+$900
Loans	+$810	Deposits	+$810

By making an $810 loan, PNC has increased both its loans and its deposits by $810.

In loaning out the $810 in excess reserves, PNC creates a new checking account deposit of $810. The initial deposit of $1,000 in currency into Wachovia Bank has now resulted in the creation of $1,000 + $900 + $810 = $2,710 in checking account deposits. The money supply has increased by $2,710 – $1,000 = $1,710.

The process is still not finished. The person who borrows the \$810 will spend it by writing a check against his account. Whoever receives the \$810 will deposit it in her bank, which could be a Wachovia branch or a PNC branch or a branch of some other bank. That new bank—if it's not PNC—will send the check to PNC and will receive \$810 in new reserves. That new bank will have an incentive to loan out 90 percent of these reserves—keeping 10 percent to meet the legal requirement—and the process will go on. At each stage, the additional loans being made and the additional deposits being created are shrinking by 10 percent, as each bank has to withhold that amount as required reserves. We can use a table to show the total increase in checking account deposits set off by your initial deposit of \$1,000. The dots in the table represent additional rounds in the money creation process:

BANK	INCREASE IN CHECKING ACCOUNT DEPOSITS	
Wachovia	\$1,000	
PNC	+ 900	(= 0.9 × \$1,000)
Third Bank	+ 810	(= 0.9 × \$900)
Fourth Bank	+ 729	(= 0.9 × \$810)
•	+ •	
•	+ •	
•	+ •	
Total change in checking account deposits	= \$10,000	

The Simple Deposit Multiplier

Simple deposit multiplier The ratio of the amount of deposits created by banks to the amount of new reserves.

Your initial deposit of \$1,000 increased the reserves of the banking system by \$1,000 and led to a total increase in checking account deposits of \$10,000. The ratio of the amount of deposits created by banks to the amount of new reserves is called the **simple deposit multiplier**. In this case, the simple deposit multiplier is equal to \$10,000/\$1,000 = 10. Why 10? How do we know that your initial \$1,000 deposit ultimately leads to a total increase in deposits of \$10,000?

There are two ways to answer this question. First, each bank in the process is keeping reserves equal to 10 percent of its deposits. For the banking system as a whole, the total increase in reserves is \$1,000—the amount of your original currency deposit. Therefore, the system as a whole will end up with \$10,000 in deposits, because \$1,000 is 10 percent of \$10,000.

A second way to answer the question is by deriving an expression for the simple deposit multiplier. The total increase in deposits equals:

$$\$1{,}000 + [0.9 \times \$1{,}000] + [(0.9 \times 0.9) \times \$1{,}000] + [(0.9 \times 0.9 \times 0.9) \times \$1{,}000] + \ldots$$

Or:

$$\$1{,}000 + [0.9 \times \$1{,}000] + [0.9^2 \times \$1{,}000] + [0.9^3 \times \$1{,}000] + \ldots$$

Or:

$$\$1{,}000 \times (1 + 0.9 + 0.9^2 + 0.9^3 + \ldots).$$

The rules of algebra tell us that an expression like the one in the parentheses sums to:

$$\frac{1}{1-0.9}.$$

Simplifying further, we have:

$$\frac{1}{0.10} = 10.$$

So:

$$\text{Total increase in deposits} = \$1{,}000 \times 10 = \$10{,}000.$$

Note that 10 is equal to 1 divided by the required reserve ratio, *RR*, which in this case is 10 percent, or 0.10. This gives us another way of expressing the simple deposit multiplier:

$$\text{Simple deposit multiplier} = \frac{1}{RR}.$$

This formula makes it clear that the higher the required reserve ratio, the smaller the simple deposit multiplier. With a required reserve ratio of 10 percent, the simple deposit multiplier is 10. If the required reserve ratio were 20 percent, the simple deposit multiplier would fall to 1/0.20, or 5. We can use this formula to calculate the total increase in checking account deposits from an increase in bank reserves due to, for instance, currency being deposited in a bank:

$$\text{Change in checking account deposits} = \text{Change in bank reserves} \times \frac{1}{RR}.$$

For example, if $100,000 in currency is deposited in a bank and the required reserve ratio is 10 percent, then:

$$\text{Change in checking account deposits} = \$100{,}000 \times \frac{1}{0.10} = \$100{,}000 \times 10 = \$1{,}000{,}000.$$

Solved Problem | **13-3**

Showing How Banks Create Money

Suppose you deposit $5,000 in currency into your checking account at a branch of PNC Bank, which we will assume has no excess reserves at the time you make your deposit. Also assume that the required reserve ratio is 0.10.

a. Use a T-account to show the initial effect of this transaction on PNC's balance sheet.

b. Suppose that PNC makes the maximum loan it can from the funds you deposited. Use a T-account to show the initial effect on PNC's balance sheet from granting the loan. Also include in this T-account the transaction from question (a).

c. Now suppose that whoever took out the loan in question (b) writes a check for this amount and that the person receiving the check deposits it in Wachovia Bank. Show the effect of these transactions on the balance sheets of PNC Bank and Wachovia Bank *after the check has been cleared.* On the T-account for PNC Bank, include the transactions from questions (a) and (b).

d. What is the maximum increase in checking account deposits that can result from your $5,000 deposit? What is the maximum increase in the money supply? Explain.

SOLVING THE PROBLEM:

Step 1: **Review the chapter material.** This problem is about how banks create checking account deposits, so you may want to review the section "Using T-Accounts to Show How a Bank Can Create Money," which begins on page 441.

Step 2: Answer question (a) by using a T-account to show the impact of the deposit. Keeping in mind that T-accounts show only the changes in a balance sheet that result from the relevant transaction and that assets are on the left side of the account and liabilities are on the right side, we have:

PNC Bank

Assets		Liabilities	
Reserves	+$5,000	Deposits	+$5,000

Because the bank now has your $5,000 in currency in its vault, its reserves (and, therefore, its assets) have risen by $5,000. But this transaction also increases your checking account balance by $5,000. Because the bank owes you this money, the bank's liabilities have also risen by $5,000.

Step 3: Answer question (b) by using a T-account to show the impact of the loan. The problem tells you to assume that PNC Bank currently has no excess reserves and that the required reserve ratio is 10 percent. This requirement means that if the bank's checking account deposits go up by $5,000, the bank must keep $500 as reserves and can loan out the remaining $4,500. Remembering that new loans usually take the form of setting up, or increasing, a checking account for the borrower, we have:

PNC Bank

Assets		Liabilities	
Reserves	+$5,000	Deposits	+$5,000
Loans	+$4,500	Deposits	+$4,500

The first line of the T-account shows the transaction from question (a). The second line shows that PNC has loaned out $4,500 by increasing the checking account of the borrower by $4,500. The loan is an asset to PNC because it represents a promise by the borrower to make certain payments spelled out in the loan agreement.

Step 4: Answer question (c) by using T-accounts for PNC and Wachovia to show the impact of the check clearing. We now show the effect of the borrower having spent the $4,500 he received as a loan from PNC. The person who received the $4,500 check deposits it in her account at Wachovia. We need two T-accounts to show this:

PNC Bank

Assets		Liabilities	
Reserves	+$500	Deposits	+$5,000
Loans	+$4,500		

Wachovia Bank

Assets		Liabilities	
Reserves	+$4,500	Deposits	+$4,500

Look first at the T-account for PNC. Once Wachovia sends the check written by the borrower to PNC, PNC loses $4,500 in reserves and Wachovia gains $4,500 in reserves. The $4,500 is also deducted from the account of the borrower. PNC is now satisfied with the result. It received a $5,000 deposit in currency from you. When that money was sitting in the bank vault, it wasn't earning any interest for PNC. Now $4,500 of the $5,000 has been loaned out and is earning interest. These interest payments allow PNC to cover its costs and earn a profit, which it has to do to remain in business.

Wachovia now has an increase in deposits of $4,500, resulting from the check deposited by the contractor, and an increase in reserves of $4,500. Wachovia is in the same situation as PNC was in question (a): It has excess reserves as a result of this transaction and a strong incentive to lend them out in order to earn some interest.

Step 5: Answer question (d) by using the simple deposit multiplier formula to calculate the maximum increase in checking account deposits and the maximum increase in the money supply. The simple deposit multiplier expression is (remember that *RR* is the required reserve ratio):

$$\text{Change in checking account deposits} = \text{Change in bank reserves} \times \frac{1}{RR}.$$

In this case, bank reserves rose by $5,000 as a result of your initial deposit, and the required reserve ratio is 0.10, so:

$$\text{Change in checking account deposits} = \$5{,}000 \times \frac{1}{0.10} = \$5{,}000 \times 10 = \$50{,}000.$$

Because checking account deposits are part of the money supply, it is tempting to say that the money supply has also increased by $50,000. Remember, though, that your $5,000 in currency was counted as part of the money supply while you had it, but it is not included when it is sitting in a bank vault. Therefore:

$$\text{Change in the money supply} = \text{Increase in checking account deposits} - \text{Decline in currency in circulation} = \$50{,}000 - \$5{,}000 = \$45{,}000.$$

YOUR TURN: For more practice, do related problem 3.9 on page 463 at the end of the chapter.

>> End Solved Problem 13-3

The Simple Deposit Multiplier versus the Real-World Deposit Multiplier

The story we have told about the way an increase in reserves in the banking system leads to the creation of new deposits and, therefore, an increase in the money supply has been simplified in two ways. First, we assumed that banks do not keep any excess reserves. That is, we assumed that when you deposited $1,000 in currency into your checking account at Wachovia Bank, Wachovia loaned out $900, keeping only the $100 in required reserves. In fact, banks often keep at least some excess reserves to guard against the possibility that many depositors may simultaneously make withdrawals from their accounts. The more excess reserves banks keep, the smaller the deposit multiplier. Imagine an extreme case where Wachovia keeps your entire $1,000 as reserves. If Wachovia does not loan out any of your deposit, the process described earlier of loans leading to the creation of new deposits, leading to the making of additional loans, and so on will not take place. The $1,000 increase in reserves will lead to a total increase of $1,000 in deposits, and the deposit multiplier will be only 1, not 10.

Second, we assumed that the whole amount of every check is deposited in a bank; no one takes any of it out as currency. In reality, households and firms keep roughly constant the amount of currency they hold relative to the value of their checking account balances. So, we would expect to see people increasing the amount of currency they hold as the balances in their checking accounts rise. Once again, think of the extreme case. Suppose that when Wachovia makes the initial $900 loan to the borrower who wants to buy a used car, the seller of the car cashes the check instead of depositing it. In that case, PNC does not receive any new reserves and does not make any new loans. Once again, the $1,000 increase in your checking account at Wachovia is the only increase in deposits, and the deposit multiplier is 1.

The effect of these two factors is to reduce the real-world deposit multiplier to about 2.5. That means that a $1 increase in the reserves of the banking system results in about a $2.50 increase in deposits.

Although the story of the deposit multiplier can be complicated, the key point to bear in mind is that the most important part of the money supply is the checking account balance component. When banks make loans, they increase checking account balances, and the money supply expands. Banks make new loans whenever they gain reserves. The whole process can also work in reverse. If banks lose reserves, they reduce their outstanding loans and deposits, and the money supply contracts.

We can summarize these important conclusions:

1. Whenever banks gain reserves, they make new loans, and the money supply expands.
2. Whenever banks lose reserves, they reduce their loans, and the money supply contracts.

13.4 LEARNING OBJECTIVE

13.4 | Discuss the three policy tools the Federal Reserve uses to manage the money supply.

The Federal Reserve System

Many people are surprised to learn that banks do not keep in their vaults all the funds that are deposited into checking accounts. In fact, in May 2007, the total amount of checking account balances in all banks in the United States was $606 billion, while total reserves were only $42 billion. The United States, like nearly all other countries, has a *fractional reserve banking system.* In a **fractional reserve banking system**, banks keep less than 100 percent of deposits as reserves. When people deposit money in a bank, the bank loans most of the money to someone else. What happens, though, if depositors want their money back? This would seem to be a problem because banks have loaned out most of the money and can't get it back easily.

Fractional reserve banking system A banking system in which banks keep less than 100 percent of deposits as reserves.

In practice, though, withdrawals are usually not a problem for banks. On a typical day, about as much money is deposited as is withdrawn. If a small amount more is withdrawn than deposited, banks can cover the difference from their excess reserves or by borrowing from other banks. Sometimes depositors lose confidence in a bank when they question the value of the bank's underlying assets, particularly its loans. Often, the reason for a loss of confidence is bad news, whether true or false. When many depositors simultaneously decide to withdraw their money from a bank, there is a **bank run**. If many banks experience runs at the same time, the result is a **bank panic**. It is possible for one bank to handle a run by borrowing from other banks, but if many banks simultaneously experience runs, the banking system may be in trouble.

Bank run A situation in which many depositors simultaneously decide to withdraw money from a bank.

Bank panic A situation in which many banks experience runs at the same time.

A *central bank,* like the Federal Reserve in the United States, can help stop a bank panic by acting as a *lender of last resort.* In acting like a lender of last resort, a central bank makes loans to banks that cannot borrow funds elsewhere. The bank can use these loans to pay off depositors. When the panic ends and the depositors put their money back in their accounts, the bank can repay the loan to the central bank.

Making the Connection

The 2001 Bank Panic in Argentina

We saw at the beginning of this chapter that Argentina suffered a bank panic in 2001. Some unusual aspects of the Argentine banking system made it very difficult for the Argentine central bank to act as a lender of last resort. As an alternative policy to stop the bank panic, the Argentine government limited the amount of Argentine currency that depositors could withdraw to $1,000 per account per month. Consumers cut back on their spending because much of the money in their bank accounts could not be withdrawn. Firms like McDonald's experienced declining sales as the country's recession worsened.

The inability of the Argentine central bank to act as a lender of last resort resulted from a decision made by the Argentine government in 1991 to fix the value of the Argentine peso relative to the U.S. dollar at one to one. This policy was meant to restore public faith in the ability of the Argentine currency to retain its value. Argentina had suffered through several periods of high inflation. In 1990, the inflation rate had been a staggering 2,300 percent. These inflationary episodes had caused the purchasing power of the currency to decline rapidly. Although the policy of fixing the value of the peso against the dollar was successful in greatly reducing inflation, it ultimately placed the banking system in an awkward situation. After 1991, Argentine banks were encouraged to take in U.S. dollar deposits and to make U.S. dollar loans, and U.S. dollars were legally recognized as a means of payment within Argentina. By 1994, 60 percent of time deposits and 50 percent of loans were in U.S. dollars. The Argentine central bank was allowed to issue pesos only in exchange for dollars, which limited its ability to provide pesos to banks experiencing a bank run.

The Argentine central bank was unable to stop the bank panic of 2001.

By 2000, many observers had begun to doubt the ability of the Argentine government to maintain the one-to-one exchange rate. As a result, Argentine households and firms, as well as foreign investors, began moving funds out of pesos and into dollars. By late 2001, fully 80 percent of time deposits in Argentine banks were in dollars rather than in pesos. In addition, many depositors began withdrawing money from their accounts. Forty-seven of the top 50 Argentine banks experienced major withdrawals by December 2001. In January 2002, the crisis was ended when the government abandoned its commitment to the one-to-one exchange rate between the peso and the dollar and decreed that dollar deposits in banks would be converted to peso deposits at a rate of 1.4 pesos to the dollar. Although some financial stability was restored, the damage to the banking system from the crisis contributed to a decline in real GDP of 11.5 percent during 2002.

Source: Kathryn M. E. Dominguez and Linda Tesar, "International Borrowing and Macroeconomic Performance in Argentina," in Sebastian Edwards, ed., *Capital Controls and Capital Flows in Emerging Economies: Policies, Practices, and Consequences*, Chicago: University of Chicago Press, 2007.

YOUR TURN: Test your understanding by doing related problem 4.7 on page 464 at the end of this chapter.

The Organization of the Federal Reserve System

Bank panics lead to severe disruptions in business activity because neither households nor firms can gain access to their accounts. Not surprisingly, in the United States, each bank panic in the late nineteenth and early twentieth centuries was accompanied by a recession. With the intention of putting an end to bank panics, in 1913, Congress passed the Federal Reserve Act setting up the Federal Reserve System—often referred to as "the Fed." The system began operation in 1914. The Fed acts as a lender of last resort to banks and as a bankers' bank, providing services such as check clearing to banks. The Fed also takes actions to control the money supply.

The Fed's first test as a lender of last resort came in the early years of the Great Depression of the 1930s, when many banks were hit by bank runs as depositors pulled funds out of checking and savings accounts. Although the Fed had been established to act as a lender of last resort, Fed officials were worried that many of the banks experiencing runs had made bad loans and other investments. The Fed believed that making loans to banks that were in financial trouble because of bad investments might reduce the incentive bank managers had to be careful in their investment decisions. Partly due to the Fed's unwillingness to act as a lender of last resort, more than 5,000 banks failed during the early 1930s. Today, many economists are critical of the Fed's decisions in the early 1930s because they believe these decisions made the Great Depression more severe. In 1934, Congress took action to set up the Federal Deposit Insurance Corporation (FDIC), to insure deposits in most banks up to a limit, which is currently $100,000 per deposit. Deposit insurance has largely stopped bank panics because it has reassured depositors that their deposits are safe even if their bank goes out of business. Today, acting as a lender of last resort is no longer the most important activity of the Fed.

To aid the Fed in carrying out its responsibilities, Congress divided the country into 12 Federal Reserve districts, as shown in Figure 13-3. Each district has its own Federal Reserve bank, which provides services to banks in that district. The real power of the Fed, however, lies in Washington, DC, with the Board of Governors. There are seven members of the Board of Governors, who are appointed by the president of the United States to 14-year, nonrenewable terms. Board members come from banking, business, and academic backgrounds. One of the seven board members is appointed chairman for a four-year, renewable term. Chairmen of the Board of Governors since World War II have come from various backgrounds, including Wall Street (William McChesney Martin), academia (Arthur Burns and Ben Bernanke), business (G. William Miller), public service (Paul Volcker), and economic forecasting (Alan Greenspan).

How the Federal Reserve Manages the Money Supply

Although Congress established the Fed to stop bank panics by acting as a lender of last resort, today a more important activity for the Fed is managing the money supply. As we

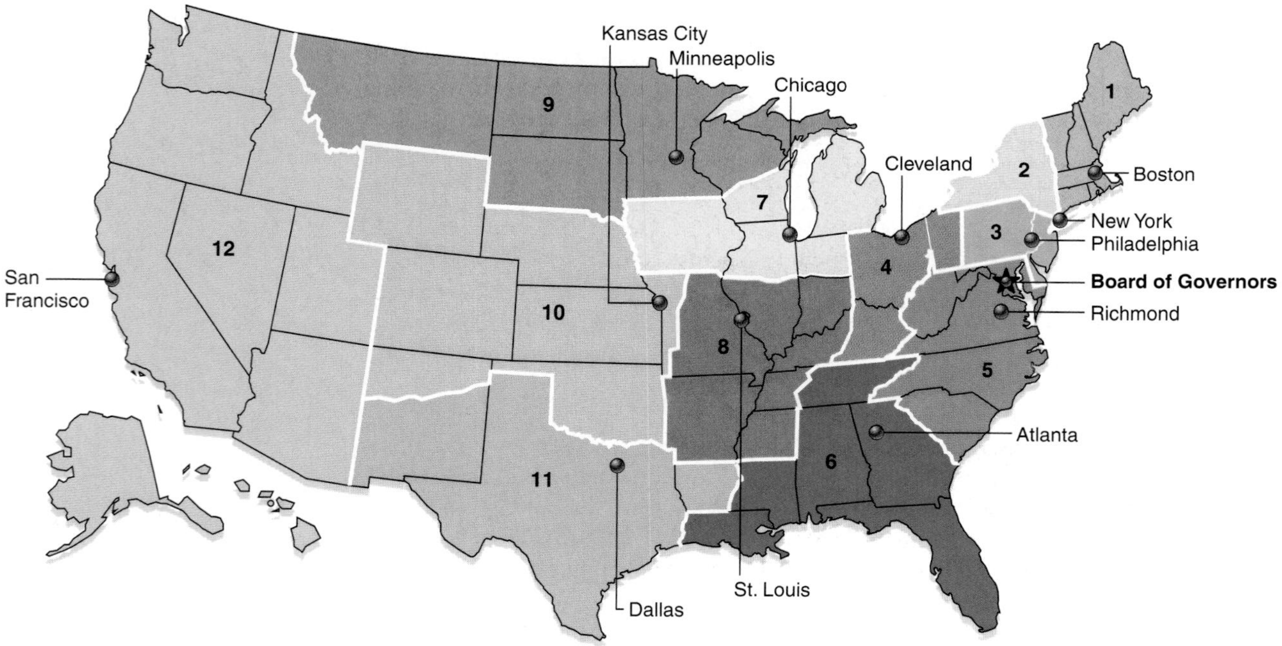

Figure 13-3 | Federal Reserve Districts

The United States is divided into 12 Federal Reserve districts, each of which has a Federal Reserve bank. The real power within the Federal Reserve System, however, lies in Washington, DC, with the Board of Governors.

Source: Board of Governors of the Federal Reserve System.

will discuss in more detail in Chapter 14, managing the money supply is part of **monetary policy**, which the Fed undertakes to pursue macroeconomic objectives.

Monetary policy The actions the Federal Reserve takes to manage the money supply and interest rates to pursue macroeconomic policy objectives.

To manage the money supply, the Fed uses three *monetary policy tools*:

1. Open market operations
2. Discount policy
3. Reserve requirements

Remember that the most important component of the money supply is checking account deposits. Not surprisingly, all three of the Fed's policy tools are aimed at affecting the reserves of banks as a means of changing the volume of checking account deposits.

Open Market Operations Eight times per year, the **Federal Open Market Committee (FOMC)** meets in Washington, DC, to discuss monetary policy. The committee has 12 members: the seven members of the Federal Reserve's Board of Governors, the president of the Federal Reserve Bank of New York, and four presidents from the other 11 Federal Reserve banks. These four presidents serve one-year rotating terms on the FOMC.

Federal Open Market Committee (FOMC) The Federal Reserve committee responsible for open market operations and managing the money supply in the United States.

The U.S. Treasury borrows money by selling bills, notes, and bonds. Remember that the *maturity* of a financial asset is the period of time until the purchaser receives payment of the face value or principal. Usually, bonds have face values of $1,000. Treasury bills have maturities of 1 year or less, Treasury notes have maturities of 2 years to 10 years, and Treasury bonds have maturities of 30 years. To increase the money supply, the FOMC directs the *trading desk*, located at the Federal Reserve Bank of New York, to *buy* U.S. Treasury securities—most frequently bills but sometimes notes or bonds—from the public. When the sellers of the Treasury securities deposit the funds in their banks, the reserves of banks rise. This increase in reserves starts the process of increasing loans and checking account deposits that increases the money supply. To decrease the money supply, the FOMC directs the trading desk to *sell* Treasury securities. When the buyers of the Treasury securities pay for them with checks, the reserves of their banks fall. This decrease in reserves starts a contraction of loans and checking account deposits that reduces the money supply. The buying and selling of Treasury securities is called **open market operations**.

Open market operations The buying and selling of Treasury securities by the Federal Reserve in order to control the money supply.

There are three reasons the Fed conducts monetary policy principally through open market operations. First, because the Fed initiates open market operations, it completely controls their volume. Second, the Fed can make both large and small open market operations. Third, the Fed can implement its open market operations quickly, with no administrative delay or required changes in regulations. Many other central banks, including the European Central Bank and the Bank of Japan, also use open market operations to conduct monetary policy.

The Federal Reserve is responsible for putting the paper currency of the United States into circulation. Recall that if you look at the top of a dollar bill, you see the words "Federal Reserve Note." When the Fed takes actions to increase the money supply, commentators sometimes say that it is "printing more money." The main way the Fed increases the money supply, however, is not by printing more money but by buying Treasury securities. Similarly, to reduce the money supply, the Fed does not set fire to stacks of paper currency. Instead, it sells Treasury securities. We will spend more time discussing how and why the Fed manages the money supply in Chapter 14, when we discuss monetary policy.

Discount Policy The loans the Fed makes to banks are called **discount loans**, and the interest rate it charges on the loans is called the **discount rate**. When a bank receives a loan from the Fed, its reserves increase by the amount of the loan. By lowering the discount rate, the Fed can encourage banks to take additional loans and thereby increase their reserves. With more reserves, banks will make more loans to households and firms, which will increase checking account deposits and the money supply. Raising the discount rate will have the reverse effect.

Discount loans Loans the Federal Reserve makes to banks.

Discount rate The interest rate the Federal Reserve charges on discount loans.

The Fed doesn't control discount policy as completely as it controls open market operations, and changing discount policy is much more difficult than changing open market operations because banks must decide whether to accept discount loans. The volume of discount loans is generally small except when the Fed is actively acting as a lender of last resort, as it did, for example, in the aftermath of the U.S. stock market crash of October 1987, the September 11, 2001, terrorist attacks, and the turmoil in the subprime mortgage markets in August 2007. In practice, the Fed prefers to limit discount loans to helping banks that experience temporary problems with deposit withdrawals rather than to use them to increase or decrease the money supply. Outside the United States, central banks such as the European Central Bank and the Bank of Japan use discount lending both as a monetary policy tool and as a means of mitigating financial crises.

Reserve Requirements When the Fed reduces the required reserve ratio, it converts required reserves into excess reserves. For example, suppose a bank has $100 million in checking account deposits and the required reserve ratio is 10 percent. The bank will be required to hold $10 million as reserves. If the Fed reduces the required reserve ratio to 8 percent, the bank will need to hold only $8 million as reserves. The Fed has converted $2 million worth of reserves from required to excess. This $2 million is now available for the bank to lend out. If the Fed *raises* the required reserve ratio from 10 percent to 12 percent, it would have the reverse effect.

The Fed changes reserve requirements much more rarely than it conducts open market operations or changes the discount rate. Because changes in reserve requirements require significant alterations in banks' holdings of loans and securities, frequent changes would be disruptive. Also, because reserves earn no interest, the use of reserve requirements to manage the money supply effectively places a tax on banks' deposit-taking and lending activities, which can be costly for the economy.

Putting It All Together: Decisions of the Nonbank Public, Banks, and the Fed

Using its three tools—open market operations, the discount rate, and reserve requirements—the Fed has substantial influence over the money supply, but that influence is not absolute. Two other actors—the nonbank public and banks—also influence the money supply.

The nonbank public—households and firms—must decide how much money to hold as deposits in banks. The larger the money holdings in deposits, the greater the reserves of banks and the more money the banking system can create. The smaller the money holdings in deposits, the lower the reserves of banks and the less money the banking system can create. In addition, the Fed can influence, but does not control, the amount bankers decide to lend. Banks create money only if they lend their reserves. If bankers retain excess reserves, they make a smaller volume of loans and create less money.

The roles of the nonbank public and banks in the money supply process do not mean that the Fed lacks meaningful control of the money supply. The Fed's staff monitors information on banks' reserves and deposits every week, and the Fed can respond quickly to shifts in behavior by depositors or banks. The Fed can therefore steer the money supply close to the level it desires.

13.5 LEARNING OBJECTIVE

13.5 | Explain the quantity theory of money and use it to explain how high rates of inflation occur.

The Quantity Theory of Money

People have been aware of the connection between increases in the money supply and inflation for centuries. In the sixteenth century, the Spanish conquered Mexico and Peru and shipped large quantities of gold and silver back to Spain. The gold and silver were minted into coins and spent across Europe to further the political ambitions of the Spanish kings. Prices in Europe rose steadily during these years, and many observers discussed the relationship between this inflation and the flow of gold and silver into Europe from the Americas.

Connecting Money and Prices: The Quantity Equation

In the early twentieth century, Irving Fisher, an economist at Yale, formalized the connection between money and prices using the *quantity equation*:

$$M \times V = P \times Y.$$

The equation states that the money supply (M) multiplied by the *velocity of money* (V) equals the price level (P) multiplied by real output (Y). Fisher defined the **velocity of money**, often referred to simply as "velocity," as the average number of times each dollar of the money supply is used to purchase goods and services included in GDP. Rewriting the original equation by dividing both sides by M, we have the equation for velocity:

Velocity of money The average number of times each dollar in the money supply is used to purchase goods and services included in GDP.

$$V = \frac{P \times Y}{M}.$$

We can use M1 to measure the money supply, the GDP price deflator to measure the price level, and real GDP to measure real output. Then the value for velocity for 2006 was:

$$V = \frac{1.161 \times \$11{,}415 \text{ billion}}{\$1{,}366 \text{ billion}} = 9.7$$

This result tells us that, on average during 2006, each dollar of M1 was spent about 10 times on goods or services included in GDP.

Because velocity is *defined* to be equal to $(P \times Y)/M$, we know that the quantity equation must always hold true: The left side *must* be equal to the right side. A theory is a statement about the world that might possibly be false. Therefore, the quantity equation is not a theory. Irving Fisher turned the quantity equation into the **quantity theory of money** by asserting that velocity was constant. He argued that the average number of times a dollar is spent depends on how often people get paid, how often they do their grocery shopping, how often businesses mail bills, and other factors that do not change very often. Because this assertion may be true or false, the quantity theory of money is, in fact, a theory.

Quantity theory of money A theory of the connection between money and prices that assumes that the velocity of money is constant.

The Quantity Theory Explanation of Inflation

The quantity equation gives us a way of showing the relationship between changes in the money supply and changes in the price level, or inflation. To see this relationship more clearly, we can use a handy mathematical rule that states that an equation where variables are multiplied together is equal to an equation where the *growth rates* of these variables are *added* together. So, we can transform the quantity equation from:

$$M \times V = P \times Y$$

to:

Growth rate of the money supply + Growth rate of velocity =
Growth rate of the price level (or inflation rate) + Growth rate of real output.

This way of writing the quantity equation is more useful for investigating the effect of changes in the money supply on the inflation rate. Remember that the growth rate for any variable is just the percentage change in the variable from one year to the next. The growth rate of the price level is just the inflation rate, so we can rewrite the quantity equation to help us understand the factors that determine inflation:

Inflation rate = Growth rate of the money supply +
Growth rate of velocity – Growth rate of real output.

If Irving Fisher was correct that velocity is constant, then the growth rate of velocity will be zero. That is, if velocity is, say, always 9.7, then its percentage change from one year to the next will always be zero. This assumption allows us to rewrite the equation one last time:

Inflation rate = Growth rate of the money supply – Growth rate of real output.

This equation leads to the following predictions:

1. If the money supply grows at a faster rate than real GDP, there will be inflation.
2. If the money supply grows at a slower rate than real GDP, there will be deflation. (Recall that *deflation* is a decline in the price level.)
3. If the money supply grows at the same rate as real GDP, the price level will be stable, and there will be neither inflation nor deflation.

It turns out that Irving Fisher was wrong in asserting that the velocity of money is constant. From year to year, there can be significant fluctuations in velocity. As a result, the predictions of the quantity theory of money do not hold every year, but most economists agree that the quantity theory provides a useful insight into the long-run relationship between the money supply and inflation: *In the long run, inflation results from the money supply growing at a faster rate than real GDP.*

High Rates of Inflation

Why do governments allow high rates of inflation? The quantity theory can help us to understand the reasons for high rates of inflation, such as that experienced in Argentina during the 1980s. Very high rates of inflation—in excess of hundreds or thousands of percentage points per year—are known as *hyperinflation*. Hyperinflation is caused by central banks increasing the money supply at a rate far in excess of the growth rate of real GDP. A high rate of inflation causes money to lose its value so rapidly that households and firms avoid holding it. If the inflation becomes severe enough, people stop using paper currency, so it no longer serves the important functions of money discussed earlier in this chapter. Economies suffering from high inflation usually also suffer from very slow growth, if not severe recession.

Given the dire consequences that follow from high inflation, why do governments allow it by expanding the money supply so rapidly? The main reason is that governments often want to spend more than they are able to raise through taxes. Developed countries, such as the United States, can usually bridge gaps between spending and taxes by borrowing through selling bonds to the public. Developing countries often have difficulty selling bonds because the public is skeptical of their ability to pay back the money. If they are unable to sell bonds to the public, governments in developing countries will force their central banks to purchase them. As we discussed previously, when a central bank buys bonds, the money supply will increase.

High Inflation in Argentina

The link between rapid money growth and high inflation was evident in the experience of Argentina during the 1980s. Panel (a) of Figure 13-4 shows rates of growth of the money supply and the inflation rate in Argentina in the years from 1981 to 1991. Both the average annual growth rate of the money supply and the average annual inflation

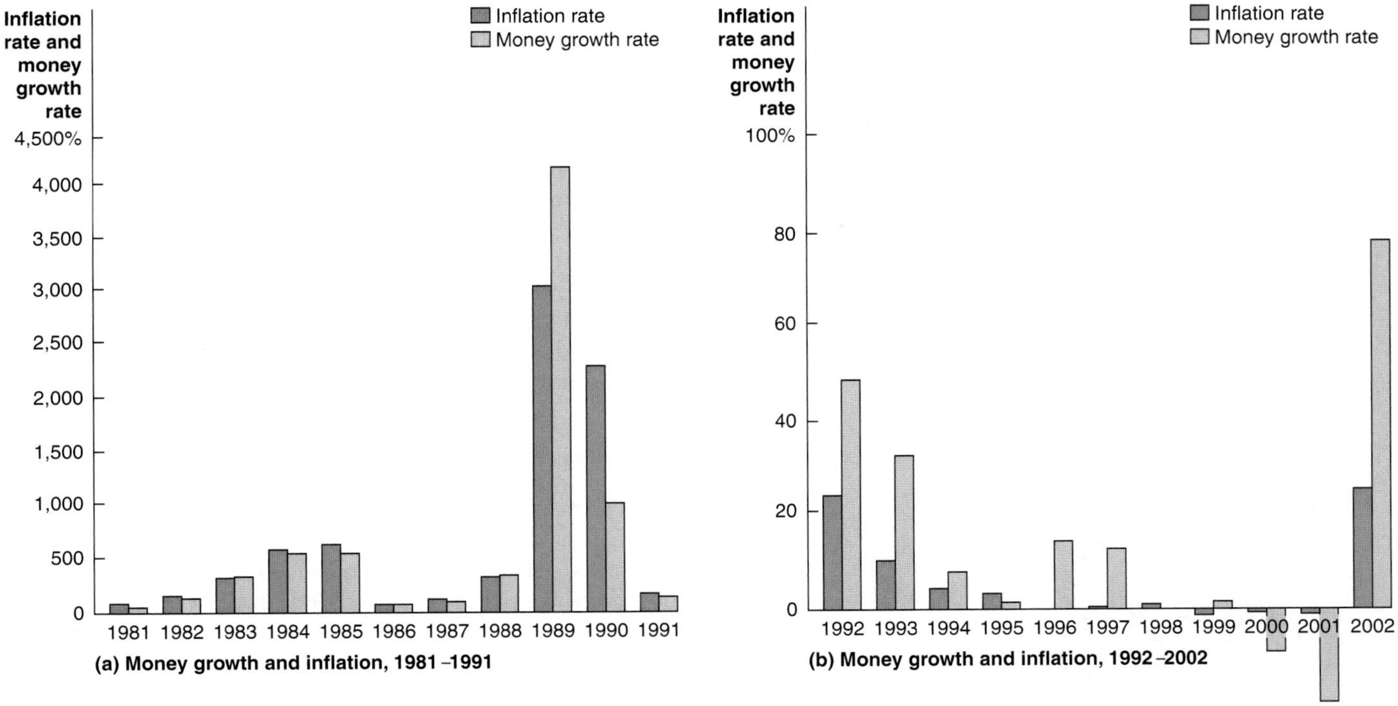

Figure 13-4 | Money Growth and Inflation in Argentina

Panel (a) shows rates of growth of the money supply and the inflation rate in Argentina in the years from 1981 to 1991. Both the average annual growth rate of the money supply and the average annual inflation rate from 1981 to 1990 were greater than 750 percent. In 1991, the Argentine government enacted a new policy that fixed the exchange rate of the peso versus the U.S. dollar at one to one. As panel (b) shows, the new policy greatly reduced increases in the money supply and the inflation rate. (Notice that the scale of panel (b) is different from the scale of panel (a), which partly disguises the fall in money growth and inflation.)

Source: International Monetary Fund.

rate from 1981 to 1990 were greater than 750 percent. With prices rising so quickly, Argentine currency could not fulfill the normal functions of money. Not surprisingly, the Argentine economy struggled during these years, with real GDP in 1990 ending up 6 percent lower than it had been in 1981.

This weak economic performance was particularly frustrating to many people in Argentina because early in the twentieth century, the country had had one of the highest standards of living in the world. In 1910, only the United States and Great Britain had higher levels of real GDP per capita than Argentina. In U.S.-made films of the 1920s and 1930s, the rich foreigner was often from Argentina.

It was clear to policymakers in Argentina that the only way to bring inflation under control was to limit increases in the money supply. As we saw in the *Making the Connection* on page 449, in 1991, the Argentine government enacted a new policy that fixed the exchange rate of the peso versus the U.S. dollar at one to one. In addition, the Argentine central bank was allowed to issue pesos only in exchange for dollars. As panel (b) in Figure 13-4 shows, the new policy greatly reduced increases in the money supply and the inflation rate. (Notice that the scale of panel (b) is different from the scale of panel (a), which partly disguises the fall in money growth and inflation.) Economic growth also revived, with real GDP increasing at an average annual rate of almost 6 percent from 1991 to 1998. Unfortunately, though, Argentina had not come to grips with several underlying economic problems, perhaps the most important of which was the continuing gap between government expenditures and tax receipts.

By 2000, many observers expected that the Argentine government would not be able to maintain the one-to-one exchange rate between the peso and the U.S. dollar. As Argentine firms and households, along with foreign investors, began exchanging pesos for dollars, the Argentine money supply declined. The money supply declined by 9 percent in 2000 and by an additional 20 percent in 2001. Argentina experienced falling prices, or deflation, during both years, along with falling real GDP. Finally, in January 2002, the Argentine government abandoned its commitment to the one-to-one exchange rate between the peso and the dollar, and the money supply increased rapidly. During 2002, the money supply increased by nearly 80 percent, and deflation was transformed to an inflation rate of 25 percent. Although the inflation rate declined over the next few years, Argentina continues to struggle to keep its money supply from growing at rates likely to result in high inflation.

During the hyperinflation of the 1920s, people in Germany used paper currency to light their stoves.

Making the Connection

The German Hyperinflation of the Early 1920s

When Germany lost World War I, a revolution broke out that overthrew Kaiser Wilhelm II and installed a new government known as the Weimar Republic. In the peace treaty of 1919, the Allies—the United States, Great Britain, France, and Italy—imposed payments called *reparations* on the new German government. The reparations were meant as compensation to the Allies for the damage Germany had caused during the war. It was very difficult for the German government to use tax revenue to cover both its normal spending and the reparations.

The German government decided to pay for the difference between its spending and its tax revenues by selling bonds to the central bank, the Reichsbank. After a few years, the German government fell far behind in its reparations payment. In January 1923, the French government sent troops into the German industrial area known as the Ruhr to try to collect the payments directly. German workers in the Ruhr went on strike, and the German government decided to support them by paying their salaries. Raising the funds to do so was financed by an inflationary monetary policy—the German government sold bonds to the Reichsbank, thereby increasing the money supply.

The inflationary increase in the money supply was very large: The total number of marks—the German currency—in circulation rose from 115 million in January 1922 to 1.3 billion in January 1923 and then to 497 billion *billion*, or 497,000,000,000,000,000,000, in December 1923. Just as the quantity theory predicts, the result was a staggeringly high rate of inflation. The German price index that stood at 100 in 1914 and 1,440 in January 1922 had risen to 126,160,000,000,000 in December 1923. The German mark became worthless. The German government ended the hyperinflation by (1) negotiating a new agreement with the Allies that reduced its reparations payments, (2) reducing other government expenditures and raising taxes to balance its budget, and (3) replacing the existing mark with a new mark. Each new mark was worth 1 trillion old marks. The German central bank was also limited to issuing a total of 3.2 billion new marks.

These steps were enough to bring the hyperinflation to an end—but not before the savings of anyone holding the old marks had been wiped out. Most middle-income Germans were extremely resentful of this outcome. Many historians believe that the hyperinflation greatly reduced the allegiance of many Germans to the Weimar Republic and may have helped pave the way for Hitler and the Nazis to seize power 10 years later.

Source: Thomas Sargent, "The End of Four Big Hyperinflations," in *Rational Expectations and Inflation*, New York: Harper and Row, 1986.

YOUR TURN: Test your understanding by doing related problem 5.7 on page 465 at the end of this chapter.

Continued from page 431

Economics in YOUR Life!

At the beginning of the chapter, we asked you to consider whether you would like to live in an economy in which the purchasing power of money rose every year. The first thing to consider when thinking about the advantages and disadvantages of this situation is that the only way for the purchasing power of money to increase is for the price level to fall; in other words, *deflation* must occur. Because the price level in the United States hasn't fallen over the course of a year since the 1930s, most people alive today have experienced only rising price levels—and declining purchasing power of money. Would replacing rising prices with falling prices necessarily be a good thing? It might be tempting to say yes, because if you have a job, then your salary will buy more goods and services each year. But, in fact, just as a rising price level results in most wages and salaries rising each year, a falling price level is likely to mean falling wages and salaries each year. So, it is likely that, on average, people would not see the purchasing power of their incomes increase, even if the purchasing power of any currency they hold would increase. There can also be a significant downside to deflation, particularly if the transition from inflation to deflation happens suddenly. In Chapter 8, we defined the real interest rate as being equal to the nominal interest rate minus the inflation rate. If an economy experiences deflation, then the real interest rate will be greater than the nominal interest rate. A rising real interest rate can be bad news for anyone who has borrowed, including homeowners who may have substantial mortgage loans. So, you are probably better off living in an economy experiencing mild inflation rather than one experiencing deflation.

Conclusion

Money plays a key role in the functioning of an economy by facilitating trade in goods and services and by making specialization possible. Without specialization, no advanced economy can prosper. Households and firms, banks, and the central bank (the Federal Reserve in the United States) are participants in the process of creating the money supply. In Chapter 14, we will explore how the Federal Reserve uses monetary policy to promote its economic objectives.

An Inside Look at Policy on the next page discusses how China's central bank is trying to control the money supply by slowing bank lending.

Using Reserve Requirements to Slow Bank Lending in China

WALL STREET JOURNAL, APRIL 30, 2007

China Lifts Bank Reserves in Bid to Cool Growth

a For the seventh time in less than a year, China's central bank raised the share of deposits banks must keep on reserve as the government struggles to soak up capital and keep the country's economy from overheating.

The move, which was announced yesterday and takes effect May 15, follows accelerated economic growth and an uptick in inflation indicators. The government announced this month that gross domestic product, or the total value of goods and services produced, expanded at a faster-than-expected 11.1% in the first quarter from a year earlier.

Economists had expected the government to take further measures to tighten money supply around tomorrow's May Day holiday and said that in coming weeks the People's Bank of China could implement even more measures—including a rate increase—to contain upward pressure on prices and slow growth from the blistering pace of the first quarter.

The central bank said on its Web site yesterday that the increase in reserve ratio is aimed at "strengthening the management of liquidity in the banking system" and guiding "the reasonable growth of credit."

b Still, economists said increases to the reserve ratio have so far achieved little, if any, of their desired effect. The newly announced increase will bring the reserve-requirement ratio—the share of deposits that lenders must keep with the central bank—up half a percentage point to 11% for most banks. The increase, in theory, reduces the amount available to banks to lend, though in practice many Chinese banks already keep more than the minimum on reserve.

"The past two years of experience in China has shown that [reserve-ratio] changes are an ineffective policy tool to control monetary expansion," Hong Liang, a Hong Kong–based Goldman Sachs economist, said in a research note after the increase was announced. Such ratio increases are "simply not binding on banks' capabilities to lend," Ms. Liang said.

Behind the flush liquidity in the domestic economy is China's booming trade surplus, or margin by which exports exceed imports, and the central bank's intervention to keep the value of the domestic currency from appreciating too quickly as a result. The central bank pays out yuan to banks to buy their dollars, pumping cash into the economy.

Because many investors believe the reserve-requirement increase signals the government's resolve to continue employing tightening measures, the move could cause traders to push domestic shares lower in trading today—the last day China's markets are open before a weeklong holiday. But any selling is likely to be limited, analysts said.

"The People's Bank tightened at this juncture to give the markets a little time to digest this increase," said Jing Ulrich, chairwoman of China equities at J.P. Morgan & Co. "This one hike alone won't trigger a major selloff."

c The acceleration in China's economic growth, driven in significant part by bank lending to new investment projects, has forced Beijing to pull a variety of monetary-policy levers since last year. It has also enacted administrative measures to cool sectors such as property and steel, which threaten to push prices higher. The latest reserve-ratio increase is the second in a month.

China's consumer-price index rose 3.3% in March and 2.7% in the first quarter, compared with a year earlier. That pickup has sparked concerns that after muted inflation in recent years, rising production capacity might no longer be able to counterbalance demand, and a surge in prices could be ahead for the world's fastest-growing major economy.

"If the inflation rate continues to climb, if the momentum of fixed-asset investment growth doesn't slow down, and if the asset prices rise too quickly, the central bank definitely will tighten further," said Yu Yongding, a professor and former member of central bank's monetary-policy committee.

Source: Rick Carew and J. R. Wu, "China Lifts Bank Reserves in Bid to Cool Growth," Wall Street Journal, *April 30, 2007, p. A2. Reprinted by permission of the* Wall Street Journal *via Copyright Clearance Center.*

Key Points in the Article

This article discusses how China's central bank has attempted to slow the growth of bank lending—and, hence, the money supply—by raising banks' reserve requirement. As of May 15, 2007, China's central bank had raised the ratio seven times in less than a year. Although changing the required reserve ratio can be a relatively disruptive monetary policy tool, the central bank is using it to slow the growth of China's economy. In the first quarter of 2007, real GDP grew at an annual rate of 11.1 percent, which is probably to be sustained without causing the inflation rate to increase. The central bank's efforts to reduce bank lending have been largely ineffective because the reserve requirements are not binding; most banks already hold more than the required reserve amount. And, ironically, this is because the supply of bank reserves is growing, thanks to the exchange-rate policies of China's central bank. Finally, the article notes that China's central bank is right to be concerned because China's consumer price index rose 2.7 percentage points more in the first quarter of 2007 than it did in the first quarter of 2006.

Analyzing the News

a China's central bank has used reserve requirements—a monetary policy tool that the U.S. Federal Reserve rarely uses today—for the seventh time in less than 12 months in order to slow the growth of bank lending in China. As you read in this chapter, changes in reserve requirements can be disruptive to banks because they necessitate significant changes in banks' holdings of loans and securities. A bank that has no excess reserves will be forced to reduce its holdings of loans and securities if the required reserve ratio is increased. Nonetheless, the Chinese government continues to raise reserve requirements as it attempts to slow the economy, which grew at a very rapid annual rate of 11.1 percent in the first quarter of 2007. By comparison, the U.S. economy grew at an annual rate of 1.3 percent in the same quarter. China's policymakers are concerned that a high rate of growth in the money supply will cause the inflation rate to increase.

b As of May 15, 2007, the required reserve ratio for most Chinese banks will be 11 percent. Nonetheless, the government's attempt to reduce bank lending by raising reserve requirements has been relatively ineffective for two reasons. First, the reserve requirement is not binding because many of China's banks already hold more than the minimum amount of required reserves. So, raising the required reserve ratio has little effect on these banks' lending practices. Second, bank reserves have been rising in part due to China's large trade surplus. And, ironically, this trade surplus is, to some extent, the product of the Chinese government's strategy of fixing the value of its currency—the yuan—to the U.S. dollar. Since the mid-1990s, the Chinese government has purchased U.S. dollars—and, consequently, sold yuan—in the foreign exchange market in order to keep the yuan from increasing in value against the U.S. dollar. This pattern is shown in the figure, which plots the Chinese yuan/U.S. dollar foreign exchange rate. By keeping the value of the yuan nearly fixed against the dollar, China effectively keeps the dollar-price of its exports relatively low. Because Chinese exporters are accumulating large amounts of dollars, when these dollars are exchange for yuan they ultimately end up in Chinese banks in the form of bank reserves.

c Recent data on inflation has China's monetary policymakers concerned. In particular, China's consumer price index rose 2.7 percentage points more in the first quarter of 2007 than it did in the first quarter of 2006. Most economists agree that this inflation has occurred because the growth in China's aggregate demand is outpacing the growth in its aggregate supply. This is precisely what the quantity theory, which you read about in this chapter, predicts: In the long run, inflation results from the money supply growing at a faster rate than real GDP.

Thinking Critically About Policy

1. Suppose China's reserve requirement were binding. Explain how a rise in the required reserve ratio would slow bank lending in China.
2. In light of the success that the United States has had with open market operations, why doesn't China use a similar tool to buy yuan in the open market and, hence, slow the growth of bank reserves that way?

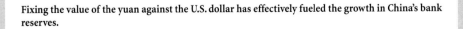

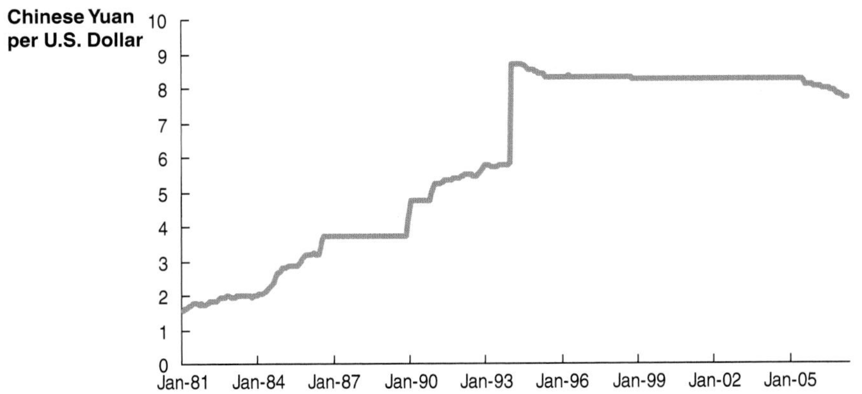

Fixing the value of the yuan against the U.S. dollar has effectively fueled the growth in China's bank reserves.

Key Terms

13.1 LEARNING OBJECTIVE 13.1 | Define money and discuss its four functions, **pages 432–435.**

What Is Money and Why Do We Need It?

Summary

A *barter economy* is an economy that does not use money and in which people trade goods and services directly for other goods and services. Barter trade occurs only if there is a *double coincidence of wants*, where both parties to the trade want what the other one has. Because barter is inefficient, there is strong incentive to use **money**, which is any **asset** that people are generally willing to accept in exchange for goods or services or in payment of debts. An *asset* is anything of value owned by a person or a firm. A *commodity money* is a good used as money that also has value independent of its use as money. Money has four functions: It is a medium of exchange, a unit of account, a store of value, and a standard of deferred payment. The *gold standard* was a monetary system under which the government produced gold coins and paper currency that were convertible into gold. The gold standard collapsed in the early 1930s. Today, no government in the world issues paper currency that can be redeemed for gold. Instead, paper currency is **fiat money**, which has no value except as money.

myeconlab Get Ahead of the Curve Visit www.myeconlab.com to complete these exercises online and get instant feedback.

Review Questions

1.1 A baseball fan with an Albert Pujols baseball card wants to trade it for a Derek Jeter baseball card, but everyone the fan knows who has a Jeter card doesn't want a Pujols card. What do economists call the problem this fan is having?

1.2 What is the difference between commodity money and fiat money?

1.3 What are the four functions of money? Can something be considered money if it does not fulfill all four functions?

Problems and Applications

1.4 The English economist Stanley Jevons described a world tour during the 1880s by a French singer, Mademoiselle Zélie. One stop on the tour was a theater in the Society Islands, part of French Polynesia in the South Pacific. She performed for her usual fee, which was one-third of the receipts. This turned out to be three pigs, 23 turkeys, 44 chickens, 5,000 coconuts, and "considerable quantities of bananas, lemons, and oranges." She estimated that all of this would have had a value in France of 4,000 francs. According to Jevons, "as Mademoiselle could not consume any considerable portion of the receipts herself, it became necessary in the meantime to feed the pigs and poultry with the fruit." Do the goods Mademoiselle Zélie received as payment fulfill the four functions of money described in the chapter? Briefly explain.

Source: W. Stanley Jevons, *Money and the Mechanism of Exchange*, New York: D. Appleton and Company, 1889, pp. 1–2.

1.5 In the late 1940s, the Communists under Mao Zedong were defeating the government of China in a civil war. The paper currency issued by the Chinese government was losing much of its value, and most businesses refused to accept it. At the same time, there was a paper shortage in Japan. During these years, Japan was still under military occupation by the United States, following its defeat in World War II. Some of the U.S. troops in Japan realized that they could use dollars to buy up vast amounts of paper currency in China, ship it to Japan to be recycled into paper, and make a substantial profit. Under these circumstances, was the Chinese paper currency a commodity money or a fiat money? Briefly explain.

1.6 In the 1970s, Pol Pot, the dictator of Cambodia, proclaimed that he intended to do away with money in his country because money represents the decadence of the West (Western Europe and the United States). Historically, did money only exist in the West? What effect would the elimination of money have on the economy?

1.7 According to a news story, during 2007, businesses in the city of Magdeburg, Germany, were printing their own currency called the Urstromtaler. The lawyer who started the currency was quoted as saying, "All the businesses have signed contracts, and it's official. We have our own banknotes and we have an issuing office in the city centre." The new currency is issued at a rate of one for one against the euro: Anyone bringing euros to the issuing office in the city will receive the same number of Urstomtalers in exchange. Although issuing this local currency is apparently technically illegal, the German government has taken no action. Unlike euros, the local currency no longer has value after a certain date, which means consumers have an incentive to spend it quickly. Does this local German currency fulfill the four functions of money described in the chapter? Briefly explain.

Source: Tristana Moore, "Germans Take Pride in Local Money," BBC News, February 6, 2007.

1.8 **(Related to the *Making the Connection* on page 435)** According to Peter Heather, a historian at the University of Oxford, during the Roman Empire, the German tribes east of the Rhine River produced no coins of their own but used Roman coins instead:

> Although no coinage was produced in Germania, Roman coins were in plentiful circulation and could easily have provided a medium of exchange (already in the first century, Tacitus tells us, Germani of the Rhine region were using good-quality Roman silver coins for this purpose).

a. What is a medium of exchange?
b. What does the author mean when he writes that Roman coins could have provided the German tribes with a medium of exchange?
c. Why would any member of a German tribe have been willing to accept a Roman coin from another member of the tribe in exchange for goods or services when the tribes were not part of the Roman Empire and were not governed by Roman law?

Source: Peter Heather, *The Fall of the Roman Empire: A New History of Rome and the Barbarians*, New York: Oxford University Press, 2006, p. 89.

>> End Learning Objective 13.1

13.2 LEARNING OBJECTIVE 13.2 | Discuss the definitions of the money supply used in the United States today, **pages 436–440.**

How Is Money Measured in the United States Today?

Summary

The narrowest definition of the money supply in the United States today is **M1**, which includes currency, checking account balances, and traveler's checks. A broader definition of the money supply is **M2**, which includes everything that is in M1, plus savings accounts, small-denomination time deposits (such as certificates of deposit (CDs)), money market deposit accounts in banks, and noninstitutional money market fund shares.

myeconlab Get Ahead of the Curve Visit www.myeconlab.com to complete these exercises online and get instant feedback.

Review Questions

2.1 What is the main difference between the M1 and M2 definitions of the money supply?

2.2 Why does the Federal Reserve use two definitions of the money supply rather than one?

Problems and Applications

2.3 Briefly explain whether each of the following is counted in M1.
a. The coins in your pocket
b. The funds in your checking account
c. The funds in your savings account
d. The traveler's check that you have left over from a trip
e. Your Citibank Platinum MasterCard

2.4 **(Related to *Solved Problem 13-2* on page 439)** Suppose you have $2,000 in currency in a shoebox in your closet. One day, you decide to deposit the money in a checking account. Briefly explain how this will affect M1 and M2.

2.5 **(Related to *Solved Problem 13-2* on page 439)** Suppose you decide to withdraw $100 in currency from your checking account. What is the effect on M1? Ignore any actions the bank may take as a result of your having withdrawn the $100.

2.6 **(Related to the *Don't Let This Happen to You!* on page 439)** Briefly explain whether you agree or disagree with the following statement: "I recently read that more than half of the money issued by the government is actually held by people in foreign countries. If that's true, then the United States is less than half as wealthy as government statistics indicate."

2.7 The paper currency of the United States is technically called "Federal Reserve notes." The following excerpt is from the Federal Reserve Act: "Federal reserve notes . . . shall be redeemed in lawful money on demand at the Treasury Department of the United States, in the city of Washington, District of Columbia, or at any Federal Reserve bank." If you took a $20 bill to the Treasury Department or a Federal Reserve bank, with what type of "lawful money" is the government likely to redeem it?

2.8 **(Related to the *Making the Connection* on page 437)** There are currently about 1.4 billion pennies in circulation. Suppose the proposal of economist François Velde to make the current penny worth five cents were adopted. What would be the effect on the value of M1? Is this change likely to have much impact on the economy? (*Hint:* According to the information given in this chapter, what is the current value of M1?)

Source: Austan Goolsbee, "Now That a Penny Isn't Worth Much, It's Time to Make It Worth 5 Cents," *New York Times*, February 1, 2007.

>> End Learning Objective 13.2

13.3 LEARNING OBJECTIVE 13.3 | Explain how banks create money, **pages 440–448.**

How Do Banks Create Money?

Summary

On a bank's balance sheet, *reserves* and loans are assets, and deposits are liabilities. **Reserves** are deposits that the bank has retained rather than loaned out or invested. **Required reserves** are reserves that banks are legally required to hold. The fraction of deposits that banks are required to keep as reserves is called the **required reserve ratio**. Any reserves banks hold over and above the legal requirement are called **excess reserves**. When a bank accepts a deposit, it keeps only a fraction of the funds as reserves and loans out the remainder. In making a loan, a bank increases the checking account balance of the borrower. When the borrower uses a check to buy something with the funds the bank has loaned, the seller deposits the check in his bank. The seller's bank keeps part of the deposit as reserves and loans out the remainder. This process continues until no banks have excess reserves. In this way, the process of banks making new loans increases the volume of checking account balances and the money supply. This money creation process can be illustrated with T-accounts, which are stripped-down versions of balance sheets that show only how a transaction changes a bank's balance sheet. The **simple deposit multiplier** is the ratio of the amount of deposits created by banks to the amount of new reserves. An expression for the simple deposit multiplier is $1/RR$.

myeconlab Get Ahead of the Curve Visit www.myeconlab.com to complete these exercises online and get instant feedback.

Review Questions

3.1 What are the largest asset and the largest liability of a typical bank?

3.2 Suppose you decide to withdraw $100 in cash from your checking account. Draw a T-account showing the effect of this transaction on your bank's balance sheet.

3.3 Give the formula for the simple deposit multiplier. If the required reserve ratio is 20 percent, what is the maximum increase in checking account deposits that will result from an increase in bank reserves of $20,000?

Problems and Applications

3.4 The following is from a newspaper story on local, or community, banks: "Community banks . . . are awash in liabilities these days, and they couldn't be happier about it." To which "liabilities" does the story refer? Why would these banks be happy about being "awash" in these liabilities?

Source: Christian Millman, "Bank Deposits on the Rise as People Flee the Stock Market," (Allentown, Pennsylvania) *Morning Call*, August 11, 2002, pp. D1, D4.

3.5 The president of a local bank described deposits this way: "That's the fuel we use to be able to go out and make loans and mortgages." Briefly explain what he means.

Source: Christian Millman, "Bank Deposits on the Rise as People Flee the Stock Market," (Allentown, Pennsylvania) *Morning Call*, August 11, 2002, pp. D1, D4.

3.6 The following is from an article on community banks: "Their commercial-lending businesses, funded by their stable deposit bases, make them steady earners."

What is commercial lending? In what sense are loans "funded" by deposits?

Source: Karen Richardson, "Clean Books Bolster Traditional Lenders," *Wall Street Journal*, April 30, 2007, p. C1.

3.7 "Most of the money supply of the United States is created by banks making loans." Briefly explain whether you agree or disagree with this statement.

3.8 Would a series of bank runs in a country decrease the total quantity of M1? Wouldn't a bank run simply move funds in a checking account to currency in circulation? How could that movement of funds decrease the quantity of money?

3.9 **(Related to *Solved Problem 13-3* on page 445)** Suppose you deposit $2,000 in currency into your checking account at a branch of Bank of America, which we will assume has no excess reserves at the time you make your deposit. Also assume that the required reserve ratio is 0.20.

a. Use a T-account to show the initial impact of this transaction on Bank of America's balance sheet.

b. Suppose that Bank of America makes the maximum loan it can from the funds you deposited. Using a T-account, show the initial impact of granting the loan on Bank of America's balance sheet. Also include on this T-account the transaction from (a).

c. Now suppose that whoever took out the loan in (b) writes a check for this amount and that the person receiving the check deposits it in a branch of Citibank. Show the effect of these transactions on the balance sheets of Bank of America and Citibank *after the check has been cleared.* (On the T-account for Bank of America, include the transactions from [a] and [b].)

d. What is the maximum increase in checking account deposits that can result from your $2,000 deposit? What is the maximum increase in the money supply? Explain.

3.10 Consider the following simplified balance sheet for a bank.

Assets		Liabilities	
Reserves	$10,000	Deposits	$70,000
Loans	$66,000	Stockholders' equity	$6,000

a. If the required reserve ratio is 10 percent, how much in excess reserves does the bank hold?

b. What is the maximum amount by which the bank can expand its loans?

c. If the bank makes the loans in (b), show the *immediate* impact on the bank's balance sheet.

3.11 **(Related to the *Don't Let This Happen to You!* on page 441)** Briefly explain whether you agree or disagree with the following statement: "Assets are things of value that people own. Liabilities are debts. Therefore, a bank will always consider a checking account deposit to be an asset and a car loan to be a liability."

3.12 "Banks don't really create money, do they?" was the challenge that a retired professor of economics was known to have used in his upper-division American economic history course to ascertain what his students remembered from introductory macroeconomics about the creation of money. He reported that few students were confident enough or remembered enough to reply correctly to his question. How would you reply?

» End Learning Objective 13.3

13.4 LEARNING OBJECTIVE 13.4 | Discuss the three policy tools the Federal Reserve uses to manage the money supply, **pages 448–452.**

The Federal Reserve System

Summary

The United States has a **fractional reserve banking system** in which banks keep less than 100 percent of deposits as reserves. In a **bank run**, many depositors decide simultaneously to withdraw money from a bank. In a **bank panic**, many banks experience runs at the same time. The **Federal Reserve System** ("the Fed") is the central bank of the United States. It was originally established in 1913 to stop bank panics, but today its main role is to carry out *monetary policy*. **Monetary policy** refers to the actions the Federal Reserve takes to manage the money supply and interest rates to pursue macroeconomic policy objectives. The Fed's three monetary policy tools are open market operations, discount policy, and reserve requirements. **Open market operations** are the buying and selling of Treasury securities by the Federal Reserve. The loans the Fed makes to banks are called **discount loans**, and the interest rate the Fed charges on discount loans is the **discount rate**. The **Federal Open Market Committee (FOMC)** meets in Washington, DC, eight times per year to discuss monetary policy.

Review Questions

4.1 Why did Congress decide to set up the Federal Reserve System in 1913? Today, what is the most important role of the Federal Reserve in the U.S. economy?

4.2 What are the policy tools the Fed uses to control the money supply? Which tool is the most important?

Problems and Applications

4.3 The text explains that the United States has a "fractional reserve banking system." Why do most depositors seem to be unworried that banks loan out most of the deposits they receive?

4.4 Suppose that you are a bank manager, and the Federal Reserve raises the required reserve ratio from 10 percent to 12 percent. What actions would you need to take? How would your actions and those of other bank managers end up affecting the money supply?

4.5 Reserve requirements have been referred to as a "tax on bank profits." Briefly explain whether you agree. How would your answer change if the Fed began paying interest on banks' reserve accounts?

4.6 Suppose that the Federal Reserve makes a $10 million discount loan to the First National Bank by increasing FNB's account at the Fed.

a. Use a T-account to show the impact of this transaction on FNB's balance sheet. Remember that the funds a bank has on deposit at the Fed count as part of its reserves.

b. Assume that before receiving the discount loan, FNB has no excess reserves. What is the maximum amount of this $10 million that FNB can lend out?

c. What is the maximum total increase in the money supply that can result from the Fed's discount loan? Assume that the required reserve ratio is 10 percent.

4.7 **(Related to the *Making the Connection* on page 449)** Argentina suffered a severe bank panic in 2001. The United States has not suffered a bank panic since the 1930s. What differences between the Argentine and U.S. financial systems can account for their differing vulnerability to bank panics?

» End Learning Objective 13.4

13.5 LEARNING OBJECTIVE 13.5 | Explain the quantity theory of money and use it to explain how high rates of inflation occur, **pages 452–457.**

The Quantity Theory of Money

Summary

The *quantity equation* relates the money supply to the price level: $M \times V = P \times Y$, where M is the money supply, V is the *velocity of money*, P is the price level, and Y is real output. The **velocity of money** is the average number of times each dollar in the money supply is spent during the year. Economist Irving Fisher developed the **quantity theory of money**, which assumes that the velocity of money is constant. If the quantity theory of money is correct, the inflation rate should equal the rate of growth of the money supply minus the rate of growth of real output. Although the quantity theory of money is not literally correct because the velocity of money is not constant, it is true that in the long run, inflation results from the money supply growing faster than real GDP. When governments attempt to raise revenue by selling large quantities of bonds to the central bank, the money supply will increase rapidly, resulting in a high rate of inflation.

Review Questions

5.1 What is the quantity theory of money? How does the quantity theory explain why inflation occurs?

5.2 What is hyperinflation? Why do governments sometimes allow it to occur?

Problems and Applications

5.3 If the money supply is growing at a rate of 6 percent per year, real GDP is growing at a rate of 3 percent per year, and velocity is constant, what will the inflation rate be? If velocity is increasing 1 percent per year instead of remaining constant, what will the inflation rate be?

5.4 Suppose that during one period, the velocity of money is constant and during another period, it undergoes large fluctuations. During which period will the quantity theory of money be more useful in explaining changes in the inflation rate? Briefly explain.

5.5 The following is from an article in the *Wall Street Journal*: "[Japan's] money supply is surging. If that doesn't curtail Japan's debilitating price deflation, a lot of economics textbooks may need to be rewritten."
   a. What is "price deflation"?
   b. If rapid increases in the money supply don't stop deflation, why will economics textbooks need to be rewritten?
   c. (This is a more difficult question.) Why might price deflation in Japan be "debilitating"? (*Hint:* What reaction might consumers have to price deflation?)

   Source: Peter Landers, "Japan Shows Vague Signs of Recovery," *Wall Street Journal*, March 5, 2002.

5.6 **(Related to the *Chapter Opener* on page 430)** During the Civil War, the Confederate States of America printed lots of its own currency—Confederate dollars—to fund the war. By the end of the war, nearly 1.5 billion paper dollars had been printed by the Confederate government. How would such a large quantity of Confederate dollars have affected the value of the Confederate currency? With the war drawing to an end, would Southerners have been as willing to use and accept Confederate dollars? How else could they have made exchanges?

   Source: Textual Transcript of Confederate Currency, Federal Reserve Bank of Richmond.

5.7 **(Related to the *Making the Connection* on page 456)** During the German hyperinflation of the 1920s, many households and firms in Germany were hurt economically. Did you think any groups in Germany benefited from the hyperinflation? Briefly explain.

5.8 In the summer of 2006, the African country of Zimbabwe decided to change its currency. At the end of the day on August 21, 2006, the old dollar would no longer be legal tender. It would be replaced with new currency, with each new dollar worth 1,000 times what the old dollar was worth. According to a newspaper article "Under the changeover rules, individuals were permitted to exchange a limit of 100 million old Zimbabwe dollars ($40) for new currency in a single transaction each week since Aug. 1." Predict what happened to prices in Zimbabwe in terms of the old dollar as the August 21 deadline approached. What would the government of Zimbabwe hope to gain from swapping a new currency for an old currency?

   Source: "Zimbabwe Swaps Currency Amid Runaway Inflation," *Wall Street Journal*, August 21, 2006.

5.9 An article in the *Economist* on Zimbabwe, described conditions in summer 2007: "inflation is hovering around 4,500%, and eight Zimbabweans in ten do not have formal jobs." Is there a connection between the very high inflation rate and the high rate of unemployment? Briefly explain.

   Source: "Rumblings Within," *Economist*, June 21, 2007.

>> End Learning Objective 13.5

Chapter 14

Monetary Policy

Monetary Policy, Toll Brothers, and the Housing Market

Few firms experienced such dramatic swings in sales as homebuilder Toll Brothers, Inc., did between 2001 and 2007. In March 2001, the U.S. economy moved into recession. During a typical recession, sales of new homes decline sharply as unemployment increases and incomes fall. Homebuilders are usually among the businesses hit hardest during recessions. For example, during the recession of 1974–1975, spending on residential construction declined by more than 30 percent. Homebuilders fared even worse during the recessions of 1980–1982, when spending on residential construction plummeted by more than 40 percent.

So, when the recession began in 2001, Toll Brothers should have experienced a decline in sales. But look at the following excerpt from the company's report to shareholders for the third quarter of 2001:

> Amid continuing sluggishness in the U.S. economy, Toll Brothers once again posted record results. Thanks to hard work and efficient planning and the [housing] market's ability to weather the downturn, we have just completed the best third quarter and first nine months in our history.

Other homebuilders also did unexpectedly well during 2001, as spending on residential construction actually *rose* by 5 percent. The success of Toll Brothers during 2001 was not the result of good luck but rather of a policy decision made by the Federal Reserve's

Federal Open Market Committee (FOMC). In early 2001, the members of the FOMC concluded that a recession was about to begin and implemented an expansionary monetary policy to keep the recession as short and mild as possible. By driving down interest rates, the Fed succeeded in heading off what some economists had predicted would be a prolonged and severe recession. Low interest rates made borrowing to buy a new home less expensive, and millions of families responded, flooding Toll Brothers with orders.

A few years later, the situation for Toll Brothers and other homebuilders looked very different. The strong housing market of 2001 had turned into a housing "bubble" by 2005. In a housing bubble, prices soar to levels that are not sustainable, and homebuilders buy more land and erect more houses than they end up being able to sell for a profit. In February 2007, Toll Brothers reported a 67 percent drop in its profits for the previous quarter and warned investors that neither the housing market nor the firm's profitability would likely improve any time

soon. This time, the Federal Reserve did not intervene to lower interest rates and rescue the housing market. As we will see in this chapter, in addition to being concerned about recessions, the Fed tries to keep the inflation rate at a low level. During 2006 and 2007, the inflation rate was at or above the level the Fed considers acceptable. Lowering interest rates might worsen inflation if it led to a large increase in spending by households and firms. In late 2007, the Fed was straining to preserve the balance between restraining inflation on the one hand and keeping the economy from tumbling into recession on the other hand.

AN INSIDE LOOK AT POLICY on **page 498** compares the effects of a slowing housing market on the United States and Europe.

Sources: Judy Lam and Michael Corkery, "Toll Brothers Net Falls 67%; Outlook Is Cut," *Wall Street Journal*, February 23, 2007, p. A3; and Shawn Tully, "Toll Brothers: The New King of the Real Estate Boom," *Fortune*, April 5, 2005.

LEARNING Objectives

After studying this chapter, you should be able to:

14.1 Define **monetary policy** and describe the Federal Reserve's **monetary policy goals**, page 468.

14.2 Describe the Federal Reserve's monetary policy targets and explain how **expansionary** and **contractionary monetary policies** affect the **interest rate**, page 470.

14.3 Use aggregate demand and aggregate supply graphs to show the **effects** of **monetary policy** on **real GDP** and the **price level**, page 477.

14.4 Discuss the Fed's setting of **monetary policy targets**, page 490.

14.5 Assess the arguments for and against the **independence** of the **Federal Reserve**, page 494.

Economics in YOUR Life!

Should You Buy a House During a Recession?

If you are like most college students, buying a house is one of the farthest things from your mind. But suppose you think forward a few years to when you might be married and maybe even (gasp!) have children. Leaving years of renting apartments behind, you are considering buying a house. But, suppose that according to an article in the *Wall Street Journal*, a majority of economists are predicting that a recession is likely to begin soon. What should you do? Would this be a good time or a bad time to buy a house? As you read the chapter, see if you can answer these questions. You can check your answers against those we provide at the end of the chapter. **Continued on page 497**

In Chapter 13, we saw that banks play an important role in creating the money supply. We also saw that the Fed manages the money supply to achieve its policy goals. As we will see in this chapter, the Fed has four policy goals: (1) price stability, (2) high employment, (3) economic growth, and (4) stability of financial markets and institutions. In this chapter, we will explore how the Federal Reserve decides which *monetary policy* actions to take to achieve its goals.

14.1 LEARNING OBJECTIVE

14.1 | Define monetary policy and describe the Federal Reserve's monetary policy goals.

What Is Monetary Policy?

In 1913, Congress passed the Federal Reserve Act, creating the Federal Reserve System ("the Fed"). The main responsibility of the Fed was to make discount loans to banks suffering from large withdrawals by depositors. In other words, the Fed was charged with preventing the bank panics you learned about in Chapter 13. As a result of the Great Depression of the 1930s, Congress amended the Federal Reserve Act to give the Federal Reserve's Board of Governors broader responsibility to act "so as to promote effectively the goals of maximum employment, stable prices, and moderate long-term interest rates."

Since World War II, the Federal Reserve has carried out an active *monetary policy*. **Monetary policy** refers to the actions the Fed takes to manage the money supply and interest rates to pursue its macroeconomic policy objectives.

Monetary policy The actions the Federal Reserve takes to manage the money supply and interest rates to pursue its macroeconomic policy objectives.

The Goals of Monetary Policy

The Fed has set four *monetary policy goals* that are intended to promote a well-functioning economy:

1. Price stability
2. High employment
3. Economic growth
4. Stability of financial markets and institutions

We briefly consider each of these goals.

Price Stability As we have seen in previous chapters, rising prices erode the value of money as a medium of exchange and a store of value. Especially after inflation rose dramatically and unexpectedly during the 1970s, policymakers in most industrial countries have price stability as a policy goal. Figure 14-1 shows that from the early 1950s until 1968, the inflation rate remained below 4 percent per year. Inflation was above 4 percent for most of the 1970s. In early 1979, the inflation rate increased to more than 10 percent, where it remained until late 1981, when it began to rapidly fall back to the 4 percent range. From 1992 until late 2005, the inflation rate was below 4 percent. The relatively high inflation rates of late 2005 and early 2006 caused concern at the Fed.

The inflation rates during the years 1979–1981 were the highest the United States has ever experienced during peacetime. When Paul Volcker became chairman of the Federal Reserve's Board of Governors in August 1979, he made fighting inflation his top policy goal. Alan Greenspan, who succeeded Volcker in August 1987, and Ben Bernanke, who succeeded Greenspan in January 2006, continued to focus on inflation. Volcker, Greenspan, and Bernanke argued that if inflation is low over the long run, the Fed will have the flexibility it needs to lessen the impact of recessions. And many economists agree.

High Employment High employment, or a low rate of unemployment, is another monetary policy goal. Unemployed workers and underused factories and office buildings reduce GDP below its potential level. Unemployment causes financial distress and

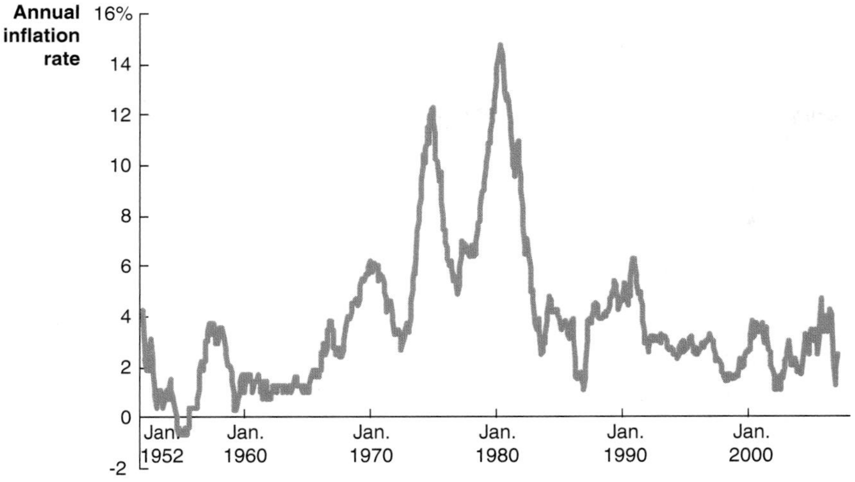

Figure 14-1

The Inflation Rate, 1952–2006

For most of the 1950s and 1960s, the inflation rate in the United States was 4 percent or less. During the 1970s, the inflation rate increased, peaking during 1979–1981, when it averaged more than 10 percent. From 1992 until late 2005, the inflation rate was less than 4 percent. The inflation rates were relatively high in late 2005 and early 2006.

Note: The inflation rate is measured as the percentage increase in the consumer price index (CPI) from the same month in the previous year.

Source: Bureau of Labor Statistics.

decreases self-esteem for workers who lack jobs. The goal of high employment extends beyond the Fed to other branches of the federal government. At the end of World War II, Congress passed the Employment Act of 1946, which stated that it was the "responsibility of the Federal Government . . . to foster and promote . . . conditions under which there will be afforded useful employment, for those able, willing, and seeking to work, and to promote maximum employment, production, and purchasing power."

Economic Growth We discussed in Chapters 9 and 10 the importance of economic growth to raising living standards. Policymakers aim to encourage *stable* economic growth because stable growth allows households and firms to plan accurately and encourages the long-run investment that is needed to sustain growth. Policy can spur economic growth by providing incentives for saving to ensure a large pool of investment funds, as well as by providing direct incentives for business investment. Policies to increase saving and investment may be better carried out by Congress and the president than by the Fed, however. For example, Congress and the president can change the tax laws to increase the return to saving and investing. In fact, some economists question whether the Fed can play a role in promoting economic growth beyond attempting to meet its goals of price stability and high employment. These economists note that high employment typically occurs only when real GDP is near potential GDP and growing at a sustained rate. So, in attaining its goal of high employment, the Fed will also have promoted economic growth. Similarly, most economists believe that economic growth is generally slow during periods of high inflation. So, in achieving price stability, the Fed will also be promoting economic growth.

Stability of Financial Markets and Institutions When financial markets and institutions are not efficient in matching savers and borrowers, resources are lost. Firms with the potential to produce goods and services valued by consumers cannot obtain the financing they need to design, develop, and market those products. Savers waste resources looking for satisfactory investments. The Fed promotes the stability of financial markets and institutions so that an efficient flow of funds from savers to borrowers will occur. The Fed's response to problems in financial markets has averted financial panics. For example, following the stock market crash of 1987, the terrorist attacks of September 11, 2001, and the turmoil in the market for subprime mortgages during August 2007, the Fed's willingness to rapidly increase the volume of discount loans reassured financial markets and promoted financial stability.

In the next section, we will look at how the Fed attempts to attain its monetary policy goals. Although the Fed has multiple monetary policy goals, during most periods, the most important goals of monetary policy have been price stability and high employment. In the remainder of this chapter, we will focus on these two goals.

14.2 LEARNING OBJECTIVE

14.2 | Describe the Federal Reserve's monetary policy targets and explain how expansionary and contractionary monetary policies affect the interest rate.

The Money Market and the Fed's Choice of Monetary Policy Targets

The Fed's objective in undertaking monetary policy is to use its policy tools to achieve its monetary policy goals. Recall from Chapter 13 that the Fed's policy tools are open market operations, discount policy, and reserve requirements. At times, the Fed encounters conflicts between its policy goals. For example, as we will discuss later in this chapter, the Fed can raise interest rates to reduce the inflation rate. But, as we saw in Chapter 12, higher interest rates typically reduce household and firm spending, which may result in slower growth and higher unemployment. So, a policy that is intended to achieve one monetary policy goal, such as lower inflation, may have an adverse effect on another policy goal, such as high employment. Some members of Congress have introduced legislation that would force the Fed to focus almost entirely on achieving price stability, and many economists support such a focus. Although so far this legislation has not passed Congress, the debate has gained momentum within the Federal Reserve.

Monetary Policy Targets

The Fed tries to keep both the unemployment and inflation rates low, but it can't affect either of these economic variables directly. The Fed cannot tell firms how many people to employ or what prices to charge for their products. Instead, the Fed uses variables, called *monetary policy targets*, that it can affect directly and that, in turn, affect variables that are closely related to the Fed's policy goals, such as real GDP, employment, and the price level. The two main monetary policy targets are the money supply and the interest rate. As we will see, the Fed typically uses the interest rate as its policy target.

The Demand for Money

The Fed's two monetary policy targets are related in an important way. To see this relationship, we first need to examine the demand and supply for money. Figure 14-2 shows the demand curve for money. The interest rate is on the vertical axis, and the quantity of money is on the horizontal axis. Here we are using the M1 definition of money, which equals currency in circulation plus checking account deposits. Notice that the demand curve for money is downward sloping.

To understand why the demand curve for money is downward sloping, consider that households and firms have a choice between holding money and holding other

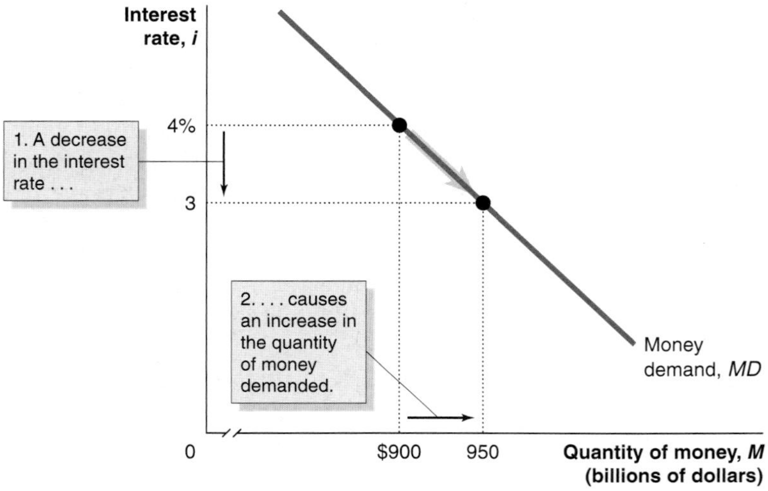

Figure 14-2

The Demand for Money

The money demand curve slopes downward because lower interest rates cause households and firms to switch from financial assets like U.S. Treasury bills to money. All other things being equal, a fall in the interest rate from 4 percent to 3 percent will increase the quantity of money demanded from $900 billion to $950 billion. An increase in the interest rate will decrease the quantity of money demanded.

financial assets, such as U.S. Treasury bills. Money has one particularly desirable characteristic: You can use it to buy goods, services, or financial assets. Money also has one undesirable characteristic: It earns either no interest or a very low rate of interest. The currency in your wallet earns no interest, and the money in your checking account earns either no interest or very little interest. Alternatives to money, such as U.S. Treasury bills, pay interest but have to be sold if you want to use the funds to buy something. When interest rates rise on financial assets such as U.S. Treasury bills, the amount of interest that households and firms lose by holding money increases. When interest rates fall, the amount of interest households and firms lose by holding money decreases. Remember that *opportunity cost* is what you have to forgo to engage in an activity. The interest rate is the opportunity cost of holding money.

We now have an explanation for why the demand curve for money slopes downward: When interest rates on Treasury bills and other financial assets are low, the opportunity cost of holding money is low, so the quantity of money demanded by households and firms will be high; when interest rates are high, the opportunity cost of holding money will be high, so the quantity of money demanded will be low. In Figure 14-2, a decrease in interest rates from 4 percent to 3 percent causes the quantity of money demanded by households and firms to rise from $900 billion to $950 billion.

Shifts in the Money Demand Curve

We saw in Chapter 3 that the demand curve for a good is drawn holding constant all variables, other than the price, that affect the willingness of consumers to buy the good. Changes in variables other than the price cause the demand curve to shift. Similarly, the demand curve for money is drawn holding constant all variables, other than the interest rate, that affect the willingness of households and firms to hold money. Changes in variables other than the interest rate cause the demand curve to shift. The two most important variables that cause the money demand curve to shift are real GDP and the price level.

An increase in real GDP means that the amount of buying and selling of goods and services will increase. This additional buying and selling increases the demand for money as a medium of exchange, so the quantity of money households and firms want to hold increases at each interest rate, shifting the money demand curve to the right. A decrease in real GDP decreases the quantity of money demanded at each interest rate, shifting the money demand curve to the left. A higher price level increases the quantity of money required for a given amount of buying and selling. Eighty years ago, for example, when the price level was much lower and someone could purchase a new car for $500 and a salary of $30 per week put you in the middle class, the quantity of money demanded by households and firms was much lower than today, even adjusting for the effect of the lower real GDP and smaller population of those years. An increase in the price level increases the quantity of money demanded at each interest rate, shifting the money demand curve to the right. A decrease in the price level decreases the quantity of money demanded at each interest rate, shifting the money demand curve to the left. Figure 14-3 illustrates shifts in the money demand curve.

How the Fed Manages the Money Supply: A Quick Review

Having discussed money demand, we now turn to money supply. In Chapter 13, we saw how the Federal Reserve manages the money supply. Eight times per year, the FOMC meets in Washington, DC. If the FOMC decides to increase the money supply, it orders the trading desk at the Federal Reserve Bank of New York to purchase U.S. Treasury securities. The sellers of these Treasury securities deposit the funds they receive from the Fed in banks, which increases the banks' reserves. The banks loan out most of these reserves, which creates new checking account deposits and expands the money supply. If the FOMC decides to decrease the money supply, it orders the trading desk to sell Treasury securities, which decreases banks' reserves and contracts the money supply.

Figure 14-3

Shifts in the Money Demand Curve

Changes in real GDP or the price level cause the money demand curve to shift. An increase in real GDP or an increase in the price level will cause the money demand curve to shift from MD_1 to MD_2. A decrease in real GDP or a decrease in the price level will cause the money demand curve to shift from MD_1 to MD_3.

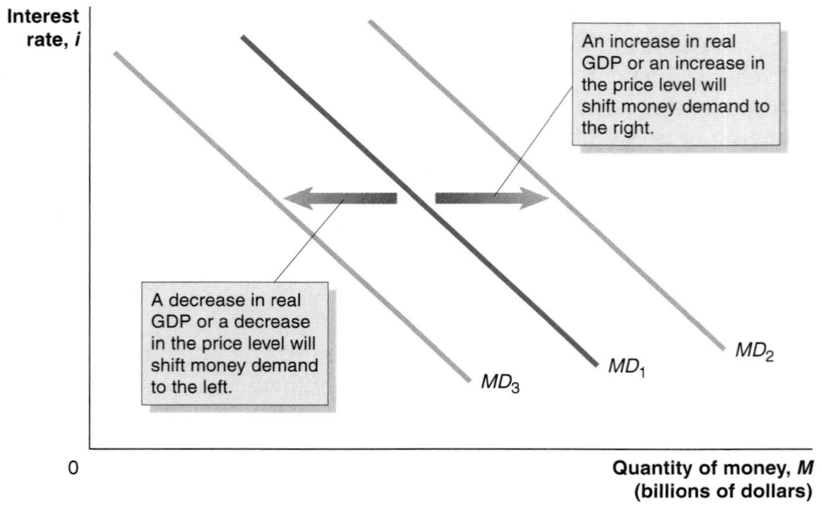

Equilibrium in the Money Market

In Figure 14-4, we include both the money demand and money supply curves. We can use this figure to see how the Fed affects both the money supply and the interest rate. For simplicity, we assume that the Federal Reserve is able to completely fix the money supply (although, in fact, the behavior of the public and banks can also affect the money supply). Therefore, the money supply curve is a vertical line, and changes in the interest rate have no effect on the quantity of money supplied. Just as with other markets, equilibrium in the *money market* occurs where the money demand curve crosses the money supply curve. If the Fed increases the money supply, the money supply curve will shift to the right, and the equilibrium interest rate will fall. In Figure 14-4, when the Fed increases the money supply from \$900 billion to \$950 billion, the money supply curve shifts from MS_1 to MS_2, and the equilibrium interest rate falls from 4 percent to 3 percent.

In the money market, the adjustment from one equilibrium to another equilibrium is a little different from the adjustment in the market for a good. In Figure 14-4, the money market is initially in equilibrium with an interest rate of 4 percent and a money supply of \$900 billion. When the Fed increases the money supply by \$50 billion, households and firms have more money than they want to hold at an interest rate of 4 percent. What do households and firms do with the extra \$50 billion? They are most likely to use the money to buy short-term financial assets, such as Treasury bills. Short-term financial

Figure 14-4

The Impact on the Interest Rate When the Fed Increases the Money Supply

When the Fed increases the money supply, households and firms will initially hold more money than they want, relative to other financial assets. Households and firms buy Treasury bills and other financial assets with the money they don't want to hold. This increase in demand drives up the prices of these assets and drives down their interest rates. Eventually, interest rates will fall enough that households and firms will be willing to hold the additional money the Fed has created. In the figure, an increase in the money supply from \$900 billion to \$950 billion causes the money supply curve to shift to the right, from MS_1 to MS_2, and causes the equilibrium interest rate to fall from 4 percent to 3 percent.

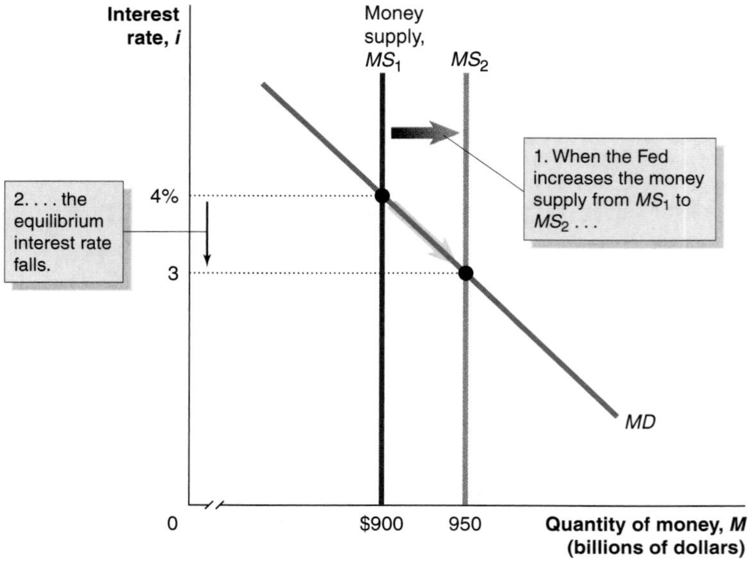

assets have maturities—the date when the last payment by the seller is made—of one year or less. By buying short-term assets, households and firms drive up their prices and drive down their interest rates.

To see why an increasing demand for Treasury bills will lower their interest rate, recall from Chapter 5 that *the prices of financial assets and their interest rates move in opposite directions.* Suppose you buy a U.S. Treasury bill today for $962 that matures in one year, at which time the Treasury will pay you $1,000. The government sells Treasury bills at a price below their face value of $1,000. The difference between the price of the bill and its $1,000 face value represents the return to investors for lending their money to the Treasury. In this case, you will earn $38 in interest on your investment of $962. The interest rate on the Treasury bill is:

$$\left(\frac{\$38}{\$962}\right) \times 100 = 4\%.$$

Now suppose that many households and firms increase their demand for Treasury bills. This increase in demand will have the same effect on Treasury bills that an increase in the demand for apples has on apples: The price will rise. Suppose the price of Treasury bills rises from $962 to $971. Now if you buy a Treasury bill, you will receive only $29 in interest on your investment of $971. The interest rate on the Treasury bill is now:

$$\left(\frac{\$29}{\$971}\right) \times 100 = 3\%.$$

Therefore, as the price of a Treasury bill increases, the interest rate on the Treasury bill falls.

As the interest rate on Treasury bills and other financial assets falls, the opportunity cost of holding money also falls. Households and firms move down the money demand curve. Eventually the interest rate will have fallen enough that households and firms are willing to hold the additional $50 billion worth of money the Fed has created, and the money market will be back in equilibrium. To summarize: *When the Fed increases the money supply, the short-term interest rate must fall until it reaches a level at which households and firms are willing to hold the additional money.*

Figure 14-5 shows what happens when the Fed decreases the money supply. The money market is initially in equilibrium, at an interest rate of 4 percent and a money supply of $900 billion. If the Fed decreases the money supply to $850 billion, households

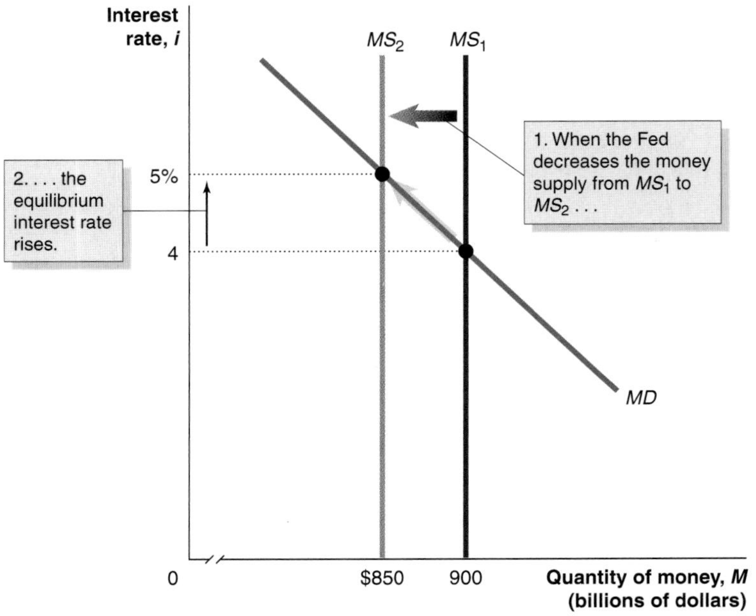

Figure 14-5

The Impact on Interest Rates When the Fed Decreases the Money Supply

When the Fed decreases the money supply, households and firms will initially hold less money than they want, relative to other financial assets. Households and firms will sell Treasury bills and other financial assets, reducing their prices and increasing their interest rates. Eventually, interest rates will rise to the point at which households and firms will be willing to hold the smaller amount of money that results from the Fed's actions. In the figure, a reduction in money supply from $900 billion to $850 billion causes the money supply curve to shift to the left, from MS_1 to MS_2, and causes the equilibrium interest rate to rise from 4 percent to 5 percent.

and firms will be holding less money than they would like—relative to other financial assets—at an interest rate of 4 percent. To increase their money holdings, they will sell Treasury bills and other financial assets. The increased supply of Treasury bills for sale will decrease their prices and increase their interest rates. Rising short-term interest rates increase the opportunity cost of holding money, causing households and firms to move up the money demand curve. Equilibrium is finally restored at an interest rate of 5 percent.

Solved Problem | 14-2

The Relationship between Treasury Bill Prices and Their Interest Rates

What is the price of a Treasury bill that pays $1,000 in one year, if its interest rate is 4 percent? What is the price of the Treasury bill if its interest rate is 5 percent?

SOLVING THE PROBLEM:

Step 1: **Review the chapter material.** This problem is about the relationship between Treasury bill prices and interest rates, so you may want to review the section "Equilibrium in the Money Market," which begins on page 472.

Step 2: **Use the formula for calculating interest rates to determine the Treasury bill price when the interest rate is 4 percent.** In this situation, the interest rate will be equal to the percentage increase from the initial purchase price of the bill to the $1,000 buyers will receive in one year. We can set up the problem like this, where P is the purchase price of the Treasury bill:

$$\left(\frac{\$1{,}000 - P}{P}\right) \times 100 = 4.$$

Dividing both sides by 100 and multiplying both sides by P, we get:

$$\$1{,}000 - P = 0.04P,$$

or:

$$\$1{,}000 = 1.04P,$$

or:

$$\frac{\$1{,}000}{1.04} = P,$$

or, rounding to the nearest dollar:

$$P = \$962.$$

Step 3: **Use the formula for calculating interest rates to determine the Treasury bill price when the interest rate is 5 percent.** We can apply the same formula to find the price when the interest rate is 5 percent:

$$\left(\frac{\$1{,}000 - P}{P}\right) \times 100 = 5.$$

Once again, dividing both sides by 100 and multiplying both sides by P, we get:

$$\$1{,}000 - P = 0.05P,$$

or:

$$\$1{,}000 = 1.05P,$$

or:

$$\frac{\$1{,}000}{1.05} = P,$$

or:

$$P = \$952.$$

EXTRA CREDIT: The interest rate on a Treasury bill or other financial asset is also called its *yield*. It's important to remember that prices of financial assets and their yields move in opposite directions. Consider this excerpt from the credit market column in the *Wall Street Journal*: "The benchmark 10-year [U.S. Treasury] note was down . . . $5 per $1,000 face value, to . . . [$964.69]. Its yield rose to 4.955% from 4.892% Thursday, as yields move inversely to prices." A similar reminder that a bond's yield moves inversely to its price appears in this newspaper column every day. Any fact that the *Wall Street Journal* feels is important enough to remind its readers of every day is probably worth remembering!

Source: Laurence Norman, "Bond Prices Decline on Mixed U.S. Data," *Wall Street Journal*, June 2, 2007.

YOUR TURN: For more practice, do problem 2.6 on page 501 at the end of this chapter.

>> End Solved Problem 14-2

A Tale of Two Interest Rates

In Chapter 9, we discussed the loanable funds model of the interest rate. In that model, the equilibrium interest rate was determined by the demand and supply for loanable funds. Why do we need two models of the interest rate? The answer is that the loanable funds model is concerned with the *long-term real rate of interest*, and the money-market model is concerned with the *short-term nominal rate of interest*. The long-term real rate of interest is the interest rate that is most relevant when savers consider purchasing a long-term financial investment such as a corporate bond. It is also the rate of interest that is most relevant to firms that are borrowing to finance long-term investment projects such as new factories or office buildings, or to households that are taking out mortgage loans to buy new homes.

When conducting monetary policy, however, the short-term nominal interest rate is the most relevant interest rate because it is the interest rate most affected by increases and decreases in the money supply. Often—but not always—there is a close connection between movements in the short-term nominal interest rate and movements in the long-term real interest rate. So, when the Fed takes actions to increase the short-term nominal interest, usually the long-term real interest rate also increases. In other words, as we will discuss in the next section, when the interest rate on Treasury bills rises, the real interest rate on mortgage loans usually also rises, although sometimes only after a delay.

Choosing a Monetary Policy Target

As we have seen, the Fed uses monetary policy targets to affect economic variables such as real GDP or the price level, which are closely related to the Fed's policy goals. The Fed chooses the money supply or the interest rate as its monetary policy target. As Figure 14-5 shows, the Fed is capable of affecting both. The Fed has generally focused more on the interest rate than on the money supply. After 1980, deregulation and financial innovations, including paying interest on checking accounts and the introduction of money market mutual funds, have made M1 less relevant as a measure of the medium of exchange. These developments led the Fed to rely for a time on M2, a broader measure of the money supply that had a more stable historical relationship to economic growth.

Even this relationship broke down in the early 1990s. In July 1993, then Fed Chairman Alan Greenspan informed the U.S. Congress that the Fed would cease using M1 or M2 targets to guide the conduct of monetary policy. The Fed has correspondingly increased its reliance on interest rate targets.

There are many different interest rates in the economy. For purposes of monetary policy, the Fed has targeted the interest rate known as the *federal funds rate*. In the next section, we discuss the federal funds rate before examining how targeting the interest rate can help the Fed achieve its monetary policy goals.

The Importance of the Federal Funds Rate

Recall from Chapter 13 that every bank must keep 10 percent of its checking account deposits above a certain threshold as reserves, either as currency held in the bank or as deposits with the Fed. Banks receive no interest on their reserves, so they have an incentive to invest reserves above the 10-percent minimum. Banks that need additional reserves can borrow in the *federal funds market* from banks that have reserves available. The **federal funds rate** is the interest rate banks charge on loans in the federal funds market. The loans in the federal funds market are usually very short term, often just overnight.

Federal funds rate The interest rate banks charge each other for overnight loans.

Despite the name, the federal funds rate is not set administratively by the Fed. Instead, the rate is determined by the supply of reserves relative to the demand for them. Because the Fed can increase and decrease the supply of bank reserves through open market operations, it can set a target for the federal funds rate and come very close to hitting it. The FOMC announces a target for the federal funds rate after each meeting. In Figure 14-6, the orange line shows the Fed's targets for the federal funds rate since 1997. The jagged green line represents the actual federal funds rate on a weekly basis.

The federal funds rate is not directly relevant for households and firms. No households or firms, except banks, can borrow or lend in the federal funds market. However, changes in the federal funds rate usually result in changes in interest rates on other short-term financial assets, such as Treasury bills, and changes in interest rates on long-term financial assets, such as corporate bonds and mortgages. The effect of a change in the federal funds rate on long-term interest rates is usually smaller than it is on short-term interest rates, and the effect may occur only after a lag in time. Although a majority of economists support the Fed's choice of the interest rate as its monetary policy target, some economists believe the Fed should concentrate on the money supply instead. We will discuss the views of these economists later in this chapter.

Figure 14-6

Federal Funds Rate Targeting, January 1997–May 2007

The Fed does not set the federal funds rate, but its ability to increase or decrease bank reserves quickly through open market operations keeps the actual federal funds rate close to the Fed's target rate. The orange line is the Fed's target for the federal funds rate, and the jagged green line represents the actual value for the federal funds rate on a weekly basis.

Source: Board of Governors of the Federal Reserve System.

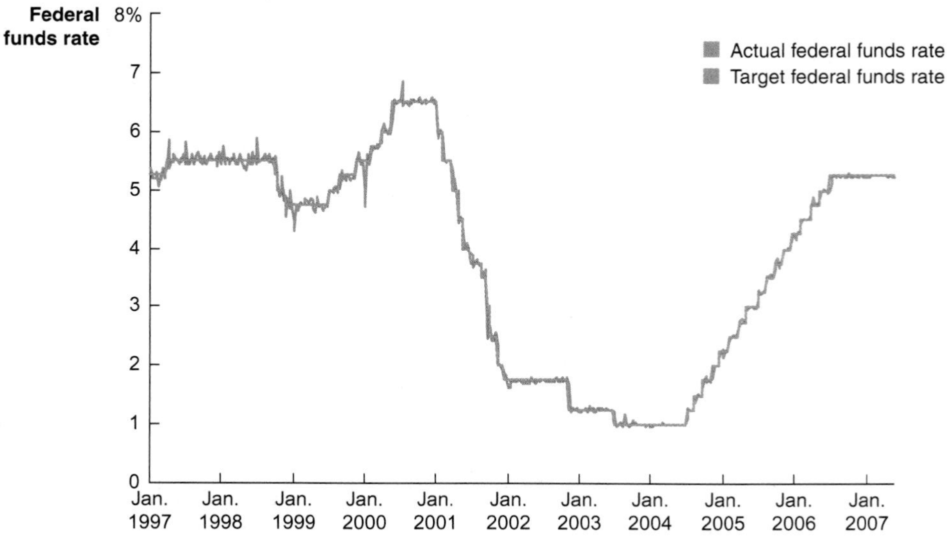

14.3 LEARNING OBJECTIVE

14.3 | Use aggregate demand and aggregate supply graphs to show the effects of monetary policy on real GDP and the price level.

Monetary Policy and Economic Activity

Remember that the Fed uses the federal funds rate as a monetary policy target because it has good control of the federal funds rate through open market operations and because it believes that changes in the federal funds rate will ultimately affect economic variables that are related to its monetary policy goals. Here it is important to consider again the distinction between the nominal interest rate and the real interest rate. Recall that we calculate the real interest rate by subtracting the inflation rate from the nominal interest rate. Ultimately, the ability of the Fed to use monetary policy to affect economic variables such as real GDP depends on its ability to affect real interest rates, such as the real interest rates on mortgages and corporate bonds. Because the federal funds rate is a short-term nominal interest rate, the Fed sometimes has difficulty affecting long-term real interest rates. Nevertheless, for purposes of the following discussion, we will assume that the Fed is able to use open market operations to affect long-term real interest rates.

How Interest Rates Affect Aggregate Demand

Changes in interest rates affect *aggregate demand*, which is the total level of spending in the economy. Recall from Chapter 12 that aggregate demand has four components: consumption, investment, government purchases, and net exports. Changes in interest rates will not affect government purchases, but they will affect the other three components of aggregate demand in the following ways:

- ***Consumption.*** Many households finance purchases of consumer durables, such as automobiles and furniture, by borrowing. Lower interest rates lead to increased spending on durables because they lower the total cost of these goods to consumers by lowering the interest payments on loans. Higher interest rates raise the cost of consumer durables, and households will buy fewer of them. Lower interest rates also reduce the return to saving, leading households to save less and spend more. Higher interest rates increase the return to saving, leading households to save more and spend less.

- ***Investment.*** Firms finance most of their spending on machinery, equipment, and factories out of their profits or by borrowing. Firms borrow either from the financial markets by issuing corporate bonds or from banks. Higher interest rates on corporate bonds or on bank loans make it more expensive for firms to borrow, so they will undertake fewer investment projects. Lower interest rates make it less expensive for firms to borrow, so they will undertake more investment projects. Lower interest rates can also increase investment through their impact on stock prices. As interest rates decline, stocks become a more attractive investment relative to bonds. The increase in demand for stocks raises their price. An increase in stock prices sends a signal to firms that the future profitability of investment projects has increased. By issuing additional shares of stocks, firms can acquire the funds they need to buy new factories and equipment, thereby increasing investment.

  Finally, spending by households on new homes is also part of investment. When interest rates on mortgage loans rise, the cost of buying new homes rises, and fewer new homes will be purchased. When interest rates on mortgage loans fall, more new homes will be purchased.

- ***Net exports.*** Recall that net exports are equal to spending by foreign households and firms on goods and services produced in the United States minus spending by U.S. households and firms on goods and services produced in other countries. The value of net exports depends partly on the exchange rate between the dollar and foreign currencies. When the value of the dollar rises, households and firms in other countries will pay more for goods and services produced in the United States, but U.S. households and firms will pay less for goods and services produced in other countries. As a result, the United States will export less and import more, so net exports fall. When the value of the dollar falls, net exports will rise. If interest rates in the United States rise relative to interest rates in other countries, investing in U.S. financial assets will become more desirable, causing foreign investors to increase their demand for dollars, which will increase the value of the dollar. As the value of the dollar increases, net exports will fall. If interest rates in the United States decline relative to interest rates in other countries, the value of the dollar will fall, and net exports will rise.

New home sales dropped 40 percent between July 2005 and March 2007.

Making the Connection

The Inflation and Deflation of the Housing Market "Bubble"

We have seen that low interest rates helped boost demand for housing during the 2001 recession and for several years thereafter. By 2005, however, many economists argued that a "bubble" had formed in the housing market. As we discussed in Chapter 5, the price of any asset reflects the returns the owner of the asset expects to receive. For example, the price of a share of stock reflects the profitability of the firm issuing the stock because the owner of a share of stock has a claim on the firm's profits and its assets. Many economists believe, however, that sometimes a stock market bubble can form when the prices of stocks rise above levels that can be justified by the profitability of the firms issuing the stock. Bubbles end when enough investors decide stocks are overvalued and begin to sell. Why would an investor be willing to pay more for a share of stock than would be justified by its underlying value? There are two main explanations: The investor may be caught up in the enthusiasm of the moment and, by failing to gather sufficient information, may overestimate the true value of the stock; or the investor may expect to profit from buying stock at inflated prices if the investor can sell the stock at an even higher price before the bubble bursts.

The price of a house should reflect the value of the housing services the house provides. We can use the rents charged for comparable houses in the area to measure the value of housing services. By 2005, some economists argued that in some cities, the prices of houses had risen so much that monthly mortgage payments were far above the monthly rent on comparable houses. In addition, in some cities, there was an increase in the number of buyers who did not intend to live in the houses they purchased but were using them as investments. Like stock investors during a stock market bubble, these housing investors were expecting to make a profit by selling houses at a higher price than they had paid for them, and they were not concerned about whether the prices of the houses were above the value of the housing services provided. Changes in the mortgage market also fueled the housing bubble. In particular, "subprime" mortgages and "exotic" mortgages became more widespread. A subprime mortgage is a mortgage granted to a borrower whose credit history is not very good, perhaps because of late bill payments. In 2007, about 15 percent of existing mortgages were subprime. An exotic mortgage might allow a borrower to make loan payments at a very low interest rate—or perhaps a zero interest rate—for several years, before having to make payments at a much higher rate for the remaining life of the mortgage. Many borrowers who took out these mortgages probably would not have otherwise been able to afford a home or would have purchased a much lower-priced home. But these new mortgages increased the risk that in the future, the borrowers would not be able to make payments on their loans, thereby defaulting on them.

During 2006 and 2007, it was clear that the air was rapidly escaping from the housing bubble. The following figure shows new home sales for each month from January 2000 through April 2007. New home sales rose by 60 percent between January 2000 and July 2005 and then fell by 40 percent between July 2005 and March 2007. Sales of existing homes followed a similar pattern. Although some housing markets, such as Manhattan and Houston, remained strong, prices of new and existing homes in most markets began to decline, and the inventory of unsold homes offered for sale soared. Some home buyers with subprime mortgages began having trouble making their loan payments. Between mid-2005 and mid-2007, the percentage of delinquent subprime loans doubled. When lenders foreclosed on some of these loans, the homes were offered for sale by the lenders, causing housing prices to decline further. In addition, some mortgage lenders that had concentrated on making subprime loans suffered heavy losses and went out of business, and most banks and other lenders tightened the requirements for borrowers. These factors made it more difficult for potential home-buyers to obtain mortgages, further depressing the market.

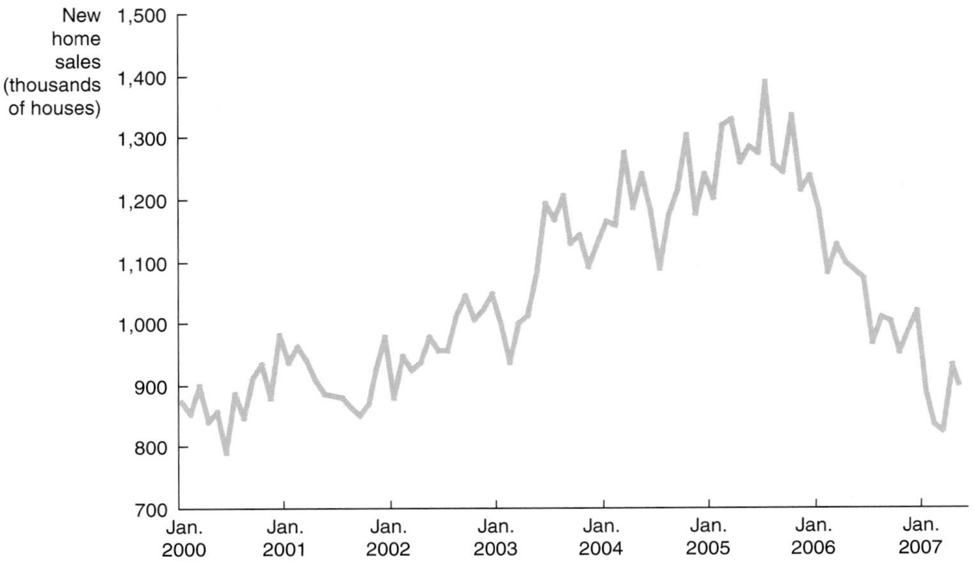

Note: The data are in thousands and are seasonally adjusted at an annual rate.

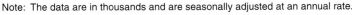

Source: U.S. Bureau of the Census.

The decline in the housing market affected other markets as well. With home prices falling, consumption spending on furniture, appliances, and home improvements declined as many households found it more difficult to borrow against the value of their homes. According to one estimate, more than 300,000 jobs related to housing were lost between March 2006 and May 2007. All told, the decline in the housing market may have reduced the growth rate of real GDP by 1 percentage point.

The deflation of the housing bubble left the Fed in a dilemma. Reducing the target for the federal funds rate might bring down mortgage interest rates and help increase spending on new homes, thereby stimulating aggregate demand and reducing the likelihood of a recession. But, with the inflation rate running higher than the Fed would like, lower interest rates might also undermine progress toward price stability. Through mid-2007, the Fed was proceeding cautiously, leaving the target for the federal funds rate unchanged, at 5.25 percent, for nearly a year.

Source: James R. Hagerty, Jonathan Karp, and Mark Whitehouse, "Economists See Housing Slump Enduring Longer," *Wall Street Journal*, June 9, 2007, p. A1.

YOUR TURN: Test your understanding by doing related problems 3.17, 3.18, and 3.19 on page 504 at the end of this chapter.

The Effects of Monetary Policy on Real GDP and the Price Level: An Initial Look

In Chapter 12, we developed the *aggregate demand and aggregate supply model* to explain fluctuations in real GDP and the price level. In the basic version of the model, we assume that there is no economic growth, so the long-run aggregate supply curve does not shift. In panel (a) of Figure 14-7, we assume that the economy is in short-run equilibrium at point *A*, where the aggregate demand curve (AD_1) intersects the short-run aggregate supply curve (*SRAS*). Real GDP is below potential real GDP, as shown by the *LRAS* curve, so the economy is in recession, with some firms operating below normal capacity and some workers having been laid off. To reach its goal of high employment, the Fed needs to carry out an **expansionary monetary policy** by increasing the money supply and decreasing interest rates. Lower interest rates cause an increase in consumption, investment, and net exports, which shifts the aggregate demand curve to the right, from AD_1 to AD_2. Real GDP increases from $12.2 trillion to potential GDP of $12.4 trillion, and the price level rises from 98 to 100 (point *B*). The policy successfully returns real GDP to its potential level. Rising production leads to increasing employment, allowing the Fed to achieve its goal of high employment.

Expansionary monetary policy The Federal Reserve's increasing the money supply and decreasing interest rates to increase real GDP.

In panel (b) of Figure 14-7, the economy is in short-run equilibrium at point *A*, with real GDP of $12.4 trillion, which is above potential real GDP of $12.2 trillion. With some firms producing beyond their normal capacity and the unemployment rate very low, wages and prices are increasing. To reach its goal of price stability, the Fed needs to carry out a **contractionary monetary policy** by decreasing the money supply and increasing rates. Higher interest rates cause a decrease in consumption, investment, and net exports, which shifts the aggregate demand curve from AD_1 to

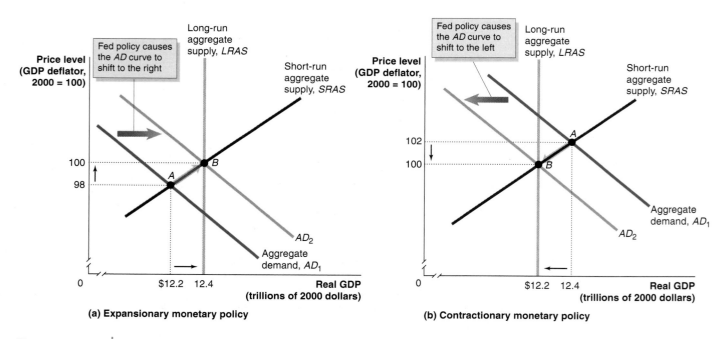

Contractionary monetary policy The Federal Reserve's adjusting the money supply to increase interest rates to reduce inflation.

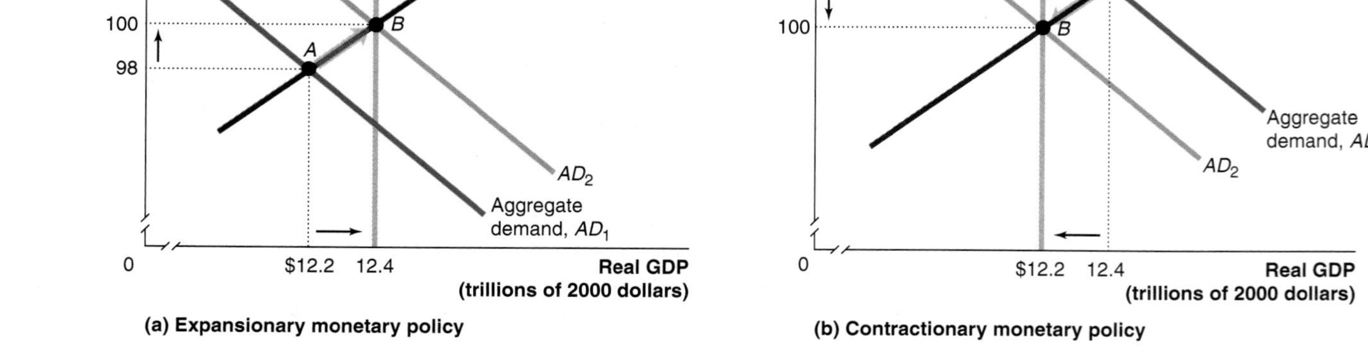

Figure 14-7 | Monetary Policy

In panel (a), the economy begins in recession at point *A*, with real GDP of $12.0 trillion and a price level of 100. An expansionary monetary policy causes aggregate demand to shift to the right, from AD_1 to AD_2, increasing real GDP from $12.0 trillion to $12.2 trillion and the price level from 98 to 100 (point *B*). With real GDP back at its potential level, the Fed can meet its goal of high employment. In panel (b), the economy begins at point *A*, with real GDP at $12.4 trillion and the price level at 102. Because real GDP is greater than potential GDP, the economy experiences rising wages and prices. A contractionary monetary policy causes aggregate demand to shift to the left, from AD_1 to AD_2, decreasing real GDP from $12.4 trillion to $12.2 trillion and the price level from 102 to 100 (point *B*). With real GDP back at its potential level, the Fed can meet its goal of price stability.

AD_2. Real GDP decreases from \$12.4 trillion to \$12.0 trillion, and the price level falls from 102 to 100 (point *B*). Why would the Fed want to intentionally cause real GDP to decline? Because in the long run, real GDP cannot continue to remain above potential GDP. Attempting to keep real GDP above potential GDP would result in rising inflation. As aggregate demand declines and real GDP returns to its potential level, upward pressure on wages and prices will be reduced, allowing the Fed to achieve its goal of price stability.

We can conclude that the Fed can use monetary policy to affect the price level and, in the short run, the level of real GDP, allowing it to attain its two most important policy goals: high employment and price stability.

The Effects of Monetary Policy on Real GDP and the Price Level: A More Complete Account

The overview of monetary policy we just finished contains a key idea: The Fed can use monetary policy to affect aggregate demand, thereby changing the price level and the level of real GDP. The account is simplified, however, because it ignores two important facts about the economy: (1) The economy experiences continuing inflation, with the price level rising every year, and (2) the economy experiences long-run growth, with the *LRAS* curve shifting to the right every year. In Chapter 12, we developed a *dynamic aggregate demand and aggregate supply model* that took these two facts into account. In this section, we use the dynamic model to gain a more complete understanding of monetary policy. Let's briefly review the dynamic model: Recall from Chapter 12 that over time, the U.S. labor force and U.S. capital stock will increase. Technological change will also occur. The result will be an increase in potential real GDP, which we show by the long-run aggregate supply curve shifting to the right. These factors will also result in firms supplying more goods and services at any given price level in the short run, which we show by the short-run aggregate supply curve shifting to the right. During most years, the aggregate demand curve will also shift to the right, indicating that aggregate expenditure will be higher at every price level. There are several reasons aggregate expenditure usually increases: As population grows and incomes rise, consumption will increase over time. Also, as the economy grows, firms expand capacity, and new firms are established, increasing investment spending. Finally, an expanding population and an expanding economy require increased government services, such as more police officers and teachers, so government purchases will expand.

During certain periods, however, *AD* does not increase enough during the year to keep the economy at potential GDP. This slow growth in aggregate demand may be due to households and firms becoming pessimistic about the future state of the economy, leading them to cut back their spending on consumer durables, houses, and factories. Other possibilities exist, as well: The federal government might decide to balance the budget by cutting back its purchases, or recessions in other countries might cause a decline in U.S. exports. In Figure 14-8, in the first year, the economy is in equilibrium, at potential real GDP of \$12.0 trillion and a price level of 100 (point *A*). In the second year, *LRAS* increases to \$12.4 trillion, but *AD* increases only to $AD_{2(\text{without policy})}$, which is not enough to keep the economy in macroeconomic equilibrium at potential GDP. If the Fed does not intervene, the short-run equilibrium will occur at \$12.3 trillion (point *B*). The \$100 billion gap between this level of real GDP and potential real GDP at $LRAS_2$ means that some firms are operating at less than their normal capacity. Incomes and profits will fall, firms will begin to lay off workers, and the unemployment rate will rise.

The economists at the Federal Reserve closely monitor the economy and continually update forecasts of future levels of real GDP and prices. When these economists anticipate that aggregate demand is not growing fast enough to allow the economy to remain at full employment, they present their findings to the FOMC, which decides whether circumstances require a change in monetary policy. For example, suppose that the FOMC meets and considers a forecast from the staff indicating that during the following year a

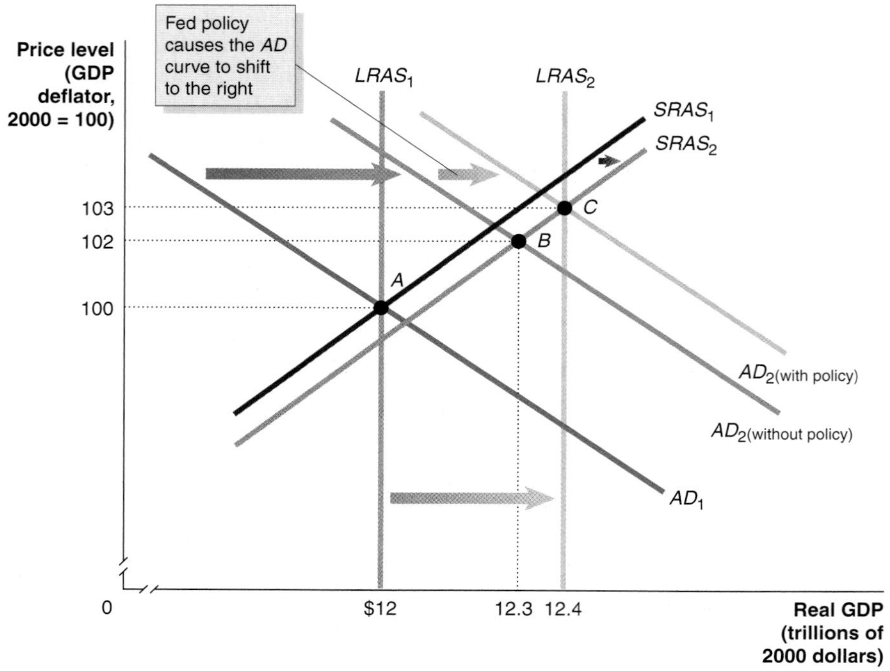

Figure 14-8 | An Expansionary Monetary Policy

The economy begins in equilibrium at point *A*, with real GDP of $12.0 trillion and a price level of 100. Without monetary policy, aggregate demand will shift from AD_1 to $AD_{2(\text{without policy})}$, which is not enough to keep the economy at full employment because long-run aggregate supply has shifted from $LRAS_1$ to $LRAS_2$. The economy will be in short-run equilibrium at point *B*, with real GDP of $12.3 trillion and a price level of 102. By lowering interest rates, the Fed increases investment, consumption, and net exports sufficiently to shift aggregate demand to $AD_{2(\text{with policy})}$. The economy will be in equilibrium at point *C*, with real GDP of $12.4 trillion, which is its full employment level, and a price level of 103. The price level is higher than it would have been if the Fed had not acted to increase spending in the economy.

gap of $100 billion will open between equilibrium real GDP and potential real GDP. In other words, the situation shown in Figure 14-8 will occur. The FOMC may then decide to carry out an expansionary monetary policy to lower interest rates to stimulate aggregate demand. The figure shows the results of a successful attempt to do this: *AD* has shifted to the right, and equilibrium occurs at potential GDP (point *C*). The Fed will have successfully headed off the falling incomes and rising unemployment that otherwise would have occurred.

Notice that in Figure 14-8, the expansionary monetary policy caused the inflation rate to be higher than it would have been. Without the expansionary policy, the price level would have risen from 100 to 102, so the inflation rate for the year would have been 2 percent. By shifting the aggregate demand curve, the expansionary policy caused the price level to increase from 102 to 103, raising the inflation rate from 2 percent to 3 percent.

Making the Connection | The Fed Responds to the Terrorist Attacks of September 11, 2001

When the Fed was founded, its main purpose was to make discount loans to banks suffering from deposit withdrawals. Today, discount loans have become relatively less important in the operations of the Fed. For example, the average weekly amount of discount loans outstanding in 2001 through September 11 was only $34 million. This volume of discount loans is very small compared with total bank reserves of more than $66 *billion*.

Still, discount loans remain an effective way for the Fed to make funds quickly available to banks in an emergency. The banks can use these funds to provide cash or loans to households and firms. The day after the terrorist attacks of September 11, 2001, the Fed made massive discount loans to banks. Discount loans rose from $99 million on September 5 to $45.5 *billion* on September 12, or to 500 times their normal level. In the end, households and firms did not withdraw excessive amounts from their bank accounts following the attacks, and the volume of discount loans returned to normal levels very quickly. By September 19, discount loans had fallen to $2.6 billion, and by September 26, they had fallen to only $20 million. The Fed had also relied on discount loans to cushion the banking and financial systems from potential instability during the stock market crash of 1987, the Y2K difficulties of late 1999, and the subprime mortgage crisis of 2007.

Although the modern Fed concentrates on its objectives for inflation and economic growth, which it implements through open market operations, it still retains its original purpose of dealing with potential financial panics. For this purpose, discount loans are an effective tool.

The day after the terrorist attacks of September 11, 2001, the Fed made massive discount loans to banks and succeeded in preventing a financial panic. Alan Greenspan, pictured here, was the chairman of the Fed at the time of the attacks.

Source: Federal Reserve Board of Governors, *Statistical Release H.4.1*, various weekly issues.

YOUR TURN: Test your understanding by doing related problem 3.21 on page 504 at the end of this chapter.

Can the Fed Eliminate Recessions?

Figure 14-8 shows an expansionary monetary policy that performs so well that no recession actually takes place. The Fed manages to shift the *AD* curve to keep the economy continually at potential GDP. In fact, however, this ideal is very difficult for the Fed to achieve. Keeping recessions shorter and milder than they would otherwise be is usually the best the Fed can do. The recession of 2001 shows the Fed performing about as well as it can in the real world. Let's review the events leading up to the 2001 recession and the actions the Fed took in response.

In spring 2000, stock prices began to decline. Hardest hit were the dot-coms because online retailing failed to grow as rapidly as many Wall Street analysts had predicted. As we saw in Chapter 12, when stock prices fall, the wealth of households declines, and, as a result, consumption falls. At the same time, many firms began to cut their expenditure on information technology.

On December 19, 2000, at the last FOMC meeting of the year, the committee left the target for the federal funds rate unchanged, although committee members believed the risk of recession had increased. Within a few days, increasing evidence indicated that the growth of aggregate demand was slowing, and the committee held a telephone conference meeting on January 3, 2001, four weeks before its regularly scheduled meeting. During the telephone conference, the committee decided to reduce the target for the federal funds rate from 6.5 percent to 6 percent. The committee continued to reduce the federal funds target at subsequent meetings. By December 2001, it had reduced the rate to 1.75 percent. Further decreases brought the federal funds rate to 1 percent in June 2003, the lowest it had been in more than 40 years.

Falling interest rates were not enough to head off a recession, which began in March 2001. The recession was milder than many economists had expected, despite the impact of the September 11, 2001, terrorist attacks. Real GDP declined only during two quarters in 2001, and GDP was actually higher for 2001 as a whole than it had been during 2000. We saw in Chapter 12 that the recovery from the recession was weaker than had been expected. The unemployment rate rose from 4.3 percent at the beginning of the recession to 5.6 percent at the end of the recession and to a peak of 6.3 percent in June 2003. Even at its peak, though, this was a relatively low unemployment rate compared to the more severe recessions of the post–World War II period, such as the 1981–1982 recession, when the unemployment rate was above 10 percent. Household purchases of consumer durables and new homes remained strong during 2001, keeping real GDP from falling too far below its potential level. Many homebuilders, like Toll Brothers, enjoyed a surprisingly good year in 2001. Although home building is usually hit hard during recessions, new home construction increased by more than 2 percent, from less than 1.57 million units in 2000 to more than 1.60 million units in 2001.

Although the Fed was able to use expansionary monetary policy successfully to reduce the severity of the 2001 recession, it was unable to entirely eliminate it. In fact, the Fed has no realistic hope of "fine-tuning" the economy to eliminate the business cycle and achieve absolute price stability.

Using Monetary Policy to Fight Inflation

In addition to using monetary policy to reduce the severity of recessions, the Fed can also use a contractionary monetary policy to keep aggregate demand from expanding so rapidly that the inflation rate begins to increase. Figure 14-9 shows the situation during 1999 and 2000, when the Fed faced this possibility. During 1999, the economy was at equilibrium beyond potential GDP, although the inflation rate for the entire year was only about 1.5 percent. By December, Alan Greenspan and other members of the FOMC were worried that aggregate demand was increasing so rapidly that the inflation rate would begin to accelerate. In fact, during the last three months of 1999, inflation

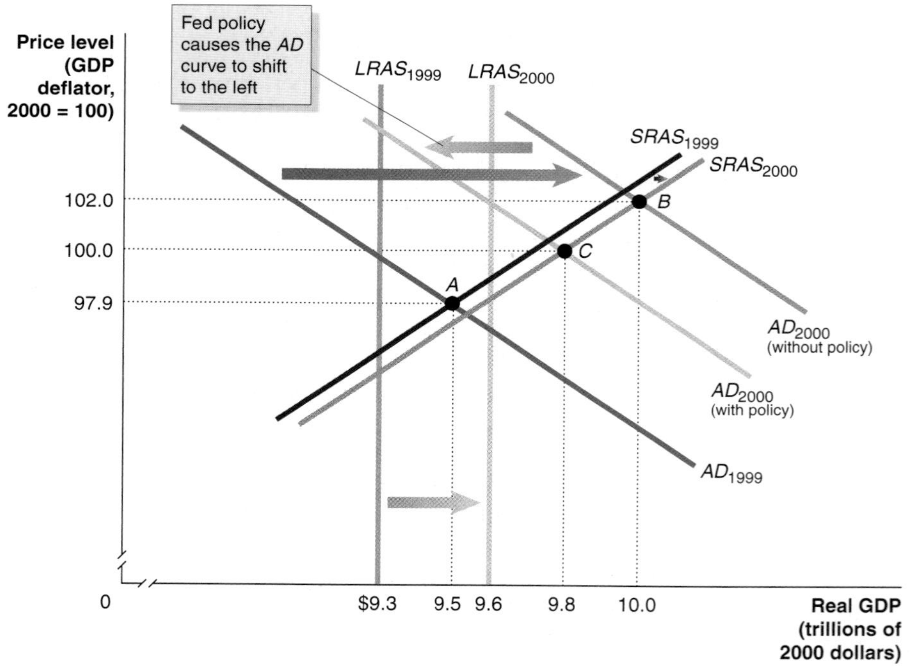

Figure 14-9 | A Contractionary Monetary Policy in 2000

The economy began 1999 in equilibrium at point *A*, with real GDP of $9.5 trillion and a price level of 97.9. From 1999 to 2000, potential real GDP increased from $9.3 trillion to $9.6 trillion, as long-run aggregate supply increased from $LRAS_{1999}$ to $LRAS_{2000}$. The Fed raised interest rates because it believed aggregate demand was increasing too rapidly. Without the increase in interest rates, aggregate demand would have shifted from AD_{1999} to $AD_{2000(\text{without policy})}$, and the new short-run equilibrium would have occurred at point *B*. Real GDP would have been $10.0 trillion—$200 billion higher than it actually was—and the price level would have been 102.0. The increase in interest rates resulted in aggregate demand increasing only to $AD_{2000(\text{with policy})}$. Equilibrium occurred at point *C*, with real GDP of $9.8 trillion and the price level rising only to 100.0.

had increased to an annual rate of about 2.5 percent. The FOMC issues a statement after each meeting that summarizes the committee's views on the current state of the economy and gives some indication of how monetary policy might change in the near future. After its meeting on December 21, 1999, the FOMC included the following remarks in its statement:

> The Committee remains concerned with the possibility that over time increases in demand will continue to exceed the growth in potential supply. . . . Such trends could foster inflationary imbalances that would undermine the economy's exemplary performance. . . . At its next meeting the Committee will assess available information on the likely balance of supply and demand, conditions in financial markets, and the possible need for adjustment in the stance of policy to contain inflationary pressures.

At its next meeting, on February 2, 2000, the committee raised the target for the federal funds rate from 5.5 percent to 5.75 percent. According to the minutes of the meeting:

> The Committee's decision . . . was intended to help bring the growth of aggregate demand into better alignment with the expansion of sustainable aggregate supply in an effort to avert rising inflationary pressures in the economy.

The committee raised the target for the federal funds rate twice more in following meetings, until it reached 6.5 percent in May, where it remained for the rest of 2000. Although it is impossible to know exactly what would have happened during 2000 without the Fed's policy change, Figure 14-9 presents a plausible scenario. The figure shows that without the Fed's actions to increase interest rates, aggregate demand would have shifted farther to the right, and equilibrium would have occurred at a level of real GDP that was even further beyond the potential level. The price level would have risen from 97.9 in 1999 to 102.0 in 2000, meaning that the inflation rate would have been above 4 percent. Because the Fed kept aggregate demand from increasing as much as it otherwise would have, equilibrium occurred closer to potential real GDP, and the price level in 2000 rose to only 100.0, keeping the inflation rate to a little over 2 percent. Notice that in this case, as with its policy actions during the 2001 recession, the Fed was unable to fine-tune the economy: In both 1999 and 2000, real GDP was above its potential level.

Solved Problem | **14-3**

The Effects of Monetary Policy

The hypothetical information in the following table shows what the values for real GDP and the price level will be in 2011 if the Fed does *not* use monetary policy.

YEAR	POTENTIAL REAL GDP	REAL GDP	PRICE LEVEL
2010	$13.3 trillion	$13.3 trillion	140
2011	13.7 trillion	13.6 trillion	142

a. If the Fed wants to keep real GDP at its potential level in 2011, should it use an expansionary policy or a contractionary policy? Should the trading desk buy Treasury bills or sell them?

b. Suppose the Fed's policy is successful in keeping real GDP at its potential level in 2011. State whether each of the following will be higher or lower than if the Fed had taken no action:

   i. Real GDP

   ii. Potential real GDP

   iii. The inflation rate

   iv. The unemployment rate

c. Draw an aggregate demand and aggregate supply graph to illustrate your answer. Be sure that your graph contains *LRAS* curves for 2010 and 2011; *SRAS* curves for 2010 and 2011; *AD* curve for 2010 and 2011, with and without monetary policy action; and equilibrium real GDP and the price level in 2011, with and without policy.

SOLVING THE PROBLEM:

Step 1: Review the chapter material. This problem is about the effects of monetary policy on real GDP and the price level, so you may want to review the section "The Effects of Monetary Policy on Real GDP and the Price Level: A More Complete Account," which begins on page 481.

Step 2: Answer question (a) by explaining how the Fed can keep real GDP at its potential level. The information in the table tells us that without monetary policy, the economy will be below potential real GDP in 2011. To keep real GDP at its potential level, the Fed must undertake an expansionary policy. To implement an expansionary policy, the trading desk needs to buy Treasury bills. Buying Treasury bills will increase reserves in the banking system. Banks will increase their loans, which will increase the money supply and lower the interest rate.

Step 3: Answer question (b) by explaining the effect of the Fed's policy. policy is successful, real GDP in 2011 will increase from the level given in the table of $13.3 trillion to its potential level of $13.7 trillion. Potential real GDP is not affected by monetary policy, so its value will not change. Because the level of real GDP will be higher, the unemployment rate will be lower than it would have been without policy. The expansionary monetary policy shifts the *AD* curve to the right, so short-run equilibrium will move up the short-run aggregate supply curve (*SRAS*), and the price level will be higher.

Step 4: Answer question (c) by drawing the graph. Your graph should look similar to Figure 14-8.

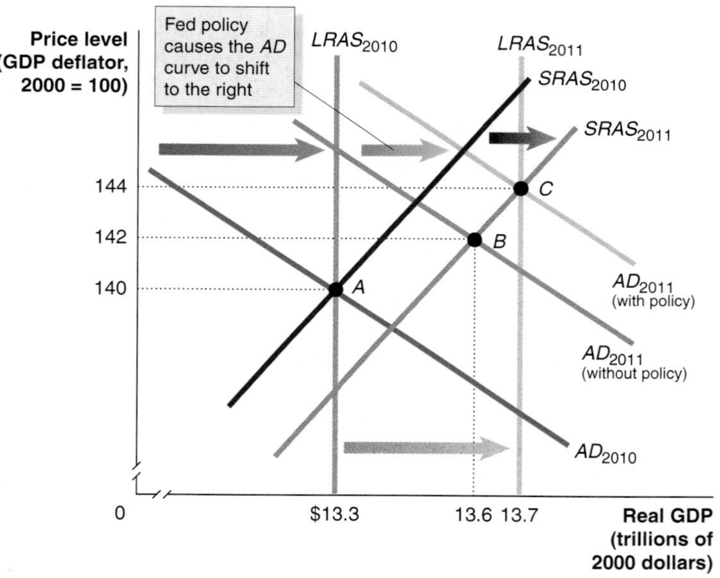

The economy starts in equilibrium in 2010 at point *A*, with the *AD* and *SRAS* curves intersecting along the *LRAS* curve. Real GDP is at its potential level of $13.3 trillion, and the price level is 140. Without monetary policy, the *AD* curve shifts to $AD_{2011(\text{without policy})}$, and the economy is in short-run equilibrium at point *B*. Because potential real GDP has increased from $13.3 trillion to $13.7 trillion, short-run equilibrium real GDP of $13.6 trillion is below the potential level. The price level has increased from 140 to 142. With policy, the *AD* curve shifts to $AD_{2011(\text{with policy})}$, and the economy is in equilibrium at point *C*. Real GDP is at its potential level of $13.7 trillion. We don't have enough information to be sure of the new equilibrium price level.

We do know that it will be higher than 142. The graph shows the price level rising to 144. Therefore, without policy, the inflation rate in 2011 would have been about 1.4 percent. With policy, it will be about 2.9 percent.

EXTRA CREDIT: It's important to bear in mind that in reality, the Fed is unable to use monetary policy to keep real GDP exactly at its potential level, as this problem suggests. In a later section, we will discuss some of the difficulties the Fed encounters in conducting monetary policy.

YOUR TURN: For more practice, do problem 3.12 and 3.13 on page 503 at the end of this chapter.

>> End Solved Problem 14-3

A Summary of How Monetary Policy Works

Table 14-1 compares the steps involved in expansionary and contractionary monetary policies. We need to add a very important qualification to this summary. At every point, we should add the phrase "relative to what would have happened without the policy." Table 14-1 is isolating the impact of monetary policy, *holding constant all other factors affecting the variables involved.* In other words, we are invoking the *ceteris paribus condition,* discussed in Chapter 3. This point is important because, for example, a contractionary monetary policy does not cause the price level to fall. As Figure 14-9 on page 484 shows, a contractionary monetary policy causes the price level *to rise by less than it would have without the policy.* One final note on terminology: An expansionary monetary policy is sometimes referred to as a *loose* or an *easy* policy. A contractionary monetary policy is sometimes referred to as a *tight* policy.

TABLE 14-1 | Expansionary and Contractionary Monetary Policies

FOMC orders an expansionary policy	→	The money supply increases and interest rates fall	→	Investment, consumption, and net exports all increase	→	The *AD* curve shifts to the right	→	Real GDP and the price level rise

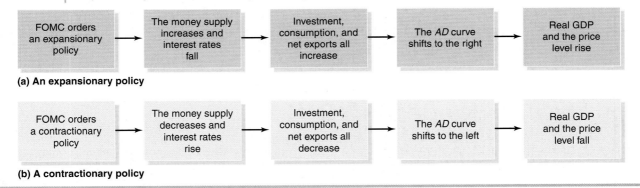

(a) An expansionary policy

FOMC orders a contractionary policy	→	The money supply decreases and interest rates rise	→	Investment, consumption, and net exports all decrease	→	The *AD* curve shifts to the left	→	Real GDP and the price level fall

(b) A contractionary policy

Making the Connection

Why Does Wall Street Care about Monetary Policy?

You have probably seen newspaper headlines similar to these:

"Fed Rate Cut Fuels Stock Gains"
"Stocks Fall in Anticipation of Fed Rate Increase"
"Worries of Fed Rate Increase Send Stocks Lower"

Before most meetings of the FOMC, newspapers report stock traders' predictions of possible Fed actions and whether those actions will cause stock prices to increase or decrease. Some Wall Street analysts are known as *Fed watchers* because they study the Fed and attempt to forecast future changes in the target for the federal funds rate. Why

The stock market reacts when the Fed either raises or lowers interest rates.

do changes in the federal funds rate affect the stock market? There are two main explanations. In thinking about both explanations, remember that changes in the federal funds rate usually cause changes in other interest rates.

The first reason that stock prices react to the Fed raising or lowering interest rates is because changes in interest rates affect the economy. As we have seen, lower interest rates usually result in increases in real GDP. Fundamentally, the value of a share of stock depends on the profitability of the firm that issued the stock. When real GDP is increasing, the profitability of many firms is also increasing. Stock prices tend to rise when investors expect that the Fed will be lowering interest rates to stimulate the economy. When investors expect that the Fed will be raising interest rates to slow down an economy at risk of rising inflation, stock prices tend to fall.

The second reason that stock prices react to changes in interest rates is that changes in interest rates make it more or less attractive for people to invest in stock rather than in other financial assets. Investors look for the highest return possible on their investments, holding constant the risk level of the investments. If the interest rates on Treasury bills, bank certificates of deposit, and corporate bonds are all low, an investment in stocks will be more attractive. When interest rates are high, an investment in stocks will be less attractive.

YOUR TURN: Test your understanding by doing related problem 3.22 on page 504 at the end of this chapter.

Can the Fed Get the Timing Right?

The Fed's ability to quickly recognize the need for a change in monetary policy is a key to its success. If the Fed is late in recognizing that a recession has begun or that the inflation rate is increasing, it may not be able to implement a new policy soon enough to do much good. In fact, if the Fed implements a policy too late, it may actually destabilize the economy. To see how this can happen, consider Figure 14-10. The straight line represents the long-run growth trend in real GDP in the United States. On average, real GDP grows about 3.5 percent per year. The actual path of real GDP differs from the underly-

Don't Let This Happen to **YOU!**

Remember That with Monetary Policy, It's the Interest Rates—Not the Money—That Counts

It is tempting to think of monetary policy working like this: If the Fed wants more spending in the economy, it increases the money supply, and people spend more because they now have more money. If the Fed wants less spending in the economy, it decreases the money supply, and people spend less because they now have less money. In fact, that is *not* how monetary policy works. Remember the important difference between money and income: The Fed increases the money supply by buying Treasury bills. The sellers of the Treasury bills have just exchanged one asset—Treasury bills—for another asset—a check from the Fed; the sellers have *not* increased their income. Even though the money supply is now larger, no one's income has increased, so no one's spending should be affected.

It is only when this increase in the money supply results in lower interest rates that spending is affected. When interest rates are lower, households are more likely to buy new homes and automobiles, and businesses are more likely to buy new factories and computers. Lower interest rates also lead to a lower value of the dollar, which lowers the prices of exports and raises the prices of imports, thereby increasing net exports. It isn't the increase in the money supply that has brought about this additional spending; *it's the lower interest rates.* To understand how monetary policy works, and to interpret news reports about the Fed's actions, remember that it is the change in interest rates, not the change in the money supply, that is most important.

YOUR TURN: Test your understanding by doing related problem 3.14 on page 503 at the end of this chapter.

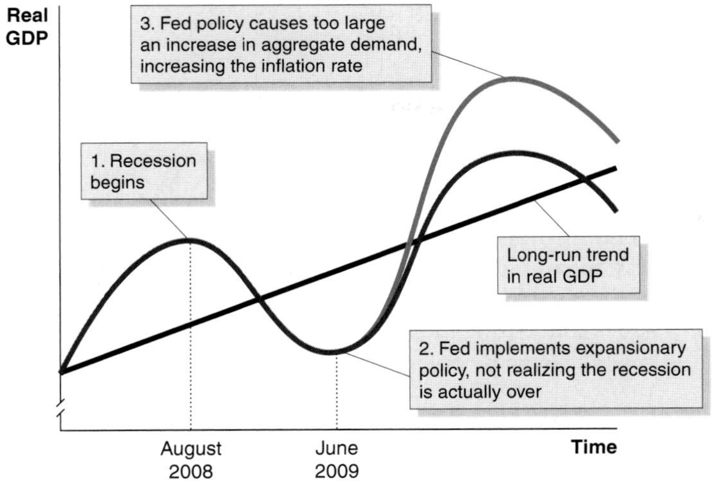

Figure 14-10 | The Effect of a Poorly Timed Monetary Policy on the Economy

The upward-sloping straight line represents the long-run growth trend in real GDP. The red curving line represents the path real GDP takes because of the business cycle. If the Fed implements a change in monetary policy too late, real GDP will follow the blue curving line. The Fed's expansionary monetary policy results in too great an increase in aggregate demand during the next expansion, which causes an increase in the inflation rate.

ing trend because of the business cycle, which is shown by the red curving line. As we saw in Chapter 9, the actual business cycle is more irregular than the stylized cycle shown here.

Suppose that a recession begins in August 2008. Because it takes months for economic statistics to be gathered by the Commerce Department, the Census Bureau, the Bureau of Labor Statistics, and the Fed itself, there is often a *lag*, or delay, before the Fed recognizes that a recession has begun. Then it takes time for the Fed's economists to analyze the data. Finally, in June 2009, the FOMC concludes that the economy is in recession and begins an expansionary monetary policy. As it turns out, June 2009 is actually the trough of the recession, meaning that the recession has already ended, and an expansion has begun. In these circumstances, the Fed's expansionary policy is not needed to end the recession. The increase in aggregate demand caused by the Fed's lowering interest rates is likely to push the economy beyond potential real GDP and cause a significant acceleration in inflation. Real GDP ends up following the path indicated by the curving blue line. The Fed has inadvertently engaged in a *procyclical policy*, which increases the severity of the business cycle, as opposed to a *countercyclical policy*, which is meant to reduce the severity of the business cycle, and which is what the Fed intends to use.

It is not unusual for employment or manufacturing production to decline for a month or two in the middle of an expansion. Distinguishing these minor ups and downs from the beginning of a recession is difficult. The National Bureau of Economic Research (NBER) announces dates for the beginning and ending of recessions that are generally accepted by most economists. An indication of how difficult it is to determine when recessions begin and end is that the NBER generally makes its announcements only after a considerable delay. The NBER did not announce that a recession had begun in March 2001 until November 2001, which is the same month it later determined the recession had ended. It did not announce that a recession had begun in July 1990 until April 1991, which was one month *after* it later determined the recession had ended. Failing to react until well after a recession has begun (or ended) can be a serious problem for the Fed.

14.4 LEARNING OBJECTIVE

14.4 | Discuss the Fed's setting of monetary policy targets.

A Closer Look at the Fed's Setting of Monetary Policy Targets

We have seen that in carrying out monetary policy, the Fed changes its target for the federal funds rate depending on the state of the economy. Is using the federal funds rate as a target the best way to conduct monetary policy? If the Fed targets the federal funds rate, how should it decide what the target level should be? In this section, we consider some important issues concerning the Fed's targeting policy.

Should the Fed Target the Money Supply?

Some economists have argued that rather than use an interest rate as its monetary policy target, the Fed should use the money supply. Many of the economists who make this argument belong to a school of thought known as *monetarism*. The leader of the monetarist school was Nobel laureate Milton Friedman, who was critical of the Fed's ability to correctly time changes in monetary policy.

Friedman and his followers favored replacing *monetary policy* with a *monetary growth rule*. Ordinarily, we expect monetary policy to respond to changing economic conditions: When the economy is in recession, the Fed reduces interest rates, and when inflation is increasing, the Fed raises interest rates. A monetary growth rule, in contrast, is a plan for increasing the money supply at a constant rate that does not change in response to economic conditions. Friedman and his followers proposed a monetary growth rule of increasing the money supply every year at a rate equal to the long-run growth rate of real GDP, which is 3.5 percent. If the Fed adopted this monetary growth rule, it would stick to it through changing economic conditions.

But what happens under a monetary growth rule if the economy moves into recession? Shouldn't the Fed abandon the rule to drive down interest rates? Friedman argued that the Fed should stick to the rule even during recessions because, he believed, active monetary policy destabilizes the economy, increasing the number of recessions and their severity. By keeping the money supply growing at a constant rate, Friedman argued, the Fed would greatly increase economic stability.

Although during the 1970s some economists and politicians pressured the Federal Reserve to adopt a monetary growth rule, most of that pressure has disappeared in recent years. A key reason is that the fairly close relationship between movements in the money supply and movements in real GDP and the price level that existed before 1980 has become much weaker. Since 1980, the growth rate of M1 has been unstable. In some years, it has grown more than 10 percent, while in other years, it has actually fallen. Yet despite these wide fluctuations in the growth of M1, growth in real GDP has been fairly stable, and inflation has remained low.

Why Doesn't the Fed Target Both the Money Supply and the Interest Rate?

Most economists believe that an interest rate is the best monetary policy target, but, as we have just seen, other economists believe the Fed should target the money supply. Why doesn't the Fed satisfy both groups by targeting both the money supply and an interest rate? The simple answer to this question is that the Fed can't target both at the same time. To see why, look at Figure 14-11, which shows the money market.

Remember that the Fed controls the money supply, but it does not control money demand. Money demand is determined by decisions of households and firms as they weigh the trade-off between the convenience of money and its low interest rate compared with other financial assets. Suppose the Fed is targeting the interest rate and

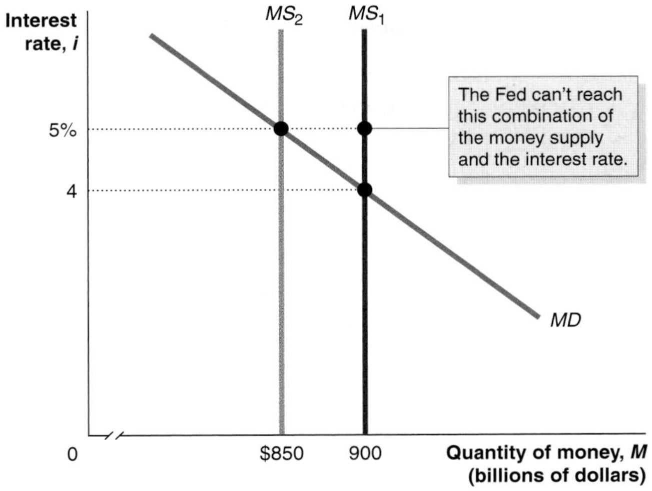

Figure 14-11 | The Fed Can't Target Both the Money Supply and the Interest Rate

The Fed is forced to choose between using either an interest rate or the money supply as its monetary policy target. In this figure, the Fed can set a target of a money supply of $900 billion or a target of an interest rate of 5 percent, but it can't have both because only combinations of the interest rate and the money supply that represent equilibrium in the money market are possible.

decides, given conditions in the economy, that the interest rate should be 5 percent. Or, suppose the Fed is targeting the money supply and decides that the money supply should be $900 billion. Figure 14-11 shows that the Fed can bring about an interest rate of 5 percent, or a money supply of $900 billion, but it can't bring about both. The point representing an interest rate of 5 percent and a money supply of $900 billion is not on the money demand curve, so it can't represent an equilibrium in the money market. Only combinations of the interest rate and the money supply that represent equilibrium in the money market are possible.

The Fed has to choose between targeting an interest rate and targeting the money supply. For most of the period since World War II, the Fed has chosen an interest rate target.

The Taylor Rule

How does the Fed choose a target for the federal funds rate? The discussions at the meetings of the FOMC can be complex, and they take into account many economic variables. John Taylor of Stanford University has analyzed the factors involved in Fed decision making and developed the **Taylor rule** to explain federal funds rate targeting. The Taylor rule begins with an estimate of the value of the equilibrium real federal funds rate, which is the federal funds rate—adjusted for inflation—that would be consistent with real GDP being equal to potential real GDP in the long run. According to the Taylor rule, the Fed should set the target for the federal funds rate so that it is equal to the sum of the inflation rate, the equilibrium real federal funds rate, and two additional terms. The first of these additional terms is the *inflation gap*—the difference between current inflation and a target rate; the second is the *output gap*—the percentage difference between real GDP and potential real GDP. The inflation gap and output gap are each given "weights" that reflect their influence on the federal funds target rate. With weights of 1/2 for both gaps, we have the following Taylor rule:

Taylor rule A rule developed by John Taylor that links the Fed's target for the federal funds rate to economic variables.

Federal funds target rate = Current inflation rate +
Real equilibrium federal funds rate + (1/2) × Inflation gap + (1/2) × Output gap.

The Taylor rule includes expressions for the inflation gap and the output gap because the Fed is concerned about both inflation and fluctuations in real GDP. Taylor demonstrated that if the equilibrium real federal funds rate is 2 percent and the target rate of inflation is 2 percent, the preceding expression does a good job of explaining changes in the Fed's target for the federal funds rate. Consider an example in which the current inflation rate is 1 percent, and real GDP is 1 percent below potential real GDP. In that case, the inflation gap is 1 percent − 2 percent = −1 percent, and the output gap is also −1 percent. Inserting these values in the Taylor rule, we can calculate the predicted value for the federal funds target rate:

$$\text{Federal funds target rate} = 1\% + 2\% + ((1/2) \times -1\%) + ((1/2) \times -1\%) = 2\%.$$

The Taylor rule accurately predicted changes in the federal funds target during the period of Alan Greenspan's leadership of the Federal Reserve. For the period of the late 1970s and early 1980s, when Paul Volcker was chairman of the Federal Reserve, the Taylor rule predicts a federal funds rate target *lower* than the actual target used by the Fed. This indicates that Chairman Volcker kept the federal funds rate at an unusually high level to bring down the very high inflation rates plaguing the economy in the late 1970s and early 1980s. In contrast, using data from the chairmanship of Arthur Burns from 1970 to 1978, the Taylor rule predicts a federal funds rate target *higher* than the actual target. This indicates that Chairman Burns kept the federal funds rate at an unusually low level during these years, which can help explain why the inflation rate grew worse.

Although the Taylor rule does not account for changes in the target inflation rate or the equilibrium interest rate, many economists view the rule as a convenient way to analyze the federal funds target.

Should the Fed Target Inflation?

Inflation targeting Conducting monetary policy so as to commit the central bank to achieving a publicly announced level of inflation.

Over the past decade, many economists and central bankers, including the current Fed chairman, Ben Bernanke, have proposed using *inflation targeting* as a framework for carrying out monetary policy. With **inflation targeting**, the central bank commits to conducting policy to achieve a publicly announced inflation target of, for example, 2 percent. Inflation targeting need not impose an inflexible rule on the central bank. The central bank would still be free, for example, to take action in case of a severe recession. Nevertheless, monetary policy goals and operations would focus on inflation and inflation forecasts. Inflation targeting has been adopted by the central banks of New Zealand (1989), Canada (1991), the United Kingdom (1992), Finland (1993), Sweden (1993), and Spain (1994), and by the European Central Bank. Inflation targeting has also been used in some newly industrializing countries, such as Chile, South Korea, Mexico, and South Africa, as well as in some transition economies in Eastern Europe, such as the Czech Republic, Hungary, and Poland. Experience with inflation targeting has varied, but typically, the move to inflation targeting has been accompanied by lower inflation (sometimes at the cost of temporarily higher unemployment).

Should the Fed adopt an inflation target? Arguments in favor of inflation targeting focus on four points. First, as we have already discussed, in the long run, real GDP returns to its potential level, and potential real GDP is not affected by monetary policy. Therefore, in the long run, the Fed can have an impact on inflation but not on real GDP. Having an explicit inflation target would draw the public's attention to this fact. Second, by announcing an inflation target, the Fed would make it easier for households and firms to form accurate expectations of future inflation, improving their planning and the efficiency of the economy. Third, an announced inflation target would help institutionalize good U.S. monetary policy. It would be less likely that abrupt changes in policy would occur as members join and leave the FOMC. Finally, an inflation target would promote accountability for the Fed by providing a yardstick against which its performance could be measured.

Inflation targeting also has opponents, who typically raise three points. First, having a numerical target for inflation reduces the flexibility of monetary policy to address other policy goals. Second, inflation targeting assumes that the Fed can accurately forecast future inflation rates, which is not always the case. Finally, holding the Fed accountable only for an inflation goal may make it less likely that the Fed will achieve other important policy goals.

The Fed's performance in the 1980s, 1990s, and 2000s, even without a formal inflation target, has generally received high marks from economists. The 1990s, for example, saw low inflation and a substantial economic expansion. In recent years, the Fed has acted to head off the threat of future inflation before it can become established. Even without a formal inflation target, the Fed has been successful at building public support for the idea that low inflation is important to the efficient performance of the economy. The Fed's strategy is not without risk, however. The Fed's prestige during the past two decades has been dependent on public trust in the effectiveness of Fed leadership in containing inflation while maintaining economic growth. But the Fed's leadership changes over time, which highlights what may be a need for more formal procedures to reassure both the public and elected officials about the continuity of policy. As Ben Bernanke assumed the chairmanship of the Fed in early 2006, his support for inflation targeting has increased the chances that the Fed would adopt such a policy.

Making the Connection

How Does the Fed Measure Inflation?

In recent years, the Federal Reserve has put increased emphasis on the goal of price stability. The Fed has therefore had to consider carefully the best way to measure the inflation rate. As we saw in Chapter 8, the consumer price index (CPI) is the most widely used measure of inflation. But we also saw that the CPI suffers from biases that cause it to overstate the true underlying rate of inflation. An alternative measure of changes in consumer prices can be constructed from the data gathered to calculate GDP. We saw in Chapter 7 that the GDP deflator is a broad measure of the price level that includes the price of every good or service that is in GDP. Changes in the GDP deflator are not a good measure of inflation experienced by the typical consumer, worker, or firm, however, because the deflator include prices of goods, such as industrial equipment, that are not widely purchased. The *personal consumption expenditures price index* (PCE) is a measure of the price level that is similar to the GDP deflator, except it includes only the prices of goods from the consumption category of GDP.

In 2000, the Fed announced that it would rely more on the PCE than on the CPI in tracking inflation. The Fed noted three advantages that the PCE has over the CPI:

1. The PCE is a so-called chain-type price index, as opposed to the market-basket approach used in constructing the CPI. As we saw in Chapter 8, because consumers shift the mix of products they buy each year, the market-basket approach makes the CPI overstate actual inflation. A chain-type price index allows the mix of products to change each year.
2. The PCE includes the prices of more goods and services than the CPI, so it is a broader measure of inflation.
3. Past values of the PCE can be recalculated as better ways of computing price indexes are developed and as new data become available. This allows the Fed to better track historical trends in the inflation rate.

In 2004, the Fed announced that it would begin to rely on a subcategory of the PCE: the so-called core PCE, which excludes food and energy prices. Prices of food and energy tend to fluctuate up and down for reasons that may not be related to the causes of general inflation and that cannot easily be controlled by monetary policy. Oil prices, in particular, have moved dramatically up and down in recent years. Therefore, a price index that includes food and energy prices may not give a clear view of underlying trends in inflation. The following graph shows movements in the CPI, the PCE, and the core PCE over a 10-year period. Although the three measures of inflation move roughly together, the core PCE has been more stable than the others. If you want to know what the Fed thinks the current inflation rate is, the best idea is to look at data on the core PCE. These data are published monthly by the Bureau of Economic Analysis.

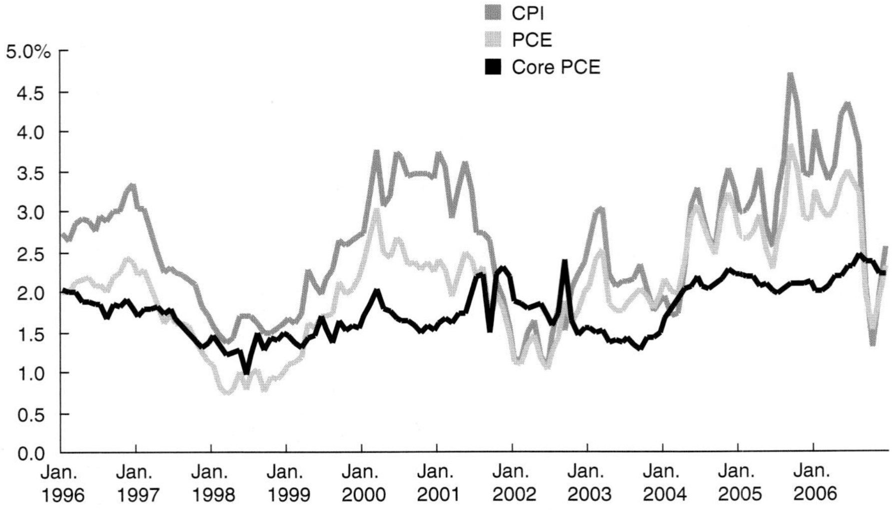

Sources: Bureau of Economic Analysis; and Bureau of Labor Statistics.

YOUR TURN: Test your understanding by doing related problem 4.7 on page 505 at the end of this chapter.

14.5 LEARNING OBJECTIVE

14.5 | Assess the arguments for and against the independence of the Federal Reserve.

Is the Independence of the Federal Reserve a Good Idea?

In our discussion of monetary policy, we have made no mention of Congress or the president. In fact, the Fed conducts monetary policy independently of them. The president nominates and the Senate confirms the seven members of the Fed's Board of Governors, but because members serve 14-year terms, they are insulated from political pressure. The seven members of the Board of Governors, along with five presidents of the Federal Reserve banks, make up the Federal Open Market Committee. The FOMC determines the monetary policy of the United States without the input of Congress or the president.

The Fed's political independence is reinforced by its financial independence. As we have discussed, when the FOMC wants to increase the money supply and decrease interest rates, it buys Treasury securities. To decrease the money supply and increase interest rates, it sells Treasury securities. Because a growing economy requires increases in the money supply, the Fed buys more Treasury securities than it sells.

Currently, the Fed owns more than $750 billion worth of Treasury securities. The interest it receives from these Treasury securities means that, unlike any other agency of the federal government, it does not have to ask Congress for the funds it needs to operate.

The Fed does not, however, have absolute independence. The U.S. Constitution contains no provision for a central bank. The authority of the Fed comes from legislation passed by Congress and signed by the president. Congress and the president are free at any time to pass new legislation to reorganize the Fed or even to abolish it. So, it is unlikely that the Fed would pursue a monetary policy that was strongly opposed by the president and a large majority in Congress. In addition, most Fed chairmen have attempted to remain in regular contact with other members of the government.

Nevertheless, the Fed is able to formulate monetary policy without taking into account the wishes of Congress and the president, unless it chooses to. Since the founding of the Fed in 1914, debate has occurred about whether the independence of the Fed is a good idea.

The Case for Fed Independence

The main reason to keep the Fed—or any country's central bank—independent of the rest of the government is to avoid inflation. Whenever a government is spending more than it is collecting in taxes, it must borrow the difference by selling bonds. The governments of many developing countries have difficulty finding anyone other than their central bank to buy their bonds. The more bonds the central bank buys, the faster the money supply grows, and the higher the inflation rate will be. Even in developed countries, governments that control their central banks may be tempted to sell bonds to the central bank rather than to the public.

Another fear is that if the government controls the central bank, it may use that control to further its political interests. It is difficult in any democratic country for a government to be reelected at a time of high unemployment. If the government controls the central bank, it may be tempted just before an election to increase the money supply and drive down interest rates to increase production and employment. In the United States, for example, a president who had direct control over the Fed might be tempted to increase the money supply just before running for reelection, even if this led in the long run to higher inflation and accompanying economic costs.

We might expect that the more independent a country's central bank is, the lower the inflation rate in the country, and the less independent a country's central bank, the higher the inflation rate. Alberto Alesina and Lawrence Summers, economists at Harvard University, tested this idea by comparing the degree of central bank independence and the inflation rate for 16 high-income countries during the years 1955–1988. Figure 14-12 shows the results.

Countries with highly independent central banks, such as the United States, Switzerland, and Germany, had lower inflation rates than countries whose central banks had little independence, such as New Zealand, Italy, and Spain. In the past few years, New Zealand and Canada have granted their banks more independence, at least partly to better fight inflation.

The Case against Fed Independence

In democracies, elected representatives usually decide important policy matters. In the United States, however, monetary policy is not decided by elected officials. Instead, it is decided by the unelected FOMC. Only rarely has anyone served on the FOMC who has ever held any elected office. The members are usually academic economists or people with careers in banking, finance, or other areas of business. Because those deciding monetary policy do not have to run for election, they are not accountable for their actions to the ultimate authorities in a democracy: the voters.

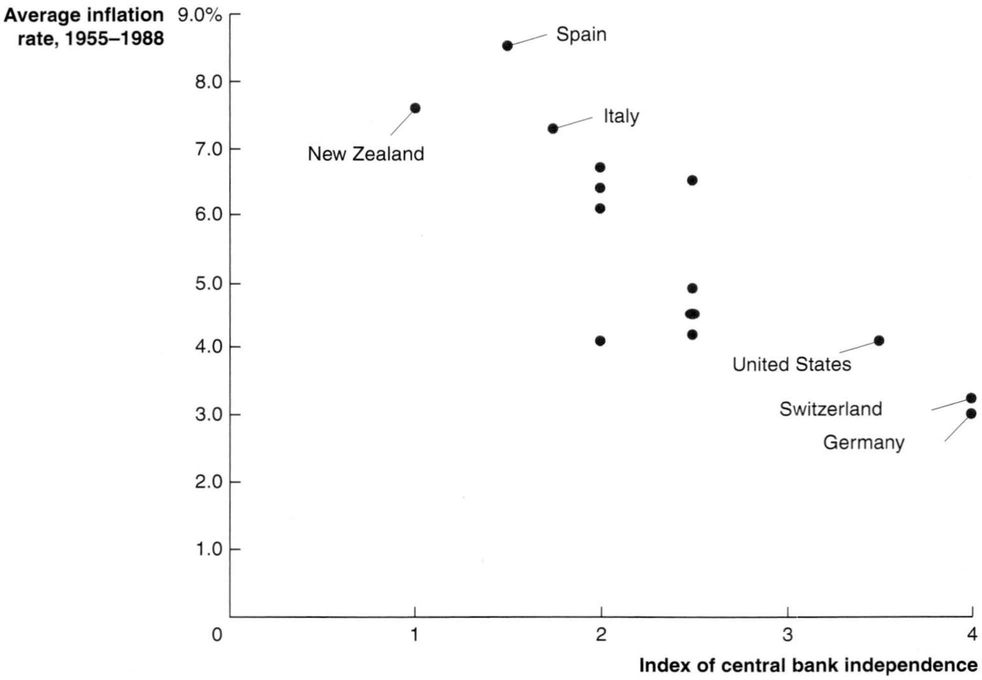

Figure 14-12 | The More Independent the Central Bank, the Lower the Inflation Rate

For 16 high-income countries, the greater the degree of central bank independence from the rest of the government, the lower the inflation rate. Central bank independence is measured by an index ranging from 1 (minimum independence) to 4 (maximum independence). During these years, Germany had a high index of independence of 4 and a low average inflation rate of just over 3 percent. New Zealand had a low index of independence of 1 and a high average inflation rate of over 7 percent.

Source: Alberto Alesina and Lawrence H. Summers, "Central Bank Independence and Macroeconomic Performance: Some Comparative Evidence," *Journal of Money, Credit and Banking*, Vol. 25, No. 2, May 1993, pp. 151–162.

Some economists and politicians argue that the Fed should operate like other parts of the executive branch of government. Under this proposal, the members of the Board of Governors would serve only as long as the president wanted them to, as do members of the president's cabinet today. That way, if the president didn't like the current monetary policy, he would have the authority to dismiss the members of the Board of Governors and appoint others in their place. When the president ran for reelection, the voters would have an opportunity to express their approval or disapproval of his monetary policy.

The Fed's independence from the rest of the government, coupled with the Fed's decision-making process, has concentrated power in the hands of the chairman. The chairman has only 1 vote in 7 on the Board of Governors and only 1 vote in 12 on the FOMC. Nevertheless, the very strong tradition at the Fed is that the chairman plays a predominant role in setting policy.

The Fed has never set out any specific guidelines regarding when it will adopt a particular monetary policy. The Fed adopts an expansionary policy when the chairman and the FOMC decide that the economy is in danger of moving into recession. The chairman's recommendations for a policy change are based on his own experience, on the analysis prepared by the Fed's economists, and on discussions with other members of the FOMC. The Fed adopts a contractionary policy when the chairman and FOMC decide that there is a threat of rising inflation. In either case, the decision to change policy depends in part on the personal judgment of the chairman. Most economists would say that monetary policy has been successful during the years since 1979, but some economists suggest that greater transparency about the Fed's objectives would help lock in future good performance.

In periods like the 1970s, when the performance of the U.S. economy was poor, proposals to reduce the independence of the Fed gained support. On balance, though, the U.S. economy has performed well during the past 25 years, which has greatly reduced discontent with the Fed's structure. At this point, it appears unlikely that Congress would consider legislation to reduce the independence of the Fed.

Continued from page 467

Economics in YOUR Life!

At the beginning of this chapter, we asked whether buying a house during a recession is a good idea. Clearly, there are many considerations to keep in mind when buying a house, which is the largest purchase you are likely to make in your lifetime. Included among these considerations are the price of the house relative to other comparable houses in the neighborhood, whether house prices in the neighborhood have been rising or falling, and the location of the house relative to stores, work, and good schools. Also important, though, is the interest rate you will have to pay on the mortgage loan you would need in order to buy the house. As we have seen in this chapter, during a recession, the Fed often takes actions to lower interest rates. So, mortgage rates are typically lower during a recession than at other times. You may well want to take advantage of these low interest rates to buy a house during a recession. But, recessions are also times of rising unemployment, and you would not want to make a commitment to borrow a lot of money for 15 or more years if you were in significant danger of losing your job. We can conclude, then, that if your job seems secure, buying a house during a recession may actually be a good idea.

Conclusion

Monetary policy is one way governments pursue goals for inflation, employment, and financial stability. Many journalists and politicians refer to the chairman of the Federal Reserve as second only to the president of the United States in his ability to affect the U.S. economy. Congress and the president, however, also use their power over spending and taxes to try to stabilize the economy. In the next chapter, we discuss how *fiscal policy*—changes in government spending and taxes—affect the economy.

Read *An Inside Look at Policy* on the next page for a comparison of how a slowing housing market affects the United States and Europe.

An Inside **LOOK** at Policy

Housing Market Slowdown Affects the United States and Europe Very Differently

WALL STREET JOURNAL, APRIL 20, 2007

Slowing Housing Market Isn't Big Worry in Europe

Europe's decade-long boom in house prices is coming to an end, much as in the U.S. But on Europe's side of the pond, the slowing property market isn't triggering the same concerns that it could stall the wider economy.

More-conservative lending practices, a smaller rise in interest rates and a lack of home-equity withdrawals mean that most of Europe isn't seeing the big pickup in mortgage defaults and bankruptcies that is worrying economists in the U.S. The difference is showing up in growth forecasts for the world's two biggest economies, as well as in interest-rate policies that have driven the euro to near-record highs against the dollar.

a While worrying property-market data have prompted economists to cut U.S. growth forecasts lately, the International Monetary Fund last week increased its projection for euro-zone growth this year to 2.3%. That is a shade faster than the IMF's 2.2% forecast for the U.S., which Europe has been trailing for years.

Far from considering interest-rate cuts to ease borrowers' burdens, the European Central Bank, which sets monetary policy for the 13 countries that use the euro, signaled last week that it is likely to increase its key rate to 4% in June, while further increases could follow, making the euro more attractive.

"There'll be some problems in the housing market, but they'll be very localized, and we won't see anything like the contagion we've seen in the U.S." said Julian Callow, chief European economist for Barclays Capital in London.

Spain, one of the euro zone's most vibrant property markets, saw home prices last year slip from years of double-digit percentage growth to post a 9.1% annual increase; Spanish bank BBVA predicts prices will rise between 3% and 5% this year. Fellow euro-zone hot spot France has seen house prices more than double since 1997, but the annual rate is expected to drop below 5% this year. Irish and Italian house prices are also slowing in the wake of similar booms.

But while Spain, Ireland and the U.K. are potential trouble spots, most economists don't worry that a slowing housing market will spur a broader slowdown in euro-zone consumer spending.

b In part, that is because banks in most of Europe—in contrast to those in the U.S. and the U.K.—don't offer home-equity withdrawal. As a result, most Europeans can't treat their houses like giant automated-teller machines, relying on rising property values to free up cash to go shopping. Consumer spending in such places as France or Italy depends more on changes in employment levels and wages, which are expected to rise steadily this year in the euro zone.

Mortgage markets also help explain the U.S.–European contrast. The vast majority of existing euro-zone mortgages are still of the long-term, fixed-rate variety. Until recently, the U.S.'s profile was similar. But in 2006, as much as 45% of new mortgages sold in the U.S., when measured by dollar value, were adjustable rate. As a result, when the U.S. Federal Reserve changes its key lending rate, mortgage owners feel it in their pockets quickly.

In continental Europe, there has also been far less proliferation of the innovative interest-only or hybrid loans that helped spur the U.S. boom. Subprime mortgages—loans made to home buyers with poor credit records—are also rare in Europe, removing a major source of concern.

"There's just been much less innovation in financial instruments," says Mr. Callow of Barclays Capital.

c Interest rates are another key difference. Since the U.S. Federal Reserve's key lending rate bottomed out at a historical low of 1% in June 2003, the Fed has raised it 17 times, to 5.25%—making money more than five times as expensive to borrow. The ECB has raised its key lending rate, too, but by a factor of less than two—to 3.75% from a low of 2% a few years ago. So most European homeowners aren't getting pinched as hard as Americans.

To be sure, some European property markets are starting to cause concern. In Spain, more than 700,000 new houses were built last year, more than in Germany and France combined, even though those two countries together have more than three times as many residents. Spaniards tend to take out variable-interest mortgages, exposing them to rate changes, and Spanish banks have been more lax about mortgage terms, allowing buyers to borrow more.

Source: Rick Carew and J. R. Wu, "Slowing Housing Market Isn't Big Worry in Europe," Wall Street Journal, April 20, 2007. Reprinted by permission of the Wall Street Journal via Copyright Clearance Center.

Key Points in the Article

This article discusses the macroeconomic effects of housing market slowdowns in the United States and Europe. Although the prices of houses are increasing more slowly in both economies, only the U.S. economy has slowed as a result of this weakness. Because of the housing market slowdown, economists have lowered their 2007 forecasts for U.S. economic growth to 2.2 percent, while they have raised their forecasts for euro-zone growth to 2.3 percent. (The "euro zone" is the 13 countries of Europe that use the euro as a common currency.) This article attributes these very different macroeconomic responses to the prevalence of home-equity loans and adjustable-rate mortgages in the United States, as well as the Federal Reserve's relatively aggressive contractionary monetary policy.

Analyzing the News

a The United States and the European Monetary Union experienced a housing boom over the past decade, as home prices in some regions of both economies appreciated by more than 10 percent annually. However, by the first half of 2007, house-price appreciation began to weaken on both sides of the Atlantic, and many economists declared that these twin booms had come to an end. While the end of the housing boom has slowed the U.S. economy, it has had a smaller effect on the European economy. Economists have recently raised their forecasts for euro-zone growth to 2.3 percent, marking the first time in many years that euro-zone growth has outpaced U.S. growth.

b While home-equity loans are readily available to U.S. homeowners, they are not readily available to euro-zone homeowners. This is important because a home-equity loan allows a homeowner to borrow against—and, in effect, spend—the difference between the values of a home and the amount of the mortgage loan on the home. Therefore, in an economy in which home equity loans are prevalent, consumption spending may rise and fall with house prices; however, in an economy where home equity loans are not prevalent, consumption spending may not be much affected by changes in house prices. According to the article, the weak housing market slowed consumption spending in the United States, but had relatively little effect on consumption spending in the euro-zone economy.

Adjustable-rate mortgages—which offer borrowers mortgage rates that rise and fall with other interest rates in the economy—are also readily available to U.S. homeowners, they are not readily available to euro-zone homeowners. This is important because, over the past few years, both the U.S. Federal Reserve and the European Central Bank implemented monetary policies that raised interest rates. While these higher rates have increased interest payments for U.S. homeowners with adjustable-rate mortgages, the higher rates did not affect European homeowners.

c Finally, although the Federal Reserve and the European Central Bank both implemented policies that raised interest rates, the Federal Reserve implemented a relatively larger and more abrupt increase in interest rates. This pattern is shown in the figure, which plots the U.S. federal funds rate and the euro interbank offered rate, both of which represent the rates that banks charge one another for overnight reserves. In the United States, the federal funds rate rose from a relatively low 1 percent to a relatively high 5.25 percent from June 2003 to May 2007; meanwhile, in the euro zone, the interbank rate rose from 2 percent to a relatively moderate 4 percent. According to the article, this difference in interest rate increases is due to the Fed's relatively more contractionary monetary policy and helps explain why the U.S. economy grew relatively more slowly during 2006 and 2007 compared to Europe.

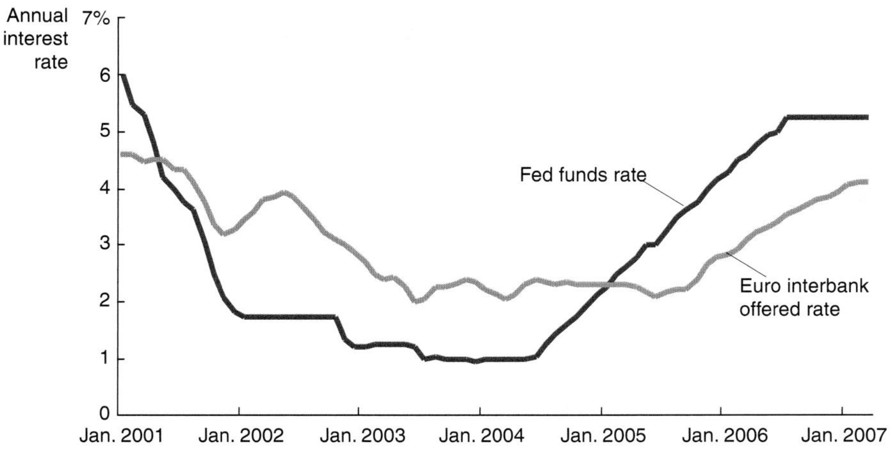

Monetary policy has been relatively more contractionary in the United States than in the euro zone during the past few years.

Thinking Critically About Policy

1. Compare the effects on aggregate demand of a contractionary monetary policy when adjustable-rate mortgages are prevalent in the economy versus when they are not.
2. Most economists agree that the effectiveness of monetary policy—for example, the extent to which a central bank must raise interest rates in order to slow an economy—varies with the economy's degree of openness. Is monetary policy relatively more or less effective in an open economy, as opposed to a closed economy? Briefly explain why.

Key Terms

Contractionary monetary policy, p. 480
Expansionary monetary policy, p. 480
Federal funds rate, p. 476
Inflation targeting, p. 492
Monetary policy, p. 468
Taylor rule, p. 491

14.1 LEARNING OBJECTIVE 14.1 | Define monetary policy and describe the Federal Reserve's monetary policy goals, **pages 468–469.**

What Is Monetary Policy?

Summary

Monetary policy is the actions the Fed takes to manage the money supply and interest rates to pursue its macroeconomic policy objectives. The Fed has set four *monetary policy goals* that are intended to promote a well-functioning economy: price stability, high employment, economic growth, and stability of financial markets and institutions.

myeconlab Get Ahead of the Curve Visit www.myeconlab.com to complete these exercises online and get instant feedback.

Review Questions

1.1 When Congress established the Federal Reserve in 1913, what was its main responsibility? When did Congress broaden the Fed's responsibilities?

1.2 What are the Fed's four monetary policy goals?

Problems and Applications

1.3 When the Federal Reserve was founded in 1913, why did Congress see the Fed's primary responsibility as making discount loans to banks?

1.4 Why is price stability one of the Fed's monetary policy goals? What problems can high inflation rates cause for the economy?

1.5 A Federal Reserve official argues that at the Fed, "the objectives of price stability and low long-term interest rates are essentially the same objective." Briefly explain his reasoning.

Source: William Poole, "Understanding the Fed," *Federal Reserve Bank of St. Louis Review*, Vol. 89, No. 1, January/February 2007, p. 4.

1.6 Stock prices rose rapidly in the late 1990s and then fell rapidly beginning in early 2000. Housing prices in many parts of the country rose rapidly in the early 2000s and then declined to some extent beginning in 2006. Some economists have argued that rapid increases and decreases in the prices of assets such as shares of stock or houses can damage the economy. Currently, stabilizing asset prices is not one of the Federal Reserve's policy goals. In what ways would a goal of stabilizing asset prices be different from the four goals listed on page 468? Do you believe that stabilizing asset prices should be added to the list of the Fed's policy goals? Briefly explain.

>> End Learning Objective 14.1

14.2 LEARNING OBJECTIVE 14.2 | Describe the Federal Reserve's monetary policy targets and explain how expansionary and contractionary monetary policies affect the interest rate, **pages 470–476.**

The Money Market and the Fed's Choice of Monetary Policy Targets

Summary

The Fed's *monetary policy targets* are economic variables that it can affect directly and that in turn affect variables such as real GDP and the price level that are closely related to the Fed's policy goals. The two main monetary policy targets are the money supply and the interest rate. The Fed has most often chosen to use the interest rate as its monetary policy target. The Federal Open Market Committee announces a target for the **federal funds rate** after each meeting. The federal funds rate is the interest rate banks charge each other for overnight loans. To fight a recession, the Fed conducts an *expansionary policy* by increasing the money supply. The increase in the money supply lowers the interest rate. To reduce the inflation rate, the Fed conducts a *contractionary monetary policy* by adjusting the money supply to increase the interest rate. In a graphical analysis of the money market, an *expansionary monetary policy* shifts the money supply curve to the right, causing a movement down the money demand curve and a new equilibrium at a lower interest rate. A contractionary policy shifts the money supply curve to the left, causing a movement up the money demand curve and a new equilibrium at a higher interest rate.

Review Questions

2.1 What is a monetary policy target? Why does the Fed use policy targets?

2.2 Draw a demand and supply graph showing equilibrium in the money market. Suppose the Fed wants to lower the equilibrium interest rate. Show on the graph how the Fed would accomplish this objective.

2.3 Explain the effect an open market purchase has on the equilibrium interest rate.

2.4 What is the federal funds rate? What role does it play in monetary policy?

Problems and Applications

2.5 A "basis point" is one one-hundredth of a percentage point. If an interest rate increases by 50 basis points, it has gone up by one-half of a percentage point. "Monetary aggregates" are measures of the money supply, such as M1 and M2. A Federal Reserve publication from February 2002 made the following observation: "As the economy slipped into recession last year, the FOMC reduced its target level for the overnight federal funds rate by 475 basis points to 1.75 percent. Also during the year, growth of the monetary aggregates jumped sharply."

a. If the target for the federal funds rate was reduced by 475 basis points, to 1.75 percent, what was its original level?

b. Is there a connection between the federal funds rate falling and the money supply increasing? Briefly explain.

Source: Richard G. Anderson, "Interpreting Monetary Growth," *Monetary Trends*, Federal Reserve Bank of St. Louis, February 2002.

2.6 **(Related to *Solved Problem 14-2* on page 474)** Suppose the interest rate is 2 percent on a Treasury bill that will pay its owner $1,000 when it matures in one year.

a. What is the price of the Treasury bill?

b. Suppose that the Fed engages in open market sales resulting in the interest rate on one-year Treasury bills rising to 3 percent. What will the price of these bills be now?

2.7 In this chapter, we depict the money supply curve as a vertical line. Is there any reason to believe the money supply curve might actually be upward sloping? (*Hint:* Think about the role of banks in the process of creating the money supply.) Draw a money demand and money supply graph with an upward-sloping money supply curve. Suppose that households and firms decide they want to hold more money at every interest rate. Show the result on your graph. What is the impact on the size of M1? How does this differ from the impact if the money supply curve were a vertical line?

2.8 If the Federal Reserve purchases $100 million worth of U.S. Treasury bills from the public, predict what will happen to the money supply. Explain your reasoning.

2.9 A 2004 editorial in the *New York Times* made the following observation about the federal funds rate: "The Federal Reserve Board announced yesterday that it would keep its overnight interest rate where it has been for nine months—at 1 percent, its lowest level since 1958. Factor in inflation, and Alan Greenspan is essentially lending money at a loss." What is another name for the "overnight interest rate" mentioned in this editorial? Do you agree with the author of this editorial that the Federal Reserve lends money at this interest rate? Briefly explain.

Source: "The Cost of Cheap Money," *New York Times*, March 17, 2004.

>> End Learning Objective 14.2

14.3 LEARNING OBJECTIVE 14.3 | Use aggregate demand and aggregate supply graphs to show the effects of monetary policy on real GDP and the price level, **pages 477–489.**

Monetary Policy and Economic Activity

Summary

An **expansionary monetary policy** lowers interest rates to increase consumption, investment, and net exports. This increased spending causes the aggregate demand curve (*AD*) to shift out more than it otherwise would, raising the level of real GDP and the price level. An expansionary monetary policy can help the Fed achieve its goal of high employment. A **contractionary monetary policy** raises interest rates to decrease consumption, investment, and net exports. This decreased spending causes the aggregate demand curve to shift out less than it otherwise would, reducing both the level of real GDP and the inflation rate below what they would be in the absence of policy. A contractionary monetary policy can help the Fed achieve its goal of price stability.

Review Questions

3.1 How does an increase in interest rates affect aggregate demand? Briefly discuss how each component of aggregate demand is affected.

3.2 If the Fed believes the economy is about to fall into recession, what actions should it take? If the Fed believes the inflation rate is about to increase, what actions should it take?

Problems and Applications

3.3 A newspaper headline in early 2002 read, "Companies Invest as Interest Rates Are at a 40-Year Low." Explain the connection between this headline and the monetary policy pursued by the Federal Reserve during that time.

Source: Brendan Murray, "Companies Invest as Interest Rates Are at a 40-Year Low," Bloomberg News, March 28, 2002.

3.4 **(Related to the *Chapter Opener* on page 466)** In an article in the *Wall Street Journal* in March 2002, Lawrence Yun, senior economist for the National Association of Realtors, was quoted as saying, "In the current [2001] brief recession, the housing-market indicators were in record territories." Economists normally expect that during a recession, the housing market does badly because of rising unemployment and falling incomes. Why did the housing market do so well during the 2001 recession?

Source: Erin Schulte, "Housing's Strength Raises Another Bubble Concern," *Wall Street Journal*, March 29, 2002.

3.5 **(Related to the *Chapter Opener* on page 466)** An article in the *New York Times* in March 2002 reported that the housing market had been surprisingly strong during the previous year. According to the article, "In trying to explain the resilience of the housing market in the face of rising unemployment, shrinking stock portfolios and a soft economy, economists start with the Federal Reserve." Why start with the Federal Reserve in trying to explain the strength of the housing market during a recession?

Source: Daniel Altman, "Economy's Rock: Homes, Homes, Homes," *New York Times*, March 30, 2002.

3.6 In December 2001, some Fed officials were worried that the U.S. economy might make only a slow recovery from the 2001 recession. An article in the *New York Times* quoted the views of these officials as follows:

> The main force inhibiting a strong comeback, Fed officials say, is the perception among businesses that the rates of return available to them from investing in new equipment remain too low given the uncertainty about demand for their products, the overall health of the economy and the risks associated with the campaign against terrorism.

How might firms' expectations that the rates of return on new investments are too low make monetary policy less effective in ending a recession?

Source: Richard W. Stevenson and Louis Uchitelle, "Fed Now Says '02 Recovery to Be Gradual," *New York Times*, December 4, 2001.

3.7 According to an article in the *New York Times*, an official at the Bank of Japan had the following explanation of why monetary policy was not pulling the country out of recession: "Despite recent major increases in the money supply, he said, the money stays in banks." Explain what the official meant by the phrase "the money stays in banks." Where does the money go if an expansionary monetary policy is successful?

Source: James Brooke, "Critics Say Koizumi's Economic Medicine Is a Weak Tea," *New York Times*, February 27, 2002.

3.8 According to an April 2007 article in the *Wall Street Journal*:

> In February . . . [Japan's] gauge of core consumer prices slipped 0.1% from a year earlier. . . . The Bank of Japan said last year it would regard prices as stable if they rose from zero to 2% a year. . . . The Bank of Japan's target for short-term interest rates is just 0.5%, compared with the Federal Reserve's 5.25% target for the U.S. and the European Central Bank's 3.75% for the euro zone. . . . "It will be very difficult for the BOJ [Bank of Japan] to raise interest rates when prices are below the range it defines as stable," says Teizo Taya, special counselor for the Daiwa Institute of Research and a former BOJ policy board member.

a. What is the term for a falling price level?
b. Why would the Bank of Japan, the Japanese central bank, be reluctant to raise its target for short-term interest rates if the price level is falling?
c. Why would a country's central bank consider a falling price level to be undesirable?

Source: Yuka Hayashi, "Japan's Consumer Prices May Threaten Economy," *Wall Street Journal*, April 25, 2007, p. A6.

3.9 According to an article in the *Wall Street Journal*, in mid-2007, many investors were expecting that the Federal Reserve would lower its target of the federal funds rate. But the article said that after the most recent meeting of the Federal Open Market Committee, "the Federal Reserve signaled continued wariness on inflation, leaving interest rates unchanged and giving no sign it is inching toward an interest-rate cut."

a. What does "continued wariness on inflation" mean?
b. If the Fed is wary of inflation, why might it be reluctant to lower the target for the federal funds rate?

Source: Greg Ip, "Inflation Risk Keeps Fed on Alert," *Wall Street Journal*, May 10, 2007, p. A3.

3.10 Most of the countries of Western Europe use a common currency, the euro, and have a common monetary policy determined by the European Central Bank. An article in the *Economist* magazine noted the following:

> The European Central Bank (ECB) raised its key interest rate by 0.25 percentage points, to 4%. The bank has now raised rates eight times since December 2005. . . . Inflation is, for the moment, on the ECB's target: consumer prices rose by 1.9% in the year to May.

If the inflation rate is on the ECB's target, why would the ECB be increasing interest rates?

Source: "Overview," *Economist*, June 7, 2007.

3.11 William McChesney Martin, who was Federal Reserve chairman from 1951 to 1970, was once quoted as saying, "The role of the Federal Reserve is to remove the punchbowl just as the party gets going." What did he mean?

3.12 **(Related to *Solved Problem 14-3* on page 485)** Use the following graph page to answer the questions.

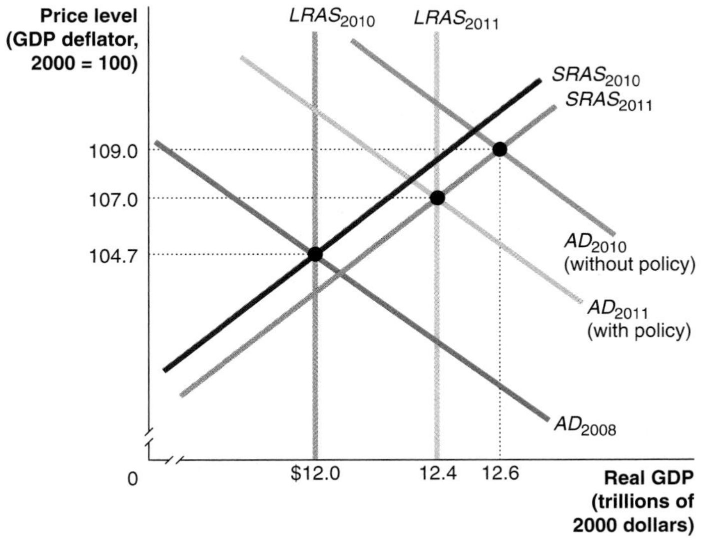

a. If the Fed does not take any policy action, what will be the level of real GDP and the price level in 2011?
b. If the Fed wants to keep real GDP at its potential level in 2011, should it use an expansionary policy or a contractionary policy? Should the trading desk be buying Treasury bills or selling them?
c. If the Fed takes no policy action, what will be the inflation rate in 2011? If the Fed uses monetary policy to keep real GDP at its full-employment level, what will be the inflation rate in 2011?

3.13 **(Related to *Solved Problem 14-3* on page 485)** The hypothetical information in the following table shows what the situation will be in 2011 if the Fed does *not* use monetary policy:

YEAR	POTENTIAL REAL GDP	REAL GDP	PRICE LEVEL
2010	$12.8 trillion	$12.8 trillion	140
2011	13.3 trillion	13.4 trillion	147

a. If the Fed wants to keep real GDP at its potential level in 2011, should it use an expansionary policy or a contractionary policy? Should the trading desk be buying T-bills or selling them?
b. If the Fed's policy is successful in keeping real GDP at its potential level in 2011, state whether each of the following will be higher, lower, or the same as it would have been if the Fed had taken no action:
   i. Real GDP
   ii. Potential real GDP
   iii. The inflation rate
   iv. The unemployment rate
c. Draw an aggregate demand and aggregate supply graph to illustrate your answer. Be sure that your graph contains *LRAS* curves for 2010 and 2011; *SRAS* curves for 2010 and 2011; *AD* curves for 2010 and 2011, with and without monetary policy action; and equilibrium real GDP and the price level in 2011, with and without policy.

3.14 **(Related to the *Don't Let This Happen to You!* on page 488)** Briefly explain whether you agree or disagree with the following statement: "The Fed has an easy job. Say it wants to increase real GDP by $200 billion. All it has to do is increase the money supply by that amount."

3.15 Some businesspeople believe that the active monetary policy of the Fed makes the economy less stable rather than more stable. Writing in the *New York Times*, T. J. Rodgers, chief executive of Cypress Semiconductor, argued:

> There is a fundamental flaw in the Fed's operational assumption that it can know enough about the future to fine-tune the economy without continually making mistakes. Events likely to alter the economy—wars, severe winters, technology breakthroughs and so on—are not predictable. . . . Fed action is just as likely to exacerbate an economic problem as it is to mitigate it.

Do you agree with Mr. Rodgers's argument? Explain.

Source: T. J. Rodgers, "A Computer Would Do Better than the Fed," *New York Times*, April 7, 2001.

3.16 The following appears in a Federal Reserve publication:

> In practice, monetary policymakers do not have up-to-the-minute, reliable information about the state of the economy and prices. Information is limited because of lags in the publication of data. Also, policymakers have less-than-perfect understanding of the way the economy works, including the knowledge of when and to what extent policy actions will affect aggregate demand. The operation of the economy changes over time, and with it the response of the economy to policy measures. These limitations add to uncertainties in the policy process and make determining the appropriate setting of monetary policy . . . more difficult.

If the Fed itself admits that there are many obstacles in the way of effective monetary policy, why does it still engage in active monetary policy rather than use a monetary growth rule, as suggested by Milton Friedman and his followers?

Source: Board of Governors of the Federal Reserve System, *The Federal Reserve System: Purposes and Functions*, Washington, DC, 1994.

3.17 **(Related to the *Making the Connection* on page 478)** In a speech in mid-2007, Federal Reserve Chairman Ben Bernanke made the following observation:

> Real gross domestic product has expanded a little more than 2 percent over the past year, compared with an average annual growth rate of 3-3/4 percent over the preceding three years. The cooling of the housing market is an important source of this slowdown.

a. What did Bernanke mean by "the cooling of the housing market"?
b. How would the cooling of the housing market contribute to slower economic growth?

Source: Ben Bernanke, "The Subprime Mortgage Market," speech delivered at the Federal Reserve Bank of Chicago's 43rd Annual Conference on Bank Structure and Competition, Chicago, May 17, 2007.

3.18 **(Related to the *Making the Connection* on page 478)** Federal Reserve Chairman Ben Bernanke has defined *subprime mortgages* this way: "Subprime mortgages are loans made to borrowers who are perceived to have high credit risk, often because they lack a strong credit history or have other characteristics that are associated with high probabilities of default." Why would some lenders be willing to grant mortgages to borrowers "who are perceived to have credit risk"? Why might many borrowers have been particularly willing to take on mortgage debt during the early 2000s, even if their credit was not very good? What risks to the economy might this type of lending involve?

Source: Ben Bernanke, "The Subprime Mortgage Market," speech delivered at the Federal Reserve Bank of Chicago's 43rd Annual Conference on Bank Structure and Competition, Chicago, May 17, 2007.

3.19 **(Related to the *Making the Connection* on page 478)** At the beginning of 2005, Robert Toll, CEO of Toll Brothers, argued that the United States was not experiencing a housing bubble. Instead, he argued that higher house prices reflected restrictions imposed by local governments on building new houses. He argued that the restrictions resulted from "NIMBY"—"Not in My Back Yard"—politics. Many existing homeowners are reluctant to see nearby farms and undeveloped land turned into new housing developments. As a result, according to Toll, "Towns don't want anything built." Why would the factors mentioned by Robert Toll cause housing prices to rise? How would it be possible to decide whether these factors or a bubble was the cause of rising housing prices?

Source: Shawn Tully, "Toll Brothers: The New King of the Real Estate Boom," *Fortune*, April 5, 2005.

3.20 In 1975, Ronald Reagan stated that inflation "has one cause and one cause alone: government spending more than government takes in." Briefly explain whether you agree.

Source: Edward Nelson, "Budget Deficits and Interest Rates," *Monetary Trends*, Federal Reserve Bank of St. Louis, March 2004.

3.21 **(Related to the *Making the Connection* on page 482)** Some economists and members of Congress have argued that because of deposit insurance, bank runs and bank panics no longer occur, and the Fed no longer needs to act as a lender of last resort. Therefore, the Federal Reserve Act should be amended to eliminate the ability of the Fed to make discount loans. Briefly evaluate this argument.

3.22 **(Related to the *Making the Connection* on page 487)** The following is from an article in the *Wall Street Journal*:

> The immediate catalyst for yesterday's gains [in stock prices] was a Federal Reserve report. . . . Some investors interpreted the comments to mean that if the economy proves resilient, the Fed won't stifle it with a rate increase and if it proves weaker than expected, the Fed might even cut rates.

Why would stock prices increase if investors believe that the Federal Reserve will not be raising interest rates and may even be cutting them?

Source: Peter A. McKay and E. S. Browning, "S&P Joins Record Club," *Wall Street Journal*, May 31, 2007, p. C1.

>> End Learning Objective 14.3

14.4 LEARNING OBJECTIVE 14.4 | Discuss the Fed's setting of monetary policy targets, **pages 490–494.**

A Closer Look at the Fed's Setting of Monetary Policy Targets

Summary

Some economists have argued that the Fed should use the money supply, rather than an interest rate, as its monetary target. Milton Friedman and other monetarists argued that the Fed should adopt a monetary growth rule of increasing the money supply every year at a fixed rate. Support for this proposal declined after 1980 because the relationship between movements in the money supply and movements in real GDP and the price level weakened. John Taylor has analyzed the factors involved in Fed decision making and developed the *Taylor rule* for federal funds targeting. The *Taylor rule* links the Fed's target for the federal funds rate to economic variables. Over the past decade, many economists and central bankers have expressed significant interest in using **inflation targeting**, under which monetary policy is conducted to commit the central bank to achieving a publicly announced inflation target. A number of foreign central banks have adopted inflation targeting, but the Fed has not. The Fed's performance in the 1980s, 1990s, and early 2000s generally received high marks from economists, even without formal inflation targeting.

myeconlab Get Ahead of the Curve — Visit www.myeconlab.com to complete these exercises online and get instant feedback.

Review Questions

4.1 What is a monetary rule, as opposed to a monetary policy? What monetary rule would Milton Friedman have liked the Fed to follow? Why has support for a monetary rule of the kind advocated by Friedman declined since 1980?

4.2 For more than 20 years, the Fed has used the federal funds rate as its monetary policy target. Why doesn't it target the money supply at the same time?

Problems and Applications

4.3 Suppose that the equilibrium real federal funds rate is 2 percent, and the target rate of inflation is 2 percent. Use the following information and the Taylor rule to calculate the federal funds rate target:

Current inflation rate = 4 percent

Potential real GDP = $14.0 trillion

Real GDP = $14.14 trillion

4.4 According to an article in the *Economist*:

> Calculations by David Mackie, of J.P. Morgan, show that virtually throughout the past six years, interest rates in the euro area have been lower than a Taylor rule would have prescribed, refuting the popular wisdom that the [European Central Bank] cares less about growth than does the Fed.

Why would keeping interest rates unusually low be an indication that the European Central Bank was very concerned about economic growth rather than inflation?

Source: "The European Central Bank: Haughty Indifference, or Masterly Inactivity?" *Economist*, July 14, 2005.

4.5 This chapter states, "Experience with inflation targeting has varied, but typically, the move to inflation targeting has been accompanied by lower inflation (sometimes at the cost of temporarily higher unemployment)." Why might a move to inflation targeting temporarily increase the unemployment rate?

4.6 William Poole, the president of the Federal Reserve Bank of St. Louis in 2007 stated, "Although my own preference is for zero inflation properly managed, I believe that a central bank consensus on some other numerical goal of reasonably low inflation is more important than the exact number." Briefly explain why the economy might gain the benefits of an explicit inflation target even if the target chosen is not a zero rate of inflation.

Source: William Poole, "Understanding the Fed," *Federal Reserve Bank of St. Louis Review*, Vol. 89, No. 1, January/February 2007, p. 4.

4.7 **(Related to the *Making the Connection* on page 493)** If the core PCE is a better measure of the inflation rate than is the CPI, why is the CPI more widely used? In particular, can you think of reasons why the federal government uses the CPI when deciding how much to increase Social Security payments to retired workers to keep the purchasing power of the payments from declining?

>> End Learning Objective 14.4

14.5 LEARNING OBJECTIVE 14.5 | Assess the arguments for and against the independence of the Federal Reserve, **pages 494–497.**

Is the Independence of the Federal Reserve a Good Idea?

Summary

The Fed conducts monetary policy without input from Congress or the president. It uses the interest it earns from purchasing U.S. Treasury bills to avoid asking Congress for the funds it needs to operate. However, the Fed's independence is not absolute because Congress and the president can pass legislation at any time to reorganize, or even abolish, it. Advocates of Fed independence argue that isolating it from political pressure allows it to choose policies in the best interest of the economy. Internationally, countries with more independent central banks tend to have lower inflation rates. Opponents of Fed independence argue that concentrating so much power in the hands of unelected officials is inconsistent with democratic principles.

myeconlab Get Ahead of the Curve Visit www.myeconlab.com to complete these exercises online and get instant feedback.

Review Questions

5.1 In what ways is the Federal Reserve more independent of the executive branch of the federal government than other agencies, such as the Environmental Protection Agency? Why did the Federal Reserve Act of 1913 give so much independence to the Fed?

5.2 What arguments do economists make in favor of reducing the independence of the Fed? What arguments do economists make in favor of maintaining the independence of the Fed?

Problems and Applications

5.3 The president of the United States appoints the comptroller of the currency and the secretary of the Treasury. Until passage of the Banking Act of 1935, these officials were both members of the Board of Governors of the Federal Reserve System. How would having these two presidential appointees on the board be likely to affect monetary policy? Would it be a good idea if they were still on the board?

5.4 An article in the *Economist* observes:

> Central-bank independence became a reality when politicians finally accepted that it was economically foolish for them to manage interest rates. . . . By setting the bankers free [from government control] . . . many countries have restrained inflation and become less prone to economic swings.

Do you agree that it is "economically foolish" for politicians, rather than the central bank, to control interest rates? Briefly explain. How has "setting the bankers free" from control by the government allowed countries to restrain inflation?

Source: "Central Banks: An Italian Comedy," *Economist*, September 29, 2005.

5.5 In early 2007, Venezuelan president Hugo Chávez announced that the country's central bank would be stripped of its independence. What impact would you predict that this action will have on the inflation rate in Venezuela? Briefly explain.

5.6 Although the Federal Reserve is formally independent of Congress and the president, Burton Abrams, an economist at the University of Delaware, has recently studied recordings of conversations between President Richard Nixon and his aides and between President Nixon and Federal Reserve Chairman Arthur Burns that indicate that President Nixon may have had significant influence on monetary policy. These conversations indicate that President Nixon brought considerable pressure to bear on Chairman Burns to increase the rate of growth of the money supply in late 1971 and early 1972 in advance of the presidential election to be held in November 1972 (in which President Nixon would be running for reelection). At one point, President Nixon told an aide: "War is going to be declared if he [Burns] doesn't come around." What did Nixon hope to gain from the Federal Reserve increasing the rate of growth of the money supply during the months before his reelection campaign?

Source: Burton A. Abrams, "How Richard Nixon Pressured Arthur Burns: Evidence from the Nixon Tapes," *Journal of Economic Perspectives*, Vol. 20, No. 4, Fall 2006, pp. 177–188.

>> End Learning Objective 14.5

Chapter 15

Fiscal Policy

A Boon for H&R Block

Just before the deadline for paying federal income taxes in 2007, a *Wall Street Journal* article warned that "Last minute changes in the law are helping make an already difficult tax season one of the trickiest in memory." Actually, the difficulties taxpayers had filling out their federal income tax forms in 2007 was not that unusual. For instance, the offices of professional tax preparers were also very busy in spring 2002 because millions of taxpayers were having a difficult time completing their income tax forms that year as well. Congress and the president had used the *discretionary fiscal policy* of cutting income taxes to increase household spending. Their goal was to help pull the economy out of the 2001 recession. Because most taxpayers would not see the money from the tax cut until they filed their tax returns in early 2002, the federal government decided to mail out checks during summer 2001 for the amount each taxpayer would receive. Single taxpayers received a check for $300, and married taxpayers received a check for $600.

A new line on the tax form was meant to give taxpayers an opportunity to claim their tax cut if they had not received it the previous summer. Many taxpayers found the instructions confusing and either incorrectly claimed an additional $300 or $600 or decided they needed the help of a professional tax preparer.

Probably the best-known professional tax preparation firm is H&R Block. In 1946, 24-year old Henry Bloch started the United Business Company, which provided accounting services to small businesses in Kansas City, Missouri. When the local office of the United States Internal Revenue Service (IRS) announced in 1955 that it would no longer provide free preparation of individual income tax forms, Henry and his brother Richard recognized an entrepreneurial opportunity. They founded a new firm, H&R Block, dedicated to preparing individual income tax returns. When the IRS announced that it would stop offering any tax preparation services at its New York City offices in 1956, the Blochs decided to expand to that city by opening seven offices close to existing IRS offices. By 2007, the firm employed more than 80,000 tax preparers to prepare more than 19.5 million tax returns a year and earned revenue of $4.9 billion.

The tax laws have become increasingly complicated. In 1955, when H&R Block was founded, the 1040 individual income tax form had 16 pages of instructions. In 2007, there were 199 pages of instructions. Even Albert Einstein supposedly remarked, "The hardest thing in the world to understand is the income tax." It is not surprising that millions of Americans have given up filling out their own income tax forms, or have to rely on software such as Intuit's TurboTax or H&R Block's TaxCut.

The tax laws are complicated because Congress and the president change them repeatedly to achieve economic and social policy goals. As we will see, some changes in tax law are the result of discretionary fiscal policy and are intended to achieve macroeconomic goals of high employment, economic growth, and price stability. Other changes in tax law are intended to achieve goals such as energy conservation.

AN INSIDE LOOK AT POLICY on **page 538** describes the debate in Congress over the alternative minimum tax (AMT).

Source: Tom Herman, "Don't Cheat (Yourself) on Taxes," *Wall Street Journal*, March 21, 2007, p. D1.

LEARNING Objectives

After studying this chapter, you should be able to:

15.1 Define **fiscal policy**, page 510.

15.2 Explain how **fiscal policy** affects **aggregate demand** and how the government can use fiscal policy to stabilize the economy, page 514.

15.3 Explain how the **government purchases** and **tax multipliers** work, page 518.

15.4 Discuss the **difficulties** that can arise in **implementing fiscal policy**, page 523.

15.5 Define federal **budget deficit** and **federal government debt** and explain how the federal budget can serve as an **automatic stabilizer**, page 527.

15.6 Discuss the effects of **fiscal policy** in the **long run**, page 532.

APPENDIX Apply the **multiplier formula**, page 546.

Economics in YOUR Life!

What Would You Do with $500?

Suppose that the federal government announces that it will immediately mail you, and everyone else in the economy, a $500 tax rebate. In addition, you expect that in future years, your taxes will also be $500 less than they would otherwise have been. How will you respond to this increase in your disposable income? What effect will this tax rebate likely have on equilibrium real GDP in the short run? As you read the chapter, see if you can answer these questions. You can check your answers against those we provide at the end of the chapter. >> **Continued on page 537**

In Chapter 14, we discussed how the Federal Reserve uses monetary policy to pursue macroeconomic policy goals, including price stability and high employment. In this chapter, we will explore how the government uses *fiscal policy*, which involves changes in taxes and government purchases, to achieve similar policy goals. As we have seen, in the short run, the price level and the levels of real GDP and total employment in the economy depend on aggregate demand and short-run aggregate supply. The government can affect the levels of both aggregate demand and aggregate supply through fiscal policy. We will explore how Congress and the president decide which fiscal policy actions to take to achieve their goals. We will also discuss the disagreements among economists and policymakers over the effectiveness of fiscal policy.

15.1 LEARNING OBJECTIVE

15.1 | Define fiscal policy.

Fiscal Policy

Since the end of World War II, the federal government has been committed under the Employment Act of 1946 to intervening in the economy "to promote maximum employment, production, and purchasing power." As we saw in Chapter 14, the Federal Reserve closely monitors the economy, and the Federal Open Market Committee meets eight times per year to decide whether to change monetary policy. Less frequently, Congress and the president also make changes in taxes and government purchases to achieve macroeconomic policy objectives, such as high employment, price stability, and high rates of economic growth. Changes in federal taxes and spending that are intended to achieve macroeconomic policy objectives are called **fiscal policy**.

Fiscal policy Changes in federal taxes and purchases that are intended to achieve macroeconomic policy objectives, such as high employment, price stability, and high rates of economic growth.

What Fiscal Policy Is and What It Isn't

In the United States, the federal, state, and local governments all have responsibility for taxing and spending. Economists restrict the term *fiscal policy* to refer only to the actions of the federal government. State and local governments sometimes change their taxing and spending policies to aid their local economies, but these are not fiscal policy actions because they are not intended to affect the national economy. The federal government makes many decisions about taxes and spending, but not all of these decisions are fiscal policy actions because they are not intended to achieve macroeconomic policy goals. For example, a decision to cut the taxes of people who buy hybrid cars is an environmental policy action, not a fiscal policy action. Similarly, the defense and homeland security spending increases in the years after 2001 to fund the war on terrorism and the wars in Iraq and Afghanistan were part of defense and homeland security policy, not fiscal policy.

Automatic Stabilizers versus Discretionary Fiscal Policy

There is an important distinction between *automatic stabilizers* and *discretionary fiscal policy*. Some types of government spending and taxes, which automatically increase and decrease along with the business cycle, are referred to as **automatic stabilizers**. The word *automatic* in this case refers to the fact that changes in these types of spending and taxes happen without actions by the government. For example, when the economy is expanding and employment is increasing, government spending on unemployment insurance payments to workers who have lost their jobs will automatically decrease. During a recession, as employment declines, this type of spending will automatically increase. Similarly, when the economy is expanding and incomes are rising, the amount the government collects in taxes will increase as people pay additional taxes on their higher incomes. When the economy is in recession, the amount the government collects in taxes will fall.

Automatic stabilizers Government spending and taxes that automatically increase or decrease along with the business cycle.

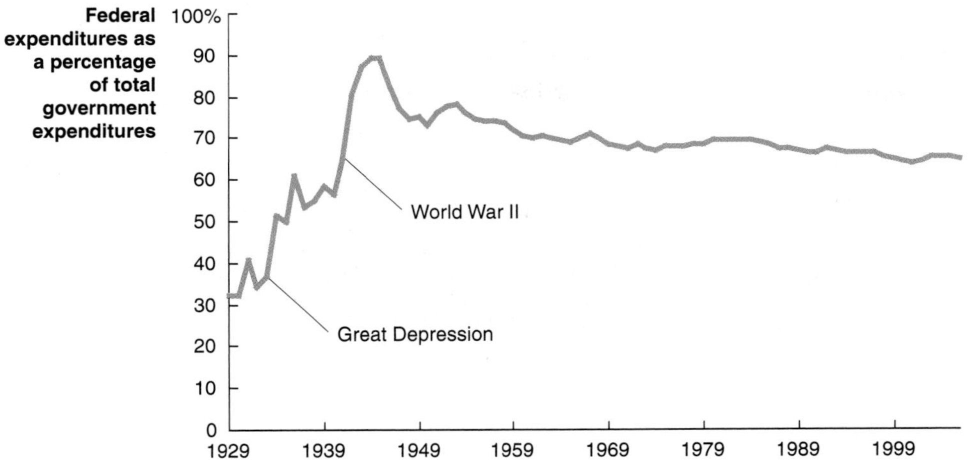

Figure 15-1

The Federal Government's Share of Total Government Expenditures, 1929–2006

Until the Great Depression of the 1930s, the majority of government spending in the United States occurred at the state and local levels. Since World War II, the federal government's share of total government expenditures has been between two-thirds and three-quarters.

Source: Bureau of Economic Analysis.

With discretionary fiscal policy, the government is taking actions to change spending or taxes. The tax cuts Congress passed in 2001 are an example of a discretionary fiscal policy action.

An Overview of Government Spending and Taxes

To provide a context for understanding fiscal policy, it is important to understand the big picture of government taxing and spending. Before the Great Depression of the 1930s, the majority of government spending took place at the state and local levels. As Figure 15-1 shows, the size of the federal government expanded significantly during the crisis of the Great Depression. Since World War II, the federal government's share of total government expenditures has been between two-thirds and three-quarters.

Economists often measure government spending relative to GDP. Remember that there is a difference between federal government *purchases* and federal government *expenditures*. When the federal government purchases an aircraft carrier or the services of a Federal Bureau of Investigation (FBI) agent, it receives a good or service in return. Federal government expenditures include purchases plus all other federal government spending. As Figure 15-2 shows, federal government *purchases* as a percentage of GDP have actually been falling since the end of the Korean War in the early 1950s. Total federal *expenditures* as a percentage of GDP rose from 1950 to the early 1990s and fell from 1992 to 2001, before rising again. The decline in expenditures between 1992 and 2001 was partly the result of the end of the Cold War between the Soviet Union and the United States, which allowed for a substantial reduction in defense spending. Real federal government spending on national defense declined from \$479 billion in 1990 to \$365 billion in 1998, before rising again to \$493 billion in 2006 in response to the war on terrorism and the wars in Iraq and Afghanistan.

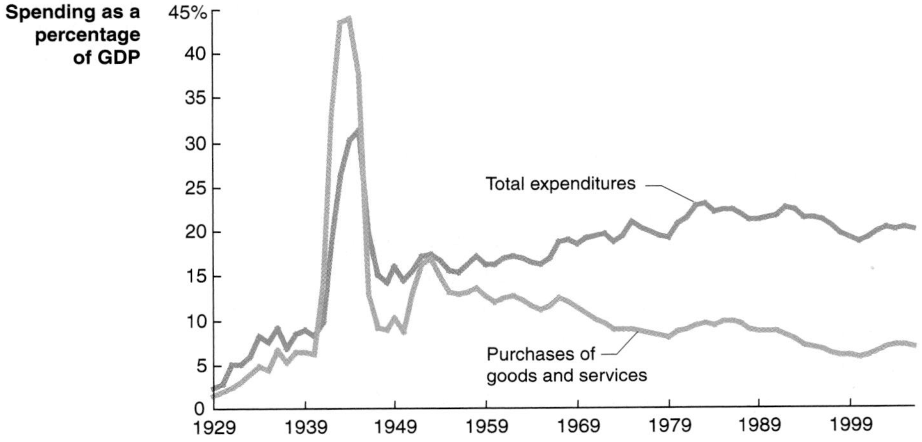

Figure 15-2

Federal Purchases and Federal Expenditures as a Percentage of GDP, 1950–2006

As a fraction of GDP, the federal government's *purchases* of goods and services have been declining since the Korean War in the early 1950s. Total *expenditures* by the federal government—including transfer payments—as a fraction of GDP slowly rose from 1950 through the early 1990s and fell from 1992 to 2001, before rising again.

Source: Bureau of Economic Analysis.

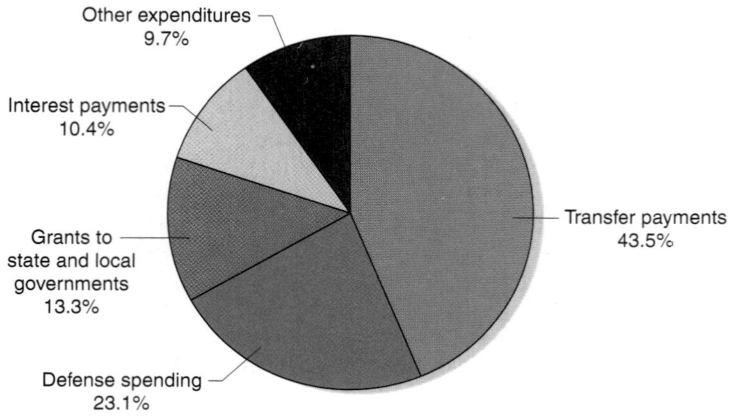

Figure 15-3 | Federal Government Expenditures, 2006

Federal government *purchases* can be divided into defense spending—which makes up about 23 percent of the federal budget—and spending on everything else the federal government does—from paying the salaries of FBI agents, to operating the national parks, to supporting scientific research—which makes up less than 10 percent of the budget. In addition to purchases, there are three other categories of federal government *expenditures*: interest on the national debt, grants to state and local governments, and transfer payments. Transfer payments have risen from about 25 percent of federal government expenditures in the 1960s to about 44 percent in 2006.

Source: Bureau of Economic Analysis.

In addition to purchases, there are three other categories of federal government expenditures: *interest on the national debt*, *grants to state and local governments*, and *transfer payments*. Interest on the national debt represents payments to holders of the bonds the federal government has issued to borrow money. Grants to state and local governments are payments made by the federal government to support government activity at the state and local levels. For example, to help reduce crime, Congress and the Clinton administration implemented a program of grants to local governments to hire more police officers. The largest and fastest-growing category of federal expenditures is transfer payments. Some of these programs, such as Social Security and unemployment insurance, began in the 1930s. Others, such as Medicare, which provides health care to the elderly, or the food stamps and Temporary Assistance for Needy Families programs, which are intended to aid the poor, began in the 1960s or later.

Figure 15-3 shows that in 2006, transfer payments were about 44 percent of federal government expenditures. In the 1960s, transfer payments were only about 25 percent of federal government expenditures. As the U.S. population ages, federal government spending on the Social Security and Medicare programs will continue to increase, causing transfer payments to rise above 50 percent of federal government expenditures by 2010. Figure 15-3 shows that spending on most of the federal government's day-to-day activities—including running federal agencies such as the Environmental Protection Agency, the FBI, the National Park Service, and the Immigration and Naturalization Service—makes up less than 10 percent of federal government expenditures.

Figure 15-4 shows that in 2006, the federal government raised about 42 percent of its revenue from the individual income tax. Payroll taxes to fund the Social Security and Medicare programs raised 36 percent of federal revenues. The tax on corporate profits raised about 15 percent of federal revenues. The remaining 7 percent of federal revenues were raised from sales taxes on certain products, such as cigarettes and gasoline, from tariffs on products imported from other countries, and from other sources, such as payments by companies that cut timber on federal lands.

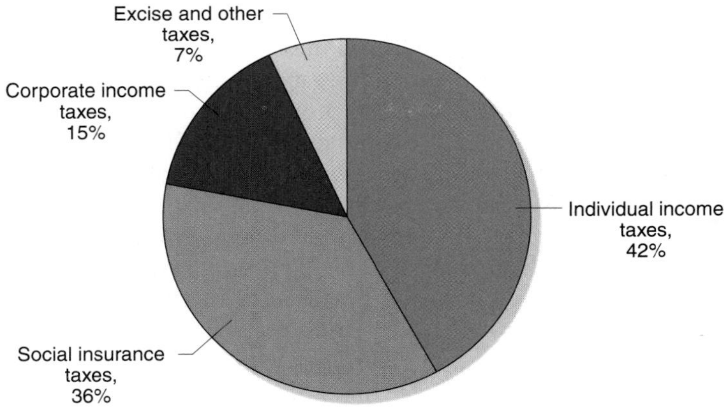

Figure 15-4 | Federal Government Revenue, 2006

In 2006, the individual income tax raised about 42 percent of the federal government's revenues. The corporate income tax raised about 15 percent of revenue. Payroll taxes to fund the Social Security and Medicare programs have risen from less than 10 percent of federal government revenues in 1950 to more than 36 percent in 2006. The remaining 7 percent of revenues were raised from sales taxes, tariffs on imports, and other fees.

Note: The sales and other taxes category includes a small amount of other revenue received by the federal government.

Source: Bureau of Labor Statistics.

Making the Connection | Is Spending on Social Security and Medicare a Fiscal Time Bomb?

Social Security, established in 1935 to provide payments to retired workers, began as a "pay-as-you-go" system, meaning that payments to current retirees were paid from taxes collected from current workers. In the early years of the program, many workers were paying into the system, and there were relatively few retirees. For example, in 1940, more than 35 million workers were paying into the system, and only 222,000 people were receiving benefits—a ratio of more than 150 workers to each beneficiary. In those early years, most retirees received far more in benefits than they had paid in taxes. For example, the first beneficiary was a legal secretary named Ida May Fuller. She worked for three years while the program was in place and paid total taxes of only $24.75. During her retirement, she collected $22,888.92 in benefits.

Will the federal government be able to keep the promises made by the Social Security and Medicare programs?

The Social Security and Medicare programs have been a great success in reducing poverty among elderly Americans, but in recent years, the ability of the federal government to finance current promises has been called into doubt. After World War II, the United States experienced a "baby boom" as birth rates rose and remained high through the early 1960s. Falling birth rates after 1965 have meant long-run problems for the Social Security system, as the number of workers per retiree has continually declined. Currently, there are only about three workers per retiree, and that ratio will probably decline to two workers per retiree in the coming decades. Congress has attempted to deal with this problem by raising the age to receive full benefits from 65 to 67 and by increasing payroll taxes. In 1940, the combined payroll tax paid by workers and firms was 2 percent; in 2007, it was 15.3 percent.

Under the Medicare program, which was established in 1965, the federal government provides health care coverage to people age 65 and over. The long-term financial situation for Medicare is also a cause for concern. As Americans live longer and as new—and expensive—medical procedures are developed, the projected expenditures under the Medicare program will eventually far outstrip projected tax revenues. The federal government also faces increasing expenditures under the Medicaid program, which is administered by state governments and provides health care coverage to low-income people. In 2006, federal spending on Social Security, Medicare, and Medicaid was 8.5 percent of GDP. As the following graph shows, forecasts by the Congressional Budget Office show spending on these three programs rising to 15.2 percent of GDP in 2030 and 19.0 percent of GDP by 2050. In other words, by 2050, the federal government will be spending, as a fraction of GDP, as much on these three programs as it currently does on all programs. Over the coming decades, the gap between the benefits projected to be paid under the Social Security and Medicare programs and projected tax revenues is a staggering $72 *trillion*, or more than five times the value of GDP in 2007. If current projections are accurate, policymakers are faced with the choice of significantly restraining spending on these programs, greatly increasing taxes on households and firms, or implementing some combination of reductions in spending increases and higher taxes. The alternatives will all clearly involve considerable pain. A report from the Congressional Budget Office concluded, "Even if taxation reached levels that were unprecedented in the United States, current spending policies could become financially unsustainable."

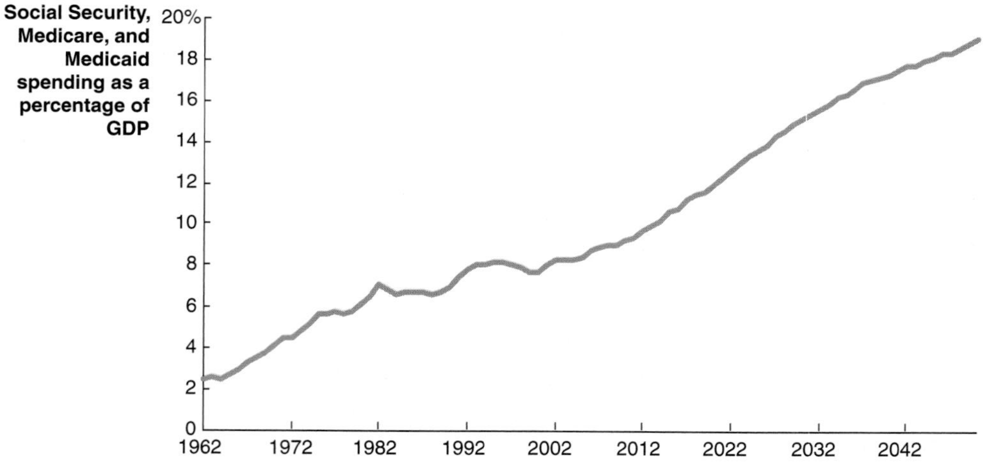

Note: The graph gives the Congressional Budget Office's "intermediate projection" of future spending.

A lively political debate has taken place over the future of the Social Security and Medicare programs. Some policymakers have proposed increasing taxes to fund future benefit payments. The tax increases needed, however, could be as much as 50 percent higher than current rates, and tax increases of that magnitude could discourage work effort, entrepreneurship, and investment, thereby slowing economic growth. There have also been proposals to slow the rate of growth of future benefits, while guaranteeing benefits to current recipients. While this strategy would avoid the need to raise taxes significantly, it would also require younger workers to save more for their retirement. Some economists and policymakers have argued for slower benefit growth for higher-income workers while leaving future benefits unchanged for lower-income workers.

Whatever changes are ultimately made, for young people, the debate over Social Security and Medicare is among the most important policy issues.

Sources: Congressional Budget Office, *The Budget and Economic Outlook: Fiscal Years 2008 to 2017*, January 2007; "The 2005 Annual Report of the Board of Trustees of the Federal Old-Age and Survivors Insurance and Disability Insurance Trust Funds," 109th Congress, 1st Session, House Document 109-18, April 5, 2005; Congressional Budget Office, *The Long-Term Budget Outlook*, December 2005; and the Social Security Administration Web site (www.ssa.gov).

YOUR TURN: Test your understanding by doing related problems 1.6 and 1.7 on page 540 at the end of this chapter.

15.2 LEARNING OBJECTIVE

15.2 | Explain how fiscal policy affects aggregate demand and how the government can use fiscal policy to stabilize the economy.

The Effects of Fiscal Policy on Real GDP and the Price Level

The federal government uses stabilization policy to offset the effects of the business cycle on the economy. We saw in Chapter 14 that the Federal Reserve carries out monetary policy through changes in the money supply and interest rates. Congress and the president carry out fiscal policy through changes in government purchases and taxes. Because changes in government purchases and taxes lead to changes in aggregate demand, they can affect the level of real GDP, employment, and the price level. When the economy is in a recession, *increases* in government purchases or *decreases* in taxes will increase aggregate demand. As we saw in Chapter 12, the inflation rate may increase when real GDP is beyond potential GDP. Decreasing government purchases or raising taxes can slow the growth of aggregate demand and reduce the inflation rate.

Expansionary and Contractionary Fiscal Policy: An Initial Look

Expansionary fiscal policy involves increasing government purchases or decreasing taxes. An increase in government purchases will increase aggregate demand directly because government expenditures are a component of aggregate demand. A cut in taxes has an indirect effect on aggregate demand. Remember from Chapter 7 that the income households have available to spend after they have paid their taxes is called *disposable income.* Cutting the individual income tax will increase household disposable income and consumption spending. Cutting taxes on business income can increase aggregate demand by increasing business investment.

Figure 15-5 shows the results of an expansionary fiscal policy using the basic version of the aggregate demand and aggregate supply model. In this model, there is no economic growth, so the long-run aggregate supply curve does not shift. Notice that this figure is very similar to Figure 14-8 on page 482, which showed the effects of an expansionary monetary policy. The goal of both expansionary monetary policy and expansionary fiscal policy is to increase aggregate demand relative to what it would have been without the policy.

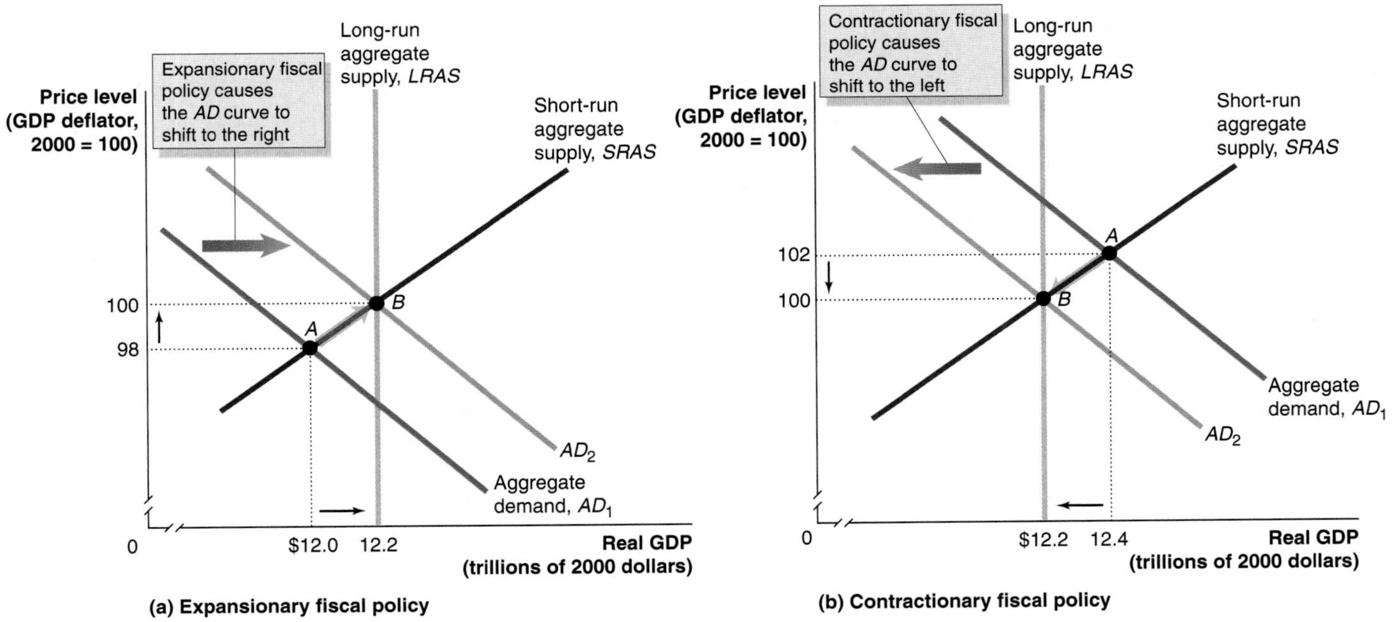

Figure 15-5 | Fiscal Policy

In panel (a), the economy begins in recession at point *A*, with real GDP of $12.0 trillion and a price level of 98. An expansionary fiscal policy will cause aggregate demand to shift to the right, from AD_1 to AD_2, increasing real GDP from $12.0 trillion to $12.2 trillion and the price level from 98 to 100 (point *B*). In panel (b), the economy begins at point *A*, with real GDP at $12.4 trillion and the price level at 102. Because real GDP is greater than potential GDP, the economy will experience rising wages and prices. A contractionary fiscal policy will cause aggregate demand to shift to the left, from AD_1 to AD_2, decreasing real GDP from $12.4 trillion to $12.2 trillion and the price level from 102 to 100 (point *B*).

In panel (a) of Figure 15-5, we assume that the economy is in short-run equilibrium at point *A*, where the aggregate demand curve (AD_1) intersects the short-run aggregate supply curve (*SRAS*). Real GDP is below potential real GDP, so the economy is in recession, with some firms operating below normal capacity and some workers having been laid off. To bring real GDP back to potential GDP, Congress and the president increase government purchases or cut taxes, which will shift the aggregate demand curve to the right, from AD_1 to AD_2. Real GDP increases from $12.0 trillion to potential GDP of $12.2 trillion, and the price level rises from 98 to 100 (point *B*). The policy has successfully returned real GDP to its potential level. Rising production will lead to increasing employment, reducing the unemployment rate.

Contractionary fiscal policy involves decreasing government purchases or increasing taxes. Policymakers use contractionary fiscal policy to reduce increases in aggregate demand that seem likely to lead to inflation. In panel (b) of Figure 15-5, the economy is in short-run equilibrium at point *A*, with real GDP of $12.4 trillion, which is above potential real GDP of $12.2 trillion. With some firms producing beyond their normal capacity and the unemployment rate very low, wages and prices will be increasing. To bring real GDP back to potential GDP, Congress and the president decrease government purchases or increase taxes, which will shift the aggregate demand curve from AD_1 to AD_2. Real GDP falls from $12.4 trillion to $12.2 trillion, and the price level falls from 102 to 100 (point *B*).

We can conclude that Congress and the president can attempt to stabilize the economy by using fiscal policy to affect the price level and the level of real GDP.

Using Fiscal Policy to Influence Aggregate Demand: A More Complete Account

In this section, we use the *dynamic model of aggregate demand and aggregate supply* to gain a more complete understanding of fiscal policy. To briefly review the dynamic model, recall that over time, potential real GDP increases, which we show by the long-run aggregate supply curve shifting to the right. The factors that cause the *LRAS* curve to shift also cause firms to supply more goods and services at any given price level in the short run, which we show by the short-run aggregate supply curve shifting to the right. Finally, during most years, the aggregate demand curve will also shift to the right, indicating that aggregate expenditure will be higher at every price level.

Figure 15-6 shows the results of an expansionary fiscal policy using the dynamic aggregate demand and aggregate supply model. Notice that this figure is very similar to Figure 14-10 on page 489, which showed the effects of an expansionary monetary policy. The goal of both expansionary monetary policy and expansionary fiscal policy is to increase aggregate demand relative to what it would have been without the policy.

In the hypothetical situation shown in Figure 15-6, the economy begins in equilibrium at potential real GDP of $12.0 trillion and a price level of 100 (point *A*). In the second year, *LRAS* increases to $12.4 trillion, but *AD* increases only to $AD_{2(\text{without policy})}$, which is not enough to keep the economy in macroeconomic equilibrium at potential GDP. Let's assume that the Fed does not react to the situation with an expansionary monetary policy. In that case, without an expansionary fiscal policy of spending increases or tax reductions, the short-run equilibrium will occur at $12.3 trillion (point *B*). The $100 billion gap between this level of real GDP and the potential level means that some firms are operating at less than their full capacity. Incomes and profits will be falling, firms will begin to lay off workers, and the unemployment rate will rise.

Increasing government purchases or cutting taxes can shift aggregate demand to $AD_{2(\text{with policy})}$. The economy will be in equilibrium at point *C*, with real GDP of $12.4 trillion, which is its potential level, and a price level of 103. The price level is higher than it would have been if expansionary fiscal policy had not been used.

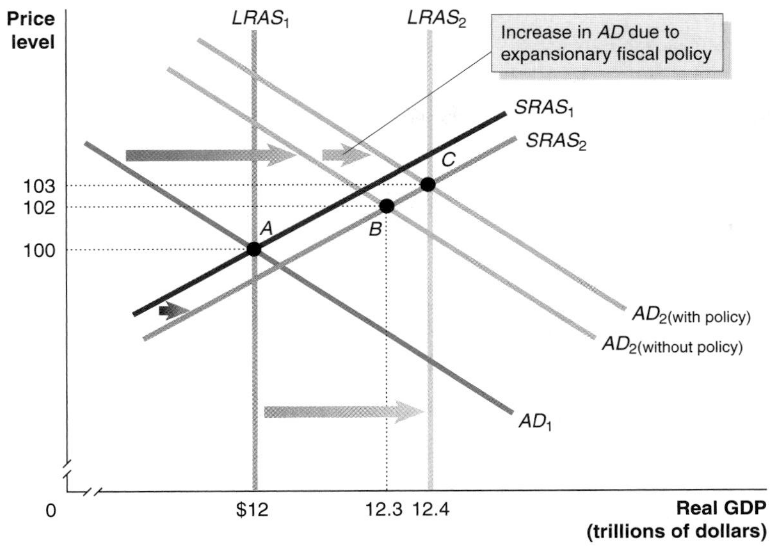

Figure 15-6

An Expansionary Fiscal Policy

The economy begins in equilibrium at point *A*, at potential real GDP of $12.0 trillion and a price level of 100. Without an expansionary policy, aggregate demand will shift from AD_1 to $AD_{2(\text{without policy})}$, which is not enough to keep the economy at potential GDP because long-run aggregate supply has shifted from $LRAS_1$ to $LRAS_2$. The economy will be in short-run equilibrium at point *B*, with real GDP of $12.3 trillion and a price level of 102. Increasing government purchases or cutting taxes will shift aggregate demand to $AD_{2(\text{with policy})}$. The economy will be in equilibrium at point *C*, with real GDP of $12.4 trillion, which is its potential level, and a price level of 103. The price level is higher than it would have been if expansionary fiscal policy had not been used.

Contractionary fiscal policy involves decreasing government purchases or increasing taxes. Policymakers use contractionary fiscal policy to reduce increases in aggregate demand that seem likely to lead to inflation. In Figure 15-7, the economy again begins at potential real GDP of $12.0 trillion and a price level of 100 (point *A*). Once again, *LRAS* increases to $12.4 trillion in the second year. In this scenario, the shift in aggregate demand to $AD_{2(\text{without policy})}$ results in a short-run macroeconomic equilibrium beyond potential GDP (point *B*). If we assume, once again, that the Fed does not respond to the situation with a contractionary monetary policy, the economy will experience a rising inflation rate. Decreasing government purchases or increasing taxes can keep real GDP from moving beyond its potential level. The result, shown in Figure 15-7, is that in the new equilibrium at point *C*, the inflation rate is 3 percent rather than 5 percent.

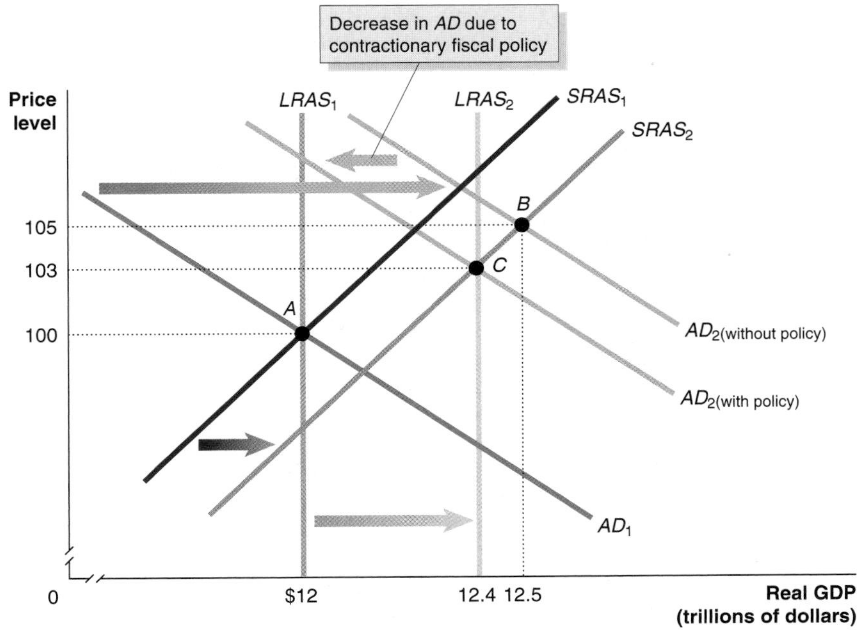

Figure 15-7

A Contractionary Fiscal Policy

The economy begins in equilibrium at point *A*, with real GDP of $12.0 trillion and a price level of 100. Without a contractionary policy, aggregate demand will shift from AD_1 to $AD_{2(\text{without policy})}$, which results in a short-run equilibrium beyond potential GDP at point *B*, with real GDP of $12.5 trillion and a price level of 105. Decreasing government purchases or increasing taxes can shift aggregate demand to $AD_{2(\text{with policy})}$. The economy will be in equilibrium at point *C*, with real GDP of $12.4 trillion, which is its potential level, and a price level of 103. The inflation rate will be 3 percent as opposed to the 5 percent it would have been without the contractionary fiscal policy.

TABLE 15-1

Countercyclical Fiscal Policy

PROBLEM	TYPE OF POLICY	ACTIONS BY CONGRESS AND THE PRESIDENT	RESULT
Recession	Expansionary	Increase government spending or cut taxes	Real GDP and the price level rise.
Rising inflation	Contractionary	Decrease government spending or raise taxes	Real GDP and the price level fall.

A Summary of How Fiscal Policy Affects Aggregate Demand

Table 15-1 summarizes how fiscal policy affects aggregate demand. Just as we did with monetary policy, we must add a very important qualification to this summary of fiscal policy: The table isolates the impact of fiscal policy *by holding constant monetary policy and all other factors affecting the variables involved.* In other words, we are again invoking the *ceteris paribus* condition we discussed in Chapter 3. This point is important because, for example, a contractionary fiscal policy does not cause the price level to fall. A contractionary fiscal policy causes the price level *to rise by less than it would have without the policy,* which is the situation shown in Figure 15-7.

15.3 LEARNING OBJECTIVE

15.3 | Explain how the government purchases and tax multipliers work.

The Government Purchases and Tax Multipliers

Suppose that during a recession, the government decides to use discretionary fiscal policy to increase aggregate demand by spending $100 billion more on constructing subway systems in several cities. How much will equilibrium real GDP increase as a result of this

Don't Let This Happen to **YOU!**

Don't Confuse Fiscal Policy and Monetary Policy

If you keep in mind the definitions of *money, income,* and *spending,* the difference between monetary policy and fiscal policy will be clearer. A common mistake is to think of monetary policy as the Fed fighting recessions by increasing the money supply so people will have more money to spend and to think of fiscal policy as Congress and the president fighting recessions by spending more money. In this view, the only difference between fiscal policy and monetary policy would be the source of the money.

To understand what's wrong with the descriptions of fiscal policy and monetary policy just given, first remember that the problem during a recession is not that there is too little *money* —currency plus checking account deposits— but too little *spending.* There may be too little spending for a number of reasons. For example, households may cut back on their spending on cars and houses because they are pessimistic about the future. Firms may cut back their spending because they have lowered their estimates of the future profitability of new machinery and factories. Or the major trading partners of the United States—such as Japan and Canada—may be suffering from recessions, which cause households and firms in those countries to cut back their spending on U.S. products.

The purpose of expansionary monetary policy is to lower interest rates, which in turn increases aggregate demand. When interest rates fall, households and firms are willing to borrow more to buy cars, houses, and factories. The purpose of expansionary fiscal policy is to increase aggregate demand either by having the government directly increase its own purchases or by cutting taxes to increase household disposable income and, therefore, consumption spending.

Just as increasing or decreasing the money supply does not have any direct effect on government spending or taxes, increasing or decreasing government spending or taxes will not have any direct effect on the money supply. Fiscal policy and monetary policy have the same goals, but they have different effects on the economy.

YOUR TURN: Test your understanding by doing related problem 2.5 on page 541 at the end of this chapter.

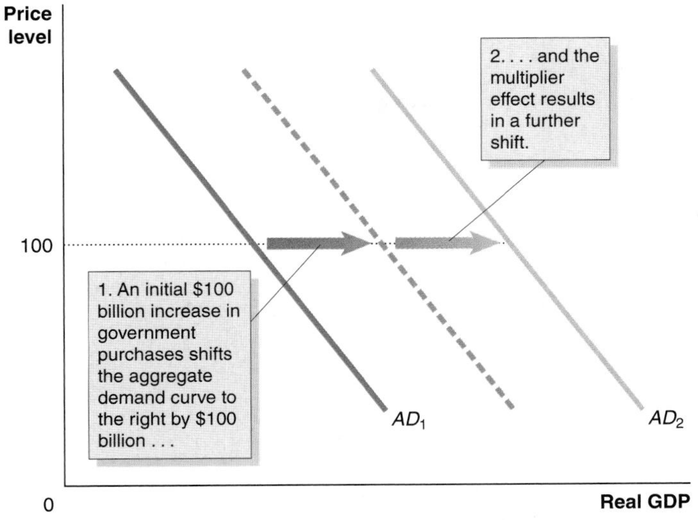

Figure 15-8

The Multiplier Effect and Aggregate Demand

An initial increase in government purchases of $100 billion causes the aggregate demand curve to shift to the right from AD_1 to the dotted *AD* curve and represents the impact of the initial increase of $100 billion in government purchases. Because this initial increase raises incomes and leads to further increases in consumption spending, the aggregate demand curve will ultimately shift further to the right, to AD_2.

increase in government purchases? We know that the answer is greater than $100 billion because we know the initial increase in aggregate demand will lead to additional increases in income and spending. To build the subways, the government hires private construction firms. These firms will hire more workers to carry out the new construction projects. Newly hired workers will increase their spending on cars, furniture, appliances, and other products. Sellers of these products will increase their production and hire more workers, and so on. At each step, real GDP and income will rise, thereby increasing consumption spending and aggregate demand.

Economists refer to the initial increase in government purchases as *autonomous* because it does not depend on the level of real GDP. The increases in consumption spending that result from the initial autonomous increase in government purchases are *induced* because they are caused by the initial increase in autonomous spending. Economists refer to the series of induced increases in consumption spending that result from an initial increase in autonomous expenditures as the **multiplier effect.**

Multiplier effect The series of induced increases in consumption spending that results from an initial increase in autonomous expenditures.

Figure 15-8 illustrates how an increase in government purchases affects the aggregate demand curve. The initial increase in government purchases causes the aggregate demand to shift to the right because total spending in the economy is now higher at every price level. The shift to the right from AD_1 to the dotted *AD* curve represents the impact of the initial increase of $100 billion in government purchases. Because this initial increase in government purchases raises incomes and leads to further increases in consumption spending, the aggregate demand curve will ultimately shift from AD_1 all the way to AD_2.

To understand the multiplier effect, let's start with a simplified analysis in which we assume that the price level is constant. In other words, initially we will ignore the effect of an upward-sloping *SRAS*. Figure 15-9 shows how spending and real GDP increase over a number of periods, beginning with the initial increase in government purchases in the first period, holding the price level constant. The initial spending in the first period raises real GDP and total income in the economy by $100 billion. How much additional consumption spending will result from $100 billion in additional income? We know that in addition to increasing their consumption spending on domestically produced goods, households will save some of the increase in income, use some to pay income taxes, and use some to purchase imported goods, which will have no direct effect on spending and production in the U.S. economy. In Figure 15-9, we assume that in the second period, households increase their consumption spending by one-half of the increase in income from the first period—or by $50 billion. This spending in the second period will, in turn, increase real GDP and income by an additional $50 billion. In the third period, consumption spending will increase by $25 billion, or one-half of the $50 billion increase in income from the second period.

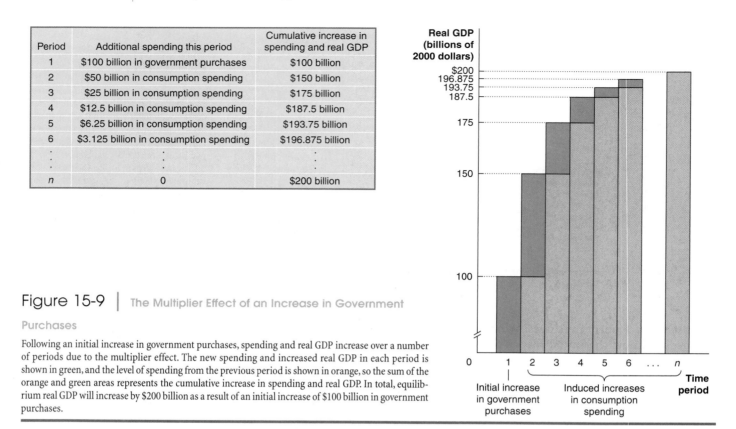

Period	Additional spending this period	Cumulative increase in spending and real GDP
1	$100 billion in government purchases	$100 billion
2	$50 billion in consumption spending	$150 billion
3	$25 billion in consumption spending	$175 billion
4	$12.5 billion in consumption spending	$187.5 billion
5	$6.25 billion in consumption spending	$193.75 billion
6	$3.125 billion in consumption spending	$196.875 billion
⋮	⋮	⋮
n	0	$200 billion

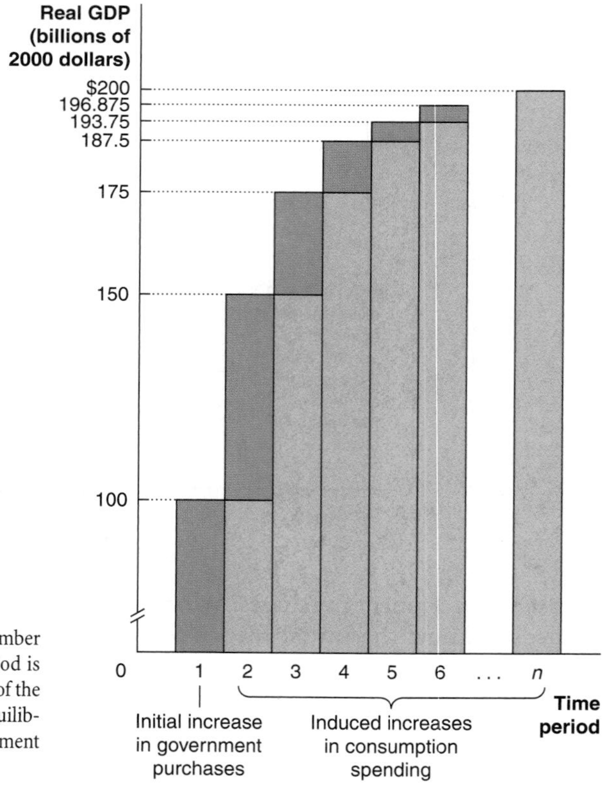

Figure 15-9 | The Multiplier Effect of an Increase in Government Purchases

Following an initial increase in government purchases, spending and real GDP increase over a number of periods due to the multiplier effect. The new spending and increased real GDP in each period is shown in green, and the level of spending from the previous period is shown in orange, so the sum of the orange and green areas represents the cumulative increase in spending and real GDP. In total, equilibrium real GDP will increase by $200 billion as a result of an initial increase of $100 billion in government purchases.

The multiplier effect will continue through a number of periods, with the additional consumption spending in each period being half of the income increase from the previous period. Eventually, the process will be complete, although we cannot say precisely how many periods it will take, so we simply label the final period *n* rather than give it a specific number. In the graph in Figure 15-9, the new spending and increased real GDP in each period is shown in green, and the level of spending from the previous period is shown in orange, so the sum of the orange and green areas represents the cumulative increase in spending and real GDP.

How large will the total increase in equilibrium real GDP be as a result of the initial increase of $100 billion in government purchases? The ratio of the change in equilibrium real GDP to the initial change in government purchases is known as the *government purchases multiplier*:

$$\text{Government purchases multiplier} = \frac{\text{Change in equilibrium real GDP}}{\text{Change in government purchases}}.$$

Economists have estimated that the government purchases multiplier has a value of about 2. Therefore, an increase in government purchases of $100 billion should increase equilibrium real GDP by $2 \times \$100$ billion = $200 billion. We show this in Figure 15-9 by having the cumulative increase in real GDP equal $200 billion.

Tax cuts also have a multiplier effect. Cutting taxes increases the disposable income of households. When household disposable income rises, so will consumption spending. These increases in consumption spending will set off further increases in real GDP and income, just as increases in government purchases do. Suppose we consider a change in taxes of a specific amount—say, a tax cut of $100 billion—with the tax *rate* remaining unchanged. The expression for this tax multiplier is:

$$\text{Tax multiplier} = \frac{\text{Change in equilibrium real GDP}}{\text{Change in taxes}}.$$

The tax multiplier is a negative number because changes in taxes and changes in real GDP move in opposite directions: An increase in taxes reduces disposable income, consumption, and real GDP, and a decrease in taxes raises disposable income, consumption, and real GDP. For example, if the tax multiplier is −1.6, a $100 billion *cut* in taxes will increase real GDP by −1.6 × −$100 billion = $160 billion. We would expect the tax multiplier to be smaller in absolute value than the government purchases multiplier. To see why, think about the difference between a $100 billion increase in government purchases and a $100 billion decrease in taxes. The whole of the $100 billion in government purchases results in an increase in aggregate demand. But households will save rather than spend some portion of a $100 billion decrease in taxes, and spend some portion on imported goods. The fraction of the tax cut that households save or spend on imports will not increase aggregate demand. Therefore, the first period of the multiplier process will see a smaller increase in aggregate demand than occurs when there is an increase in government purchases, and the total increase in equilibrium real GDP will be smaller.

The Effect of Changes in Tax Rates

A change in tax *rates* has a more complicated effect on equilibrium real GDP than does a tax cut of a fixed amount. To begin with, the value of the tax rate affects the size of the multiplier effect. The higher the tax rate, the smaller the multiplier effect. To see why, think about the size of the additional spending increases that take place in each period following an increase in government purchases. The higher the tax rate, the smaller the amount of any increase in income that households have available to spend, which reduces the size of the multiplier effect. So, a cut in tax rates affects equilibrium real GDP through two channels: (1) A cut in tax rates increases the disposable income of households, which leads them to increase their consumption spending, and (2) a cut in tax rates increases the size of the multiplier effect.

Taking into Account the Effects of Aggregate Supply

To this point, as we discussed the multiplier effect, we assumed that the price level was constant. We know, though, that because the *SRAS* curve is upward sloping, when the *AD* curve shifts to the right, the price level will rise. As a result of the rise in the price level, equilibrium real GDP will not increase by the full amount the multiplier effect indicates. Figure 15-10 illustrates how an upward-sloping *SRAS* curve affects the size

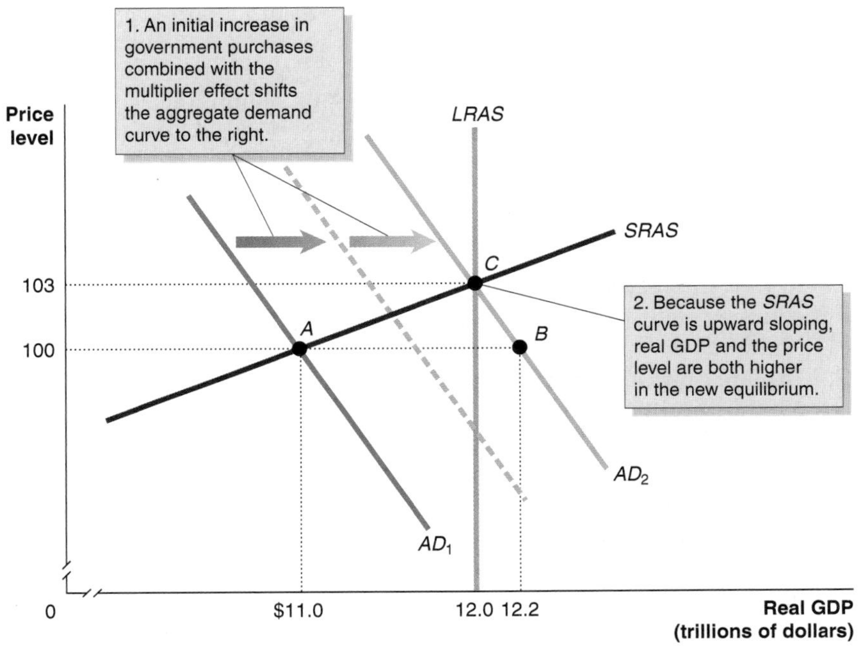

Figure 15-10

The Multiplier Effect and Aggregate Supply

The economy is initially at point *A*. An increase in government purchases causes the aggregate demand to shift to the right, from AD_1 to the dotted *AD* curve. The multiplier effect results in the aggregate demand curve shifting further to the right, to AD_2 (point *B*). Because of the upward-sloping supply curve, the shift in aggregate demand results in a higher price level. In the new equilibrium at point *C*, both real GDP and the price level have increased. The increase in real GDP is less than indicated by the multiplier effect with a constant price level.

of the multiplier. To keep the graph relatively simple, assume that the *SRAS* and *LRAS* curves do not shift. The economy starts at point *A*, with real GDP below its potential level. An increase in government purchases shifts the aggregate demand curve from AD_1 to the dotted *AD* curve. Just as in Figure 15-8, the multiplier effect causes a further shift in aggregate demand to AD_2. If the price level remained constant, real GDP would increase from $11.0 trillion at point *A* to $12.2 trillion at point *B*. However, because the *SRAS* curve is upward sloping, the price level rises from 100 to 103, reducing the total quantity of goods and services demanded in the economy. The new equilibrium occurs at point *C*, with real GDP having risen to $12.0 trillion, or by $200 billion less than if the price level had remained unchanged. We can conclude that the actual change in real GDP resulting from an increase in government purchases or a cut in taxes will be less than indicated by the simple multiplier effect with a constant price level.

The Multipliers Work in Both Directions

Increases in government purchases and cuts in taxes have a positive multiplier effect on equilibrium real GDP. Decreases in government purchases and increases in taxes also have a multiplier effect on equilibrium real GDP, only in this case, the effect is negative. For example, an increase in taxes will reduce household disposable income and consumption spending. As households buy fewer cars, furniture, refrigerators, and other products, the firms that sell these products will cut back on production and begin laying off workers. Falling incomes will lead to further reductions in consumption spending. A reduction in government spending on defense would set off a similar process of decreases in real GDP and income. The cutback would be felt first by defense contractors selling directly to the government, but then it would spread to other firms.

We look more closely at the government purchases multiplier and the tax multiplier in the appendix to this chapter.

Solved Problem | 15-3

Fiscal Policy Multipliers

Briefly explain whether you agree or disagree with the following statement: "Real GDP is currently $12.2 trillion, and potential real GDP is $12.5 trillion. If Congress and the president would increase government purchases by $300 billion or cut taxes by $300 billion, the economy could be brought to equilibrium at potential GDP."

SOLVING THE PROBLEM:

Step 1: Review the chapter material. This problem is about the multiplier process, so you may want to review the section "The Government Purchases and Tax Multipliers," which begins on page 518.

Step 2: Explain how the necessary increase in purchases or cut in taxes is less than $300 billion because of the multiplier effect. The statement is incorrect because it neglects the multiplier effect. Because of the multiplier effect, an increase in government purchases or a decrease in taxes of less than $300 billion is necessary to increase equilibrium real GDP by $300 billion. For instance, assume that the government purchases multiplier is 2 and the tax multiplier is −1.6. We can then calculate the necessary increase in government purchases as follows:

$$\text{Government purchases multiplier} = \frac{\text{Change in equilibrium real GDP}}{\text{Change in government purchases}}$$

$$2 = \frac{\$300 \text{ billion}}{\text{Change in government purchases}}$$

$$\text{Change in government purchases} = \frac{\$300 \text{ billion}}{2} = \$150 \text{ billion.}$$

And the necessary change in taxes:

$$\text{Tax multiplier} = \frac{\text{Change in equilibrium real GDP}}{\text{Change in taxes}}$$

$$-1.6 = \frac{\$300 \text{ billion}}{\text{Change in taxes}}$$

$$\text{Change in taxes} = \frac{\$300 \text{ billion}}{-1.6} = -\$187.5 \text{ billion.}$$

YOUR TURN: For more practice, do related problem 3.5 on page 542 at the end of this chapter.

>> End Solved Problem 15-3

15.4 LEARNING OBJECTIVE

15.4 | Discuss the difficulties that can arise in implementing fiscal policy.

The Limits of Using Fiscal Policy to Stabilize the Economy

Poorly timed fiscal policy, like poorly timed monetary policy, can do more harm than good. As we discussed in Chapter 14, it takes time for policymakers to collect statistics and identify changes in the economy. If the government decides to increase spending or cut taxes to fight a recession that is about to end, the effect may be to increase the inflation rate. Similarly, cutting spending or raising taxes to slow down an economy that has actually already moved into recession can make the recession longer and deeper.

Getting the timing right can be more difficult with fiscal policy than with monetary policy for two main reasons. Control over monetary policy is concentrated in the hands of the Federal Open Market Committee, which can change monetary policy at any of its meetings. By contrast, the president and a majority of the 535 members of Congress have to agree on changes in fiscal policy. The delays caused by the legislative process can be very long. For example, in 1962, President John F. Kennedy concluded that the U.S. economy was operating below potential GDP and proposed a tax cut to stimulate aggregate demand. Congress eventually agreed to the tax cut—but not until 1964.

Once a change in fiscal policy has been approved, it takes time to implement the policy. Suppose Congress and the president agree to increase aggregate demand by spending $30 billion more on constructing subway systems in several cities. It will probably take at least several months to prepare detailed plans for the construction. Local governments will then ask for bids from private construction companies. Once the winning bidders have been selected, they will usually need several months to begin the project. Only then will significant amounts of spending actually take place. This delay may push the spending beyond the end of the recession that the spending was intended to fight.

The events of 2001 showed that it is possible to change fiscal policy in a timely manner. When President George W. Bush came into office in January 2001, he immediately proposed a tax cut. Congress passed the tax cut, and the president signed it into law in early June 2001. As mentioned at the beginning of this chapter, the federal government put the tax cut into effect by mailing checks to taxpayers during summer 2001. This increase in household disposable income helped increase consumption spending and contributed in part to the 2001 recession being short and relatively mild. The 2002 and 2003 tax cuts President Bush proposed were also approved quickly. But Congress and the president use fiscal policy relatively infrequently because they are well aware of the timing problem. The Fed plays a larger role in stabilizing the economy because it can quickly change monetary policy in response to changing economic conditions.

Does Government Spending Reduce Private Spending?

In addition to the timing problem, using increases in government purchases to increase aggregate demand presents another potential problem. We have been assuming that when the federal government increases its purchases by $30 billion, the multiplier effect will cause the increase in aggregate demand to be greater than $30 billion. However, the size of the multiplier effect may be limited if the increase in government purchases causes one of the nongovernment, or private, components of aggregate expenditures—consumption, investment, or net exports—to fall. A decline in private expenditures as a result of an increase in government purchases is called **crowding out**.

Crowding out A decline in private expenditures as a result of an increase in government purchases.

Crowding Out in the Short Run

First, consider the case of a temporary increase in government purchases. Suppose the federal government decides to fight a recession by spending $30 billion more this year on subway construction. When the $30 billion has been spent, the program will end, and government spending will drop back to its previous level. As the spending takes place, income and real GDP will increase. These increases in income and real GDP will cause households and firms to increase their demand for currency and checking account balances to accommodate the increased buying and selling. Figure 15-11 shows the result, using the money market graph introduced in Chapter 14.

Figure 15-11

An Expansionary Fiscal Policy Increases Interest Rates

If the federal government increases spending, the demand for money will increase from Money demand$_1$ to Money demand$_2$ as real GDP and income rise. With the supply of money constant, at $950 billion, the result is an increase in the equilibrium interest rate from 3 percent to 5 percent, which crowds out some consumption, investment, and net exports.

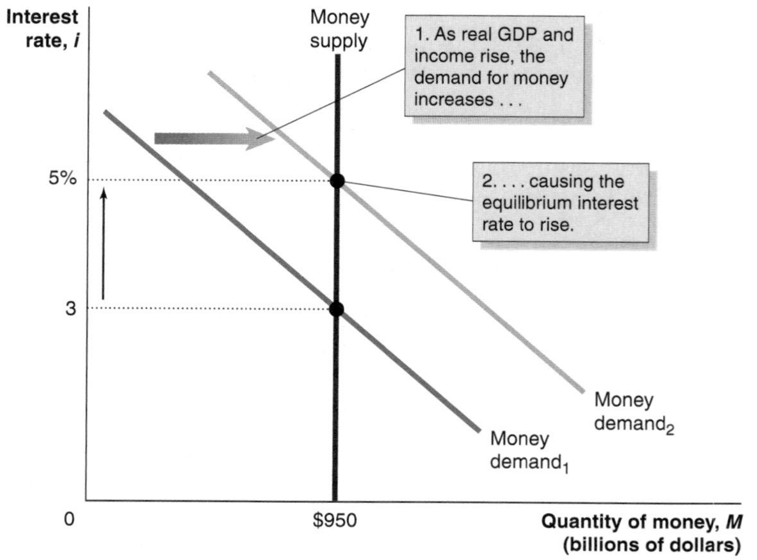

At higher levels of real GDP and income, households and firms demand more money at every level of the interest rate. When the demand for money increases, the equilibrium interest rate will rise. Higher interest rates will result in a decline in each component of private expenditures. Consumption spending and investment spending will decline because households will borrow less to buy cars, furniture, and appliances, and firms will borrow less to buy factories, computers, and machine tools. Net exports will also decline because higher interest rates in the United States will attract foreign investors. German, Japanese, and Canadian investors will want to exchange the currencies of their countries for U.S. dollars to invest in U.S. Treasury bills and other U.S. financial assets. This increased demand for U.S. dollars will cause an increase in the exchange rate between the dollar and other currencies. When the dollar increases in value, the prices of U.S. products in foreign countries rise—causing a reduction in U.S. exports—and the prices of foreign products in the United States fall—causing an increase in U.S. imports. Falling exports and rising imports mean that net exports are falling.

The greater the sensitivity of consumption, investment, and net exports to changes in interest rates, the more crowding out will occur. In a deep recession, many firms may be so pessimistic about the future and have so much excess capacity that investment spending falls to very low levels and is unlikely to fall much further, even if interest rates rise. In this case, crowding out is unlikely to be a problem. If the economy is close to potential GDP, however, and firms are optimistic about the future, then an increase in interest rates may result in a significant decline in investment spending.

Figure 15-12 shows that crowding out may reduce the effectiveness of an expansionary fiscal policy. The economy begins in short-run equilibrium at point *A*, with real GDP at $12.2 trillion. Real GDP is below potential GDP, so the economy is in recession. Suppose that Congress and the president decide to increase government purchases to bring the economy back to potential GDP. In the absence of crowding out, the increase in government purchases would shift aggregate demand to $AD_{2(\text{no crowding out})}$ and bring the economy to equilibrium at real GDP of $12.4 trillion, which is the potential level of GDP (point *B*). But the higher interest rate resulting from the increased government purchases reduces consumption, investment, and net exports, causing aggregate demand to shift back to $AD_{2(\text{crowding out})}$. The result is a new short-run equilibrium at point *C*, with real GDP of $12.3 trillion, which is $100 billion short of potential GDP.

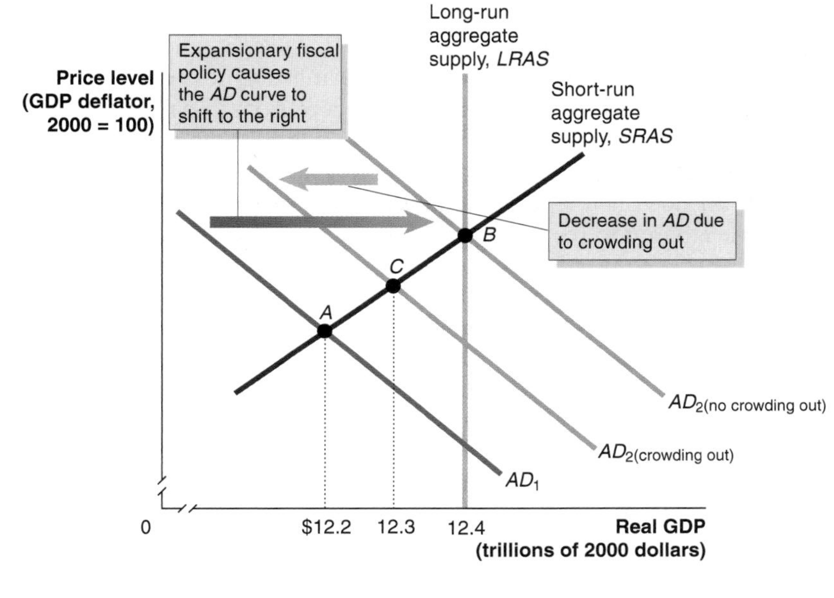

Figure 15-12

The Effect of Crowding Out in the Short Run

The economy begins in a recession with real GDP of $12.2 trillion (point *A*). In the absence of crowding out, an increase in government purchases would shift aggregate demand to $AD_{2(\text{no crowding out})}$ and bring the economy to equilibrium at potential real GDP of $12.4 trillion (point *B*). But the higher interest rate resulting from the increased government purchases reduces consumption, investment, and net exports, causing aggregate demand to shift to $AD_{2(\text{crowding out})}$. The result is a new short-run equilibrium at point *C*, with real GDP of $12.3 trillion, which is $100 billion short of potential real GDP.

Crowding Out in the Long Run

Most economists agree that in the short run, an increase in government spending results in partial, but not complete, crowding out. What is the long-run effect of a *permanent* increase in government spending? In this case, most economists agree that the result is complete crowding out. In the long run, the decline in investment, consumption, and net exports exactly offsets the increase in government purchases, and aggregate demand remains unchanged. To understand crowding out in the long run, recall from Chapter 12 that *in the long run, the economy returns to potential GDP*. Suppose that the economy is currently at potential GDP and that government purchases are 35 percent of GDP. In that case, private expenditures—the sum of consumption, investment, and net exports—will make up the other 65 percent of GDP. If government purchases are increased permanently to 37 percent of GDP, in the long run, private expenditures must fall to 63 percent of GDP. There has been complete crowding out: Private expenditures have fallen by the same amount that government purchases have increased. If government spending is taking a larger share of GDP, then private spending must take a smaller share.

An expansionary fiscal policy does not have to cause complete crowding out in the short run. If the economy is below potential real GDP, it is possible for both government purchases and private expenditures to increase. But in the long run, any permanent increase in government purchases must come at the expense of private expenditures. Keep in mind, however, that it may take several—possibly many—years to arrive at this long-run outcome.

Recent research shows that, surprisingly, the health of people who are temporarily unemployed may improve.

Making the Connection | Is Losing Your Job Good for Your Health?

Recessions cause lost output and cyclical unemployment, which reduce welfare. It makes sense, then, that monetary and fiscal policies that shorten recessions would increase welfare. Someone experiencing cyclical unemployment will clearly experience declining income. Will the unemployed also suffer from declining health? For many years, most economists believed that they would. If this belief were correct, effective macroeconomic policies would improve welfare by both raising the incomes and improving the health of people who might otherwise be cyclically unemployed.

Recently, however, Christopher Ruhm, an economist at the University of North Carolina, Greensboro, has found substantial evidence that during recessions, the unemployed may on average experience improving health. Ruhm analyzed data gathered by the federal Centers for Disease Control. He found that during recessions, people tend to smoke less, drink less alcohol, eat a healthier diet, lose weight, and exercise more. As a result, death rates and sickness rates decline during business cycle recessions and increase during business cycle expansions. Why do recessions apparently have a positive impact on health? The reasons are not completely clear, but Ruhm offers several possibilities. The unemployed may have more time available to exercise, prepare healthy meals, and visit the doctor. Temporary joblessness also may reduce the workplace stress that some people attempt to relieve by smoking and drinking alcohol. In addition, during a recession, traffic congestion and air pollution decline, which may reduce deaths from coronary heart disease. In fact, Ruhm estimates that during business cycle expansions, a one percent decline in the unemployment rate is associated with an additional 3,900 deaths from heart disease.

Ruhm has found that health problems, such as cancer, that tend to develop over many years, are not affected by the business cycle. In addition, unlike physical health, mental health apparently does decline during recessions and improve during expansions. It is important to understand that Ruhm's research is analyzing the effects on health of temporary fluctuations in output and employment during the business cycle.

Over the long-run, economic research has shown that rising incomes result in better health.

The results of the new research on health and the business cycle do not mean that the federal government should abandon using monetary and fiscal policy to stabilize the economy. Although the physical health of the unemployed may, on average, increase during recessions, their incomes and their mental health may decline. No one doubts that losing your job can be a heavy blow, as the rising suicide rate during recessions shows. So, most economists would still agree that a successful policy that reduced the severity of the business cycle would improve average well-being in the economy.

Sources: Christopher J. Ruhm, "A Healthy Economy Can Break Your Heart," forthcoming, *Demography*, 2007; Christopher J. Ruhm, "Healthy Living in Hard Times," *Journal of Health Economics*, Vol. 24, No. 2, March 2005, pp. 341–363; and Christopher J. Ruhm, "Are Recessions Good for Your Health?" *Quarterly Journal of Economics*, Vol. 115, No. 2, May 2000, pp. 617–650.

YOUR TURN: Test your understanding by doing related problem 4.7 on page 543 at the end of this chapter.

15.5 LEARNING OBJECTIVE

15.5 | Define federal budget deficit and federal government debt and explain how the federal budget can serve as an automatic stabilizer.

Deficits, Surpluses, and Federal Government Debt

The federal government's budget shows the relationship between its expenditures and its tax revenue. If the federal government's expenditures are greater than its revenue, a **budget deficit** results. If the federal government's expenditures are less than its tax revenue, a **budget surplus** results. As with many other macroeconomic variables, it is useful to consider the size of the surplus or deficit relative to the size of the overall economy. Figure 15-13 shows that, as a percentage of GDP, the largest deficits of the twentieth century came during World Wars I and II. During major wars, higher taxes only partially offset massive increases in government expenditures, leaving large

Budget deficit The situation in which the government's expenditures are greater than its tax revenue.

Budget surplus The situation in which the government's expenditures are less than its tax revenue.

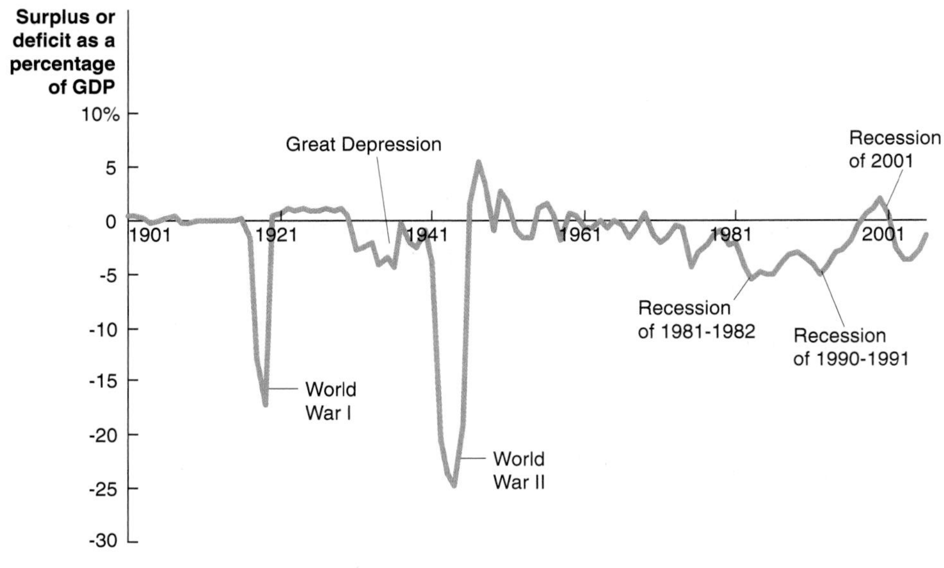

Figure 15-13

The Federal Budget Deficit, 1901–2006

During wars, government spending increases far more than tax revenues, increasing the budget deficit. The budget deficit also increases during recessions, as government spending increases and tax revenues fall.

Sources: *Budget of the United States Government, Fiscal Year 2003, Historical Tables*, Washington, DC: U.S. Government Printing Office, 2002; and Bureau of Economic Analysis.

budget deficits. Figure 15-13 also shows large deficits during recessions. During recessions, government spending increases and tax revenues fall, increasing the budget deficit. In 1970, the federal government entered into a long period of continuous budget deficits. From 1970 through 1997, the federal government's budget was in deficit every year. From 1998 through 2001, there were four years of budget surpluses. The recession of 2001, tax cuts, and increased government spending on homeland security and the wars in Iraq and Afghanistan helped keep the budget in deficit in the years after 2001.

How the Federal Budget Can Serve as an Automatic Stabilizer

The federal budget deficit sometimes increases during recessions because of discretionary fiscal policy actions. Discretionary increases in spending or cuts in taxes to increase aggregate demand during a recession will increase the budget deficit. For example, the decision to cut taxes during 2001 reduced federal revenues, holding constant other factors that affect the budget. As we saw earlier, in many recessions no significant fiscal policy actions are taken. In fact, most of the increase in the federal budget deficit during recessions takes place without Congress and the president taking any action because of the effects of the *automatic stabilizers* we briefly mentioned earlier in this chapter.

Deficits occur automatically during recessions for two reasons: First, during a recession, wages and profits fall, causing government tax revenues to fall. Second, the government automatically increases its spending on transfer payments when the economy moves into recession. The government's contribution to the unemployment insurance program will increase as unemployment rises. Spending will also increase on programs to aid poor people, such as the food stamps, Temporary Assistance for Needy Families, and Medicaid programs. These spending increases take place without Congress and the president taking any action. Existing laws already specify who is eligible for unemployment insurance and these other programs. As the number of eligible persons increases during a recession, so does government spending on these programs.

Because budget deficits automatically increase during recessions and decrease during expansions, economists often look at the *cyclically adjusted budget deficit or surplus*, which can provide a more accurate measure of the effects on the economy of the government's spending and tax policies than the actual budget deficit or surplus. The **cyclically adjusted budget deficit or surplus** measures what the deficit or surplus would be if the economy were at potential GDP. An expansionary fiscal policy should result in a cyclically adjusted budget deficit, and a contractionary fiscal policy should result in a cyclically adjusted budget surplus.

Cyclically adjusted budget deficit or surplus The deficit or surplus in the federal government's budget if the economy were at potential GDP.

Automatic budget surpluses and deficits can help to stabilize the economy. When the economy moves into a recession, wages and profits fall, which reduces the taxes that households and firms owe the government. In effect, households and firms have received an automatic tax cut, which keeps their spending higher than it otherwise would have been. In a recession, workers who have been laid off receive unemployment insurance payments, and households whose incomes have dropped below a certain level become eligible for food stamps and other government transfer programs. As a result of receiving this extra income, these households will spend more than they otherwise would have spent. This extra spending helps reduce the length and severity of the recession. Many economists argue that lack of an unemployment insurance system and other government transfer programs contributed to the severity of the Great Depression. During the Great Depression, workers who lost their jobs saw their wage incomes drop to zero and had to rely on their savings, what they could borrow, or what they received from private charities. As a result, many cut back drastically on their spending, which made the downturn worse.

When GDP increases above its potential level, households and firms have to pay more taxes to the federal government, and the federal government makes fewer transfer payments. Higher taxes and lower transfer payments cause total spending to rise by less than it otherwise would have, which helps reduce the chance that the economy will experience higher inflation.

Making the Connection

Did Fiscal Policy Fail during the Great Depression?

Modern macroeconomics began during the 1930s with publication of *The General Theory of Employment, Interest, and Money* by John Maynard Keynes. One conclusion many economists drew from Keynes's book was that an expansionary fiscal policy would be necessary to pull the United States out of the Great Depression. When Franklin D. Roosevelt became president in 1933, federal government expenditures increased, and there was a federal budget deficit each remaining year of the decade, except for 1937. The U.S. economy recovered very slowly, however, and did not reach potential real GDP again until the outbreak of World War II in 1941.

Although government spending increased during the Great Depression, the cyclically adjusted budget was in surplus most years.

Some economists and policymakers at the time argued that because the economy recovered slowly despite increases in government spending, fiscal policy had been ineffective. In separate studies, economists E. Cary Brown of MIT and Larry Peppers of Washington and Lee University argued that, in fact, fiscal policy had not been expansionary during the 1930s. The following table provides the data supporting the arguments of Brown and Peppers (all variables in the table are nominal rather than real). The second column shows federal government expenditures increasing from 1933 to 1936, falling in 1937, and then increasing in 1938 and 1939. The third column shows a similar pattern, with the federal budget being in deficit each year after 1933, with the exception of 1937. The fourth column, though, shows that in each year after 1933, the federal government ran a cyclically adjusted budget *surplus*. Because the level of income was so low and the unemployment rate was so high during these years, tax collections were far below what they would have been if the economy had been at potential GDP. As the fifth column shows, in 1933 and again in the years 1937 to 1939, the cyclically adjusted surpluses were quite large relative to GDP.

YEAR	FEDERAL GOVERNMENT EXPENDITURES (BILLIONS OF DOLLARS)	ACTUAL FEDERAL BUDGET DEFICIT OR SURPLUS (BILLIONS OF DOLLARS)	CYCLICALLY ADJUSTED BUDGET DEFICIT OR SURPLUS (BILLIONS OF DOLLARS)	CYCLICALLY ADJUSTED BUDGET DEFICIT OR SURPLUS AS A PERCENTAGE OF GDP
1929	$2.6	$1.0	$1.24	1.20%
1930	2.7	0.2	0.81	0.89
1931	4.0	–2.1	–0.41	–0.54
1932	3.0	–1.3	0.50	0.85
1933	3.4	–0.9	1.06	1.88
1934	5.5	–2.2	0.09	0.14
1935	5.6	–1.9	0.54	0.74
1936	7.8	–3.2	0.47	0.56
1937	6.4	0.2	2.55	2.77
1938	7.3	–1.3	2.47	2.87
1939	8.4	–2.1	2.00	2.17

Although President Roosevelt did propose many new government spending programs, he had also promised during the 1932 presidential election campaign to balance the federal budget. He achieved a balanced budget only in 1937, but his reluctance to allow the actual budget deficit to grow too large helps explain why the cyclically adjusted budget remained in surplus. Many economists today would agree with E. Cary Brown's conclusion: "Fiscal policy, then, seems to have been an unsuccessful recovery device in the 'thirties—not because it did not work, but because it was not tried."

Sources: E. Cary Brown, "Fiscal Policy in the 'Thirties: A Reappraisal," *American Economic Review*, Vol. 46, No. 5, December 1956, pp. 857–879; Larry Peppers, "Full Employment Surplus Analysis and Structural Changes," *Explorations in Economic History*, Vol. 10, Winter 1973, pp. 197–210; and Bureau of Economic Analysis.

YOUR TURN: Test your understanding by doing related problem 5.9 on page 544 at the end of this chapter.

Solved Problem | **15-5**

The Effect of Economic Fluctuations on the Budget Deficit

The federal government's budget deficit was $207.8 billion in 1983 and $185.4 billion in 1984. A student comments, "The government must have acted during 1984 to raise taxes or cut spending or both." Do you agree? Briefly explain.

SOLVING THE PROBLEM:

Step 1: Review the chapter material. This problem is about the federal budget as an automatic stabilizer, so you may want to review the section "How the Federal Budget Can Serve as an Automatic Stabilizer," which begins on page 528.

Step 2: Explain how changes in the budget deficit can occur without Congress and the president acting. If Congress and the president take action to raise taxes or cut spending, the federal budget deficit will decline. But the deficit will also decline automatically when GDP increases, even if the government takes no action. When GDP increases, rising household incomes and firm profits result in higher tax revenues. Increasing GDP also usually means falling unemployment, which reduces government spending on unemployment insurance and other transfer payments. So, you should disagree with the comment. A falling deficit does not mean that the government *must* have acted to raise taxes or cut spending.

EXTRA CREDIT: Although you don't have to know it to answer the question, GDP did increase from $3.5 trillion in 1983 to $3.9 trillion in 1984.

>> End Solved Problem 15-5

YOUR TURN: For more practice, do related problem 5.6 on page 543 at the end of this chapter.

Should the Federal Budget Always Be Balanced?

Although many economists believe that it is a good idea for the federal government to have a balanced budget when the economy is at potential GDP, few economists believe that the federal government should attempt to balance its budget every year. To see why economists take this view, consider what the government would have to do to keep the budget balanced during a recession, when the federal budget automatically moves into deficit. To bring the budget back into balance, the government would have to raise taxes or cut spending, but these actions would reduce aggregate demand, thereby making the recession worse. Similarly, when GDP increases above its potential level, the budget automatically moves into surplus. To eliminate this surplus, the government would have to cut taxes or increase government spending. But these actions would increase aggregate demand, thereby increasing GDP further beyond potential GDP and raising the risk of higher inflation. To balance the budget every year, the government might have to take actions that would destabilize the economy.

Some economists argue that the federal government should normally run a deficit, even at potential GDP. When the federal budget is in deficit, the U.S. Treasury sells bonds to investors to raise the funds necessary to pay the government's bills. Borrowing to pay the bills is a bad policy for a household, firm, or government when the bills are for current expenses, but it is not a bad policy if the bills are for long-lived capital goods. For instance, most families pay for a new home by taking out a 15- to 30-year mortgage. Because houses last many years, it makes sense to pay for a house out of the income the family makes over a long period of time rather than out of the income received in the year the house is bought. Businesses often borrow the funds to buy machinery, equipment, and factories by selling 30-year corporate bonds. Because these capital goods generate profits for the businesses over many years, it makes sense to pay for them over a period of years as well. By similar reasoning, when the federal government contributes to the building of a new highway, bridge, or subway, it may want to borrow funds by selling Treasury bonds. The alternative is to pay for these long-lived capital goods out of the tax revenues received in the year the goods were purchased. But that means that the taxpayers in that year have to bear the whole burden of paying for the projects, even though taxpayers for many years in the future will be enjoying the benefits.

The Federal Government Debt

Every time the federal government runs a budget deficit, the Treasury must borrow funds from investors by selling Treasury securities. For simplicity, we will refer to all Treasury securities as "bonds." When the federal government runs a budget surplus, the Treasury pays off some existing bonds. Figure 15-13 on page 527 shows that there are many more years of federal budget deficits than years of federal budget surpluses. As a result, the total number of Treasury bonds has grown over the years. The total value of U.S. Treasury bonds outstanding is referred to as the *federal government debt* or, sometimes, as the *national debt.* Each year the federal budget is in deficit, the federal government debt grows. Each year the federal budget is in surplus, the debt shrinks.

Figure 15-14 shows federal government debt as a percentage of GDP over the past 100 years. The ratio of debt to GDP increased during World Wars I and II and the

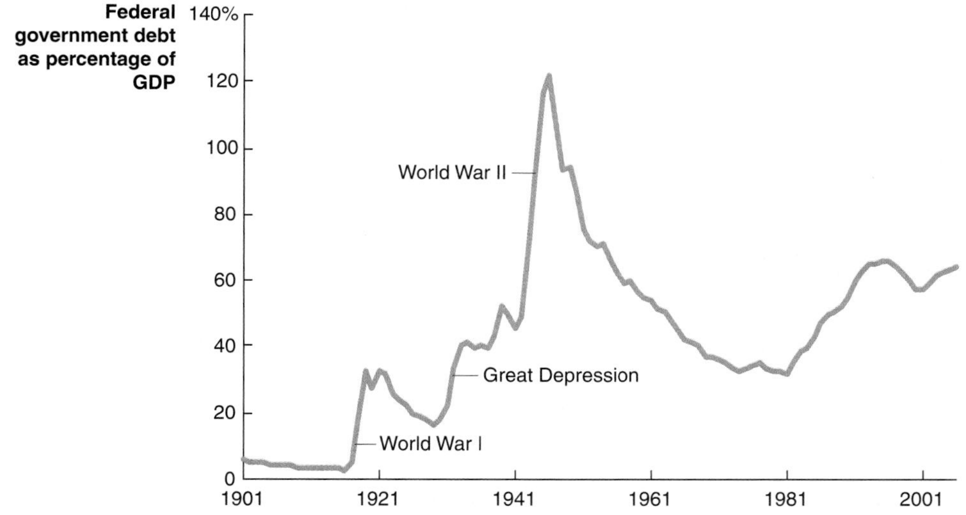

Figure 15-14

The Federal Government Debt, 1901–2006

The federal government debt increases whenever the federal government runs a budget deficit. The large deficits incurred during World Wars I and II, the Great Depression, and the 1980s and early 1990s increased the ratio of debt to GDP.

Sources: U.S. Bureau of the Census, *Historical Statistics of the United States, Colonial Times to 1970*, Washington, DC: U.S. Government Printing Office, 1975; *Budget of the United States Government, Fiscal Year 2003, Historical Tables*, Washington, DC: U.S. Government Printing Office, 2002; and Federal Reserve Bank of St. Louis, *National Economic Trends*, June 2007.

Great Depression, reflecting the large government budget deficits of those years. After the end of World War II, GDP grew faster than the debt until the early 1980s, which caused the ratio of debt to GDP to fall. The large budget deficits of the 1980s and early 1990s sent the debt-to-GDP ratio climbing. The budget surpluses of 1998 to 2001 caused the debt-to-GDP ratio to fall, but it rose again with the return of deficits beginning in 2002.

At the end of June 2007, the federal government debt was $8.9 trillion, but more than half of this debt was actually held by agencies of the federal government, including the Federal Reserve. In effect, the Treasury had borrowed more than half the debt from other agencies of the federal government. It may seem strange that other agencies of the federal government have purchased more than half of the bonds, or debt, issued by the Treasury. This has happened for two reasons. First, as discussed in Chapter 13, the Federal Reserve increases the money supply by buying Treasury bonds. As the economy grows, the Fed provides additional money to households and firms by adding more and more Treasury bonds to its holdings. By the end of June 2007, the Fed had accumulated $791 billion worth of Treasury bonds. Second, the impact of the baby boom on the Social Security and Medicare systems has led the *Social Security and Medicare trust fund* to acquire $3.9 trillion worth of Treasury debt. When the baby boomers retire, the trust fund will sell these bonds to make payments to retirees.

Is Government Debt a Problem?

Debt can be a problem for a government for the same reasons that debt can be a problem for a household or a business. If a family has difficulty making the monthly mortgage payment, it will have to cut back spending on other things. If the family is unable to make the payments, it will have to *default* on the loan and will probably lose their house. The federal government is in no danger of defaulting on its debt. Ultimately, the government can raise the funds it needs through taxes to make the interest payments on the debt. If the debt becomes very large relative to the economy, however, the government may have to raise taxes to high levels or cut back on other types of spending to make the interest payments on the debt. Interest payments are currently about 10 percent of total federal expenditures. At this level, tax increases or significant cutbacks in other types of federal spending are not required.

In the long run, a debt that increases in size relative to GDP can pose a problem. As we discussed previously, crowding out of investment spending may occur if an increasing debt drives up interest rates. Lower investment spending means a lower capital stock in the long run and a reduced capacity of the economy to produce goods and services. This effect is somewhat offset if some of the government debt was incurred to finance improvements in *infrastructure*, such as bridges, highways, and ports; to finance education; or to finance research and development. Improvements in infrastructure, a better-educated labor force, and additional research and development can add to the productive capacity of the economy.

15.6 LEARNING OBJECTIVE

15.6 | Discuss the effects of fiscal policy in the long run.

The Effects of Fiscal Policy in the Long Run

Some fiscal policy actions are intended to meet short-run goals of stabilizing the economy. Other fiscal policy actions are intended to have long-run effects by expanding the productive capacity of the economy and increasing the rate of economic growth. Because these policy actions primarily affect aggregate supply rather than aggregate demand, they are sometimes referred to as *supply-side economics*. Most fiscal policy actions that attempt to increase aggregate supply do so by changing taxes to increase the incentives to work, save, invest, and start a business.

The Long-Run Effects of Tax Policy

Tax wedge The difference between the pretax and posttax return to an economic activity.

The difference between the pretax and posttax return to an economic activity is known as the **tax wedge**. The tax wedge applies to the *marginal tax rate*, which is the fraction of each additional dollar of income that must be paid in taxes. For example, the U.S. federal income tax has several tax brackets, which are the income ranges within which a tax rate applies. In 2007, for a single taxpayer, the tax rate was 10 percent on the first $7,825 earned during a year. The tax rate rose for higher income brackets, until it reached 35 percent on income earned above $349,700. Suppose you are paid a wage of $20 per hour. If your marginal income tax rate is 25 percent, then your after-tax wage is $15, and the tax wedge is $5. When discussing the model of demand and supply in Chapter 3, we saw that increasing the price of a good or service increases the quantity supplied. So, we would expect that reducing the tax wedge by cutting the marginal tax rate on income would result in a larger quantity of labor supplied because the after-tax wage would be higher. Similarly, we saw in Chapter 9 that a reduction in the income tax would increase the after-tax return to saving, causing an increase in the supply of loanable funds, a lower equilibrium interest rate, and an increase in investment spending. In general, economists believe that the smaller the tax wedge for any economic activity—such as working, saving, investing, or starting a business—the more of that economic activity that will occur.

We can look briefly at the effects on aggregate supply of cutting each of the following taxes:

- ***Individual income tax.*** As we have seen, reducing the marginal tax rates on individual income will reduce the tax wedge faced by workers, thereby increasing the quantity of labor supplied. Many small businesses are *sole proprietorships*, whose profits are taxed at the individual income tax rates. Therefore, cutting the individual income tax rates also raises the return to entrepreneurship, encouraging the opening of new businesses. Most households are also taxed on their returns from saving at the individual income tax rates. Reducing marginal income tax rates, therefore, also increases the return to saving.

- ***Corporate income tax.*** The federal government taxes the profits earned by corporations under the corporate income tax. In 2007, most corporations faced a marginal corporate tax rate of 35 percent. Cutting the marginal corporate income tax rate would encourage investment spending by increasing the return corporations receive from new investments in equipment, factories, and office buildings. Because innovations are often embodied in new investment goods, cutting the corporate income tax can potentially increase the pace of technological change.

- ***Taxes on dividends and capital gains.*** Corporations distribute some of their profits to shareholders in the form of payments known as *dividends*. Shareholders also may benefit from higher corporate profits by receiving *capital gains*. A capital gain is the change in the price of an asset, such as a share of stock. Rising profits usually result in rising stock prices and capital gains to shareholders. Individuals pay taxes on both dividends and capital gains (although the tax on capital gains can be postponed if the stock is not sold). As a result, the same earnings are, in effect, taxed twice: once when corporations pay the corporate income tax on their profits and a second time when the profits are received by individual investors in the form of dividends or capital gains. Economists debate the costs and benefits of a separate tax on corporate profits. With the corporate income tax remaining in place, one way to reduce the "double taxation" problem is to reduce the taxes on dividends and capital gains. These taxes were, in fact, reduced in 2003, and currently the marginal tax rates on dividends and capital gains are well below the top marginal tax rate on individual income. Lowering the tax rates on dividends and capital gains increases the supply of loanable funds from household to firms, increasing saving and investment and lowering the equilibrium real interest rate.

Tax Simplification

In addition to the potential gains from cutting individual taxes, there are also gains from tax simplification. As we saw at the beginning of the chapter, the complexity of the tax code has created a whole industry of tax preparation services, such as H&R Block. The tax code is extremely complex and is almost 3,000 pages long. The Internal Revenue Service estimates that taxpayers spend more than 6.4 billion hours each year filling out their tax forms, or about 45 hours per tax return. Households and firms have to deal with more than 480 tax forms to file their federal taxes. It is not surprising that there are more H&R Block offices around the country than Starbucks coffeehouses.

If the tax code were greatly simplified, the economic resources currently used by the tax preparation industry would be available to produce other goods and services. In addition to wasting resources, the complexity of the tax code may also distort the decisions made by households and firms. For example, the tax rate on dividends has clearly affected whether corporations pay dividends. When Congress passed a reduction in the tax on dividends in 2003, many firms—including Microsoft—began paying a dividend for the first time. A simplified tax code would increase economic efficiency by reducing the number of decisions households and firms make solely to reduce their tax payments.

The flat tax would simplify tax preparation.

Making the Connection

Should the United States Adopt the "Flat Tax"?

In thinking about fundamental tax reform, some economists and policymakers have advocated simplifying the individual income tax by adopting a "flat tax." A flat tax would replace the current individual income tax system, with its many tax brackets, exemptions, and deductions, with a new system containing few, or perhaps no, deductions and exemptions and a single tax rate.

The proposal received publicity in the United States during the 2000 presidential election campaign, when candidate Steve Forbes proposed that the tax system be changed so that a family of four would pay no taxes on the first $36,000 of income and be taxed at a flat rate of 17 percent on income above that level. Under Forbes's proposal, corporate profits would also be taxed at a flat rate of 17 percent. The marginal tax rate of 17 percent is well below the top marginal tax rates on individual and corporate income. During the campaign, Forbes declared, "The flat tax would be so simple, you could fill out your tax return on a postcard."

In 1994, Estonia became the first country to adopt a flat tax when it began imposing a single tax rate of 26 percent on individual income. As the table shows, a number of other countries in Eastern Europe have followed Estonia's lead. Although all these countries have a flat tax rate on income, they vary in the amount of annual income they allow to be exempt from the tax and on which income is taxable. For example, Estonia does not tax corporate profits directly, although it does tax dividends paid by corporations to shareholders.

COUNTRY	FLAT TAX RATE	YEAR FLAT TAX WAS INTRODUCED
Estonia	26%	1994
Lithuania	33	1994
Latvia	25	1995
Russia	13	2001
Serbia	14	2003
Ukraine	13	2004
Slovakia	19	2004
Georgia	12	2005
Romania	16	2005

Governments in Eastern Europe are attracted by the simplicity of the flat tax. It is easy for taxpayers to understand and easy for the government to administer. The result has been greater compliance with the tax code. A study of the effects of Russia's moving to a flat tax found that, before tax reform, Russians whose incomes had placed them in the two highest tax brackets had on average been reporting only 52 percent of their income to the government. In 2001, with the new single 13 percent tax bracket in place, these high-income groups on average reported 68 percent of their income to the government.

In the United States and Western Europe, proponents of the flat tax have focused on the reduction in paperwork and compliance cost and the potential increases in labor supply, saving, and investment that would result from a lower marginal tax rate. Opponents of the flat tax believe it has two key weaknesses. First, they point out that many of the provisions that make the current tax code so complex were enacted for good reasons. For example, currently taxpayers are allowed to deduct from their taxable income the interest they pay on mortgage loans. For many people, this provision of the tax code reduces the after-tax cost of owning a home, thereby aiding the government's goal of increasing home ownership. Similarly, the limited deduction for educational expenses increases the ability of many people to further their or their children's educations. The tax deduction of up to $3,150 in 2006 for the purchase of hybrid cars that combine an electric motor with a gasoline-powered engine was intended to further the goal of reducing air pollution and oil consumption. These and other deductions would be eliminated under most flat tax proposals, thereby reducing the ability of the government to pursue some policy goals. Second, opponents of the flat tax believe that it would make the distribution of income more unequal by reducing the marginal tax rate on high-income taxpayers. Because high-income taxpayers now can sometimes use the intricacies of the tax code to shelter some of their income from taxes, it is unclear whether the amount of taxes paid by high-income people actually would decrease under a flat tax.

Sources: "The Case for Flat Taxes," *Economist*, April 14, 2005; and Juan Carlos Conesa and Dirk Krueger, "On the Optimal Progressivity of the Income Tax Code," *Journal of Monetary Economics*, Vol. 53, No. 7, October 2006, pp. 1425–1450.

YOUR TURN: Test your understanding by doing related problem 6.7 on page 545 at the end of this chapter.

The Economic Effect of Tax Reform

We can analyze the economic effects of tax reduction and simplification by using the aggregate demand and aggregate supply model. Figure 15-15 shows that without tax changes, the long-run aggregate supply curve will shift from $LRAS_1$ to $LRAS_2$. This shift

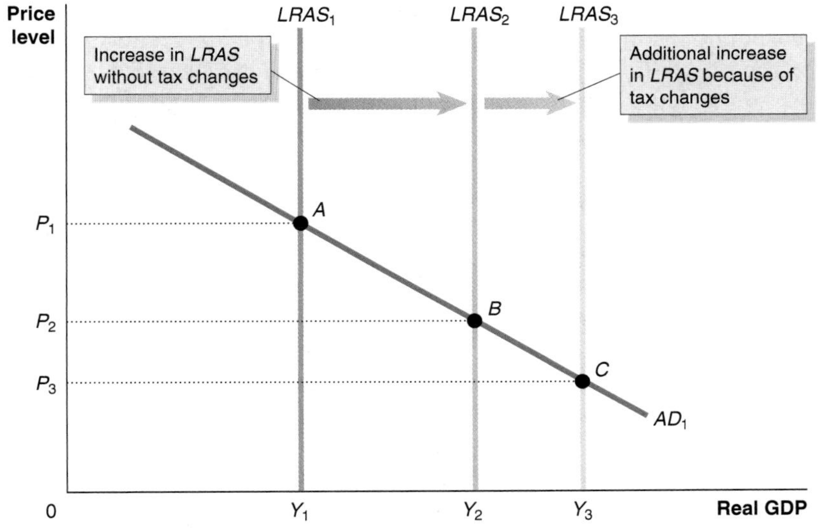

Figure 15-15

The Supply-Side Effects of a Tax Change

The economy's initial equilibrium is at point A. With no tax change, long-run aggregate supply shifts to the right, from $LRAS_1$ to $LRAS_2$. Equilibrium moves to point B, with the price level falling from P_1 to P_2 and real GDP increasing from Y_1 to Y_2. With tax reductions and simplifications, long-run aggregate supply shifts further to the right, to $LRAS_3$, and equilibrium moves to point C, with the price level falling to P_3 and real GDP increasing to Y_3.

represents the increases in the labor force and the capital stock and the technological change that would occur even without tax reduction and simplification. As we know from our discussion of the *AD–AS* model in Chapter 12, during any year, the aggregate demand and short-run aggregate supply curves will also shift. To focus on the impact of tax changes on aggregate supply, we will ignore the short-run aggregate supply curve, and we will assume that the aggregate demand remains unchanged, at AD_1. In this case, equilibrium moves from point *A* to point *B*, with real GDP increasing from Y_1 to Y_2 and the price level decreasing from P_1 to P_2.

If tax reduction and simplification are effective, the economy will experience increases in labor supply, saving, investment, and the formation of new firms. Economic efficiency will also be improved. Together these factors will result in an increase in the quantity of real GDP supplied at every price level. We show the effects of the tax changes in Figure 15-15 by a shift in the long-run aggregate supply curve to $LRAS_3$. With aggregate demand remaining unchanged, the equilibrium in the economy moves from point *A* to point *C* (rather than to point *B*, which is the equilibrium without tax changes), with real GDP increasing from Y_1 to Y_3 and the price level decreasing from P_1 to P_3. An important point to notice is that compared with the equilibrium without tax changes (point *B*), the equilibrium with tax changes (point *C*) occurs at a lower price level and a higher level of real GDP. We can conclude that the tax changes have benefited the economy by increasing output and employment while at the same time reducing the price level.

Clearly, our analysis is unrealistic because we have ignored the changes in aggregate demand and short-run aggregate supply that will actually occur. How would a more realistic analysis differ from the simplified one in Figure 15-15? The change in real GDP would be the same because in the long run, real GDP is equal to its potential level, which is represented by the long-run aggregate supply curve. The results for the price level would be different, however, because we would expect both aggregate demand and short-run aggregate supply to shift to the right. The likeliest case is that the price level would end up higher in the new equilibrium than in the original equilibrium. However, because the position of the long-run aggregate supply curve is further to the right as a result of the tax changes, the increase in the price level will be smaller; that is, the price level at point *C* is likely to be lower than at point *B*, even if it is higher than at point *A*, although—as we will discuss in the next section—not all economists would agree. We can conclude that a successful policy of tax reductions and simplifications will benefit the economy by increasing output and employment and, at the same time, may result in smaller increases in the price level.

How Large Are Supply-Side Effects?

Most economists would agree that there are supply-side effects to reducing taxes: Decreasing marginal income tax rates will increase the quantity of labor supplied, cutting the corporate income tax will increase investment spending, and so on. The magnitude of the effects is subject to considerable debate, however. For example, some economists argue that the increase in the quantity of labor supplied following a tax cut will be limited because many people work a number of hours set by their employers and lack the opportunity to work additional hours. Similarly, some economists believe that tax changes have only a small effect on saving and investment. In this view, saving and investment are affected much more by changes in income or changes in expectations of the future profitability of new investment due to technological change or improving macroeconomic conditions than they are by tax changes.

Economists who are skeptical of the magnitude of supply-side effects believe that tax cuts have their greatest impact on aggregate demand rather than on aggregate supply. In their view, focusing on the impact of tax cuts on aggregate demand, while ignoring any impact on aggregate supply, yields accurate forecasts of future movements in real GDP and the price level, which indicates that the supply-side effects must be small. If tax changes have only small effects on aggregate supply, it is unlikely that they will reduce the size of price increases, as they did in the analysis in Figure 15-15.

Ultimately, the size of the supply-side effects of tax policy can be resolved only through careful study of the effects of differences in tax rates on labor supply and saving and investment decisions. Some recent studies have arrived at conflicting conclusions, however. For example, a study by Nobel laureate Edward Prescott of Arizona State University concludes that the differences between the United States and Europe with respect to the average number of hours worked per week and the average number of weeks worked per year are due to differences in taxes. The lower marginal tax rates in the United States compared with Europe increase the return to working for U.S. workers and result in a larger quantity of labor supplied. But another study by Alberto Alesina and Edward Glaeser of Harvard University and Bruce Sacerdote of Dartmouth College argues that the more restrictive labor market regulations in Europe explain the shorter work weeks and longer vacations of European workers and that differences in taxes have only a small effect.

As in other areas of economics, over time, differences among economists in their estimates of the supply-side effects of tax changes may narrow as additional studies are undertaken.

>> Continued from page 509

Economics in YOUR Life!

At the beginning of the chapter we posed the question: How will you respond to a $500 tax rebate? and What effect will this tax rebate likely have on equilibrium real GDP in the short run? This chapter has shown that tax cuts increase disposable income, and, when there is a permanent increase in disposable income, consumption spending increases. So, you will likely respond to a permanent $500 increase in your disposable income by increasing your spending. In addition, this chapter has also shown that tax cuts such as this one have a multiplier effect on the economy. That is, an increase in consumption spending sets off further increases in real GDP and income. So, if the economy is not already at potential GDP, this tax rebate will likely increase equilibrium real GDP in the short run.

Conclusion

In this chapter, we have seen how the federal government uses changes in government purchases and taxes to achieve its economic policy goals. We have seen that economists debate the effectiveness of discretionary fiscal policy actions intended to stabilize the economy. Congress and the president share responsibility for economic policy with the Federal Reserve. In Chapter 16, we will discuss further some of the challenges that the Federal Reserve encounters as it carries out monetary policy. In Chapters 17 and 18, we will look more closely at the international economy, including how monetary and fiscal policy are affected by the linkages between economies.

Read *An Inside Look at Policy* on the next page for a discussion of the debate in Congress about the alternative minimum tax (AMT).

Can Congress Afford to Fix the Alternative Minimum Tax?

WALL STREET JOURNAL, APRIL 14, 2007

Congress's Taxing Hurdle: The AMT

The alternative minimum tax originally was created to prevent the wealthy from using heavy deductions to legally avoid paying income tax. But because it is not adjusted for inflation, the tax increasingly ensnares upper-middle-class taxpayers who never were intended to be its targets.

Repealing the tax is supported by members of Congress but is costly. The government could lose $1 trillion in revenue over the next decade if it were eliminated. That has Congress looking at a partial repeal and also at ways to ramp up tax collections by, among other things, trying to close the estimated $290 billion "tax gap"—the difference between what taxpayers should have paid and what they actually pay.

While the alternative minimum tax means a significant boost in the tax bills of many Americans, proposals to close the tax gap—by increasing resources for the tax collector—could be costly for many, too. Here's what's at stake:

(a) What is the alternative minimum tax? The AMT is a separate system from the regular income tax, and it operates under many different rules. There are two rates—26% and 28%. Some popular deductions that many people claim under the regular system, such as state and local taxes, aren't allowed under the AMT. Because of the AMT, taxpayers at certain income levels have to figure out their taxes both ways and pay the higher amount.

How many people are affected? Four million taxpayers will pay the AMT in their 2006 taxes, but that could rise to 23 million for taxes filed next year. Those who pay the tax face an average increase in their tax bill of $6,800.

The problem has become more pronounced because President Bush's tax cuts lowered income-tax obligations for those who pay through the regular tax system without addressing the growing numbers that are subject to the alternative minimum tax.

(b) Who is most likely to get hit by the AMT? The tax tends to hit those with annual incomes between $100,000 and $500,000 the most, but it could reach some who earn as little as $50,000 to $75,000 on next year's taxes. White-collar professionals in high-tax states like California and in the Northeast tend to bear the brunt of the tax, because it doesn't give credits for state and local taxes. Taxpayers with large families or high medical expenses also are hit harder because it doesn't provide credits for dependents and has a higher threshold for deductions for medical expenses.

What will Congress do? In past years, Congress and the president have prevented the growing reach of the AMT with a series of one-year fixes. Congress passed such a fix for taxes filed this year, but hasn't passed one yet for next year's taxes. Democrats have suggested that they want to permanently overhaul the tax, but because they have passed pay-as-you-go spending rules, the government would have to pay for the lost revenue by increasing taxes or cutting spending. Ultimately, Congress may defer action until after the 2008 election, when it also will consider the fate of the Bush tax cuts.

If Congress boosts the resources of the Internal Revenue Service, who will be affected? The difference between what taxpayers should have paid and what they actually paid on time was $345 billion in 2001. After enforcement efforts, it collected $55 billion, leaving a net gap of $290 billion. The IRS estimates the overall compliance rate at about 84%.

(c) President Bush's budget for the 2008 fiscal year proposes a $410 million spending increase for compliance programs in order to bring in $29 billion in increased taxes over the next decade. Congress might increase that even more.

As a result, the number of families who are audited could rise. Right now, about 1% of all filings are audited. The odds of an audit are higher for those with higher incomes. Around 6% of individuals with an annual income exceeding $1 million were audited last year.

Small businesses and the self-employed are estimated to be the largest source of the tax gap, and therefore would likely bear the brunt of more aggressive enforcement efforts. One proposal would require banks to report to the IRS merchants' annual credit-card payments so that the IRS could compare the tax returns of small businesses with the payments to determine any underreporting of income. Small-business groups are fighting back by arguing that more intrusive regulation would add to their already high tax-preparation costs.

Source: Nick Timiraos, "Congress's Taxing Hurdle: The AMT," Wall Street Journal, *April 14, 2007, p. A7. Reprinted by permission of the* Wall Street Journal *via Copyright Clearance Center.*

Analyzing the News

(a) The AMT is an income tax that Congress established in 1970 to ensure that high-income individuals do not take advantage of deductions and exemptions to reduce or eliminate their income tax liability. The AMT operates alongside the traditional income tax so that individuals must pay the AMT if it exceeds their standard income tax liability. For example, in 2006, individuals who were subject to the AMT paid, on average, $6,800 more in taxes than they would have under the traditional income tax. In recent years, the AMT has come under scrutiny from taxpayers and Congress. This is, in part, because Congress has not adjusted the AMT's tax brackets for inflation, as is done with the regular income tax. In other words, the AMT taxes individuals' nominal incomes as if they were real incomes. Therefore, as the average price level in the economy rises, so does the number of middle-income individuals who are subject to the AMT. In 2006, about 4 million taxpayers were subject to the AMT. However, under current tax law, this number is likely to rise substantially in 2007 and beyond. The figure charts the estimated numbers of individuals who will be subject to the AMT in the future if Congress does not change the current tax law.

(b) Until recently, individuals earning between $100,000 and $500,000 have been the group most likely to pay the AMT. However, because the AMT does not adjust for inflation, economists expect the tax to apply in 2007 to individuals who earn between $50,000 and $75,000. Moreover, because the AMT does not credit individuals for any state and local income taxes they pay, those living in California and the Northeast—where state and local taxes are highest—are disproportionately affected by the AMT. Because the AMT does not allow individuals to claim dependents—such as their children or other persons these individuals support financially—or deduct as many health expenses, those with large families and medical expenses are also disproportionately affected. To date, Congress has addressed these problems on a year-by-year basis. This is why the number of taxpayers affected by the AMT has so far not increased substantially. Although many in Congress support a permanent overhaul of the AMT, action on reform has been slow. An overhaul of the AMT would reduce tax revenue, and the current Congress operates under pay-as-you-go rules, which require that any reduction in revenue must be offset by either an increase in revenue elsewhere or a reduction in spending.

(c) One way for Congress to offset the revenue lost from permanently overhauling the AMT is to improve tax compliance—in other words, to collect taxes from the roughly 16 percent of those who owe but do not pay their taxes. President Bush's budget for 2008 allocates $400 million to improve compliance; the administration expects these improvements to enable the IRS to collect an estimated $29 billion of heretofore uncollected taxes. Efforts to improve compliance include increasing the number of audits and regulating small businesses more closely.

Key Points in the Article

This article discusses the alternative minimum tax (AMT), which Congress established in order to ensure that wealthy individuals pay a minimum amount of income tax. In recent years, the AMT has come under scrutiny from taxpayers and Congress because middle-income households are increasingly subject to the AMT, which, unlike the regular income tax, does not adjust income brackets for inflation. Although Congress wants to permanently overhaul, if not eliminate, the AMT, it may not be able to do so. This is because the current Congress operates under pay-as-you-go rules, which require that any reduction in revenue be offset by either an increase in revenue elsewhere or a reduction in spending. Eliminating the AMT would reduce revenue that would be politically difficult to replace.

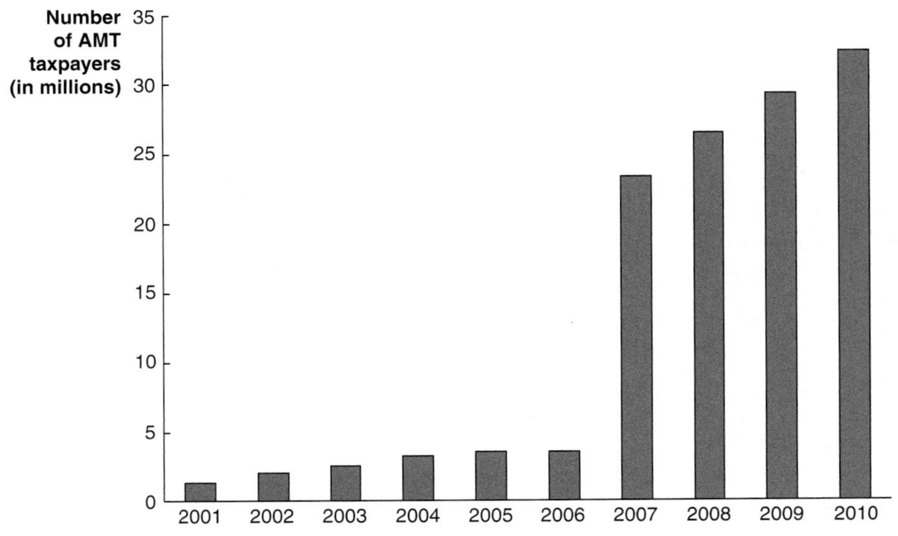

The number of taxpayers affected by the AMT will increase substantially under current U.S. tax laws.

Thinking Critically About Policy

1. Suppose that Congress passes—and the president signs into law—increased spending for an expansionary fiscal policy. All else being equal, is the policy's effect on aggregate demand relatively larger or smaller if a pay-as-you-go rule is in effect? Briefly explain your reasoning.
2. Suppose that Congress announces that it will not renew President Bush's 2001 tax cuts when they expire in 2010. How is this announcement likely to affect aggregate demand today?

Key Terms

Automatic stabilizers, p. 510
Budget deficit, p. 527
Budget surplus, p. 527
Crowding out, p. 524
Cyclically adjusted budget deficit or surplus, p. 528
Fiscal policy, p. 510
Multiplier effect, p. 519
Tax wedge, p. 533

15.1 LEARNING OBJECTIVE 15.1 | Define fiscal policy, **pages 510–514.**

Fiscal Policy

Summary

Fiscal policy involves changes in federal taxes and purchases that are intended to achieve macroeconomic policy objectives. **Automatic stabilizers** are government spending and taxes that automatically increase or decrease along with the business cycle. Since World War II, the federal government's share of total government expenditures has been between two-thirds and three-quarters. Federal government *expenditures* as a percentage of GDP rose from 1950 to the early 1990s and fell between 1992 and 2001, before rising again. Federal government *purchases* have declined as a percentage of GDP since the end of the Korean War in the early 1950s. The largest component of federal expenditures is transfer payments. The largest source of federal government revenue is social insurance taxes, which are used to fund the Social Security and Medicare systems.

myeconlab Get Ahead of the Curve Visit www.myeconlab.com to complete these exercises online and get instant feedback.

Review Questions

1.1 What is fiscal policy? Who is responsible for fiscal policy?

1.2 What is the difference between fiscal policy and monetary policy?

1.3 What is the difference between federal purchases and federal expenditures? Are federal purchases higher today than they were in 1960? Are federal expenditures higher today than they were in 1960?

Problems and Applications

1.4 Why have federal government expenditures been increasing more rapidly than federal government purchases? What effect will the increasing average age of the U.S. population have on federal government purchases in the coming years?

1.5 From the discussion in this chapter, which source of government revenue shown in Figure 15-4 on page 513 is likely to increase the most in the future? Briefly explain.

1.6 **(Related to the *Making the Connection* on page 513)** According to a Congressional Budget Office report:

> The baby boomers will start becoming eligible for Social Security retirement benefits in 2008, when the first members of that generation turn 62. As a result, the annual growth rate of Social Security spending is expected to increase from about 4.5 percent in 2008 to 6.5 percent by 2017.

Who are the "baby boomers"? Why should their retirement cause such a large increase in the growth rate of spending by the federal government on Social Security?

Source: Congressional Budget Office, *The Budget and Economic Outlook: Fiscal Years 2008 to 2017*, January 2007, p. xiii.

1.7 **(Related to the *Making the Connection* on page 513)** According to a Congressional Budget Office report, "The number of people age 65 or older will more than double by 2050, and the number of adults under age 65 will increase by about 16 percent." Briefly explain what the implications of these facts are for federal government spending as a percentage of GDP in 2050.

Source: Congressional Budget Office, *The Budget and Economic Outlook: Fiscal Years 2008 to 2017*, January 2007, p. 10.

>> End Learning Objective 15.1

15.2 LEARNING OBJECTIVE 15.2 | Explain how fiscal policy affects aggregate demand and how the government can use fiscal policy to stabilize the economy, **pages 514–518.**

The Effects of Fiscal Policy on Real GDP and the Price Level

Summary

To fight recessions, Congress and the president can increase government purchases or cut taxes. This expansionary policy causes the aggregate demand curve to shift out more than it otherwise would, raising the level of real GDP and the price level. To fight rising inflation, Congress and the president can decrease government purchases or raise taxes. This contractionary policy causes the aggregate demand curve to shift out less than it otherwise would, reducing the increase in real GDP and the price level.

myeconlab Get Ahead of the Curve Visit www.myeconlab.com to complete these exercises online and get instant feedback.

Review Questions

2.1 What is an expansionary fiscal policy? What is a contractionary fiscal policy?

2.2 If Congress and the president decide an expansionary fiscal policy is necessary, what changes should they make in government spending or taxes? What changes should they make if they decide a contractionary fiscal policy is necessary?

Problems and Applications

2.3 Briefly explain whether you agree or disagree with the following statements: "An expansionary fiscal policy involves an increase in government purchases or an increase in taxes. A contractionary fiscal policy involves a decrease in government purchases or a decrease in taxes."

2.4 Identify each of the following as (i) part of an expansionary fiscal policy, (ii) part of a contractionary fiscal policy, or (iii) not part of fiscal policy.

a. The corporate income tax rate is increased.
b. Defense spending is increased.
c. Families are allowed to deduct all their expenses for daycare from their federal income taxes.
d. The individual income tax rate is decreased.
e. The State of New Jersey builds a new highway in an attempt to expand employment in the state.

2.5 **(Related to the *Don't Let This Happen to You!* on page 518)** Briefly explain whether you agree with the following remark: "Real GDP is $250 billion below its full-employment level. With a multiplier of 2, if Congress and the president increase government purchases by $125 billion or the Fed increases the money supply by $125 billion, real GDP can be brought back to its full-employment level."

2.6 Use the graph to answer the following questions.

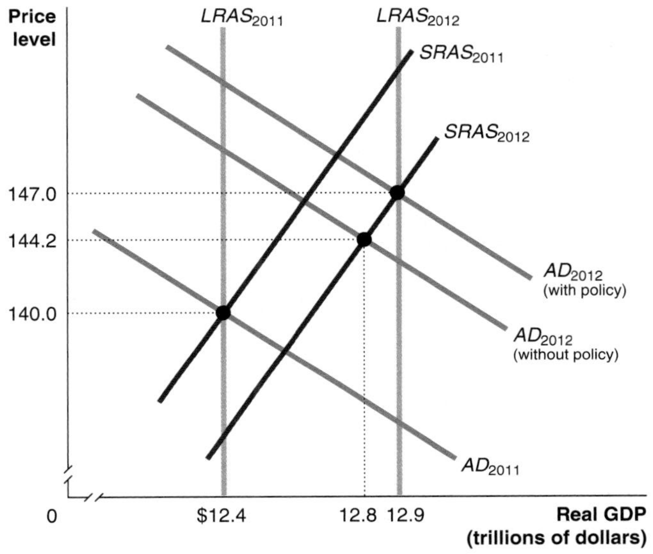

a. If the government does not take any policy actions, what will be the values of real GDP and the price level in 2012?
b. If the government purchases multiplier is 2, how much will government purchases have to be increased to bring real GDP to its potential level in 2012? (Assume that the multiplier value takes into account the impact of a rising price level on the multiplier effect.)
c. If the tax multiplier is −1.6, how much will taxes have to be cut to bring real GDP to its potential level in 2012? (Again, assume that the multiplier value takes into account the impact of a rising price level.)
d. If the government takes no policy actions, what will be the inflation rate in 2012? If the government uses fiscal policy to keep real GDP at its potential level, what will be the inflation rate in 2012?

>> End Learning Objective 15.2

15.3 LEARNING OBJECTIVE 15.3 | Explain how the government purchases and tax multipliers work, **pages 518–523.**

The Government Purchases and Tax Multipliers

Summary

Because of the **multiplier effect**, an increase in government purchases or a cut in taxes will have a multiplied effect on equilibrium real GDP. The *government purchases multiplier* is equal to the change in equilibrium real GDP divided by the change in government purchases. The *tax multiplier* is equal to the change in equilibrium real GDP divided by the change in taxes. Increases in government purchases and cuts in taxes have a positive multiplier effect on equilibrium real GDP. Decreases in government purchases and increases in taxes have a negative multiplier effect on equilibrium real GDP.

myeconlab Get Ahead of the Curve Visit www.myeconlab.com to complete these exercises online and get instant feedback.

Review Questions

3.1 Why does a $1 increase in government purchases lead to more than a $1 increase in income and spending?

3.2 Define the government purchases multiplier and the tax multiplier.

Problems and Applications

3.3 In *The General Theory of Employment, Interest, and Money*, John Maynard Keynes wrote this:

> If the Treasury were to fill old bottles with banknotes, bury them at suitable depths in disused coal mines which are then filled up to the surface with town rubbish, and leave it to private enterprise . . . to dig the notes up again . . . there need be no more unemployment and, with the help of the repercussions, the real income of the community . . . would probably become a good deal greater than it is.

Which important macroeconomic effect is Keynes discussing here? What does he mean by "repercussions"? Why does he appear unconcerned if government spending is wasteful?

3.4 Suppose that real GDP is currently $13.1 trillion, potential real GDP is $13.5 trillion, the government purchases multiplier is 2, and the tax multiplier is –1.6.

a. Holding other factors constant, by how much will government purchases need to be increased to bring the economy to equilibrium at potential GDP?

b. Holding other factors constant, by how much will taxes have to be cut to bring the economy to equilibrium at potential GDP?

c. Construct an example of a *combination* of increased government spending and tax cuts that will bring the economy to equilibrium at potential GDP.

3.5 **(Related to *Solved Problem 15-3* on page 522)** Briefly explain whether you agree or disagree with the following statement: "Real GDP is currently $12.7 trillion, and potential real GDP is $12.5 trillion. If Congress and the president would decrease government purchases by $200 billion or increase taxes by $200 billion, the economy could be brought to equilibrium at potential GDP."

3.6 If the short-run aggregate supply curve (*SRAS*) were a horizontal line, what would be the impact on the size of the government purchases and tax multipliers?

>> End Learning Objective 15.3

15.4 LEARNING OBJECTIVE 15.4 | Discuss the difficulties that can arise in implementing fiscal policy, **pages 523–527.**

The Limits of Using Fiscal Policy to Stabilize the Economy

Summary

Poorly timed fiscal policy can do more harm than good. Getting the timing right with fiscal policy can be difficult because obtaining approval from Congress for a new fiscal policy can be a very long process and because it can take months for an increase in authorized spending to actually take place. Because an increase in government purchases may lead to a higher interest rate, it may result in a decline in consumption, investment, and net exports. A decline in private expenditures as a result of an increase in government purchases is called **crowding out**. Crowding out may cause an expansionary fiscal policy to fail to meet its goal of keeping the economy at potential GDP.

myeconlab Get Ahead of the Curve Visit www.myeconlab.com to complete these exercises online and get instant feedback.

Review Questions

4.1 Which can be changed more quickly: monetary policy or fiscal policy? Briefly explain.

4.2 What is meant by crowding out? Explain the difference between crowding out in the short run and in the long run.

Problems and Applications

4.3 In a column published in the *Wall Street Journal* on July 19, 2001, David Wessel wrote, "Most economic forecasters don't foresee recession this year or next." In fact, a recession had already begun in March 2001. Does this tell us anything about the difficulty of Congress and the president implementing a fiscal policy that stabilizes rather than destabilizes the economy?

Source: David Wessel, "Economic Forecasting in Three Steps," *Wall Street Journal*, July 19, 2001, p. A1.

4.4 Figure 15-11 on page 524 shows the equilibrium interest rate rising as the demand for money increases. Describe what must be happening in the market for Treasury bills.

4.5 Some economists argue that because increases in government spending crowd out private spending, increased government spending will reduce the long-run growth rate of real GDP.

a. Is this most likely to happen if the private spending being crowded out is consumption spending, investment spending, or net exports? Briefly explain.

b. In terms of its effect on the long-run growth rate of real GDP, would it matter if the additional government spending involves (i) increased spending on highways and bridges or (ii) increased spending on the national parks? Briefly explain.

4.6 In his column in the *Wall Street Journal*, David Wessel wrote, "Global financial markets, politicians, corporate executives and ordinary Americans have confidence in [the Federal Reserve chairman's] ability to steer the U.S. economy, particularly during times of crisis." But isn't it Congress and the president, and not the chairman of the Fed, who steer the U.S. economy? Briefly discuss.

Source: David Wessel, "Four Hard-to-Predict Factors That Will Shape the Economy," *Wall Street Journal*, April 4, 2002.

4.7 **(Related to the *Making the Connection* on page 526)** Why might the effects on health of a temporary increase or decrease in income be different than the effects of a permanent increase or decrease?

>> End Learning Objective 15.4

15.5 LEARNING OBJECTIVE 15.5 | Define federal budget deficit and federal government debt and explain how the federal budget can serve as an automatic stabilizer, **pages 527–532.**

Deficits, Surpluses, and Federal Government Debt

Summary

A **budget deficit** occurs when the federal government's expenditures are greater than its tax revenues. A **budget surplus** occurs when the federal government's expenditures are less than its tax revenues. The budget deficit automatically increases during recessions and decreases during expansions. The automatic movements in the federal budget help to stabilize the economy by cushioning the fall in spending during recessions and restraining the increase in spending during expansions. The **cyclically adjusted budget deficit or surplus** is the deficit or surplus in the federal government's budget if the economy were at potential GDP. The federal government debt is the value of outstanding bonds issued by the U.S. Treasury. More than half of the national debt is actually owned by other federal agencies. The national debt is a problem if interest payments on it require taxes to be raised substantially or require other federal expenditures to be cut.

Review Questions

5.1 In what ways does the federal budget serve as an automatic stabilizer for the economy?

5.2 What is the cyclically adjusted budget deficit or surplus? Suppose that the economy is currently at potential GDP and the federal budget is balanced. If the economy moves into recession, what will happen to the federal budget?

5.3 Why do few economists argue that it would be a good idea to balance the federal budget every year?

5.4 What is the difference between the federal budget deficit and federal government debt?

5.5 In the United States, why is more than half of federal government debt actually owned by the federal government?

Problems and Applications

5.6 **(Related to *Solved Problem 15-5* on page 530)** The federal government's budget deficit was $221.4 billion in 1990 and $269.2 billion in 1991. What does this information tell us about fiscal policy actions that Congress and the president took during these years?

5.7 The following is from an article in the *Wall Street Journal*: "The Treasury Department said it expected to borrow a net $1 billion during the April-to-June quarter—not repay a net $89 billion, as it said it would earlier this year." Why does the Treasury Department borrow? When the Treasury "repays," who is it repaying? Why would the Treasury say it was going to repay debt and then end up borrowing?

Source: Rebecca Christie and Deborah Lagomarsino, "U.S. Debt Is Set to Rise in Quarter as Tax Receipts Come Up Short," *Wall Street Journal*, April 30, 2002.

5.8 The federal government calculates its budget on a fiscal year that begins each year on October 1 and ends on the following September 30. At the beginning of the 1997 fiscal year, the Congressional Budget Office (CBO) forecast that the federal budget deficit would be $127.7 billion. The actual budget deficit for fiscal 1997 was only $21.9 billion. Federal expenditures were $30.3 billion less than the CBO had forecast, and federal revenue was $75.5 billion more than the CBO had forecast.

a. Is it likely that the economy grew faster or slower during fiscal 1997 than the CBO had expected? Explain your reasoning.

b. Suppose that Congress and the president were committed to balancing the budget each year. Does what happened during 1997 provide any insight into difficulties they might run into in trying to balance the budget every year?

5.9 **(Related to the *Making the Connection* on page 529)** The following is from a message by President Hoover to Congress, dated May 5, 1932:

> I need not recount that the revenues of the Government as estimated for the next fiscal year show a decrease of about $1,700,000,000 below the fiscal year 1929, and inexorably require a broader basis of taxation and a drastic reduction of expenditures in order to balance the Budget. Nothing is more necessary at this time than balancing the Budget.

Do you think President Hoover was correct in saying that, in 1932, nothing was more necessary than balancing the federal government's budget? Explain.

5.10 Nobel laureate Paul Samuelson, an economist at MIT, argued that "it was harmful to let a large budget surplus develop in the weak 1959–60 revival and thereby help to choke off that recovery." Why would a large budget surplus "choke off" a recovery from economic recession? What could the federal government have done to have kept a large budget surplus from developing?

Source: Paul A. Samuelson, "Economic Policy for 1962," *American Economic Review*, Vol. 44, No. 1 (February 1962), p. 6.

5.11 In testifying before Congress in 2003, then Federal Reserve Chairman Alan Greenspan observed, "There is no question that if you run substantial and excessive deficits over time you are draining savings from the private sector." What did Greenspan mean by "draining savings from the private sector"? How might this be bad for the economy?

Source: Martin Crutsinger, "Greenspan Warns of Rising Deficits," Associated Press, July 17, 2003.

5.12 An editorial in the *Wall Street Journal* declares that: "We don't put much stock in future budget forecasts because they depend on so many variables." What variables would a forecast of future federal budget deficits depend on? What is it about these variables that makes future budget deficits difficult to predict?

Source: "Fiscal Revelation," *Wall Street Journal*, February 6, 2007, p. A 16.

5.13 According to an article in the *Wall Street Journal* "U.S. tax revenue for fiscal 2006, . . . is expected to be 5%—or $115 billion—higher, than the administration projected in February. Largely as a result, the budget deficit is expected to be $296 billion this year, instead of $423 billion." Why would higher than expected tax revenues cause the budget deficit to be smaller than expected? What might make tax revenues be higher than expected? (Hint: For one possibility, note the title of the article given in the source line below.)

Source: Greg Ip and Deborah Solomon, "As Bigger Piece of Economic Pie Shifts to Wealthiest, U.S. Deficit Heads Downward," *Wall Street Journal*, July 17, 2006, p. A2.

5.14 During 2003, China ran large government budget deficits to stimulate its economy. The *Wall Street Journal* quoted an official in China's ministry of finance as saying, "The proactive fiscal policy has brought some negative effects because it has squeezed out the private investor." What did the official mean by a "proactive fiscal policy"? Why would such a policy "squeeze out" the private investor? Does that mean the policy should not have been used?

Source: Karby Leggett and Kathy Chen, "China's Rising Debt Raises Questions about the Future," *Wall Street Journal*, January 20, 2003.

5.15 A political columnist wrote the following:

> Today . . . the main purpose [of government's issuing bonds] is to let craven politicians launch projects they know the public, at the moment, would rather not fully finance. The tab for these projects will not come due, probably, until after the politicians have long since departed for greener (excuse the expression) pastures.

Do you agree with this commentator's explanation for why some government spending is financed through tax receipts and other government spending is financed through borrowing, by issuing bonds? Briefly explain.

Source: Paul Carpenter, "The Bond Issue Won't Be Repaid by Park Tolls," *(Allentown, PA) Morning Call*, May 26, 2002, p. B1.

>> End Learning Objective 15.5

15.6 LEARNING OBJECTIVE 15.6 | Discuss the effects of fiscal policy in the long run, **pages 532–537.**

The Effects of Fiscal Policy in the Long Run

Summary

Some fiscal policy actions are intended to have long-run effects by expanding the productive capacity of the economy and increasing the rate of economic growth. Because these policy actions primarily affect aggregate supply rather than aggregate demand, they are sometimes referred to as *supply-side economics*. The difference between the pretax and posttax return to an economic activity is known as the **tax wedge**. Economists believe that the smaller the tax wedge for any economic activity—such as working, saving, investing, or starting a business—the more of that economic activity will occur. Economists debate the size of the supply-side effects of tax changes.

myeconlab Get Ahead of the Curve Visit www.myeconlab.com to complete these exercises online and get instant feedback.

Review Questions

6.1 What is meant by supply-side economics?

6.2 What is the "tax wedge"?

Problems and Applications

6.3 **(Related to the *Chapter Opener* on page 508)** It would seem that both households and businesses would benefit if the federal income tax were simpler and tax forms were easier to fill out. Why then have the tax laws become increasingly complicated?

6.4 Suppose a political candidate hired you to develop two arguments in favor of a flat tax. What two arguments would you advance? Alternatively, if you were hired to develop two arguments against the flat tax, what two arguments would you advance?

6.5 Suppose that an increase in marginal tax rates on individual income affects both aggregate demand and aggregate supply. Briefly describe the effect of the tax increase on equilibrium real GDP and the equilibrium price level. Will the changes in equilibrium real GDP and the price level be larger or smaller than they would be if the tax increase affected only aggregate demand? Briefly explain.

6.6 An editorial in the *Wall Street Journal* in early 2007 observed: "The other news you won't often hear concerns the soaring tax revenues in the wake of the 2003 supply-side tax cuts. Tax collections have risen by $757 billion, among the largest revenue gushers in history." What is a "supply-side" tax cut? How would a supply-side tax cut lead to higher tax revenues? Would a supply-side tax cut always result in higher tax revenues?

Source: "Fiscal Revelation," *Wall Street Journal*, February 6, 2007.

6.7 **(Related to the *Making the Connection* on page 534)** As the Czech Republic considered converting to a flat tax, an editorial in the *Wall Street Journal* noted, "If the [Czech] Prime Minister manages to push his plans through a divided parliament in June, it would bring to 14 the number of single-rate tax systems in the world, all but four of them in Eastern Europe. (Hong Kong, Iceland, Mongolia and Kyrgyzstan are the exceptions.)" Why would the countries of eastern Europe and the other small countries mentioned be more likely to adopt a flat tax than the United States, Canada, Japan, or the countries of Western Europe?

Source: "Flat Czechs," *Wall Street Journal*, April 13, 2007.

>> End Learning Objective 15.6

Appendix

A Closer Look at the Multiplier

LEARNING OBJECTIVE

Apply the multiplier formula.

In this chapter, we saw that changes in government purchases and changes in taxes have a multiplied effect on equilibrium real GDP. In this appendix, we will build a simple economic model of the multiplier effect. When economists forecast the effect of a change in spending or taxes, they often rely on *econometric models*. As we saw in the appendix to Chapter 11, an econometric model is an economic model written in the form of equations, where each equation has been statistically estimated, using methods similar to those used in estimating demand curves, as briefly described in Chapter 3. In this appendix, we will start with a model similar to the one we used in the appendix to Chapter 11.

An Expression for Equilibrium Real GDP

We can write a set of equations that includes the key macroeconomic relationships we have studied in this and previous chapters. It is important to note that in this model, we will be assuming that the price level is constant. We know that this is unrealistic because an upward-sloping *SRAS* curve means that when the aggregate demand curve shifts, the price level will change. Nevertheless, our model will be approximately correct when changes in the price level are small. It also serves as an introduction to more complicated models that take into account changes in the price level. For simplicity, we also start out by assuming that taxes, T, do not depend on the level of real GDP, Y. We also assume that there are no government transfer payments to households. Finally, we assume that we have a closed economy, with no imports or exports. The numbers (with the exception of the *MPC*) represent billions of dollars:

(1) $C = 1{,}000 + 0.75(Y - T)$	Consumption function
(2) $I = 1{,}500$	Planned investment function
(3) $G = 1{,}500$	Government purchases function
(4) $T = 1{,}000$	Tax function
(5) $Y = C + I + G$	Equilibrium condition

The first equation is the consumption function. The marginal propensity to consume, or *MPC*, is 0.75, and 1,000 is the level of autonomous consumption, which is the level of consumption that does not depend on income. We assume that consumption depends on disposable income, which is $Y - T$. The functions for planned investment spending, government spending, and taxes are very simple because we have assumed that these variables are not affected by GDP and, therefore, are constant. Economists who use this type of model to forecast GDP would, of course, use more realistic planned investment, government purchases, and tax functions.

Equation (5)—the equilibrium condition—states that equilibrium GDP equals the sum of consumption spending, planned investment spending, and government purchases. To calculate a value for equilibrium real GDP, we need to substitute equations (1) through (4) into equation (5). This substitution gives us the following:

$$Y = 1{,}000 + 0.75(Y - 1{,}000) + 1{,}500 + 1{,}500$$
$$= 1{,}000 + 0.75Y - 750 + 1{,}500 + 1{,}500.$$

We need to solve this equation for Y to find equilibrium GDP. The first step is to subtract $0.75Y$ from both sides of the equation:

$$Y - 0.75Y = 1{,}000 - 750 + 1{,}500 + 1{,}500.$$

Then, we solve for Y:

$$0.25Y = 3{,}250$$

or:

$$Y = \frac{3{,}250}{0.25} = 13{,}000.$$

To make this result more general, we can replace particular values with general values represented by letters:

(1) $C = \bar{C} + MPC(Y - T)$	Consumption function
(2) $I = \bar{I}$	Planned investment function
(3) $G = \bar{G}$	Government purchases function
(4) $T = \bar{T}$	Tax function
(5) $Y = C + I + G$	Equilibrium condition

The letters with "bars" represent fixed, or *autonomous*, values that do not depend on the values of other variables. So, $\bar{C}$ represents autonomous consumption, which had a value of 1,000 in our original example. Now, solving for equilibrium, we get:

$$Y = \bar{C} + MPC(Y - \bar{T}) + \bar{I} + \bar{G}$$

or:

$$Y - MPC(Y) = \bar{C} - (MPC \times \bar{T}) + \bar{I} + \bar{G}$$

or:

$$Y(1 - MPC) = \bar{C} - (MPC \times \bar{T}) + \bar{I} + \bar{G}$$

or:

$$Y = \frac{\bar{C} - (MPC \times \bar{T}) + \bar{I} + \bar{G}}{1 - MPC}.$$

A Formula for the Government Purchases Multiplier

To find a formula for the government purchases multiplier, we need to rewrite the last equation for changes in each variable rather than levels. Letting Δ stand for the change in a variable, we have:

$$\Delta Y = \frac{\Delta\bar{C} - (MPC \times \Delta\bar{T}) + \Delta\bar{I} + \Delta\bar{G}}{1 - MPC}.$$

If we hold constant changes in autonomous consumption spending, planned investment spending, and taxes, we can find a formula for the government purchases multiplier, which is the ratio of the change in equilibrium real GDP to the change in government purchases:

$$\Delta Y = \frac{\Delta G}{1 - MPC}$$

or:

$$\text{Government purchases multiplier} = \frac{\Delta Y}{\Delta G} = \frac{1}{1 - MPC}.$$

For an *MPC* of 0.75, the government purchases multiplier will be:

$$\frac{1}{1 - 0.75} = 4.$$

A government purchases multiplier of 4 means that an increase in government spending of $10 billion will increase equilibrium real GDP by 4 × $10 billion = $40 billion.

A Formula for the Tax Multiplier

We can also find a formula for the tax multiplier. We start again with this equation:

$$\Delta Y = \frac{\Delta\bar{C} - (MPC \times \Delta\bar{T}) + \Delta\bar{I} + \Delta\bar{G}}{1 - MPC}.$$

Now we hold constant the values of autonomous consumption spending, planned investment spending, and government purchases, but we allow the value of taxes to change:

$$\Delta Y = \frac{-MPC \times \Delta T}{1 - MPC}.$$

Or:

$$\text{The tax multiplier} = \frac{\Delta Y}{\Delta T} = \frac{-MPC}{1 - MPC}.$$

For an *MPC* of 0.75, the tax multiplier will be:

$$\frac{-0.75}{1 - 0.75} = -3.$$

The tax multiplier is a negative number because an increase in taxes causes a decrease in equilibrium real GDP, and a decrease in taxes causes an increase in equilibrium real GDP. A tax multiplier of −3 means that a decrease in taxes of $10 billion will increase equilibrium real GDP by −3 × −$10 billion = $30 billion. In this chapter, we discussed the economic reasons for the tax multiplier being smaller than the government spending multiplier.

The "Balanced Budget" Multiplier

What will be the effect of equal increases (or decreases) in government purchases and taxes on equilibrium real GDP? At first, it might appear that the tax increase would exactly offset the government purchases increase, leaving real GDP unchanged. But we have just seen that the government purchases multiplier is larger (in absolute value) than the tax multiplier. We can use our formulas for the government purchases multiplier and the tax multiplier to calculate the net effect of increasing government purchases by $10 billion at the same time that taxes are increased by $10 billion:

$$\text{Increase in real GDP from the increase in government purchases} = \$10 \text{ billion} \times \frac{1}{1 - MPC}$$

$$\text{Decrease in real GDP from the increase in taxes} = \$10 \text{ billion} \times \frac{-MPC}{1 - MPC}$$

So, the combined effect equals:

$$\$10 \text{ billion} \times \left[\left(\frac{1}{1 - MPC}\right) + \left(\frac{-MPC}{1 - MPC}\right)\right]$$

or:

$$\$10 \text{ billion} \times \left(\frac{1 - MPC}{1 - MPC}\right) = \$10 \text{ billion}.$$

The balanced budget multiplier is, therefore, equal to $(1 - MPC)/(1 - MPC)$, or 1. Equal dollar increases and decreases in government purchases and in taxes lead to the same dollar increase in real GDP in the short run.

The Effects of Changes in Tax Rates on the Multiplier

We now consider the effect of a change in the tax *rate*, as opposed to a change in a fixed amount of taxes. Changing the tax rate actually changes the value of the multiplier. To see this, suppose the tax rate is 20 percent, or 0.2. In that case, an increase in household income of $10 billion will increase *disposable income* by only $8 billion [or $10 billion × (1 − 0.2)]. In general, an increase in income can be multiplied by $(1 - t)$ to find the increase in disposable income, where t is the tax rate. So, we can rewrite the consumption function as:

$$C = \bar{C} + MPC(1 - t)Y.$$

We can use this expression for the consumption function to find an expression for the government purchases multiplier using the same method we used previously:

$$\text{Government purchases multiplier} = \frac{\Delta Y}{\Delta G} = \frac{1}{1 - MPC(1 - t)}.$$

We can see the effect of changing the tax rate on the size of the multiplier by trying some values. First, assume that $MPC = 0.75$ and $t = 0.2$. Then:

$$\text{Government purchases multiplier} = \frac{\Delta Y}{\Delta G} = \frac{1}{1 - 0.75(1 - 0.2)} = \frac{1}{1 - 0.6} = 2.5.$$

This value is smaller than the multiplier of 4 that we calculated by assuming that there was only a fixed amount of taxes (which is the same as assuming that the marginal tax *rate* was zero). This multiplier is smaller because spending in each period is now reduced by the amount of taxes households must pay on any additional income they earn. We can calculate the multiplier for an *MPC* of 0.75 and a lower tax rate of 0.1:

$$\text{Government purchases multiplier} = \frac{\Delta Y}{\Delta G} = \frac{1}{1 - 0.75(1 - 0.1)} = \frac{1}{1 - 0.675} = 3.1.$$

Cutting the tax rate from 20 percent to 10 percent increased the value of the multiplier from 2.5 to 3.1.

The Multiplier in an Open Economy

Up to now, we have assumed that the economy is closed, with no imports or exports. We can consider the case of an open economy by including net exports in our analysis. Recall that net exports equal exports minus imports. Exports are determined primarily by factors—such as the exchange value of the dollar and the levels of real GDP in other countries—that we do not include in our model. So, we will assume that exports are fixed, or autonomous:

$$\text{Exports} = \overline{\textit{Exports}}.$$

Imports will increase as real GDP increases because households will spend some portion of an increase in income on imports. We can define the *marginal propensity to import* (*MPI*) as the fraction of an increase in income that is spent on imports. So, our expression for imports is:

$$\text{Imports} = MPI \times Y.$$

We can substitute our expressions for exports and imports into the expression we derived earlier for equilibrium real GDP:

$$Y = \overline{C} + MPC(1 - t)Y + \overline{I} + \overline{G} + [\overline{\textit{Exports}} - (MPI \times Y)],$$

where the expression $\overline{\textit{Exports}} - (MPI \times Y)$ represents net exports. We can now find an expression for the government purchases multiplier by using the same method as we did previously:

$$\text{Government purchases multiplier} = \frac{\Delta Y}{\Delta G} = \frac{1}{1 - [MPC(1 - t) - MPI]}.$$

We can see the effect of changing the value of the marginal propensity to import on the size of the multiplier by trying some values of key variables. First, assume $MPC = 0.75$, $t = 0.2$, and $MPI = 0.1$. Then:

$$\text{Government purchases multiplier} = \frac{\Delta Y}{\Delta G} = \frac{1}{1 - (0.75(1 - 0.2) - 0.1)} = \frac{1}{1 - 0.5} = 2.$$

This value is smaller than the multiplier of 2.5 that we calculated by assuming that there were no exports or imports (which is the same as assuming that the marginal propensity to import was zero). This multiplier is smaller because spending in each period is now reduced by the amount of imports households buy with any additional income they earn. We can calculate the multiplier with $MPC = 0.75$, $t = 0.20$, and a higher *MPI* of 0.2:

$$\text{Government purchases multiplier} = \frac{\Delta Y}{\Delta G} = \frac{1}{1 - (0.75(1 - 0.2) - 0.2)} = \frac{1}{1 - 0.4} = 1.7.$$

Increasing the marginal propensity to import from 0.1 to 0.2 decreases the value of the multiplier from 2 to 1.7. We can conclude that countries with a higher marginal propensity to import will have smaller multipliers than countries with a lower marginal propensity to import.

It is always important to bear in mind that the multiplier is a short-run effect which assumes that the economy is below the level of potential real GDP. In the long run, the economy is at potential real GDP, so an increase in government purchases causes a decline in the nongovernment components of real GDP, but it leaves the level of real GDP unchanged.

The analysis in this appendix is simplified compared to what would be carried out by an economist forecasting the effects of changes in government purchases or changes in taxes on equilibrium real GDP in the short run. In particular, our assumption that the price level is constant is unrealistic. However, looking more closely at the determinants of the multiplier has helped us see more clearly some important macroeconomic relationships.

LEARNING OBJECTIVE Apply the multiplier formula, **pages 546–551.**

myeconlab Get Ahead of the Curve Visit www.myeconlab.com to complete these exercises online and get instant feedback.

Problem and Applications

15A.1 Assuming a fixed amount of taxes and a closed economy, calculate the value of the government purchases multiplier, the tax multiplier, and the balanced budget multiplier if the marginal propensity to consume equals 0.6.

15A.2 Calculate the value of the government purchases multiplier if the marginal propensity to consume equals 0.8, the tax rate equals 0.25, and the marginal propensity to import equals 0.2.

15A.3 Show on a graph the change in the aggregate demand curve resulting from an increase in government purchases if the government purchases multiplier equals 2. Now, on the same graph, show the change in the aggregate demand curve resulting from an increase in government purchases if the government purchases multiplier equals 4.

15A.4 Using your understanding of the multiplier process, explain why an increase in the tax rate would decrease the size of the government purchases multiplier. Similarly, explain why a decrease in the marginal propensity to import would increase the size of the government purchases multiplier.

>> End Appendix Learning Objective

Inflation, Unemployment, and Federal Reserve Policy

Why Does Whirlpool Care about Monetary Policy?

How does inflation affect monetary policy, and how does monetary policy affect inflation? Testifying before Congress in March 2007, Federal Reserve Chairman Ben Bernanke said the following:

> In regard to monetary policy, the Federal Open Market Committee has left its target for the federal funds rate unchanged, at 5-1/4 percent, since last June. To date, the incoming data have supported the view that the current stance of policy is likely to foster sustainable economic growth and a gradual ebbing in core inflation. Because core inflation is above the levels most conducive to the achievement of sustainable growth and price stability, the Committee indicated in the statement following its recent meeting that its predominant policy concern remains the risk that inflation will fail to moderate as expected.

In other words, the Fed was hoping that its current target for the federal funds rate was high enough to keep the inflation declining, but not so high as to push the economy into recession.

We saw in Chapter 3 when introducing the model of demand and supply that the ability of firms to increase prices is determined partly by microeconomic factors. This statement by Chairman Bernanke indicates that macroeconomic factors, including monetary policy, also play a role.

For example, during 2005, with the housing boom in full swing and demand for appliances growing rapidly, Whirlpool was able to increase the prices of its products from 5 percent to 10 percent. But by 2007, the macroeconomic environment was not as strong for Whirlpool. The housing bubble had burst, with home sales declining in most parts of the country. Most new homes contain new built-in appliances, and many buyers of existing homes also buy at least some new appliances. Fewer home sales during 2006 and 2007 meant less demand for the appliances Whirlpool sells. During the first three months of 2007, Whirlpool's sales in the United States declined by 9.5 percent, while at the same time, the rising cost of raw materials, including oil-based products and metals, led the firm to raise prices. Falling demand and rising costs is not a good combination for any firm.

Whirlpool was founded in 1911 by brothers Louis, Frederick, and Emory Upton. In 2006, Whirlpool, headquartered in Benton Harbor, Michigan, had 73,000 employees and $18 billion in annual sales. In 2001 and the following years, Whirlpool clearly benefited from the effects of monetary policy. As we saw in Chapter 14, expansionary monetary policy in 2001 and several years thereafter resulted in low real interest rates on home mortgage loans, which led to the boom in residential housing construction. As Chairman Bernanke's testimony indicates, however, by 2007, the Fed was attempting to balance the slowdown in economic growth caused by the bursting of the housing bubble and rising oil prices against the fear that inflation might remain high. As Whirlpool's situation showed, a slowdown in the growth of aggregate demand coupled with an aggregate supply shock can lead to slower growth in GDP and increases in the price level.

AN INSIDE LOOK AT POLICY on **page 576** discusses new research about the role the public's expectations of future inflation play in determining the inflation rate.

Sources: "Testimony of Chairman Ben S. Bernanke Before the Joint Economic Committee, U.S. Congress," March 28, 2007; and Ilan Brat and Henry Sanderson, "Whirlpool Likely to Keep Lift from Global Sales," *Wall Street Journal*, April 25, 2007, p. C8.

LEARNING Objectives

After studying this chapter, you should be able to:

16.1 Describe the **Phillips curve** and the nature of the **short-run trade-off** between **unemployment** and **inflation**, page 554.

16.2 Explain the relationship between the **short-run** and **long-run Phillips curves**, page 559.

16.3 Discuss how **expectations** of the **inflation rate** affect monetary policy, page 564.

16.4 Use a Phillips curve graph to show how the **Federal Reserve** can permanently **lower** the **inflation rate**, page 567.

Economics in YOUR Life!

How Big of a Raise Should You Ask For?

Suppose that you meet with your boss to discuss your raise for next year. One factor in deciding how big an increase to request is your expectation of what the inflation rate will be. If the Federal Reserve pledges to keep the unemployment rate at 3 percent in the long run, what effect will this pledge have on the size of the raise you request? As you read this chapter, see if you can answer this question. You can check your answer against the one we provide at the end of the chapter.

>> **Continued on page 575**

As we saw in Chapter 14, two of the Federal Reserve's monetary policy goals are price stability and high employment. These goals can sometimes be in conflict, however. Chairman Bernanke's testimony indicates that in 2007 the Fed was concerned that economic growth was slowing but was reluctant to cut the target for the federal funds rate for fear that inflation would remain above acceptable levels. An important consideration for the Fed is that in the short run, there can be a trade-off between unemployment and inflation: Lower unemployment rates can result in higher inflation rates. In the long run, however, this trade-off disappears, and the unemployment rate is independent of the inflation rate. In this chapter, we will explore the relationship between inflation and unemployment in both the short run and the long run, and we will discuss what this relationship means for monetary policy.

16.1 LEARNING OBJECTIVE

16.1 | Describe the Phillips curve and the nature of the short-run trade-off between unemployment and inflation.

The Discovery of the Short-Run Trade-off between Unemployment and Inflation

Unemployment and inflation are the two great macroeconomic problems the Fed must deal with in the short run. As we saw in Chapter 12, when aggregate demand increases, unemployment usually falls and inflation rises. When aggregate demand decreases, unemployment usually rises and inflation falls. As a result, there is a *short-run trade-off* between unemployment and inflation: Higher unemployment is usually accompanied by lower inflation, and lower unemployment is usually accompanied by higher inflation. As we will see later in this chapter, this trade-off exists in the short run—a period that may be as long as several years—but disappears in the long run.

Although today the short-run trade-off between unemployment and inflation plays a role in the Fed's monetary policy decisions, this trade-off was not widely recognized until the late 1950s. In 1957, New Zealand economist A. W. Phillips plotted data on the unemployment rate and the inflation rate in Great Britain and drew a curve showing their average relationship. Since that time, a graph showing the short-run relationship between the unemployment rate and the inflation rate has been called a **Phillips curve**. (Phillips actually measured inflation by the percentage change in wages rather than by the percentage change in prices. Because wages and prices usually move together, this difference is not important to our discussion.) Figure 16-1 shows a graph similar to the

Phillips curve A curve showing the short-run relationship between the unemployment rate and the inflation rate.

Figure 16-1

The Phillips Curve

A. W. Phillips was the first economist to show that there is usually an inverse relationship between unemployment and inflation. Here we can see this relationship at work: In the year represented by point *A*, the inflation rate is 4 percent and the unemployment rate is 5 percent. In the year represented by point *B*, the inflation rate is 2 percent and the unemployment rate is 6 percent.

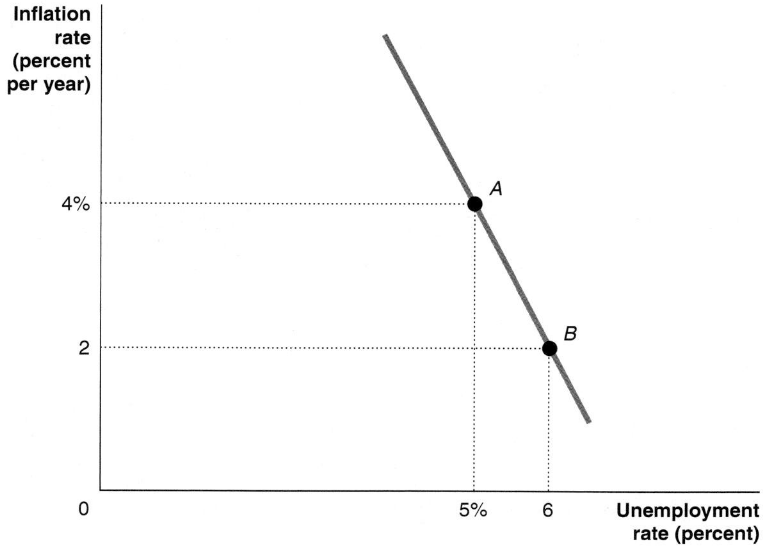

one Phillips prepared. Each point on the Phillips curve represents a possible combination of the unemployment rate and the inflation rate that might be observed in a given year. Point *A* represents a year in which the inflation rate is 4 percent and the unemployment rate is 5 percent, and point *B* represents a different year in which the inflation rate is 2 percent and the unemployment rate is 6 percent. Phillips documented that there is usually an *inverse relationship* between unemployment and inflation. During years when the unemployment rate is low, the inflation rate tends to be high, and during years when the unemployment rate is high, the inflation rate tends to be low.

Explaining the Phillips Curve with Aggregate Demand and Aggregate Supply Curves

The inverse relationship between unemployment and inflation that Phillips discovered is consistent with the aggregate demand and aggregate supply analysis we developed in Chapter 12. Figure 16-2 shows the factors that cause this inverse relationship.

Panel (a) shows the aggregate demand and aggregate supply *(AD–AS)* model from Chapter 12, and panel (b) shows the Phillips curve. For simplicity, in panel (a), we are using the basic *AD–AS* model, which assumes that the long-run aggregate supply curve and the short-run aggregate supply curve do not shift. Assume that the economy in 2011 is at point *A*, with real GDP of $14.0 trillion and a price level of 100. If there is weak growth in aggregate demand, in 2012, the economy moves to point *B*, with real GDP of $14.3 trillion and a price level of 102. The inflation rate is 2 percent and the unemployment rate is 6 percent, which corresponds to point *B* on the Phillips curve in panel (b). If there is strong growth in aggregated demand, in 2012, the economy moves to point *C*, with real GDP of $14.5 trillion and a price level of 104. Strong aggregate demand growth results in a higher inflation of 4 percent but a lower unemployment rate of 5 percent.

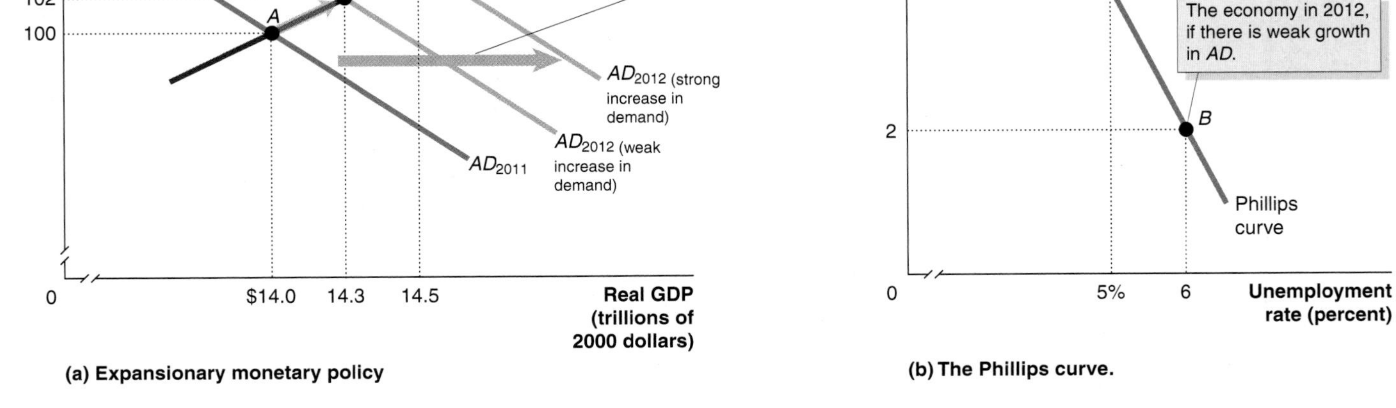

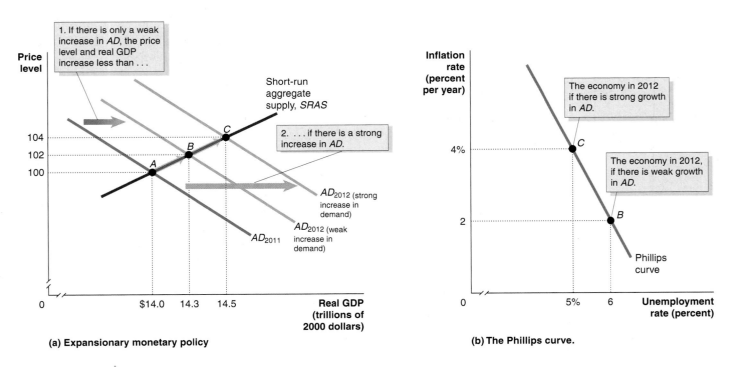

Figure 16-2 | Using Aggregate Demand and Aggregate Supply to Explain the Phillips Curve

In panel (a), the economy in 2011 is at point *A*, with real GDP of $14.0 trillion and a price level of 100. If there is weak growth in aggregate demand, in 2012, the economy moves to point *B*, with real GDP of $14.3 trillion and a price level of 102. The inflation rate is 2 percent and the unemployment rate is 6 percent, which corresponds to point *B* on the Phillips curve in panel (b). If there is strong growth in aggregated demand, in 2012, the economy moves to point *C*, with real GDP of $14.5 trillion and a price level of 104. Strong aggregate demand growth results in a higher inflation rate of 4 percent but a lower unemployment rate of 5 percent. This combination of higher inflation and lower unemployment is shown as point *C* on the Phillips curve in panel (b).

This combination of higher inflation and lower unemployment is shown as point *C* on the Phillips curve in panel (b).

To summarize, the *AD–AS* model indicates that slow growth in aggregate demand leads to both higher unemployment and lower inflation. This relationship explains why there is a short-run trade-off between unemployment and inflation, as shown by the downward-sloping Phillips curve. The *AD–AS* model and the Phillips curve are different ways of illustrating the same macroeconomic events. The Phillips curve has an advantage over the *AD–AS* model, however, when we want to analyze explicitly *changes* in the inflation and unemployment rates.

Is the Phillips Curve a Policy Menu?

Structural relationship A relationship that depends on the basic behavior of consumers and firms and remains unchanged over long periods.

During the 1960s, some economists argued that the Phillips curve represented a *structural relationship* in the economy. A **structural relationship** depends on the basic behavior of consumers and firms and remains unchanged over long periods. Structural relationships are useful in formulating economic policy because policymakers can anticipate that these relationships are constant—that is, the relationships will not change as a result of changes in policy.

If the Phillips curve were a structural relationship, it would present policymakers with a reliable menu of combinations of unemployment and inflation. Potentially, policymakers could use expansionary monetary and fiscal policies to choose a point on the curve that had lower unemployment and higher inflation. They could also use contractionary monetary and fiscal policies to choose a point that had lower inflation and higher unemployment. Because many economists and policymakers in the 1960s viewed the Phillips curve as a structural relationship, they believed it represented a *permanent trade-off between unemployment and inflation.* As long as policymakers were willing to accept a permanently higher inflation rate, they would be able to keep the unemployment rate permanently lower. Similarly, a permanently lower inflation rate could be attained at the cost of a permanently higher unemployment rate. As we discuss in the next section, however, economists came to realize that the Phillips curve did *not*, in fact, represent a permanent trade-off between unemployment and inflation.

Is the Short-Run Phillips Curve Stable?

During the 1960s, the basic Phillips curve relationship seemed to hold because a stable trade-off appeared to exist between unemployment and inflation. In the early 1960s, the inflation rate was low, and the unemployment rate was high. In the late 1960s, the unemployment rate had declined, and the inflation rate had increased. Then in 1968, in his presidential address to the American Economic Association, Milton Friedman of the University of Chicago argued that the Phillips curve did *not* represent a *permanent* trade-off between unemployment and inflation. At almost the same time, Edmund Phelps of Columbia University published an academic paper making a similar argument. Friedman and Phelps noted that economists had come to agree that the long-run aggregate supply curve was vertical (a point we discussed in Chapter 12). If this observation were true, the Phillips curve could not be downward sloping in the long run. A critical inconsistency existed between a vertical long-run aggregate supply curve and a long-run Phillips curve that is downward sloping. Friedman and Phelps argued, in essence, that there is no trade-off between unemployment and inflation in the long run.

The Long-Run Phillips Curve

Natural rate of unemployment The unemployment rate that exists when the economy is at potential GDP.

To understand the argument that there is no permanent trade-off between unemployment and inflation, first recall that the level of real GDP in the long run is also referred to as *potential real GDP.* At potential real GDP, firms will operate at their normal level of capacity, and everyone who wants a job will have one, except the structurally and frictionally unemployed. Friedman defined the **natural rate of unemployment** as the unemployment rate that exists when the economy is at potential GDP. The actual unem-

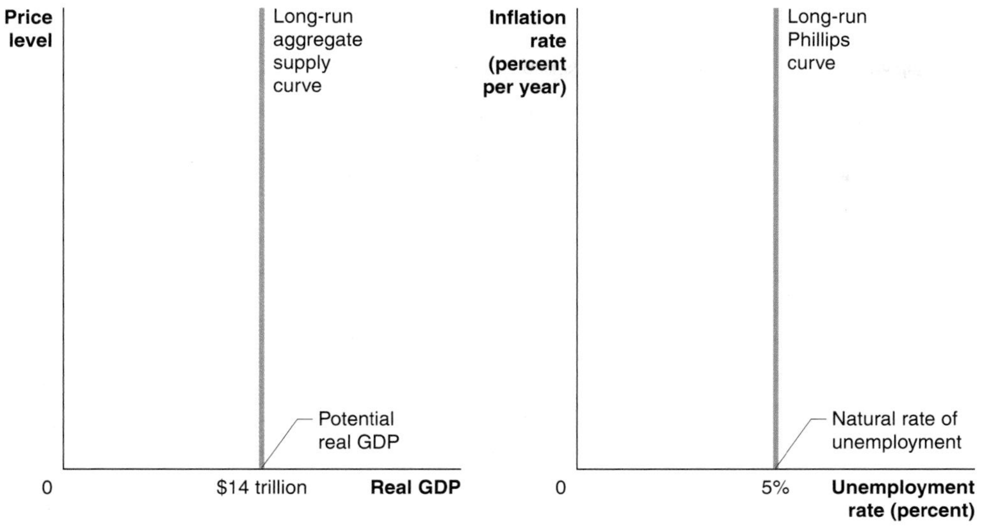

Figure 16-3

A Vertical Long-Run Aggregate Supply Curve Means a Vertical Long-Run Phillips Curve

Milton Friedman and Edmund Phelps argued that there is no trade-off between unemployment and inflation in the long run. If real GDP automatically returns to its potential level in the long run, the unemployment rate must return to the natural rate of unemployment in the long run. In this figure, we assume that potential real GDP is $14.0 trillion and the natural rate of unemployment is 5 percent.

ployment rate will fluctuate in the short run but will always come back to the natural rate in the long run. In the same way, the actual level of real GDP will fluctuate in the short run but will always come back to its potential level in the long run.

In the long run, a higher or lower price level has no effect on real GDP because real GDP is always at its potential level in the long run. In the same way, in the long run, a higher or lower inflation rate will have no effect on the unemployment rate because the unemployment rate is always equal to the natural rate in the long run. Figure 16-3 illustrates Friedman's conclusion that the long-run aggregate supply curve is a vertical line at the potential real GDP, and *the long-run Phillips curve is a vertical line at the natural rate of unemployment.*

The Role of Expectations of Future Inflation

If the long-run Phillips curve is a vertical line, *no trade-off exists between unemployment and inflation in the long run.* This conclusion seemed to contradict the experience of the 1950s and 1960s, which showed a stable trade-off between unemployment and inflation. Friedman argued that the statistics from those years actually showed only a short-run trade-off between inflation and unemployment.

The short-run trade-off existed—but only because workers and firms sometimes expected the inflation rate to be either higher or lower than it turned out to be. Differences between the expected inflation rate and the actual inflation rate could lead the unemployment rate to rise above or dip below the natural rate. To see why, consider a simple case of General Motors negotiating a wage contract with the United Automobile Workers (UAW) union. Remember that both General Motors and the UAW are interested in the real wage, which is the nominal wage, corrected for inflation. Suppose, for example, that General Motors and the UAW agree on a wage of $31.50 per hour to be paid during 2012. Both General Motors and the UAW expect that the price level will increase from 100 in 2011 to 105 in 2012, so the inflation rate will be 5 percent. We can calculate the real wage General Motors expects to pay and the UAW expects to receive as follows:

$$\text{Real wage} = \frac{\text{Nominal wage}}{\text{Price level}} \times 100 = \frac{\$31.50}{105} \times 100 = \$30.$$

But suppose that the actual inflation rate turns out to be higher or lower than the expected inflation rate of 5 percent. Table 16-1 shows the effect on the actual real wage. If the price level rises only to 102 during 2012, the inflation rate will be 2 percent, and the actual real wage will be $30.88, which is higher than General Motors and

TABLE 16-1

The Impact of Unexpected Price Level Changes on the Real Wage

NOMINAL WAGE	EXPECTED REAL WAGE	ACTUAL REAL WAGE	
	Expected P_{2012} = 105	Actual P_{2012} = 102	Actual P_{2012} = 108
	Expected inflation = 5%	Actual inflation = 2%	Actual inflation = 8%
\$31.50	$\frac{\$31.50}{105} \times 100 = \$30$	$\frac{\$31.50}{102} \times 100 = \$30.88$	$\frac{\$31.50}{108} \times 100 = \$29.17$

the UAW had expected. With a higher real wage, General Motors will hire fewer workers than it had planned to at the expected real wage of \$30. If the inflation rate is 8 percent, the actual real wage will be \$29.17, and General Motors will hire more workers than it had planned. If General Motors and the UAW expected a higher or lower inflation rate than actually occurred, other firms and workers probably made the same mistake.

If actual inflation is higher than expected inflation, actual real wages in the economy will be lower than expected real wages, and many firms will hire more workers than they had planned to hire. Therefore, the unemployment rate will fall. If actual inflation is lower than expected inflation, actual real wages will be higher than expected; many firms will hire fewer workers than they had planned to hire, and the unemployment rate will rise. Table 16-2 summarizes this argument.

Friedman and Phelps concluded that *an increase in the inflation rate increases employment (and decreases unemployment) only if the increase in the inflation rate is unexpected.* Friedman argued that in 1968, the unemployment rate was 3.6 percent rather than 5 percent only because the inflation rate of 4 percent was above the 1 percent to 2 percent inflation that workers and firms had expected: "There is always a temporary trade-off between inflation and unemployment; there is no permanent trade-off. The temporary trade-off comes not from inflation per se, but from unanticipated inflation."

TABLE 16-2

The Basis for the Short-Run Phillips Curve

IF . . .	THEN . . .	AND . . .
actual inflation is greater than expected inflation,	the actual real wage is less than the expected real wage,	the unemployment rate falls.
actual inflation is less than expected inflation,	the actual real wage is greater than the expected real wage,	the unemployment rate rises.

Will her wage increases keep up with inflation?

Making the Connection

Do Workers Understand Inflation?

A higher inflation rate can lead to lower unemployment if *both* workers and firms mistakenly expect the inflation rate to be lower than it turns out to be. But this same result might be due to firms forecasting inflation more accurately than workers do or to firms understanding better the effects of inflation. Some large firms employ economists to help them gather and analyze information that is useful in forecasting inflation. Many firms also have human resources or employee compensation departments that gather data on wages paid at competing firms and analyze trends in compensation. Workers generally rely on much less systematic information about wages and prices. Workers also often fail to realize a fact we discussed in Chapter 8: *Expected inflation increases the value of total production and the value of total income by the same amount.* Therefore, although not all wages will rise as prices rise, inflation will increase the average wage in the economy at the same time that it increases the average price.

Robert Shiller, an economist at Yale University, conducted a survey on inflation and discovered that, although most economists believe an increase in inflation will lead quickly to an increase in wages, a majority of the general public thinks otherwise. In one question, Shiller asked how "the effect of general inflation on wages or salary relates to your own experience and your own job." The most popular response was: "The price increase will create extra profits for my employer, who can now sell output for more; there will be no effect on my pay. My employer will see no reason to raise my pay."

Shiller also asked the following question:

> Imagine that next year the inflation rate unexpectedly doubles. How long would it probably take, in these times, before your income is increased enough so that you can afford the same things as you do today? In other words, how long will it be before a full inflation correction in your income has taken place?

Eighty-one percent of the public answered either that it would take several years for the purchasing power of their income to be restored or that it would never be restored.

If workers fail to understand that rising inflation leads over time to comparable increases in wages, then when inflation increases, in the short run, firms can increase wages by less than inflation without needing to worry about workers quitting or their morale falling. Once again, we have a higher inflation rate, leading in the short run to lower real wages and lower unemployment. In other words, we have an explanation for a downward-sloping short-run Phillips curve.

Source: Robert J. Shiller, "Why Do People Dislike Inflation?" in *Reducing Inflation: Motivation and Strategy*, Christina D. Romer and David H. Romer, eds., Chicago: University of Chicago Press, 1997.

YOUR TURN: Test your understanding by doing related problems 1.12 and 1.13 on page 579 at the end of this chapter.

16.2 LEARNING OBJECTIVE

16.2 | Explain the relationship between the short-run and long-run Phillips curves.

The Short-Run and Long-Run Phillips Curves

If there is both a short-run Phillips curve and a long-run Phillips curve, how are the two curves related? We can begin answering this question with the help of Figure 16-4, which represents macroeconomic conditions in the United States during the 1960s. In the late

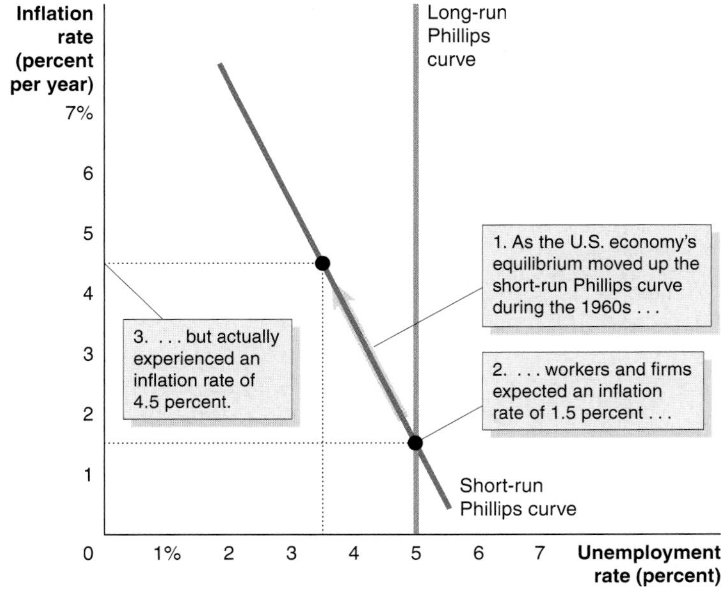

Figure 16-4

The Short-Run Phillips Curve of the 1960s and the Long-Run Phillips Curve

In the late 1960s, U.S. workers and firms were expecting the 1.5 percent inflation rates of the recent past to continue. However, expansionary monetary and fiscal policies moved the short-run equilibrium up the short-run Phillips curve to an inflation rate of 4.5 percent and an unemployment rate of 3.5 percent.

1960s, workers and firms were still expecting the inflation rate to be about 1.5 percent, as it had been from 1960 to 1965. Expansionary monetary and fiscal policies, however, had moved the short-run equilibrium up the short-run Phillips curve to an inflation rate of 4.5 percent and an unemployment rate of 3.5 percent. This very low unemployment rate was possible only because the real wage rate was unexpectedly low.

Once workers and firms began to expect that the inflation rate would continue to be about 4.5 percent, they changed their behavior. Firms knew that only nominal wage increases of more than 4.5 percent would increase real wages. Workers realized that unless they received a nominal wage increase of at least 4.5 percent, their real wage would be falling. Higher expected inflation rates had an impact throughout the economy. For example, as we saw in Chapter 13, when banks make loans, they are interested in the *real interest rate* on the loan. The real interest rate is the nominal interest rate minus the expected inflation rate. If banks need to receive a real interest rate of 3 percent on home mortgage loans and expect the inflation rate to be 1.5 percent, they will charge a nominal interest rate of 4.5 percent. If banks revise their expectations of the inflation rate to 4.5 percent, they will increase the nominal interest rate they charge on mortgage loans to 7.5 percent.

Shifts in the Short-Run Phillips Curve

The new, higher expected inflation rate can become *embedded* in the economy, meaning that workers, firms, consumers, and the government all take the inflation rate into account when making decisions. The short-run trade-off between unemployment and inflation now takes place from this higher, less favorable level, as shown in Figure 16-5.

As long as workers and firms expected the inflation rate to be 1.5 percent, the short-run trade-off between unemployment and inflation was the more favorable one shown by the lower Phillips curve. Along this Phillips curve, an inflation rate of 4.5 percent was enough to drive down the unemployment rate to 3.5 percent. Once workers and firms adjusted their expectations to an inflation rate of 4.5 percent, the short-run trade-off deteriorated to the one shown by the higher Phillips curve. At this higher expected inflation rate, the real wage rose, causing some workers to lose their jobs, and the economy's equilibrium returned to the natural rate of unemployment of 5 percent, but now with an

Figure 16-5

Expectations and the Short-Run Phillips Curve

By the end of the 1960s, workers and firms had revised their expectations of inflation from 1.5 percent to 4.5 percent. As a result, the short-run Phillips curve shifted up, which made the short-run trade-off between unemployment and inflation worse.

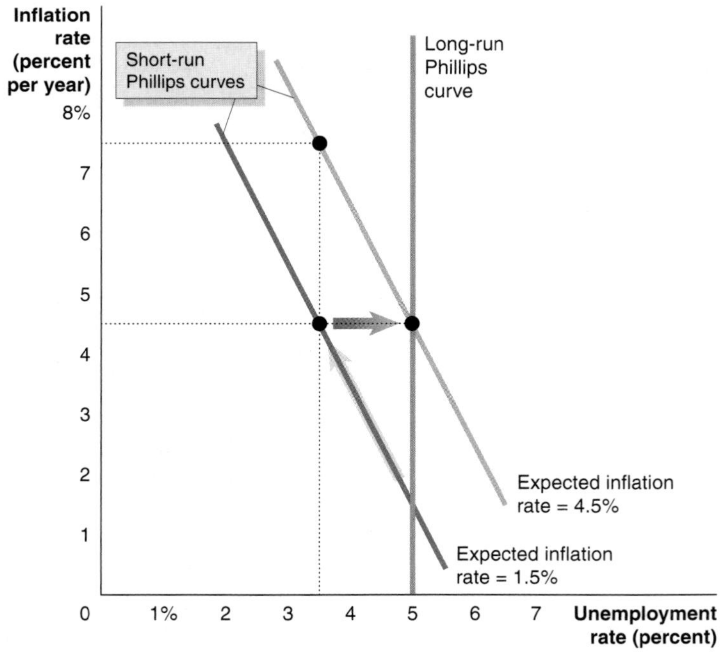

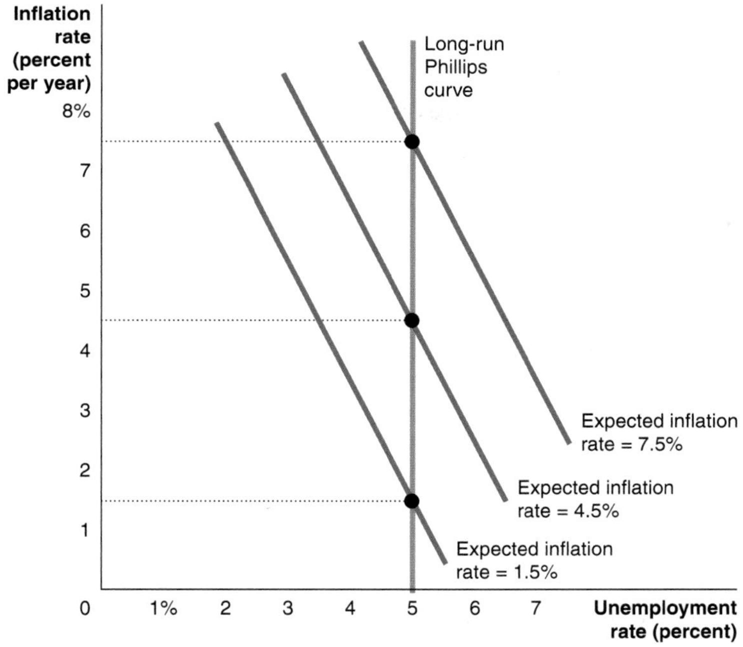

Figure 16-6

A Short-Run Phillips Curve for Every Expected Inflation Rate

There is a different short-run Phillips curve for every expected inflation rate. Each short-run Phillips curve intersects the long-run Phillips curve at the expected inflation rate.

inflation rate of 4.5 percent rather than 1.5 percent. On the higher short-run Phillips curve, an inflation rate of 7.5 percent would be necessary to reduce the unemployment rate to 3.5 percent. An inflation rate of 7.5 percent would keep the unemployment rate at 3.5 percent only until workers and firms revised their expectations of inflation up to 7.5 percent. In the long run, the economy's equilibrium would return to the 5 percent natural rate of unemployment.

As Figure 16-6 shows, there is a short-run Phillips curve for every level of expected inflation. Each short-run Phillips curve intersects the long-run Phillips curve at the expected inflation rate.

How Does a Vertical Long-Run Phillips Curve Affect Monetary Policy?

By the 1970s, most economists accepted the argument that the long-run Phillips curve is vertical. In other words, economists realized that the common view of the 1960s had been wrong: It was *not* possible to buy a permanently lower unemployment rate at the cost of a permanently higher inflation rate. The moral of the vertical long-run Phillips curve is that *in the long run, there is no trade-off between unemployment and inflation.* In the long run, the unemployment rate always returns to the natural rate, no matter what the inflation rate is.

Figure 16-7 shows that the inflation rate is stable only when the unemployment rate is equal to the natural rate. If the Federal Reserve were to attempt to use expansionary monetary policy to push the economy to a point such as *A*, where the unemployment rate is below the natural rate, the result would be increasing inflation as the economy moved up the short-run Phillips curve. If the economy remained below the natural rate long enough, the short-run Phillips curve would shift up as workers and firms adjusted to the new, higher inflation rate. During the 1960s and 1970s, the short-run Phillips curve did shift up, presenting the economy with a more unfavorable short-run trade-off between unemployment and inflation.

If the Federal Reserve used contractionary policy to push the economy to a point such as *B*, where the unemployment rate is above the natural rate, the inflation rate would decrease. If the economy remained above the natural rate long enough, the short-run Phillips curve would shift down as workers and firms adjusted to the new, lower inflation

Figure 16-7

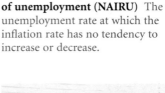

The Inflation Rate and the Natural Rate of Unemployment in the Long Run

The inflation rate is stable only if the unemployment rate equals the natural rate of unemployment (point *C*). If the unemployment rate is below the natural rate (point *A*), the inflation rate increases, and, eventually, the short-run Phillips curve shifts up. If the unemployment rate is above the natural rate (point *B*), the inflation rate decreases, and, eventually, the short-run Phillips curve shifts down.

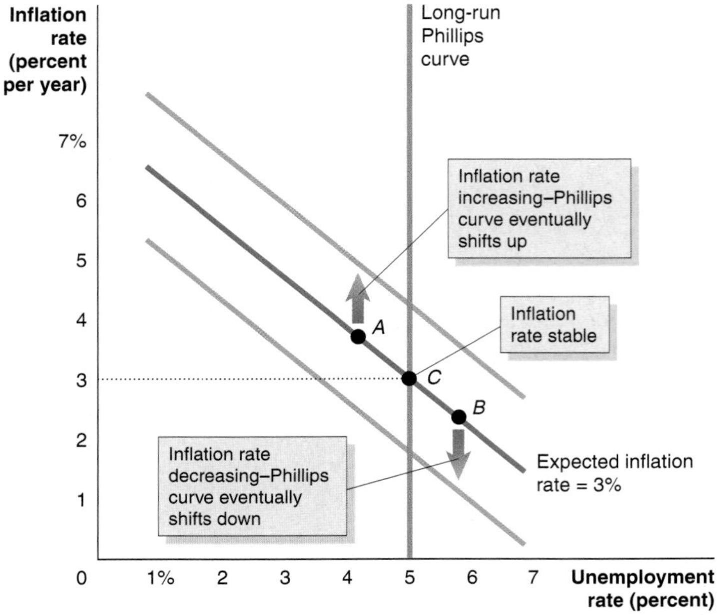

rate. Only at a point such as *C*, where the unemployment rate is equal to the natural rate, will the inflation rate be stable. As a result, the natural rate of unemployment is sometimes called the **nonaccelerating inflation rate of unemployment (NAIRU)**. We can conclude this: *In the long run, the Federal Reserve can affect the inflation rate but not the unemployment rate.*

Nonaccelerating inflation rate of unemployment (NAIRU) The unemployment rate at which the inflation rate has no tendency to increase or decrease.

Making the Connection | Does the Natural Rate of Unemployment Ever Change?

What makes the natural rate of unemployment increase or decrease?

Life would be easier for the Federal Reserve if it knew exactly what the natural rate of unemployment was and if that rate never changed. Unfortunately for the Fed, the natural rate does change over time. Remember that at the natural rate of unemployment, only frictional and structural unemployment remain. Frictional or structural unemployment can change—thereby changing the natural rate—for several reasons:

- ***Demographic changes.*** Younger and less skilled workers have higher unemployment rates, on average, than do older and more skilled workers. Because of the baby boom, the United States had an unusually large number of younger and less skilled workers during the 1970s and 1980s. As a result, the natural rate of unemployment rose from about 5 percent in the 1960s to about 6 percent in the 1970s and 1980s. As the number of younger and less skilled workers declined as a fraction of the labor force during the 1990s, the natural rate returned to about 5 percent.
- ***Labor market institutions.*** As we discussed in Chapter 8, labor market institutions such as the unemployment insurance system, unions, and legal barriers to firing workers can increase the economy's unemployment rate. Because many European countries have generous unemployment insurance systems, strong unions, and restrictive policies on firing workers, the natural rate of unemployment in most Europeans countries has been well above the rate in the United States.
- ***Past high rates of unemployment.*** Evidence indicates that if high unemployment persists for a period of years, the natural rate of unemployment may increase. When

workers have been unemployed for longer than a year or two, their skills deteriorate, they may lose confidence that they can find and hold a job, and they may become dependent on government payments to survive. Robert Gordon, an economist at Northwestern University, has argued that in the late 1930s, so many U.S. workers had been out of work for so long that the natural rate of unemployment may have risen to more than 15 percent. He has pointed out that even though the unemployment rate in the United States was 17 percent in 1939, the inflation rate did not change. Similarly, many economists have argued that the high unemployment rates experienced by European countries during the 1970s increased their natural rates of unemployment.

YOUR TURN: Test your understanding by doing related problem 2.7 on page 581 at the end of this chapter.

Solved Problem | **16-2**

Changing Views of the Phillips Curve

Writing in a Federal Reserve publication, Bennett McCallum, an economist at Carnegie Mellon University, argues that during the 1970s, the Fed was "acting under the influence of 1960s academic ideas that posited the existence of a long-run and exploitable Phillips-type tradeoff between inflation and unemployment rates." What does he mean by a "long-run and exploitable Phillips-type trade-off"? How would the Fed have attempted to exploit this long-run trade-off? What would be the consequences for the inflation rate?

SOLVING THE PROBLEM:

Step 1: **Review the chapter material.** This problem is about the relationship between the short-run and long-run Phillips curves, so you may want to review the section "The Short-Run and Long-Run Phillips Curves," which begins on page 559.

Step 2: **Explain what a "long-run exploitable Phillips-type tradeoff" means.** A "long-run exploitable Phillips-type tradeoff" means a Phillips curve that in the long run is downward sloping rather than vertical. An "exploitable" trade-off is one that the Fed could take advantage of to *permanently* reduce unemployment at the expense of higher inflation or to permanently reduce inflation at the expense of higher unemployment.

Step 3: **Explain how the inflation rate will accelerate if the Fed tries to exploit a long-run trade-off between unemployment and inflation.** As we have seen, during the 1960s, the Fed conducted expansionary monetary policies to move up what it thought was a stationary short-run Phillips curve. By the late 1960s, these policies resulted in very low unemployment rates. In the long run, there is no stable trade-off between unemployment and inflation. Attempting to permanently keep the unemployment rate at very low levels leads to a rising inflation rate, which is what happened in the late 1960s and early 1970s.

Source: Bennett T. McCallum, "Recent Developments in Monetary Policy Analysis: The Roles of Theory and Evidence," Federal Reserve Bank of Richmond, *Economic Quarterly*, Winter 2002, p. 73.

YOUR TURN: For more practice, do related problem 2.4 on page 580 at the end of this chapter.

>> End Solved Problem 16-2

16.3 LEARNING OBJECTIVE

16.3 | Discuss how expectations of the inflation rate affect monetary policy.

Expectations of the Inflation Rate and Monetary Policy

How long can the economy remain at a point that is on the short-run Phillips curve, but not on the long-run Phillips curve? It depends on how quickly workers and firms adjust their expectations of future inflation to changes in current inflation. The experience in the United States over the past 50 years indicates that how workers and firms adjust their expectations of inflation depends on how high the inflation rate is. There are three possibilities:

- ***Low inflation.*** When the inflation rate is low, as it was during most of the 1950s, the early 1960s, the 1990s, and the early 2000s, workers and firms tend to ignore it. For example, if the inflation rate is low, a restaurant may not want to pay for printing new menus that would show slightly higher prices.
- ***Moderate but stable inflation.*** For the four-year period from 1968 to 1971, the inflation rate in the United States stayed in the narrow range between 4 percent and 5 percent. This rate was high enough that workers and firms could not ignore it without seeing their real wages and profits decline. It was also likely that the next year's inflation rate would be very close to the current year's inflation rate. In fact, workers and firms during the 1960s acted as if they expected changes in the inflation rate during one year to continue into the following year. People are said to have *adaptive expectations* of inflation if they assume that future rates of inflation will follow the pattern of rates of inflation in the recent past.
- ***High and unstable inflation.*** Inflation rates above 5 percent during peacetime have been rare in U.S. history, but the inflation rate was above 5 percent every year from 1973 through 1982. Not only was the inflation rate high during these years, it was also unstable—rising from 6 percent in 1973 to 11 percent in 1974, before falling below 6 percent in 1976 and rising again to 13.5 percent in 1980. In the mid-1970s, Nobel laureate Robert Lucas of the University of Chicago and Thomas Sargent of New York University argued that the gains to forecasting inflation accurately had dramatically increased. Workers and firms that failed to correctly anticipate the fluctuations in inflation during these years could experience substantial declines in real wages and profits. Therefore, Lucas and Sargent argued, people should use all available information when forming their expectations of future inflation. Expectations formed by using all available information about an economic variable are called **rational expectations**.

Rational expectations Expectations formed by using all available information about an economic variable.

The Effect of Rational Expectations on Monetary Policy

Lucas and Sargent pointed out an important consequence of rational expectations: An expansionary monetary policy would not work. In other words, there might not be a trade-off between unemployment and inflation, even in the short run. By the mid-1970s, most economists had accepted the idea that an expansionary monetary policy could cause the actual inflation rate to be higher than the expected inflation rate. This gap between actual and expected inflation would cause the actual real wage to fall below the expected real wage, and the unemployment rate would be pushed below the natural rate. The economy's short-run equilibrium would move up the short-run Phillips curve.

Lucas and Sargent argued that this explanation of the Phillips curve assumed that workers and firms either ignored inflation or used adaptive expectations in making their forecasts of inflation. If workers and firms have rational expectations, they will use all

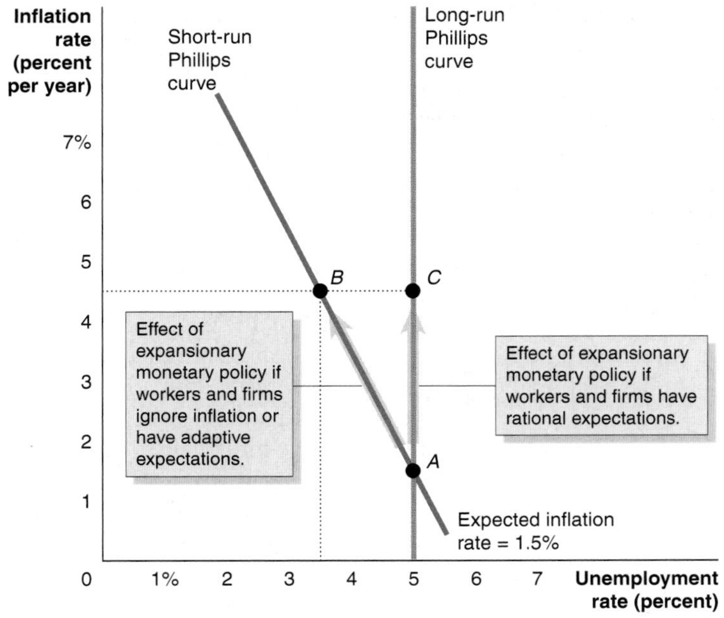

Figure 16-8

Rational Expectations and the Phillips Curve

If workers and firms ignore inflation, or if they have adaptive expectations, an expansionary monetary policy will cause the short-run equilibrium to move from point *A* on the short-run Phillips curve to point *B*; inflation will rise, and unemployment will fall. If workers and firms have rational expectations, an expansionary monetary policy will cause the short-run equilibrium to move up the long-run Phillips curve from point *A* to point *C*. Inflation will still rise, but there will be no change in unemployment.

available information, *including knowledge of the effects of Federal Reserve policy.* If workers and firms know that an expansionary monetary policy will raise the inflation rate, they should use this information in their forecasts of inflation. If they do, an expansionary monetary policy will not cause the actual inflation rate to be above the expected inflation rate. Instead, the actual inflation rate will equal the expected inflation rate, the actual real wage will equal the expected real wage, and the unemployment rate will not fall below the natural rate.

Figure 16-8 illustrates this argument. Suppose the economy begins at point *A*, where the short-run Phillips curve intersects the long-run Phillips curve. The actual and expected inflation rates are both equal to 1.5 percent, and the unemployment rate equals the natural rate of 5 percent. Then suppose the Fed engages in an expansionary monetary policy. If workers ignore inflation or if they form their expectations adaptively, the expansionary monetary policy will cause the actual inflation rate to be higher than the expected inflation rate, and the short-run equilibrium will move from point *A* on the short-run Phillips curve to point *B*. The inflation rate will rise to 4.5 percent, and the unemployment rate will fall to 3.5 percent. The decline in unemployment will be only temporary, however. Eventually, workers and firms will adjust to the fact that the actual inflation rate is 4.5 percent, not the 1.5 percent they had expected. The short-run Phillips curve will shift up, and the unemployment rate will return to 5 percent at point *C*.

Lucas and Sargent argued that if workers and firms have rational expectations, they will realize that the Fed's expansionary policy will result in an inflation rate of 4.5 percent. Therefore, as soon as the new policy is announced, workers and firms should adjust their expectations of inflation from 1.5 percent to 4.5 percent. There will be no temporary decrease in the real wage, leading to a temporary increase in employment and real GDP. Instead, the short-run equilibrium will move immediately from point *A* to point *C* on the long-run Phillips curve. The unemployment rate will never drop below 5 percent, and the *short-run* Phillips curve will be vertical.

Is the Short-Run Phillips Curve Really Vertical?

The claim by Lucas and Sargent that the short-run Phillips curve was vertical and that an expansionary monetary policy could not reduce the unemployment rate below the natural rate surprised many economists. An obvious objection to the argument of Lucas and Sargent was that the record of the 1950s and 1960s seemed to show that there was a short-run trade-off between unemployment and inflation and that, therefore, the short-run Phillips curve was downward sloping and not vertical. Lucas and Sargent argued that the apparent short-run trade-off was actually the result of *unexpected* changes in monetary policy. During those years, the Fed did not announce changes in policy, so workers, firms, and financial markets had to *guess* when the Fed had begun using a new policy. In that case, an expansionary monetary policy might cause the unemployment rate to fall because workers and firms would be taken by surprise, and their expectations of inflation would be too low. Lucas and Sargent argued that a policy that was announced ahead of time would not cause a change in unemployment.

Many economists have remained skeptical of the argument that the short-run Phillips curve is vertical. The two main objections raised are that (1) workers and firms actually may not have rational expectations, and (2) the rapid adjustment of wages and prices needed for the short-run Phillips curve to be vertical will not actually take place. Many economists doubt that people are able to use information on the Fed's monetary policy to make a reliable forecast of the inflation rate. If workers and firms do not know what impact an expansionary monetary policy will have on the inflation rate, the actual real wage may still end up being lower than the expected real wage. Also, firms may have contracts with their workers and suppliers that keep wages and prices from adjusting quickly. If wages and prices adjust slowly, then even if workers and firms have rational expectations, an expansionary monetary policy may still be able to reduce the unemployment rate in the short run.

Real Business Cycle Models

During the 1980s, some economists, including Nobel laureates Finn Kydland of Carnegie Mellon University and Edward Prescott of Arizona State University, argued that Robert Lucas was correct in assuming that workers and firms formed their expectations rationally and that wages and prices adjust quickly, but that he was wrong in assuming that fluctuations in real GDP are caused by unexpected changes in the money supply. Instead, they argued that fluctuations in "real" factors, particularly *technology shocks*, explained deviations of real GDP from its potential level. Technology shocks are changes to the economy that make it possible to produce either more output—a positive shock—or less output—a negative shock—with the same number of workers, machines, and other inputs. Real GDP will be above its previous potential level following a positive technology shock and below its previous potential level following a negative technology shock. Because these models focus on real factors—rather than on changes in the money supply—to explain fluctuations in real GDP, they are known as **real business cycle models**.

Real business cycle models Models that focus on real rather than monetary explanations of fluctuations in real GDP.

The approach of Lucas and Sargent and the real business cycle models are sometimes grouped together under the label *the new classical macroeconomics* because these approaches share the assumptions that people have rational expectations and that wages and prices adjust rapidly. Some of the assumptions of the new classical macroeconomics are similar to those held by economists before the Great Depression of the 1930s. John Maynard Keynes, in his 1936 book *The General Theory of Employment, Interest, and Money*, referred to these earlier economists as "classical economists." Like the classical economists, the new classical macroeconomists believe that the economy will normally be at its potential level.

Economists who find the assumptions of rational expectations and rapid adjustment of wages and prices appealing are likely to accept the real business cycle model approach. Other economists are skeptical of these models because the models explain recessions as being caused by negative technology shocks. Negative technology shocks are uncommon and, apart from the oil price increases of the 1970s, real business cycle theorists have had difficulty identifying shocks that would have been large enough to cause recessions. Some economists have begun to develop real business cycle models that allow for the possibility that changes in the money supply may affect the level of real GDP. If real business cycle models continue to develop along these lines, they may eventually converge with the approaches used by the Fed.

16.4 LEARNING OBJECTIVE

16.4 | Use a Phillips curve graph to show how the Federal Reserve can permanently lower the inflation rate.

How the Fed Fights Inflation

We have already seen that the high inflation rates of the late 1960s and early 1970s were due in part to the Federal Reserve's attempts to keep the unemployment rate below the natural rate. By the mid-1970s, the Fed also had to deal with the inflationary impact of the OPEC oil price increases. By the late 1970s, as the Fed attempted to deal with the problem of high and worsening inflation rates, it received conflicting policy advice. Many economists argued that the inflation rate could be reduced only at the cost of a temporary increase in the unemployment rate. Followers of the Lucas–Sargent rational expectations approach, however, argued that a painless reduction in the inflation rate was possible. Before analyzing the actual policies used by the Fed, we can look at why the oil price increases of the mid-1970s made the inflation rate worse.

The Effect of a Supply Shock on the Phillips Curve

As we saw in Chapter 12, the increases in oil prices in 1974 resulting from actions by the Organization of Petroleum Exporting Countries (OPEC) caused the short-run aggregate supply curve to shift to the left. This shift is shown in panel (a) of Figure 16-9. (For simplicity, in this panel, we use the basic rather than dynamic *AD–AS* model.) The result was a higher price level and a lower level of real GDP. On a Phillips curve graph—panel (b) of Figure 16-9—we can shift the short-run Phillips curve up to show that the inflation rate and unemployment rate both increased.

As the Phillips curve shifted up, the economy moved from an unemployment rate of about 5 percent and an inflation rate of about 5.5 percent in 1973 to an unemployment

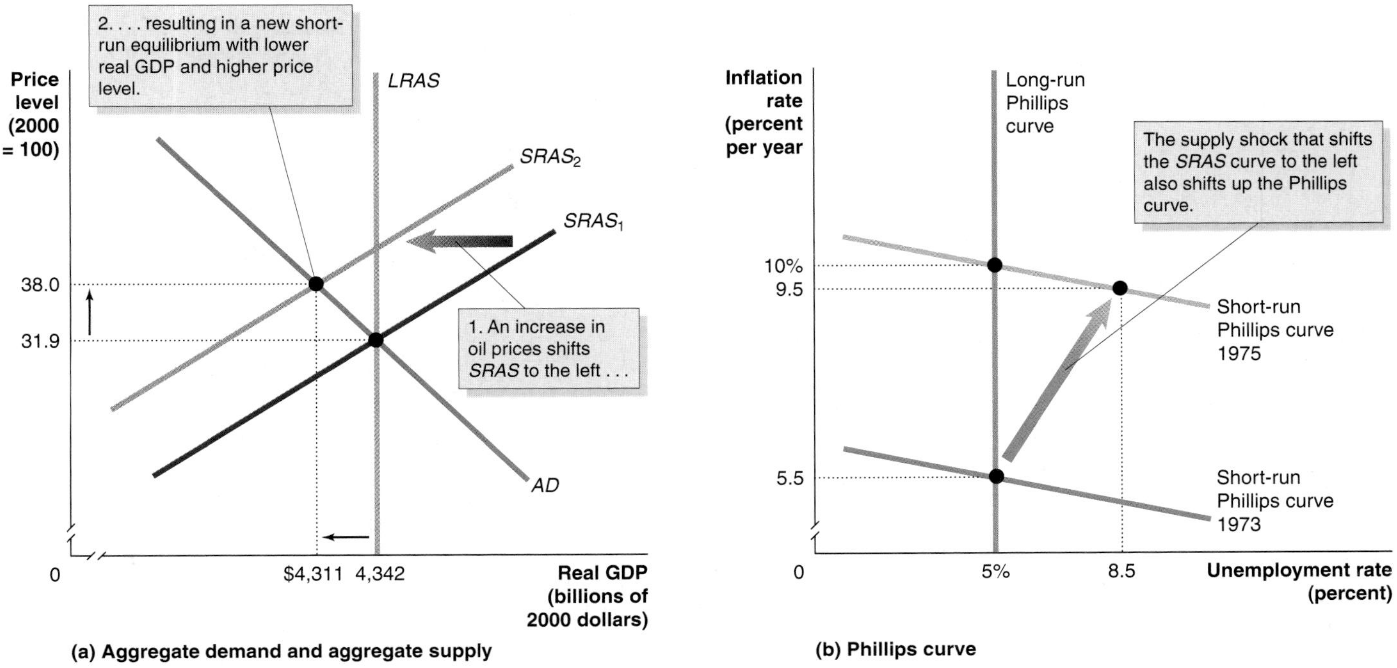

Figure 16-9 | A Supply Shock Shifts the *SRAS* and the Short-Run Phillips Curve

When OPEC increased the price of a barrel of oil from less than \$3 to more than \$10, in panel (a), the *SRAS* curve shifted to the left. Between 1973 and 1975, real GDP declined from \$4,342 billion to \$4,311 billion, and the price level rose from 31.9 to 38.0. Panel (b) shows that the supply shock shifted up the Phillips curve. In 1973, the U.S. economy had an inflation rate of about 5.5 percent and an unemployment rate of about 5 percent. By 1975, the inflation rate had risen to about 9.5 percent and the unemployment rate to about 8.5 percent.

rate of 8.5 percent and an inflation rate of about 9.5 percent in 1975. This combination of rising unemployment and rising inflation placed the Federal Reserve in a difficult position. If the Fed used an expansionary monetary policy to fight the high unemployment rate, the *AD* curve would shift to the right, and the economy's equilibrium would move up the short-run Phillips curve. Real GDP would increase, and the unemployment rate would fall—but at the cost of higher inflation. If the Fed used a contractionary monetary policy to fight the high inflation rate, the *AD* curve would shift to the left, and the economy's equilibrium would move down the short-run Phillips curve. As a result, real GDP would fall, and the inflation rate would be reduced—but at the cost of higher unemployment. In the end, the Fed chose to fight high unemployment with an expansionary monetary policy, even though that decision worsened the inflation rate.

Paul Volcker and Disinflation

By the late 1970s, the Federal Reserve had gone through a two-decade period of continually increasing the rate of growth of the money supply. In August 1979, President Jimmy Carter appointed Paul Volcker as chairman of the Board of Governors of the Federal Reserve System. Along with most other economists, Volcker was convinced that high inflation rates were inflicting significant damage on the economy and should be reduced. To reduce inflation, Volcker decided to reduce the annual growth rate of the money supply. This contractionary monetary policy raised interest rates, causing a decline in aggregate demand. Figure 16-10 uses the Phillips curve model to analyze the movements in unemployment and inflation from 1979 to 1989.

The Fed's contractionary monetary policy shifted the economy's short-run equilibrium down the short-run Phillips curve, lowering the inflation rate from 11 percent in

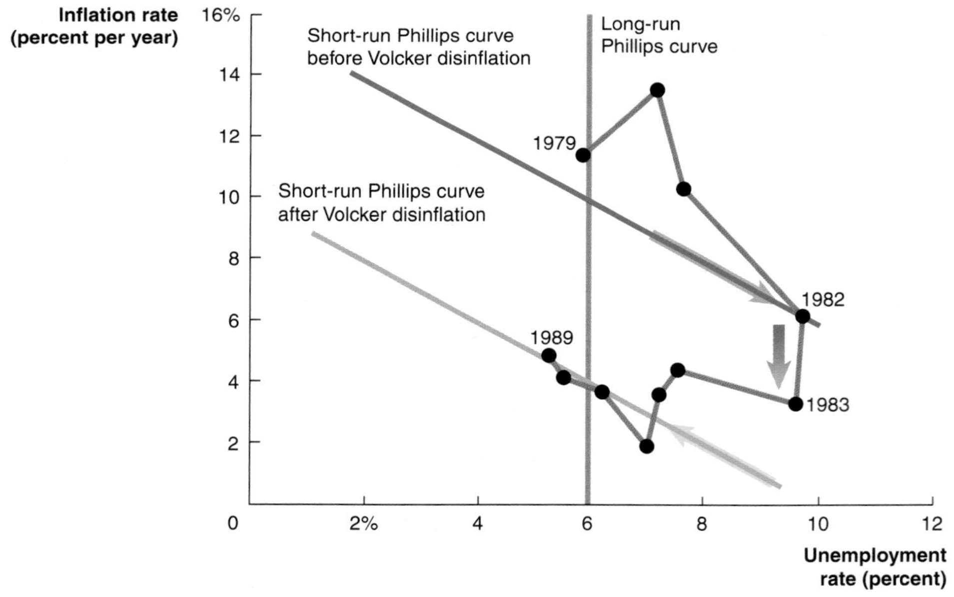

Figure 16-10 | The Fed Tames Inflation, 1979–1989

The Fed, under Chairman Paul Volcker, began fighting inflation in 1979 by reducing the growth of the money supply, thereby raising interest rates. By 1982, the unemployment rate had risen to 10 percent, and the inflation rate had fallen to 6 percent. As workers and firms lowered their expectations of future inflation, the short-run Phillips curve shifted down, improving the short-run trade-off between unemployment and inflation. This adjustment in expectations allowed the Fed to switch to an expansionary monetary policy, which by 1987 brought the economy back to the natural rate of unemployment, with an inflation rate of about 4 percent. The orange line shows the actual combinations of unemployment and inflation for each year from 1979 to 1989. Note that during these years, the natural rate of unemployment was estimated to be about 6 percent.

1979 to 6 percent in 1982—but at a cost of raising the unemployment rate from 6 percent to 10 percent. As workers and firms lowered their expectations of future inflation, the short-run Phillips curve shifted down, improving the short-run trade-off between unemployment and inflation. This adjustment in expectations allowed the Fed to switch to an expansionary monetary policy. By 1987, the economy was back to the natural rate of unemployment, which during these years was about 6 percent. The orange line in Figure 16-10 shows the actual combinations of unemployment and inflation for each year from 1979 to 1989.

Under Volcker's leadership, the Fed had reduced the inflation rate from more than 10 percent to less than 5 percent. The inflation rate has generally remained below 5 percent ever since. A significant reduction in the inflation rate is called **disinflation**. In fact, this episode is often referred to as the "Volcker disinflation." The disinflation had come at a very high price, however. From September 1982 through June 1983, the unemployment rate was above 10 percent. This period is the only one since the end of the Great Depression of the 1930s when unemployment has been above 10 percent in the United States.

Disinflation A significant reduction in the inflation rate.

Some economists argue that the Volcker disinflation provided evidence against the view that workers and firms have rational expectations. Volcker's announcement in October 1979 that he planned to use a contractionary monetary policy to bring down the inflation rate was widely publicized. If workers and firms had had rational expectations, we might have expected them to have quickly reduced their expectations of future inflation. The economy should have moved smoothly down the long-run Phillips curve. As we have seen, however, the economy moved down the existing short-run Phillips curve, and only after several years of high unemployment did the Phillips curve shift down. Apparently, workers and firms had adaptive expectations—only changing their expectations of future inflation after the current inflation rate had fallen.

Robert Lucas and Thomas Sargent argue, however, that a less painful disinflation would have occurred if workers and firms had *believed* Volcker's announcement that he was fighting inflation. The problem was that previous Fed chairmen had made similar promises throughout the 1970s, but inflation had continued to get worse. By 1979, the credibility of the Fed was at a low point. Some support for Lucas's and Sargent's argument comes from surveys of business economists at the time, which showed that they also reduced their forecasts of future inflation only slowly, even though they were well aware of Volcker's announcement of a new policy.

Don't Let This Happen to **YOU!**

Don't Confuse Disinflation with Deflation

Disinflation refers to a decline in the *inflation rate*. *Deflation* refers to a decline in the *price level*. Paul Volcker and the Federal Reserve brought about a substantial disinflation in the United States during the years between 1979 and 1983. The inflation rate fell from over 11 percent in 1979 to below 5 percent in 1984. Yet even in 1984, there was no deflation: The price level was still rising—but at a slower rate.

The last period of significant deflation in the United States was in the early 1930s during the Great Depression. The following table shows the consumer price index for those years:

YEAR	CONSUMER PRICE INDEX	DEFLATION RATE
1929	17.1	—
1930	16.7	–2.3%
1931	15.2	–9.0
1932	13.7	–9.9
1933	13.0	–5.1

Because the price level fell each year from 1929 to 1933, there was deflation.

YOUR TURN: Test your understanding by doing related problem 4.5 on page 582 at the end of this chapter.

Solved Problem | 16-4

Using Monetary Policy to Lower the Inflation Rate

Consider the following hypothetical situation: The economy is currently at the natural rate of unemployment of 5 percent. The actual inflation rate is 6 percent and, because it has remained at 6 percent for several years, this is also the rate that workers and firms expect to see in the future. The Federal Reserve decides to reduce the inflation rate permanently to 2 percent. How can the Fed use monetary policy to achieve this objective? Be sure to use a Phillips curve graph in your answer.

SOLVING THE PROBLEM:

Step 1: **Review the chapter material.** This problem is about using a Phillips curve graph to show how the Fed can fight inflation, so you may want to review the section "Paul Volcker and Disinflation," which begins on page 568.

Step 2: **Explain how the Fed can use monetary policy to reduce the inflation rate.** To reduce the inflation rate significantly, the Fed will have to raise the target for the federal funds rate. Higher interest rates will reduce aggregate demand, raise unemployment, and move the economy's equilibrium down the short-run Phillips curve.

Step 3: **Illustrate your argument with a Phillips curve graph.** How much the unemployment rate would have to rise to drive down the inflation rate from 6 percent to 2 percent depends on the steepness of the short-run Phillips curve. Here we have assumed that the unemployment rate would have to rise from 5 percent to 7 percent.

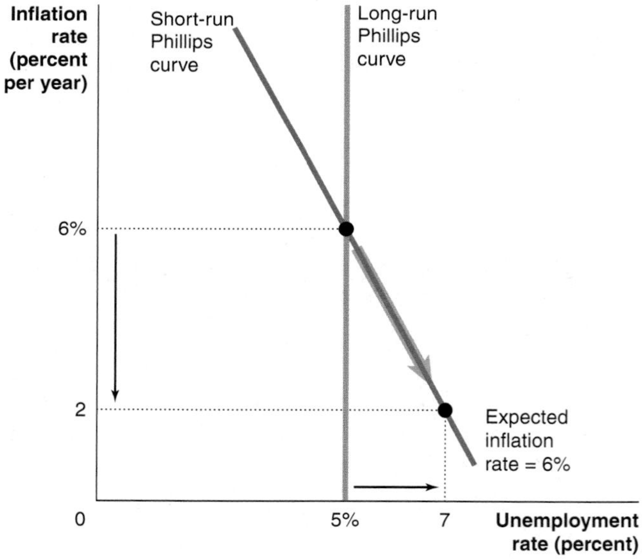

Step 4: **Show on your graph the reduction in the inflation rate from 6 percent to 2 percent.** For the decline in the inflation rate to be permanent, the expected inflation rate has to decline from 6 percent to 2 percent. We can show this on our graph:

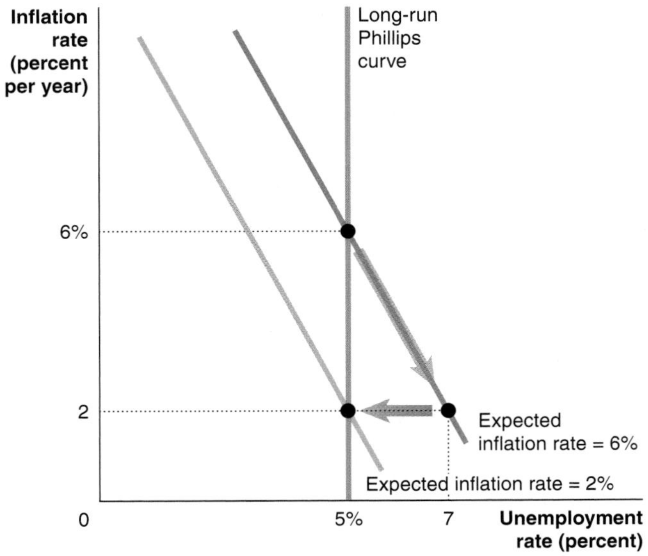

Once the short-run Phillips curve has shifted down, the Fed can push the economy back to the natural rate of unemployment with an expansionary monetary policy. This policy is similar to the one carried out by the Fed after Paul Volcker became chairman in 1979. The downside to these policies of disinflation is that they lead to significant increases in unemployment.

EXTRA CREDIT: A follower of the new classical macroeconomics approach would have a more optimistic view of the consequences of using monetary policy to lower the inflation rate from 6 percent to 2 percent. According to this approach, the Fed's policy announcement should cause people to immediately revise downward their expectations of future inflation from 6 percent to 2 percent. The economy's short-run equilibrium would move directly down the long-run Phillips curve from an inflation rate of 6 percent to an inflation rate of 2 percent, while keeping the unemployment rate constant at 5 percent. For the reasons discussed in this chapter, many economists are skeptical that disinflation can be brought about that painlessly.

YOUR TURN: For more practice, do related problems 4.7 and 4.8 on page 583 at the end of this chapter.

>> End Solved Problem 16-4

Alan Greenspan and the Importance of a Credible Monetary Policy

President Ronald Reagan appointed Alan Greenspan to succeed Paul Volcker as Fed chairman in 1987. Like Volcker, Greenspan was determined to keep the inflation rate low. Table 16-3 shows that the average annual inflation rate was lower during Greenspan's term than it was during the terms of his three most immediate predecessors. The low inflation rates continued under Ben Bernanke, Greenspan's successor. Under Greenspan's leadership of the Fed, inflation was reduced nearly to the low levels experienced during the term of Chairman William McChesney Martin in the 1950s and 1960s. As we discussed in Chapter 10, beginning in the mid-1990s, the U.S. economy experienced an increase in the growth of labor productivity. By increasing the capacity of the economy, productivity growth caused a more rapid increase in potential GDP. The greater capacity of the economy to produce goods and services at every price level contributed to the low rates of inflation experienced in the United States during the late 1990s and early 2000s.

TABLE 16-3

The Record of Fed Chairmen and Inflation

FEDERAL RESERVE CHAIRMAN	TERM	AVERAGE ANNUAL INFLATION RATE DURING TERM
William McChesney Martin	April 1952–January 1970	2.0%
Arthur Burns	February 1970–January 1978	6.5
G. William Miller	March 1978–August 1979	9.2
Paul Volcker	August 1979–August 1987	6.2
Alan Greenspan	August 1987–January 2006	3.1
Ben Bernanke	January 2006–	2.9

Note: Data for Bernanke are through August 2007.

De-emphasizing the Money Supply

We saw in Chapter 13 that during the 1980s and 1990s, the close relationship between growth in the money supply and inflation broke down. Before 1987, the Fed would announce annual targets for how much M1 and M2 would increase during the year. In February 1987, near the end of Paul Volcker's term, the Fed announced that it would no longer set targets for M1. In July 1993, Alan Greenspan announced that the Fed also would no longer set targets for M2. Instead, the Federal Open Market Committee (FOMC) has relied on setting targets for the federal funds rate to meet its goals of price stability and high employment.

The Importance of Fed Credibility

The Fed learned an important lesson during the 1970s: Workers, firms, and investors in stock and bond markets have to view Fed announcements as credible if monetary policy is to be effective. As inflation worsened throughout the late 1960s and 1970s, the Fed announced repeatedly that it would take actions to reduce inflation. In fact, inflation rose. These repeated failures to follow through on announced policies had greatly reduced the Fed's credibility by the time Paul Volcker took office in August 1979. The contractionary monetary policy that the Fed announced in October 1979 had less impact on the expectations of workers, firms, and investors than it would have had if the Fed's credibility had been greater. It took a severe recession to convince people that this time, the inflation rate really was coming down. Only then were workers willing to accept lower nominal wage increases, banks willing to accept lower interest rates on mortgage loans, and investors willing to accept lower interest rates on bonds.

Over the past two decades, the Fed has taken steps to enhance its credibility. Most importantly, whenever a change in Fed policy has been announced, the change has actually taken place. In addition, Greenspan revised the previous Fed policy of keeping secret the target for the federal funds rate. Since February 1994, any change in the target rate has been announced at the conclusion of the FOMC meeting at which the change is made. In addition, the minutes of the FOMC meetings are now made public after a brief delay. Finally, in February 2000, the Fed helped make its intentions for future policy clearer by announcing at the end of each FOMC meeting whether it considered the economy in the future to be at greater risk of higher inflation or of recession. During Greenspan's terms as Fed chairman, the U.S. economy experienced only two brief recessions and no periods of high inflation.

Monetary Policy Credibility after Greenspan

Even now, debate continues over policies to increase the Fed's credibility. Some economists and policymakers believe that central banks are more credible if they adopt and follow rules. A *rules strategy* for monetary policy involves the central bank's following specific and publicly announced guidelines for policy. This strategy requires that when the central bank chooses a rule, it follows the rule, whatever the state of the economy. For example, the Fed might commit to increasing the money supply 5 percent each year, regardless of whether the economy enters a recession or suffers a financial crisis. (Note that support among economists for a monetary growth rule of this type has declined over the past 25 years.) The rule the Fed adopts should apply to variables that the Fed can control. For example, a rule stating that the Fed was committed to maintaining the growth rate of real GDP at 4 percent per year would not be useful because the Fed has no direct control over GDP.

Economists and policymakers who oppose the rules strategy support a *discretion strategy* for monetary policy. With a discretion strategy, the central bank should adjust monetary policy as it sees fit to achieve its policy goals, such as price stability and high employment. This approach differs from the rules strategy in that it allows the Fed to adjust its policy based on changes in the economy. In practice, the Fed has generally followed a discretion strategy.

Many economists believe a middle course between a rules strategy and a discretion strategy is desirable. In this view, the central bank should be free to make adjustments in policy as long as the adjustments are stated as part of the rules. The *Taylor rule*, which we discussed in Chapter 14, is an example of a modified rule of this type, although it has never been adopted explicitly by the Fed. According to the Taylor rule, the Fed should set the target for the federal funds rate according to an equation that includes the inflation rate, the equilibrium real federal funds rate, the "inflation gap," and the "output gap." Even a modified rule isn't foolproof. Rules are credible because they reduce central bank flexibility, thereby giving firms, workers, and investors more confidence that the central bank will actually do what it says it will do. But the same lack of flexibility that can make a rule credible can also limit the central bank's ability to respond during a financial crisis, such as a stock market crash.

Most economists believe the best way to achieve commitment to rules is to remove political pressures on the central bank. When the central bank is free of political pressures, the public is more likely to believe the central bank's announcements. In the early 2000s, many economists also suggested that the Federal Reserve should be more transparent about its objectives for inflation, a call embraced by Greenspan's successor, Ben Bernanke.

A Failure of Credibility at the Bank of Japan

Is it possible for the inflation rate to be too *low*? The answer is yes, particularly if inflation becomes deflation. Since the early 1990s, the Japanese economy has been plagued by slow growth and significant periods of *deflation*—or a falling price level. Deflation can contribute to slow growth by raising real interest rates, increasing the real value of debts, and causing consumers to postpone purchases in the hope of experiencing even lower prices in the future. The Bank of Japan attempted to end deflation and spur economic growth by using expansionary monetary policy to drive down interest rates and stop deflation.

By 1999, the Bank of Japan had reduced the target interest rate on overnight bank loans—the equivalent of the U.S. federal funds rate—to zero. Because Japan was experiencing deflation, however, the *real* interest rate on these loans was greater than zero. The real interest rate on mortgages and long-term bonds also remained too high to stimulate the increase in investment spending needed to bring the Japanese economy back to potential GDP. Why was the Bank of Japan unable to end deflation and reduce real interest rates? Some economists argue that the key problem was that the Bank of Japan's policies lacked credibility. Because firms, workers, and participants in financial markets doubted the Bank of Japan's willingness to continue an expansionary monetary policy long enough to end the deflation, the price level continued to fall, and real interest rates remained high. In fact, this view was reinforced when the Bank of Japan raised the target interest rate on overnight bank loans in August 2000, even though deflation continued. The lack of credibility also may have stemmed in part from the unwillingness of the Bank of Japan to state an explicit target for inflation. An explicit inflation rate target of, say, 2 percent may have caused firms, workers, and investors to raise their expectations of inflation, which could have brought the deflation to an end. Some officials at the Bank of Japan also appeared reluctant to pursue too aggressive an expansionary policy for fear of reigniting the inflation in stock prices and real estate prices that Japan had experienced in the 1980s.

Although deflation was not the only reason economic growth in Japan was so weak, failing to end deflation made other problems, such as reform of the banking system, harder to manage. The Bank of Japan's failure of credibility helps to explain its weak performance compared with the performance of the Federal Reserve during the same period.

Federal Reserve Policy and Whirlpool's "Pricing Power"

We saw in the chapter opener that in early 2007, Whirlpool was suffering from declining sales of appliances in the United States at the same time that its cost were rising as raw materials prices increased. The success of any firm, particularly a firm like Whirlpool that produces consumer durables, will be determined partly by its ability to compete against rival firms and partly by macroeconomic conditions. The strength of Whirlpool's competitive position in the home appliance market was shown by its ability to acquire rival appliance maker Maytag in 2006 and by its ability to expand sales and market share in Europe and Latin America.

During and immediately after the recession of 2001, Whirlpool had clearly benefited from the effects of expansionary monetary policy. As we discussed in Chapter 9, during a typical business cycle recession, consumers reduce expenditures on new homes and on durable goods, such as household appliances. Whirlpool has a double exposure to recession because it may lose direct sales to consumers buying new or replacement appliances and also sales to builders buying appliances to be included in new home construction. In 2001 and the following years, expansionary monetary policy lessened the effects of recession by lowering interest rates. As we saw in Chapter 14, spending on new housing actually increased during 2001, as did Whirlpool's sales. Whirlpool acknowledged the importance of monetary policy to its performance in its 2004 annual report: "Consumer demand remained strong throughout 2004 as low interest rates in the United States helped maintain the momentum of new housing starts."

But in 2007, both Whirlpool and the Fed were caught in a dilemma: The declining housing market caused Whirlpool's sales to decline, while rising raw materials prices meant that its costs were increasing. Raising appliance prices to offset rising costs could further damage sales. The Fed was wrestling with a similar problem at the macroeconomic policy level: It might have been led to reduce the target for the federal funds rate to offset the sharp decline in the housing market but was reluctant to do so because the inflation rate was still above the level consistent with meeting the Fed's goal of price stability. By mid-2007, it was unclear whether the Fed would be able to succeed in its policy of cooling off the economy enough to restrain inflation while still avoiding a recession.

>> Continued from page 553

Economics in YOUR Life!

At the beginning of the chapter, we posed this question: If the Federal Reserve pledges to keep the economy's long-run unemployment rate below 3 percent, what effect will this pledge have on the size of the raise you request? To answer this question, recall that the long-run, or natural, rate of unemployment is determined by the economy's long-run aggregate supply curve, not monetary policy, and is probably about 5 percent. The Federal Reserve's attempt to keep the economy's long-run unemployment rate below its natural level will cause the inflation rate to increase and eventually raise the public's expectations of future inflation and, by doing so, will keep inflation relatively high. Therefore, you should ask your boss for a relatively large wage increase in order to preserve the future purchasing power of your wage.

Conclusion

The workings of the contemporary economy are complex. The attempts by the Federal Reserve to keep the U.S. economy near the natural rate of unemployment with a low rate of inflation have not always been successful. Economists continue to debate the best way for the Fed to proceed.

An Inside Look at Policy on the next page discusses new research from the Federal Reserve which indicates that inflation is driven largely by the public's expectation of inflation.

The Fed Rethinks the Phillips Curve

WALL STREET JOURNAL, FEBRUARY 26, 2007

Policy Makers at Fed Rethink Inflation's Roots

For decades, a simple rule has governed how the Federal Reserve views the nation's economy: When unemployment falls too low, inflation goes up, and vice versa.

a But Fed officials have rethought that notion. They believe it takes a far bigger change in unemployment to affect inflation today than it did 25 years ago. Now, when inflation fluctuates, they are far more likely to blame temporary factors, such as changes in oil prices or rents, than a change in the jobless rate.

One explanation for why inflation is influenced less by changes in unemployment is that the American public has come to expect inflation to remain stable. When inflation moves up or down, it is less likely to get stuck at the new level because companies and workers don't factor the change into their expectations—or their behavior. Another explanation is that the Fed is better at adjusting interest rates in anticipation of swings in unemployment before those swings can affect inflation.

This new view of the economy, formed in recent years, helps explain why the Fed stopped raising interest rates last summer while core inflation, which excludes food and energy prices, was rising. And it helps explain why the Fed is reluctant to cut rates now even though it sees inflation edging lower over the next two years. . . .

b In the late 1950s, economists discovered a tendency for inflation to rise when unemployment was low and to fall when unemployment was high. At lower unemployment rates, they concluded, companies paid more to attract scarce workers and recouped the higher wage costs by raising prices. This relationship was shown on a chart called the Phillips Curve, after Alban William Phillips, one of the first economists to identify it.

In the 1960s, American presidents and Fed officials sought to exploit the Phillips Curve by letting inflation edge higher in exchange for lower unemployment. But in the late 1960s economists Milton Friedman, who died last year, and Edmund Phelps, both of whom would later become Nobel laureates, independently deduced that the reduction in unemployment would be temporary.

Once workers began to expect higher inflation, they would want higher wages. In the long run, the economists argued, unemployment would gravitate to some "natural" level no matter what inflation did.

Although economists concluded there wasn't a *long-run* tradeoff between inflation and unemployment, they still believed there could be a *short-run* tradeoff. From 1979 to 2003, Fed Chairman Paul Volcker and his successor, Alan Greenspan, exploited this idea, periodically using interest rates to push unemployment higher to achieve lasting reductions in inflation.

But even as they were doing so, the short-run impact of unemployment on inflation began to diminish. Though the trend has been under way for 25 years, only recently has intensive research by Fed economists and others incorporated it into mainstream thinking. . . .

Core inflation, now running at a 2.2% rate by the Fed's preferred measure, remains higher than the 2% ceiling most Fed officials are comfortable with. But Janet Yellen, president of the Federal Reserve Bank of San Francisco, noted earlier this year that over the past decade, when inflation has drifted away from the 1.75% to 2% range, it has later reverted to it. For this reason it "may move down from its elevated level faster than many forecasters expect. . . ."

c Mr. Phelps says the new thinking on the Phillips Curve doesn't change the implications of his Nobel-winning work. If the Fed never responded to higher inflation, consumers and businesses eventually would begin to expect higher inflation, and "then the game is up."

Fed officials agree. While a given drop in unemployment is less likely to spark inflation, the potential is still there. The Fed's staff estimates it takes up to twice as much additional unemployment to achieve a percentage drop in inflation as it did before 1984. "Imbalances between demand and potential supply [may] be slow to show through convincingly to inflation, but when they do, they may be costly to correct," Fed Vice Chairman Donald Kohn said in late 2005.

That's one reason the Fed, though it expects core inflation to ease this year, isn't relaxing. With unemployment currently 4.6%, at or below the Fed's view of its natural rate, inflation may edge up after the temporary impacts of energy and rent subside. That could require the Fed to raise interest rates enough to push unemployment up sharply and bring inflation down.

Source: Greg Ip, "Policy Makers at Fed Rethink Inflation's Roots," Wall Street Journal, February 26, 2007. Reprinted by permission of the Wall Street Journal via Copyright Clearance Center.

Key Points in the Article

This article discusses new economic research from the Federal Reserve that indicates that inflation is influenced to a large extent by the public's expectation of future inflation, as well as by temporary factors, including changes in oil prices and housing rents. These findings have led Federal Reserve researchers to rethink the shape of the short-run Phillips curve because the findings suggest that the inflation rate has become less sensitive to changes in the unemployment rate.

Analyzing the News

a New economic research indicates that when temporary factors increase inflation, inflation is less likely to remain elevated for long. Why? The U.S. public—including both workers and firms—has come to expect stable inflation over time. So, when a temporary factor increases inflation, workers and employers do not alter their expectations of future inflation; instead, they expect inflation to return to its original level. These findings have also led Federal Reserve researchers to rethink the shape of the short-run Phillips curve. In particular, the Fed is relatively less concerned today that a fall in the unemployment rate will fuel inflation.

b Shortly after A. W. Phillips identified the tendency for inflation and unemployment rates to move in opposite directions, economic policymakers sought to exploit this tendency. In the 1960s, Milton Friedman and Edmund Phelps made the case that such a trade-off does not exist in the long run. Both economists reasoned that the unemployment rate ultimately returns to its natural level, which is determined by the economy's long-run aggregate supply curve; hence, the Phillips curve does not represent a structural relationship. Friedman and Phelps argued that, in the long run, a relatively high inflation rate only raises the public's expectations of future inflation and, by doing so, keeps inflation relatively high. This pattern is shown in the figure, where the inflation rate is 2 percent when the economy's unemployment rate equals the natural rate of unemployment of 5 percent (point *A*); however, if the economy's unemployment rate is 4 percent, which is below its natural rate of unemployment, the inflation rate increases to 3 percent (point *B*) and, eventually, the short-run Phillips curve shifts up so that the economy returns to its natural rate of unemployment (point *C*).

c According to the Fed's estimates, to achieve a 1-percentage-point reduction in inflation today, the unemployment must rise by twice as much as it would have before 1984. So, the short-run Phillips curve is effectively flatter than it once was. Nonetheless, Fed researchers agree that their findings underscore Friedman's and Phelps's early work on the role of expectations in determining inflation. That is, a monetary policy that seeks to lower unemployment below its natural rate will ultimately only increase inflation.

Thinking Critically About Policy

1. According to this new Federal Reserve research, would a temporary increase in the inflation rate brought about by Fed policy have a larger or smaller immediate effect on unemployment today than it would have had decades ago?
2. Suppose the U.S. public does not believe that the Federal Reserve's commitment to maintain price stability is credible. Would this situation strengthen or weaken the Fed's ability to lower the unemployment rate below its natural rate?

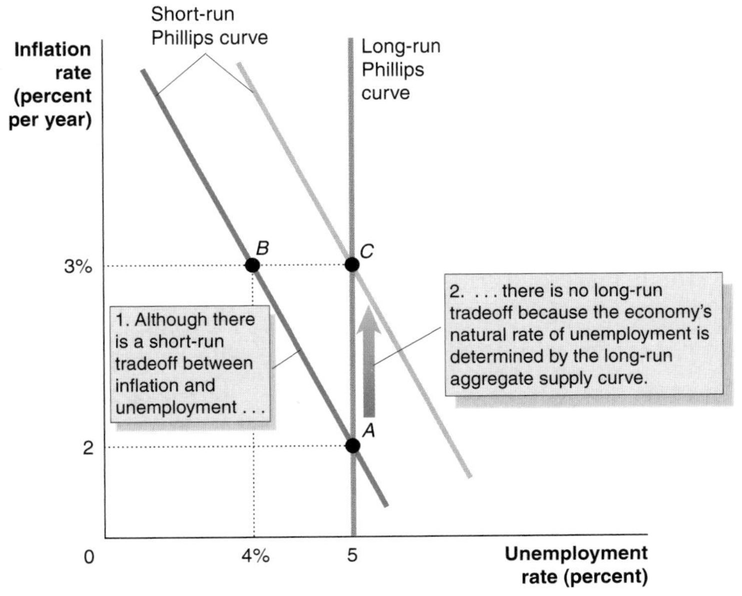

The short- and long-run Phillips curves.

Key Terms

Disinflation, p. 569
Natural rate of unemployment, p. 556
Nonaccelerating inflation rate of unemployment (NAIRU), p. 562
Phillips curve, p. 554
Rational expectations, p. 564
Real business cycle models, p. 566
Structural relationship, p. 556

16.1 LEARNING OBJECTIVE 16.1 | Describe the Phillips curve and the nature of the short-run trade-off between unemployment and inflation, **pages 554–559.**

The Discovery of the Short-Run Trade-off between Unemployment and Inflation

Summary

The **Phillips curve** illustrates the short-run trade-off between the unemployment rate and the inflation rate. The inverse relationship between unemployment and inflation shown by the Phillips curve is consistent with the aggregate demand and aggregate supply analysis developed in Chapter 11. The *AD–AS* model indicates that slow growth in aggregate demand leads to both higher unemployment and lower inflation, and rapid growth in aggregate demand leads to both lower unemployment and higher inflation. This relationship explains why there is a short-run trade-off between unemployment and inflation. Many economists initially believed that the Phillips curve was a **structural relationship** that depended on the basic behavior of consumers and firms and that remained unchanged over time. If the Phillips curve were a stable relationship, it would present policymakers with a menu of combinations of unemployment and inflation from which they could choose. Nobel laureate Milton Friedman argued that there is a **natural rate of unemployment**, which is the unemployment rate that exists when the economy is at potential GDP and to which the economy always returns. As a result, there is no trade-off between unemployment and inflation in the long run, and the long-run Phillips curve is a vertical line at the natural rate of unemployment.

myeconlab Get Ahead of the Curve Visit www.myeconlab.com to complete these exercises online and get instant feedback.

Review Questions

1.1 What is the Phillips curve? Draw a graph of a short-run Phillips curve.

1.2 What actions should the Fed take if it wants to move from a point on the short-run Phillips curve representing high unemployment and low inflation to a point representing lower unemployment and higher inflation?

1.3 Why did economists during the early 1960s think of the Phillips curve as a "policy menu"? Were they correct to think of it in this way? Briefly explain.

1.4 Why did Milton Friedman argue that the Phillips curve did not represent a permanent trade-off between unemployment and inflation? In your answer, be sure to explain what Friedman meant by the "natural rate of unemployment."

Problems and Applications

1.5 In fall 2003, the economy had not yet returned to the natural rate of unemployment following the end of the recession of 2001. An article in the *Wall Street Journal* noted the following:

> Perhaps the best cure for [unemployed workers'] woes would be a return to the unusually strong economy of the late 1990s, when unemployment fell so low that employers couldn't be picky. President Bush and Federal Reserve Chairman Alan Greenspan are working on that, [using] tax cuts and interest-rate cuts.

a. Which of these two actions (tax cuts and interest-rate cuts) is fiscal policy and which is monetary policy?
b. Briefly explain how tax cuts and interest-rate cuts reduce unemployment.

Source: David Wessel, "Clues to the Cure for Unemployment Begin to Emerge," *Wall Street Journal*, October 13, 2003.

1.6 Use the graphs in the next column to answer the following questions.

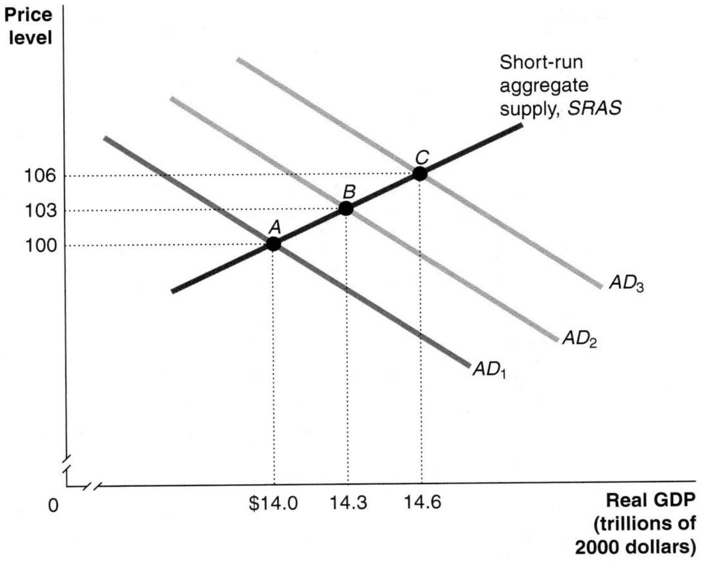

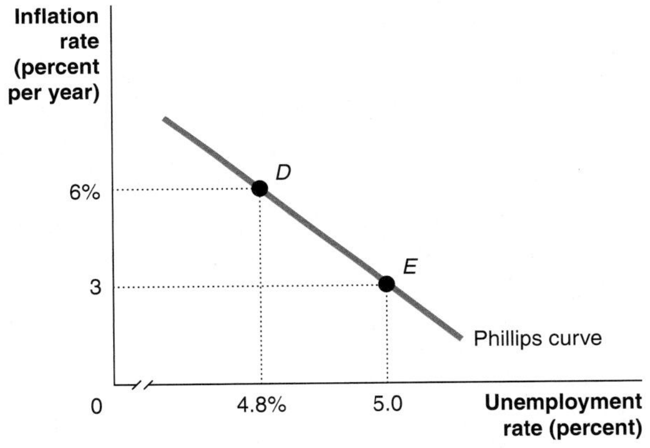

a. Briefly explain which point on the Phillips curve graph represents the same economic situation as point *B* on the aggregate demand and aggregate supply graph.

b. Briefly explain which point on the Phillips curve graph represents the same economic situation as point *C* on the aggregate demand and aggregate supply graph.

1.7 Given that the Phillips curve is derived from the aggregate demand and aggregate supply model, why use the Phillips curve analysis? What benefits does the Phillips curve analysis offer compared to the *AD–AS* model?

1.8 Briefly explain whether you agree or disagree with the following statement: "Any economic relationship that changes as economic policy changes is not a structural relationship."

1.9 In macroeconomics courses in the 1960s and early 1970s, some professors taught that one of the U.S. political parties was willing to have higher unemployment in order to achieve lower inflation and that the other major political party was willing to have higher inflation in order to achieve lower unemployment. Why might such views of the trade-off between inflation and unemployment have existed in the 1960s? Why are such views rare today?

1.10 General Juan Perón, the former dictator of Argentina, once said of the labor market in his country, "Prices have gone up the elevator, and wages have had to use the stairs." In this situation, what was happening to real wages in Argentina? Was unemployment likely to have been relatively high or relatively low?

Source: Robert J. Shiller, "Why Do People Dislike Inflation?" in Christina D. Romer and David H. Romer, eds., *Reducing Inflation: Motivation and Strategy*, Chicago: University of Chicago Press, 1997.

1.11 This chapter argues that if the price level increases, over time, the average wage should increase by the same amount. Why is this true?

1.12 **(Related to the *Making the Connection* on page 558)** Robert Shiller asked a sample of the general public and a sample of economists the following question: "Do you agree that preventing high inflation is an important national priority, as important as preventing drug abuse or preventing deterioration in the quality of our schools?" Fifty-two percent of the general public, but only 18 percent of economists, fully agreed. Why does the general public believe inflation is a bigger problem than economists do?

1.13 **(Related to the *Making the Connection* on page 558)** When Shiller asked a sample of the general public what they thought caused inflation, the most frequent answer he received was "greed." Do you agree that greed causes inflation? Briefly explain.

1.14 **(Related to the *Chapter Opener* on page 552)** Why would Whirlpool Corporation pay more attention than most other firms to the Federal Reserve raising or lowering interest rates? In other words, why do interest rates particularly affect Whirlpool?

1.15 Use the following information to draw a graph showing the short-run and long-run Phillips curves:
Natural rate of unemployment = 5 percent
Current rate of unemployment = 4 percent
Expected inflation rate = 4 percent
Current inflation rate = 6 percent
Be sure your graph shows the point where the short-run and long-run Phillips curves intersect.

>> End Learning Objective 16.1

16.2 LEARNING OBJECTIVE 16.2 | Explain the relationship between the short-run and long-run Phillips curves, **pages 559–563.**

The Short-Run and Long-Run Phillips Curves

Summary

There is a short-run trade-off between unemployment and inflation only if the actual inflation rate differs from the inflation rate that workers and firms had expected. There is a different short-run Phillips curve for every expected inflation rate. Each short-run Phillips curve intersects the long-run Phillips curve at the expected inflation rate. With a vertical long-run Phillips curve, it is not possible to buy a permanently lower unemployment rate at the cost of a permanently higher inflation rate. If the Federal Reserve attempts to keep the economy below the natural rate of unemployment, the inflation rate will increase. Eventually, the expected inflation rate will also increase, which causes the short-run Phillips curve to shift up and pushes the economy back to the natural rate of unemployment. The reverse happens if the Fed attempts to keep the economy above the natural rate of unemployment. In the long run, the Federal Reserve can affect the inflation rate but not the unemployment rate.

Review Questions

2.1 What is the relationship between the short-run Phillips curve and the long-run Phillips curve?

2.2 Why is it inconsistent to believe that the long-run aggregate supply curve is vertical and the long-run Phillips curve is downward sloping?

Problems and Applications

2.3 In 1968, Herbert Stein, who would later serve on President Nixon's Council of Economic Advisers, wrote, "Some who would opt for avoiding inflation would say that in the long run such a policy would cost little, if any, additional unemployment." Was Stein correct? Did most economists in 1968 agree with him? Briefly explain.

Source: Herbert Stein, *The Fiscal Revolution in America*, Chicago: University of Chicago Press, 1969, p. 382.

2.4 **(Related to *Solved Problem 16-2* on page 563)** In a speech in September 1975, then Fed chairman Arthur Burns said the following:

> There is no longer a meaningful trade-off between unemployment and inflation. In the current environment, a rapidly rising level of consumer prices will not lead to the creation of new jobs. . . . Highly expansionary monetary and fiscal policies might, for a short time, provide some additional thrust to economic activity. But inflation would inevitably accelerate—a development that would create even more difficult economic problems than we have encountered over the past year.

How do Burns's views in this speech compare with the views at the Fed in the late 1960s? Why do you think he specifically says "in the current environment" there is no trade-off between unemployment and inflation?

Source: Arthur F. Burns, "The Real Issues of Inflation and Unemployment," in Federal Reserve Bank of New York, *Federal Reserve Readings on Inflation*, February 1979.

2.5 In testifying before Congress, former Federal Reserve Chairman Alan Greenspan remarked, "The challenge of monetary policy is to interpret data on the economy and financial markets with an eye to anticipating future inflationary forces and to countering them by taking action in advance." Why should the Fed take action in anticipation of inflation becoming worse? Why not just wait until the increase in the inflation rate has occurred?

Source: Nicoletta Batini and Andrew G. Haldane, "Forward-Looking Rules for Monetary Policy," in John B. Taylor, ed., *Monetary Policy Rules*, Chicago: University of Chicago Press, 1999, p. 157.

2.6 **(Related to the *Chapter Opener* on page 552)** In the same congressional testimony quoted in the chapter opener, Federal Reserve Chairman Ben Bernanke said:

> Another significant factor influencing medium-term trends in inflation is the public's expectations of inflation. These expectations have an important bearing on whether transitory influences on prices, such as changes in energy costs, become embedded in wage and price decisions and so leave a lasting imprint on the rate of inflation.

What did Bernanke mean when he said that the public's expectations of inflation could "become embedded in wage and price decisions"? What would be the effect on the short-run Phillips curve of the public coming to expect a higher inflation rate?

Source: "Testimony of Chairman Ben S. Bernanke Before the Joint Economic Committee, U.S. Congress," March 28, 2007.

2.7 (Related to the *Making the Connection* on page 562) An article in the *Economist* magazine discussing the natural rate of unemployment, makes the observation: "'Natural' does not mean optimal." Do you agree that the natural rate of unemployment is not the optimal rate of unemployment? In your answer, be sure to explain what you mean by *optimal.*

Source: "A Natural Choice," *Economist*, October 12, 2006.

>> End Learning Objective 16.2

16.3 LEARNING OBJECTIVE 16.3 | Discuss how expectations of the inflation rate affect monetary policy, **pages 564–566.**

Expectations of the Inflation Rate and Monetary Policy

Summary

When the inflation rate is moderate and stable, workers and firms tend to have *adaptive expectations.* That is, they form their expectations under the assumption that future inflation rates will follow the pattern of inflation rates in the recent past. During the high and unstable inflation rates of the mid- to late 1970s, Robert Lucas and Thomas Sargent argued that workers and firms would have *rational expectations.* **Rational expectations** are formed by using all the available information about an economic variable, including the effect of the policy being used by the Federal Reserve. Lucas and Sargent argued that if people have rational expectations, expansionary monetary policy will not work. If workers and firms know that an expansionary monetary policy is going to raise the inflation rate, the actual inflation rate will be the same as the expected inflation rate. Therefore, the unemployment rate won't fall. Many economists remain skeptical of Lucas and Sargent's argument in its strictest form. **Real business cycle models** focus on "real" factors—technology shocks—rather than changes in the money supply to explain fluctuations in real GDP.

myeconlab Get Ahead of the Curve Visit www.myeconlab.com to complete these exercises online and get instant feedback.

Review Questions

3.1 Why do workers, firms, banks, and investors in financial markets care about the future rate of inflation? How do they form their expectations of future inflation? Do current conditions in the economy have any bearing on how they form their expectations?

3.2 What does it mean to say that workers and firms have rational expectations?

3.3 Why did Robert Lucas and Thomas Sargent argue that the Phillips curve might be vertical in the short run? What difference would it make for monetary policy if they were right?

Problems and Applications

3.4 During a time when the inflation rate is increasing each year for a number of years, are adaptive expectations or rational expectations likely to give the more accurate forecasts? Briefly explain.

3.5 An article in the *Economist* notes: "A government's inability to demonstrate sincerity in achieving low inflation can . . . lead consumers to make high inflation a self-fulfilling prophecy." What does "a government's inability to demonstrate sincerity in achieving low inflation" mean in terms of Fed policy? If consumers have rational expectations, why will this policy failure make high inflation a self-fulfilling prophecy?

Source: "Cycles and Commitment," *Economist*, October 10, 2004.

3.6 Would a monetary policy intended to bring about disinflation cause a greater increase in unemployment if workers and firms have adaptive expectations or if they have rational expectations? Briefly explain.

3.7 If both the short-run and long-run Phillips curves are vertical, what will be the effect on the inflation rate and the unemployment rate of an expansionary monetary policy? Use a Phillips curve graph to illustrate your answer.

3.8 An article in the *Wall Street Journal* contained the following about the views of William Poole, the president of the Federal Reserve Bank of St. Louis:

> Mr. Poole said both inflation expectations and the output gap—the spare room the economy has between what it's producing and what it could potentially produce—go into the inflation process. But "inflation expectations . . . trump the gap. If inflation expectations were to rise, that development by itself would tend to drag the inflation rate up . . . and it might take a very long time before the (output gap) would be able to offset what's going on with inflation expectations."

a. Explain using the short-run and long-run Phillips curves what Poole meant in saying that both inflation expectations and the output gap affect the current inflation rate.
b. In terms of Phillips curve analysis, what are the implications of Poole's claim that "it might take a very long time before the (output gap) would be able to offset what's going on with inflation expectations"?
c. Why might inflation expectations be slow to respond to the output gap?

Source: Greg Ip, "Fed Policy Maker Warns of Rising Inflation," *Wall Street Journal*, June 6, 2006.

>> End Learning Objective 16.3

16.4 LEARNING OBJECTIVE 16.4 | Use a Phillips curve graph to show how the Federal Reserve can permanently lower the inflation rate, **pages 567–575.**

How the Fed Fights Inflation

Summary

Inflation worsened through the 1970s. Paul Volcker became Fed chairman in 1979, and, under his leadership, the Fed used contractionary monetary policy to reduce inflation. A significant reduction in the inflation rate is called **disinflation**. This contractionary monetary policy pushed the economy down the short-run Phillips curve. As workers and firms lowered their expectations of future inflation, the short-run Phillips curve shifted down, improving the short-run trade-off between unemployment and inflation. This change in expectations allowed the Fed to switch to an expansionary monetary policy to bring the economy back to the natural rate of unemployment. During Alan Greenspan's terms as Fed chairman, inflation remained low, and the credibility of the Fed increased. Some economists and policymakers believe a central bank's credibility is increased if it follows a *rules strategy* for monetary policy, which involves the central bank's following specific and publicly announced guidelines for policy. Other economists and policymakers support a *discretion strategy* for monetary policy, under which the central bank adjusts monetary policy as it sees fit to achieve its policy goals, such as price stability and high employment.

myeconlab Get Ahead of the Curve Visit www.myeconlab.com to complete these exercises online and get instant feedback.

Review Questions

4.1 What was the "Volcker disinflation"? What happened to the unemployment rate during the period of the Volcker disinflation?

4.2 Why does Ben Bernanke believe that the credibility of the Fed's policy announcements is particularly important?

Problems and Applications

4.3 According to an article in *BusinessWeek*, many workers who retired in the year 2000 expected to live off the interest they would receive from bank certificates of deposit or money market mutual funds. "Then came disinflation—and a steep fall in interest rates." What is disinflation and why should it lead to a fall in interest rates?

Source: Peter Coy, "The Surprise Threat to Nest Eggs," *BusinessWeek*, July 28, 2003.

4.4 Marvin Goodfriend, an economist at Carnegie Mellon University, argues that one of the advances in macroeconomic thinking since 1979 is "the proven power of monetary policy to reduce and stabilize inflation and inflation expectations at a low rate." How has monetary policy proven its power to reduce inflation and inflation expectations?

Source: Marvin Goodfriend, "The Monetary Policy Debate Since October 1979: Lessons for Theory and Practice," Federal Reserve Bank of St. Louis *Review*, March/April 2005, Vol. 87, No. 2, Part 2, pp. 243–262.

4.5 **(Related to the *Don't Let This Happen to You!* on page 569)** Look again at the table on prices during the early 1930s in the *Don't Let This Happen to You!* Was there disinflation during 1933? Briefly explain.

4.6 Suppose the current inflation rate and the expected inflation rate are both 4 percent. The current unemployment rate and the natural rate of unemployment are both 5 percent. Use a Phillips curve graph to show the effect on the economy of a severe supply shock. If the Federal Reserve keeps monetary policy unchanged, what will happen eventually to the unemployment rate? Show this on your Phillips curve graph.

4.7 **(Related to *Solved Problem 16-4* on page 570)** Suppose the inflation rate has been 15 percent for the past four years. The unemployment rate is currently at the natural rate of unemployment of 5 percent. The Federal Reserve decides that it wants to permanently reduce the inflation rate to 5 percent. How can the Fed use monetary policy to achieve this objective? Be sure to use a Phillips curve graph in your answer.

4.8 **(Related to *Solved Problem 16-4* on page 570)** In 1995, some economists argued that the natural rate of unemployment was 6 percent. Then Fed Chairman Alan Greenspan was convinced that the natural rate was actually about 5 percent. If Greenspan had accepted the view that the natural rate was 6 percent, how might monetary policy have been different during the late 1990s?

4.9 The following statement appeared in an article in the *Wall Street Journal* in early 2007, when it was unclear whether the Fed would soon raise the target for the federal funds rate: "Federal Reserve officials appear to believe unemployment can go lower than they previously thought without generating inflation, a potentially important shift that some economists think could make interest-rate increases this year less likely."

a. Does this statement have anything to do with the Fed's estimate of the natural rate of unemployment? Briefly explain.

b. Why would the author of this article believe that the Fed's changed views would have an impact on how likely the Fed was to raise the target for the federal funds rate?

Source: Greg Ip, "Fed Suggests It Is Loosening Employment–Inflation Link," *Wall Street Journal*, February 16, 2007, p. A2.

4.10 According to an article in the *Wall Street Journal*, "J.P. Morgan Chase economist Michael Feroli finds that in the past two decades it has taken a far larger drop in the jobless rate to boost inflation by one percentage point than it did in the previous 25 years." If this economist is correct, has the short-run Phillips curve become steeper during the past 25 years or less steep? If true, would this fact have any implications for monetary policy? Briefly explain.

Source: Greg Ip, "Fed Sees Inflation Rise as Fleeting," *Wall Street Journal*, August 4, 2006, p. A2.

4.11 Would a rules strategy for monetary policy be more important to increasing the credibility of the Federal Reserve during the 1970s or today? Briefly explain.

4.12 Robert Lucas was recently quoted as saying: "In practice, it is much more painful to put a modern economy through a deflation than the monetary theory we have would lead us to expect. I take this to mean that we have 'price stickiness.'" What does Lucas mean by "the monetary theory we have"? What events may have led him to conclude that it is more painful to reduce the inflation rate than theory would predict? Why does he conclude the U.S. economy apparently has "price stickiness"?

Source: Paul A. Samuelson and William A. Barnett, eds., *Inside the Economist's Mind: Conversations with Eminent Economists*, Malden, MA: Blackwell Publishing, 2007, p. 63.

>> End Learning Objective 16.4

Chapter 17

Macroeconomics in an Open Economy

NewPage Paper versus China

Mark Suwyn is the CEO of NewPage, a paper manufacturer headquartered in Dayton, Ohio. NewPage specializes in the glossy paper used in catalogs and magazines. At one time, the most important competition for NewPage came from U.S.-based firms. In recent years, though, the firm's strongest competitors have been Chinese firms. Chinese exports of glossy paper to the United States in 2006 were 10 times higher than they were in 2002. Chinese firms have the advantage of paying their workers the equivalent of about $2.10 per hour, while U.S. firms pay their workers at least 10 times as much. In addition, NewPage claims that Chinese firms have received subsidies from the Chinese government in the form of special tax breaks and low-cost loans. Under existing international trade agreements, governments are not allowed to subsidize firms that export to other countries, and NewPage filed a complaint with the U.S. Department of Commerce. According to Suwyn, "We've had to shut down machines and lay off people because [Chinese firms] are dumping product way below their costs." In March 2007, the Department of Commerce announced that in response to NewPage's complaint, it was imposing tariffs of 10 percent to 20 percent on imports of glossy paper from China. Although U.S. paper manufacturers such as NewPage applauded the tariffs, U.S. publishing firms that use glossy paper complained that their costs would rise and U.S. consumers would face rising prices for magazines and other publications.

Of course, Chinese firms were exporting much more than just paper to the United States. In 2006, total Chinese exports to the United States were $287 billion, while Chinese imports from the United States were only $52 billion. The Chinese government has found that high levels of exports have led to political problems not only with the United States but also with Japan and the countries of the European Union. As we will see in this chapter, any country that has a high level of net exports must also have a high level of *net foreign investment.* When the foreign investment takes the form of buying foreign stocks and bonds, relatively little political friction usually results. But when the foreign investment takes the form of purchasing foreign firms, it can result in political difficulties. For example, in 2005, Chinese firms attempted to buy the U.S. oil company Unocal Corporation and the U.S. appliance maker Maytag. Ultimately, neither purchase was successful, and Cnooc, the Chinese oil company that failed to buy Unocal, blamed the political environment in the United States and "the unprecedented political opposition."

AN INSIDE LOOK on **page 606** discusses why most global investors aren't worried about America's current account deficit.

Sources: James Hanah, "U.S. Paper Mills See Glimmer of Hope," *Charlotte Observer*, June 8, 2007; Gregg Hitt, "U.S. Sets New China Duties," *Wall Street Journal*, March 31, 2007, p. A3; and Matt Pottinger, Russell Gold, Michael M. Phillips, and Kate Linebaugh, "Cnooc Drops Offer for Unocal, Exposing U.S.–Chinese Tensions," *Wall Street Journal*, August 3, 2005, p. A1.

LEARNING Objectives

After studying this chapter, you should be able to:

17.1 Explain how the **balance of payments** is calculated, page 586.

17.2 Explain how **exchange rates** are determined and how changes in exchange rates affect the **prices** of **imports** and **exports**, page 590.

17.3 Explain the **saving and investment equation**, page 597.

17.4 Explain the effect of a **government budget deficit** on **investment** in an **open economy**, page 601.

17.5 Discuss the difference between the effectiveness of **monetary and fiscal policy** in an **open economy** and in a **closed economy**, page 604.

Economics in YOUR Life!

The South Korean Central Bank and Your Car Loan

Suppose that you are shopping for a new car, which you plan to finance with a loan from a local bank. One morning, as you head out the door to visit another automobile dealership, you hear the following newsflash on the radio: "The Bank of Korea, South Korea's central bank, announces it will sell its large holdings of U.S. Treasury bonds." What effect will the Bank of Korea's decision to sell its U.S. Treasury bonds likely have on the interest rate that you pay on your car loan? As you read this chapter, see if you can answer this question. You can check your answer against the one we provide at the end of the chapter. » **Continued on page 605**

In Chapter 6, we looked at the basics of international trade. In this chapter, we look more closely at the linkages among countries at the macroeconomic level. Countries are linked by trade in goods and services and by flows of financial investment. We will see how policymakers in all countries take these linkages into account when conducting monetary and fiscal policy.

17.1 LEARNING OBJECTIVE

17.1 | Explain how the balance of payments is calculated.

The Balance of Payments: Linking the United States to the International Economy

Open economy An economy that has interactions in trade or finance with other countries.

Closed economy An economy that has no interactions in trade or finance with other countries.

Balance of payments The record of a country's trade with other countries in goods, services, and assets.

Today, consumers, firms, and investors routinely interact with consumers, firms, and investors in other economies. A consumer in France may use a computer produced in the United States, listen to music on a CD player made in Japan, and wear a sweater made in Italy. A firm in the United States may sell its products in dozens of countries around the world. An investor in London may sell a U.S. Treasury bill to an investor in Mexico City. Nearly all economies are **open economies** and have extensive interactions in trade or finance with other countries. Open economies interact by trading goods and services and by making investments in each other's economies. A **closed economy** has no interactions in trade or finance with other countries. No economy today is completely closed. A few countries, such as North Korea, have very limited economic interactions with other countries.

The best way to understand the interactions between one economy and other economies is through the *balance of payments*. The **balance of payments** is a record of a country's trade with other countries in goods, services, and assets. Just as the U.S. Department of Commerce is responsible for collecting data on the GDP, it is also responsible for collecting data on the balance of payments. Table 17-1 shows the balance of payments for the United States in 2006. Notice that the table contains three "accounts": the *current account*, the *financial account*, and the *capital account*.

The Current Account

Current account The part of the balance of payments that records a country's net exports, net investment income, and net transfers.

The **current account** records *current*, or short-term, flows of funds into and out of a country. The current account for the United States includes imports and exports of goods and services (*net exports*), income received by U.S. residents from investments in other countries, income paid on investments in the United States owned by residents of other countries (*net investment income*), and the difference between transfers made to residents of other countries and transfers received by U.S. residents from other countries (*net transfers*). If you make a donation to a charity caring for orphans in Afghanistan, it would be included in net transfers. Any payments received by U.S. residents are positive numbers in the current account, and any payments made by U.S. residents are negative numbers in the current account.

Balance of trade The difference between the value of the goods a country exports and the value of the goods a country imports.

The Balance of Trade Part of the current account is the **balance of trade**, which is the difference between the value of the goods a country exports and the value of the goods a country imports. The balance of trade is the largest item in the current account and is often a topic politicians and the media discuss. If a country exports more than it imports, it has a *trade surplus*. If it exports less than it imports, it has a *trade deficit*. In 2006, the United States had a trade deficit of $838 billion. In the same year, Japan had a trade surplus of $68 billion, and China had a trade surplus of $232

TABLE 17-1

The Balance of Payments of the United States, 2006 (billions of dollars)

CURRENT ACCOUNT		
Exports of goods	$1,023	
Imports of goods	–1,861	
Balance of trade		–838
Exports of services	423	
Imports of services	–343	
Balance of services		80
Income received on investments	650	
Income payments on investments	–614	
Net income on investments		–36
Net transfers		–90
Balance on current account		–812
FINANCIAL ACCOUNT		
Increase in foreign holdings of assets in the United States	1,860	
Increase in U.S. holdings of assets in foreign countries	–1,055	
Balance on financial account		805
BALANCE ON CAPITAL ACCOUNT		**–4**
Statistical discrepancy		11
Balance of payments		0

Source: U.S. Department of Commerce, *Survey of Current Business*, August 2007.

billion. Figure 17-1 shows imports and exports of goods between the United States and its trading partners and between Japan and its trading partners. The data show that the United States ran a trade deficit in 2006 with all its major trading partners and with every region of the world. Japan ran trade deficits with China, the Middle East, and Africa and trade surpluses with other regions. (Note that exports from the United States to Japan in panel (a) of Figure 17-1 should equal imports by Japan from the United States in panel (b). That the two numbers are different is an indication that international trade statistics are not measured exactly.)

Net Exports Equals the Sum of the Balance of Trade and the Balance of Services In previous chapters, we saw that *net exports* is a component of aggregate expenditures. Net exports is not explicitly shown in Table 17-1, but we can calculate it by adding together the balance of trade and the balance of services. The *balance of services* is the difference between the value of the services a country exports and the value of the services a country imports. Notice that, technically, net exports is *not* equal to the current account balance because the current account balance also includes net investment income and net transfers. But these other two items are relatively small, so it is often a convenient simplification to think of net exports as equal to the current account balance, as we will see later in this chapter.

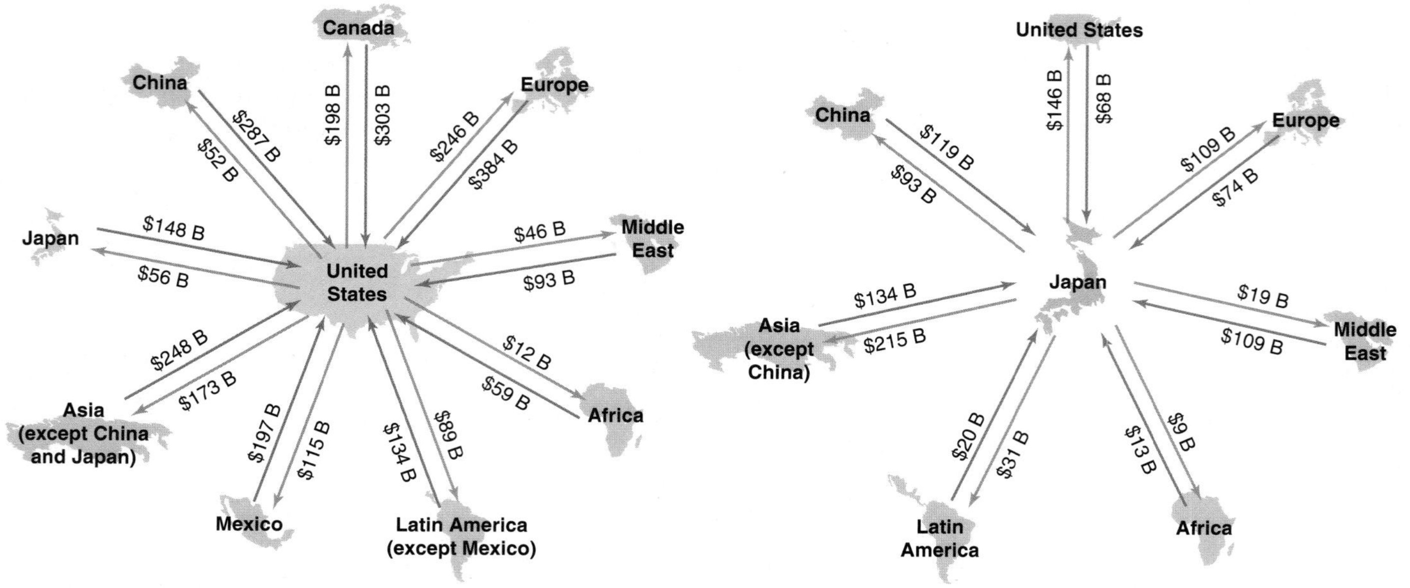

(a) Trade flows for the United States (in billions of dollars)

(b) Trade flows for Japan (in billions of dollars)

Figure 17-1 | Trade Flows for the United States and Japan, 2006

Panel (a) shows that in 2006, the United States ran a trade deficit with all its major trading partners and with every region of the world. Panel (b) shows that Japan ran trade deficits with China, the Middle East, and Africa, and trade surpluses with other regions. In each panel, the green arrows represent exports from the United States or Japan, and the red arrows represent imports.

Note: Japanese data are converted from yen to dollars at the average 2006 exchange rate of 116.31 yen per dollar.
Sources: U.S. International Trade Commission; and Japanese Ministry of Finance.

The Financial Account

Financial account The part of the balance of payments that records purchases of assets a country has made abroad and foreign purchases of assets in the country.

The **financial account** records purchases of assets a country has made abroad and foreign purchases of assets in the country. The financial account records long-term flows of funds into and out of a country. There is a *capital outflow* from the United States when an investor in the United States buys a bond issued by a foreign company or government or when a U.S. firm builds a factory in another country. There is a *capital inflow* into the United States when a foreign investor buys a bond issued by a U.S. firm or by the government or when a foreign firm builds a factory in the United States. Notice that we are using the word *capital* here to apply not just to physical assets, such as factories, but also to financial assets, such as shares of stock. When firms build or buy facilities in foreign countries, they are engaging in *foreign direct investment*. When investors buy stock or bonds issued in another country, they are engaging in *foreign portfolio investment*.

Net foreign investment The difference between capital outflows from a country and capital inflows, also equal to net foreign direct investment plus net foreign portfolio investment.

Another way of thinking of the balance on the financial account is as a measure of *net capital flows*, or the difference between capital inflows and capital outflows. (Here we are omitting a few transactions included in the capital account, as discussed in the next section.) A closely related concept to net capital flows is **net foreign investment**, which is equal to capital outflows minus capital inflows. Net capital flows and net foreign investment are always equal but have opposite signs: When net capital flows are positive, net foreign investment is negative, and when net capital flows are negative, net foreign investment is positive. Net foreign investment is also equal to net foreign direct investment plus net foreign portfolio investment. Later in this chapter, we will use the relationship between the balance on the financial account and net foreign investment to understand an important aspect of the international economic system.

The Capital Account

A third, less important, part of the balance of payments is called the *capital account*. The **capital account** records relatively minor transactions, such as migrants' transfers—which consist of goods and financial assets people take with them when they leave or enter a country—and sales and purchases of nonproduced, nonfinancial assets. A nonproduced, nonfinancial asset is a copyright, patent, trademark, or right to natural resources. The definitions of the financial account and the capital account are often misunderstood because the capital account prior to 1999 recorded all the transactions included now in both the financial account and the capital account. In other words, capital account transactions went from being a very important part of the balance of payments to being a relatively unimportant part. Because the balance on what is now called the capital account is so small, for simplicity we will ignore it in the remainder of this chapter.

Capital account The part of the balance of payments that records relatively minor transactions, such as migrants' transfers, and sales and purchases of nonproduced, nonfinancial assets.

Why Is the Balance of Payments Always Zero?

The sum of the current account balance, the financial account balance, and the capital account balance equals the balance of payments. Table 17-1 shows that the balance of payments for the United States in 2006 was zero. It's not just by chance that this balance was zero; *the balance of payments is always zero.* Notice that the current account balance in 2006 was –$812 billion. This value is not quite equal (with opposite sign) to the balance on the financial account, which was $805 billion. To make the balance on the current account equal the balance on the financial account, the balance of payments includes an entry called the *statistical discrepancy.* (Remember that we are ignoring the balance on the capital account. If we included the balance on the capital account, we would say that the statistical discrepancy takes on a value equal to the difference between the current account balance and the sum of the balance on the financial account and the balance on the capital account.)

Why does the U.S. Department of Commerce include the statistical discrepancy entry to force the balance of payments to equal zero? The department knows that the sum of the current account balance and the financial account balance must equal zero. If the sum does not equal zero, some imports or exports of goods and services or some capital inflows or capital outflows were not measured accurately.

To understand why the balance of payments must equal zero every year, consider the following: In 2006, the United States spent $812 billion more on goods, services, and other items in the current account than it received. What happened to that $812 billion? We know that every dollar of that $812 billion was used by foreign individuals or firms to invest in the United States or was added to foreign holdings of dollars. We know this because logically there is nowhere else for the dollars to go: If the dollars weren't spent on U.S. goods and services—and we know they weren't because in that case they would have shown up in the current account—they must have been spent on investments in the United States or not spent at all. Dollars that aren't spent are added to foreign holdings of dollars. Changes in foreign holdings of dollars are known as *official reserve transactions.* Foreign investment in the United States or additions to foreign holdings of dollars both show up as positive entries in the U.S. financial account. Therefore, a current account deficit must be exactly offset by a financial account surplus, leaving the balance of payments equal to zero. Similarly, a country that runs a current account surplus, such as China or Japan, must run a financial account deficit of exactly the same size. If a country's current account surplus is not exactly equal to its financial account deficit, or if a country's current account deficit is not exactly equal to its financial account surplus, some transactions must not have been accounted for. The statistical discrepancy is included in the balance of payments to compensate for these uncounted transactions.

Solved Problem 17-1

Understanding the Arithmetic of Open Economies

Test your understanding of the relationship between the current account and the financial account by evaluating the following assertion by a political commentator: "The industrial countries are committing economic suicide. Every year, they invest more and more in developing countries. Every year, more U.S., Japanese, and European manufacturing firms move their factories to developing countries. With extensive new factories and low wages, developing countries now export far more to the industrial countries than they import."

SOLVING THE PROBLEM:

Step 1: **Review the chapter material.** This problem is about the relationship between the current account and the capital account, so you may want to review the section "Why Is the Balance of Payments Always Zero?" which begins on page 589.

Step 2: **Explain the errors in the commentator's argument.** The argument sounds plausible. It would be easy to find similar statements to this one in recent books and articles by well-known political commentators. But the argument contains an important error: The commentator has failed to understand the relationship between the current account and the financial account. The commentator asserts that developing countries are receiving large capital inflows from industrial countries. In other words, developing countries are running financial account surpluses. The commentator also asserts that developing countries are exporting more than they are importing. In other words, they are running current account surpluses. As we have seen in this section, it is impossible to run a current account surplus *and* a financial account surplus simultaneously. A country that runs a current account surplus *must* run a financial account deficit and vice versa.

EXTRA CREDIT: Most emerging economies that have received large inflows of foreign investment during the past decade, such as South Korea, Thailand, and Malaysia, have run current account deficits: They import more goods and services than they export. Emerging economies, such as Singapore, that run current account surpluses also run financial account deficits: They invest more abroad than other countries invest in them.

The point here is not obvious, otherwise it wouldn't confuse so many intelligent politicians, journalists, and political commentators. Unless you understand the relationship between the current account and the financial account, you won't be able to understand a key aspect of the international economy.

YOUR TURN: For more practice, do related problems 1.7, 1.8, and 1.9 on page 608 at the end of this chapter.

>> End Solved Problem 17-1

17.2 LEARNING OBJECTIVE

17.2 | Explain how exchange rates are determined and how changes in exchange rates affect the prices of imports and exports.

The Foreign Exchange Market and Exchange Rates

A firm that operates entirely within the United States will price its products in dollars and will use dollars to pay suppliers, workers, interest to bondholders, and dividends to

Don't Let This Happen to **YOU!**

Don't Confuse the Balance of Trade, the Current Account Balance, and the Balance of Payments

The terminology of international economics can be tricky. Remember that the *balance of trade* includes only trade in goods; it does not include services. This observation is important because the United States, for example, usually imports more *goods* than it exports, but it usually exports more *services* than it imports. As a result, the U.S. trade deficit is almost always larger than the current account deficit. The *current account balance* includes the balance of trade, the balance of services, net investment income, and net transfers. Net investment income and net transfers are much smaller than the balance of trade and the balance of services.

Even though the *balance of payments* is equal to the sum of the current account balance and the financial account balance—and must equal zero—you may sometimes see references to a balance of payments "surplus" or "deficit." These references have two explanations. The first is that the person making the reference has confused the balance of payments with either the balance of trade or the current account balance. This is a very common mistake. The second explanation is that the person is not including official reserve transactions in the financial account. If we separate changes in U.S. holdings of foreign currencies and changes in foreign holdings of U.S. dollars from other financial account entries, the current account balance and the financial account balance do not have to sum to zero, and there can be a balance of payments surplus or deficit. This may sound complicated—and it is! But don't worry. How official reserve transactions are accounted for is not crucial to understanding the basic ideas behind the balance of payments.

YOUR TURN: Test your understanding by doing related problem 1.6 on page 608 at the end of this chapter.

shareholders. A multinational corporation, in contrast, may sell its product in many different countries and receive payment in many different currencies. Its suppliers and workers may also be spread around the world and may have to be paid in local currencies. Corporations may also use the international financial system to borrow in a foreign currency. During the 1990s, for example, many large firms located in East Asian countries, such as Thailand and South Korea, received dollar loans from foreign banks. When firms make extensive use of foreign currencies, they must deal with fluctuations in the exchange rate.

Nominal exchange rate The value of one country's currency in terms of another country's currency.

The **nominal exchange rate** is the value of one country's currency in terms of another country's currency. Economists also calculate the *real exchange rate*, which corrects the nominal exchange rate for changes in prices of goods and services. We discuss the real exchange rate later in this chapter. The nominal exchange rate determines how many units of a foreign currency you can purchase with \$1. For example, the exchange rate between the U.S. dollar and the Japanese yen can be expressed as ¥100 = \$1. (This exchange rate can also be expressed as how many U.S. dollars are required to buy 1 Japanese yen: \$0.01 = ¥1.) The market for foreign exchange is very active. Every day, the equivalent of more than \$1 trillion worth of currency is traded in the foreign exchange market. The exchange rates that result from this trading are reported each day in the business or financial sections of most newspapers.

Banks and other financial institutions around the world employ currency traders, who are linked together by computer. Rather than exchange large amounts of paper currency, they buy and sell deposits in banks. A bank buying or selling dollars will actually be buying or selling dollar bank deposits. Dollar bank deposits exist not just in banks in the United States but also in banks around the world. Suppose that the Credit Lyonnais bank in France wishes to sell U.S. dollars and buy Japanese yen. It may exchange U.S. dollar deposits that it owns for Japanese yen deposits owned by the Deutsche Bank in Germany. Businesses and individuals usually obtain foreign currency from banks in their own country.

The financial pages of most newspapers provide information on exchange rates.

Making the Connection

Exchange Rates in the Financial Pages

The business pages of most newspapers list the exchange rates between the dollar and other important currencies. The exchange rates in the following table are for June 13, 2007. The euro is the common currency used by 13 European countries, including France, Germany, and Italy.

EXCHANGE RATE BETWEEN THE DOLLAR AND THE INDICATED CURRENCY

CURRENCY	UNITS OF FOREIGN CURRENCY PER U.S. DOLLAR	U.S. DOLLARS PER UNIT OF FOREIGN CURRENCY
Canadian dollar	1.067	0.937
Japanese yen	122.650	0.008
Mexican peso	10.919	0.092
British pound	0.507	1.972
Euro	0.752	1.330

Notice that the expression for the exchange rate stated as units of foreign currency per U.S. dollar is the *reciprocal* of the exchange rate stated as U.S. dollars per unit of foreign currency. So, the exchange rate between the U.S. dollar and the British pound can be stated as either 0.507 British pounds per U.S. dollar or 1/0.507 = 1.972 U.S. dollars per British pound.

Banks are the most active participants in the market for foreign exchange. Typically, banks buy currency for slightly less than the amount for which they sell it. This spread between the buying and selling prices allows banks to cover their expenses from currency trading and to make a profit. Therefore, when most businesses and individuals buy foreign currency from a bank, they receive fewer units of foreign currency per dollar than would be indicated by the exchange rate printed in the newspaper.

Source: *Wall Street Journal*, June 13, 2007.

YOUR TURN: Test your understanding by doing related problem 2.5 on page 609 at the end of this chapter.

The market exchange rate is determined by the interaction of demand and supply, just as other prices are. Let's consider the demand for U.S. dollars in exchange for Japanese yen. There are three sources of foreign currency demand for the U.S. dollar:

1. Foreign firms and households who want to buy goods and services produced in the United States.
2. Foreign firms and households who want to invest in the United States either through foreign direct investment—buying or building factories or other facilities in the United States—or through foreign portfolio investment—buying stocks and bonds issued in the United States.
3. Currency traders who believe that the value of the dollar in the future will be greater than its value today.

Equilibrium in the Market for Foreign Exchange

Figure 17-2 shows the demand and supply of U.S. dollars for Japanese yen. Notice that as we move up the vertical axis in Figure 17-2, the value of the dollar increases relative to the value of the yen. When the exchange rate is ¥150 = $1, the dollar is worth 1.5 times as much relative to the yen as when the exchange rate is ¥100 = $1. Consider, first, the demand curve for dollars in exchange for yen. The demand curve has the normal downward slope. When the value of the dollar is high, the quantity of dollars demanded will be low. A Japanese investor will be more likely to buy a $1,000 bond

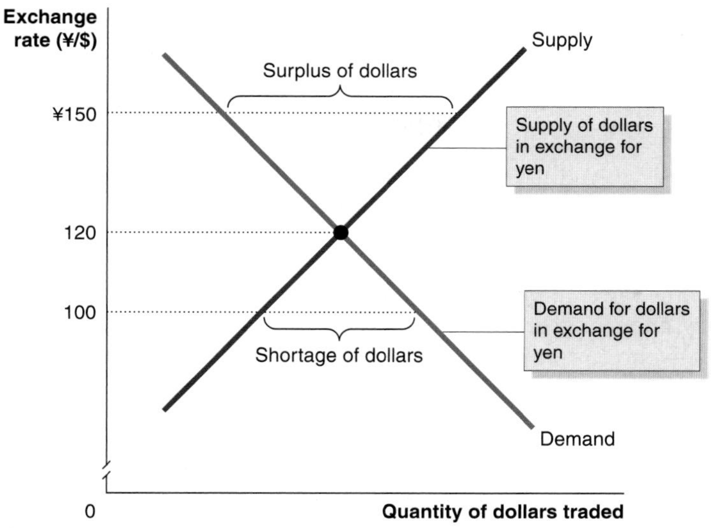

Figure 17-2

Equilibrium in the Foreign Exchange Market

When the exchange rate is ¥150 to the dollar, it is above its equilibrium level, and there will be a surplus of dollars. When the exchange rate is ¥100 to the dollar, it is below its equilibrium level, and there will be a shortage of dollars. At an exchange rate of ¥120 to the dollar, the foreign exchange market is in equilibrium.

issued by the U.S. Treasury when the exchange rate is ¥100 = $1 and the investor pays only ¥100,000 to buy $1,000 than when the exchange rate is ¥150 = $1 and the investor must pay ¥150,000. Similarly, a Japanese firm is more likely to buy $150 million worth of microchips from Intel Corporation when the exchange rate is ¥100 = $1 and the microchips can be purchased for ¥15 billion than when the exchange rate is ¥150 = $1 and the microchips cost ¥22.5 billion.

Consider, now, the supply curve of dollars in exchange for yen. The supply curve has the normal upward slope. When the value of the dollar is high, the quantity of dollars supplied in exchange for yen will be high. A U.S. investor will be more likely to buy a ¥200,000 bond issued by the Japanese government when the exchange rate is ¥200 = $1 and he needs to pay only $1,000 to buy ¥200,000 than when the exchange rate is ¥100 = $1 and he must pay $2,000. The owner of a U.S. electronics store is more likely to buy ¥20 million worth of television sets from the Sony Corporation when the exchange rate is ¥200 = $1 and she only needs to pay $100,000 to purchase the televisions than when the exchange rate is ¥100 = $1 and she must pay $200,000.

Don't Let This Happen to **YOU!**

Don't Confuse What Happens When a Currency Appreciates with What Happens When It Depreciates.

One of the more confusing aspects of exchange rates is that they can be expressed in two ways. We can express the exchange rate between the dollar and the yen either as how many yen can be purchased with $1 or as how many dollars can be purchased with ¥1. That is, we can express the exchange rate as ¥100 = $1 or as $0.01 = ¥1. When a currency appreciates, it increases in value relative to another currency. When it depreciates, it decreases in value relative to another currency.

If the exchange rate changes from ¥100 = $1 to ¥120 = $1, the dollar has appreciated and the yen has depreciated because it now takes more yen to buy $1. If the exchange rate changes from $0.01 = ¥1 to $0.015 = ¥1, however, the dollar has depreciated and the yen has appreciated because it now takes more dollars to buy ¥1. This situation can appear somewhat confusing because the exchange rate seems to have "increased" in both cases. To determine which currency has appreciated and which has depreciated, it is important to remember that an appreciation of the domestic currency means that it now takes *more* units of the foreign currency to buy one unit of the domestic currency. A depreciation of the domestic currency means it takes *fewer* units of the foreign currency to buy one unit of the domestic currency. This observation holds no matter which way we express the exchange rate.

YOUR TURN: Test your understanding by doing related problem 2.4 on page 609 at the end of the chapter.

As in any other market, equilibrium occurs in the foreign exchange market where the quantity supplied equals the quantity demanded. In Figure 17-2, ¥120 = $1 is the equilibrium exchange rate. At exchange rates above ¥120 = $1, there will be a surplus of dollars and downward pressure on the exchange rate. The surplus and the downward pressure will not be eliminated until the exchange rate falls to ¥120 = $1. If the exchange rate is below ¥120 = $1, there will be a shortage of dollars and upward pressure on the exchange rate. The shortage and the upward pressure will not be eliminated until the exchange rate rises to ¥120 = $1. Surpluses and shortages in the foreign exchange market are eliminated very quickly because the volume of trading in major currencies such as the dollar and the yen is very large, and currency traders are linked together by computer.

Currency appreciation An increase in the market value of one currency relative to another currency.

Currency depreciation A decrease in the market value of one currency relative to another currency.

Currency appreciation occurs when the market value of a country's currency increases relative to the value of another country's currency. **Currency depreciation** occurs when the market value of a country's currency decreases relative to the value of another country's currency.

How Do Shifts in Demand and Supply Affect the Exchange Rate?

Shifts in the demand and supply curves cause the equilibrium exchange rate to change. Three main factors cause the demand and supply curves in the foreign exchange market to shift:

1. Changes in the demand for U.S.-produced goods and services and changes in the demand for foreign-produced goods and services
2. Changes in the desire to invest in the United States and changes in the desire to invest in foreign countries
3. Changes in the expectations of currency traders about the likely future value of the dollar and the likely future value of foreign currencies

Shifts in the Demand for Foreign Exchange Consider how the three factors listed above will affect the demand for U.S. dollars in exchange for Japanese yen. During an economic expansion in Japan, the incomes of Japanese households will rise, and the demand by Japanese consumers and firms for U.S. goods will increase. At any given exchange rate, the demand for U.S. dollars will increase, and the demand curve will shift to the right. Similarly, if interest rates in the United States rise, the desirability of investing in U.S. financial assets will increase, and the demand curve for dollars will also shift to the right. Some buyers and sellers in the foreign exchange market are *speculators*. **Speculators** buy and sell foreign exchange in an attempt to profit from changes in exchange rates. If a speculator becomes convinced that the value of the dollar is going to rise relative to the value of the yen, the speculator will sell yen and buy dollars. If the current exchange rate is ¥120 = $1, and the speculator is convinced that it will soon rise to ¥140 = $1, the speculator could sell ¥600,000,000 and receive $5,000,000 (= ¥600,000,000/¥120) in return. If the speculator is correct and the value of the dollar rises against the yen to ¥140 = $1, the speculator will be able to exchange $5,000,000 for ¥700,000,000 (= $5,000,000 × ¥140), leaving a profit of ¥100,000,000.

Speculators Currency traders who buy and sell foreign exchange in an attempt to profit from changes in exchange rates.

To summarize, the demand curve for dollars shifts to the right when incomes in Japan rise, when interest rates in the United States rise, or when speculators decide that the value of the dollar will rise relative to the value of the yen.

During a recession in Japan, Japanese incomes will fall, reducing the demand for U.S.-produced goods and services and shifting the demand curve for dollars to the left. Similarly, if interest rates in the United States fall, the desirability of investing in U.S. financial assets will decrease, and the demand curve for dollars will shift to the left. Finally, if speculators become convinced that the future value of the dollar will be lower than its current value, the demand for dollars will fall, and the demand curve will shift to the left.

Shifts in the Supply of Foreign Exchange The factors that affect the supply curve for dollars are similar to those that affect the demand curve for dollars. An economic expansion in the United States increases the incomes of Americans and increases their demand for goods and services, including goods and services made in Japan. As U.S. consumers and firms increase their spending on Japanese products, they must supply dollars in exchange for yen, which causes the supply curve for dollars to shift to the right. Similarly, an increase in interest rates in Japan will make financial investments in Japan more attractive to U.S. investors. These higher Japanese interest rates will cause the supply of dollars to shift to the right, as U.S. investors exchange dollars for yen. Finally, if speculators become convinced that the future value of the yen will be higher relative to the dollar than it is today, the supply curve of dollars will shift to the right as traders attempt to exchange dollars for yen.

A recession in the United States will decrease the demand for Japanese products and cause the supply curve for dollars to shift to the left. Similarly, a decrease in interest rates in Japan will make financial investments in Japan less attractive and cause the supply curve of dollars to shift to the left. If traders become convinced that the future value of the yen will be lower relative to the dollar, the supply curve will also shift to the left.

Adjustment to a New Equilibrium The factors that affect the demand and supply for currencies are constantly changing. Whether the exchange rate increases or decreases depends on the direction and size of the shifts in the demand curve and supply curve. For example, as Figure 17-3 shows, if the demand curve for dollars in exchange for Japanese yen shifts to the right by more than the supply curve does, the equilibrium exchange rate will increase.

Some Exchange Rates Are Not Determined by the Market

To this point, we have assumed that exchange rates are determined in the market. This assumption is a good one for many currencies, including the U.S. dollar, the euro, the Japanese yen, and the British pound. Some currencies, however, have *fixed exchange rates* that do not change over long periods. For example, for more than 10 years, the value of the Chinese yuan was fixed against the U.S. dollar at a rate of 8.28 yuan to the dollar. As we will discuss in more detail in Chapter 18, a country's central bank has to intervene in the foreign exchange market to buy and sell its currency to keep the exchange rate fixed.

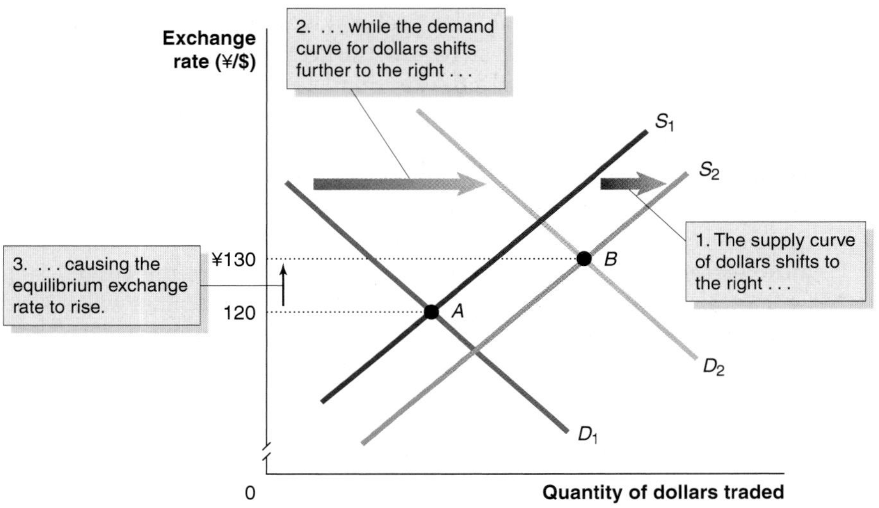

Figure 17-3

Shifts in the Demand and Supply Curve Resulting in a Higher Exchange Rate

Holding other factors constant, an increase in the supply of dollars will decrease the equilibrium exchange rate. An increase in the demand for dollars will increase the equilibrium exchange rate. In the case shown in this figure, the demand curve and the supply curve have both shifted to the right. Because the demand curve has shifted to the right by more than the supply curve, the equilibrium exchange rate has increased from ¥120 to $1 at point *A* to ¥130 to $1 at point *B*.

How Movements in the Exchange Rate Affect Exports and Imports

When the market value of the dollar increases, the foreign currency price of U.S. exports rises, and the dollar price of foreign imports falls. For example, suppose that initially the market exchange rate between the U.S. dollar and the euro is \$1 = €1. In that case, an Apple iPod Nano that has a price of \$200 in the United States will have a price of €200 in France. A bottle of French wine that has a price of €50 in France will have a price of \$50 in the United States. Now suppose the market exchange rate between the U.S. dollar and the euro changes to \$1.20 = €1. Because it now takes more dollars to buy a euro, the dollar has *depreciated* against the euro, and the euro has *appreciated* against the dollar.

The depreciation of the dollar has decreased the euro price of the iPod from €200 to \$200/(1.20 dollars/euro) = €167. The dollar price of the French wine has risen from \$50 to €50 × 1.20 dollars/euro = \$60. As a result, we would expect more iPods to be sold in France and less French wine to be sold in the United States. To generalize, we can conclude that a depreciation in the domestic currency will increase exports and decrease imports, thereby increasing net exports. As we saw in previous chapters, net exports is a component of aggregate demand. If the economy is currently below potential GDP, then, holding all other factors constant, a depreciation in the domestic currency should increase net exports, aggregate demand, and real GDP. An appreciation in the domestic currency should have the opposite effect: Exports should fall, and imports should rise, which will reduce net exports, aggregate demand, and real GDP.

Solved Problem | 17-2

The Effect of Changing Exchange Rates on the Prices of Imports and Exports

In March 2001, the average price of goods imported into the United States from Canada fell 3.3 percent. This decline was the largest since the federal government began gathering such statistics in 1992. Is it likely that the value of the U.S. dollar appreciated or depreciated versus the Canadian dollar during this period? Is it likely that the average price in Canadian dollars of goods exported from the United States to Canada during March 2001 rose or fell?

SOLVING THE PROBLEM:

Step 1: **Review the chapter material.** This problem is about changes in the value of a currency, so you may want to review the section "How Movements in the Exchange Rate Affect Exports and Imports," which appears on this page.

Step 2: **Explain whether the value of the U.S. dollar appreciated or depreciated against the Canadian dollar.** We know that if the U.S. dollar appreciates against the Canadian dollar, it will take more Canadian dollars to purchase one U.S. dollar, and, equivalently, fewer U.S. dollars will be required to purchase one Canadian dollar. A Canadian consumer or business will need to pay more Canadian dollars to buy products imported from the United States: A good or service that had been selling for 100 Canadian dollars will now sell for more than 100 Canadian dollars. A U.S. consumer or business will have to pay fewer U.S. dollars to buy products imported from Canada: A good or service that had been selling for 100 U.S. dollars will now sell for fewer than 100 U.S. dollars. We can conclude that if the price of goods imported into the United States from Canada fell, the value of the U.S. dollar must have appreciated versus the Canadian dollar.

Step 3: **Explain what happened to the average price in Canadian dollars of goods exported from the United States to Canada.** If the U.S. dollar appreciated relative to the Canadian dollar, the average price in Canadian dollars of goods exported from the United States to Canada will have risen.

YOUR TURN: For more practice, do related problem 2.9 on page 610 at the end of this chapter.

>> End Solved Problem 17-2

The Real Exchange Rate

We have seen that an important factor in determining the level of a country's exports to and imports from another country is the relative prices of each country's goods. The relative prices of two countries' goods are determined by two factors: the relative price levels in the two countries and the nominal exchange rate between the two countries' currencies. Economists combine these two factors in the *real exchange rate*. The **real exchange rate** is the price of domestic goods in terms of foreign goods. Recall that the price level is a measure of the average prices of goods and services in an economy. We can calculate the real exchange rate between two currencies as:

Real exchange rate The price of domestic goods in terms of foreign goods.

$$\text{Real exchange rate} = \text{Nominal exchange rate} \times \left(\frac{\text{Domestic price level}}{\text{Foreign price level}}\right).$$

Notice that changes in the real exchange rate reflect both changes in the nominal exchange rate and changes in the relative price levels. For example, suppose that the exchange rate between the U.S. dollar and the British pound is \$1 = £1, the price level in the United States is 100, and the price level in the United Kingdom is also 100. Then the real exchange rate between the dollar and the pound is:

$$\text{Real exchange rate} = 1 \text{ pound/dollar} \times \left(\frac{100}{100}\right) = 1.00.$$

Now suppose that the nominal exchange rate increases to 1.1 pounds per dollar, while the price level in the United States rises to 105 and the price level in the United Kingdom remains 100. In this case, the real exchange rate will be:

$$\text{Real exchange rate} = 1.1 \text{ pound/dollar} \times \left(\frac{105}{100}\right) = 1.15.$$

The increase in the real exchange rate from 1.00 to 1.15 tells us that the prices of U.S. goods and services are now 15 percent higher than they were relative to British goods and services.

Real exchange rates are reported as index numbers, with one year chosen as the base year. As with the consumer price index, the main value of the real exchange rate is in tracking changes over time—in this case, changes in the relative prices of domestic goods in terms of foreign goods.

17.3 LEARNING OBJECTIVE

17.3 | Explain the saving and investment equation.

The International Sector and National Saving and Investment

Having studied what determines the exchange rate, we are now ready to explore further the linkages between the U.S. economy and foreign economies. Until 1970, U.S. imports and exports were usually 4 percent to 5 percent of GDP. As Figure 17-4 shows, imports and exports are now more than twice as large a fraction of U.S. GDP. The figure also shows that since 1975, imports have consistently been larger than exports, meaning that net exports have been negative.

Figure 17-4

U.S. Imports and Exports, 1970–2006

Imports and exports are much larger fractions of GDP today than they were before 1970. Imports have increased faster than exports, which has made net exports negative every year since 1975.

Source: U.S. Bureau of Economic Analysis.

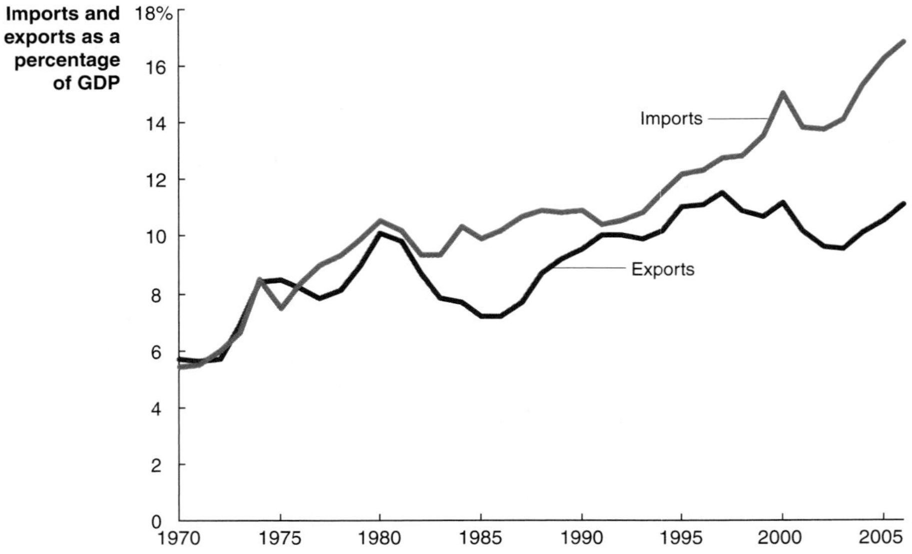

Net Exports Equal Net Foreign Investment

If your spending is greater than your income, what can you do? You can sell some assets—maybe those 20 shares of stock in the Walt Disney Company your grandparents gave you—or you can borrow money. A firm can be in the same situation: If a firm's costs are greater than its revenues, it has to make up the difference by selling assets or by borrowing. A country is in the same situation when it imports more than it exports. The country must finance the difference by selling assets—such as land, office buildings, or factories—or by borrowing.

In other words, for any country, a current account deficit must be exactly offset by a financial account surplus. When a country sells more assets to foreigners than it buys from foreigners, or when it borrows more from foreigners than it lends to foreigners—as it must if it is running a current account deficit—the country experiences a net capital inflow and a financial account surplus. Remember that net exports is roughly equal to the current account balance. Remember also that the financial account balance is roughly equal to net capital flows, which are in turn equal to net foreign investment but with the opposite sign. To review these two points, look again at Table 17-1 on page 587, which shows that the current account balance is determined mainly by the balance of trade and the balance of services, and the financial account is equal to net capital flows. Also, remember the definition of net foreign investment.

When imports are greater than exports, net exports are negative, and there will be a net capital inflow as people in the United States sell assets and borrow to pay for the surplus of imports over exports. Therefore, net capital flows will be equal to net exports (but with the opposite sign), and net foreign investment will also be equal to net exports (and with the same sign). Because net exports are usually negative for the United States, in most years, the United States must be a net borrower from abroad, and U.S. net foreign investment will be negative.

We can summarize this discussion with the following equations:

$$\text{Current account balance} + \text{Financial account balance} = 0$$

or:

$$\text{Current account balance} = -\text{Financial account balance}$$

or:

$$\text{Net exports} = \text{Net foreign investment.}$$

This equation tells us, once again, that countries such as the United States that import more than they export must borrow more from abroad than they lend abroad: If net exports are negative, net foreign investment will also be negative by the same amount. Countries such as Japan and China that export more than they import must lend abroad more than they borrow from abroad: If net exports are positive, net foreign investment will also be positive by the same amount.

Domestic Saving, Domestic Investment, and Net Foreign Investment

As we saw in Chapter 9, the total saving in any economy is equal to saving by the private sector plus saving by the government sector, which we called *public saving*. When the government runs a budget surplus by spending less than it receives in taxes, it is saving. When the government runs a budget deficit, public saving is negative. Negative saving is also known as *dissaving*. We can write the following expression for the level of saving in the economy:

National saving = Private saving + Public saving

or:

$$S = S_{\text{private}} + S_{\text{public}}.$$

Private saving is equal to what households have left of their income after spending on consumption goods and paying taxes (for simplicity, we assume that transfer payments are zero):

Private saving = National income − Consumption − Taxes

or:

$$S_{\text{private}} = Y - C - T.$$

Public saving is equal to the difference between government spending and taxes:

Government saving = Taxes − Government spending

or:

$$S_{\text{public}} = T - G.$$

Finally, remember the basic macroeconomic equation for GDP or national income:

$$Y = C + I + G + NX.$$

We can use this last equation, our definitions of private and public saving, and the fact that net exports equal net foreign investment to arrive at an important relationship, known as the **saving and investment equation**:

Saving and investment equation An equation that shows that national saving is equal to domestic investment plus net foreign investment.

National saving = Domestic investment + Net foreign investment

or:

$$S = I + NFI.$$

This equation is an *identity* because it must always be true, given the definitions we have used.

The saving and investment equation tells us that a country's saving will be invested either domestically or overseas. If you save $1,000 and use the funds to buy a bond issued by General Motors, GM may use the $1,000 to renovate a factory in the United States (I) or to build a factory in China (NFI) as a joint venture with a Chinese firm.

Solved Problem 17-3

Arriving at the Saving and Investment Equation

Use the definitions of private and public saving, the equation for GDP or national income, and the fact that net exports must equal net foreign investment to arrive at the saving and investment equation.

SOLVING THE PROBLEM:

Step 1: **Review the chapter material.** This problem is about the saving and investment equation, so you may want to review the section "Domestic Saving, Domestic Investment, and Net Foreign Investment," which begins on page 599.

Step 2: **Derive an expression for national saving (S) in terms of national income (Y), consumption (C), and government purchases (G).** We can bring together the four equations we need to use:

1. $S_{private} = Y - C - T$
2. $S_{public} = T - G$
3. $Y = C + I + G + NX$
4. $NX = NFI$

Because national saving (S) appears in the saving and investment equation, we need to find an equation for it in terms of the other variables. Adding equation 1. plus equation 2. yields national saving:

$$S = S_{private} + S_{public} = (Y - C - T) + (T - G) = Y - C - G.$$

Step 3: **Use the result from step 2 to derive an expression for national saving in terms of investment (I) and net exports (NX).** Because GDP (Y) does not appear in the saving and investment equation, we need to substitute the expression for it given in equation 3.:

$$S = (C + I + G + NX) - C - G$$

and simplify:

$$S = I + NX.$$

Step 4: **Use the results of steps 2 and 3 to derive the saving and investment equation.** Finally, substitute net foreign investment for net exports:

$$S = I + NFI.$$

YOUR TURN: For more practice, do related problem 3.8 on page 611 at the end of this chapter.

>> End Solved Problem 17-3

A country such as the United States that has negative net foreign investment must be saving less than it is investing domestically. To see this, rewrite the saving and investment equation by moving domestic investment to the left side:

$$S - I = NFI.$$

If net foreign investment is negative—as it is for the United States nearly every year—domestic investment (I) must be greater than national saving (S).

The level of saving in Japan has been well above domestic investment. The result has been high levels of Japanese net foreign investment. For example, Japanese automobile companies Toyota, Honda, and Nissan have all constructed factories in the United States. Sony purchased the Columbia Pictures film studio. Japanese investors are also estimated to hold more than $200 billion worth of U.S. Treasury bonds. Japan has made many similar investments in countries around the world, which has sometimes caused resentment in these countries. There were some protests in the United States in the 1980s, for example, when Japanese investors purchased the Pebble Beach golf course in California and the Rockefeller Center complex in New York City.

Japan needs a high level of net exports to help offset a low level of domestic investment. When exports of a product begin to decline and imports begin to increase, governments are often tempted to impose tariffs or quotas to reduce imports. (See Chapter 6 to review tariffs and quotas and their negative effects on the economy.) In fact, many Japanese firms have been urging the Japanese government to impose trade restrictions on exports from China.

17.4 LEARNING OBJECTIVE

17.4 | Explain the effect of a government budget deficit on investment in an open economy.

The Effect of a Government Budget Deficit on Investment

The link we have just developed among saving, investment, and net foreign investment can help us understand some of the effects of changes in a government's budget deficit. When the government runs a budget deficit, national saving will decline unless private saving increases by the amount of the budget deficit, which is unlikely. As the saving and investment equation ($S = I + NFI$) shows, the result of a decline in national saving must be a decline in either domestic investment or net foreign investment. Why, though, does an increase in the government budget deficit cause a fall in domestic investment or net foreign investment?

To understand the answer to this question, remember that if the federal government runs a budget deficit, the U.S. Treasury must raise an amount equal to the deficit by selling bonds. To attract investors, the Treasury may have to raise the interest rates on its bonds. As interest rates on Treasury bonds rise, other interest rates, including those on corporate bonds and bank loans, will also rise. Higher interest rates will discourage some firms from borrowing funds to build new factories or to buy new equipment or computers. Higher interest rates on financial assets in the United States will attract foreign investors. Investors in Canada, Japan, or China will have to buy U.S. dollars to be able to purchase bonds in the United States. This greater demand for dollars will increase their value relative to foreign currencies. As the value of the dollar rises, exports from the United States will fall, and imports to the United States will rise. Net exports and, therefore, net foreign investment will fall.

When a government budget deficit leads to a decline in net exports, the result is sometimes referred to as the *twin deficits*, which refers to the possibility that a government budget deficit will also lead to a current account deficit. The twin deficits idea first became widely discussed in the United States during the early 1980s when the federal government ran a large budget deficit that resulted in high interest rates, a high exchange value of the dollar, and a large current account deficit.

Figure 17-5 shows that in the early 1980s, the United States had large federal budget deficits and large current account deficits. The figure also shows, however, that the twin deficits idea does not match the experience of the United States after 1990. The large federal budget deficits of the early 1990s occurred at a time of relatively small current

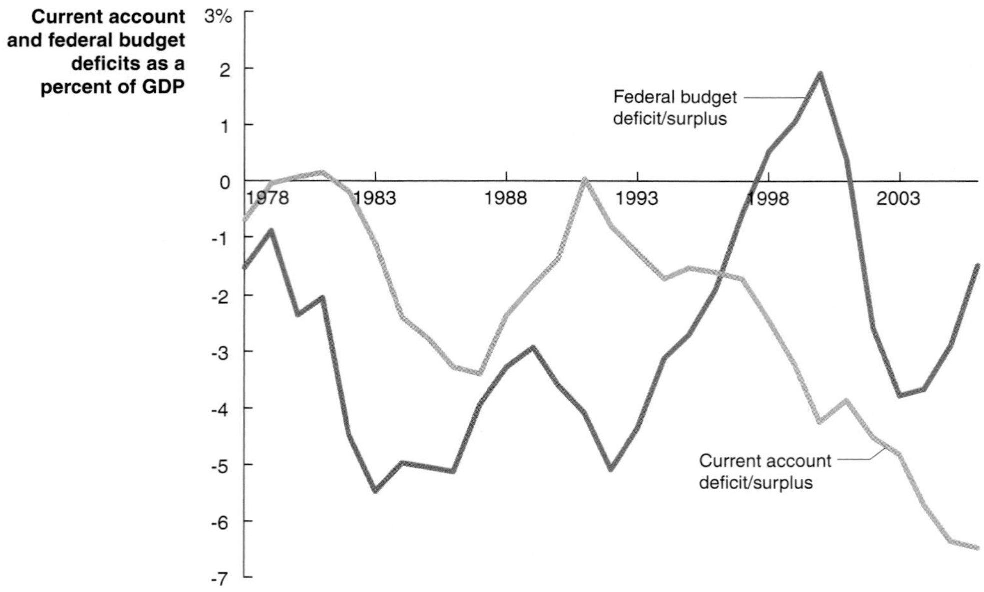

Figure 17-5 | The Twin Deficits, 1978–2006

During the early 1980s, large federal budget deficits occurred at the same time as large current account deficits, but twin deficits did not occur in the 1990s.
Source: U.S. Bureau of Economic Analysis.

account deficits, and the budget surpluses of the late 1990s occurred at a time of then-record current account deficits. Both the current account deficit and the federal budget deficit increased in the early 2000s, but the federal budget deficit declined in the mid-2000s, while the current account deficit continued to increase.

The experience of other countries also shows only mixed support for the twin deficits idea. Germany ran large budget deficits and large current account deficits during the early 1990s, but both Canada and Italy ran large budget deficits during the 1980s without running current account deficits. The saving and investment equation shows that an increase in the government budget deficit will not lead to an increase in the current account deficit, provided that either private saving increases or domestic investment declines. According to the twin deficits idea, when the federal government ran budget surpluses in the late 1990s, the current account should also have been in surplus, or at least the current account deficit should have been small. In fact, the increase in national saving due to the budget surpluses was more than offset by a sharp decline in private saving, and the United States ran very large current account deficits.

Making the Connection

Why Is the United States Called the "World's Largest Debtor"?

The following graph shows the current account balance as a percentage of GDP for the United States for the period 1950–2006. The United States has had a current account deficit every year since 1982, with the exception of 1991. Between 1950 and 1975, the United States ran a current account deficit in only five years. Many economists believe that the current account deficits of the 1980s were closely related to the federal budget deficits of those years. High interest rates attracted foreign investors to U.S. bonds, which raised the exchange rate between the dollar and foreign currencies. The high exchange rate reduced U.S. exports and increased imports, leading to current account deficits.

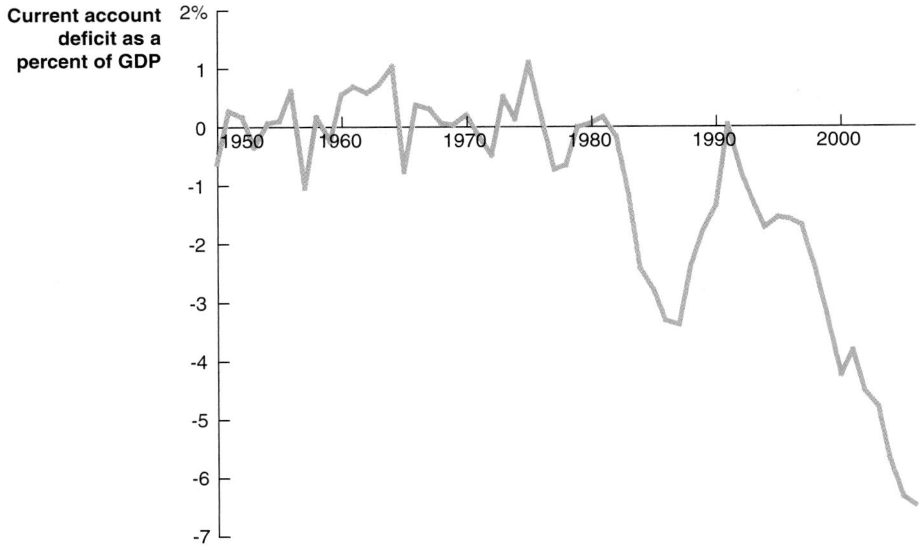

Source: Bureau of Economic Analysis.

As the federal budget deficit narrowed in the mid-1990s and disappeared in the late 1990s, the foreign exchange value of the dollar remained high—and large current account deficits continued—because foreign investors persisted in investing in the United States despite low interest rates. In the late 1990s, a number of countries around the world, such as South Korea, Indonesia, Brazil, and Russia, suffered severe economic problems. In a process known as a *flight to quality*, many investors sold their investments in those countries and bought investments in the United States. In addition, the strong performance of the U.S. stock market through the spring of 2000 attracted many investors. Finally, the sharp decline in private saving in the United States during the late 1990s also contributed to the U.S. current account deficit.

Large current account deficits have resulted in foreign investors purchasing large amounts of U.S. assets.

Do persistent current account deficits represent a problem for the United States? Current account deficits result in U.S. net foreign investment being negative. Each year, foreign investors accumulate many more U.S. assets than U.S. investors accumulate foreign assets. At the end of 2006, foreign investors owned about \$2.7 trillion more of U.S. assets—such as stocks, bonds, and factories—than U.S. investors owned of foreign assets, which is why the United States is sometimes called "the world's largest debtor." But the continued willingness of foreign investors to buy U.S. stocks and bonds and foreign companies to build factories in the United States can be seen as a vote of confidence in the strength of the U.S. economy and the buying power of U.S. consumers. With private saving rates having declined in the United States to historically low levels, only the continued flow of funds from foreign investors has made it possible for the United States to maintain the high levels of domestic investment required for economic growth.

YOUR TURN: Test your understanding by doing related problem 4.6 on page 612 at the end of this chapter.

17.5 LEARNING OBJECTIVE

17.5 | Discuss the difference between the effectiveness of monetary and fiscal policy in an open economy and in a closed economy.

Monetary Policy and Fiscal Policy in an Open Economy

When we discussed monetary and fiscal policy in Chapters 14 and 15, we did not emphasize that the United States is an open economy. Now that we have explored some of the links between economies, we can look at the difference between how monetary and fiscal policy work in an open economy as opposed to a closed economy. Economists refer to the ways in which monetary and fiscal policy affect the domestic economy as *policy channels*. An open economy has more policy channels than does a closed economy.

Monetary Policy in an Open Economy

When the Federal Reserve engages in an expansionary monetary policy, it buys Treasury securities to lower interest rates and stimulate aggregate demand. In a closed economy, the main effect of lower interest rates is on domestic investment spending and purchases of consumer durables. In an open economy, lower interest rates will also affect the exchange rate between the dollar and foreign currencies. Lower interest rates will cause some investors in the United States and abroad to switch from investing in U.S. financial assets to investing in foreign financial assets. This switch will lower the demand for the dollar relative to foreign currencies and cause its value to decline. A lower exchange rate will decrease the price of U.S. products in foreign markets and increase the price of foreign products in the United States. As a result, net exports will increase. This additional policy channel will increase the ability of an expansionary monetary policy to affect aggregate demand.

When the Fed wants to reduce the rate of economic growth to reduce inflation, it engages in contractionary monetary policy. The Fed sells Treasury securities to increase interest rates and reduce aggregate demand. In a closed economy, the main effect is once again on domestic investment spending and purchases of consumer durables. In an open economy, higher interest rates will lead to a higher foreign exchange value of the dollar. The prices of U.S. products in foreign markets will increase, and the prices of foreign products in the U.S. will fall. As a result, net exports will fall. The contractionary policy will have a larger impact on aggregate demand, and therefore it will be more effective in slowing down the growth in economic activity. To summarize: *Monetary policy has a greater impact on aggregate demand in an open economy than in a closed economy.*

Fiscal Policy in an Open Economy

To engage in an expansionary fiscal policy, the federal government increases its purchases or cuts taxes. Increases in government purchases directly increase aggregate demand. Tax cuts increase aggregate demand by increasing household disposable income and business income, which results in increased consumption spending and investment spending. An expansionary fiscal policy may result in higher interest rates. In a closed economy, the main effect of higher interest rates is to reduce domestic investment spending and purchases of consumer durables. In an open economy, higher interest rates will also lead to an increase in the foreign exchange value of the dollar and a decrease in net exports. Therefore, in an open economy, an expansionary fiscal policy may be less effective because the *crowding out effect* may be larger. In a closed economy, only consumption and investment are crowded out by an expansionary fiscal policy. In an open economy, net exports may also be crowded out.

The government can fight inflation by using a contractionary fiscal policy to slow the rate of economic growth. A contractionary fiscal policy cuts government purchases or raises taxes to reduce household disposable income and consumption spending. It also reduces the federal budget deficit (or increases the budget surplus), which may lower interest rates. Lower interest rates will increase domestic investment and purchases of consumer durables, thereby offsetting some of the reduction in government spending and increases in taxes. In an open economy, lower interest rates will also reduce the foreign exchange value of the dollar and increase net exports. Therefore, in an open economy, a contractionary fiscal policy will have a smaller impact on aggregate demand and therefore will be less effective in slowing down an economy. In summary: *Fiscal policy has a smaller impact on aggregate demand in an open economy than in a closed economy.*

>> Continued from page 585

Economics in YOUR Life!

At the beginning of the chapter, we posed this question: What effect will the Bank of Korea's decision to sell its U.S. Treasury bonds likely have on the interest rate that you pay on your car loan? To sell its holdings of Treasury bonds, South Korea's central bank may have to offer them at a lower price. When the prices of bonds fall, the interest rates on them rise. As the interest rates on U.S. Treasury bonds increase, the interest rates on corporate bonds and bank loans, including car loans, may also increase. So, the decision of the Bank of Korea has the potential to increase the interest rate you pay on your car loan. In practice, the interest rate on your car loan is likely to be affected only if the Bank of Korea sells a very large number of bonds and if investors consider it likely that other foreign central banks may soon do the same thing. The basic point is important, however: Economies are interdependent, and interest rates in the United States are not determined entirely by the actions of people in the United States.

Conclusion

At one time, U.S. policymakers—and economics textbooks—ignored the linkages between the United States and other economies. In the modern world, these linkages have become increasingly important, and economists and policymakers must take them into account when analyzing the economy. In the next chapter, we will discuss further how the international financial system operates.

Read *An Inside Look* on the next page for a discussion of how the U.S. current account deficit affects global investors.

An Inside **LOOK**

Can the U.S. Current Account Deficit Be Sustained?

ECONOMIST, MARCH 15, 2007

Sustaining the Unsustainable

Sour subprime mortgages, sluggish retail sales, the spectre of a broader retreat in credit and consumer spending. These are the American shadows that spooked investors across the globe this week, once again sending share prices tumbling from Manhattan to Mumbai.

(a) For years, the longest shadow of all was cast by America's imposing current-account deficit. But in these fretful times, no one seems to be fretting much about the country's heavy reliance on foreign funding. New figures released on March 14th showed that Americans spent some $857 billion more than they produced in 2006, the equivalent of 6.5% of GDP, and a new record. . . .

China's government, one of America's best creditors, has announced it is seeking a better return on a chunk of its foreign-exchange reserves. It will create a new investment agency, which looks sure to diversify some of the central bank's assets out of the American Treasury bonds that now dominate its portfolio. . . .

(b) None of this had much effect on the dollar. Measured on a trade-weighted basis, it has fallen by a mere 0.04% since the recent financial turbulence began on February 27th. And as investors yawn at America's deficit, so too do policymakers. A year ago, finance ministers and central bankers from the G7 group of big, rich countries promised to take "vigorous action" to resolve the imbalances between the world's savers (particularly China, Japan and the oil exporters) and borrowers (especially America). The IMF was hoping to reinvent itself as the overseer of this grand macroeconomic bargain. A year later the venture has fizzled. . . .

What explains this nonchalance? By some measures, the world is already rebalancing. The dollar after all has fallen by 16% from its 2002 peak in real terms. Compared with the previous quarter, America's current-account deficit shrank in the last three months of 2006 and was below $200 billion for the first time in more than a year. . . . That decline owes a lot to lower oil prices. But even excluding oil, America's trade balance seems to be stabilising as exports boom and imports slow. . . . A few years ago most economists argued that the spectacle of poor countries bankrolling America's deficits was the perverse and unsustainable consequence of American profligacy. Economic theory suggested that capital should flow from rich countries to poor ones, and that America could not increase its foreign borrowing forever. Empirical studies showed that deficits of more than 5% of GDP caused trouble.

Since then, economists have vied with each other to overturn this orthodoxy. Indeed, rejecting the conventional wisdom is now itself entirely conventional, as Jeffrey Frankel, an economist at Harvard University, has pointed out. . . .

In 2005 Ben Bernanke, now chairman of the Federal Reserve, pointed out that global interest rates were oddly low, suggesting a glut of saving abroad, not a shortfall of saving at home, was responsible for the flow of capital to America.

More recent papers have picked up similar threads, arguing that imbalances might prove to be both more persistent and less perverse than once thought. A study last summer by three economists at the IMF, for instance, showed that poor countries which export capital have grown faster than those which rely on importing it from abroad.

(c) One reason may be the feebleness of their financial markets. That is a thesis explored by Ricardo Caballero and Emmanuel Farhi of the Massachusetts Institute of Technology, as well as Pierre-Olivier Gourinchas of the University of California, Berkeley. They point out that emerging economies have been frantically accumulating real assets, such as assembly lines and office towers, but their generation of financial assets has not kept pace. Thanks to weak property rights, fear of expropriation and poor bankruptcy procedures, many newly rich countries are unable to create enough trustworthy claims on their future incomes. Lacking vehicles for saving at home, the thrifty buy assets abroad instead. In China, Mr. Caballero argues, this is done indirectly through the state, which buys foreign securities, such as Treasuries, then issues bonds of its own, which are held by Chinese banks, companies and households.

Because emerging economies' supply of financial instruments is so unreliable, people may hoard more of them as a precautionary measure. Firms and households fear they will not be able to borrow to tide themselves over bad times, therefore they choose to save for a rainy day instead. Because they cannot transfer purchasing power from the future to the present, they must store it from the past. . . .

Source: "Sustaining the Unsustainable," Economist, *March 15, 2007. Reprinted by permission of the* Economist *via Copyright Clearance Center.*

account deficits can last only as long as foreigners are willing to hold the deficit country's currency, which typically decreases in value as its supply in the world market increases. For example, the U.S. current account deficit in 2006 was $857 billion, or 6.5 percent of U.S. GDP.

Key Points in the Article

This article discusses the U.S. balance of payments and, in particular, the country's large current account deficit. The U.S. current account deficit in 2006 was $857 billion, or 6.5 percent of U.S. GDP. The article explains why economists have long argued that large current account deficits are unsustainable and why some economists believe that the U.S. current account deficit may prove to be the exception to this rule.

Analyzing the News

a Most macroeconomists contend that large deficits in a country's current account—the part of the balance of payments that records a country's net exports, net investment income, and net transfers—are unsustainable. This is because a country's current account deficit is matched by foreigners' (net) purchases of the country's real and financial assets. Hence, current account deficits can last only as long as foreigners are willing to hold the deficit country's currency, which typically decreases in value as its supply in the world market increases. For example, the U.S. current account deficit in 2006 was $857 billion, or 6.5 percent of U.S. GDP.

b As the U.S. current account deficit increases, so does the supply of U.S. dollars in the foreign exchange market. And, as you read in this chapter, an increase in the supply of dollars decreases the foreign exchange value of the dollar. Nonetheless, despite the growing U.S. current account deficit and, the resulting increase in the supply of U.S. dollars, the foreign exchange value of the U.S. dollar has not fallen as much as most economists and policymakers had expected. This pattern is shown in the figure below, where the trade-weighted exchange value of the U.S. dollar remained relatively stable through 2005 and 2006, during which time the U.S. current account deficit continued to increase. (The trade-weighted exchange rate shows the value of the U.S. dollar against an average of other countries' currencies, with the average determined by how much trade the United States does with each country.) This apparent resilience of the U.S. dollar has—for better or worse—eased the concerns of policymakers.

c Economists have developed several theories that explain why the U.S. dollar remains so resilient and, consequently, the United States continues to run a current account deficit. One explanation focuses on the fact that many investors in developing countries are unable to buy stocks and bonds issued by domestic firms because relatively weak property rights and court systems have made it difficult for financial markets to function in these countries So, investors in developing countries who wish to buy stocks and bonds have chosen to invest abroad, particularly in the United States. This explains, in part, foreigners' willingness to hold U.S. dollars, despite the enormous current account deficit of the United States.

Thinking Critically

1. Suppose the foreign exchange value of the U.S. dollar fell to an extent that reflected the country's large current account deficit. What segment of the U.S. economy would, all else being equal, benefit from such an adjustment? Why?
2. As you read in this article, the United States has a larger trade deficit with China than with any other country. How would China's economy be affected by a significant decline in the value of the U.S. dollar? Briefly explain your reasoning.

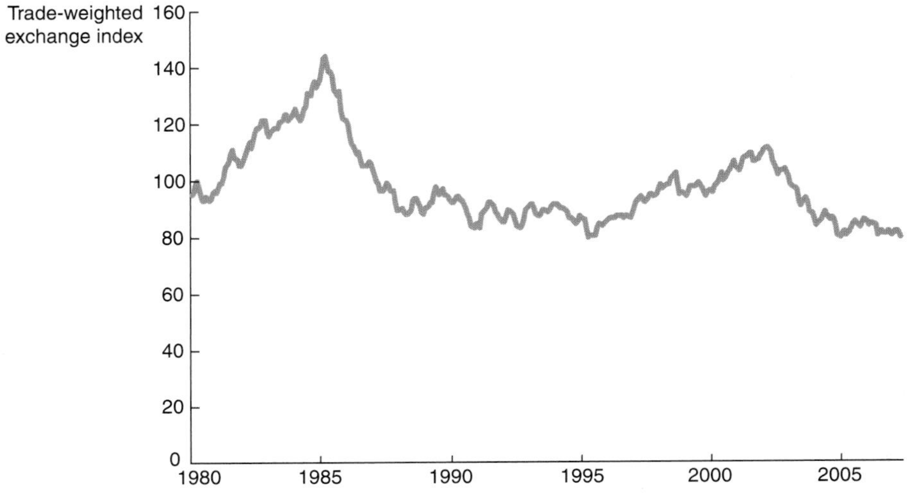

U.S. trade-weighted exchange index: Major currencies.
Source: Board of Governors of the Federal Reserve System.

Key Terms

Balance of payments, p. 586
Balance of trade, p. 586
Capital account, p. 589
Closed economy, p. 586
Currency appreciation, p. 594
Currency depreciation, p. 594
Current account, p. 586
Financial account, p. 588
Net foreign investment, p. 588
Nominal exchange rate, p. 591
Open economy, p. 586
Real exchange rate, p. 597
Saving and investment equation, p. 599
Speculators, p. 594

17.1 LEARNING OBJECTIVE 17.1 | Explain how the balance of payments is calculated, **pages 586–590.**

The Balance of Payments: Linking the United States to the International Economy

Summary

Nearly all economies are **open economies** that trade with and invest in other economies. A **closed economy** has no transactions in trade or finance with other economies. The **balance of payments** is the record of a country's trade with other countries in goods, services, and assets. The **current account** records a country's net exports, net investment income, and net transfers. The **financial account** shows investments a country has made abroad and foreign investments received by the country. The **balance of trade** is the difference between the value of the goods a country exports and the value of the goods a country imports. **Net foreign investment** is the difference between capital outflows from a country and capital inflows. The **capital account** is a part of the balance of payments that records relatively minor transactions. Apart from measurement errors, the sum of the current account and the financial account must equal zero. Therefore, the balance of payments must also equal zero.

myeconlab Get Ahead of the Curve Visit www.myeconlab.com to complete these exercises online and get instant feedback.

Review Questions

1.1 What is the relationship among the current account, the financial account, and the balance of payments?

1.2 What is the difference between net exports and the current account balance?

1.3 Explain why you agree or disagree with the following statement: "The United States has run a balance of payments deficit every year since 1982."

Problems and Applications

1.4 In 2006, France had a current account deficit of $46 billion. Did France experience a net capital outflow or a net capital inflow during 2006? Briefly explain.

1.5 Use the information in the following table to prepare a balance of payments account, like the one shown in Table 17-1 on page 587. Assume that the balance on the capital account is zero.

Increase in foreign holdings of assets in the United States	$1,181
Exports of goods	856
Imports of services	–256
Statistical discrepancy	?
Net transfers	–60
Exports of services	325
Income received on investments	392
Imports of goods	–1,108
Increase in U.S. holdings of assets in foreign countries	–1,040
Income payments on investments	–315

1.6 **(Related to the *Don't Let This Happen to You!* on page 591)** In 2006, Germany had a trade surplus of €162.2 billion and a current account balance of €116.6 billion. Explain how Germany's current account surplus could be smaller than its trade surplus. In 2006, Germany's balance on financial account was –€146.3 billion. Shouldn't Germany's balance on financial account have been the same size as its balance on current account, but with the opposite sign?

1.7 **(Related to *Solved Problem 17-1* on page 590)** Is it possible for a country to run a trade deficit and a financial account deficit simultaneously? Briefly explain.

1.8 **(Related to *Solved Problem 17-1* on page 590)** Suppose we know that a country has been receiving large inflows of foreign investment. What can we say about its current account balance?

1.9 **(Related to *Solved Problem 17-1* on page 590)** The United States ran a current account surplus every year during the 1960s. What must have been true about the U.S. financial account balance during those years?

1.10 The only year since 1982 that the United States has run a current account surplus was 1991. In that year, Japan made a large payment to the United States to help pay for the Gulf War. Explain the connection between these two facts. (*Hint:* Where would Japan's payment to the United States appear in the balance of payments?)

1.11 According to this chapter, the U.S. trade deficit is almost always larger than the U.S. current account deficit. Why is this true?

1.12 According to an article in *BusinessWeek*, "The U.S. is depending on an ever-rising influx of foreign funds to pay for all the imported automobiles, TVs, and clothing that U.S. consumers crave." Convert this sentence into a statement about changes in the U.S. current account and the U.S. financial account.

Source: Rich Miller and David Fairlamb, "The Greenback's Setback: Cause for Concern?" *BusinessWeek*, May 20, 2002, p. 44.

>> End Learning Objective 17.1

17.2 LEARNING OBJECTIVE 17.2 | Explain how exchange rates are determined and how changes in exchange rates affect the prices of imports and exports, **pages 590–597.**

The Foreign Exchange Market and Exchange Rates

Summary

The **nominal exchange rate** is the value of one country's currency in terms of another country's currency. The exchange rate is determined in the foreign exchange market by the demand and supply of a country's currency. Changes in the exchange rate are caused by shifts in demand or supply. The three main sets of factors that cause the supply and demand curves in the foreign exchange market to shift are changes in the demand for U.S.-produced goods and services and change in the demand for foreign-produced goods and services; changes in the desire to invest in the United States and changes in the desire to invest in foreign countries; and changes in the expectations of currency traders—particularly **speculators** —concerning the likely future values of the dollar and the likely future values of foreign currencies. **Currency appreciation** occurs when a currency's market value increases relative to another currency. **Currency depreciation** occurs when a currency's market value decreases relative to another currency. The **real exchange rate** is the price of domestic goods in terms of foreign goods. The real exchange rate is calculated by multiplying the nominal exchange rate by the ratio of the domestic price level to the foreign price level.

Review Questions

2.1 If the exchange rate between the Japanese yen and the U.S. dollar expressed in terms of yen per dollar is ¥110 = $1, what is the exchange rate when expressed in terms of dollars per yen?

2.2 Suppose that the current exchange rate between the dollar and the euro is 1.1 euros per dollar. If the exchange rate changes to 1.2 euros per dollar, has the euro appreciated or depreciated against the dollar?

2.3 What are the three main sets of factors that cause the supply and demand curves in the foreign exchange market to shift?

Problems and Applications

2.4 (Related to the *Don't Let This Happen to You!* on page 593) If we know the exchange rate between Country A's currency and Country B's currency and we know the exchange rate between Country B's currency and Country C's currency, then we can compute the exchange rate between Country A's currency and Country C's currency.

a. Suppose the exchange rate between the Japanese yen and the U.S. dollar is currently ¥120 = $1 and the exchange rate between the British pound and the U.S. dollar is £0.60 = $1. What is the exchange rate between the yen and the pound?

b. Suppose the exchange rate between the yen and dollar changes to ¥130 = $1 and the exchange rate between the pound and dollar changes to £0.50 = $1. Has the dollar appreciated or depreciated against the yen? Has the dollar appreciated or depreciated against the pound? Has the yen appreciated or depreciated against the pound?

2.5 (Related to the *Making the Connection* on page 592) Beginning January 1, 2002, 12 of the 15 member countries of the European Union eliminated their own individual currencies and began using a new common currency, the euro. For a three-year period from January 1, 1999, through December 31, 2001, these 12 countries priced goods and services in terms of both their own currencies and the euro. During this period, the value of their currencies was fixed against each other and against the euro. So during this time, the dollar had an exchange rate against each of these currencies and against the euro. The information in the following table shows the fixed exchange rates of four European currencies against the euro and their exchange rates against the U.S. dollar on March 2, 2001. Use the information on the next page to calculate the exchange rate between the dollar and the euro (in euros per dollar) on March 2, 2001.

CURRENCY	UNITS PER EURO (FIXED)	UNITS PER U.S. DOLLAR (AS OF MARCH 2, 2001)
German mark	1.9558	2.0938
French franc	6.5596	7.0223
Italian lira	1,936.2700	2,072.8700
Portuguese escudo	200.4820	214.6300

2.6 Graph the demand and supply of U.S. dollars for euros and label each axis. Show graphically and explain the effect of an increase in interest rates in Europe by the European Central Bank (ECB) on the demand and supply of dollars and the resulting change in the exchange rate of euros for U.S. dollars.

2.7 Graph the demand and supply of U.S. dollars for euros and label each axis. Show graphically and explain the effect of an increase in U.S. government budget deficits that increase U.S. interest rates on the demand and supply of dollars and the resulting change in the exchange rate of euros for U.S. dollars. Why might the change in the exchange rate lead to a current account deficit?

2.8 Use the graph to answer the following questions.

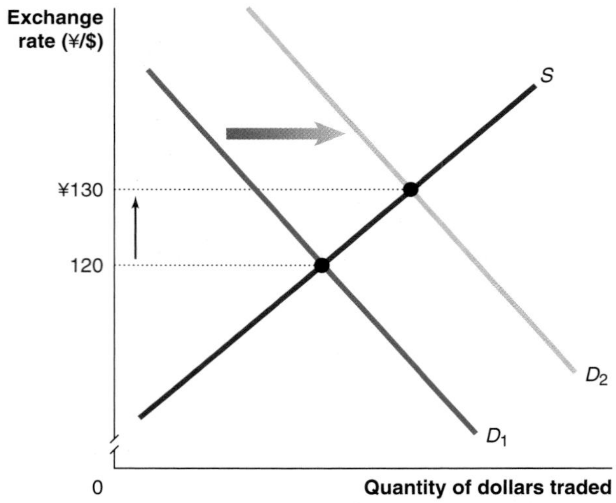

a. Briefly explain whether the dollar appreciated or depreciated against the yen.

b. Which of the following events could have caused the shift in demand shown in the graph?
   i. Interest rates in the United States have declined.
   ii. Income rises in Japan.
   iii. Speculators begin to believe the value of the dollar will be higher in the future.

2.9 **(Related to *Solved Problem* 17-2 on page 596)** When a country's currency appreciates, is this generally good news or bad news for the country's consumers? Is it generally good news or bad news for the country's businesses? Explain your reasoning.

2.10 The following appeared in an article in the *Wall Street Journal*: ". . . Japanese exporters got a lift from the sagging yen."

a. What does the reporter mean by a "sagging yen"?

b. Why would the yen's sagging help Japanese exporters?

Source: Tim Annett, "Housing Still Hurting," *Wall Street Journal*, February 22, 2007.

2.11 **(Related to the *Chapter Opener* on page 584)** Some U.S. firms, such as the paper manufacturer NewPage, argued that the Chinese government was keeping the value of the yuan artificially low against the dollar, which gave Chinese exporters an advantage when selling their products in the United States. Why would a low value of the yuan in exchange for the dollar help Chinese firms exporting to the United States?

2.12 Phil Treadway is president and owner of Erie Molded Plastics, Inc., which is located in Erie, Pennsylvania, and makes electrical connectors and plastic bottle caps. Treadway was quoted as follows in the *New York Times*: "Our customers have a market without borders, and we know that. We can compete against China's low labor costs. . . . But we cannot compete with them if they have a 20 percent to 40 percent currency advantage." What does Treadway mean by a "currency advantage"? How would a currency advantage make it hard for his firm to compete with Chinese firms?

Source: Elizabeth Becker and Edmund L. Andrews, "Currency of China Is Emerging as Tough Business Issue in U.S.," *New York Times*, August 26, 2003.

>> End Learning Objective 17.2

17.3 LEARNING OBJECTIVE 17.3 | Explain the saving and investment equation, **pages 597–601.**

The International Sector and National Saving and Investment

Summary

A current account deficit must be exactly offset by a financial account surplus. The financial account is equal to net capital flows, which is equal to net foreign investment but with the opposite sign. Because the current account balance is roughly equal to net exports, we can conclude that net exports will equal net foreign investment. National saving is equal to private saving plus government saving. Private saving is equal to national income minus consumption and minus taxes. Government saving is the difference between taxes and government spending. As we saw in previous chapters, GDP (or national income) is equal to the sum of investment, consumption, government spending, and net exports. We can use this fact, our definitions of private and government saving, and the fact that net exports equal net foreign investment, to arrive at an important relationship known as the **saving and investment equation**: $S = I + NFI$.

Review Questions

3.1 Explain the relationship between net exports and net foreign investment.

3.2 What is the saving and investment equation? If national saving declines, what will happen to domestic investment and net foreign investment?

3.3 If a country saves more than it invests domestically, what must be true of its net foreign investment?

Problems and Applications

3.4 Writing in the *Wall Street Journal*, David Wessel makes the following observation:

> Trend one: The U.S. has been buying more than $1 billion a day more from the rest of the world than it has been selling. . . . Trend two: Foreigners have been investing more than $1 billion a day of their savings in U.S. stocks, bonds, office towers, factories, and companies.

Is it coincidence that both of his "trends" involve $1 billion per day? Briefly explain.

Source: David Wessel, "Pain from the Dollar's Decline Will Mostly Be Felt Overseas," *Wall Street Journal*, June 13, 2002.

3.5 In 2006, domestic investment in Japan was 24.1 percent of GDP, and Japanese net foreign investment was 3.9 percent of GDP. What percentage of GDP was Japanese national saving?

3.6 In 2006, France's net foreign investment was negative. Which was larger in France in 2006: national saving or domestic investment? Briefly explain.

3.7 Briefly explain whether you agree with the following statement: "Because in 2006 national saving was a smaller percentage of GDP in the United States than in the United Kingdom, domestic investment must also have been a smaller percentage of GDP in the United States than in the United Kingdom."

3.8 **(Related to *Solved Problem 17-3* on page 600)** Look again at Solved Problem 17-3, in which we derived the saving and investment equation $S = I + NX$. In deriving this equation, we assumed that national income was equal to Y. But Y only includes income *earned* by households. In the modern U.S. economy, households receive substantial transfer payments—such as Social Security payments and unemployment insurance payments—from the government. Suppose that we define national income to be equal to $Y + TR$, where TR equals government transfer payments, and we also define government spending to be equal to $G + TR$. Show that after making these adjustments, we end up with the same saving and investment equation.

3.9 Use the saving and investment equation to explain why the United States experienced large current account deficits in the late 1990s.

3.10 Former Congressman and presidential candidate Richard Gephardt once proposed that tariffs be imposed on imports from countries with which the United States has a trade deficit. If this proposal were enacted and if it were to succeed in reducing the U.S. current account deficit to zero, what would be the likely effect on domestic investment spending within the United States? Assume that no other federal government economic policy is changed. (*Hint:* Use the saving and investment equation to answer this question.)

3.11 **(Related to the *Chapter Opener* on page 584)** Suppose that the U.S. government decides to raise tariffs on Chinese exports of paper to the United States even higher. Discuss the impact on the following:

a. U.S. paper manufacturers
b. Chinese paper manufacturers
c. U.S. consumers
d. U.S. net exports
e. U.S. net foreign investment

3.12 According to an article in *BusinessWeek*, "In the past year, foreign purchases of stocks and bonds are down 24%, and foreign direct investment is off 63%. . . . And a key victim is the dollar, down 12% vs. the euro and 10% vs. the yen." From the U.S. point of view, do the changes mentioned in the first sentence represent an increase or a decrease in net foreign investment? Why would this change in net foreign investment cause the exchange value of the dollar to decline?

Source: James C. Cooper and Kathleen Madigan, "The Twin Deficits Are Back—And as Dangerous as Ever," *BusinessWeek*, July 8, 2002, pp. 29–30.

>> End Learning Objective 17.3

17.4 LEARNING OBJECTIVE 17.4 | Explain the effect of a government budget deficit on investment in an open economy, **pages 601–603.**

The Effect of a Government Budget Deficit on Investment

Summary

When the government runs a budget deficit, national saving will decline unless private saving increases by the full amount of the budget deficit, which is unlikely. As the saving and investment equation ($S = I + NFI$) shows, the result of a decline in national saving must be a decline in either domestic investment or net foreign investment.

Review Questions

4.1 What happens to national saving when the government runs a budget surplus? What is the twin deficits idea? Did it hold for the United States in the 1990s? Briefly explain.

4.2 Why were the early and mid-1980s particularly difficult times for U.S. exporters?

Problems and Applications

4.3 Writing in the April 1997 issue of *International Economic Trends*, published by the Federal Reserve Bank of St. Louis, economist Michael Pakko observed the following:

> The current account . . . reached a deficit of $165 billion in 1996, second only to the deficit of $167 billion in 1987. . . . The evidence suggests that strong investment demand underlies the current economic expansion. Since the recession of 1990–91, real fixed investment spending has been growing at a rate of 6.9 percent . . . compared to 2.6 percent growth of GDP. . . . Only time will tell what the payoff to these investments will be, but they do give some reason to interpret the U.S. current account deficit with less apprehension.

Why should the fact that investment spending in the United States has been strong reduce apprehension about the size of the current account deficit? What does the current account deficit have to do with investment spending?

4.4 Lee Morgan, chairman of Caterpillar, was quoted in 1985 as saying this of his company's difficulties in exporting: "We believe that there should be a 25% to 30% improvement in the exchange rate with the Japanese yen, because U.S. manufacturers are finding themselves disadvantaged by that amount." When Morgan talked about an "improvement" in the exchange rate between the dollar and the yen, did he want the dollar to exchange for more yen or for fewer yen? Why was the exchange value of the dollar particularly high during the mid-1980s?

4.5 The text states, "The budget surpluses of the late 1990s occurred at a time of then-record current account deficits." Holding everything else constant, what would the likely impact have been on domestic investment in the United States if the current account had been balanced instead of being in deficit?

4.6 **(Related to the *Making the Connection* on page 602)** Why might "the continued willingness of foreign investors to buy U.S. stocks and bonds and foreign companies to build factories in the United States" result in the United States running a current account deficit?

>> End Learning Objective 17.4

17.5 LEARNING OBJECTIVE 17.5 | Discuss the difference between the effectiveness of monetary and fiscal policy in an open economy and in a closed economy, **pages 604–605.**

Monetary Policy and Fiscal Policy in an Open Economy

Summary

When the Federal Reserve engages in an expansionary monetary policy, it buys government bonds to lower interest rates and increase aggregate demand. In a closed economy, the main effect of lower interest rates is on domestic investment spending and purchases of consumer durables. In an open economy, lower interest rates will also cause an increase in net exports. When the Fed wants to slow the rate of economic growth to reduce inflation, it engages in a contractionary monetary policy. With a contractionary policy, the Fed sells government bonds to increase interest rates and reduce aggregate demand. In a closed economy, the main effect is once again on domestic investment and purchases of consumer durables. In an open economy, higher interest rates will also reduce net exports. We can conclude that monetary policy has a greater impact on aggregate demand in an open economy than in a closed economy. To engage in an expansionary fiscal policy, the government increases government spending or cuts taxes. An expansionary fiscal policy can lead to higher interest rates. In a closed economy, the main effect of higher interest rates is on domestic investment spending and spending on consumer durables. In an open economy, higher interest rates will also reduce net exports. A contractionary fiscal policy will reduce the budget deficit and may lower interest rates. In a closed economy, lower interest rates increase domestic investment and spending on consumer durables. In an open economy, lower interest rates also increase net exports. We can conclude that fiscal policy has a smaller impact on aggregate demand in an open economy than in a closed economy.

Review Questions

5.1 Why does monetary policy have a greater effect on aggregate demand in an open economy than in a closed economy?

5.2 Why does fiscal policy have a smaller impact in an open economy than in a closed economy?

Problems and Applications

5.3 What is meant by a "policy channel"? Why would an open economy have more policy channels than a closed economy?

5.4 Suppose that Federal Reserve policy leads to higher interest rates in the United States.
 a. How will this policy affect real GDP in the short run if the United States is a closed economy?
 b. How will this policy affect real GDP in the short run if the United States is an open economy?
 c. How will your answer to part b change if interest rates also rise in the countries that are the major trading partners of the United States?

5.5 An economist remarks, "In the 1960s, fiscal policy would have been a better way to stabilize the economy, but now I believe that monetary policy is better." What has changed about the U.S. economy that might have led the economist to this conclusion?

5.6 Suppose the federal government increases spending without also increasing taxes. In the short run, how will this action affect real GDP and the price level in a closed economy? How will the affects of this action differ in an open economy?

>> End Learning Objective 17.5

Chapter 18

The **International Financial System**

Molson Coors Deals with Fluctuating Exchange Rates

In 2004, two of North America's oldest brewers, Molson, Inc., based in Montreal, Canada, and Adolph Coors Company, based in Golden, Colorado, officially announced their plans to merge and create Molson Coors Brewing Company. Today, the combined company is the fifth-largest brewer in the world. It employs nearly 10,000 people, generates annual sales of nearly $6 billion, and operates breweries in Canada, the United Kingdom, and Golden, Colorado. The company sells 40 brands of beer in 30 markets across North America, Latin America, Europe, and Asia. Some of its most familiar brands are Molson Canadian and Carling, the best-selling beers in Canada and the United Kingdom, respectively, as well as Coors Original, Coors Light, Keystone, and Zima XXX. Because the company sells in many different markets, it is vulnerable to fluctuations in the foreign exchange value of the U.S. dollar. In its 2006 annual report to shareholders, the company noted that it faced risk from "exchange rate exposure which could materially and adversely affect [the company's] operating results." The "exchange rate exposure" results from Molson Coors earning revenue and incurring costs in several currencies, particularly the U.S. dollar, the Canadian dollar, and the British pound. When the company converts its profits in the United Kingdom, Canada, and other countries into dollars, the amount of profits it earns depends on how many dollars it receives in exchange for those other currencies. For example, if the value of the dollar falls relative to the British pound, then Molson Coors' profits will rise because it receives more dollars when it converts the pounds it earns in the United Kingdom into U.S. dollars.

Before its merger with Coors, Molson had faced a different kind of exposure to fluctuating exchange rates. Molson had purchased the Montreal Canadiens hockey team in 1957. During the time Molson owned the team, it had to deal with a problem posed by a provision in the labor agreement between the National Hockey League and its players. This agreement required Molson to pay the Canadiens players in U.S. dollars rather than in Canadian dollars. Because the Canadiens play most of their games in the United States, many of the team's other expenses also had to be paid in U.S. dollars. Most of the team's revenues from ticket sales and local television and radio broadcasts, however, were received in Canadian dollars.

Unfortunately for Molson, the value of the Canadian dollar declined by more than 25 percent against the U.S. dollar during the last 10 years before it sold the Canadiens in 2001. In 1991, one Canadian dollar exchanged for $0.87. By 2001, one Canadian dollar exchanged for only $0.65. In U.S. dollars, the total salary payroll for Canadiens players rose from $10 million in 1991 to $38 million in 2001. If the exchange rate between the Canadian and U.S. dollars had been the same in 2001 as it was in 1991, the Canadiens payroll would have cost Molson 43.7 million

Canadian dollars. Because of the decline in the value of the Canadian dollar, Molson actually had to pay 58.5 million to meet the Canadiens' payroll. In this chapter, we will explore why exchange rates fluctuate and how central banks sometimes intervene to try to control movements in exchange rates.

AN INSIDE LOOK AT POLICY on **page 634** discusses whether governments should try to limit speculation in currencies.

Sources: Molson Coors Brewing Company, *Annual Report: 2006*; and "Lessons from a Lockout," *Economist*, July 21, 2005.

LEARNING Objectives

After studying this chapter, you should be able to:

18.1 Understand how different **exchange rate systems** operate, page 616.

18.2 Discuss the **three key features** of the current **exchange rate system**, page 617.

18.3 Discuss the growth of **international capital markets**, page 631.

APPENDIX Explain the **gold standard** and the **Bretton Woods system**, page 641.

Economics in YOUR Life!

Exchange Rate Risk in Your Life

Suppose that you decide to take a job in Spain. Your plan is to work there for the next 10 years, build up some savings, and then return to the United States. As you prepare for your move, you read that economists expect the average productivity of Spanish firms to grow faster than the average productivity of U.S. firms over the next 10 years. If economists are correct, then, all else being equal, will the savings that you accumulate (in euros) be worth more or less in U.S. dollars than it would have been worth without the relative gains in Spanish productivity? As you read this chapter, see if you can answer this question. You can check your answer against the one we provide at the end of the chapter. » **Continued on page 633**

A key fact about the international economy is that the exchange rates among the major currencies fluctuate. These fluctuations have important consequences for firms, consumers, and governments. In Chapter 17, we discussed the basics of how exchange rates are determined. We also looked at the relationship between a country's imports and exports, as well as at capital flows into and out of a country. In this chapter, we will look further at the international financial system and at the role central banks play in the system.

18.1 LEARNING OBJECTIVE

18.1 | Understand how different exchange rate systems operate.

Exchange Rate Systems

Floating currency The outcome of a country allowing its currency's exchange rate to be determined by demand and supply.

Exchange rate system An agreement among countries on how exchange rates should be determined.

Managed float exchange rate system The current exchange rate system, under which the value of most currencies is determined by demand and supply, with occasional government intervention.

Fixed exchange rate system A system under which countries agree to keep the exchange rates among their currencies fixed.

A country's exchange rate can be determined in several ways. Some countries simply allow the exchange rate to be determined by demand and supply, just as other prices are. A country that allows demand and supply to determine the value of its currency is said to have a **floating currency**. Some countries attempt to keep the exchange rate between their currency and another currency constant. For example, China kept the exchange rate constant between its currency, the yuan, and the U.S. dollar, from 1994 until 2005, when it announced it would allow greater exchange-rate flexibility. When countries can agree on how exchange rates should be determined, economists say that there is an **exchange rate system**. Currently, many countries, including the United States, allow their currencies to float most of the time, although they will occasionally intervene to buy and sell their currency or other currencies to affect exchange rates. In other words, many countries attempt to *manage* the float of their currencies. As a result, the current exchange rate system is a **managed float exchange rate system**.

Historically, the two most important alternatives to the managed float exchange rate system were the *gold standard* and the *Bretton Woods system*. These were both **fixed exchange rate systems**, where exchange rates remained constant for long periods. Under the gold standard, a country's currency consisted of gold coins and paper currency that the government was committed to redeem for gold. When countries agree to keep the value of their currencies constant, there is a fixed exchange rate system. The gold standard was a fixed exchange rate system that lasted from the nineteenth century until the 1930s.

Under the gold standard, exchange rates were determined by the relative amounts of gold in each country's currency, and the size of a country's money supply was determined by the amount of gold available. To rapidly expand its money supply during a war or an economic depression, a country would need to abandon the gold standard. Because of the Great Depression, by the mid-1930s, most countries, including the United States, had abandoned the gold standard. Although during the following decades there were occasional discussions about restoring the gold standard, no serious attempt to do so occurred.

A conference held in Bretton Woods, New Hampshire, in 1944 set up an exchange rate system in which the United States pledged to buy or sell gold at a fixed price of $35 per ounce. The central banks of all other members of the new Bretton Woods system pledged to buy and sell their currencies at a fixed rate against the dollar. By fixing their exchange rates against the dollar, these countries were fixing the exchange rates among their currencies as well. Unlike under the gold standard, neither the United States nor any other country was willing to redeem its paper currency for gold domestically. The United States would redeem dollars for gold only if they were presented by a foreign central bank. Fixed exchange rate regimes can run into difficulties because exchange rates are not free to adjust quickly to changes in demand and supply for currencies. As

Don't Let This Happen to YOU!

Remember That Modern Currencies Are Fiat Money

Although the United States has not been on the gold standard since 1933, many people still believe that somehow gold continues to "back" U.S. currency. The U.S. Department of the Treasury still owns billions of dollars worth of gold bars, most of which are stored at the Fort Knox Bullion Depository in Kentucky. (Even more gold is stored in a basement of the Federal Reserve Bank of New York, which holds about one-quarter of the world's gold supply—almost 10 percent of all the gold ever mined. This gold, however, is entirely owned by foreign governments and international agencies.) The gold in Fort Knox no longer has any connection to the amount of paper money issued by the Federal Reserve. As we saw in Chapter 13, U.S. currency—like the currencies of other countries—is fiat money, which means it has no value except as money. The link between gold and money that existed for centuries has been broken in the modern economy.

YOUR TURN: Test your understanding by doing related problem 1.3 on page 636 at the end of this chapter.

we will see in the next section, central banks often encounter difficulty if they are required to keep an exchange rate fixed over a period of years. By the early 1970s, the difficulty of keeping exchange rates fixed led to the end of the Bretton Woods system. The appendix to this chapter contains additional discussion of the gold standard and the Bretton Woods system.

18.2 LEARNING OBJECTIVE

18.2 | Discuss the three key features of the current exchange rate system.

The Current Exchange Rate System

The current exchange rate system has three important aspects:

1. The United States allows the dollar to float against other major currencies.
2. Most countries in Western Europe have adopted a single currency, the **euro**.
3. Some developing countries have attempted to keep their currencies' exchange rates fixed against the dollar or another major currency.

Euro The common currency of many European countries.

We begin our discussion of the current exchange rate system by looking at the changing value of the dollar over time. In discussing the value of the dollar, we can look further at what determines exchange rates in the short run and in the long run.

The Floating Dollar

Since 1973, the value of the U.S. dollar has fluctuated widely against other major currencies. Panel (a) of Figure 18-1 shows the exchange rate between the U.S. dollar and the Canadian dollar between 1973 and 2006, and panel (b) shows the exchange rate between the U.S. dollar and the Japanese yen for the same years. Remember that the dollar increases in value when it takes more units of foreign currency to buy $1, and it falls in value when it takes fewer units of foreign currency to buy $1. From the beginning of 1973 to the end of 2006, the U.S. dollar lost about 60 percent in value against the yen, while it increased about 15 percent in value against the Canadian dollar.

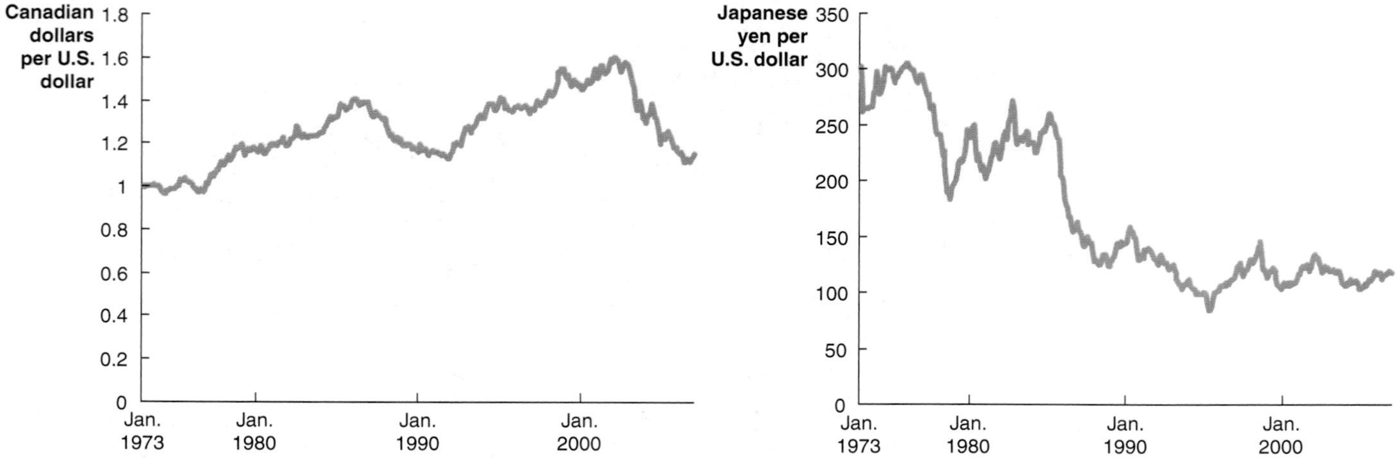

(a) The exchange rate between the Canadian dollar and the U.S. dollar.

(b) The exchange rate between the Japanese yen and the U.S. dollar.

Figure 18-1 | U.S. Dollar–Canadian Dollar and U.S. Dollar–Yen Exchange Rates, 1973–2006

Panel (a) shows that since the end of the Bretton Woods system in 1973, the U.S. dollar has gained value against the Canadian dollar. Panel (b) shows that during the same period, the U.S. dollar has lost value against the Japanese yen.

Source: Federal Reserve Board of Governors.

The Toronto Blue Jays have benefited from the rising value of the Canadian dollar.

Making the Connection

The Toronto Blue Jays Gain from the Rising Value of the Canadian Dollar

In December 2000, the Canadian firm Rogers Communications, Inc., purchased the Toronto Blue Jays baseball team from Interbrew, a Canadian beer company. Rogers is based in Toronto and is the largest provider of cable television in Canada. We saw at the beginning of this chapter that Molson was hurt as the value of the Canadian dollar declined against the U.S. dollar for most of the period from 1991 to 2001, during which Molson owned the Montreal Canadiens ice hockey team. A close look at panel (a) of Figure 18-1 shows that Rogers was in a much better situation than Molson because after 2000, the number of Canadian dollars necessary to buy one U.S. dollar was declining; that is, the value of the Canadian dollar was rising. When Rogers bought the Blue Jays in December 2000, one Canadian dollar exchanged for $0.66. By May 2007, one Canadian dollar exchanged for $0.91, an increase of more than 35 percent.

Like the Canadiens, the Blue Jays have to pay their players in U.S. dollars and, because all the other major league baseball teams play in the United States, most of the Blue Jays' expenses for travel and lodging for their players also must be paid in U.S. dollars. In 2007, the total salary payroll for Blue Jays players was 82 million U.S. dollars. If the exchange rate between the Canadian and U.S. dollars had remained what it had been in December 2000, the Blue Jays payroll would have cost Rogers 125 million Canadian dollars. Because the Canadian dollar had risen in value against the U.S. dollar, Rogers actually only had to pay 90 million Canadian dollars. Rogers' other U.S. dollar expenses for the Blue Jays were correspondingly lower, and the firm benefited from the rise in the value of the Canadian dollar in other ways as well. The Blue Jays play spring training games in Dunedin, Florida. The high value of the Canadian dollar led many more Canadians to travel to Florida and buy tickets to the games there. Between 2004 and 2005 alone, ticket sales rose by nearly 33 percent. Overall, the Blue Jays improved from losing 71 million Canadian dollars in 2001 to making a profit of 33 million Canadian dollars in 2006. A team official attributed 70 percent of the improvement in the team's financial situation to the stronger Canadian dollar. In 2007, Blue Jays president Paul Godfrey was quoted as saying: "We check the box scores first, then we check the attendance, and then we check the dollar." Of course, the Blue

Jays remained vulnerable to the possibility that the Canadian dollar could again decline in value.

Sources: Joe Christensen, "Baseball Insider," Knight Ridder Tribune Business News, May 27, 2007; Rob Neyer, "Good Young Pitchers in Toronto's System," ESPN.com, August 8, 2005; and Alan Snel, "Springing Back," *Tampa Tribune*, March 14, 2005.

YOUR TURN: Test your understanding by doing related problem 2.7 on page 637 at the end of this chapter.

What Determines Exchange Rates in the Long Run?

Over the past 30 years, why did the value of the U.S. dollar fall against the Japanese yen but rise against the Canadian dollar? In the short run, the two most important causes of exchange rate movements are changes in interest rates—which cause investors to change their views of which countries' financial investments will yield the highest returns—and changes in investors' expectations about the future values of currencies. Over the long run, other factors are important in explaining movements in exchange rates.

The Theory of Purchasing Power Parity It seems reasonable that, in the long run, exchange rates should be at a level that makes it possible to buy the same amount of goods and services with the equivalent amount of any country's currency. In other words, the purchasing power of every country's currency should be the same. The idea that in the long run, exchange rates move to equalize the purchasing powers of different currencies is referred to as the theory of **purchasing power parity**.

Purchasing power parity The theory that in the long run, exchange rates move to equalize the purchasing powers of different currencies.

To make the theory of purchasing power parity clearer, consider a simple example. Suppose that a Hershey candy bar has a price of $1 in the United States and £1 in the United Kingdom and that the exchange rate is $1 per pound. In that case, at least with respect to candy bars, the dollar and the pound have equivalent purchasing power. If the price of a Hershey bar increases to £2 in the United Kingdom but stays at $1 in the United States, the exchange rate will have to change to £2 per $1 in order for the pound to maintain its relative purchasing power. As long as exchange rates adjust to reflect purchasing power, it will be possible to buy a Hershey bar for $1 in the United States or to exchange $1 for £2 and buy the candy bar in the United Kingdom.

If exchange rates are not at the values indicated by purchasing power parity, it appears that there are opportunities to make profits. For example, suppose a Hershey candy bar sells for £2 in the United Kingdom and $1 in the United States, and the exchange rate between the dollar and the pound is £1 = $1. In this case, it would be possible to exchange £1 million for $1 million and use the dollars to buy 1 million Hershey bars in the United States. The Hershey bars could then be shipped to the United Kingdom, where they could be sold for £2 million. The result of these transactions would be a profit of £1 million (ignoring any shipping costs). In fact, if the dollar–pound exchange rate does not reflect the purchasing power for many products—not just Hershey bars—this process could be repeated until extremely large profits were made. In practice, though, as people attempted to make these profits by exchanging pounds for dollars, they would bid up the value of the dollar until it reached the purchasing power exchange rate of £2 = $1. Once the exchange rate reflected the purchasing power of the two currencies, there would be no further opportunities for profit. This mechanism appears to guarantee that exchange rates will be at the levels determined by purchasing power parity.

Three real-world complications, though, keep purchasing power parity from being a complete explanation of exchange rates, even in the long run:

- ***Not all products can be traded internationally.*** Where goods are traded internationally, profits can be made whenever exchange rates do not reflect their purchasing power parity values. However, more than half of all goods and services produced in the United States and most other countries are not traded internationally. When goods are not traded internationally, their prices will not be the same in every country. For instance, suppose that the exchange rate is £1 for $1, but the price for having a cavity filled by a dentist is twice as high in the United States as it is in the United Kingdom. In this case, there is no way to buy up the low-priced British service and resell it in the United States. Because many goods and services are not traded internationally, exchange rates will not reflect exactly the relative purchasing powers of currencies.

- ***Products and consumer preferences are different across countries.*** We expect the same product to sell for the same price around the world, but if a product is similar but not identical to another product, their prices might be different. For example, a 3-ounce Hershey candy bar may sell for a different price in the United States than does a 3-ounce Cadbury candy bar in the United Kingdom. Prices of the same product may also differ across countries if consumer preferences differ. If consumers in the United Kingdom like candy bars more than do consumers in the United States, a Hershey candy bar may sell for more in the United Kingdom than in the United States.

- ***Countries impose barriers to trade.*** Most countries, including the United States, impose *tariffs* and *quotas* on imported goods. A **tariff** is a tax imposed by a government on imports. A **quota** is a limit on the quantity of a good that can be imported. For example, the United States has a quota on imports of sugar. As a result, the price of sugar in the United States is much higher than the price of sugar in other countries. Because of the quota, there is no way to buy up the cheap foreign sugar and resell it in the United States.

Tariff A tax imposed by a government on imports.

Quota A government-imposed limit on the quantity of a good that can be imported.

Making the Connection | The Big Mac Theory of Exchange Rates

In a lighthearted attempt to test the accuracy of the theory of purchasing power parity, the *Economist* magazine regularly compares the prices of Big Macs in different countries. If purchasing power parity holds, you should be able to take the dollars required to buy a Big Mac in the United States and exchange them for the amount of foreign currency needed to buy a Big Mac in any other country. The following table is for February 2007, when Big Macs were selling for an average price of $3.22 in the United States. The implied exchange rate shows what the exchange rate would be if purchasing power parity held for Big Macs. For example, a Big Mac sold for ¥280 in Japan and $3.22 in the United States, so for purchasing power parity to hold, the exchange rate should have been ¥280/$3.22, or ¥87 = $1. The actual exchange rate in February 2007 was ¥121 = $1. So, on Big Mac purchasing power parity grounds, the yen was *undervalued* against the dollar by 28 percent (((¥121 − ¥87)/¥121) × 100 = 28 percent). That is, if Big Mac purchasing power parity held, it would have taken 28 percent fewer yen to buy a dollar than it actually did.

Could you take advantage of this difference between the purchasing power parity exchange rate and the actual exchange rate to become fabulously wealthy by buying up low-priced Big Macs in Tokyo and reselling them at a higher price in San Francisco? Unfortunately, the low-priced Japanese Big Macs would be a soggy mess by the time you got them to San Francisco. The fact that Big Mac prices are not the same around the world illustrates one reason why purchasing power parity does not hold exactly: Many goods are not traded internationally.

Is the price of a Big Mac in Beijing the same as the price of a Big Mac in Chicago?

COUNTRY	BIG MAC PRICE	IMPLIED EXCHANGE RATE	ACTUAL EXCHANGE RATE
Argentina	8.25 pesos	2.56 pesos per dollar	3.11 pesos per dollar
Japan	280 yen	87 yen per dollar	121 yen per dollar
Britain	1.99 pounds	0.62 pound per dollar	0.51 pound per dollar
Switzerland	6.30 Swiss francs	1.96 Swiss francs per dollar	1.25 Swiss francs per dollar
Indonesia	15,900 rupiahs	4,398 rupiahs per dollar	9,100 rupiahs per dollar
Canada	3.63 Canadian dollars	1.13 Canadian dollars per U.S. dollar	1.18 Canadian dollars per U.S. dollar
China	11.0 yuan	3.42 yuan per dollar	7.77 yuan per dollar

Source: "The Big Mac Index," *Economist*, February 1, 2007.

YOUR TURN: Test your understanding by doing related problem 2.13 on page 637 at the end of this chapter.

Solved Problem | **18-2A**

Calculating Purchasing Power Parity Exchange Rates Using Big Macs

Fill in the missing values in the following table. Remember that the implied exchange rate shows what the exchange rate would be if purchasing power parity held for Big Macs. Assume that the Big Mac is selling for $3.22 in the United States. Explain whether the U.S. dollar is overvalued or undervalued relative to each currency and predict what will happen in the future to each exchange rate. Finally, calculate the implied exchange rate between the Polish zloty and the Brazilian real and explain which currency is overvalued in terms of Big Mac purchasing power parity.

COUNTRY	BIG MAC PRICE	IMPLIED EXCHANGE RATE	ACTUAL EXCHANGE RATE
Brazil	6.40 reals		2.13 reals per dollar
Poland	6.90 zlotys		3.01 zlotys per dollar
South Korea	2,900 won		942 won per dollar
Czech Republic	52.1 korunas		21.6 korunas per dollar

SOLVING THE PROBLEM:

Step 1: **Review the chapter material.** This problem is about the theory of purchasing power parity as illustrated by prices of Big Macs, so you may want to review the sections "The Theory of Purchasing Power Parity," which begins on page 619, and the Making the Connection "The Big Mac Theory of Exchange Rates," which begins on page 620.

Step 2: **Fill in the table.** To calculate the purchasing power exchange rate, divide the foreign currency price of a Big Mac by the U.S. price. For example, the implied exchange rate between the Brazilian real and the U.S. dollar is 6.40 reals/$3.22, or 1.99 reals per dollar.

COUNTRY	BIG MAC PRICE	IMPLIED EXCHANGE RATE	ACTUAL EXCHANGE RATE
Brazil	6.40 reals	1.99 reals per dollar	2.13 reals per dollar
Poland	6.90 zlotys	2.14 zlotys per dollar	3.01 zlotys per dollar
South Korea	2,900 won	901 won per dollar	942 won per dollar
Czech Republic	52.1 korunas	16.2 korunas per dollar	21.6 korunas per dollar

Step 3: **Explain whether the U.S. dollar is overvalued or undervalued against the other currencies.** The dollar is overvalued if the actual exchange rate is greater than the implied exchange rate. In this case, the dollar is overvalued against all four of these currencies. This overvaluation would lead us to predict that the value of the dollar should fall in the future.

Step 4: **Calculate the implied exchange rate between the zloty and the real.** The implied exchange rate between the zloty and the real is 6.90 zlotys/6.40 reals, or 1.08 zlotys per real. We can calculate the actual exchange rate by taking the ratio of zlotys per dollar to reals per dollar: 3.01 zlotys/2.13 reals, or 1.41 zlotys per real. The zloty is undervalued relative to the real.

EXTRA CREDIT: Because the Big Mac is a nontraded good, it's not surprising that prices differ from country to country. Nevertheless, the fact that comparing Big Mac prices indicates that the dollar was overvalued relative to the currencies of most countries is at least a small piece of evidence that the dollar was likely to decline in the period after February 2007.

Source: "The Big Mac Index," *Economist*, February 1, 2007.

>> End Solved Problem 18-2A

YOUR TURN: For more practice, do related problem 2.14 on page 638 at the end of this chapter.

The Four Determinants of Exchange Rates in the Long Run We can take into account the shortcomings of the theory of purchasing power parity to develop a more complete explanation of how exchange rates are determined in the long run. There are four main determinants of exchange rates in the long run:

- ***Relative price levels.*** The purchasing power parity theory is correct in arguing that in the long run, the most important determinant of exchange rates between two countries' currencies is their relative price levels. If prices of goods and services rise faster in Canada than in the United States, the value of the Canadian dollar has to decline to maintain demand for Canadian products. Over the past 30 years, prices in Canada have risen faster on average than prices in the United States, while prices in Japan have risen more slowly. This difference in inflation rates is a key reason the U.S. dollar has gained value against the Canadian dollar while losing value against the Japanese yen.
- ***Relative rates of productivity growth.*** When the productivity of a firm increases, it is able to produce more goods and services using fewer workers, machines, or other inputs. The firm's costs of production fall, and usually so do the prices of its products. If the average productivity of Japanese firms increases faster than the average productivity of U.S. firms, Japanese products will have relatively lower prices than U.S. products, which increases the quantity demanded of Japanese products relative to U.S. products. As a result, the value of the yen should rise against the dollar. For most of the period from the early 1970s to the early 1990s, Japanese productivity increased faster than U.S. productivity, which contributed to the fall in the value of the dollar versus the yen. However, between 1992 and 2007, U.S. productivity increased faster than Japanese productivity.
- ***Preferences for domestic and foreign goods.*** If consumers in Canada increase their preferences for U.S. products, the demand for U.S. dollars will increase relative to the demand for Canadian dollars, and the U.S. dollar will increase in value relative to the Canadian dollar. During the 1970s and 1980s, many U.S. consumers increased their preferences for Japanese products, particularly automobiles and consumer electronics. This greater preference for Japanese products helped to increase the value of the yen relative to the dollar.
- ***Tariffs and quotas.*** The U.S. sugar quota forces firms like Hershey Foods Corporation to buy expensive U.S. sugar rather than less expensive foreign sugar. The quota increases the demand for dollars relative to the currencies of foreign sugar producers and, therefore, leads to a higher exchange rate. Changes in tariffs and quotas have not been a significant factor in explaining trends in the U.S. dollar–Canadian dollar or U.S. dollar–yen exchange rates.

Because these four factors change over time, the value of one country's currency can increase or decrease by substantial amounts in the long run. These changes in exchange rates can create problems for firms. A decline in the value of a country's currency lowers the foreign currency prices of the country's exports and increases the prices of imports. An increase in the value of a country's currency has the reverse effect. Firms can be both helped and hurt by exchange rate fluctuations. For example, the 10 percent decline in the value of the U.S. dollar against the Canadian dollar between 2005 and 2007 helped Coors Molson sell more Coors beer in Canada, but it hurt the firm's sales of Molson beer in the United States.

The Euro

A second key aspect of the current exchange rate system is that most western European countries have adopted a single currency. After World War II, many of the countries of western Europe wanted to more closely integrate their economies. In 1957, Belgium, France, West Germany, Italy, Luxembourg, and the Netherlands signed the Treaty of Rome, which established the European Economic Community, often referred to as the European Common Market. Tariffs and quotas on products being shipped within the Common Market were greatly reduced. Over the years, Britain, Sweden, Denmark, Finland, Austria, Greece, Ireland, Spain, and Portugal joined the European Economic Community, which was renamed the European Union (EU) in 1991. By 2007, 25 countries were members of the EU.

EU members decided to move to a common currency beginning in 1999. Three of the 15 countries that were then members of the EU—the United Kingdom, Denmark, and Sweden—decided to retain their domestic currencies. The move to a common currency took place in several stages. On January 1, 1999, the exchange rates of the 12 (now 13) participating countries were permanently fixed against each other and against the common currency, the *euro*. At first the euro was a pure *unit of account*. No euro currency was actually in circulation, although firms began quoting prices in both domestic currency and euros. On January 1, 2002, euro coins and paper currency were introduced, and on June 1, 2002, the old domestic currencies were withdrawn from circulation. Figure 18-2 shows the countries in the EU that have adopted the euro.

Figure 18-2

Countries Adopting the Euro

The 13 member countries of the European Union that have adopted the euro as their common currency as of 2007 are shaded with red hatch marks. The members of the EU that have not adopted the euro are colored tan. Countries in white are not members of the EU.

A new European Central Bank (ECB) was also established. Although the central banks of the member countries continue to exist, the ECB has assumed responsibility for monetary policy and for issuing currency. The ECB is run by a governing council that consists of a six-member executive board—appointed by the participating governments—and the governors of the central banks of the 13 member countries that have adopted the euro. The ECB represents a unique experiment in allowing a multinational organization to control the domestic monetary policies of independent countries.

Economists are divided over whether the creation of the euro will help growth in the EU countries. Having a common currency makes it easier for consumers and firms to buy and sell across borders. It is no longer necessary for someone in France to exchange francs for marks in order to do business in Germany. This change should reduce costs and increase competition. However, the participating countries are no longer able to run independent monetary policies. In addition, with fixed exchange rates, the value of one country's currency cannot fall during a recession, thereby expanding net exports to help revive aggregate demand. The experiences of the countries using the euro will provide economists with additional information on the costs and benefits to countries from using the same currency.

Making the Connection

Was the Euro Undervalued or Overvalued in 2007?

Whether a currency is undervalued or overvalued can have both economic and political significance. As we saw in Chapter 17, a declining exchange rate can boost a country's exports and reduce its imports; a rising exchange rate can have the opposite effect. In 2007, whether some country's currencies were chronically undervalued against the dollar became a political issue in the United States. A bill was introduced in the Senate that would punish countries whose exchange rates were "fundamentally misaligned" against the dollar. The bill seemed to be aimed at China because some politicians and economists argued that the Chinese government was taking actions to keep the Chinese yuan undervalued against the dollar. An undervalued yuan would make it easier for Chinese firms to export to the United States and harder for U.S. firms to export to China.

But is it easy to tell whether a country's currency is undervalued or overvalued against another country's currency? In fact, it is very difficult. One possible approach would be to use the model of purchasing power parity we discussed earlier in this chapter. But, as we have seen, we only expect purchasing power parity to explain exchange rates in the long run, so it does not provide a good guide to whether a currency is correctly valued at any particular time. Because investment firms buy and sell different currencies, they have an interest in knowing whether currencies are correctly valued. Economist Stephen Jen of the investment firm Morgan Stanley has analyzed whether the euro is undervalued or overvalued against the dollar. The graph on the next page shows movements in the exchange rate between the dollar and the euro from January 2002 through May 2007.

Determining whether a currency is undervalued or overvalued can be difficult.

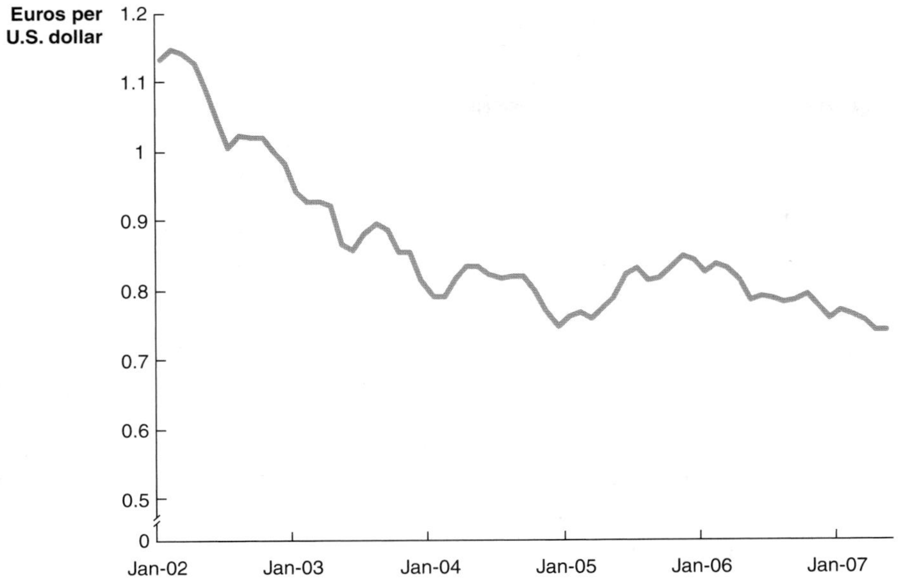

During this period, the value of the dollar declined from 1.13 euros to 0.74 euros, or by about 35 percent. Is this decline justified by changing economic conditions, or had the euro become overvalued (and, therefore, the dollar undervalued)? To see, Jen studied which economic variables had been correlated with exchange rate movements in the past. He then used current values of these variables, including productivity growth rates and the relative prices of imports and exports, to determine whether the euro was undervalued or overvalued. To account for the uncertainty in determining whether an exchange rate is at its "fair value," Jen constructed 13 estimates of what the euro's value should be. These estimates ranged from a low of 0.98 euros to the dollar to a high of 0.78 euros to the dollar. Because Jen's highest estimate was lower than the actual value of 0.74 euros to the dollar, he concluded that the euro was overvalued.

Jen's estimates have a very wide range, but even so, not every economist would agree with his conclusion that the euro is overvalued. This uncertainty in assessing the value of the euro indicates the practical difficulty of determining whether a currency is undervalued or overvalued.

Source: "Misleading Misalignments," *Economist*, June 21, 2007.

YOUR TURN: Test your understanding by doing related problem 2.17 on page 638 at the end of this chapter.

Pegging against the Dollar

A final key aspect of the current exchange rate system is that some developing countries have attempted to keep their exchange rates fixed against the dollar or another major currency. Having a fixed exchange rate can provide important advantages for a country that has extensive trade with another country. When the exchange rate is fixed, business planning becomes much easier. For instance, if the South Korean won increases in value relative to the dollar, Hyundai, the Korean car manufacturer, may have to raise the dollar price of cars it exports to the United States, thereby reducing sales. If the exchange rate between the Korean won and the dollar is fixed, Hyundai's planning is much easier.

In the 1980s and 1990s, an additional reason for having fixed exchange rates developed. During those decades, the flow of foreign investment funds to developing countries, particularly those in East Asia, increased substantially. It became possible for firms in countries such as Korea, Thailand, Malaysia, and Indonesia to borrow dollars directly from foreign investors or indirectly from foreign banks. For example, a Thai firm might borrow U.S. dollars from a Japanese bank. If the Thai firm wants to build a new factory in Thailand with the borrowed dollars, it has to exchange the dollars for the equivalent amount of Thai currency, the baht. When the factory opens and production begins, the Thai firm will be earning the additional baht it needs to exchange for dollars to make the interest payments on the loan. A problem arises if the value of the baht falls against the dollar. Suppose that the exchange rate is 25 baht per dollar when the firm takes out the loan. A Thai firm making an interest payment of $100,000 dollars per month on a dollar loan could buy the necessary dollars for 2.5 million baht. But if the value of the baht declines to 50 baht to the dollar, it would take 5 million baht to buy the dollars necessary to make the interest payment. These increased payments might be a crushing burden for the Thai firm. The government of Thailand would have a strong incentive to avoid this problem by keeping the exchange rate between the baht and the dollar fixed.

Finally, some countries feared the inflationary consequences of a floating exchange rate. When the value of a currency falls, the prices of imports rise. If imports are a significant fraction of the goods consumers buy, a fall in the value of the currency may significantly increase the inflation rate. During the 1990s, an important part of Brazil's and Argentina's anti-inflation policies was a fixed exchange rate against the dollar. (As we will see, though, there are difficulties with following a fixed exchange rate policy, and, ultimately, both Brazil and Argentina abandoned fixed exchange rates.)

Pegging The decision by a country to keep the exchange rate fixed between its currency and another currency.

The East Asian Exchange Rate Crisis of the Late 1990s When a country keeps its currency's exchange rate fixed against another country's currency, it is **pegging** its currency. It is not necessary for both countries involved in a peg to agree to it. When a developing country has pegged the value of its currency against the dollar, the responsibility for maintaining the peg has been entirely with the developing country.

Countries attempting to maintain a peg can run into problems, however. We saw in Chapter 4 that when the government fixes the price of a good or service, the result can be persistent surpluses or shortages. Figure 18-3 shows the exchange rate between the

Figure 18-3

By 1997, the Thai Baht Was Overvalued against the Dollar

The government of Thailand pegged the value of the baht against the dollar to make it easier for Thai firms to export to the United States and to protect Thai firms that had taken out dollar loans. The pegged exchange rate of $0.04 per baht was well above the equilibrium exchange rate of $0.03 per baht. In the example in this figure, the overvalued exchange rate created a surplus of 70 million baht, which the Thai central bank had to purchase with dollars.

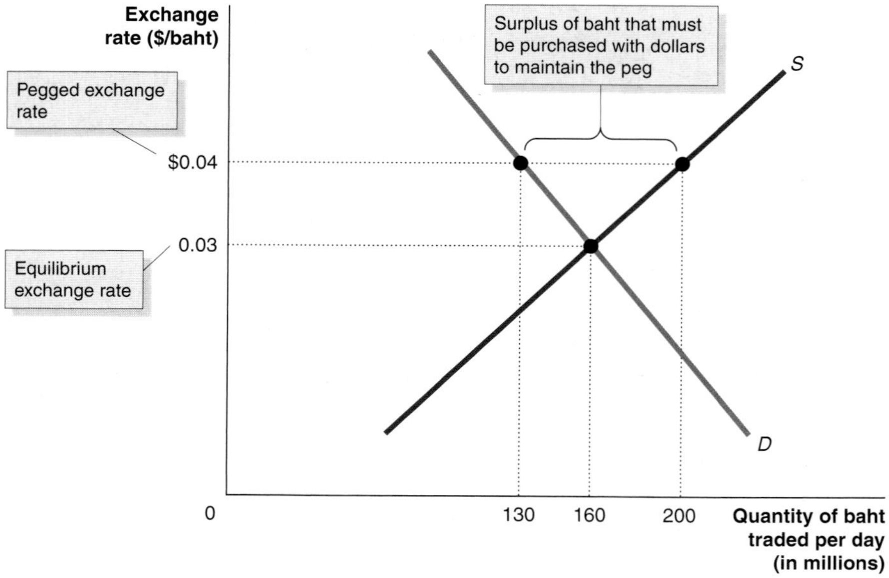

dollar and the Thai baht. The figure is drawn from the Thai point of view, so we measure the exchange rate on the vertical axis as dollars per baht. The figure represents the situation in the 1990s when the government of Thailand pegged the exchange rate between the dollar and the baht above the equilibrium exchange rate as determined by demand and supply. A currency pegged at a value above the market equilibrium exchange rate is said to be *overvalued.* A currency pegged at a value below the market equilibrium exchange rate is said to be *undervalued.*

Pegging made it easier for Thai firms to export products to the United States and protected Thai firms that had taken out dollar loans. The pegged exchange rate was 25.19 baht to the dollar, or about $0.04 to the baht. By 1997, this exchange rate was well above the market equilibrium exchange rate of 35 baht to the dollar, or about $0.03 to the baht. The result was a surplus of baht on the foreign exchange market. To keep the exchange rate at the pegged level, the Thai central bank, the Bank of Thailand, had to buy these baht with dollars. In buying baht with dollars, the Bank of Thailand gradually used up its holdings of dollars, or its *dollar reserves.* To continue supporting the pegged exchange rate, the Bank of Thailand borrowed additional dollar reserves from the International Monetary Fund (IMF). It also raised interest rates to attract more foreign investors to investments in Thailand, thereby increasing the demand for the baht. The Bank of Thailand took these actions even though allowing the value of the baht to decline against the dollar would have helped Thai firms exporting to the United States by reducing the dollar prices of their goods. The Thai government was afraid of the negative consequences of abandoning the peg even though it had led to the baht being overvalued.

Although higher domestic interest rates helped attract foreign investors, they made it more difficult for Thai firms and households to borrow the funds they needed to finance their spending. As a consequence, domestic investment and consumption declined, pushing the Thai economy into recession. International investors realized that there were limits to how high the Bank of Thailand would be willing to push interest rates and how many dollar loans the IMF would be willing to extend to Thailand. They began to speculate against the baht by exchanging baht for dollars at the official, pegged exchange rate. If, as they expected, Thailand was forced to abandon the peg, they would be able to buy back the baht at a much lower exchange rate, making a substantial profit. Because these actions by investors make it more difficult to maintain a fixed exchange rate, they are referred to as *destabilizing speculation.* Figure 18-4 shows the results of this destabilizing speculation. The decreased demand for baht shifted the demand curve for

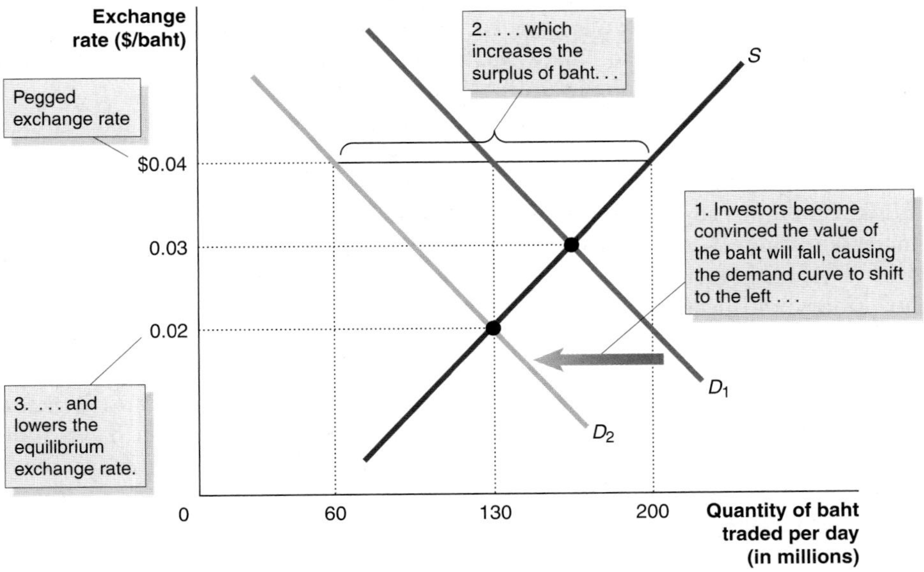

Figure 18-4

Destabilizing Speculation against the Thai Baht

In 1997, the pegged exchange rate of $0.04 = 1 baht was above the equilibrium exchange rate of $0.03 = 1 baht. As investors became convinced that Thailand would have to abandon its pegged exchange against the dollar and allow the value of the baht to fall, they decreased their demand for baht from D_1 to D_2. The new equilibrium exchange rate became $0.02 = 1 baht. This increased the quantity of baht the Bank of Thailand had to purchase in exchange for dollars from 70 million per day to 140 million to defend the pegged exchange rate. The *destabilizing speculation* by investors caused Thailand to abandon its pegged exchange rate in July 1997.

baht from D_1 to D_2, increasing the quantity of baht the Bank of Thailand needed to buy in exchange for dollars.

Foreign investors also began to sell off their investments in Thailand and exchange the baht they received for dollars. This *capital flight* forced the Bank of Thailand to run through its dollar reserves. Dollar loans from the IMF temporarily allowed Thailand to defend the pegged exchange rate. Finally, on July 2, 1997, Thailand abandoned its pegged exchange rate against the dollar and allowed the baht to float. Thai firms that had borrowed dollars were now faced with interest payments that were much higher than they had planned. Many firms were forced into bankruptcy, and the Thai economy plunged into a deep recession.

Many currency traders became convinced that other East Asian countries, such as South Korea, Indonesia, and Malaysia, would have to follow Thailand and abandon their pegged exchange rates. The result was a wave of speculative selling of these countries' currencies. These waves of selling—sometimes referred to as *speculative attacks* —were difficult for countries to fight off. Even if a country's currency was not initially overvalued at the pegged exchange rate, the speculative attacks would cause a large reduction in the demand for its currency. The demand curve for its currency would shift to the left, which would force the country's central bank to quickly run through its dollar reserves. Within the space of a few months, South Korea, Indonesia, the Philippines, and Malaysia abandoned their pegged currencies. All these countries also plunged into recession.

The Decline in Pegging Following the disastrous events experienced by the East Asian countries, the number of countries with pegged exchange rates declined sharply. Most countries that continue to use pegged exchange rates are small and trade primarily with one, much larger, country. So, for instance, several Caribbean countries continue to peg against the dollar, and several former French colonies in Africa that formerly pegged against the French franc now peg against the euro. Overall, the trend has been toward replacing pegged exchange rates with managed floating exchange rates.

The Chinese Experience with Pegging As we discussed in Chapter 10, in 1978, China began to move away from central planning and toward a market system. The result was a sharp acceleration in economic growth. Real GDP per capita grew at a rate of 6.5 percent per year between 1979 and 1995, and at the very rapid rate of 9.1 percent per year between 1996 and 2006. An important part of Chinese economic policy was the decision in 1994 to peg the value of the Chinese currency, the yuan, to the dollar at a fixed rate of 8.28 yuan to the dollar. Pegging against the dollar ensured that Chinese exporters would face stable dollar prices for the goods they sold in the United States. By the early 2000s, many economists argued that the yuan was undervalued against the dollar, possibly significantly so. Many U.S. firms claimed that the undervaluation of the yuan gave Chinese firms an unfair advantage in competing with U.S. firms.

To support the undervalued exchange rate, the Chinese central bank had to buy large amounts of dollars with yuan. By 2005, the Chinese government had accumulated more than $700 billion, a good portion of which it had used to buy U.S. Treasury bonds. In addition, China was coming under pressure from its trading partners to allow the yuan to increase in value. Chinese exports of textile products were driving some textile producers out of business in Japan, the United States, and Europe. China has also begun to export more sophisticated products, including televisions, personal computers, and cell phones. Politicians in other countries were anxious to protect their domestic industries from Chinese competition, even if the result was higher prices for domestic consumers. The Chinese government was reluctant to revalue the yuan, however, because it believed high levels of exports were needed to maintain rapid economic growth. The Chinese economy needs to create as many as 20 million new nonagricultural jobs per year to keep up with population growth and the shift of workers from rural areas to cities. Because of China's large holdings of dollars, it will also incur significant losses if the yuan increases in value.

By July 2005, the pressure on China to revalue the yuan had become too great. The government announced that it would switch from pegging the yuan against the dollar to linking the value of the yuan to the average value of a basket of currencies including the dollar, the Japanese yen, the euro, the Korean won, and several other currencies. The immediate effect was a fairly small increase in the value of the yuan from 8.28 to the dollar to 8.11 to the dollar. The Chinese central bank declared that it had switched from a peg to a managed floating exchange rate. Some economists and policymakers were skeptical, however, that much had actually changed because the initial increase in the value of yuan had been small and because the Chinese central bank did not explain the details of how the yuan would be linked to the basket of other currencies. Two years later, in mid-2007, the value of the yuan had increased to 7.62 to the dollar. But this limited increase made it clear that the value of the yuan was still not very responsive to changes in demand and supply in the foreign exchange markets.

Making the Connection | Crisis and Recovery in South Korea

Korea spent the first part of the twentieth century as a colony of Japan. In 1945, at the end of World War II, Korea was divided into Communist North Korea and democratic South Korea. North Korea's invasion of South Korea in June 1950 set off the Korean War, which devastated South Korea, before ending in 1953. Despite these difficult beginnings, by the 1960s, the South Korean economy was growing rapidly. As one of the *newly industrializing countries*, South Korea was a model for other developing countries.

To make it easier for firms like Hyundai to export to the United States and to protect firms that had taken out dollar loans, the South Korean government pegged the value of its currency, the won, to the U.S. dollar. Following Thailand's decision in July 1997 to abandon its peg, large-scale destabilizing speculation took place against the won. Foreign investors scrambled to sell their investments in Korea and to convert their won into dollars. South Korea was unable to defend the peg and allowed the won to float in October 1997.

Like other countries that underwent an exchange rate crisis, South Korea had attempted to maintain the value of the won by raising domestic interest rates. The result was a sharp decline in aggregate demand and a severe recession. However, unlike other East Asian countries—particularly Thailand and Indonesia—that made only slow progress in recovering from exchange rate crises, South Korea bounced back rapidly. The figure shows that after experiencing falling real GDP through 1999, South Korea quickly returned to high rates of growth.

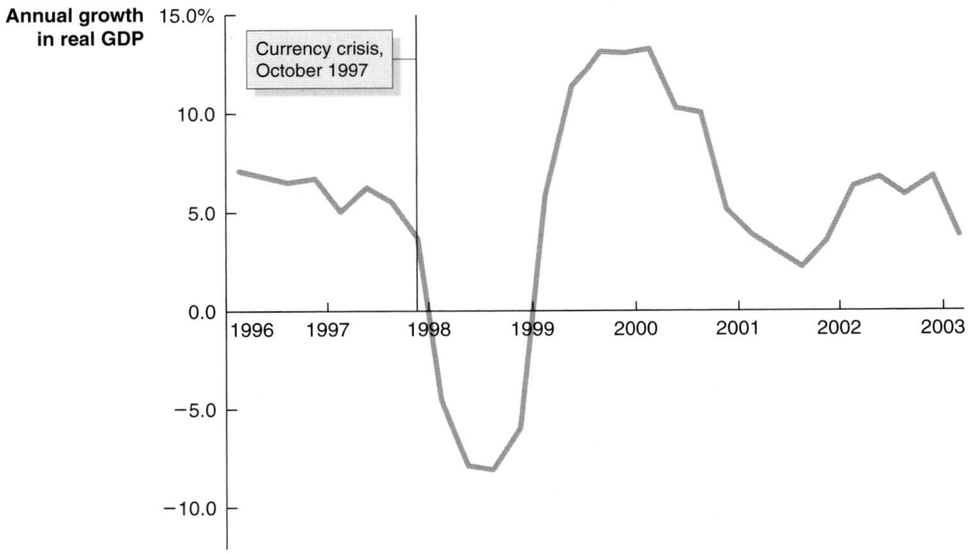

Why was the performance of South Korea so much better than that of other East Asian countries? Jahyeong Koo and Sherry L. Kiser, economists at the Federal Reserve Bank of Dallas, cite several factors:

- South Korea benefited from a $21 billion loan from the IMF in December 1997. This loan helped stabilize the value of the won.
- Even though South Korean banks were badly hurt in the crisis and cut back their loans, South Korean firms were able to obtain financing for investment projects from the stock and bond markets.
- The South Korean labor market was flexible enough to allow wage reductions, which offset some of the negative impact of the crisis on corporate profits.

South Korean firms remain saddled with large debts, and the Korean banking system has yet to fully recover. But South Korea was able to emerge from its exchange rate crisis without suffering the political and social upheavals that occurred in countries such as Indonesia.

Sources: Korea National Statistical Office; and Jahyeong Koo and Sherry L. Kiser, "Recovery from a Financial Crisis: The Case of South Korea," Federal Reserve Bank of Dallas *Economic and Financial Review*, Fourth Quarter 2001.

YOUR TURN: Test your understanding by doing related problem 2.28 on page 639 at the end of this chapter.

Solved Problem | 18-2B

Coping with Fluctuations in the Value of the U.S. Dollar

Analyze the following excerpt from an article in the *New York Times*: "Some economists say that if the flow of capital into the United States dries up, the dollar could fall sharply in value, reigniting the threat of inflation and putting pressure on the Fed to raise interest rates."

Use a foreign exchange market graph in your analysis and be sure to explain what the value of the dollar has to do with the U.S. inflation rate, as well as why a falling value of the dollar puts pressure on the Fed to raise interest rates.

SOLVING THE PROBLEM:

Step 1: **Review the chapter material.** This problem is about the determinants of exchange rates, so you may want to review the section "The Current Exchange Rate System," which begins on page 617.

Step 2: **Draw the graph.** Draw a graph to show the effect of a decline in the flow of capital into the United States. "Flow of capital into the United States" refers to foreign investors engaging in portfolio investment (such as buying U.S. stocks and bonds) or direct investment (such as building factories in the United States). To invest in the United States, foreign investors must exchange their currencies for dollars. If they decide to cut back on investing in the United States, their demand for dollars will fall. This reduction is shown in the following figure by the shift from D_1 to D_2. The equilibrium exchange falls from ¥130 = $1 to ¥120 = $1.

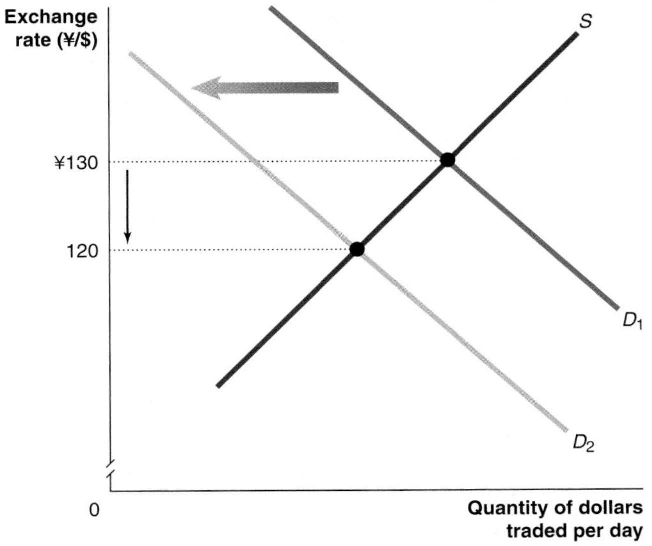

Step 3: **Explain why a falling value of the dollar puts pressure on the Fed to raise interest rates.** If the value of the dollar falls, the prices of imports will rise. Rising import prices add to the inflation rate. If the Fed wanted to increase the value of the dollar (or keep it from falling further), it would raise interest rates to make U.S. financial investments more attractive to foreign investors. In the graph, this would result in shifting the demand for dollars back to the right.

Source: Richard W. Stevenson, "Dollar Falls as Top Official Casts Doubts on Intervention," *New York Times*, May 2, 2002.

YOUR TURN: For more practice, do related problem 2.29 on page 639 at the end of this chapter.

>> End Solved Problem 18-2B

18.3 LEARNING OBJECTIVE

18.3 | Discuss the growth of international capital markets.

International Capital Markets

One important reason exchange rates fluctuate is that investors seek out the best investments they can find anywhere in the world. For instance, if Chinese investors increase their demand for U.S. Treasury bills, the demand for dollars will increase, and the value of the dollar will rise. But if interest rates in the United States decline, foreign investors may sell U.S. investments, and the value of the dollar will fall.

Shares of stock and long-term debt, including corporate and government bonds and bank loans, are bought and sold on *capital markets.* Before 1980, most U.S. corporations raised funds only in U.S. stock and bond markets or from U.S. banks. U.S. investors rarely invested in foreign capital markets. In the 1980s and 1990s, European governments removed many restrictions on foreign investments in financial markets. It became possible for U.S. and other foreign investors to freely invest in Europe and for European investors to freely invest in foreign markets. Improvements in communications and computer technology made it possible for U.S. investors to receive better and more timely information about foreign firms and for foreign investors to receive better information about U.S. firms. The growth in economies around the world also made more savings available to be invested.

Although at one time the U.S. capital market was larger than all other capital markets combined, this is no longer true. Today there are large capital markets in Europe and Japan, and there are smaller markets in Latin America and East Asia. The three most important international financial centers today are New York, London, and Tokyo. Each day, the *Wall Street Journal* provides data not just on the Dow Jones Industrial Average

Figure 18-5

Growth of Foreign Portfolio Investment in the United States

Since 1995, a large rise has occurred in foreign purchases of bonds issued by U.S. corporations and by the federal government. Falling stock prices in the United States caused a fall in foreign purchases of corporate stocks in the years immediately after 2001. By 2006, however, foreign investment in these securities was at record levels.

Sources: International Monetary Fund, *International Capital Markets*, August 2001; and U.S. Department of the Treasury, *Treasury Bulletin*, June 2007.

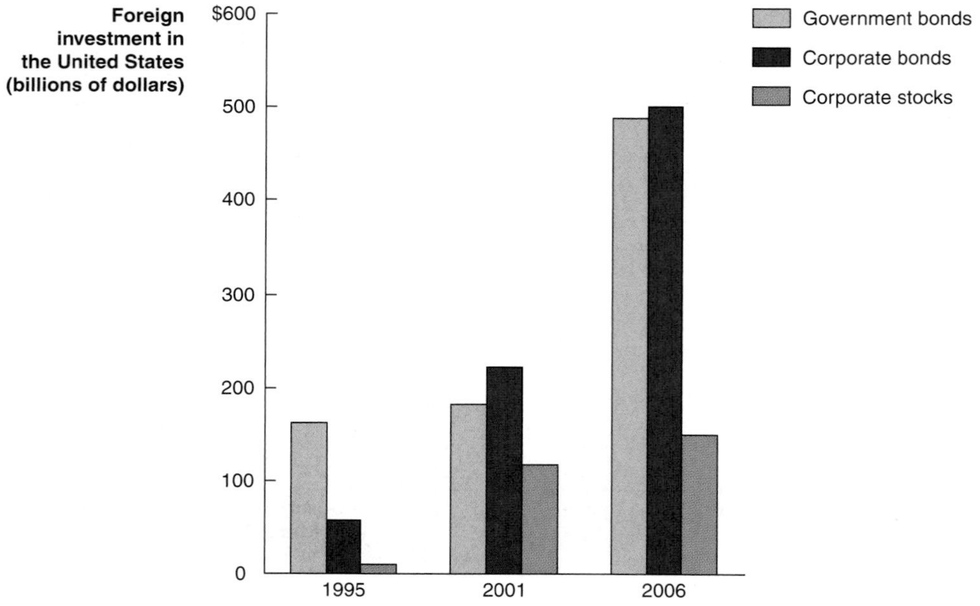

and the Standard & Poor's 500 stock indexes of U.S. stocks but also on the Nikkei 225 average of Japanese stocks, the FTSE 100 index of stocks on the London Stock Exchange, and the Euro STOXX 50 index of European stocks. By 2007, corporations, banks, and governments raised more than $1 trillion in funds on global financial markets.

Beginning in the 1990s, the flow of foreign funds into U.S. stocks and bonds—or *portfolio investments*—increased substantially. As Figure 18-5 shows, a dramatic increase in foreign purchases of bonds issued by corporations and by the federal government has occurred since 1995. Even though falling stock prices in the United States caused a fall in foreign purchases of corporate stocks in the years immediately after 2001, by 2006, foreign investment in these securities was at record levels.

Figure 18-6 shows the distribution of foreign portfolio investment in the United States by country. Investors in the United Kingdom accounted for more than 40 percent of all foreign purchases of U.S. stocks and bonds. Investors in China accounted for 10 percent, and investors in Japan accounted for 5 percent.

The globalization of financial markets has helped increase growth and efficiency in the world economy. Now it is possible for the savings of households around the world to be channeled to the best investments available. It is also possible for firms in nearly every country to tap the savings of foreign households to gain the funds needed for expansion. No longer are firms forced to rely only on the savings of domestic households to finance investment.

Figure 18-6

The Distribution of Foreign Purchases of U.S. Stocks and Bonds by Country, 2006

Investors in the United Kingdom accounted for more than 40 percent of all foreign purchases of U.S. stocks and bonds, while investors in China accounted for 10 percent, and investors in Japan accounted for 5 percent.

Source: U.S. Department of the Treasury, *Treasury Bulletin*, June 2007.

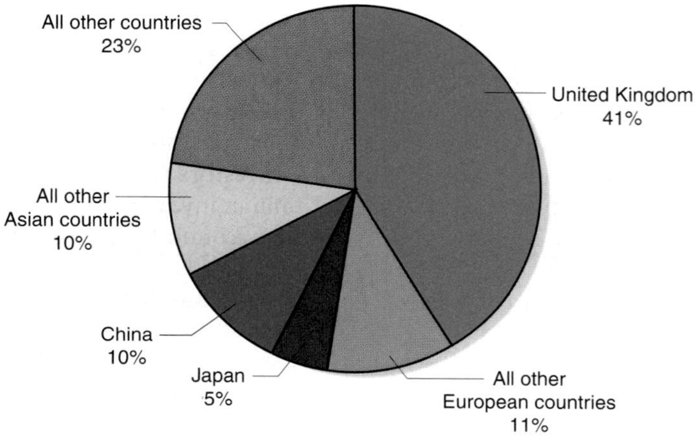

Continued from page 615

Economics in YOUR Life!

At the beginning of the chapter, we posed this question: If economists are correct about the relative rates of average productivity growth between Spain and the United States in the next decade, then, all else being equal, will the savings that you accumulate (in euros) be worth more or less in U.S. dollars than it would have been worth without the relative gains in Spanish productivity? To answer this question, we saw in this chapter that when the average productivity of firms in one country increases faster than the average productivity of firms in another country, the value of the faster-growing country's currency should—all else being equal—rise against the slower-growing country's currency. Of course, Spain is only one of the 13 countries using the euro, so the impact of productivity increases in Spain on the value of the euro may not be large. But the savings that you accumulate in euros while you are in Spain are likely to be worth more in U.S. dollars than they would have been worth without the gains in Spanish productivity.

Conclusion

Fluctuations in exchange rates continue to cause difficulties for firms and governments. From the gold standard to the Bretton Woods system to currency pegging, governments have attempted to find a workable system of fixed exchange rates. Fixing exchange rates runs into the same problems as fixing any price: As demand and supply shift, surpluses and shortages will occur unless the price adjusts. Most of the countries of Western Europe are attempting to avoid this problem by using a single currency. Economists are looking closely at the results of that experiment.

Read *An Inside Look at Policy* on the next page for a discussion of whether governments should try to limit speculation in currencies.

An Inside **LOOK** at Policy

Should the International Financial System Limit Currency Speculation?

WALL STREET JOURNAL, APRIL 5, 2007

Can Asia Control the "Hot Money"?

Asian finance officials plan to meet in Thailand Thursday, and high on the agenda: doing something about the money pouring into their countries from foreign investors, so it doesn't whipsaw their economies on the way back out.

(a) Capital-control regulations can be controversial. Last year when Thailand slapped controls on moving foreign investments out of the country, Thai shares fell a record 15% in one day as overseas investors fled.

Yet many foreign investors are starting to warm to the idea of controls on "hot money"—speculative investors who move in and out quickly. Analysts say limited restrictions help prevent highflying markets from collapsing if foreigners decide to suddenly pull up stakes, potentially causing economic damage. . . .

Increased restriction would be a step back from the trend of the past decade or so toward more-open markets. That move toward openness to money from abroad has helped make stock markets in India, Brazil and Russia some of the best performers in the world. . . .

(b) Some U.S. mutual-fund managers say the sort of controls they consider potentially helpful are those that would target hot money but wouldn't necessarily disrupt longer-term investors. These restrictions cover a range of measures intended to manage speculative investment flows. In Brazil, for instance, there is a tax on some transactions of securities sold within 30 days of being bought. In India, foreigners are restricted from participating in some of the domestic derivative markets, while foreign investors in Argentina are subject to a 180-day minimum holding period for all debt purchases. . . .

In Vietnam, where Hanoi is grappling with what many analysts say is a stock-market bubble that threatens to burst, some investors say they would actually welcome state action. "You'd want the government to prevent a stock-market meltdown," says Cliff Quisenberry, who manages the Eaton Vance Structured Emerging Markets Fund and invests in Vietnamese stocks. "Controls may be useful."

When Thailand's shares tanked late last year, after the government tried to make it tougher for foreigners to move money out of the country, Mark Headley, of Matthews International Capital Management in San Francisco, says he viewed it as a buying opportunity. This despite the fact that he has been burned in the past: In 1998, he was among the investors whose money got trapped inside Malaysia when the government there barred foreigners from repatriating funds amid the Asian economic crisis then unfolding.

Today Mr. Headley takes a more benign view of Thailand's actions. He says the new Thai government was worried about a strengthening currency hurting Thai exporters, "and they panicked. That's profoundly different from Malaysia, where they were trying to stick it to foreign investors." Thailand later rolled back its restrictions slightly. . . .

(c) "Where Malaysia tried to keep foreigners from getting out, the controls today are aimed at keeping overeager money from coming in," he says. "That's a big difference." Not to everyone, however. Some say any government interference is bound to create inefficiencies and is doomed to fail. "It takes a sure policy-making hand to avoid trouble," says Stuart Schweitzer, global-markets strategist for JP Morgan Private Bank. "Markets do a better job." . . .

Not all investment restrictions are done for the same reason. Colombia in 2004 imposed a one-year "residency requirement" that prevented investors from withdrawing their money from the country for 12 months. The stated rationale was to prevent hot-money flows from causing the Colombian peso to appreciate. But analysts say it was really a bow to political pressure from exporters, who wanted the currency to stay weak.

The currency appreciated anyway because direct foreign investment in Colombian companies continued. When the stock market started to tumble last year, the government abruptly removed the lockup rule in hopes of luring foreign fund managers back.

Three months after Thailand's move, officials scrapped restrictions on stock investors. But controls on currency trading remain. Some think those controls may actually have helped the country weather more recent market turbulence. . . .

Source: Craig Karmin, "Can Asia Control the 'Hot Money'?" Wall Street Journal, April 5, 2007, p. C1. Reprinted by permission of the Wall Street Journal via Copyright Clearance Center.

Key Points in the Article

This article discusses government-imposed capital controls, which restrict foreign investors' ability to speculate in a country's financial markets. Although foreign investors have typically resisted capital controls, a growing number of them now support some form of controls on very short-term investment flows, which can disrupt the returns of relatively long-term foreign investors. Most investors, however, continue to believe that capital controls are bad for the international financial system, which, they contend, allocates capital most efficiently when it is run by markets rather than governments.

Analyzing the News

a Private investors in the international financial system have typically resisted government-imposed capital controls designed to limit hot money—large flows of speculative foreign portfolio investments that quickly enter and exit a country's financial markets. Any government restrictions on foreign investors' ability to sell a country's stocks, bonds, or currency make it less likely that foreign investors will buy these assets. Recently, the Thai government imposed a so-called 30 percent withholding rule that required foreigners to deposit 30 percent of their foreign portfolio investments in non-interest-earning accounts at the central bank for one year. Foreigners demonstrated their opposition to the withholding rule by pulling their funds from the country. Although the Thai government later exempted stocks and some other types of investments from the rule, it has left the capital control largely in place.

Hot money enters a country's economy through its foreign exchange market; that is, speculators must buy the country's currency in order to buy the country's financial assets. Speculators buy a country's currency when they believe the currency—or the financial investments denominated in that currency—will increase in value. This pattern is shown in the figure, where the demand curve for Thai baht shifts to the right from D_1 to D_2, and the value of the baht increases from \$0.03 to \$0.06. Similarly, speculators sell a country's currency when they believe it will decrease in value.

b Hot money flows can disrupt the returns of other foreign investors who intend to invest in a country's assets over a long period of time. A growing number of foreign investors support some form of capital controls on short-term flows while agreeing that long-term foreign portfolio investments and foreign direct investments should remain exempt from such controls. For example, Brazil taxes foreign investors who hold select securities for less than 30 days; meanwhile, Argentina requires that foreign investors hold debt securities, such as bonds, for a minimum of 180 days. Of course, another reason some foreign investors tolerate or even support capital controls may be that foreign portfolio investments in many of these countries with capital controls are earning very high returns. If these high returns were to deteriorate, foreign investors' support for capital controls might fade.

c Capital controls today differ from those that governments imposed even a decade ago. While today's controls seek to keep speculators from entering the financial systems of these countries, earlier controls sought to keep speculators from exiting them. In other words, today, countries such as Thailand are trying to stave off a run-up in the values of their currencies, rather than avoid a collapse in their currencies' value.

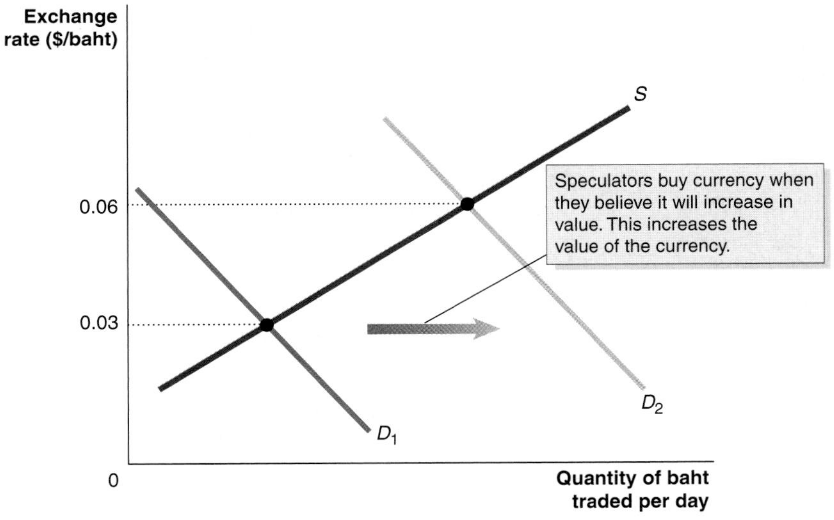

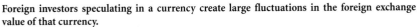

Foreign investors speculating in a currency create large fluctuations in the foreign exchange value of that currency.

Thinking Critically About Policy

1. Suppose a small, open-economy, such as Thailand, imposes capital controls so that foreign investors who buy its currency must hold it for at least two years. Would a contractionary monetary policy, with the central bank effectively raising interest rates to slow the growth rate of GDP, be relatively more or less effective as a result of the capital controls? Briefly explain your reasoning.
2. Why do governments impose short-term capital controls on foreign portfolio investment rather than on foreign direct investment?

Key Terms

Euro, p. 617	Fixed exchange rate system, p. 616	Managed float exchange rate system, p. 616	Purchasing power parity, p. 619
Exchange rate system, p. 616	Floating currency, p. 616	Pegging, p. 626	Quota, p. 620
			Tariff, p. 620

18.1 LEARNING OBJECTIVE 18.1 | Understand how different exchange rate systems operate, **pages 616–617.**

Exchange Rate Systems

Summary

When countries agree on how exchange rates should be determined, economists say that there is an **exchange rate system**. A **floating currency** is the outcome of a country allowing its currency's exchange rate to be determined by demand and supply. The current exchange rate system is a **managed float exchange rate system** under which the value of most currencies is determined by demand and supply, with occasional government intervention. A **fixed exchange rate system** is a system under which countries agree to keep the exchange rates among their currencies fixed. Under the gold standard, the exchange rate between two currencies was automatically determined by the quantity of gold in each currency. By the end of the Great Depression of the 1930s, every country had abandoned the gold standard. Under the Bretton Woods system, which was in place between 1944 and the early 1970s, the United States agreed to exchange dollars for gold at a price of $35 per ounce. The central banks of all other members of the system pledged to buy and sell their currencies at a fixed rate against the dollar.

myeconlab Get Ahead of the Curve Visit www.myeconlab.com to complete these exercises online and get instant feedback.

Review Questions

1.1 What is an exchange rate system? What is the difference between a fixed exchange rate system and a managed float exchange rate system?

1.2 How were exchange rates determined under the gold standard? How did the gold standard differ from the Bretton Woods system?

Problems and Applications

1.3 **(Related to the *Don't Let This Happen to You!* on page 617)** Briefly explain whether you agree with the following statement: "The Federal Reserve is limited in its ability to issue paper currency by the amount of gold the federal government has in Fort Knox. To issue more paper currency, the government first has to buy more gold."

1.4 The United States and most other countries abandoned the gold standard during the 1930s. Why would the 1930s have been a particularly difficult time for countries to have remained on the gold standard? (*Hint:* Think about the macroeconomic events of the 1930s and about the possible problems with carrying out an expansionary monetary policy while remaining on the gold standard.)

1.5 If a country is on the gold standard, what is likely to happen to the country's money supply if new gold deposits are discovered in the country, as happened in the United States with the gold discoveries in California in 1849? Is this change in the money supply desirable? Briefly explain.

>> End Learning Objective 18.1

18.2 LEARNING OBJECTIVE 18.2 | Discuss the three key features of the current exchange rate system, **pages 617–631.**

The Current Exchange Rate System

Summary

The three key aspects of the current exchange rate system are: (1) the U.S. dollar floats against other major currencies; (2) most countries in western Europe have adopted a common currency; and (3) some developing countries have fixed their currencies' exchange rates against the dollar or against another major currency. Since 1973, the value of the U.S. dollar has fluctuated widely against other major currencies. The theory of **purchasing power parity** states that in the long run, exchange rates move to equalize the purchasing power of different currencies. This theory helps to explain some of the long-run movements in the value of the U.S. dollar relative to other currencies. Purchasing power parity does not provide a complete explanation of movements in exchange rates for several reasons, including the existence of *tariffs* and *quotas*. A **tariff** is a tax imposed by a government on imports. A **quota** is a government-imposed limit on the quantity of a good that can be imported. Currently, 13 countries of the European Union use a common currency, known as the **euro**. The experience of the countries using the euro will provide economists with information on the costs and benefits to countries from using the same currency. When a country keeps its currency's exchange rate fixed against another country's currency, it is **pegging** its currency. Pegging can result in problems similar to the problems countries encountered with fixed exchange rates under the Bretton Woods system. If investors become convinced that a country pegging its exchange rate will eventually allow the exchange rate to decline to a lower level, the demand curve for the currency will shift to the left. This illustrates the difficulty of maintaining a fixed exchange rate in the face of destabilizing speculation.

Review Questions

2.1 What is the theory of purchasing power parity? Does it give a complete explanation for movements in exchange rates in the long run? Briefly explain.

2.2 Briefly describe the four determinants of exchange rates in the long run.

2.3 Which European countries currently use the euro as their currency? Why did these countries agree to replace their previous currency with the euro?

2.4 What does it mean when one currency is "pegged" against another currency? Why do countries peg their currencies? What problems can result from pegging?

2.5 If you owned a firm in Indonesia and wanted to export your product to the United States, would you like the Indonesian government to peg the value of the rupiah against the dollar? Briefly explain.

2.6 Briefly describe the Chinese experience with pegging the yuan.

Problems and Applications

2.7 **(Related to the *Making the Connection* on page 618)** Suppose you are a baseball player for the Toronto Blue Jays, and your salary is paid in U.S. dollars. If you and your family live in Toronto, would you be helped or hurt by an increase in the value of the Canadian dollar relative to the U.S. dollar? Briefly explain.

2.8 Consider this newspaper report: "DuPont said that soft currencies overseas, particularly in Europe and Asia, had dragged down its sales 2 percent worldwide, ultimately costing it $35 million in net income." What is a "soft currency"? Why would soft currencies overseas hurt DuPont's sales?

Source: Danny Hakim and Greg Winter, "G.M. Official Says Dollar Is Too Strong," *New York Times*, August 9, 2001.

2.9 Consider this statement: "It usually takes more than 100 yen to buy 1 U.S. dollar and more than 1.5 dollars to buy 1 British pound. These values show that the United States must be a much wealthier country than Japan, and that the United Kingdom must be wealthier than the United States." Do you agree with this reasoning? Briefly explain.

2.10 The following is from an article in the *Wall Street Journal*:

> In Japan, demand for videogame machines is declining. In the past three years, the number of videogame players sold there has declined by more than 8%, while more household members say they are not interested in playing, according to an annual survey by the Japanese industry group Computer Entertainment Supplier's Association. Sales of both hardware and software have fallen about 20% to 496.5 billion yen ($4.3 billion) in 2005 from 623.2 billion yen ($5.7 billion) in 2000, according to the group.

a. According to the information in this article, what was the exchange rate between the yen and the dollar in 2000? What was the exchange rate between the yen and the dollar in 2005?

b. Was the change in the yen–dollar exchange rate between 2000 and 2005 good news or bad news for Japanese firms, such as Sony, that export video game consoles to the United States? Was the change in the yen–dollar exchange rate good news or bad news for U.S. consumers who buy Sony video game consoles? Briefly explain.

Source: Yukari Iwatani Kane and Nick Wingfield, "Amid Videogame Arms Race, Nintendo Slows Things Down," *Wall Street Journal*, November 2, 2006, p. A1.

2.11 An article in the *Wall Street Journal* is headlined "Pain from the Dollar's Decline Will Mostly Be Felt Overseas." Briefly explain the reasoning behind this headline.

Source: David Wessel, "Pain from the Dollar's Decline Will Mostly Be Felt Overseas," *Wall Street Journal*, June 13, 2002.

2.12 According to the theory of purchasing power parity, if the inflation rate in Australia is higher than the inflation rate in New Zealand, what should happen to the exchange rate between the Australian dollar and the New Zealand dollar? Briefly explain.

2.13 **(Related to the *Making the Connection* on page 620)** Look again at the table on page 621 that shows the prices of Big Macs and the implied and actual exchange rates. Indicate which countries listed in the table have undervalued currencies versus the U.S. dollar and which have overvalued currencies.

2.14 **(Related to *Solved Problem 18-2A* on page 621)** Fill in the missing values in the following table. Assume that the Big Mac is selling for $3.22 in the United States. Explain whether the U.S. dollar is overvalued or undervalued relative to each currency and predict what will happen in the future to each exchange rate. Finally, calculate the implied exchange rate between the Russian ruble and the New Zealand dollar and explain which currency is overvalued in terms of Big Mac purchasing power parity.

COUNTRY	BIG MAC PRICE	IMPLIED EXCHANGE RATE	ACTUAL EXCHANGE RATE
Chile	1,670 pesos		544 pesos per dollar
Estonia	30 kroons		12.0 kroons per dollar
Russia	49.0 rubles		26.5 rubles per dollar
New Zealand	4.60 New Zealand dollars		1.45 New Zealand dollars per U.S. dollar

2.15 Britain decided not to join with other European Union countries and use the euro as its currency. One British opponent of adopting the euro argued, "It comes down to economics. We just don't believe that it's possible to manage the entire economy of Europe with just one interest rate policy. How do you alleviate recession in Germany and curb inflation in Ireland?" What interest-rate policy would be used to alleviate recession in Germany? What interest-rate policy would be used to curb inflation in Ireland? What does adopting the euro have to do with interest-rate policy?

Source: Alan Cowell, "Nuanced Conflict Over Euro in Britain," *New York Times*, June 22, 2001.

2.16 When the euro was introduced in January 1999, the exchange rate was $1.19 per euro. In June 2007, the exchange rate was $1.34 per euro. Was this change in the dollar–euro exchange rate good news or bad news for U.S. firms exporting goods and services to Europe? Was it good news or bad news for European consumers buying goods and services imported from the United States? Briefly explain.

2.17 **(Related to the *Making the Connection* on page 624)** Suppose that Stephen Jen is correct that the euro was overvalued relative to the dollar in mid-2007. Would we then expect that in the future, the euro would exchange for more dollars or for fewer dollars? Would this movement in the euro be good news or bad news for European firms that export to the United States? Briefly explain.

2.18 Construct a numeric example that shows how an investor could have made a profit by selling Thai baht for dollars in 1997.

2.19 The following statement is from an article in the *New York Times*: "Government action to support [its] currency cannot be effective in the long run if it runs counter to the collective judgment of the financial markets." What does it mean to say a government is taking action to "support" its currency? Do you agree with the conclusion that this action is not effective in the long run if it runs counter to the judgment of financial markets? Briefly explain.

Source: Richard W. Stevenson, "Dollar Falls as Top Official Casts Doubts on Intervention," *New York Times*, May 2, 2002.

2.20 Use the graph to answer the following questions.

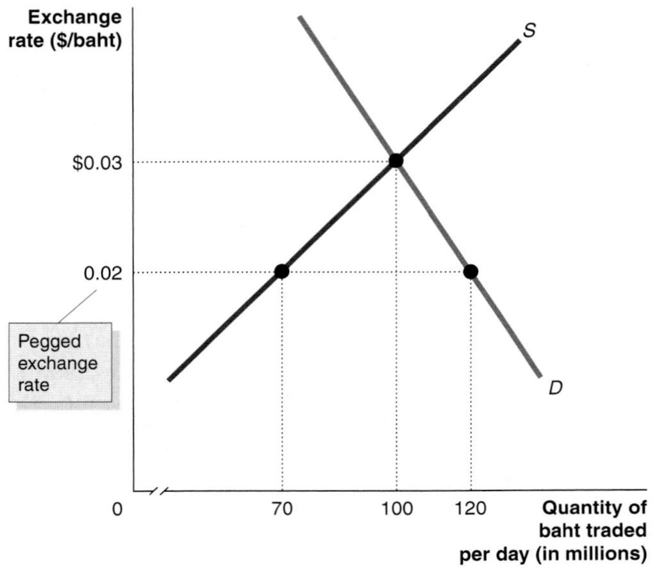

a. According to the graph, is there a surplus or a shortage of baht in exchange for U.S. dollars? Briefly explain.
b. To maintain the pegged exchange rate, will the Thai central bank need to buy baht in exchange for dollars or sell baht in exchange for dollars? How many baht will the Thai central bank need to buy or sell?

2.21 For many years, Argentina suffered from high rates of inflation. As part of its program to fight inflation, in the 1990s, the Argentine government pegged the value of the Argentine peso to the U.S. dollar at a rate of one peso per dollar. In January 2002, the government decided to abandon the peg and allow the peso to float. Just before the peg was abandoned, firms in Buenos Aires posted signs urging customers to come in and shop and take advantage of the "Last 72 Hours of One to One." What was likely to happen to the exchange rate between the dollar and the peso when Argentina abandoned the peg? Why would customers find it better to shop before the peg ended than after?

Source: Larry Rohter, "Argentina Unlinks Peso from Dollar, Bracing for Devaluation," *New York Times*, January 7, 2002.

2.22 The *Economist* observed the following: "In Argentina, many loans were taken out in dollars: this had catastrophic consequences for borrowers once the peg collapsed." What does it mean that Argentina's "peg collapsed"? Why was this catastrophic for borrowers in Argentina who had taken out dollar loans?

Source: "Spoilt for Choice," *Economist*, June 3, 2002.

2.23 According to the *Economist*, during the period in which Argentina pegged the value of its currency to the dollar, "Argentina's monetary policy was, in effect, made in Washington and was often inappropriate for Argentina's needs." Explain the sense in which Argentina's monetary policy was made in Washington during those years.

Source: "Spoilt for Choice," *Economist*, June 3, 2002.

2.24 A newspaper story discussing the effects of a decline in the exchange value of the dollar contained the following two observations:

a. "The weaker dollar will also mean higher inflation in this country."
b. "The biggest danger in coming months is that a declining dollar will make foreigners less willing to invest in the United States."

Explain whether you agree or disagree with these two observations.

Source: Martin Crutsinger, "Mighty Dollar Fading," Associated Press, May 30, 2002.

2.25 Suppose that a developing country pegs the value of its currency against the U.S. dollar. Further, suppose that the exchange rate between the dollar and the yen and between the dollar and the euro increases. What will be the impact on the ability of the developing country to export goods and services to Japan and Europe? Briefly explain.

2.26 Graph the demand and supply of Chinese yuan for U.S. dollars and label each axis. To maintain its pegged exchange rate, the Chinese central bank used yuan to buy large quantities of U.S. dollars. Indicate whether the pegged exchange rate was above or below the market equilibrium exchange rate and show on the graph the quantity of yuan the Chinese central bank would have to supply each trading period.

2.27 According to a newspaper story, "American manufacturers contend the yuan is undervalued by as much as 40 percent. . . . The [Bush] administration is under growing pressure to take a get-tough approach with the Chinese in light of soaring trade deficits. They include an imbalance of $233 billion last year with China alone, the largest ever recorded with a single country." What does it mean to say the yuan is undervalued? Why would American manufacturers be concerned that the yuan is undervalued? How does the yuan exchange rate affect the balance of trade in the United States and China?

Source: Martin Crutsinger, "Beijing Prodded on Currency Issue," *Houston Chronicle*, June 20, 2007.

2.28 **(Related to the *Making the Connection* on page 629)** The following is from an article in the *Wall Street Journal* on changes in the Korean economy:

> The biggest is a change in where Korean companies are finding growth. It is no longer just the U.S. and Europe, markets where Samsung, Hyundai and other big exporters have long focused on. Instead, it is in places like China, central Asia and the Middle East. . . . The broader trend is that global economic growth is less tied to the U.S., a phenomenon that has been called "decoupling."

If the trend identified in this article is correct, what are the implications for the policy of the Korean government with respect to the dollar–won exchange rate?

Source: Evan Ramstad, "Korean Stock Rally Shows a Different Picture," *Wall Street Journal*, June 19, 2007, p. C3.

2.29 **(Related to *Solved Problem 18-2B* on page 630)** An article in the *Wall Street Journal* stated the following:

> Romania's central bank vowed to intervene to defend the country's currency, the leu. . . . But traders said authorities will have to work quickly to maintain confidence in the currency. . . . With reserves at just $1.59 billion . . . the central bank's arsenal for staving off further speculation is limited.

Is it likely that the Romanian central bank was trying to defend an exchange rate that is above or below the exchange rate that would prevail in the absence of intervention? Draw a graph to illustrate your answer. Briefly explain what traders would have to gain by speculating against the leu and what the Romanian central bank's dollar reserves have to do with its ability to defend the value of the Romanian currency.

Source: John Reed, "Romania Vows to Defend Currency if Necessary," *Wall Street Journal*, March 19, 1999.

2.30 **(Related to the *Chapter Opener* on page 614)** For 35 years, the Montreal Expos played major league baseball in the French-speaking Canadian province of Quebec, before relocating in 2005 to Washington, DC. All but one of the other 29 major league baseball teams were based in cities in the United States. Before they moved to Washington (and became the Nationals), an analysis of the Expos contained the following observation: "Numerous factors, from the language barrier to the floating Canadian dollar, conspire to make baseball in Quebec a difficult proposition." What is meant by a "floating" Canadian dollar? Why would a floating Canadian dollar make it difficult to operate a major league baseball team in Montreal?

Source: Jeff Bower et al., *Baseball Prospectus, 2002*, Washington, DC: Brassey, 2002, p. 358.

2.31 **(Related to the *Chapter Opener* on page 614)** In 2001, Molson, a Canadian firm, sold the Montreal Canadiens ice hockey team to George Gillett, Jr., a U.S. ski resort operator. What was a key problem that Molson encountered in operating the Canadiens? Would Gillett, as a U.S. citizen, be better able to deal with this problem? Briefly explain.

>> End Learning Objective 18.2

18.3 LEARNING OBJECTIVE 18.3 | Discuss the growth of international capital markets, **pages 631–633.**

International Capital Markets

Summary

A key reason that exchange rates fluctuate is that investors seek out the best investments they can find anywhere in the world. Since 1980, the markets for stocks and bonds have become global. Foreign purchases of U.S. corporate bonds and stocks and U.S. government bonds have increased greatly just in the period since 1995. As a result, firms around the world are no longer forced to rely only on the savings of domestic households for funds.

Review Questions

3.1 What were the main factors behind the globalization of capital markets in the 1980s and 1990s?

3.2 Are foreign investors more likely to buy U.S. government bonds, U.S. corporate bonds, or U.S. corporate stocks?

Problems and Applications

3.3 Why are foreign investors more likely to invest in U.S. government bonds than in U.S. corporate stocks and bonds?

3.4 The text states that "the globalization of financial markets has helped increase growth and efficiency in the world economy." Briefly explain which aspects of globalization help to increase growth in the world economy.

>> End Learning Objective 18.3

Appendix

The Gold Standard and the Bretton Woods System

LEARNING OBJECTIVE

Explain the gold standard and the Bretton Woods system.

It is easier to understand the current exchange rate system by considering further two earlier systems: the gold standard and the Bretton Woods system, which together lasted from the early nineteenth century through the early 1970s.

The Gold Standard

As we saw in this chapter, under the gold standard, the currency of a country consisted of gold coins and paper currency that could be redeemed in gold. Great Britain adopted the gold standard in 1816, but as late as 1870, only a few nations had followed. In the late nineteenth century, however, Great Britain's share of world trade had increased, as had its overseas investments. The dominant position of Great Britain in the world economy motivated other countries to adopt the gold standard. By 1913, every country in Europe, except Spain and Bulgaria, and most countries in the Western Hemisphere had adopted the gold standard.

Under the gold standard, the exchange rate between two currencies was automatically determined by the quantity of gold in each currency. If there was one-fifth of an ounce of gold in a U.S. dollar and one ounce of gold in a British pound, the price of gold in the United States would be \$5 per ounce, and the price of gold in Britain would be £1 per ounce. The exchange rate would be \$5 = £1.

The End of the Gold Standard

From a modern point of view, the greatest drawback to the gold standard was that the central bank lacked control of the money supply. The size of a country's money supply depended on its gold supply, which could be greatly affected by chance discoveries of gold or by technological change in gold mining. For example, the gold discoveries in California in 1849 and Alaska in the 1890s caused rapid increases in the U.S. money supply. Because the central bank cannot determine how much gold will be discovered, it lacks the control of the money supply necessary to pursue an active monetary policy. During wartime, countries usually went off the gold standard to allow their central banks to expand the money supply as rapidly as was necessary to pay for the war. Britain abandoned the gold standard at the beginning of World War I in 1914 and did not resume redeeming its paper currency for gold until 1925.

When the Great Depression began in 1929, governments came under pressure to abandon the gold standard to allow their central banks to pursue active monetary policies. In 1931, Great Britain became the first major country to abandon the gold standard.

A number of other countries also went off the gold standard that year. The United States remained on the gold standard until 1933, and a few countries, including France, Italy, and Belgium, stayed on even longer. By the late 1930s, the gold standard had collapsed.

The earlier a country abandoned the gold standard, the easier time it had fighting the Depression with expansionary monetary policies. The countries that abandoned the gold standard by 1932 suffered an average decline in production of only 3 percent between 1929 and 1934. The countries that stayed on the gold standard until 1933 or later suffered an average decline of more than 30 percent. The devastating economic performance of the countries that stayed on the gold standard the longest during the 1930s is the key reason no attempt was made to bring back the gold standard in later years.

The Bretton Woods System

In addition to the collapse of the gold standard, the global economy had suffered during the 1930s from tariff wars. The United States had started the tariff wars in June 1930 by enacting the Smoot-Hawley Tariff, which raised the average U.S. tariff rate to more than 50 percent. Many other countries raised tariffs during the next few years, leading to a collapse in world trade.

As World War II was coming to an end, economists and government officials in the United States and Europe concluded that they had to restore the international economic system to avoid another depression. In 1947, the United States and most other major countries, apart from the Soviet Union, began participating in the General Agreement on Tariffs and Trade (GATT), under which they worked to reduce trade barriers. The GATT was very successful in sponsoring rounds of negotiations among countries, which led to sharp declines in tariffs. U.S. tariffs dropped from an average rate of more than 50 percent in the early 1930s to an average rate of less than 2 percent today. In 1995, the GATT was replaced by the World Trade Organization (WTO), which has similar objectives.

The effort to develop a new exchange rate system to replace the gold standard was more complicated than establishing the GATT. A conference held in Bretton Woods, New Hampshire, in 1944 set up a system in which the United States pledged to buy or sell gold at a fixed price of $35 per ounce. The central banks of all other members of the new **Bretton Woods system** pledged to buy and sell their currencies at a fixed rate against the dollar. By fixing their exchange rates against the dollar, these countries were fixing the exchange rates among their currencies as well. Unlike under the gold standard, neither the United States nor any other country was willing to redeem its paper currency for gold domestically. The United States would redeem dollars for gold only if they were presented by a foreign central bank. The United States continued the prohibition, first enacted in the early 1930s, against private citizens owning gold, unless they were jewelers or rare coin collectors. The prohibition was not lifted until the 1970s, when it again became possible for Americans to own gold as an investment.

Bretton Woods system An exchange rate system that lasted from 1944 to 1971, under which countries pledged to buy and sell their currencies at a fixed rate against the dollar.

Under the Bretton Woods system, central banks were committed to selling dollars in exchange for their own currencies. This commitment required them to hold *dollar reserves.* If a central bank ran out of dollar reserves, it could borrow them from the newly created **International Monetary Fund (IMF)**. In addition to providing loans to central banks that were short of dollar reserves, the IMF would oversee the operation of the system and approve adjustments to the agreed-on fixed exchange rates.

International Monetary Fund (IMF) An international organization that provides foreign currency loans to central banks and oversees the operation of the international monetary system.

Under the Bretton Woods system, a fixed exchange rate was known as a *par exchange rate.* If the par exchange rate was not the same as the exchange rate that would have been determined in the market, the result would be a surplus or a shortage. For example, Figure 18A-1 shows the exchange rate between the dollar and the British pound. The figure is drawn from the British point of view, so we measure the exchange rate on the vertical axis as dollars per pound. In this case, the par exchange rate between the dollar and the pound is above the equilibrium exchange rate as determined by supply and demand.

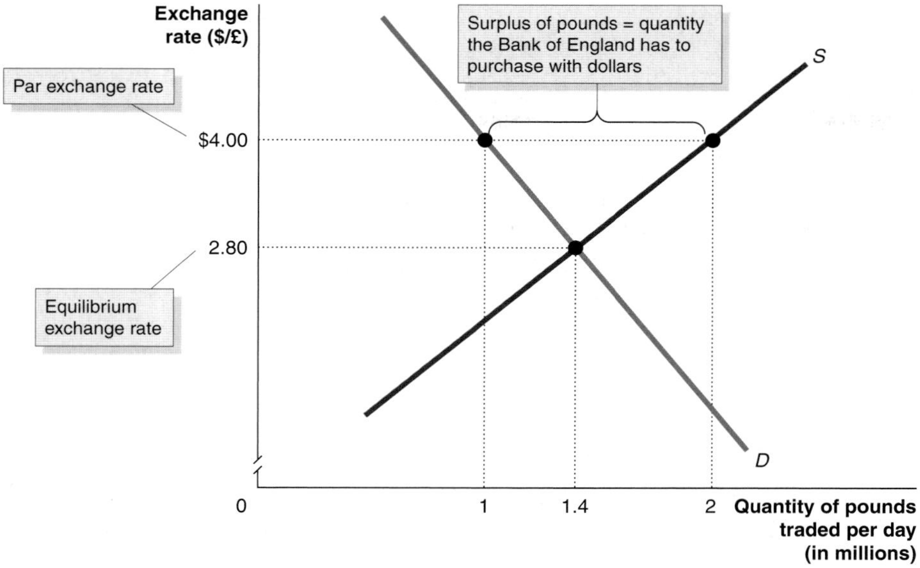

Figure 18A-1

A Fixed Exchange Rate above Equilibrium Results in a Surplus of Pounds

Under the Bretton Woods system, if the par exchange rate was above equilibrium, the result would be a surplus of domestic currency in the foreign exchange market. If the par exchange rate was below equilibrium, the result would be a shortage of domestic currency. In the figure, the par exchange rate between the pound and the dollar is $4 = £1, whereas the equilibrium exchange rate is $2.80 = £1. This gap forces the Bank of England to buy £1 million per day in exchange for dollars.

In this example, at the par exchange rate of $4 per pound, the quantity of pounds demanded by people wanting to buy British goods and services or wanting to invest in British assets is smaller than the quantity of pounds supplied by people who would like to exchange them for dollars. As a result, the Bank of England must use dollars to buy the surplus of £1 million per day. Only at an exchange rate of $2.80 per pound would the surplus be eliminated. If the par exchange rate were below the equilibrium exchange rate, there would be a shortage of domestic currency in the foreign exchange market.

A persistent shortage or surplus of a currency under the Bretton Woods system was seen as evidence of a *fundamental disequilibrium* in a country's exchange rate. After consulting with the IMF, countries in this position were allowed to adjust their exchange rates. In the early years of the Bretton Woods system, many countries found that their currencies were *overvalued* versus the dollar, meaning that their par exchange rates were too high. A reduction in a fixed exchange rate is a **devaluation**. An increase in a fixed exchange rate is a **revaluation**. In 1949, there was a devaluation of several currencies, including the British pound, reflecting the fact that those currencies had been overvalued against the dollar.

Devaluation A reduction in a fixed exchange rate.

Revaluation An increase in a fixed exchange rate.

The Collapse of the Bretton Woods System

By the late 1960s, the Bretton Woods system faced two severe problems. The first was that after 1963, the total number of dollars held by foreign central banks was larger than the gold reserves of the United States. In practice, most central banks—the Bank of France was the main exception—rarely redeemed dollars for gold. But the basis of the system was a credible promise by the United States to redeem dollars for gold if called upon to do so. By the late 1960s, as the gap between the dollars held by foreign central banks and the gold reserves of the United States grew larger and larger, the credibility of the U.S. promise to redeem dollars for gold was called into question.

The second problem the Bretton Woods system faced was that some countries with undervalued currencies, particularly West Germany, were unwilling to revalue their currencies. Governments resisted revaluation because it would have increased the prices of their countries' exports. Many German firms, such as Volkswagen, put pressure on the government not to endanger their sales in the U.S. market by raising

Figure 18A-2

West Germany's Undervalued Exchange Rate

The Bundesbank, the German central bank, was committed under the Bretton Woods system to defending a par exchange rate of $0.27 per deutsche mark (DM). Because this exchange rate was lower than what the equilibrium market exchange rate would have been, there was a shortage of deutsche marks in the foreign exchange market. The Bundesbank had to supply deutsche marks equal to the shortage in exchange for dollars. The shortage in the figure is equal to 1 billion deutsche marks per day.

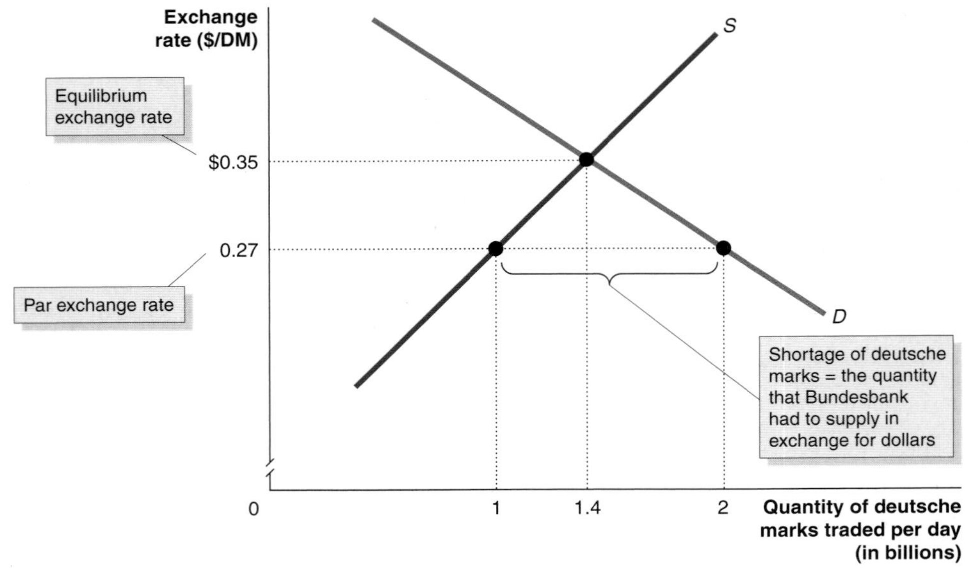

the exchange rate of the deutsche mark against the dollar. Figure 18A-2 shows the situation faced by the German government in 1971. The figure takes the German point of view, so the exchange rate is expressed in terms of dollars per deutsche mark.

Under the Bretton Woods system, the Bundesbank, the German central bank, was required to buy and sell deutsche marks for dollars at a rate of $0.27 per deutsche mark. The equilibrium that would have prevailed in the foreign exchange market if the Bundesbank had not intervened was about $0.35 per deutsche mark. Because the par exchange rate was below the equilibrium exchange rate, the quantity of deutsche marks demanded by people wanting to buy German goods and services or wanting to invest in German assets was greater than the quantity of deutsche marks supplied by people who wanted to exchange them for dollars. To maintain the exchange rate at $0.27 per deutsche mark, the Bundesbank had to buy dollars and sell deutsche marks. The number of deutsche marks supplied by the Bundesbank was equal to the shortage of deutsche marks at the par exchange rate.

By selling deutsche marks and buying dollars to defend the par exchange rate, the Bundesbank was increasing the West German money supply, risking an increase in the inflation rate. Because Germany had suffered a devastating hyperinflation during the 1920s, the fear of inflation was greater in Germany than in any other industrial country. No German government could survive politically if it allowed a significant increase in inflation. Knowing this fact, many investors in Germany and elsewhere became convinced that eventually, the German government would have to allow a revaluation of the mark.

Capital controls Limits on the flow of foreign exchange and financial investment across countries.

During the 1960s, most European countries, including Germany, relaxed their *capital controls*. **Capital controls** are limits on the flow of foreign exchange and financial investment across countries. The loosening of capital controls made it easier for investors to *speculate* on changes in exchange rates. For instance, an investor in the United States could sell $1 million and receive about 3.7 million deutsche marks at the par exchange rate of $0.27 per deutsche mark. If the exchange rate rose to $0.35 per deutsche mark, the investor could then exchange deutsche marks for dollars, receiving $1.3 million at the new exchange rate: a return of 30 percent on an initial $1 million investment. The more convinced investors became that Germany would have to allow a revaluation, the more dollars they exchanged for deutsche marks. Figure 18A-3 shows the results.

The increased demand for deutsche marks by investors hoping to make a profit from the expected revaluation of the mark shifted the demand curve for marks to the right, from D_1 to D_2. Because of this expectation, the Bundesbank had to increase the

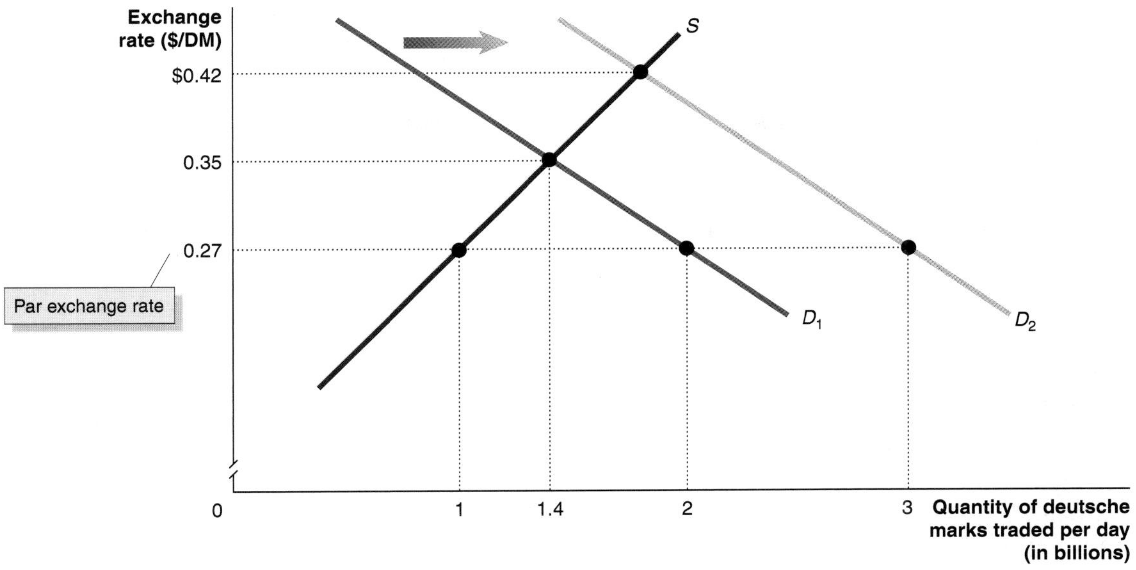

Figure 18A-3 | Destabilizing Speculation against the Deutsche Mark, 1971

In 1971, the par exchange rate of $0.27 = DM1 was below the equilibrium exchange rate of $0.35 = DM1. As investors became convinced that West Germany would have to revalue the deutsche mark, they increased their demand for marks from D_1 to D_2. The new equilibrium exchange rate became $0.42 = DM1. This increase in demand raised the quantity of marks the Bundesbank had to supply in exchange for dollars to defend the par exchange rate from DM1 billion to DM2 billion per day.

marks it supplied in exchange for dollars, raising further the risk of inflation in Germany. As we saw in the chapter, because these actions by investors make it more difficult to maintain a fixed exchange rate, they are referred to as *destabilizing speculation*. By May 1971, the Bundesbank had to buy more than $1 billion per day to support the fixed exchange rate against the dollar. Finally, on May 5, the West German government decided to allow the mark to float. In August, President Richard Nixon decided to abandon the U.S. commitment to redeem dollars for gold. Attempts were made over the next two years to reach a compromise that would restore a fixed exchange rate system, but by 1973, the Bretton Woods system was effectively dead.

Key Terms

Bretton Woods system, p. 642
Capital controls, p. 644
Devaluation, p. 643
International Monetary Fund (IMF), p. 642
Revaluation, p. 643

LEARNING OBJECTIVE Explain the gold standard and the Bretton Woods system, **pages 641–645.**

myeconlab Get Ahead of the Curve Visit www.myeconlab.com to complete these exercises online and get instant feedback.

Review Questions

18A.1 What determined the exchange rates among currencies under the gold standard? Why did the gold standard collapse?

18A.2 Briefly describe how the Bretton Woods system operated.

18A.3 What is the difference between a devaluation and a revaluation?

18A.4 What are capital controls?

18A.5 What role did the International Monetary Fund play in the Bretton Woods system?

18A.6 What is destabilizing speculation? What role did it play in the collapse of the Bretton Woods system?

Problems and Applications

18A.7 Suppose that under the gold standard, there was one-fifth of an ounce of gold in a U.S. dollar and one ounce of gold in a British pound. Demonstrate that if the exchange rate between the dollar and the pound was \$4 = £1, rather than \$5 = £1, you could make unlimited profits by buying gold in one country and selling it in the other. If the exchange rate was \$6 = £1, how would your strategy change? For simplicity, assume that there was no cost to shipping gold from one country to the other.

18A.8 An article in the *Economist* observes that "Enthusiasm for the gold standard evaporated in the 1930s, when it made dreadful conditions worse." How did the gold standard make dreadful conditions worse during the 1930s?

Source: "Heading for a Fall, by Fiat?" *Economist*, February 26, 2004.

18A.9 According to an article in the *Economist*, when most countries left the gold standard in the 1930s, in South Africa, "the mining industry flourished." Briefly explain why the end of the gold standard might be good news for the owners of gold mines.

Source: "Johannesburg," *Economist*, August 18, 2004.

18A.10 By the mid-1960s, the price of gold on the London market had increased to more than \$35 per ounce. (Remember that it was not legal during these years for investors in the United States to own gold.) Would this have happened if foreign investors had believed that the U.S. commitment to buy and sell gold at \$35 per ounce under the Bretton Woods system would continue indefinitely? Briefly explain.

18A.11 An article in the *New York Times* states that during the 1970s, the "United States abandon[ed] the gold standard, a decision that sent the yen rocketing." Is the author of this article correct that the United States abandoned the gold standard in the 1970s? What action of the United States during the 1970s would have caused the value of the yen to rise against the dollar?

Source: Ken Belson, "Did He Fiddle While Japan Burned?" *New York Times*, February 26, 2003.

18A.12 An article summarizing the United Kingdom's experience with the gold standard makes the following statement about an event in August 1927: "The New York Federal Reserve Bank cuts its rediscount rate to 3.5% from 4%, partly in order to help the U.K. to stay on the gold standard." Why would a fall in interest rates in the United States help the United Kingdom to stay on the gold standard?

Source: Worth Civils, "A History of the Pound: 1925–2007," *Wall Street Journal*, April 18, 2007.

18A.13 One economist has argued that the East Asian exchange rate crisis of the late 1990s was due to "the simple failure of governments to remember the lessons from the breakdown of the Bretton Woods System." What are the lessons from the breakdown of the Bretton Woods system? In what sense did the East Asian governments fail to learn these lessons?

Source: Thomas D. Willett, "Crying for Argentina," *Milken Institute Review*, Second Quarter 2002, p. 54.

18A.14 An article in the *Wall Street Journal* argues that "The Bretton Woods system ran into trouble in the 1960s, in part because U.S. trade deficits mounted." Why would increases in the U.S. trade deficit cause problems for the Bretton Woods system?

Source: Jon E. Hilsenrath and Mary Kissel, "Currency Decision Marks Small Shift toward Flexibility," *Wall Street Journal*, July 22, 2005.

18A.15 Thomas Mayer, an economist at the German bank, Deutsche Bank, wrote that "following the breakup of the Bretton Woods system that had kept the mark tied to the U.S. dollar, the Bundesbank adopted a monetary policy strategy that allowed it to keep its eyes on ensuring price stability in the long run." Why might keeping the mark tied to the value of the dollar have made it difficult for the Bundesbank to pursue a policy of price stability?

Source: Thomas Mayer, "Euro Down," *Wall Street Journal*, July 21, 2005.

18A.16 In 2007, Jean-Claude Trichet, the president of the European Central Bank, argued that "the [Bretton Woods] system's collapse in the '70s seriously threatened the process of economic integration in Europe. However, Europe's leaders rose to the challenge." Why would the collapse of the Bretton Woods system have threatened economic integration in Europe? How did the European countries eventually replace the system?

Source: Jean-Claude Trichet, "Europe Turns 50," *Wall Street Journal*, March 23, 2007, p. A11.

>> End Appendix Learning Objective

Glossary

A

Absolute advantage The ability of an individual, a firm, or a country to produce more of a good or service than competitors, using the same amount of resources.

Accounting profit A firm's net income measured by revenue minus operating expenses and taxes paid.

Adverse selection The situation in which one party to a transaction takes advantage of knowing more than the other party to the transaction.

Aggregate demand and aggregate supply model A model that explains short-run fluctuations in real GDP and the price level.

Aggregate demand curve A curve that shows the relationship between the price level and the quantity of real GDP demanded by households, firms, and the government.

Aggregate expenditure (*AE*) The total amount of spending in the economy: the sum of consumption, planned investment, government purchases, and net exports.

Aggregate expenditure model A macroeconomic model that focuses on the relationship between total spending and real GDP, assuming that the price level is constant.

Allocative efficiency A state of the economy in which production represents consumer preferences; in particular, every good or service is produced up to the point where the last unit provides a marginal benefit to consumers equal to the marginal cost of producing it.

Antitrust laws Laws aimed at eliminating collusion and promoting competition among firms.

Arrow impossibility theorem A mathematical theorem that holds that no system of voting can be devised that will consistently represent the underlying preferences of voters.

Asset Anything of value owned by a person or a firm.

Asymmetric information A situation in which one party to an economic transaction has less information than the other party.

Autarky A situation in which a country does not trade with other countries.

Automatic stabilizers Government spending and taxes that automatically increase or decrease along with the business cycle.

Autonomous expenditure An expenditure that does not depend on the level of GDP.

Average fixed cost Fixed cost divided by the quantity of output produced.

Average product of labor The total output produced by a firm divided by the quantity of workers.

Average revenue (*AR*) Total revenue divided by the quantity of the product sold.

Average tax rate Total tax paid divided by total income.

Average total cost Total cost divided by the quantity of output produced.

Average variable cost Variable cost divided by the quantity of output produced.

B

Balance of payments The record of a country's trade with other countries in goods, services, and assets.

Balance of trade The difference between the value of the goods a country exports and the value of the goods a country imports.

Balance sheet A financial statement that sums up a firm's financial position on a particular day, usually the end of a quarter or year.

Bank panic A situation in which many banks experience runs at the same time.

Bank run A situation in which many depositors simultaneously decide to withdraw money from a bank.

Barrier to entry Anything that keeps new firms from entering an industry in which firms are earning economic profits.

Behavioral economics The study of situations in which people make choices that do not appear to be economically rational.

Black market A market in which buying and selling take place at prices that violate government price regulations.

Bond A financial security that represents a promise to repay a fixed amount of funds.

Brand management The actions of a firm intended to maintain the differentiation of a product over time.

Bretton Woods System An exchange rate system that lasted from 1944 to 1971, under which countries pledged to buy and sell their currencies at a fixed rate against the dollar.

Budget constraint The limited amount of income available to consumers to spend on goods and services.

Budget deficit The situation in which the government's expenditures are greater than its tax revenue.

Budget surplus The situation in which the government's expenditures are less than its tax revenue.

Business cycle Alternating periods of economic expansion and economic recession.

Business strategy Actions taken by a firm to achieve a goal, such as maximizing profits.

C

Capital account The part of the balance of payments that records relatively minor transactions, such as migrants' transfers, and sales and purchases of nonproduced, nonfinancial assets.

Capital controls Limits on the flow of foreign exchange and financial investment across countries.

Capital Manufactured goods that are used to produce other goods and services.

Cartel A group of firms that collude by agreeing to restrict output to increase prices and profits.

Cash flow The difference between the cash revenues received by a firm and the cash spending by the firm.

Catch-up The prediction that the level of GDP per capita (or income per capita) in poor countries will grow faster than in rich countries.

Centrally planned economy An economy in which the government decides how economic resources will be allocated.

***Ceteris paribus* ("all else equal")** The requirement that when analyzing the relationship between two variables—such as price and quantity demanded—other variables must be held constant.

Circular-flow diagram A model that illustrates how participants in markets are linked.

Closed economy An economy that has no interactions in trade or finance with other countries.

Coase theorem The argument of economist Ronald Coase that if transactions costs are low, private bargaining will result in an efficient solution to the problem of externalities.

Collusion An agreement among firms to charge the same price or otherwise not to compete.

Command and control approach An approach that involves the government imposing quantitative limits on the amount of pollution firms are allowed to emit or requiring firms to install specific pollution control devices.

Commodity money A good used as money that also has value independent of its use as money.

Common resource A good that is rival but not excludable.

Comparative advantage The ability of an individual, a firm, or a country to produce a good or service at a lower opportunity cost than competitors.

Compensating differentials Higher wages that compensate workers for unpleasant aspects of a job.

Competitive market equilibrium A market equilibrium with many buyers and many sellers.

Complements Goods and services that are used together.

Constant returns to scale The situation when a firm's long-run average costs remain unchanged as it increases output.

Consumer price index (CPI) An average of the prices of the goods and services purchased by the typical urban family of four.

Consumer surplus The difference between the highest price a consumer is willing to pay and the price the consumer actually pays.

Consumption function The relationship between consumption spending and disposable income.

Consumption Spending by households on goods and services, not including spending on new houses.

Contractionary monetary policy The Federal Reserve's adjusting the money supply to increase interest rates to reduce inflation.

Cooperative equilibrium An equilibrium in a game in which players cooperate to increase their mutual payoff.

Copyright A government-granted exclusive right to produce and sell a creation.

Corporate governance The way in which a corporation is structured and the effect a corporation's structure has on the firm's behavior.

Corporation A legal form of business that provides the owners with limited liability.

Coupon payment An interest payment on a bond.

Cross-price elasticity of demand The percentage change in quantity demanded of one good divided by the percentage change in the price of another good.

Crowding out A decline in private expenditures as a result of an increase in government purchases.

Currency appreciation An increase in the market value of one currency relative to another currency.

Currency depreciation A decrease in the market value of one currency relative to another currency.

Current account The part of the balance of payments that records a country's net exports, net investment income, and net transfers.

Cyclical unemployment Unemployment caused by a business cycle recession.

Cyclically adjusted budget deficit or surplus The deficit or surplus in the federal government's budget if the economy were at potential GDP.

D

Deadweight loss The reduction in economic surplus resulting from a market not being in competitive equilibrium.

Deflation A decline in the price level.

Demand curve A curve that shows the relationship between the price of a product and the quantity of the product demanded.

Demand schedule A table showing the relationship between the price of a product and the quantity of the product demanded.

Demographics The characteristics of a population with respect to age, race, and gender.

Derived demand The demand for a factor of production that is derived from the demand for the good the factor produces.

Devaluation A reduction in a fixed exchange rate.

Direct finance A flow of funds from savers to firms through financial markets, such as the New York Stock Exchange.

Discount loans Loans the Federal Reserve makes to banks.

Discount rate The interest rate the Federal Reserve charges on discount loans.

Discouraged workers People who are available for work but have not looked for a job during the previous four weeks because they believe no jobs are available for them.

Diseconomies of scale The situation when a firm's long-run average costs rise as the firm increases output.

Disinflation A significant reduction in the inflation rate.

Dividends Payments by a corporation to its shareholders.

Dominant strategy A strategy that is the best for a firm, no matter what strategies other firms use.

Dumping Selling a product for a price below its cost of production.

E

Economic discrimination Paying a person a lower wage or excluding a person from an occupation on the basis of an irrelevant characteristic such as race or gender.

Economic efficiency A market outcome in which the marginal benefit to consumers of the last unit produced is equal to its marginal cost of production and in which the sum of consumer surplus and producer surplus is at a maximum.

Economic growth The ability of an economy to produce increasing quantities of goods and services.

Economic growth model A model that explains growth rate changes in real GDP per capita in the long run.

Economic loss The situation in which a firm's total revenue is less than its total cost, including all implicit costs.

Economic model A simplified version of reality used to analyze real-world economic situations.

Economic profit A firm's revenues minus all its costs, implicit and explicit.

Economic rent (or pure rent) The price of a factor of production that is in fixed supply.

Economic surplus The sum of consumer surplus and producer surplus.

Economic variable Something measurable that can have different values, such as the wages of software programmers.

Economics The study of the choices people make to attain their goals, given their scarce resources.

Economies of scale The situation when a firm's long-run average costs fall as it increases output.

Efficiency wage A higher-than-market wage that a firm pays to increase worker productivity.

Elastic demand Demand is elastic when the percentage change in quantity demanded is *greater* than the percentage change in price, so the price elasticity is *greater* than 1 in absolute value.

Elasticity A measure of how much one economic variable responds to changes in another economic variable.

Endowment effect The tendency of people to be unwilling to sell a good they already own even if they are offered a price that is greater than the price they would be willing to pay to buy the good if they didn't already own it.

Entrepreneur Someone who operates a business, bringing together the factors of production—labor, capital, and natural resources—to produce goods and services.

Equity The fair distribution of economic benefits.

Euro The common currency of many European countries.

Excess burden The efficiency loss to the economy that results from a tax causing a reduction in the quantity of a good produced; also known as the deadweight loss.

Excess reserves Reserves that banks hold over and above the legal requirement.

Exchange rate system An agreement among countries on how exchange rates should be determined.

Excludability The situation in which anyone who does not pay for a good cannot consume it.

Expansion path A curve that shows a firm's cost-minimizing combination of inputs for every level of output.

Expansion The period of a business cycle during which total production and total employment are increasing.

Expansionary monetary policy The Federal Reserve's increasing the money supply and decreasing interest rates to increase real GDP.

Explicit cost A cost that involves spending money.

Exports Goods and services produced domestically but sold to other countries.

External economies Reductions in a firm's costs that result from an increase in the size of an industry.

Externality A benefit or cost that affects someone who is not directly involved in the production or consumption of a good or service.

F

Factor markets Markets for the factors of production, such as labor, capital, natural resources, and entrepreneurial ability.

Factors of production Labor, capital, natural resources, and other inputs used to produce goods and services.

Federal funds rate The interest rate banks charge each other for overnight loans.

Federal Open Market Committee (FOMC) The Federal Reserve committee responsible for open market operations and managing the money supply in the United States.

Federal Reserve System The central bank of the United States.

Fiat money Money, such as paper currency, that is authorized by a central bank or governmental body and that does not have to be exchanged by the central bank for gold or some other commodity money.

Final good or service A good or service purchased by a final user.

Financial account The part of the balance of payments that records purchases of assets a country has made abroad and foreign purchases of assets in the country.

Financial intermediaries Firms, such as banks, mutual funds, pension funds, and insurance companies, that borrow funds from savers and lend them to borrowers.

Financial markets Markets where financial securities, such as stocks and bonds, are bought and sold.

Financial system The system of financial markets and financial intermediaries through which firms acquire funds from households.

Fiscal policy Changes in federal taxes and purchases that are intended to achieve macroeconomic policy objectives, such as high employment, price stability, and high rates of economic growth.

Fixed costs Costs that remain constant as output changes.

Fixed exchange rate system A system under which countries agree to keep the exchange rates among their currencies fixed.

Floating currency The outcome of a country allowing its currency's exchange rate to be determined by demand and supply.

Foreign direct investment (FDI) The purchase or building by a corporation of a facility in a foreign country.

Foreign portfolio investment The purchase by an individual or a firm of stocks or bonds issued in another country.

Fractional reserve banking system A banking system in which banks keep less than 100 percent of deposits as reserves.

Free market A market with few government restrictions on how a good or service can be produced or sold or on how a factor of production can be employed.

Free riding Benefiting from a good without paying for it.

Free trade Trade between countries that is without government restrictions.

Frictional unemployment Short-term unemployment that arises from the process of matching workers with jobs.

G

Game theory The study of how people make decisions in situations in which attaining their goals depends on their interactions with others; in economics, the study of the decisions of firms in industries where the profits of each firm depend on its interactions with other firms.

GDP deflator A measure of the price level, calculated by dividing nominal GDP by real GDP and multiplying by 100.

Globalization The process of countries becoming more open to foreign trade and investment.

Government purchases Spending by federal, state, and local governments on goods and services.

Gross domestic product (GDP) The market value of all final goods and services produced in a country during a period of time, typically one year.

H

Horizontal merger A merger between firms in the same industry.

Human capital The accumulated knowledge and skills that workers acquire from education and training or from their life experiences.

I

Implicit cost A nonmonetary opportunity cost.

Imports Goods and services bought domestically but produced in other countries.

Income effect The change in the quantity demanded of a good that results from the effect of a change in price on consumer purchasing power, holding all other factors constant.

Income elasticity of demand A measure of the responsiveness of quantity demanded to changes in income, measured by the percentage change in quantity demanded divided by the percentage change in income.

Income statement A financial statement that sums up a firm's revenues, costs, and profit over a period of time.

Indifference curve A curve that shows the combinations of consumption bundles that give the consumer the same utility.

Indirect finance A flow of funds from savers to borrowers through financial intermediaries such as banks. Intermediaries raise funds from savers to lend to firms (and other borrowers).

Industrial Revolution The application of mechanical power to the production of goods, beginning in England around 1750.

Inelastic demand Demand is inelastic when the percentage change in quantity demanded is *less* than the percentage change in price, so the price elasticity is *less* than 1 in absolute value.

Inferior good A good for which the demand increases as income falls and decreases as income rises.

Inflation targeting Conducting monetary policy so as to commit the central bank to achieving a publicly announced level of inflation.

Interest rate The cost of borrowing funds, usually expressed as a percentage of the amount borrowed.

Intermediate good or service A good or service that is an input into another good or service, such as a tire on a truck.

International Monetary Fund (IMF) An international organization that provides foreign currency loans to central banks and oversees the operation of the international monetary system.

Inventories Goods that have been produced but not yet sold.

Investment Spending by firms on new factories, office buildings, machinery, and additions to inventories, and spending by households on new houses.

Isocost line All the combinations of two inputs, such as capital and labor, that have the same total cost.

Isoquant A curve that shows all the combinations of two inputs, such as capital and labor, that will produce the same level of output.

K

Keynesian revolution The name given to the widespread acceptance during the 1930s and 1940s of John Maynard Keynes's macroeconomic model.

L

Labor force The sum of employed and unemployed workers in the economy.

Labor force participation rate The percentage of the working-age population in the labor force.

Labor productivity The quantity of goods and services that can be produced by one worker or by one hour of work.

Labor union An organization of employees that has the legal right to bargain with employers about wages and working conditions.

Law of demand The rule that, holding everything else constant, when the price of a product falls, the quantity demanded of the product will increase, and when the price of a product rises, the quantity demanded of the product will decrease.

Law of diminishing marginal utility The principle that consumers experience diminishing additional satisfaction as they consume more of a good or service during a given period of time.

Law of diminishing returns The principle that, at some point, adding more of a variable input, such as labor, to the same amount of a fixed input, such as capital, will cause the marginal product of the variable input to decline.

Law of supply The rule that, holding everything else constant, increases in price cause increases in the quantity supplied, and decreases in price cause decreases in the quantity supplied.

Liability Anything owed by a person or a firm.

Limited liability The legal provision that shields owners of a corporation from losing more than they have invested in the firm.

Long run The period of time in which a firm can vary all its inputs, adopt new technology, and increase or decrease the size of its physical plant.

Long-run aggregate supply curve A curve that shows the relationship in the long run between the price level and the quantity of real GDP supplied.

Long-run average cost curve A curve showing the lowest cost at which a firm is able to produce a given quantity of output in the long run, when no inputs are fixed.

Long-run competitive equilibrium The situation in which the entry and exit of firms has resulted in the typical firm breaking even.

Long-run economic growth The process by which rising productivity increases the average standard of living.

Long-run supply curve A curve that shows the relationship in the long run between market price and the quantity supplied.

Lorenz curve A curve that shows the distribution of income by arraying incomes from lowest to highest on the horizontal axis and indicating the cumulative fraction of income earned by each fraction of households on the vertical axis.

M

M1 The narrowest definition of the money supply: The sum of currency in circulation, checking account deposits in banks, and holdings of traveler's checks.

M2 A broader definition of the money supply: M1 plus savings account balances, small-denomination time deposits, balances in money market deposit accounts in banks, and noninstitutional money market fund shares.

Macroeconomics The study of the economy as a whole, including topics such as inflation, unemployment, and economic growth.

Managed float exchange rate system The current exchange rate system, under which the value of most currencies is determined by demand and supply, with occasional government intervention.

Marginal analysis Analysis that involves comparing marginal benefits and marginal costs.

Marginal benefit The additional benefit to a consumer from consuming one more unit of a good or service.

Marginal cost The change in a firm's total cost from producing one more unit of a good or service.

Marginal product of labor The additional output a firm produces as a result of hiring one more worker.

Marginal productivity theory of income distribution The theory that the distribution of income is determined by the marginal productivity of the factors of production that individuals own.

Marginal propensity to consume (*MPC*) The slope of the consumption function: The amount by which consumption spending changes when disposable income changes.

Marginal propensity to save (*MPS*) The change in saving divided by the change in disposable income.

Marginal rate of substitution (*MRS*) The slope of an indifference curve, which represents the rate at which a consumer would be willing to trade off one good for another.

Marginal rate of technical substitution (*MRTS*) The slope of an isoquant, or the rate at which a firm is able to substitute one input for another while keeping the level of output constant.

Marginal revenue (*MR*) Change in total revenue from selling one more unit of a product.

Marginal revenue product of labor (*MRP*) The change in a firm's revenue as a result of hiring one more worker.

Marginal tax rate The fraction of each additional dollar of income that must be paid in taxes.

Marginal utility (*MU*) The change in total utility a person receives from consuming one additional unit of a good or service.

Market A group of buyers and sellers of a good or service and the institution or arrangement by which they come together to trade.

Market demand The demand by all the consumers of a given good or service.

Market economy An economy in which the decisions of households and firms interacting in markets allocate economic resources.

Market equilibrium A situation in which quantity demanded equals quantity supplied.

Market failure A situation in which the market fails to produce the efficient level of output.

Market for loanable funds The interaction of borrowers and lenders that determines the market interest rate and the quantity of loanable funds exchanged.

Market power The ability of a firm to charge a price greater than marginal cost.

Marketing All the activities necessary for a firm to sell a product to a consumer.

Median voter theorem The proposition that the outcome of a majority vote is likely to represent the preferences of the voter who is in the political middle.

Menu costs The costs to firms of changing prices.

Microeconomics The study of how households and firms make choices, how they interact in markets, and how the government attempts to influence their choices.

Minimum efficient scale The level of output at which all economies of scale are exhausted.

Mixed economy An economy in which most economic decisions result from the interaction of buyers and sellers in markets but in which the government plays a significant role in the allocation of resources.

Monetarism The macroeconomic theories of Milton Friedman and his followers; particularly the idea that the quantity of money should be increased at a constant rate.

Monetary growth rule A plan for increasing the quantity of money at a fixed rate that does not respond to changes in economic conditions.

Monetary policy The actions the Federal Reserve takes to manage the money supply and interest rates to pursue macroeconomic policy objectives.

Money Assets that people are generally willing to accept in exchange for goods and services or for payment of debts.

Monopolistic competition A market structure in which barriers to entry are low and many firms compete by selling similar, but not identical, products.

Monopoly A firm that is the only seller of a good or service that does not have a close substitute.

Monopsony The sole buyer of a factor of production.

Moral hazard The actions people take after they have entered into a transaction that make the other party to the transaction worse off.

Multinational enterprise A firm that conducts operations in more than one country.

Multiplier effect The series of induced increases in consumption spending that results from an initial increase in autonomous expenditure.

Multiplier The increase in equilibrium real GDP divided by the increase in autonomous expenditure.

N

Nash equilibrium A situation in which each firm chooses the best strategy, given the strategies chosen by other firms.

Natural monopoly A situation in which economies of scale are so large that one firm can supply the entire market at a lower average total cost than can two or more firms.

Natural rate of unemployment The normal rate of unemployment, consisting of frictional unemployment plus structural unemployment.

Net exports Exports minus imports.

Net foreign investment The difference between capital outflows from a country and capital inflows, also equal to net foreign direct investment plus net foreign portfolio investment.

Network externalities The situation where the usefulness of a product increases with the number of consumers who use it.

New classical macroeconomics The macroeconomic theories of Robert Lucas and others, particularly the idea that workers and firms have rational expectations.

New growth theory A model of long-run economic growth which emphasizes that technological change is influenced by economic incentives and so is determined by the working of the market system.

Nominal exchange rate The value of one country's currency in terms of another country's currency.

Nominal GDP The value of final goods and services evaluated at current-year prices.

Nominal interest rate The stated interest rate on a loan.

Nonaccelerating inflation rate of unemployment (NAIRU) The unemployment rate at which the inflation rate has no tendency to increase or decrease.

Noncooperative equilibrium An equilibrium in a game in which players do not cooperate but pursue their own self-interest.

Normal good A good for which the demand increases as income rises and decreases as income falls.

Normative analysis Analysis concerned with what ought to be.

O

Oligopoly A market structure in which a small number of interdependent firms compete.

Open economy An economy that has interactions in trade or finance with other countries.

Open market operations The buying and selling of Treasury securities by the Federal Reserve in order to control the money supply.

Opportunity cost The highest-valued alternative that must be given up to engage in an activity.

P

Partnership A firm owned jointly by two or more persons and not organized as a corporation.

Patent The exclusive right to a product for a period of 20 years from the date the product is invented.

Payoff matrix A table that shows the payoffs that each firm earns from every combination of strategies by the firms.

Pegging The decision by a country to keep the exchange rate fixed between its currency and another currency.

Perfectly competitive market A market that meets the conditions of (1) many buyers and sellers, (2) all firms selling identical products, and (3) no barriers to new firms entering the market.

Perfectly elastic demand The case where the quantity demanded is infinitely responsive to price, and the price elasticity of demand equals infinity.

Perfectly inelastic demand The case where the quantity demanded is completely unresponsive to price, and the price elasticity of demand equals zero.

Personnel economics The application of economic analysis to human resources issues.

Per-worker production function The relationship between real GDP per hour worked and capital per hour worked, holding the level of technology constant.

Phillips curve A curve showing the short-run relationship between the unemployment rate and the inflation rate.

Pigovian taxes and subsidies Government taxes and subsidies intended to bring about an efficient level of output in the presence of externalities.

Positive analysis Analysis concerned with what is.

Potential GDP The level of GDP attained when all firms are producing at capacity.

Poverty line A level of annual income equal to three times the amount of money necessary to purchase the minimal quantity of food required for adequate nutrition.

Poverty rate The percentage of the population that is poor according to the federal government's definition.

Present value The value in today's dollars of funds to be paid or received in the future.

Price ceiling A legally determined maximum price that sellers may charge.

Price discrimination Charging different prices to different customers for the same product when the price differences are not due to differences in cost.

Price elasticity of demand The responsiveness of the quantity demanded to a change in price, measured by dividing the percentage change in the quantity demanded of a product by the percentage change in the product's price.

Price elasticity of supply The responsiveness of the quantity supplied to a change in price, measured by dividing the percentage change in the quantity supplied of a product by the percentage change in the product's price.

Price floor A legally determined minimum price that sellers may receive.

Price leadership A form of implicit collusion where one firm in an oligopoly announces a price change, which is matched by the other firms in the industry.

Price level A measure of the average prices of goods and services in the economy.

Price taker A buyer or seller that is unable to affect the market price.

Principal–agent problem A problem caused by an agent pursuing his own interests rather than the interests of the principal who hired him.

Prisoners' dilemma A game in which pursuing dominant strategies results in noncooperation that leaves everyone worse off.

Private benefit The benefit received by the consumer of a good or service.

Private cost The cost borne by the producer of a good or service.

Private good A good that is both rival and excludable.

Producer price index (PPI) An average of the prices received by producers of goods and services at all stages of the production process.

Producer surplus The difference between the lowest price a firm would be willing to accept and the price it actually receives.

Product markets Markets for goods—such as computers—and services—such as medical treatment.

Production function The relationship between the inputs employed by a firm and the maximum output it can produce with those inputs.

Production possibilities frontier (*PPF*) A curve showing the maximum attainable combinations of two products that may be produced with available resources and current technology.

Productive efficiency The situation in which a good or service is produced at the lowest possible cost.

Profit Total revenue minus total cost.

Progressive tax A tax for which people with lower incomes pay a lower percentage of their income in tax than do people with higher incomes.

Protectionism The use of trade barriers to shield domestic firms from foreign competition.

Public choice model A model that applies economic analysis to government decision making.

Public franchise A designation by the government that a firm is the only legal provider of a good or service.

Public good A good that is both nonrivalrous and nonexcludable.

Purchasing power parity The theory that in the long run, exchange rates move to equalize the purchasing powers of different currencies.

Q

Quantity demanded The amount of a good or service that a consumer is willing and able to purchase at a given price.

Quantity supplied The amount of a good or service that a firm is willing and able to supply at a given price.

Quantity theory of money A theory of the connection between money and prices that assumes that the velocity of money is constant.

Quota A numeric limit imposed by a government on the quantity of a good that can be imported into the country.

R

Rational expectations Expectations formed by using all available information about an economic variable.

Real business cycle model A macroeconomic model that focuses on real, rather than monetary, causes of the business cycle.

Real exchange rate The price of domestic goods in terms of foreign goods.

Real GDP The value of final goods and services evaluated at base-year prices.

Real interest rate The nominal interest rate minus the inflation rate.

Recession The period of a business cycle during which total production and total employment are decreasing.

Regressive tax A tax for which people with lower incomes pay a higher percentage of their income in tax than do people with higher incomes.

Rent seeking The attempts by individuals and firms to use government action to make themselves better off at the expense of others.

Required reserve ratio The minimum fraction of deposits banks are required by law to keep as reserves.

Required reserves Reserves that a bank is legally required to hold, based on its checking account deposits.

Reserves Deposits that a bank keeps as cash in its vault or on deposit with the Federal Reserve.

Revaluation An increase in a fixed exchange rate.

Rivalry The situation that occurs when one person's consuming a unit of a good means no one else can consume it.

Rule of law The ability of a government to enforce the laws of the country, particularly with respect to protecting private property and enforcing contracts.

S

Saving and investment equation An equation that shows that national saving is equal to domestic investment plus net foreign investment.

Scarcity The situation in which unlimited wants exceed the limited resources available to fulfill those wants.

Separation of ownership from control A situation in a corporation in which the top management, rather than the shareholders, control day-to-day operations.

Short run The period of time during which at least one of a firm's inputs is fixed.

Shortage A situation in which the quantity demanded is greater than the quantity supplied.

Short-run aggregate supply curve A curve that shows the relationship in the short run between the price level and the quantity of real GDP supplied by firms.

Shutdown point The minimum point on a firm's average variable cost curve; if the price falls below this point, the firm shuts down production in the short run.

Simple deposit multiplier The ratio of the amount of deposits created by banks to the amount of new reserves.

Social benefit The total benefit from consuming a good or service, including both the private benefit and any external benefit.

Social cost The total cost of producing a good or service, including both the private cost and any external cost.

Sole proprietorship A firm owned by a single individual and not organized as a corporation.

Speculators Currency traders who buy and sell foreign exchange in an attempt to profit from changes in exchange rates.

Stagflation A combination of inflation and recession, usually resulting from a supply shock.

Stock A financial security that represents partial ownership of a firm.

Stockholders' equity The difference between the value of a corporation's assets and the value of its liabilities; also known as net worth.

Structural relationship A relationship that depends on the basic behavior of consumers and firms and remains unchanged over long periods.

Structural unemployment Unemployment arising from a persistent mismatch between the skills and characteristics of workers and the requirements of jobs.

Substitutes Goods and services that can be used for the same purpose.

Substitution effect The change in the quantity demanded of a good that results from a change in price making the good more or less expensive relative to other goods, holding constant the effect of the price change on consumer purchasing power.

Sunk cost A cost that has already been paid and cannot be recovered.

Supply curve A curve that shows the relationship between the price of a product and the quantity of the product supplied.

Supply schedule A table that shows the relationship between the price of a product and the quantity of the product supplied.

Supply shock An unexpected event that causes the short-run aggregate supply curve to shift.

Surplus A situation in which the quantity supplied is greater than the quantity demanded.

T

Tariff A tax imposed by a government on imports.

Tax incidence The actual division of the burden of a tax between buyers and sellers in a market.

Tax wedge The difference between the pretax and posttax return to an economic activity.

Taylor rule A rule developed by John Taylor that links the Fed's target for the federal funds rate to economic variables.

Technological change A change in the quantity of output a firm can produce using a given quantity of inputs.

Technology The processes a firm uses to turn inputs into outputs of goods and services.

Terms of trade The ratio at which a country can trade its exports for imports from other countries.

Total cost The cost of all the inputs a firm uses in production.

Total revenue The total amount of funds received by a seller of a good or service, calculated by multiplying price per unit by the number of units sold.

Trade The act of buying or selling.

Trade-off The idea that because of scarcity, producing more of one good or service means producing less of another good or service.

Tragedy of the commons The tendency for a common resource to be overused.

Transactions costs The costs in time and other resources that parties incur in the process of agreeing to and carrying out an exchange of goods or services.

Transfer payments Payments by the government to individuals for which the government does not receive a new good or service in return.

Two-part tariff A situation in which consumers pay one price (or tariff) for the right to buy as much of a related good as they want at a second price.

U

Underground economy Buying and selling of goods and services that is concealed from the government to avoid taxes or regulations or because the goods and services are illegal.

Unemployment rate The percentage of the labor force that is unemployed.

Unit-elastic demand Demand is unit-elastic when the percentage change in quantity demanded is *equal to* the percentage change in price, so the price elasticity is equal to 1 in absolute value.

Utility The enjoyment or satisfaction people receive from consuming goods and services.

V

Value added The market value a firm adds to a product.

Variable costs Costs that change as output changes.

Velocity of money The average number of times each dollar in the money supply is used to purchase goods and services included in GDP.

Vertical merger A merger between firms at different stages of production of a good.

Voluntary exchange The situation that occurs in markets when both the buyer and seller of a product are made better off by the transaction.

Voluntary export restraint (VER) An agreement negotiated between two countries that places a numeric limit on the quantity of a good that can be imported by one country from the other country.

Voting paradox The failure of majority voting to always result in consistent choices.

W

Winner's curse The idea that the winner in certain auctions may have overestimated the value of the good, thus ending up worse off than the losers.

World Trade Organization (WTO) An international organization that oversees international trade agreements.

Company Index

Subject Index

Key terms and the page number on which they are defined appear in **boldface**.

Credits

Photo

Chapter 1, *pages 2, 3, 19*, © Phototex/Sipa Press/0501050124; *page 13*, Brian Lee, CORBIS–NY.

Chapter 2, *pages 36, 37, 59*, © Car Culture/CORBIS, All Rights Reserved; *page 41*, Getty Images, Inc.; *page 51 top*, Jupiter Images Picturequest–Royalty Free; *right*, Dan Lim, Masterfile Corporation; *bottom*, Photolibrary.com; *left*, David Young Wolff, Getty Images Inc.–Stone Allstock; *page 53*, © Apple Computer/Court Mast/Handout/Reuters/Corbis; *page 55*, Imagination Photo Design.

Chapter 3, *pages 66, 67, 91*, © Glow Images/Alamy; *page 72*, Getty Images, Inc; *page 75*, Getty Images, Inc.

Chapter 4, *pages 98, 99, 123*, © Ambient Images Inc./Alamy; *page 113*, Neil Guegan, Corbis Zefa Collection; *page 119*, Bill Aron, PhotoEdit, Inc.

Chapter 5, *pages 136, 137, 155*, AP Wide World Photos; *page 139*, Ed Pritchard, Getty Images Inc.–Stone Allstock; *page 147*, David McIntyre, Black Star.

Chapter 6, *pages 170, 171*, David R. Frazier, Photolibrary, Inc., Alamy Images; *page 174*, © Chung Sung-Jun/Getty Images; *page 182*, Ron Sherman, Photographer; *page 191*, Pallava Bagla, Corbis/Sygma; *page 193*, AP Wide World Photos; *page 208*, Michael Newman, PhotoEdit Inc.

Chapter 7, *pages 212, 213*, © Joe Raedle/Getty Images; *page 217 left*, Eric Gevaert, Shutterstock; *top*, Jupiter Images Picturequest–Royalty Free; *right*, Bill Aron, PhotoEdit Inc.; *bottom*, Photolibrary.com; *center*, Yoshio Tomii, SuperStock, Inc.; *page 219*, Stephan Savoia, AP Wide World Photos; *page 223*, John Maier, Jr., The Image Works.

Chapter 8, *pages 238, 239*, Philippe Wojazer/Reuters, Landov LLC; *page 244*, The Kobal Collection/NBC TV; *page 250*, © Andre Durand/AFP/Getty Images, Inc.; *page 253*, Spencer Grant, PhotoEdit Inc.

Chapter 9, *pages 274, 275, 303*, John Froschauer, AP Wide World Photos; *page 289*, © John Springer Collection/CORBIS All Rights Reserved.

Chapter 10, *pages 308, 309*, Getty Images, Inc.; *page 311*, Authors Image, Alamy Images Royalty Free; *page 313*, Katsumi Kasahara, AP Wide World Photos; *page 318*, Lionel Cironneau, AP Wide World Photos; *page 334*, AP Wide World Photos.

Chapter 11, *pages 346, 347, 381*, AP Wide World Photos; *page 368*, Bloomberg News, Landov LLC; *page 373*, Minnesota Historical Society/CORBIS.

Chapter 12, *pages 390, 391*, Kristine Larsen; *page 396*, Toyota Motor Sales, USA, Inc.; *page 416*, Junji Kurokawa, AP Wide World Photos; *page 428*, © Bettmann/CORBIS All Rights Reserved.

Chapter 13, *pages 430, 431*, Robert Fried, Alamy Images; *page 435*, Reuters/Russell Boyce, Reuters Limited; *page 437*, Tom Stack, Tom Stack & Associates, Inc.; *page 449*, Daniel Luna, AP Wide World Photos; *page 456*, Corbis/Bettmann.

Chapter 14, *pages 466, 467, 499*, Mike Mergen/Bloomberg News, Landov LLC; *page 478*, Seth Joel, Getty Images Inc.–Photographer's Choice Royalty Free; *page 483*, © Reuters/Larry Downing/Corbis; *page 488*, UPI Photo/Monika Graff.

Chapter 15, *pages 508, 509, 539*, Getty Images, Inc.; *page 513*, Paddy Eckersley, ImageState/International Stock; *page 526*, Getty Images, Inc.; *page 529*, AP Wide World Photos; *page 534*, © JLP/Jose L. Pelaez/Corbis.

Chapter 16, *pages 552, 553*, Michael Fein/Bloomberg News, Landov LLC; *page 558*, Photonica/Getty Images, Inc.; *page 562*, David J. Green, Alamy Images.

Chapter 17, *pages 584, 585, 607*, Nicole Gearhart, AP Wide World Photos; *page 592*, Getty Images, Inc.; *page 603*, AP Wide World Photos.

Chapter 18, *pages 614, 615*, © REUTERS/Andy Clark/Landov; *page 618*, Winslow Townson, AP Wide World Photos; *page 620*, Ng Han Guan, AP Wide World Photos; *page 624*, Incrocci, Alberto, Getty Images Inc.–Image Bank.

Text

Chapter 1, *page 5*, "In Estonia, Paying Women to Have Babies Is Paying Off" by Marcus Walker from *Wall Street Journal*, October 20, 2006, p. A1. Copyright © 2006 Dow Jones. Reprinted by permission of Dow Jones via Copyright Clearance Center; *page 18*, "Nightmare Scenarios" from *The Economist*, October 7, 2006. Copyright © 2006 *The Economist*. Reprinted by permission of *The Economist* via Copyright Clearance Center.

Chapter 2, *page 58*, Jim Duplessis, "BMW Expects Turnaround," *Knight Ridder Tribune Business News*, January 25, 2007, p. 1. Reprinted by permission of The Permissions Group.

Chapter 3, *page 90*, "Apple Coup: How Steve Jobs Played Hardball in iPhone Birth" by Armol Sharma, Nick Wingfield, and Li Yuan from *Wall Street Journal*, February 17, 2007, p. A1. Copyright © 2007 Dow Jones. Reprinted by permission of Dow Jones via Copyright Clearance Center.

Chapter 4, *page 122*, Diane Wedner, "The Landlords: Two Sides of a Coin," *Los Angeles Times*, Jan. 14, 2007, p. K1. Copyright © 2007 Los Angeles Times. Reprinted by permission.

Chapter 5, *page 145*, "Stock Prices from Abercrombie and Fitch" from *Wall Street Journal*, March 6, 2007. Copyright © 2007 Dow Jones. Reprinted by permission of Dow Jones via Copyright Clearance Center; *page 154*, Michael Liedtke, "Google CEO, Co-Founders Get $1 Salary," Associated Press, April 4, 2007, 4:52PM ET version. Available at: http://hosted.ap.org/dynamic/stories/G/GOOGLE_APRIL_FOOLS?SITE=TXKER&SECTION=HOME&TEMPLATE=DEFAULT&CTIME=2007-04-02-09-57-41. Reprinted by permission of Associated Press via Reprint Management Services.

Chapter 6, *page 193*, Gordon H. Hanson, "What Has Happened to Wages in Mexico Since NAFTA? Implications for Hemispheric Free Trade" in Toni Estevadeordal, Dani Rodrick, Alan Taylor Andres Velasco, eds., *FTAA and Beyond: Prospects for Integration in the Americas*, Cambridge: Harvard University Press, 2004; *page 206*, The Top 25 Multinational Corporations 2006 from "Fortune Global 500" *Fortune*, July 24, 2006. © 2007 Time Inc. All rights reserved. Reprinted by permission.

Chapter 7, *page 232*, "Economic Slowdown Slams Breaks on Trucking Sector" from *Omaha World-Herald*, January 11, 2007. Reprinted by permission.

Chapter 8, *page 266*, "Jobs Data Signal Growth Is Easing but Still Solid" from *Wall Street Journal*,

February 3, 2007. Copyright © 2007 Dow Jones. Reprinted by permission of Dow Jones via Copyright Clearance Center.

Chapter 9, *page 302*, "Chinese Aviation: On a Wing and a Prayer" from *The Economist*, February 23, 2006. Reprinted by permission of *The Economist* via Copyright Clearance Center.

Chapter 10, *page 338*, "Feeling Brighter" from *The Economist*, February 19, 2007. Reprinted by permission of *The Economist* via Copyright Clearance Center.

Chapter 11, *page 380*, "Economy Slows Buy May Hold Seeds of Growth" from *Wall Street Journal*, April 28, 2007. Copyright © 2007 Dow Jones. Reprinted by permission of Dow Jones via Copyright Clearance Center.

Chapter 12, *page 418*, "Freight Carrier Weakness Shows Retailer Uncertainty" by Daniel Machalaba and Corey Dade from *Wall Street Journal*, April 26, 2007, p. A4. Reprinted by permission of *The Wall Street Journal*, via Copyright Clearance Center.

Chapter 13, *page 458*, "China Lifts bank Reserves in Bid to Cool Growth" by Rick Carew and J.R. Wu from *Wall Street Journal*, April 30, 2007, p. A2. Reprinted by permission of *Wall Street Journal*, via Copyright Clearance Center.

Chapter 14, *page 498*, "Slowing Housing Market Isn't Big Worry in Europe" by Rick Carew and J.R. Wu from *Wall Street Journal*, April 20, 2007. Reprinted by permission of *Wall Street Journal*, via Copyright Clearance Center.

Chapter 15, *page 538*, "Congress's Taxing Hurdle: The AMT" by Nick Timiraos, from *Wall Street Journal*, April 14, 2007, p. A7. Reprinted by permission of *The Wall Street Journal*, via Copyright Clearance Center.

Chapter 16, *page 576*, "Policy Makers at Fed Rethink Inflation's Roots" by Greg Ip, from *Wall Street Journal*, February 26, 2007. Reprinted by permission of *Wall Street Journal* via Copyright Clearance Center.

Chapter 17, *page 606*, "Sustaining the Unsustainable," from *The Economist*, March 15, 2007. Reprinted by permission of *The Economist* via Copyright Clearance Center

Chapter 18, *page 634*, "Can Asia Control the 'Hot Money' " by Craig Karmin from *Wall Street Journal*. April 5, 2007, p. C1. Reprinted by permission of *Wall Street Journal* via Copyright Clearance Center.

We use **business examples** to explain economic concepts. This table highlights the topic and **real-world** company introduced in the chapter-opening vignette and revisited throughout the chapter. This table also lists the companies that appear in our *Making the Connection* and *An Inside Look* features.

Chapter Title	Chapter Opener	Making the Connection	An Inside Look
CHAPTER 1			
Economics: Foundations and Models	What Happens When U.S. High-Technology Firms Move to China?	Will Women Have More Babies if the Government Pays Them To? • When Economists Disagree: A Debate over Outsourcing	Should the United States Worry about High-Tech Competition from India and China? Source: Economist
CHAPTER 2			
Trade-offs, Comparative Advantage, and the Market System	Managers Making Choices at BMW	Trade-offs: Hurricane Katrina, Tsunami Relief, and Charitable Giving • A Story of the Market System in Action: How Do You Make an iPod? • Property Rights in Cyberspace: YouTube and MySpace	BMW Managers Change Production Strategy Source: Knight Ridder Tribune Business News
CHAPTER 3			
Where Prices Come From: The Interaction of Demand and Supply	Apple and the Demand for iPods	Why Supermarkets Need to Understand Substitutes and Complements • Companies Respond to a Growing Hispanic Population • Apple Forecasts the Demand for iPhones and other Consumer Electronics • The Falling Price of LCD Televisions	How Does the iPhone Help Apple and AT&T? Source: WSJ
CHAPTER 4			
Economic Efficiency, Government Price Setting, and Taxes	Should the Government Control Apartment Rents?	The Consumer Surplus from Satellite Television • Price Floors in Labor Markets: The Debate over Minimum Wage Policy • Does Holiday Gift Giving Have a Deadweight Loss? • Is the Burden of the Social Security Tax Really Shared Equally between Workers and Firms?	Is Rent Control a Lifeline or Stranglehold? Source: Los Angeles Times
CHAPTER 5			
Firms, the Stock Market, and Corporate Governance	Google: From Dorm Room to Wall Street	What's in a "Name"? Lloyd's of London Learns about Unlimited Liability the Hard Way • Following Abercrombie & Fitch's Stock Price in the Financial Pages • A Bull in China's Financial Shop	Executive Compensation at Google Source: Associated Press
CHAPTER 6			
Comparative Advantage and the Gains from International Trade	Is Using Trade Policy to Help U.S. Industries a Good Idea?	How Expanding International Trade Has Helped Boeing • Why Is Dalton, Georgia, the Carpet-Making Capital of the World? • The Unintended Consequences of Banning Goods Made with Child Labor • Has NAFTA Helped or Hurt the U.S. Economy?	The United States and South Korea Reach a Trade Deal Source: New York Times

Chapter Title	Chapter Opener	Making the Connection	An Inside Look
CHAPTER 7			
GDP: Measuring Total Production and Income	Increases in GDP Help Revive American Airlines	Spending on Homeland Security • How the Underground Economy Hurts Developing Countries • Did World War II Bring Prosperity?	Trucking Industry Depends on the Goods—Not Services—Component of GDP Source: Omaha World-Herald
CHAPTER 8			
Unemployment and Inflation	Alcatel-Lucent Contributes to Unemployment	What Explains the Increase in "Kramers"? • How Should We Categorize the Unemployment at Alcatel-Lucent? • Why Does Costco Pay Its Workers So Much More Than Wal-Mart Does? • Why a Lower Inflation Rate Is Like a Tax Cut for Alcatel-Lucent's Bondholders	Making Sense of Employment Data Source: WSJ
CHAPTER 9			
Economic Growth, the Financial System, and Business Cycles	Growth and the Business Cycle at Boeing	The Connection between Economic Prosperity and Health • What Explains Rapid Economic Growth in Botswana? • Ebenezer Scrooge: Accidental Promoter of Economic Growth? • Who Decides if the Economy Is in a Recession?	China's Airlines Are Failing to Translate Rapid Growth into Profits Source: Economist
CHAPTER 10			
Long-Run Economic Growth: Sources and Policies	MySpace Meets the Chinese Economic Miracle	Why Did the Industrial Revolution Begin in England? • The Benefits of an Earlier Start: Standards of Living in China and Japan • Why Did the Soviet Union's Economy Fail? • Globalization and the Spread of Technology in Bangladesh	Entrepreneurship and Sustained Economic Growth in Europe Source: Economist
CHAPTER 11			
Output and Expenditure in the Short Run	Fluctuating Demand at Cisco Systems	Cisco Rides the Roller Coaster of Information Technology Spending • Business Attempts to Control Inventories, Then … and Now • The Multiplier in Reverse: The Great Depression of the 1930s	Consumer Spending and Business Inventories Send Positive Signals about GDP Source: WSJ
CHAPTER 12			
Aggregate Demand and Aggregate Supply Analysis	The Fortunes of FedEx Follow the Business Cycle	In a Global Economy, How Can You Tell the Imports from the Domestic Goods? • Does Rising Productivity Growth Reduce Employment? • Do Oil Shocks Still Cause Recessions?	Profits at UPS Signal Slow Growth in the U.S. Economy Source: WSJ

Chapter Title	Chapter Opener	Making the Connection	An Inside Look
CHAPTER 13			
Money, Banks, and the Federal Reserve System	McDonald's Money Problems in Argentina	Money without a Government? The Strange Case of the Iraqi Dinar • Do We Still Need the Penny? • The 2001 Bank Panic in Argentina • The German Hyperinflation of the Early 1920s	Using Reserve Requirements to Slow Bank Lending in China Source: WSJ
CHAPTER 14			
Monetary Policy	Monetary Policy, Toll Brothers, and the Housing Market	The Inflation and Deflation of the Housing Market "Bubble" • The Fed Responds to the Terrorist Attacks of September 11, 2001 • Why Does Wall Street Care about Monetary Policy? • How Does the Fed Measure Inflation?	Housing Market Slowdown Affects the United States and Europe Very Differently Source: WSJ
CHAPTER 15			
Fiscal Policy	A Boon for H&R Block	Is Spending on Social Security and Medicare a Fiscal Time Bomb? • Is Losing Your Job Good for Your Health? • Did Fiscal Policy Fail during the Great Depression? • Should the United States Adopt the "Flat Tax"?	Can Congress Afford to Fix the Alternative Minimum Tax? Source: WSJ
CHAPTER 16			
Inflation, Unemployment, and Federal Reserve Policy	Why Does Whirlpool Care about Monetary Policy?	Do Workers Understand Inflation? • Does the Natural Rate of Unemployment Ever Change?	The Fed Rethinks the Phillips Curve Source: WSJ
CHAPTER 17			
Macroeconomics in an Open Economy	NewPage Paper versus China	Exchange Rates in the Financial Pages • Why Is the United States Called the "World's Largest Debtor"?	Can the U.S. Current Account Deficit Be Sustained? Source: Economist
CHAPTER 18			
The International Financial System	Molson Coors Deals with Fluctuating Exchange Rates	The Toronto Blue Jays Gain from the Rising Value of the Canadian Dollar • The Big Mac Theory of Exchange Rates • Was the Euro Undervalued or Overvalued in 2007? • Crisis and Recovery in South Korea	Should the International Financial System Limit Currency Speculation? Source: WSJ